THE SALE OF GOODS

THE SALE OF GOODS

SECOND EDITION

M.G. BRIDGE

Professor of Law, London School of Economics, Barrister

OXFORD
UNIVERSITY PRESS

OXFORD
UNIVERSITY PRESS

Great Clarendon Street, Oxford OX2 6DP

Oxford University Press is a department of the University of Oxford.
It furthers the University's objective of excellence in research, scholarship,
and education by publishing worldwide in

Oxford New York

Auckland Cape Town Dar es Salaam Hong Kong Karachi
Kuala Lumpur Madrid Melbourne Mexico City Nairobi
New Delhi Shanghai Taipei Toronto

With offices in

Argentina Austria Brazil Chile Czech Republic France Greece
Guatemala Hungary Italy Japan Poland Portugal Singapore
South Korea Switzerland Thailand Turkey Ukraine Vietnam

Oxford is a registered trade mark of Oxford University Press
in the UK and in certain other countries

Published in the United States
by Oxford University Press Inc., New York

© Michael Bridge, 2009

First published 2009

British Library Cataloguing in Publication Data

Data available

Library of Congress Cataloging-in-Publication Data

Bridge, M. G. (Michael G.)
The sale of goods / M. G. Bridge. — 2nd ed.
p. cm.
Includes index.
ISBN 978-0-19-955977-0
(acid-free paper) 1. Sales—Great Britain. I. Title.
KD1650 .B75 2009
346.4207' 2—dc22   2009000254

Typeset by Cepha Imaging Private Ltd, Bangalore, India
Printed in Great Britain
on acid-free paper by
CPI Antony Rowe, Chippenham, Wiltshire

ISBN 978-0-19-955977-0

1 3 5 7 9 10 8 6 4 2

FOREWORD

John Bunyan's opinion, that buying in the cheapest market and selling in the dearest was knavery in disguise, accords little with human realities. But it provides a backdrop to the legal rules which, although designed to facilitate sale, at the same time offer some protection against exploitation for both buyers and sellers. This book contains a thorough discussion of the English law of sale, its case law and statutory basis, with reference to the comparable law of other common law jurisdictions. Professor Bridge is a master of the subject. He sets the rules governing sale, especially on formation and breach, in their contractual context. While acknowledging that sales law is partly applied contract law, however, he also brings to bear his deep knowledge of personal property law. It may be a matter of regret, but English sales law has important property elements embedded in it. Without a knowledge of this legal derivation, some of the statutory rules can never be fully appreciated. Professor Bridge also has reference to relevent legal regimes such as trade descriptions and consumer protection legislation.

But this is not simply a black letter account of English sales law. First, professor Bridge has an extensive knowledge of the context in which sales law operates. There is the obvious difference between commercial and consumer sales, and the rules sometimes differ for the two, both in their form and operation. Professor Bridge raises the issue of just how long commercial and consumer sales can fall under the same legal umbrella. There is another point about context with commercial sales. The American scholar, Karl Llewellyn, the force behind the Uniform Commercial Code, contended that English sales law began as farmers' law, and that while it might include rules for the sale of horses, it had a majestic ignorance of commerce. As an expert in the sale of international commodities Professor Bridge knows that many of the statutory rules laid down for domestic sales are varied for international commodities sales by the standard form contracts of international trade associations. That backdrop to the operation of sales law in practice is made good use of throughout the book. Professor Bridge also touches on other realities in international sales such as letters of credit and bills of lading, which are brought to bear in the discussion of matters such as payment and the seller's obligations.

Further, policy is never far from the surface of Professor Bridge's exposition. This involves explaining the implications of particular judicial decisions, and sometimes a criticism of the court for failing to appreciate these. There is also a good account of the rationale of the statutory rules, with discussion of the relevant Law Commission background to more recent changes. Perhaps most importantly, Professor Bridge explains the contending policy considerations behind a particular body of law. Drawing the line as to whether termination rights lie for breach of contract is a good example, where professor Bridge discusses a range of issues such as using termination rights to engender contract compliance, the futility of imprisoning parties in a contract no longer wanted, and underlining certainty and forward planning.

This second edition of *The Sale of Goods* is thus very much to be welcomed. It represents the mature reflections of a scholar with a profound knowledge of the subject, both domestically and internationally. The extensive footnotes, with their reference to the relevant literature and law reform material, can be used as a springboard for further analysis. This student, the practitioner, the policy-maker and, dare I say it, the judge, will all learn from this book.

The Honorary Mr Justice Cranston
Royal Courts of Justice
October 2008

PREFACE

Eleven years have passed since the first edition of this book. In that time, the law has substantially changed. This edition is nearly half as long again as the previous edition, partly due to an extension of the range of coverage of existing subject and partly due to an addition of new subjects. There is now a separate chapter on exemption clauses and new material on penalty clauses, risk in consumer sales, additional remedies in consumer sales, and title reservation in insolvency. The sections dealing with letters of credit and innocent misrepresentation have undergone a particularly substantial expansion, but discussion of the following subjects is also appreciably longer: bills of sale; body parts; computer software; co-ownership; frustration; negligent misstatement; defective products; credit cards; contractual termination; cure; interest and late payment; and gain-based damages.

The order of chapter has been altered somewhat and the layout of the book changed, so that, with the aid of paragraph headings and numbers, the material can more easily be located. Although more comprehensive than the first edition, the character of the book as one dealing with the domestic law of sale remains unchanged. The law of international sale is drawn on so far as it provides an aid to understanding the domestic law, but international sale remains the subject of a complementary text of mine with this publisher, *The International Sale of Goods: Law and Practice* (2nd edn, Oxford, 2007).

On the statutory and regulatory front, a major alteration to the structure of the Sale of Goods Act 1979 occurred with the Sale and Supply of Goods to Consumer Regulations 2002. The other most significant statutory and regulatory changes since the first edition are the Contracts (Rights of Third Parties) Act 1999 (whose impact on sale of goods law may more clearly emerge in the coming years), the Late Payment of Commercial Debts (Interest) Act 1998, the Electronic Commerce (EC Directive) Regulations 2002, the Consumer Protection (Distance Selling) Regulations 2000, and the Consumer Protection from Unfair Trading Regulations 2008. Much of this change is drawn from European Community Directives.

Perhaps the most important case law developments over the past eleven years comprise the following: *Customs and Excise Commissioners v Everwine Ltd* (passing of property); *Atari Corp (UK) Ltd v Electronoc Boutique Stores Ltd* (sale or return);

Great Peace Shipping Ltd v Tsavliris (mistake); *Shogun Finance Ltd v Hudson* (mistake); *Forthright Finance Ltd v Carlyle Finance Ltd* (title transfer); *Michael Gerson (Leasing) Ltd v Wilkinson* (title transfer); *Montrod Ltd v Grundkotter Fleischvertriebs-GmbH* (letters of credit); *Czarnikow-Rionda Sugar Trading Inc. v Standard Bank London Ltd* (letters of credit); *Mahonia Ltd v JP Morgan Chase Bank* (letters of credit); *Stevenson v Rogers* (implied terms); *Office of Fair Trading v Lloyd's Bank plc* (credit cards); *JH Ritchie Ltd v Lloyd* (acceptance); *Clegg v Andersson* (acceptance); *Sempra Metals Ltd v Inland Revenue Commissioners* (interest); *Attorney General v Blake* (damages); *The Golden Victory* (damages); *The Achilleas* (damages); and *Bence Graphics International Ltd v Fasson UK Ltd* (damages).

Last but not least, the promulgation in July 2007 of UCP 600, the latest edition of the Uniform Customs and Practice on Documentary Credits, has resulted in major changes to the text.

I wish also to record my gratitude for all the assistance and encouragement that I received from Oxford University press in completing this new edition.

Michael Bridge
31 October 2008

PREFACE TO THE FIRST EDITION

The origins of this work lie in a book that I wrote on the Faculty of Law of McGill University, Montreal. It was entitled *Sale of Goods* (1988) and addressed the subject from a Canadian perspective. Thanks to Oxford University Press, I have been able to 'patriate' this book but have, in the process, produced much more than an update of that 1988 book. Large parts of the book have been extensively rewritten; relatively few sentences have emerged from the process unscathed. There have of course been a substantial number of changes in sales law in the last decade, which is somewhat surprising given the relative paucity of case law in a mature subject. The most important developments have been statutory ones, notably the Sale and Supply of Goods Act 1994 and the Sale of Goods (Amendment) Act 1995. The former recasts the old merchantable quality implied term, the Act in rechristening that term points to the fundamental shifts in the pattern of sale transactions that have occurred in the last hundred years or so. The latter statute, introducing a major proprietary reform, creates interests by way of tenancy in common in bulk goods, a matter of no small interest to the bulk commodities trade but not confined to that trade.

The focus of this work is the English law of sale. A series of statutory reforms of the last thirty years have given it an identity separate from its counterparts in other Commonwealth jurisdictions. It is with some regret that I note the passing of as *ius commune* of sale in common law countries. The old American Uniform Sales Act was modeled by Williston on our Sale of Goods Act 1893. It disappeared with the arrival of Article 2 of the Uniform Commercial Code in the 1950s. But there was no practice of citing American cases in this country, so the rupture was more differences in drafting techniques. English statutory definitions referred to above, together with major changes in the receiving countries, such as Australia's Trade Practices Act, will create difficulties of transferring authorities between jurisdictions, even as the courts of this country show a refreshing willingness to look overseas for inspiration. This disintegration of sales law is, nevertheless, inevitable if it is to keep pace with the society in which it is embedded: the law of sale is not a museum piece. This is very much a book on the English law of sale. It should be consulted with care by those interested in the Scots treatment of the subject since, in important respects relevant or of sufficient interest to throw light on English law.

This is a book concerned with the general, domestic law of sale. It aims, not merely to lay out the English law of sale, but also to prescribe and criticize. The best service an author can provide for the professional and scholarly communities is to furnish them with a thoroughgoing examination of principle that will equip them to understand, and not merely to know, the subject. Otherwise the book would soon become about as useful as an out-of- date railway timetable. It is therefore important to appraise the subject of sale with an evolutionary eye. Many apparent oddities in the law were accurate enough expressions of the case law codified for the first time in 1893. Understanding their origin is more than half of the way towards dealing with them. Although our Sale of Goods Act dates from 1979, it is just the 1893 Act as modified by a series of statutes, designed mainly to equip the law to deal with consumer transactions, together with a few very minor changes of style introduced for no apparent reason. The 1979 Act falls well short of a modern recasting of sales law. It is questionable how long the Act can survive in its present form as a general sales statute. The work of the Law Commission in the field adds up to a fairly compelling case for the separation of the consumer and commercial law of sale.

One of the difficulties facing a writer, dealing with sale, is knowing where to draw the line between the special law of sale and the general law of contract. As a matter of principle, this question became for me subordinate to the maximum permitted length of the manuscript. Sale is probably the most important of the special contracts; it cannot be mastered without a solid understanding of general contract law. Some account must therefore be taken of the general law, but it would be pointless to reproduce in great detail areas that had best be consulted in the general contract (and tort) textbooks. Export sales are not treated as such but case law is examined to the extent that it applies the rules concerning delivery, payment, and proprietary matters. In addition, this book deals with consumer material only in so far as it bears upon the private law relationship of seller and buyer. It cannot therefore be regarded as a consumer law text. Transactions similar to sale are referred to quite copiously but the overwhelming concern of the book is with sale itself. Finally, although it is easy to think of sales as a branch of applied law and I hope I have done justice to it.

I owe much to the support and encouragement of Richard Hart and his colleagues at Oxford University Press. Furthermore, when the process of retyping and editing was threatening to overwhelm me, I become indebted to the Nottingham University Law Department administrator, Linda Wright, who arranged for outside assistance at short notice. I also wish to record my gratitude for the efforts of Sandra Frisby, who gave me invaluable assistance as a summer research student. Finally, my thanks and apologies go to my family, who do not share my peculiar fascination with sales law but who, like any conscientious buyer, paid the price.

University of Nottingham
26 July 1996

CONTENTS—SUMMARY

CONTENTS

Contents

Contents

6. Delivery, Acceptance, and Payment

7. The Implied Terms of Description, Fitness, and Quality

TABLE OF CASES

TABLE OF STATUTES

UNITED STATES

TABLE OF INTERNATIONAL INSTRUMENTS

LIST OF ABBREVIATIONS

1878 Act	Bills of Sale Act 1878
1893 Act	Sale of Goods Act 1893
1977 Act	Unfair Contract Terms Act 1977
1979 Act	Sale of Goods Act 1979
1987 Act	Consumer Protection Act 1987
2002 Regulations	Sale and Supply of Goods to Consumers Regulations 2002, SI 2002 No. 3045
ARA ports	Amsterdam/Rotterdam/Antwerp
c. & f./CFR	cost and freight
c.i.f./CIF	cost, insurance, freight
c.o.d.	cash on delivery
CPR	Civil Procedure Rules
DEQ	delivered ex quay
DES	delivered ex ship
f.a.s./FAS	free alongside ship
f.o.b./FOB	free on board
f.o.t.	free on truck
FOSFA 22	form 22 of the Federation of Oils, Seeds and Fats Associations
GAFTA 100	form 100 of the Grain and Feed Trade Association
UCC	Uniform Commercial Code
UCP 500	Uniform Customs and Practice for Documentary Credits 1993
UCP 600	Uniform Customs and Practice for Documentary Credits 2007
UNCITRAL	United Nations Commission on International Trade Law

1

INTRODUCTION AND CONCLUSION OF THE CONTRACT

Introduction

Background to Modern Sale of Goods Legislation

Introduction.   Sale of goods is a specialized branch of the general law of con-   **1.01**
tract. Its case law has been of fundamental importance in assisting the development of the general law. In two principal respects, however, the special law of sale
of goods stands apart from general contract law. First, unlike most nominate contracts, sale involves a conveyance of the seller's property interest in the goods in
favour of the buyer, which, together with the abundance of reported sales decisions, lends a degree of autonomy to this branch of the law. Secondly, and quite
strikingly in view of the paucity of statutes in general contract law, sale has its own
statutory code, the Sale of Goods Act 1979, which is for the most part a reworking
of its 1893 predecessor. Far from separating sales law from the general law of contract, a reference to it is directed by the Act where none other of its provisions apply.[1]
Yet the process of reabsorption of sale by the general law, prompted by the gaps that
appear in a code over time and by the mass of decisions that encrust particular

---

[1] S. 62(2).

provisions of the Act, is disguised by the way that syllabuses and textbook writers have delineated sale as a category apart.

1.02 **Evolution of sale of goods law.** Most of the law of sale, a branch of commercial law, is the product of nineteenth-century developments.[2] Prior to this, Lord Mansfield had fostered the integration of the law merchant into the common law by making the latter responsive to the customs and usages of the former,[3] just as Lord Holt, a half century earlier, had laid the foundation of the common law treatment of negotiable instruments.[4] Nevertheless, the major features of the modern law of sale, such as the passing of property and risk, the implied terms of description, fitness for purpose, and merchantable quality, and the remedies for breach of contract were laid down in a series of nineteenth-century judgments ranging from the time of Lord Ellenborough to Lord Blackburn. The enactment in 1893 of the Sale of Goods Act[5] was the coping-stone of this development and was part of a broad operation to codify important areas of commercial law.[6]

1.03 **Characteristic transactions.** A consequence of this course of progression is that the present Sale of Goods Act 1979, a re-enactment of the 1893 Act with inter-vening amendments and minor statutory changes, faithfully reflects the type of sale agreement that preoccupied the courts in that century. This case law was mainly concerned with small commodities agreements and the sale of goods for industrial use and consumption. It can be traced into the provisions of the 1893 Act. Large-scale commodities agreements on forward delivery terms involving the transfer of documents find no mention in the 1893 Act or even in its 1979 succes-sor. Further, the difficulties experienced in reforming the statutory provisions on the implied terms, discharge for breach, and acceptance, dealt with by the Sale and Supply of Goods Act 1994, are rooted in the fact that the law was not codified on the basis of decisions arising out of the dealings in consumer durables and com-plex manufactured goods that are prominent in modern case law.[7]

1.04 **Sale of Goods Act 1979.** The Sale of Goods Act 1979 cannot be described as an attempt to revise the law of sale to meet late twentieth-century conditions. The law therein was not overhauled and subjected to the rigorous scrutiny needed for such a task. Rather, a number of important, though, in the greater scheme of things, incidental, reforms of the 1960s and 1970s were consolidated alongside a

---

[2] K. Llewellyn (1939) 52 *Harv LR* 725, 740–6.
[3] W. S. Holdsworth, *A History of English Law* (1903 *et seq.*, Methuen and Sweet & Maxwell, 17 vols.), xii (1938), 524–42.
[4] *Ibid.*, vi (1924), 519–22.
[5] 56 & 57 Vict., cap. 71.
[6] See Rodger (1992) 109 *LQR* 570.
[7] K. Sutton (1969) 7 *Alta LR* 130, 173; Lord Diplock, (1981) 15 *UBC LR* 371, 373–4.

few minor changes of drafting style.[8] Those reforms affected the definition of the implied terms of title, description, merchantable quality, and fitness for purpose; the ability of the seller to exclude these obligations; the relationship between the buyer's right to examine the goods and to reject them if they are defective; and the exceptions to the rule of *nemo dat quod non habet*. Further changes of similar importance, advocated by the Law Commission,[9] were implemented by the Sale and Supply of Goods Act 1994 without changing the original structure inherited from the 1893 Act. In addition, a Sale of Goods (Amendment) Act 1994 was passed to abolish the rule of market overt in the transfer of title to goods, followed in 1995 by another Sale of Goods (Amendment) Act, which permitted prepaying buyers to acquire an undivided interest in identified bulk goods. In 2002, an EC Directive[10] was transposed in the form of regulations.[11] These gave consumer buyers additional rights in respect of non-conforming goods and made some alterations to the rules on the transfer of risk and satisfactory quality. The regulations introduced new provisions in the Sale of Goods Act[12] by way of an implant, a new Part 5A ('Additional Rights of Buyer in Consumer Cases'). This legislative technique, which may have been unavoidable in the absence of a thorough recasting of the Sale of Goods Act, has caused significant damage to the structure of the Act. Part 5A sits in the Act in a thoroughly unintegrated way, laying out for consumer buyers an almost completely separate remedial path from the one already in the Act which, if they so choose, consumer buyers remain free to take.

Presumptive law. Any discussion of the merits of a radical revision of sales law **1.05** should start from the position that the Sale of Goods Act is largely presumptive and rarely mandatory. Those with a mind to exclude or vary its provisions are, for the most part, unimpeded in their efforts, though the combined force of statutory inertia and contractual brevity should not be underestimated. It cannot be said that an archaic statute, essentially Victorian, is stifling commerce. Even if there were any truth in this, commerce is resilient enough to absorb such an irritant in the way that an oyster envelopes a grain of sand. In any case, an ageing statute increasingly defers to case law responsive to changes in commercial practice.[13] Set against these considerations, the argument that the Sale of Goods Act has lost its

---

8 See *Stevenson v Rogers* [1999] QB 1028, 1040 (Potter LJ): 'The Act of 1979 forms a single code; however, that is upon the basis simply that it consolidates and enacts within one statute and without material amendment a number of disparate statutes previously governing the field of sale of goods.' The learned judge went on to say that a consolidating Act was not more than 'the sum of its parts' and that, if doubt as to any of its provisions arose, they were to be construed as if they had remained in the earlier Act or Acts: *ibid*.

9 *Sale and Supply of Goods* (Law Com. No. 160, 1987).

10 EC Directive on the sale of consumer goods and associated guarantees (1999/44/EC).

11 Sale and Supply of Goods to Consumers Regulations, SI 2002 No. 3045.

12 Under powers contained in s. 2(2) of the European Communities Act 1972.

13 G. Gilmore (1948) 57 *Yale LJ* 1341.

shape and is out of date does not seem strong enough to merit the time needed by law reform agencies and Parliament to produce a new Act for the twenty-first century. Nevertheless, the introduction of Part 5A has so thoroughly compromised the structure of the Sale of Goods Act, revealing in the process of its insertion some of the more archaic features of the Act[14] and pointing to the continuing difficulty of holding within the bounds of one statute provisions dealing with commercial and with consumer sales, that a case can now be made for a thorough statutory revision.[15] This revision might even take the form of separate statutes for commercial and consumer sales. There is, however, a danger that the modern style of statutory drafting will in the process obliterate the simpler style of the late nineteenth century, which is still evident in the Sale of Goods Act today. The Act is not a regulatory Act; a statutory style that trusts the courts to work in harmony with the Act is appropriate to this area of law. Any new legislation should be closer in style to the Arbitration Act 1996 than to the Consumer Credit Act 1974, at least in so far as that legislation is dedicated to commercial sale of goods contracts.

1.06 **International harmonization.**   Account should be taken of the work that has taken place on the unification of the law of international sale,[16] which began in the 1930s under the auspices of the Institute for the Unification of Private Law. These efforts resumed after the Second World War in the 1950s and produced two conventions that were adopted at a diplomatic conference sponsored by the Dutch Government. The conventions dealt with the formation of international sale of goods contracts and with the law governing the sales themselves. Neither convention was successful: the United States and socialist and developing states were not active in the process. A fresh reform initiative was taken by the United Nations Commission on International Trade Law (UNCITRAL), which culminated in a 1978 draft Convention on International Sale of Goods that was unanimously approved at a diplomatic conference held in Vienna in 1980. The Convention has now been adopted by seventy-one countries, accounting for the greater part of world trade, and the isolation of the United Kingdom, which has so far failed to adopt the Convention, is becoming increasingly obvious. Drawing from a wide array of civil and common law experience, and responsive to the commercial needs of different types of economies, the Convention rests upon the inherited wisdom and authority of no particular legal system. Its influence, radiated through the medium of the EC Directive on consumer sales and associated guarantees,[17] is already apparent in English law in the provisions of Part 5A of the Sale of

---

[14] See M. Bridge, 'Do We Need a New-Sale of Goods Act?' in J. Lowry and L. Mistelis (eds), *Commercial Law: Perspectives and Practice* (Butterworths LexisNexis, 2006), 15–47

[15] M. Bridge (2003) 119 *LQR* 173.

[16] For an historical account of these developments, see J. Honnold, *Uniform Law for International Sales* (3rd edn, Kluwer, 1999).

[17] 1999/44/EC.

Goods Act. UNCITRAL provides a documentary service about the national case law interpreting the Convention[18] but there is no authoritative supranational source to provide *amicus curiae* opinions. The most active national courts and tribunals have set the tone for the Convention's future interpretation. English courts have therefore had no part to play in the interpretation of the Convention, and will continue not to do so if the United Kingdom remains outside the Convention, apart perhaps from the occasional case where they might be called upon to apply, as the applicable law of a contract, a law that incorporates the Convention.

Code and Common Law

Drafting style and complexity.   A legitimate criticism of the common law is that   **1.07** its finely calibrated character, responsive to infinite shades of practical reality, is purchased at the cost of a complexity that places its comprehension beyond the reach of all but a select number of academics, judges, and practitioners.[19] The complexity of modern case law complements the complexity of modern statutes. It is salutary to compare in the 1979 Act the pristine sections of the 1893 Act with additions made in the last quarter-century: the former are open-textured and simple, while the latter are contorted by the draftsman's attempts to provide for every eventuality. The 1893 Act was consequent upon the simplification of procedure and the abolition of the forms of action,[20] together with the substitution of a mass of judge-made legal rules for the unrecorded factual judgments of juries.[21] It is a compendium of clear rules that has come under stress in modern conditions as the pendulum between law and fact has swung increasingly in favour of the latter, a tendency due in no small part to the infusion of the common law with a benevolent judicial discretion at the expense of legal inflexibility.[22] The Sale of Goods Act 1893 recorded a process that over the nineteenth century had substituted a network of legal rules for a laconic and unsystematic mass of jury decisions.[23] The line between fact and law has been redrawn in modern times in favour of the former, although this has come too late for the civil jury, now almost completely disappeared.

---

18 CLOUT: Case Law on Uncitral Texts. There is also an information service organized by Pace University of New York available on the Internet: see <http://cisgw3.law.pace.edu>.

19 See the criticisms of Lord Diplock about the cost and needless complexity of modern legal argument fuelled by the multiple citation of authority in, e.g., *Lambert v Lewis* [1982] AC 225.

20 Holdsworth, n. 3 above, ix (3rd edn, 1944), 247–335.

21 The virtues of a clear rule are promoted in M. Chalmers (1903) 19 *LQR* 10; Holdsworth, n. 3 above, xi (1938), 315–18.

22 P. S. Atiyah (1980) 65 *Iowa LR* 1249.

23 The right to terminate for breach was firmly established as a matter of law by cases such as *Bentsen v Taylor, Sons & Co. (No. 2)* [1893] 2 QB 274. Perhaps the best-known example is the laying down of rules governing remoteness of damage in contract; see *Hadley v Baxendale* (1854) 9 Ex. 341; A.W.B. Simpson (1979) 46 *U Chi LR* 533.

1.08 **Codification.** Confidence in statutory codes as universal solvents is inversely proportional to the number of years that have passed since their enactment; the same holds true for civilian codes. The Sale of Goods Act may not be a code in the sense understood by a civilian jurist, since it is confined to a special contract (sale) and permits penetration by the general uncodified law to fill its lacunae, but it can rightly be called a codification for the conscious attempt to summarize rather than reform the antecedent case law.[24] Unlike a statute such as the Consumer Credit Act 1974, which manufactures its own concepts and largely consigns the antecedent case law to oblivion, the Sale of Goods Act is very much a creature of the common law that it summarized. A thorough understanding of the Act cannot be attained without a journey to the case law that prompted the statutory provisions, however much this might be deplored by those who argue that statutes supply a fresh start and wholly supersede earlier case law.

1.09 **Earlier case law.** Be that as it may, the classic approach to a codifying statute, uttered in the full and optimistic flush of the statute's youth, is given by Lord Herschell in respect of the Bills of Exchange Act 1882,[25] like the Sale of Goods Act 1893 a product of Sir Mackenzie Chalmers's draftsmanship. He said that the starting point should be the natural meaning of the statutory text itself, 'uninfluenced by any considerations derived from the previous state of the law', and that recourse should be had to the antecedent case law only in exceptional cases, for example, if the text was unclear or if it adopted a term of art that could be clarified by a discussion of the cases. Besides the economy of effort that comes with not 'roaming over a vast sea of authorities', the court also avoids the risk of misreading provisions of a reforming or clarifying nature, not literally based upon earlier cases.[26]

1.10 **Modern divergence.** But in our legal tradition, the accretion of case law impedes direct access to the text and the text itself becomes absorbed eventually by the common law. The words of Lord Herschell might have seemed to lack currency in the case of sale were it not for the introduction of a statutory definition of merchantable quality in 1973, renamed with some modification as satisfactory quality in 1994. This has prompted two divergent judicial approaches to its interpretation: the one seeking an answer to its meaning in the text itself, and the other looking to the case law on which it was modelled.[27] Since the current definition of satisfactory

---

[24] Chalmers, n. 21 above.

[25] *Bank of England v Vagliano Bros* [1891] AC 107. For a defence of the merits of the Sale of Goods Act in promoting legal simplicity, see A. Diamond, (1968) 31 *MLR* 361, 368–70.

[26] But for references to the Sale of Goods Act 1893 codifying rather than the reforming law, see e.g. *Bristol Tramways & Carriage Co. Ltd v Fiat Motors Ltd* [1910] 2 KB 831, 836; *Harris v Tong* (1930) 65 OLR 133, 137 (Can.); *Healing Sales Pty Ltd v Inglis Electrix Pty Ltd* (1968) 121 CLR 584, 612 (Windeyer J).

[27] For a statement of the need to examine pre-codification authorities, see *M/S Aswan Engineering Establishment Co. v Lupdine Ltd* [1987] 1 WLR 1. For the opposite view, see *Rogers v Parish Motors*

quality is hardly a definition at all but an open-ended list of criteria that a court might consult in determining whether goods are of satisfactory quality, the arguments against consulting former case law are unconvincing, though such case law if consulted ought be looked at with care. Further, an argument in favour of turning from time to time to the pre-1893 case law is that the provisions of the Act are sometimes based upon common law reasoning that is now outmoded. Chalmers faithfully recorded the law as he saw it, though it should be understood that certain changes were made to the 1893 Act in its progression through Parliament. Condensing sales law as it did, the Sale of Goods Act encouraged later observers to see as flaws in the Act rules that were a perfect reflection of the contemporary law that had been codified.[28] A similar judgment is that Chalmers, the author of the highly successful Bills of Exchange Act 1882, nodded when he laid out the inferior Sale of Goods Act 1893.[29] With continuing imaginative and informed interpretation, the Act can be brought back into line with contemporary contract law, but the price paid for this is that the Act can no longer in places be read for an understanding of the modern position.[30] Sale of goods law and contract law alike are dynamic and must respond to changing patterns of commercial activity. On occasion, the resolution of a modern problem may need the antecedents of the statutory text to be scrutinized with no small care. To understand the pedigree of sales law is not to practise legal antiquarianism.

Sale of Goods Act and Common Law

Background common law.   The Sale of Goods Act is less than a code, for section **1.11** 62(2) directs a reference to the general law when the Act itself is silent:[31]

> The rules of the common law, including the law merchant, except in so far as they are inconsistent with the provisions of this Act, and in particular the rules relating to the

---

(Scarborough) Ltd [1987] 2 All ER 232 (Mustill LJ) and *Marimpex Mineralöl Handels GmbH v Louis Dreyfus et Cie GmbH* [1995] 1 Lloyd's Rep. 167, 179. Assuming the latter approach to an unhelpful statutory definition, how should a court dealing with 'satisfactory quality' approach cases decided under the 'old' s. 14(6) definition of merchantable quality? See further the examination of the pre-1973 authorities in *Cehave NV v Bremer Handelsgesellschaft mbH* [1976] QB 44.

[28] The Ontario Law Reform Commission, *Report on Sale of Goods* (1979), i, 23–4, refers to a number of rules as 'original defects'. But, to take one example, the 'artificial restrictions on the remedies of a buyer in a sale of specific goods' were in fact a faithful reflection of a lingering *caveat emptor* ethic.

[29] L. C. B. Gower, Foreword to P. S. Atiyah, *The Sale of Goods* (Pitman, 1963) ('perhaps, his least happy effort'). A similar judgment is that of K. Llewellyn, who referred to the Act as drafted 'not by Blackburn nor by Bramwell, nor yet by Hamilton or Kennedy, but by merely an able lawyer who knew his Bills and Notes': (1937) 37 *Col LR* 341, 409.

[30] A good test is to read s. 48 on the seller's right of resale and then to consider whether it even comes close to the modern understanding of contractual termination.

[31] M. Chalmers, *The Sale of Goods Act, 1893, Including the Factors Acts, 1889 & 1890* (4th edn, Butterworths, 1899), 6:

> [T]he contract of sale . . . [i]n part . . . is governed by principles peculiar to itself, and in part by principles common to all [consensual and bilateral] contracts . . . The Act, except incidentally,

law of principal and agent and the effect of fraud, misrepresentation, duress or coercion, mistake or other invalidating cause, apply to contracts for the sale of goods.

1.12 This section shows that the Act was never designed to be comprehensive and inward-looking; rather, it expresses a framework of mainly presumptive rules complementing the general law.[32] A number of sections state that the intention of the parties is paramount,[33] thereby emphasizing the parties are free to strike their own bargain.[34] Sales law and general contract law are both affected by forces abridging contractual freedom, and by the need to strike a reasonable balance between contractual autonomy and contractual regulation.

1.13 **Flexibility.** Section 62(2) has proved its value in the past when enabling courts to avoid inflexibility in the Sale of Goods Act. Thus section 7 was not applied in one case where the goods had never existed and therefore could not be said to have perished for the purpose of initial impossibility;[35] and the Act's classification of implied contractual terms as conditions and warranties was held in another case not to impede the application of intermediate stipulation analysis to express terms of the contract.[36] Applied in this corrective fashion, section 62(2) works to prevent the divergence of sales law from an evolving general law.

Equity

1.14 **Meaning of 'common law'.** In another respect, however, section 62(2) has fostered just such a divergence. It makes no reference to the rules of equity. Does 'the rules of common law' mean common law and equity as opposed to statute, or common law in the narrower sense that excludes equity? The question has proved to be particularly troubling in the areas of equitable proprietary interests and, in certain Commonwealth jurisdictions, the equitable rule of innocent misrepresentation.[37]

---

deals only with the first-mentioned principles. The principles of law which govern the contract of sale, in common with all other consensual contracts, are outside its scope. But they are saved by sect. [62(2)].

[32] Introduction to the first edition of Chalmers, *ibid.*, and reproduced in all subsequent editions of the work: 'Sale is a consensual contract, and the Act does not seek to prevent the parties from making any bargain they please. Its object is to lay down clear rules for the case where the parties have either formed no intention, or failed to express it.'

[33] Particularly apparent in Part IV (Performance of the Contract).

[34] Expressed most strongly by Jessel MR in *Printing and Numerical Registering Co. v Sampson* (1875) LR 19 Eq. 462, 465:

[I]f there is one thing which more than another public policy requires it is that men of full age and competent understanding shall have the utmost liberty of contracting, and that their contracts when entered into freely and voluntarily shall be held sacred and shall be enforced by Courts of justice.

[35] *McRae v Commonwealth Disposals Commission* (1951) 84 CLR 377.

[36] *Cehave NV v Bremer Handelsgesellschaft mbH*, n. 27 above.

[37] *Riddiford v Warren* (1901) 20 NZLR 572; *Watt v Westhoven* [1933] VLR 458.

Innocent misrepresentation. The issue concerning innocent misrepresentation **1.15** is whether the lenient equitable test for an actionable misrepresentation, that a statement merely induce the making of a contract,[38] or the common law rule, that it induce in the mind of the listener a fundamental mistake,[39] applies to sale of goods agreements. In England, the matter has long been settled in favour of the equitable view.[40] But the New Zealand Court of Appeal in *Riddiford v Warren*[41] took the opposite view for these reasons. First, innocent misrepresentation had never formed part of sales law before sale was codified, as opposed to reformed, by statute. The reference in section 62(2) to 'misrepresentation' was therefore to the common law rule. Moreover, a lenient misrepresentation rule could subvert the statutory scheme of contractual terms and remedies for breach.[42] We shall see later in this text that English courts have moved by other means to prevent such subversion from occurring and that some modest degree of judicial control has been granted by statute so as to prevent a contract from being rescinded in some cases.[43] Secondly, the issue was not to be resolved in accordance with the rule that, in cases of conflict between law and equity, the rules of equity shall prevail. There was no conflict to resolve since innocent misrepresentation had never been extended to 'mercantile contracts for the sale of goods' in the years before the fusion of law and equity.

Evolving law. However faithful *Riddiford v Warren* may have been to the pre- **1.16** code law of sale, it is motivated by the regrettable view that the Sale of Goods Act froze the living law. Chalmers may well have believed that sales law had reached the acme of its development before the Act, but a sensible view of the draftsman's intention would see section 62(2) as incorporating the general law as it exists from time to time so as to retain the affinity between sale of goods law and the general law of contract.

Equitable property. An approach similar to the one in *Riddiford v Warren* has **1.17** exercised a more general and lasting appeal in respect of the transfer of equitable proprietary rights between seller and buyer. In contrast with its laconic treatment

---

[38] *Redgrave v Hurd* (1881) 20 Ch D 1; *Torrance v Bolton* (1872) LR 8 Ch. App. 118.
[39] *Kennedy v Panama, New Zealand and Australian Royal Mail Co. Ltd* (1867) LR 2 QB 580.
[40] See, e.g., the example of *Naughton v O'Callaghan* [1990] 3 All ER 191, where the issue does not rate a mention.
[41] *Riddiford v Warren*, n. 37 above.
[42] *Watt v Westhoven*, n. 37 above, 463: 'Much of the language, and the arrangement in which the Act has codified the common law, would have to be revised to accommodate a doctrine whereby every warranty could become a condition, and every inducing statement not warranted would be a condition also.' The approach taken in this case to misrepresentation in s. 62(2) was rejected in *Graham v Freer* (1980) 35 SASR 424 (Full Ct.). See also Law Reform Commission of New South Wales, *Sale of Goods* (Report No 51, 1987), paras 2.1 *et seq.*
[43] *Leaf v International Galleries* [1950] 2 KB 86; M. G. Bridge (1986) 20 *UBC LR* 53; see Ch. 10 below.

of common law misrepresentation, the Act deals at length with the passing of the legal, or general, property in goods.[44] A buyer who has obtained this general property may, if the seller becomes insolvent before delivery, assert this property right against the seller's creditors, secured and unsecured. A buyer unable to show that such a conveyance has taken place, but to whom equitable proprietary rights have been transferred, would receive upon the seller's insolvency equivalent protection.[45] Despite nineteenth-century authority favouring the buyer, the dominant view in the twentieth century has been that there is no room in sale of goods law for the passing of implied equitable proprietary rights.[46] The question why some equitable rules have been incorporated in sales law while others, in the interest of commercial stability and convenience, have not, has not received a thorough judicial explanation.

1.18 **Other equitable principles.** In numerous other respects, equity plays an uncontroversial part in contemporary sales law. Any argument that promissory estoppel,[47] injunctive relief,[48] and rectification,[49] to name just three examples, are excluded by the Act would receive short shrift. Other equitable institutions, such as relief against forfeiture,[50] remain of doubtful scope in sale of goods cases, not because of anything in the Act but because their own doctrinal limitations may restrict their operation. The problem of equity's relationship with the common law centres today, not so much upon the scope of the Act, but rather upon the extent to which equitable rules and institutions are free to develop by expansion or even by retraction after the administrative fusion of the two systems.[51] This in turn presents the questions whether such a refurbished equity is greatly different from a common law renewed by an infusion of discretion and sensitivity to particular fact, and whether the two systems are converging to produce a unification of substantive law.

---

[44] See Ch. 3 below.

[45] *McEntire v Crossley Bros.* [1895] AC 457, 461; *Madell v Thomas* [1891] 1 QB 230, 238.

[46] *Re Wait* [1927] 1 Ch. 606; *Leigh and Sillavan Ltd v Aliakmon Shipping Co. Ltd* [1986] AC 785.

[47] The rule has been applied in numerous commodities cases as a last ditch attempt to curb the application of the strict law on termination for breach: e.g., *Société Italo-Belge pour le Commerce et l'Industrie v Palm and Vegetable Oils (Malaysia) Sdn. Bhd.* [1981] 2 Lloyd's Rep. 695; *Peter Cremer v Granaria BV* [1981] 2 Lloyd's Rep. 583; *Bremer Handelsgesellschaft mbh v Finagrain, Cie Commerciale Agricole et Financière SA* [1981] 2 Lloyd's Rep. 259; *Bremer Handelsgesellschaft mbh v C. Mackprang Jnr.* [1979] 2 Lloyd's Rep. 221.

[48] e.g., *Sky Petroleum Ltd v VIP Petroleum Ltd* [1974] 1 WLR 576.

[49] *United States of America v Motor Trucks Ltd* [1924] AC 203; *FE Rose (London) Ltd v WH Pim Jnr. & Co. Ltd* [1953] 2 QB 450.

[50] *Stockloser v Johnson* [1954] 1 QB 476; *Barton Thompson & Co. Ltd v Stapling Machines Co.* [1966] Ch. 499; *Sport Internationaal Bussum BV v Inter-Footwear Ltd* [1984] 1 WLR 776.

[51] *United Scientific Holdings Ltd v Burnley Borough Council* [1978] AC 904; *Federal Commerce & Navigation Co. Ltd v Molena Alpha Inc.* [1978] QB 927, 974; Goodhart and Jones (1980) 43 *MLR* 489.

Law Merchant

Meaning of law merchant.   Section 62(2) explicitly incorporates the rules of the   **1.19**
law merchant. The law merchant was the source of the unpaid seller's right of
stoppage in transit[52] and it continues still to invigorate the common law.[53] The
law merchant is not, however, some body of immutable, supranational law proceeding from the will of a higher sovereign, or even an all-encompassing *opinio
juris*, but rather the sum of trade usages and customs practised from time to time
and upon which commercial parties are presumed to conduct their dealings.[54]
These are binding either as implied terms of the contract or because they colour
its interpretation; they may therefore be ousted by a contrary agreement.[55] In
modern times, the proliferation of standard-form agreements has diminished the
scope for implied terms based upon trade usage,[56] so that in a very real sense now
the law merchant is the totality of standard forms.

Inconsistency with Act.   Section 62(2) would exclude the law merchant where   **1.20**
it is inconsistent with the Act. To understand how far this reservation hampers the
law merchant, it is necessary to quantify the mandatory content of the Sale of
Goods Act. It cannot be that the law merchant is excluded every time the Act lays
down presumptive rules of agreement, for this would concede it a very small role
to the law merchant[57] and would create an inconsistency between trade usages and
other sources of express and implied terms. Since the binding force of trade usage
itself depends upon presumptive agreement, the inroads it makes into the Act are
surely as great as those made by inconsistent express and implied terms. The rules
regarding the passing of property and risk in c.i.f. contracts,[58] inconsistent with
the presumptive rules of the Act, may be regarded as binding on the parties by
virtue of either implied agreement or of trade usage.

Mandatory provisions.   But there are provisions in the Act that may not be   **1.21**
excluded by the parties. Parties may not provide for the general property in

---

    [52] *Gibson v Carruthers* (1841) 8 M & W 321; see Ch. 11 below.
    [53] Lord Devlin, *Samples of Lawmaking* (OUP, 1962), 'The Relation between Commercial Law
and Commercial Practice' (Lecture 2); L. Trakman, *The Law Merchant: The Evolution of Commercial
Law* (Fred B. Rothman & Co., 1983).
    [54] *Goodwin v Robarts* (1875) LR 10 Ex. 337; *Edelstein v Schuler & Co.* [1902] 2 KB 144. For the
requirement that custom must be reasonable, see *Produce Brokers Co. v Olympia Oil and Cake Co.*
[1916] 2 KB 296, 298.
    [55] *Palgrave, Brown & Son Ltd v SS Turid (Owners)* [1922] 1 AC 397; *Brown v Byrne* (1854) 2 E
& B 703 (reluctance to find inconsistency between established custom and bill of lading).
    [56] Lord Devlin, n. 53 above.
    [57] Since rules of presumptive agreement are particularly apparent in the area of delivery, where
trade usage is most likely to intrude, the point speaks for itself.
    [58] See, e.g., *Comptoir d'Achat et du Boerenbond Belge S/A v Luis de Ridder Lda* [1949] AC 293;
see Ch. 6 below. See generally M. Bridge, *International Sale of Goods[:] Law and Practice* (2nd edn,
OUP, 2007).

unascertained goods to pass to the buyer before the goods become ascertained;[59] any inconsistent trade usage should be excluded under section 62(2). The Act also deals with the proprietary relationship between original owner and subsequent transferee in a group of sections dealing with the rule of *nemo dat quod non habet* and its exceptions.[60] These may not be excluded by the agreement of seller and buyer. The law merchant has been relied upon in the past to extend the scope of the negotiability principle to novel types of securities.[61] Were it to manufacture new exceptions to the *nemo dat* rule, this would be in contravention of the comprehensive scheme of title resolution laid down in the Act and so could not be recognized.

Conclusion of the Contract

1.22 Scope.   This section of the chapter is devoted to certain aspects of the contractual formation process that merit attention in a specialist sale of goods text. No attempt will be made to dispose of matters that had best be left to the general contract texts. Mention will be made here of formalities and electronic commerce; of special statutory provision for abuses and potential abuses in the process of concluding a sale of goods contract, particularly in the case of distance selling; and of offer and acceptance, contractual capacity and certainty, to the extent that they are dealt with specifically in the Sale of Goods Act.

Formalities

1.23 Writing requirement.   Between 1677 and 1954, sale of goods agreements for goods exceeding £10 in value could be enforced only if they were evidenced by a note or memorandum of the agreement signed by the party against whom enforcement was sought. Two statutory exceptions to this writing requirement existed: where the buyer had actually received and accepted the goods; and where the buyer had made some advance payment.[62] These exceptions created for sale of goods contracts an extended equivalent of the equitable doctrine of part-performance applicable to contracts involving the sale of land, the existence of which was recognized by statute[63] before the writing requirement was tightened for land in such a way as to leave no room for the continuing existence of part-performance.[64]

---

[59] S. 16; see Ch. 3 below.
[60] Ss. 21–26.
[61] *Goodwin v Robarts*, n. 54 above (scrip); *Edelstein v Schuler & Co., ibid.* (bearer bonds).
[62] This provision originated as s. 17 of the Statute of Frauds 1677, 29 Car. II, cap. 3, and was re-enacted with changes as s. 4 of the Sale of Goods Act 1893.
[63] S. 40(2) of the Law of Property Act 1925.
[64] Law of Property (Miscellaneous Provisions) Act 1989.

The writing requirement for sale of goods gave rise to a body of very complex law,[65] which was severely criticized by Stephen and Pollock in one of the most polemical law review articles ever written.[66] In 1954, the need for writing was abolished by the Law Reform (Enforcement of Contracts) Act.[67] The current position, as expressed in section 4 of the Sale of Goods Act 1979, is that no formal requirements of any kind are exacted for sale of goods agreements under the Act, which may be concluded in any way that evidences the appropriate contractual intention. Section 4, however, is without prejudice to other statutes imposing formal requirements that extend to certain sale of goods agreements.

Bills of sale. Statutes imposing formal requirements on contracts of sale of goods include the Bills of Sale Acts 1878–91.[68] Briefly, these statutes promote two quite different policies: they protect needy debtors against certain types of grasping behaviour by creditors, and they supposedly protect outside creditors from the deceptive appearances created when a debtor appears to be in unencumbered possession of chattels, but in reality has signed away his rights to a particular creditor. The Bills of Sale Act 1878 applies to absolute (that is, non-security) bills of sale and deals with the second of the two policies stated above.[69] It imposes a most demanding formal and written procedure once the parties to a bill of sale have decided to reduce their agreement to writing.[70] A wide variety of document is caught by the statutory definition of a bill of sale;[71] it is by no means confined to

1.24

---

[65] The writing requirement is still in existence in a number of Commonwealth jurisdictions; see M. G. Bridge, *Sale of Goods* (Butterworths, Toronto, 1988), 75–95.

[66] (1885) 1 *LQR* 1.

[67] S. 1.

[68] Bills of Sale Act 1878; Bills of Sale Act (1878) Amendment Act 1882; Bills of Sale Act 1890; Bills of Sale Act 1891.

[69] The Bills of Sale Act (1878) Amendment Act 1882 governs security bills of sale (in effect, chattel mortgages) and pursues both policies.

[70] *Newlove v Shrewsbury* (1888) 21 QBD 41; *Charlesworth v Mills* [1892] AC 231. The Acts do not themselves demand that the agreement take a written form.

[71] Bills of sale legislation is confined in its operation to 'personal chattels' (defined in s. 4 of the Bills of Sale Act 1878). The definition of 'bill of sale' in s. 4 of the 1878 Act is a lengthy one, which, focused on the types of documents in nineteenth-century use rather than upon their defining features, is not as helpful as it ought to be in contemporary conditions:

> The expression 'bill of sale' shall include bills of sale, assignments, transfers, declarations of trust without transfer, inventories of goods with receipt thereto attached, or receipts for purchase moneys of goods, and other assurances of personal chattels, and also powers of attorney, authorities, or licenses to take possession of personal chattels as security for any debt, and also any agreement, whether intended or not to be followed by the execution of any other instrument, by which a right in equity to any personal chattels, or to any charge or security thereon, shall be conferred, but shall not include the following documents; that is to say, assignments for the benefit of the creditors of the person making or giving the same, marriage settlements, transfers or assignments of any ship or vessel or any share thereof, transfers of goods in the ordinary course of business of any trade or calling, bills of sale of goods in foreign parts or at sea, bills of lading, India warrants, warehouse-keepers' certificates, warrants or orders for the delivery of goods, or any other documents used in the

agreements that borrow the form of a sale of goods contract. The bill must set forth the consideration for which it is given and must be duly attested and registered.[72] Attestation is carried out by a solicitor who—and this has to be expressed in the attestation statement—explains the effect of the bill of sale to the grantor of the bill.[73] The bill, together with every schedule or inventory annexed to or referred to in the bill, has to be filed with the registrar[74] within seven clear working days after the grant of the bill.[75] In addition to the bill, there must be filed with the registrar: a true copy of the bill, as well as of any schedule or inventory; every attestation of the execution of the bill, together with an affidavit of the time the bill was given and of its due execution and attestation; and a description of the residence and occupation of the person giving the bill and of every attesting witness to the bill of sale. According to section 8, an unregistered bill of sale is deemed to be fraudulent and void as regards the property in or right to possession of chattels comprised in the bill of sale as against trustees in bankruptcy, sheriffs, and execution creditors. Nevertheless, the limited effect of such voidness must be appreciated. In so far as a transaction takes effect between two parties as 'a prior and independent bargain', the bill of sale itself not being a part of the bargain, the transaction will not be avoided because of the subsequent grant of a void bill of sale.[76] In modern times, there are unsurprisingly few registered absolute bills of sale and the statutory repeal of the legislation would probably leave little mark on the law.[77] In so far as registration under the 1878 Act counters the reputed ownership of the grantor of the bill of sale, the continuing existence of the Act cannot be justified after the repeal of the doctrine of reputed ownership in bankruptcy matters in the insolvency legislation of the 1980s. The Bills of Sale Act 1878 serves no worthwhile purpose and should be repealed for absolute bills of sale. Its survival may owe something to its integration with the Bills of Sale (1878) Amendment Act 1882 in governing security bills of sale. Until something can be done with security bills of sale, the 1878 Act remains of some relevance to absolute bills of sale.

---

ordinary course of business as proof of the possession or control of goods, or authorising or purporting to authorise, either by indorsement or by delivery, the possessor of such document to transfer or receive goods thereby represented . . .

The essence of a bill of sale is that it grants a property interest in 'personal chattels' and a licence to the grantee to take possession: see A. Diamond (1960) 23 *MLR* 399, 402.

[72] S. 8 of the 1878 Act.

[73] S. 10(1) of the 1878 Act.

[74] Defined in s. 11 of the 1878 Act.

[75] Registration must also be renewed at least every five years: s. 11 of the 1878 Act.

[76] *Ramsay v Margrett* [1894] 2 QB 18.

[77] The subject is dealt with in specialist texts; see especially *Halsbury's Laws of England* (4th edn., Title: 'Bills of Sale' by R. M. Goode, Butterworths, 1992). It is rare for an issue to arise concerning absolute bills of sale, but see, e.g., *Koppel v Koppel* [1966] 1 WLR 802.

Consumer credit.   Formalities are also prescribed for those sale of goods con-   **1.25**
tracts that are also regulated consumer credit agreements under the Consumer
Credit Act 1974.[78] The powers of the Secretary of State to make regulations dealing with the form and content of agreements are laid down in section 60 of the
Act. The regulations made are required to deal, *inter alia*, with the rights and
duties under the agreement, the amount and rate of the total charge for credit and
the protection and remedies available to the consumer under the Act.[79] Particular
mention is made in section 60(2) of the power to regulate the manner in which
specific information is included or excluded in documents and to ensure that
specified information is brought to the attention of the consumer.[80] Section 61 of
the Act also requires regulated agreements to be signed by the consumer and by or
on behalf of the credit provider. The document signed must contain all the terms
of the agreement, other than implied terms.[81] The consumer must also receive a
copy of the agreement when he signs it, if at that time it becomes an executed
agreement; if it is not executed at that time, then a copy of the executed agreement
must be delivered within seven days following the making of the agreement.[82]
The consumer is also entitled to be notified of his rights of cancellation and of
the manner in which they may be exercised if the agreement is a cancellable one.[83]
A failure to comply with the above requirements means that the agreement is
not properly executed, which in turn means that it may be enforced only with a
court order.[84]

Unsolicited Goods

Deemed gift of unsolicited goods.   The Unsolicited Goods and Services   **1.26**
Act 1971[85] was passed to deal with one particular abusive practice in the formation of contracts,[86] namely, the practice of inertia selling, by which goods were

---

[78] A regulated agreement is an agreement between a creditor and a debtor who is an 'individual'.
The credit supplied, if the individual is acting for business purposes, must not exceed £25,000 (ss. 8
and 16B of the Consumer Credit Act 1974). For consumers, the £25,000 upper limit was removed
with effect from 6 April 2008, but s. 16A, which came into effect on 6 April 2008, allows for regulations to be made to exclude high net worth debtors from the provisions of the Act.

[79] S. 60(1).

[80] S. 60(3). The Office of Fair Trading may waive requirements in regulations in individual cases
where compliance is impracticable and consumers are not prejudiced by the waiver: s. 60(3), (4).

[81] S. 61(1).

[82] Ss. 62–63. This is modified for cancellable agreements: s. 63(3).

[83] S. 64. The time provision is the same as under ss. 62–63. A failure to comply with the requirement of giving notice within seven days, where applicable, may be waived by the Office of Fair
Trading if regulations give the Office of Fair Trading the power to do so: s. 64(4).

[84] S. 65(1). Enforcement includes retaking goods: s. 65(2).

[85] Amended by the Unsolicited Goods and Services (Amendment) Act 1975 and partly repealed
by the Consumer Protection (Distance Selling) Regulations 2000, SI 2000 No. 2334.

[86] Other abusive practices are dealt with by the Consumer Protection from Unfair Trading
Regulations 2008, SI 2008 No. 1277 (discussed in Ch. 8 below), which repealed Part II of the Fair

sent without prior request to recipients with the accompanying information that they were to be considered sold at the stated price unless the recipients declared in time their intention not to buy the goods. There is little doubt that many recipients, whether through inertia or a less-than-perfect understanding of the principles of contract formation, paid the demanded price and kept the goods. The civil consequences of sending unsolicited goods are no longer dealt with by the 1971 Act but now come under the Consumer Protection (Distance Selling) Regulations 2000.[87] The key provision is regulation 24, which provides that, as between the sender and the unwilling recipient, the latter may 'use, deal with or dispose of the goods as if they were an unconditional gift to him'[88] and the sender's rights in the goods shall be extinguished.[89] It is not clear what the position would be if the recipient's first response is to have nothing to do with the goods and even to demand that the sender take back the goods. If the recipient has agreed to return the goods, then the civil consequences of sending unsolicited goods no longer apply.[90] In the absence of an agreement to return, the better view, given the need to protect recipients and to free them from the burden of taking legal advice, is that the recipient is free to revert to his statutory right to treat the sending of the goods as a gift. The Regulations do say that the sender's rights in the goods are extinguished, without providing that this extinguishment is conditional on the recipient choosing to treat the goods as a gift. A further difficulty is that the Regulations do not say the the goods are a gift, but rather confer upon the recipient a type of statutory immunity when using, dealing, or disposing of the goods. It does not follow that this provision would protect a donee to whom the recipient makes a gift of the goods, though a sale of the goods by the recipient might confer an effective title on the buyer outside the Regulations.[91] If the recipient were simply to abandon the goods, it is also unclear whether the sender could claim the goods as an owner with the right to immediate possession, though the apparently unconditional provision that the sender's rights in the goods are extinguished

---

Trading Act 1973, under which the Director General of Fair Trading exercised powers to combat such abuses. The list of commercial practices deemed unfair in the 2008 Regulations includes pyramid promotional schemes (Sch. 1 para. 14). Pyramid selling and other trading schemes are also the subject of regulation under the Trading Schemes Regulations 1997, SI 1997 No. 30, made under the Trading Schemes Act 1996, which amended Part XI of the Fair Trading Act 1973.

[87] SI 2000 No. 2334 (as am. by SI 2004 No. 2095 and SI 2005 No. 689).

[88] Reg. 24(2).

[89] Reg. 24(3).

[90] Reg. 24(1)(c). This would mean that the rights of the sender in the goods, previously extinguished under reg. 24(3), are revived. The revival should be prospective: an agreement to return the goods should not allow the sender to treat prior conduct of the recipient as a conversion of or trespass to the goods.

[91] Under s. 21(2)(b), an awkwardly worded provision that would protect the 'validity' of a contract of sale concluded by someone exercising a common law or statutory power of sale: see Ch. 5 below. The recipient of unsolicited goods may be treated as someone exercising a statutory power of sale so far as he acts within the immunity conferred by reg. 24(3).

seems to indicate that this is not the case. The sender would therefore have to compete with the rest of the world to acquire ownership of the goods by capture. This solution might also resolve the above problem of the donee, who could be considered as having acquired ownership by capture.

Other provisions.   Before the civil consequences laid down in regulation 24 can   **1.27**
apply, a number of conditions have to be satisfied.[92] First, the goods have to be sent with a view to the recipient acquiring them. This would protect the sender if the goods were mistakenly sent to the wrong person or to the wrong address. The recipient would need to think long and hard about treating the goods as a gift if there were a possibility, which might be based on evidence not available to the recipient, that a mistake of this kind had occurred. Secondly, the sender is protected if the recipient had no reasonable cause to believe that the goods were sent for the purpose of acquisition by a trade or business. Circumstances could arise where it is no easy matter for the recipient to read the mind of the sender.[93] Thirdly, the recipient must not have requested the goods or have agreed to return them. Finally, the Regulations make it an offence, without reasonable cause to believe there is a right to payment, to demand or claim payment, or to threaten legal or collection proceedings or place a recipient on a blacklist.[94]

Electronic Commerce

Contract formation.   With one exception, contracts concluded by electronic   **1.28**
means follow orthodox rules of contract formation, which will not be repeated here. The entry of data on a website accompanied by the selection of the appropriate box or boxes would, in an entirely orthodox way, be treated as an offer when there is a commitment being made to purchase; the operator of the website would then accept and would communicate electronically the acceptance to the person inputting the data. The provisions of the Electronic Commerce (EC Directive) Regulations 2002,[95] nevertheless, contain provisions of particular interest concerning the process of contract formation. They are designed to promote the proper functioning of the internal market to the minimum extent that intervention in this way accords with the principle of proportionality.[96] A 'service provider' providing a commercial communication as part of an 'information society

---

[92] Reg. 24(1).

[93] The burden of proof is presumably on the recipient.

[94] Reg. 24(4), (5). The same offences remain in the unrepealed s. 2 of the Unsolicited Goods and Services Act 1971 (as amended).

[95] SI 2002 No. 2013, transposing Directive 2000/31/EC of the European Parliament and of the Council on certain legal aspects of information society services, in particular electronic commerce, in the Internal Market (Directive on electronic commerce).

[96] Recital (10).

service'[97] must, *inter alia*, ensure that that communication is 'clearly identifiable as a commercial communication', 'clearly identify the person on whose behalf the commercial communication is made', and 'clearly identify as such any promotional offer (including any discount, premium or gift) and ensure that any conditions which must be met to qualify for it are easily accessible, and presented clearly and unambiguously'.[98] Furthermore, 'any unsolicited commercial communication sent by him by electronic mail' must be 'clearly and unambiguously identifiable as such as soon as it is received'.[99] In addition, a service provider is required, where a contract is to be concluded by 'electronic means', to state in 'a clear, comprehensible and unambiguous manner' the 'different technical steps to follow to conclude the contract', 'whether or not the concluded contract will be filed by the service provider and whether it will be accessible', 'the technical means for identifying and correcting input errors prior to the placing of the order',[100] and 'the languages offered for the conclusion of the contract'.[101] The Regulations also require that a service provider shall make available to the other party terms and conditions that are applicable to the contract in a way that permits that other party to store and reproduce those terms and conditions.[102] The Regulations require also a certain response to offers made to service providers, who must acknowledge receipt of the order without undue delay and by electronic means[103] and also make available 'appropriate, effective and accessible technical means' allowing the other party to identify and correct input errors prior to placing the order.[104] The order is deemed to be received when the addressee is able to access it, which is an orthodox statement of the position in general contract law, and the same goes for the 'acknowledgment of receipt', which is a communication with no special significance in

---

[97] A service provider is defined as a person providing 'information society services': reg. 2(1). There are cross-references in reg. 2(1) to EC Directives to clarify the meaning of information society services, but the key point for present purposes is that the expression includes the sale of goods online: see recital (18) of Directive 2000/31/EC, n. 95 above.

[98] Reg. 7.

[99] Reg. 8.

[100] The word 'order' in this provision, reg. 9(1)(c), means a contractual offer, but it does not have that meaning elsewhere in the Regulations (apart from reg. 11(1)(b)).

[101] Reg. 9(1) These provisions do not apply to contracts concluded by an exchange of emails or equivalent electronic communications: reg. 9(4).

[102] Reg. 9(3). There is no provision made here for an action for damages for breach of a statutory duty but an order may be sought from the court to require compliance on the part of the service provider: reg. 14.

[103] Reg. 11(1)(a).

[104] Reg. 11(1)(b). There is no provision here for an action for damages for breach of a statutory duty. The word 'order' in this provision, reg. 11(1)(b), means a contractual offer, but it does not have that meaning elsewhere in the Regulations (apart from reg. 9(1)(c)).

general contract law.[105] That acknowledgement of receipt can also be provided in the form of performance of the contract by the services provider.[106]

Remedies. An action for damages for breach of a statutory duty exists in a num- **1.29**
ber of cases in the Regulations.[107] The exception to orthodox rules of contract formation referred to above concerns a rule that, with the aid of a statutory remedy of rescission,[108] inhibits the formation of a contract concluded imperfectly by electronic means. As stated above, regulation 11(1)(b) states that a service provider must make available to the other party 'appropriate, effective and accessible technical means allowing him to identify and correct input errors prior to the placing of the order'. If the service provider fails to comply with regulation 11(1)(b), persons entering into a contract with the service provider are entitled to rescind the contract, subject to the discretion of the court that rescission should not be allowed.[109] The Regulations do not define 'rescission' but the mischief behind the provisions in question points strongly to a treatment of the contract as though it had never been made.

Auctions

Formation principles. Although Part II of the Sale of Goods Act is entitled **1.30**
'Formation of the Contract', the only provision dealing with the formation of contracts,[110] section 57 on auction sales, is located elsewhere in the Act. Section 57(2), in providing that the contract is concluded when the auctioneer announces this by the fall of the hammer or in some other customary way, codifies one of the earliest common law rules on contract formation.[111] The bidder consequently makes the offer which, in accordance with ordinary contract principle, the auctioneer is free to accept or refuse.[112] The contract concluded in this way relates to the particular lot announced to be the subject of the bidding, unless this

---

[105] Reg. 11(2)(a).

[106] Reg. 11(2)(b). The provisions of reg. 11 do not apply to contracts concluded by an exchange of emails or equivalent communications: reg. 11(3). Parties who are not consumers may exclude the operation of reg. 11: reg. 11(1).

[107] Reg. 13. The relevant provisions mentioned above are regs 7, 8, 9(1), and 11(1)(a).

[108] Cf cases of cancellation in consumer cases, discussed below.

[109] Reg. 15. This is not unlike the discretion to declare a contract subsisting in s. 2(2) of the Misrepresentation Act 1967; see Ch. 8 below.

[110] There is arguably another provision, s. 2(3), which provides that a contract of sale may be absolute or conditional. The occurrence of a condition may arrest the conclusion of a contract; see Ch. 2 below.

[111] See *Payne v Cave* (1789) 3 TR 148. On auction sales generally, see F. Meisel and B. W. Harvey, *Law and Practice of Auctions* (3rd edn, OUP, 2006).

[112] *British Car Auctions v Wright* [1972] 3 All ER 462. In so-called 'Dutch' auctions, the auctioneer announces the price for which he is willing to sell, starting high and continuing in a downwards direction until someone is prepared to buy at the stated price. The auctioneer is thus making an offer and the successful bidder an acceptance.

presumptive rule is displaced in the circumstances.[113] There is an exception to the binding nature of a contract concluded by the auctioneer's announcement. It arises where bidders have been notified that the auction is subject to a reserve or upset price.[114] If a sale is announced by the auctioneer below this price, it has been held[115] that an auctioneer refusing to complete the contract in these circumstances may not be sued by the successful bidder for breach of his warranty of authority.[116] The auctioneer also clearly lacks the actual authority to bind the principal. Furthermore, having notified the reserve price, the auctioneer cannot bind the principal on the ground of apparent authority.

1.31 **Seller's right to bid.** Besides an auction being notified as subject to a reserve or upset price, it may also be notified as subject to a right to bid by or on behalf of the seller.[117] Where a right to bid is thus reserved, the seller, or any single person in his stead, is entitled to bid at the auction.[118] If no such notification is made, it is unlawful for the seller to bid or to employ someone else to bid.[119] An auctioneer, moreover, who knowingly takes such a bid also acts unlawfully.[120] The Act goes on to provide that a sale concluded after an unlawful bid may be treated as fraudulent by the buyer.[121]

1.32 **Reserve price.** A number of questions about reserve prices and rights to bid arise under the Sale of Goods Act. First, it is not clear from the Act what the position is where a reserve price has not been notified but the auctioneer withdraws the goods. The Act does not as such say that withdrawal of the goods is wrongful. Nevertheless, it has been held that the auctioneer is liable on a collateral contract to sell to the highest bidder. The consideration for the auctioneer's promise to sell to the highest bidder may be seen in the detriment incurred by an offeror making a bid that was liable to be accepted, or in the benefit accruing to the auctioneer of increased attendance at the auction.[122] The same collateral contract liability should arise where the goods are knocked down to the seller or his agent.[123] Section 57(2), in accordance with normal contract principle, states that the contract of sale is concluded on the fall of the hammer or in some other customary manner, but this

---

[113] S. 57(1).
[114] S. 57(3).
[115] In *McManus v Fortescue* [1907] 2 KB 1.
[116] Under the rule in *Collen v Wright* (1857) 8 E & B 647.
[117] S. 57(3). The right to bid must be 'reserved expressly'.
[118] S. 57(6).
[119] S. 57(4).
[120] *Ibid.*
[121] S. 57(5).
[122] *Barry v Davies* [2000] 1 WLR 1962, following *Warlow v Harrison* (1859) 1 E & B 309. The award of damages is on the same market basis as an award against a non-delivering seller: *Barry v Davies*, above, 1969.
[123] *Warlow v Harrison*, n. 122 above.

provision does not affect the collateral contract claim. Secondly, where an auction is not subject to reserve, the Act does not provide for all consequences of an unlawful bid being made by or on behalf of the seller or knowingly accepted by the auctioneer. The Act does deal with the case of the successful bidder, but does not deal with other disappointed bidders. Since they will have been outbid by the successful bidder, they would seem not to have suffered any loss as a result of any breach by the auctioneer of a collateral undertaking to sell to the highest bidder.[124] Thirdly, whilst the successful bidder may treat the 'sale' as fraudulent when an unlawful bid has been made,[125] there is some doubt whether 'sale' should be understood in the same way as it is elsewhere in the Act, where it is distinguished from an 'agreement to sell'.[126] Common sense would require 'sale' to be read broadly to include also contracts of sale so that the seller could not recover damages from a non-accepting buyer who has made a successful bid.[127] Fourthly, although the successful bidder should be able to rescind the contract of sale for fraud, after an unlawful bid, in accordance with the limits imposed for rescission in fraud cases, the question of damages is not so easy where, for example, the buyer has lost the right to rescind. Presumably, damages would lie in the tort of deceit against the seller, but it is not clear whether only the seller would be liable or whether the auctioneer would also be liable, with joint and several liability between the two. Section 57(5) deems the sale to be fraudulent and not the behaviour of those acting unlawfully in making or permitting bids when the auction is conducted. The auctioneer is not a party to the contract of sale.[128] Although section 57(5) as such may not impose liability on the auctioneer, the auctioneer's conduct may be fraudulent at common law. Where damages are awarded, they should be on the normal fraud scale, which is for all direct losses arising out of entry into the contract.[129]

---

[124] It does not follow that a collateral contract to sell to the highest bidder is made only with the person who turns out to be the highest bidder.

[125] S. 57(4), (5).

[126] See s. 2(4). It is likely that an agreement to sell exists, where payment has not yet been made, because of an intention that the property shall pass only upon payment.

[127] It would make little sense to require the buyer to pay before taking proceedings.

[128] For other legislation on abusive auction practices, see the Mock Auctions Act 1961 (criminal penalties) and the Auctions (Bidding Agreements) Acts of 1927 and 1969 (bidding rings). Under s. 3 of the 1969 Act, a seller may avoid the contract of sale where there has been a bidding agreement, involving at least one dealer (who need not be the person making the successful bid), by which one or more parties to the agreement undertake not to bid. If restitution of the goods is not made to the seller, then all parties to the bidding agreement are jointly and severally liable to the seller for loss caused by the operation of the bidding agreement.

[129] See Ch. 8 below.

Cancellation of the Contract and Early Termination

1.33 **Consumer credit transactions.** For regulated conditional sales, as well as for other regulated agreements, the Consumer Credit Act grants rights of cancellation (or cooling-off) in certain circumstances,[130] a subject dealt with also by the Consumer Protection (Distance Selling Regulations) 2000.[131] Under the Act, where an agreement is cancellable, the consumer has a cooling-off period of five days[132] from the delivery to him of a copy of the unexecuted agreement or notice to him of the existence of rights of cancellation. For practical purposes, these two starting points are the same, since an improperly executed agreement, which would include one that did not give notice of cancellation rights, is not enforceable against the consumer.[133] For transactions involving goods, a cancellable agreement is one where antecedent negotiations include oral representations made in the presence of the consumer by the negotiator (typically, a dealer under a three-party conditional sale arrangement) or an agent of the negotiator, and the unexecuted agreement is signed by the consumer at the premises of the other party or of a negotiator.[134] Cancelling the agreement means that the agreement never was concluded.[135] The effect of cancellation is that money paid by the consumer and credit advanced to the consumer are recoverable.[136] The consumer entitled to the recovery of money paid has a lien on any goods supplied until repaid,[137] but in the meantime has a duty to take reasonable care of the goods.[138] The consumer's duty to restore the goods is to do so at his own premises,[139] though he may undertake to have them transported elsewhere.[140] If the consumer has traded in goods by way of part-exchange allowance, he is entitled to recover the allowance unless the part-exchange goods are returned to him in substantially the same condition within ten days of the date of cancellation.[141] Where credit has already been advanced to the

---

130 Ss. 67–73.

131 SI 2000 No. 2334 (as am. by SI 2004 No. 2095 and SI 2005 No. 689). See generally G. G. Howells and S. Weatherill, *Consumer Protection Law* (2nd edn, Ashgate, 2005); J. K. Macleod, *Consumer Sales Law* (2nd edn., Routledge-Cavendish, 2007), Ch. 8.

132 In special cases, 14 days: ss. 64(4), 68(b).

133 Ss. 64(1), 65.

134 S. 67. If the consumer is still in possession of goods under the cancelled agreement, he has a lien on those goods pending receipt of the part-exchange goods or of the part-exchange allowance: s. 73(5). If it has not already done so, title to the part-exchange goods vests in the negotiator when the consumer is paid the part-exchange allowance: s. 73(6).

135 Subject to contrary provision in the Act: s. 69(4). Where goods are supplied on an emergency basis or worked by the consumer into land so as to become fixtures, it is only the credit aspect of the transaction that is cancelled: s. 69(2).

136 Ss. 70–71.

137 S. 70(2).

138 S. 72(4). A failure to perform this duty is actionable as a breach of statutory duty: s. 72(11).

139 S. 72(5).

140 S. 72(6).

141 S. 73(2).

consumer, the agreement remains in force for the repayment of that sum with interest,[142] except that the consumer is free from having to pay any interest if he repays the advance within one month of serving the notice of cancellation.[143]

Distance selling. The Consumer Protection (Distance Selling) Regulations **1.34** 2000[144] transpose an EC Directive on the protection of consumers in respect of distant transactions.[145] In respect of goods, the Regulations apply to contracts for the supply of goods[146] to a consumer[147] made under an organized distance sales scheme by a supplier[148] who uses exclusively one or more means of distance communication.[149] Apart from exceptional cases,[150] consumers have a right to cancel sale of goods contracts.[151] The period in the standard case runs for seven working days beginning with the day after the day the consumer receives the goods,[152] but it depends on the supplier complying with the requirement that stipulated information, which includes information about cancellation rights,[153] be given to the consumer either prior to the contract or in good time and before delivery.[154] Otherwise, if the information is provided within the three months beginning on

---

[142] S. 71(1).

[143] S. 71(2).

[144] N. 131 above. So far as contract terms are inconsistent with the protection given to the consumer by the Regulations, they are void: reg. 25.

[145] Directive 97/7/EC of the European Parliament and the Council of 20 May 1997 (OJ No. L144 of 4.6.97, p 19). The Regulations do not transpose Art. 10 of that Directive. The Directive in earlier drafts may be seen at [1992] OJ C156/14 and [1993] OJ C308/18, and the Commission Recommendation at [1992] OJ L156/21.

[146] There are exempt transactions, but the only relevant transactions for the purposes of this book are auction sales, sales conducted through a public payphone, and sales made through an automated vending machine or premises: reg 5(1).

[147] Defined as 'any natural person who, in contracts to which these Regulations apply, is acting for purposes which are outside his business': reg. 3. A business is defined as including a trade or profession: *ibid.*

[148] The supplier must act in a commercial or professional capacity: reg. 3 ('supplier').

[149] Regs 3–4. Distance communication is any means that does not require the simultaneous presence of the supplier and the consumer: reg. 3. An indicative list of means of distance communication is contained in Sch. 1 to the Regulations.

[150] Reg. 13 (exceptions to the right to cancel). The sale of goods cases included here are sales of goods that are perishable or personalized for the buyer or made to the buyer's specifications; sales of newspapers, periodicals, or magazines; sales of audio or video recordings or of computer software if they are unsealed by the consumer; and sales where the price depends on fluctuations in the financial markets not controlled by the supplier. The reference to financial markets points to 'goods' having a broader meaning than it does in English law under the Sale of Goods Act 1979 (cf *R (on the application of Khatun) v Newham LBC* [2005] EWCA Civ 55; [2005] QB 37). The Regulations also provide that they are only partly applicable to certain contracts (regs. 7–20 are disapplied), including contracts for the supply of food, beverages, and other goods intended for everyday consumption, supplied by regular roundsmen to the consumer's residence or workplace: reg. 6.

[151] The method of giving the notice is dealt with by reg. 10.

[152] Reg. 11(2), referring back to reg. 8.

[153] The information has to be supplied in writing or another durable medium available and accessible to the consumer: reg. 8(1). See also reg. 11(3).

[154] Reg. 8(1).

the day after the consumer receives the goods, the seven-day cancellation period starts on the day following the consumer's receipt of the information.[155] Where neither of the two above periods apply, the period ends three months and seven working days after the day on which the consumer receives the goods.[156] The information referred to above relates first of all to the right of cancellation, and concerns the conditions and procedures for exercising the right of cancellation, including notification of the consumer's duty to return the goods where a term of the contract so requires and information about whether it is the consumer or the supplier who under the Regulations bears the cost of recovering the goods or returning them to the supplier.[157] In addition, the running of the cancellation period depends upon the supply of information concerning the geographical address of the supplier's place of business to which complaints should be made, after-sales services and guarantees and, for contracts of more than one year's duration or of unspecified duration, the conditions governing the right of cancellation.[158] There is also a requirement under the Regulations that other information be provided in the case of distance contracts,[159] but the failure to give this information does not govern the exercise of cancellation rights.[160]

1.35 **Distance selling: effects of cancellation.** The effects of cancellation under the Regulations bear some resemblance to the effects of cancellation under the

---

[155] Reg. 11(3).

[156] Reg. 11(4). Since none of the three cancellation periods starts with or depends in any way upon the date of conclusion of the contract, it seems impossible to make sense of reg. 11(1): '... [T]he cancellation period in the case of contracts for the supply of goods begins with the day on which the contract is concluded and ends as provided for in paragraphs (2) to (5).' Where the goods are received by a third party, the third party's receipt of the goods is deemed to be the consumer's receipt in paras (2) to (4): reg. 11(5).

[157] Regs 7(a)(vi) and 8(2)(b).

[158] Reg. 8(2)(c)–(e). Cancellation under reg. 8(2)(e) seems to be used in a different sense to mean termination.

[159] This information, to be supplied either prior to the contract or in good time and before delivery, comprises information concerning: the identity of the supplier and, if payment is made in advance, the address of the supplier; a description of the main characteristics of the goods; the price of the goods; delivery costs; arrangements for payment, delivery or performance; the cost of using means of distance communication; the period for which the offer or price remains valid; where appropriate, the minimum duration of the contract; and the intention, if it exists, to supply substitute goods if the designated goods are unavailable and to bear the cost of that substitution: reg. 7(1). The information must be 'clear and comprehensible', due regard being had to 'the principle of goods faith in commercial transactions and the principles governing the protection of those who are unable to give their consent such as minors': reg. 7(2). The supplier's commercial purpose should be made clear: reg. 7(3). A supplier making a telephone communication should also make its identity and commercial purpose clear at the beginning of the call: reg. 11(4) (e.g., 'I want to sell you double-glazing', not 'I want to interest you in energy savings').

[160] The Regulations do not create an offence for failing to supply this information, but provision is made for complaints to enforcement authorities and for the seeking of injunctions to prevent breaches of the Regulations: regs 26–27. Provision is also made for the giving of undertakings in lieu of injunctions: regs 28–29.

Consumer Credit Act 1974. First of all, the contract is generally treated as if it had not been made.[161] The supplier must return moneys paid no later than thirty days from the beginning of the day on which notice of cancellation was given,[162] though the supplier may levy a charge for the return of the goods where the cost of this should have been but was not borne by the consumer.[163] Cancellation of the supply contract entails also cancellation of a related credit agreement.[164] The consumer on cancellation is bound to restore the goods; during the period that the goods were in his possession, he is deemed to have been bound to retain in his possession and take reasonable care of them.[165] The consumer's duty to deliver the goods is a duty to make them available at his own premises and his duty to take reasonable care ceases after the twenty-one days following the date on which notice of cancellation was given if he receives no request to make the goods available.[166] If the consumer was bound to return the goods and not just to make them available, the twenty-one-day period becomes a six-month period.[167] A consumer who fails to comply with his obligations concerning the restitution or return of the goods is liable to an action for breach of statutory duty.[168] If the consumer has provided goods in part-exchange, these must be returned to him within ten days starting from the date of cancellation, unless the consumer is to recover instead the part-exchange allowance.[169] Upon receipt of the allowance, title to the goods vests in the supplier if it has not already done so.[170]

Doorstep sales. Doorstep selling is a practice that can give rise to abuses taking **1.36** the form of denial of choice and harassment in the formation of contracts. For some years after the Consumer Credit Act 1974 was enacted, with its introduction of cancellation rights for regulated consumer credit agreements, no legislation provided cancellation rights for sales that lacked a credit element. This omission was rectified by the Consumer Protection (Cancellation of Contracts Concluded away from Business Premises) Regulations 1987,[171] which adopted an

---

[161] Reg. 10(2).

[162] Reg. 14(1), (3) (return of moneys paid by or on behalf of the consumer).

[163] Reg. 14(5), except where the consumer exercises a right to reject the goods under, e.g., s. 14 of the Sale of Goods Act: reg. 14(6), or where the term requiring the consumer to return the goods is an unfair term under the Unfair Terms in Consumer Contracts Regulations 1999, SI 1999 No. 2083.

[164] Reg. 15. For the repayment of credit and interest after the cancellation of a related credit agreement, see reg. 16.

[165] Reg. 17(2), (3). The consumer's obligations are discharged if he sends or delivers the goods the goods to a person to whom he could have given a cancellation notice (reg. 17(5)), whereupon his obligation of reasonable care ceases (reg. 17(6)).

[166] Reg. 17(4), (7).

[167] Reg. 17(8).

[168] Reg. 17(10).

[169] Reg. 18(2).

[170] Reg. 18(4).

[171] SI 1987 No. 2117, am. by SI 1988 No. 958 and SI 1998 No. 3050.

EEC Directive to protect consumers in respect of contracts negotiated away from business premises.[172] The Regulations apply to contracts for the supply of goods or services between a consumer[173] and a trader[174] made in any one of four cases: during an unsolicited visit[175] made by a trader to the home of the consumer or another person or to the consumer's place of work; during a visit by a trader at the consumer's express request where the goods or services are different from those for which the consumer requested the visit and the consumer could not reasonably have known that the supply of those other goods or services formed part of the trader's business activities; during an excursion organized by the trader away from his business premises; after the consumer has made an offer to purchase goods or services in any one of the three preceding cases.[176] Where the Regulations apply,[177] a contract may not be enforced against a consumer unless a written notice of cancellation rights with additional information and a cancellation form is delivered to the consumer,[178] who, within seven days of the making the contract, may serve a notice of cancellation on the trader or other person identified in the trader's written notice.[179] A contract term inconsistent with a provision in the Regulations for the protection of consumers is void.[180] The Regulations also contain a number of offences, liabilities, and defences.[181]

1.37 **Doorstep selling: effects of cancellation.**   A contract that is cancelled is deemed never to have been concluded.[182] So far as sale of goods contracts are concerned, the consumer is entitled to recover money that has been paid and has a lien over

---

[172] Council Directive 85/577/EEC of 20 December 1985, [1985] OJ L372/31.

[173] Reg. 2: "'consumer" means a person, other than a body corporate, who, in making a contract to which these Regulations apply, is acting for purposes which can be regarded as outside his business.'

[174] Reg. 2: "'trader" means a person who, in making a contract to which these Regulations apply, is acting for the purposes of his business, and anyone acting in the name or on behalf of such a person.'

[175] Defined in reg. 3(3).

[176] Reg. 3.

[177] Certain contracts are excepted, including contracts for the supply of food, drink, and other consumables supplied by regular roundsmen; contracts for the sale of goods in a catalogue readily available before the contract and containing a prominent notice of cancellation rights; and contracts where the payments are low (£35): reg. 3(2).

[178] Reg. 4(1). The notice must be delivered when the contract is made or the consumer makes the offer, as the case may be: reg. 4(4). In addition to a statement that the consumer has a right of cancellation, the information required comprises the name of the trader, the trader's reference number, code or other details, the name and address of the person to whom notice of cancellation must be given, and a statement that the consumer may use the cancellation form if he wishes.

[179] Reg. 4(5).

[180] Reg. 10.

[181] Regs.4A–4H.

[182] Reg. 4(6) (subject to exceptions in the Regulations).

goods supplied for the recovery of the money.[183] With certain exceptions,[184] the consumer is under a duty to restore those goods.[185] Restoration means making the goods available at the consumer's premises further to the trader's written request,[186] though the consumer may instead return the goods.[187] Until restoration or return occurs, the consumer is under a duty to take reasonable care of the goods[188] and is liable for breach of statutory duty if he does not do so.[189] If the trader has taken part-exchange goods, these must be returned in substantially the same condition within ten days running from the date of cancellation or else the consumer is entitled to recover from the trader the part-exchange allowance.

Early termination.   Consumers have statutory rights to terminate ahead of time   **1.38** certain types of regulated agreements under the Consumer Credit Act 1974, including conditional sale contracts.[190] The consumer may terminate the contract with prospective effect at any time before the final payment falls due,[191] except where title to the goods has been transferred to someone other than the debtor under the regulated agreement.[192] Upon early termination, the consumer must pay the amount by which one half of the total price exceeds the aggregate of moneys due and paid immediately before termination, unless the contract calls for a lesser sum to be paid or makes no provision for payment at all.[193]

Capacity

Scope.   Part II of the Sale of Goods Act contains limited provision on contractual   **1.39** capacity. It has nothing to say about corporate capacity.[194] Section 3 deals only with the purchase of 'necessaries', leaving all other matters arising in connection with

---

[183] Reg. 5. The consumer also has a lien over the goods for the return of part-exchange goods or the payment of the part-exchange allowance: reg. 8(3).

[184] Reg. 7(2) (perishable goods; consumable goods that are consumed prior to cancellation; goods supplied to meet an emergency; goods that have become fixtures or accessions).

[185] Reg. 7(1).

[186] Reg. 7(3).

[187] Reg. 7(4).

[188] Reg. 7(1), (5). The duty of reasonable care runs for twenty-one days after the cancellation, unless within that time the trader serves a request in writing for the restoration of the goods: reg. 7(6).

[189] Reg. 7(8).

[190] Termination statements are dealt with by s. 103.

[191] S. 99(1), (2). The property in the goods thereupon immediately revests in the previous owner: s. 99(5).

[192] S. 99(4).

[193] S. 100(1). The court, moreover, may require a lesser amount to be paid if satisfied that the loss caused to the creditor by early termination is less than the amount payable under s. 100(1): s. 100(3). A greater amount may be payable by a debtor who has failed to take reasonable care of the goods: s. 100(4).

[194] See *Palmer's Company Law* (ed. by G. K. Morse, Sweet & Maxwell, looseleaf), i, Pts 2–3.

capacity to buy and sell and matters of property to the general law.[195] Section 3 applies only to minors and persons who are not competent to contract as a result of drunkenness.[196] A minor is someone who has not yet attained the age of 18.[197] According to section 3(2), the incapacitated person must pay a reasonable price for necessaries that are sold and delivered. This raises three major points. First, 'necessaries' are defined in general terms by section 3(3) as 'goods suitable both to the condition in life of the minor' or other incapacitated person and to his actual requirements at the time of the sale and delivery. The definition has been particularly hard to apply in the case of minors. The question whether goods are necessaries is a mixed question of law and fact, so that there must be some evidence on which a finding to that effect can be made.[198] It is the seller who carries the burden of proving that the goods are necessaries[199] and, given the nature of the test, it will often be a difficult burden to discharge. The seller will have to show that the goods are necessaries, having regard not only to the condition in life of the minor, but also to the minor's existing provision of goods of that kind.[200]

1.40 **Common law cases.**   Secondly, section 3(2) applies only to necessaries 'sold and delivered'. Where the goods have not yet been delivered, or have been delivered but the property has not yet passed to the buyer, the common law applies and does not give a clear answer to the question whether either or both of the seller and buyer are bound.[201] Since the minor lacks capacity to contract,[202] there is no reason to give the protection of a binding contract to a seller who can help himself by refusing to deliver, or by taking proceedings for the recovery of goods, in which he has reserved the general property, against a minor unlawfully retaining possession.

---

[195] See the standard contract texts.

[196] Section 3(2) formerly applied also to mental incapacity. The same rule is now to be found in the Mental Capacity Act 2005, s. 7(1). According to s. 2(1), 'a person lacks capacity in relation to a matter if at the material time he is unable to make a decision for himself in relation to the matter because of an impairment of, or a disturbance in the functioning of, the mind or brain'.

[197] The Family Law Reform Act 1969 reduced the age from 21 and so, to a large extent, eliminated the problem of minors' contracts.

[198] *Ryder v Wombwell* (1868) LR 4 Ex. 32.

[199] *Ibid.*; *Nash v Inman* [1908] 2 KB 1.

[200] *Nash v Inman*, n. 199 above. For the difficulties of a seller who lacks knowledge, see *Johnstone v Marks* (1887) 19 QBD 509. For details of nineteenth-century case law showing the consumer needs of sons of the nobility, see G. H. Treitel, *The Law of Contract* (12th edn by E. Peel, Sweet & Maxwell, 2007), 568–9.

[201] See *Nash v Inman*, n. 199 above; *Roberts v Gray* [1913] 1 KB 520 (services). But an incapacitated person able to show that he did not understand what he was doing may at his option avoid the contract: *Hart v O'Connor* [1985] AC 1000.

[202] The position of mentally incapable buyers is different. If the seller is unaware of the mental disorder, he need not rely upon s. 3 but may enforce the contract at common law: *Baxter v Portsmouth* (1826) 5 B & C 170. Otherwise, the contract may be avoided by the mentally incapable party: *Imperial Loan Co. v Stone* [1892] 1 QB 599. A drunkard is liable on a contract at common law unless his condition is so extreme as to be known to the other party: *Gore v Gibson* (1843) 13 M & W 623.

Nor is there any reason to give the minor a right to compel further performance of the contract by demanding that the seller deliver the goods or convey the property in them. Thirdly, the contractual price is displaced by the reference to a reasonable price. That is consistent with the price recoverable on a restitutionary basis under the old count of goods sold and delivered.[203] It is not necessarily predicated upon a binding contract. Section 3(2) does not include the count of goods bargained and sold, applicable where the property had passed but delivery had not yet been made. A seller dealing with a minor in these circumstances is protected by the unpaid seller's right of retention in section 39 and the right of resale in section 48. Such a seller does not need the protection of a personal action as well. Section 3 can therefore be rationalized as minimal legislative intervention designed to avert an unjustified enrichment of the minor. It would take a modern rationalization of the law to interpret it as a partial codification of the law dealing with the enforcement of contracts against minors.

Unstated Price

General.   Section 8(1) of the Sale of Goods Act, after making the uncontrover-   **1.41**
sial point that the parties are at liberty to settle the price in the contract, goes on to say that it 'may be left to be fixed in a manner agreed by the contract, or may be determined by the course of dealing between the parties'.[204] Section 8(2) then states that the buyer must pay a reasonable price[205] where 'the price is not determined as mentioned in sub-section (1)'. There is an ambiguity at the heart of this provision which captures the difficulty of knowing how far the law is prepared to go in enforcing uncertain contracts for the sale of goods. The question is whether the word 'determined' is to be read as 'actually determined' or as 'to be determined'. If it is the former, then section 8(2) is literally capable of application to cases where the parties have prescribed a method of determining the price,[206] but for one reason or another the agreed machinery has broken down. If section 8(2) bears the latter meaning, however, it will apply only where the contract fails to create machinery for establishing the price. It will thus certainly apply where the contract says nothing at all about the price; arguably, it will also apply where the price is indirectly described in terms of a current or future standard that is treated

---

203 Discussed in the context of contractual certainty, text accompanying nn. 208–13 below.

204 If the contract gives the seller a discretion to settle the price, that discretion is not unconfined. In a case dealing with the sale of financial assets by the seller upon default by the buyer, *Socimer International Bank Ltd v Standard Bank London Ltd* [2008] EWCA Civ 116; [2008] 1 Lloyd's Rep. 558, Rix LJ said at [66]: '[A] decision maker's discretion will be limited, as a matter of necessary implication, by matters of honesty, good faith and genuineness, and the need for the absence of arbitrariness, capriciousness, perversity and irrationality.' This obligation fell short of an objective valuation of the assets.

205 Defined in the usual way in s. 8(3) as dependent upon the particular circumstances.

206 With the exception of the particular method dealt with by s. 9.

as though it were self-executing, such as a 'fair price' or a 'reasonable price'. As the law has developed, it seems likely that the former approach is correct, at least to the extent that the contractual relations of the parties are well enough defined for there to be a binding contract at common law to which section 8(2) can apply.[207]

1.42 **Executed and executory contracts.** Section 8(2) was codified on the basis of a number of nineteenth-century authorities where nothing was said about the price.[208] In most of these decisions, the seller's consideration had actually been executed, by delivery of the goods to the buyer or to an agent of the buyer, such as a carrier. Where this had occurred, it was not necessary to assess the buyer's liability in terms of any special or express contract between them. Indeed, it could be assumed that there was no special contract to embarrass resolution of the matter, which was handled off the contract in the *indebitatus* count of goods sold and delivered. The buyer was rendered liable in a price action, and an amount was adjudged owing that was the reasonable, fair, or market value of the goods at the time of their delivery.[209] So far, this line of development would not extend to cases where the seller wished to pursue a damages action for non-acceptance under an executory contract. This decisive step was taken in *Hoadly v M'Laine*,[210] where a carriage was manufactured to the buyer's specifications[211] and the buyer held liable, on the basis of the reasonable value of the carriage, in a damages action.[212] Doubts have nevertheless been expressed in Australia in modern times about whether section 8(2) should apply to executory contracts.[213]

1.43 **Non-price items.** Section 8 deals with only one source of uncertainty in a sale of goods contract, the amount of the price. It does not deal with elements such as the amounts of delivery and payment that have to be made under an instalment contract, or the time and place of delivery,[214] which are left to the common law.[215]

---

[207] A problem of an obvious chicken-and-egg character raised in *May & Butcher Ltd v The King* (1929) [1934] 2 KB 17 note.

[208] See in particular *Valpy v Gibson* (1847) 4 CB 837; *Acebal v Levy* (1834) 10 Bing. 376.

[209] See text preceding n. 207 above.

[210] (1834) 10 Bing. 482.

[211] And was thus not a standard market item where the seller might have been expected to find another buyer.

[212] Carrying the law beyond the more restrictive statements in *Acebal v Levy*, n. 208 above, 382, by Tindal CJ, who also gave the judgment in *Hoadly v M'Laine*, n. 210 above.

[213] *Hall v Busst* (1960) 104 CLR 206, 233–4 (Menzies J). Menzies J was prepared to distinguish *Hoadly* as a work and materials contract, so that the buyer would be liable in a restitutionary *quantum meruit* action for a reasonable price on completion of the work. Windeyer J, dissenting on a different point in *Hall v Busst*, supported *Hoadly* and the reading it directed of s. 8(2). To this effect, see also *Wenning v Robinson* (1964) 64 SR(NSW) 157; *Montana Mustard Seed Co. v Gates* (1963) 42 WWR 303 (Can.).

[214] See, e.g., *Hillas & Co. Ltd v Arcos Ltd* (1932) 147 LT 503; *Custom Motors Ltd v Dwinell* (1975) 61 DLR (3d) 342.

[215] See the general contract texts.

The prevailing approach is for the courts to strive for the enforcement of agreements, on the ground that a transaction intended to be binding should as far as possible be upheld: *verba sunt intelligenda ut res magis valeat quam pereat*.[216] They are particularly likely to adopt this attitude in the case of 'mutual dealings arising out of a specialist trade'.[217] In additon, the old distinction between executory and executed contracts survives to the extent that a greater judicial willingness to enforce an incomplete agreement is likely to be presented in executed consideration cases,[218] if only because the prejudice suffered by the claimant if the defendant is released from his undertaking will probably be greater in such a case.[219] A court is likely to enforce a contract even if sense cannot be made of one of its terms, if that term is plainly unimportant or meaningless,[220] but will not thus intervene if the term is important and sense cannot be made of it,[221] or if a particular method of valuation chosen by the parties has broken down and was not necessarily designed to produce the fair or reasonable price that would be reached by the trier of fact.[222]

Agreements to agree. One particular stumbling block to enforcement in the **1.44** past has been the assertion that the courts will not intervene where the price is to be settled by the parties themselves at a future date, on the ground that an agreement to agree is not a contract known to law.[223] In some cases, there may be a binding agreement even though something is left to be agreed between the parties in the future. In one case, an agreement where the quantity of goods was left to

216 *Hillas & Co. Ltd v Arcos Ltd*, n. 214 above; *Pagnan SpA v Feed Products Ltd* [1987] 2 Lloyd's Rep. 601 (Bingham J); *Mamidoil-Jetoil Greek Petroleum Co SA v Okta Crude Oil Refinery (No. 1)* [2001] EWCA Civ 406; [2001] 2 Lloyd's Rep 76 (where the authorities are reviewed in detail). See also *iSoft Group plc v Misys Holdings Ltd* [2002] EWHC 2094 (Ch) at [72]–[80]; *Northern Foods Ltd v Focal Foods Ltd* [2001] EWCA Civ 1262.
217 *iSoft Group plc v Misys Holdings Ltd* [2003] EWCA Civ 229 at [43] (Buxton LJ).
218 *British Bank for Foreign Trade v Novinex Ltd* [1949] 1 KB 623.
219 *Foley v Classique Coaches Ltd* [1934] 2 KB 1; *Mack & Edwards (Sales) Ltd v McPhail Bros* (1968) 112 SJ 211.
220 e.g., *Nicolene Ltd v Simmonds* [1953] 1 QB 543 ('the usual conditions of acceptance apply').
221 e.g., *Scammell v Ouston* [1941] AC 251 ('balance of purchase price can be had on hire purchase terms').
222 See, e.g., *Re Nudgee Bakery Pty Ltd's Agreement* [1971] Qd. R 24, where a five-year contract for flour requirements prescribed payment at the maximum level permitted by a regulatory contract without providing for the case where the statute was repealed. Also *Kidston v Sterling and Pitcairn Ltd* (1920) 61 SCR 193 (Can: parties could not agree on what they meant by 'market price' in seven-year supply contract, except that it did not mean the market price).
223 *May & Butcher Ltd v The King*, n. 207 above. See also *Courtney and Fairbairn Ltd v Tolaini Bros. (Hotels) Ltd* [1975] 1 WLR 297. *May & Butcher* was distinguished in a case involving a lease with an option to purchase the reversion at a price to be agreed, not by the parties themselves, but by valuers appointed by each of the parties: *Sudbrook Trading Estate Ltd v Eggleton* [1983] 1 AC 444; see also *Queensland Electricity Generating Board v New Hope Collieries Pty Ltd* [1989] 1 Lloyd's Rep. 205.

future agreement was upheld as a binding contract.[224] The prohibition on enforcing an agreement to agree is a shibboleth that should not command unswerving support in a modern and flexible law of contract. This is particularly so where the parties intend to be contractually bound on terms that are fair and reasonable[225] and the consequences of holding otherwise would be unduly prejudicial to one of them,[226] or where they are dealing at arm's length in goods that are traded on a market, so that they may be presumed likely to arrive in any event at a price directed by market forces. According to Rix LJ in *Mamidoil-Jetoil Greek Petroleum Co SA v Okta Crude Oil Refinery (No. 1)*:

> There is, in my view, implicit support here for the doctrine that in a commercial contract, which, when dealing with the future and sometimes the long-term future of necessity leaves certain matters such as price to be worked out over time, an arbitration clause assists the Court to find sufficient certainty by means of the implication of what is reasonable. Which is not to say, that the Court will not itself provide the dispute resolution machinery, even in the absence of an arbitration clause.[227]

Furthermore, the *May & Butcher* objection that section 8(2) of the Sale of Goods Act is brought into play only when an agreement passes the test of a binding contract at common law[228] may be countered in the following way. Section 62(2) introduces common law contract rules into sale of goods contracts only to the extent that these are not inconsistent with the provisions of the Act. Since the prohibition on enforcing agreements to agree appears to contradict the literal wording of section 8(1) and (2), it would seem that such agreements should be enforced in accordance with the terms of the section, whatever might be the position under the general law of contract.[229]

1.45   **Agreements to negotiate.**   The rule that an agreement to agree is unenforceable has given rise to difficulties where parties have entered into an agreement to negotiate. In *Walford v Miles*,[230] Lord Ackner treated an agreement to negotiate as just as lacking in certainty as an agreement to agree. He stated, however, that an agreement

---

[224] *F & G Sykes (Wessex) Ltd v Fine Fare Ltd* [1967] 1 Lloyd's Rep. 53 (buyer's requirements over five years of 30–80,000 broiler chickens with the precise figure to 'be agreed'). See also *Global Container Lines Ltd v State Black Sea Shipping Co.* [1997] EWCA Civ 3007; [1999] 1 Lloyd's Rep.127.

[225] *Queensland Electricity Generating Board v New Hope Collieries Pty Ltd*, n. 223 above. See also *Alstom Signalling Ltd v Jarvis Facilities Ltd* [2004] EWHC 1232 (TCC) (court to settle 'differences').

[226] Especially the case in output and requirements contracts where one party's needs or capacity are monopolized by the other.

[227] n. 216 above at [67]. See also *BJ Aviation Ltd v Pool Aviation Ltd* [2002] EWCA Civ 163; [2002] 2 P.&C.R. 25 at [23] (noting also that a court cannot imply a term inconsistent with that which has been agreed).

[228] A similar problem presents itself with the Vienna Convention on Contracts for the International Sale of Goods 1980: compare Arts 14 and 55.

[229] There is a problem with interpreting the Act in this way: the Act does not as such define 'contract', which arguably should be interpreted according to the general law.

[230] [1992] 2 AC 128.

to use best endeavours to agree would not be open to the same objection,[231] but went on to say that an agreement to negotiate in good faith was 'repugnant to the adversarial position of the parties when involved in negotiations' and thus too uncertain to be enforced.[232] The general bar on giving effect to agreements to negotiate means that a clause seeking to lock the seller of a business into negotiations for the sale of that business over a stated period cannot be enforced,[233] despite the prejudice that this might cause negotiating parties who have sunk costs into the negotiation process,[234] though the same objection does not apply where the clause (a 'lock-out clause') precludes the vendor from opening competing discussions with the third parties over a stipulated period.[235] There are, moreover, cases of long-term supply contracts, where a contract containing a future price negotiation clause has been acted upon and the courts have exceptionally given effect to the negotiation clause by treating it as indicating in market conditions a reasonable price.[236] This is consistent with the view that declaring a contract unenforceable for lack of certainty is a last resort. The court will do its best to find substitute machinery for the agreement to agree.[237] In *Queensland Electricity Generating Board v New Hope Collieries Pty Ltd*,[238] critical elements in the pricing formula for coal were to be the subject of fresh negotiation five years into a fifteen-year supply agreement. The Privy Council held that the parties had impliedly agreed to use reasonable endeavours and, failing agreement, to do all that was reasonably necessary to procure the appointment of an arbitrator to resolve the issue. There was plainly an intention to enter into binding legal relations and it was implicit in the agreement that the new pricing structure was to be fair and reasonable.

Third-party valuation. Section 9 of the Sale of Goods Act deals with contracts **1.46** where the price is to be settled by a third-party valuer. Subsection (1) deals with

---

231 But an undertaking to use best endeavours to reach agreement has been held to be too uncertain to enforce: *Little v Courage Ltd* [1995] CLC 164, 169; *London & Regional Investments Limited v TBI plc* [2002] EWCA Civ 355; *Multiplex Constructions (UK) Ltd v Cleveland Bridge UK Ltd* [2006] EWHC 1341 (TCC) at [633]–[638].

232 *Ibid.*, 138. Cf *Petromec Inc. v Petroleo Brasiliero SA Petrobas (No. 3)* [2005] EWCA Civ 891; [2006] 1 Lloyd's Rep. 121 at [120]–[121] (whilst an implied obligation to negotiate in good faith is unenforceable, it may be that an express undertaking to negotiate in good faith is, especially where it is entered into under an already binding contract).

233 *Walford v Miles*, n. 230 above.

234 It is common for a preliminary contract to contain a break clause, by which the professional fees of the prospective purchaser will be reimbursed if the prospective vendor breaks off negotiations, but the fees may not exceed a conventional limit, for otherwise they would amount to unlawful financial assistance under the Companies Act 1985, ss. 151 *et seq.* (due to be replaced by Companies Act 2006, ss. 677 *et seq.* at a date to be appointed).

235 *Pitt v PHH Asset Management Ltd* [1994] 1 WLR 327.

236 See *Rafsanjan Pistachio Producers Co-operative v Kaufmanns Ltd* (Unreported, 19 December 1997).

237 *iSoft Group plc v Misys Holdings Ltd*, n. 216 at [75].

238 n. 223 above.

two cases. First, where the valuation machinery breaks down because the designated valuer cannot or will not do the job, the agreement is avoided.[239] Secondly, where the machinery thus breaks down but a part or all of the goods are delivered to and appropriated by the buyer,[240] the buyer is bound to pay a reasonable price on the basis of an *indebitatus* count for goods sold and delivered.[241] Section 9(2) then goes on to create a special statutory action in damages where either the buyer or the seller is at fault in causing the valuation machinery to break down: it could, for example, deal with a case where one of the parties refuses to carry out an undertaking to name one of two agreed joint valuers.[242] There is no justification for the special treatment in section 9 of this one aspect of contractual formation. It would be better to allow such issues to be resolved by the general law of contract, or by a sufficiently general statutory text that embraced other examples of obstructive behaviour in the bargaining process. This would allow the law to develop unimpeded by a nineteenth-century approach to formation in one corner of the law. There seems every reason nowadays to apply a fair or reasonable price where two parties each appoint a valuer but the machinery breaks down because of one of those valuers;[243] yet section 9(1) states that the agreement is avoided.

---

[239] S. 9(1) codifies *Cooper v Shuttleworth* (1856) 25 LJ Ex. 114.
[240] The property, it seems, would thereupon pass.
[241] This codifies *Clark v Westrope* (1856) 18 CB 765.
[242] S. 9(2) would reverse the actual result in *Vickers v Vickers* (1867) LR 4 Eq. 529, 535–6 (Page-Wood V-C: 'this particular case . . . tries the principle to the utmost').
[243] Cf *Sudbrook Trading Estate Ltd v Eggleton*, n. 223 above.

2

DEFINITION AND SUBJECT MATTER OF THE SALE OF GOODS CONTRACT

Introduction. Section 2(1) defines a sale of goods contract for the purpose of **2.01** the Act as one 'whereby the seller transfers or agrees to transfer the property in the goods for a money consideration called the price'. Sale is to be distinguished from other contracts in that it involves the transfer of ownership (that is, the property) in goods (as opposed to other items) for money (as opposed to some other type of consideration). Ownership is a notion that should be treated with some care in personal property law. For present purposes,[1] it may be seen as the best available possessory right to a thing. If any of these three elements of ownership, goods, or money is absent, the contract will not be one of sale of goods for the purpose of the Act, no matter how similar in spirit it may be to such a contract. The fate of such cognate transactions will be dealt with later in this chapter.

---

[1] Discussed in the text accompanying nn. 213–18 below.

35

Definition of 'Goods'

2.02 **Definition of 'goods'.** These are defined by section 61(1) as including 'all personal chattels other than things in action and money' and in particular 'emblements, industrial growing crops, and things attached to or forming part of the land which are agreed to be severed before sale or under the contract of sale'. Personal chattels consist of what remains of property after land and chattels real (leasehold interests in land) are abstracted.[2] Once things in action[3] and money[4] are also removed, the personal chattels that may be the subject of a sale of goods agreement consist of those tangible, movable items that we call things in possession.[5] The definition of goods therefore embraces all personal chattels (with the above exceptions). Large and unusual items such as ships[6] and aircraft,[7] certainly personal chattels, are therefore dealt with by the Act,[8] from whose provisions special statute may depart in their case.[9] The particular mention of various types of crop and agricultural produce in the above definition needs to be explained in the light of the legislative history governing the observance of forms in sales of land and of goods.

2.03 **Writing requirement.** Before 1954, contracts for the sale of goods above a certain value had to be evidenced in writing. This requirement, introduced in section 17 of the Statute of Frauds 1677 for the sale of 'goods, wares and merchandizes' (not defined in the statute),[10] was continued by section 5 of the Sale of Goods Act 1893 for 'goods', defined in terms almost identical to those used in the 1979 Act. Section 4

---

[2] For the common law distinction between personalty and realty, see J. Williams, *Principles of the Law of Personal Property etc.* (14th edn, by T. Cyprian Williams, Sweet & Maxwell, 1894), 1–6.

[3] So called because rights in them cannot physically be vindicated by taking possession and so depend upon legal proceedings. See *Torkington v Magee* [1902] 2 KB 427, 430. Lord Blackburn said the expression extended to 'all personal chattels that are not in possession': *Colonial Bank v Whinney* (1886) 11 App. Cas. 426, 439–40.

[4] Hard to classify as a thing in possession or a thing in action: see M. Bridge, *Personal Property Law* (3rd edn, OUP, 2002), 9–10.

[5] The expression 'goods' is used and defined in a large number of statutes with divergent purposes. The definition in the Fair Trading Act 1973, s. 137(2), is especially wide in including 'buildings and other structures'. Decisions on the meaning of goods under such statutes must therefore be approached with some caution.

[6] *Behnke v Bede Shipping Co. Ltd* [1927] 1 KB 649; *McDougall v Aeromarine of Emsworth Ltd* [1958] 3 All ER 431.

[7] See *United Dominions Trust (Commercial) Ltd v Eagle Aircraft Services Ltd* [1968] 1 All ER 104.

[8] For ships see *Sirius Shipping Corpn v The Ship Sunrise* [2006] NSWSC 398; cf. *Hooper v Gumm* (1867) 2 Ch. App. 282, 290 (Turner LJ). Ships are, however, excluded by the Vienna Convention on the International Sale of Goods 1980, Art. 2(e).

[9] Note the provisions governing the register of ships and their ownership: Merchant Shipping Act 1995, ss. 8–16.

[10] The words 'wares and merchandizes' seem to add nothing to 'goods'.

of the Statute of Frauds also required writing for the sale of 'lands, tenements and hereditaments or any interest in or concerning them' (again not defined). It was superseded by a similar requirement in section 40 of the Law of Property Act 1925, which defined land in lengthy terms, specifically referring to buildings and minerals.[11] When section 40 was repealed by the Law of Property (Miscellaneous Provisions) Act 1989, which introduced a more stringent writing rule, land itself was not defined in the new Act.

Crops and Natural Produce

Goods and land.   For writing purposes, it is important to distinguish goods   **2.04** and land,[12] since contracts concerning the latter are invalid if not in writing. Unfortunately, a reading of the case law and the definition of 'goods' in the Sale of Goods Act suggests that crops and other agricultural produce are capable of being both goods and land. In principle, things attached to land form part of the land: thus, while a conveyance of land does not include chattels upon the land, attached things, even if not expressly listed, will pass to the transferee.[13] It is commonly contemplated that crops and natural produce will be severed, at seasonal intervals in the case of crops, and treated as goods. Where severance is contemplated pursuant to contract, the question is whether the contract must comply with section 2 of the 1989 Act or might be made by informal means, as is permitted by the Sale of Goods Act. It cannot safely be assumed that, just because such items are 'goods' for the purpose of the latter Act, a contract for their sale need not satisfy any writing requirement for land. Had the sanction for non-compliance with the writing requirement for land remained unenforceability, it might have been arguable that the plaintiff should have been allowed to characterize and enforce the contract as one for the sale of goods: the Sale of Goods Act in section 60 states that rights and liabilities declared by the Act may be enforced by action. But the Law of Property (Miscellaneous Provisions) Act 1989 now provides that a contract for the disposition of an interest in land 'can only be made in writing'.[14] To allow such a contract to be enforced just because it is also a sale of goods contract is too sharp an inroad into a recently enacted statute to be a permissible outcome of litigation.

Nineteenth-century Case Law

Characterizing crops and produce.   The nineteenth-century cases characteriz-   **2.05** ing crops and produce as either goods or land are difficult to follow and summarize. Abinger CB once said that no general rule laid down in one case was not

---

[11]   S. 205(1)(ix).

[12]   M. Bridge (1986) 64 *Can. Bar Rev.* 58.

[13]   *Saunders v Pilcher* [1949] 2 All ER 1097; *Dyck v Dyck* [1926] 3 WWR 762 (Can.); *Shewchuk v Seafred (No. 2)* [1927] 2 WWR 207 (Can.).

[14]   S. 2.

contradicted in another.[15] Numerous criteria were brought into play in Statute of Frauds cases: whether it was the buyer or the seller who was to sever growing things from the soil;[16] the putting of those things into a deliverable state and the intention of the parties to pass the property in them before or after severance;[17] the practical necessity of the buyer having an interest in the land in order to enter upon it and effect a severance;[18] the introduction of human labour into the growing process;[19] the intention of the parties to have mature growths severed immediately after the contract so that after the contract the soil would serve only as a natural warehouse;[20] and the collateral issues of whether for the purpose of execution of judgments the growing things would have been treated as goods, and whether for the purpose of descent on death they would have gone to the next-of-kin (goods) or the heir-at-law (land).[21] Implicit in some of these older authorities is a confusion between contract and conveyance, namely that because the property in future crops cannot pass before they come into existence, so a contract for their sale cannot concern goods. Further, the application of multiple criteria in some cases compounds the difficulty of stating the law, and the sparseness of reasoning in others encourages a search for an overarching rule that fits the results, if not the reasoning in the cases.

2.06 **Passing of property.** Lord Blackburn was responsible for the central position given to the passing of property in sales law. In a magisterial classification of the cases, he said that, if the property in growing things was to pass after severance, the contract was one of sale of goods; but if it was to pass before severance, it was not a sale of goods contract at all and might or might not concern land under section 4 of the Statute of Frauds.[22] Although early editions of *Benjamin* supported this thesis,[23] there was only partial backing for it in the cases, which are more fully explained as follows.

2.07 *Fructus naturales.* In the case of *fructus naturales*, the spontaneous growth of the soil such as timber or grass, the contract disposed of an interest in land if

---

[15] *Rodwell v Phillips* (1842) 9 M & W 501, 505.

[16] *Evans v Roberts* (1826) 5 B & C 829.

[17] *Smith v Surman* (1829) 9 B & C 561.

[18] *Crosby v Wadsworth* (1805) 6 East 602 as discussed in *Evans v Roberts*, n. 16 above; *Jones v Flint* (1839) 10 A & E 753.

[19] *Evans v Roberts*, n. 16 above; *Scorell v Boxall* (1827) 1 Y & J 396.

[20] *Parker v Staniland* (1809) 11 East 362; Sjt. Williams's notes to *Duppo v Mayo* (1670) 1 Wms. Saund. 275, 276 (6th edn, by E. V. Williams, 1845). These reports were edited on various occasions, and it is the last edition, subsequently incorporated in the English Reports, that is referred to here.

[21] *Rodwell v Phillips*, n. 15 above; *Scorell v Boxall*, n. 19 above; *Evans v Roberts*, n. 16 above; *Jones v Flint*, n. 18 above.

[22] *Blackburn on Sale* (2nd edn, by W. C. Graham, Stevens, 1885), 4–15.

[23] e.g., J. P. Benjamin, *A Treatise on the Law of Sale of Personal Property* (2nd edn, Sweet & Maxwell, 1873), 91–3.

the buyer was to sever,[24] and of an interest in goods if the seller was to sever.[25] But the cases consistent with this distinction rely upon other reasons: if the seller severed, the contract could be seen as reserving in him a controlling intention to pass the property only after the growing things acquired the identity of goods upon severance;[26] if the buyer severed, he could be seen as needing at least a limited proprietary interest in the land in order to carry out that purpose.[27]

Fructus industriales. These consist of fruits and crops grown by the labour of **2.08** the agricultural year. They were treated as goods no matter who was responsible for their severance,[28] even if they were not in a mature state at the contract date.[29] The probable reason was that a buyer did not need anything so enduring as an interest in land to achieve a purpose whose success depended upon dispatch.[30] Where the crops were mature at the date of the contract and had to be severed immediately, there was the further reason that the soil had no more to give and served merely as a natural warehouse for the crops.[31] Any divergence between *fructus naturales* and *fructus industriales* was narrowed by the controversial decision in *Marshall v Green*,[32] which extended the warehouse principle to *fructus naturales*.

Statutory Definition

Extended statutory meaning. Interpreted literally, the statutory definition of **2.09** 'goods' set out above significantly extended the definition to be drawn from the cases. This definition clearly gives support to the Blackburn proprietary thesis and, though not explicitly, is by virtue of its width consistent with the natural warehouse principle in *Marshall v Green*.[33] In practical terms, any extension of the definition would lie in the area of *fructus naturales* where the buyer severs. It is hard

---

[24] *Smith v Surman*, n. 17 above; *Evans v Roberts*, n. 16 above; *Emmerson v Heelis* (1809) 2 Taunt. 38 (extended to *fructus industriales*).

[25] *Crosby v Wadsworth*, n. 18 above; *Scorell v Boxall*, n. 19 above; *Carrington v Roots* (1837) 2 M & W 248.

[26] *Smith v Surman*, n. 17 above.

[27] *Crosby v Wadsworth*, n. 18 above; *Jones v Flint*, n. 18 above.

[28] *Evans v Roberts*, n. 16 above; *Parker v Staniland*, n. 20 above; *Warwick v Bruce* (1813) 2 M & S 205; *Jones v Flint*, n. 18 above; *Sainsbury v Matthews* (1838) 4 M & W 334; Sjt. Williams's notes to *Duppo v Mayo*, n. 20 above. But see the inconsistent results in *Rodwell v Phillips*, n. 15 above, and *Emmerson v Heelis*, n. 24 above; also the result in *Waddington v Briscoe* (1801) 2 B & P 452, where the speculative nature of a contract for the supply of crops encouraged a disapproving court to deny the exemption from stamp duty accorded by the Stamp Act, 55 Geo. 3, cap. 184, to contracts for the sale of goods, wares, and merchandise.

[29] *Evans v Roberts*, n. 16 above; *Jones v Flint*, n. 18 above; *Sainsbury v Matthews* (1838) 4 M & W 334; n. 28 above. This was also the view of Scrutton LJ in *English Hop Growers Ltd v Dering* [1928] 1 KB 174, 178–9.

[30] *Jones v Flint*, n. 18 above.

[31] *Parker v Staniland*, n. 20 above.

[32] (1875) 1 CPD 35.

[33] *Ibid.*

to say what the draftsman meant when inserting the expression 'industrial growing crops' but it seems designed to serve as the Scots equivalent of *fructus industriales*,[34] just as 'emblements' has come loosely to mean the same thing.[35]

2.10 Literal interpretation. English decisions based on the statutory definition give some support for the view that it should be given its literal meaning. It seems to have been assumed in *Kursell v Timber Operators and Contractors Ltd*[36] that the grant to a buyer of a licence to sever timber in a Latvian forest over a fifteen-year period was a transaction caught by the Sale of Goods Act. A contract permitting the buyer to enter land and sever timber was regarded in *James Jones & Sons Ltd v Earl of Tankerville*[37] as a sale of goods contract and thus amenable to specific performance under the Sale of Goods Act. In contrast, the Privy Council, construing a New Zealand tax statute in *Kauri Timber Co Ltd v Commissioner of Taxes*,[38] held that a buyer's right to cut and haul timber was an interest in land: the natural warehouse principle in *Marshall v Green*[39] could not be applied since the contract required a lengthy occupation of the land by the buyer until the timber reached maturity. Further, an Australian court has held that a contract conferring the right to enter land to harvest nuts from trees conferred a profit à prendre, and was not a contract of sale of goods since the buyer was under no obligation to sever.[40] The Court of Appeal in *Saunders v Pilcher*[41] held that a conveyance of land to a buyer included also the natural produce growing on the land, but it was not denied that the scope of 'goods' had been extended by the Act. There seems no reason to doubt that crops and natural produce might be the subject of both a sale of land and sale of goods agreement.

2.11 Straightforward interpretation. It is submitted that the definition of 'goods' should be given a straightforward reading and the Act be applied even to cases where the buyer, pursuant to an obligation to do so, effects severance of natural produce, with the possible exception of contracts where the buyer is given an interest in land pending a lengthy maturing of the produce. Difficulties may arise

---

[34] But the expression is not a term of art in Scots law: *Benjamin's Sale of Goods* (7th edn, by A. G. Guest, Sweet & Maxwell, 2006), para. 1–093; see also *Boskabelle Ltd v Laird* [2006] ScotCS CSOH 173.
[35] Chalmers used emblements and *fructus industriales* interchangeably: M. Chalmers, *The Sale of Goods Act, 1893, Including the Factors Acts, 1889 & 1890* (4th edn, Butterworths, 1899), 117. But see the technical meaning of emblements in *Benjamin's Sale of Goods*, above, para. 1–093.
[36] [1927] 1 KB 298.
[37] [1909] 2 Ch. 440.
[38] [1913] AC 771, not cited in *Kursell*, n. 36 above. See also *Mohanlal Hargovind of Jubbulpore v Commissioner of Income Tax, Central Provinces and Berar, Nagpur* [1949] AC 521, applying the *Kauri* case.
[39] n. 32 above.
[40] *Warren v Nut Farms of Australia Pty Ltd* [1981] WAR 134.
[41] [1949] 2 All ER 1097.

where the definitions of goods and land overlap: we have seen that this may happen with regard to the writing requirement. There may also be a title dispute between a purchaser of land and a purchaser of goods. This is unlikely to be a problem apart from cases where the seller of crops or produce that have attained maturity then sells the land before the crops or produce have been severed. A similar difficulty could arise with fixtures. Where property has a dual existence as land and goods, the rule of *nemo dat quod non habet,* together with its exceptions, could resolve title disputes.[42] Statutory rules for the registration of interests in land may have to be followed by the buyer of crops or produce if his interest is to be asserted successfully against a later buyer of the land.

Fixtures

Meaning of fixtures.   Chattels attached to land have long been treated as land **2.12** for various legal purposes.[43] They vest in the owner of the land once they are so attached to the land as to comply with the legal test of a fixture and accompany the land when it is conveyed.[44] Whether a chattel becomes a fixture depends upon a dual test consisting of a factual element and an intentional element: the degree of attachment of the chattel to the land and the object and purpose of the attachment.[45] The role accorded to intention, however, is limited. It must be apparent from the degree and the object of annexation that the intention of the parties, the owner of the chattel and the owner of the land, is that ownership should be retained by the owner of the chattel.[46] That intention must be 'apparent' and 'patent for all to see'.[47] Where an engine was bolted to the floor through iron plates set in newly poured concrete to prevent it from rocking, and a plate was attached to the engine stating it to be the property of the owner of the engine, this was held not to be sufficient to prevent the treatment of the engine as a fixture.[48] The mirror image of this approach is presented by objects that the parties seek to treat as a fixture. An intention to treat a chattel as though it were land, in circumstances where it can readily be disconnected from the land and moved elsewhere, will not suffice to have the chattel treated as a fixture.[49] An object that cannot be removed from the

---

[42] A radically different approach would treat the acquirer of an interest in land as paramount in all cases: see Ontario Law Reform Commission, *Report on Sale of Goods* (1979), i, 70.

[43] H. Bennett, 'Attachment of Chattels to Land' in N. Palmer and E. McKendrick (eds), *Interests in Goods* (2nd edn, LLP, 1998); M. Bridge, *Personal Property Law* (3rd edn, OUP, 2002), 104–6.

[44] *Lavery v Pursell* (1889) 39 Ch. D 508; *Lee v Risdon* (1816) 7 Taunt. 188.

[45] *Hellawell v Eastwood* (1851) 6 Ex. 295.

[46] *Hobson v Gorringe* [1897] 1 Ch 182, 193.

[47] *Ibid.*, approving Blackburn J in *Holland v Hodgson* (1872) LR 7 CP 328; see also *Melluish v BMI (No. 3) Ltd* [1996] AC 454, 473.

[48] *Hobson v Gorringe*, n. 46 above; see also *Reynolds v Ashby & Son* [1904] AC 466.

[49] *Chelsea Yacht and Boat Co. Ltd v Pope* [2000] 1 WLR 1941 (houseboat). But the occupation of a permanently moored boat may be treated as rateable occupation of the licensed riverbed for

land without its destruction will be treated as a fixture.[50] An object whose attachment to the land is temporary, however, may for that reason retain its character as a chattel even though it is firmly secured to the land.[51] Overall, however, the test of a fixture is not easy to apply or predict in its application.[52] In addition, even if a chattel becomes a fixture in this way, as between a landlord and a tenant it may be a tenant's fixture or a landlord's fixture.[53] Those fixtures in the former category attached by the tenant under the lease may be removed by the tenant, pursuant to a common law right, at the end of the lease, whereupon they are reinvested with the character of chattels.[54] Consistently with this entitlement, an agreement by a tenant to transfer this right of severance is not treated as disposing of an interest in land; nor is it treated as a sale of goods agreement.[55]

2.13 **Sale of fixtures by land owner.**   There is surprisingly little authority for the case where the owner of land agrees to sell fixtures to a buyer whilst retaining ownership of the land itself. Before the enactment of the Sale of Goods Act, it might have been useful to ask whether fixtures were akin to growing crops and who was to sever them, and whether it was significant that the parties might or might not have intended the property in them to pass before severance. In *Lavery v Pursell*,[56] Chitty J held that a contract permitting a buyer to sever building materials from land concerned land for the purpose of section 4 of the Statute of Frauds. In one Canadian case, where it was the seller who was to sever a saw-mill together with its machinery at the end of the logging season, the court surprisingly concluded that the contract concerned land.[57] Regardless of whether it is the seller or the buyer who is to sever, the definition of 'goods' in the Sale of Goods Act is broad enough to embrace all sales of a fixture to be severed from land under the contract. Given the cautionary purposes served by the Law of Property (Miscellaneous Provisions) Act 1989, which do not appear to be in play where a building is dismantled and sold, it is submitted that a narrow view should be taken of land where fixtures are separated from the soil and that a contract capable of being classified as a sale of goods contract under the Sale of Goods Act should not at the same time be a contract for the sale of an interest in land under the 1989 Act.

---

the purpose of paying rates: *Rudd v Cinderella Rockerfellas Ltd* [2003] EWCA Civ 529; [2003] 1 WLR 2423.

   [50] *Elitestone Ltd v Morris* [1997] 1 WLR 687.
   [51] *Billing v Pill* [1954] 1 QB 70 (removable hut and larceny).
   [52] See the conflicting results in two cases involving cinema seats: *Lyon & Co v London City and Midland Bank* [1903] 2 KB 135; *Vaudeville Electric Cinema Ltd v Muriset* [1923] 2 Ch. 328.
   [53] *Halsbury's Laws of England* (4th edn, Butterworths, 1994), xxviii(1) (Title: 'Landlord and Tenant'), paras. 143 *et seq.*
   [54] *Bain v Brand* (1876) 1 App. Cas. 762.
   [55] *Lee v Gaskell* (1876) 1 QBD 700; *Devine v Callery* (1917) 40 OLR 505 (Can.).
   [56] n. 44 above.
   [57] *McPherson v US Fidelity and Guaranty Co.* (1914) 33 OLR 524 (Can.).

Minerals and Energy

Similarity to *fructus naturales*.   Similar principles apply where the buyer extracts   **2.14**
minerals under a contract of sale. The closest analogy is with *fructus naturales*,
where it is the buyer who severs. Despite the breadth of the statutory definition,
however, there seems to be great reluctance to treat contracts for buyer severance
other than as sale of land agreements,[58] the justification apparently being that the
words in the definition of goods 'attached to or forming part of the land' ought to
be read *eiusdem generis* with emblements and industrial growing crops. The natural warehouse principle of *Marshall v Green*[59] will not serve to extend the definition of goods for items like minerals that have never derived sustenance from the
land. Thus in *Morgan v Russell & Sons*,[60] the sale of a heap of slag and cinders resting on the land was held to dispose of an interest in land. In rejecting the statutory
extension of the definition of 'goods', this approach is restrictive and out of line
with other types of thing attached to or part of land.

Energy.   The sale of energy, which will usually take the form of oil, gas, or elec-   **2.15**
tricity, presents more problems. Oil is conventionally bought and sold in crude
and refined versions, subject to the Sale of Goods Act. So far as other types of
energy amount to tangible, physical personalty, there should be no difficulty in
treating it as goods under the Sale of Goods Act, provided that the relationship
between seller and buyer is one of private contract.[61] The sale of bottled gas is
clearly governed by the Act.[62] There is every reason why the sale of gas transported
by pipeline should also be governed by the Act. Even if the gas is acquired under a
gas lease permitting the buyer to extract gas from the ground, the Sale of Goods
Act should be applied on its terms to the transaction.[63] Similarly, the supply of

---

[58] See British Columbia Law Reform Commission, *Report on the Statute of Frauds* (1977), 11.
Royalty agreements are treated, however, as involving neither a sale of goods nor a sale of land:
Emerald Resources Ltd v Sterling Oil Properties Management Ltd (1969) 3 DLR (3d) 630, affd. (1971)
15 DLR (3d) 356 (Can.).

[59] n. 32 above.

[60] [1909] 1 KB 357; see also *Mills v Stokman* (1967) 116 CLR 61; *McNeil v Corbett* (1907) 39
SCR 608 (Can.); *Saskatoon Sand & Gravel v Steve* (1973) 40 DLR (3d) 248 (Can.) (gravel to be
extracted by the buyer).

[61] For a discussion of statutory entitlement ousting private sale, see *Pfizer Corpn v Minister of
Health* [1965] AC 512. A compulsory purchase of railway equipment was held not to be a sale for
the purpose of income tax legislation in *Kirkness v John Hudson & Co Ltd* [1955] AC 696.

[62] *Marleau v People's Gas Supply Co. Ltd* [1940] 4 DLR 433 (Can.); *Bradshaw v Boothe's Marine
Ltd* [1973] 2 OR 646 (Can.); *Britvic Soft Drinks Ltd v Messer UK Ltd* [2002] 1 Lloyd's Rep. 20.

[63] The supply of power (whether in the form of 'gas, electricity or any other motive power')
was treated as occurring under a sale, and therefore attracting fitness for purpose liability, in *Bentley
Bros v Metcalfe & Co.* [1906] 2 KB 548, though the court was uncertain about the precise definition
of the subject matter. The supply of any form of power, heating, refrigeration, or ventilation is treated
as a supply of goods, rather than services for VAT purposes: Value Added Tax Act 1994, Sch. 34,
para 3.

running water should be regarded as a contract of sale of goods,[64] especially if it is metered, the quantity recorded and a unit price paid. Old issues concerning the classification of the contract by reference to whether it is the seller or the buyer who is to sever should not encumber a straightforward reading of the Act.[65] It is certainly possible to commit the tort of conversion by extracting gas without permission.[66] As for other types of formless energy, one Canadian case accepts that steam for heating purposes was tangible personalty under a tax statute, but its supply took place under a contract for services since the residue of steam was returned to the supplier in the form of a vapour.[67] As tangible personalty, the steam supplied should be treated as goods if the subject of a sale. The supply of other formless things such as electricity should be seen as a sale of goods transaction if capable of being bought and sold.[68] The Sale of Goods Act, if applicable, is likely to add little to a contract for the supply of electricity that is not already provided for in the general law of contract. This inclusive approach would bring the Sale of Goods Act into line with other legislation. Electricity has been treated in England as a 'product' for the purpose of the Consumer Protection Act 1987, which defines 'product' as meaning goods or electricity.[69] In unfair contract terms regulations,[70] originating like the Act in an EC Directive and drawing on a broader European sense of 'goods', it has been recognized that 'goods' should not be confined to its Sale of Goods Act meaning.[71]

Body Parts

2.16 **Goods.** In this developing area of law, the focus has not been mainly on whether a contract for the sale of parts of the human body is a contract of sale of goods for the purpose of the Sale of Goods Act. There are vital preliminary questions to be

---

[64] *Hamilton v Papakura District Council* [2002] UKPC 9 (where the applicability of the New Zealand Sale of Goods Act 1908 was assumed).

[65] There is no reference to the Sale of Goods Act, however, in *Erie County Natural Gas and Fuel Co. Ltd v Carroll* [1911] AC 105, but this concerned an appeal from Ontario and Ontario did not codify the law of sale of goods until 1920; see also *Tilbury Town Gas Co. Ltd v Maple City Oil and Gas Co. Ltd* (1915) 35 OLR 186 (Can.).

[66] *Erie County Natural Gas and Fuel Co. Ltd v Carroll*, n. 65 above, 116 (trover).

[67] *Re Social Services Tax Act* (1970) 74 WWR 246 (Can.).

[68] The question whether a supply of electricity was covered by an exemption from a taxing clause provided for agreements 'for or relating to the sale of goods' was left open in *County of Durham Electrical Power Distribution Co. v IRC* [1909] 2 KB 604; another taxing clause was applicable. A county court has decided that electricity is not goods for the purpose of companies legislation (s. 108(4) of the Companies Act 1948): *East Midlands Electricity Board v Grantham* [1980] CLY 271. Electricity is excluded from the Vienna Convention on the International Sale of Goods 1980, Art. 2(f), and is differentiated from goods in the definition of 'product' in the Consumer Protection Act 1987, s. 1(2) ('any goods or electricity').

[69] S. 1(2).

[70] See Ch. 9 below.

[71] *R (on the application of Khatun) v Newham LBC* [2005] EWCA Civ 55; [2005] QB 37.

resolved, namely, whether parts of the human body are capable of ownership[72] and whether contracts for their disposition are illegal under statute.[73] The general rule is that the law does not recognize a property right in a corpse or a part thereof,[74] but there is an exception if the body or its part has been processed or treated by human skill by way, for example, of stuffing or embalming.[75] For centuries, human hair has been bought and sold without controversy;[76] and it is a commonplace that human skeletons are owned by medical students and bought and sold accordingly. A property right in such items may be protected with the aid of the property torts.[77] The existence of a property right is a necessary precondition for a contract of sale of goods, for otherwise the seller could not perform one of the primary obligations of the seller of goods, which is to transfer the general property to the buyer. So far as a human part may be treated as property, it should naturally be sub-classified as goods.

Public policy and illegality.   There is nevertheless the likelihood that a contract **2.17** for the sale of body parts may be illegal, so that whether the transaction is in the first case a sale of goods contract may be a matter of little consequence. Transplant surgery has shown that body organs have a transfer value, whether they come from corpses or from living transferors. Legislative recognition has been given to the need to protect vulnerable people. The Human Tissue Act 2004 establishes a scheme whereby activities in relations to 'relevant material'[78] are prohibited unless they are on a statutory list and are the subject of the appropriate consent.[79] The Act also makes it a trafficking offence to conduct various activities in relation to human tissue, for example, commercial dealings in human material for transplantation.[80]

Implications of selling.   In those countries with a broader sense than English **2.18** law of what constitutes an enforceable contract for the sale of human tissue, the

---

[72] See R. Hardcastle, *Law and the Human Body: Property Rights, Ownership and Control* (Hart, 2007); D. Meyers, *The Human Body and the Law* (3rd edn, Aldine De Gruyter, 2006), Ch. 5.

[73] See generally G. Dworkin and I. Kennedy (1993) 1 *Medical LR* 291.

[74] *R v Kelly* [1999] QB 621, 630–1. Hence there can be no tortious liability for wrongful interference with a body: *Re Organ Group Litigation* [2005] EWHC 644 (QB); [2005] QB 506 at [128].

[75] *R v Kelly*, n. 74 above; *Dobson v North Tyneside Health Authority* [1997] 1 WLR 596; *Doodeward v Spence* (1908) 6 CLR 406; see also *Williams v Williams* (1882) 20 Ch. D. 659, 662–3. These exceptional cases are referred to as examples of 'work and skill' in *Re Organ Group Litigation*, n. 74 above at [160].

[76] But there does not appear to be any process carried out other than the removal of the hair from the living person.

[77] *Doodeward v Spence*, n. 75 above (detinue—the preserved foetus of a two-headed child stillborn 40 years previously).

[78] Defined as material other than gametes which consists of or includes human cells, except for embryos outside the human body and hair and nails from the body of a living person: s. 53.

[79] Ss. 1 and 5 and Sch. 1. The list in Sch. 1 does not include sale.

[80] In s. 32. Transplantation includes transfusion: s. 54(3).

extent of the seller's liability has caused acute difficulties. North American case law has dealt with the responsibilities of a supplier of blood,[81] a matter of great importance if the blood carries hepatitis or is HIV-infected. In one Canadian case, the court, for unclear reasons, held that a doctor supplying HIV-infected semen for artificial insemination did not owe the recipient the strict warranty obligations of a seller of goods.[82] Another Canadian case concluded that a hospital patient, not billed for the cost of blood supplied, did not provide a money consideration; consequently, the Sale of Goods Act did not apply.[83] Furthermore, it held, the fact that blood fell outside normal commercial channels of distribution made the case an inappropriate one for fashioning common law warranties akin to the strict implied terms in the Sale of Goods Act.[84] In England, though blood may not lawfully be sold, its supply can give rise to liability in tort. Blood has been recognized as a product for the purpose of the Consumer Protection Act 1987.[85]

Things in Action and Money

2.19 **Shares.**   The statutory definition of 'goods' excludes things in action and money, which is consistent with the pre-Act case law. This exclusion would affect documentary intangibles, which are documents that express an obligation, such as a right to receive payment or delivery, which itself is a thing in action. For this reason, shares in a company (unless for special reasons the share certificates themselves have become collectors' items and are bought and sold accordingly) are not goods under the Act. A share is an intangible proprietary right in a company measured by a sum of money.[86] In *Colonial Bank v Whinney*,[87] shares were found to be things in action under bankruptcy legislation. Lord Blackburn thought they were personal chattels but not goods; they were outside section 17 of the Statute of Frauds[88] since the property in them did not pass by delivery. In accordance with the express language of the Act, however, an undivided interest in goods may be the subject matter of a sale of goods contract.[89]

---

[81] e.g. *Perlmutter v Beth David Hospital* (1954) 123 NE 2d 792 (services not sale); *Reilly v King County Central Blood Bank Inc.* (1972) 492 P 2d 246 (sale); R. Magnusson, 'Proprietary Rights in Human Tissue' in N. E. Palmer and E. McKendrick (eds), n. 43 above, 46–8. For Australian authority on the question whether blood can be 'goods', see *E v Australian Red Cross Society* (1991) 105 ALR 53; *PQ v Australian Red Cross Society* [1992] 1 VR 19.

[82] *ter Neuzen v Korm* (1993) 103 DLR (4th) 473.

[83] *Pittman Estate v Bain* (1994) 112 DLR (4th) 257.

[84] *Quaere* the position under the Supply of Goods and Services Act 1982, s. 1? Would it depend upon whether the patient was receiving NHS or private treatment?

[85] *A v National Blood Authority (No. 2)* [2001] 3 All ER 289.

[86] See *Borland's Trustee v Steel Bros & Co. Ltd* [1901] 1 Ch. 279, 288.

[87] (1886) 11 App. Cas. 426.

[88] See also *Duncuft v Albrecht* (1841) 12 Sim. 189, 198.

[89] Discussed in the text accompanying nn. 93–102 below.

Money.   Money itself may not be goods, for otherwise the exchange of money   **2.20**
for a money consideration called the price could be regarded as a sale of goods
contract instead of a loan or a moneylending agreement, clearly a more natural
representation of the transaction.[90] Where, nevertheless, currency and bank notes
have attributes enhancing their face value,[91] rarity for example, these additional
attributes may be sufficient to give them the character of goods for the purpose of
the Act. Again, if money is treated as a commodity instead of a medium of
exchange, authority exists for treating the money as goods, at least for the purpose
of a special statute.[92]

Shares in Goods[93]

Part owners.   According to section 2(2): 'There may be a contract of sale between   **2.21**
one part owner and another.' The parties may be joint tenants or tenants in common and their interests may arise in varying degrees. More difficult is the case, not
covered by section 2(2), where a co-owner wishes to sell an undivided share in
goods to an outside buyer, since it was held, before the Sale of Goods (Amendment)
Act 1995, that an undivided share is not goods but a chose in action for the
purpose of bills of sale legislation.[94] There are also licensing cases holding that
members of unincorporated associations do not buy the drinks supplied to them
but obtain on terms a distribution of the property owned by the association.[95]
For contracts concluded before the implementation of the Sale of Goods Act
(Amendment) 1995,[96] the position is as follows. The effect of section 2(2) is to
modify the definition of goods to admit shares disposed of between co-owners.
The provisions of the Sale of Goods Act thus apply to such contracts, with the

---

[90] Similarly, gaming chips in a casino are not goods: *Lipkin Gorman v Karpnale Ltd* [1991] 2 AC
548, 575. (The chips are simply a convenient mechanism for facilitating gambling with money. The
property in the chips as such remains in the club, so that there is no question of a gambler buying
the chips from the club when he obtains them for cash.)

[91] *Moss v Hancock* [1899] 2 QB 111 (restitution of stolen property, which would not be ordered
if the sovereigns had passed in currency). See also statements about the difference between goods
and currency in *Banque Belge pour l'Etranger v Hambrouck* [1921] 1 KB 321, 326, 329 (recovery of
stolen money not yet passed into currency).

[92] *R v Vanek* [1969] 2 OR 724 (Can.) (bags of silver coin under export licence statute). Naturally,
the mischief of individual statutes will have an enlarging or diminishing effect on the scope of
'goods'.

[93] See Law Commission, *Sale of Goods Forming Part of a Bulk* (Law Com. No. 215, 1993);
L. S. Sealy and R. J. A. Hooley, *Text and Materials in Commercial Law* (3rd edn, Butterworths
LexisNexis 2003), 298–300.

[94] *Re Sugar Properties (Derisley Wood) Ltd* [1988] BCLC 146.

[95] *Graff v Evans* (1882) 8 QBD 373; *Trebanog Working Men's Club & Institute Ltd v Macdonald*
[1940] 1 KB 576. The light thrown on the civil aspect of sale of goods by tax, licensing, and criminal
cases is often unilluminating.

[96] Taking effect on 19 Sept. 1995.

presumable exception of section 16,[97] since otherwise the contract under section 2(2) could never be executed. Where a co-owner's share in goods is the subject of a contract with an outside buyer, section 2(2) does not apply. Nevertheless, by common law analogy,[98] the relevant provisions of the Sale of Goods Act could be applied to a contract concerning the sale of an undivided share.[99]

2.22 **Undivided shares.** Where the Sale of Goods (Amendment) Act 1995 applies, the position now is that an undivided share in goods is within the definition of goods in the Sale of Goods Act. This is accomplished by the addition to that definition of the words 'and an undivided share in goods'.[100] The distinction between a contract for the sale of an undivided share and a contract for the sale of a quantity of goods to be drawn from a specific bulk, however, remains. Furthermore, where the subject matter of a contract is a share in an existing identified bulk, this is defined as specific goods,[101] with the result that section 16 again will have no application. A more difficult case is that of the bulk that is subsequently identified to the contract, for in that case the undivided share in the bulk cannot be treated as specific goods.[102]

Computer Software

2.23 **Software.** Computer hardware is obviously goods and it has been said that a contract for the sale of both hardware and software (but not software alone) is a contract of sale of goods.[103] In *St Albans City and District Council v International Computers Ltd*,[104] the contract concerned bespoke software containing a database that was provided under an agreement for the supply of a computer system. At trial, the judge was of the view that the software was 'probably' goods for the purpose of the Sale of Goods Act since '[p]rograms are . . . of necessity contained in some physical medium'.[105] In the Court of Appeal, Sir Iain Glidewell went further when saying that the disk carrying the program was goods under the Act, though the program itself was not. Taking into account the possibility that the program might be directly transferred under a licensing agreement to a customer's computer

---

[97] Which requires as a matter of law that the contract goods be first ascertained before the property in them can pass to the buyer.

[98] S. 62(2).

[99] Again, s. 16 should be excluded. See Law Com. No. 215, n. 93 above, paras 2.5–6; see Ch. 3 below.

[100] S. 2(c) of the 1995 Act amending s. 61(1) of the Sale of Goods Act; see further Ch. 3 below.

[101] S. 2(d) of the 1995 Act amending s. 61(1) of the Sale of Goods Act.

[102] On this point, see Ch. 3 below.

[103] *Toby Constructions Products Pty Ltd v Computer Bar (Sales) Pty Ltd* [1983] 2 NSWLR 48. The Sale of Goods Act has been applied to the sale of a computer system: *Rubicon Computer Systems Ptd v United Paints Ltd* [2000] 2 TCLR 453; also to the sale of hard disk drives: *Amstrad plc v Seagate Technology Inc.* (1987) 86 BLR 34. See generally S. Green and D. Saidor [2007] *JBL* 161.

[104] [1996] 4 All ER 481. See G. Gretton [1996] *JBL* 524.

[105] [1995] FSR 686, 699.

system without the ownership of any disk changing hands, he was of the view that the transaction would fall outside the Sale of Goods Act and outside the Supply of Goods and Services Act 1982 as well.[106]

Strict liability. The real question in *St Albans* was whether the supplier of 2.24 software owes the due care obligation of the supplier of services or the strict obligations of the seller of goods.[107] Sir Iain Glidewell was of the view that the licensor's standard of liability should be the same as that of a seller of goods under section 14 of the Sale of Goods Act and that, as a matter of common law implication into the contract, the parties 'must have intended' that a standard of strict liability should apply. This approach surpasses the business efficacy approach to implied terms[108] and owes more to a desire for uniformity of liability across the wide range of supply of goods and of intangible property than to an assessment of what contracting parties genuinely intend. Under the Sale of Goods Act, a book would certainly be regarded as goods but information or advice therein would probably be subject to a due care standard. It might be the case, however, that a distinction would be drawn between the presentation of material as fact and its presentation as authorial judgment. It is one thing for an author to assert that software is not goods; it is quite a different thing to claim that the past participle of the French verb 'vendre' is 'vendé' instead of 'vendu'. It may be, nevertheless, that strict liability should apply only in those cases of factual inaccuracy that would bespeak negligence in any case, so that the importance of any distinction between different levels of liability would fall away.

Ancillary software. A further distinction might be drawn between software that 2.25 serves the purpose of using goods, like the satellite navigation system in a car, and goods that are provided so that software might be used. A computer hardware system would be an example of the latter case. For the purpose of the seller's liability under section 14, where goods are provided with a manual without which they cannot be used, the manual is regarded as one with the goods it accompanies, so that the two taken together attract strict liability under section 14.[109] Computer software designed to perform tasks such as running an accounts system or a council tax operation performs a task that might once have been performed by a professional

---

[106] The definition of goods in the Supply of Goods and Services Act 1982, s. 18, is the same as that in the Sale of Goods Act 1979, s. 61(1). In *SAM Business Systems Ltd v Hedley and Co.* [2002] EWHC 2733 (TCC), the court at [52] considered that a contract for the supply of developed (not bespoke) software was covered by the Supply of Goods and Services Act 1982 and attracted strict liability under s. 4. See also *Astea (UK) Ltd v Time Group Ltd* [2003] EWHC 725 (TCC) at [35]. Cf *Brocket v DGS Retail Ltd* [2004] CLY 3269 (county court applied the Sale of Goods Act to the supply of software packages)

[107] Discussed in Ch. 7 below.

[108] *The Moorcock* (1889) 14 PD 64.

[109] See *Wormell v RHM Agriculture (East) Ltd* [1986] 1 WLR 336.

supplying professional services, subject to liability based on the negligence stand-ard. It is not at all obvious that in such a case liability for non-performing software should be strict. The standard of liability certainly ought not to depend upon whether the software comes with a disk or not.[110] A contract for the supply of soft-ware has been said to be *sui generis*,[111] so an authoritative decision needs to be taken whether liability should be strict or fault-based. The quality and fitness of the disk for embodying software is nevertheless perfectly appropriate for strict liability under the Supply of Goods and Services Act 1982.[112]

A 'Money Consideration Called the Price'

2.26 **General.** A contract of sale of goods under the 1979 Act is one where the buyer pays a money consideration called the price. There is no reason why a contract should not be one of sale of goods just because the currency of payment is for-eign.[113] Certain difficulties arise where goods are exchanged or traded in for other goods: these will be examined below, when the sale of goods contract is compared to similar transactions. The present purpose is to distinguish money from similar forms of payment.

2.27 **Legal tender.** The most obvious forms of money are coins and bank notes, in other words legal tender. In the United Kingdom, coinage is issued exclusively by the Royal Mint in accordance with Treasury permission.[114] In England and Wales, banknotes are issued exclusively by the Bank of England,[115] the denominations and overall amounts being the subject of Treasury approval.[116] It should be no objection to the buyer's consideration consisting of money that it be in a

---

[110] In cases decided under the Vienna Convention on the International Sale of Goods 1980, where the definition of goods cannot be assumed to be the same as it is under the Sale of Goods Act, the major question that has arisen in the case law is not whether liability should be strict or fault-based, nor whether the Convention goes beyond sales to embrace licensing agreements, but whether a contract for the sale of software consists preponderantly of the supply of labour or other services so as to fall outside the Convention under Art. 3. The cases seem to have settled on the view that standard software amounts to goods but that bespoke software may be the subject of a contract for the labour or other services. The Convention does not explicitly recognize a category of contracts corresponding to the work and materials contract of English law and therefore has nothing to say on the question whether software can be 'materials'; see M. Bridge, *International Sale of Goods[:] Law and Practice* (2nd edn, OUP, 2007), 519–20.
[111] *Beta Computers (Europe) Ltd v Adobe Systems (Europe) Ltd* 1996 SLT 604, 609 (Lord Penrose).
[112] See s. 1.
[113] *Daewoo Australia Pty Ltd v Suncorp-Metway Ltd* [2000] NSWSC 35; (2000) 33 ACSR 481 (Aust.) at [21]; see also *The Halcyon the Great* [1975] 1 WLR 515 (lawful 'sale' in foreign currency by Admiralty Marshall).
[114] Coinage Act 1971, ss. 2–3, 9.
[115] Bank Charter Act 1844.
[116] Currency and Bank Notes Act 1954; Currency Act 1983.

foreign currency. The essence of money for present purposes is that it is a freely circulating medium of exchange.[117]

Money's worth.   A clear and liquidated financial advantage accruing to the   **2.28**
'seller' will not, however, amount to money as such: money is not the same as money's worth. Thus an agreement to transfer leasehold land in return for the transferee agreeing to assume substantial rent payments has been held not to be a sale.[118] Similarly, the transferor of shares paid with shares in the transferee company (who alternatively might have taken a stated money price for the transferred shares) does not sell them to the transferee.[119] But it is no objection to the characterization of an agreement as one of sale that the buyer pays with a cheque or banker's draft, for here the instrument serves as conditional payment[120] until the bank, acting as agent for the buyer, puts the seller in funds with the amount of the cheque or draft. The instrument itself may not be money but it is the means by which the seller obtains money.

Instruments and absolute payment.   An instrument may be given in payment   **2.29**
for goods supplied where it serves as absolute and not conditional payment. It has been held in one old case[121] that the contract is not one of sale but one of barter (or exchange) of the instrument against the goods. The buyer of seven pipes of Guernsey red wine paid the seller with a bill of exchange drawn by one stranger on another and due on a later date, without recourse against the buyer if the bill were dishonoured. When the bill became due, it was dishonoured by the drawee, whereupon the seller brought action against the buyer in debt on one of the old money counts, namely, for goods sold and delivered. The seller's action failed because the goods had been bartered and not sold; the buyer had never undertaken to pay a money sum. Accepting that the buyer in the above case was not liable to pay when the drawee defaulted, it does not necessarily follow that the contract may not be treated as one of sale. An alternative argument is that the payment of the money consideration is entrusted under the contract to a third party

---

117 See *Moss v Hancock*, n. 91 above; also Case 7/78 *R v Thompson* [1978] ECR 2247 (ECJ) (Krugerrands and UK coin not goods under EEC Treaty).
118 *Robshaw Bros Ltd v Mayer* [1957] Ch. 125. It is questionable that it is a binding contract at all as opposed to a gift with a burden attached to it: see *Thomas v Thomas* (1842) 2 QB 851. A promise of land for the extinguishment of an antecedent debt was held not to be a sale in *Simpson v Connolly* [1953] 1 WLR 911.
119 *Re Westminster Property Group Plc* [1984] 1 WLR 1117, approved [1985] 1 WLR 676.
120 *Currie v Misa* (1875) LR 10 Ex. 153, 163, reversed other grounds (1876) 1 App. Cas. 554; *Re Romer & Haslam* [1893] 2 QB 286, 296, 300, 303; *Royal Securities Corpn Ltd v Montreal Trust Co.* (1966) 57 DLR (2d) 666.
121 *Read v Hutchinson* (1813) 3 Camp. 352. See also *McGlynn v Hastie* (1918) 44 OLR 190 (Can.: barter of hogs for cheque drawn by third party on bank).

but that the seller takes the risk of third-party default and so may not have recourse to the buyer in that event.[122]

2.30 **Trading checks.** The above approach may be useful in dealing with the relationships arising out of the use of trading checks, which are vouchers issued by a lender to a borrower and used by the latter, who trades them in for goods at certain nominated retail outlets, pursuant to arrangements between those outlets and the lender.[123] The borrower uses the checks exactly as though they are cash, yet they lack the universality of money. In *Davis v Customs and Excise Commissioners*,[124] the court concluded that a contract of sale had been entered into between the borrower and the retailer, so that value added tax could be levied. Moreover, the court also rejected the argument that there had been a sale of goods by the retailer to the lender, but delivered at the latter's request to the borrower.

Credit Cards and Other Cards

2.31 **Use of credit cards.** The above case is of assistance in analysing the relationships arising out of the acquisition of goods by means of a bank credit card.[125] The card-holding buyer presents the card in payment to a seller, who has pre-existing arrangements with the issuer of the card to accept the use of the card in payment.[126] Until quite recently, the seller would make a graphite impression of the card on a sales voucher signed by the cardholder. The seller would then retain a copy of the voucher, present a copy to the customer, and then send a third copy to the issuer, who would pay the face amount less an agreed commission.[127] The current practice is for the card to be 'swiped' or read on a credit card terminal linked to the card issuer, which captures information from the card. The customer will then receive a copy of the till receipt, after either signing the receipt or inserting a personal identification number (PIN) on the credit card terminal. There is no need for the customer to present the card physically to a distant seller. Instead, details of the card may be given over the telephone or entered online in an internet transaction, in both cases with the addition of a security number inscribed on

---

[122] A variation of this is that both parties are discharged if the cheque is dishonoured: see s. 2(3) (a contract of sale may be absolute or conditional).

[123] See the Crowther Committee Report on *Consumer Credit* (HMSO, London, 1971, Cmnd 4596), i, Ch. 2.4.1 *et seq.*

[124] [1975] 1 WLR 204.

[125] M. Bridge (1977) 28 *NILQ* 382. The expression 'bank credit card' signifies a card other than one that is issued by the seller itself as a means of identifying customers who have an existing account and as a convenient means of recording sales on credit.

[126] This is a so-called three-party system. There is also a four-party system, whereby a so-called merchant-acquirer (who recruits the seller to the credit card network) is interposed for payment purposes between the seller and the card issuer. See the description in *Office of Fair Trading v Lloyds TSB Bank Plc* [2004] EWHC 2600 (Comm) at [5]; also *Landcore Services Ltd v Barclays Bank Plc* [2008] EWHC 1264 (Ch).

[127] As described by Millett J in *Re Charge Card Services Ltd* [1987] 1 Ch. 150, 156.

the back of the card. From the cardholder's point of view, it is like a deferred cash transaction, with payment of the sale price eventually being made to the issuer. The card issuer will not invoice the cardholder until the seller has presented a claim for reimbursement.

Credit cards and money consideration.   It is sometimes loosely said that the **2.32** credit card is the equivalent of a money consideration, but the reality is that a credit card, like a cheque drawn on a bank account, is the means by which a money consideration can be paid to the seller by the credit card issuer.[128] Where goods are supplied in return for a credit card payment, the contract is one of sale of goods.[129] The payment mechanism for bank credit cards differs from payment by means of a cheque drawn by a buyer on his bank in that, whereas the cardholder always draws on a line of credit provided by the issuer, a buyer paying by cheque receives credit only if the account on which the cheque is drawn is in debit or is a special loan account. The bank credit card differs in terms of degree from trading checks in that many fewer sellers will accept trading checks than credit cards.

Discounted payment.   Unlike the case of trading checks, where the seller receives **2.33** payment from the lender without having commission deducted, the seller is paid less than the face amount of the transaction by the card issuer. While the grant of a commission from seller to issuer comes close to being a notorious fact, the amount of it is not, and there is usually no disclosure of either by the issuer to the cardholder. The contract between seller and cardholder should remain nonetheless a contract of sale of goods, with the presentation of the credit card constituting the agreed method of paying the price.[130]

Problem issues.   Certain problems, however, remain. First, there is the question **2.34** of contractual certainty, which is a problem in that most cardholders never know the final price received by the seller.[131] This is unlikely to matter in practice, since certainty is usually a problem in executory contracts and one of the advantages of bank credit cards is that they accelerate the execution of contracts. A second problem concerns the liability of the cardholder to the seller if the issuer fails to pay the seller. This is a small risk, but it has been settled that, as a matter of construction, the cardholder and seller agree on a paymaster, the issuer, with no recourse against

---

[128] See *Re Charge Card Services Ltd* [1989] Ch. 497, 509 ('payment by use of the card').

[129] *Re Charge Card Services Ltd*, n. 127 above, 164.

[130] A contract of sale of goods is defined in s.2(1) as one in which the seller agrees to transfer the property in goods to the buyer for a money consideration: it does not say that the price must come from the buyer. The buyer's duty to pay (s. 27) may be 'negatived or varied' (s. 55(1)) so that the seller looks to a third party instead for payment. For the joint and several liability of that third party for misrepresentations and breaches of contract by the seller, see Consumer Credit Act 1974, ss. 56 and 75 and Ch. 8 below.

[131] See Ch. 1 above.

the cardholder if the issuer defaults.[132] In this respect, bank credit card payment differs from payment by means of a cheque or under a banker's letter of credit.[133] The ruling thus given that payment by credit card constitutes absolute and not conditional payment is not inconsistent with treating the credit card, not as a money consideration in itself, but as the means by which the seller obtains a money consideration. Absolute payment means that seller and cardholder have agreed that, when the cardholder selects the card issuer as the paymaster, the seller shall have no recourse to the cardholder if the card issuer fails. The use of the credit card as a means of obtaining payment, therefore, would not prevent the contract between seller and cardholder from being one of sale of goods.[134] Thirdly, if the view is taken that the issuer is the agent of the cardholder in effecting payment to the seller, it might be argued that the undisclosed commission by seller to card issuer is a secret profit which the agent issuer should disgorge to its principal, the cardholder.[135] Any such difficulty, if it arises, could be resolved if issuers took it upon themselves to make full and frank disclosure of their discounts to their cardholders.[136] If it should be argued that the strict rules on secret profits ought to apply only to those agents who negotiate the formation and terms of contracts, which card issuers do not, it must be said that the law supports no such distinction. In addition, card issuers come within the spirit of the rules governing secret profits. They hold out to sellers that acceptance of their credit cards will increase business volume and their commission has a manifest tendency to drive up selling prices at the expense of cardholders, who may be denied the cash discounts sometimes given to other buyers or surcharged for using a credit card.

2.35 **Other cards.** The use of a cheque guarantee card to make payment by cheque raises no issues concerning the characterization of the transaction concluded between seller and buyer. Such issues as arise concern mainly the relationship between the seller and the bank that has issued the card.[137] Debit cards can be used to make automated transfers from an account to which they are linked, which results in a simultaneous depletion of the cardholder's account and crediting of the seller's account. They therefore serve as a means of paying a money consideration to the seller which is faster than drawing a cheque on the bank account.[138] They differ from cheques in that the seller will pay a small fixed sum by way of

---

[132] *Re Charge Card Services Ltd*, n. 128 above.

[133] *WJ Alan & Co. v El Nasr Export and Import Co.* [1972] 2 QB 189.

[134] n. 130 above.

[135] On agency and secret profits, see *Bowstead on Agency* (18th edn, by F. M. B. Reynolds, Sweet & Maxwell, 2006), paras 6–079 to 6–097 and Art. 49; *Phipps v Boardman* [1967] 2 AC 46; *Keogh v Dalgety* (1916) 22 CLR 402; *Aas v Bentham* [1891] 2 Ch. 144.

[136] *Hippisley v Knee Bros* [1905] 1 KB 1.

[137] See *First Sport Ltd v Barclays Bank plc* [1993] 1 WLR 129.

[138] It is common for the same plastic card to serve as a debit card, as a cheque guarantee card, and as a cash card allowing the holder to withdraw cash from bank terminals.

deduction from the amount of the transaction credited to the seller by the bank. The amount thus deducted will be less than the amount of commission paid by the seller to the issuer of a credit card. Smart cards[139] do need to be assessed in terms of the money consideration. Smart cards can perform a wide variety of functions, one of which, not fully developed in the United Kingdom, is that of electronic purse:[140] a digital chip on the card can be charged with value, either once and for all or on a renewable basis, by the cardholder, who pays value for the charging to be done.[141] When used off-line at authorized terminals, typically for small transactions, the amount of the transaction is deducted from the value stored on the card. The smart card is thus a convenient substitute for cash itself and should be treated as a money consideration under the Sale of Goods Act. The card is issued by a financial institution, such as a bank, which may reimburse the seller in respect of the value transferred under this and other transactions. Alternatively, the seller may simply take the value received from a card and transfer it for value to another card that is being recharged or to its own supplier.

Trading Stamps

Money consideration. Finally, similar problems are posed by trading stamps **2.36** accumulated on certain purchases and then later surrendered for goods. The supply of goods for stamps was examined in a Canadian case, where the court appears to have concluded that the surrender of intrinsically worthless trading stamps for goods was a barter contract and not a sale of goods.[142] The trading stamps could not therefore be seen as a money consideration. A similar approach underlay legislation, now repealed, that was passed on the assumption that it was necessary to ensure that the supply of goods in return for trading stamps attracts the same obligations concerning description, fitness, and quality of the goods as are laid down by the Sale of Goods Act.[143] If the issuer is paid for the stamps before or when they are issued by retailers to their customers, then this payment is divorced from any subsequent transaction involving the surrender of accumulated stamps by those

---

[139] See R. J. A. Hooley, 'Payment in a Cashless Society', in B. A. K. Rider, *The Realm of Company Law—a Collection of Papers in Honour of Professor Leonard Sealy* (Kluwer Law International, 1998), discussing the relationships of the various parties involved in the 'handling' of electronic money, including participating banks and the originator of the electronic money.

[140] A smart card is not the only way to create an electronic purse: L. S. Sealy and R. J. A. Hooley, *Commercial Law[:] Text, Cases and Materials* (3rd edn, Butterworths LexisNexis, 2003), 780.

[141] For this reason, since the cardholder is not the recipient of credit, the smart card should not be treated as a credit token under s.14(1) of the Consumer Credit Act 1974.

[142] *R v Langley* (1899) 31 OR 295.

[143] Trading Stamps Act 1964. The Act was repealed by the Regulatory Reform (Trading Stamps) Order 2005, SI 2005 No. 871, subject to a saving provision in reg. 3. Previously, trading stamp transactions were excepted contracts under the Supply of Goods and Services Act 1982, but the Order removed the exception in the 1982 Act (ss. 1(2)(c), 6) so that the Act, otherwise applicable on its terms, could be applied to trading stamp transactions.

customers in return for goods. It cannot therefore be said that the supplier of the goods receives stamps in order to recover the price of goods supplied from some other paymaster. The stamps themselves lack the currency of money, so, though perhaps they are money's worth, they are not money.[144]

Basic Statutory Distinctions

2.37　**General.**　The implementation of the Sale of Goods Act is based on sets of key definitions. These definitions are of major importance in the application of the passing of property rules. The sale of goods is a hybrid of contract and conveyance in which the contractual and proprietary aspects of the transaction are virtually inseparable, in contrast with the sale of land where the contract and the convey-ance are formally and chronologically distinct.[145] Under the Sale of Goods Act, the passing of property from seller to buyer is the fulcrum on which depend issues as diverse as the incidence of risk, the impact of frustration, the seller's entitlement to recover as a debt the unpaid price, and the rights of buyer and seller in the event of the other's bankruptcy. As this last item shows, the passing of property does not merely provide the key to the resolution of contract problems between the parties *inter se*; it also affects strangers to the contract and may be significant for certain statutory, non-sale purposes where it is important to identify the owner of the goods. The definitions in the Sale of Goods Act do not bear upon the passing of property as an end in itself, but rather as a medium through which contractual rights and liabilities are resolved.

Contract and Conveyance

2.38　**'Contract of sale'.**　The Act defines 'contract of sale' as comprised of 'an agree-ment to sell' and 'a sale'.[146] The former is merely the description of the contract at the executory stage; the latter, in its pure form, refers to the actual conveyance of the goods, though sometimes it designates the cumulation of contract and conveyance arrived at when the contract is executed. Consistent with this latter usage is section 2(6): 'An agreement to sell becomes a sale when the time elapses or the conditions are fulfilled subject to which the property in the goods is to be transferred.' Section 2(4) recognizes that, under some contracts of sale, the property in the goods passes automatically by virtue of the conclusion of the

---

[144] Similarly, gambling chips are not money: *CHT Ltd v Ward* [1965] 2 QB 63,79 ('People do not game in order to win chips; they game in order to win money. The chips are not money or money's worth; they are mere counters or symbols used for the convenience of all concerned in the gaming'), approved in *Lipkin Gorman v Karpnale Ltd* [1991] 2 AC 548, 575.

[145] M. Bridge (1986) 20 *UBC LR* 53.

[146] S. 2(1), (4)–(5).

contract itself: 'Where under a contract of sale the property in the goods is transferred from the seller to the buyer the contract is called a sale.' Here, the contract and conveyance are thoroughly fused and inseparable. According to section 2(5) on the other hand: 'Where under a contract of sale the transfer of the property in the goods is to take place at a future time or subject to some condition later to be fulfilled the contract is called an agreement to sell.' In this case, the contract and conveyance may be chronologically distinct, but the absence of forms in the passing of property in goods renders it just an incident in the performance of the contract.

'Sale'.   The Act also provides in section 61(1) that '"sale" includes a bargain and   **2.39**
sale as well as a sale and delivery', which has no practical significance in modern conditions. This is an unexplained reference to the old common (or *indebitatus*) counts of goods bargained and sold and goods sold and delivered.[147] These counts were simplified actions identifying in abbreviated form the circumstances in which the seller could maintain a debt action for the price. Briefly, if the seller were unable to fit his case into either of these counts, he could not sue in debt but was generally limited to a damages action against the buyer for non-acceptance. The factor uniting the two counts was the passing of property in the goods: the count of goods bargained and sold applied where the property had passed, usually on the conclusion of the contract, but delivery had not occurred; the count of goods sold and delivered lay when the property passed at a later time and delivery had been made. It was always possible for the seller to maintain a right to sue in debt if he stipulated in the contract that the buyer was to pay for the goods at a date prior to the passing of property: the buyer's duty to pay thus became a condition precedent to the seller's duty to convey the goods to the buyer.[148] To succeed in his debt action, however, the seller would have to continue holding himself ready and willing to convey the goods to the buyer on the eventual payment of the price, and would be disqualified if he conveyed the goods to a third party in the meantime.[149] These rules establishing the scope of the seller's debt action are preserved, albeit in different language, in section 49 of the Act.

Significance of sale.   Broadly speaking, sale is the event on which a seller's breach   **2.40**
of contract action passes from damages to debt, though in the latter instance the seller has always been free to elect to sue for damages instead.[150] Sale is also significant in determining whether a buyer denied delivery of the goods may pursue an

---

[147] E. Bullen and S. Leake, *Precedents of Pleadings in Personal Actions in the Superior Courts of the Common Law* (3rd edn, Sweet & Maxwell, 1868), 35–40.

[148] See Sjt. Williams's notes to *Pordage v Cole* (1669) 1 Wms. Saund. 319, Rule 1; *Dunlop v Grote* (1845) 2 C & K 153.

[149] *Laird v Pim* (1841) 7 M & W 478; *Lamond v Davall* (1847) 9 QB 1030.

[150] S. 50.

action in the tort of conversion; such a buyer may thereby succeed in establishing the right to immediate possession[151] needed for bringing an action of this kind. A right to immediate possession does not necessarily follow the passing of property to the buyer, for example, where the buyer has not yet paid and payment is a contractual condition of delivery.[152] Conversely, a buyer may already be in possession of goods though the property has not yet passed under the contract of sale. The buyer's possession of the goods will support an action in trespass or conversion against a third-party tortfeasor, or against a seller who is guilty of a wrongful interference with the goods.[153] A buyer with the right to immediate possession may, where the seller has wrongfully not delivered, elect to sue for damages for non-delivery instead of in conversion. Commonly, there will be little difference between these two actions since the rules on specific delivery in tort have been aligned with the rules on specific performance in contract, with the result that specific delivery is rarely awarded to the buyer.[154] The greater frequency of the seller's debt action for the price, when contrasted with the buyer's correlative action for the recovery of the goods themselves, is explicable on the ground that debt is not a discretionary remedy[155] and that specific delivery has been infected by the discretionary limitations of specific performance.

Conditional Contracts

2.41 **Meaning of conditional contract.**   The Act also provides in section 2(3), a very general provision of no particular significance dealing with an important and complex matter, that a 'contract of sale may be absolute or conditional'. This provision may refer either to a contract whose existence or whose performance turns

---

[151] *Marquess of Bute v Barclays Bank Ltd* [1955] 1 QB 202; *Rodgers v Kennay* (1846) 9 QB 594, 596; *Jarvis v Williams* [1955] 1 WLR 71; *International Factors Ltd v Rodriguez* [1979] QB 351. Although the right to immediate possession may suffice for conversion, the better view is that possession at the time of the wrong is needed for trespass: F. Pollock and R. Wright, *An Essay on Possession in the Common Law* (Clarendon Press, 1888), 28; *Penfold's Wines Pty Ltd v Elliott* (1946) 74 CLR 204; see also E. H. Warren (1936) 49 *Harv LR* 1084.
[152] *Lord v Price* (1874) LR 9 Ex. 54. In *Chinery v Viall* (1860) 5 H & N 288, where sheep had been bought on credit and left in the possession of the seller *qua* agent, the buyer had title to sue without payment or tender of payment. In actions against the seller where the property has passed but the unpaid seller has a lien for the price, the unlawful action of the seller will terminate the lien and endow the buyer with the right to immediate possession so as to be able to sue the seller in conversion: *Gurr v Cuthbert* (1843) 12 LJ Ex. 309. A mere contractual expectancy of receiving goods is not equivalent to the right to immediate possession of them: see *Jarvis v Williams*, n. 151. It may be, however, that the property need not have passed for a buyer in conversion to have the right to immediate possession: *International Factors Ltd v Rodriguez*, n. 151 above.`
[153] *The Winkfield* [1902] P 42; *Wilson v Lombank Ltd* [1963] 1 WLR 1294; *Healing (Sales) Pty Ltd v Inglis Electrix Pty Ltd* (1968) 121 CLR 584 (also a breach of the quiet possession warranty in s. 12(2)(b): *Chinery v Viall*, n. 152 above.
[154] *Cohen v Roche* [1927] 1 KB 169 (specific delivery); *Behnke v Bede Shipping Co. Ltd* [1927] 1 KB 649 (specific performance); see Ch. 11 below.
[155] *White and Carter (Councils) Ltd v McGregor* [1962] AC 413.

upon the occurrence or non-occurrence of a 'condition',[156] a word which is quite possibly the most ambiguous in the contract lexicon.[157] The conclusion of a binding contract may be held up pending the occurrence of a condition external to the contract.[158] Or one or more obligations of a binding contract may be suspended until a condition internal to the contract has been fulfilled.[159] The advantage of the latter type of condition is that, if there has been performance, it can be dealt with under the terminated contract instead of on a restitutionary basis. Where there is an internal condition, it may be non-promissory, in that neither party has undertaken that it will or will not occur.[160] Nevertheless, a non-promissory condition may accompanied by an obligation of varying degrees requiring a party to take steps to assist or not to impede its occurrence.[161] The condition may be promissory in the sense of its occurrence being guaranteed, so that the party bound is answerable in damages while the other is entitled to discharge himself from the contract.[162] In the case of well-established conditions of this sort, the practice is firmly entrenched in English law of conflating the condition, in the sense of an

---

[156] The effect of a condition on the contract is a matter of construction: *North Sea Energy Holdings NV v Petroleum Authority of Thailand* [1997] 2 Lloyd's Rep. 418, 427–8.

[157] See S. Stoljar (1953) 69 *LQR* 485.

[158] As in the 'subject to contract' cases: *Winn v Bull* (1877) 7 Ch. D 29; *Von Hatzfeldt-Wildenberg v Alexander* [1912] 1 Ch. 284, 288–89; *Astra Trust v Adams & Williams* [1969] 1 Lloyd's Rep. 89; *Thoresen & Co (Bangkok) Ltd v Fathom Marine Co. Ltd* [2004] EWHC 167 (Comm); [2004] 1 Lloyd's Rep. 622 (sale of boats: 'subject details' equivalent to subject to contract). See also *Aberfoyle Plantations Ltd v Cheng* [1960] AC 115 (no contract of sale concluded when condition that vendor obtain renewal of seven leases was not fulfilled by the due date).

[159] *Pym v Campbell* (1856) 6 E. & B. 379 (agreement to purchase share of invention did not come into force until a designated third party had approved the invention). See also *Total Gas Marketing Ltd v Arco British Ltd* [1998] 2 Lloyd's Rep. 209 (duties of delivery and acceptance under a gas supply agreement dependent upon the seller entering into an allocation agreement with third parties). On the implied obligation of parties to cooperate with respect to the occurrence of conditions, see *Mackay v Dick* (1881) 6 App. Cas. 251; *AV Pound & Co. Ltd v MW Hardy & Co. Inc.* [1956] AC 588; *Phoebus D Kyprianou v Cyprus Textiles Ltd* [1958] 2 Lloyd's Rep. 60, 64; *North Sea Energy Holdings NV v Petroleum Authority of Thailand*, n. 156 above, 430. See also *Cie Noga d'Importation et d'Exportation SA v Abacha (No. 3)* [2002] EWCA Civ 1142; [2003] 1 WLR 307 at [94]–[108] (Rix LJ) on the effect of non-cooperation by one party on the condition.

[160] It was a common practice in the days of sail for certain overseas contracts to be concluded on 'to arrive' terms, according to which the contract was conditional upon the safe arrival of the ship in the port of discharge. Safe arrival would therefore be a condition precedent to further performance of the contract. The seller was not liable in the event of the goods failing to reach their destination and the buyer was not bound to pay the price; see *Calcutta and Burmah Steam Navigation Co. v De Mattos* (1863) 32 LJQB 322, affd. (1864) 33 LJQB 214; *Hollis Bros & Co. Ltd v White Sea Timber Trust Ltd* [1936] 3 All ER 895. But the courts leant against interpreting contracts to exculpate the non-delivering seller: *Fragano v Long* (1825) 4 B & C 219.

[161] *Habton Farms v Nimmo* [2003] EWCA Civ 68; [2004] QB 1 (sale of racehorse 'subject to veterinary inspection and approval of x-rays in the USA').

[162] *Trans Trust SPRL v Danubian Trading Co. Ltd* [1952] 2 QB 297. This is the sense in which the word is used in the sections dealing with the termination of the contract for breach and with the seller's duties in respect of title, description, fitness, and quality of the goods.

event, and the promise relating to it.[163] The obligee is entitled to terminate the contract when the other party fails to fulfil the condition. Where the performance of a contract is dependent upon compliance with a condition, this may also have an effect on the passing of the property.[164] A common example is a conditional sale contract whereby the buyer obtains possession of the goods and agrees to pay the price by deferred instalments, the property passing upon payment of the final instalment. A similar example is the supply of goods on reservation of title terms.

Existing and Future Goods

2.42 **Forward selling.** Section 5(1) of the Act states: 'The goods which form the subject of a contract of sale may be either existing goods, owned or possessed by the seller, or goods to be manufactured or acquired by him after the making of the contract of sale, in this Act called future goods.' This distinction between existing and future goods comprises the universe of goods: all goods are either one or the other and may not be both. Goods that are in existence but are not yet owned by the seller are, for the purposes of the Act, treated as future goods.[165] The significance of section 5(1) and the remaining provisions of section 5 is as follows. First of all, section 5(1) resolves any doubt that future goods may lawfully be the subject of a contract of sale.[166] The common law has not always been sympathetic to futures and forward delivery trading[167] and, as stated above, there has also been a discernible tendency to confuse an impossible conveyance of future goods with a feasible agreement to convey future goods once they become existing goods. This point is reinforced by section 5(2), which provides that the seller's acquisition of future goods may depend upon a contingency.[168] Whether the seller will be liable in the event that he does not acquire the goods is a different matter: that depends upon the construction of the contract.[169] It is a characteristic feature of modern

---

[163] This is the sense in which the word 'condition' is understood in ss. 11–15 of the Sale of Goods Act.

[164] See Ch. 3 below.

[165] e.g., the goods at the date of the contract in *Varley v Whipp* [1900] 1 QB 513.

[166] *Ajello v Worsley* [1898] 1 Ch. 274.

[167] As an example of a number of early sale of goods cases, see *Lorymer v Smith* (1822) 1 B & C 1, 2. The Statute of Frauds (Amendment) Act (Lord Tenterden's Act) 1828, 9 Geo. IV, cap. 14, s. 7, reproduced in substance as s. 5(2) of the Sale of Goods Act, recognized the existence of such contracts as binding sale of goods agreements. For the exploded belief that such contracts were wagers on commodity prices, see *Bryan v Lewis* (1826) Ry. & Moo. 386. See also K. Llewellyn (1937) 37 *Col. LR* 341, 351 n. 21 (reference to 16th-century market regulations and the forbidden practice of forestalling).

[168] It seems to be a particular application of s. 2(3), though s. 5(2) does not deny the possibility of a seller warranting that future goods will become existing goods.

[169] *Watts v Friend* (1858) 10 B & C 446; *Hale v Rawson* (1858) 4 CB(NS) 85. For the *buyer* claiming a contractual right not to take future goods, see *Messervey v Central Canada Canning Co.* [1923] 3 WWR 365; *Wingold v William Looser & Co. Ltd* [1951] 1 DLR 429.

commodities trading that abstract futures may be the subject of a contract of sale with the possibility that a physical delivery will be made at the due date but the greater likelihood that a settlement will be made in favour of the party who read the market correctly between the contract date and the delivery date.[170] Alternatively, contracting parties may agree on physical delivery at a future date but, for one of various reasons, will substitute a financial settlement in favour of the party who has read the market correctly for physical delivery.[171] In both of these cases, the parties perform as though the contract were one for the settlement of financial differences instead of a true sale of goods contract. A number of questions are posed by such transactions, including whether the contract is one of sale of goods at all, whether the contract is a lawful one and whether the contract is a regulated one. The question whether a contract is truly one of sale or one for the payment of financial differences seems not to be a significant one: the provisions of the Sale of Goods Act relevant to such a contract could apply directly or by analogy. The Gambling Act 2005 permits gambling activity if it is conducted in accordance with the regulatory scheme laid down in the Act or with the Financial Services and Markets Act 2000. A contract of sale of goods is regulated if in fact it amounts to the carrying on of a regulated activity under the Financial Services and Markets Act 2000.[172]

Passing of property. Secondly, section 5(1) leads into section 5(3). Taken **2.43** together, the two provisions establish that a contract is not invalidated just because the subject matter does not exist as defined by the Act.[173] Although the contract may be valid, section 5(3) makes it clear that there can be no passing of property in future goods.[174] This provision recognizes the physical impossibility of the seller transferring the property in goods that do not exist, or that exist but are not

---

[170] For the conversion of a paper contract into a contract calling for the delivery of oil, see *Nissho Iwai Petoleum Co. Inc. v Cargill International SA* [1993] 1 Lloyd's Rep. 80.

[171] See *Gebruder Metelmann GmbH & Co KG v NBR (London) Ltd* [1984] 1 Lloyd's Rep. 614, 523 (explaining the operation of the terminal market in sugar); *Pagnan (R) & Fratelli v Schouten (NGJ) NV (The Filipinas I)* [1973] 1 Lloyd's Rep 349 (contract performed by matching resale and payment of price difference).

[172] See M. Bridge, n. 110 above, 31–2, discussing *CR Sugar Trading Ltd v China National Sugar & Alcohol Group Corpn* [2003] 1 Lloyd's Rep. 179. That case concerned the grant of put options for the sale of sugar on f.o.b. terms which the parties never intended should be exercised. It was held that the parties were carrying on an investment business for the purposes of the Financial Services Act 1986, which preceded the Financial Services and Markets Act 2000. The net cast by the latter statute is potentially very wide: it extends to futures, defined in a way that catches forward delivery contracts—'[r]ights under a contract for the sale of a commodity or property of any description under which delivery is to be made at a future date' (Sch. 2, para. 2).

[173] See also s. 5(2) and n. 167 above.

[174] *Lunn v Thornton* (1845) 1 CB 379; *Belding v Read* (1865) 3 H & C 955, 961 ('there cannot be a prophetic conveyance').

owned by him.[175] Furthermore, a purported present conveyance of future goods will not automatically be converted by the Act or by common law into an effective conveyance at the moment future goods become existing goods. Even if the seller purports to transfer the property in future goods before they become existing goods, he will be treated as having undertaken to transfer the property once they become existing goods by manufacture or acquisition as the case may be.[176] At common law, it has always been impossible to direct the passing of property in goods at some future date without performing a fresh act of conveyance.[177] Nevertheless, a category of goods with a potential existence, such as the unborn young of particular animals or the crop of a particular field owned by the seller, has long been recognized at common law as an exception to this rule, so that a fresh conveyance is not needed when the goods come into existence.[178] This common law exception is the general rule in equity which, looking on that as done which ought to be done, transmits automatically the equitable property in goods, in response to a purported present conveyance, once the goods have come into existence.[179] The equitable rule, however, does not assist volunteers, namely those who have given no consideration for the purported present conveyance.[180] As will be discussed in a later chapter,[181] it was never clear to what extent these equitable rules applied to ordinary contracts of sale that were not designed as part of a scheme to provide security for a loan. Furthermore, as the present authorities hold, it seems that the Sale of Goods Act concedes no part or very little part to equitable rules concerning the passing of property.[182]

Specific and Unascertained Goods

2.44 Definitions. Specific goods are those 'identified and agreed on at the time a contract of sale is made'.[183] The Act also makes references to unascertained

---

[175] But note that s. 5(1) appears to include, in the definition of existing goods, goods that the seller possesses but does not own. It may be that the seller of such goods may, prior to acquiring ownership from the third-party owner, divest himself of the whole of his entitlement in the goods on the proprietary transfer (see Ch. 3 below). As soon as the seller acquires proprietary rights from the owner, the buyer's title would then be automatically fed. The seller's contractual responsibility in respect of that transfer, however, would fall under s. 12.

[176] In accordance with s. 27.

[177] *Lunn v Thornton*, n. 174 above; *Langton v Higgins* (1859) 4 H & N 402. The same effect would be achieved if the buyer took possession under a licence to seize: *Congreve v Evetts* (1854) 10 Ex. 298; *Hope v Hayley* (1856) 5 E & B 830.

[178] *Grantham v Hawley* (1603) Hob. 132; *Grass v Austin* (1882) 7 OAR 511 (Can.).

[179] *Holroyd v Marshall* (1862) 10 HLC 191; *Tailby v Official Receiver* (1888) 13 App. Cas. 523; *Collyer v Isaacs* (1881) 19 Ch. D 342.

[180] *Re Ellenborough* [1903] 1 Ch. 697.

[181] See Ch. 3 below.

[182] *Ibid.*; *Re Wait* [1927] 1 Ch. 606.

[183] S. 61(1). This now includes an 'undivided share, specified as a fraction or percentage, of goods identified and agreed on' at the contract date: see the definition of specific goods in s. 61(1) of the Sale of Goods Act (as am. by s. 2(d) of the Sale of Goods (Amendment) Act 1995).

goods,[184] which are nowhere defined. By inference, however, unascertained goods are all those goods that, at the date of the contract, are not specific goods. Although the Act is clear that these goods cannot be specific,[185] goods that subsequently become ascertained so as to acquire some of the properties of specific goods are occasionally and loosely referred to as specific goods.[186] Just as the distinction between existing and future goods exhausts all goods at the contract date, so too does the distinction between specific and unascertained goods. But the two sets of distinctions do not quite rotate on the same axis. Existing goods may be either specific or unascertained, while future goods are nearly always unascertained and specific goods are almost always existing goods. An identified second-hand reaper owned and possessed by a third party at the contract date, and thus future goods, was regarded as specific goods in *Varley v Whipp*.[187] A more difficult case is that of goods, not yet physically in existence, such as a contract for the sale of a manufacturing seller's entire output over a stated, future period. If that output cannot be measured at the contract date, the question is whether it has been 'identified'; it would seem to have been 'agreed on'. Identification supposes a process of ascertaining uniqueness that is certain. The treatment of an entire future output as specific goods will depend upon whether courts are prepared to invoke the principle of subsequent ascertainment (*id certum est quod certum reddi potest*). The words 'at the time a contract of sale is made' point away from the application of this principle and towards the treatment of the future output as unascertained goods. A contract to sell a fungible item possessed in bulk by a seller in his store room will involve goods that are both existing and unascertained. A contract to sell a fungible item that the seller intends to manufacture in bulk will involve goods that are both future and unascertained. A contract for the sale of a fungible item often will not stipulate whether the goods to be supplied are existing or future goods, leaving the seller with the choice of appropriating either to the contract.

Quasi-specific Goods

Unascertained goods and specific bulk.   Two refinements have to be introduced **2.45** to the distinction between specific and unascertained goods. First, the parties may contract for the sale of unascertained goods but limit the seller's power of selection to a specific bulk. A seller may be required to supply widgets from the stock currently in his store room just as, in an example used by Chalmers,[188] a seller may

---

[184] Ss. 16 and 18, Rule 5. They are also referred to in their later ascertained state in ss. 17(1) and 52.

[185] See also *Re Wait*, n. 182 above, 630.

[186] e.g., *Waren Import Gesellschaft Krohn & Co. v Toepfer (Alfred C) (The Vladimir Ilich)* [1975] 1 Lloyd's Rep 322, 328.

[187] [1900] 1 QB 513. See also *Bannerman v Barlow* (1908) 7 WLR 859 (Can.); *JI Case Threshing Machine Co. v Fee* (1909) 10 WLR 70 (Can.).

[188] n. 35 above, 19–20 ('five dozen of the '74 champagne wine in my cellar'); see *Howell v Coupland* (1876) 1 QBD 258.

undertake to supply a number of bottles of a particular vintage of wine from the larger stock currently lying in his cellar. Despite sometimes being described as specific goods,[189] these quasi-specific goods remain in principle unascertained goods since it cannot be said of any particular widget or bottle in the larger stock whether it has been identified and agreed upon at the contract date. The seller's power of selection may be constrained in varying degrees between the cases of unlimited selection and quasi-specific goods. A seller, for example, may have to supply amber durum wheat shipped from a Pacific Coast port in July. Although these are not quasi-specific goods, the seller's choice is limited: he may not tender to the buyer amber durum wheat of the same quality as the contract demands shipped from a Great Lakes port in a different month.

2.46 **Quasi-specific goods in the Act.** Quasi-specific goods cannot be treated as specific goods where the Act lays down particular rules for specific goods, as it does for example in sections 6–7 for initial and subsequent impossibility of performance arising out of the perishing of goods.[190] Indeed, the Act itself makes it plain that the passing of property rules for specific goods cannot be applied to quasi-specific goods.[191] Yet this hybrid category of quasi-specific goods has certain of the characteristics of specific goods and, even if a provision of the Act does not apply to it, careful thought should be given to the application of that provision by analogy or as the statutory expression of a broader and relevant common law principle.

Ascertained Goods

2.47 **Effect of ascertainment.** The second refinement concerns ascertained goods which appear to defy the binary classification of goods as specific or unascertained. Ascertained goods, along with specific goods, are eligible for specific performance.[192] Ascertained goods do not exist in that state at the contract date: they are goods initially unascertained that have subsequently been identified to the contract.[193] At that date, the impediment to the passing of property in unascertained goods, laid down by the Act and motivated by the same consideration of impossibility that prevents the property passing in future goods, is lifted.

Summary

2.48 **Significance of distinction between specific and unascertained.** The distinction between specific and unascertained goods formerly had a dramatic impact

---

[189] e.g., *Howell v Coupland,* n. 188 above.

[190] *HR and S Sainsbury Ltd v Street* [1972] 1 WLR 834.

[191] S. 16. See also *Re Wait,* n. 182 above.

[192] S. 52.

[193] *Re Wait,* n. 182 above, 630 (Atkin LJ). On ascertainment, see Ch. 3 below.

on the incidence of contractual rights and duties. It is much less important nowadays.[194] In principle, as the Act maintains, the property in specific goods passes at the contract date and in unascertained goods at a later date.[195] Judicial interpretation of the relevant provisions has blunted this distinction in the area of the passing of property, partly at least to avoid the application of the now-repealed rule that specific goods could never be rejected by the buyer if the property in them had already passed.[196] The distinction retains its force in the contractual areas of discharge for initial and subsequent impossibility.[197] For much of the nineteenth century, the distinction was important for the incidence of the seller's obligations concerning the quality and fitness of goods. The rule of *caveat emptor* was more effective in diluting the obligations of the seller of specific goods than those of the seller of unascertained goods.[198] This discrepancy showed a tendency to diminish during the course of the nineteenth century, though it persisted to a lesser degree in a disguised form in the Act.[199]

General and Special Property

Definitions. A sale of goods contract requires the seller to transfer the 'property' **2.49** in goods to the buyer:[200] 'property' is defined as 'the general property in goods and not merely a special property'.[201] No definition is given for 'special property'.

Ownership and conversion. Personal property law is vague on the definition of **2.50** its basic concepts. The Sale of Goods Act does not speak of ownership, and for a good reason. At common law, proprietary rights are protected from tortious interference by means of personal actions requiring the plaintiff to be in possession or have the right to immediate possession at the time of the wrong.[202] Before the

---

194 The distinction did not feature in the draft bill attached to the Ontario Law Reform Commission, *Report on Sale of Goods* (1979). A periphrastic reference to a hybrid of specific and ascertained goods emerges in the Canadian Uniform Sale of Goods Act, s. 92(2)(a) ('a contract that requires for its performance goods identified when the contract is made or goods that have been subsequently identified to the contract with the consent of both parties'). See Alberta Institute of Law Research and Reform, *The Uniform Sale of Goods Act 1982* (Report No. 38), 203–4.
195 S. 18, Rule 1, Rule 5.
196 Misrepresentation Act 1967, s. 4(1).
197 Ss. 6–7.
198 See Ch. 7 below.
199 In the former presumptive denial of rejection rights in the case of specific goods.
200 S. 2(1).
201 S. 61(1).
202 *The Winkfield* [1902] P 42; *Marquess of Bute v Barclays Bank Ltd* [1955] 1 QB 202. According to F. Pollock and R. Wright, n. 151 above, 5, 'so feeble and precarious was property without possession, or rather without possessory remedies . . . that Possession largely usurped not only the substance but the name of Property'. For the recovery in damages of the full value of the chattel by the bailee, see *The Winkfield*, above, and *The Joanna Vatis* [1922] P 92. Owners out of possession were given a new remedy in the form of an action on the case for damage done to their reversionary interest in *Mears v London and South Western Railway Co. Ltd* (1862) 11 CB (NS) 850.

enactment of the Torts (Interference with Goods) Act 1977, the position was as follows. A plaintiff succeeded in a conversion action because his possessory right was superior to the defendant's.[203] The judgment operated finally as between the parties to the action without having an *in rem* effect on strangers. Only in exceptional cases was the defendant permitted to resist the plaintiff's possession-based claim by pointing to the superior possessory right (the *ius tertii*) of a third party.[204] Such relativity of right as between plaintiff and defendant[205] hardly accorded with anything so absolute as ownership.[206] It was quite consistent with this lack of absoluteness that delivery up of the disputed thing was not available as a remedy until quite recent times;[207] even today, it is infrequently awarded.[208]

2.51 **Abolition of *ius tertii*.** The 1977 Act abolished the *ius tertii* defence and promoted the joinder of multiple actions involving the same disputed goods.[209] It also made provision for the avoidance of the overcompensation that came with the award of full damages to plaintiffs with only a limited possessory interest; the defendant was concomitantly protected from multiple liabilities exceeding the value of the goods.[210] The 1977 changes may betoken the start of a movement towards absolute ownership going beyond the text of the Act itself; they do not affect the earlier[211] provisions of the Sale of Goods Act.

2.52 **Meaning of general property.** The general property in goods can therefore be understood as encapsulating the best possessory right there can be in the contract goods, a possessory right that is good against the whole world. If even such a possessory right seems fugitive, it should be remembered that goods, in contrast with land, which is permanent and ineradicable, have always been regarded at common law as transient and so hardly deserving of the complex

---

[203] *Buckley v Gross* (1863) 3 B & S 566; *Bird v Town of Fort Frances* [1949] OR 292 (Can.).

[204] Where the defendant had not interfered with the plaintiff's possession and was not the plaintiff's bailee: *Leake v Loveday* (1842) 4 M & G 972; *Biddle v Bond* (1865) 6 B & S 225. A defendant unable to plead the *ius tertii* might yet defend the action on the authority of the true owner: *Biddle v Bond*, above; *Rogers Sons & Co. v Lambert & Co.* [1891] 1 QB 318. He could also plead eviction by title paramount: *Ross v Edwards* (1895) 73 LT 100.

[205] *Waverley Borough Council v Fletcher* [1996] QB 334, 345: '[T]he English law of ownership and possession . . . is not a system of identifying absolute entitlement, but of priority of entitlement' (Auld LJ). See also *Costello v Chief Constable of Derbyshire* [2001] EWCA Civ 381; [2001] 1 WLR 1437.

[206] The language of ownership is probably attributable to the influence of 19th-century factors legislation; see generally G. Battersby and A.D. Preston (1972) 35 *MLR* 268.

[207] Common Law Procedure Act 1854, s. 78.

[208] See Ch. 11 below; *General and Finance Facilities Ltd v Cook's Cars (Romford) Ltd* [1963] 2 All ER 314. For a case where the court exercised its discretion in favour of the plaintiff, see *Howard E Perry & Co. Ltd v British Railways Board* [1980] 1 WLR 1375 ('Steel is gold').

[209] Ss. 8–9.

[210] Ss. 5(3), 7.

[211] In the sense that they were brought forward from the 1893 Act.

proprietary structure (the doctrine of estates) that is capable of dividing land in a multiple fashion among various owners and over time.[212] Quite simply, the general property in goods is the most exalted interest that the law deems personal property fit to have: nothing more enduring is necessary for a species of property that does not last forever.

Sale of limited interest.   Despite this modest statement of the general property,   **2.53** it may not be the interest that the buyer and seller have agreed that the former shall have. It is common for a limited interest to be the subject of a sale agreement,[213] even an interest that is precarious to a degree unknown by the parties.[214] Notwithstanding such shortcomings in the seller's proprietary interest, the contract should still be regarded as one governed by the Sale of Goods Act. To reach this result, the above definition of general property needs to be modified. For the contract to be one of sale, it is necessary for the seller to transfer or agree to transfer the whole of his interest in the goods, and not reserve a part of that interest unconditionally or direct the buyer to hold the goods on bailment terms,[215] for a bailee's interest is but a special property in the goods.[216] The difference between general and special property will nevertheless in certain cases appear to be quantitative,[217] but that is hardly unusual given the extent to which the notion of relativity of right has pervaded this area of law. In the last resort, what matters is the scope of the interest that the seller warrants will be transferred and not the interest the seller succeeds in transferring.[218]

---

[212] J. Williams, n. 2 above, 44.

[213] S. 2(2) deals with sales beween part owners.

[214] S. 12(3) permits limited title sales.

[215] But a contract can still be one of sale if the buyer is charged with redeeming a carrier's lien by paying outstanding freight or with redeeming a pledge advance: see *Franklin v Neate* (1844) 13 M&W 481.

[216] *The Odessa* [1916] AC 145 (terminology criticized); *Nyberg v Handelaar* [1892] 2 QB 202; *Donald v Suckling* (1866) LR 1 QB 585; O. W. Homes, *The Common Law* (Little Brown, 1881), 242. For the proprietary interest of a commercial pledgee of documents of title, see *Burdick v Sewell* (1884) 13 QBD 157, 174 (Bowen LJ dissenting), reversed *sub nom. Sewell v Burdick* (1884) 10 App. Cas. 74, 92–3 (Lord Blackburn); *Harper v Godsell* (1870) LR 5 QB 422, 426 (Blackburn J) (delivery warrants); *The Orteric* [1920] AC 724.

[217] e.g., the lease of goods for a period equal to their useful life. From an early date, a finder has been considered to hold the chattel under the terms of a deemed bailment, yet where the true owner is not to be found it is in practical terms indefeasible; see W. Laidlaw (1931) 16 *Cornell LQ* 286, 287. The same idea was implicit in the 14th-century extension of the writ of detinue to finders: Williams, n. 2 above, 16. See also *Newman v Bourne and Hollingsworth* (1915) 31 TLR 209.

[218] 'The purpose of the contract [of sale] is that the seller divests himself of all proprietary rights in the thing sold in favour of the buyer': M. Chalmers, n. 35 above, 3. Cf Atkin LJ's statement that 'there can be no sale of goods at all which the seller has no right to sell': *Rowland v Divall* [1923] 2 KB 500, 507, criticized in Ch. 5 below.

The Contract of Sale and Related Transactions Involving Goods

2.54 **General.** Though the issue is rather less important than it used to be, it may still be important for various reasons to distinguish sale of goods contracts from related contracts involving the transfer of goods. It should not be forgotten, however, that much of the Sale of Goods Act consists of *prima facie* rules, departed from in numerous types of sale contracts, and of duties that may be excluded subject to external statutory controls. Furthermore, section 62(2) exists to prevent the divergence of sales law from the general law of contract.

2.55 **Issues.** The scope of the Act may present itself in different contexts. No longer do sale of goods contracts have to be evidenced in writing when related contracts need not be.[219] Furthermore, as regards the quality and fitness of goods supplied under transfer contracts akin to sale, such as work and materials contracts, the courts displayed a willingness at common law to mimic the statutory terms of fitness and quality even before these were enacted in the Supply of Goods and Services Act 1982. Nevertheless, the rules in the Act on the passing of property and on the seller's action for the price find no statutory counterpart in legislation dealing with related contracts. These rules may be applied by analogy outside the Act, an expedient adopted for the implied terms of quality and fitness before these were expressly enacted in separate legislation. What precisely is meant by application by analogy is a different matter. A statute might serve as a policy inspiration for innovation in the common law.[220] It might even be argued that cases outside the Sale of Goods Act fall within the equity of the statute.[221] These approaches hardly fit a codifying statute like the Sale of Goods Act which, in its 1893 form, drew upon case law that also sustained contracts akin to sale of goods. The Act in this respect may be regarded as evidence of the common law that applied to related contracts, or the common law that would have developed had it not been cut off by the process of enactment and confined to sale of goods, the most important of a group of like transactions. The enactment of a codifying statute should not be relied upon to prevent the cross-pollination between sale and related contracts that would certainly have occurred if sales law had remained uncodified.

---

[219] The writing requirement was repealed by the Law Reform (Enforcement of Contracts) Act 1954, s. 1.

[220] *The Queen in Right of Canada v Saskatchewan Wheat Pool* (1983) 143 DLR (3d) 9; *Bhadauria v Board of Governors of Seneca College* (1979) 105 DLR (3d) 707, revd (1981) 124 DLR (3d) 193. This process may lead to the expansion at common law of tenancy in common principles boosted by statutory changes to the Sale of Goods Act (principally ss. 20A–B) introduced in the mid-1990s. See the discussion below of loans for consumption.

[221] J. Landis, 'Statutes and the Sources of Law' in *Harvard Legal Essays* (Harvard University Press, 1934). See also J. Landis (1965) 2 *Harv J of Leg.* 7.

Work and Materials Contracts

Range of contracts.   Work and materials[222] contracts fall within a spectrum run-   **2.56**
ning from the supply of services to sale of goods. A contract to supply services,
such as transport or dry-cleaning, is not a sale of goods contract. Nor is it a work
and materials contract.[223] There are, however, few contracts for services where
only labour is supplied: even a dry-cleaner supplies wire coat hangers. Work and
materials differ from services in that goods supplied are integral, not collateral, to
the supplier's performance. At the other end of the spectrum, a sale of goods contract may include services, for example, the sale of a kitchen appliance with a
labour and parts warranty, or the sale of a fixture which the seller agrees to disman-
tle prior to delivery.[224] Labour is inherent in the manufacture and distribution of
goods, so the distinction between sale of goods and work and materials is one of
degree.

Interplay of labour and goods.   It is therefore necessary to explore the conjunc-   **2.57**
tion of labour and goods before drawing a line between sale of goods and work and
materials. Labour and goods may be blended in an integrated way in the manufacturing process, as where a painter produces a portrait in oils[225] and a dentist
a set of dentures.[226] Or the labour may be collateral to goods that are made serviceable, as where a plumber installs a furnace[227] or a garage fits replacement parts in
a car.[228] Sometimes labour is both integral and collateral, as where boilers are built
and then installed.[229] In so far as labour and goods are capable of being separated,

---

222 An expression preferred herein to labour and materials and work and labour.

223 But the two are sometimes confused: *Grouse Mountain Resorts Ltd v Bank of Montreal* (1960)
25 DLR (2d) 371. For a discussion of the difference between services contracts and work and materials contracts, see *Foster Wheeler Wood Group Engineering Ltd v Chevron UK Ltd* [1996] QB 381 at
[87] *et seq.* (as to whether the doctrine of abatement applied to the contract).

224 *Underwood v Burgh Castle Brick Co.* [1992] 1 KB 343.

225 *Robinson v Graves* [1935] 1 KB 579 (work and materials); *Isaacs v Hardy* (1884) Cab. &
El. 287 (sale of goods). In such cases, the law tends towards work and materials: *Dodd and Dodd v
Wilson* [1949] 2 All ER 691 (inoculation of cattle). But see *Philip Head & Sons Ltd v Showfronts Ltd*
[1970] 1 Lloyd's Rep. 140 (installation of carpet).

226 *Lee v Griffin* (1861) 1 B & S 272 (sale); *Samuels v Davis* [1943] 1 KB 526 (sale). See also
Marcel (Furriers) Ltd v Tapper [1953] 1 All ER 15 (sale of fur jacket made to order); *Deta Nominees
Pty Ltd v Viscount Plastic Products Pty Ltd* [1979] VR 167 (sale of custom-built manufacturing dies);
Lockett v A and M Charles Ltd [1938] 4 All ER 170; *Gee v White Spot Ltd* (1986) 7 BCLR (2d) 235
(Can.) (sale of restaurant meal).

227 *British American Paint Co. v Fogh* (1915) 24 DLR 61 (*semble* sale, but out of line with other
authorities).

228 *Stewart v Reavell's Garage* [1952] 2 QB 545 (work and materials); *GH Myers & Co. v Brent
Cross Service Co.* [1934] 1 KB 46 (work and materials); *Sterling Engine Works v Red Deer Lumber Co.*
(1920) 51 DLR 509 (work and materials).

229 *Anglo-Egyptian Navigation Co. v Rennie* (1875) LR 10 CP 271 (work and materials). See also
Clark v Bulmer (1843) 11 M & W 243 (installation of engine: work and materials); *Fairbanks Soap
Co. v Sheppard* [1953] 1 SCR 314 (Can.) (building of machinery: work and materials); *Wolfenden v
Wilson* (1873) 33 UCQB 442 (Can.: manufacture and installation of tombstone: sale *sed quaere?*).

it might be argued that the Sale of Goods Act should be applied to that part of the transaction concerning goods, the remainder being governed by a separate regime.[230] The abolition of the writing requirement and the enactment of the Supply of Goods and Services Act 1982 have created the opportunity to move away from contractual classification questions and ask more specific questions about the different incidents of contracts on a sliding scale of variation.[231] Where labour and goods are inseparably blended, the Act could be applied to the ingredients used, if not to the overall product. Support for this type of partial application of the Sale of Goods Act, however, is hardly at all in evidence in the case law.[232]

2.58 **Possible tests.** If a transaction concerning the product of labour and goods must be classified definitively as a sale of goods or supply of work and materials, the choice seems to lie among three possible tests. First, the transaction may be seen in substance or essence as one or the other; secondly, a comparative value test may be applied to determine whether the goods or the labour have the greater financial value; or thirdly, the transaction may be seen as a sale of goods contract if the property in some goods is conveyed and these goods are not wholly incidental to the transaction. Drawing the line between sale of goods and work and materials has in the past been distorted in favour of the latter by the judicial desire in some cases to avoid the old writing requirement for sale of goods.

2.59 **Substance of the transaction.** In *Lee v Griffin*,[233] the plaintiff dentist contracted to prepare two sets of false teeth. When his patient died before payment, her executor, citing the absence of writing, declined to pay. The contract was held to be one of sale of goods and thus unenforceable. Blackburn J purportedly applied a substance test, but considered it satisfied if the property in goods was transferred by one party to the other. The breadth of his approach is evident in the example he gives of the sculptor who, despite all his art and labour,[234] is a seller of the statue he makes. The comparative value test was firmly rejected by the court,[235] which also excluded from the category of sale supplies of collateral goods, such as the

---

[230] It has been recognized that a transaction may be mixed: *Hyundai Heavy Industries Co. Ltd v Papadopoulos* [1980] 1 WLR 1129 (contract for sale of ship to be built contained features making it akin to work and materials and services contracts); *Stocznia Gdanska SA v Latvian Shipping Co* [1998] 1 WLR 574, 588–89. See also *Pritchett & Gold v Currie* [1916] 2 Ch. 515 (sale of storage battery later to be installed); *Matheson v Meredith* (1955) 1 DLR (2d) 332. Cf. *H Parsons (Livestock) Ltd v Uttley, Ingham & Co. Ltd* [1978] QB 791. But shipbuilding contracts have usually been treated as sale of goods contracts: *Reid v Macbeth & Gray* [1904] AC 223; *McDougall v Aeromarine of Emsworth Ltd* [1958] 3 All ER 431.

[231] Such as: how strict is the liability of a garage when installing new parts? Or when checking existing parts?

[232] But see *Borek v Hooper* (1994) 18 OR (2d) 470 (Can.), discussed below.

[233] n. 226 above; see the thorough review in *Deta Nominees, ibid*.

[234] Exceeding in value the materials.

[235] 'I do not think that the test to apply to these cases is whether the value of the work exceeds that of the materials': n. 226 above, 278.

paper used by an attorney for an opinion and the book produced by the printer.[236] It is hard to see why these are excluded by the letter of the test applied by Blackburn J, who was plainly yielding to the imperative of an impressionistic judgment guided by some sense of substance.

Comparative value.   The leading modern statement of the law, *Robinson v* **2.60** *Graves*,[237] concerned a contract to paint a portrait of the defendant's future wife, which was held to be one of work and materials. The reasoning is unpersuasive and the court is unsure whether it is applying or departing from *Lee v Griffin*,[238] a case hard to distinguish on its facts. Some emphasis was placed on the degree of co-operation required of the sitter as tending towards work and materials, but the same could be said of a patient whose mouth is modelled for dentures. The core of the decision in *Robinson*, however, was that a contract was in substance one for work and materials where the value of the skill well exceeded that of the accompanying materials.[239] This pragmatic blend of language accepted and rejected in *Lee v Griffin* is unproductive of precision and encourages the search for differences of degree between, for example, a photographer who produces quick passport photographs[240] and one who prints portraits, or between a society painter and a street artist. In defence of *Robinson*, however, the court seemed unwilling to allow an unconscientious contract-breaker to put up the defence of non-compliance with the sale of goods writing requirement.

Materials supplied by customer.   A particular difficulty along the line between **2.61** work and materials and sale of goods occurs in those cases where materials are supplied by a customer to be made up into a new product. The supply of the new product by the manufacturer is unlikely to be treated as a sale of goods if no goods of the manufacturer are used in the process.[241] The position is more complicated if the manufacturer's own goods are added to the customer's. There is support for the view that such a contract is one of sale,[242] but this conclusion would be unattainable if the customer never intended to convey the property in his materials to the manufacturer and the preponderance of the materials came from the customer rather than the manufacturer. In this case, the manufacturer's materials would, under the rule of accession, vest in the customer once they were irrevocably

---

[236] *Ibid.*, 277–8. But see *Canada Bank Note Engraving and Printing Co. v Toronto Railway Co.* (1895) 21 OAR 462 (Can.) (printing of a special debenture form a sale of goods), purportedly applying *Lee v Griffin*, n. 226 above.

[237] n. 225 above. Criticized trenchantly in *Deta Nominees*, n. 226 above.

[238] n. 226 above.

[239] n. 225 above, 585–6 and 589–90.

[240] Cf *R v Howarth* [1920] 2 WWR 1043 (Can.) (sale of enlarged photograph).

[241] One possibility is a contract for services, but the property in new goods vests under the *specificatio* rule in the manufacturer, so a work and materials contract (at least) ought to be required if the property is later to be transferred to the supplier of the materials.

[242] *Dixon v London Small Arms Co. Ltd* (1876) 1 App. Cas. 632, *per* Lord Penzance.

attached to the customer's materials[243] and there would be nothing to convey to the customer.

2.62 **Practical importance.**   To a large extent, the repeal of the writing requirement has robbed this issue of any practical significance. Even before the enactment of the Supply of Goods and Services Act 1982, the House of Lords in *Young & Marten Ltd v McManus Childs Ltd*[244] was prepared to extend by analogy implied terms of fitness and quality in the Sale of Goods Act to related transactions, since it would be invidious for the strength of warranty rights to be determined by the side of the line on which a transaction fell.[245] In the Canadian case of *Borek v Hooper*,[246] a painting was commissioned to fill a particular space in the purchaser's home. The painting cracked and the court, ruling in favour of the purchaser, applied a common law warranty of fitness for purpose, not to the painting as such, but to the materials used. It is unlikely that the Supply of Goods and Services Act 1982 Act would permit such a distinction between the ingredients and the final product, but it would probably be immaterial in most cases. Modern legislation also enacts a standard of due care for the supply of services[247] so that, whilst the line between sale of goods and work and materials may not be important for warranty reasons, the line between services and goods will be.[248]

Barter and Trade-in Agreements

2.63 **Analysis.**   Where goods are supplied in return for goods, the transaction is one of barter (or exchange).[249] A similar conclusion follows where goods are exchanged for labour[250] or for some consideration other than a money consideration. The absence of a money consideration means it is not a sale of goods and so the rules

---

[243] *Scott Maritimes Pulp Ltd v BF Goodrich Canada Ltd* (1977) 72 DLR (3d) 680. The issue was not resolved in *Simplex Machine Co. Ltd v McLellan, McFeely & Co. Ltd* [1928] 3 WWR 255 (Can.).

[244] [1969] 1 AC 454. See also *GH Myers & Co. v Brent Cross Service Co.* n. 228 above; *Watson v Buckley Osborne Garrett & Co. Ltd* [1940] 1 All ER 174; *Stewart v Reavell's Garage*, n. 228 above; *Hart v Bell Telephone Co. of Canada Ltd* (1976) 26 OR (2d) 218 (Can.). Cf *Helicopter Sales (Australia) Pty Ltd v Rotor-Work Pty Ltd* (1974) 132 CLR 1.

[245] Lord Upjohn in *Young & Marten*, n. 244 above, 473 ('most unsatisfactory, illogical, and indeed a severe blow to any idea of a coherent system of common law').

[246] (1994) 18 OR (2d) 470 (Can.).

[247] Supply of Goods and Services Act 1982, s. 13.

[248] See Ch. 7 below.

[249] *Pearce v Brain* [1929] 2 KB 310. The Sale of Goods Bill originally contained a provision applying its provisions *mutatis mutandis* to contracts of exchange, but this was deleted in the House of Commons Select Committee: Chalmers, n. 35 above, 5.

[250] See *Doyle v East* [1972] 1 WLR 1080 (land); *Robshaw Bros Ltd v Mayer* [1957] Ch. 125. Cf *Koppel v Koppel* [1966] 1 WLR 802 (where the passing of property rules in the Sale of Goods Act 1979 were applied to a contract for services in return for goods).

governing actions for the price will not apply.[251] Extending these rules by analogy will not assist a plaintiff if a liquidated money value cannot be assigned to the undelivered goods. It is sometimes possible to construe a barter as back-to-back sales with a mutual set-off of the prices owed, but this may only be done if a cash-value can be assigned to the subject matter of the transaction.[252] In some running account agreements, the periodic striking of a settlement figure should give the supplier in credit a debt action.[253] Some transactions may be analysed as requiring the recipient of goods to pay cash subject to an option to supply goods instead.[254] This inference will be a likely one if a cash price is first agreed before the buyer is given the option.[255]

Trade-in.   Trade-in agreements, as well as the similar promotional agreements   **2.64** under which money and vouchers are supplied for goods, merit a separate mention. Lord Reid was of the view that the party giving the mixed consideration in a promotional transaction was not a buyer of goods,[256] but the Act does not require an exclusively money consideration. If the seller's consideration (goods) may be leavened with some labour, it ought to follow that the buyer's consideration (money) may be supplemented with some goods. Suppose the seller of a new car wishes to sue for the price a defaulting buyer who agreed to pay with cash and a trade-in. This should be permissible if a price was agreed and the buyer given the option, as is usually the case, of paying a stated amount in the form of the trade-in.[257] A buyer who defaults is thereby not exercising his option to pay part of the price in kind. A further complex problem in trade-in transactions is whether both parties deal in the dual capacities of buyer and seller. If this is the case, the dealer will be entitled to the benefit of whatever implied terms might be available if he were the buyer of the trade-in vehicle. The liability of trade sellers being greater than private sellers,[258] this question is more significant if the

---

[251] *Harrison v Luke* (1845) 14 M & W 139; *WJ Albutt & Co. v Riddell* [1930] 4 DLR 111; *R v Langley* (1899) 31 OR 295 (Can.). Since the contract of exchange or barter is governed by s. 1 of the Supply of Goods and Services Act 1982 ('a contract under which one person transfers or agrees to transfer the property in goods'), the implied terms of title, description, satisfactory quality, and fitness for purpose are to be found in that Act (ss. 2–4).

[252] e.g., *Aldridge v Johnson* (1857) 7 E & B 855; *Messenger v Greene* [1937] 2 DLR 26 (goods exchanged at 'regular prices'); *Saxty v Wilkin* (1843) 11 M & W 622; *Hands v Burton* (1808) 9 East 349; *Flynn v Mackin & Mahon* [1974] IR 101; but see *Davey v Paine Bros (Motors) Ltd* [1954] NZLR 1122 (explicable on apparent authority grounds).

[253] e.g., *Ingram v Shirley* (1816) 1 Stark 185.

[254] *South Australian Insurance Co. Ltd v Randell* (1869) LR 3 PC 101 and similar cases discussed below.

[255] *Gordon v Hipwell* [1951] 2 DLR 733.

[256] *Chappell & Co. Ltd v Nestlé Co. Ltd* [1960] AC 87, 109. Cf *Buckley v Lever Bros* [1953] OR 704; see also *Mason & Risch v Christner* (1920) 48 OLR 8 (Can.).

[257] See *GJ Dawson (Clapham) Ltd v Dutfield* [1936] 2 All ER 232; see also *Forsyth v Jervis* (1816) 1 Stark 437. A trade-in was, however, treated as an exchange in *Davey v Paine* [1954] NZLR 1122.

[258] Since s. 14(2), (3) only applies to sales in the course of a business.

trade-in supplier is also in the motor trade. It should not unduly strain matters to regard both parties as sellers under back-to-back transactions with a set-off and out-standing cash balance.[259]

Bailment Agreements

2.65 **Meaning of bailment.** Bailment is a transaction in which possession of goods is transferred from bailor to bailee, whether for a fixed, determinable, or indeterminate term, on the understanding that the goods will be returned at the end of the term, or transferred to or held on behalf of someone else at the bailor's direction.[260] In those cases where the bailee pays hire for the enjoyment of the goods, it is his acquisition of only a special property that distinguishes the bailment from a sale.[261] The distinction between sale and bailment fades away in practical terms, where depreciating goods are hired to a bailee for the rest of their useful life, or under that form of bailment called hire purchase where a purchase option is given to the bailee. Bailment is usually a consensual relationship[262] which in most cases flows from a contract between bailor and bailee, though in some cases it is gratuitous.[263] Sometimes the bailor will pay the bailee for his services in relation to the goods; sometimes the bailee will pay the bailor for his enjoyment of them. It is the latter of these cases that approximates more to a sale of goods agreement, from which it is to be distinguished by the transfer under the bailment of only a special property in the goods in return for a sum called hire, representing not the value of the goods themselves but the value of their use.

Hire Purchase

2.66 **Similarity to sale.** Hire purchase[264] is functionally similar to conditional sale, a transaction plainly covered by the Sale of Goods Act.[265] Both transactions permit

---

[259] This was done in *Smith v Billard* (1922) 55 NSR 502 (Can.), even though there had been no valuation of the trade-in. Cf. *Mason & Risch*, n. 256 above.

[260] N. E. Palmer, *Bailment* (2nd edn, Sweet & Maxwell, 1991); W. Jones, *An Essay on the Law of Bailment* (1781); G. Paton, *Bailment in the Common Law* (Stevens, 1952); *Motor Mart Ltd v Webb* [1958] NZLR 773.

[261] But see *Motor Mart*, n. 260 above, where the court treated a conditional sale agreement as a bailment: *sed quaere*? See also the reservation of title cases discussed in Ch. 3 below.

[262] With the exception of involuntary bailment, and quasi-bailments such as that based upon a finding.

[263] Despite attempts to fit it into a contract mould, it is submitted that this is the better rationalization, on the facts presented, of *Bainbridge v Firmstone* (1838) 8 A & E 743. See C. Davidge (1925) 41 *LQR* 433 and Sir F. Pollock's sharp observation, *ibid.*, 440.

[264] R. Goode, *Hire Purchase Law and Practice* (2nd edn, Butterworths, 1970); A. G. Guest, *The Law of Hire Purchase* (Sweet & Maxwell, 1966).

[265] Except in the case of s. 25(1) of the Act and conditional sale agreements as defined by the Consumer Credit Act: s. 25(2) of the Sale of Goods Act. The Consumer Credit Act 1974 introduces also, for regulatory purposes, the so called 'credit-sale agreement'(see s. 189(1)), but this has no significance for the purpose of the Sale of Goods Act.

the possession and enjoyment of goods on credit in the expectation of paying the contract price over time. Hire purchase developed in the furtherance of statutory avoidance. As a credit-granting transaction, permitting the hirer to enjoy goods before paying for them in full, hire purchase was distinguishable from a security bill of sale and free from bills of sale legislation prescribing stiff formalities and registration procedures.[266] Furthermore, it was not a type of loan, and so the bailor finance companies were free from the Moneylenders Acts. Hire purchase was useful to finance companies, too, in that the hirer in possession was not treated as someone who had 'agreed to buy' the goods,[267] so as to have the power to pass a good title to a third-party purchaser under the buyer in possession exception[268] to the rule of *nemo dat quod non habet*.[269] In contrast, a conditional purchaser was someone who had agreed to buy and who therefore had that disposing power.[270]

Sham and artificial transactions.   Unlike hire purchase, a security bill of sale   **2.67** involves the sale of goods to a lender defeasible upon the repayment of the loan.[271] Although the law condones artificial transactions, so long as the parties to the transaction do what they say they are doing,[272] it does not permit parties to enter into wholly fictitious 'sham' transactions.[273] For that reason, transactions taking the form of a sale to a financier with a bailment back on hire purchase terms have often in the past been struck down as unregistered security bills of sale,[274] perhaps with greater alacrity than now would be the case. In contrast, hire purchase is an agreement based on the acquisition of goods by the hirer and structured around the payment of hire for the goods in instalments, with an option to purchase, exercisable for usually a nominal sum, after all the instalments of hire have been paid.[275] As the agreement proceeds to term so that, as very often is the case, the value of the goods exceeds the amount of hire not yet paid, it makes commercial

---

[266] *McEntire v Crossley Bros* [1895] AC 457.

[267] *Helby v Matthews* [1895] AC 471.

[268] S. 25(1) of the Sale of Goods Act 1979 and s. 9 of the Factors Act 1889.

[269] See Ch. 5 below.

[270] *Lee v Butler* [1893] 2 QB 318.

[271] The transaction in *Beckett v Tower Assets Co.* [1891] 1 QB 1 was held not to be a chattel mortgage, where the lender first bought the goods at a friendly distress sale before returning the goods to the borrower on hire purchase terms. See also *Manchester, Sheffield and Lincolnshire Railway Co. v North Central Wagon Co.* (1888) 13 App. Cas. 554, 567–8; *WJ Albutt & Co. Ltd v Riddell*, n. 251 above; *Re Estate of Smith & Hogan Ltd* [1932] SCR 661 (Can.).

[272] e.g., *Welsh Development Agency v Export Finance Co.* [1992] BCLC 148. This is what is meant in English law by the rule that the law looks at the substance of the transaction; see *North Central Wagon Co. v Brailsford* [1962] 1 WLR 1288.

[273] e.g., *Re George Inglefield Ltd* [1933] Ch. 1.

[274] See n. 260 above; *Re Watson* (1890) 25 QBD 27; *Polsky v S and A Services* [1951] 1 All ER 185; *North Central Wagon Co. v Brailsford*, above; *Stoneleigh Finance Ltd v Phillips* [1965] 2 QB 537; *Snook v West Riding Investments Ltd* [1967] 1 QB 786.

[275] *Helby v Matthews* [1895] AC 471.

sense to acquire the general property in the goods for a nominal sum when the last instalment of hire has been paid.[276] Nevertheless, no matter how irresistible may be the economic argument in favour of exercising the option to purchase as the final instalment draws near, the hirer is still not, and never does become, someone who has 'agreed to buy' the goods.[277] Even the exercise of the option itself, which brings about an instant sale,[278] cannot import any prior undertaking to buy. Until special hire purchase legislation was introduced many decades after the development of hire purchase,[279] the bailor's title was secure against good faith purchasers from the hirer.[280]

2.68 **Modern developments.** The nature of hire purchase was settled in the early cases. Nevertheless, some further attention was given to its nature in *Forthright Finance Ltd v Carlyle Finance Ltd*, where the contract required the 'hirer' to pay all of the instalments and thus deemed him to have exercised a hirer's option to purchase, 'unless [he] has told the owner before that time that such is not the case'. Despite the quit option given to the 'hirer', criticized as 'specious', the agreement was held to be one of conditional sale.[281] It can fairly be said that there is a commitment to purchase under a contract of this nature, so long as the quit option has not been exercised. When the argument was consequently pressed in another case [282] that a supposed hire-purchase contract should be treated as one of conditional sale where the option was for a nominal amount, the court rejected it. The judge, referring to *Forthright Finance*, said: 'The peculiar feature there was that, instead of there being an option to purchase, there is a clause which deemed the option to have been exercised if the payments were made and the hirer there had to indicate that he was not going to take the goods in order to prevent

---

[276] *Warman v Southern Counties Car Finance Corpn* [1949] 2 KB 576, 582. In accordance with the economic purpose of the transaction, the hirer is usually liable to maintain the hire for a minimum period, having to face a minimum payments clause if desiring to withdraw from the agreement before that date. This minimum sum is a primary alternative to the hire that was agreed to be paid over the instalment period. See *Associated Distributors Ltd v Hall* [1938] KB 83; *Bridge v Campbell Discount Co. Ltd* [1962] AC 600. It is not a liquidated damages clause, and thus not open to scrutiny as a penalty. The rule against penalties applies only to secondary obligations liability: *Protector Endowment Loan & Annuity Co. v Grice* (1880) 5 QBD 592; *Wallingford v Directors, &c, of the Mutual Society* (1880) 5 App. Cas. 685; *Re Emerald Christmas Tree Co.* (1979) 105 DLR (3d) 75. Confined to the improper commutation of primary into secondary liability, the rule against penalties does not exist to police the fairness of contracts; see further Ch. 12 below.

[277] *Helby v Matthews*, n. 267 above; *Lee v Butler* [1893] 2 QB 318. Cf. *RE MEL Industries Ltd* (1981) 121 DLR (3d) 103.

[278] The sale option should qualify as a contract of sale of goods under s. 2(1) of the Sale of Goods Act (see *Mountford v Scott* [1975] Ch. 258), and is a sale under s. 2(4) as opposed to an agreement to sell under s. 2(5).

[279] Part III of the Hire Purchase Act 1964, as am. by the Consumer Credit Act 1974.

[280] *Helby v Matthews*, n. 267 above; see Ch. 5 below.

[281] [1997] 4 All ER 90.

[282] *Close Asset Finance v Care Graphics Machinery Ltd* [2000] CCLR 43 (unpaginated).

that happening. That is not the case in the instant case, which has the standard option to purchase, albeit for a nominal amount.' The approach taken in earlier hire purchase cases was therefore reaffirmed and *Forthright Finance* was not taken to have altered the legal understanding of hire purchase contracts.

Pledge

Meaning of pledge.   Pledge is a form of bailment[283] in which possession of goods **2.69** or documents of title to goods is granted to a pledgee as security for a loan.[284] This loan is not comparable to the price paid by a buyer since, unlike the payments made by a hirer, it is not related to the use and enjoyment of the pledge itself by the pledgee. The pledgee has only a special property;[285] consequently, the analogy with sale is slender. At common law, the pledgee may sell the pledge if the pledgor defaults on repayment of the loan, though any surplus realized will have to be turned over to the pledgor.[286] The general property, therefore, never passes to the pledge.

Sale or Return and Sale on Approval

General.   A more compelling analogy with sale of goods is afforded by those **2.70** bailments called sale or return and sale on approval in which the bailee obtains possession with an option to buy the goods at a stated price, no hire being paid in the meantime. In a sale or return, a potential buyer acquires the goods with an eye to their resale, a common arrangement in certain businesses such as bookselling. Sale on approval refers to the acquisition of goods for the personal enjoyment of the potential buyer, a transaction familiar to stamp-collecting juveniles. Legislation hostile to the sending of unsolicited goods[287] has reduced certain types of sales on approval.

Formation of contract.   Though they may ripen into a sale and although the **2.71** parties may be subject to an innominate contract in the meantime,[288] in neither type of bailment has the bailee 'bought or agreed to buy' the goods.[289] The Sale of

---

283 *Coggs v Bernard* (1703) 2 Ld. Raym. 909.

284 *Chitty on Contracts*, (29th edn, by H. G. Beale, Sweet & Maxwell, 2004); N. E. Palmer, n. 260 above; E. I. Sykes and S. Walker, *The Law of Securities* (5th edn, Law Book Co., 1993).

285 *Carter v Wake* (1877) 4 Ch. D 605; *Sewell v Burdick*, n. 216 above, 93.

286 *Ex p. Hubbard* (1886) 17 QBD 690, 698; *Halliday v Holgate* (1868) LR 3 Ex. 299; *Burdick v Sewell*, n. 216 above, 174 (Bowen LJ). Pledge is described as a security halfway between a lien and a mortgage by Willes J in *Halliday v Holgate*, above, 302. For the position governing that type of pledging known as pawnbroking, see the Consumer Credit Act 1974, ss. 114–121.

287 The Unsolicited Goods and Services Act 1971, as amended by the Unsolicited Goods and Services (Amendment) Act 1975 and partly repealed by the Consumer Protection (Distance Selling) Regulations 2000, SI 2000 No. 2334; see Ch. 1, above.

288 *Atari Corp (UK) Ltd v Electronic Boutique Stores (UK) Ltd* [1998] QB 539.

289 In this respect, the position is like hire purchase, discussed above. Cf. *Marten v Whale* [1917] 2 KB 480, where the party in possession was not so under 'a mere option to buy'.

Goods Act deals with sale or return and sale on approval in section 18, Rule 4, which lays down certain rules for the formation of a contract of sale pursuant to the option given by the bailor.[290] Upon conclusion of the contract, the seller's property passes immediately to the buyer, which is consistent with the presumptive rule that the property in specific goods passes to the buyer at the contract date. These bailments should be distinguished from those defeasible sales where the buyer is entitled to return the goods and annul the sale within certain limits, including time. Such transactions are regular sales unless and until the buyer's divesting option is exercised.[291] The option to return the goods may involve placing the interim risk of loss on the buyer,[292] but the presumptive rule seems to put the risk on the seller in the absence of special language in the agreement.[293]

2.72 Extended rejection rights. Defeasible sales of this type may be barely distinguishable from sales where the buyer is given wider rights of rejection than those arising under the Act.[294] Suppose a buyer rejects goods under a provision in the contract allowing him to do so if he is not satisfied with the goods. As a matter of construction, it may be difficult to determine whether the buyer determines the contract because of a discharging breach by the seller or pursuant to a non-promissory condition, his own lack of satisfaction. Only in the former case will the buyer be entitled to damages. The further the buyer goes beyond the entitlement given by the Act, it is submitted, the more should a court tend to construe as non-promissory the event giving rise to the right of rejection.

Loans for Consumption

2.73 General. The relation between sale and bailment emerges in a number of cases, mainly from the Commonwealth, involving grain stored for a period in grain elevators prior to one of three events: its eventual return to the depositor; the return of an equivalent quantity and standard of grain;[295] and the sale of the grain to the elevator company.[296] The depositor's objective will normally be the sale of the grain, though he may simply want it stored or treated prior to its use for seeding and animal feed purposes. If the producer sells the grain, this may occur some time after its initial deposit in the elevator.

---

[290] See Ch. 3 below.

[291] *The Vesta* [1921] 1 AC 774; *Ward v Cormier* (1910) 39 NBR 567 (Can.).

[292] The custom of the trade imposed it on the buyer in *Bevington & Morris v Dale & Co. Ltd* (1902) 7 Com. Cas. 12.

[293] *Elphick v Barnes* (1880) 5 CPD 321, following *Head v Tattersall* (1872) LR 7 Ex. 7.

[294] *Patterson v Lane* (1921) 60 DLR 252.

[295] The grain is inspected and graded for this purpose.

[296] The depositor may have a sale option; cf sale or return where the option is exercised by the buyer. Or the elevator company may exercise a purchase option on the producer's failure to remove the grain or its equivalent amount by a certain date.

Substituting the goods.   Where under the agreement the grain is deposited in a   **2.74**
special bin, isolated from other depositors' grain, the contract gives rise to a bailment,[297] even though a later sale may be contemplated. The general property in
the grain remains in the bailor. Until recently,[298] it could have been said with some
confidence that grain commingled as part of a common stock vests in the elevator
company, whose obligation to return an equivalent amount under what is a contract of barter is in the nature of a debt obligation and not a proprietary matter.
Unlike Roman law, where the real contract of *mutuum* constituted a loan of fun-
gibles for consumption,[299] the common law of bailment required a return of the
very goods bailed, in their original or altered form.[300] Consequently, a loan of cattle, to be returned, either as the original cattle or their comparable substitutes,
with a number of their young, was held not to be a bailment.[301]

Bailment and agreed mixing.   In *Mercer v Craven Grain Storage Co*,[302] however,   **2.75**
the House of Lords, in a summary judgment appeal, concluded in abbreviated
terms and without considering prior authority that a bailment survived an agreed
mixing where the bailee had authority to extract goods from the common stock
and substitute other goods for them.[303] In that case, the bailors sometimes removed
their grain from storage to execute sale transactions and sometimes ordered the
bailee to deliver directly to buyers. The case concerned an action in conversion[304]
by the bailors against the bailee, which had exceeded its authority to sell by disposing of grain for less than the minimum stipulated price and was in no financial
position to pay the proceeds to the bailor. Bailment arrangements of the above
sort would involve the treatment of the various bailors as tenants in common of
the commingled goods, liable to share rateably the losses arising from any shrinkage

---

[297] *Isaac v Andrew* (1877) 28 UCCP 40 (Can.); *Cargo v Joyner* (1899) 4 Terr. LR 64 (Can.);
Lawlor v Nicol (1898) 12 Man. LR 244 (Can.).

[298] See now the House of Lords decision in *Mercer v Craven Grain Storage Ltd* [1994] CLC 328;
L. Smith (1995) 111 *LQR* 10.

[299] In *Wincanton Ltd v P&O Trans European Ltd* [2001] CLC 962 at [12]–[24], *mutuum* is treated
as giving rise to a personal obligation to redeliver the equivalent thing, to be inferred generally in the
case of consumables, but only where the contract so provides in the case of non-consumables.

[300] *Chapman Bros v Verco Bros and Co. Ltd* (1933) 49 CLR 306; *South Australian Insurance Co.
Ltd v Randell* (1869) LR 3 PC 101. See also *Wincanton Ltd v P&O Trans European Ltd*, n. 299 above
at [19] and [23] (pallets delivered by A to B, thence, with A's consent, by B to C); N. E. Palmer,
Bailment, n. 260 above, 135: 'What is necessary is that the goods themselves, whether in altered
or original form, should be returnable and not merely some other goods of equivalent character or
value. There must be a clear physical heredity between what has been delivered to the bailee and
what must be returned.'

[301] *Crawford v Kingston* [1952] OR 714 (Can.). Cf *Harding v Commissioner of Inland Revenue*
[1977] 1 NZLR 337.

[302] n. 298 above; see also *Busse v Edmonton Grain & Hay Co. Ltd* [1932] 1 WWR 296.

[303] The bailment agreement contained a clause reserving title in the bailors.

[304] The principal point was whether the bailee had an arguable defence to the bailors' claim that
they had sold the grain without authority. Apart from this, the bailors, to succeed in conversion,
would need to show a right to immediate possession stemming from their retained ownership.

in the bulk. A particular bailor's percentage entitlement, moreover, in the case of a fluctuating common stock, would have to be measured against the lowest intermediate balance existing after the date of deposit.[305] Subject to that, any reduction in the stock after the time of the deposit would be shared by the bailor with other interested parties, including the bailee, and a wrongdoing bailee with a proprietary interest in the stock would have the reduction charged in full, and not rateably, against his interest.[306]

2.76 **Tenancy in common.** The principle of tenancy in common, successfully pressed by the bailors in *Mercer*, had earlier been invoked sparingly by the common law,[307] and was seemingly inconsistent with the bailee having the freedom to deal beneficially with the common stock.[308] Tenancy in common was to be found where the owner of goods was not privy to their mixing by a bailee, which might occur accidentally[309] or through the actions of a wrongdoer, often a bailee.[310] Furthermore, where the depositor knew no more than that his goods might be mixed with those of an identical kind belonging to others, the transaction gave rise to a tenancy in common between this depositor and others on the ground that the depositor had not done enough to surrender his property interest in full.[311] In *Re Stapylton Fletcher Ltd*,[312] certain buyers of vintage wine authorized the seller to hold their wine in the seller's different capacity as warehouseman. The goods having been ascertained,[313] the buyers' property in the wine survived the removal of the wines from the seller's trading stacks and its storage commingled with the wines of others in warehouse stacks. Although there was nothing in the warehouse stacks to indicate ownership of particular bottles or cases, the seller's meticulous stock record was valuable evidence of an intention that the buyers were not to be divested of property rights by the fact of commingling in this way. In addition to *Mercer*, tenancy in common has in effect been incorporated in modern reforms of the Sale

---

305 See L. Smith, *The Law of Tracing* (OUP, 1997), 80–5.

306 *Ibid.*, and see below. See also *Mercer v Craven Grain Storage Ltd*, n. 298 above at 329: 'The storage society was guilty of conversion if it allowed the mix to be so depleted by withdrawals that the balance remaining was not sufficient to satisfy the demands of the plaintiffs.'

307 *Laurie and Morewood v Dudin and Sons* [1926] 1 KB 223. Cf *Inglis v Stock* (1885) 10 App. Cas. 263, 267.

308 *Chapman Bros v Verco Bros and Co. Ltd*, n. 300 above.

309 *Spence v Union Marine Insurance Co.* (1868) LR 3 CP 427.

310 *Indian Oil Corpn v Greenstone Shipping SA* [1988] QB 345, departing from earlier dicta of Lord Moulton in *FS Sandeman & Sons v Tyzack and Branfoot Steamship Co. Ltd* [1913] AC 680, penalizing the wrongdoer by vesting the whole of the commingled goods in the person whose goods were wrongfully mixed; see P. Matthews [1981] *CLP* 159.

311 See *Re Stapylton Fletcher Ltd* [1994] 1 WLR 1181.

312 *Ibid.*

313 Under s. 16: discussed in Ch. 3 below.

of Goods Act,[314] which could give tenancy in common an added impetus at common law and outside the terms of the Act itself.

Bailment and tenancy in common.   There seems no good reason why principles **2.77** of bailment and tenancy in common might not be combined. Goods are commonly stored in bulk prior to sale, with no intention on the part of any of the depositors to transfer the general property in their goods to the storage company.[315] If the storage company is given an authority to dispose of the goods, there seems no reason why the conferment of this authority should expropriate the depositor. Where goods have been delivered on retention of title terms, the grant of an authority or permission to the buyer to sub-sell the goods does not serve to expropriate the seller.[316] Moreover, if the storage company as agent were given authority to acquire substitute goods and replenish the common stock, there is no reason why this act of feeding the common stock should not serve to transfer a proprietary interest to the depositor.[317]

Intention.   It is not clear to what extent the inference of tenancy in common at **2.78** common law is dependent upon intention, whether it is express[318] or implied.[319] Consequently, it is difficult to know how far the *Mercer* decision may be taken outside its immediate facts, given the brief treatment that the subject received in the House of Lords. Assuming the relevance of an intention that the depositor should be a tenant in common or should retain a proprietary entitlement, and that a bailment leading to a tenancy in common will not be inferred from the simple mixing of goods with the consent of the depositor, complex problems could arise from multiple deposits of different types. If there are a number of depositors, only some of whom have the requisite intention, then the warehouse would presumably

---

[314] By the Sale of Goods (Amendment) Act 1995, discussed in Ch. 3 below. The expression tenancy in common is not expressly used in the Act but the proprietary rights in an identified bulk created by the legislation is a tenancy in common right.

[315] e.g., *Sterns Ltd v Vickers Ltd* [1923] 1 KB 78.

[316] See Ch. 5.

[317] If the storage company repurchases as agent, then the property in the goods might be transferred directly to the depositor under the contract of sale. That general property would survive as a tenancy in common entitlement from the point the goods are submerged in the common stock: *Re Stapylton Fletcher Ltd*, n. 311 above. Otherwise, if the storage company purchases the goods as a principal, the relationship between the depositor and storage company might be classified as one of sale, with the proceeds of the earlier sale, if not previously remitted to the depositor, being offset against the depositor's duty to pay the price. Or it might be an innominate contract of the kind dealt with by the Supply of Goods and Services Act 1982, with the passing of property rules in the Sale of Goods Act brought in by way of analogy. The application of these rules by way of analogy might be the best explanation for why s. 18 Rule 1 of the Sale of Goods Act 1979 was applied to a contract for the transfer of goods in return for services: *Koppel v Koppel* [1966] 1 WLR 802.

[318] As in *Mercer* (the reservation of title clause), n. 298 above.

[319] As in *Re Stapylton Fletcher Ltd*, n. 311 above.

stand in for those who fail to show the requisite intention to retain an interest by way of tenancy in common.

2.79 **Practical issues.** The practical problems arising out of commingled bailment cases concern principally the risk of loss, by fire for example, and the insolvency of the bailee. Where the general property is transferred to the warehouse or elevator company, as would happen in the case of an exchange or sale of the goods, the risk of loss will pass to transferee but the risk of insolvency will be assumed by the transferor. The position is reversed if there is a bailment. It is probably easier to insure against fire than someone else's insolvency, and the spate of insolvencies in recent times means that developments like the *Mercer* case are a source of encouragement to those depositing goods for storage and similar purposes.[320] Tenancy in common, on the other hand, is not needed to effectuate sales by the bailor of goods that have been deposited in a common stock. Whether the bailor has a surviving proprietary right or not, the consent and cooperation of the bailee in delivering the goods to the buyer, in the process transferring the general property in the goods to the buyer, should suffice for the bailor selling the goods to have the right to sell them as required by section 12 of the Sale of Goods Act.[321] There is no need for the bailee to be a party to the contract of sale or for the bailee to be more than a ministerial agent in assisting performance of the contract.

Gift

2.80 **Gift and contract.** Unlike the civil law, the common law does not treat a gift as a species of contract. Rather, it is a gratuitous conveyance of the general property complete upon delivery,[322] coupled with an intention on the donor's part to vest the general property in the donee. Neither at common law nor under the statute does the donor owe duties in respect of title, description, satisfactory quality, or fitness.[323] A promise to give, unless made by way of deed,[324] is unenforceable at common law for lack of consideration. Furthermore, equity will not perfect an

---

[320] The decision in *Mercer* has significant implications for the securities market where fungible securities are commonly transferred under a 'repo' (sale and repurchase) scheme, whereby the enhanced repurchase price represents the equivalent of interest on the advance to the transferor made when the transferor transfers the securities under the sale leg of the transaction to the transferee. There is no expectation that the self-same securities will be returned to the transferor when the repurchase leg of the transaction takes place.

[321] Ch. 5 below.

[322] *Irons v Smallpiece* (1819) 2 B & Ald. 551; *Re Ridgway* (1885) 15 QBD 447; *Cochrane v Moore* (1890) 25 QBD 57; *Re Cole* [1964] Ch. 175. Alternatively, a gift may be completed by deed without delivery: *Cochrane v Moore*, above.

[323] This is the case even if the gift comes with an artifical consideration in the form of a deed: s. 1(2)(d) of the Supply of Goods and Services Act 1982.

[324] Which demonstrates the vestigial hold of the old writ of covenant.

imperfect gift and so will not intervene by, for example, inferring a fictitious trust in favour of the donee.[325]

Promotional Schemes

Goods with gifts.   The distinction between gift and sale emerges under certain   **2.81** promotional schemes where the buyer obtains a 'gift' with the contract goods. *Esso Petroleum Co. Ltd v Customs and Excise Commissioners*[326] involved the supply of coins celebrating a sporting event with the purchase of a minimum quantity of petrol. The question was whether the coins had been produced for 'general sale', in which case their supply would attract purchase tax. The various analytical possibilities were that the coins were the subject of a gift, or were supplied under an innominate collateral contract separate from the sale of the petrol, or were sold to the customer together with the petrol for the same money consideration. On the first possibility, tax could not be levied in the absence of any contractual obligation relating to the coins. Nor could it be levied on the second possibility, since the customer's consideration, entry into the main contract of sale, was not itself a money consideration, which meant that the coins had not been sold. Only on the third possibility would tax be payable. By a majority,[327] the House of Lords held that tax was not payable, the majority of four being equally divided between the first two possibilities.[328] It is submitted that the court should clearly have preferred the second. The first hypothesis would not meet the legitimate complaints of qualifying customers denied the coins after buying the petrol, and oil companies are not benevolent institutions. The third possibility was rightly rejected: the garages were seeking to expand their petrol sales, not to diversify their trading activities.

Agency Agreements

Buyer or agent.   It may be uncertain whether goods are delivered to a recipient   **2.82** in his capacity as buyer or as agent on behalf of the remitting principal. The classification of a relationship as one of agency or of sale depends upon the construction of the underlying agreement and is therefore a question of law.[329] There are various reasons why classifying the relationship may be important, including whether

---

[325] *Richards v Delbridge* (1874) LR 18 Eq. 11; *Jones v Lock* (1865) 1 Ch. App 25.

[326] [1976] 1 WLR 1. For a detailed description of various Esso promotional schemes, see *Esso Petroleum Co Ltd v Addison* [2003] EWHC 1130 (Comm) at [20]–[30].

[327] Lord Fraser dissented. *Chappell & Co. Ltd v Nestlé Co. Ltd* [1960] AC 87 does not help to solve the problem since in that case the mixed consideration came from the buyer and not the seller.

[328] Lords Wilberforce and Simon took the view that there was a collateral contract (second hypothesis) while Viscount Dilhorne and Lord Russell came down in favour of gift (first hypothesis).

[329] *WT Lamb & Sons v Goring Brick Co.* [1932] 1 KB 710; see also *Snelgrove v Ellingham Colliery* (1881) 45 JP 408.

the recipient is entitled to the protection afforded to commercial agents upon the termination of a commercial agency.[330] A buyer may wish to rescind a contract for a fraudulent misrepresentation committed by someone further up the distribution chain, possible if that person was the undisclosed principal of the apparent seller but not otherwise.[331] Or a problem of title transfer may arise in which it is important to know in what capacity a person is in possession of goods.[332] In construing the agreement, a court, though guided by the label chosen by the parties, will not be bound by their characterization of the relationship. Parties' conduct is more important than what they say.[333] Where a contract described the plaintiffs as 'sole selling agents' of the defendants' bricks, the price to be paid by them not being fixed but settled at 90 per cent of the retail price paid by builder customers, the conclusion was that the agent was really a buyer.[334] Nevertheless, despite the relationship between the parties being a question of substance rather than form, the difficulty of drawing the line between sale and agency ensures that, sham transactions apart, the description by the parties of their own relationship will pay an important part in the court's classification of the relationship.[335]

2.83 **Relevant circumstances.** Subject to the parties' own description of their relationship, courts are guided by the circumstances of the case in classifying that relationship, but not all the circumstances are helpful. Agents establish privity of contract between their customers and their principals; this is a consequence and not a diagnostic test of agency.[336] A similar case is that of the person asked to procure goods for another at a price not exceeding a stated figure. If that person is an agent, he owes his principal a duty of diligence to acquire the goods as cheaply as possible, accounting for any savings made.[337] Since any such duty to account will be consequent on the relationship being one of sale or agency, the existence of the duty cannot be a diagnostic tool. Any relevant circumstances considered will

---

[330] The Commercial Agents (Council Directive) Regulations 1993, SI 1993 No. 3053. See *Mercantile International Group plc v Chuan Soon Huat Industrial Group Ltd* [2002] EWCA Civ 128; [2002] 1 All ER (Comm.) 788.

[331] *Garnac Grain Co. Inc. v HMF Faure & Fairclough Ltd* [1966] 1 QB 650, affirmed [1968] AC 1130 note. The buyer was held to be purchasing so as to resell the goods to the original seller.

[332] *Weiner v Harris* [1910] 1 KB 285.

[333] *WT Lamb & Sons v Goring Brick Co.*, n. 329 above; *International Harvester Co. of Australia Pty Ltd v Carrigan's Hazeldene Pastoral Co.* (1958) 100 CLR 644; *Ex p. White* (1871) LR 6 Ch. App 397, 399, affirmed *sub nom. John Towle & Co. v White* (1873) 29 LT 78, 79.

[334] *WT Lamb & Sons v Goring Brick Co.*, n. 329 above; see also *WY McCarter, Burr Co. Ltd v Harris* (1922) 70 DLR 420.

[335] *Mercantile International Group plc v Chuan Soon Huat Industrial Group Ltd*, n. 330 above, especially at [30] (noting the absence of such documentation in *Ex p. White*, above n. 333, and *AMB Imballaggi Plastici SRL v Pacflex Ltd* [1999] 2 All ER (Comm.) 249).

[336] For the possibility that the property in goods passes through a commission agent without privity of contract being established between principal and third party, see *Ireland v Livingstone* (1874) LR 5 HL 395.

[337] *Ireland v Livingstone*, n. 336 above.

have to be weighed, which lends an unpredictable character to the law. Perhaps the most helpful indication of agency is the degree of control exercised by one party over the activities of another,[338] though in certain cases, as where a manufacturer wishes to preserve the integrity of its distribution network, sellers may have considerable control over buyers.[339] A close integration of two businesses, common with exclusive distributorships and output and requirements contracts, will not necessarily influence judicial interpretation in favour of agency.[340] The freedom of a recipient of goods to determine the date of payment and the amount of the price when passing the goods on, whilst having to pay the consignor a fixed price and at a fixed date, is indicative but not determinative of the relationship between consignor and recipient being one of sale.[341] Indeed, it has been stated that someone may be an agent even if he is allowed to retain any surplus over a minimum sale figure.[342] If a person receiving goods is paid a percentage of the mark-up instead of being exposed to the market with its advantages and disadvantages, this points towards agency.[343] Likewise if he need not pay for them until paid in turn by his customer.[344] It is quite possible for a court to conclude that a relationship of agency arises between consignor and recipient, but that the agent enters into separate collateral contracts with principal and third party containing duties that themselves are not indicative of an agency relationship.[345]

Security Agreements

Form of security agreement.   Certain security agreements borrow the form of a   **2.84**
contract of sale. Though similar in economic purpose to a conditional sale, which certainly comes under the Sale of Goods Act, a security bill of sale is accorded special treatment precisely because it is a sale only in formal terms. It consists of an outright sale by a mortgagor who remains at all material times in possession of the goods, the conveyance to the mortgagee buyer being defeasible on the occurrence of a condition, namely the repayment in full of the loan made by mortgagee to mortgagor.[346] Since the use and enjoyment of the goods by the mortgagee is not

---

338   *Weiner v Harris*, n. 332 above.

339   *Dunlop Pneumatic Tyre Co. Ltd v Selfridge & Co. Ltd* [1915] AC 847.

340   *Decro-Wall International SA v Practitioners in Marketing Ltd* [1971] 2 All ER 216. Similarly, franchise agreements.

341   *Ex p. White*, above n. 333, at 403, 405.

342   *Ex p. Bright* (1879) 10 Ch. D 566: but other factors favoured agency in the illustration given by Jessel MR.

343   *Weiner v Harris*, n. 332 above; *AMB Imballaggi Plastici SRL v Pacflex Ltd*, above n. 335.

344   *Ibid.*

345   *Mercantile International Group plc v Chuan Soon Huat Industrial Group Ltd*, n. 330 above at [19], [36] and [40], where the agent conducted its own independent refund policy and its own marketing support, and did not account to the principal for proceeds of sale received from third-party buyers.

346   *Keith v Burrows* (1876) 1 CPD 722, 731.

contemplated by the parties, it would be inappropriate to apply the provisions of the Act regarding, for example, delivery, quality, fitness, and damages.[347] Hence section 62(4) of the Act provides: 'The provisions of this Act about contracts of sale do not apply to a contract in the form of a contract of sale which is intended to operate by way of mortgage, charge, pledge, or other security.'

2.85 **Limited application of Act.** The question is whether section 62(4) excludes the operation of the whole of the Act or only those provisions that operate between buyer and seller *inter se*. Excluded from the latter group would be those sections concerning title transfer arising out of a contract of sale but concerning disputes between parties who are not buyer and seller. If a conditional buyer is in principle a buyer in possession under section 25 of the Act,[348] and thus able to overreach the seller's title when disposing of the goods to a good-faith transferee, it is difficult to see why the grantor of a security bill of sale should not be a seller left in possession of the goods by the buyer under section 24 with similar disposing powers.[349] Both conditional sales and security bills may be used to acquire goods on financed terms and both pose the risk of deception of third parties by the party given or left in possession by the owner of the goods. Section 62(4) can be sensibly confined to the terms of the contract of sale so as to give disposing power to the grantor of the bill. Further, had the draftsman sought to exclude the whole Act, it would have been easy enough to say just that by omitting the words 'about contracts of sale'.

2.86 **Title-based schemes.** The question of sale or security sometimes arises too in respect of title-based schemes that serve as security whilst retaining the form of sale, for example, a sale of goods followed by a resale or leaseback. The question that often arises in such transactions is whether the transaction is a disguised charge void for want of registration as a company charge.[350] A sale and resale arrangement was struck down for this reason in *Re Curtain Dream plc*,[351] because the documents as drafted made reference to interest and a credit line. It was never contemplated that the buyer would ever take possession of the goods, and the original seller remained in possession at all times under the terms of an agreement to repurchase, under which the interests of the reseller out of possession were

---

[347] The mortgagee may previously have sold the goods to the mortgagor before taking back a security bill of sale. The initial sale would thus be a genuine sale and governed by the Act in the usual way.

[348] Subject to the position in consumer contracts, discussed in Ch. 5 below.

[349] But there is no provision in consumer legislation excepting security bills of sale from s. 24 of the Sale of Goods Act.

[350] See s. 395 of the Companies Act 1985, which will be repealed when the relevant provisions of the Companies Act 2006 (ss. 860–61 and 874) are brought into force (the expected date is 1 October 2009).

[351] [1990] BCLC 925.

protected by a reservation of title clause. On one view, as long as the language is clear and the parties follow the steps laid down in the documentation for a sale and a resale, a transaction of this nature will be recognized. Nevertheless, a transaction built up as a sale followed by an automatic resale if a prescribed condition is met (payment of the enhanced repurchase price) looks too much like a mortgage ('once a mortgage, always a mortgage') for this conclusion to be safely reached.

3

THE PASSING OF PROPERTY

Introduction.   Sale of goods law deals with a hybrid transaction that consists of   **3.01**
contract and conveyance. In contrast with the sale of land, sale of goods is informal and fast-moving. Consequently, the sequence of contract and conveyance is
not as clearly differentiated as it is in the case of sale of land. The passing of property in goods affects contractual rights and duties. It is the fulcrum on which
depend issues as diverse as the seller's entitlement to sue for the price[1] and the incidence of risk of loss or casualty to the goods.[2] The passing of property may also
have an incidental effect on the remedies of the parties, including specific performance. Until the law was changed in 1967,[3] the buyer's right of rejection was
affected by whether the property in specific goods had passed at the time of the
contract. The passing of property is also of prime significance in defining the position of buyer and seller on the other's insolvency. The whereabouts of the property
may affect third parties as it touches upon liability in conversion,[4] insurable

---

[1] S. 49(1).

[2] S. 20.

[3] Misrepresentation Act, s. 4(1); see Ch. 10 below.

[4] The claimant must show possession or the right to immediate possession at the time of the tort.
The incidence of property will also come into play in the adjustment of complex liabilities: Torts
(Interference with Goods) Act 1977, ss. 7–9.

interest, liability to tax, criminal responsibility,[5] and the amenability of the goods to execution and insolvency creditors.[6] Lord Blackburn was largely responsible for the central position occupied by the passing of property in sales law.[7] A century later, Karl Llewellyn, a proponent of legal realism and the principal architect of the American Uniform Commercial Code, trenchantly criticized the 'lump' concept of title (or property), namely the use of property to resolve divergent issues by mechanical means without heeding the different functional requirements of these issues.[8] There are signs of the 'narrow issue thinking' he favoured in cases on risk, where practicalities are allowed to override legal doctrine. But, to take other examples, functional thinking does not seem much in evidence in actions for the price and the rights of pre-paying buyers when the seller becomes insolvent.

The Rule Structure

3.02 General. The passing of property was first permitted by manual delivery and then by a deed of transfer. It was only some considerable time later that it could be accomplished purely in accordance with the intention of the contracting parties.[9] Even though, in principle, the passing of property was thus emancipated from physical delivery, in practice the two events largely coincide. Subject to that, the passing of property in accordance with the intention of the parties is today the dominant rule. The paramountcy of intention is established in section 17 but the parties' intention is checked in the case of unascertained and future goods, where the property may only pass once the goods become respectively ascertained or existing.[10] A purported present sale will not automatically become a sale once the goods become existing goods;[11] the parties must also agree their unconditional appropriation to the contract. The same result should hold true for a purported sale of unascertained goods, though section 16 does not explicitly say so. These rules have been supplemented by provisions introduced by the Sale of Goods (Amendment) Act 1995, notably section 20A. It is now possible for an undivided

---

[5] e.g., *Edwards v Ddin* [1976] 1 WLR 942.

[6] *Re Wait* [1927] 1 Ch. 606; *Carlos Federspiel & Co SA v Charles Twigg & Co. Ltd* [1957] 1 Lloyd's Rep. 240.

[7] As the full title of his treatise, usually known as *Blackburn on Sale*, shows: *A Treatise on the Effect of the Contract of Sale on the Legal Rights of Property and Possession in Goods, Wares and Merchandise* (1845).

[8] 'Through Title to Contract and a Bit Beyond' (1938) 15 *NYU LR* 159.

[9] *Cochrane v Moore* (1890) 25 QBD 57. The rule in Scots law, to which the provisions of ss. 17 and 18 of the Sale of Goods Act are an exception, is that delivery is required: *Burnett's Trustee v Grainger* [2004] UKHL 8 at [12].

[10] S. 16 (unascertained goods); s. 5(3) (sale of future goods treated as agreement to sell).

[11] *Lunn v Thornton* (1845) 1 CB 379. There is an exception for goods with a potential existence: *Grantham v Hawley* (1615) Hob. 132, discussed Ch. 2, above.

share to pass to the buyer by way of tenancy in common where the buyer has paid and the goods are to come from a bulk that has been identified to the contract at or subsequent to the contract date.[12] The Act is unclear on the process by which the buyer's interest in the bulk is transformed into the general property in ascertained and unconditionally appropriated goods. This is discussed below.

Intention. Except where the seller gives up possession but retains the property in the goods as security for the payment of the price, it is relatively uncommon for buyer and seller to express their intention concerning the passing of property. The Act encourages an inquiry into 'the terms of the contract, the conduct of the parties and the circumstances of the case'[13] but sets out in section 18 presumptive rules of intention if such inquiry is fruitless. By these rules,[14] the property in specific goods passes at the contract date, unless the goods have to be put in a deliverable state, or the seller has to weigh, measure, or test them to determine the price. In sale or return and similar transactions, the property passes as soon as the contract is concluded because the goods are necessarily specific at that time. Unascertained and future goods are dealt with together in the one rule, which requires their 'unconditional appropriation' to the contract by one party with the 'assent' of the other; a particular application of the rule is then given for the case where a carrier is employed to deliver the goods.   **3.03**

Reserving the right of disposal. Tacked on to this scheme of rules, but in a way that is not clearly linked to the previous set of rules on the passing of property, is section 19. This provision deals with cases where the seller 'reserve[s] the right of disposal' of goods,[15] whether specific or later 'appropriated' to the contract, that are delivered to the buyer or to a carrier or other bailee. Before the Act, it was not clear whether such action by the seller reserved in him the property in the goods or asserted the continuance of a lien over them, at least in those cases where the seller retained control of shipping documents.[16] This lack of clarity is evident in the failure of section 19 to state bluntly that the seller retains the property and to integrate section 19 into the scheme of the preceding sections.   **3.04**

Related contracts. As for contracts involving the transfer of goods that are not contracts of sale, such as barter contracts and work and materials contracts, there is a distinct shortage of authority on the passing of property from transferor to   **3.05**

---

12 S. 1(3) of the 1995 Act, adding a new s. 20A to the Sale of Goods Act with effect from 19 Sept. 1995.

13 S. 17(2). 'It is impossible to imagine a clause more vague than this, but I think it correctly represents the state of the authorities when the Act was passed': *Varley v Whipp* [1900] 1 QB 513, 517 (Channell J).

14 Discussed in the text accompanying nn. 18 *et seq.* below.

15 *James v The Commonwealth* (1939) 62 CLR 339.

16 Ontario Law Reform Commission, *Report on Sale of Goods* (1979), ii, 342–4.

transferee. It is likely that the rules of the Sale of Goods Act would be applied,[17] a court being perhaps not too astute to say that this is done as a matter of analogy.

Specific Goods

Section 18, Rules 1–3

Section 18, Rule 1

3.06 **General rule.** Section 18, Rule 1, provides: 'Where there is an unconditional contract for the sale of specific goods in a deliverable state[18] the property in the goods passes to the buyer when the contract is made, and it is immaterial whether the time of payment or the time of delivery, or both, be postponed.'[19] The closing words appear to limit severely the chance of finding a contrary implied intention.[20] Yet, in modern times, the courts have been prepared to find a way round this presumptive rule,[21] which is founded on the fiction that a delivery of the goods to the buyer is deemed to have occurred upon the conclusion of the contract.[22] There is some small justification for the rule if the parties are *inter praesentes* and all that is left to do is for the buyer to carry away the goods.[23] The presumptive rule is that delivery occurs at the seller's place of business,[24] where the specific goods will usually be found, and the seller may exercise a lien to prevent the buyer from taking away the goods before payment if credit is not allowed under the contract.[25] Here, a fusion of the contract and the conveyance may well accord with the expectations of the parties. But the goods may be elsewhere and delivery may be delayed, and these variations cause the fiction to break down. Until quite recent times, section 18, Rule 1, was applied almost as an ineluctable

---

[17] *Koppel v Koppel* [1966] 1 WLR 802 (barter). Cf *Flynn v Mackin & Mahon* [1974] IR 101.
[18] The meaning of 'deliverable state' is discussed under Rule 2, below.
[19] *Tarling v Baxter* (1827) 6 B & C 360; *Simmons v Swift* (1826) 5 B & C 857; *Martindale v Smith* (1841) 1 QB 389; *Gilmour v Supple* (1858) 11 Moo. PC 551; *Sweeting v Turner* (1871) LR 7 QB 310, 313; *Koppel v Koppel,* n. 17 above, 811. The place where the property passes is where the goods happen to be at the contract date: *Badische Anilin und Soda Fabrik v Hickson* [1906] AC 419.
[20] On the search for intention, see *Re Anchor Line (Henderson Bros.) Ltd* [1937] Ch. 1.
[21] They were encouraged to do so by the old s. 11(1)(c) of the 1893 Act which, before its amendment by s. 4(1) of the Misrepresentation Act 1967, in concert with s. 18, Rule 1 deprived the buyer of specific goods of the right of rejection for breach of condition where the property passed at the contract date.
[22] *Dixon v Yates* (1833) 5 B & Ad. 313, 340: 'The very appropriation of the chattel is equivalent to delivery by the vendor, and the assent of the vendee to take the specific chattel, and to pay the price, is equivalent to his accepting possession' (Parke B).
[23] *Tarling v Baxter,* n. 19 above ('where there is an immediate sale and nothing remains to be done by the vendor as between him and the vendee' (Bayley J)).
[24] S. 29(2).
[25] S. 39(1)(a); see Ch. 11 below.

rule of law, consistently with the declared immateriality of postponing delivery or payment. It has also been applied though the seller had further duties to perform, such as cutting standing hay[26] and delivering the goods to a carrier.[27] The property has been held to pass with the fall of the auctioneer's hammer, despite the unknown reputation of the successful bidder.[28] It has also passed despite the goods being in the hands of a bailee who has not yet attorned to the buyer.[29]

Inconsistent intention.   The existence of an inconsistent intention ousting section 18, Rule 1, was considered at length in *Re Anchor Line (Henderson Brothers) Ltd*[30] where the buyers of an electric crane on instalment terms were to have 'the entire charge and responsibility for the crane'. They were to pay a 'deferred purchase price'; references were made to the 'completion of the purchase'; and the instalments covered 'interest' and 'depreciation'. On the liquidation of the buyers, the court held the property remained with the sellers. More recently, an inconsistent intention has been said to be quite easily found;[31] there was little formal authority underpinning this statement at the time it was made, but support for it is growing[32] and it is in tune with a modern concern with insolvency and with the abundance of property-retention devices in instalment and deferred payment contracts. The presumptive rule in section 18, Rule 1, is not as strong today as it used to be. **3.07**

Former effect of rule.   Perhaps the most important reason for easing the strictness of Rule 1 was its earlier role[33] in preventing the buyer of specific goods from rejecting them if the seller committed a discharging breach of contact. If the property passed at the contract date, the buyer was denied rejection rights altogether. Initially it was a question of a buyer, having paid, whose abstract enjoyment of the general property meant he could never assert the total failure of consideration that was necessary to ground an action to recover the money.[34] This was because the **3.08**

---

26 *Tarling v Baxter*, n. 19 above.

27 *Craig v Beardmore* (1904) 7 OLR 674 (Can.).

28 *Dennant v Skinner* [1948] 2 KB 164. Cf *Dobson v General Accident Fire and Life Assurance Corpn plc* [1990] 1 QB 274, where the court avoided passing of property issues in holding that a loss could be claimed under a theft clause in an insurance policy where goods were delivered in return for a stolen, and therefore valueless, building society cheque.

29 *Richardson v Gray* (1869) 29 UCQB 360 (Can.).

30 n. 20 above.

31 *RV Ward Ltd v Bignall* [1967] 1 QB 534, 545 (Diplock LJ).

32 See also *Minister for Supply and Development v Servicemen's Co-operative Joinery Manufacturers Ltd* (1952) 82 CLR 621, 635, 640; *Orix Australia Corp. Ltd v Peter Donnelly Automotive Pty Ltd* [2007] NSWSC 977 (stipulation for payment on delivery of specific goods treated as reservation of title clause); *Michael Gerson (Leasing) Ltd v Wilkinson* [2001] QB 514 at [49] ('inconceivable' that a finance company would pass the property to an outright purchaser before payment) and [57]; *Habton Farms v Nimmo* [2003] EWCA Civ 68; [2004] QB 1 at [118].

33 n. 21 above.

34 See, e.g., *Hunt v Silk* (1804) 5 East 449; *Street v Blay* (1831) 2 B & Ad 456.

contract had first to be rescinded *ab initio* before such an action could be maintained.[35] Oddly, the denial of rejection was then extended to cases where the buyer had not yet paid when he sought to reject, since no sensible distinction could be drawn between non-paying and prepaying buyers.[36] The apparent result was the complete denial of rejection and termination rights where the property in specific goods had passed to the buyer.[37] It was never clear why the same result should not also apply where the property passed in ascertained goods.[38] This position was preserved in statutory amber when the Sale of Goods Act was first enacted in 1893, at a time when developments in the general law of contract were destroying the logical underpinnings of the position.[39]

3.09 **Exceptions to rule.** Judicial assaults on the combined effect of section 18, Rule 1, and the old section 11(1)(c) focused on language in the latter provision permitting its ouster by a contrary intention; they also raked over the meaning in Rule 1 of 'unconditional' and 'deliverable state' in decisions that are still relevant in the application of the rule. This approach began with *Varley v Whipp*,[40] where the contract was for a second-hand self-binding reaper, new the previous season, when it had cut fifty to sixty acres, and currently at Upton where it had not been seen by the buyer. When the machine arrived by rail at its destination, the buyer found it to be old and much-used. According to Channell J, who did not explain why, the property had not passed since the contract was not 'unconditional'.[41] One possible interpretation of this ambiguous word is that the contract contains no

---

[35] *Weston v Downes* (1778) 1 Dougl 23; *Towers v Barrett* (1786) 1 TR 133. The common law process of rescission was not flexible enough to allow for a minor monetary adjustment. Cf the American position: S. Williston (1901) 14 *Harv LR* 317, 421, and American Law Institute, *Restatement of the Law of Contracts* (1939), §349, as reformulated in broader discretionary language in *Restatement of the Law Second [:] Contracts* (1982), §384(2)(b).

[36] *Street v Blay*, n. 34 above.

[37] Subject to a contrary term in the contract: see *Head v Tattersall* (1872) LR 7 Ex. 7; *Rowland v Divall* [1923] 2 KB 500 (Atkin LJ).

[38] But see *Perkins v Bell* [1893] 1 QB 193, 198 (right of rejection lost with passing of property). One view was that the appropriation of non-conforming ascertained goods did not pass the property, since the buyer had not assented to the appropriation of such goods: *Ollett v Jordan* [1918] 2 KB 41. Note that, for unascertained goods, the presumptive rule (Rule 5) turns on the appropriation of goods that conform to the contract description. The idea behind this was to preserve the buyer's right of examination (see Ch. 10 below) notwithstanding the prior delivery of the goods to the carrier as the buyer's agent. This view can be seen also in Atkin LJ's opinion that the property in c.i.f. goods does not pass upon the documentary transfer if the buyer has not had the opportunity to examine: *Hardy v Hillerns & Fowler* [1923] 2 KB 490, 499; see also M. G. Bridge (1986) 20 *UBC LR* 53, 100, n. 23.

[39] e.g. the modern orthodoxy of prospective contractual termination: *Heyman v Darwins Ltd* [1942] AC 356; *Photo Production Ltd v Securicor Transport Ltd* [1980] AC 827; *Johnson v Agnew* [1980] AC 367.

[40] n. 13 above.

[41] *Ibid.*, 517.

promissory conditions,[42] which is a rather implausible creature. Less implausible is a contract that contains no promissory conditions that have been breached by the seller, which may have been what Channell J had in mind. One suggestion is that the commission of a discharging breach by the seller prevents the property passing,[43] but there is nothing explicit in the Act to the effect that the passing of property is dependent upon compliance by the seller with the promissory conditions that the goods are fit for their purpose or are of satisfactory quality. The idea that 'unconditional' refers to the absence of a breach of promissory condition by the seller may be narrowed further to breaches of the description condition in section 13.[44] In the case of specific goods, the description condition requires the seller to tender goods that conform to their contractual identity,[45] a test consonant with that employed in cases of common law mistake. Hardly an exacting obligation, this would be breached where the goods supplied were different in kind from those called for by the contract. In most specific goods contracts, where the goods are seen by buyer and seller, there is normally little prospect of the description obligation being breached, but the goods in *Varley v Whipp* had never been seen by the buyer and their variance from the contract language was so marked that it could truly be said that the goods supplied were not the contract goods.

'Unconditional'.   Nevertheless, the word 'unconditional' has to be construed as   **3.10**
it appears in section 18, Rule 1, and not just as it might be understood in the judgment of Channell J. Its likely meaning is that it connotes an event that the parties have expressly or impliedly intended to mark the passing of property.[46] Such an event is one that may or must happen after the contract date. In section 18, Rules 2–3, the property in specific goods presumptively passes when various acts of weighing, testing, and putting the goods into a deliverable state have been carried out. These, it is submitted, are events of the kind also referred to in more general terms in section 18, Rule 1, under the umbrella word 'unconditional'. Other events could be found in the express or implied agreement of the parties, which a modern court might be readier to find in the teeth of the strong language of Rule 1. It might be agreed, for example, that the property will pass only after the buyer has had a chance to inspect or test the goods[47] or upon the clearance

---

[42] See *Taylor v Combined Buyers Ltd* [1924] NZLR 627; *Armaghdown Motors Ltd v Gray* [1963] NZLR 518.

[43] *Varley v Whipp*, n. 13 above.

[44] Cf *Vigers Bros v Sanderson Bros* [1901] 1 QB 608, 612, where the court restricted a clause providing for the passing of property to 'goods which come within the meaning of the contract'.

[45] See Ch. 7 below.

[46] It does not relate to conditions that have no bearing on the passing of property: *Classic Automobiles of London v L Aura Holdings Inc.* [1997] EWCA Civ 2724.

[47] Cf *Head v Tattersall*, n. 37 above.

of a cheque used by the buyer in payment.[48] A conditional sale contract expressly providing that the property in goods shall pass once the buyer has paid the final instalment is a very clear case of a contract that is not unconditional.[49]

Section 18, Rule 2

3.11 **Deliverable state.**   Section 18, Rule 1, also requires the goods to be in a 'deliverable state', defined as 'such a state that the buyer would under the contract be bound to take delivery of them'.[50] This requirement may be seen as a specific instance of a conditional contract. It should be read with section 18, Rule 2, which provides that if specific goods have to be put in a deliverable state, the property presumptively passes when this is done and the buyer has notice thereof. In the cause of giving rights of rejection to the buyer of specific goods, it has been argued in the past[51] that goods are not in a deliverable state if the buyer is entitled to reject them because of the seller's discharging breach, for in such a case the buyer is not bound to take delivery. This approach is uncomfortably circular and is not good law. With the statutory changes in 1967 enhancing the rejection rights of buyers of specific goods, it is no longer needed for their protection.[52]

3.12 **Actions of the seller.**   The words 'deliverable state' can now sensibly be confined to the performance by the seller of duties, such as packing, repair, dismantling, and servicing between the contract date and delivery. This state of affairs is dealt with by section 18, Rule 2.[53] In *Underwood Ltd v Burgh Castle Cement and Brick Syndicate*,[54] the seller of a horizontal condensing engine was to put it free on rail in London. The machine weighed thirty tons and was bolted to and embedded in concrete, and so had to be detached and dismantled before delivery to the carrier. Until this was done, it was in no state to be delivered.[55] Goods are not prevented

---

[48] See *Godts v Rose* (1855) 17 CB 229; *Shepherd v Harrison* (1871) LR 5 HL 116; *Kidd v Harden* [1924] 3 WWR 293 (Can.).

[49] See *McEntire v Crossley Bros Ltd* [1895] AC 457.

[50] This requirement also appears in Rule 5(1), discussed below.

[51] P. S. Atiyah (1956) 19 *MLR* 315.

[52] If the goods are not in a deliverable state, does it mean that the buyer may reject a tender of them even if the seller has not committed a breach of condition and call upon the seller first to put them in a deliverable state? If so, the unfulfilled requirement under the contract that the seller put the goods into a deliverable state would supply a defence to a seller's claim for damages for non-acceptance. For the connection between rejecting a tender of goods and termination, and between rejection and cure, see Ch. 10.

[53] If such activities are to be performed by the buyer, as in *Kursell v Timber Operators and Contractors Ltd* [1927] 1 KB 298, the case will come under the general language of s. 18, Rule 1.

[54] [1922] 1 KB 343.

[55] *Ibid.*, 345 (Bankes LJ): 'A "deliverable state" does not depend upon the mere completeness of the subject matter in all its parts. It depends on the actual state of the goods at the date of the contract and the state in which they are to be delivered by the terms of the contract.' See also *Wilde v Fedirko* [1920] 1 WWR 866 (Can.); *McDill v Hilson* [1920] 2 WWR 877 (Can.) (seller agreed to polish furniture already paid for by buyer). It would be interesting to see if a court would so readily apply

from being in a deliverable state just because the seller has yet to deliver them to a carrier: they do not have to be in a *delivered* state for the property to pass. Nor will the passing of property be delayed under Rule 2 if certain acts have to be performed by a third party, for example by a warehouseman as agent for the buyer.[56]

Notice. Once goods have been put into a deliverable state, the buyer must be given notice of this before the property will pass under Rule 2.[57] This notice is actual and not constructive, so in one case the property did not pass when the seller completed repairs to a car but failed to inform the buyer.[58] Like any other presumptive rule, however, Rule 2 may be excluded by contrary agreement. This occurred in *Young v Matthews*[59] where 1.3 million bricks were sold in return for the surrender by the buyer of a bill of exchange drawn on the seller. The seller's foreman pointed to three clamps of finished, burning, and unbaked bricks from which delivery was to be made and responded yes to the question: 'Do I clearly understand that you are prepared, and will hold and deliver this said quantity of bricks?' The seller became bankrupt before delivery, but the court held that the property in the bricks had already passed to the buyer despite their not being in a deliverable state, a result in accord with the unusual circumstances of the case.[60] In a case involving the sale of heavy second-hand machinery, the property was held to pass upon payment being made, although the machines still had to be dismantled ready for delivery. The parties had shown an implied intention contrary to Rule 2.[61]

Section 18, Rule 3

Weighing, measuring, and testing. Section 18, Rule 3, provides that where, under a contract for the sale of specific goods in a deliverable state, the seller has to 'weigh, measure, test or do some other act or thing for the purpose of ascertaining the price', the property will not pass until this act has been done and the buyer given notice.[62] This rule, said to be 'somewhat hastily adopted from the civil law',[63] was firmly established at common law before the codification of sale.

3.13

3.14

---

s. 18, Rule 2, where the risk of damage to the goods is not the issue but rather the insolvency of the seller.

[56] *Rugg v Minett* (1809) 11 East 210.

[57] Notice was introduced into the original Sale of Goods Bill on a Scottish suggestion that it would be unfair to put the risk on a buyer who did not know that the property had passed.

[58] *Jerome v Clements Car Sales Ltd* [1958] OR 738.

[59] (1866) LR 2 CP 127.

[60] The court was generous: the goods had not been ascertained from bulk (see K. Llewellyn (1938) 15 *NYU LR* 159, 172, n. 20). Estoppel would not assist the buyer in view of the seller's insolvency.

[61] See *Broadcrest CD Ltd v Ruddock* 2000 WL 1881420.

[62] Like the rest of the rule, notice can be dispensed with by contrary intention: *Martineau v Kitching* (1872) LR 7 QB 436, 449; *Begert v Parry* (1922) 70 DLR 233.

[63] *Blackburn on Sale* (2nd edn, by J.C. Graham, Stevens, 1885), 175.

In *Rugg v Minett*,[64] where the buyer bought at auction two lots of turpentine, whose contents could only be determined once another twenty-five lots had been topped up from the two lots, the property did not pass until this was done. Likewise, the property in a stack of bark sold at so much a ton did not pass where it had to be weighed 'and the concurrence of the seller in the act of weighing was necessary'.[65] Even where the contract is an entire one, it has been held that the property may pass in some of the goods though not the residue when the seller's acts are incomplete.[66]

3.15 **Nature of actions.** If the measurements have been taken leaving only mechanical arithmetical tasks to be performed, the property will pass.[67] Furthermore, the acts in Rule 3 are concerned with ascertaining the price and so the rule does not apply where a lump sum for the goods, unaffected by the acts to be performed, has already been agreed.[68] Rule 3 does not apply if the acts in question, even if connected with ascertaining the price, are those of the buyer or of a sub-buyer.[69]

Sale or Return and Sale on Approval

3.16 **General.** According to section 18, Rule 4, where goods are sent on approval or on sale or return or similar terms, the property will pass when the buyer 'signifies his approval or acceptance to the seller or does any other act adopting the transaction'. Alternatively, it will pass if the buyer retains the goods, without notifying the seller of his rejection of them, beyond either a reasonable time or the time stipulated by the seller for the return of the goods. The difference between a sale on approval and a sale or return transaction is not clear-cut, though the former case seems primarily to deal with the acquisition of goods for personal use or consumption, and the latter with the acquisition of goods with a view to resale. It is not necessarily the case, however, that sale or return is for the purpose of resale[70] and the true distinction between the two transactions may lie in the active duty to return goods on sale or return,[71] as opposed to making them available to the bailor in the case of a sale on approval.

---

[64] n. 56 above.

[65] *Simmons v Swift*, n. 19 above. See also *Logan v Le Mesurier* (1847) 6 Moo. PC 116; *Gilmour v Supple*, n. 19 above; *Acraman v Morrice* (1849) 8 CB 449: *R v Tideswell* [1905] 2 KB 273, 277 (no larceny where goods are counted and then a false number returned by the buyer in collusion with the seller's agent).

[66] *Rugg v Minett*, n. 56 above.

[67] *Tansley v Turner* (1835) 2 Bing. NC 151.

[68] *Hansen v Meyer* (1805) 6 East 614, 627; *Alexander v Gardner* (1835) 1 Bing (NC) 671; *Lockhart v Pannell* (1873) 22 UCCP 597 (Can.).

[69] *Turley v Bates* (1863) 2 H & C 200; *Nanka-Bruce v Commonwealth Trust* [1926] AC 77.

[70] *Poole v Smith's Car Sales (Balham) Ltd* [1962] 1 WLR 744, 747–8.

[71] For the requirement that the goods be returned, see *Kirkham v Attenborough* [1897] 1 QB 201, 203; *Poole v Smith's Car Sales (Balham) Ltd*, n. 70 above.

Function of rules. Although expressed in terms of passing of property, these are **3.17**
rules that have two principal functions. First, they deal in an elliptical fashion with
the formation of a contract of sale, yet refer to the parties as 'seller' and 'buyer' before
any contract of sale has been concluded. Secondly, they state that the property passes
as soon as the contract of sale is concluded. Until that moment arrives, there is no
contract of sale as defined by the Sale of Goods Act, since the 'buyer'[72] has not yet
bought or agreed to buy the goods. Prior to the contract of sale, the goods are held
on contractual bailment terms,[73] the bailee having an option to purchase them.
The nature of this bailment relationship between the potential buyer and the
potential seller was examined by the Court of Appeal in *Atari Corp (UK) Ltd v
Electronic Boutique Stores (UK) Ltd*,[74] where there was unanimity that the bailment was a contractual one.[75] One consequence of this analysis was that the
acceptance provided for in Rule 4 converted the bailment contract into a sale of
goods contract.[76] Another consequence, which does not inevitably follow from
analysing the bailment as contractual, is that the bailor may not withdraw the
offer to sell the goods to the bailee pending the bailee's acceptance of it in one of
the ways laid down in Rule 4.[77] It is not immediately obvious what consideration
is provided by the bailee to give rise to an irrevocable offer to sell the goods by the
bailor. It is an unlikely construction of such a relationship that, in the absence of
express provision, the bailee undertakes to promote sales of the goods to sub-buyers
or otherwise limits its freedom in deciding whether to accept or reject the bailor's
offer. Nevertheless, so far as sale or return provides a vehicle for financing the
acquisition of stock-in-trade, which it does in certain industries, there is business
sense in treating the relationship between the parties as a contractual one, pending
its incremental conversion into a contract of sale as quantities of goods are accepted
at intervals when being sold on to sub-buyers. Sale or return may be the subject of
a master agreement containing obligations to deliver and take delivery of quantities of goods from time to time, which should resolve any difficulty of consideration that might arise before individual contracts of sale are concluded.

Defeasible sales. To be distinguished from contractual bailments of this sort are **3.18**
contracts of sale in which the buyer is given a wide right of rejection of the goods
within a stated period. Although the contract of bailment in *Atari Corp (UK) Ltd
v Electronic Boutique Stores (UK) Ltd*[78] called for payment before the option date,

---

[72] Note: the language of seller and buyer will be used in this discussion of Rule 4 even where the arrangement under which the goods are delivered has not yet become a contract of sale.
[73] *Atari Corp (UK) Ltd v Electronic Boutiques Stores (UK) Ltd* [1998] QB 539.
[74] n. 73 above.
[75] See also *Kirkham v Attenborough*, n. 71 above, 204 (Lord Esher MR).
[76] See Auld LJ, n. 73 above at 551. This view needs some adaptation for the case where severable quantities of a single consignment of goods are accepted at varying intervals.
[77] See Phillips LJ, n. 73 above at 548.
[78] n. 73 above.

it was not interpreted as a defeasible contract of sale. Where a binding but defeasible contract of sale has been concluded, the buyer's entitlement to put the goods back on the seller may evidence an intention to delay the passing of property (and perhaps also the risk) until the buyer runs out of time to exercise his right of rejection.[79]

3.19 **Issues.** The issues arising under Rule 4 are not usually (though they may be) those at stake when the passing of property is considered, such as the incidence of risk and the insolvency of either party, and the seller's right to sue for the price. The most common issue is a title dispute between the seller and a transferee by way of sale or pledge from the buyer, where the buyer disposes of the goods without paying the seller. It is in the seller's interest to argue that the buyer did not accept his offer in accordance with Rule 4 and so retained the status of bailee; consequently, the property did not pass to the 'buyer' who was therefore as a mere bailee unable to transmit title to the transferee. The transferee will be concerned to argue that a contract of sale was concluded between a seller and a buyer; the property passed and accordingly a general or special property was transferred by buyer to transferee under the later disposition.

The Buyer's Acceptance

3.20 **Forms of acceptance.** The acceptance of the buyer that concludes the contract of sale and thus triggers the conveyance under Rule 4 may take three forms: first, a declared acceptance like any other contractual acceptance; secondly, conduct that is consistent with an intention to accept the offer; and thirdly, retention of the goods beyond the time stipulated by the seller or beyond a reasonable time. This last mode of acceptance is difficult to reconcile with the rule that a contract may not be concluded by the offeree's silence.[80] The preoccupation of Rule 4 with title transfer issues, and its failure to refer explicitly to contract formation, encourages a rather literal reading of the rule at the expense of orthodox contract principle. The provisions of the Act may, of course, override the rules of common law contract. Nevertheless, since section 18, Rule 4, fails to state that the seller can stipulate for acceptance by silence, and since there is no contract of sale before the buyer's acceptance, Rule 4 should as far as possible be read in harmony with contract

---

[79] *Elphick v Barnes* (1880) 5 CPD 321 is a case of this kind. *Quaere* the binding character of the contract where the buyer's right of rejection appears to be unfettered as it was in *Elphick*? In French law, such potestative (or self-enabling) clauses in contracts are null and void: C. civ. Arts. 1170, 1174.

[80] *Felthouse v Bindley* (1862) 11 CB(NS) 869, affd (1863) 7 LT 835. But see *Atari Corp (UK) Ltd v Electronic Boutique Stores (UK) Ltd*, n. 73 above, which treats the formation of the contract of sale as succeeding a previously binding contract of bailment. There is an argument that the rules of contract formation ought not to be applied so strictly where the issue is whether a bailment contract has been transformed into a contract of sale.

formation rules,[81] especially since the buyer is exercising an option.[82] The buyer's acceptance by effluxion of time should only arise if his retention of the goods can plausibly be interpreted as conduct evincing an intention to accept, bolstered perhaps by previous arrangements between the parties or by what was said by the seller when possession of the goods was given to the buyer. Taking possession of goods is a consensual act that can supply the necessary conduct, whereas receipt of a contractual offer is a passive affair. Even if the rules of contract formation were designed to give way to special statutory provision in this case, Rule 4 does not permit a seller to practise inertia selling on the buyer by sending goods without prior request and unilaterally defining the time of acceptance.[83] Its wording turns upon 'delivery' to the buyer, which requires a *voluntary* transfer of possession.

Approval and adoption.   The first mode of acceptance in Rule 4, signifying the   **3.21** buyer's approval or acceptance, needs no comment,[84] but the second mode, performing an act adopting the transaction, has proved troublesome. In *Kirkham v Attenborough*,[85] where the language of the Act was criticized, the 'transaction' in Rule 4 was interpreted as the agreement of sale proposed by the seller when bailing the goods to the buyer. When the latter, who had received the goods on sale or return terms, pledged them with the defendant pawnbroker, he was held thereupon to have adopted the transaction. At the very moment of the pledge, the property in the goods passed from the seller to the buyer, and the special property in turn to the defendant transferee.[86] Consequently, the special property conveyed in turn by the buyer to the pawnbroker was strong enough to resist the demands of the seller. In *Kirkham*, the court did not interpret the buyer's behaviour in terms of an objective intention to accept the seller's offer; rather, the court was impressed by the fact that his action was inconsistent with his 'free power'[87] to return the goods. Besides drifting somewhat from the orthodoxy of contract formation, this approach does not sit well with authority that an unauthorized sub-pledge is not as such an act of conversion.[88] Similarly, apart from any fraudulent intentions of the bailee, the pledge of goods may always be redeemed and the goods returned

---

81 Cf *May and Butcher Ltd v The King* [1934] 2 KB 17 note (HL), for the view that the reasonable price rule in s. 8(1) cannot be invoked until an agreement passes the threshold test of a binding contract at common law. The rules of the common law continue to apply to contracts of sale of goods if they are not inconsistent with the provisions of the Act; s. 62(2).
82 Cf *Holwell Securities Ltd v Hughes* [1974] 1 WLR 155.
83 On the sending of unsolicited goods, see Ch. 1 above.
84 Acceptance should not have the special meaning given to it for the purposes of s. 35.
85 n. 71 above, followed in *London Jewellers Ltd v Attenborough* [1934] 2 KB 206.
86 *Whitehorn Bros v Davison* [1911] 1 KB 463.
87 n. 85 above, 203 (Esher MR). See also *ibid.*, 204 (Lopes LJ), and the bailee's 'free control [over the goods] so as to be in a position to return them'.
88 *Donald v Suckling* (1866) LR 1 QB 585.

within the stated time or a reasonable time. The *Kirkham* approach might also be better suited to a sale or return where the buyer sub-sells,[89] since a sub-sale is the very transaction contemplated by the sale or return. It seems less suited to a pledge or to any disposition of the goods under a sale on approval, which contemplates that the buyer will use and consume the goods.

3.22 **Sub-bailment.** Further light is cast on the adopting act in *Genn v Winkel*,[90] a case involving two further sub-bailments of the goods on sale or return terms, which lends support for the following two propositions. First, the adoption by a sub-bailee of a proposed sale will feed adoptions back up the bailment chain, so that the bailee may become bound as a buyer of the goods even if not aware of the sub-bailee's adopting act. If the sub-bailment itself were seen as equivalent to a pledge in inhibiting the bailee's 'free power' to return the goods, then consistency with *Kirkham v Attenborough* would require a sale to be concluded earlier at the moment of sub-bailment, unless the bailor authorized the sub-bailment. More consistent with *Kirkham* is the second proposition from *Genn v Winkel*, that once the offer of a sub-bailment takes place on terms permitting the sub-bailee to retain the goods beyond the time for acceptance given to the bailee, then the bailee thereby adopts the bailor's offer and becomes the buyer of the goods.[91] So, if A bails goods on sale or return terms to B for fourteen days and B sub-bails the goods to C for a period stated to be longer or capable of being longer, B will at the point of sub-bailment be deemed to have accepted A's offer.

3.23 **Personal use.** A further difficulty of adoption concerns the bailee who makes personal use of the goods. Where the transaction is a sale on approval, some degree of use is contemplated by the nature of the arrangement but not, it is submitted, such use as appreciably diminishes the value of the goods, at least in the absence of clear permission to the contrary. If the transaction is one of sale or return, the transaction may on its construction permit the bailee to allow potential sub-buyers some degree of use of the goods for trial purposes. But a sale or return arrangement may become a sale if the bailee makes an unauthorized personal use of the goods.[92] Any assertion of title going beyond the authority to act conferred by the bailor ought to be sufficient to adopt the transaction.[93]

---

[89] Cf *Re Florence* (1879) 10 Ch D 591, 593 (sale or return bailee does not sell the goods as owner but as the holder of an option).

[90] (1912) 107 LT 434.

[91] *Ibid.*, (Buckley LJ).

[92] Consider the conduct of the bailee's salesmen in *Poole v Smith's Car Sales (Balham) Ltd* [1962] 1 WLR 744 using the car for their own purposes.

[93] Like conversion but without the restricting effect of s. 11(3) of the Torts (Interference with Goods) Act 1977 (denial of title alone is not a conversion); see *Astley Industrial Trust v Miller* [1968] 2 All ER 36—registering the car.

Reasonable time. The lapse of a reasonable time, arising under the third mode **3.24**
of acceptance in Rule 4, was considered in *Poole v Smith's Cars (Balham) Ltd*,[94]
where the court, in holding that the time had elapsed under a sale or return
between two car dealers, considered a number of factors, including the declining
second-hand car market at that time of the year, the rapid depreciation of the car,
the bailor's repeated requests for the return of the car, and the evidently temporary
('holiday arrangement') character of the bailment. The question is one of fact and
degree. The reasonable time in Rule 4 may elapse after the bailee has become
bankrupt. The risk of this is not assumed by the bailor, so the failure of the bailee
or his trustee in bankruptcy to return the goods will not mean that the property in
the goods passes to the bailee as buyer and thence to the trustee.[95]

Bailee's negligence. A bailee who is negligent in looking after the goods during **3.25**
the option period should not thereby be seen as adopting the transaction,[96] but
will be liable in tort as a negligent bailee and in that capacity will bear the burden
of disproving personal negligence.[97] A mechanical application of section 18, Rule
4, should not be used to justify substituting an absolute contractual obligation for
a duty of care in negligence, by deeming a contract of sale to be concluded by the
passage of time where the bailee is unable to return destroyed goods. The result
should be the same if the accident to the goods happens down a bailment chain.[98]
A more difficult case is dishonesty down the bailment chain. In *Ray v Barker*,[99] the
bailee was held to have adopted the transaction as a consequence of a fraudulent
pledge further down the chain. Since the bailee trusts to the integrity and credit
of the sub-bailee, however, it is surely appropriate to say that he undertakes
qua the bailor to accept the risk of default of the sub-bailee, and of subsequent
sub-bailees too.

Signifying non-approval. The passage of time, whether prescribed or reasona- **3.26**
ble, is interrupted when the bailee signifies to the bailor that he is not approving
or adopting the transaction. In *Atari Corp (UK) Ltd v Electronic Boutique Stores
(UK) Ltd*,[100] the court treated such conduct as equivalent to the rejection of the
offer of sale.[101] In that case, the bailee of a quantity of computer games had distributed them to a number of its stores and had sold some of them before taking the

---

[94] n. 92 above; see also *Moss v Sweet* (1851) 16 QB 493.
[95] *Re Ferrier* [1944] Ch. 295.
[96] e.g., by retaining destroyed goods or goods that have had to be repaired beyond a reasonable
time.
[97] *Houghland v RR Low (Luxury Coaches) Ltd* [1962] 1 QB 694.
[98] *Genn v Winkel*, n. 90 above, 109 (Vaughan Williams LJ).
[99] (1879) 4 Ex. D 279.
[100] n. 73 above.
[101] Although s. 35 is not mentioned in the case, there are similarities between rejection under
that section and rejection of the offer under s.18, Rule 4 (see Auld LJ, n. 73 above, 551).

decision not to continue stocking the game. The bailee therefore gave notice that it intended to return the remaining games, though at the time it was unable to state how many games would be returned and the remaining games themselves had not been gathered at a central point. The bailee's notice was effective even though it had failed to pay the price that had fallen due, some of the games had been purchased, and the precise number of games for collection by the bailor[102] was not stated. Provided the goods were available for collection within a reasonable time,[103] a generic notice was sufficient; the number of games being returned was capable of subsequent ascertainment.

Exclusion of Rule 4

3.27 **Contrary agreement.** Since it is based upon presumed intention, Rule 4 can be displaced by contrary agreement. The lesson of *Kirkham v Attenborough* was learnt by the bailor of jewellery in *Weiner v Gill*[104] where the agreement on which goods were bailed on sale or return, stated: '[G]oods had on approbation or on sale or return remain the property of Samuel Weiner until such goods are settled for or charged.' This displayed a contrary intention, allowing the bailor to assert his title against the defendant pledgee. But *Weiner v Gill* was not the last word on the battle between bailor and innocent transferee. As will later be shown, words like 'sale or return' are not conclusive of the nature of a transaction if the court believes that on its true construction the agreement is one of agency, where the principal who owns the disputed goods is liable to be challenged by the innocent transferee on different grounds.[105] Rule 4 has been excluded elsewhere because the plain intention of the parties was that the property should only pass on a cash payment.[106] If the bailee declares an intention not to accept the offer, his subsequent conduct in relation to the goods has been held not to be an acceptance,[107] though it could be a conversion of them.

---

[102] The bailor did not claim that the goods had to be physically returned to them (n. 73 above, Waller LJ at 544 and Phillips LJ at 549, the latter citing *Ornstein v Alexandra Furnishing Co.* (1895) 12 TLR 128)) and the sale or return agreement evidenced in fax messages imposed no such requirement. An analogy with s. 36 would therefore make the bailee's notice effective if it made the goods available for collection by the bailor.

[103] A bailee failing to hand over the goods at that time would commit the tort of conversion according to Waller LJ: n. 73 above, 546. It is submitted, however, that delay by the bailee should be treated no more strictly in this type of bailment than in other types.

[104] [1906] 2 KB 574.

[105] *Weiner v Harris* [1910] 1 KB 285, discussed in Ch. 5 below. For the difference between sale or return and agency, see *Re Nevill* (1870) LR 6 Ch. App. 397. See also *WT Lamb & Sons v Goring Brick Co. Ltd* [1932] 1 KB 710, *The Kronprinzessin Cecilie* (1917) 33 TLR 292, and the cases on reservation of title, discussed in the text accompanying nn. 296 *et seq.* below.

[106] *Percy Edwards Ltd v Vaughan* (1910) 26 TLR 545; see also *Whitehorn Bros v Davison*, n. 86 above, 483–4.

[107] *Swenson v Lavigne* [1925] 3 DLR 681; see also *Ellis v Mortimer* (1805) 1 B & P NR 257.

Unascertained and Future Goods

Ascertainment and Existence

General.   Although the intention of the parties is paramount in the passing of **3.28**
property, this is subject to the goods having become existing and ascertained.[108]
Since the enactment of section 20A, introduced by the Sale of Goods (Amendment)
Act 1995, a buyer will in some cases acquire as tenant in common an undivided
share in a bulk before ascertainment of the particular goods that the seller intends
to deliver under the contract.[109] The incidents of this tenancy in common, which
is anyway confined to special cases, are somewhat different from the general property in the goods that the buyer acquires once the rules in sections 16–19 of the
Act have been satisfied. Consequently, although the 1995 tenancy in common
rules have in a practical sense modified the law on ascertainment and the significance of ascertainment, the established position in the Sale of Goods Act will first
be considered before attention is turned to the 1995 changes.

Existence.   Some assistance is given by the Act in determining when future **3.29**
goods come into existence, namely, upon their manufacture or acquisition by the
seller.[110] Crops and produce in an immature state should also be future goods;
hence the property in grapes still on the vine will not pass.[111] In a contract for the
sale of a ship to be built, it is common for parties to stipulate that the property in
the inchoate structure will pass as it is added to from time to time,[112] and nothing
in sections 5 and 16 is inconsistent with such an intention. Courts have been
reluctant to give effect to clauses providing that the property will pass in materials
fashioned for a ship, even before they become part of the ship by accession,[113] possibly because the contract is for the sale of a ship and not of building materials,
which before attachment constitute future goods.[114] In the absence of contractual

---

[108] Ss. 5(3) and 16.

[109] Discussed in the text accompanying nn. 204 *et seq.* below. The Act does not in fact explicitly
use the language of tenancy in common.

[110] S. 5(1).

[111] *Orr v Danforth Wine Co.* [1936] OWN 306 (Can.).

[112] *Clarke v Spence* (1836) 4 A & E 448; *Seath v Moore* (1886) 11 App. Cas. 350; *Reid v MacBeth
& Gray* [1904] AC 223; *Sir James Laing & Sons Ltd v Barclay, Curle & Co. Ltd* [1908] AC 35; *Re Blyth
Shipbuilding & Dry Docks Co. Ltd* [1926] Ch. 494. In the absence of such a clause, there appears
to be 'a strong *prima facie* presumption' against the passing of property in incomplete work: *Seath
v Moore*, above, 370 (Lord Blackburn); *Sir James Laing & Sons*, above. See also *Re Royal Bank of
Canada and Saskatchewan Telecommunications* (1985) 20 DLR (4th) 415.

[113] *Seath v Moore*, n. 112 above, and *Re Blyth Shipbuilding, ibid.* (where this seems to be treated
as a rule of law).

[114] But it may be possible to provide for the property to pass in unattached parts by clear drafting:
North Western Shipping & Towage Co. v Commonwealth Bank of Australia Ltd (1993) 118 ALR 453,
481 (Fed. CA).

provision, the property will pass in materials when they are incorporated in the ship.[115]

Ascertainment

3.30 **Identification.** Not defined by the Act, ascertainment[116] occurs once goods have subsequently been identified to the contract.[117] Goods bought in by a seller with the intention of fulfilling a sale obligation, which thereby become existing goods, may not yet be ascertained. That will happen when they are identified to the particular contract at hand by a process of earmarking such as labelling or packaging.[118] If the seller merely promises or represents that he holds the agreed goods for the buyer, this is not enough to ascertain the goods from the seller's existing or after-acquired stock. This was the position in *Re Goldcorp Exchange Ltd,*[119] where a seller misled investors into believing that, when they paid for precious metals, the seller would store the appropriate quantity on their behalf in a vault free of charge. The seller's statements did not as such identify to the contract existing metals in the seller's possession answering to the contract description or future metals coming in, in which latter case there was the added difficulty of not knowing how such metals could be identified amongst a range of competing contracts of sale.

3.31 **Bulk portion.** Goods will be treated as unascertained even if they are a fungible portion of a specific or ascertained bulk, at least until separation occurs.[120] Another way of putting it is that the relevant quantity is not appropriated to the contract before separation.[121] The property, for example, did not in one case pass in a quantity of newsprint where the seller retained an unascertained portion.[122] A graphic

---

[115] *Anglo-Egyptian Navigation Co. v Rennie* (1875) LR 10 CP 271; *Petromec Inc. v Petrolas Brasileiro SA Petrobas* [2004] EWHC 1180 (Comm); [2005] 1 Lloyd's Rep 219 at [36], affirmed without reference to this point at [2005] EWCA Civ 891; [2006] 1 Lloyd's Rep. 121. Both cases concerned contracts for work and materials but the principle should be the same. It was also held in the latter case that the property in equipment brought on board the ship had passed even though the equipment had not yet been irrevocably incorporated in the structure of the ship: *ibid.*

[116] See the discussion in Law Commission, *Sale of Goods Forming Part of a Bulk* (Law Com. No. 215, 1993) Part II.

[117] *Re Wait*, n. 6 above; *Thames Sack & Bag Co. Ltd v Knowles & Co. Ltd* (1918) 88 LJKB 585; *Re Western Canada Pulpwood & Lumber Co.* [1929] 3 WWR 544.

[118] For a laxer approach to ascertainment in cases where goods of the type and quantity agreed to be sold are then warehoused rather than delivered to the buyer, see *Re Stapylton Fletcher Ltd* [1994] 1 WLR 1181, discussed below.

[119] [1995] 1 AC 74; see also *Re London Wine Co. (Shippers) Ltd* (1979) [1986] PCC 121.

[120] *Gillett v Hill* (1834) 2 Cr. & M 530; *Swanwick v Sothern* (1839) 9 A & E 895; *Campbell v Mersey Docks and Harbour Board* (1863) 14 CB(NS) 412; *Boswell v Kilborn* (1858) 15 Moo. PC 309; *Jenkyns v Usborne* (1844) 7 Man. & Gr. 678.

[121] *Healy v Howlett & Sons* [1917] 1 KB 337.

[122] *Ross v Eby* (1877) 28 UCCP 316 (Can.).

illustration of this approach is *Re Wait*,[123] where Wait agreed to sell to the buyer on c.i.f. Avonmouth terms 500 tons of Western White Wheat from a parcel of 1,000 tons shipped by one of Wait's own suppliers on the *m.v 'Challenger'*.[124] Although the buyer paid the contract sum, no property in the goods passed for reasons expressed by Atkin LJ as follows: '[N]o 500 tons of wheat have ever been earmarked, identified or appropriated as the wheat to be delivered . . . under the contract. The buyers have never received any bill of lading, warrant, delivery order or any document of title representing the goods.'[125] *Re Wait* would therefore support the passing of property to a buyer of the 1,000-ton bulk receiving the bill of lading against payment but not to two cash-paying buyers of 500 tons each.[126]

Passive ascertainment.   The buyer of goods contained in a specific or ascer-   **3.32** tained bulk was sometimes fortunate even before the enactment of section 20A in 1995. In one case, ascertainment of the buyer's share occurred by exhaustion when it was isolated after other orders from the same bulk had been executed by delivery.[127] In another case, the buyers would have failed, but for the happy accident of buying from a different seller the remainder of the goods left in the specific bulk with their own unascertained portion.[128] It would have been an exercise in legal pedantry to deny the buyers on the ground that neither contractual portion had been ascertained when the two taken together had been.

Sale of share.   There is no need to fulfil the requirements of section 16 where the   **3.33** contract is for the sale of an undivided share in specific goods belonging to the seller, rather than a severable quantity of goods in that bulk.[129] Formerly, this was because the contract was not a sale of goods contract. The new definition of 'goods'[130] includes an undivided share in goods. This means that contracts for the sale of undivided shares are now governed by the Sale of Goods Act. If they are contracts for undivided shares in specific goods, they are treated as contracts for

---

[123] n. 6 above.
[124] Note the disagreement between Atkin LJ, who thought that any parcel of 500 tons on the *Challenger* could have been tendered, regardless of the identity of the shipper, and Sargant LJ, who thought the opposite. The latter was surely correct given the clause in the contract naming the particular shipper and releasing Wait in the event of his named shipper failing to perform.
[125] n. 6 above, 629.
[126] For the difficulties posed by s. 16 to the modern practice of bulk shipments of commodities, see B. Davenport [1986] *LMCLQ* 4, discussing the Dutch case of *The Gosforth*, 20 Feb. 1985, Rotterdam Comm. Ct., unreported.
[127] *Wait & James v Midland Bank* (1926) 31 Com. Cas. 172.
[128] *Karlshamns Oljefabriker v Eastport Navigation Co. Ltd (The Elafi)* [1982] 1 All ER 208. This result, and the one in *Wait & James*, is incorporated in s. 1(2) of the Sale of Goods (Amendment) Act 1995, amending the rules on unconditional appropriation by adding a new s. 18, Rule 5(3),(4), to the Sale of Goods Act 1979.
[129] Law Com. No. 215, paras. 2.5–6.
[130] In s. 61(1) of the Sale of Goods Act as amended by s. 2(c) of the Sale of Goods (Amendment) Act 1995.

specific goods[131] and will therefore remain unaffected by section 16 of the Sale of Goods Act. The property in an undivided share of specific goods can therefore pass without payment being made by the buyer and thus otherwise than by means of section 20A.[132] A contract for the sale of an undivided share of specific goods remains different, therefore, from a contract for the sale of unascertained goods in a specific bulk. The latter is now treated, for the purpose only of overcoming the barrier to the passing of property in section 16, as though it were a contract for the sale of an undivided share.

3.34 **Undivided share in unascertained goods.**   A more difficult case is presented by a contract for the sale of an undivided share in unascertained goods, such as a 1/64 share of a ship yet to be built. Section 16 is now applicable to such a case but section 20A does not on its terms apply, since it concerns only contracts for the sale of a 'specified quantity' of unascertained goods. In this case, there is no clear way to avoid the conclusion that, as a result of legislative change, the property can never pass in such cases, except by means of an act of transfer effected once the goods have come into existence. In other cases, such as the (unlikely) contract for the sale of half of a cargo to be shipped at a future date, it may be possible to arrive at a 'quantity', whether the amount to be shipped is known in advance or not. The goods shipped will be capable of enumeration and their parts fungible. Whereas one soya bean in a shipment may be interchangeable with another, however, the same cannot be said for the parts of a ship.

Overcoming Section 16

3.35 **Attempts to avoid Section 16.**   The seller in *Re Wait* did not provide the buyer with a delivery document of any kind, though in c.i.f. contracts payment is usually net cash against shipping documents. Suppose, however, that a seller performs all his personal obligations[133] under a contract where the goods are held in an undivided bulk by a carrier or warehouseman.[134] The buyer of unascertained goods may benefit from a personal estoppel against a third party,[135] such as a

---

131 Pursuant to s. 2(d) of the 1995 Act amending s. 61(1) of the Sale of Goods Act.

132 For the distinction between subject matter and shares thereof, in the constitution of a trust and the application of the certainty rule, compare *Re London Wine Co. (Shippers) Ltd*, n. 119 above, with *Hunter v Moss* [1994] 1 WLR 452, criticized by D. Hayton (1994) 110 *LQR* 335; see also *Holland v Newbury* [1997] 2 BCLC 369.

133 The seller may, of course, be in breach for non-delivery if a third party, such as a ware-house-man, fails to do something, e.g., attorn to the buyer.

134 See the sympathetic approach to the buyer of the Canadian court in *Coffey v Quebec Bank* (1869) 20 UCCP 110, 113, affirmed (1869) 20 UCCP 555. Cf. *Re Rose* [1952] Ch. 499 (gift of shares and equitable interest in donee prior to registration of transfer by company).

135 Because the estoppel gives rise to a personal right (*see Re London Wine Co. (Shippers) Ltd*, n. 119 above) the insolvency of a seller renders worthless any estoppel against him: *Re Goldcorp Exchange Ltd*, n. 119 above.

warehouseman who attorns to the buyer[136] when the buyer's quantity has not yet been ascertained. May the seller's performance of his obligations also give rise to proprietary entitlement? In one case concerning the risk of adulteration of white spirit, the Court of Appeal departed from the 'lump' concept of title in holding that, notwithstanding the property remaining in the seller, the risk had passed to the buyer from the time when the buyer could have called for delivery of his portion of the bulk.[137] It does not necessarily follow, however, that the same approach could or should be adopted in cases of seller insolvency. Yet Blackburn J once said that he was 'very much inclined to struggle very hard' to prevent the 'monstrous hardship' of a windfall benefit to the seller's creditors in such circumstances.[138] Before the enactment in 1995 of section 20A, attempts to assist buyers by overcoming the section 16 impediment to the passing of property were made with the assistance of equitable ideas[139] and the common law notion of tenancy in common.[140] These attempts proved unsuccessful.

Equitable Property Rights

Pre-Act authorities. Although *Re Wait* is an apparently decisive authority **3.36** against the buyer acquiring equitable rights to the contract goods by operation of law,[141] it is worth tracing the antecedent law before the case is considered at length. Before the codification of sale, the Privy Council had held that a seller purportedly negotiating a non-negotiable bill of lading in favour of a bank had nevertheless succeeded in conveying an equitable title.[142] Although not a case of unascertained goods, this decision was significant in applying equitable proprietary principles where the seller had intended but failed to transfer a legal proprietary right. It might yet be significant where a seller transfers a bill of lading to an undivided part of a bulk with the intention of passing the general property in the quantity covered by the bill of lading to the buyer.[143] There were other pre-codification decisions from which a buyer of unascertained goods could draw considerable comfort. In *Hoare*

---

[136] See *Laurie and Morewood v Dudin and Sons* [1926] 1 KB 223; *Woodley v Coventry* (1863) 2 H & C 64; *Knights v Wiffen* (1870) LR 5 QB 660; *Henderson v Williams* [1895] 1 QB 521.

[137] *Sterns Ltd v Vickers Ltd* [1923] 1 KB 78.

[138] *Martineau v Kitching* (1872) LR 7 QB 436, 454.

[139] Rejected in *Re Wait* [1927] 1 Ch. 606, discussed below. See Law Reform Commission of Western Australia, *Discussion Paper on Equitable Rules in Contracts for the Sale of Goods* (Project no. 89, 1995), Ch. 4 (especially paras 4.35 *et seq.*).

[140] The buyer's argument to this effect was implicitly rejected, presumably because of its inconsistency with s. 16, by the Court of Appeal in *Laurie and Morewood v Dudin and Sons*, n. 136 above. Cf *Inglis v James Richardson & Sons* (1913) 29 OLR 229 (Can.).

[141] It was not challenged head on in *Re Goldcorp Exchange Ltd*, n. 119 above; see also *Re Stapylton Fletcher Ltd*, n. 118 above.

[142] *CP Henderson & Co. v Comptoir d'Escompte de Paris* (1873) LR 5 PC 253.

[143] The transfer of a bill of lading carries with it the property rights intended by the transferor: *Sewell v Burdick* (1884) 10 App. Cas. 74. On the failure of the law prior to 1995 to satisfy commercial expectations, see Law Com. No. 215, paras 3.3–4.

v Dresser,[144] a broker, acting as the *del credere* agent of a seller of three cargoes of timber, accepted a number of the seller's drafts, in return receiving copies of the charterparties of two of the vessels carrying the goods and the promise of bills of lading when the loading was completed. The House of Lords held that he acquired an equitable interest in the goods upon loading even though he never received the bills of lading. Furthermore, in the leading case of *Holroyd v Marshall*,[145] a textile manufacturer, as security for a debt, assigned by way of mortgage[146] all present and future machinery in the mill until the debt was paid. The House of Lords held that the creditor had automatically acquired an equitable interest in the future machinery upon its acquisition by the debtor, since a court of equity would order the performance of the contract to assign the machinery. At law, a deed assigning future property was, to the extent of that property, void in law[147] and a fresh conveyance of each item of machinery would be required as and when it came into existence.

3.37 **Promise to assign.** Equity gave effect to a purported present assignment of future property by treating it as a promise to assign the goods.[148] Treating that as done which ought to be done, equity viewed the contract to assign as a perfected assignment as soon as it was able to 'fasten upon' the goods, that is, upon their coming into existence.[149] Even if this event occurred during the assignor's insolvency, the equitable assignment would take effect.[150] An issue never adequately resolved was whether the promise to convey had to be linked to the completed assignment by compliance with the doctrine of specific performance. In *Holroyd v Marshall*,[151] Lord Westbury said that the assignee was entitled to relief provided the contract was such 'as a court of equity would direct to be specifically performed'.[152] On the face of it, this limitation would give little scope for equitable assignment in commercial sales contracts where goods almost always lack the unique quality needed if the discretionary remedy of specific performance is to be successfully invoked.[153] Furthermore, the law is also reluctant to grant specific performance outside cases of specific or ascertained goods.[154]

---

[144] (1859) 7 HLC 290.

[145] (1862) 10 HLC 191.

[146] A defeasible sale: *Keith v Burrows* (1876) 1 CPD 722.

[147] *Lunn v Thornton* (1845) 1 CB 379; explained as an application of the maxim *nemo dat quod non habet* by Willes J (*arguendo*) in *Chidell v Galsworthy* (1859) 6 CB (NS) 471, 473.

[148] See P. Matthews [1981] *LMCLQ* 40.

[149] *Tailby v Official Receiver* (1888) 13 App. Cas. 523.

[150] *Collyer v Isaacs* (1881) 19 Ch. D 342. But it would not apply to property coming into the hands of a bankrupt upon his discharge from bankruptcy: *ibid*.

[151] n. 145 above.

[152] *Ibid.*, 211.

[153] The limitation would surely exclude the (run-of-the-) mill machinery in *Holroyd v Marshall*, n. 145 above.

[154] See s. 52 of the Sale of Goods Act and *Re Wait*, n. 123 above.

Specific performance issues.   Lord Westbury, nevertheless, gave as an example   **3.38**
of a valid equitable assignment a contract for the sale of 'five hundred chests of the
particular kind of tea which is now in my warehouse in Gloucester',[155] which, not
without some ambiguity, is a contract for the supply of an unascertained part of a
specific bulk. This example, using commonplace goods, tells against taking too
literally the reference to specific performance, and alone should be enough to
refute the argument that equitable rights may only be assigned where the remedy
of specific performance is available. Yet Lord Westbury's example was phrased in
another report quite differently as one for the sale, not of an unascertained part of
a specific bulk, but of specific goods.[156] Even if the claimant is able to surmount
the specific performance barrier, however high it is erected, more recent authority
denies that the availability of specific performance necessarily means that the
buyer has an equitable interest in the subject matter of the contract.[157] In the later
case of *Tailby v Official Receiver*, Lord Westbury's specific performance limitation
was interpreted as confined to the particular example he used to show that equitable
rights are more than shadowy things.[158] Another attempt to neutralize Lord
Westbury's words came in a case where Cotton LJ stated that the specific performance limitation applied only where the contract was wholly executory and not where
the assignee had already performed his part of the bargain, for in such a case damages
would not be an adequate remedy.[159] Prior to the passing of the Sale of Goods Act in
1893, the prospects for a prepaying buyer therefore appeared encouraging.

Re Wait

The transaction.   The effect of the Act on equitable proprietary rights in sales law   **3.39**
was considered in *Re Wait*.[160] The prompt date for payment by the buyer was thirty-
three days after Wait had sight of the bill of lading (which covered the whole parcel
of 1,000 tons) from his own seller. Although this seemed a normal c.i.f. contract,
where the buyer might have demanded a documentary tender that included a bill of
lading,[161] the buyer paid the seller after being invoiced for the agreed sum without

---

[155] n. 145 above, 209.
[156] The Law Journal report records 'a contract to sell *the* five hundred chests of a particular kind
of tea which are now in my warehouse in Gloucester' (emphasis added): (1862) 33 LJ Ch 193, 196.
Predictably, the resultant ambiguity was relied upon in *Re Wait*, n. 6 above, to attack the notion of
equitable property rights in sales law.
[157] *Re London Wine Co. Ltd*, n. 119 above; *Re Stapylton Fletcher Ltd*, n. 118 above.
[158] n. 149 above, 545–8 (Lord Macnaghten).
[159] *Re Clarke* (1887) 36 Ch. D 348, 352; see also Buckley LJ in *Swiss Bank Corpn v Lloyds Bank
Ltd* [1982] AC 584, 595 (Buckley LJ). For conflicting statements on whether the defendant's insolvency should incline a court to grant specific performance, see *Anders Utkilens Rederei A/S v O/Y
Louise Stevedoring Co. A/B* [1985] 2 All ER 669, 674 (it should not) and *Eximenco Handels AG v
Partredereit Oro Chief* [1983] 2 Lloyd's Rep. 509, 521 (it should); see further Ch. 11 below.
[160] n. 6 above, strongly criticized by Sir. F. Pollock (1927) 43 *LQR* 293. For delivery terms see the
text accompanying n. 123 above.
[161] *Quaere* a bill of lading that dealt with an unascertained portion of a larger bulk?

receiving a bill of lading or indeed any other delivery document. Wait hypothecated the bill of lading to his bank as security for his overdraft and paid the price received from the buyer into his general account. The bank, acting unilaterally, transferred this credit item a few days later into a separate loan account that had been debited with the sum advanced to Wait upon the hypothecation. Before delivery of the 500 tons could be made to the buyer, Wait was made bankrupt and the official receiver's representative obtained the bill of lading by discharging the debt from the loan account, thus leaving the buyer's payment as a credit. At no material time did the 500 tons due to the buyer ever become separated from bulk.

3.40 **Summary.** The trial judge declined to award specific performance of the contract but held that the buyer's payment was trust money earmarked for a special purpose and so should be repaid to the buyer.[162] The Divisional Court in Bankruptcy, however, ordered specific performance but the Court of Appeal by a majority overturned the award on the ground that the goods had never become 'specific or ascertained' for the purpose of section 52 and specific performance.[163] It further held that the buyer had no equitable property in the 1,000 ton bulk.[164] No argument relating to a trust of the purchase money was made by the buyer by the time the action reached this stage.

3.41 **Reasons of majority.** Of the majority judges, Lord Hanworth MR pointed to the specific performance limitation in Lord Westbury's judgment in *Holroyd v Marshall*[165] and held also, in effect, that an equitable appropriation would have to pass the test of ascertainment in section 16.[166] Atkin LJ too referred to Lord Westbury and held also there could be no equitable assignment of the buyer's 500 tons enforceable by equitable lien or charge over the 1,000 ton bulk arising from 'the mere sale[167] or agreement to sell'.[168] The Act was a complete codification of property rights arising out of the contract of sale:

> It would have been futile in a code intended for commercial men to have created an elaborate structure of rules dealing with rights at law, if at the same time it was

---

[162] For such a trust to arise, the buyer's money must be sufficiently dedicated to the purpose of acquiring the goods that it not may be mingled with the seller's other moneys and it must be returned if the dedicated purpose cannot be performed: see M. Bridge (1992) 12 *OJLS* 333 and the case law therein discussed, including *Barclays Bank Ltd v Quistclose Investments Ltd* [1970] AC 567 and *Re Kayford Ltd* [1975] 1 All ER 604. In *Re Goldcorp Exchange Ltd*, n. 119 above, the buyer's argument that his money was received by the seller in the capacity of fiduciary failed because the buyer's purpose in making payment was to fulfil his sale obligations and there was no restriction imposed on the use by the seller of the money.

[163] n. 6 above, 616–21 and 630–4.

[164] Before the trial judge, the buyer had also claimed a charge over the bulk to secure repayment of the purchase money.

[165] n. 145 above.

[166] n. 6 above, 622.

[167] *Quaere* s. 2(4)?

[168] n. 6 above, 636.

intended to leave, subsisting with the legal rights, equitable rights inconsistent with, more extensive, and coming into existence earlier than the rights so carefully set out in the various sections of the Code.[169]

Furthermore, to grant the relief sought by the buyer would 'also appear to embarrass to a most serious degree the ordinary operations of buying and selling goods, and the banking operations which attend them'.[170] Despite Atkin LJ's concerns, however, it is surely not too important to worry about the bank advancing money to the seller against a pledge of the shipping documents.[171] If the bank has notice of the equitable interest granted to the buyer, it is forewarned and can take its own precautions; and if it is not aware of this interest, its own special legal property will prevail against or override[172] the buyer's equitable interest.

3.42

Express equitable rights.   Atkin LJ did concede that a 'seller or a purchaser may, of course, create any equity he pleases by way of charge, equitable assignment or any other dealing with or disposition of the goods, the subject matter of sale; and he may of course create such equity as one of the terms expressed in the contract of sale'.[173] No such special provision had in his view been made in the present case.[174] Nor did he feel drawn to intervene in favour of the buyer on grounds so inherently vague as dishonesty (or, supposedly, equitable fraud). The general hostility of Atkin LJ's remarks towards the equitable infiltration of commercial law, however, has succeeded in concealing his concession that the parties could create equitable rights under a contract of sale if they put their minds to it in the proper way. But to the extent that equitable rights would create real impediments to the operation of the seller's activities, as they would if they encumbered a portion of the seller's trading stock,[175] a court would require a great deal of persuading that equitable rights were genuinely intended by the parties.[176]

3.43

Reasons for dissent.   Sargant LJ, dissenting in *Re Wait*,[177] plainly believed that Wait had appropriated the particular cargo of 1,000 tons from which to fulfil his

3.44

---

169 *Ibid.*, 635–6.

170 *Ibid.*, 629–30. Note also his criticism of the difficulty in determining when an equitable property passed to the buyer: *ibid.*, 635.

171 His concern was that the efficacy of a seller's pledge of the shipping documents with a bank would be undermined if the bank's knowledge of the existence of a contract of sale were to be treated as knowledge of equitable interests arising thereunder: *ibid.*, 639–40. Why should it?

172 Depending upon whether the pledge precedes the equitable assignment or vice versa.

173 n. 6 above, 636. This concession is not referred to by Lord Brandon in *Leigh and Sillavan Ltd v Aliakmon Shipping Ltd* [1986] AC 785, 812–13, when he adopts Atkin LJ's views on the need to exclude equitable proprietary principles from the scope of the Sale of Goods Act. The concession, however, is mentioned explicitly by Lord Mustill in *Re Goldcorp Exchange Ltd*, n. 119 above, where he too adopts Atkin LJ's views.

174 n. 6 above, 635.

175 The seller could not deal freely with stock the subject of a trust.

176 *Re Goldcorp Exchange Ltd*, n. 119 above, 91, 96–7.

177 n. 6 above, especially 644–7, 655–6.

sale obligations to the buyer. He considered that an equitable interest would have passed to the buyer from the time of appropriation if the buyer had agreed to buy the whole of the 1,000-ton bulk, and the same conclusion should follow on the present facts, since in both cases it would be fraud or dishonesty for the seller to divert the wheat from the contract with the buyer.[178] Equitable assignment, in his view, was not tied to the doctrine of specific performance and, though the 500 tons had never been ascertained, they were nevertheless ascertainable at the time when it was sought to enforce the contract.[179] Finally, the Sale of Goods Act had not put paid to equitable interests arising out of sale of goods contracts and the equitable assignment could be implemented by specific performance since the goods in question could be regarded as 'specific goods' under section 52.

3.45 **Effect of *Re Wait*.**   For practical purposes, *Re Wait* put an end to the idea of an implied equitable assignment in sale of goods,[180] despite a majority view that the result would have been different if the seller had undertaken to deliver the buyer's 500 tons out of the 1,000 tons for which he held a bill of lading.[181] Recent confirmation of the effect of *Re Wait* comes from the Privy Council decision in *Re Goldcorp Exchange Ltd*,[182] which also stands for a refusal to infer a fiduciary relationship from ordinary contractual dealings or to impose constructive trust, equitable lien, and restitutionary proprietary rights simply because the seller has failed to abide by his promises and representations regarding the holding of earmarked goods for the buyer. From the buyer's point of view, this case was weaker on its facts than *Re Wait*, since there was no question of an identified bulk to be charged with equitable rights.

Tenancy in Common

3.46 **Co-ownership.**   It is noteworthy that the Law Commission, when it considered the problem of insolvency and bulk goods, recommended a reform favouring the prepaying buyer based, not upon equitable ideas, but upon the common law doctrine of tenancy in common. Such a buyer, unless the parties otherwise agreed, would obtain an undivided share in an identified bulk, until his share was separated in the normal course.[183] The Commission's proposal was that tenants

---

[178] On this point, see also *Clark v Scottish Imperial Insurance Co.* (1879) 4 SCR 192 (Can.) (Ritchie J).

[179] See also Bowen LJ in *Re Clarke*, n. 159 above, 355.

[180] But see *Electrical Enterprises Pty Ltd v Rodgers* (1989) 15 NSWLR 473, where the court gave the seller of goods an equitable (non-possessory) lien over them, declining to follow the *Re Wait* view that the Sale of Goods Act fully codified property rights. See also *International Finance Corpn v DSNL Offshore Ltd* [2005] EWHC 1844; [2007] 2 All ER (Comm.) 305, discussed below n. 236.

[181] Hanworth MR and Sargant LJ. Atkin LJ insisted, against a plain reading of the contract, that the seller could have tendered from any shipment on board the *Challenger*.

[182] N. 119 above; McKendrick (1994) 110 *LQR* 514.

[183] The Commission's proposals, in line with the views of consultants, were confined to sales out of a particular bulk: Law Com. No. 215, n. 116 above, paras. 3.10 and 4.1. For discussion of the

in common of the bulk would share rateably any shrinkage of the bulk, but that any of them removing or receiving his contract quantity from the bulk should be protected from liability to other tenants suffering a shortfall.[184] The recommendations of the Law Commission were enacted as changes to the Sale of Goods Act in 1995,[185] though the expression 'tenancy in common' appears nowhere in the legislation.

Intention and co-ownership. The position before the 1995 changes, where **3.47** there was a specific or ascertained bulk and various unsatisfied buyers therefrom, was that those buyers could not be treated without more ado as tenants in common of the undivided bulk.[186] It was not enough that the seller's creditors would obtain a windfall benefit from the accident of non-ascertainment from the bulk, or that the buyers had a common interest, or at least no adversity of interest, in the face of the seller's insolvency. Nevertheless, in *Re Stapylton Fletcher Ltd*,[187] decided after the Law Commission report, it was held that, just as a tenancy in common can be imposed by law in the case of a wrongful mixing of goods,[188] so there was nothing to prevent the parties impliedly or expressly agreeing for the seller to hold the buyer's goods mixed in common with those of other buyers as their relationship was converted from one of sale into one of storage.[189] In that case, sellers of wine located in one of their warehouses, exercising rigorous stock controls, conscientiously segregated cases of wine that they held in stock, the subject of various contract of sales, by removing the wine from their ordinary trading stacks and transferring it to their warehouse stacks.[190] Even though there was no evidence that individual buyers' wines had been earmarked and isolated from the same wines of other buyers for the purpose of or in the process of transfer into the warehouse stacks, the court held first that the wines of those buyers had thereby been ascertained under section 16. Consequently, the way was open for the property to pass to individuals in accordance with the intention of the parties before the wines were submerged in a common warehouse pool. The test of ascertainment was to be understood differently where sellers made a constructive delivery to themselves as warehousemen as opposed to an actual delivery to the buyer.[191]

---

report and the working paper, see A. Hudson [1989] *LMCLQ* 420; R. Bradgate and F. White [1994] *LMCLQ* 315.

[184] *Ibid.*, paras. 4.19–21.

[185] Discussed below.

[186] *Laurie and Morewood v Dudin and Sons* [1926] 1 KB 223; *Karlshamns Oljefabriker v Eastport Navigation Corpn (The Elafi)* [1982] 1 All ER 208, 214. See Law Com. No. 215, n. 116 above, paras. 2.4 and 2.7.

[187] n. 118 above; N. Campbell [1996] *JBL* 199.

[188] See *Indian Oil Corpn v Greenstone Shipping SA* [1988] QB 345.

[189] *Quaere* a tenancy in common between the seller and one or more buyers?

[190] *Re London Wine Co. Ltd*, n. 119 above, was distinguished by the existence of a defined bulk coupled with this process of segregation: n. 187 above, 1194.

[191] n. 118 above, 1199.

A less controversial feature of the case was the next step taken by the court, namely, the inference from the parties' conduct of a tenancy in common of the wine in the warehouse stacks. This conclusion was reached even though the cases of wine in those stacks were not allocated to particular warehousing contracts and there was nothing to show to which warehousing contract cases of a particular type and vintage of wine belonged. The meticulous records of the warehouse, however, revealed the names of those who were entitled in gross to share those cases. In the event of loss or breakages in the common warehouse pool, each buyer would bear the burden rateably with the other tenants in common according to their respective shares. The tenancy in common result in this case is equally applicable to goods delivered by the seller and mingled with identical or compatible goods of the buyer, in circumstances where the seller does not intend to pass the property in the goods to the buyer.[192]

3.48 **Ascertainment by documentary means.** The interpretation of the seller's actions in the above case as amounting to ascertainment was generous to the buyers, but the way that the court in *Re Stapylton Fletcher Ltd* dealt with the sale of other, *en primeur*, wines ordered from foreign growers in the names of individual buyers was more generous still. A stock certificate accompanied the wines into a bonded warehouse and the sellers recorded the entitlements of individual buyers in a master index. The sellers then notified the warehouse of the individual buyers' entitlements. At no material time did the sellers physically touch, move or separate the wines in a way that could be construed as ascertainment under individual contracts of sale, yet the court treated the sellers' actions as amounting to ascertainment. The Court of Appeal in *Customs and Excise Commissioners v Everwine Ltd*[193] noted that the sellers at no time held wines of their own in the bulk designated for their various buyers and limited the effect of *Re Stapylton Fletcher Ltd*. In *Everwine*, the buyers acquired no property rights because the goods destined for them did not exhaust all of the stocks in the name of the sellers in the bonded warehouse. The documentary actions of the seller in a case like *Re Stapylton Fletcher Ltd*, therefore, will be an effective ascertainment only if the seller has no goods of its own or if its own goods have first been physically separated from those destined for buyers. Moreover, the response of the court in *Everwine* suggests that *Re Stapylton Fletcher Ltd*, in its application to the *en primeur* wines, might be open to challenge in a higher court. In any case, the special features of *Re Stapylton Fletcher Ltd* render it of little assistance in cases like *Re Wait*, where the application of section 20A[194] is likely to provide more assistance to buyers.

---

[192] See P. Watts (1990) 106 *LQR* 552, discussing *Coleman v Harvey* [1989] 1 NZLR 723; A. Hudson [1991] *LMCLQ* 23.
[193] [2003] EWCA Civ 953. The case concerned the evasion of excise duty and s. 20A was raised at a late stage of the proceedings and not pursued in the Court of Appeal.
[194] Discussed below.

Buyers and Insolvent Sellers

Reasons for assisting buyer. Before we turn to the 1995 amendments to the   **3.49**
Sale of Goods Act, it is useful to consider a further aspect of the case for intervention on behalf of the buyer. If section 16 may not be applied[195] in a way favourable
to the buyer, then any intervention on his behalf, by means of equitable rules or
by statutory means, should not be a matter of mere legal technique under broad
rubrics such as 'fraud' and 'dishonesty'. It should as a matter of principle be asked
why the buyer should rank ahead of the insolvent seller's other creditors.[196] The
Law Commission did assert that 'insolvency law has to accept the rules of property
law as it finds them'[197] and implied that removing anomalies from existing law
does not interfere with the rules of distribution on insolvency.[198] But it is difficult
to see a proposed major reform, prompted by a report dealing with the problems
raised by a long-established body of law, as responding to a mere anomaly. There
is much to be said in this area of law for confronting the issue of insolvency head
on. The best starting point for preferring the prepaying buyer is Atkin LJ's statement in *Re Wait*:

> If a seller of goods delivers them to a buyer before payment, trusting to receive pay-
> ment in due course, and the buyer becomes bankrupt, the seller is restricted to a
> proof, and can assert no beneficial interest in the goods. There seems no particular
> reason why a different principle should prevail where a buyer hands the price to the
> seller before delivery of the goods trusting to receive delivery in due course. In both
> cases credit is given to the debtor, and the buyer and the seller take the well known
> risk of the insolvency of their customer.[199]

A seller who delivers the goods before payment is well able to see the risk and
guard against it by reserving the general property. The prepaying buyer is not so
well positioned and may be unaware that his goods form an undifferentiated part
of a bulk.[200] A matter of critical importance raised in this passage is whether 'credit'
is granted by the prepaying buyer to the seller or, more accurately, whether the
buyer advances money to the seller with the intention of financing the latter's
business, accepting the risk of relegation to the status of an unsecured creditor if
he does not actively bargain for a security. In *Re Wait*, the buyer did not advance
the price to permit Wait to obtain the goods from his shipper. The contract was an
ordinary c.i.f. transaction contemplating the transfer of the general property,
through the medium of the bill of lading, against payment. It is arguable that the
adventitious circumstance of the contract quantity being submerged in a larger

---

[195] As it was in *Re Stapylton Fletcher Ltd*, n. 118 above.
[196] See *Re Goldcorp Exchange Ltd*, n. 119 above, 99.
[197] Law Com. No. 215, n. 116 above, para. 3.19.
[198] *Ibid.*
[199] n. 6 above, 640.
[200] Or that there is even a bulk: *Re Goldcorp Exchange Ltd*, n. 119 above.

bulk baffled the expectations of the parties that the buyer would become the owner of the contract goods upon payment. Credit is not the practice in commodity transactions and a case can be made for intervention in favour of the buyer where otherwise the seller's creditors would obtain a windfall benefit. Those who take an insolvency risk commonly charge a premium commensurate with the risk, which is not the case with prepaying buyers of part of a bulk cargo.

3.50 **Instalment sales.** It is easily overlooked that one example of a prepaying buyer who does not extend credit to the seller, and indeed receives it from the seller, is the buyer on instalment terms, where the seller retains the general property until payment in full has been made. Canadian cases on conditional sales, seemingly attracted by the analogy of a security bill of sale where the grantor has an equity of redemption in the goods, support the view that an equitable or other limited interest, measured by the instalments paid from time to time, passes to the buyer.[201] These cases are consistent in approach with English hire purchase cases, allowing the finance company, in a conversion action against a third-party tortfeasor, to recover only damages limited to the unpaid balance on the hire purchase agreement.[202] The normal conversion award, based upon the value of the goods, would be more consistent with the *legal* structure of the hire purchase agreement, under which the finance company retains the full beneficial and legal ownership until the hirer can and does exercise the option to purchase.[203]

Sale of Goods (Amendment) Act 1995

3.51 **Statutory change.** Rather than build upon notions of equitable proprietary entitlement, the Sale of Goods (Amendment) Act 1995[204] implemented the above tenancy in common proposals of the Law Commission. Since the amendments and additions it made to the Sale of Goods Act[205] do not expressly use the language of tenancy in common, however, it cannot be taken to codify all circumstances where a tenancy in common will arise. There is no reason why a buyer

---

[201] *CC Motor Sales Ltd v Chan* [1926] SCR 485, 491; *Workmen's Compensation Board v US Steel Corpn* (1956) 5 DLR (2d) 184; *Commercial Credit Corpn v Niagara Finance Corpn* [1940] SCR 420; *Rogerson Lumber Co. Ltd v Four Seasons Chalet Ltd* (1980) 29 OR (2d) 193. See also the old system of lien notes: A. Hogg (1924) 2 *Can. Bar Rev* 491.

[202] *Belvoir Finance Co. Ltd v Stapleton* [1971] 1 QB 210; *Wickham Holdings Ltd v Brooke House Motors Ltd* [1967] 1 All ER 117.

[203] Other examples showing that the law does not stop at the formal structure of hire purchase include *Whiteley v Hilt* [1918] 2 KB 808 (assignability of option rights); *Transag Haulage Ltd v Leyland DAF Finance plc* [1994] BCC 356 (relief against forfeiture); Consumer Credit Act 1974, ss. 90, 132 (limits on the right of repossession).

[204] J. Ulph [1996] *LMCLQ* 93; L. Gullifer [1999] *LMCLQ* 93; R. Goode, *Commercial Law* (3rd edn, Penguin, 2004), 209–13, 220–8; N. E. Palmer and E. McKendrick, *Interests in Goods* (2nd edn, LLP, 1998), Ch.16.

[205] These are to be found in ss. 16, 18(3), (4), 20A, 20B, and 61(1) ('bulk', 'delivery', 'goods', 'specific goods').

might not invoke tenancy in common outside the legislation, though it is unlikely that a buyer will have to do so and unlikely that a court will accede to a tenancy in common claim that does not fulfil the requirements of the Act. According to section 20A of the Sale of Goods Act 1979, where 'the goods or some of them form part of a bulk', the buyer acquires an 'undivided share in the bulk' and becomes an owner in common of the bulk[206] unless the parties agree otherwise.

Required conditions. Three conditions have to be satisfied before this proprietary interest arises. First, there must exist a 'bulk', which is defined as 'a mass or collection of goods of the same kind which . . . is contained in a defined space or area . . . and is such that any goods in the bulk are interchangeable with any other goods therein of the same number or quantity'.[207] The requirement is that goods be of the same kind, and not of the same kind, grade, and quality. Crude oil, for example, may be mixed, accidentally or otherwise, in different grades to produce a hybrid blend. There is no reason why this event should prevent a buyer from acquiring a co-ownership right, even though it may be practically impossible to extract from the blend goods of the description bound for the buyer under the contract. The crude oil that has been mixed remains crude oil. If the blend is not in conformity with the contract requirements, the buyer may be able to terminate the contract consequent upon a breach of section 13 or 14 of the Sale of Goods Act, but the existence of a right to terminate ought not to prevent the property first passing to the buyer in the relevant undivided share. A further point is that there must be limits to what constitutes a defined space or area. A defined space will usually and without undue difficulty be referable to a named warehouse or ship, but a defined area could be large enough for a real difficulty to arise in applying section 20A. A pragmatic interpretation of this phrase would combine its operation to cases where the size of the bulk can be computed by practical means. If this cannot be done, it is hard to see how the area can be treated as a 'defined' one. The second condition for a proprietary interest is that this bulk must be identified in the contract or by subsequent agreement between the parties. A difficult case, common in international commodity sales, is that of the seller who issues a notice of appropriation (or declaration of shipment) indicating that the buyer's goods will come from a named ship. The notice will give the date or approximate date of the relevant bill of lading. Of itself, this notice may not sufficiently identify a particular hold of the ship or portion of the ship's cargo. Unless the reference in the notice to the ship is judged sufficient to identify the bulk, an undivided share

3.52

---

[206] Evidently with other buyers in the same position and/or the seller, to the extent that the seller retains an interest in the bulk.
[207] S. 61(1).

may therefore not pass to the buyer.[208] This difficulty will in practice be resolved by compliance with the third condition, demanded by section 20A before the buyer will acquire an undivided share, which is that the buyer must have made payment for that share. In international commodity sales where goods are shipped in bulk and documents are exchanged for payment before the bulk is broken, payment will usually be made against the transfer to the buyer of a ship's delivery order containing an undertaking by the ship to deliver a stated quantity of goods to the holder of the order.[209] The undertaking of the ship to surrender the relevant cargo, which makes the delivery order effective, will have been given upon the surrender by the seller to the ship of one or more bills of lading. The receipt by the buyer of the delivery order will therefore be predicated upon the identification of the bulk by that bill of lading.

3.53 **The buyer's share.** Certain matters deriving from the implementation of the above provisions of the 1995 Act are dealt with in the same legislation. First of all, the size of the buyer's share is stated by section 20A(3) to be a rateable one, corresponding to the ratio between the bulk and the quantity of the goods for which payment has been made by the buyer.[210] The buyer's ratio, thus expressed in quantitative terms, would therefore not take account of a change in the quality or type of the bulk produced by a mixing of different grades or qualities. This means that the buyer should be able to claim a quantity whose overall quality is higher than the contract quality, if the blending process has produced a grade superior to the buyer's contractual entitlement, but only a lower quality if the resultant grade is inferior to the buyer's entitlement. In this latter case, the buyer who affirms the contract after a breach of condition by the seller will have a damages claim under section 53 of the Sale of Goods Act. In cases of part-payment, the legislation provides that any 'delivery' out of the bulk to such a buyer will be 'ascribed' to that payment.[211] Under sections 20A and 20B, 'delivery' has the extended meaning of 'such appropriation of goods to the contract as results in property to the goods being transferred to the buyer'[212] and so can take place without possession being transferred physically or constructively to the buyer.[213] The effect of this part-payment rule is that any undivided share that the buyer might have in the remaining bulk

---

[208] Cf the views of Atkin LJ, expressed in *Re Wait*, n. 6 above, that the sellers could have performed the contract out of any cargo on the *Challenger*, and not just that portion of the cargo for which they held a bill of lading: discussed at n. 103 above.

[209] For the meaning of which see Ch. 6 below.

[210] The buyer's share may therefore increase incrementally as payment is progressively made. The size of the buyer's share corresponds directly to the size of the part-payment (a unit pricing approach): s. 20A(6).

[211] S. 20A(5)

[212] See the definition of 'delivery' in s. 61(1), as amended by s. 2(b) of the 1995 Act.

[213] Subject to the application of s. 18, Rule 5.

will be diminished[214] to the extent of the goods paid for and delivered and in effect substituted by the general property in those goods.[215] The buyer's property interest, whether it takes the form of an undivided share or the property in goods or both, will not by virtue of sections 20A–B exceed the payment made, except for those cases where separation leads to a passing of the general property in an amount that exceeds the equivalent of payment made by the buyer.

Shrinkage. The next matter arising from section 20A concerns shrinkage in the **3.54** bulk, which could occur for various reasons including natural wastage, theft, or default of the seller, will be borne rateably by the various tenant buyers according to the size of their respective shares in the bulk. Section 20A(4) does not explicitly address the position of a co-owning immediate seller, whether or not responsible for the shrinkage. Nor does it deal with persons other than the immediate seller, such as a seller at the head of a sales string, who may have shipped additional goods to avoid deadfreight charges to the shipowner and may not have onsold them. If section 20A(4) is given a literal reading, it would allow the buyers' individual shares to start to abate only at the point when the bulk is no longer large enough to accommodate all their entitlements. This would mean that any shrinkage in the bulk would first be implicitly attributed to the immediate seller and head seller (where relevant). This result would expropriate these sellers and is therefore wrong in principle. Section 20A(4), it is submitted, should be interpreted as expressing a particular case of a broader co-ownership principle and therefore open to supplementation by the common law.[216] The expropriation of the immediate seller could not be justified as a matter of risk allocation since the allocation of risk cannot be used in respect of goods that are not the subject of the particular contract, and the seller's unappropriated and unseparated goods are not the subject of any of the contracts of sale. As far as the immediate seller does not remove his own portion from the bulk but is negligent as a bailee in conserving the bulk, there is similarly no good reason to attribute that negligence first of all to the seller's own portion. The appropriate response would be to give the other co-owners an action in negligence against the bailee seller, just as would be the case if the bailee were a third party.

Deliveries out of bulk. A further aspect of section 20A concerns the effect **3.55** of deliveries[217] out of the bulk to individual buyers. These deliveries may override the undivided shares of co-owners to whom delivery has not been made.

---

214 And those of other co-owners increased.
215 See discussion below.
216 Common law principles would reach the same result as s. 20A(4), at least in the case of an innocent seller: *Spence v Union Marine Insurance Co.* (1868) LR 3 CP 427; M. Bridge, *Personal Property Law* (3rd edn, Clarendon Law, 2002), 110–11.
217 In the extended sense referred to above.

Section 20B(1)(a) of the Sale of Goods Act provides that co-owners are deemed to consent to such deliveries out of the bulk to fellow co-owners entitled to receive such delivery. A buyer receiving delivery in full in this way is not required to indemnify fellow co-owners, who will therefore bear a disproportionately large share of any shrinkage that has occurred in the bulk.[218] Similarly, this consent of co-owners of the bulk extends under section 20B(1)(b) to 'any dealing with or removal, delivery or disposal of the goods' by one of their number, 'so far as the goods fall within that co-owner's undivided share in the bulk at the time of the removal, dealing, delivery or disposal'. This broad provision could include dealings between a buyer and a sub-buyer. It could also include the case of a seller, with rights of co-ownership in the bulk, who allows a buyer to have delivery of goods in the bulk when that buyer's failure to pay means that he has acquired no co-ownership rights under section 20A(2). The reason why the seller can be treated as a co-owner for the purposes of section 20B(1)(b) is that, as soon as the first buyer acquires an interest in the bulk, the seller necessarily surrenders ownership of the whole bulk in return for a lesser co-ownership interest in the bulk. The seller thus implicitly 'becomes an owner in common of the bulk' under section 20A(2), even though that provision explicitly confers co-ownership rights on the buyer and not on the seller. The delivery of the contract goods in full to a non-paying buyer despite shrinkage would not be within the deemed consent of other co-owners of the bulk under section 20B(1)(b). That provision does no more than allow the co-owner of the bulk to deal with and separate his share: the consent of the other co-owners extends only to the size of the co-owner's share 'at the time of the removal, dealing, delivery or disposal'.[219] If, at the buyer's request, the delivery is made by the seller directly to a sub-buyer, it might appear that the sub-buyer's rights are limited in the way prescribed by section 20B(1)(b). Nevertheless, it is possible to bring this case within section 20B(1)(a) provided the buyer has paid in full. This is done by treating the delivery to the sub-buyer as a truncated process of delivery to the buyer and sub-delivery to the sub-buyer, a process that has been recognized for the purposes of section 25 and should be recognized here.[220] The sub-buyer would therefore succeed to the position of the buyer. A sub-buyer taking direct delivery from the seller should be no worse off than a buyer taking delivery. This interpretation does not deprive section 20B(1)(b) of practical effect. It can still apply, for example, to a seller who retains a share and either removes that original, pre-shrunken share or directs a bailee to deliver to him that share.

---

[218] S. 20B(3)(a). But co-owning buyers are free to agree otherwise amongst themselves: s. 20B(3)(b). Unless they all contract with the seller on the same standard form making such provision, it is unlikely that such a bargain will be struck.

[219] Whether the sub-buyer's entitlement could be expanded with the aid of s. 25(2) is discussed in Ch. 5 below.

[220] *Four Point Garage Ltd v Carter* [1985] 3 All ER 12; *E & S Ruben Ltd v Faire* [1949] 1 KB 254.

Protecting third parties.   Section 20B(2) goes on to state that '[n]o cause of **3.56** action shall accrue to anyone against a person by reason of that person having acted in accordance with' a delivery to an owner in common of goods to the extent of his share, or removal, delivery or disposal by an owner in common to the extent of his share. This provision protects third parties assisting in these transactions, especially those occurring under section 20B(1)(a), where a co-owning buyer receives more than his entitlement. Section 20B(2) amounts largely to an abundance of caution, since carriers, warehousemen, and stevedores are already protected at common law from liability in conversion when performing actions that, so far as they know, have no transfer of title implications.[221] There are limits to the protection afforded by section 20B(2). A carrier may be protected who has delivered the full bill of lading quantity to a cargo receiver, notwithstanding the shrunken bulk, but a carrier who signs a bill of lading for a certain amount will still be liable to deliver that amount to the holder of the bill of lading.[222] Finally, the contractual rights of a buyer benefiting from the various proprietary rights conferred by sections 20A–B remain unaffected by the legislation.[223]

Undivided shares and general property.   Additional features arising from the **3.57** 1995 changes to the Sale of Goods Act should also be mentioned. First, although it does not say so explicitly, the Act creates an interim position in the passing of property from seller to buyer: the buyer's undivided share as tenant in common of the bulk will fall between having no property rights and having the general property in the contract goods. It can normally be expected that, with the separation of the buyer's goods from the identified bulk, the requirements for the passing of the general property will either already have occurred or will thereupon occur. The general property in such cases will therefore supersede the buyer's undivided interest. Suppose, however, that the test for the passing of the general property, whether prescribed in the contract or arising under section 18, Rule 5,[224] has not been satisfied. Once the buyer's contractual portion has been separated, the buyer can no longer have an undivided interest in the bulk. If the contract contains a provision that the property will only pass upon payment in full, and the buyer pays half of the contract price, it is possible that the buyer will qualify for an undivided interest corresponding to half of his contractual entitlement. If that entitlement were to disappear as a result of the actions of the seller or an agent of the seller, in separating the buyer's portion, it would be most unsatisfactory for the buyer to be deprived altogether of proprietary rights. A likely construction of the contract, however, is that the reservation of title clause manifests a contrary

---

[221] *Hollins v Fowler* (1875) LR 7 HL 457 (Blackburn J.).
[222] M. Bridge, *International Sale of Goods* (2nd edn., OUP, 2007), Ch. 10.
[223] S. 20B(3)(c) (e.g. any action against the seller for non-delivery of agreed goods would remain).
[224] Discussed below.

intention to the acquisition by the buyer of an undivided interest in common. An undivided interest is acquired under section 20A once the conditions laid down in the section are met *and* 'unless the parties agree otherwise'. A more difficult case is where section 18, Rule 5, might require physical delivery to the buyer, the contract is silent on the passing of property, and separation of the buyer's portion occurs before physical delivery to the buyer. Such might occur, for example, where the seller's contract undertakes to transport and deliver a quantity of goods on shore. It would be a curious property right of the buyer's if it could be unilaterally divested by the seller when separating the buyer's portion. The seller would thus invest himself with the general property in the goods by his own act. The most practicable solution to this problem would be to recall that section 18, Rule 5, is a rule of presumptive intention. If there is nothing to repel the acquisition by the buyer of an undivided interest under section 20A, this could be seen as excluding Rule 5 and impliedly providing instead for the general property to pass to the buyer upon separation.

3.58 **Undivided shares and passive ascertainment.** The second additional feature concerns the relationship between the new sections 18, Rule 5(3), (4), and 20A. Although a buyer will not acquire an undivided interest under the latter provision until payment is made, once the bulk is exhausted by other buyers' claims, leaving only the non-paying buyer with a claim to receive goods from that bulk, the property in the remaining goods would pass to that buyer pursuant to section 18, Rule 5(3), (4). The unpaid seller, however, would have the protection of a lien over the goods until payment is made.[225] It may seem curious that section 20A does not give a non-paying buyer an undivided share leaving the seller to be protected by that same lien. Section 18 Rule 5(3), (4), however, will apply only where the seller does not reserve the right of disposal under section 19, which an unpaid seller is likely to do in cases where section 18, Rule 5(3), (4), might come into play.

3.59 **Contrary intention.** A third feature is the reference in section 20A to the parties showing a contrary intention. It is clear enough that this intention can negative the creation of a buyer's undivided interest, but less clear whether it can provide for an undivided interest in circumstances, for example, where the buyer has not paid, where the full requirements of the section have not been met. Section 20A(2) allows for a contrary intention only '[w]here this section applies'. The requirements of the section are that a bulk be identified and that the buyer have paid at least a part of the price. Whilst the parties would be free to allocate a full, undivided interest to a buyer who has made part-payment, they would not be free to make any provision for an undivided interest if the buyer has paid nothing. There seems no reason in principle why such a distinction ought to be drawn, but the

---

[225] Sale of Goods Act, s. 39(1)(a).

language of the section appears to make the distinction unavoidable. There is every reason, however, why the parties should not be free to dispense with the requirement of a bulk: they are, after all, not free to dispense with ascertainment under section 16. The reason for this is that 'a priori common sense dictates that the buyer cannot acquire title until it is known to what goods the title relates'; the buyer is defeated 'not by some arid legal technicality but by what Lord Blackburn called "the very nature of things"'.[226]

Undivided share and 'goods'. A fourth feature of the 1995 changes, as noted **3.60** earlier, is that an undivided interest is now defined as goods under the Sale of Goods Act 1979. This does not mean that a sub-buyer (who may not yet have paid) of unascertained goods in a bulk automatically becomes the buyer of an undivided share just because the buyer acquires an undivided share in the bulk upon payment. The distinction between the sale of an undivided share and the sale of unascertained goods in a specific or identified bulk remains. That distinction is built upon and preserved in the amended Sale of Goods Act.

Overseas comparison. The 1995 Act may usefully be compared to a 1993 **3.61** reform to the British Columbia Sale of Goods Act.[227] This reform grants to a consumer buyer,[228] to the extent of any prepayment made, a 'lien' against goods in the seller's possession and destined for sale, the property in which has not passed to a different buyer, as correspond with the contract description or (where relevant) any sample of the goods. There is no need for any bulk to be appropriated to the contract, a clear point of departure from the amended Sale of Goods Act 1979. Furthermore, it is not clear whether this 'lien' is of an equitable or common law nature; it seems to be *sui generis*. The scheme of the legislation is as follows. First, a 'trustee-in-bankruptcy'[229] with no knowledge of the lien is not liable for dealings with the goods. Secondly, the lien is discharged when goods are 'appropriated'[230] to a 'sale'.[231] Thirdly, the buyer's lien ranks ahead of 'other security interests'[232] under the province's modern personal property security legislation, which has abandoned any distinction between common law and equitable interests.

---

226 *Re Goldcorp Exchange Ltd*, n. 119 above, 90.

227 The Consumer Protection Statutes Amendment Act SBC, c. 1993, s. 27, adding ss. 73–80 to the Sale of Goods Act RSBC 1979, c. 370. See the comment by the Chairman of the British Columbia Law Reform Commission (A. Close) at (1995) 25 *Can Bus LJ* 127 and the criticism of the draft proposal by M. Bridge at (1989) 5 *Banking and Finance LR* 171.

228 One who buys 'primarily for personal, family or household purposes'. The reform is designed to deal with mail order and similar transactions.

229 This includes sheriffs, liquidators, and even receivers.

230 It is not clear what this means under the legislation.

231 Contract of sale or sale properly so called? *Semble*, the buyer under this 'sale' need not have paid. *Quaere*, sales by trustees, liquidators, and (some) receivers acting as agents of the insolvent seller, and by sheriffs and (other) receivers who do not act in that capacity?

232 Which includes mortgages, charges, and title reservations.

Fourthly, the buyer's lien, as against other buyers' similar liens, is treated as in the nature of a tenancy in common in that the shortage of any available goods to satisfy all liens entails the rateable abatement of the buyers' several claims. Fifthly, the equitable principles of marshalling govern in the case of competing buyers' liens, so that a buyer's lien will be released in favour of other buyers' liens to the extent that that buyer has other security (broadly defined) to reinforce his claim to goods or the return of his purchase price. A final point to note about this legislation is that the buyer does not merely have a lien over the seller's goods but also a lien over 'any account in a savings institution in which the seller usually deposits the proceeds of sale'. There is thus no need to comply with the requirements of a *Quistclose* trust;[233] the interesting question of how such a lien is to be reconciled with a competing claim by that savings institution falls outside the scope of this text. It should be noted that the two liens, over goods and accounts, both apply in securing either the performance of the contract by the delivery of goods or the reimbursement of any money prepaid.[234]

Unconditional Appropriation

3.62 **Presumptive rule.** Once the embargo placed by section 16 on the passing of property is lifted, by the goods becoming ascertained,[235] the way is open for the property to pass according to the intention of the parties.[236] Failing an actual intention, the presumptive intention in section 18, Rule 5(1), is as follows:

> Where there is a contract for the sale of unascertained or future goods by description, and goods of that description and in a deliverable state are unconditionally

---

[233] Referred to at n. 162 above.

[234] The seller decides whether to perform or repay. This appears to give him in all cases where the liens exist an option to terminate contracts of sale, subject to the buyer's right to claim damages for breach of contract if the prepaid money is returned.

[235] Likewise the embargo on future goods in s. 5(3) lifted when they become existing goods.

[236] Although a purchaser's equitable lien over goods for moneys prepaid by the purchaser has not generally found favour in English law, support for the acquisition of such a right by operation of law is to be found in *International Finance Corpn v DSNL Offshore Ltd* [2005] EWHC 1844; [2007] 2 All ER (Comm.) 305. That case concerned an oil company that concluded a contract for labour and materials with a contractor, with ownership of the installation manufactured by the latter to pass to the oil company upon completion. Instead of the contractor paying for the supply of parts by a third party and then invoicing the oil company, it was agreed that the oil company would pay the third party directly (though the contract for the sale of the parts remained between the third party and the contractor). In view of the fact that the parts had 'characteristics specifically designed for the requirements of the purchaser' (*ibid.*, at [60]), and the facility with which the oil company could have obtained an injunction to prevent the parts being used otherwise than on the installation (had it ever been necessary to do so), the oil company acquired an equitable lien in the parts for which it had paid. The equitable lien existed even where the labour and materials contract fell within the Sale of Goods Act (*sic*): *ibid.*, at [60]. No such lien would arise in the case of 'ordinary commercial goods': *ibid.*, at [49] (applying *Transport and General Credit Corpn v Morgan* [1939] Ch 531, 546). The reasoning in this case, if correct (it is difficult to reconcile with *Re Wait*, n. 6 above), could apply just as well to a simple bilateral case where a purchaser prepays the seller for goods that are or become ascertained; see also *Hewett v Court* (1983) 149 CLR 639, on which the court in *International Finance* relied.

appropriated to the contract, either by the seller with the assent of the buyer or by the buyer with the assent of the seller, the property in the goods then passes to the buyer; and the assent may be express or implied, and may be given either before or after the appropriation is made.

It is possible, where ascertainment from an agreed bulk is delayed, for an agreed unconditional appropriation to be held in suspense until the act of ascertainment occurs.[237] A review of the case law fails to reveal a differential application of the rule depending upon the issue at stake, whether it is a matter of risk, or the seller's bankruptcy, or the seller's entitlement to sue for the price. Indeed, attempts by litigants to manipulate the rule according to context once attracted disparaging comment in the Privy Council.[238] Yet it cannot be said that the approach to unconditional appropriation has been wholly consistent in the cases: as will be seen, much depends upon the seller's delivery obligations. The passing of property, as shown by Rule 5(1), is a consensual act. Indeed, it is shaped almost as a contract within the contract of sale, with one of the parties offering particular goods to another, who then accepts them.[239]

Appropriation. Appropriation is an ambiguous word and the case law is unhelp- **3.63**
ful in elucidating it. Baron Parke once ascribed to it three meanings in a well-known but obscure passage.[240] To isolate the meaning of the word, it helps for analytical purposes to define three stages in the passing of property in unascertained goods: first, an appropriation by one party; secondly, a further act by that same party that renders the appropriation unconditional; and thirdly, the assent of the non-appropriating party (whether to the appropriation or the making of it unconditional is not clear, but unlikely to be significant). Subject to one exception,[241] appropriation *simpliciter* appears to mean only the ascertainment of the goods.[242] A seller would thus appropriate from existing stock by setting aside goods intended for the fulfilment of a particular sale contract. Appropriation from future stock would be accomplished, for example, upon the later receipt of stock specially bought in for a particular resale commitment, or upon the completion by a

---

[237] See *The Elafi* [1982] 1 All ER 208. This has been confirmed by legislation: s. 1(2) of the Sale of Goods (Amendment) Act 1995, adding a new s. 18, Rule 5(3),(4), to the 1979 Act.

[238] *Gilmour v Supple*, n. 19 above.

[239] This contractual feature is not as well developed here as it has been for sale of land where the contract of sale may merge in the later conveyance.

[240] *Wait v Baker* (1848) 2 Ex. 1, 8–9:

> The word appropriation may be understood in different senses. It may mean a selection on the part of the vendor, where he has the right to choose the article which he has to supply in performance of his contract. . . . Or the word may mean, that both parties have agreed that a certain article shall be delivered in pursuance of the contract, and yet the property may not pass in either case. . . . 'Appropriation' may also be used in another sense . . . viz. where both parties agree upon the specific article in which the property is to pass, and nothing remains to be done in order to pass it.

[241] See the use of the word in c.i.f. sales discussed in the next para. below.

[242] This would correspond to the first of Baron Parke's meanings, n. 240 above.

manufacturing seller of a production run set up for a particular buyer, or upon a set-ting aside of goods out of a general consignment bought in or manufactured.

3.64 **International sales.** In certain international sales conducted on c.i.f terms, appropriation works as follows. Goods are said to be appropriated to the contract when the seller passes on to the buyer details of their shipment, including the identity of the ship, in a notice of appropriation (or declaration of shipment). It is common for goods to be thus appropriated when they are an unascertained part of a larger bulk thereby rendered specific, such as 10,000 tonnes of soya bean meal from the 50,000 tonnes on board the named ship. This process of appropriation, unlike the examples of appropriation given above, locks the seller in to delivering goods from that ship, but they can be any 10,000 tonnes therein.[243] The property in the goods, even if ascertained from the bulk,[244] will not usually pass by virtue of this appropriation,[245] but the seller will have lost his contractual freedom to appropriate to the contract goods from any other source.

3.65 **Unconditional.** The next step is to determine what it is about an appropriation that makes it unconditional.[246] There are two broad alternative approaches. First, if an appropriation takes place when particular goods are applied to the contract, it is unconditional if the seller's decision is, or later becomes, demonstrably a firm one. Secondly, an appropriation becomes unconditional when a seller puts it out of his physical power to reverse the effect of the appropriation. The former approach is based upon the idea of election.[247] The appropriation of a cargo by a c.i.f. seller, who thereby loses his contractual freedom to supply goods from an alternative source,[248] would be unconditional if Rule 5 turned on election. The effect of the unconditional appropriation, however, might be inhibited by the non-ascertainment of the buyer's quantity or by a reservation by the seller under

---

[243] Subject to the right, if it exists, to substitute another appropriation.

[244] As where the seller appropriates the entire contents of a particular hold.

[245] Because the seller will reserve the right of disposal under s. 19 until payment is made: discussed in the text accompanying nn. 296 *et seq.* below.

[246] In view of reservation of the right of disposal in s. 19 (discussed below), little attention has been paid under Rule 5 to the making of an appropriation that is conditional. See, however, cases where arguments have been unsuccessfully advanced that, where there is a physical delivery of goods further to a c.i.f. contract, the passing of property in the goods is dependent upon a later tender of the shipping documents, no longer serving their original purpose because of the physical delivery, being a compliant one: *Huyton SA v Peter Cremer GmbH and Co* [1999] 1 Lloyd's Rep. 620, 633; *Trafigura Beheer BV v BCL Trading GmbH* [2002] EWCA Civ 251 at [28]; *Cie Noga d'Importation et d'Exportation SA v Abacha (No. 3)* [2002] EWCA Civ 1142; [2003] 1 WLR 307 at [94]–[108] (Rix LJ).

[247] *Heyward's Case* (1595) 2 Co. Rep. 35a. For the modern definition of election, see *Peyman v Lanjani* [1985] Ch. 457, discussed in Ch. 6 below.

[248] But see *Borrowman, Phillips & Co. v Free & Hollis* (1878) 4 QBD 500 for the view that the appropriation of a cargo that does not comply with the contract is binding on the seller only if the buyer accepts it. *Sed quaere?*

section 19 of his right of disposal. Similarly, election may explain the Canadian case where the manufacturer of certain cars was bound to deliver them to a carrier and, before doing so, prepared drafts for the buyer with accompanying invoices and certificates identifying the cars by serial number. The buyers accepted the drafts and, though the cars were never delivered, the court held that they had been unconditionally appropriated to the contract.[249] Consistent too with the election approach is *Pignataro v Gilroy,*[250] where the seller sold a quantity of rice by sample, the sample having earlier been inspected by the buyer at the seller's premises. The bulk of the goods were to be removed by the buyer from the seller's premises and the court stated that the necessary appropriation had occurred when the seller notified the buyer that the goods were ready for collection. Elsewhere, an appropriation[251] effective to pass the property has been found when the seller filled containers supplied by the buyer, even though the goods were not delivered to the carrier.[252] In both cases, however, the goods were to be supplied from a specific bulk[253] and the result is consistent with the c.i.f. example given above. These cases involve one or both of the following: a contractual commitment to deliver from a specific bulk and a statement to the buyer that the appropriation has been made.

Tentative or final selection. Outside the above cases, the election approach is **3.66** open to the criticism that little separates a mere appropriation from one that is unconditional, and that it begs the question whether a setting aside by the seller is tentative or final. A further criticism is that it is difficult to police such an approach if there is no external display of the seller's binding choice of goods. The result in other cases accords with the view that an appropriation becomes unconditional only when the seller is physically unable to change his mind.[254] This may explain the view of Atkin J in *Stein, Forbes & Co. v County Tailoring Co.*[255] that the appropriation of a seller who does not mean the buyer to have the goods before payment

---

[249] *Hayes Bros Buick-Opel-Jeep Inc. v Canada Permanent Trust Co.* (1976) 15 NBR (2d) 166.

[250] [1919] 1 KB 459. The goods were deliverable on *ex* warehouse terms, for the meaning of which see *Fisher Reeves and Co. Ltd v Armour and Co. Ltd* [1920] 3 KB 614.

[251] The word 'unconditional' is not used, which is typical of the pre-Act authorities. This makes *Wait v Baker*, n. 240 above, difficult to apply today. The word is also absent in s. 19(1).

[252] *Aldridge v Johnson* (1857) 7 E & B 855; *Langton v Higgins* (1859) 4 H & N 402. See also *Bacardi-Martini Beverages Ltd v Thomas Hardy Packaging Ltd* [2002] 1 Lloyd's Rep. 62 at [49] (bottles and labels, as well as promotional material, supplied by the buyer).

[253] The whole bulk in the case of *Langton*, above.

[254] See *Edwards v Ddin*, n. 5 above (property passed when petrol fed into the tank of the defendant's car). Cf. *R v Thomas* [1928] 2 WWR 608 (passing of property conditional upon payment being made); *Addy v Blake* (1887) 19 QBD 478; *Noblett v Hopkinson* [1905] 2 KB 214. As for the possibility that a tenancy in common arises in a commingled mass, see P. Watts (1990) 106 *LQR* 552.

[255] (1916) 88 LJKB 448.

is only a conditional one.[256] Further, in *Carlos Federspiel & Co. SA v Charles Twigg & Co. Ltd*,[257] the seller, who had been paid by the buyer, was bound to ship a quantity of bicycles and tricycles at a UK port, and so had packed the goods into crates labelled with the buyer's name and address. The seller was awaiting a ship bound for a Central American port when a receiver was sent in by one of the seller's creditors. Consequently, delivery never took place. Pearson J held that the property had not passed[258] and stated that unconditional appropriation[259] occurs with the last act of the seller's performance under the contract. The result in this case was difficult to avoid, given that section 18, Rule 5(2), presumptively has the property passing when the seller delivers the goods to a carrier.[260] The performance of the seller's last act is tantamount to delivery or constructive delivery. The constructive delivery that occurs where a third-party bailee attorns to the buyer, which puts a change of mind beyond the reach of the seller, marks the moment when the property passes.[261] Constructive delivery may also be found where the seller holds the goods as bailee for the buyer. This accommodates the above cases of the buyer's containers, where a constructive (more accurately a fictitious) delivery was found in the act of filling them.[262] The container cases were explained in *Re Stapylton Fletcher Ltd*[263] as cases where the seller constituted himself a bailee of the contract goods. In *Re Stapylton Fletcher Ltd*, the court held that certain goods had been unconditionally appropriated to a sale contract when they were removed from the seller's trading stock and then shortly afterwards mixed with similar goods destined for other buyers and held by the seller on warehouse terms.

Unconditional Appropriation and Sections 20A–B

3.67   **Effect of undivided share on unconditional appropriation.**   Although sections 20A–B are not couched in the language of unconditional appropriation, it must be asked what effect they might have on the existing understanding of unconditional

---

256 See also *Godts v Rose* (1855) 17 CB 229. But that seller could be protected by a lien and does not need the general property as such.

257 [1957] 1 Lloyd's Rep. 240. *Quaere* the seller who ships goods under the terms of a sea waybill entitling him, as against the carrier, to change the identity of the named consignee when the goods are in transit?

258 Cf. the Canadian case of *NEC Corpn v Steintron Electronics Ltd* (1985) 50 CBR (NS) 91, where, on similar facts, the court held that the property had passed since the seller in practice always shipped out goods already addressed to the named buyer.

259 Pearson J speaks of appropriation but means unconditional appropriation.

260 *Quaere* the seller who packs and labels the goods but who uses his own employee to deliver them at the buyer's premises?

261 *Laurie and Morewood v Dudin and Sons* [1926] 1 KB 223; *Wardar's Import and Export Co. Ltd v W Norwood & Sons Ltd* [1968] 2 QB 663.

262 *Langton v Higgins*, n. 252 above (Bramwell B); *Aldridge v Johnson, ibid.* (Crompton J).

263 n. 118 above.

appropriation in section 18, Rule 5.[264] As stated above, a buyer, to the extent of any payment made, acquires an undivided interest by way of tenancy in common in 'a bulk which has been identified either in the contract or by subsequent agreement between the parties'.[265] The Act defines 'bulk' as a 'mass or collection of goods of the same kind', whose components are interchangeable and which is 'confined in a defined space or area'.[266] Suppose that in *Carlos Federspiel & Co. SA v Charles Twigg & Co. Ltd*[267] there had been two prepaying Costa Rican buyers and they had both been informed by the sellers that their goods, bicycles of the same type, had been set aside and were awaiting shipment in the sellers' loading bay. It is arguable that this would amount to the agreed identification of a bulk so as to confer a proprietary interest on each buyer. This conclusion would be easier to reach if the crates were not addressed and were so positioned that the two parcels of goods were not separated. If only one buyer were informed of the readiness of the goods for dispatch, only that buyer, on the face of it, could claim that there is an identified bulk.

Identification of bulk by subsequent agreement. Suppose now that the sellers **3.68** failed to inform either buyer that his goods were in the loading bay. This prompts the question what is meant by identification 'either in the contract or by subsequent agreement'. Section 18, Rule 5(1), permits unconditional appropriation with an added assent to amount to a transfer of the property in the goods; as we shall see, that assent is frequently implied in advance of the appropriation. This is an implied agreement of sorts, but it might be difficult to see a similar passive response by the buyer to a seller's message as the basis for a 'subsequent agreement' under section 20A. It could not easily be seen either as an identification 'in the contract'. Finally, if there is only one quantity of goods laid out in the loading bay for only one buyer, who is informed that the goods are ready for shipment, it is not easy to see that the goods constitute a 'bulk', but it seems perverse to deny such buyer a proprietary interest if, in the case outlined above, two buyers together had each an undivided interest. It would also be odd to deny an interest to the two buyers on the ground that their goods had been separated and identified to each of them so as not to form a commingled mass. The incoherence between the 1995 changes and the existing law on unconditional appropriation seems destined to cause future trouble. A relaxation of section 16 and its requirement of ascertainment, following upon the enactment of section 20A, does not sit easily with a continuing strict approach to section 18, Rule 5.

---

[264] See also the above discussion of the gap between the separation from bulk of goods the subject of a buyer's undivided interest and the unconditional appropriation of those goods.

[265] S. 20A of the Sale of Goods Act as added by s. 1(3) of the 1995 Act.

[266] S. 61 of the Sale of Goods Act as added by s. 2(a) of the 1995 Act.

[267] n. 257 above.

Scope of Rule 5(1)

3.69 **Deliverable state.** Rule 5(1) requires the goods to be in 'a deliverable state', which here has the same meaning as in Rule 1.[268] Rule 5(1) was not satisfied where carpets, brought to the buyer's premises, had not yet been fitted by the seller.[269] It has been said that the goods must answer to the contractual description if the property is to pass under Rule 5.[270] The scope of description used to be larger for unascertained than for specific goods. In recent years, there has been a discernible tendency to diminish the scope of description so that, far from embracing all the stated attributes of unascertained goods, it is confined for specific and unascertained goods alike to the identity of the goods.[271] Consequently, the property will not often nowadays be prevented from passing under Rule 5(1) by a failure to meet the contractual description. Where the buyer's assent to an unconditional appropriation by the seller is implied, which is quite common, the justification for the above approach to description is that the buyer does not authorize the seller to appropriate to the contract goods not conforming to the basic standard of the contractual description. The property will not pass if the seller tenders goods other than the agreed contract quantity.[272] Courts are also markedly reluctant to recognize that the property in goods the subject of an entire contract passes incrementally as they are delivered into the hands of a carrier.[273]

---

[268] Discussed in the text accompanying nn. 53–6 above.

[269] *Philip Head & Sons Ltd v Showfronts Ltd* [1970] 1 Lloyd's Rep. 140. See also *Pritchett & Gold v Currie* [1916] 1 Ch. 515; *Hendy Lennox Ltd v Grahame Puttick Ltd* [1984] 1 WLR 485; *Anderson v Morice* (1876) 1 App. Cas. 713 (Lord Blackburn: incomplete loading of ship), *sed quaere?* since the section speaks of deliverable and not delivered state. In contracts for the sale of bottled drinks in public houses, it has been held for the purpose of environmental regulations that the property passes in the bottle as well as in its contents at the time the publican selects the particular bottle on the shelf and regardless of whether the customer drinks from a glass or takes the bottle away: *R (on the application of Valpac Ltd) v Environment Agency* [2002] EWHC 1510 (Admin); [2002] Env. LR 36 at [33]. The buyer, however, may not confidently insist on having the bottle: 'Even though, with the consent of the buyer, the drink may be served in a glass and the publican may himself throw away the bottle, it is still the customer's bottle. The legal nature of the sale is not affected by the fact that, for the purposes of maintaining order, a publican may insist on retaining a bottle or having it returned, should that be necessary to avoid disturbance': *ibid.*, at [36]. Given the circumstances of the transaction, including the fact that the customer will not yet have paid, the conclusion that property passes in the bottle at all, and if so at the point of selection by the publican, is open to some doubt: see *Geddling v Marsh* [1920] 1 KB 668, 672.

[270] *Vigers v Sanderson* [1901] 1 KB 608; *Hammer and Barrow v Coca-Cola* [1962] NZLR 723, 731.

[271] Discussed in Ch. 7 below.

[272] *Cunliffe v Harrison* (1851) 6 Ex. 903; *Levy v Green* (1859) 1 E & E 969.

[273] *Bryans v Nix* (1839) 4 M & W 775; *Anderson v Morice*, n. 269 above. See, however, *Colonial Insurance Co. of New Zealand v Adelaide Marine Insurance Co.* (1886) 12 App. Cas. 128, where the court was plainly concerned to give the buyer an insurable interest in cargo loaded from time to time. The courts have not denied the incremental passing of property as goods are removed from storage: *Rohde v Thwaites* (1827) 6 B & C 388; *Aldridge v Johnson*, n. 252 above.

Assent

Nature of assent. Rule 5(1) requires the assent of one party to the other's uncon- **3.70**
ditional appropriation.[274] It may take the form of an authority given by the buyer
to the seller to appropriate, as where the contract calls for payment against shipping documents,[275] or it may be given by a third party, such as the carrier,[276] acting
thus as agent for the buyer. A seller delivering to a carrier other than the one nominated by the buyer will therefore not have the buyer's assent to the unconditional
appropriation.[277] The assent is often implied: in *Pignataro v Gilroy*,[278] a portion of
the contract goods were in storage at a wharf. The buyer paid for the goods by
cheque and requested a delivery order. One possible assent of the buyer was this
request, preceding the seller's unconditional appropriation in notifying the buyer
that the goods were ready to be taken away. The court preferred, however, to find
the buyer's assent in doing nothing for a month after being notified by the seller
that the goods were ready. This is evidently unsatisfactory, so far as it does not precisely date the moment when the property (and hence also the risk in this case)
had passed to the buyer. A better approach would have been to find an implied
assent after the passing of a reasonable time for the buyer to collect the goods.
Even in those cases where it is implied, the assent is real enough:[279] an unlawful
repudiation of the contract by the buyer will effectively withdraw his assent to an
unconditional appropriation by the seller.[280] Denied the buyer's cooperation in
the passing of property, the seller is unable to sue for the price as a debt[281] and must
be content with a damages action for non-acceptance of the goods. The absence
of an earlier assent by the buyer has prevented the property from passing, even
though the goods have been marked in some way with the buyer's name.[282] Where
the assent given is express and takes place after the seller has appropriated the
goods, that act of appropriation is more likely to be treated as unconditional than
a similar appropriation preceded by an implied assent.[283]

---

[274] See *Godts v Rose*, n. 256 above; *Campbell v Mersey Docks and Harbour Board* (1863) 14
CB(NS) 412, 415–16.

[275] *Ginner v King* (1890) 7 TLR 140.

[276] *Blackburn on Sale* (2nd edn, by J. C Graham, Stevens, 1885), 139–40.

[277] *Copp v Rhindress* (1921) 67 DLR 782; *Pullan v Speizman* (1921) 67 DLR 365.

[278] n. 250 above.

[279] See *Jenner v Smith* (1869) LR 4 CP 270; *Atkinson v Bell* (1828) 8 B & C 277.

[280] *Sells Ltd v Thomson Stationery Ltd* (1914) 6 WWR 731 (Can.); *Butterick Publishing Co. v
White & Walker* (1914) 6 WWR 1394 (Can.); *Mason & Risch Ltd v Christner* (1918) 44 OLR 146,
affd. (1920) 48 OLR 8 (Can.) (revocation of seller's agency to make unconditional appropriation).

[281] *White & Carter (Councils) Ltd v McGregor* [1962] AC 413.

[282] *Xenos v Wickham* (1867) LR 2 HL 296, 316; *Mucklow v Mangles* (1808) 1 Taunt 318. Or
designed for the buyer's special use: *Atkinson v Bell*, n. 279 above.

[283] See *Xenos v Wickham*, n. 282 above; *Donaghy's Rope and Twine Co. v Wright Stephenson & Co.*
(1906) 25 NZLR 641.

3.71 **Assent and examination.**   Assent needs to be considered in connection with the buyer's right of examination of the goods,[284] which has had an impact on both the passing of property and the buyer's right to reject non-conforming goods. In the nineteenth century, it was common to assert that the buyer lost his right to reject by failing to examine the goods at or before delivery. If such an examination did take place, it could be regarded as providing the buyer's assent to the seller's unconditional appropriation of the goods.[285] The relaxation of the buyer's right of examination, so as to permit it and a concomitant rejection of the goods to take place upon their arrival, may explain why, until it became clear that the passing of the property was no bar to a later rejection of the goods,[286] some courts held that the property did not pass before examination.[287] Examination may therefore have encouraged courts generally to conclude that the property passed later rather than sooner in the case of unascertained goods.

3.72 **Types of delivery.**   The different delivery obligations of the seller have a bearing upon the moment property passes. We have seen that where the buyer is to take delivery of the goods from the seller's premises, a number of cases hold that the property passes even before such delivery takes place. Where the seller undertakes personally to deliver the goods to the buyer's establishment or residence, there appears to be no general rule, the property in some cases passing before delivery[288] and in others upon delivery to the buyer at destination.[289] The passing of property upon delivery is a likely construction where the sale is not on credit terms and the buyer is to pay upon receipt of the goods.

Rule 5(2) and Carriers

3.73 **Independent carrier.**   Where an independent carrier is employed by the parties, the position is dealt with by Rule 5(2) in these terms:

> Where, in pursuance of the contract, the seller delivers the goods to the buyer or to a carrier or other bailee or custodier (whether named by the buyer or not) for the purpose of transmission to the buyer, and does not reserve the right of disposal, he is to be taken to have unconditionally appropriated the goods to the contract.

Though its relationship to Rule 5(1) is not expressly stated, Rule 5(2) appears to be a particular application of the former rule. With its reference to the right

---

[284] S. 34; discussed in Ch. 10 below.

[285] *Naugle Pole & Tie Co. v Wilson* [1929] 3 WWR 730. Examination could also be assent to a later ascertainment from a specific bulk: *Rohde v Thwaites*, n. 273 above. Cf. *Wardar's Import and Export Co. Ltd v W Norwood & Sons Ltd* [1968] 2 QB 663.

[286] *Colonial Insurance Co. of New Zealand v Adelaide Marine Insurance Co*, n. 273 above; *McDougall v Aeromarine of Emsworth Ltd* [1958] 1 WLR 1126.

[287] e.g., *Perkins v Bell* [1893] 1 QB 193.

[288] *Pletts v Beattie* [1896] 1 QB 519; *Furby v Hoey* [1947] 1 All ER 206.

[289] *Noblett v Hopkinson* [1905] 2 KB 214 (*semble*); *Caradoc Nurseries Ltd v Marsh* (1959) 19 DLR (2d) 491; *Coupland v Elmore* [1928] 1 WWR 380; *R v Chappus* (1920) 48 OLR 189 (Can.).

of disposal,[290] Rule 5(2) could fairly be read as meaning that the property passes no later than delivery to the carrier, leaving Rule 5(1) satisfied if, for example, the buyer has expressly assented to an appropriation before the goods are placed in the carrier's hands. Nevertheless, the effect of enacting Rule 5(2) in specific terms is to make it hard to argue that the property passes before delivery.[291] It may pass, of course, after delivery if the seller still has duties to perform.[292] In Canadian decisions dealing with a seller's delivery duty expressed as f.o.b. the place of destination, the courts have decisively rejected the argument that the expression f.o.b. is designed only to indicate that the seller is to pay for the cost of carriage.[293] Instead, they have held that the term indicates an intention to defer the passing of property.[294] Rule 5(2) applies only to carriers and not to warehouses. Consequently, where goods are deposited by the seller in a warehouse, the property should not pass then but later, when the warehouse attorns to the buyer, and not later still when the buyer collects the goods from the warehouse.[295]

Reserving the Right of Disposal

General. The purpose of section 19 is to counter the presumptive passing of **3.74** property rules in section 18, which it does by stating that contracting for the sale of specific goods, or appropriating[296] goods to a contract for unascertained goods, will not pass the property if the seller reserves the right of disposal. The draftsman might simply have left the matter to be determined by an application of the intention rule in section 17, which overrides the presumptive rules in section 18, but the additional text in section 19 has the merit of avoiding doubts about implied intention. The reservation of the right of disposal most often concerns unascertained goods and delays the passing of property after a delivery or constructive

---

[290] See s. 19 (shipping documents transferred after delivery to carrier).

[291] *Carlos Federspiel & Co. SA v Charles Twigg & Co. Ltd*, n. 257 above; *Atkinson v Plimpton* (1903) 6 OLR 566 (Can.); *William Blackley Ltd v Elite Costumes Ltd* (1905) 9 OLR 382. The Post Office is a carrier for this purpose: *Badische Anilin und Soda Fabrik v Basle Chemical Works* [1898] AC 200; *T Comedy (UK) Ltd v Easy Managed Transport Ltd* [2007] EWHC 611; [2007] 2 Lloyd's Rep. 297 at [47]. The rule is, of course, subject to a contrary intention: *Mooney v Lipka* [1926] 4 DLR 647; *National Coal Board v Gamble* [1959] 1 QB 11. The court declined to find a contrary intention where it was the seller's practice to insure goods dispatched to its customers in *H. B. McGuiness Ltd v Dunford* (1958) 13 DLR (2d) 622.

[292] *National Coal Board v Gamble*, n. 291 above (weighing the goods).

[293] *Winnipeg Fish Co. v Whitman Fish Co.* (1909) 41 SCR 453; *Steel Co. of Canada Ltd v The Queen* [1955] SCR 161; *Beaver Specialty Ltd v Donald H Bain Ltd* (1973) 39 DLR (3d) 574. If the delivery term were f.o.b. the place of shipment, the buyer would have to arrange and pay for freight.

[294] See also *Re Grainex Canada Ltd* (1987) 34 DLR (4th) 646.

[295] *Laurie and Morewood v Dudin and Sons* [1926] 1 KB 223; *Wardar's Import and Export Co. Ltd v W Norwood & Sons Ltd* [1968] 2 QB 663.

[296] *Sc.* unconditional appropriation.

delivery, since delivery is normally the event upon which the property passes in such cases. But it can also affect specific goods where, in those cases where the property passes at the date of the contract, the reservation must take place by the terms of the contract and therefore before delivery.[297] Where the contract is for unascertained goods, the seller may reserve the right of disposal unilaterally by taking the requisite action. If a seller reserves the right of disposal when he was bound, under the contract, to appropriate the goods unconditionally on delivering them to the carrier, the seller's action will be no less effective as a reservation for that reason.[298]

3.75 **International sales.** Reserving the right of disposal is commonly done in documentary international sales of unascertained goods taking place on f.o.b., c.i.f., or similar terms, the very case contemplated by the section.[299] Despite delivery to the carrier, who is presumptively the agent of the buyer,[300] the property will normally pass when shipping documents are subsequently tendered to the buyer in return for payment in full.[301] A more prolonged form of security for payment is the conditional sale, whereby the property passes upon payment of the last instalment due under the contract. Unlike the functionally similar hire purchase and equipment leasing transactions, this transaction is governed by the Sale of Goods Act. In recent years, trade suppliers of goods have developed an appreciation of their rights under the Sale of Goods Act. The practice has grown of sellers expressly

---

[297] *Re Shipton, Anderson & Co. and Harrison & Co.* [1915] 3 KB 676 ('payment cash within seven days against transfer order'). Reserving the right of disposal of specific goods may not happen after the contract date if the property has already passed: *Dennant v Skinner* [1948] 2 KB 164; *Sirius Shipping Corp. v The Ship Sunrise* [2006] NSWSC 398. The seller does not have the unilateral right to divest the buyer of the general property. Section 19(1) deals with both specific goods and unascertained goods (the former being referred to in explicit terms). It permits the seller to reserve the right of disposal by the terms of the contract, which can presumably be done for unascertained goods as well as for specific goods, and by the terms of the appropriation of the goods to the contract after the contract has been concluded. The case of appropriation can only refer to unascertained goods since no appropriation of specific goods takes place after the contract date: specific goods are attached to the contract from the contract date and do not need to be appropriated to it.

[298] *Gabarron v Kreeft* (1875) LR 10 Ex. 274. See also *The San Nicholas* [1976] 1 Lloyd's Rep. 8, where the contract provided for the property to pass upon shipment but the sellers took out a bill of lading providing for delivery to their own order. Lord Denning thought there was at least a *prima facie* case that the property in the goods passed upon the transfer of the bill of lading. If it were argued that firmer evidence of an intention to reserve the right of disposal is needed where a seller's action is contrary to the provisions of the contract, the response would be that having a bill of lading drawn to the seller's own order is the very case of reservation dealt with in s.19(2).

[299] S. 19(2), (3).

[300] This is true of f.o.b. contracts (*Wait v Baker*, n. 240 above) but clearly a fiction in the case of c.i.f. buyers (see Ch. 6 below). See *Scottish & Newcastle International Ltd v Othon Ghalanos* [2006] EWCA Civ 1750; [2007] 2 Lloyd's Rep. 341, affirmed [2008] UKHL 11; [2008] 1 Lloyd's Rep. 462.

[301] *Mitsui & Co. Ltd v Flota Mercante Grancolombiana SA (The Ciudad de Pasto)* [1988] 2 Lloyd's Rep. 208 (f.o.b.); *Transpacific Eternity SA v Kanematsu Corpn (The Antares III)* [2002] 1 Lloyd's Rep. 233, 236 (f.a.s.).

retaining the property in goods after delivery. In order to bridge the gap between the short commercial life of the contract goods and the eventual date of payment, sellers have also sought by a variety of drafting devices to acquire rights in goods made by the buyer with the aid of the contract goods, or in the proceeds of a sub-sale of these or the original contract goods.[302]

Reasons for reservation. Where the seller reserves the right of disposal after delivering the goods to the carrier, the normal reason is that the seller is seeking security for the payment of the price,[303] though there are other reasons. For example, a seller may wish to pledge the bill of lading issued by the carrier as security for a loan bridging the period between delivery and payment by the buyer,[304] or may wish for tactical reasons to delay as long as possible the appropriation of the goods to contracts with different consignees.[305] **3.76**

Reservation and bills of lading. In international sales, reserving the right of disposal occurs most often in the presumptive case set out in section 19(2), namely where an order bill of lading[306] naming the seller (or an agent, such as a bank) as consignee is issued by the carrier and retained by the seller.[307] A seller taking a bill of lading in this form is free to endorse it at a later date in favour of the buyer, who will need it to take delivery of the goods from the carrier at the port of discharge. It is a question of fact whether a particular seller's behaviour accords with this presumed intention.[308] In *The Albazero*, Brandon J at first instance[309] saw ample evidence to rebut any presumption that the sellers had reserved the right of disposal in order to secure payment by the buyers. The sellers, a major oil company, **3.77**

---

302 Discussed in the text accompanying nn. 359 *et seq*, below.

303 *Wait v Baker*, n. 240 above. Where the contract allows credit to the buyer, the passing of property rules in ss.17–18 will apply in the normal way, even though the seller may still control the bill of lading after the property passes in accordance with those sections: *Scottish & Newcastle International Ltd v Othon Ghalanos Ltd*, n. 300 above at [19].

304 *The Albazero* [1977] AC 774; *Ross T Smyth & Co. Ltd v TD Bailey, Son & Co.* [1940] 3 All ER 60.

305 *The Albazero*, n. 304 above (Brandon J).

306 Though the statutory presumption does not apply in such cases, a seller on the facts is likely to reserve the right of disposal when retaining other delivery documents such as delivery warrants and orders which, though not documents of title at common law, are in fact effective means of securing delivery from carriers and other bailees. Another case is where the seller consigns goods to himself under a non-negotiable waybill, reserving the right to give the carrier fresh delivery instructions.

307 Before the enactment of the statutory presumption, the Court of Exchequer Chamber in *Browne v Hare* (1859) 4 H & N 822 had declined to overturn a jury finding that the taking out of a bill of lading 'unto shippers' order or their assigns' did not show an intention to reserve the general property. The approach of the court was coloured by its view that a seller who reserved the right of disposal could not be said to have shipped the goods *free* on board as required by the contract, a view that would not be entertained today: see *Mitsui & Co. Ltd v Flota Mercante Grancolombiana SA (The Ciudad de Pasto)*, n. 301 above, 213.

308 *Browne v Hare*, n. 307 above. The reservation must not occur too late or the seller will be taken to have unconditionally appropriated the goods: *Ogle v Atkinson* (1814) 5 Taunt. 759.

309 n. 304 above, 799.

did not intend to pledge the bill of lading or tender it for cash payment from the buyer; the oil had been sold on credit; and sellers and buyers were associated companies. Nevertheless, because the stated destination in the bill of lading was 'Gibraltar for orders', whereas the contractual destination was Antwerp, Brandon J concluded, in view of the sellers' manifest desire to keep for as long as possible their strategic freedom to divert the cargo to another customer at a different port of discharge, that the presumed intention in section 19(2) to reserve the right of disposal had not been rebutted.

Nature of the Seller's Reservation

3.78 **Reserving seller's rights.**   Section 19 does not say precisely what is the proprietary effect of reserving the right of disposal, and the lack of explicit connection between this section and the previous sections dealing with the passing of property is curious. If securing payment of the price were the only reason for this arrangement, it might plausibly be argued that the unpaid seller needs no more than a lien[310] over the shipping documents after unconditionally appropriating the goods on delivery to the carrier. The bill of lading is the only effective way in which the goods can be constructively handled in transit[311] and the carrier is both entitled and bound to deliver the goods only to the lawful holder of the bill of lading.[312] Even if the property has passed to the buyer, an unpaid seller would be able to rescind the contract and resell the goods in the circumstances provided for by section 48[313] and would be able to negotiate the bill of lading made out in his name to a second buyer. The problem with this reasoning is that, if a lien were all that the seller obtained, one would expect to see section 19 refer explicitly to lien and the section itself located in that part of the Act dealing with the real rights of the unpaid seller. Further, in the case of a seller who pledges shipping documents, a lien interest in the underlying goods would not be enough because a lien is not transferable[314] and the pledgee would obtain no interest in the goods for the advance to the seller.[315] Hence, it makes sense for such a seller to retain the general property when reserving the right of disposal. Moreover, a seller who has not appropriated the goods to a particular contract of sale when the bill of lading is

---

[310] S. 41.

[311] But by notices of appropriation, the goods may be made the subject of repeated c.i.f. contracts in string trading conditions.

[312] See Ch. 6 below.

[313] See Ch. 11 below.

[314] *Donald v Suckling* (1866) LR 1 QB 585; *Franklin v Neate* (1844) 13 M & W 481 (but see the discussion of mercantile agency and the factor's lien: see Ch. 9 below). A lienee cannot sell the lien, nor may it be taken in execution by a sheriff: *Legg v Evans* (1840) 6 M & W 36. Although a lienee has no power of sale at common law (*Thames Iron Works Co. v Patent Derrick Co.* (1860) 1 J & H 93), a seller in these cicumstances would resort to the power of sale in s. 48.

[315] *Van Casteel v Booker* (1848) 2 Ex. 691.

issued cannot but be treated as having reserved the general property.[316] Although the requirements of sections 16–18 for the passing of property have not been met, it should be noted that such a seller will often be factually or legally committed to tendering the shipping documents under a particular contract. For example, a seller with an unappropriated shipment in hand and an f.o.b. contract to perform may not be able to find another shipment for that contract within the time allowed by the contract for delivery, or may not be able to find another cargo on the same ship, which was nominated by the buyer and has now left port. In some circumstances, the act of shipping goods that accord with a particular contract may be seen as an election by the seller to appropriate the shipment to that contract.[317] It should be otherwise if the seller has more than one contract to perform under which this shipment could have been made. In a c.i.f. string, a seller relaying a notice of appropriation becomes contractually committed to supply documents concerning goods on the named ship.

General property.   The cases recognizing that the seller has reserved the right of **3.79** disposal usually treat the seller as having retained the general property in full,[318] the implication being that the buyer has no proprietary interest. As will later be seen, the buyer in such cases commonly bears the risk from an earlier date and therefore has an insurable interest in the goods, which may be referred to ambiguously as though it were a property interest.[319] In a minority of cases the buyer is recognized as having at least some interest in the goods by way of a derogation from any general property of the seller.[320] One case refers to the seller as having (only) a 'hold' over the goods, going beyond the 'right to retain possession' and involving a power of resale on default by the buyer.[321] A modern court is unlikely to hold that a seller reserves anything less than the general property.

Rebuttable presumption.   If, nevertheless, it were felt that in some cases the **3.80** seller needs no more than a lien over the shipping documents then, instead of trying to diminish the proprietary effects of reserving the right of disposal, an alternative approach would be to deny that the seller has reserved the right of disposal at all. The rebuttable presumption in section 19(2) has been stated to be a weak

---

316 *The Albazero*, n. 304 above.

317 *Wait v Baker*, n. 240 above, 9 (500 qtrs of barley).

318 *James v The Commonwealth*, n. 15 above, 378; *Wait v Baker*, n. 240 above; *Mirabita v Imperial Ottoman Bank* (1878) 3 Ex. D 164 (Cotton LJ); *The Miramichi* [1915] P 71; *The Prinz Adalbert* [1917] AC 586. In *Ross T Smyth*, n. 304 above, 68, Lord Wright thought it essential.

319 This seems the best explanation of the judgment of Bramwell LJ in *Mirabita*, above.

320 In *Van Casteel v Booker*, n. 315 above, where the goods had been loaded on the buyer's own ship, the court was content to say only that the reserving seller had preserved his right of stoppage *in transitu*.

321 *Ogg v Shuter* (1875) 1 CPD 47, 50–1 (Lord Cairns LC).

one where payment is the only goal sought.[322] It has been rebutted where the seller's purpose in taking out an order bill of lading in his own name was because he feared the buyer would reject the goods and so wished to make certain he had an insurable interest in them.[323] But the presumption was not rebutted in one case, where the seller procured from the master of the buyer's own ship a bill of lading deliverable to order.[324]

Non-statutory Examples of Reservation

3.81 **Additional cases of reservation.** Outside the express language of section 19(2), the right of disposal was held to have been reserved where the seller refused to comply with the contract by shipping goods on the buyer's account, but instead procured the issuance of the bill of lading naming a fictitious person as consignee.[325] A reservation has also been recognized where goods are stated in the bill of lading to be simply deliverable to order.[326] Where the bill of lading is made out to buyer or order, the act of the seller in retaining possession of the bill of lading in this form is likely to be treated as a reservation,[327] but not if the evidence shows the seller intended the buyer to have the general property.[328] As a matter of principle, there is something to be said for the view that the seller thereby retains only a lien over the shipping documents since, while the contract remains on foot, the goods cannot be appropriated to any other contract of sale. Nevertheless, while still the holder of the bill of lading, the seller may indorse the bill so as to require the carrier to deliver to a different named consignee.[329] There seems no reason, therefore, to distinguish different cases of reservation of the right of disposal according to the identity of the named consignee.

---

[322] *The Parchim* [1918] AC 157, 170–1, referred to as decided on 'very special facts' in *The Kronprinsessan Margareta* [1921] 1 AC 486, 516 (Lord Sumner).

[323] *Joyce v Swann* (1864) 17 CBNS 84; see also *The Albazero*, n. 304 above.

[324] *Van Casteel v Booker*, n. 315 above: seller's right of stoppage therefore preserved when otherwise it would have been lost since a delivery to the buyer's ship is a delivery to the buyer; see also *Turner v Liverpool Docks Trustees* (1851) 6 Ex. 453.

[325] *Gabarron v Kreeft*, n. 298 above.

[326] *James v The Commonwealth*, n. 15 above, 380; *Shepherd v Harrison* (1871) LR 5 HL 116, 128, 131; *Van Casteel v Booker*, n. 315 above.

[327] *Hansson v Hamel and Horley Ltd* [1922] 2 AC 36, 43 (Lord Sumner); *The Kronprinsessan Margareta*, n. 322 above. Note that in *Arnhold Karberg & Co. v Blythe Green Jourdain & Co.* [1915] 2 KB 379, 387, Scrutton J states that in such a case the buyer acquires the general property on tendering the price whereas, in other cases where the right of disposal is reserved, the property passes upon payment.

[328] *Ladenburg & Co. v Goodwin, Ferreira & Co.* [1912] 3 KB 275: also stating that the transfer of the general property did not affect the right of stoppage in transit for non-payment.

[329] *Mitchell v Ede* (1840) 11 Ad. & E 888, 903; *Elder Dempster Lines Ltd v Zaki Ishag* [1983] 2 Lloyd's Rep. 548, 555.

Bill of Lading and Bill of Exchange

Conditional passing of property.   Even if the bill of lading is delivered to the   **3.82**
buyer, it does not follow that the seller thereby surrenders the right of disposal.
Section 19(3) states that, where the seller transmits the bill of lading to the buyer
together with a draft bill of exchange for the price, the buyer must return the bill
of lading if he does not accept the draft.[330] This refers to a practice not current in
modern times. Section 19(3) makes no distinction between bills of lading naming
the buyer as consignee and those naming the seller as consignee. It further provides that the property in the goods does not pass to the buyer who wrongfully
retains the bill of lading. The difficulty with the language of section 19(3) is that
it leaves open the possibility that the property may have been transferred to the
buyer, only to be retransferred to the seller, possibly with retrospective effect,
when the buyer wrongfully retains the bill of lading. The case law on which the
provision is based are more precise in holding that the seller's intention to pass the
property to the buyer is conditional upon the buyer's acceptance of the draft.[331] In
this regard, the proprietary consequences of a bill of lading being indorsed and
delivered depend upon the intention of the transferor.[332] The seller may intend
not to pass the property to the buyer[333] unil the draft has been accepted, though
there is a strong presumption that this was intended where the seller indorses and
delivers a bill of lading to the buyer.[334] Even if it were held under section 19(3) that
no property interest passes to the buyer on the indorsement and delivery of a bill
of lading, the buyer would be a buyer in possession of a document of title and thus
empowered to transfer good title to a *bona fide* purchaser.[335]

Reservation of Title Clauses

Express clauses.   In domestic sales, it is common for unpaid sellers to reserve the   **3.83**
right of disposal after delivery to the buyer by means of a *Romalpa* clause, which
takes its name from the leading modern case that focused attention on the seller's
right of reservation.[336] The practice developed because unpaid sellers, permitting

---

[330] The buyer has no lien over the bill of lading for any freight paid: *Rew v Payne Douthwaite* (1885) 53 LT 932.

[331] *Shepherd v Harrison*, n. 326 above; *Brandt v Bowlby* (1831) 2 B & Ad. 932; *Jenkyns v Brown* (1849) 14 QB 496; *Wilmshurst v Bowker* (1841) LJCP 161. Cf *Key v Colesworth* (1852) 7 Ex. 594.

[332] *Sewell v Burdick* (1884) 10 App. Cas. 74; *Sanders Bros v Maclean & Co.* (1883) 11 QBD 327; *Burgos v Nascimento* (1908) 11 LT 71; *The Orteric* [1920] AC 274.

[333] *Leigh and Sillavan Ltd v Aliakmon Shipping Ltd* [1986] AC 785.

[334] *Dracachi v Anglo-Egyptian Navigation Co.* (1868) LR 3 CP 190; rebutted in *Aliakmon Shipping*, n. 333 above.

[335] Under s. 25(1) of the Sale of Goods Act or s. 9 of the Factors Act 1889; see *Cahn v Pockett's Bristol Channel Steam Packet Co. Ltd* [1899] 1 QB 643.

[336] *Aluminium Industrie Vaassen BV v Romalpa Aluminium Ltd* [1976] 1 WLR 676. See generally G. McCormack, *Reservation of Title* (2nd edn, Sweet & Maxwell, 1995); S. Wheeler, *Reservation*

the property to pass in the conventional way under section 18, find themselves at a disadvantage upon the insolvency of the buyer. The first call on the buyer's assets will come from secured and preference creditors, and the seller will join other unsecured creditors in receiving on average a very small insolvency dividend hardly worth the expense of lodging a proof with the buyer's liquidator or trustee in bankruptcy.[337] The great advantage to a seller of reserving the general property in the goods is that, until the property passes, no ownership rights vest in the buyer and therefore the goods cannot fall within a security granted by the buyer, before or after the contract of sale is concluded, to one or more creditors, or vest in the liquidator or trustee. A further advantage is that a property reservation clause need not be registered in the way that a security by way of charge or mortgage has to be if a secured creditor is to be able to assert his rights against third parties and the liquidator or trustee of the grantor of the security.[338]

3.84 **Extended reservation.** An inherent limitation on the seller's rights is that goods supplied tend to depreciate, or else they have an ephemeral existence, quite possibly acquired on a 'just in time basis', before being resold or consumed or transformed in identity by the buyer. To counter this limitation, sellers have drafted clauses purporting: (a) to reserve by an 'all moneys' clause the general property in goods supplied until the whole of the buyer's indebtedness to the seller, and not just the price owed for the goods supplied, has been paid off; (b) to reserve rights in goods newly manufactured by the buyer that incorporate the goods supplied by the seller; (c) to claim the proceeds of sale of goods resold by the buyer, whether these are the original goods or new goods manufactured by the buyer.[339] In summary, sellers have been successful with adequately drafted clauses (including all moneys clauses) to the extent of the original goods supplied, but have failed in their attempts to reserve property rights in money proceeds and newly manufactured goods. They have been unable to persuade courts that these extended rights are truly reserved rights as opposed to rights granted by the buyer, with the consequence that courts have characterized sellers' efforts as charges. Since unpaid sellers invariably fail to register these extended rights as charges,[340] they are

---

of Title Clauses (OUP, 1991); *Palmer's Company Law* (G. K. Morse (ed.), Sweet & Maxwell, looseleaf), iii, ch. 13; L. S. Sealy and R. J. A. Hooley, *Text and Materials in Commercial Law* (3rd edn, Butterworths, 2003), 428–46; N. E. Palmer (1993) 6 *J of Cont. Law* 175.

[337] The treatment given to unsecured creditors is criticized as a 'raw deal' by Templeman LJ in *Borden (UK) Ltd v Scottish Timber Products Ltd* [1981] Ch. 25, 42.

[338] Companies Act 1985, ss. 395 *et seq*. Ss. 395 *et seq*. will be superseded at a date to be appointed (currently expected to be 1 October 2009) by ss. 860 *et seq*. of the Companies Act 2006. Unless the Secretary of State exercises powers to issue regulations under s. 894, the current registration regime will remain unchanged.

[339] For a more elaborate classification of these clauses, see G. McCormack, n. 336 above, 2.

[340] This is because (a) the preparation of documents for registration is expensive; (b) the Companies Act and the rules of priority, together, do not lend themselves to a single registration for

worthless in the event of the buyer's insolvency or receivership. This is understood, if not always stated in the cases: a seller unsuccessful in reserving the general property is plainly seen to have lost despite the empty compensation of having a charge over the assets of the buyer. A further complicating feature of *Romalpa* litigation, rendering it difficult to make universal statements, is that the scope of the seller's rights may be affected by concessions made in the course of litigation and by the particular language used in the clause.

Simple reservation.   Where the contract goods remain in the buyer's possession **3.85** in an unaltered state, the courts have given effect to a simple reservation clause, even if the buyer is given liberty to transform or consume the goods before payment is made.[341] This accords with sections 17–19 of the Sale of Goods Act, which make it plain that the property in goods originally unascertained cannot pass to the buyer without the cooperation of the seller.[342] Provided the seller's intention is clear, it does not matter if other parts of a clause expressing this intention operate as a charge on the buyer's assets.[343] No particular words need be used by the seller, for example, describing the buyer as an agent, bailee,[344] or fiduciary. If, however, the seller purports to reserve 'equitable or beneficial ownership', this has been held to be a charge.[345] The reason is that the clause amounts to an outright transfer of the general property to the buyer, coupled with a grant back to the seller of the beneficial ownership in the goods. The premise given for this two-stage analysis, that the bare legal title cannot directly be conveyed to the buyer, is not as a matter of principle to be reconciled with the decision of the House of Lords in *Abbey National Building Soc. v Cann*,[346] that the equitable interest of a mortgagee building society in a dwelling was carved out of the ownership of the dwelling before

---

multiple supplies of goods; and (c) the seller would, in any event, obtain only the protection of a weak floating charge with limited enforcement rights and a subordinated standing in the event of the buyer's insolvency

341 *Romalpa*, n. 336 above; *Clough Mill Ltd v Martin* [1985] 1 WLR 111.

342 The seller must either unconditionally appropriate the goods or must assent to an unconditional appropriation by the buyer. Where it is the buyer who assents, the assent is often implied, but an implied assent by the seller is less likely in the nature of things. Note also that s. 19(1) refers to the seller reserving the right of disposal 'by the terms of the contract *or appropriation*' (emphasis added). Even if the seller has contracted to pass the property to the buyer at an earlier date, yet his action in reserving the right of disposal may be effective to inhibit the passing of property; see R. Bradgate [1988] *JBL* 477.

343 *Clough Mill Ltd. v Martin*, n. 341 above.

344 An inappropriate way to describe a buyer in possession: *E Pfeiffer Weinkellerei-Weinenkauf GmbH v Arbuthnot Factors Ltd* [1988] 1 WLR 150; *Borden (UK) Ltd v Scottish Timber Products Ltd*, n. 337 above (Bridge LJ). *Aliter Clough Mill Ltd v Martin*, n. 341 above, 116 (Robert Goff LJ).

345 *Re Bond Worth Ltd* [1980] Ch. 228.

346 [1991] 1 AC 56, overruling *Church of England Building Soc. v Piskor* [1954] Ch. 533. See R. Gregory (1990) 106 *LQR* 551. But *Re Bond Worth Ltd*, n. 345 above, was said to survive *Abbey National Building Soc. v Cann* in *Stroud Architectural Systems Ltd v John Laing Construction Ltd* [1994] BCC 18.

the proprietary residue[347] vested directly in the buyer granting the mortgage. There was no *scintilla temporis* in which full legal and beneficial ownership vested in the buyer before the grant to the building society. Nevertheless, the pitfall presented by *Re Bond Worth Ltd*[348] is easily avoided if the clause by one means or another makes it plain that the seller is reserving the general property in the goods.[349]

All-moneys Clauses

3.86 **Effect of clause.** An all-moneys clause, by which the seller reserves the general property until all the buyer's indebtedness to the seller is paid off, will be effective. The rules in the Sale of Goods Act making the passing of property a matter of contractual intention are not confined to payment of the contract price. This was confirmed by the House of Lords in *Armour v Thyssen Edelstahlwerke AG*.[350] Where a seller supplies the buyer on a recurring basis, it means that past indebtedness can always be brought forward and attached to any goods of the seller in the buyer's possession, even if part or the whole of the price for these goods has been paid. The use of all moneys clauses also deprives of significance in proprietary terms the allocation of part-payments by the buyer to particular contracts of sale, since the part-payment of itself does not lift the reservation of title from any particular goods.[351] The effectiveness of the all moneys approach to reservation demands that the clause be inserted in all contracts for the supply of goods to the buyer since the seller cannot know in what order the buyer will consume those supplies. It was the view of the House of Lords in *Armour* that a seller availing himself of his reservation rights and repossessing the goods was under no obligation to account to the buyer for any surplus realized on resale exceeding the buyer's indebtedness.[352] This is certainly the case where the seller terminates the contract of sale for the buyer's discharging breach,[353] but it has been said that a seller will have to account for any surplus in the (unlikely) event of the contract remaining on foot at all times.[354] A seller is most likely to realize a surplus where durable

---

[347] The bare legal title plus the equity of redemption.

[348] n. 345 above.

[349] It should avoid any reference to equitable or beneficial ownership.

[350] [1991] AC 339.

[351] The rule is that the creditor has the right to appropriate payment to a particular debt if the paying debtor does not do so: *Cory Bros and Co. Ltd v Owners of the Turkish Steamship Mecca (The Mecca)* [1897] AC 286. In building contracts, where progress payments are made for supplies, particular difficulties are presented when those payments are not allocated to particular supplies; see *P4Ltd v United Integrated Solutions Plc* [2006] EWHC 2640 (TCC).

[352] Cf the position of a mortgagee.

[353] *Clough Mill Ltd v Martin*, n. 341 above. But a buyer unable to recover surplus value might have a restitutionary right to the recovery of excessive sums paid: Robert Goff LJ, *ibid*.

[354] *Ibid*. Robert Goff LJ attributes the seller's duty to account to an implied term in the contract. But it is not easy to see why the implication of such a term should be necessary to give business

items have been supplied on various occasions under the terms of all moneys clauses, or where part of the price of appreciating goods has been paid.[355] Any attempt to make the seller account for a surplus comes close to treating him as a mortgagee realizing his security and to treating the reservation itself as a registrable charge.

Forfeiture relief.   The above view of the seller's entitlement to retain resale moneys, applicable to all moneys and simple reservation clauses, is entirely orthodox: the effect of the clause is that the seller reserves the full legal property until the attached condition has been met by the buyer. The buyer does not have a property interest in the goods, though there may, in rare circumstances, be relief from forfeiture of his possessory interest given to a buyer prepared to pay the sum due.[356] To succeed, the buyer[357] must show that the principal purpose of the reservation clause was to secure payment of the price by the buyer pursuant to the contract. This requirement should not pose a great problem in practice, but the buyer will usually be in severe difficulties in further showing a substantial windfall to the seller over and above the sum due under the contract.[358]   **3.87**

Altered Goods

Attachment.   For the reservation clause to remain effective, the goods have to retain their identity, which will be lost if they are irrevocably attached to a larger chattel or if they are so altered by the manufacturing process that they cannot be said to be the goods supplied by the seller. In the case of irrevocable attachment (or *accessio*), the rule is that ownership of the lesser thing vests in the owner of the greater thing. In *Hendy Lennox (Industrial Engines) Ltd v Grahame Puttick Ltd,*[359] the incorporation of diesel engines identified by serial numbers in generator sets did not amount to *accessio* because the process could be reversed by several hours' work without damaging the separated parts. Where goods are altered in the manufacturing process and lose their identity, it is a case of *specificatio*, and the operator, whose labour brings about the alteration, becomes the owner.[360] It is a question of degree whether the goods have been sufficently altered to lose their identity. Thus the identity of the goods supplied is lost where fibre is worked into yarn and   **3.88**

---

efficacy to the contract or why it should apply only if the contract has not been terminated; see also N. E. Palmer (1993) 6 *J of Cont. Law* 175, 182–3.

[355]   *Clough Mill Ltd v Martin*, n. 341 above (Robert Goff LJ).
[356]   See Ch. 11 below.
[357]   More likely administrator or liquidator bringing proceedings in the buyer's name.
[358]   *Transag Haulage Ltd v Leyland DAF Finance plc* [1994] BCC 356.
[359]   [1984] 2 All ER 152.
[360]   *Chaigley Farms Ltd v Crawford, Kaye & Grayshire Ltd* [1996] BCC 957.

subsequently into carpet,[361] leather is cut and stitched into handbags,[362] and resin incorporated in chipboard.[363] Some generosity to the unpaid seller is to be found in one case deciding that logs retained their identity despite being cut into planks[364] and in another that goods surrender their original identity when they lose all significant value as raw materials, the implication being that some degree of transformation by the buyer's efforts is not fatal to that original identity.[365] Where goods are supplied and blended by the buyer with identical goods, then, subject to a tenancy in common argument, it will be difficult for the seller to assert that a title retention clause remains effective.[366]

Tracing Claims

3.89 **Right to trace.** Apart from attempts by sellers to draft clauses giving them rights in new goods manufactured by the buyer and in the money proceeds of sales of goods, tracing claims have been made by the unpaid seller to new goods and to money proceeds. In *Aluminium Industrie Vaassen BV v Romalpa Aluminium Ltd*,[367] the seller of aluminium foil was held entitled to trace into the money proceeds from sales of the foil even though nothing was explicitly said in the contract about these proceeds. The court found between the buyer and the seller a fiduciary relationship, as required to trace in equity.[368] Roskill LJ, in particular, saw nothing inconsistent in a buyer disposing of the foil to a sub-buyer as principal whilst acting as the seller's agent or bailee.[369]

3.90 **Bailees and tracing.** *Romalpa* is a flawed decision. The seller conceded that the buyer held the foil as a bailee,[370] and it seems to have been assumed that bailees and agents receive proceeds as fiduciaries in all cases. It was stated in later cases that bailees only presumptively received proceeds as fiduciaries[371] and, more recently,

---

361 *Re Bond Worth Ltd*, n. 345 above.

362 *Re Peachdart Ltd* [1984] Ch. 131. The leather was said to lose its identity when by a process of cutting it was appropriated to the manufacturing process so as to lose its identity as leather, but this was expressed as a matter of party intention rather than as the rule of property law that it should be: *ibid*, 142.

363 *Borden (UK) Ltd v Scottish Timber Products Ltd*, n. 337 above.

364 *Pongakawa Sawmill Ltd v New Zealand Forest Products Ltd* [1992] 3 NZLR 304.

365 *Modelboard Ltd v Outer Box Ltd* [1992] BCC 945.

366 But see *Forsyth International (UK) Ltd v Silver Shipping Co. Ltd (The Saetta)* [1994] 1 WLR 1334, 1338, where it was common ground between the parties that the title retention clause of a supplier of bunker fuels was still good against a charterer purchasing the fuels, even though (*semble*) the fuels were mixed with bunker fuels already on board ship.

367 n. 336 above.

368 See *Re Diplock* [1948] Ch. 465; *Chase Manhattan Bank NA v Israel-British Bank Ltd* [1981] Ch. 105; *Bank of America v Arnell* [1999] Lloyd's Rep. Bank. 399.

369 n. 336 above, 690.

370 *Re Bond Worth Ltd*, n. 345 above ('of crucial importance').

371 *Hendy Lennox (Industrial Engines) Ltd v Grahame Puttick Ltd* [1984] 2 All ER 152, referring to *Boardman v Phipps* [1967] AC 46, 127 (Lord Upjohn) and *Re Coomber* [1911] 1 Ch. 723; see also L. Sealy [1962] CLJ 69.

even the existence of a presumption has been doubted.[372] In *Borden (UK) Ltd v Scottish Timber Products Ltd*,[373] the court declined to trace the resin into the chipboard so as to give the seller a shared interest in the final product. The liberty given to the buyer to consume the resin in the manufacturing process was held to be inconsistent with a bailment relationship between the parties,[374] so that no fiduciary relationship could exist between them. It was, moreover, impossible to regard the buyer as acting as agent for the seller.[375] Had such a relationship existed, tracing might present an 'intractable problem' in a case where, for example, goods consisted of the seller's resin and the buyer's woodchip and labour. '[I]n quantifying the proportion of the value of the manufactured product which the tracer could claim as properly attributable to his ingredient', it might be impossible to do this for the fluctuating values over time of the various ingredients in manufactured goods.[376] The case was far removed from that of an homogeneous mixture, as where a sovereign is added to a bag containing already one thousand sovereigns and a successful tracing claim to one thousand sovereigns would yield a charge over the thousand and one sovereigns for that amount.[377]

Modern tracing developments. The common law rules for following assets **3.91** would not have availed the seller in *Borden* since the common law will not follow assets into a mixed fund.[378] Nevertheless, possible developments in the law of tracing should be borne in mind. Lord Millett has powerfully argued that 'there is nothing legal or equitable about the tracing process. There is thus no sense in retaining different rules for tracing at law and in equity. One set of tracing rules is enough.'[379] If this logic were to be adopted as English law, it would dispense with any need for a fiduciary relationship to enforce a tracing claim. Surrendering to the new orthodoxy that tracing is merely the process for asserting a pre-existing claim[380] might turn out to have incalculable consequences in commercial matters unless tracing were limited to cases where the original goods have been erased or alienated by a wrongful act.

---

[372] *Re Andrabell Ltd* [1984] 3 All ER 407; see also *E Pfeiffer Weinkellerei-Weinenkauf GmbH v Arbuthnot Factors Ltd* [1988] 1 WLR 150. On the difficulty of establishing a fiduciary relationship in an ordinary sale contract see *Re Goldcorp Exchange Ltd*, n. 119 above; *Compaq Computer Ltd v Abercorn Group Ltd* [1991] BCC 484.

[373] n. 337 above.

[374] Following *South Australian Insurance Co. v Randell* (1869) LR 3 PC 101. But Bridge LJ does contemplate a bailment arising in respect of unused resin: *ibid*, 35.

[375] *Ibid*, 38 (Bridge LJ).

[376] *Ibid*, 42 (Bridge LJ) See also Templeman LJ, *ibid*, 43.

[377] The illustration given in *Re Hallett's Estate* (1880) 13 Ch D 696, 711 and discussed in *Borden (UK) Ltd v Scottish Timber Products Ltd*, n. 337 above, 40–1 (Bridge LJ).

[378] *Banque Belge pour l'Etranger v Hambrouck* [1921] 1 KB 321; *Agip (Africa) Ltd v Jackson* [1991] Ch 547.

[379] *Foskett v McKeown* [2001] 1 AC 102, 128.

[380] *Ibid*, 128–9 (Lord Millett); *Trustees of the Property of FC Jones & Son v Jones* [1997] Ch 159, 171–2 (Millett LJ).

Extended Title Reservation

3.92 **Recharacterizing extended reservation clauses.** A reservation of title clause may go beyond the rights of the seller to the original goods and extend to the money proceeds of those goods, to new goods, or to the money proceeds of new goods. The cases demonstrate that it is a matter of 'looking to the substance and reality of the transaction'[381] to determine whether the label chosen by the parties is appropriate. More recent case law on the distinction between fixed and floating charges has made it plain that the parties may be free contractually to define their rights and duties but it is for the courts to characterize the nature of the agreement or interest that they have created.[382] There is every reason to adopt the same approach to the characterization of extended reservation of title clauses so far as they seek to confer rights on the seller to new goods and money proceeds. If in fact the buyer is given liberty to deal with the goods supplied in the ordinary course of business, then credence will not be given to the language of agency or fiduciary relationship adopted in the contract of sale. As expressed by Mummery J in *Compaq Computer Ltd v Abercorn Group Ltd*:[383] 'When [the buyer] sold [the seller's goods] which it had not paid for to subpurchasers it did not sell as bailee, agent, fiduciary or trustee. It did not sell in breach of any fiduciary obligation. [The buyer] sold [the seller's goods] lawfully on its own account, vesting full legal and beneficial title in [the seller's goods] in its subpurchasers. It sold [the seller's goods] without reference to [the seller], when it liked, at what prices it liked and on what terms it liked, in the hope of making a profit for itself.'

3.93 **Creation of new goods.** It was stated above that a seller, relying upon a simple reservation clause, may not trace the goods once they lose their identity in the manufacturing process. But what is the effect of a clause that purports to reserve in the seller the general property in those newly manufactured goods? Robert Goff LJ in *Clough Mill Ltd v Martin*[384] gave considerable comfort to the draftsmen of such extended clauses. That case involved various consignments of yarn that had not lost their identity, but the reservation clause stated that the ownership of the yarn 'shall be and remain with' the seller even if the yarn were 'incorporated in or used as material for other goods'. Robert Goff LJ had difficulty seeing why such a clause, vesting the property in new goods in the seller from the moment of their creation, amounted to the conferment by the buyer of a right on the seller by way of charge, even though, but for the clause, the rules of property law would have vested ownership of the new goods in the buyer. With respect, this reasoning is hard to support. It is the essence of a successful reservation clause that its effects

---

[381] *Compaq Computer Ltd v Abercorn Group Ltd*, n. 372 above, 493.
[382] *Agnew v Commissioner of Inland Revenue* [2001] 2 AC 710, 725.
[383] n. 372 above, 496.
[384] n. 341 above.

require no proprietary input from the buyer: the seller declines to participate in the process of an assented to unconditional appropriation that would pass the property to the buyer under section 18, Rule 5. The clause referred to by Robert Goff LJ requires the buyer to surrender property rights to the new goods conferred by the rules of *accessio* and *specificatio*.[385] Furthermore, a different view of the matter was taken by Buckley LJ in *Borden (UK) Ltd v Scottish Timber Products Ltd*,[386] who thought it 'impossible' for the seller to reserve the property in a new item that 'originates' with the buyer. In this area of law, results speak louder than words. Robert Goff LJ himself went on to say that the above clause was in fact a charge. It gave no credit for any value added by the buyer in the form of labour and materials, and the learned judge could not believe the parties intended the seller would have the windfall benefit that would accrue under a reservation clause in a contract terminated for the buyer's discharging breach.[387] The prospect of two suppliers of raw materials, each relying upon a clause like that in *Clough Mill*, also pointed to its treatment as a charge, despite the 'violence' this did to the language used.[388] It has even been asserted that, if the rights of the seller are to be found in the very language of a reservation of title clause, then the source of the seller's rights is the clause and not the equitable principles that might have been applied in the absence of the clause.[389] This conclusion would have the clause characterized as giving rise to a registrable charge.

Money proceeds.   The remaining area of difficulty concerns the money pro-   **3.94**
ceeds of sub-sales of the goods[390] by the buyer. In *Aluminium Industrie Vaassen BV v Romalpa Aluminium Ltd*,[391] a quantity of aluminium foil was supplied under a contract containing a clause providing that 'ownership . . . will only be transferred to purchaser when he has met all that is owing' to the seller. The clause also stated that the buyer was 'fiduciary owner' of new goods made with the foil and had to 'hand over . . . claims' against sub-buyers to the seller. This clause was not apt to cover the money proceeds of the original foil, which was the subject of a tracing claim instead.[392] Later cases, dealing with express proceeds clauses extending to

---

[385] As well as in cases of commingling.

[386] n. 337 above, 46.

[387] See also *Re Peachdart Ltd*, n. 362 above (where the parties, supplier of leather and manufacturer of handbags, 'must have intended' a charge); *Specialist Plant Services Ltd v Braithwaite* [1987] BCLC 1; *Ian Chisholm Textiles Ltd v Griffiths* [1994] BCC 96.

[388] *Clough Mill Ltd v Martin*, n. 341 above (Robert Goff LJ).

[389] *Tatung (UK) Ltd v Galex Telesure Ltd* (1989) 5 BCC 325, 334–35 (Phillips J) (a case on the money proceeds of original goods).

[390] No appreciable difference exists in the treatment of clauses concerning the money proceeds of original goods and clauses concerning the money proceeds of new goods, except that if the seller's rights in new goods are considered to arise by way of charge, then it follows that any rights in the proceeds of new goods also arise by way of charge: *Tatung (UK) Ltd v Galex Telesure Ltd* (1989) 5 BCC 325, 332.

[391] n. 336 above.

[392] Discussed above.

the proceeds of new goods, have set down conditions to be satisfied if these clauses are not to be treated as registrable charges. These constraints, in practical terms impossible to satisfy,[393] drive home the message that it is not for the parties to deem their relationship to be a fiduciary one or one of agency if in objective commercial terms they are conducting an arm's-length sale.[394]

3.95 **Requirements for successful proceeds clauses.**   The conditions required for a successful proceeds clause are as follows. First, the seller must require the proceeds to be kept segregated from other assets of the buyer.[395] Secondly, to the extent the seller's interest in the proceeds is defeasible upon payment of the contract price, that interest will be regarded as a charge.[396] Thirdly, any requirement that the buyer shall account only for such proceeds as equal the price due under the sale contract will be regarded as inconsistent with the beneficial interest in the proceeds vesting first in the seller.[397] Fourthly, language in the sale contract requiring the seller to transfer or pass on claims against sub-buyers is not consistent with the seller's claim that those rights were vested in him from the date of their creation.[398] Fifthly, a fixed period of credit that does not match the cycle in which the buyer receives the proceeds of a resale will tend towards the conclusion that a proceeds clause amounts to a charge.[399] The obstacles facing the seller seeking a non-registrable interest in money proceeds seem insuperable.

Insolvency and Title Reservation

3.96 **Receivership.**   The rights of a seller reserving title to the goods supplied are subject to controls laid down in the Insolvency Act 1986, primarily in Schedule B1 to

---

[393] '[I] is almost inevitable . . . that where the contract seeks to confer upon the seller a right to look for satisfaction of the price to property which is worth more than that amount (or to a sum of money which exceeds the price which is owed), the courts will construe the transaction as one involving a charge': L. S. Sealy and R. J. A. Hooley, *Text and Materials in Commercial Law* (3rd edn, Butterworths LexisNexis, 2003), 434.

[394] Cf. the more lenient attitude of the courts in other areas of the law relating to charges: *Welsh Development Agency v Export Finance Co. Ltd* [1992] BCLC 48, with which contrast *Curtain Dream plc v Churchill Merchanting Ltd* [1990] BCC 341.

[395] *Hendy Lennox (Industrial Engines) Ltd v Grahame Puttick Ltd*, n. 371 above; *Re Andrabell Ltd*, n. 372 above.

[396] *Tatung (UK) Ltd v Galex Telesure Ltd*, n. 389 above; *Compaq Computer Ltd v Abercorn Group Ltd*, n. 372 above.

[397] *Re Andrabell Ltd*, n. 372 above; *Pfeiffer Weinkellerei-Weinenkauf GmbH v Arbuthnot Factors Ltd, ibid.* Cf *Associated Alloys v CAN 001 452 106 Pty Ltd* (2000) 202 CLR 568, where the Australian High Court recognized in its own terms a clause, consistent with the doctrine of certainty in the law of trusts, that the buyer held on trust for the seller such portion of the resale price of the goods as corresponded to the buyer's indebtedness to the seller under the contract of sale. This decision is not likely to be followed in English cases.

[398] *E Pfeiffer Weinkellerei-Weinenkauf GmbH v Arbuthnot Factors Ltd*, n. 372 above.

[399] *Re Andrabell Ltd*, n. 372 above.

the Act.[400] The office of administrator was created in the Insolvency Act 1986, primarily to deal with cases where no dominant secured creditor existed with a floating charge[401] over the whole or substantially the whole of a debtor company's assets. It was the practice for secured creditors of this type to reserve the power to appoint, in the name of the debtor company, a receiver and manager with a mandate to pay the secured creditor and to exercise extensive powers of management as might be needed for the particular case. Receivers and managers appointed in this way were designated administrative receivers in the Insolvency Act, which conferred on them special statutory powers to accomplish their task.[402] The Act also set out in a schedule a list of powers to deal with the company's property and affairs comparable to the powers that would in any case have been conferred on the administrative receiver by well-drawn security documents.[403] Administrative receivers, however, were not granted the power to interfere with reservation of title rights.[404] This power, however, was granted to administrators.[405]

Administration.   Under the Insolvency Act 1986, an administrator might be **3.97** appointed by the court to achieve one or more stated goals, the principal ones for present purposes being the survival of the company as a going concern and the achievement of a greater break-up value of the company than would be possible in a liquidation. The exercise of management powers and the continuing use of assets subject to reservation of title rights were seen as necessary if the administrator was to achieve those goals. When the Insolvency Act was amended in 2002, the administrator was given the following goals: '(a) rescuing the company as a going concern, or (b) achieving a better result for the company's creditors as a whole than would be likely if the company were wound up (without first being in administration), or (c) realising property in order to make a distribution to one or more secured or preferential creditors'.[406] Furthermore, apart from special cases, including existing debentures allowing for the appointment of administrative receivers, no new appointments of administrative receivers could be made.[407] Nevertheless, administrators, formerly only appointed in court, could now be the subject of an out-of-court appointment. The administrator was subjected to a duty to weigh the interests of all creditors of the company in administration, but it does not seem that the modified procedure has had a major impact on outcomes for

---

[400] Inserted by the Enterprise Act 2002, s. 248 and Sch.16.
[401] Or a combination of floating and fixed charges.
[402] Insolvency Act 1986, ss. 230 *et seq.* (powers of office-holders).
[403] Insolvency Act 1986, Sch.1.
[404] But see how such a power might indirectly arise if the administrative receiver gave the necessary undertakings to reservation of title creditors: *Lipe Ltd v Leyland Daf Ltd* [1993] BCC 385 (cf *UCA France Champignon v Fisher Foods Ltd* [2002] EWHC 1906 (QB); [2003] BPIR 299).
[405] The current provisions are now in Sch. B1 to the Insolvency Act.
[406] Sch. B1, para. 3, as added by the Enterprise Act 2002.
[407] Insolvency Act 1986, ss.72A–H (as added by the Enterprise Act 2002, s.250).

secured creditors. More importantly, for present purposes, the replacement of administrative receivers by administrators has meant that creditors with security over substantially the whole of a debtor company's assets can appoint an out-of-court administrator with the added power to prevent the enforcement of reservation of title rights.

3.98 **Moratorium.** The Insolvency Act creates a moratorium on the enforcement of reservation of title rights while the company is in administration: '[n]o step may be taken to repossess goods in the company's possession under a hire-purchase agreement' except with the consent of the administrator or the permission of the court.[408] A 'hire-purchase agreement' is broadly defined to include a reservation of title agreement.[409] In cases where an application is made to the court for the appointment of an administrator, there is further provision for an interim moratorium pending the appointment of the administrator.[410] Once appointed, the administrator has the power to dispose of 'hire-purchase' property as if the rights of the reserver of title were vested in the debtor company.[411] The net proceeds of the disposal, however, must be applied to the payment of the debt owed to the 'hire-purchase' creditor, along with, where relevant, any further sum needed to arrive at the figure of a market value disposal of the property.

---

[408] Para. 43(3).

[409] Para. 111(1).

[410] Para. 44. For similar temporary powers that arise in favour of the directors of certain types of company when they propose a voluntary arrangement, see Insolvency Act 1986 (as amended by the Insolvency Act 2000), Sch. A1.

[411] Para. 72.

4

RISK, MISTAKE, AND FRUSTRATION

General.   Risk and frustration may conveniently be treated in proximity since   **4.01**
the operation of frustration is bounded by the transfer of risk. Risk is associated
with the price: it determines when the buyer must pay for goods accidentally
damaged, lost, or destroyed. Where a contract is frustrated, it is automatically
discharged.[1] The primary effect of this is to excuse the party, usually the seller,
whose performance is affected by the frustrating event from liability for breach of
contract. The buyer would, even without the dissolving effect of frustration on the
contract, usually have the defence of the seller's non-performance of a condition precedent.[2] Although the passage of risk to the buyer ousts the operation of frustration,

---

[1] *Hirji Mulji v Cheong Yue Steamship Co. Ltd* [1926] AC 497; *Bank Line Ltd v Arthur Capel & Co.*
[1919] AC 435; *Tamplin Steamship Co. Ltd v Anglo-Mexican Petroleum Co.* [1916] 2 AC 397. The
treatment of frustration in this text is necessarily limited. For further detail, consult the standard
contract texts.
[2] e.g. the hirer of the music hall in *Taylor v Caldwell* (1863) 3 B & S 826 need not have benefited
from an implied condition, that the concert hall continue to exist, excusing both parties when the
hall burnt down. It would be enough that the owner, unable to tender the hall to the hirer, could not
comply with the condition precedent to the hirer's duty to pay. The burning down of the hall could
be raised as a defence by the owner if sued by the hirer for failing to make the hall available as agreed.
A similar approach to this is adopted by Art. 79 of the Vienna Convention on the International Sale

frustration may still be in issue when risk remains with the seller. The real significance of risk is not where it lies, on seller or buyer, but rather whether it has been
transferred to the buyer.[3] Since mistake[4] also deals with the same subject matter
of material mishap to the goods, there is a tendency to apply it with the same
degree of rigour as frustration as a contractual dispensing agent. It is therefore
convenient to treat mistake and frustration in sequence. It is just possible for there
also to be a degree of intersection between mistake and risk, though it is unlikely
that any contract on its construction will transfer to the buyer the risk of loss
occurring before the contract is even concluded.

Risk

4.02 Introduction.   Risk is dealt with in four sections of the Sale of Goods Act[5] which,
though concerned with the location of risk between buyer and seller, is not at all
explicit about its contractual consequences. Risk, not defined in the Sale of Goods
Act, is a proprietary notion that has to be translated into the language of contractual rights and duties:[6]

> The truth is that risk is a derivative, and essentially negative, concept—an elliptical
> way of saying that either or both of the primary obligations of one party shall be
> enforceable, and that those of the other party shall be deemed to have been dis-
> charged, even though the normally prerequisite conditions have not been satisfied.
> That is to say, the legal consequences attaching to 'the risk' fall to be defined purely in
> terms of the parties' other duties and the corresponding rights and remedies: the seller's
> right to claim the price, and the buyer's right to resist payment or demand its return; and
> the right to claim damages (for non-delivery, non-acceptance, or breach of warranty of
> quality) or to resist such a claim.

Meaning of Risk

4.03 Events of risk.   Goods may suffer casualty, by Act of God or the actions of
third parties, in the form of damage, destruction, or loss, in circumstances where
neither seller nor buyer is at fault or contractually responsible for the casualty.

---

of Goods 1980, which in stated conditions 'exempts' from liability the non-performing party, leaving the other party's position to be determined by the performance and avoidance rules elsewhere
stated in the Convention.

  [3] See the discussion of frustration below.
  [4] Largely confined in this text to initial impossibility. For further detail, consult the standard
contract texts.
  [5] Ss. 7, 20, 32(3), and 33. It also appears inferentially in s. 32(2), where the buyer may displace
the allocation of risk if the seller makes an unreasonable contract with the carrier on behalf of the
buyer.
  [6] L. Sealy [1972B] *Camb. LJ* 225, 226–7. On risk, see also Lawson (1949) 65 *LQR* 352;
D. Fitzgerald (1996) 9 *J of Cont. Law* 206.

This may occur, for example, because goods are destroyed or damaged by an accidental fire while in the possession of a bailee, such as a warehouseman. Or the bailee's negligence may be responsible for the casualty. There is no finite list of events that trigger the doctrine of risk, but risk should be understood in rather specific terms and not as being confluent with the general notion of contractual risk. The risk of currency devaluation borne by the seller is not a risk that affects the goods. The risk of technological obsolescence of computer equipment, which may or may not engage the seller's liability for supplying goods that are fit for purpose and of satisfactory quality,[7] is not casualty for present purposes. On the other hand, the requisition of the goods by governmental action should, like other forms of loss, come within this proprietary notion of risk.

Risk on seller.   If the risk of loss remains with the seller, the seller cannot call on   **4.04** the buyer to pay the price or sue for damages for the buyer's refusal to accept a tender of ashes or damaged goods.[8] The buyer is entitled to refuse a tender of defective goods and, if delivery has already occurred before the casualty to the goods, he will hold the goods or what remains of them at the disposal of the seller.[9] If the property has passed to the buyer while the risk remains with the seller, a possible though infrequent occurrence, the property, having passed only conditionally, will revest in the seller.[10] Further, if the buyer has already paid the price but the risk remains with the seller, he may recover this as money had and received on a failure of consideration.[11] Despite its baneful effect in the past on the buyer's right to reject specific goods for breach of condition,[12] the passing of property has not prejudiced the buyer's claim where the risk has remained with the seller.[13] If the buyer elects to retain damaged but serviceable goods, or a lesser quantity than that agreed, there is authority supporting his recovery of a portion of the price paid.[14]

---

7 S. 14(2), (3).

8 Whether the seller would be liable for damages for non-delivery depends upon the operation of frustration.

9 Subject to contrary agreement, the buyer need not return the goods to the seller: s. 36.

10 *Head v Tattersall* (1872) LR 7 Ex. 7; *May v Conn* (1911) 23 OLR 102 (Can.); Sealy, n. 6 above, 239.

11 S. 54; see *Fitt v Cassanet* (1842) 4 M&G 898 (recovery of deposit). The buyer's right to recover moneys paid may arise consequent upon either termination for breach by the seller, or discharge for frustration, if the seller is able to plead successfully that the event that damages or destroys the goods is a frustrating event. The buyer's action to recover money prepaid will be subject to the Law Reform (Frustrated Contracts) Act 1943, which in s. 1(2) authorizes the court if it considers it just to do so to award the seller some or all of the prepaid moneys if the seller has incurred expenses. This provision, however, does not apply in the case of specific goods the subject of an agreement to sell where the risk remains with the seller: see s. 2(5)(c).

12 See Ch. 3 above.

13 *Head v Tattersall*, n. 10 above, 14.

14 In the breach case of *Ebrahim Dawood Ltd v Heath Ltd* [1961] 2 Lloyd's Rep. 512, where the buyer, electing to keep some of the goods tendered under the now-repealed s. 30(3), was allowed to recover that portion of the price corresponding to the rejected goods. See also *Devaux v Connolly*

And if in such a case he has not yet paid, the buyer would presumably pay the agreed price subject to an abatement for the affected goods.

4.05 **Risk on buyer.** If the risk of loss is on the buyer, the seller may sue for the price even though not fulfilling the normal preconditions for maintaining a price action.[15] He will be unable to make a tender of conforming goods, which is presumptively demanded before the buyer can be called upon to pay,[16] and if the risk is on the buyer but the property remains with the seller, he may be unable to appropriate the goods to the contract with the assent of the buyer, so as to comply with the usual requirement of a price action that the property has passed.[17] Besides the seller being deemed to have fulfilled all conditions precedent to an action for the price, the effect of risk being on the buyer is that he may not sue for damages for non-delivery[18] or for breach of warranty of quality.[19] Furthermore, where goods are supplied on sale or return or on approval and the parties agree that the risk shall lie with the potential buyer, the effect of transferring the risk to the buyer is to bring into existence a contract of sale.[20]

4.06 **Risk and future events.** In some instances, the buyer's duty to pay may be conditioned either as to time or amount by an event that can no longer occur as a result of the accident to the goods. This requires some adjustment to the parties' rights and duties under the contract to accommodate the transfer of risk. If the buyer was bound to pay so many days after delivery, which cannot now occur,[21] it seems reasonable to date this obligation from the time when delivery should otherwise have probably occurred.[22] Sometimes, the exact quantity of the goods on arrival or delivery serves to quantify the price. In *Martineau v Kitching*,[23] the risk of loss of sugar loaves destroyed in a fire was on the buyer. Each loaf weighed between thirty-eight and forty-two pounds and the practice was for the buyer to pay on the prompt date either a sum equivalent to the actual weight, if delivery had already been made, or an approximate sum to be subsequently adjusted. The fire destroyed any chance of calculating the actual weight of the loaves but the buyer was bound to pay a sum 'ascertain[ed] . . . as nearly as you can'.[24] A similar

---

(1849) 8 CB 640; *Behrend v Produce Brokers Ltd* [1920] 3 KB 530; *Westdeutsche Landesbank v Islington LBC* [1994] 1 WLR 938; Sealy, n. 6 above.

15 *Habton Farms v Nimmo* [2003] EWCA Civ 68; [2004] QB 1 at [72].
16 S. 28 in concert with the various conditions dealing with description, fitness, and quality.
17 S. 49(1).
18 The seller will not 'wrongfully' have refused or neglected to deliver under s. 51(1).
19 S. 53.
20 See *Bevington & Morris v Dale & Co. Ltd* (1902) 7 Com. Cas. 12.
21 Cf *Alexander v Gardner* (1835) 1 Bing. NC 671.
22 Sealy, n. 6 above, prefers payment to be made in 'a reasonable time'.
23 (1872) LR 7 QB 436.
24 *Ibid.*, 456.

case involved the arrival weight of a cargo of ice,[25] where the buyer's liability was to pay 'fair estimation of its value'[26] at the time the ship went down.

Allocation of Risk

Transfer of risk.   The main provision on the transfer of risk is section 20(1):   **4.07**

> Unless otherwise agreed, the goods remain at the seller's risk until the property in them is transferred to the buyer, but when the property in them is transferred to the buyer the goods are at the buyer's risk whether delivery has been made or not.

Presumptively, therefore, risk and property march hand in hand[27] though there is   **4.08** authority that the two should be separated where this accords with the common intention of the parties, an intention that should readily be inferred when a yoking together of property (especially the presumptive rule in section 18, Rule 1) and risk would produce an inconvenient or unjust result.[28] The Sale of Goods Act, in linking the passing of risk to the passing of property, has been criticized for ignoring insurance realities, in particular that the person in possession of goods is nearly always the one better placed to insure them.[29] There is much force in this since delivery, which is the voluntary transfer of possession, is usually a visible event.[30] But the rule in section 20(1) is only a presumptive one and the modern law on the passing of property ties it in with delivery, so any statutory reform associating risk with possession rather than property would yield modest results in practice.

Consumer cases.   When the Directive on certain aspects of the sale of consumer   **4.09** goods and associated guarantees[31] was transposed as the Sale and Supply of Goods to Consumers Regulations,[32] the opportunity was taken to alter the basic rule for the transfer of risk in consumer cases. Where the buyer deals as a consumer,[33] section 20(4) provides that the goods are at the seller's risk until delivery is made, any provision to contrary effect in section 20(1) having to be 'ignored'. If delivery were capable of being constructive for present purposes, there would be many

---

[25] *Castle v Playford* (1872) LR 7 Ex. 98.

[26] *Ibid.*, 99.

[27] It is common in the cases for the property first to be located prior to ascertaining risk. Occasionally, risk will be located first by a court searching for the whereabouts of property.

[28] *Martineau v Kitching*, n. 23 above; *Sterns Ltd v Vickers Ltd* [1923] 1 KB 78; K. Llewellyn (1938) 15 *NYU LR* 159. See also Lord Normand in *Comptoir d'Achat et du Boerenbond SA v Luis de Ridder Lda (The Julia)* [1949] AC 293, 319, referring to the buyer having 'an immediate and practical interest in the goods' in those cases where risk precedes property.

[29] P. S. Atiyah, *The Sale of Goods* (11th edn, by J. N. Adams, Longman, 2005), 358.

[30] An obvious exception is constructive delivery, e.g., where a warehouseman attorns to a new bailor.

[31] Directive 1999/44/EC of the European Parliament and of the Council.

[32] SI 2002 No. 3045 (which came into force on 31 March 2003).

[33] This has the same meaning that it has in the Unfair Contract Terms Act (see Ch. 9 below): s. 61(5A) (added by Sch. 2, para 5(9)(c) of the Sale and Supply of Goods Act 1994).

cases where no conflict existed between the two provisions. But another provision, section 32(4), introduced at the same time as section 20(4), makes it clear that, where the seller is authorized or required to 'send' the goods to the buyer, then delivery of the goods to the carrier is not delivery to the buyer.[34] Section 32(4) applies so that, where for example a courier or the post office is used to transport goods to the consumer, risk will pass to the consumer only on actual receipt of the goods by the consumer. The effect of the new provisions, therefore, is to prevent a consumer buyer, who is unlikely to carry insurance for goods in transit, from being unfairly surprised.[35] The constitutional basis of sections 20(4) and 32(4), however, is not entirely clear. The European Communities Act 1972 allows for regulations to be made 'for the purpose of implementing any Community obligation of the United Kingdom, or enabling any such obligation to be implemented . . .'[36] and 'for the purpose of dealing with matters arising out of or related to any such obligation or rights . . .'.[37] The Directive provides that 'the seller must deliver goods to the consumer that are in conformity with the contract of sale'. The Directive does not define delivery (or non-conformity) but the indications are that it means actual receipt by the consumer buyer. This is because, for the purpose of the minimum limitation period of two years[38] and of the presumption that goods are non-conforming at the time of delivery if a non-conformity appears within six months of delivery,[39] the Directive makes reference to the 'time of delivery'. Time should not start to run before the consumer has a chance to see and examine the goods, which will in the great majority of cases be upon actual receipt of the goods. The Directive also states in recital 17: 'Whereas the references to the time of delivery do not imply that Member States have to change their rules on the passing of risk.' This provision at first glance points away from any obligation on Member States, as is required if section 2(2) of the European Communities Act is to take effect, to alter established rules on risk. Nevertheless, the rule concerning the seller's duty to deliver conforming goods does require the seller to absorb transit risk if delivery is taken to mean actual delivery. Moreover, recital 17 can be understood as permitting the law of Member States to require the buyer in possession of goods to absorb the risk of destruction or loss of goods that is not due to

---

[34] See *Independiente Ltd v Music Trading On-Line (HK) Ltd* [2007] EWHC 533 (Ch); [2007] FSR 21.

[35] See in support of a rule like s. 20(4) Ontario Law Reform Commission, *Report on Sale of Goods* (1979), i, 267. It may be that this position was recognized informally in commercial practice by sellers not charging consumer buyers with the risk of loss or damage in transit: R. Cranston, *Consumers and the Law* (2nd edn, Weidenfeld & Nicholson, 1984), 169 (referring to customer good will). It is common for buyers to pay an additional sum representing, not just postage and packing, but also insurance.

[36] S. 2(2)(a).

[37] S. 2(2)(b).

[38] Art. 5(1).

[39] Art. 5(3).

the seller's earlier failure to deliver conforming goods. Understood in this way, recital 17 says nothing about the incidence of risk before the buyer is in actual receipt of the goods. On that basis, sections 20(4) and 32(4) may be seen as mandated by the Directive.[40]

Risk and third party bailees. The refusal of the common law to permit the property to pass in an ascertainable but unascertained part of a specific bulk has already been noted.[41] Were the law to insist dogmatically on risk accompanying the general property, a seller might bear the risk of loss of goods lying in a warehouse for months after abandoning all pretensions to deal with them. A willingness has therefore been shown to separate the passing of property and the transfer of risk. In *Sterns Ltd v Vickers Ltd*,[42] the sellers sold 120,000 gallons of white spirit out of a 200,000 gallon bulk kept in their name in a warehouse. The sellers procured from the warehouse a delivery warrant addressed to the order of the buyer. The buyer indorsed the warrant to a sub-buyer, who appeared at the warehouse several months later with it, only to discover a deterioration in the quality of the spirit affecting its specific gravity. This seems to have been due to the wrongful behaviour of the warehouse company in topping up the tank with spirit of a different specific gravity. It was understood, in both the sale and sub-sale transactions, that storage costs and insurance charges should be borne by buyer and sub-buyer, respectively. In an action by the sellers, the court held that the risk of deterioration had passed to the buyer. The property in the goods, not yet in the buyer,[43] would doubtless have passed on payment and transfer of the warrant but for the non-separation of the 120,000 gallons. Further, the sellers, in procuring from the warehouse a warrant addressed to the buyer, which bound the warehouse to the buyer,[44] had performed their delivery obligation and there was nothing more for them to do under the contract.[45] The buyer could have collected the spirit at any time thereafter.

4.10

---

[40] Cf. *Benjamin's Sale of Goods* (7th edn, by A. G. Guest, Sweet & Maxwell, 2006), para. 6–014.

[41] Ch. 3 above.

[42] n. 28 above.

[43] It is noteworthy that on similar facts Blackburn J in *Martineau v Kitching*, n. 23 above, 454, would strive to prevent the passing of property from producing an artificial solution in both risk and insolvency cases. In his view, it would be a 'monstrous hardship' for the buyer in a case like *Martineau* to have to lodge an insolvency proof: 'I should be very much inclined to struggle very hard to find any legal reason for saying that, though the risk remained in the sellers, yet the property had passed to the buyers as soon as they made payment.'

[44] The warehouse had thus attorned to the buyer, but not to the sub-buyer; see Ch. 6 below. A delivery warrant is not a document of title at common law: *ibid*. Consequently, endorsees have no rights against the issuer of the warrant in the absence of attornment. A warrant is, however, a document of title in the extended statutory sense for the purpose of exceptions to the *nemo dat* rule of title transfer: Ch. 5 below.

[45] n. 28 above, 85 (Scrutton LJ). Although the buyer, in transferring the delivery order to the sub-buyer, might also be said to have done all that was required under the contract, the failure of the

4.11 **The bailee's undertaking to deliver.** The above willingness to separate risk and property was absent in *Healy v Howlett & Sons*.[46] In that case, the seller of fish caught off the west coast of Ireland consigned to his own order 190 boxes of mackerel, which included an unascertained portion of twenty boxes that he had agreed to sell to the London buyer. Because of a delay in the rail journey to Dublin, the fish missed the scheduled Holyhead boat and had deteriorated to the point of unacceptable quality when the seller's agent at Holyhead, about half way into the transit, separated the buyer's boxes. An invoice sent too late, after the conclusion of the contract, put the 'sole risk' on the buyer, but this document was rightly disregarded. It seemed that the seller consigned the fish to his own order as far as Holyhead only to conceal from competitors the identity of his buyers. But for the delayed separation of the buyer's boxes, the property would probably have passed to the buyer when the fish began its journey in Ireland and before it missed the boat.[47] An arguable case existed that the buyer should have borne the risk of deterioration but the court, seemingly drawn by the supposed indivisibility of property and risk, ruled otherwise. The buyer in *Sterns* had the benefit of the warehouse company's direct undertaking to deliver the goods, so the seller, when procuring the warranty, had constructively delivered the goods. The carrier in *Healy*, however, gave no undertaking to the buyer to deliver the goods to the buyer. The difference between the two cases, therefore, may turn not so much on what the seller did to effectuate delivery but on whether the buyer had direct recourse to the third party on the latter's undertaking.

4.12 **Undivided shares.** When the Sale of Goods Act was amended in the mid-1990s to allow for the buyer to acquire an undivided share in identified bulk goods under section 20A,[48] no amendments were made to section 20 to provide for the transfer of risk to be presumptively linked to the passing of an undivided share. Nor, when a contract for the sale of an undivided share in goods was made a contract of sale of goods and thus subject to the Sale of Goods Act,[49] was any similar change made to section 20. Section 20 should not in terms apply to these cases. The 'property' in section 20 means the general property[50] and the Act was not amended to treat the holder of an undivided share as having the general property in goods or in any

---

buyer thus to confer on the sub-buyer direct rights against the warehouse does not make the transfer of risk to the sub-buyer a foregone conclusion. Yet it would not be sensible to leave the goods at the buyer's risk for months after the sub-buyer has received an indorsed delivery order, unless the point is made that in such circumstances the buyer should procure from the warehouse a fresh delivery order in the name of the sub-buyer and thus an attornment to the sub-buyer.

[46] [1917] 1 KB 337.

[47] The report does not record the shipping terms or the incidence of the duty to pay freight to the carrier(s), though the quoted price probably included the cost of carriage.

[48] See Ch. 3 above.

[49] *Ibid.*

[50] S. 61(1).

part of goods. As seen in the case of *Sterns Ltd v Vickers Ltd*,[51] the common law had already fashioned a solution for the case of undivided shares, though it had necessarily done so by means of constructive delivery rather than by reference to proprietary notions. On the facts of *Sterns*, however, an undivided share in the goods stored would probably now have arisen in favour of the buyer.[52] It may be significant that section 20 was not amended so as presumptively to pass the risk once the buyer acquired an undivided share; an amendment in those terms might have been seen as a retrograde step. In the case of unascertained goods, the property will in fact normally pass upon delivery, so the presumptive rule in section 20 turns in practical terms on the transfer of possession, rather than the passing of property. An amendment to section 20 to accommodate undivided shares, if expressed in proprietary terms, would not have reflected the importance of constructive delivery, and if expressed in terms of constructive delivery, would have jarred with the existing content of section 20. The failure to amend section 20 may be seen as offering some support for the view that the transfer of risk should not be recognized as turning upon the passing of property rather than the transfer of possession. In consequence, the approach taken in *Sterns* should be suitable in cases where an undivided share arises under section 20A. Where there is no interest, because the buyer has not paid, or there is a diminished interest because the buyer has paid only part of the price, then *Sterns* should apply even if section 20A does not. This is subject to contrary intention. In most of the cases where an undivided interest exists in favour of the buyer, the particular common law rules on the transfer of risk in f.o.b. and c.i.f. contracts deriving from settled intention and practice will govern. Risk in such cases is transferred on or as from shipment.[53] Had there been any amendment in general terms to section 20, then, assuming its language to have been presumptive like the rest of section 20, it would thus have been excluded by contrary intention.

Risk and Quality Obligations

Transit and deterioration. A difficult practical problem concerns perishable 4.13 goods that deteriorate in transit. Normally, when goods are delivered to the carrier, the risk will pass at that time.[54] When perishable goods arrive at their destination unfit for consumption, it may be difficult to know whether this is due to

---

[51] n. 28 above.

[52] But the result in *Sterns* does not as such depend upon payment by the buyer, whereas s. 20A grants an undivided share to a buyer only when and to the extent that the buyer has paid.

[53] Discussed in the text accompanying nn. 88 *et seq*. below.

[54] Either because of the combined presumptive effects of ss. 18, Rule 5, and 20, or because the parties to a documentary sale on f.o.b., c.i.f., or similar terms have expressly or impliedly provided for the risk to pass when the goods are shipped and the property at a later date when the shipping documents are transferred against payment.

the seller's breach of contract in not shipping goods that are of satisfactory quality and fit for the buyer's purpose or to an event that occurred in transit while the goods were at the buyer's risk. It depends on the evidence going to the state of the goods upon shipment. The goods must then have been capable of standing the rigours of a normal voyage and of satisfying fitness and quality standards for a reasonable period thereafter so as to allow for disposal.[55] The burden, as in any case where the buyer claims the goods to be unsatisfactory or unfit for purpose, is on the buyer to show they are not capable of withstanding the voyage.[56] This means identifying the cause of the damage, or the causes, and showing that this cause or causes lies within the seller's sphere of responsibility.[57] In *Mash & Murrell Ltd v Joseph I Emmanuel Ltd*,[58] the seller of Cyprus spring potatoes shipped c. & f. Liverpool was held liable at trial for the fact that upon arrival they were found to be unfit for consumption. The evidential difficulties in arriving at such a finding should not be underestimated. The decision was reversed on appeal because the voyage had not been normal: the damage to the potatoes had occurred as a result of their lying unventilated in a port of call for five days. The risk therefore fell upon the buyer.[59]

4.14 **Long voyage.** Where the transit is unusually long, the buyer will on similar grounds bear the risk of loss attributable to the length of the voyage, unless the buyer's stated purpose embraces a voyage of this length[60] or the seller expressly warrants that the goods will stand a 'long haul'.[61] Where the court is faced with a conflict between findings that the goods were sound when shipped and that nothing unusual occurred in transit, it is likely as a matter of evidence that any extraordinary deterioration in the goods will be put down to a hidden flaw in them, and thus be made the responsibility of the seller.[62] In international sales forms, however, it is common for the contract to stipulate that a certificate of inspection will

---

[55] *Healy v Howlett & Sons*, n. 46 above (Ridley J).

[56] *AB Kemp Ltd v Tolland* [1956] 2 Lloyd's Rep. 681.

[57] *Ibid.*

[58] [1961] 1 WLR 862, revd. on the facts [1962] 1 WLR 16. See also *Beer v Walker* (1877) 46 LJQB 677; *Ollett v Jordan* [1918] 2 KB 41, 47 (Atkin LJ); *AB Kemp Ltd v Tolland*, n. 56 above; *Hardwick Game Farm v Suffolk Agricultural and Poultry Producers' Association Ltd* [1964] 2 Lloyd's Rep. 227, 270; *Oleificio Zucchi SpA v Northern Sales Ltd* [1965] 2 Lloyd's Rep. 496, 517; *Georgetown Seafoods Ltd v Usen Fisheries Ltd* (1977) 78 DLR (3d) 542; *Gatoil International Inc. v Tradax Petroleum Ltd* [1985] 1 Lloyd's Rep. 350. Cf *Cordova Land Co. Ltd v Victor Bros Inc.* [1966] 1 WLR 793, where the court drew a distinction between perishable goods like potatoes, where description and quality standards might have to be met by the goods on arrival, and goods like the present animal hides, where this was not the case.

[59] See also *Davidson v Bigelow & Hood Ltd* [1923] 1 DLR 1175.

[60] For the purpose of s. 14(3): discussed in Ch. 7 below.

[61] e.g., *Tregunno v Aldershot Distributing Co-operative Co. Ltd* [1943] OR 795 (Can.). A similar result follows if the buyer is responsible for the mode of carriage and the damage to the goods stems from the chosen mode: *Kelly, Douglas & Co. Ltd v Pollock* (1958) 14 DLR (2d) 526.

[62] *Barnes v Waugh* (1906) 41 NSR 38 (Can.)

be conclusive evidence as to their quality upon shipment, the object being to direct an aggrieved buyer away from the seller and in the direction of the carrier or the insurance company.[63] In such sales, furthermore, evidence about the condition of the goods upon shipment may be found in the bill of lading, which may state that the goods were or appeared to be in good condition, or which may be claused to indicate they were defective.

Risk and Carriage

Unreasonable contract of carriage.   Even if the risk is on the buyer while the **4.15** goods are in transit, the seller may still be liable if loss or deterioration is due to an unreasonable contract of carriage made by the seller with the carrier. According to section 32(2):

> Unless otherwise authorised by the buyer, the seller must make such contract with the carrier on behalf of the buyer as may be reasonable having regard to the nature of the goods and the other circumstances of the case; and if the seller omits to do so, and the goods are lost or damaged in course of transit, the buyer may decline to treat the delivery to the carrier as a delivery to himself or may hold the seller responsible in damages.[64]

Where the seller in one case could, for the same freight charge, have put the goods on rail at the carrier's risk, subject only to the reasonable burden of the carrier inspecting the packing, it was unreasonable to ship at the buyer's risk.[65] In one Canadian case, a seller who, in breach of the contract of sale, failed to stipulate with the railway carrier that cabbages should be carried in heated wagons was held liable when they suffered frost damage after being left unheated in a railway siding.[66] Since the carrier was never under an obligation to keep the railway wagons heated, the buyer's only recourse was against the defaulting seller. A seller who does make a proper contract does not, of course, guarantee that the carrier will comply and does not answer for the carrier's breach of the contract of carriage.[67] The seller, moreover, does not guarantee that the buyer will have a remedy against the carrier if the goods are damaged or lost, since the carrier will enjoy defences and limitations of liability under international conventions.[68]

---

[63] See M. Bridge, *The International Sale of Goods[:] Law and Practice* (2nd edn, OUP, 2007), 52–7.

[64] S. 32(4) requires s. 32(2) to be 'ignored' if the buyer deals as a consumer. Since s. 32(2) is a rule favouring buyers, s. 32(4) is explicable only as making it quite clear that the risk cannot pass to a consumer buyer before actual receipt, so whatever the seller might have done to make a reasonable contract of carriage is not relevant.

[65] *T Young & Sons v Hobson and Partner* (1949) 65 TLR 365.

[66] *BC Fruit Market Ltd v National Fruit Co.* (1921) 59 DLR 87.

[67] *Van Zonnefeld & Co. v Gilchrist* (1915) 8 OWN 4 (Can.).

[68] See Carriage of Goods by Sea Act 1971, Sch. (Hague–Visby Rules).

4.16 **Choice of remedies.** Section 32(2) should apply regardless of whether the seller contracts with the carrier as principal or as agent for the buyer.[69] The provision gives the buyer a choice of remedies. If the buyer chooses to regard the seller as having failed to deliver, this should mean that the buyer may decline to pay the price or, having paid it, recover the price as on a failure of consideration. The buyer thereby puts the risk back on the seller. The buyer should also have an action for damages for non-delivery. The buyer's exercise of this first remedy is tantamount to treating the seller's action as a discharging breach of the contract of sale, and it would appear not to depend upon the degree of damage suffered by the goods in transit. But the buyer's rights under section 32(2), it is submitted, should depend on there being a causal link between the seller's default and the buyer's prejudice, which will be absent in those cases where the buyer could have corrected that default before the damage was done.[70] Where the buyer elects to sue for damages, this seems to assume an affirmation of the contract. There is no reason to suppose that the measure of damages is anything other than that under section 53.[71]

4.17 **Sending the goods by sea.** Similar to section 32(2) in drawing on the seller's default is section 32(3), which establishes the presumptive rule that, where goods are 'sent' by sea by seller to buyer, in circumstances where insurance is usually carried, a failure by the seller to give such 'notice' as to enable the buyer to insure the goods in transit[72] means that the goods will be at the seller's risk.[73] This provision comes from Scots law[74] and does not sit comfortably with English practice in the area of international documentary sales on c.i.f. and f.o.b. terms. In such contracts, the risk is on the buyer from shipment,[75] which is the case dealt with by section 32(3). That provision is ousted by contrary implication in the case of

---

[69] The former will be the case with c.i.f. contracts (see *Houlder & Bros Co. Ltd v Commissioner of Public Works* [1908] AC 276, 290) and the latter would apply in the case of certain f.o.b. contracts (see Devlin J's classification in *Pyrene Co. Ltd v Scindia Navigation Co. Ltd* [1954] 2 QB 402).

[70] *Mayhew v Scott Fruit Co.* (1921) 21 DLR 54 9 (goods dispatched to wrong address and buyer doing nothing about it).

[71] Discussed in Ch. 12 below.

[72] The notice may be given after the transit commences but in time for the particular risk to be covered: *Re Weis & Co. Ltd and Credit Colonial et Commercial (Antwerp)* [1916] 1 KB 346 (seizure of goods in transit by belligerent State).

[73] Although the provision as such is clearly confined to sea transit, it may well be that a common law analogue would be fashioned under s. 62(2) for other forms of transport such as multimodal transportation. Again, this rule is disapplied in the case of buyers who deal as consumers. Section 32(4) qualifies s. 32(3) in the same way that it qualifies s. 32(2): see n. 64 above.

[74] *Wimble, Sons & Co. v Rosenberg & Sons* [1913] 3 KB 743 (Hamilton LJ).

[75] In c.i.f. contracts, the cargo may be appropriated to the contract after shipment, whereupon the risk passes retrospectively to the buyer. Discussed in the text accompanying nn. 97 *et seq.* below.

c.i.f. contracts, since insurance is the responsibility of the seller.[76] It should apply
to c. & f. contracts, at least in those cases where the seller is not contractually
bound to take out insurance for the buyer's account. It is, however, awkward in
c. & f. cases to speak of goods being 'sent' to the buyer instead of the seller tendering a shipping document issued under a contract of carriage. A similar awkwardness is present with f.o.b. contracts, where delivery to the carrier on shipment is
tantamount to delivery to the buyer since the carrier is presumptively the buyer's
agent.[77]

F.o.b. difficulties. The difficulty in applying section 32(3) to f.o.b. contracts **4.18**
came to a head in the leading case of *Wimble Sons & Co. v Rosenberg & Sons*.[78] It
concerned a contract for the sale of 200 bags of rice f.o.b. Antwerp, under which
the sellers, informed after the contract date that Odessa was the destination, were
responsible for shipping as required by the buyers and were left to select the ship.[79]
Information about the ship was first sent to the buyers four days after the ship
foundered upon leaving harbour. The buyers had not yet effected insurance since
it was their practice to do so only after notification of the name of the ship on which
the goods were loaded. They refused to pay, citing the sellers' non-compliance with
section 32(3). By a majority decision, the Court of Appeal found for the sellers.
Of the two judges who held that section 32(3) applied to f.o.b. contracts,[80]
Vaughan Williams LJ thought that section 32(3) required an actual notice, which
was not dispensed with because the buyer might already have sufficient knowledge to insure.[81] Buckley LJ, on the other hand, thought the requirements of the
provision could be and had been met in the shape of the knowledge already
possessed by the buyers. Hamilton LJ agreed with Buckley LJ on this point,[82]
though his preference was for holding that section 32(3) had no application to
f.o.b. contracts. So there were clear (though differently constituted) majorities
that the provision applied, that no formal notice was required, and that the buyers
had sufficient knowledge. They knew the port of discharge and did not need to

---

[76] *Law and Bonar Ltd v British American Tobacco Co. Ltd* [1916] 2 KB 605. But it might apply
in the unlikely case of a buyer wanting a usual type of insurance cover going beyond the insurance
required under a c.i.f. contract: *ibid.*, 608–9.

[77] S. 32(1).

[78] n. 74 above.

[79] Presumptively the f.o.b. buyer selects the ship: see *Pyrene Co. Ltd v Scindia Navigation Co. Ltd*
[1954] 2 QB 402.

[80] Vaughan Williams and Buckley LJJ. The former stated that 'the word "send" covers every
obligation of the seller in reference to effecting or securing the arrival of the goods . . . at their destination'. The latter thought 'send' was equivalent to transmit or dispatch. Dissenting on this point,
Hamilton LJ thought that the sellers could not send the goods to the buyers by sea when they had
already delivered the goods to the buyers' agent, the carrier, upon shipment.

[81] On the facts, his lordship thought the buyer did not already know enough.

[82] See also *Northern Steel and Hardware Co. Ltd v John Batt and Co. (London) Ltd* (1917) 33 TLR
516.

know the name of the ship since they could have effected insurance on an Odessa voyage by a ship or ships to be declared.

4.19 **Seller's risk agreement.** Sometimes the seller 'agrees to deliver . . . at his own risk' the goods to some place other than where they are when sold.[83] In such a case, section 33 states a presumptive rule that this assumption of risk does not include 'any risk of deterioration in goods necessarily incident to the course of transit'.[84] This provision should apply where the seller's agreement to assume the risk is express or implied, or where in accordance with the presumptive rule in section 20(1) the risk remains with the seller. Section 33, with its limited allocation of necessary risk to the seller, should not be read so as to detract from the broader allocation of risk to the seller under the special provisions of section 32(2) and (3). In particular, section 33 should not be allowed to undermine the normal rule that, where the risk is on the buyer, the seller must still ship goods that will not in a normal transit deteriorate to the point of non-conformity to the contract.[85] It would be odd if the seller's quality obligations were to be diluted just because the risk of loss had been assumed by the seller under section 33.

4.20 **Necessary incident.** Section 33 is based on a case where a quantity of iron dispatched by canal rusted in transit.[86] It was held that this was a necessary incident of canal transport and so had to be borne by the buyer. In modern conditions, a different result should follow where the goods can be packed or treated to obviate such a risk by a method usual in the trade, or where they must be so dealt with to ensure that on arrival they are to pass the tests of fitness and quality laid down by the implied terms in section 14 of the Act.[87] Peaches cannot be expected to be as fresh on arrival as on shipment, but they can be expected to be fit for human consumption on distribution to consumers through the normal retail channels.[88] The word 'necessarily' is likely to be quite strictly interpreted nowadays and it is hard to imagine a modern instance of the application of the section.

---

[83] *Quaere* does 'sold' refer to contract or conveyance? It makes more sense to say the former, though the latter accords with the technical language of the Act.

[84] Oddly, this rule, as unlikely as it is ever to be applied in modern conditions, is not disapplied in the case of buyers who deal as consumers.

[85] *Winnipeg Fish Co. v Whitman Fish Co.* (1909) 41 SCR 453; *Georgetown Seafoods Ltd v Usen Fisheries Ltd* (1977) 78 DLR (3d) 542.

[86] *Bull v Robison* (1854) 10 Ex. 342; see also *Lewis v Barré* (1901) 14 Man. LR 32 (Can.).

[87] In *Bull v Robison*, n. 86 above, the goods were admittedly unmerchantable on arrival, but a modern water shipment of equivalent length would surely require shipment below deck by the seller or in a container, methods denied to a 19th-century canal shipment by barge.

[88] *Mash & Murrell Ltd v Joseph I Emmanuel Ltd* [1961] 1 WLR 862; *Beer v Walker* (1877) 46 LJQB 677.

Risk and Export Sales

General.   As stated earlier, risk presumptively passes to the buyer on shipment,   **4.21**
when the services of an independent carrier are used, because that is when the
property in the goods presumptively passes. This will not be the case with those
contracts where the seller undertakes to deliver the goods to the buyer in the country of destination, whether from the ship itself (*ex* ship) or at some inland point
such as a warehouse (arrival). In such cases, the risk will be on the seller during
transit.[89] With other shipping terms, such as c.i.f. and f.o.b., the property will not
normally pass until payment is made on the documentary exchange.[90] It is nevertheless settled that the risk impliedly passes as from shipment in c.i.f.[91] and on
shipment in f.o.b.[92] contracts. The difference in formulation stems from the common case of shipment in an f.o.b. contract being made when the identity of the
buyer is already known, whereas shipment commonly occurs before the goods are
appropriated to a c.i.f. contract and sometimes even before the c.i.f. contract is
concluded. It can therefore be transferred retrospectively in c.i.f. contracts. One
possible meaning of shipment is that it occurs at the time and point when the
goods cross the ship's rail,[93] but a preferable view is that it happens when the seller's
duty regarding the physical delivery of the goods to the carrier has been accomplished.[94] There is ground for saying that the transfer of risk should be detached
from any technical meaning of shipment. If exceptionally the contract of sale permits the seller to tender to the buyer a 'received for shipment' bill of lading,[95] it is
arguable that this alters the nature of the seller's loading responsibilities, so that
the risk might pass before the goods are placed on board. No authority, however,
supports this proposition. Perhaps the most principled approach to the matter is to
regard the risk as being transferred at the moment when the carrier becomes responsible for the goods and thus protected by insurance cover and able to benefit from

---

[89] *Yangtse Insurance Asscn v Lukmanjee* [1918] AC 585, 589 (Lord Sumner).

[90] The f.o.b. seller may, even if consigning the goods to a named buyer, reserve the right of
disposal: see Ch. 3 above.

[91] *Comptoir d'Achat et du Boerenbond Belge S/A v Luis de Ridder Lda (The Julia)* [1949] AC 293;
Biddell Bros v E Clemens Horst Co. [1911] 1 KB 934; see Bridge, n. 63 above, 369–70, 374–8.

[92] *Stock v Inglis* (1884) 12 QBD 564; *The Parchim* [1918] AC 157, 168; see Bridge, n. 63 above,
364–7.

[93] Criticized in the f.o.b. case of *Pyrene Co. Ltd v Scindia Navigation Co. Ltd*, n. 79 above.

[94] Certain variations on the f.o.b. contract require the seller not merely to load the goods or cause
them to be loaded, but to go further and see to it that they are stowed below or stowed below and
trimmed. Again, in a case where a quantity of rice in bags had to be loaded, shipment under an entire
contract was treated as incomplete until the entire quantity had been loaded: *Anderson v Morice*
(1875) LR 10 CP 609, affirmed (1876) 1 App. Cas. 713. There is an argument that, if the contract
of sale permits the seller to tender to the buyer a 'received for shipment' bill of lading, which it might
do in some c.i.f. cases, the risk might therefore pass before the goods are placed on board.

[95] It might do for some c.i.f. contracts, though not for f.o.b. contracts in view of the nature of the
seller's loading responsibilities. Discussed further in Ch. 6 below.

limitations of liability under international conventions,[96] though the matter cannot be regarded as settled and an express provision to this effect on the transfer of risk is to be preferred.

4.22 **C.i.f. contracts.** In c.i.f. contracts, the consequences of the risk being on the buyer as from shipment are even today not thoroughly resolved. In *Couturier v Hastie*,[97] the seller was not permitted to recover the price on a tender of shipping documents relating to a cargo of specific goods that had perished before the conclusion of the contract. This decision therefore supports the view that in a c.i.f. contract the retrospective transfer of the risk of loss to the buyer will stop at the contract date. But the decision does not rule out a similar backdating of the risk of damage, as opposed to loss, and it does not prevent the parties from making whatever contractual provision for the allocation of risk they wish as long as they sufficiently demonstrate their intentions. The c.i.f. buyer will have a valuable insurance policy as well as the prospect, as successor to the seller's rights and obligations under the contract of carriage, of an action against the carrier. Yet the allocation of the risk of pre-contract loss is an unlikely construction of a contract for unascertained goods where the seller is aware of the loss before concluding the contract or before even appropriating the goods. The courts are reluctant to treat c.i.f. contracts as purely sales of documents.[98] If such a seller had a range of c.i.f. buyers from whom to select the recipient of the shipping documents, there is the further complication of deciding the principles on which such a selection might be made. And if the seller actually knew of the loss before entering into the particular contract of sale, any construction that the buyer must be satisfied with only the documents would to all intents and purposes be untenable.

---

[96] See *Benjamin's Sale of Goods*, n. 40 above, para. 20–090. See the Hague–Visby Rules as set out in the Carriage of Goods by Sea Act 1971, Sch.

[97] (1853) 9 Ex. 102, affirmed (1856) 5 HLC 673.

[98] See *Arnhold Karberg & Co. v Blyth, Green, Jourdain & Co.* [1916] 1 KB 495, where Scrutton J at first instance states that 'a c.i.f. sale is not a sale of goods, but a sale of documents relating to goods' ([1915] 2 KB 379, 388). In the Court of Appeal, Bankes and Warrington LJJ state, however, that a c.i.f. contract is a sale of goods to be performed by the delivery of documents (above, 510, 514). McCardie J in *Manbre Saccharine Co. Ltd v Corn Products Co. Ltd* [1919] 1 KB 198, 203, referred to the difference of opinion in *Arnhold Karberg* as 'one of phrase only', saying for his part that delivery in a c.i.f. contract was effected by a delivery of goods and not documents (*ibid.*, 202). In *James Finlay & Co. Ltd v NV Kwik Hoo Tong Handel Maatschappij* [1929] 1 KB 400, 407–8, Scrutton LJ thought it unnecessary to say whether a c.i.f. contract was a sale of goods or of documents, but he still thought there was a lot to be said for the documents view. See also *Ross T Smyth & Co. Ltd v TD Bailey, Sons & Co.* [1940] 3 All ER 60, 68, where Lord Wright stated that a c.i.f. contract was a sale of goods contract, and *Hindley & Co. Ltd v East Indian Produce Co. Ltd* [1973] 2 Lloyd's Rep. 515, where a c. & f. contract was stated to be a sale of goods contract to be performed by the delivery of documents. On balance, this is the preferred view, with the addition that the documents in question should evidence that the seller has entered into proper contracts of carriage and insurance. The transfer of the documents should also be effective in assigning to the buyer rights under the above contracts.

C.i.f. and post-contract perishing. Suppose the seller appropriates to the **4.23**
contract a cargo that perishes after the contract date but before the appropriation.
At first sight, the c.i.f. risk rule requires the buyer to bear the loss,[99] but it has been
powerfully argued that the risk should remain with the seller, seemingly regardless
of whether the seller knew of the loss before the notice of appropriation.[100]
Certainly, if the seller did know of the loss at that time, the difficulty mentioned
above of discovering on what basis a seller with a number of purchasers should
single one of them out makes itself felt again. Authorities dealing with c.i.f. contracts containing prohibition clauses, where the seller's capacity to perform across
a wide contractual front is impaired by a governmental embargo on shipment,
appear to favour any reasonable action by the seller in apportioning whatever
performance capability he retains amongst his various buyers.[101] This approach,
which may usefully be adapted to unappropriated damaged cargoes and to partly
damaged bulk cargoes destined for numerous buyers, could also be adopted for
lost cargoes. To say that a seller may not appropriate a lost cargo strikes at the principle of retrospective risk allocation, though some room would still be left for that
principle if retrospectivity were permitted to apply to damaged as opposed to lost
cargoes. It would in many cases be impracticable to conduct a minute evidentiary
inquiry in order to discover whether damage to cargo occurred before or after
appropriation.

Retrospectivity and lost cargoes. There is case law support for retrospective risk **4.24**
allocation in the case of lost cargoes. In *C Groom Ltd v Barber*,[102] the sellers appropriated a cargo of Hessian cloth on board the *City of Winchester* to their contract
with the buyer the day before the ship, which had been sunk two weeks previously,
was posted as a loss at Lloyd's. Atkin J held that the seller was entitled to be paid
against a tender of the usual shipping documents even if the goods had not been
'appropriated' at that time. He stated that on the facts there had apparently been
no appropriation, but, since he was refuting the seller's argument that the buyer
had to be in a position to pass the property in the goods upon the documentary
tender, it is clear that he was talking of appropriation in the proprietary sense, and
not in the sense of attaching a descriptive source to the contract goods. In *Manbre*

99 See *Produce Brokers Co. Ltd v Olympia Oil Co. Ltd* [1917] 1 KB 320, 329–30 (Scrutton LJ),
disapproving *Re Olympia Oil and Cake Co. and Producers Co.* [1915] 1 KB 253 (Div. Ct.), but revd.
on other grounds [1916] 1 AC 314; J. Feltham [1975] *JBL* 273. The judgment of Scrutton LJ,
above, has been explained as turning on the construction of the particular contract: *Benjamin's Sale
of Goods*, n. 40 above, para. 19–083.
100 *Benjamin's Sale of Goods*, n. 40 above, para. 19–082.
101 See *Westfälische Central-Genossenschaft GmbH v Seabright Chemicals Ltd* (unreported), cited
in *Bremer Handelsgesellschaft mbH v Continental Grain Co.* [1983] 1 Lloyd's Rep. 269; M. Bridge,
'The 1973 Mississippi Floods: "Force Majeure" and Export Prohibition' in E. McKendrick (ed.),
Force Majeure and Frustration of Contract (2nd edn, LLP, 1995).
102 [1915] 1 KB 316.

Saccharine Co. Ltd v Corn Products Co. Ltd,[103] the sellers, with knowledge of the loss of the ship, appropriated a quantity of corn starch on the *Algonquin* to their contract with the buyers. The buyer's defence pointed to the significance of the seller's knowledge. Curiously, however, McCardie J did not focus on this point in his judgment and was content to hold that the sellers were entitled to be paid against documents representing a cargo lost before tender.[104]

4.25 **String sales.** Cargoes are commonly sold on c.i.f. terms in string. Where the practice of the trade is content with an insurance policy covering certain risks, there seems little reason for halting the loss before the string is fully formed. Otherwise, a seller, who may have carefully matched his purchase and sale commitments, thus avoiding a speculative long or short position in the market, would be left with an insurance policy covering loss and a possible breach of contract action for non-delivery against him by a buyer to whose contract he cannot now appropriate a cargo. Nevertheless, the Divisional Court in *Re Olympia Oil and Cake Co. Ltd*[105] held that the seller could not appropriate a lost cargo.[106] When the same case went before the Court of Appeal at a later stage of its confused judicial and arbitral existence, under the name of *Produce Brokers Co. Ltd v Olympia Oil and Cake Co. Ltd*,[107] Scrutton LJ stated in trenchant terms that the earlier decision was wrong.[108] Furthermore, the Court of Appeal upheld an arbitral finding that there was a custom in the oil seed trade by which a buyer had to accept an appropriation originating with the head seller even if the intermediate seller knew of the loss before appropriating the cargo to the contract with the buyer.

4.26 **Insurance shortfall.** The difficulties in this area arise, not because buyers dislike having to claim under an insurance policy (for it is usually the case in commodities sales to insure in excess of the contract value), but because the lost cargoes question arose during the First World War. At that time, war risk was not covered in many c.i.f. contracts[109] and the insurance rights of a buyer of a cargo lost through enemy action were therefore worth nothing. The problem could still arise with any risk falling outside the customary insurance obligations of the c.i.f. seller or where a rising market produces a loss in excess of the insurance value.

---

[103] n. 98 above.

[104] The seller had taken out war risk insurance but the insured value, though markedly higher than the contract price, was lower than the market price at the date of the appropriation.

[105] n. 99 above.

[106] Two members of the court (Shearman and Avory JJ) thought the fact of the cargo being lost before appropriation was enough, while the third, Rowlatt J, based his decision in favour of the buyer on the ground that the seller knew of the loss at the time of the appropriation.

[107] n. 99 above.

[108] *Ibid.*, 330.

[109] Sometimes war risk was expressly stated to be for the buyer's account; *C Groom Ltd v Barber*, n. 102 above.

Risk and Breach of Contract

General.   Where the seller commits a discharging breach of contract, the   **4.27**
relation of this to risk poses a problem. Suppose damage to or destruction of the
goods is due to the very breach committed by the seller. A car, for example, is
destroyed in an accident caused by a defect in its steering. The modern view is that
the passing of the property to the buyer is no bar to its revesting in the seller when
the goods are lawfully rejected by the buyer.[110] It could equally be said that the
transfer of risk is no bar to rejection. The seller cannot seriously argue against the
buyer's right of rejection (or notional rejection of lost goods) in the above case on
the ground that the buyer bore the risk, because this would nullify the buyer's
rights of rejection and contractual termination.

Unconnected breach.   Where, however, the goods are damaged or destroyed for   **4.28**
reasons unconnected with the seller's discharging breach, the position is more
complex. If the buyer would have rejected the goods on discovering the breach,
there is an argument that it would be unreasonable to oblige him to bear the
interim risk. It might also be argued somewhat tenuously that the property in
goods that fail to accord with the contract description will not pass to the buyer
under the presumptive rule in section 18, Rule 5, since it cannot be said that the
buyer assents to their unconditional appropriation to the contract.[111] In *Head v
Tattersall*,[112] the seller of a horse warranted that it had hunted with the Bicester
hounds and undertook to take it back if, by a certain date, the buyer should discover this was not so. The buyer found out in time that the horse was an imposter,
but not before it had died. The court decided that the buyer was entitled to recover
the price. It is not clear whether the seller had as such committed a breach of contract or whether the buyer's discovery was a non-promissory condition precedent
to his right to reclaim the money, but the difference between the two should not
affect the location of the interim risk.

Criticism.   The reversal of risk in a less exotic case than *Head v Tattersall* appears   **4.29**
more questionable, especially since, nowadays, the buyer's right of rejection
may endure for a significant period beyond the point and time of delivery.[113]
Furthermore, to leave the risk with the buyer avoids a very difficult speculation,

---

[110] *RV Ward Ltd v Bignall* [1967] 1 QB 534. On the property passing only conditionally in such
a case, see *Colonial Insurance Co. of New Zealand v Adelaide Marine Insurance Co.* (1886) 12 App.
Cas. 128; *Hardy & Co. v Hillerns and Fowler* [1923] 2 KB 490, 499 (Atkin LJ); *Kwei Tek Chao v
British Traders & Shippers Ltd* [1954] 2 QB 459, 487–8; *McDougall v Aeromarine of Emsworth Ltd*
[1958] 3 All ER 431, 437.

[111] See Ch. 3 above.

[112] (1872) LR 7 Ex. 7. See also *Vitol SA v Esso Australia Ltd (The Wise)* [1989] 1 Lloyd's Rep. 96
(vessel damaged by missile but seller had loaded less than the agreed contractual quantity), reversed
on different grounds [1989] 2 Lloyd's Rep. 451.

[113] See Ch. 10 above.

informed by self-serving argument from the buyer, about whether the buyer would or would not have gone on to reject the goods. Finally, there is the insurance argument that a buyer should insure goods in his possession and the seller may reasonably not have insurance coverage. This argument weighed heavily with a New Zealand court, which ruled that the risk of accidental fire rested on the buyer who, at the relevant time, had not decisively rejected the goods for their failure to conform to sample.[114] The court conceded that upon rejection a defeasible property in the buyer could revest in the seller, so its decision is not based upon a mechanical attachment of property and risk. In addition, the court did not deprive the buyer of the right to reject because of the buyer's delay in exercising it, so the decision cannot be explained away on that ground.[115] On balance, unless the contract expressly or impliedly permits the buyer to reverse the risk, which is a possible interpretation of *Head v Tattersall*, it is submitted that the risk of interim loss arising from events not connected with the non-conforming character of the goods should remain with the buyer.[116] In many cases, this point of principle will not need to be settled: the event that damages or destroys the goods will prevent the buyer from proving the existence of a discharging breach.

Risk and Delayed Delivery

4.30   **Fault and causation.**   Section 20(1), which states the presumptive date of transfer of the risk to the buyer, is subject to the contrary intention of the parties. It is also ousted under section 20(2) 'where delivery has been delayed through the fault of either buyer or seller'. In that event, 'the goods are at the risk of the party at fault as regards any loss which might not have occurred but for such fault'.[117] It is submitted that 'might' cannot be read as mere conjecture: the party on risk should have to prove on the balance of probabilities, in the normal way, that the loss would not have occurred but for the delay.

4.31   **Buyer as owner.**   Section 20(2) contemplates two types of case: first, where the property (and hence the risk) has passed to the buyer, as presumptively it does

---

114   *Canterbury Seed Co. Ltd v JG Ward Farmers' Association Ltd* (1895) 13 NZLR 96. See also A. Hudson 'Conformity of Goods on Passing of Risk' in D. Feldman and F. Meisel (eds), *Corporate and Commercial Law* (Lloyd's of London Press, 1996).

115   The fire occurred four days after the buyers' letter failed unequivocally to state a rejection of the goods. In the court's opinion, n. 114 above, 110: 'Until the vendors were informed of the election so to divest [the property, consequent upon rejection] they would not be expected to insure the goods or be justified in dealing with them.'

116   But see *Vitol SA v Esso Australia Ltd (The Wise)*, n. 112 above (where the seller would not be left without insurance cover).

117   This provision does not apply where the buyer deals as a consumer. In this case, the goods remain at the seller's risk until delivery takes place: s. 20(4). There is no just reason why the buyer should be favoured in this way, unless the provision recognizes implicitly that the seller may have and should have insurance cover whilst the goods are in his possession.

with specific goods at the date of the contract,[118] but the buyer has been prevented by a defaulting seller from taking delivery; and secondly, where the property in the goods (and hence the risk) remain with the seller, who is unable to pass the property by unconditional appropriation to the buyer because of the latter's delay.[119] There is little case law. Both examples of the provision would seem to be most necessary in a legal system that links together risk and property indissolubly, which is not the case under the Sale of Goods Act. The first example is also of reduced significance because of the modern judicial reluctance to hold that the property in specific goods passes before delivery.[120] It has, nevertheless, been applied where a c.i.f. seller interferes with the discharge by the carrier of goods to the buyer.[121] Even though a c.i.f. contract does not as such require the seller to 'deliver' the goods to the buyer,[122] the bill of lading contract, under which the buyer acquires rights against the carrier, does indeed require the carrier to deliver the goods to the buyer,[123] and the seller who persuades the carrier not to do so is guilty of delaying delivery to the buyer.

Seller as owner. The second case dealt with by section 20(2) was applied in **4.32** *Demby Hamilton & Co. Ltd v Barden*,[124] which concerned the delivery by instalments of apple juice sold by sample and a buyer who was at fault in not issuing delivery instructions. The great difficulty of complying with the sample except by furnishing each instalment from the same bulk led the court to the conclusion that the buyer could not delay the seller in the expectation that stocks on hand would be sold to other buyers and the buyer's demands met from stocks newly manufactured by the seller. There had, in effect, been an appropriation of a particular bulk to the contract, though, because of non-ascertainment, the property had not, and could not have, passed in the undelivered instalments. Consequently, when the balance of the contract quantity became putrid, the buyer bore the loss. A difficult case to defend is the Canadian case which left on the seller the risk of loss where, had the buyer taken timely delivery, the agreed horses would have been somewhere other than the place where they contracted the disease that killed them.[125]

---

[118] S. 18, Rule 1, in conjunction with s. 20(1).

[119] A related provision here is s. 37(1), which applies where the buyer has not within a reasonable time responded to the seller's request to take delivery (see Ch. 6). The defaulting buyer is 'liable to the seller for any loss occasioned by his neglect or refusal to take delivery'.

[120] See Ch. 3 above.

[121] *Gatoil International Inc. v Tradax Petroleum Ltd* [1985] 1 Lloyd's Rep. 350.

[122] See *Congimex Cia Geral SARL v Tradax Export SA* [1983] 1 Lloyd's Rep. 250; see also Bridge, n. 63 above, 126–7.

[123] See Ch. 6 below.

[124] [1949] 1 All ER 435; see also the extension in *Gillespie v Hamm* (1899) 4 Terr. LR 78 (Can.: delay in payment by conditional buyer in possession).

[125] *Collins v Wilson* [1922] 3 WWR 1086. If the disease was caused by the neglect of the seller, then s. 20(3) or a common law extension of it (see below) should be applied.

4.33 **Specific goods and specific bulks.**   Section 20(2) is therefore most likely to be applied to specific goods or to unascertained goods in a larger bulk, the bulk having been specific at the date of the contract or ascertained by subsequent appropriation. The provision recognizes, by transferring only that portion of the risk attributable to delay, that the risk may be divided between seller and buyer.[126] If the risk is displaced under section 20(2), it does not merely release from his obligations the party freed from the risk. This party may also sue for the price or damages for non-acceptance (if he is the seller), or sue to recover the price or damages for non-delivery (if he is the buyer).[127] In the latter case, the seller is unlikely to be assisted by the frustration defence since the loss or damage will be the product of his own culpable delay.[128]

4.34 **Bailee's liability.**   Section 20(3) preserves the responsibility of the buyer or seller as bailee notwithstanding the allocation of risk elsewhere in the section.[129] The bailee of goods must take reasonable care of them and bears the burden of demonstrating that such care has been taken.[130] This provision will certainly apply where possession is transferred or retained for purposes collateral to the contract of sale.[131] More loosely, section 20(3), or an equivalent common law principle,[132] will apply wherever there is a separation of possession and risk under a contract of sale. The result in section 20(3) can sometimes be reached by other means. For example, the risk of loss to goods in the seller's possession may, because of the buyer's delay, have been transferred under section 20(2). In this case, the answer to the problem of the careless seller/owner can be found in the words of section 20(2) itself: the loss or damage to the goods cannot be attributed to the buyer who delays taking delivery. Further, suppose that, under section 20(1), the risk has passed to the buyer but not yet the property. The seller's quality and fitness obligations

---

[126] For another example of divided risk, see *Rugg v Minett* (1809) 11 East 210. See also *Petromec Inc v Petroleo Brasiliero SA Petrobas (No. 1)* [2003] EWHC 179 (Comm), affirmed [2004] EWCA Civ 156; [2004] 1 Lloyd's Rep. 629 (series of sales and charters of oil platform, culminating in sub-bareboat charter, with payments to be made according to a discounting formula if platform became a total loss).

[127] *Allied Mills Ltd v Gwydir Valley Oilseeds Pty Ltd* [1978] 2 NSWLR 26.

[128] *Joseph Constantine Steamship Line Ltd v Imperial Smelting Corpn Ltd* [1942] AC 154.

[129] Section 20(4) states that s. 20(3) 'must be ignored' where the buyer deals as a consumer and that the seller retains the risk until 'delivery to the consumer' takes place. The reference in s. 20(4) to s. 20(3) is odd because s. 20(3) does not need to be ignored to effectuate s. 20(4). There is no conflict between the two provisions.

[130] *Travers & Sons v Cooper* [1915] 1 KB 73, 90 (Kennedy LJ); *Brook's Wharf and Bull Wharf v Goodman Bros* [1937] 1 KB 534, 538–39; *Houghland v RR Low (Luxury Coaches) Ltd* [1962] 1 QB 695; *Port Swettenham Authority v TW Wu & Co. Sd. Bhd.* [1979] AC 580 (Malaysian Contracts Ordinance); *Sutcliffe v Chief Constable of West Yorkshire* [1996] RTR 86.

[131] *Wiehe v Dennis Bros* (1913) 29 TLR 250: the sellers retained a Shetland pony called 'Tiny' so it could continue to collect for 'Our Dumb Friends League' at the Olympia Horse Show.

[132] The seller retaining the general property in the goods cannot aptly be regarded as a bailee for the buyer.

should prevail over the transfer of risk and prevent him from charging the buyer with the consequences of his own carelessness; he may also be liable in damages for non-delivery or defective delivery.

Risk and Third-party Tortfeasors

Right of action against third party. A buyer to whom the risk of loss or damage **4.35** is transferred will suffer the effect of tortious damage committed by third parties for whom the seller is not responsible. It is well settled that the buyer who bears the risk, but has neither property nor possession, has an insurable interest in the goods.[133] But such a buyer has very real difficulties in suing the third party in tort. The tort of trespass requires the claimant to have been in possession of the goods at the time the third party interferes with them, while a claimant suing in conversion must have had either possession or the right to immediate possession at the time of the wrongful act.[134] For negligence, the claimant must have either the property or possession.[135] Unlike conversion, where damages are usually calculated according to the value of the goods at the date of conversion,[136] damages in negligence will measure the actual injury suffered by the claimant. These should, however, come to the full value of the goods, notwithstanding the claimant having only the possession but not the property, if the claimant bears the risk as between himself and the other party to a contract of sale.[137]

Actions against carriers. The question of risk and standing to sue in tort poses **4.36** the greatest problems in the area of ocean transport where the carrier is guilty of losing, damaging, or misdelivering the goods. To accommodate c.i.f. and related contracts, provision was made by the Bills of Lading Act 1855 for the statutory transfer to the buyer of the benefits and burdens of the contract of carriage taken out by the seller.[138] Because this transfer took place in narrowly defined circumstances, and the law on the subject was not reformed until the Carriage of Goods Act 1992, it meant that a buyer who could not sue the carrier for breach of contract was driven instead to seek an action in tort. In *Margarine Union GmbH v Cambay Prince Steamship Co. Ltd*,[139] the buyer of goods to whom the risk had passed was denied an action in negligence when the carrier transported copra in an unfumigated vessel. At the time of the carrier's wrongdoing, the buyer had no

---

[133] *Inglis v Stock* (1885) 10 App. Cas. 263; *The Parchim* [1918] AC 157.

[134] See M. Bridge, *Personal Property Law* (3rd edn, Clarendon Law, 2002), Ch. 3.

[135] *Leigh and Sillavan Ltd v Aliakmon Shipping Ltd* [1986] AC 785.

[136] *General & Finance Facilities Ltd v Cook's Cars (Romford) Ltd* [1963] 1 WLR 644.

[137] *Quaere* the effect of the defendant's ability to plead the *ius tertii* in consequence of s. 8 of the Torts (Interference with Goods) Act 1977?

[138] S. 1.

[139] [1969] 1 QB 219. Assumed to be correct in *Karlshamns Oljefabriker v Eastport Navigation Co. Ltd (The Elafi)* [1982] 1 All ER 208.

proprietary interest in the copra. The law of tort, apart from exceptional cases, will not permit the recovery of damages for economic loss, such as that suffered by a buyer in having to pay the seller the price of lost or damaged goods. Nevertheless, the risk-bearing c.i.f. buyer was permitted to recover in *Schiffhart & Kohlen GmbH v Chelsea Maritime Ltd*[140] on the ground that a c.i.f. buyer was within the reasonable contemplation of the negligent carrier and there were no reasons of a policy nature to preclude recovery.

4.37 **Retrenchment.** As part of a general clampdown on recovery in the tort of negligence for economic loss, the House of Lords in *Leigh and Sillavan Ltd v Aliakmon Shipping Ltd*[141] refused an action to the risk-bearing buyer and signalled in the most emphatic terms a return to *Margarine Union*. In the Court of Appeal,[142] where the buyer was similarly denied, it had been emphasized by the majority that allowing the buyer to sue the carrier in tort would permit him to evade the limitations on liability imposed by the Hague Rules for contract actions against carriers,[143] and would disturb the economic balance between the relations of buyer and seller and of carrier and cargo-owner.[144] In the House of Lords, the buyer was sacrificed in the general interest of certainty of tort liability. The court was attracted by the prospect of a bright line separating liability and immunity in tort, and it saw such a line in the rule denying economic loss recovery to a claimant in consequence of property damage caused by the defendant to a third party.

4.38 **Transfer of bill of lading and property.** The buyer in *Leigh and Sillivan* was unable to sue in contract under the Bills of Lading Act 1855, because the bill of lading had been indorsed in favour of and delivered to the buyer, not to transfer the general property, but to permit the buyer as agent for the seller to collect and warehouse the goods at the port of discharge. The buyer and seller had initially contracted on c. & f. terms before varying their contract to provide for delivery *ex* warehouse on arrival of the goods. Consistently with the contract being initially a c.& f. contract, the risk of damage in transit remained upon the buyer notwithstanding the variation. In the court's view, the buyer at the moment of variation ought to have secured an assignment of the seller's contract rights against the carrier or else an undertaking by the seller to sue the carrier on behalf of the buyer in the event of damage to the cargo. There was not truly any gap in the law that had to be filled by an extension of tort liability since the buyer could have obtained

---

[140] [1982] QB 481, followed in *The Nea Tyhi* [1982] 1 Lloyd's Rep. 608.

[141] n. 135 above.

[142] [1985] QB 350.

[143] The same limitations are imposed by the Hague–Visby Rules (Art. IV *bis*(1)) in the case of tort actions against carriers. Although the report in *Aliakmon Shipping* does not say so, the country of shipment (South Korea) was not a party to the Brussels Convention adopting the Visby amendments.

[144] n. 142 above, 367 and 397.

protection from contract law. Furthermore, the House of Lords refused to accede even to a duty of care made subject to the carrier's contractual defences against the seller contained in the bill of lading.

Carrier's immunity.   As much as one sympathizes with the court's yearning for **4.39** simple law, the result gives the carrier a windfall immunity. It also imposes an unrealistically high standard of legal circumspection on international traders in unusual circumstances demanding rapid action. If the immunity of negligent stevedores is predicated upon the integral nature of contracts involved in the distribution and carriage of goods overseas,[145] it is difficult to see why this integrality should not also be recognized in the interest of buyers in circumstances like those arising in *Leigh and Sillavan Ltd v Aliakmon Shipping Ltd.*[146] The opening up, by the Carriage of Goods by Sea Act 1992, of contractual actions against the carrier to a wide range of buyers[147] is designed to prevent problems of this kind from arising in the future. Nevertheless, if there are gaps in the coverage of the Act,[148] experience in this area of commercial activity shows they will be discovered in litigation sooner rather than later.

Frustration

General.   Frustration deals with contracts that have become impossible, whether **4.40** factually or commercially, to perform and with contracts that may no longer be performed because supervening illegality, not present at the time they were concluded, prevents their being performed. Despite the similarity between discharge for breach and discharge for frustration, in respect of the degree of impairment of the expectation of the party awaiting performance, the effect of a frustrating event is that the contract is automatically discharged. Since the doctrine of frustration operates within a narrow compass, and does not extend to very many cases where commercial practicality and expectation supports relief from performance, it is common practice for *force majeure* and similar clauses to expand the circumstances in which relief, whether temporary or permanent, might be given.[149] *Force majeure*

---

[145] *New Zealand Shipping Co. Ltd v AM Satterthwaite & Co. Ltd (The Eurymedon)* [1975] AC 154.

[146] n. 135 above.

[147] The most striking feature of s. 2(1) of the Act is that the right to sue the carrier is unhitched from the passing of property. It may be exercised by the holder of a bill of lading, by the person to whom delivery is to be made under a non-negotiable sea waybill, and by the holder of a ship's delivery order.

[148] See S. Baughen [1994] *JBL* 62. The Act does not apply where shipment is effected under the terms of a mate's receipt which is not superseded by a later document, or where goods are shipped under a bill of lading which is later lost.

[149] There may be particular reasons why a *force majeure* clause is not used. In long-term oil and gas sales, a distinction is drawn between a supply agreement and a depletion agreement. In the

clauses are very much tailored for the particular type of contract. Although it may rightly be said that a failure to take account of them gives an unbalanced account of the circumstances in which contracting parties are relieved from performing contracts, *force majeure* clauses cannot be considered as an undifferentiated whole, though certain common features may be observed.

4.41 **Sale of Goods Act.** The Sale of Goods Act treats explicitly only a small portion of the law on frustration of contracts. The relevant provision is section 7: 'Where there is an agreement to sell specific goods and subsequently the goods, without any fault on the part of seller or buyer, perish before the risk passes to the buyer, the agreement is avoided.'[150] There are no reported cases bearing directly upon the section. It applies only to agreements to sell specific goods. When section 18, Rule 1, was applied less flexibly than it is now, the presumptive contract for specific goods was a sale and not an agreement to sell, since the property in the goods was considered to pass at the date of the contract. Moreover, section 7 treats only one supervening event, namely, the perishing of the goods. This includes both the physical destruction of the goods and any drastic change that alters their commercial identity.[151] Section 7 does not deal with unascertained goods, nor, probably, with unascertained goods from a specific bulk. Even if the seller is able to tender goods differing in no material respect from the agreed specific goods, he may not do so: specific goods are unique and irreplaceable, even if their exact counterparts can be found elsewhere.

Frustration and Risk

4.42 **Relationship of risk to frustration.** As section 7 is formulated, its relationship to risk is unclear. Risk in section 20 is directed mainly to the question whether the buyer has to pay the price, whereas frustration usually answers the question whether the seller, unable to make a conforming tender of goods, is released from paying damages to the buyer. If the risk remains with the seller by virtue of section 20(1), it should not be assumed that the parties intended that the seller should answer to the buyer for the accident to the goods. Risk has two meanings that ought not to be confused: first, the statutory meaning in the Sale of Goods

---

former, the oil and gas is not sourced from a particular place and the supplier is not protected by a *force majeure* clause. In the latter, the supplies come from a particular field whose quantities can only be estimated and which is to be exhausted. In depletion contracts, it is the practice to have a *force majeure* clause: see *Shell UK Ltd v Commissioners for Her Majesty's Revenue and Customs* [2007] UKSPC SPC00624 at [56].

[150] See the criticisms of the Ontario Law Reform Commission, n. 35 above, ii, 366–8.

[151] For the meaning of which, see the insurance case of *Asfar & Co. Ltd v Blundell* [1896] 1 QB 123, where the dates at the bottom of the river could no longer be described as dates and could only be used for distilling industrial alcohol. See also *Turnbull v Rendell* (1908) 27 NZLR 1067 (where the seller should have been held to warrant that 'table potatoes' were still capable of answering that description).

Act that determines whether the buyer should still pay despite the accident to the goods; and secondly, the meaning it has when the contract upon its construction visits the harsh consequences of an event more or less upon the designated risk-bearer. The Sale of Goods Act is only concerned with the *transfer* of risk and the effect this has upon the buyer's obligations. It does not deal with the broader reaches of contractual risk-allocation. If the contract were explicitly to place the risk of loss upon the seller, this would go beyond the limited effect of section 20(1), which is that the risk would not have passed to the buyer. The contractual clause may well signify the parties' intention that the seller shall be liable in damages for an inability to tender conforming goods; the statutory provision merely entails that the buyer need not pay the price.

Buyer on risk. A related question concerns the buyer to whom the risk of loss **4.43** has passed. Section 7 is explicitly excluded in this case. The clear implication is that the contract would not be frustrated if the goods perished in the circumstances covered by section 7. If, however, the contract were held to be frustrated upon the perishing of the goods, the transfer of risk would still be effective to a degree, but it would be confined to damage or loss falling outside the notion of perishing in section 7. This is, if not an impossible construction of sections 7 and 20(1), at least an unlikely one. Where the buyer has both risk and possession, the above implication that the buyer bears the loss is even stronger and where, in addition to these two, the buyer also has the general property, the implication that the contract remains on foot is irresistible.

Events outside section 7. If the supervening event is one with which section 7 **4.44** is not concerned, such as a governmental embargo on trading or a requisition of goods,[152] risk in the Sale of Goods Act sense will not provide a solution to the problem where it remains with the seller. In some cases, it may not solve the problem where the risk has been transferred to the buyer. If the doctrine of risk does not determine the incidence of liability, the contractual liability of the buyer or seller will be determined by ordinary principles of contractual construction and frustration. In *Kursell v Timber Operators and Contractors Ltd*,[153] the contract was for the sale of all the trees of stated dimensions in a Latvian forest. The forest was nationalized and the court concluded that the property (and therefore also the risk) in the trees had not passed to the buyer since the trees were not in a deliverable state under section 18, Rule 1. In consequence, the contract was held to be frustrated. Even if the property, and seemingly also the risk, had passed,

---

[152] Governmental requisition was treated as perishing 'in a sense' in *Re Shipton, Anderson & Co. and Harrison & Co.* [1915] 3 KB 676, where the problem was solved by the court construing the particular contract. Governmental acts are invariably made the subject of express *force majeure* and prohibition of export clauses in international commodities contracts.

[153] [1927] 1 KB 298.

Scrutton LJ was of the view that the doctrine of frustration would still operate given that so much remained to be done under the contract. The contract had a full fifteen years to run, during which the buyer was to have had the use of the seller's sawmill and plant when felling the trees. If this view is correct, it would surely govern only in exceptional circumstances like those in *Kursell*.

Frustration and Fault

4.45 **Effect of fault.**   Section 7 does not apply where specific goods perish owing to the fault of buyer or seller. As seen above, the fault of either party in delaying delivery will subject that party to the risk arising from the delay.[154] Where this results in the transfer of the risk of loss to the buyer, both his fault and the transfer of risk will prevent the implementation of section 7. Where the seller is responsible for the delay, his fault blocks the application of the section. In neither case should the party at fault be able to take comfort from general contractual principles, for there is no relief given for self-induced frustration.[155] Delay, as provided for by section 20(2), should be considered as fault in section 7 whenever delivery is not taken or made at the contractually agreed time, whether this is a fixed date or a reasonable period.

4.46 **Seller's and buyer's liability.**   If the seller is negligent in losing or damaging the goods in his possession, he should be liable in damages for non-delivery. Any argument that liability ought to be in the tort of negligence founders if the buyer did not have the property in the goods at the time.[156] If the negligence is that of the buyer in possession, the buyer should have to pay the price if the risk or the property has passed. If neither has passed, then one possibility is that the buyer will be liable in damages for non-acceptance. This depends upon treating a buyer who refuses to pay as having infringed his section 27 obligation to 'accept and pay for' the goods. Acceptance by the buyer, in other words, would be complete only upon payment and the buyer would be amenable to a damages claim by the seller for non-acceptance under section 50 if he refused to pay. The alternative possibility is that the buyer is liable to pay damages for negligence. If the goods are a total loss as a result of the buyer's negligence, it is likely that the price and the contractual and tortious measures of damages will all yield the same or approximately the same sum.[157]

---

[154] S. 20(2).

[155] *Joseph Constantine Steamship Line Ltd v Imperial Smelting Corpn Ltd* [1942] AC 154.

[156] See discussion in the text accompanying nn. 133 *et seq*. above.

[157] An indemnity and an expectation valuation of the article will produce different results only in the case of non-market items: L. L. Fuller and A. Perdue (1936) 46 *Yale LJ* 52.

Frustration and Quality Obligations

Relationship of frustration and quality obligations. Another difficulty **4.47**
concerns the relationship between the seller's fitness and quality obligations (in
section 14)[158] and section 7. In *Horn v Minister of Food*,[159] a farmer agreed to sell
a specific clamp of potatoes, thirty-three tons in weight, on terms providing for
delivery instructions over a five–seven-month period starting from the contract
date. The contract recognized that the potatoes would suffer some deterioration
but imposed a duty on the seller to cover them so as to minimize that deterioration. When a seam of rot was discovered in the potatoes some five months after the
contract date, the buyers refused to give delivery instructions. The seller's action
against the buyers[160] succeeded since, though the goods were not of merchantable
quality, the parties had by their agreement substituted for this obligation a duty
on the seller to take reasonable care of the potatoes, which had been duly
performed. The court might equally have said that the risk of post-contract deterioration had been transferred contractually to the buyers, although the property
was to pass only upon delivery. It had to rule out section 7 to reach the result it did,
on the questionable ground that, though all thirty-three tons of potatoes had
rotted before delivery, the potatoes were still potatoes and so could not be said to
have perished.[161] A better view, it is submitted, was that the outright destruction
of the potatoes was at the risk of the buyers owing to their delay in giving delivery
instructions, section 20(2) thus overriding section 7 because of the buyers' fault.
Alternatively, the court might have said simply that the parties had displayed a
contrary intention ousting section 7.[162]

Deterioration and seller's risk. Apart from special facts like those in *Horn*, deteri- **4.48**
oration in perishable goods between the contract date and delivery is likely to be
at the risk of the seller, who will consequently be liable for supplying unfit or
unsatisfactory goods. Where there is accidental loss or destruction of specific
goods for reasons not connected with natural decaying processes, the seller should
normally be able to invoke the frustration principle in section 7, or an equivalent
common law provision.[163]

---

[158] See Ch. 7 below.
[159] [1948] 2 All ER 1036.
[160] It seems to have been for the price, though it is not easy to see how the seller qualified for the
right to sue for the price under s. 49.
[161] Cf n. 151 above.
[162] Assuming it may be excluded: see discussion on s. 6 below.
[163] If the goods have not perished.

Section 7 and Foresight

4.49 **Effect of foreseeability.**   Nothing in section 7 precludes its application simply because the risk of perishing was foreseen by the parties at the contract date. Just because a risk is foreseen does not mean that the parties have implicitly agreed that the seller shall bear responsibility for it.[164] A failure to make explicit provision for an event may signify hope that it will not occur or an inability to reach agreement about it. But it may also in some cases amount to an implicit allocation of risk ousting the application of the doctrine of frustration. For example, a seller who undertakes to sell a herd of cattle, despite a nearby outbreak of foot-and-mouth disease, to a distant buyer unaware of the disease, should, if the cattle become infected or are slaughtered, be prevented from relying upon section 7 and compelled to pay damages for non-delivery. Section 7 could, with a little difficulty, be treated as impliedly excluded. In such a case, a court is very unlikely to conclude both that the property in the herd passed at the contract date to the buyer under section 18, Rule 1, and that the risk passed simultaneously under section 20.

Partial and Temporary Frustration

4.50 **Automatic discharge.**   The orthodox position, enacted by section 7, is that frustration operates automatically to discharge both parties prospectively from the contract. The effect of frustration is therefore visited upon the whole contract and not just upon the particular obligation affected by the outside event. A different approach would be to exempt from liability in damages the party whose performance is affected, whilst the other party would be able to oppose that non-performance to his own duty to perform and, in a sufficiently serious case, claim the right to terminate the contract.[165] This approach has not been taken by English law. This is unfortunate in that it denies flexibility to a court where the impossibility of performance is only temporary or partial in effect. If the seller cannot deliver the whole of the agreed specific goods because a portion has perished, why should not the buyer be able to demand delivery, even if the seller is in no position to demand acceptance of the remainder? If a contract calls for the delivery of the goods on a certain date and a governmental embargo of temporary duration prevents delivery on that date, why should not either party, even in the absence of contractual provision, demand performance when the embargo is lifted on the ground that the contract has only been suspended?[166] If suspension were

---

[164] *Ocean Tramp Tankers Corpn. v VO Sovfracht (The Eugenia)* [1964] 2 QB 226.

[165] See Art. 79 of the Vienna Convention on the International Sale of Goods Convention 1980. Where it is the seller, for example, who is exempted under this provision, the buyer will in an appropriate case still claim avoidance of the contract for fundamental breach under Art. 25.

[166] On suspension generally, see J. Carter 'Suspending Contract Performance for Breach' in J. Beatson and D. Friedmann (eds), *Good Faith and Fault in Contract Law* (OUP, London, 1995).

permitted at common law, this might depend upon whether the time of delivery was of the essence of the contract. The principle that frustration automatically discharges contracts receives its strongest expression from a line of cases on supervening illegality, where public policy prevented either party from demanding partial or delayed performance of the contract.[167] The justification for applying this rule to other cases of frustration is not self-evident.

Difficulties with automatic discharge.   The drawbacks to the orthodox position can be seen in two decisions dealing with the partial perishing of future goods to be derived from a specific location, a case that falls outside section 7. In *Howell v Coupland*,[168] a farmer agreed to sell '200 tons of regent potatoes grown on land belonging to [the farmer] in Whaplode'. When the contract was made, twenty-five of the Whaplode acres had been sown with potatoes and the remaining forty-three acres were later sown. A disease subsequently attacked the crop, through no fault of the farmer. The eighty tons of potatoes that were produced were delivered to the buyer who nevertheless brought an action for non-delivery of the remaining 120 tons. The Court of Appeal found an implied condition precedent to the farmer's duty to deliver that the potatoes should not have been destroyed for reasons beyond the control of the farmer: 'It was not an absolute contract of delivery under all circumstances, but a contract to deliver so many potatoes, of a particular kind, grown on a specific place, if deliverable from that place.'[169]

4.51

Construction of contract.   A notable feature of the decision is the room it leaves for the construction of the contact. If the potatoes had been damaged rather than destroyed by the disease, again through no fault of the farmer, they would not have been in a deliverable state, so the farmer would not be liable for non-delivery or able to insist that the buyer take them in their damaged state. No issue arose as to the buyer's or seller's right to insist on delivery of the eighty tons grown, for delivery had already occurred. In the court below,[170] Blackburn J said there was an implied term of the contract that each party should be free if the crop perished. If the contract were entire and indivisible, this would mean that neither party could have compelled delivery of the eighty tons. If the contract, however, could be interpreted to require delivery of a part crop, then the farmer would only have been *pro tanto* released by the supervening event. The buyer would not have been entitled to demand 120 tons of potatoes from another source. The clear description given in the contract to the potatoes would have precluded that.

4.52

---

[167] *Hirji Mulji v Cheong Yue Steamship Co. Ltd* [1926] AC 497; *Bank Line Ltd v Arthur Capel & Co.* [1919] AC 435; *Tamplin Steamship Co. Ltd v Anglo-Mexican Petroleum Co.* [1916] 2 AC 397. On partial and temporary frustration, see G. H. Treitel, *Frustration and Force Majeure* (Sweet & Maxwell, London, 1994), Ch. 5.

[168] (1874) LR 9 QB 462, affirmed (1876) 1 QBD 258.

[169] *Ibid.* 261.

[170] n. 168 above.

4.53 **Seller's duty to deliver lesser quantity.** The seller's duty to deliver the lesser quantity was clarified nearly one-hundred years later in *HR & S Sainsbury Ltd v Street*,[171] which concerned a contract for the whole of the 1970 harvest of feed barley, estimated by the parties at 'about 275 tons', to be grown on the defendant's farm. In a bad harvest, only 140 tons were grown and the farmer wished to be released from the contract to find another buyer for his barley at the higher prevailing market rate. The buyer, disclaiming any right to sue for short delivery, recovered damages for non-delivery of the barley actually grown. According to the court, section 7 did not apply for it dealt only with goods existing at the contract date. Rather, the relevant provision was section 5(2), which states that '[t]here may be a contract for the sale of goods the acquisition of which by the seller depends on a contingency'. Nevertheless, this provision was almost certainly drawn to prevent contracts to sell future goods from being treated as unlawful wagers on commodity prices, and to allow parties to buy and sell goods on an arrival basis.[172] A better approach would be to admit the common law under section 62(2) and construe the contract to reach the result.

4.54 **Buyer's option or obligation?** The court's decision, that the buyer could call for delivery of the reduced crop, is not clear whether this is a matter of option or obligation on the buyer's part,[173] although the market price made it an option that any buyer would want to exercise. The court constructed an implied condition from 'the presumed intention of reasonable men' that the buyer was entitled to delivery. Presumably, if there had been a glut leading to a fall in the market, the same presumed intention should have permitted the seller to call on the buyer to accept at the contract price a harvest in excess of 275 tons.[174] The decision is to be welcomed for admitting the flexibility that comes with construction of the contract and for not holding that the contract was automatically frustrated. The common law of frustration surrenders more easily to the contrary intention of the parties than does the unyielding language of section 7.

4.55 **Delayed performance.** A similar constructive approach could be applied to delayed performance. Since the common law does not rewrite contracts, it will not impose a suspension on contracting parties where no warrant exists for this in the contract.[175] In commercial sales contracts, the time of delivery is normally of

---

[171] [1972] 1 WLR 834.

[172] See *Hale v Rawson* (1858) 4 CB(NS) 85.

[173] Cf UCC Art. 2–613(b) (buyer's option).

[174] If the estimate were the seller's, there would probably be an implied term that it be a reasonable one.

[175] *Sanschagrin v Echo Flour Mills Co.* [1922] 3 WWR 694 (Can.). Contractual suspension is a common feature of *force majeure* clauses in international commodity sales forms: see M. Bridge, 'The 1973 Mississippi Floods: "Force Majeure" and Export Prohibition' in E. McKendrick (ed.), *Force Majeure and Frustration of Contract* (2nd edn, LLP, 1995).

the essence of the contract.[176] The buyer may, however, waive timely performance by the seller,[177] in which case the seller may not insist the contract is discharged for his own breach.[178] Where the delay is due to causes for which the seller is not responsible, it may be that contractual performance by the seller is impossible, even though the contract is not frustrated according to the stringent common law test. There may be, for example, a condition of a particular contract that the goods be put on rail on a stated date and, owing to industrial action, the cancellation of rail services on that date. In such a case, even though time is of the essence, the buyer ought to be able, though not bound, to waive timely performance, while the seller has a defence to an action for damages for late delivery.[179] Eventually, either a temporary restraint upon performance will be lifted or the delay will mature into a frustrating delay.[180] On the construction of some contracts, it might be possible to say that time is not of the essence, or that the performance period is elastic, where the delay is due to events for which the seller is not contractually responsible.[181] In such a case, the seller would also be entitled to insist that the contract remain on foot.

Price apportionment and instalment delivery.   Partial frustration can emerge in **4.56** another guise too. Suppose specific goods are to be delivered in more than one instalment, payment to occur after all deliveries have been made. After some instalments have been delivered, the remainder perish in a frustrating incident before the risk passes to the buyer. In the perhaps unlikely event of the contract being construed as entire and indivisible, delivery in full is a condition precedent to the buyer's duty to pay the price, which leaves no room for apportioning the price under the contract. If still in possession of the goods, the buyer has the option under section 30(1) of the Sale of Goods Act of rejecting them or retaining and paying for them at the contract rate.[182] This provision, which enacts a form of implied contract on *quantum valebant* terms, avoids the need to consider whether retaining the goods is a matter of option or obligation for the buyer, a point not clarified by the law on partial frustration.[183] If the goods have been disposed of or consumed by the buyer before the frustrating incident, section 30(1) would not apply, since it contemplates the buyer accepting the goods notwithstanding the

---

176 See Ch. 6 below.

177 *Charles Rickards Ltd v Oppenhaim* [1950] 1 KB 616.

178 Discharge is at the injured buyer's election: *Photo Production Ltd v Securicor Transport Ltd* [1980] AC 827.

179 See G. H. Treitel, *The Law of Contract* (12th edn, by E. Peel, Sweet & Maxwell, 2007), 931–3, for a discussion of cases of temporary unavailability of the subject matter of the contract.

180 *Jackson v Union Marine Insurance Co. Ltd* (1875) LR 10 CP 125.

181 e.g., *Brenner v Consumers Metal Co.* (1917) 41 OLR 534 (Can.: delivery 'as soon as possible').

182 There is no good reason to confine this provision to cases of breach of contract.

183 See discussion of *Sainsbury v Street*, n. 171 above.

short delivery. Nor would there be any scope for section 1(3) of the Law Reform (Frustrated Contracts) Act 1943 which, upon a frustration of the contract, requires the recipient of a 'valuable benefit' to pay a 'just sum', since the Act has no application to contracts for specific goods frustrated by the perishing of the goods.[184] The provisions of the Act could, however, apply to other frustrating events, such as governmental requisition,[185] in which event payment at the contract rate is probably the most likely outcome. As for the case where a portion of the specific goods perish, whether or not the contract as a whole is sufficiently disturbed for it to be frustrated, a court seeking a just result is likely to make a restitutionary award based upon the contract rate.

4.57 **Payment exceeding buyer benefit.** The same case of specific goods where a part of the goods perish also causes difficulties if the buyer has paid a portion or the whole of the agreed price in excess of any benefit received before the event destroying the remainder of the goods. On the face of it, the buyer is not able to demonstrate the total failure of consideration needed to support an action for money had and received. It has nevertheless been argued that the effect of the risk being on the seller means that the seller cannot retain a sum in excess of the benefit conferred upon the buyer.[186] It is doubtful that so much can be read into the fact that the risk has not yet passed to the buyer,[187] but predictable that a modern court will strive to avoid an unjustified enrichment of the seller and fashion a result akin to what could have been achieved under the 1943 Act had it been applicable.[188]

4.58 **Pro-rating goods in short supply.** The final problem arising out of partial frustration concerns the seller of goods from a specific bulk or location who, owing to a supervening event such as governmental requisition or prohibition of export, has not or cannot procure sufficient goods of the contract description to satisfy all of his contractual commitments. May the seller fulfil those contracts that he can, pleading that the remainder are frustrated? Or is the seller obliged to perform the contracts in order of seniority? Or may or must the seller apportion such goods as he has or can procure amongst all of his outstanding contracts? There is high

---

[184] S. 2(5)(c). Or to specific goods contracts where the risk has passed to the buyer or indeed to any contracts to which s. 7 of the Sale of Goods Act applies.

[185] Provided the risk has not passed to the buyer: *ibid*.

[186] Atiyah, n. 29 above, 367. *Aliter* Treitel, n. 179 above, 1141–2.

[187] See the discussion on risk above.

[188] A number of authorities sanction the recovery of a part of the prepaid price where the consideration has partly failed, as where the seller fails to deliver all of the agreed goods or where the buyer rejects some of the goods for misdescription. See *Devaux v Connolly* (1849) 8 CB 640; *Biggerstaff v Rowatt's Wharf Ltd* [1896] 2 Ch. 93, 100, 105; *Behrend & Co. Ltd v Produce Brokers Co. Ltd* [1920] 3 KB 530, 535; *Ebrahim Dawood Ltd v Heath Ltd* [1961] 2 Lloyd's Rep. 512; *Westdeutsche Landesbank Girozentrale v Islington LBC* [1994] 1 WLR 938. The number of such claims is likely to rise in consequence of the increased rights of partial rejection introduced by the Sale and Supply of Goods Act 1994: see Ch. 10 below.

authority consistent with the view that, if a seller chooses to fulfil some of his contracts in full to the exclusion of the rest, he cannot plead frustration of the contracts he does not perform, since the frustration is self-induced.[189] This places the seller in an invidious position. A series of cases dealing with governmental prohibition of shipment, all based upon contract forms that contain express prohibition clauses, would appear to protect the seller against the self-induced frustration argument and sanction any reasonable behaviour on the seller's part in response to his various legal, as opposed to moral, commitments.[190] This might, depending on the circumstances, involve a *pro rata* allocation amongst all of the seller's contracts.[191] These prohibition clauses did not then and do not now deal in detail with the partly capable seller. The result they support could sensibly extend to all cases, whether or not the contract contains an express clause, where the seller has properly incurred a range of contractual commitments before the supervening event.[192]

Frustration and Unascertained Goods

Availability in the market.   Section 7 does not deal with unascertained goods **4.59** from a specific bulk or with generic goods whose source of supply is delimited by the contract.[193] The orthodox view is that the seller of unascertained goods can always go to market to buy in fresh supplies if the anticipated source dries up.[194] Likewise, a buyer will be unable to plead frustration if the markets he had in mind for distributing the goods become closed to him.[195] Just as a seller is not prevented from buying in merely because of a steep rise in commodity prices,[196] so a buyer

---

[189] *Maritime National Fish Ltd v Ocean Trawlers Ltd* [1935] AC 524; *J Lauritzen AS v Wijsmuller BV (The Super Servant Two)* [1990] 1 Lloyd's Rep. 1.

[190] *Bremer Handelsgesellschaft mbH v Continental Grain Co.* [1983] 1 Lloyd's Rep. 269, 282; *Intertradex SA v Lesieur-Tourteaux SARL* [1977] 2 Lloyd's Rep. 146, 155, [1978] 2 Lloyd's Rep. 509, 513; *Bremer Handelsgesellschaft mbH v Vanden-Avenne Izegem PVBA* [1978] 2 Lloyd's Rep. 109, 115, 128, 131; *Bremer Handelsgesellschaft mbH v C Mackprang Jnr.* [1979] 1 Lloyd's Rep. 221, 224; *Westfälische Centrale Genossenschaft GmbH v Seabright Chemicals Ltd* (unreported), cited in *Bremer Handelsgesellschaft mbH v Continental Grain Co.*, above; *Pancommerce SA v Veecheema BV* [1982] 1 Lloyd's Rep. 645, reversed on other grounds [1983] 2 Lloyd's Rep. 304.

[191] Bridge, n. 175 above.

[192] Cf *The Super Servant Two*, n. 189 above.

[193] e.g. soya bean meal of US origin shipped from a Gulf of Mexico port within a stated period.

[194] *Blackburn Bobbin Co. v TW Allen & Sons* [1918] 2 KB 467; *Exportelisa SA v Giuseppe Figli Soc. Coll.* [1978] 1 Lloyd's Rep. 433. See also *Ross T Smyth & Co. Ltd (Liverpool) v WN Lindsay Ltd (Leith)* [1953] 1 WLR 1289.

[195] *Congimex Cia Geral de Comercia SARL v Tradax Export SA* [1983] 1 Lloyd's Rep. 250 (buyer of goods c.i.f. Lisbon unable to land them could still tranship them or have them oncarried to another country); *Wingold v William Looser & Co. Ltd* [1951] 1 DLR 429; *Atlantic Paper Stock Ltd v St Anne-Nackawic Pulp & Paper Co.* [1976] 1 SCR 580 (Can.).

[196] See *Davis Contractors Ltd v Fareham Urban District Council* [1956] AC 696; *Samuel v Black Lake Asbestos and Chrome Co. Ltd* (1920) 48 OLR 561 (Can.: unprofitability due to increased cost of mineral abstraction).

can always find another market if he incurs the necessary expense or reduces his prices sufficiently. The law of frustration gives relief from impossibility, not economic hardship. If a more generous measure of relief is sought by the parties, then an express clause to that effect should be inserted in the contract.[197]

4.60 **Agreed source of supply.** If, however, the contractually stipulated source of supply cannot provide the goods, as where potatoes were to come from a particular field where the crop failed[198] or flour was to come from a mill that burned,[199] the contract will be frustrated.[200] If the contractually agreed method of shipment or delivery becomes impossible, the contract will also be frustrated.[201] Neither party may unilaterally alter contractual shipment or delivery terms, even if the alteration imposes a lesser burden on the other party.[202] Where a method of shipment or delivery is contemplated by the parties rather than required by the contract, the contract will be frustrated only if its foundation has been altered in a way that satisfies the stringent common law test. One party's factual expectation regarding performance does not constitute the legal basis for performance. For this reason, a c.i.f. Hamburg contract for the sale of a quantity of Sudanese groundnuts shipped from a Red Sea port was held not to be frustrated when the consequence of the closure of the Suez Canal was that the groundnuts had to endure a journey two or three times as long *via* the Cape of Good Hope.[203] The failure of a source of supply contemplated by only one of the parties will not frustrate the contract;[204] where the source is contemplated by both parties, the event will have to satisfy the common law test for frustration.[205]

4.61 **Third-party suppliers.** A particular difficulty is presented when the seller's source of supply is a third-party supplier which itself is prevented from performing

---

[197] See essays by A. Berg, M. Furmston, and E. McKendrick in E. McKendrick (ed.), n. 175 above.

[198] *Howell v Coupland*, n. 168 above.

[199] *Sanschagrin v Echo Flour Mills Co.* [1922] 3 WWR 694 (Can.). See also *Re Badische Co. Ltd* [1921] 2 Ch. 331 (supervening illegality); *E Hulton and Co. Ltd v Chadwick and Taylor Ltd* (1918) 34 TLR 230.

[200] See also *CTI Group Inc. v Transclear SA* [2008] EWCA Civ 856 at [23].

[201] See *Nickoll & Knight v Ashton, Edridge & Co.* [1901] 2 KB 126; *Vancouver Milling & Grain Co. Ltd v CC Ranch Co. Ltd* [1924] 2 DLR 569; *Brenner v Consumers Metal Co.*, n. 181 above.

[202] *Maine Shipping Co. v Sutcliffe* (1918) 87 LJKB 382. *A fortiori* the party whose performance has become impossible cannot be required to provide an alternative and more onerous performance: *Nile Co. for the Export of Crops v H & JM Bennett (Commodities) Ltd* [1986] 1 Lloyd's Rep. 555 (buyer stopped by governmental act from paying cash against documents not bound to open an irrevocable letter of credit instead).

[203] *Tsakiroglou & Co. Ltd v Noblee Thorl GmbH* [1962] AC 93. Cf *Holland American Metal Corpn v Goldblatt* [1953] OR 112 (Can.).

[204] *Blackburn Bobbin Co. v TW Allen & Sons*, n. 194 above ('Finnish birch timber' could have come from existing stocks in England when imports from Finland became impossible).

[205] Cf *Re Badische Co. Ltd* (supervening illegality), n. 199 above; *E Hulton and Co. Ltd v Chadwick and Taylor Ltd, ibid.*

the supply contract. In *CTI Group Inc. v Transclear SA*,[206] the buyers knew that the sellers' ability to obtain a cargo of cement might be impeded by the opposition of a monopolist in the country of import. The sellers made various attempts to procure a cargo but these proved unavailing. Reversing a finding in the tribunal below that the contract of sale had thus become impossible to perform, the court held that that the sellers were liable for non-delivery because they had assumed the risk of a failure of supply. They might have guarded against this risk by entering into a binding contract with suppliers of their own prior to incurring a commitment to the buyers or by making their own obligation to deliver conditional upon the availability to them of goods.[207] The Court of Appeal dismissed the appeal, stressing that mere impossibility of performance was not sufficient in some cases to amount to frustration of the contract.[208] In the court below, the buyers argued in the alternative that the sellers should be held liable because the fault of their own suppliers could be attributed to them under the contract of sale. This argument, however, did not apply on the facts because the sellers had not entered into a binding contract with suppliers of their own, hence there was no supplier fault to be attributed to the sellers. That said, the ground on which the sellers were held liable is in principle preferable to some principle of attributed fault or vicarious liability. The failure of the seller's source of supply in the *CTI* case was a highly foreseeable one, but the impact of foreseeability on the application of the doctrine of frustration is hard to assess.[209] The more foreseeable the risk, the less likely it is that relief will be granted to the seller or buyer as the case may be since the failure of the contract to deal with the matter is likely to be regarded as resting on an implied agreement that the risk of the event occurring should lie where it falls.[210] Even a foreseeable risk, however, might prove to have so much greater an impact on the contract than the parties foresaw that the contract should be discharged for frustration.[211]

Express Clauses

General.   The strict character of the common law doctrine of frustration, allied **4.62** to its unwieldy practical application, make it an unsatisfactory vehicle for dealing with events that disturb the performance of the contract. In addition, though it is

---

[206] [2007] EWHC 2070 (Comm); [2008] All E.R. (Comm) 192, affirmed [2008] EWCA Civ 856.

[207] At both instances, the court relied on *Lebeaupin v Crispin & Co* [1920] 2 K.B. 714, *Re Thornett and Fehr and Yuills Ltd* [1921] 1 K.B. 219, *Intertradex SA v Lesieur Tourteaux SARL* [1978] 2 Lloyd's Rep. 509, and *Atisa SA v Aztec AG* [1983] 2 Lloyd's Rep. 579.

[208] n. 200 above at [14] and [27].

[209] See the discussion of specific goods above.

[210] *Krell v Henry* [1903] 2 KB 740, 752; see also *Larrinaga & Co. v Société Franco-Américaine des Phosphates de Médulla* (1923) 92 LJKB 455.

[211] See *WJ Tatem Ltd v Gamboa* [1939] 1 KB 132.

an improvement on the position at common law, the Law Reform (Frustrated Contracts) Act 1943,[212] whilst establishing useful default rules for dealing with the consequences of frustration in a wide variety of circumstances, cannot of its nature be preferable to express contractual provision tailored to the particular contract.

4.63 *Force majeure* **and prohibition of export.** The standard clauses used in the commodities trades have through successive drafts over many decades refined the description and effects of the stipulated events that disturb the performance of the contract.[213] Taking as an example the *force majeure* clause in GAFTA 100,[214] it exempts the seller from liability for delay in shipping the goods, 'occasioned' by 'Act of God, strike, lockout, riot or civil commotion, combination of workmen, breakdown of machinery, fire, or any cause comprehended in the term "force majeure"'. A seller[215] apprehending delay for any of these reasons is required to serve on the buyer a timely notice stating the reasons for the anticipated delay[216] and, if seeking an extension of the shipment period, a further notice. Where shipment is delayed for thirty days, the buyer has the option of then cancelling the contract, or else the contract is extended for a further thirty days, at the end of which the contract is 'void' if shipment is 'prevented'. It is one thing for the seller's delay to be excused within the sixty-day period and another for the seller to claim avoidance at the end of that period. Ultimately, in those cases where the buyer does not cancel after thirty days—in which case, it would seem, the parties are both released without further liability—the contract is avoided if shipment is 'prevented' by the *force majeure* event. To demonstrate prevention, the seller has a higher bar to negotiate than the one which sets the extension period running in the first place. A seller claiming an extension may, therefore, be unable to claim that the contract has been avoided and will thus be open to a claim by the buyer under the default clause in the contract.[217] Prior to avoidance or not, the *force majeure* clause amounts to a check on the rule that the time of delivery in commercial

---

[212] Discussed below.

[213] For a more extensive treatment of these clauses, see Bridge, n. 63 above, 321–9; Bridge, n. 175 above.

[214] Form 100 of the Grain and Feed Trade Association (a c.i.f contract for the shipment of feeding stuffs in bulk), cl. 19.

[215] The clause in fact provides for notices to be given by shippers, but since c.i.f. contracts commonly occur in string trading conditions, with particular shipments being resold on multiple occasions, subsequent sellers, just as they adopt those shipments that are made when performing subsales, may also adopt a shipper's *force majeure* notice: see *Tradax Export SA v Andre & Cie SA* [1976] 1 Lloyd's Rep. 416, 422.

[216] GAFTA 100 does not state the consequences of failing to serve this notice but the failure to give notice under a prohibition clause was treated as the breach of an intermediate stipulation by the House of Lords in *Bremer Handelsgesellschaft mbH v Vanden-Avenne Izegem PVBA*, n. 190 above.

[217] Cl. 23.

contracts of sale is of the essence of the contract.[218] Neither the clause nor the rest of the contract form makes provision for the consequences of avoidance, except to say that the seller is not liable to pay damages for non-shipment. Furthermore, since contracts of this nature are essentially cash-on-delivery contracts, it is unlikely that the expenses and benefits provisions of the Law Reform (Frustrated Contracts) Act 1943 will be brought into play, with the consequence that any losses will lie where they fall. The effect of avoidance after sixty days should therefore be the same as the effect of cancellation after thirty days. In the case of 'prohibition of export or in any case of executive or legislative act' by the government at the port of shipment that 'restricts shipment',[219] a separate clause provides that the contract shall be cancelled.[220] As with *force majeure*, the seller is required to advise the buyer without delay.[221]

Other cases.   *Force majeure* clauses used in international sales forms outside the   **4.64** commodities markets increasingly use language drawn from the Vienna Convention on the International Sale of Goods 1980 and, before that, Article 2 of the American Uniform Commercial Code, in granting relief from a failure to perform where that failure was due to an impediment beyond the control of the non-performing party, which he could not reasonably have been expected to take into account at the date the contract was concluded and which he was not reasonably able to avoid or overcome. There will frequently be a list of events that might pass the impediment test, and a well-drawn clause will, for the avoidance of doubt, list events that will not give rise to the necessary impediment. The excluded events typically relate to matters within the control of the non-performing party, such as compliance with bureaucratic requirements and the breakdown of a manufacturing seller's machinery, or events in relation to which the non-performing party could have taken precautions, for example, by hedging or by ensuring the continuing availability of raw materials. In the case of long-term supply contracts, *force majeure* clauses are particularly needed to deal with interruptions in instalments, which they may do, for example, by abating the seller's duty to deliver and the buyer's duty to take delivery, to the extent of the contractual disturbance. In addition, they may seek, however successfully, to require the party whose performance is affected to perform by alternative means and they may also provide explicitly for the seller who has a number of contracts to fulfil and who is able to perform all contracts only on a rateable basis. The lesson to draw from the variety of *force*

---

[218] See Ch. 6 below.

[219] The clause provides that a restriction of shipment is deemed to be prevention. The reasons for alleviating the burden on sellers seeking to invoke prohibition are to be found in a series of cases arising out of the Mississippi floods in 1973; see Bridge, n. 175 above.

[220] Cl. 18.

[221] The *force majeure* clause in fact lays down specific periods for the two notices of apprehended and actual delay.

majeure clauses available is that no single clause suits all cases and that the clause itself may provide the basis for negotiation between the parties to deal with the aftermath of a disturbance of the contract. The common law doctrine of frustration is best avoided for any sophisticated or complex contract.

Consequences of Frustration

4.65 **Prospective discharge.** At common law, discharge for frustration operates prospectively so that any loss lies where it falls. Contractual performance due or already rendered remains undisturbed; future liabilities are discharged. Before the landmark decision in *Fibrosa Spolka Akcyjna v Fairbairn Lawson Combe Barbour Ltd*,[222] the law worked against the interest of a prepaying buyer who received no actual benefit before the contract was frustrated. If the buyer sought to recover his money on the ground of a total failure of consideration, he was met with the successful objection that, upon the conclusion of the contract, he did receive something of value, namely, the seller's promise to supply the goods, which remained binding until the frustrating event.[223] The House of Lords in *Fibrosa* overcame this objection in holding that consideration in the formation of contracts was not to be confused with consideration in the quasi-contractual action for the recovery of money. The latter signified benefit actually received rather than benefit promised. This reasoning would still be needed for those sale of contracts falling outside the 1943 Act if the buyer is to recover money paid.[224]

4.66 **Effect of 1943 Act.** The Law Reform (Frustrated Contracts) Act 1943 modified the common law rule that frustration discharges a contract prospectively. The starting point is that moneys paid may be recovered and moneys payable before the frustrating event need no longer be paid.[225] Important exceptions are then grafted on to this rule. First, a party who has incurred expenses in performing the contract may, within the discretion of the court, retain or recover from the sum paid or payable an amount that does not exceed such sum.[226] Secondly, if one of the parties has obtained a valuable benefit, the other is entitled, again subject to the discretion of the court, to recover a sum equivalent to the value of this benefit to the party obtaining it.[227] The words of the statute clearly point to actual benefit received and not potential benefit.[228] Applied to a simple sale of goods contract, the rule that moneys paid or payable may be recovered or retained amounts to a

---

[222] [1943] AC 32, overruling *Chandler v Webster* [1904] 1 KB 593.
[223] *Chandler v Webster*, n. 222 above.
[224] See also discussion above on partial failure of consideration.
[225] S. 1(2).
[226] *Ibid*.
[227] S. 1(3). See Robert Goff J in *BP Exploration Co. (Libya) Ltd. v Hunt (No. 2)* [1979] 1 WLR 783, affirmed [1981] 1 WLR 232 and [1983] 2 AC 352.
[228] Cf Treitel, n. 179 above, 978–9.

concession to the interests of buyers, while the exceptions for benefits and expenses redress the countervailing interests of sellers.

Sale of goods and the Act.   The 1943 Act has only a limited impact upon sale of **4.67** goods contracts. First, the Act does not apply to contracts for the sale of specific goods where the goods perish.[229] Secondly, in very many simple sale of goods contracts, the rules concerning benefit and exceptions will not apply. If an executory contract for the sale of specific goods is frustrated other than by reason of the goods perishing, the buyer and seller will walk away from the contract. A buyer who has prepaid the price or a part of it will be able to recover the payment.[230] No corresponding provision is made for the seller who has delivered the goods or a part of them, but a buyer who voluntarily retains the goods will be liable to pay for any benefit received on the basis of an implied contractual or restitutionary obligation. In the case of a contract for the sale of unascertained goods, it is difficult, as seen above, to establish that the contract is frustrated at common law. The Act itself does not codify or modify the common law test for frustration. It is perhaps more likely that the expense and benefit provisions of the Act will apply to a contract for the sale of unascertained goods than to a contract for the sale of specific goods, but the likelihood of the Act operating in the former case is still low. The type of case where the Act might apply is where the seller goes to significant expense in acquiring or modifying machinery to set up a production run for the buyer and requires to be put in funds by the buyer to do so. The prepayment requirement is indicative that the buyer participates to a degree in the risk of the enterprise.[231] Nevertheless, unless the buyer obtains a factual benefit of some kind,[232] the expense and benefit provisions of the Act will not be implemented. A buyer is unlikely to obtain a factual benefit where possession is not transferred,[233] and where possession is transferred, the contract is not likely to be frustrated.

---

[229] S. 2(5)(c). This provision also specifically excepts from the Act contracts for the sale of specific goods where the risk has passed to the buyer and the goods perish (s. 7 of the Sale of Goods Act contracts). This was unnecessary, since such contracts come within the specific exception anyway.

[230] S. 1(2).

[231] Cf shipbuilding contracts, which to the extent that they are sale of goods contracts (see Ch. 2 above), are not simple sale of goods contracts. See, e.g., *Stocznia Gdanska SA v Latvian Shipbuilding Co* [1998] 1 WLR 574, applying *Hyundai Heavy Industries Co. Ltd v Papadopoulos* [1980] 1 WLR 1129 (moneys prepaid not recoverable when contract rescinded under express clause).

[232] See *Appleby v Myers* (1867) LR 2 CP 651.

[233] Cf *BP Exploration (Libya) Ltd v Hunt*, n. 227 above. If the seller provides a mixed consideration, for example services and goods, the supply of services before the goods might bring the provisions of the Act into play.

Mistake

4.68 **General.** The subject matter of mistake is dealt with in only two places in the Sale of Goods Act: first, in section 6; and secondly, in section 23, which deals with the transfer of title to goods under a voidable contract.[234] The first of these provisions deals with the case where the parties share the same misapprehension about the existence of the goods; according to older terminology, the parties' shared mistake is 'mutual'. More usually nowadays, this is referred to as a matter of 'common' mistake. The latter provision, section 23, is concerned with cases where a mistake of identity concerning one of the parties so vitiates the process of agreement that no true contractual consensus exists between the parties. It raises issues concerning the protection of ownership and the rights of good faith purchasers and will be discussed in greater detail in Chapter 5. The greater part of the law of mistake is remitted to the general law of contract; it is incorporated in sale of goods contracts by virtue of section 62(2) and is treated to a limited extent in this text. Common mistake has little part to play in the law of sale of goods. It is a source of contractual relief that tends to be resorted to when other avenues are exhausted. These other avenues include express warranty, innocent misrepresentation, and, most importantly, the implied condition of correspondence with description.[235] At times in its evolution, the last of these was stated in terms akin to the doctrine of common mistake and it was not necessarily the case, as it is now, that an action for damages for breach of contract lay when the goods failed to correspond to their condition.[236] Until recently, it might have been said that common mistake existed in two versions—a common law doctrine and an equitable doctrine, the difference between the two centring, not so much on the seriousness of the mistake needed for relief to be given, but rather on the remedial consequences of the two versions. In short, common mistake at common law renders, or is considered to render, a contract void, whereas equitable mistake was considered to render the contract voidable. Equitable mistake enjoyed an existence of fifty or so years before the Court of Appeal firmly ruled that it had no recognized existence.

4.69 **Section 6.** According to section 6: 'Where there is a contract for the sale of specific goods, and the goods without the knowledge of the seller have perished at

---

[234] Discussed in Ch. 5 below.

[235] Discussed in Ch. 7 below.

[236] The cases that demonstrate this most clearly are those dealing with the sale of bills of exchange where the transferor did not give a warranty. In *Gompertz v Bartlett* (1853) 2 E & B 849, a bill was sold without recourse. It was mistakenly believed to be a foreign bill and was not stamped. This meant that it was worthless. According to Lord Campbell CJ: 'The case is precisely as if a bar was sold as gold, but was in fact brass . . . (*ibid.*, 853).' See also *Gurney v Womersley* (1854) 4 E & B 132; *Young v Cole* (1837) 3 Bing (NC) 724 (total failure of consideration).

the time when the contract is made, the contract is void.' Section 6 is supposedly based upon *Couturier v Hastie*,[237] a case that repays careful examination. The contract was for the sale of a specific cargo of corn on board the *Kezia Page*. Unknown to the parties, the cargo had already overheated and had been sold in Tunis by the ship's master; it had thus ceased to exist for commercial purposes. The seller nevertheless demanded payment, tendering the shipping documents, which included an insurance policy, under this early version of a c.i.f. contract. The buyer refused to accept the documents and pay the price, citing the non-existence of the cargo at the contract date. Consequently, the seller sued for the price of the cargo the *del credere* agent who had negotiated the sale, the liability of this agent turning upon whether the buyer was entitled to refuse payment. The trial judge ruled that it was a condition of the contract that a cargo was in existence and capable of delivery, so the seller could not recover. Reversing this decision, the Court of Exchequer held that the seller could validly tender documents relating to goods lost before the conclusion of the contract. This decision was reversed by the Court of Exchequer Chamber, which held that the buyer had not taken the risk of casualty to the goods before the contract, and that it was the basis of the contract that the cargo was in existence at the date the contract was concluded. The seller had therefore not made a valid tender. This ruling was upheld in the House of Lords, where it was stressed that the decision turned upon the construction of the particular contract, which was conditioned on the goods being in existence at the contract date.

A case of construction. Nowhere in any of the judgments is there a reference to **4.70** mistake or voidness. The case is entirely consistent with the use of constructive conditions precedent.[238] The decision was that the seller, having failed to satisfy the condition of making a good tender, could not complain about the buyer's refusal to pay the price. It does not rule out the possibility or the presumption that sellers warrant the existence of specific goods at the contract date. The plaintiff seller's liability was never put to the test since there was no counterclaim for damages for non-delivery. Yet Chalmers interpreted *Couturier* as holding that contracts for the sale of goods that have perished at the contract date are void for mistake,[239] and this view has subsequently been followed in the case law.[240] Section 6 enacts what appears to be an inflexible rule of law making no allowance for a contrary intention that the seller should be contractually liable if by words or conduct he expressly or impliedly warrants or represents the existence of the goods.

---

237 (1853) 9 Ex. 102, affirmed (1856) 5 HLC 673.

238 According to Sir F. Pollock (Introduction to the Revised Reports, i, vi): '*Couturier* v. *Hastie* . . . shows how a large proportion of the cases which swell the rubric of relief against mistake in the text-books (with or without protest from the text-writer) are really cases of construction.'

239 *The Sale of Goods Act, 1893* (4th edn, Butterworths, 1899), 19.

240 *Barrow, Lane & Ballard Ltd v Phillip Phillips & Co.* [1929] 1 KB 574.

4.71 **Implied conditions precedent and liability.** These difficulties came to the surface in the highly persuasive decision of the Australian High Court in *McRae v Commonwealth Disposals Commission*,[241] where a government agency, inviting salvage bids, negligently asserted the existence of a specific wreck on a non-existent reef in the Pacific Ocean. Section 6 was held inapplicable on the ground that goods that never existed cannot have perished. Carefully reviewing *Couturier*, the High Court found that the common law position was based upon constructive conditions precedent and not upon the idea that certain contracts are void for mistake. Hence it declined to invoke any principle identical to the one in section 6 *via* the common law gateway of section 62(2). In *McRae*, the buyer was suing the seller for damages representing his out-of-pocket expenses in equipping a salvage expedition. The issue could not be resolved simply by holding that the seller had failed to make a good tender. Starting from the constructive principle that sellers normally warrant the existence of specific goods, the court found such a warranty had been impliedly given by the seller. It was plainly influenced by the high degree of negligence displayed by the seller, an attitude consistent with the modern tendency to introduce fault into the test of promissory intention for express warranty.[242] Similar evidence of the influence of tort law is to be found in the court's denial to the buyer of expectation damages founded on the notional value of the wreck, which was impossible to evaluate, and in its award instead of a reliance measure based upon the buyer's wasted expenses. Construction and conditions precedent are useful expedients for embodying the idea that the parties are contractually free to allocate risk in a way that produces an outcome different from the ordinary application of mistake rules.[243] The allocation of the risk of non-existence in *McRae* may be said to have been placed by the parties themselves on the defendant government agency.

4.72 **Liability in tort.** Tort law provides one way round section 6 and its apparent disallowance of contractual liability. A seller negligent in asserting the existence of goods could be held liable for negligent misstatement and subjected to a tortious measure of damages.[244] Where the seller is not negligent but plainly undertakes that the goods are in existence, it is not so easy. It may be possible to construe a collateral contract based on the seller's implied undertaking that the goods exist.

---

[241] (1951) 84 CLR 377.

[242] See Ch. 8 below. The decision of the Australian High Court was 'an entirely satisfactory conclusion': *Great Peace Shipping Ltd v Tsavliris Salvage (International) Ltd* [2002] EWCA Civ 1407; [2003] QB 679 at [80].

[243] *Associated Japanese Bank (International) Ltd v Crédit du Nord SA* [1989] 1 WLR 255, 268; *Great Peace Shipping Ltd v Tsavliris Salvage (International) Ltd*, n. 242 above at [75], [84]–[85]; *Apvodedo NV v Collins* [2008] EWHC 775 (Ch) at [36].

[244] *Hedley Byrne & Co. Ltd v Heller & Partners Ltd* [1964] AC 465. In an appropriate case, these should include the loss of an alternative expectation: *VK Mason Construction Ltd v Bank of Nova Scotia Ltd* (1985) 16 DLR (4th) 598.

Since entry into even an illegal contract has been held to be sufficient considera-tion for a collateral promise,[245] the same should hold true for entry into a void contract. Yet it is difficult to see this as other than an illusory consideration. Another possibility is to say that section 6, in common with the other contractual provisions[246] of the Sale of Goods Act, may always be excluded by a contrary agreement, express or implied. Such contrary agreement imposing liability on the seller may be found in the warranty itself. Alternatively, it may be that the parties agree that the buyer shall assume the risk of pre-contract loss. Section 55 permits the parties to exclude 'any right, duty or liability' arising by implication of law under a contract of sale. Though the rule in section 6 seems to be, if anything, the very negation of rights, duties, and liabilities, a court would probably invoke sec-tion 55 if it felt it had to avoid the effect of section 6, even though the latter provi-sion, unlike so many others in the Act, does not expressly permit a contrary intention or use the language of presumption.

Events other than perishing.   Section 6 deals only with perishing.[247] It has **4.73** nothing to say about embargoes or other forms of governmental intervention. Nor does it as such apply to the perishing of goods other than specific goods. Where unascertained goods are agreed to be sold under a broad description, it is unlikely that the unavailability of such goods to the seller would vitiate the contract. The position could be different if descriptive words closely delimit the source of the contract goods, and should most certainly be different if the seller's obligation is to supply an undivided part of a specific bulk. In all these cases falling outside section 6, the court, it is submitted, should have recourse to the common law approach espoused in *McRae*.[248]

Part perishing.   The rule in section 6 does apply to specific goods that have **4.74** perished in part. In *Barrow, Lane & Ballard Ltd v Phillip Phillips Ltd*,[249] where the contract concerned a batch of 700 bags of Chinese groundnuts lying at a wharf, 109 bags had, without the parties' knowledge, already been stolen by unknown persons. The contract was entire and indivisible, so the diminished quantity could not be used towards a proportionate abatement of the price. The court held that the contract was void and, to be consistent with principle, would have had to reach the same result if even a much smaller quantity had been stolen, at least where the seller could not make a tender within the ungenerous margins allowed by the maxim *de minimis non curat lex*. The seller consequently had to bear the risk

---

[245] *Strongman (1945) Ltd v Sincock* [1955] 2 QB 525.
[246] As opposed to those dealing with the *nemo dat* rule and title transfer: see Ch. 5 below.
[247] Discussed at n. 151 above.
[248] n. 241 above. And in the second part of Lord Atkin's speech in *Bell v Lever Bros* [1932] AC 161.
[249] n. 240 above.

of additional theft occurring after the contract date. Before the shortfall became known, the buyer had removed 150 bags from the wharf and paid a proportion of the contract price into court. Although a *quantum valebant* undertaking could not be inferred from the buyer's consumption of these bags in ignorance of the theft or thefts, a modern court would impose on a recalcitrant buyer a restitutionary duty to pay in such circumstances. In some cases, the contract might expressly or impliedly allow the seller such a wide tolerance in matters of quantity that the buyer would be liable at the contract rate for goods delivered.[250]

4.75 **Operative common mistake.** Section 6 does not deal with all cases where an operative common mistake of the parties exists but, as stated above, common mistake has little part to play in the law of sale of goods. Where the mistake concerns the goods themselves, it must concern a quality of the goods that makes them essentially different from what the parties believed them to be.[251] A common mistake, where operative, may affect the contract at common law in either of two ways. First, it may be said that the existence of the contract is dependent upon the correctness of the factual basis of the contract as understood by the parties. Secondly, it may more directly be said that the contract is void. Both approaches are evident in the speech of Lord Atkin in *Bell v Lever Bros Ltd*,[252] though the former approach has been disapproved of in modern times.[253] The implied term approach, however, is truer to the origins of common mistake and shows the kinship between common mistake and the implied condition of correspondence with description in section 13 of the Sale of Goods Act.[254] In terms of the seriousness of the mistake likely to give rise to relief, it seems that nothing turns upon which particular approach is adopted.[255] An example given by Lord Atkin in *Bell v Lever Bros Ltd* vividly captures the difficulty of establishing an operative mistake. It is the example of the painting wrongly believed by the parties to a contract of

---

[250] *Goldsborough, Mort & Co. Ltd v Carter* (1914) 19 CLR 429 (after bad weather, seller could muster only 890 sheep instead of 'about' 4,000).

[251] *Bell v Lever Bros Ltd* [1932] AC 161, 218. For an analysis of *Bell v Lever Bros*, see *Associated Japanese Bank (International) Ltd v Crédit du Nord SA* [1989] 1 WLR 255.

[252] n. 251 above.

[253] *Great Peace Shipping Ltd v Tsavliris Salvage (International) Ltd*, n. 242 above at [82]. Similarly, the treatment of frustration as dependent upon an implied condition in the contract (see *Taylor v Caldwell* (1863) 3 B & S 826) has fallen out of fashion: see Treitel, n. 179 above, 984–7. In construing a contract of guarantee respecting rental payments to be made for equipment the subject of a sale and leaseback, Steyn J in *Associated Japanese Bank (International) Ltd v Crédit du Nord SA*, n. 251 above, adopted the technique of the implied condition precedent in determining that no liability arose under the guarantee because the equipment in question was non-existent. He held that the condition precedent that the equipment be in existence could be implied on the facts either under the business efficacy approach or under the reasonable bystander approach to implied terms.

[254] Discussed in Ch. 7 below.

[255] See, e.g., the denial of equitable relief in *Magee v Pennine Insurance Co. Ltd* [1969] 2 QB 507, a case that on its facts is barely distinguishable from *Bell v Lever Bros Ltd*, n. 251 above, where relief was denied at common law.

sale to be an old master, said by Lord Atkin not to be a case of operative mistake.[256] In favour of this strict approach is that a contract, where the seller does not expressly warrant the painting to be the work of a particular artist or where the authorship of the painting is not part of the contractual description,[257] impliedly places upon the buyer the risk of authenticity. According to Lord Phillips MR in *Great Peace Shipping Ltd v Tsavliris Salvage (International) Ltd*:

> Circumstances where a contract is void as a result of common mistake are likely to be less common than instances of frustration. Supervening events which defeat the contractual adventure will frequently not be the responsibility of either party. Where, however, the parties agree that something shall be done which is impossible at the time of making the agreement, it is much more likely that, on true construction of the agreement, one or other will have undertaken responsibility for the mistaken state of affairs. This may well explain why cases where contracts have been found to be void in consequence of common mistake are few and far between.[258]

4.76 Where goods the subject of a contract have never existed, however, then, in the absence of a warranty given by the seller that the goods are in existence,[259] it seems that the mistake would be sufficiently fundamental to vitiate the contract.[260] This may be regarded as a modest extension of section 6 of the Sale of Goods Act, not applicable on its terms to goods that never existed.

4.77 **Equitable mistake.** The common law doctrine of common mistake provides no flexibility in adjusting the rights of the parties when the contract is set aside. In particular, there is no statutory equivalent of the Law Reform (Frustrated Contracts) Act 1943.[261] The driving force behind the invention of the doctrine of equitable mistake was the flexibility possessed by the court in ordering rescission on terms.[262] In *Great Peace Shipping Ltd v Tsavliris Salvage (International) Ltd*,[263] a vessel was chartered to render assistance to a another vessel in distress, the parties being mistaken about the distance separating the two vessels at the date of

---

[256] n. 251, 224. See also *Leaf v International Galleries* [1950] 2 KB 86 (authorship of painting); *Oscar Chess Ltd v Williams* [1957] 1 WLR 370, 373 (age of car). Cf *Nicholson & Venn v Smith-Marriott* (1947) 177 LT 189 (a doubtful case so far as it applies to mistake).

[257] But for the buyer's lack of reliance, the incorrect statement of authorship of a painting in *Harlingdon and Leinster Enterprises Ltd v Christopher Hull Fine Art Ltd* [1991] 1 QB 564 would have given rise to a breach of s. 13 of the Sale of Goods Act; see Ch. 7 below.

[258] n. 242 above at [85].

[259] See *McRae v Commonwealth Disposals Commission*, n. 241 above.

[260] See *Associated Japanese Bank (International) Ltd v Crédit du Nord SA*, n. 251 above. Similarly, the unusual case of the buyer purchasing his own property would give rise to relief: *Cooper v Phibbs* (1867) LR 2 HL 149.

[261] See the court's call for new legislation in *Great Peace Shipping Ltd v Tsavliris Salvage (Internationa) Ltd*, n. 242 above at [161].

[262] *Solle v Butcher* [1950] 1 KB 671. see also *Frederick E Rose (London) Ltd v William H Pim Jnr & Co Ltd* [1953] 2 QB 450 (wrong type of horsebeans).

[263] n. 242 above, affirming (2001) 151 NLJ 1696.

the contract.[264] The mistake was not sufficiently essential to render the contract void at common law. Since the doctrine of equitable mistake occupied the same field as common law mistake, moreover, its existence was incompatible with the decision of the House of Lords in *Bell v Lever Bros Ltd*.[265] A contract avoided at common law could not be rescinded on terms in equity, and a mistake not operative at common law was not operative in equity.[266] The extirpation of an equitable doctrine of common mistake in the *Great Peace* case appears to be complete and irreversible.[267]

---

[264] The vessels were 410 miles apart instead of 35.
[265] n. 251 above at [160].
[266] n. 251 above at [153].
[267] For the rejection of a jurisdiction to grant equitable relief in cases of unilateral mistake, see *Statoil ASA v Louis Dreyfus Energy Services LP* [2008] EWHC 2257 (Comm) at [105].

5

THE SELLER'S DUTY AND POWER TO TRANSFER TITLE

Introduction. This chapter is divided into two parts. First, it deals with the **5.01** contractual relations of seller and buyer and the scope of the title to the goods that under section 12 of the Sale of Goods Act the seller is obliged to invest in the buyer. Secondly, it deals with the various circumstances in which a seller of goods, lacking the right to sell them to the buyer, has yet the power to override the superior title of a third party by the act of transferring the goods to the buyer. The disparate circumstances in which a seller can achieve this amount to a substantial inroad into the rule of *nemo dat quod non habet* that no one can transfer a better title than the one that he himself possesses.

The Seller's Duty to Transfer Title

5.02 **Right to sell.** Section 12 contains a number of implied terms, the most important of which is the condition[1] that, in the case of a sale, the seller has the right to sell the goods, and that in the case of an agreement to sell he will have such a right at the time when the property is to pass. A contract of sale is an agreement to sell until the property passes, whereupon it becomes a sale, except where the passing of property at the contract date meant that it always was a sale.[2] Section 12(1) imposes two obligations on the seller where the property does not pass at the contract date: first, a promise that the seller will have the right to sell at the future date when the agreement to sell becomes a sale; and secondly, a promise springing at that future date that the seller does have the right to sell. Even if only the latter obligation had been spelt out in section 12(1), the doctrine of anticipatory repudiation would have supplied also the equivalent of the first. Under the doctrine of anticipatory repudiation, a seller clearly unable to transfer title at an agreed future date might be said to be in present breach of the latter obligation.[3] Where a seller has the capacity and the will to buy out the true owner, and thus transfer good title to the buyer at the agreed future date, there is neither a breach of the seller's implied promise that he will have the right to sell at the point of sale nor an anticipatory breach of his implied promise that he does have the right to sell. If the contract of sale is a conditional sale, and the buyer must in the meantime pay instalments to the seller, this places the buyer in an invidious position.

5.03 **Express term.** In *Barber v NWS Bank plc*,[4] the buyer of a car on conditional sale terms had the option within ten days of the contract to pay in cash the balance of the moneys due, after account was taken of the trade-in allowance. He declined to exercise the option and paid instalments for about eighteen months. Faced with difficulties in paying the instalments, he then sought to trade in the car for a cheaper car. This led to his discovery that the seller was not the owner of the car, which was still owned by a third party under a prior finance agreement. About three months later, the buyer rescinded the contract, shortly after which (it seems) the seller bought out the interest of the previous owner. An express term in the contract, that 'the property in the Goods shall pass to the Customer' upon payment in full, was conceded by the seller to amount to an express term that the seller was the owner of the goods at the contract date. This concession was regarded

---

[1] Prior to the implementation of the Supply of Goods (Implied Terms) Act 1994, the status of this term was in s. 12(1) itself. The 1994 Act introduced the cosmetic change locating the status of the term in s. 12(5A).

[2] S. 2(4)–(6); see Ch. 2 above.

[3] For prospective incapacity as repudiation, see Ch. 10 below.

[4] [1996] 1 All ER 906.

by the Court of Appeal as 'both correct and unavoidable'.[5] The court was impressed by the fact that the buyer could have paid off the balance in cash within ten days of the contract, but the report is silent on whether he could have accelerated future instalments after the ten days had elapsed. Whether he was contractually entitled to or not, he lacked the financial means to do so. The conclusion that the seller had expressly warranted its ownership at the contract date is therefore not self-evident. The decision is also open to criticism for failing to distinguish between the seller's title obligations under section 12 and the passing of property between seller and buyer: the express term concerned the former and not the latter. The court's decision does, however, possess the merit of plugging the gap in the statutory coverage of the seller's title obligations. The discussion in the case centred mainly on the status of the express term breached by the seller. It was treated as a condition of the contract, rather than an intermediate stipulation, on the ground that without it the agreement would not work. This draws attention to the failure of section 12(1) expressly to provide that a conditional seller should have the right to sell the goods at the contract date. Indeed, section 12(1) provides by implication that the seller is *not* under any such duty. It states that the seller must have a right to sell in the case of a sale, but have a right to sell only at the time when the property is to pass in the case of an agreement to sell.[6] A conditional sale is an agreement to sell.[7] The shortcomings of the provision are thrown into sharp relief by *Barber*, which indicates that a conditional sale is unworkable if it does not contain an express title term taking effect at the contract date.

Right to sell and ownership.   Section 12(1) states in general language that the seller must have a right to sell. It does not state that the seller must transfer ownership or title, nor that the seller must pass the property in the way and at the time provided for in the Act.[8] Ownership, not mentioned at all in the Act and title, apart from a mention in the marginal note to section 12, is dealt with in the sections on the *nemo dat* rule. Property is defined in section 61(1) as the general property and not a mere special property. A special property is a possessory interest of a type claimed by bailees and pledgees,[9] so that the general property refers to the whole of the seller's interest in goods without any reservation of reversionary rights of the kind made by bailor or pledgor. A contract in which the whole of a transferor's proprietary interest in goods is exchanged for a money consideration

5.04

---

[5] *Ibid.*, 910.

[6] See Ch. 2 above for the distinction between sale and agreement to sell.

[7] S. 2(5), (6).

[8] On terminology and concepts, see A. Kiralfy (1949) 12 *MLR* 424; G. Battersby and A. D. Preston (1972) 35 *MLR* 268.

[9] *Donald v Suckling* (1866) LR 1 QB 585; *Nyberg v Handelaar* [1892] 2 QB 202; O. W. Holmes, *The Common Law* (1881), 242. See *The Odessa* [1916] 1 AC 145, 155–9 (disapproval of special property terminology).

is therefore a contract of sale to which the passing of property rules in sections 16–19 apply.

5.05 **Extent of general property.** In defining the scope of section 12(1), there is no need to gauge how far the general property exceeds in scope the special property; it is a provision dealing with contractual undertakings, not conveyancing. The provision speaks of a right to sell and refrains from using terms such as ownership, title, or property. It records the seller's undertaking to transfer at the agreed time the best possessory entitlement in the world. It is hard to speak of the ownership of goods in the sense of an absolute right, good against the world. A strong argument can be made that there is no such thing as a law of property in goods:[10] proprietary entitlement is resolved through tortious actions, principally conversion and trespass *de bonis asportatis*, in which standing to sue is based upon possession or the right to immediate possession,[11] rather than upon anything called ownership; the remedy is nearly always damages rather than specific delivery of the goods;[12] and a claimant is successful who demonstrates a superior possessory entitlement to that of the defendant.[13] This point is weakened, however,

---

[10] Kiralfy, n. 8 above.

[11] E. H. Warren (1936) 49 *Harv. LR* 1084; *Jeffries v Great Western Railway Co.* (1856) 5 E & B 802; F. Pollock and R. Wright, *An Essay on Possession in the Common Law* (Clarendon Press, 1888), 5; M. G. Bridge, *Personal Property Law* (3rd edn, Clarendon Law, 2002), 62–71.

[12] Specific delivery was introduced by the Common Law Procedure Act 1854, s. 78. The remedy is rarely awarded: *General and Finance Facilities Ltd v Cook's Cars (Romford) Ltd* [1963] 1 WLR 644; *Howard Perry & Co. v British Railways Board* [1980] 1 WLR 1375 (interlocutory relief).

[13] Public policy apart (see *Parker v British Airways Board* [1982] QB 1004), a thief would be able to sue an person unlawfully interfering with his possession: see *Costello v Chief Constable of Derbyshire* [2001] EWCA Civ 381; [2001] 1 WLR 1437; *Buckley v Gross* (1863) 3 B & S 566; *Bird v Town of Fort Frances* [1949] OR 292 (Can.). There is no residual common law power that permits the police to retain property unlawfully obtained: *Webb v Chief Constable of Merseyside* [2000] QB 427. A statutory power exists to make a restitution order under the Powers of the Criminal Courts (Sentencing) Act 2000 in the case of stolen goods. Where 'a person is convicted of any offence with reference to the theft (whether or not the stealing is the gist of his offence)' (s. 148(1)(b)), the court 'may order anyone having possession or control of the stolen goods to restore them to any person entitled to receive them from him' (s. 148(2)(a)). The power is not exercised lightly. See *R v Ferguson* [1970] 1 WLR 1246, 1249:

> It is only in the plainest cases, when there can be no doubt that the money belonged to the convicted man, that the court would be justified in exercising its discretion in making an order for restitution. To do so in any case of doubt might cause the gravest injustice to a third party because the third party to whom the money may belong has no locus standi to appear before a criminal court. Nor is there any appropriate machinery available in the criminal courts for deciding the issue as to who is the true owner. Discovery is sometimes a very important part of the necessary machinery for resolving issues of that sort, and discovery for this purpose can be obtained only in the civil courts. The civil courts are the correct forum for deciding matters of that kind.

A similar power is available in summary cases under the Police (Property) Act 1897, s. 1(1) (to 'make an order for the delivery of the property to the person appearing to . . . be the owner thereof, or, if the owner cannot be ascertained, make such order with respect to the property as . . . may seem meet'). A similar restriction exists on the exercise of the court's discretion: *Raymond Lyons & Co. Ltd v Metropolitan Police Commissioner* [1975] QB 321, 326 ('summary procedure . . . not to be

by the Torts (Interference with Goods) Act 1977,[14] which seeks to reduce overcompensation and to encourage all interested parties to join in the litigation.[15] Subject to this, ownership is relative rather than absolute.[16] It is unusual for documents to be kept recording changes of ownership of goods, and the common law does not lend itself to the view that restrictive covenants and encumbrances can attach themselves to goods[17] so as to follow them through changes of ownership.[18]

Pre-Act cases. Early cases on the inference of express warranty[19] show the courts **5.06** have long found contractual promises in representations of ownership made by sellers. Nevertheless, some resistance to the universal inference of an implied undertaking, arising from the mere fact of sale, survived until well into the nineteenth century. This resistance seems to have been fuelled by *caveat emptor* thinking, the idea being that the buyer should secure an express undertaking, and was expressed at length by Baron Parke in *Morley v Attenborough*.[20] A pawnbroker was held not to have undertaken to transfer outright ownership when selling an unredeemed pledge, a result that might also be reached today.[21] According to Parke B, the seller of unascertained goods gave such an undertaking, but a seller of specific goods did so only in two cases: first, where trade custom required it and, secondly, where it could readily be inferred from the nature of the seller's business, such as that of retail shopkeeper.[22] The reason for the absence of a general undertaking for specific goods was that, formerly, such sales had occurred in market overt, where the buyer's acquisition of clear title meant that no such undertaking was needed.[23] Later authorities, however, thought the exceptions had consumed the general rule[24] and this was the position first codified in 1893.

---

used in difficult cases involving tricky questions of title or large sums of money'). See also the Police and Criminal Evidence Act 1984 (as amended), ss. 19 and 22 (seizure and retention); Proceeds of Crime Act 2002 (as amended), s. 6 (confiscation orders), applied in *Crown Prosecution Service (Nottinghamshire) v Rose* [2008] EWCA Crim 239.

[14] Ss. 5(4), 7–8.

[15] The now-repealed market overt exception to the rule of *nemo dat quod non habet* in the text accompanying nn. 153–64 below, created the nearest thing to an absolute title in effacing all earlier titles.

[16] See also CPR 19.5A.

[17] Kiralfy, n. 8 above.

[18] Mortgage and conditional sale are both based upon the notion of undivided ownership, transferred in the first case and retained in the second. Of course, this notion is qualified by equitable ideas, which also support charges on personalty.

[19] *Crosse v Gardner* (1688) Carth. 90, *sub nom. Cross v Garret* at 3 Mod. 261; *Medina v Stoughton* (1699) 1 Salk. 210, 1 Ld. Raym. 593.

[20] (1849) 3 Ex. 500.

[21] S. 12(3).

[22] n. 20 above, 509 *et seq.*

[23] *Ibid.*, 511.

[24] *Sims v Marryat* (1851) 17 QB 281; J. P. Benjamin, *A Treatise on the Sale of Personal Property* (2nd American edn, Sweet & Maxwell, 1873), 522–3; see also *Eicholz v Bannister* (1864) 17 CB(NS) 708.

Title and Failure of Consideration

5.07 **Fundamental obligation.** While section 12(1) formally states the seller's undertaking that he has a right to sell as a condition, also the case for fitness and satisfactory quality in section 14, this undertaking is in some ways treated as a matter of fundamental obligation transcending even a contractual condition. In *Rowland v Divall*,[25] the defendant seller sold a car to the plaintiff dealer, who paid cash, repainted the car, and drove it from Sussex to Dorset. He exhibited it in his showroom for two months and then sold it to a local buyer, who in turn used it for two months before it was repossessed by the police as a stolen car. The dealer reimbursed the buyer and brought the present action to recover from the defendant, not damages, but his own purchase money as on a total failure of consideration.[26] The defendant pleaded that the dealer's intermediate enjoyment of the car over the four-month period amounted to the receipt of a benefit precluding any rescission of the contract *ab initio*, a necessary precondition to a failure of consideration action.[27] The court, nevertheless, found a failure of consideration.[28] Rejecting the seller's assertion that a benefit, even if not the one bargained for, could preclude rescission and thus the failure of consideration action,[29] the court equated enjoyment with lawful enjoyment.[30] Consequently, the buyer's precarious and unlawful possession was no impediment to the action.[31]

5.08 **Criticism.** The court's decision amounts to treating wasting assets as bought for the abstract enjoyment of title rather than for consumption—a dubious proposition—for that is all that separates lawful enjoyment from unlawful enjoyment. The reasoning proves too much. It could not tenably be argued to

---

[25] [1923] 2 KB 500. See G. H. Treitel (1967) 30 *MLR* 139, 146–9; M. Bridge, 'The Title Obligations of the Seller of Goods', in N. Palmer and E. McKendrick (eds), *Interests in Goods* (2nd edn, Lloyds of London Press, 1998); Lord Goff of Chieveley and G. Jones, *The Law of Restitution* (7th edn, Sweet & Maxwell, 2007), 512–14.

[26] Such a claim, sanctioned by s. 54, is to a degree independent of an action for breach of the undertaking in s. 12(1) and has links with standard common law mistake authorities like *Kennedy v Panama, New Zealand and Australian Royal Mail Co.* (1867) LR 2 QB 580; *Gompertz v Bartlett* (1853) 2 E & B 849; and *Gurney v Womersley* (1854) 4 E & B 133. This type of action in title cases was sanctioned by Erle CJ in *Eicholz v Bannister*, n. 24 above; see also *Australian Credit Corpn v Ross* [1983] 2 VLR 319.

[27] *Weston v Downes* (1778) 1 Dougl. 23; *Towers v Barrett* (1786) 1 TR 133; *Hunt v Silk* (1804) 5 East 449.

[28] n. 25 above, 523–4 (Bankes LJ in particular). Curiously, s. 54 is not mentioned in the case.

[29] *Taylor v Hare* (1805) 1 B & PNR 260.

[30] See also *Rover International Ltd v Cannon Film Sales Ltd* [1989] 1 WLR 912, 925; *David Securities Pty Ltd v Commonwealth Bank of Australia* (1992) 175 CLR 353, 381–83; *Baltic Exchange Co. v Dixon* (1993) 176 CLR 344, 351. In the case of a contract validly concluded, recovery of money on the basis of a total failure of consideration has been said to turn on 'a failure by one contracting party to perform any part of his essential obligation under the contract': *Guinness Mahon & Co. v Kensington and Chelsea Royal Borough Council* [1999] QB 215, 240.

[31] Atkin LJ added an estoppel argument that the seller could not plead the buyer's enjoyment of a benefit: n. 25 above, 507.

similar effect that goods are bought only so that they can be enjoyed as fit for the buyer's purpose or as of satisfactory quality. *Rowland v Divall* may thus be seen as the other side of the coin to the now-repealed rule preventing the buyer of specific goods from rejecting them and terminating the contract once the property has passed.[32] Just as the passing of property no longer prevents the rejection of specific goods, so the seller's failure to vest a lawful title in the buyer should no longer be treated as a total failure of consideration if there has in fact been a clear enjoyment derived from the goods. This is not to deny that there may be cases where the buyer obtains no benefit, as where the seller is unable to transfer even possession to a prepaying buyer. The receipt of any benefit broadly of the kind bargained for ought to preclude an action for the recovery of the price if the goods have been accepted.[33] *Rowland v Divall* sidesteps the acceptance and *ex post facto* warranty rules in the Sale of Goods Act,[34] when the better solution would have been to remit the buyer to a damages claim amounting to the price paid minus the benefit.[35]

Alteration of position.   Even if the buyer is considered as having received no benefit, a further question that now arises, in the light of the House of Lords decision in *Lipkin Gorman v Karpnale*,[36] is whether a seller who has acted in good faith may raise the defence of alteration of position against a claim for repayment of the price in the form of an action for money had and received.[37] *Lipkin Gorman* was the case of a void contract, but nothing in that case precludes the recognition of the change of position defence in a case where the buyer terminates the contract for breach because the seller is in breach of the title obligation in section 12(1). A seller successfully invoking the change of position defence would have to show that he had incurred expenditure that he would not have incurred but for the receipt of the price. This would be no easy matter to prove for a seller like the one in *Rowland v Divall*, buying and selling cars on a regular basis. Furthermore, even a seller able to prove an alteration of position would have to pay over value surviving, such as the value of depreciated goods bought with the buyer's money.[38] The defence of alteration of position lies because and to the extent that it would be

5.09

---

32 Ch. 10 below.

33 See *Taylor v Hare*, n. 29 above; *Linz v Electric Wire Co. of Palestine* [1948] AC 371 (shares); *Lawes v Purser* (1856) 6 E & B 930 (patent).

34 Ch. 10 below.

35 There may in some cases be a damages claim for the loss of resale profit and for the cost of defending an action in conversion by the true owner.

36 [1991] 2 AC 548.

37 This argument was summarily rejected on the facts in *Barber v NWS Bank plc* n. 4 above, where the defendant conditional seller had paid money received for the contract goods to its own supplier.

38 See Lord Templeman and his illustrations of the purchased car and the round the world trip: n. 36 above, 560.

unjust or unfair in some cases to require the payee to return money paid.[39] In *Lipkin Gorman*, Lord Goff was at pains to say that the defence of alteration of position would not avail a 'wrongdoer',[40] but it is not clear whether a wrongdoer includes one who, without personal fault, is in breach of section 12(1). It is submitted that the context of Lord Goff's speech, with its accompanying references to bad faith, to good faith and to 'innocent' donees, suggests that the defence ought not to be precluded in section 12(1) cases where the seller has acted in good faith. Furthermore, it might be argued that a buyer invoking section 12(1) and the seller's breach ought to abide by the normal consequences of a breach of condition as these are spelt out in section 35, which would ordinarily lead to a claim for damages for breach of an *ex post facto* warranty.[41]

5.10 **Failure of consideration and acceptance.** *Rowland v Divall* is also a troublesome case for the way that failure of consideration arguments become confused with the issue whether the buyer was precluded from rejecting the goods for a breach of condition after accepting them, together with the related issue of whether a buyer could reject goods if unable to place them at the disposal of the seller. An undiscoverable latent defect of title should be no more potent than a latent defect of quality in prolonging the buyer's rejection period.[42] Scrutton LJ chose to dispose of the seller's objection, so far as it related to rejection as opposed to rescission *ab initio*, by asserting that it hardly lay in the seller's mouth to complain of the buyer's inability to return the goods when this very inability stemmed from the seller's breach of section 12(1).[43] Atkin LJ conjured up a section 11(4) implied agreement ousting the acceptance rules in section 35 and also asserted that 'there can be no sale of goods at all which the seller has no right to sell',[44] thus ousting the very applicability of those acceptance rules.[45] This latter expedient is

---

[39] n. 36 above, 560.

[40] *Ibid.*, 580.

[41] See Ch. 12.

[42] See Ch. 10 below. Subject to one point below, where the buyer obtains nothing of any value under the contract, the failure of consideration claim should generally lie. See *Kwei Tek Chao v British Overseas Traders and Shippers Ltd* [1954] 2 QB 459, 476–7 (bills of lading a nullity); *South West Water Services Ltd v International Computers Ltd* [1999] BLR 420 (failure of computer system to work). But the receipt of something that has no value should be a rare event. See *Yeoman Credit Ltd v Apps* [1962] 2 QB 508, 521 (buyer obtained something of value). In *Stocznia Gdanska SA v Latvian Shipping Co.* [1998] UKHL 9; [1998] 1 WLR 574, Lord Goff stressed that it was not the absence of *receipt* of something valuable that gave rise to a claim for the recovery of money on a total failure of consideration, but that the defendant could not be said to have executed any part of the consideration for which payment was made. This has implications for sellers and buyers in a *Rowland v Divall* type of case where the seller prepares and delivers goods to the buyer.

[43] *Rowland v Divall*, n. 25 above, 505–6.

[44] *Ibid.*, 507. He added an estoppel argument, that the seller could not plead the buyer's enjoyment of a benefit: *ibid.*

[45] A similar view, that there can be no sale if the seller does not own the goods, is to be found in *Mallett & Son (Antiques) Ltd v Roger* [2005] IEHC 131.

unfortunate, for what is surely significant in the characterization of contracts of sale is what the seller promised to do, rather than succeeded in doing. A pursuit of the latter approach would find in the very breach of section 12(1) the circumstances of its own exclusion.[46] The seller intended to divest himself totally of his interest in the goods and successfully accomplished this.

Buyer's windfall benefit.   The major drawback to *Rowland v Divall*, whether **5.11** rationalized as a failure of consideration leading to rescission *ab initio* or as a belated and irregular rejection for breach of condition, is that the buyer obtains an unpaid-for benefit, a result stigmatized as unjust.[47] On the facts of the case itself, rough justice may have been done, since the buyer did not pursue a damages claim, whether for loss of profit or for damage to his business reputation arising from the sale of a stolen car. Further, he had bought out the true owner for an undisclosed amount.[48] But an application of the reasoning in *Rowland v Divall* has led to buyers in later cases receiving free and lengthy periods of beneficial use.[49] Any objection that the possession of such buyers is precarious and that they are at risk of being sued in conversion can be met by factoring any loss thereby suffered into a damages claim against the seller.[50]

Nature of rescission.   A flaw in the failure of consideration argument in *Rowland* **5.12** *v Divall* is that it draws from an outmoded view of rescission *ab initio* as a necessary complement to a price recovery action, otherwise now refuted in the law of restitution.[51] This view highlights a logical inconsistency in combining a claim, denying the existence of the contract, for the return of the price with an action for damages on the contract. A buyer terminating a contract in the orthodox way may recover the price paid as part of a rolled-up damages award that adjusts the consequence of termination.[52] If the doctrine of failure of consideration is denied application, on the ground that the Sale of Goods Act adequately protects the buyer's position by means of section 12(1) and the damages and rejection remedies associated

---

[46] Although this approach undermines a damages claim on the contract, it does not have the same effect on a failure of consideration action.

[47] Law Reform Committee, *Twelfth Report (Transfer of Title to Chattels)* (1966, Cmnd. 2958), 15.

[48] Bankes LJ considered this irrelevant: see the report at [1923] All ER 270, 272.

[49] *Butterworth v Kingsway Motors Ltd* [1954] 1 WLR 1086 (10½ months); *McNeill v Associated Car Markets Ltd* (1962) 35 DLR (2d) 581 (nearly 20 months); *Barber v NWS Bank plc*, n. 4 above (22 months).

[50] Canadian cases have offset against successful claims for the recovery of money on a failure of consideration amounts representing the benefit obtained by the buyer from the use of the goods: *F & B Transport Ltd v White Truck Sales Manitoba Ltd* (1964) 47 DLR (2d) 419, affirmed (1965) 49 DLR (2d) 670; *Wiebe v Butchart's Motors Ltd* [1949] 4 DLR 838.

[51] *Fibrosa Spolka Akcyjna v Fairbairn Lawson Combe Barbour Ltd* [1943] AC 32, overruling *Chandler v Webster* [1904] 1 KB 493.

[52] In effect, this happened in *Mason v Burningham* [1949] 2 KB 545.

with it,[53] the problem of the buyer's free benefit[54] could then be resolved by confining the buyer who has accepted the goods to an appropriate award of damages.

5.13   Damages.   Even here, nevertheless, the notion of unlawful enjoyment should not be allowed to distort the assessment of damages. Yet in the hire purchase case of *Warman v Southern Counties Car Finance Corpn*[55] this is what happened. A hirer, who had plainly elected to sue the finance company for damages, for breach of an *ex post facto* implied warranty that it had title to the goods, was allowed to recover as damages the sum of all instalments paid, on the ground that his option to purchase the goods was valueless.[56] This approach should be resisted. In favour of the application of section 35 in the normal way, remitting the buyer to a damages action in section 12(1) where a benefit has been enjoyed, is the absence of a particular problem evident in other cases of non-conforming goods. Unlike goods that are unfit, section 12(1) cases do not face having to decide which of the parties should have the burden of dealing with unwanted goods. The goods may function perfectly adequately but have been repossessed by the true owner. *Rowland v Divall* represents the pathological survival of archaic ideas in a contract law that has witnessed in modern times the establishment of contractual termination on a firm, prospective basis.[57]

5.14   Law reform.   The response of law reform agencies is interesting to a problem that is now too entrenched to be resolved other than by statutory means. In a 1968 working paper,[58] the Law Commission recommended the implementation of the Law Reform Committee's earlier recommendation that the buyer give credit for any benefit received.[59] The final report, however, recommended that a study of the law of restitution be done before any amendment to section 12.[60] A 1975 working paper on restitution recommended reform subject to resolving a number of ensuing practical problems.[61] The 1983 report that followed, however, decided to defer a final recommendation on section 12 until further work on sale reform had

---

[53] But see *Northwest Co. Ltd v Merland Oil Co. of Canada Ltd* [1936] 2 WWR 577.

[54] Unlikely to arise where the buyer is still within the s. 35 acceptance period.

[55] [1949] 2 KB 576.

[56] The same approach is taken in *Australian Credit Corpn v Ross* [1983] 2 VLR 319; *Shoard v Palmer* (1989) 98 FLR 402.

[57] *Photo Production Ltd v Securicor Transport Ltd* [1980] AC 827; *Johnson v Agnew* [1980] AC 367.

[58] Law Commission (WP No. 18), *Provisional Proposals Relating to Amendments to Sections 12–15 of the Sale of Goods Act 1893 etc.*

[59] *Transfer of Title to Chattels* n. 47 above, 15.

[60] Law Commission (Law Com. No. 24), *First Report on Exemption Clauses in Contract*, para. 12.

[61] Law Commission (WP No. 65), *Law of Contract[:] Pecuniary Restitution on Breach of Contract*, paras 57–8.

been done.[62] The working paper on sale in the same year provisionally recommended that a buyer's recovery of the full price should be subject to a judicial discretion where there had been a significant use of the goods.[63] But the tide favouring reform turned with the final report of the Law Commission on *Sale and Supply of Goods*,[64] which recommended that nothing be done. First of all, any reform would be procedurally difficult to implement where there was a chain of transactions.[65] Secondly, the Law Commission could not see why the buyer should pay the seller for the use of someone else's goods. One response to this is to point to the outcome in *Butterworth v Kingsway Motors Ltd*.[66] Another is that the contract is still a sale of goods contract under which the seller has transferred the general property to the buyer. It is not to the point that the buyer proves to the hilt a breach of contract in respect of the seller's right to sell. This of itself does not justify displacing the normal rules on rejection of the goods and damages. *Rowland v Divall*, however, treats this contract for practical purposes as a nullity.[67]

Chain transactions.   Further difficulties in the application of section 12(1) to a   **5.15**
chain of transactions have been presented by *Butterworth v Kingsway Motors Ltd*.[68]
A car, subject to a hire purchase agreement, was unlawfully sold by the hirer (the fifth party) to a car dealer (the fourth party) for £1,000. The dealer in turn sold it for £1,015 to the third party, who then sold it for £1,030 to the defendant sellers, who finally sold it for £1,275 to the plaintiff. The four sales were all for cash and followed each other in rapid succession. After the plaintiff had had the use and enjoyment of the car for 10½ months, he received a letter from the finance company owner demanding possession of the car, but also giving him the option of paying off the hirer's hire purchase debt of £175 and keeping the car. The plaintiff then wrote a solicitor's letter to the defendant sellers clearly electing to put an end to the contract and demanding the return of his purchase money. About a week later, the plaintiff was informed by the finance company that the hirer had paid off the debt and that it would release the car. Nevertheless, the plaintiff continued to press the defendant sellers for the return of his money and requested instructions for the disposal of the car, which the defendants did not provide. At the date the plaintiff put an end to the contract, the car had fallen in value to £800; this figure had fallen further to £450 by the time of the action in the present case. When the plaintiff sued for the return of the price, the defendant sellers apparently claimed

---

62 Law Commission (Law Com. No. 121), *Law of Contract[:]Pecuniary Restitution on Breach of Contract*, para. 1.12.

63 Law Commission (WP No. 85), *Sale and Supply of Goods*, para. 6.7.

64 Law Commission (Law Com. No. 160) (1987), paras 6.1–5.

65 For a summary and criticism of these difficulties, see Bridge, n. 25 above, 325–7.

66 [1954] 1 WLR 1286. Discussed in the text accompanying nn. 68 *et seq.* below.

67 For an explicit holding to this effect, see *H W West Ltd v McBlain* [1950] NI 144.

68 n. 66 above. See also *Patten v Thomas* (1965) 66 SR (NSW) 458; *Lucas v Dixon* [1926] VLR 400.

over in damages for breach of section 12(1) against the third party,[69] and similar claims were made by the third party against the fourth party and by the latter against the fifth-party hirer at the head of the distribution chain. The final result was that the plaintiff buyer had the free use of the car for nearly a year, during which time it depreciated from £1,275 to £800.

5.16 Criticism of result.   This is quite unconscionable and argument enough that the transfer of ownership, as important as it is, is not the sole object of a sale of goods agreement.[70] The defendant sellers then had to absorb the car's depreciation from the date of the buyer's rescission to the trial, a matter of £350. This was treated as an incident, not so much of mitigation of damages, as of the defendants' owner-ship of the car. The remaining depreciation of £475, occurring during the plain-tiff's possession of the car, was then transmitted as a section 12(1) *ex post facto* warranty claim back up the chain to the fifth-party hirer. On any view of the mat-ter, the overall result is less than satisfactory.

5.17 Reasoning.   In deciding that the plaintiff buyer was entitled to the return of his money, Pearson J applied the rescission and failure of consideration analysis adopted in particular by Bankes LJ in *Rowland v Divall*,[71] though he stated that the result would have been the same if the matter had been treated as one of fun-damental breach entitling the buyer to treat the contract as repudiated. With respect, this understates the role that the acceptance rules in section 35 could play.[72] If the contract had not been terminated, a claim only for damages could hardly justify the return of the price in full, for reasons stated above. A rescission *ab initio* having been promptly and already self-executed by the buyer through his solicitor's letter, it was not relevant to his claim that the titles of all the sellers in the distribution chain were 'fed' (or cured) as far as the defendant sellers when the hirer later paid off the hire purchase debt and acquired the general property in the car. It was unnecessary to say whether the buyer's rescission could have been prevented if the hirer's title had been fed before this happened, and since it seemed that all other buyers had elected to pursue a damages claim, seeking neither to rescind *ab initio* nor to terminate for breach. While reluctant to express a firm opinion on the matter, Pearson J felt it would be 'extraordinary' for the buyer in such a case to rescind for a failure of consideration.[73]

---

[69] This was the explanation given in *Patten v Thomas*, n. 68 above, 464.

[70] Long-term financial leases attest to the significance of beneficial use whilst demystifying title.

[71] n. 25 above, 523–4.

[72] *Pace* the reasoning of Atkin LJ that the acceptance rules are ousted in *Rowland v Divall*, n. 25 above, 507.

[73] n. 66 above, 1295. Cf *Lucas v Dixon*, n. 68 above; *H W West Ltd v McBlain*, n. 67 above. The issue was left open by Winn LJ in *Bennett v Griffin Finance Ltd* [1967] 2 QB 46. Feeding title may be relevant outside sale in other proprietary transfers. In support of feeding, see the pledge cases of *Whitehorn Bros v Davison* [1911] 1 KB 463, 475; *Blundell-Leigh v Attenborough* [1921] 3 KB 235.

Feeding the seller's title. Since a failure of consideration claim looks to what in fact has been received under an extant contract, it seems right to rule out the action if the seller's title is fed before the rescission of the contract.[74] A claim that the contract has been terminated, allowing the buyer to recover the price as part of a post-termination damages adjustment, is a different matter. Section 12(1) recites 'an implied condition . . . that in the case of a sale [the seller] has a right to sell the goods'. Leaving aside Atkin LJ's difficulty whether they could properly be characterized as sales of goods at all, the sales in *Butterworth* were all present sales and the sellers all committed a discharging breach of condition at the moment of sale. No later feeding of title erases this breach of condition and prevents a buyer from terminating the contract, subject to section 35 and acceptance. Nevertheless, the act inconsistent with the seller's ownership[75] that all sellers in the chain performed when reselling the goods would bulk large and preserve the effect of a feeding of title. This argument probably renders unnecessary any attempt to argue the existence in this corner of sales law of a doctrine of cure that prevents the buyer from exercising rights of contractual termination.[76]   **5.18**

Two transfers. A final difficulty arising from the feeding of title concerns the seller with a defective title who makes two purported proprietary transfers and then subsequently acquires title to the goods. The question is how priority between the two earlier transferees is to be determined. In *Patten v Thomas*,[77] the hirer of a hire purchase car unlawfully sold the car and created a distribution chain like the one in *Butterworth*. The hirer subsequently paid off the finance company, but did so with moneys obtained by mortgaging the same car. At the time of this mortgage, the hirer had no title to convey to the mortgagee, but paying off the finance company appeared to feed both the mortgage and the series of sales transactions. Plainly it could not do both and the question was whether title to the car was now in the mortgagee or in the ultimate buyer. The court decided that the ultimate buyer prevailed on temporal grounds, since the sale chain was created before the mortgage. A later Queensland case[78] supports this result. The hirer of goods had unlawfully sold them to two buyers and the court, applying the equitable rule that a purported present sale of future property amounts to a covenant to convey that creates an equitable interest as soon as the property comes into existence,[79] concluded that, as between the equitable interests of the two buyers, the first in time should prevail.[80]   **5.19**

---

74 See E. P. Ellinger (1969) 5 *VUW LR* 168, 173.

75 S. 35: see Ch. 10 below.

76 See Ch. 10 below.

77 n. 68 above.

78 *Denis Geary Motors Pty Ltd v Hunter Street Finance Ltd* [1979] Qd. R 207.

79 *Tailby v Official Receiver* (1888) 13 App. Cas. 523.

80 In such a case, the superior title of the first buyer may be defeated by an application of the *nemo dat* exception in s. 24 of the Sale of Goods Act, discussed in the text accompanying nn. 433 *et seq.* below, if the seller remains in possession at the time of the second purported sale.

Limited Title Sales and Exclusion Clauses

5.20 Prohibition of exclusion. According to section 6(1)(a) of the Unfair Contract Terms Act 1977, the seller's liability in respect of the implied terms in section 12 of the Sale of Goods Act may be not be excluded or limited.[81] This prohibition extends to all contracts of sale and not just consumer transactions. Nevertheless, it is one thing to exclude or limit liability, and another for the parties to agree that 'the seller should transfer only such title as he or a third person may have'.[82] The line between a prohibited exclusion and a limited title sale is a peculiarly elusive one to draw. Before this is done, it should be asked what lies behind the outright ban on exclusion clauses under section 12 when this ban applies only to consumer transactions for the other implied terms in sections 13 to 15 of the Sale of Goods Act.

5.21 Title and fundamental breach. The Law Commission's extensive discussion of implied terms and exclusion clauses[83] is concerned only with the implied terms in sections 13–15. There is only the following statement made about section 12: 'We see no justification for varying or excluding the implied conditions and warranties imposed by section 12, save where it is clear that the seller is purporting to sell only a limited title.'[84] It is likely that this dogmatic view arose out of the title fundamentalism that inspired *Rowland v Divall*, especially the view of Atkin LJ that '[t]here can be no sale at all of goods which the seller has no right to sell'.[85] The literature predating the 1969 report[86] certainly was inspired by the idea that a breach of the terms in section 12 was a fundamental breach of contract (or a breach of a fundamental term), which at the time could not as a matter of substantive law be excluded. Largely because of the success of the Unfair Contract Terms Act 1977 in controlling certain abuses, the courts may now afford to take a more flexible view of exclusion and similar clauses, recognizing that in certain cases they play a fair role in defining the terms of the bargain and identifying the least cost insurer.[87] Indeed, it has long been recognized that exclusion clauses are central features of the contractual bargain and not merely forensic appendages brought into play

---

[81] The prohibition extends to clauses limiting the time within which a claim may be brought: *Ocean Chemical Transport Inc. v Exnor Craggs Ltd* [2000] 1 Lloyd's Rep. 446 at [28]. On exemption clauses generally, see Ch. 9.

[82] S. 12(3).

[83] In Law Com. No. 24, n. 60 above.

[84] *Ibid.*, para. 17. The Law Reform Committee, in *Transfer of Title to Chattels*, n. 47 above, had earlier seen no reason to distinguish sale and hire purchase, where a ban on exclusion already existed: para. 38.

[85] [1923] 2 KB 500, 506–7.

[86] A. Hudson (1957) 20 *MLR* 236; *ibid.*, (1961) 24 *MLR* 690; A. G. Guest (1961) 77 *LQR* 98, 100.

[87] *Photo Production Ltd v Securicor Transport Ltd* [1980] AC 827.

when a contractual dispute is resolved.[88] This principle, that clauses defining obligations and clauses excluding obligations cannot properly be distinguished, is breached by section 12(3) of the Sale of Goods Act, which attempts to do precisely that in defining limited title sales.

Identifying limited title sales.   As difficult as it is to separate limited title sales   **5.22**
and exclusions, it must be done. Perhaps the most obvious case of a limited title sale, which need not be expressed to be so in the contract but may be inferred from the circumstances, is a sale by sheriffs and bailiffs pursuant to their office,[89] where there has long been a desire to protect such officers in the exercise of their functions.[90] The common law development of the section 12 implied terms was retarded largely by such transactions. The law has also been sympathetic to secured creditors exercising powers of sale upon the debtor's default[91] and to auctioneers acting on behalf of unnamed principals.[92]

Buyer's awareness.   Another pointer to a limited title sale is the presence of cir-   **5.23**
cumstances where the buyer is or should be aware of a cloud on the seller's title.[93] An example of an implied limited title sale is where the seller functions almost as a buying agent, acquiring the goods to order and turning them over rapidly to the buyer.[94] In *Warming's Used Cars Ltd v Tucker*,[95] a used-car dealer gave a small deposit on a car to a seller and then contacted the sub-buyer, who he knew was interested in buying a car of this type. The sub-buyer drew a cheque for the balance of the price in favour of the seller and allowed a profit on the sale to the buyer, the dealer, as part of a periodical settlement of a running account between them. At all material times, the car remained on the premises of the seller before being taken to the sub-buyer's trade premises. The car turned out to be stolen and the sub-buyer's action against the dealer for breach of section 12(1)[96] was unsuccessful. The circumstances of the sale were held to negative the section 12 undertakings by the dealer.

---

[88] B. Coote, *Exception Clauses* (Sweet & Maxwell, 1970), 17. Cf *'Istros' (Owners) v F W Dahlstrom & Co.* [1931] 1 KB 247.

[89] *Peto v Blades* (1814) 5 Taunt. 657; *Chapman v Speller* (1850) 14 QB 621; *Niblett Ltd v Confectioners' Materials Co. Ltd* [1921] 3 KB 387, 401; *Payne v Elsden* (1900) 17 TLR 161.

[90] *Peto v Blades*, n. 89 above. On the protection of sheriffs and other officers, see County Courts Act 1984, s. 98 (as amended by Insolvency Act 1986, s. 183); Courts Act 2002, Sch. 7 para. 11.

[91] *Morley v Attenborough* (1849) 3 Ex. 500 (pawnbroker).

[92] *Wood v Baxter* (1883) 49 LT 45 (personal liability of auctioneer acting for unnamed principal limited to existence of his authority).

[93] *Page v Cowasjee Eduljee* (1866) LR 1 PC 127 (no liability on sale of stranded vessel by ship's master); *Northwest Co. Ltd v Merland Oil Co. of Canada Ltd* [1936] 2 WWR 577 (Can.).

[94] See *Clark v England* (1916) 10 WWR 1056 (Can.).

[95] [1956] SASR 249.

[96] Also for the implied warranty of quiet possession.

5.24 **Criticism.** The facts as presented might well have justified the conclusion that the dealer was in reality an agent purchasing on commission, leaving the field clear for an action by the 'sub-buyer' directly against the seller. Accepting that the court's characterization of the transaction was accurate, however, one objection to the outcome of the case is that a too-ready inference of a limited title sale in such circumstances runs counter to the policy of encouraging liability to pass up a distribution chain to the source of the fault in the goods. In section 12(1) cases, this will be the first unlawful seller or, if the seller is a rogue or a man of straw, the buyer who trusted that seller. An interesting question is whether the buyer under a limited title sale, who discovers that someone other than his seller was the true owner, has any recourse at all against his seller outside section 12(1). This buyer has plainly obtained nothing of value from the contract[97] so the question arises whether he can claim the recovery of any price paid, or resist paying it, on the ground that there has been a total failure of consideration. It is submitted that, in limited title sales, the buyer takes the risk of paying for something that is of no value, so that an action of this kind could not be sustained.[98]

5.25 **Express limited title.** The above discussion refers to cases where an implied limited title would be inferred. What of express contractual clauses to this effect? Clearly, in cases where an implied intention of a limited title sale would probably be inferred even without the clause, an express clause would be unlikely to be struck down as an exclusion clause. Any clause of general application in a standard form, or inserted in a contract of sale just because it might for unimaginable reasons turn out to be useful, would surely be classed as an exclusion clause. A difficult case is the car dealer with a large turnover and time only to consult the standard sources of information, sometimes fallible, concerning encumbrances of one kind or another on vehicles that are traded in. It is not at all clear that such a dealer could by standard clauses protect himself, or whether other factors could be taken into consideration, such as the consumer status of his purchaser, or the existence of any warning or explanation to the purchaser. The distinction between limited title clauses and exclusion clauses is very unsatisfactory but there is no evidence that it has caused much trouble in practice.

Range of Section 12(1)

5.26 **Beyond title.** The seller's liability under section 12(1), based on the 'right to sell', extends beyond matters of title. In *Niblett Ltd v Confectioners' Materials*

---

[97] Assuming that he has not had the use and enjoyment of the goods.

[98] An obvious exception to this would be where the seller was seeking to retain the price paid by two buyers: see *Chapman v Speller*, n. 89 above; *Northwest Co. Ltd v Merland Oil Co. of Canada Ltd*, n. 93 above.

Co. Ltd,[99] the sellers agreed to sell 3,000 cases of tinned milk bearing one or more of three brand names, including 'Nissly', a name that infringed the trade mark of a well-known manufacturer. One-third of the tins delivered bore the offending mark, and for this reason were detained by customs officials when they arrived in this country. The buyer had to remove the labels from the tins to secure their release, which greatly reduced their value. Scrutton LJ took a literal view of section 12(1): 'If a vendor can be stopped by process of law from selling he has not the right to sell.'[100] Similarly, the provision has been held to be breached where goods failed to comply with mandatory food[101] and electrical safety[102] standards. It would therefore seem generally that section 12(1) is infringed when the sale of goods amounts to a criminal offence or can be restrained by injunction.[103]

Second sale.   Section 12(1) might be taken further. Suppose a seller agrees to sell   **5.27**
specific goods to a buyer and, before the property in them passes to that buyer, agrees to sell them to a second buyer. The second buyer in such circumstances might reasonably wish not to take delivery of or retain the goods, given the possibility of becoming embroiled in a dispute with the first buyer, which might take the form of an action for interference with contractual relations. The second buyer, it is submitted, should be able to invoke section 12(1). The warranty of quiet possession in section 12(2)(b) might not afford sufficient protection. First it is only a warranty;[104] this limitation would be particularly apparent to someone wishing not to take delivery of the goods in the first place. Secondly, the first buyer's action in tort might not amount to an interference with the second buyer's possession.

Section 12(1) and *nemo dat*.   A further aspect of the seller's 'right' to sell con-   **5.28**
cerns the seller who unlawfully disposes of goods, thereby committing the tort of

---

[99] n. 89 above.

[100] Scrutton LJ had some doubt whether a limited title sale might have been intended if the contract had called only for the supply of 'Nissly' cans, *sed quaere?*

[101] *Egekvist Bakeries Inc. v Tizel* [1950] 1 DLR 585.

[102] *J Barry Winsor & Associates Ltd v Belgo-Canadian Manufacturing Co. Ltd* (1976) 76 DLR (3d) 685.

[103] In *Microbeads AG v Vinhurst Road Markings Ltd* [1975] 1 WLR 218, 221–2, Denning MR said: 'The words "a right to sell the goods" mean not only a right to pass the property . . . to the buyer, but also to confer on the buyer the undisturbed possession of the goods.'

[104] Nevertheless, in *Rubicon Computer Systems Ltd v Reliance Trading Ltd* (2000) 2 TCLR 453, the Court of Appeal held, in a case where the seller had breached its quiet possession warranty in s. 12(2)(b), that the seller's conduct amounted to a repudiation of the contract. No other term was identified as having been breached by the seller. Another unorthodox feature of the case was that the buyer's acceptance of the repudiation meant that the contract was rescinded *ab initio*: '. . .the repudiatory breach having been accepted, the contract was in effect rescinded. The parties were to be returned to the position in which they had been placed before the contract had been entered into, and that involved the respondents being entitled to the return of the purchase money, and no question arose of their having to pay the unpaid balance' (unpaginated).

conversion as against the true owner, but who does so under an exception to the rule of *nemo dat quod non habet*[105] so that the buyer obtains a title that overrides that of the true owner. The buyer, especially if purchasing goods (like cars) that are the subject of earlier recorded hire purchase or similar agreements, may find it in practical terms impossible to dispose of the goods by way of resale. Even if the buyer's quiet possession is not impaired by the finance company that retained title to the goods,[106] such a buyer has plainly suffered a loss. Moreover, while the right to sell term is a condition, the quiet possession term is a mere warranty. It is more than a little difficult to see how such a seller, committing the tort of conversion, can be said to have a 'right' to sell, as opposed to a power.

5.29 **Seller's immunity under section 12(1).** The little authority that there is, how-ever, points to the seller's freedom from liability. In *Karlhamns Oljefabriker v Eastport Navigation Corpn,*[107] the court considered a contract for the sale of a quantity of goods in a larger commingled mass. Such a contract might be an inter-mediate contract in a sales string, in respect of which contract the seller never acquires the property in the goods because the quantity in this contract, as opposed to the end contract in the string, is at no time ascertained. In the opinion of Mustill J, intermediate sellers in this position were not in breach of section 12(1) since that provision 'involves no promise about the seller's proprietary rights, only that he will be able to create the appropriate rights in the buyer'.[108] Neither this case, nor the others cited in favour of the seller, directly address the question of the *nemo dat* exception under discussion. The problem that concerned Mustill J, even if not resolved after the Sale of Goods (Amendment) Act 1995,[109] can be dealt with satisfactorily by different means. A seller of bulk commodities surely licenses buyers and sub-buyers to agree to sell parcels from the bulk, a very common occur-rence, in circumstances where that seller retains title to that bulk. In that sense, each intermediate seller has a right to sell. Furthermore, each of these intermediate contracts surely features a limited title sale that modifies anyway the effect of section 12(1). It is submitted that, because of the very real loss that a buyer might suffer when acquiring goods under the terms of a *nemo dat* exception, there is no

---

[105] Discussed in the text accompanying nn. 153 *et seq.* below.

[106] Atkin LJ said in *Niblett Ltd v Confectioners' Materials Co. Ltd*, n. 89 above, 403: 'It may be that possession would not be disturbed if the only cause of complaint was that the buyer could not dispose of the goods.'

[107] [1982] 1 All ER 208. See also *Niblett Ltd v Confectioners' Materials Co. Ltd*, n. 89 above, 401 (Atkin LJ); *R v Wheeler* (1991) 92 Cr. App. R 279 (noted by I. Brown (1992) 108 *LQR* 229) (rescission for misrepresentation refused since a buyer in these circumstances did not suffer a loss); *Benjamin's Sale of Goods* (7th edn, by A. G. Guest, 2006), para. 4.004.

[108] n. 107 above, 215.

[109] On paying his seller, each intermediate seller would acquire and be able to transmit an undivided share of the bulk: see Ch. 3 above.

case for putting a gloss on the language of section 12(1). The words should be given their literal meaning and the seller made liable.[110]

Instalment sales and third-party demands.   As stated above, the language of **5.30** section 12(1) is broad enough to embrace agreements to sell, an example of which is conditional sales under which the property passes once the buyer has paid all of the stipulated instalments of the price.[111] The seller undertakes that he will have a right to sell 'at the time when the property is to pass'. An interesting question concerns the buyer who is faced with a demand for the goods by a third party who has a superior title to that of the seller. As we shall see, the buyer's quiet possession is thus impaired but, unless the seller thereby commits an anticipatory repudiation of the above obligation in section 12(1), the buyer may not terminate the contract. If the buyer is unable to do so, then in principle the buyer must continue paying instalments as they fall due. There is in English law no broad entitlement for a party to demand that the other provide 'adequate assurance of due performance'[112] or to suspend contractual performance.[113] If the third party displaces the buyer from possession, the seller will surely have committed an anticipatory repudiation of section 12(1), although there may be cases where the seller can credibly point to negotiations with the third party likely to lead to the acquisition of that third party's rights, and hence pointing to the seller's ability to comply with section 12(1) by the time the buyer pays the last instalment. The effect of a buyer's action, taking advantage of any contractual right to accelerate payment by paying off all future instalments,[114] is hard to assess but it could accelerate a present breach of the implied condition in section 12(1) before the seller has time to pay off the third party.

Non-sale Contracts

Hire purchase.   Section 12(1) does not extend to contracts of hire and hire pur- **5.31** chase. In the latter case, the sale that usually occurs at the end of the period of hire

---

[110] In *Barber v NWS Bank plc*, n. 4 above, a seller in a position to pass a good title to the conditional buyer under Part III of the Hire Purchase Act 1964 (discussed in the text accompanying nn. 598 *et seq.* below) was held nevertheless to be in breach of an express title condition of the contract. The court, however, relied upon the language of the statute (s. 27(6)—*sed quaere?*) and not upon the argument advanced in this text, for which see also R. M. Goode, *Commercial Law* (3rd edn, Penguin, 2004), 286.

[111] See *McNeill v Associated Car Markets Ltd* (1962) 35 DLR (2d) 581; *Barber v NWS Bank plc*, n. 4 above (express clause).

[112] UCC Art. 2–609 (each contracting party guarantees that the other's performance expectation will not be impaired). Where a party reasonably feels insecure, he may suspend performance until the other provides adequate assurance that performance will be duly forthcoming and treat any failure to do so within a reasonable time as a contractual repudiation.

[113] See J. Carter, 'Suspending Contract Performance for Breach', in J. Beatson and D. Friedmann (eds.), *Good Faith and Fault in Contract Law* (OUP, 1995).

[114] Cf *Warman v Southern Counties Car Finance Corpn* [1949] 2 KB 576.

does so pursuant to an option that the hirer is not bound to exercise.[115] There is only a slight body of case law on the subject of a finance company's title obligations under a hire purchase agreement. Sometimes an agreement will contain an express undertaking that the finance company is the owner.[116] The importance of such an express undertaking will lead to its being treated as a contractual condition.[117] The functional equivalence of a hire purchase to sale has resulted in the hirer not being estopped in the same way as an ordinary bailee from denying the bailor's title.[118] There is also common law authority that the finance company is the owner at the date of the contract.[119] A better moment, if the agreement is executed before delivery, might be the date of the delivery itself.[120]

5.32 Legislation. Legislation, of general application to hire purchase contracts,[121] provides for the title obligation to spring at the moment the property is to pass under the agreement. If this legislation stood alone, without the common law authorities, it would put hirers in an intolerable predicament, not knowing whether they dare continue making payments in the hope that the finance company's title would be cleansed in due course, or even whether they might bring on the crisis by tendering all future instalments, thus bringing forward the operative date of the finance company's obligation. The combination of case law and statute, not incompatible, would appear to give the hirer the choice of dates of obligation.[122]

5.33 Hire. The obligations under a hiring agreement are established by section 7 of the Supply of Goods and Services Act 1982. The bailor does not, of course, undertake that he will have a right to sell at the moment the property is to pass, because the property does not pass, unless the parties at the end of the term agree on the sale of the goods, in which case the rules in section 12 of the Sale of Goods Act will apply. The bailor's corresponding obligation is the implied condition that he has a right to transfer possession of the goods by way of hire; alternatively, he undertakes that he will have the right to transfer possession in the case of an agreement to hire. These obligations are quite distinct from the quiet possession obligations, also owed, which protects the possession of the hirer when it is acquired.[123]

---

[115] *Lee v Butler* [1893] 2 QB 318; *Helby v Matthews* [1895] AC 471; *Belsize Motor Supply Co. v Cox* [1914] 1 KB 244.

[116] As was conceded and approved by the court in *Barber v NWS Bank plc*, n. 4 above.

[117] *Ibid*; *Karflex Ltd v Poole* [1933] 2 KB 251; *Warman v Southern Counties Car Finance Corpn*, n. 114 above.

[118] *Karflex Ltd v Poole*, n. 117 above.

[119] *Ibid.*; *Warman v Southern Counties Car Finance Corpn*, n. 114 above.

[120] *Mercantile Union Guarantee Corpn. v Wheatley* [1938] 1 KB 490.

[121] Supply of Goods (Implied Terms) Act 1973, s. 8(1)(a).

[122] A. Diamond, *Introduction to Hire Purchase Law* (2nd edn, Butterworths, 1971), 54.

[123] S. 7(2) of the 1982 Act.

Section 12 Warranties

General. Section 12(2) of the Sale of Goods Act recites two further implied **5.34** terms, this time warranties. First, there is the implied warranty that the goods are and will remain free from encumbrances before the property is to pass. This duty is subject to charges and encumbrances known or disclosed to the buyer before the date of the contract.[124] In a limited title sale, the seller further warrants that all charges or encumbrances known to him have been disclosed to the buyer before the date of the contract.[125] Secondly, there is the warranty that the buyer shall have quiet possession of the goods with the exception of disturbance arising out of such charges or encumbrances.[126] The quiet possession warranty of the seller under a limited title sale still applies to interference by the seller, by a third party whose limited title is being passed on by the seller, and by anyone claiming through the seller or such third party (apart from those claiming under a charge or encumbrance disclosed or known to the buyer at the contract date).[127] Liability for breach of the quiet possession warranty can exist alongside liability in tort for wrongful interference with the goods.[128] The case law on the quiet possession warranty is meagre and that on the encumbrance warranty more meagre still. Some guidance on the former, however, might be obtained from cases on the covenant of quiet possession in land law, since this covenant provided the model for the quiet possession warranty.[129]

Overlap. It is practically impossible to envisage a case that falls within the **5.35** encumbrance warranty but not within section 12(1) or the quiet possession warranty. For that reason alone, it is likely that the repeal of section 12(2)(a) would yield no practical consequences. It is not easy to envisage encumbrances against goods.[130] The common law has traditionally been unreceptive to the notion of covenants running with chattels.[131] Charges could include legal or equitable mortgages, as well as equitable charges.

---

[124] S. 12(2)(a). For very similar implied terms in other types of contract, see Supply of Goods (Implied Terms) Act 1973, s. 8(1)(b)(i) (hire purchase); Supply of Goods and Services Act 1982, s. 2(2)(a) (other contracts for the transfer of goods). Canadian case law has held that the registration of an encumbrance under personal property security legislation does satisfy the test of disclosure or knowledge: *Zuker v Paul* (1982) 37 OR (2d) 161 (Can.).

[125] S. 12(4). For very similar implied terms in other types of contract, see Supply of Goods (Implied Terms) Act 1973, s. 8(1)(b)(i) (hire purchase); Supply of Goods and Services Act 1982, ss. 2(2)(a) (other contracts for the transfer of goods) and 7(2) (hire—quiet possession only).

[126] S. 12(2)(b).

[127] S. 12(5).

[128] *Rubicon Computer Systems Ltd v United Paints Ltd*, n. 104 above.

[129] *Niblett Ltd v Confectioners' Materials Co. Ltd*, n. 89 above, 403.

[130] But see *Louis Dreyfus Trading Ltd v Reliance Trading Ltd* [2004] EWHC 525 (Comm); [2004] 2 Lloyd's Rep. 243 (third party's exclusivity agreement with seller).

[131] *Port Line Ltd v Ben Line Steamers* [1958] 2 QB 146, distinguishing *Lord Strathcona Steamship Co. v Dominion Coal Co.* [1926] AC 108; *Swiss Bank Corpn v Lloyds Bank Ltd* [1982] AC 584. Cf. *Law Debenture Trust Corpn v Ural Caspian Oil Corpn* [1993] 1 WLR 138, 143.

Quiet Possession

5.36 **General.** A number of quite taxing problems arise in the case of the quiet possession warranty. First, can the seller be liable if, at the contract date, even at the
date that property passes, there does not exist a cloud on the seller's title, but a
third party later interferes legitimately with the buyer's possession? Secondly, for
how long after the buyer acquires possession does the seller's guarantee last?
Thirdly, how far does the seller's liability extend? Fourthly, is the seller liable for all
or only some third-party interferences with the buyer's possession?

5.37 **Later third-party rights.** The first problem involves rights of a third party
against the contract goods springing into existence after the contract of sale.
Microbeads AG v Vinhurst Road Markings Ltd[132] concerned the sale of a number
of items of road-marking equipment by a Swiss seller to an English buyer. The
process of invention and application for letters patent being a confidential one,
neither party knew that another English company had filed an application for a
patent three years earlier and the complete specification itself two years earlier.
The completed specification was not published, and thus brought to the attention
of the outside world, until several months after the equipment had been sold and
delivered to the buyer.[133] At that time, the third party acquired patent rights to the
invention. There was no doubt that the seller had complied with the condition in
section 12(1), which was to be judged when the property passed. This occurred
before the publication of the specification. The Court of Appeal held that the
seller bore the burden of the retrospective application of the patent for the purpose of section 12(2)(b). The warranty guaranteed the buyer's quiet possession in
the future when the third party could, by taking legal action, prevent the buyer
from using the equipment. As between an innocent buyer and an innocent seller,
the loss should fall on the latter. It is a close call, but the decision seems unexceptionable; liability under section 12 is strict.[134]

5.38 **Duration of seller's liability.** The future character of section 12(2)(b) gives rise
to the second problem mentioned above: how far into the future might the seller
be liable? Compared to other obligations under the Sale of Goods Act, the quiet
possession warranty is unique in that it cannot be determined at the date of delivery whether the seller is in breach or ever will be in breach. No duration of the

---

[132] n. 103 above.

[133] In *Gencab of Canada Ltd v Murray-Jensen Manufacturing Ltd* (1980) 29 OR (2d) 552 (Can.),
the letters patent had been granted long before the contract of sale and the seller could have discovered their existence. The buyer's quiet possession was infringed when the buyer was warned of the
patent rights and even before the patent holder began proceedings.

[134] What about the supply of equipment whose use is later made unlawful under secondary
legislation dealing with health and safety? Would it depend upon whether the parent legislation had
been enacted at the date of the sale? Or whether a report recommending its enactment had been
published?

warranty is stated in its text and the presumption must be that the seller guarantees the buyer's possession as long as the buyer retains an interest in the goods. Individual acts of interference would be subject to the usual six-year limitation period[135] but, as long as the buyer retains a possessory interest in the goods,[136] a claim should arise in respect of each interference, even if it is the same third party who interferes on each occasion. Ackner LJ, in *The Playa Larga*,[137] was concerned about the prospect of endless liability on the part of sellers. In that case, the sellers sought to confine their exposure to a latent defect in their performance and to 'the time of performance', contrary to the *Microbeads* case, where the interference took place seven to ten months after the various dates of delivery and sale. Ackner LJ, however, gave some comfort to the notion that a seller should only be liable if the buyer had not accepted the goods under section 35.[138] This restriction, justified by expediency rather than by logic, would certainly cramp section 12(2)(b). The quiet possession warranty is precisely that—a warranty—and the acceptance period, often of short duration and difficult to protect, has nothing to do with the case. In the absence of qualifying legislation, there is no time limit on the seller's exposure apart from the limitation period running from the fact of interference.[139]

Sellers and sub-buyers. The exposure of the seller will cease to exist if the goods **5.39** themselves cease to exist. If the buyer disposes of them to a sub-buyer, the seller's liability should also cease. The seller does not protect the sub-buyer's quiet possession, and the quiet possession of the buyer cannot be infringed after the buyer has delivered the goods to the sub-buyer.[140] If the sub-buyer is able to sue the buyer for breach of the quiet possession warranty, the odd result is that the buyer will be unable to seek an indemnity from the seller unless able to point to another implied term in section 12 that has been breached. On the facts in *Microbeads*, if the defendant sellers had bought the road marking equipment from head sellers, they would have been unable to pass on their liability to these head sellers.

Nature of seller's action. The third problem mentioned above includes an **5.40** assessment of action on the seller's part that could make him liable for breach of the warranty. In *The Playa Larga*,[141] the seller was liable for colluding with a third

---

135 Limitation Act 1980, s. 5.

136 What about the buyer who has only a right to immediate possession?

137 *Empresa Exportadora de Azucar v Industria Azucarera Nacional SA (The Playa Larga)* [1983] 2 Lloyd's Rep. 171.

138 But the buyers in *Microbeads*, n. 103 above, had almost certainly accepted the equipment.

139 *Quaere* liability only so long as durability demands that the goods remain fit for the buyer's purpose or of satisfactory quality under s. 14?

140 A buyer out of possession, able to resist a prior owner's claim in conversion by raising a *nemo dat* exception by way of defence, would have no s. 12(2)(b) claim against the seller and, as seen above, might have no s. 12(1) claim either.

141 n. 137 above. For further instances of seller interference, see *Healing (Sales) Pty Ltd v Inglis Electrix Ltd* (1968) 121 CLR 584; *Gatoil International Inc. v Tradax Petroleum Ltd* [1985] 1 Lloyd's Rep. 350, 360–1 (unjustified exercise of lien).

party who interfered with the buyer's quiet possession. The seller participated in discussions with the Cuban Government, the consequence of which was the withdrawal from a Chilean harbour of a ship bearing a c. & f. cargo already paid for by the Chilean buyer. It would seem that the buyer's constructive possession of the cargo[142] was thus being interfered with by the seller and the Cuban Government. A seller's unlawful interference can occur where the seller interferes with the use and not just with the possession of goods, as occurred in one case where the seller of a computer system with remote access to it activated a time lock, with the result that the buyer was unable to use the system.[143]

5.41 **Identity of third-party interferer.**   The fourth problem mentioned above relates to the identity of the person interfering with the buyer's possession. As stated above, the section 12(2)(b) warranty appears to be modelled upon its sale of land equivalent, the covenant of quiet enjoyment of land. The circumstances of a sale of land, including the investigation of title by the buyer, deprive the buyer of protection if he is evicted by title paramount,[144] confining an action on the covenant to interferences by the seller. Opinions have been expressed that the quiet possession warranty in sale of goods should similarly be confined,[145] but it is settled that the very different circumstances of a sale of goods justify the imposition of liability for third-party interference.[146] A seller will be liable if, as a result of his default, a third party lawfully interferes with the buyer's possession,[147] but not where the third party is 'totally unconnected with the seller',[148] otherwise the seller

---

[142] As (*semble*) the holder of the bill of lading transferred on payment. The fact of interference with quiet possession had earlier been conceded. See also *Gatoil International Inc. v Tradax Petroleum Ltd*, n. 141 above, where a breach of s. 12(2)(b) appears to have been found in the conduct of the sellers, also the sub-charterers of the ship, in giving orders to the ship not to release the cargo at a time when the bills of lading had not come into the buyers' hands. If correct, this should be confined to interferences with a buyer's factual expectation of obtaining possession from a third party, or else the seller will be in breach whenever he is late in delivering the goods.

[143] *Rubicon Computer Systems Ltd v United Paints Ltd*, n. 104 above. It is not clear from the report whether the seller directly interfered with the computer in a physical way or disabled it remotely. Unlawful interference can arise without the seller's direct interference, as where the seller requests a third party to interfere: *The Playa Larga*, n. 137 above.

[144] *Baynes & Co. v Lloyd & Sons* [1895] 2 QB 610 (not a covenant for title); *Jones v Lavington* [1903] 1 KB 253. The reason given for this is that there exists already an action against the third-party wrongdoer: *Markham v Paget* [1908] 1 Ch 697, 716–19.

[145] *Bergfeldt v Markell* [1921] 1 WWR 453 (Can.), applying *Monforts v Marsden* (1895) 12 RPC 266, itself disapproved in *Niblett*, n. 89 above.

[146] *Mason v Burningham* [1949] 2 KB 545; *Microbeads AG v Vinhurst Road Markings Ltd*, n. 103 above; *The Playa Larga*, n. 137 above.

[147] *Gatoil International Inc. v Tradax Petroleum Ltd*, n. 141 above (shipowner exercising lien over cargo against seller as sub-character of ship). See also *Louis Dreyfus Trading Ltd v Reliance Trading Ltd* [2004] EWHC 525 (Comm); [2004] 2 Lloyd's Rep. 243 (seller's entry into exclusivity agreement with third party who obtained injunction preventing the goods from being unloaded).

[148] *The Playa Larga*, n. 137 above, 178. See also *Malzy v Eicholz* [1916] 2 KB 308 (land and third-party nuisance); *Matania v National Provincial Bank* [1936] 2 All ER 633 (nuisance committed by co-tenant and not permitted by landlord).

would be guaranteeing the buyer against burglaries and thefts, or where the claim is not a 'lawful' one.[149] Short of such extreme cases is the third party with the arguable claim, for example, the owner defeated by a *nemo dat* exception or the *Romalpa*[150] seller who mistakenly believes that the clause permits the contract goods to be repossessed from a sub-buyer. If such interference is not unreasonable, it is submitted that the seller should be liable for the third-party interference. Furthermore, if the seller is aware of the prospect of unreasonable interference by a particular claimant, and fails to warn the buyer of this or negotiate a limited title sale,[151] there is a good case for the application of section 12(2)(b).[152] An example would be the sale of jewellery by a family member who knows of the risk that another member will make an unreasonable claim against the buyer.

The *Nemo Dat* Rule and its Exceptions

Protecting ownership and commerce. A legal system concerned with the pro-   **5.42**
tection of private property, and not open to any countervailing policies, would assert with unabated vigour the maxim *nemo dat quod non habet*,[153] by which the transferee's title could never exceed the title of the transferor and would always be vulnerable to a superior title. If, on the other hand, a legal system pursued to the same degree a policy of facilitating transactions, again without countervailing policies, it would maintain that a transferee acting in good faith[154] could trust in the appearance of ownership created by possession of goods in the hands of the transferor. The common law takes an intermediate position, starting from the *nemo dat* maxim and grafting on a number of exceptions. A number of these are statutory ones enacted in response to the needs of the commercial community.[155] This pragmatic resolution of the irreconcilable demands of private property protection and the facilitation of transactions is expressed by Denning LJ as follows:[156]

> In the development of our law, two principles have striven for mastery. The first is the protection of private property: no one can give a better title than he himself possesses. The second is for the protection of commercial transactions: the person who

---

[149] *Niblett Ltd v Confectioners' Materials Co. Ltd*, n. 89 above, 403.

[150] *Aluminium Industrie Vaassen BV v Romalpa Aluminium Ltd* [1976] 1 WLR 676.

[151] The scope of a limited title sale here may be limited by the language of s. 12(5)(c), and there is the further difficulty that a limited title sale appears to be confined to cases where the seller's title is indeed limited, which is not the case here.

[152] *Pace* the confinement in *Niblett*, n. 89 above, to 'lawful' claims.

[153] Restated in s. 21(1) of the Sale of Goods Act.

[154] For a useful general discussion of the good faith purchaser doctrine, see *R Griggs Group Ltd v Evans (No. 2)* [2004] EWHC 1088 (Ch); [2005] Ch 153.

[155] R. S. T. Chorley (1932) 48 *LQR* 51.

[156] *Bishopsgate Motor Finance Corpn v Transport Brakes Ltd* [1949] AC 322, 336–7.

takes in good faith and for value without notice should get a good title. The first principle has held sway for a long time, but has been modified by the common law itself and by statute so as to meet the needs of our own times.

It would be more accurate to say that the various statutory exceptions to *nemo dat* were designed to maintain a balance between these two principles rather than redress it in favour of the facilitation of transactions. Nevertheless, the above passage reveals a conflict going far beyond the resolution of individual disputes. The clash of opposing principle should be borne in mind, even though individual cases often reveal internal inconsistency and illogicality.

5.43 Principal parties. Title chains may be of variable length, but they can be simplified to three principal actors. First, there is the owner of goods. Secondly, there is the rogue[157] who unlawfully either acquires or disposes of the goods. Thirdly, there is the innocent purchaser who acquired the goods from the rogue in good faith. The rogue disappears or is not worth suing so, as between the dispossessed owner and the transferee who has paid the rogue, the common judicial *cri de cœur* is which of these two innocent persons should suffer the consequences of the rogue's dishonesty.

5.44 Common law exception *to nem dat.* The exceptions of common law origin to the *nemo dat* rule are as follows. First, there is the voidable title rule by which a party to whom the transferor's title has defeasibly passed may in turn pass on that title to a *bona fide* purchaser.[158] This can be accomplished indefeasibly provided it is done before the first transaction is rescinded by the transferor. Secondly, until the repeal of the rule by the Sale of Goods (Amendment) Act 1995, a seller of goods in market overt could effectively transfer title to a *bona fide* purchaser.[159] The theoretical importance of this exception was that it was the only exception, of common law or statutory origin, that treated as irrelevant the details of the transaction between owner and rogue in the simplified title chain above. This exception could launder doubtful titles and created the nearest thing to absolute ownership recognized by the common law.[160] The third of these exceptions is the doctrine of apparent authority.[161] It applies where the third-party purchaser

---

[157] A title of convenience. The 'rogue' is usually dishonest but sometimes acts mistakenly and in good faith.

[158] This has been codified as s. 23 where the second transaction is a sale. The common law governs if it is a pledge or other disposition.

[159] S. 22 of the Sale of Goods Act 1979.

[160] For details of the market overt rule, see M. Bridge, *Sale of Goods* (Butterworths, Toronto, 1988), 584–9; Palmer and E. McKendrick (eds), *Interests in Goods* (2nd edn, LLP, 1998), Ch. 14 (B. Davenport and A. Ross), who write at 352: 'The only losers from the end of the special rules concerning sales in market overt are thieves and a few antique dealers who, it seems, trade in stolen goods.'

[161] Codified in s. 21(1) where the second transaction is a sale. See generally *Bowstead on Agency* (18th edn, by F. M. B. Reynolds, Sweet & Maxwell, 2006).

reasonably but incorrectly apprehends that an agent has the owner's permission to sell. Apparent authority is not to be confused with implied authority, where an agent has an actual but unexpressed authority to act. Similar to apparent authority, and commonly confused with it, is the doctrine of apparent ownership, where in limited circumstances a purchaser may reasonably equate possession in the hands of a transferor with ownership. A purchaser may often be incurious as to whether someone is in possession of goods as agent or owner.

Statutory exceptions to *nemo dat*.   There exist also a number of statutory excep-   **5.45**
tions to the *nemo dat* rule, all inspired by notions of apparent authority or owner-ship, though they are legislative extensions of a common law that inadequately protects good faith purchasers. These exceptions concern dispositions by mercan-tile agents in possession of goods, or of documents of title, with the owner's con-sent,[162] as well as dispositions by sellers[163] and buyers[164] in possession. All of the *nemo dat* exceptions that are located or partly codified in the Sale of Goods Act are circumstantially related to a contract of sale, whether because the contract between owner and rogue is one of sale or because the transfer from the rogue to the inno-cent purchaser takes the form of a sale. This amounts to less than a full legislative treatment of all the exceptions to the *nemo dat* rule. Indeed, it is by no means obvious that the Sale of Goods Act was and is the proper place to deal with title disputes: there is much to be said for a separate and comprehensive statute.

Money and negotiable instruments.   Outside the Act lies the transfer of money   **5.46**
and negotiable instruments, for these are not goods.[165] Title to money is trans-ferred once it passes in currency to a good faith purchaser.[166] Negotiable instru-ments resemble money, in that their transfer for value, by indorsement and delivery or just delivery, as the case may be, creates in the transferee an unencum-bered title, subject to a few exceptions. Negotiable documents of title are treated somewhat differently. Their negotiability consists of the freedom with which they may be transferred so as to endow the current holder with a direct right to call on a bailee to surrender the goods they represent.[167] But they are also significant, whether as common law or statutory documents of title,[168] in that their transfer may affect title to the underlying goods. Transferability and true negotiability should be distinguished, since documents of title never have the currency of money. They lack its intrinsic value and their issue does not as such affect the antecedent title chain to the goods they represent.

---

[162] Factors Act 1889, s. 2.
[163] Factors Act, s. 8; Sale of Goods Act, s. 24.
[164] Factors Act, s. 9; Sale of Goods Act, s. 25(1).
[165] See Ch. 2 above.
[166] *Miller v Race* (1758) 1 Burr. 452.
[167] Bridge, n. 11 above, 165–8.
[168] Discussed in the text accompanying nn. 387 *et seq.* below.

Sales under a Voidable Title

5.47   **General.**   Under section 23, a good faith purchaser of goods to which the seller's title is voidable acquires a 'good title'[169] if, at the time of the sale, the seller's title has not yet been avoided.[170] The section makes no reference to the rogue obtaining possession of the goods, nor to the purchaser obtaining possession from the rogue. Nor does the sale have to comply with an ordinary course of business test. In such an unlikely transaction, however, serious questions would arise in respect of the purchaser's good faith and absence of notice.

5.48   **Contract void or voidable?**   In determining the applicability of the section, the question usually asked is whether the contract under which the seller acquired title is void because of a fundamental mistake as to the rogue's identity, or whether it is merely voidable because the rogue's fraud[171] induced in the mind of the owner a lesser mistake as to the rogue's attributes, notably creditworthiness. A rogue acquires no title at all under a void contract.[172] For many decades, the leading though somewhat controversial authority was *Cundy v Lindsay*,[173] in recent years reaffirmed by a bare majority of the House of Lords in *Shogun Finance Ltd v Hudson*.[174] As the authorities developed, it became plain that a distinction was to be drawn between cases where a contract was concluded at a distance and in writing, and contracts where the parties dealt face to face, where 'the innocent party will have in mind, when considering with whom he is contracting, both the person with whom he is in contact and the third party whom he imagines that person to be'.[175] In *Cundy*, a rogue called Alfred Blenkarn rented premises at No. 37 Wood Street and No. 5 Little Love Lane. A well-established firm called W. Blenkiron and Son traded from No. 123 Wood Street. The rogue sent letters to the plaintiffs, Belfast linen manufacturers, ordering a large quantity of handkerchiefs, giving his address as '37, Wood Street . . . entrance, second door in

---

[169] This can be transferred in the normal way to a sub-purchaser even if that sub-purchaser at the time had notice of the circumstances in which the purchaser acquired title: *Peirce v London Horse and Carriage Repository Ltd* [1922] WN 170.

[170] *Cundy v Lindsay* (1878) 3 App Cas 459; *Phillips v Brooks* [1919] 2 KB 243; *Dennant v Skinner* [1948] 2 KB 164; *Robin and Rambler Coaches Ltd v Turner* [1947] 2 All ER 284; *Lewis v Averay* [1972] 1 QB 98. A similar common law principle will apply where the rogue's disposition takes the form of a pledge instead of a sale: *Whitehorn Bros v Davison* [1911] 1 KB 463; *Babcock v Lawson* (1880) 5 QBD 284. But no title at all is transferred for present purposes under a sale or return: *Truman v Attenborough* (1910) 26 TLR 601.

[171] An innocent misrepresentation would suffice.

[172] The criminal law once drew a distinction between false pretences and larceny by a trick, the latter offence corresponding to cases where any supposed contract between owner and rogue was void. See *Heap v Motorists' Advisory Agency Ltd* [1923] 1 KB 577; *Lake v Simmons* [1927] AC 487; *Whitehorn Bros v Davison*, n. 170 above.

[173] n. 170 above.

[174] [2003] UKHL 62; [2004] 1 AC 919.

[175] *Shogun Finance Ltd v Hudson*, above, n. 174 at [153] (Lord Phillips).

Little Love Lane'. He signed the letters 'A. Blenkarn & Co.' but in such a misleading way that the plaintiffs read the signature as 'A. Blenkiron & Co'. The plaintiffs, knowing W. Blenkiron and Son to be a reputable firm, dispatched the handkerchiefs to Blenkarn on credit terms. He decamped with the proceeds after selling the handkerchiefs to the innocent defendants.

No contract.   Blackburn J's decision in favour of the defendants at first instance **5.49** was overturned by the Court of Appeal; the ensuing appeal was dismissed by the House of Lords. In Lord Cairns's view, no contract existed between the plaintiffs and Alfred Blenkarn because the plaintiffs, knowing nothing of the existence of an Alfred Blenkarn,[176] intended to deal only with the 'well-known and solvent house of Blenkiron & Co'. It was all tantamount to a forgery of this firm's signature by the rogue and a later interception by the rogue of the goods sent to the firm.[177] The decision of the House of Lords appears therefore to be based on a simile inspired by the uncontested factual record of the case rather than on the facts themselves. The conclusion that the plaintiffs intended to deal only with the firm of W. Blenkiron and Son is hard to support given that neither the proper name nor the proper address of the genuine firm was used by either the rogue or the plaintiffs. It is not certain that the result would have been the same if the plaintiffs had been confused by a genuine signature from the rogue. *Cundy v Lindsay* does not as such express a rule of law that contractual offers and acceptance are enforceable only by the person to whom they are addressed. Furthermore, it was the fate of the decision that it was subsequently confined to cases where contracting parties dealt with each other at a distance.[178] Even here, it was not followed in *King's Norton Metal Co. Ltd v Edridge, Merrit & Co. Ltd* where the rogue, Wallis, gave himself the bogus corporate identity and branch offices of a fictional Hallam & Co.,[179] since an intention to deal with a non-existent entity could not be inferred.[180]

Affirmation of *Cundy v Lindsay*.   In *Shogun Finance Ltd v Hudson*, Lord Phillips **5.50** in particular laid down a principled basis for identifying cases where a mistake as to identity made a contract void *ab initio*. He did so, not by stating any bald rule of law that offers may be accepted only by those to whom they are addressed,

---

176 'Of him they knew nothing, and of him they never thought': n. 170 above, 465.

177 Lord Cairns, *ibid.* at 464.

178 But see Lord Haldane in *Lake v Simmons* [1927] AC 487.

179 (1897) 14 TLR 98, changing the emphasis from the absence of an intention to deal with the rogue to the existence of an intention to deal with some other person.

180 'If it could have been shown that there was a separate entity called Hallam and Co. [C] and another entity called Wallis [A] then the case might have come within the decision in *Cundy v Lindsay...*': *ibid.*, 99 (A. L. Smith LJ). As Lord Phillips expressed it in *Shogun Finance Ltd v Hudson*, n. 174 above at [135]: 'The plaintiffs intended to deal with whoever was using the name of Hallam & Co. Extrinsic evidence was needed to identify who that was but, once Wallis was identified as the user of that name, the party with whom the plaintiffs had contracted was established. They could not demonstrate that their acceptance of the offer was intended for anyone other than Wallis.'

but by treating the matter as one of construction dependent upon all of the circumstances of the case.[181] After reviewing the authorities, not all of which concerned mistakes as to identity,[182] he said this:

> [A] person carrying on negotiations in writing can, by describing as one of the parties to the putative agreement an individual who is unequivocally identifiable from the description, preclude any finding that the party to the putative agreement is other than the person so described. The process of construction will lead inexorably to the conclusion that the person with whom the other party intended to contract was the person thus described.[183]

In *Shogun Finance* itself, a rogue filled in a hire purchase company's standard form contract, passing himself off as Durlabh Patel. He had Patel's driver's licence, but Patel was wholly innocent of the subterfuge. The rogue forged his signature so as to match the genuine signature on the driver's licence. The admirably clear wording of the standard form made it plain that an offer was being addressed to the finance company that the latter might accept without further communication with the offeror. The finance company checked the credit rating of Patel, the register of court judgments and the electoral register, before deciding to go ahead with the transaction. The rogue obtained possession of the vehicle after writing a cheque in part-payment of the deposit, which was dishonoured. The rogue then disappeared after selling the vehicle to an innocent purchaser, whose claim to obtain good title under Part III of the Hire Purchase Act 1964 turned upon whether the rogue could be described as the 'hirer' under the hire purchase agreement. This in turn depended upon whether a hire purchase agreement had come into existence between the finance company and the rogue. After construing the documents and the surrounding circumstances, the House of Lords by a majority concluded that the hire purchase agreement was a nullity because the intention of the finance company was to deal with Patel and only Patel.[184] The dissentients

---

181 The other majority speeches are to the same effect. See Lord Hobhouse at [46] ('a question of the construction of this written document, not a question of factual investigation and evaluation') and [47] ('the written document . . . admits of only one conclusion'); Lord Walker at [183] (objective approach to offer and acceptance).

182 *Newborne v Sensolid (Great Britain) Ltd* [1954] 1 QB 45; *Homburg Houtimport BV v Agrosin Private Ltd (The Starsin)* [2003] UKHL 12; [2004] 1 AC 715.

183 n. 174 above at [161].

184 See Lord Hobhouse at [50] (no consensus ad idem between the finance company and the rogue); Lord Phillips at [167] (contract void because Patel had not authorised it); Lord Walker at [191] ('intention . . . to accept an offer made by the real Mr Patel, and no one else'). Lord Hobhouse also stated in trenchant terms at [49] a conclusive version of the parol evidence rule that has fallen out of judicial fashion. An earlier case where the same conclusion was reached is *Boulton v Jones* (1859) 2 H & N 564, where the defendant sent an order addressed to Brocklehurst at the premises where Brocklehurst did business. He had a right of set-off against Brocklehurst. Unknown to him, Brocklehurst had sold his business to Boulton, who fulfilled the order. The defendant was held not liable to pay the price. One of the dissentients in *Shogun Finance* considered *Boulton v Jones* to be rightly decided: n. 174 above at [94] (Lord Millett).

would have been prepared to overrule *Cundy v Lindsay* and saw no categorical difference between cases of written correspondence and face-to-face dealings. On one view of the dissents, there would be a strong presumption that a contract was concluded between parties dealing or in correspondence with each other.[185] On the other, slightly stronger, view, all would turn upon whether an offer was made to its recipient, as would be so in cases where there are dealings between the relevant parties, even if the offer was made by means of deception or mistake.[186]

Construing documents.   The result in *Shogun Finance* is that, where written communications pass between two parties, it is a matter of construing the documents whether it is the intention of each party to deal with the other. It did not matter in the case that the finance company would have been willing to hire the vehicle to anyone passing its credit reference and other checks and had no interest in Patel as a person in his own right. The necessary intention will not be present where it is positively one party's intention to deal with someone other than the other party to the written exchange. Where the rogue assumes the identity of a fictional person, it would seem from the reception given in the majority speeches to the *King's Norton* case that the absence of a real person of the same name permits the inference of a binding contract between rogue and victim.[187] It is not clear why this should make a difference if the issue is one of construing written correspondence. The victim in the *King's Norton* case was in correspondence with Hallam and Co. and not with the rogue Wallis. As for *Cundy v Lindsay* itself, it does not appear to withstand the rigours of the construction approach laid down by the majority in *Shogun Finance*. No rigorous checks were undertaken to ensure that the victim of the fraud was dealing with the reputable firm of W. Blenkiron and Son. The letters from the rogue came from the fictional entity of A. Blenkarn and Co. and from an address other than that of W. Blenkiron and Son. Although the formation of contracts by written correspondence is a matter of construction and not of 'factual investigation and evaluation',[188] the need to resort to extrinsic evidence in aid of construction ensures that fact remains of great importance.[189]

5.51

Face-to-face dealings.   The proposition that face-to-face dealings are different from dealings by written correspondence has survived the House of Lords decision in *Shogun Finance*,[190] even though a sharp distinction between the two cannot

5.52

---

185   n. 174 above at [24] and [33]–[37] (Lord Nicholls)
186   *Ibid.*, at [68] and [81] (Lord Millett).
187   See Lord Phillips at [135] and Lord Walker at [189].
188   Lord Hobhouse at [46].
189   Lord Phillips's speech begins at [111] with a quotation from *Fawcett v Star Car Sales Ltd* [1960] NZLR 406, 413, stating that 'the difficulty in deciding whether a mistake of identity prevents the formation of a concluded contract is a proper assessment of the facts rather than the ascertainment of the law'. It makes a further approving reference to the case at [176].
190   n. 174 above at [153] (Lord Phillips) and [187] (Lord Walker: 'strong presumption').

readily be drawn. The written correspondence in *Shogun Finance* was supplemented by fax messages and telephone calls.[191] The drawing of a categorical difference between these two cases, each with its own distinctive rule, does not further the coherence of the law on title transfer. In consequence, the position remains that transactions between rogues and owners face-to-face are significantly more likely to be held to be voidable. In *Phillips v Brooks Ltd*,[192] a rogue claiming to be Sir George Bullough, a man of substance whose existence was known to the plaintiff jeweller, bought a ring from the jeweller and paid for it with a worthless cheque. He later pledged it with the innocent defendants. The jeweller was held to have intended to deal with the person physically present,[193] so the rogue was able to pass a valid possessory title to the defendants. It was said in the later case of *Ingram v Little*[194] that parties face-to-face presumptively intend to deal with each other and that the presumption can be shifted only with difficulty.[195] The majority found in that case that the presumption had been displaced on facts justifying little more than sympathy for the plight of the unworldly owners deceived by the rogue.[196] Claiming to be a certain P. G. M. Hutchinson of Stanstead House, Caterham, the rogue was allowed by its Bournemouth owners to take away a car in return for a worthless cheque. The owners had never heard of Hutchinson, but released the car after one of them discreetly verified his existence in a telephone directory. The court finding that the owners did not intend to deal with the person physically present, the loss fell on a Blackpool car dealer who had bought the car from the rogue and who in all probability could more easily afford the loss than the owners. Devlin LJ, the dissenting judge, agreed that the presumption could be displaced, citing the case of the transaction concluded on the premises of a reputable company with someone who appeared to be representing the company but who was in fact an unauthorized rogue.[197] Nevertheless, in Devlin LJ's view, the owners' behaviour in *Ingram v Little* revealed little more than a concern for the

---

[191] n. 174 above at [173].

[192] [1919] 2 KB 253. See *Terry v Vancouver Motors U-Drive Ltd* [1942] 1 WWR 503 (Can.) (affirmed [1942] SCR 391), *per* McDonald CJBC (commenting on the difficulty of distinguishing *Cundy v Lindsay* and the unsatisfactory distinction between contracts formed by written correspondence and contracts formed face-to-face).

[193] See E. C. S. Wade (1922) 38 *LQR* 201, arguing that the property had already passed in the ring (specific goods) before the rogue announced his identity. See also *Ingram v Little* [1961] QB 31, 51, 60.

[194] n. 193 above.

[195] A rare example where the presumption would be shifted, if the modern way of putting the matter had been adopted at the time, is *Hardman v Booth* (1863) 1 H & C 803. In that case, a person was on the premises of a firm with which he did intend to contract and had no intention of contracting with a different firm represented by the person in front of him, who also happened to be an (unauthorized) employee of the firm with which he did intend to deal.

[196] See Phillimore LJ in *Lewis v Averay* [1972] 1 QB 198, 208 ('the very special and unusual facts of the case').

[197] *Hardman v Booth*, n. 195 above.

creditworthiness of the buyer, a matter of attributes rather than identity, and the extent to which they had been duped did not affect the issue.[198]

Strength of presumption. This sounder approach to the facts of the case was later vindicated by the Court of Appeal in *Lewis v Averay*.[199] In that case, a rogue obtained possession of a car under a contract of sale in return for a worthless cheque, representing himself as an actor famous for playing the television role of Robin Hood.[200] The rogue was held to have acquired a voidable title on the sale, which was transmitted to the defendant on the resale. Although Lord Denning was prepared to hold that a mistake as to identity can never render a contract void,[201] the majority of the court held that the presumption of an intention by the plaintiff to deal with the person opposite had not been displaced, a conclusion almost certain to be followed in similar cases.   **5.53**

Innocent purchaser and prior contract. In these cases, the purchaser's legal position is determined by the contract between owner and rogue of which he knows nothing. Devlin LJ in *Ingram v Little* asked: 'Why should the question whether the defendant should or should not pay the plaintiff damages for conversion depend upon voidness or voidability, and upon inferences to be drawn from a conversion in which the defendant took no part?'[202] He would have preferred a scheme of even apportionment between owner and purchaser in the case of pure misfortune, adjusted where one or the other had been guilty of negligence.[203] Nevertheless, all of the statutory extensions to apparent authority[204] turn upon the details of a relationship between owner and rogue unknown to the purchaser. Such illogicality would seem to be the natural product of the irreconcilable clash between the protection of private property and the facilitation of transactions. *Ingram v Little* was interpreted by Megaw LJ in *Lewis v Averay* as requiring the issue of void or voidable to turn on the rogue's apprehension of whether the owner's offer was being made to him or someone else.[205] This is a perfectly acceptable rendering of the principle of objectivity in contract formation,[206] though   **5.54**

---

[198] n. 193 above, 67, 69. Cf. The criticism of Lord Hobouse in *Shogun Finance*, n. 174 above, at [47].

[199] n. 196 above. In *Shogun Finance*, n. 174 above at [185], Lord Walker considered Devlin LJ's dissent to be 'unanswerable' and *Ingram v Little* to be wrongly decided.

[200] The actor's name on the cheque was misspelt: Richard Green(e).

[201] See UCC Art. 2–403(1); Law Reform Committee, *Twelfth Report (Transfer of Title to Chattels)*, n. 47 above, para. 15.

[202] n. 193 above, 73.

[203] *Ibid.*, 73–4.

[204] Mercantile agency and sellers and buyers in possession.

[205] n. 196 above, 208. Cf. A. Goodhart (1941) 57 *LQR* 228, 240.

[206] *Smith v Hughes* (1871) LR 6 QBD 597; *Tilden Rent-A-Car v Clendenning* (1978) 83 DLR (3d) 400; *Harris v Great Western Railway Co.* (1876) 1 QBD 515; *UGS Finance Ltd v National Mortgage Bank of Greece* [1964] 1 Lloyd's Rep. 446.

Megaw LJ thought it wrong that the purchaser's protection should hinge upon the rogue's apprehension.[207]

Rescission

5.55 **Avoiding the contract.**   Section 23 does not say how the owner might avoid the contract of sale before the rogue resells the goods to the innocent purchaser. The problem is a difficult one, since rogues put themselves beyond the reach of owners. If, exceptionally, the owner is able to confront the rogue, any behaviour of the owner evincing an intention to disaffirm the contract should suffice.[208] It is not clear whether the avoidance contemplated by section 23 takes place at common law or in equity. Equitable rescission *ab initio* does not in principle require judicial intervention,[209] though the court's assistance may be needed to work out its remedial consequences. Prior to the fusion of the courts of common law and equity, the common law had developed a remedy amounting to rescission *ab initio* in cases of fraud.[210] Further, whilst at common law rescission *ab initio* is no longer a permissible outcome of termination for breach,[211] the property in goods could revest in a seller by virtue of an implied resolutive condition,[212] producing the same result as in equitable rescission.

5.56 **Election.**   An owner's rescission of the contract depends upon an election to avoid the contract, which requires clear and positive evidence that the elector has chosen a particular remedy.[213] It may be that the circumstances will demand as clear evidence of the elector's choice a communication to the other party. Communication is obviously necessary too where the elector may choose to sue one of two parties but not both.[214] The elector may also have to communicate a choice of remedies if the contract fairly implies that this should occur to save the

---

[207] n. 196 above, 208.

[208] The contract was affirmed where the owner said at a police station that all he wanted was his money: *Jim Spicer Chev. Olds. Ltd v Kinniburgh* [1978] 1 WWR 253 (Can.).

[209] *Abram Steamship Co. Ltd v Westville Shipping Co. Ltd* [1923] AC 773; *Car and Universal Finance Co. Ltd v Caldwell* [1965] 1 QB 525; *Bevan v Anderson* (1957) 23 WWR 508 (Can.). But note that the right to rescind may be removed under s. 2(2) of the Misrepresentation Act 1967 (discussed in Ch. 8 below).

[210] *Clarke v Dickson* (1858) E B & E 148; *Clough v London and North Western Railway Co.* (1871) LR 7 Ex. 26.

[211] *Johnson v Agnew* [1980] AC 367; *Photo Production Ltd v Securicor Transport Ltd* [1980] AC 827.

[212] *RV Ward Ltd v Bignall* [1967] 1 QB 534.

[213] *Reese Silver Mining Co. v Smith* (1869) LR 4 HL 64, 74 (Lord Hatherley LC). See also Denning MR, at first instance, in *Car and Universal Finance Co. v Caldwell*, n. 209 above, 532. The disagreement between Lord Denning and the Court of Appeal, *ibid.*, about the need to communicate the election may be reconciled, it is submitted, by the immediately ensuing arguments in this text. Davies LJ is equivocal on the need to communicate. On the question of the elector's knowledge of the choice being made, see *Peyman v Lanjani* [1985] Ch. 457 and Ch. 6 below.

[214] *Scarf v Jardine* (1882) 7 App. Cas. 345.

other party from detrimental action. Communication, in the form of rejection, is also necessitated by section 35 of the Sale of Goods Act if the buyer does not want his retention of the goods to be seen as an acceptance of them.[215] But there are cases where the elector's choice is so vividly clear that no communication is required. One example of this is the recaption of goods;[216] another occurs in *Car and Universal Finance Co. v Caldwell*,[217] where the disappearing rogue was in no position to demand that the owner's election to avoid the contract be communicated to him.

Avoidance and third-party purchasers.   As between owner and rogue, the above   **5.57** statement appears uncontroversial, but the later involvement of an innocent purchaser raises the question whether the owner should be allowed thus to rescind when the rogue is on the loose with possession of the goods and the semblance of ownership. One response to this is that the mere investiture of the rogue with possession of the goods is not tantamount to an appearance of ownership or authority to dispose of goods. *Car and Universal Finance* does show, however, that the process of avoidance is coloured by some concern for the predicament of purchasers. In that case, as soon as the rogue's cheque was seen to be worthless, the owner notified the police and a motoring organization. A number of dubious transactions were launched in respect of the car, but the owner's action occurred before the arrival of the first good faith purchaser. Conceding that an election to rescind should normally be communicated to the other party, the court held it did not apply in the present case since the rogue had put it out of the owner's power to communicate with him. The owner's behaviour was 'the best other means possible' to an actual communication.[218] While the court was explicitly indifferent to the purchaser in working out the contractual position between owner and rogue, it is hard to believe that the same conclusion would have been reached if the owner had merely stated his position in a letter to his solicitor.

Law reform.   In 1966, the Law Reform Committee stated[219] that the decision in   **5.58** *Car and Universal Finance* had largely destroyed the value of the section 23 exception for innocent purchasers. Without weighing up the various arguments or putting section 23 into the wider context of the *nemo dat* rule with its various exceptions, the Committee recommended simply that the owner should have to communicate his rescission to the rogue, which would in most cases render inefficacious the owner's right to rescind. This recommendation was not brought into effect.

---

[215] Cfs. 48(3),(4) inferentially supporting the absence of a need to communicate in certain cases of resale.

[216] *Re Eastgate* [1905] 1 KB 465; *Car and Universal Finance Co. v Caldwell*, n. 209 above, 558 (Davies LJ).

[217] n. 209 above. See also *Newton's of Wembley Ltd v Williams* [1965] 1 QB 560.

[218] n. 209 above, 558 (Davies LJ).

[219] *Transfer of Title to Chattels*, n. 47 above, para. 16.

Burden of Proof

5.59 **Burden on owner.** Section 23 does not state whether owner or purchaser bears the burden of proof of good faith or its absence. Since the voidable title rule is an exception to *nemo dat*, one might expect the purchaser should have to show his own good faith. This seems a reasonable inference from section 23 itself: it does not refer to bad faith and it is contrary to sensible forensic practice to require the owner to prove a negative, namely, the purchaser's want of good faith.[220] Nevertheless, the Court of Appeal in *Whitehorn Bros v Davison*[221] held that the burden lay on the plaintiff owner seeking to recover goods from the defendant, since the plaintiff 'comes to displace another from the enjoyment of property'.[222] This reasoning would fall short of the owner who had already recapted the goods or sought them in interpleader proceedings.[223] It is submitted that the burden should in all cases fall on the purchaser.[224] This would be consistent with other exceptions to *nemo dat*. The purchaser, moreover, is better placed to relate the circumstances of the transaction than the owner, and the rogue is rarely to be found.

Apparent Authority and Apparent Ownership

5.60 **Sale by apparent owner or agent.** The governing provision is section 21(1), which states an exception to the *nemo dat* rule where goods are sold by someone who is neither the owner nor the owner's authorized agent and 'the owner of the goods is by his conduct precluded from denying the seller's authority to sell'. This may be taken loosely to encapsulate both apparent authority and apparent ownership. It should be noted at the outset that the goods must be 'sold' by the apparent owner or agent. Consequently, if the property does not pass under the contract of sale concluded by that person, no title will be transmitted to the purchaser. This was the result in *Shaw v Commissioner of Police of the Metropolis*,[225] where the owner of a car gave possession of it to a rogue on unusual agency terms, taking a post-dated cheque for a substantial sum that was subsequently dishonoured. The rogue agreed to sell the car to the plaintiff purchaser from whom he received a banker's draft in the agreed amount, the third party 'rightly' conceding in the present case[226] that the property in the car was not to pass until the rogue received

---

[220] On the difficulties of a party coming to court 'blindfold', see *Fowler v Lanning* [1959] 1 QB 426.
[221] [1911] 1 KB 463. The Court of Appeal considered itself bound by the *Whitehorn* rule in *Thomas v Heelas*, 27 Nov. 1986 (CAT no. 1065).
[222] n. 221 above, 481 (Buckley LJ; see also Vaughan Williams LJ at 478.
[223] But see Kennedy LJ, *ibid.*, 487, for whom the burden falls on anyone 'who comes forward to deprive another of his title to property', a proposition that should apply equally to a purchaser seeking to deprive the owner.
[224] See to this effect *Transfer of Title to Chattels*, n. 47 above, para. 25.
[225] [1987] 3 All ER 405.
[226] *Sed quaere?*

payment under the draft. The rogue attempted to present the draft for payment to a bank where he had shortly before opened an account, but that bank declined to pay cash against the draft and the rogue disappeared. It was most unlikely that the rogue would ever attempt to recover payment against the draft, so it was an 'extremely remote' possibility that the indemnity the plaintiff offered his own bank, which had issued the draft and had reimbursed the plaintiff the amount he had paid for it, would be called in. The plaintiff's only loss, therefore, was the loss of bargain. It would have been extraordinary if the plaintiff had been held entitled to retain a valuable car for nothing, and the court recoiled from a result that would have offended its sense of justice.

Apparent authority. Apparent authority exists whenever one person is pre-   **5.61**
cluded by his words or conduct from denying that another is his agent and author-ized to transact certain business with third parties.[227] A person will be so precluded if he creates the appearance that an agent with limited authority has more author-ity than in fact he possesses, but the doctrine can equally apply where no actual relationship of agency exists at all.[228] The third party must prove that he entered into dealings with the agent on the faith of an appearance created by the principal and not the agent.[229] Apparent authority is thus a particular manifestation of estoppel.[230] It is a matter of debate whether an agent with actual but not apparent authority does indeed consummate a contractual relationship directly between principal and third party, as opposed to a state of affairs that estops a principal from denying such a contractual relationship.[231] The latter would appear correct but does not explain why the apparent agent or owner is able to transfer a real title and not just its procedural simulacrum.[232]

---

[227] *Pickering v Busk* (1812) 15 East 38; *Freeman & Lockyer v Buckhurst Park Properties (Mangal) Ltd* [1964] 2 QB 480; *Hely-Hutchinson v Brayhead Ltd* [1968] 1 QB 549; *Canadian Laboratory Supplies Ltd v Engelhard Industries Ltd* [1980] 2 SCR 450, revg. in part (1977) 78 DLR (3d) 232.

[228] *Bowstead on Agency* (18th edn, by F. M. B. Reynolds, Sweet & Maxwell, 2006), para. 8–027.

[229] *Colonial Bank v Cady* (1890) 15 App. Cas. 257; *Armagas v Mundogas SA (The Ocean Frost)* [1986] AC 717; *First Energy (UK) Ltd v Hungarian International Bank Ltd* [1993] 2 Lloyd's Rep. 194, 201: 'Our law does not recognize, in the context of apparent authority, the idea of the self-authorizing agent' (Steyn LJ).

[230] *Bowstead*, n. 228 above, para. 8–029. Estoppel *per rem judicatam* is a different matter. If A sells goods to B and A is subsequently involved in proceedings with C whereby C is granted a declaration that he is the owner of the goods in question, the judgment in the A–C proceedings does not bind B if B has not been joined to those proceedings. The outcome is different if the sale to B takes place after judgment is given in the A–C proceedings; see *Powell v Wiltshire* [2004] EWCA Civ 534; [2005] QB 117.

[231] *Ibid.*

[232] *Eastern Distributors Ltd v Goldring* [1957] 2 QB 600.

5.62 **Usual authority.** Apparent authority may arise actively where a principal voluntarily[233] represents to the third party the existence of authority in the agent, but
commonly arises in a more passive form where the agent is placed by the principal
in a position that usually carries with it a certain degree of authority.[234] This will
be so where the agent is put in a nominate position that, in the experience of the
commercial world, is invested with a known authority. This usual authority would
be an implied, actual authority if the principal did not in his dealings with the
agent abridge it. But if this authority is limited and third parties not duly notified,
the usual authority that extends beyond the undisclosed abridgment of authority
will be an apparent authority that binds the principal.[235]

Estoppel by Representation

5.63 **General.** Most sale of goods cases have concerned apparent owners or agents of
a class who sometimes deal on their own account and sometimes for an undisclosed or unnamed principal. The estoppel may take the form of a representation
(words) or conduct; references are sometimes made to negligence as though it
were separate from words and conduct. It is possible, however, that an owner's
negligence may be used, not to destroy his title as such, but to found a counterclaim by a purchaser sued for conversion of the goods.

5.64 **Example.** A clear example of an estoppel by representation is *Eastern Distributors
Ltd v Goldring*.[236] The owner of a van wished to purchase a car but had insufficient
money for a deposit. When the dealer suggested that a deposit could be procured
on the security of the van, owner and dealer colluded in a scheme that led a finance
company to believe that the dealer was the owner of the van as well as of the
desired car, and that a deposit had been put down on both vehicles. The true
owner signed in blank a hire purchase proposal form and a memorandum of
agreement concerning the van, as well as a note certifying that he had taken delivery of the van. The finance company accepted this proposal but rejected the one
concerning the car. In breach of his authority from the owner of the van, the dealer
went ahead and sold the van to the finance company. Informed that the car proposal had fallen through, the owner of the van sold it to the present defendant.

---

[233] *Debs v Sibtec Developments Ltd* [1990] RTR 91 (robber procured representation by duress).
[234] A. Hornby [1961] *CLJ* 238.
[235] *Bowstead*, n. 228 above, paras 8–018, 8–026.
[236] n. 232 above. For a similar case where the true owner holds out the car dealer to a finance
company as the owner, see *Stoneleigh Finance Ltd v Phillips* [1964] 2 QB 539. See also *NZ Securities
& Finance Ltd v Wrightcars Ltd* [1976] 1 NZLR 77 (car said by owner to be 'paid for'); *Big Rock Pty
Ltd v Esanda Finance Corpn Ltd* (1992) 10 WAR 259 (mortgagee's letter stated (erroneously) that
the mortgage payments had all been made); *Shaw v Commissioner of Police of the Metropolis*, n. 225
above (owner signed a letter certifying car as sold).

Third party unaware of representation.   The issue of title to the van was resolved   **5.65**
in favour of the finance company plaintiff since, by signing the documents in
blank, the owner had knowingly armed the dealer with the means to deceive the
finance company and was privy to the representation of ownership made by the
dealer. A problem not confronted in the case is the following. How does the owner's statement cause the purchaser to be misled if the purchaser would just as much
have been misled by the dealer forging the owner's signature to the documents?
The finance company did not so much rely upon the owner as upon the established figure of the dealer. The doctrine of estoppel by representation is not, however, pitched at this level of scepticism. It is enough that the owner made the
statement and that the purchaser believed it, without the purchaser having to
believe on independently verifiable grounds that it was the owner who made the
statement.

Meaning of representation.   Difficulties may arise as to the meaning of a repre-   **5.66**
sentation made by the owner. In *Moorgate Mercantile Co. Ltd v Twitchings*,[237]
a number of finance companies were members of Hire Purchase Information Ltd,
a voluntary title registration service. The finance company claiming title to a car
disposed of by a rogue had failed to effect registration of its title. The service's
response when the purchaser consulted it was that the car was not covered by a
recorded hire purchase agreement. The House of Lords declined to inflate this
into a statement that no registrable agreement had been concluded.[238]

Estoppel by Conduct

Transfer of possession or documents.   Estoppel by conduct has caused greater   **5.67**
difficulty in the case law than estoppel by representation. The starting point is the
proposition that the mere transfer of possession of goods or the indicia of title does
not create an estoppel that the person in possession is the owner,[239] for possession
is consistent with a range of transactions from bailment to outright sale, not all of
which involve the transfer of the general property. In *Farquarson Bros and Co. v C
King and Co.*,[240] the plaintiff firm of timber merchants authorized one of its clerks
to arrange for timber sales to its known customers, and informed the warehouse
holding the timber that the clerk's delivery orders were to be honoured. The warehouse was not told, however, of the limitation on the clerk's authority to issue

---

[237] [1977] AC 890.

[238] Cl. 1 of the conditions governing the issue of information slips provided: 'All information
is given to the best knowledge and belief of H. P. Information Ltd. according to the information
contained in its records.' The service was also held not to be the agent of the finance company in
making representations: above, 902, 918, 923, 930.

[239] *Johnson v Crédit Lyonnais Co.* (1877) 3 CPD 32; *Central Newbury Car Auctions Ltd v Unity
Finance Ltd* [1957] 1 QB 371. For a case that is particularly hard on the purchaser, see *McVicar v
Herman* (1958) 13 DLR (2d) 419.

[240] [1902] AC 325.

delivery orders. The clerk therefore had constructive possession of the timber. Over a number of years, the clerk, assuming the identity of 'a phantom broker, an imaginary being [that he] created, associated and worked . . . for his own purposes under the plain and unpretentious name of Brown',[241] sold quantities of timber to the defendants. To effect the sales, he instructed the warehouse to deliver the timber to the order of Brown and, as Brown, indorsed the delivery orders in favour of the defendants. Nothing said or done by the plaintiffs amounted to a representation, to the defendants (as opposed to the warehouse), that the imaginary broker, Brown, whom the defendants never saw or inquired after, had the right to sell timber to the defendants. The plaintiffs and the defendants never came into direct contact with each other, and so the estoppel argument failed.

5.68 Example. The estoppel argument succeeded, however, in the Canadian case of *Canadian Laboratory Supplies Ltd v Engelhard Industries Ltd*,[242] where an employee of the plaintiffs, exceeding his actual authority, bought on their behalf ever-increasing amounts of platinum over several years and was able to process payment for it through the plaintiffs' accounts department at approximately sixty-day intervals. Intercepting the platinum, the employee sold most of it back to the defendant sellers as waste material, receiving sums close to the original purchase price. The employee purported to resell on behalf of an imaginary person, a scientist engaged in a confidential process. For some of the time during which the fraud was carried out, the employee was held to have purchased new platinum with the plaintiffs' authority and to have sold it back as its apparent owner in the form of waste. The dealings of the employee were seen as an integrated whole, the plaintiffs being in the invidious position of seeking to affirm the purchases of platinum but to disaffirm the resales of platinum waste.

5.69 Document of title. Despite a discredited Privy Council decision,[243] the decision in *Farquarson* that the mere transfer of possession or its constructive equivalent does not raise an estoppel also holds true if what is transferred is a document of title or other delivery instrument. The leading case is *Mercantile Bank of India Ltd v Central Bank of India Ltd,*[244] where a purchaser of groundnuts, deliverable to the order of the holder of railway receipts, pledged these receipts with the respondent bank as security for a loan. The bank transmitted the receipts to its own godown[245] keeper, who released the receipts to the purchaser for the sole purpose of collecting the groundnuts from the railway, which were then to be deposited in

---

[241] *Ibid.* 334–5 (Lord Macnaghten).
[242] n. 227 above.
[243] *Commonwealth Trust Ltd v Akotey* [1926] AC 72.
[244] [1938] AC 287.
[245] A form of warehouse.

the bank's godown.[246] The purchaser then fraudulently used the same receipts to obtain a second advance from the appellants. The purchaser was held to be able to transfer to the appellants only such title as he had, which was encumbered by the pledge to the respondent bank. The release of the railway receipts did not create an estoppel.[247]

Indicia of Title

Possession plus *indicia*.　It has been argued that the estoppel position changes if **5.70** the owner, instead of transferring just the possession of the goods or delivery documents, transfers also *indicia* of title. The notion of *indicia* of title, a vague expression, emerges in *Central Newbury Car Auctions Ltd v Unity Finance Ltd.*[248] A distinguished-looking rogue visited the plaintiff car dealers to acquire a car[249] and signed the usual hire purchase forms, leaving a car he claimed as his own, but which was the subject of a hire purchase agreement, as a trade-in and deposit. He was allowed to take away the car, as well as the logbook,[250] despite the finance company's instruction that this should not be done before it granted permission. The finance company declined the proposal, believing the prospective bailee to be a rogue. The logbook, a permanent document recording in an officially validated form the identity of the person bound from time to time to pay road tax on the vehicle, had been signed neither by the dealers[251] nor by the previous owner (whose name had been entered in it). Despite its continuity, the fact that owners almost always sign it and the practical difficulties of selling a car without it,[252] the logbook was not a document of title either at common law or under statute.[253] The rogue assumed the identity of the previous owner and signed the logbook in his name before selling the car to a purchaser,[254] who in turn sold it to the defendant finance company, which bailed it on the usual hire purchase terms to the second defendant.

---

[246] A tightly controlled form of trust receipt, where the bank's possessory interest in the documents by way of pledge is deemed to continue notwithstanding the release of the documents for a limited purpose. See *North Western Bank Ltd v John Poynter, Son & Macdonalds* [1895] AC 56 (cf. *Babcock v Lawson* (1880) 5 QBD 284); *Official Assignee of Madras v Mercantile Bank of India Ltd* [1935] AC 53; *Lloyds Bank Ltd v Bank of America National Trust and Savings Association* [1938] 2 KB 146; *Re David Allester Ltd* [1922] 2 Ch. 211.

[247] Marking the receipts would not have helped the bank to prevent the fraud, for then the rogue might have sold the goods themselves.

[248] n. 239 above.

[249] Valued at £337 10s.

[250] The vehicle registration document.

[251] The dealers were not bound to pay road tax and so their name did not appear in the book.

[252] The logbook warned that the person in whose name the vehicle was registered might not be the owner.

[253] See also *Joblin v Watkins & Roseveare (Motors) Ltd* [1949] 1 All ER 47; *Pearson v Rose & Young Ltd* [1951] 1 KB 275; *Shaw v Commissioner of Police of the Metropolis*, n. 225 above.

[254] For £20.

5.71 **Result.**   By a majority, the court held that the plaintiffs were not estopped by their conduct from denying the rogue's authority to sell.[255] This was in spite of the plausibility of the rogue and the purchaser's investigation of the files of a service recording the great majority of hire purchase agreements. The defendants' argument that the scales were tipped by a combination of the plaintiffs' negligence and the persuasive character of the logbook was unsuccessful. So far, the decision in *Central Newbury* is just another illustration of the difficulty of maintaining the estoppel argument. But the dissenting judgment of Denning LJ is significant for the bridge it establishes with a series of decisions that are practically impossible to reconcile with estoppel theory.

5.72 **Dissent.**   Denning LJ did not dispute the orthodoxy that mere careless conduct by an owner in the control of goods or their entrustment to another does not estop the owner from contesting a title derived through a rogue.[256] But he believed the situation different where the owner is induced to part with the property in the goods or the power of disposing of them, or behaves as if he had such an intention by arming a rogue with the necessary documents.[257] The owners in the present case may have intended to dispose of their property in favour of the finance company rather than the rogue, but that did not matter. What counted was the combined effect of their intention to dispose of their property and the facility with which the rogue could present himself as the owner when given the unsigned logbook together with the car. Now, this seems to have little to do with any orthodox understanding of estoppel but rather strikes new ground in finding significance in the owner's divesting behaviour *qua* a third party. Nevertheless, the dissent does come close to certain agency authorities that are hard to explain.

Inherent Agency Power

5.73 **A controversial case.**   The starting point is the controversial case of *Watteau v Fenwick*,[258] where the manager of a beer house had a limited authority to purchase stock-in-trade. It did not extend to the cigars that the manager purchased on credit from the plaintiff. There was nothing to indicate that the manager was not the owner of the beer house; indeed, the licence in his name was prominent over the door. The plaintiff seller believed the manager to be the owner, and the cigars were goods of a type usually dealt with in a beer house. Wills J relied upon the principle of usual authority in holding that the seller was entitled to recover the price of the cigars from the defendant owner of the beer house. A limitation of

---

[255] Despite the evident ease with which the rogue could reproduce the previous owner's 'signature'.

[256] He therefore accepted decisions like *Farquarson Bros and Co v C King and Co.*, n. 240 above, and *Mercantile Bank of India Ltd v Central Bank of India Ltd*, n. 244 above.

[257] n. 239 above, 381–2.

[258] [1893] 1 QB 346.

the authority usually confided to managers would not avail the principal against third parties uninformed of this limitation. Put in the alternative form, that a third party is entitled to rely upon the appearance of authority in a particular class of agent, the following difficulty presents itself: how can a third party rely upon an agent's usual authority when he does not know he is dealing with an agent?

Reasons for inherent agency power.   Some help in resolving the difficulty comes   **5.74**
from the notion of 'inherent agency power', contained in the Restatement Second on Agency,[259] which exists 'purely as a product of the agency relation'.[260] It does not depend upon authority or estoppel but is *sui generis*, and is similar to the test that a master is liable for torts committed in the course of a servant's employment.[261] The master's vicarious liability does not depend upon whether the victim of the tort is aware of the employment relationship or whether the servant is acting within his authority, which commonly he is not. Inherent agency power has been criticized as so vague that it creates more problems than it resolves,[262] but it has been promoted as consonant with notions of fairness and consistent with the practices of the business world.[263] It has also been said that inherent agency power is justified because the principal has reposed more trust in the agent than has the third party, which is hardly a reason for making the principal liable.[264] Other arguments are that the demands of business do not give the third party time to investigate an agent's authority, met by the response that this is relevant only if he knows he is dealing with an agent; that the principal must take the burden as well as benefit of an agent's activities, greeted by the retort that this can apply to the third party too; and that liability follows control, criticized as begging the question.[265]

Criticism.   On the other hand, *Watteau v Fenwick*, in compelling the principal   **5.75**
to accept both benefit and burdens of an agent's activity, prevents him from running what amounts to a limited liability company in disguise. Further, where an agent sells rather than buys, one argument, empirically difficult to demonstrate, is that agents are more likely to exceed a limited selling authority than to arrogate to themselves a selling authority that does not exist at all.[266]

---

[259] American Law Institute 1957 (Reporter: Seavey), §8A.
[260] *Ibid.*, Comment a.
[261] D. H. Bester (1972) 89 *SALJ* 49, 53.
[262] A. Conant (1968) 47 *Nebraska LR* 678, 686. See also *Bowstead on Agency*, n. 228 above, para. 8–079.
[263] Restatement Second on Agency, §§ 8A, Comment a, and 161, Comment a.
[264] J. L. Montrose (1939) 17 *Can. Bar Rev.* 693, 711 *et seq.* (criticizing Seavey).
[265] *Ibid.*
[266] The Restatement Second on Agency refers to dispositions of property by agents where the excess of authority is more formal than substantial, as where the agent departs from the authorized mode of sale: §8A, Comment b.

5.76 **Estoppel and inherent agency power.** The legal supports for inherent agency power seem somewhat fragile, but a number of estoppel authorities are actuated by the notion or something similar. Though by no means the first of these cases, *Lloyds and Scottish Finance Ltd v Williamson*[267] raises the issue squarely. An owner entrusted his car to a dealer and repairer for the purpose of repair and the solicitation of offers to purchase. The dealer exceeded his authority by lending the car to a creditor, saying the car was for sale. The owner later authorized the dealer to sell, provided a minimum cash price of £625 were remitted to him, the dealer to retain any surplus as commission. The dealer then sold the car to a friend of his creditor for £625, but the price was paid to the creditor in partial discharge of the dealer's debt. Although this method of payment prevented the dealer from acting in the ordinary course of business of a mercantile agent under section 2 of the Factors Act 1889,[268] it did not impair the estoppel argument of the purchaser, since he bought the car in the belief that the dealer was the owner. There is naturally no need for apparent owners to act in the ordinary course of business of a mercantile agent.[269]

5.77 **Result.** The Court of Appeal held that the purchaser had obtained good title to the car. The owner had impliedly authorized the dealer to sell the car as principal and had put him in a position enabling him to do so; hence the owner was estopped[270] from denying the dealer's authority[271] to sell. Now, all of this was unknown to the purchaser from whose vantage point there is no difference in appearance between a dealer with full and a dealer with limited authority to sell. The dealer's fraud, moreover, was in no way facilitated by the owner's conduct in expanding his authority beyond the authority to receive offers. The case is difficult to rationalize[272] but, it is submitted, is best explained as concerned with the inherent usual power of a car dealer to sell, the converse of the agent's power to buy in *Watteau v Fenwick*.[273]

---

[267] [1965] 1 All ER 641.

[268] See the text accompanying nn. 313 *et seq.* below.

[269] See also *Motor Credits (Hire Finance) Ltd v Pacific Motor Auctions Pty. Ltd* (1963) 109 CLR 87, affirmed on different grounds *sub nom. Pacific Motor Auctions Pty. Ltd v Motor Credits (Hire Finance) Ltd* [1965] AC 867.

[270] *Pace* para. 1 of the headnote. Salmon LJ, n. 267 above, 645, denies a 'true estoppel' but he appears to mean that the purchaser's title is real rather than metaphorical: see *Eastern Distributors Ltd v Goldring* [1957] 2 QB 600 (with which cf. *Simm v Anglo-American Telegraph Co.* (1879) 5 QBD 188, 206).

[271] The case does not separate apparent authority and apparent ownership: [1965] 1 All ER 641, 644.

[272] *Bowstead*, n. 228 above, at para. 8–129 note 34 attempts to justify it on actual authority grounds.

[273] [1893] 1 QB 436.

Documents of title cases. Thus rationalized, *Lloyds and Scottish Finance* accords **5.78** with a number of cases where instruments of title are lodged with an agent who has a limited authority to deal with them but is thus enabled to present himself as their owner.[274] It also helps to explain the reasoning of Lord Halsbury in *Henderson & Co. v Williams*,[275] the difficulty of which provoked the same judge to tumescent language in *Farquarson Bros and Co v C King and Co*.[276] In *Henderson*, the owners of a quantity of sugar lying in a warehouse were induced by the fraud of a rogue to believe that he was representing one of their established customers.[277] They instructed the warehouse to transfer the sugar to the order of the rogue who sold the goods to the plaintiff. Before paying the price, the plaintiff secured from the defendant warehouse an undertaking to hold the goods to his order. By thus attorning to the plaintiff, the warehouse incurred personal liability on an estoppel. Although the rogue had concluded no contract with the owners, Lord Halsbury and Lindley LJ[278] both went on to say that the owners had authorized the rogue to dispose of the goods. Indeed, they had intended to surrender all title to the sugar but had failed to do so only because the purported contract of sale negotiated by the rogue was a nullity. The argument is the same as the one made by Denning LJ in dissent in *Central Newbury Car Auctions Ltd v Unity Finance Ltd*.[279] Once again, one asks unavailingly how far the dealings between owners and rogue served to mislead the *bona fide* purchaser for value.

A further example. The estoppel issue was developed further in *Jerome v* **5.79** *Bentley,*[280] where a rogue called 'Major Tatham' obtained possession of a diamond ring on the ground that he had better social contacts than the owner (a jeweller). He was given a limited authority to hold the ring only for seven days and to sell it for a minimum cash price which was to be remitted to the owner, the rogue to keep any surplus as a commission.[281] In excess of his authority, the rogue sold the ring outside the seven-day period for a cash price much lower than the minimum figure. The result in favour of the owner is a perfectly orthodox application of the rule that mere possession does not create the semblance of apparent authority to sell or apparent ownership. But Donovan J went on to consider the principle in *Watteau v Fenwick*,[282] dismissing it on the ground that it applied to well-known classes of agents (including, one imagines, well-known classes of traders) with a

---

274 *Brocklesby v Temperance Building Society* [1895] AC 173; *Rimmer v Webster* [1902] 2 Ch. 163; *Fry v Smellie* [1912] 3 KB 282; *Abigail v Lapin* [1934] AC 491.
275 [1895] 1 QB 521.
276 [1902] AC 325.
277 Hence the issue of voidable title did not arise; see *Hardman v Booth* (1863) 1 H & C 803.
278 The latter with some hesitation because of *Kingsford v Merry* (1856) 1 H & N 503.
279 n. 239 above.
280 [1952] 2 All ER 14.
281 Similar to the arrangements in *Lloyds and Scottish Finance*, n. 267 above.
282 n. 258 above. He also considered *Rimmer v Webster* [1902] 2 Ch. 163.

recognized usual authority. As an itinerant socialite, 'Major Tatham' could not be said to have any usual authority. Moreover, unlike the manager in *Watteau v Fenwick*, whose authority was continuing but limited at the time of the purchase, 'Major Tatham's' authority had expired altogether at the end of the seven days, and he was thereafter to be treated as a thief of the ring. The conditions laid down by Donovan J are consistent with those met by the dealer in *Lloyds and Scottish Finance*, and one therefore has to conclude that there is some substance in the notion of inherent agency power. As will be seen, the practical effect of this development is to expand the *nemo dat* exception in section 2 of the Factors Act 1889.

Estoppel by Negligence

5.80 **Estoppel by conduct and by negligence.** Estoppel by conduct and estoppel by negligence are overlapping categories. The central issue presented by the latter is whether the rights of a *bona fide* purchaser should be affected by negligence on the part of the owner which does not add to the rogue's appearance of ownership or authority. The cases show that negligence in this context has to respond to the technical requirements of the tort of that name; that is, there must be a duty of care and a breach of that duty, as well as damage, factually caused by the breach, that does not fall outside the remoteness of damage rule. Arguments in favour of expanding estoppel by negligence have invariably relied upon a battered dictum of Ashhurst J in *Lickbarrow v Mason* [283] that 'whenever one of two innocent persons must suffer by the acts of a third, he who has enabled such third person to occasion the loss must sustain it'. Reliance on this dictum is the badge of a losing cause, for 'enabled' is much too wide.[284] As Lord Lindley once put it, 'every one who has a servant enables him to steal whatever is within his reach'.[285]

5.81 **Effect of owner's negligence.** Even if the owner has been negligent in safeguarding his interests, the *bona fide* purchaser's cause is not carried much further. As Lord Macnaghten said: '[H]ow can carelessness, however extreme, in the conduct of a man's own business preclude him from recovering his own property which has been stolen from him?'[286] This attitude has also coloured the approach taken in cases where an owner negligently entrusts or surrenders possession of goods.[287] The predicament of the *bona fide* purchaser is also compounded if there is an element

---

[283] (1787) 2 TR 63, 70.

[284] *Farquarson Bros and Co. v C King and Co.*, n. 240 above, 342 (Lindley LJ); *Central Newbury Car Auctions Ltd v Unity Finance Ltd*, n. 239 above, 388–9 (Hodson LJ).

[285] *Farquarson Bros and Co.*, n. 240 above. The inhospitability of the common law to estoppel by negligence may have been coloured by the widespread employment of domestic servants among the professional and judicial classes.

[286] *Ibid.* 335–6, citing the examples of the owner who loses a valuable dog because it is not properly chained up, and the owner of a watch who carelessly leaves it on a park bench or restaurant table.

[287] See also *Moorgate Mercantile Credit Co. Ltd v Twitchings* [1977] AC 890, 925.

of carelessness on his own part in dealing with the rogue. Lord Macnaghten put the matter as sharply as it can be put:[288]

> If it were permissible it would be interesting to inquire which of the two firms parties to this litigation was the more blameworthy from a moral point of view. The plaintiffs trusted a man whom they had long known and whom they believed to be honest. The defendants trusted a man, whom a breath of suspicion and the most ordinary inquiries would have unmasked.

As inhospitable as the legal landscape is to estoppel by negligence, the idea has excited such interest over the years that it is worth asking how it could be implemented in litigation. One way would be to give the defendant purchaser a defence to an action in conversion brought by the true owner. Unless the defendant can establish a representation, in which case negligence would appear to add nothing to the defence, the defendant is disqualified from raising the owner's negligence as a defence by section 11(1) of the Torts (Interference with Goods) Act 1977, which states that '[c]ontributory negligence is no defence in proceedings founded on conversion, or on intentional trespass to goods'. A different way of formulating the defendant's position, not ruled out by section 11(1), would be to assert that estoppel by negligence amounts to a representation by omission.[289] A negligent failure to contradict a rogue's representation of authority or ownership would itself amount to a representation that the rogue is so authorized.[290] It is hard to resist the conclusion, however, that an owner who is dispossessed by a rogue is not, except in a fictitious way, making any such representation. To condone the defence being framed in these terms, moreover, comes close to flouting section 11(1). Yet another way in which the owner's negligence can be taken into account is to say that the purchaser has no defence to an action in conversion brought by the owner but may assert a counterclaim against a negligent owner for the economic loss caused when the purchaser paid the irrecoverable price to the rogue. If the purchaser has himself been negligent too, the owner would then be able to plead by way of defence to the counterclaim the purchaser's own contributory negligence. This apportionment of loss would consummate by different means the division of loss once recommended by Lord Devlin for dividing losses between innocent owners and innocent purchasers.[291] This method of treating the purchaser's invocation of the owner's negligence was left open by Lord Wilberforce in *Moorgate*

---

[288] *Farquarson Bros and Co. v C King and Co.*, n. 240 above, 335.

[289] See *Spiro v Lintern* [1973] 1 WLR 1002; *Pacol Ltd v Trade Lines Ltd (The Henrik Sif)* [1983] 2 Lloyd's Rep. 456, 464–5; see also *Bank of Nova Scotia v Hellenic Mutual War Risks Association (Bermuda) Ltd (The Good Luck)* [1990] 1 QB 818, 891.

[290] P. S. Atiyah, *The Sale of Goods* (11th edn, by J. N. Adams, Longman, 2005), 375.

[291] Rejected by the Law Reform Committee because of the procedural complexities of its operation in a title chain: n. 47 above, 15. The present position is complex already: see *Butterworth v Kingsway Motors Ltd* [1954] 1 WLR 1286.

Mercantile Credit Co. Ltd v Twitchings,[292] but it comes very close to flouting the will of Parliament as later expressed in section 11(1). Furthermore, developments in the tort of negligence in the past decade or so make the prospects of success for such an economic loss claim appear most unpromising.[293]

5.82 **A duty owed to the world?** Be that as it may, the concept of estoppel by negligence was accepted by Blackburn J more than 100 years ago when he stated the requirement of 'the neglect of some duty that is owed to the person led into the belief, or . . . to the general public of whom that person is one, and not merely neglect of what would be prudent in respect of the party himself'.[294] In *Central Newbury Car Auctions*, Morris LJ jibbed at the notion of a duty of care owed to the world.[295] But although multiple parties might be involved in the rogue's chain of deception, in the end there is only one sale price or pledge advance secured by the rogue. The liability in negligence of manufacturers of defective goods is a duty owed to the world, though only one consumer will drink the ginger beer containing the decomposing snail.

5.83 **Requirements of the tort of negligence.** The difficulty of persuading a sceptical court of the merits of estoppel by negligence is illustrated by *Mercantile Credit Co. Ltd v Hamblin*.[296] The owner of a car, seeking an advance on the security of her car, at the dealer's suggestion signed hire purchase proposal forms in blank in the belief that they were mortgage documents. Unlike mortgage forms, hire purchase forms presented the dealer as the owner of the car. The dealer, outwardly respectable and socially known to the owner, gave her a blank cheque with instructions to fill in the amount of the loan. She later withdrew from the agreement but the hire purchase proposal had already gone through and the dealer paid for the car by the finance company. When the owner refused to pay hire purchase instalments, the finance company claimed she was estopped by her negligence from disputing the dealer's title. The Court of Appeal found for the owner, holding that the finance company had failed to show the technical requirements of negligence, in particular, the existence of a duty of care and a breach of that duty.[297] Despite the existence of a duty of care when the owner signed the forms, she was not in breach

---

292 n. 287 above, 906.

293 e.g. *Leigh and Sillavan Ltd v Aliakmon Shipping Co. Ltd* [1986] AC 785; *Muirhead v Industrial Tank Specialties Ltd* [1986] QB 507.

294 *Swan v North British Australian Co.* (1863) 2 H & C 175, 182. These words were approved by Lord Sumner in *RE Jones Ltd v Waring and Gillow Ltd* [1926] AC 670, 693. The requirement of a duty was emphasized in *Thomas Australia Wholesale Vehicle Trading Co. Ltd v Marac Finance Australia Ltd* [1985] 3 NSWLR 452.

295 [1957] 1 QB 371, 393. For the difficulties posed by duty of care, see *Mercantile Bank of India Ltd v Central Bank of India Ltd*, n. 244 above; *Rimmer v Webster* [1902] 2 Ch. 163; *Wilson v Pickering* [1946] KB 422.

296 [1965] 2 QB 242.

297 *Ibid.*, 271.

of that duty. She knew the dealer and, furthermore, the blank cheque disarmed any suspicions that she might have had. Statements were also made that the effective cause of the finance company's loss was the fraud of the dealer rather than the negligence of the owner.[298] But since the dealer's fraud is the very risk posed by the owner's negligence, this approach seems highly dubious.[299] Perhaps the most surprising feature of the case is that, though signing the forms in blank, the owner was not treated as making the statements later inserted by the dealer. Had she been regarded as making those statements, then an inquiry into negligence should not have been required.[300]

Absence of duty owed by owner. The difficulties of estoppel by negligence **5.84** came to a head in *Moorgate Mercantile Co. Ltd v Twitchings*,[301] shortly before the enactment of section 11(1) of the Torts (Interference with Goods) Act 1977, a case demonstrating 'the perennial failure of English law to develop a proper method of charging moveable property'.[302] It was the contention of the dealer who had purchased a car from a hire purchase bailee[303] after being informed that no hire purchase agreement in respect of it was on file, that the finance company owner was estopped by its negligence in failing to register the hire purchase agreement from denying the bailee's title to sell the car. The voluntary registration scheme run by Hire Purchase Information Ltd recorded about 98 per cent of all hire purchase agreements relating to motor vehicles, and was the only practical means available to dealers buying cars to ascertain whether they were encumbered by a hire purchase agreement. According to a bare majority of the House of Lords, which found in favour of the finance company, the dealer was owed no duty that registrable hire purchase agreements should actually be registered. Lord Edmund-Davies saw no reason why all careless behaviour should be elevated into a tort and no justification why non-member finance companies should be compelled by the tort of negligence to join the scheme.[304] It was also thought invidious to distinguish between finance companies that were members and finance companies that were not.[305] Nor did it make any difference that there was a common membership

---

[298] *Ibid.*, 266, 275.

[299] See *Moorgate Mercantile Co. Ltd v Twitchings*, n. 287 above, 928; *Stansbie v Troman* [1948] 2 KB 48. On severing the chain of causation in negligence, see *Weld-Blundell v Stephens* [1920] AC 956; *The Oropesa* [1943] P 32; *Home Office v Dorset Yacht Co.* [1970] AC 1004; *Knightley v Johns* [1982] 1 All ER 851.

[300] Cf the knowledge of the owner of the contents of the forms in *Eastern Distributors Ltd v Goldring* [1957] 2 QB 600.

[301] n. 287 above.

[302] *Ibid.*, 905 (Lord Wilberforce).

[303] And thus was not protected by Part III of the Hire Purchase Act 1964, discussed in the text accompanying nn. 598 *et seq.* below.

[304] n. 287 above, 919.

[305] *Ibid.* See also Lord Russell, at 930, speaking of the finance company joining the scheme 'putting its head into the noose of an estoppel' if this were to entail liability in negligence.

in the scheme of finance companies and car dealers; mere propinquity with a dealer did not impose a duty on a finance company to take care of its own property.[306] Concern was also expressed at the possibility of Hire Purchase Information Ltd, in giving selective information to the public, incurring thus a duty of care.[307] Had there been a duty of care, a failure on the part of the finance company to register would have been held to be a breach of this duty.[308]

5.85 **Risk.** Now, the dealer knew in his dealings with the scheme that there was an element of risk. Not all agreements were registered, though the lion's share was. It is scant relief to the dealer to know that mistakes like the present one occurred only rarely and that the coverage of the scheme was close to universal. The presence in life of unavoidable risks does not render any the more acceptable a further layer of avoidable risk created by the negligence of others. The dissenting speeches of Lords Wilberforce and Salmon are compelling. Lord Wilberforce was impressed by the degree of reliance by car dealers on the scheme.[309] The paradox that those joining the scheme might be disadvantaged by the imposition of a duty of care was met by the proper response they would derive countervailing advantages in the form of mutual benefits and lower administration costs.[310] It is unlikely, however, that the position established in *Twitchings* and confirmed in legislation will change in the foreseeable future.

5.86 *Non est factum.* It is interesting to note, nevertheless, a lack of consistency between this area and the law on *non est factum*. *Non est factum* is a plea that the signer of a document may enter when fundamentally mistaken about the nature of the document he signs so that it cannot be said to be his document at all. The resulting document is a nullity. The signature is commonly induced by the fraud of another and often takes the form of a disposition of property. This plea may be defeated by the negligence of a party signing a document,[311] even though the document signed is no less fundamentally different. It looks distinctly odd that an owner carelessly signing a document runs a considerable risk of disentitlement while an owner careless in other respects does not.[312]

---

306 *Ibid.*, 925–6 (Lord Fraser).

307 *Ibid.*, 927 (Lord Fraser).

308 *Ibid.*, 921 (Lord Edmund-Davies), 927 (Lord Fraser).

309 *Ibid.*, 904.

310 *Ibid.*, 906.

311 *Saunders v Anglia Building Society* [1971] AC 1004; *Marvco Color Research Ltd v Harris* [1982] 2 SCR 774 (Can.).

312 See Ontario Law Reform Commission, *Report on Sale of Goods* (1979), ii, 310–11 and the recommendation that an owner owes a duty of care when entrusting goods to others. Although the Commission divided equally on the case of a contributorily negligent purchaser, and so made no recommendation, the Uniform Sale of Goods Act adopted in 1982 by the Uniform Law Conference of Canada would allow apportionment in this case.

Mercantile Agency

Statutory extension to estoppel.   The doctrine of estoppel does little to assist   **5.87**
the *bona fide* purchaser for value. In particular, it is far from any assurance that the
purchaser may safely trust to possession as the *indicium* of title. As a result of various statutory exceptions to the *nemo dat* rule, extending the protection afforded
by the doctrine of estoppel, however, the purchaser may in certain instances repose
confidence in another's possession of goods or documents of title to goods. Besides
the separate instances of the seller and the buyer in possession of goods or documents of title, these statutory exceptions include the mercantile agent in possession in section 2 of the Factors Act 1889,[313] the provisions of which legislation are
expressly preserved in the Sale of Goods Act alongside the recital of the *nemo dat*
rule.[314] Taken together, these exceptions fall short of conferring protection in all
cases where persons are entrusted with goods.[315]

Mercantile Agents

Definition of mercantile agent.   The only reference to factors in the Factors Act   **5.88**
is in the title; the Act is by no means confined to just that class of agent.[316] According
to section 1(1): 'The expression "mercantile agent" shall mean a mercantile agent
having in the customary course of his business as such agent authority either to sell
goods or to consign goods for the purpose of sale, or to buy goods or to raise
money on the security of goods.'[317] It has been held to extend to the buyer of
goods obtaining constructive possession of goods upon the release to him of a
bill of lading on trust receipt terms.[318] This definition excludes servants and
employees,[319] carriers,[320] repairers,[321] and warehousemen,[322] all of whom as a class

---

[313] This is essentially a consolidation of earlier legislation of 1823, 1825, 1842, and 1877. For a
discussion of the history of the legislation, see *Johnson v Crédit Lyonnais Co.* (1877) 3 CPD 32; *Cole v
North Western Bank* (1875) LR 10 CP 354 (quoting Lord Tenterden's abstract of the 1823 and 1825
Acts); *Mildred, Goyeneche & Co. v Maspons* (1883) 8 App. Cas. 874; *Kaltenbach v Lewis* (1883) 24
Ch. D 54, 61 (noting the difficulty of coming to terms with evolving commerce).

[314] S. 21(1), (2)(a).

[315] *Cole v North Western Bank*, n. 313 above; *Davey v Paine Bros (Motors) Ltd* [1954] NZLR 1122.

[316] In the 19th century, a factor was a selling agent entrusted with possession of a principal's
goods for that purpose, in contrast with a broker, who might never see the goods at all. Nowadays, a
factor is someone who discounts future trade debts and offers a debt management service.

[317] *Heyman v Flewker* (1863) 13 CBNS 519, 527.

[318] *Lloyds Bank Ltd v Bank of American National Trust and Savings Asscn Ltd* [1938] 2 KB 147;
Fairfax Gerrard Holdings Ltd v Capital Bank Plc [2006] EWHC 3439 (QB); [2007] 1 Lloyd's Rep.
171, revd on different grounds [2007] EWCA Civ 1226; [2008] 1 Lloyd's Rep. 297.

[319] *Lamb v Attenborough* (1862) 1 B & S 831; *Fuentes v Montis* (1868) LR 3 CP 268, affd. (1868)
LR 4 CP 93.

[320] *Monk v Whittenbury* (1831) 2 B & Ad. 484.

[321] *Forristal v McDonald* (1883) 9 SCR 12, 17 (Can.); see also *Directors etc. of City Bank v Barrow*
(1880) 5 App. Cas. 664 (tanner).

[322] *Cole v North Western Bank*, n. 313 above; *Schafhauser v Shaffer* [1943] 3 DLR 656.

lack such authority in the customary course of their businesses. A seller who remains in possession of goods after a sale is not as such a mercantile agent.[323] The agent, nevertheless, need not fit into a well-established niche in order to be a mercantile agent; the category has in the past evolved to accommodate changing mercantile usage. For example, peripatetic jewellery salesman have been held to be mercantile agents,[324] likewise retail car dealers selling their own stock-in-trade to finance companies and private purchasers,[325] as well as second-hand vehicles entrusted to them by private individuals.[326] But car dealers always selling on their own behalf and never on behalf of a principal will not be mercantile agents.[327]

5.89 **Retail sales.**   Pitching mercantile agency at the retail sales level involves extending a mercantile idea to transactions involving buyers who themselves are not merchants and, since retail sales are often conducted in myriad ways, has meant that mercantile agency cannot be confined to a closed, nineteenth-century list of categories of mercantile agents. This extension, together with the practice adopted by certain types of mercantile agents of selling the principal's goods as though they were their own, has made it difficult to see mercantile agency as a mere extension of apparent authority or estoppel. It has also created difficulties in applying the test that the agent must act in the ordinary course of business of a mercantile agent.

5.90 **First time as agent.**   It is also clear that a person may be a mercantile agent even though this is the first time he has ever acted as such. Willes J saw no valid reason for distinguishing between the first of such an agent's principals and subsequent principals:[328]

> Assuming the case of ten persons who on ten successive days put their property for sale upon commission into the hands of another, who thereupon should think it worth his while to set up as commission-agent, it would not be easy to suggest any sound distinction between the cases of the first and the last employer, or between either of them and that of the first customer who arrived after the words 'commission-agent' had been put up over his door.

Similarly, someone may be a mercantile agent though this is the first time he has acted for the particular principal and in this particular fashion in his

---

[323] *Johnson v Crédit Lyonnais Co.,* n. 313 above.

[324] *Weiner v Harris* [1910] 1 KB 285.

[325] *Motor Credits (Hire Finance) Ltd v Pacific Motor Auctions Pty Ltd* (1963) 109 CLR 87; *WJ Albutt & Co. Ltd v Continental Guaranty Corpn of Canada Ltd* [1929] 3 WWR 292 (Can.).

[326] *Folkes v King* [1923] 1 KB 282; *Paris v Goodwin* [1954] NZLR 823; *Stadium Finance Ltd v Robbins* [1962] 2 QB 664; *Lewis v Richardson* [1936] SASR 502; *Davey v Paine Bros Motors Ltd,* n. 315 above.

[327] *Belvoir Finance Ltd v Harold G Cole & Co. Ltd* [1969] 1 WLR 1877; *Evans v Ritchie* (1964) 44 DLR (2d) 675.

[328] *Heyman v Flewker,* n. 317 above, 527; see also *Mortgage, Loan & Finance Co. of Australia Ltd v Richards* (1932) 32 SR(NSW) 50.

mercantile dealings. This was the case in *Lowther v Harris*,[329] where an art dealer who had his own antique shop was admitted to the house of his principal for the purpose of showing a collection of furniture and tapestry to prospective purchasers. He was nonetheless a mercantile agent.

Types of mercantile agent. Obviously, a combination of the informal behav- **5.91** iour of certain mercantile agents and the extension of the Factors Act to mercantile agents acting as such for the first time comes quite close to the proposition that anyone who receives goods from the owner in the capacity of agent for purposes connected with their sale is a mercantile agent. This step, however, has not been taken.[330] In the final resort, the person receiving the goods must be an agent of an established commercial type.[331] For example, in *Heap v Motorists' Advisory Agency*[332] the owner of a car entrusted it to a man calling himself Captain the Hon. Roger North for the purpose of driving it to a named friend of North's in Uxbridge looking to purchase a car. Although North later did become a car dealer, the court held that he was not a mercantile agent at the time he obtained possession of the car.[333] Similarly, in the Canadian case of *Bush v Fry*,[334] a piano was delivered to a music teacher, who was known in no other capacity, for the purpose of sale to a particular, named customer. The teacher then shipped the instrument under an assumed name to Toronto, took on that name when he came to Toronto and pledged the piano. The special *ad hoc* agency of the music teacher was held not to be a mercantile agency. Obviously, the difference between cases like these and *Lowther v Harris* depends largely on the degree to which courts are prepared to recognize novel examples of mercantile activity for the purpose of section 2 of the Factors Act.

Receipt as a Mercantile Agent

A judicial gloss on the section. It is not enough that the agent be a mercantile **5.92** agent, for he must also receive the goods in his capacity as a mercantile agent. As a Canadian judge once put it:[335]

> [N]o case has ever decided that the owner of goods is estopped merely because he has entrusted with the possession of his property a person who, being engaged in a business in the course of which he sells goods of the same kind as those which have been delivered to him as bailee, in breach of his duty, has wrongfully sold the goods of his bailor as his own. If this were so, no man could safely leave his watch with a watchmaker

---

329 [1927] 1 KB 393; *Thoresen v Capital Credit Corpn* (1964) 43 DLR (2d) 94.
330 *Jerome v Bentley*, n. 280 above.
331 *Heyman v Flewker*, n. 317 above; *Directors etc. of City Bank v Barrow*, n. 321 above.
332 [1923] 1 KB 577.
333 Cf the question whether a certain 'Major Tatham' could be said to have a usual authority for the purpose of the estoppel doctrine in *Jerome v Bentley*, n. 280 above.
334 (1887) 15 OR 12.
335 *Forristal v McDonald*, n. 321 above, 17.

who sells watches, or his carriage with a carriage maker who sells carriages, to be repaired.

This additional requirement is a judicial gloss upon section 2 of the Factors Act. It was introduced on the basis of old factors legislation, which required that the agent be 'intrusted with and in possession of'[336] the goods before the owner could be bound by their 'sale or disposition'. Cases decided under this provision required the agent to be entrusted in his capacity as a mercantile agent.[337] Although the current Factors Act substitutes for the above language a requirement that the mercantile agent obtain 'with the consent of the owner . . . possession of goods or of the documents of title to goods',[338] there still remains the judicially introduced requirement that possession be obtained *qua* mercantile agent.[339] Certain older cases[340] have held not to be a mercantile agent one who is authorised only to relay offers of purchase to the owner and not to enter into any binding contracts of sale. This is inconsistent with other authority[341] and wrong in principle, for what is important is the selling authority usually confided in such agents rather than the actual authority that is restricted between owner and agent in an undisclosed way.

5.93 **Examples.** The requirement that the mercantile agent receive *qua* mercantile agent has meant that section 2 does not apply where a finance company repossesses a vehicle and deposits it with a garage for storage purposes only.[342] Section 2 has also been held not to apply to the acquisition of a car by a car rental company, because receipt for hire does not fall within the usual authority of a mercantile agent as defined in section 1(1) of the Factors Act.[343] A mercantile agent who receives possession of goods under the terms of sale or return or sale on approval

---

[336] Factors Act 1825, s. 2.

[337] *Hellings v Russell* (1877) 33 LT 380; *Cole v North Western Bank*, n. 313 above; *Monk v Whittenbury*, n. 320 above; *Forristal v McDonald*, n. 321 above; *Directors etc. of City Bank v Barrow*, n. 321 above; *Johnson v Crédit Lyonnais Co*, n. 313 above; *Turner v Sampson* (1911) 27 TLR 200, 202.

[338] S. 2(1). Said to be effectively the same thing as entrustment: *Lake v Simmons* [1927] AC 487, 509–10; *Oppenheimer v Attenborough & Son* [1907] 1 KB 510, 516.

[339] *Astley Industrial Trust Ltd v Miller* [1968] 2 All ER 36; *Belvoir Finance Co. Ltd v Harold G Cole & Co. Ltd*, n. 327 above; *Staffs Motor Guarantee Co. Ltd v British Wagon Co. Ltd* [1934] 2 KB 305; *Kendrick v Sotheby & Co.* (1967) 111 SJ 470 (statue entrusted for purpose of obtaining a photograph signed by sculptor's widow). Cf. *Moody v Pall Mall Deposit and Forwarding Co. Ltd* (1917) 33 TLR 306; *Cahn v Pockett's Bristol Channel Steam Packet Co. Ltd* [1899] 1 QB 643, 660–1.

[340] *Biggs v Evans* [1894] 1 QB 88 (Wills J—a judgment similar to the one he gave in *Watteau v Fenwick* [1893] 1 QB 346); *Brown and Co. v Bedford Pantechnicon Co. Ltd* (1889) 5 TLR 449.

[341] *Pearson v Rose & Young Ltd* [1951] 1 KB 275, 288; *Lloyds and Scottish Finance Ltd v Williamson* [1965] 1 All ER 641.

[342] *Schafhauser v Shaffer* [1943] 3 DLR 656. It is not easy to see how a buyer obtaining a document of title on trust receipt terms (n. 318 above and accompanying text) can be seen as receiving that document in his capacity as a mercantile agent.

[343] *Astley Industrial Trust Ltd v Miller*, n. 339 above.

agreements obtains them as a potential buyer and not as an agent at all and would, if selling them to an innocent purchaser, be more accurately pictured, as between himself and the owner, as reselling rather than selling the goods.[344] Obviously, it can be a difficult question of interpretation whether the agent has received *qua* agent or *qua* potential buyer.[345] The third-party dimension has ensured that courts do not consider themselves bound by the label chosen by the parties themselves.[346]

Disposing Power of Mercantile Agents

Effect. Section 2(1) of the Factors Act states the power of a mercantile agent as follows: **5.94**

> Where a mercantile agent is, with the consent of the owner, in possession of goods or of the documents of title to goods, any sale, pledge or other disposition of the goods, made by him when acting in the ordinary course of business of a mercantile agent, shall, subject to the provisions of this Act, be as valid as if he were expressly authorised by the owner of the goods to make the same; provided that the person taking under the disposition acts in good faith, and has not at the time of the disposition notice that the person making the disposition has not authority to make the same.

This provision raises a number of points. The meaning of 'mercantile agent' and the requirement of receipt in that capacity have already been considered. First of all, though section 2(1) speaks of the 'owner', it does not launder title but rather effaces whatever title, which may be a possessory one, is vested in the party transferring possession to the mercantile agent. A limited possessory title was defeated in *Lloyds Bank Ltd v Bank of America National Trust and Savings Association,* [347] where a financing bank released to the buyers of certain goods documents of title relating to them. The buyers took the documents on trust receipt terms and were to keep the goods and their proceeds of sale separate from their other assets. Despite the buyers having the general property in the goods and the bank a possessory interest by way of a deemed continuing pledge that survived the release of the documents, the bank was held to be the owner for the purpose of section 2(1) and the buyers to be mercantile agents receiving them in that capacity. Consequently, an unauthorized but ordinary course pledge of the documents by the buyer was held to override the interest of the bank.

Possession. Possession in section 2 has the same meaning as that given to it in other areas of personal property law, that is to say, it is constituted by physical control of the goods complete with an intention to exclude others.[348] In *Lowther*   **5.95**

---

[344] *Weiner v Harris* [1910] 1 KB 285.
[345] *Ibid.*
[346] *Ibid.*
[347] [1938] 2 KB 146. See also *Beverley Acceptances Ltd v Oakley* [1982] RTR 417.
[348] *Cahn v Pockett's Bristol Channel Steam Packet Co. Ltd* [1899] 1 QB 643; Bridge, n. 11 above, 16–25.

v Harris,[349] the mercantile agent was not in possession of the furniture and tapestry while it remained in Colonel Lowther's house. Admittedly, the agent had the key and had access by permission to certain parts of the house for his personal occupation.[350] But the owner kept a secretary in the house during business hours and the court rightly held that it was not until the agent fraudulently obtained permission to remove the tapestry from the house and did so that he could be said to have acquired possession of it.[351]

5.96 **Owner's consent.** The agent's possession of the goods or documents of title must be obtained with the 'consent' of the owner.[352] Fraud alone will not destroy the owner's consent.[353] A particular difficulty that used to arise before the reform of the law of theft in 1967[354] was whether the commission of larceny by a trick[355] by the agent destroyed the consent.[356] The cases initially were divided and contrasting opinions were expressed whether the 'technicalities' of criminal law were to be introduced into commercial law.[357] Even before larceny by a trick was abolished, it was settled, however, that the owner's consent might in fact be given even to an agent who had committed larceny by a trick.[358] Central to the offence of larceny by a trick was the absence of the owner's intention to pass the property in the goods, or the power of disposing of the property, to the agent.[359] While larceny by a trick might therefore destroy the voidable title of a rogue under section 23 of the Sale of Goods Act,[360] it did not have the same effect under section 2 of the Factors Act, since the owner never intended to pass the property in the goods

---

[349] [1927] 1 KB 393.

[350] He was a 'licensee, perhaps caretaker': *ibid*.

[351] See also *Brown and Co. v Bedford Pantechnicon Co. Ltd*, n. 340 above.

[352] The consent is to the agent's possession of goods and is not an intention to pass the property in the goods to the agent: *Cahn*, n. 348 above. It must be given by the owner and not by someone in unlawful possession (*Cook v Rodgers* (1946) 46 SR(NSW) 229; *Brandon v Leckie* (1972) 29 DLR (3d) 633) or by an unauthorized agent (*WJ Albutt & Co. Ltd v Continental Guaranty Corpn of Canada Ltd*, n. 325 above.

[353] *Cole v North Western Bank*, n. 313 above, 393; *Cahn*, n. 348 above, 659.

[354] Theft Act 1967.

[355] Described as 'a most bewildering subject' in *London Jewellers Ltd v Attenborough* [1934] 2 KB 206, 213.

[356] For authority that larceny by a trick destroyed consent, see: *Oppenheimer v Frazer & Wyatt* [1907] 2 KB 50; *Heap v Motorists' Advisory Agency Ltd* [1923] 1 KB 577; *Lake v Simmons* [1926] 2 KB 51 (Atkin LJ).

[357] No: *Folkes v King* [1923] 1 KB 282, 305 (Scrutton LJ). Yes (and they are not technicalities): *Lake v Simmons*, n. 356 above, 71 (Atkin LJ) and [1927] AC 487, 509–10 (Lord Sumner).

[358] *Folkes v King*, n. 357 above (Bankes and Scrutton LJJ); *Paris v Goodwin* [1954] NZLR 823; *Pearson v Rose & Young Ltd*, n. 341 above; *Roache v Australian Mercantile Land & Finance Co. Ltd* (1966) 67 SR(NSW) 54, 66; *London Jewellers Ltd v Attenborough*, n. 355 above. The same holds true for buyers and sellers in possession: *Du Jardin v Beadman Bros Ltd* [1952] 2 QB 712; *Reed v Motors Ltd* [1926] SASR 128.

[359] *Whitehorn Bros v Davison* [1911] 1 KB 463; *Folkes v King*, n. 357 above; *London Jewellers Ltd v Attenborough*, n. 355 above; *Dennant v Skinner* [1948] 2 KB 164.

[360] Discussed above.

to the rogue agent. Indeed, he employed the agent to create an opportunity for the future transfer of the property, and in some cases would actually and genuinely be authorizing the agent to pass the property on limited terms.[361] Accordingly, a pre-occupation with larceny by a trick diverted attention from the relevant question in section 2, namely, whether the agent was in fact in possession of the goods with the owner's consent. It added nothing to mercantile agency and its abolition complements the sensible course already taken by the case law under section 2.

Evidentiary presumptions. To facilitate the forensic task of the innocent pur-   **5.97**
chaser of the goods in a title dispute with the owner, the Factors Act establishes a number of evidentiary presumptions favouring the purchaser. Someone who has the custody of the goods, or who controls someone else who has it, will be deemed to be in possession.[362] Once the mercantile agent is shown to be or to have been in possession of the goods, it will then be presumed in the absence of evidence to the contrary that this was with the owner's consent;[363] the burden of proof of showing this not to be the case is therefore on the owner. Furthermore, any consent given by the owner to the agent's possession of goods or of documents of title to goods is deemed to be given also with respect to documents of title into which those goods or documents of title are translated.[364] Thus a mercantile agent depositing his principal's goods in a warehouse and being issued with a warehouse receipt will be deemed to be in possession of the warehouse receipt with the consent of the owner, and any effective dealings with the warehouse receipt will bind the goods. Likewise, a mercantile agent who exchanges one manufacturer's warehouse receipt for another will obtain the second receipt with the consent of the owner if that was the way the first was obtained.[365] The final, and probably the most important, presumption is contained in section 2(2):

> Where a mercantile agent has, with the consent of the owner, been in possession of goods or of documents of title to goods, any sale, pledge, or other disposition, which would have been valid if the consent had continued, shall be valid notwithstanding the termination of the consent: provide that the person taking under the disposition has not at the time thereof notice that the consent has been terminated.[366]

Given the mercurial habits of disappearing rogue agents, this is a presumption that in practical terms is impossible to rebut. Its most significant effect has been in section 25 of the Sale of Goods Act which, as we shall see, by requiring the buyer

---

[361] e.g. *Folkes v King*, n. 357 above.
[362] S. 1(2).
[363] S. 2(4), discussed in *Fuentes v Montis* (1868) LR 3 CP 831.
[364] S. 2(3).
[365] *Ibid.*, overruling *Hatfield v Phillips* (1845) 14 M & W 665.
[366] This overrules *Fuentes v Montis*, n. 363 above. See now *Folkes v King*, n. 357 above, 301–2; *Pearson v Rose & Young Ltd* [1951] 1 KB 275, 288.

in possession to act in the same way as a mercantile agent, has imported the relevant provisions of the Factors Act into the interpretation of section 25.

Ordinary Course of Business

5.98 **Meaning.**   Perhaps the most difficult problem posed by section 2(1) concerns the requirement that the agent act in the ordinary course of business of a mercantile agent in selling, pledging, or otherwise disposing of the goods or documents of title. The difficulty is caused by the fact that the innocent purchaser need not realize he is dealing with a mercantile agent.[367] This development appears to stem from the practice of nineteenth-century brokers, acting on behalf of undisclosed principals, of not revealing that they were acting as agents when carrying on a business in which they commonly bought and sold on their own behalf. The leading case on the subject is *Oppenheimer v Attenborough & Son*,[368] where a diamond broker fraudulently pledged some diamonds that he had obtained for the purpose of showing to named potential purchasers. At the trial, it appeared that diamond brokers did not have a usual authority to pledge their principals' diamonds. The broker in question, however, had also transacted business for a number of years as a diamond merchant and in that capacity had pledged diamonds on a number of occasions with the defendants for short-term advances. The issue was whether the diamond broker had to act in the ordinary course of business of a diamond broker when dealing with the defendants, who did not know that the broker was acting in the capacity of a broker.

5.99 **Business-like behaviour.**   In finding for the defendant pawnbrokers, the Court of Appeal might have held that it was sufficient for the broker to behave in the ordinary course of business of a diamond merchant, which was evidently what the pawnbrokers believed him to be,[369] but it did not so hold. Instead, the court drew on the difference in language between sections 1(1) and 2(1), the former requiring an agent to have a minimum usual authority in the course of his business as 'such agent' in order to qualify as a mercantile agent under the Act, and the latter, looking to the transactions entered into by mercantile agents who had passed the threshold test in section 1(1), requiring these transactions to have been entered into in the ordinary course of business of 'a mercantile agent'. Thus stated, the language in section 2(1) is to be seen as colouring the good faith and absence of notice of the purchaser or pledgee: the mercantile agent's ordinary course of behaviour is judged by formal and general business criteria, namely, whether he

---

[367] *Oppenheimer v Attenborough & Son* [1908] 1 KB 221. See Buckley LJ's interpretation of s. 4 (at 221) and Kennedy LJ (at 231).

[368] Above.

[369] The case is not clear on this. See Buckley LJ's assumption, n. 367 above, 230, of the pawnbroker's ignorance of a diamond broker's usual authority (*sed quaere* of a large pawnbroker involved in much litigation in this period?). Kennedy LJ, *ibid.* 231, is clearer on this.

acted 'within business hours, at a proper place of business and in other respects in the ordinary way in which a mercantile agent would act'.[370]

Question of fact. The ordinary course of business is clearly a question of fact[371] **5.100** and should be interpreted according to the pattern of practice of the particular trade. *Oppenheimer v Attenborough & Son*[372] lays down in very bland terms a formal test of businesslike behaviour, which a diamond broker in one case failed to meet who persuaded a 'friend' to pledge diamonds with a pawnbroker.[373] But even general business behaviour has to be coloured by the context. For example, it may well be in the ordinary course of business for a car dealer to raise money by mortgage financing on existing stock,[374] but the same could hardly be said of an encyclopaedia salesman. It would not matter how businesslike and professional that salesman was in approaching the lender. Furthermore, the agent may not act in a way in which no responsible agent would have acted; the innocent purchaser or pledgee may truly believe that he is dealing with an owner, but the agent's behaviour must be objectively consistent with the behaviour of someone who is an agent rather than an owner. Thus section 2(1) will not apply where the agent, instead of receiving payment, permits the sum due to be set off against an indebtedness owed personally by the agent to the purchaser or pledgee.[375] Although at one time the common law did not recognize the usual authority of agents to pledge their principals' property, factors legislation responded[376] to the emergent practice of factors making advances to their principals and keeping themselves in funds by pledging the goods or documents of title until an ensuing sale.[377]

Car trade. The car trade has been a particularly fruitful source of reported cases **5.101** on the subject of ordinary course of business. It has been held without any difficulty that dealers act in the ordinary course of business when accepting an exchange

---

[370] Kennedy LJ, 230–1 (Buckley LJ). See also *Newton's of Wembley Ltd v Williams* [1965] 1 QB 560 (kerbside sale in Warren Street); *People's Credit Jewellers Ltd v Melvin* [1933] 1 DLR 498.

[371] *Jensen v Harrison* [1933] 3 WWR 669.

[372] n. 367 above.

[373] *De Gorter v George Attenborough and Son* (1904) 19 TLR 19. An auction sale was held on the facts not to be in the ordinary course in *Waddington and Sons v Neale and Sons* (1907) 96 LT 786.

[374] *Industrial Acceptance Corpn Ltd v Whiteshell Finance Corpn Ltd* (1966) 57 DLR (2d) 670.

[375] *Lloyds and Scottish Finance Ltd v Williamson* [1965] 1 All ER 641; *Biggs v Evans* [1894] 1 QB 88 (payment to agent's judgment creditor). Cf New Zealand cases where a set-off is regarded as occurring in the ordinary course of business if the purchaser believes he is contracting with someone acting on his own account: *R and E Tingey & Co. Ltd v John Chambers & Co. Ltd* [1967] NZLR 785; *Ceres Orchard Partnership v Fiatagri Australia Pty Ltd* [1995] 1 NZLR 112 (sale in the ordinary course of business not confined to what is ordinarily done in business).

[376] Factors Act 1842, s. 1.

[377] *Fuentes v Montis*, n. 363 above, 277–8; *Roache v Australian Mercantile Land & Finance Ltd*, n. 358 above, 69. See also *Oppenheimer v Attenborough & Son*, n. 367 above; *Janesich v George Attenborough and Son* (1902) 102 LT 605.

or trade-in.[378] In certain circumstances, a dealer will not sell in the ordinary course of business unless the sale is accompanied by the appropriate documents. A number of decisions hold that the car logbook, the forerunner of the present registration document, must accompany the goods if the sale of a second-hand car is to be effective under section 2(1) of the Factors Act.[379] Although the logbook, in common with the modern registration document, was not a document of title[380] and merely designated the person responsible for paying road tax, it was a permanent document lasting for the life of the car and its transfer was in practical terms a necessary incident of any transfer of the vehicle. This was not the case with the sale of a new vehicle,[381] where the registration authority might not yet have issued the logbook. The position would appear to be the same for modern registration documents, although they are not permanent in character and are reissued with each registered change of ownership. In what can only be described as an effort to assist a private owner against an innocent trade purchaser, in one case when the owner had been duped by the rogue into parting with possession of the logbook, it was held that, while the logbook may not have been 'goods' within section 1(3) of the Factors Act, the rogue should not have had it, therefore could not be said to have sold the car with it, and so the sale did not take place in the ordinary course of business.[382] The proposition has only to be stated for its logical flaws to be apparent.

5.102 **Transactions of the agent.** Section 2(1) of the Factors Act applies to the 'sale, pledge or other disposition' of the goods by the mercantile agent. If there is a sale, it must not be an accommodation sale with the agent remaining in possession of the goods at all material times and the expectation being that the agent will buy back at an elevated price reflecting the time value of the money advanced by the purchaser.[383] Auctioneers receiving goods from mercantile agents for the purpose of the sale have unsuccessfully argued that this receipt amounts to a pledge or disposition.[384] Despite the auctioneer in one case making an advance of the contingent

---

[378] *Davey v Paine Bros (Motors) Ltd* [1954] NZLR 1122; *Lewis v Richardson* [1936] SASR 502.

[379] *Pearson v Rose & Young Ltd*, n. 366 above; *Stadium Finance Ltd v Robbins* [1962] 2 QB 664. Cf *Dreverton v Regal Garage* [1998] CLY 4382, a case dealing with the modern registration document and rejecting any rule that the sale of a car without this document can never be in the ordinary course of business of a mercantile agent.

[380] *Central Newbury Car Auctions Ltd v Unity Finance Ltd* [1957] 1 QB 371; *Joblin v Watkins* [1949] 1 All ER 47 note; *Pearson v Rose & Young Ltd*, n. 366 above; *J. Sargent (Garages) Ltd v Motor Auctions (West Bromwich) Ltd* [1977] RTR 121; *Beverley Acceptances Ltd v Oakley* [1982] RTR 417.

[381] *Astley Industrial Trust Ltd v Miller* [1968] 2 All ER 36.

[382] *Stadium Finance Ltd v Robbins*, n. 379 above (Ormerod and Dankwerts LJJ); see also *Pearson v Rose & Young Ltd*, n. 366 above.

[383] *Joblin v Watkins*, n. 380 above.

[384] *Waddington and Sons v Neale and Sons*, n. 373 above. For a further discussion of 'disposition' under s. 24 of the Sale of Goods Act, see discussion in the text accompanying nn. 508 *et seq.* below.

sale price to the agent, the relationship between the two was rightly held not to amount to a pledge; the redemption of the goods by the agent was never contemplated by the parties. It has also been held that the transfer by the agent to the auctioneer cannot be treated as a disposition, since this implies a divesting of the general property in the goods in a manner akin to a sale;[385] the agent merely transfers possession to the auctioneer and has no intention of vesting any other property interest in the auctioneer.

Agent's possession. It is not clear from a reading of section 2(1) whether posses- **5.103** sion must necessarily be transferred by the mercantile agent. Obviously it must in the case of a pledge,[386] but the section does not clearly state that it should for a sale or a disposition. It does, however, refer to a 'taking under' a sale, pledge, or disposition, but this can be understood as a general reference to the nature of the property interest purportedly conferred by the agent on the transferee, which will vary according to whether he is a buyer or a pledgee. It is submitted that, like the voidable title provision of section 23, section 2(1) does not require an actual transfer of possession to the transferee in cases of sales and other dispositions. But the absence of such a transfer might colour other Factors Act questions, such as whether the transaction took place in the ordinary course of business and whether the transferee acted in good faith.

Documents of Title

Extended meaning. Section 2(1) applies to dealings in documents of title as **5.104** well as in goods. If the Act had been confined to the common law understanding of a document of title, which is satisfied only by a negotiable bill of lading,[387] the purchasers receiving delivery orders and warrants would have obtained singularly little protection. But section 1(4) of the Factors Act gives the following definition:

> The expression 'document of title' shall include any bill of lading, dock warrant, warehouse-keeper's certificate, and warrant or order for the delivery of goods, and any other document used in the ordinary course of business as proof of the possession or control of goods, or authorising or purporting to authorise, either by endorsement or by delivery, the possessor of the document to transfer or receive goods thereby represented.

---

[385] *Roache v Australian Mercantile Land & Finance Co. Ltd*, n. 358 above. See also *Suttons Motors (Temora) Pty Ltd v Hollywood Motors Pty Ltd* [1971] VR 684.

[386] But see the notional transfer under the second pledge, where the first pledge (redeemable at any time) of a bill of lading had not exhausted the value of the goods, in *Portalis v Tetley* (1867) LR 5 Eq. 140.

[387] See Ch. 6 below. See also *Gunn v Bolckow, Vaughan & Co.* (1875) LR 10 Ch. App. 491; *Cole v North Western Bank*, n. 313 above; *Official Assignee of Madras v Mercantile Bank of India Ltd* [1935] AC 53.

This definition poses the question whether a non-negotiable document, in the form of a sea waybill or a straight bill of lading, [388] for example, may be a document of title under section 1(4). This question may be approached from two angles. The first approach is to ask if the document is of a type against which the bailee in possession of goods would be expected in the ordinary course of business to surrender the goods therein represented. Such documents would go beyond a negotiable bill of lading since they would include other negotiable (that is, transferable) documents that do not confer direct rights against the bailee, namely, documents calling for delivery to the holder for the time being or bearer. The second approach assesses the character of the document as affording evidence of ownership or of authority to deal in the underlying goods.

5.105 **Non-negotiable documents.** The first approach clearly excludes most non-negotiable documents since delivery will be made by the bailee, not against any document as such, but pursuant to instructions given by the bailor.[389] Documents such as a sea waybill will name a consignee, but the bailee may be directed by the consignor to deliver to someone else instead.[390] The treatment of non-negotiable documents under the second approach is less clear. Section 1(4) of the Factors Act appears to contemplate a wider range of documents than those in negotiable form. It does refer to an entitlement to receive goods arising out of indorsement or delivery of a document, a reference to its negotiation.[391] But it also refers to the 'possessor' of a document, instead of the 'holder' we expect to see in the case of negotiable documents, and it refers separately to documents that prove possession or control of goods. On balance, it seems that a party in possession of a non-negotiable document may have a disposing power under section 2(1) of the Factors Act. One example would be an agent, to whom goods are entrusted, who consigns them under the terms of a sea waybill. As long as the goods are at sea and the carrier amenable to a change of delivery instructions, the agent's possession of the waybill would represent 'proof of possession *or control* of goods' (emphasis added). Other examples would depend upon the particular commercial context.[392]

5.106 **Negotiable documents.** Whatever may be the scope of section 2 in relation to non-negotiable documents, it should be noted too that it confers certain powers upon mercantile agents in relation to negotiable documents that could not be

---

[388] See *JI McWilliam Co. Inc. v Mediterranean Shipping Co SA (The Rafaela S)* [2005] UKHL 11; [2005] 2 AC 423.

[389] But a straight bill of lading has to be presented to the carrier: *The Rafaela S*, above.

[390] See the indirect recognition of this practice in the wording of s. 2(1)(b) of the Carriage of Goods by Sea Act 1992.

[391] See s. 11 of the Factors Act 1889.

[392] The conclusion that a non-negotiable document falls with s. 2 of the Factors Act is indirectly borne out by *Mercantile Bank of India Ltd v Central Bank of India Ltd*, n. 244 above, where the Privy Council, applying s. 178 of the Indian Contracts Act, which treats railway receipts as documents of title, was prepared to say that even a non-negotiable receipt was a document of title.

exercised by the owners themselves. Apart from the case of negotiable bills of lading, the owner of goods may not by documentary means effect a pledge of goods held by a third party except by securing from that third party an attornment in favour of the new bailor;[393] the mere endorsement or delivery of the negotiable document itself to the new holder would not operate as a pledge. But section 2(1) of the Factors Act[394] empowers a mercantile agent to make an effective pledge of the goods by negotiating a document of title,[395] even if it is not a bill of lading.[396]

Pledges

Various provisions.   The Factors Act contains a number of provisions dealing with pledges. First of all, section 3 provides that a pledge of documents of title by a mercantile agent will be deemed to be a pledge of the goods themselves. Although section 3 does not refer explicitly to mercantile agents, it is contained in a part of the Act bearing the heading 'Dispositions by Mercantile Agents' and so should be read in that context. Secondly, section 4 limits the effect of certain pledges by providing that, if a pledge of goods by a mercantile agent secures a debt incurred by the pledgor before the pledge, the effect of the pledge is confined to whatever interest the pledgor has in the goods. The origins of section 4 lie in an earlier provision dealing with pledges by factors of goods over which they had a lien.[397] Section 4 was considered in *Kaltenbach v Lewis*,[398] where a commission agent unlawfully pledged bills of lading with produce brokers as security for a short-term loan. The money was needed to pay the brokers themselves, on the following day, the price of certain shellac sold to him by the brokers. The brokers did not know that the pledges were unauthorized, and the advance was not made to secure an antecedent debt, since the price of the shellac fell due only on the following day. The reason for the restriction in section 4 is that the owner of goods is prejudiced enough by the mercantile agent's disposing powers under the Act without in effect becoming susceptible to a general lien claimed against the mercantile agent.[399] **5.107**

Specific advances.   The above prohibition on a general lien had posed problems in cases where a mercantile agent pledges his principal's goods or documents **5.108**

---

393 See Ch. 6 below.
394 In combination with s. 3.
395 As defined in s. 1(4).
396 See *Official Assignee of Madras v Mercantile Bank of India Ltd*, n. 387 above.
397 Earlier legislation also provided for the transfer of only this lien interest where the pledgee had notice that the goods did not belong to the factor. See R. Munday (1977) 6 *Anglo-Am LR* 221, 246, referring to the fifth edition of *Abbot on Shipping* as cited in *Cole v North Western Bank*, n. 313 above, 361–2. The Factors Act, in ss. 4 and 7(1), recognizes that possessory liens may be transferred or pledged, a relic of the rule that agents acting for overseas principals did not establish privity between the principal and the third party but contracted themselves with both parties. There is strong contrary authority at common law: *Donald v Suckling* (1866) LR 1 QB 585; *Franklin v Neate* (1844) 13 M & W 481.
398 (1883) 24 Ch. D 54, applying s. 3 of the 1825 Act, the predecessor of the present s. 4.
399 *Ibid.*

of title, together with other goods or documents of title, in return for one consolidated advance. An Australian court has held that the Factors Act protects only specific advances and does not permit a combined pledge for a consolidated amount that might vary from time to time.[400] This appears to be a somewhat drastic result where the amount of the pledge advance could be apportioned so as to cover the proportionate value of the principal's goods or documents of title, and where the balance in a continuing pledge account could be calculated on 'first in, first out' principles if subsequent pledge securities were added.

5.109   **General lien.**   A different approach was adopted in *Thoreson v Capital Credit Corpn Ltd*,[401] which dealt also with section 12(2) of the Factors Act, which entitles an owner to recover goods from a pledgee on reimbursing the latter the amount of the pledge advance. In that case, the British Columbia court upheld the validity of a pledge of the plaintiff's trailer where a mercantile agent consolidated his pledge account with the pledgee in return for the grant of a fresh advance. The court held that the owner was entitled to redeem his goods, a trailer, only if he paid off the whole advance secured on this and six other trailers, and not merely a rateable proportion of the advance fitting his own trailer. This is tantamount, as against the owner, to allowing the pledgee a general lien, for the amount the pledgee might have advanced on the owner's trailer alone would have fallen well short of the advance actually made. Although this recognition of a consolidated pledge does not overtly affect section 4 of the Factors Act, which declines to recognize pledges for antecedent and not future advances, it involves a departure from the approach taken in *Kaltenbach v Lewis*,[402] as well as that in the Australian case referred to above. Although the matter is not free from doubt, it is unlikely that a pledgee was ever intended to obtain the advantages under sections 4 and 12(2) of the Factors Act that were obtained by the pledgee in *Thoresen*. The better solution, it is submitted, is to apportion the pledge advance to the rateable value of the owner's goods; it is fair, though not easy to do.

Consignments

5.110   **General.**   The oldest provision in the Factors Act is section 7[403] but little is known (or remembered) of it and it attracts little textual analysis. According to section 7(1):

> Where the owner of goods has given possession of the goods to another person for the purpose of consignment or sale, or has shipped the goods in the name of another

---

[400] *Re Farmers and Settlers Co-operative Society Ltd* (1908) SR (NSW) 41, applying *Kaltenbach*, n. 398 above.
[401] (1964) 43 DLR (2d) 94.
[402] n. 398 above.
[403] S. 1 of the 1823 Act, devoted exclusively to it.

person, and the consignee of the goods has not had notice that such person is not the owner of the goods, the consignee shall, in respect of advances made to or for the use of such person, have the same lien on the goods as if such person were the owner of the goods, and may transfer any such lien to another person.

Section 7(1) raises a number of obvious difficulties of interpretation. It does not state what is meant by 'consignment', 'advances', or 'lien'. Over a century ago, Lord Blackburn said of its precursor:

> The enactment has never been altered and its provisions have, in practice, been found to work so harmoniously with the practice of merchants that I am not aware that any case has ever arisen requiring a court of law to construe it, which probably is the reason why an Act of such importance is not familiar to every one.[404]

The case in question concerned a cargo of tobacco, owned by a Cuban resident, that had been shipped by a Cuban broker to an English commission agent, on terms requiring the latter to take out marine insurance against a total loss. The question was whether the commission agent had a lien on the insurance moneys, paid upon the loss of the cargo, for the personal indebtedness to him of the Cuban broker under their running account. Lord Blackburn would have held that the commission agent had such a lien under section 7(1),[405] were it not for the fact that he had notice of the existence of the Cuban principal; it was not necessary that the principal's name be known. The reason for the denial of a lien where there was notice that the mercantile agent was not the owner was taken to be a general principle of the common law 'that it was unjust, with knowledge, to take one man's goods to pay another's debt'.[406]

Relationship to lien.   Section 7(1) was also put forward in another case by an   **5.111** auctioneer who had made an advance to a mercantile agent, whom he believed to be the owner of a piano, in contemplation of the sale of that piano.[407] It was said abruptly that section 7(1) need not be considered at all, and the reason is apparent. While an auctioneer may have a common law lien on the goods for his commission and sale expenses, he would surely have to bargain expressly for a lien in connection with any money-lending activities. If the word 'lien' were read expansively, section 7(1) would make considerable inroads into the limitations on apparent ownership and would undermine the limitations on the mercantile agent's power in section 2(1), particularly the limitations that the agent receive as a mercantile agent and act in the ordinary course of business of a mercantile agent. The greater scope of a mercantile agent's disposing power under section 7(1) is

---

[404] *Mildred, Goyeneche & Co. v Maspons* (1883) 8 App. Cas. 874, 884.
[405] Lord Fitzgerald doubted it: *ibid.*
[406] *Ibid.* 885.
[407] *Waddington and Sons v Neale and Sons* (1907) 96 LT 786.

brought out by sub-section (2), which provides that nothing in sub-section (1) limits or affects sales, pledges, and dispositions by mercantile agents.[408]

5.112 Advances. Section 7(1) seems to reflect patterns of overseas mercantile activity no longer current today. If the word 'advance' is read liberally so as to cover any disbursement or expenditure, section 7(1) may be seen as protecting the lien rights, special or general, of certain consignees acting as factors,[409] bankers,[410] calico printers,[411] and dyers.[412] A banker, for example, making advances to a consignee on the security of a bill of lading might therefore be able to claim a lien as against an undisclosed owner who is neither the named consignor (perhaps a mere forwarding agent) nor the consignee. A warehouseman might also be able to claim against such an owner in respect of his storage charges,[413] though only if 'advance' is broadly interpreted. These liens could be upheld in circumstances where the lienee's claims might fail under section 2(1).

Good Faith and Notice

5.113 General. Section 2(1) of the Factors Act requires the purchaser or pledgee taking from the mercantile agent to act in good faith and not to have notice of the mercantile agent's lack of authority. The Factors Act does not define 'good faith' but it will certainly be understood in the same way as it is in the Sale of Goods Act,[414] namely to mean honest behaviour.[415] Normally, good faith and notice will coincide,[416] for someone may not claim to be acting in good faith when he has notice of the agent's lack of authority. But if notice were to be read in an expansive fashion, a gap would be opened up between it and good faith.

5.114 Actual notice. It is rare for purchasers dealing with a mercantile agent to be made explicitly aware that the agent is acting in excess of his authority. A more likely possibility is that purchasers are actually put on notice by the circumstances of the transaction. It has been held that notice of an interest may exist where the

---

[408] Curiously, it does not mention s. 2(1).

[409] *Cowell v Simpson* (1809) 16 Ves. Jun. 258; *Rolls Razor Ltd v Cox* [1967] 1 QB 552.

[410] *Brandao v Barnett* (1846) 12 Cl. & F. 786.

[411] *Weldon v Gould* (1801) 3 Esp. 268.

[412] *Savill v Barchard* (1801) 4 Esp. 53.

[413] There are also common law means for such persons asserting rights against owners who have not bailed goods to them: see *Bowmaker Ltd v Wycombe Motors Ltd* [1946] KB 505; *Tappenden v Artus* [1964] 2 QB 185.

[414] S. 61(3). It is probably best defined as the absence of bad faith: *Mogridge v Clapp* [1892] 3 Ch. 382, 391. Kay LJ, *ibid.*, 401, defined good faith as the 'belief that all is being regularly and properly done'.

[415] See *Dodds v Yorkshire Bank Finance* [1992] CCLR 92 (Part III of the Hire Purchase Act 1964).

[416] See, e.g., their synthesized treatment in *Forsyth International (UK) Ltd v Silver Shipping Co. Ltd (The Saetta)* [1994] 1 WLR 1332, 1349–51.

transferee is wilfully blind[417] and fails to make even the most rudimentary inquiries dictated by the common sense of the circumstances.[418] Notice may also be inferred from the terms of the transaction between the mercantile agent and the transferee. It has been held that an unusually low price for an automobile could be evidence of notice,[419] especially where the purchaser is 'rather uncomfortable and suspicious',[420] but care should be taken in applying this to goods of elastic value, such as second-hand cars and to goods of whose true value the purchaser is unaware.[421] The opinion has also been expressed that 'an unusual rate of interest' levied by a pledgee might be 'strong evidence' of notice.[422] Finally, where one joint purchaser has notice, this notice is attributed also to the other joint purchaser.[423]

Constructive notice.   Apart from actual notice, attempts have at various times **5.115** been made to fix purchasers with constructive notice as a result of failing to inspect a register. The registers relevant for present purposes would be bills of sale registers, as well as the national register of company charges, particularly the latter. The common law has long been resistant to constructive notice in dealings with personal property, thus revealing a desire to permit business to be conducted expeditiously without time-consuming enquiries. Lindley LJ once said it was 'extremely important not to encourage the application of the equitable doctrines of constructive notice to honest mercantile transactions'.[424] In the case of corporate assets, such as raw materials, work-in-progress, and stock-in-trade, these would normally be encumbered by a floating charge, under the terms of which the company has an actual right to dispose of the assets in question free of the charge.[425] Consequently, even actual notice of the existence of such a charge would not fetter

---

[417] *Re Gomersall* (1875) 1 Ch. D 137; *Jones v Gordon* (1877) 2 App. Cas. 616.

[418] *Mehta v Sutton* (1913) 10 LT 529; *Patry v General Motors Acceptance Corpn of Canada Ltd* (2000) 187 DLR (4th) 99 (failure to ask questions).

[419] *Heap v Motorists' Advisory Agency*, n. 172 above. See also *Re Gomersall*, n. 417 above.

[420] *Heap*, n. 172 above.

[421] *GE Capital Bank Ltd v Rushton* [2005] EWCA Civ 1556; [2006] 1 WLR 899, at [43]. A discount of 20% on the true value in a distress sale 'gave no reason to think that [the purchaser] knew that the price he was being asked to pay was so much less than the [goods] were worth that he must have realised that something was wrong': *ibid.*, at [47].

[422] *Janesich v George Attenborough & Son* (1910) 102 LT 605.

[423] *Oppenheimer v Frazer & Wyatt* [1907] 2 KB 50.

[424] *Kaltenbach v Lewis*, n. 398 above, 78. See also *Manchester Trust v Furness* [1895] 2 QB 39; *Greer v Downs Supply Co.* [1927] 2 KB 28; *Vowles v Island Finances Ltd* [1940] 4 DLR 357; *Worcester Works Finance Ltd v Cooden Engineering Co. Ltd* [1972] 1 QB 210; *General Motors Acceptance Corpn v Hubbard* (1978) 87 DLR (3d) 39; *Feuer Leather Corpn v Frank Johnstone & Sons* [1981] Com. LR 251; *Forsyth International (UK) Ltd v Silver Shipping Co. Ltd (The Saetta)*, n. 416 above; *Joseph v Lyons* (1884) 15 QBD 280.

[425] *Re Hamilton's Windsor Ironworks* (1879) 12 Ch. D 707; *Wheatley v Silkstone and Haigh Moor Colliery Co.* (1885) 29 Ch. D 715; *Re Automatic Bottle Makers Ltd* [1926] 1 Ch. 412; *Re Bond Worth Ltd* [1980] Ch. 228. See also *National Mercantile Bank v Hampson* (1880) 5 QBD 177; *Taylor v M'Keand* (1880) 5 CPD 358.

the disposing power of a company.[426] The life blood of a company's business is the turnover of its stock-in-trade and the business would be paralysed if a chargee's interest followed the goods into the hands of the ordinary course purchaser. This would damage the commercial interests of both company and chargee. Constructive notice becomes more of an issue if the assets sold by the company are, like equipment and other permanent assets, the subject of a fixed charge or mortgage.[427] There does exist a doctrine of constructive notice, in respect of the registrable particulars of a company charge,[428] but it would appear to be confined to those who can reasonably be expected to inspect the register of company charges,[429] a category that would include creditors of the company taking security but would exclude those purchasing goods from the company in the ordinary course of business. The common law's long-standing hostility to constructive notice would come to the assistance of such purchasers. Nevertheless, in a case involving share dealings, whose relevance for sale-of-goods transactions in this area is far from clear, it has been said that a form of constructive notice, less rigorous than the doctrine that prevails in transactions involving land, imputes to a purchaser 'notice of such facts as he would have discovered if he had taken proper measures to investigate them'.[430] It is unlikely, even if such a doctrine could apply to sale of goods agreements, that it would have a practical impact on the kinds of informal transactions typically dealt with under the rubric of *nemo dat* transactions.[431]

5.116 **Burden of proof.** The burden of proof clearly lies on the purchaser to show he acted in good faith and without notice.[432] Earlier in this chapter, it was noted that the Court of Appeal placed the burden of proof on the plaintiff in proceedings arising out of the voidable title provision, section 23 of the Sale of Goods Act.

---

[426] Cf. s. 13 of the Factors Act: the disposing powers of an agent outside the Act are not to be abridged by anything in the Act.

[427] In so far as the charge or mortgage is equitable, there is of course a general *nemo dat* exception favouring the *bona fide* purchaser of the legal estate: *Pilcher v Rawlins* (1871) LR 7 Ch. App. 259, 269; *Macmillan Inc. v Bishopsgate Trust (No. 3)* [1995] 1 WLR 978, 999–1001. In the case of a legal mortgage, the purchaser will have to invoke s. 2(1) of the Factors Act or one of the other recognized common law or statutory *nemo dat* exceptions.

[428] *Wilson v Kelland* [1910] 2 Ch. 306.

[429] R. M. Goode, *Legal Problems of Credit and Security* (3rd edn, Sweet & Maxwell, 2003), 83.

[430] *Macmillan Inc. v Bishopsgate Trust (No. 3)*, n. 427 above, 1000.

[431] A surer guide is *Feuer Leather Corpn v Frank Johnstone & Sons*, n. 424 above, 253 ('no general duty on a buyer of goods in an ordinary commercial transaction to make inquiries as to the right of the seller to dispose of the goods'); *Forsyth International (UK) Ltd v Silver Shipping Co. Ltd (The Saetta)*, n. 416 above.

[432] *Oppenheimer v Frazer & Wyatt*, n. 423 above; *Heap v Motorists' Advisory Agency*, n. 172 above; *Stadium Finance Ltd v Robbins* [1962] 2 QB 664; *Suttons Motors (Temora) Pty Ltd v Hollywood Motors Pty Ltd* [1971] VR 684; *Buckland v Clarke* [1956] SR (NSW) 185 (an estoppel case); *Newton's of Wembley Ltd v Williams* [1965] 1 QB 560; *Forsyth International (UK) Ltd v Silver Shipping Co. Ltd (The Saetta)*, n. 416 above; *Fairfax Gerrard Holdings Ltd v Capital Bank Plc* [2006] EWHC 3439 (QB); [2007] 1 Lloyd's Rep. 171, revd on different grounds [2007] EWCA Civ 1226; [2008] 1 Lloyd's Rep. 297.

In all other cases of *nemo dat* exceptions, the burden of proof can confidently be said to be on the transferee asserting an interest against the owner.

The Seller in Possession

Introduction. Prior to the enactment of the Factors Act 1877, the power of a   **5.117**
seller, left in possession of the contract goods or of documents of title to those
goods, to transfer title to an innocent purchaser or pledgee was determined according to the ordinary principles of estoppel flowing from an appearance of ownership or authority. In that same year, it had been held that a seller, left in possession
of goods or of documents of title, was not to be treated as in receipt thereof as a
mercantile agent, even if otherwise he occupied the position of a mercantile
agent.[433] Responding to this decision, the 1877 Act conferred on sellers in possession of documents of title the power to convey title,[434] and this power was extended
to sellers left in possession of the goods themselves in the Factors Act 1889.[435]

Sale of Goods Act and Factors Act

Dual provisions. The relevant provision in the Sale of Goods Act is section 24:   **5.118**

> Where a person having sold goods continues or is in possession of the goods, or of
> the documents of title to the goods, the delivery or transfer by that person, or by a
> mercantile agent acting for him, of the goods or documents of title under any sale,
> pledge, or other disposition thereof, to any person receiving the same in good faith
> and without notice of the previous sale, has the same effect as if the person making
> the delivery or transfer were expressly authorised by the owner of the goods to make
> the same.

This provision is paralleled by the almost identical section 8 of the Factors Act
1889, which departs from the Sale of Goods Act provision by extending the seller's
power to the additional case where the delivery or transfer occurs 'under any *agreement for* sale, pledge, or other disposition' (emphasis added). The significance of
this extension will be discussed below.

Single code. A general question arising under the relationship between the   **5.119**
Factors and Sale of Goods Acts concerns the extent to which provisions in the
Factors Act can also be read into the interpretation of the seller and buyer in
possession exceptions to *nemo dat* in sections 24–25 of the Sale of Goods
Act. Although 'the Factors Acts of 1889 and 1890 and the Sale of Goods Act 1893
must for many purposes be treated as one code',[436] it is not clear how far this

---

[433] *Johnson v Crédit Lyonnais Co.* (1877) 3 CPD 32.
[434] S. 3.
[435] S. 8.
[436] *Worcester Works Finance Ltd v Cooden Engineering Co. Ltd* [1972] 1 QB 210, 220.

treatment goes.[437] The Factors Act definition of 'mercantile agent'[438] is repeated with more elaborate punctuation in section 26 of the Sale of Goods Act. Moreover, the definition of 'document of title' in the Sale of Goods Act[439] simply incorporates by reference the Factors Act definition of the same.[440] But there are other matters, such as the method of 'transfer' of documents of title, which are dealt with in the Factors Act[441] but not in the Sale of Goods Act. Furthermore, section 5 of the Factors Act requires consideration to support a sale, pledge, or disposition by a mercantile agent. It is not clear whether this is required also for pledges and dispositions under section 24 of the Sale of Goods Act.

5.120 **Interpretation issues.**   A similar problem relates to the very interpretation of the seller and buyer in possession provisions of the Factors Act itself. To return to section 5, this is to be found in a part of the statute under the heading 'Dispositions by Mercantile Agents'; the seller and buyer in possession sections are contained in another part headed 'Dispositions by Sellers and Buyers of Goods'. This raises the question whether the need for consideration is to be read forward into sections 8 and 9 of the Factors Act, which do not deal with dispositions by mercantile agents. The opinion has been expressed that sections 8 and 9 are not to be read subject to definitional material in the earlier part of the Factors Act.[442] This is contentious, and will be discussed below.[443]

Disposing Power of Seller

5.121 **Sale and agreement to sell.**   The first requirement of section 24 is that the seller has already 'sold' the goods. If there has been merely an agreement to sell to a first buyer, the seller will be able to transmit his title to a second buyer in accordance with normal principles and there should be no need to invoke section 24. The second buyer would in these circumstances not have to comply with section 24 at all, though, if he took with notice that the seller was in breach of the agreement to sell to the first buyer, he might be held liable to the first buyer in the tort of interference with contractual relations. Certainly, if the seller made a gift of the goods to a donee who had no notice of an agreement to sell them, the first buyer could have no complaint against the donee since the seller at all material times had retained the property in the goods.

---

[437] See the qualified support ('for some purposes') for the one-code view of Christopher Clarke LJ, discussing s. 1(2) of the Factors Act in conjunction with s. 24 of the Sale of Goods Act, in *Michael Gerson (Leasing) Ltd v Wilkinson* [2001] QB 514 at [35].

[438] S. 1(1).

[439] S. 61(1).

[440] S. 1(4).

[441] S. 11.

[442] *Inglis v Robertson* [1898] AC 616, 629–30.

[443] The Law Reform Committee in 1966, Cmnd. 2958, recommended without discussion the repeal of ss. 8–9 of the Factors Act.

Equitable property.   A more taxing question concerns the first buyer who has   **5.122**
acquired an equitable property in or a charge on the goods. Atkin LJ in *Re Wait*[444]
was prepared to allow the contracting parties to bargain for such rights, though
the House of Lords has interpreted *Re Wait* somewhat sweepingly as an outright
denial of equitable proprietary principles in sales law.[445] Assuming that a buyer
could acquire an equitable entitlement in goods later made the subject of a second
sale, a second buyer for value without notice would override the first seller's equitable interest in any event, on general principles of equity without having to pray
in aid section 24. Where general equitable principles and section 24 part company, however, is in the statutory requirement that the second buyer take delivery
of the goods. No such requirement is exacted in equity if a second purchaser of the
legal estate is to override the equitable interest of an earlier purchaser.

Conditional sale.   Since section 24 requires that the seller has 'sold' the goods, it   **5.123**
follows that the section will not govern if the first contract is a conditional sale
agreement, for until the property passes to the buyer there is no sale.[446] But in
Vowles v Island Finances Ltd,[447] a car dealer agreed to sell a car on conditional sale
terms and then assigned his interest in the car as well as the benefit of the agreement to the defendant finance company. Before the conditional buyer took delivery of the car, the dealer sold the car to the plaintiff, a *bona fide* cash-paying buyer,
who did take delivery. While the conditional sale itself was not a sale, the court
concluded that the assignment to the finance company amounted to a sale and in
consequence the *bona fide* purchaser obtained a good title under section 24.

Chattel Mortgages

Seller as mortgagor.   One question that cannot easily be answered is whether   **5.124**
section 24 applies in the case of a seller who has borrowed money on the security
of a mortgage of goods. A chattel mortgage is modelled on a sale of the goods by
mortgagor to mortgagee, which sale is defeasible by a resolutive condition, namely
payment in full of the sum owed.[448] On the face of it, the mortgagor retaining
possession after executing a mortgage is a seller in possession. If this view is correct, it would balance the relationship between sections 24 and 25. A financier
taking a mortgage interest in a seller's goods would be vulnerable under section 24
to dealings by the seller. If finance were advanced to a borrower on conditional sale
terms, the financier would again be vulnerable, but this time under section 25,

---

[444] [1927] 1 Ch. 606.
[445] *Leigh and Sillavan Ltd v Aliakmon Shipping Co. Ltd* [1986] AC 785.
[446] S. 2(4).
[447] [1940] 4 DLR 357.
[448] *Keith v Burrows* (1876) 1 CPD 722.

since the borrower is a buyer in possession.[449] If *bona fide* purchasers dealing with commercial sellers are, as a class, deserving of protection, they should not be prejudiced by the fact that the seller's goods are financed on mortgage as opposed to conditional sale terms.

5.125 **Interpretation of section 62(4).** An argument against applying section 24 in the case of chattel mortgages arises from section 62(4) of the Sale of Goods Act: 'The provisions of this Act about contracts of sale do not apply to a transaction in the form of a contract of sale which is intended to operate by way of mortgage, pledge, charge, or other security.' On the face of this, chattel mortgages are therefore excluded from section 24. Charges are certainly excluded since they are not modelled on a sale; indeed, the chargor merely encumbers assets without conveying a property interest to the chargee.[450] If mortgages, however, were to be excluded from section 24, it would have been much easier and more natural to provide that the Act *simpliciter*, rather than its contract of sale provisions, does not apply to them. Section 62(4) can be given a coherent meaning if it is read so as to exclude two-party sales issues flowing from the beneficial and absolute passing of property and delivery from seller to buyer. There seems little reason to extend to chattel mortgagees rights concerning the delivery of the goods and their quality characteristics when the goods are never delivered to the mortgagee and the expectation of the parties is that the security will eventually be lifted. On this reading, section 62(4) could be denied application to three-party title problems. Indeed, the *nemo dat* provisions are not naturally housed in a sale of goods statute and could just as easily have been made the subject of a special title transfer statute. Moreover, there is no equivalent to section 62(4) in the Factors Act and therefore nothing to inhibit a straightforward interpretation of section 8, the equivalent of section 24 of the Sale of Goods Act.

5.126 The cases do not reveal a concern with the above problem and the reason is not difficult to find. Section 24 could serve a practical purpose only in the case of goods subject to a fixed legal mortgage, for reasons stated above. The law does not recognize fixed mortgages and charges over stock-in-trade in so far as they leave the company free, as for practical reasons they must, to dispose of stock beneficially in the ordinary course of its business. In these circumstances, a purported fixed security would be recharacterized as a floating security, where the company would have authority to dispose of its assets in the ordinary course of business.[451]

---

[449] S. 25(2)(b) excludes from the scope of the section only those conditional sale contracts that pass the test of a consumer credit agreement laid down in the Consumer Credit Act 1974. It does not exclude commercial contracts of the type under discussion.

[450] *Re Bond Worth Ltd* [1980] Ch. 228; *Carreras Rothmans Ltd v Freeman Mathews Treasure Ltd* [1985] Ch. 207.

[451] See *Re Yorkshire Woolcombers Association Ltd* [1903] 2 Ch. 284, affirmed *sub nom. Illingworth v Houldsworth* [1904] AC 355; *Re Bond Worth Ltd*, n. 450 above. See also the absence of creditor

A live problem would present itself if the seller were seeking to dispose of equipment the subject of a legal mortgage. For reasons stated above, it is submitted that a sale of such equipment to a *bona fide* buyer should fall within section 24.

Constructive Possession

Reasons for protecting third party. The requirement in section 24 that the **5.127** seller be in possession of the goods or documents of title will normally be satisfied by the seller having actual possession. Some difficulty arises where the seller's possession is constructive,[452] a bailee holding the goods on his behalf. The purpose behind section 8 of the Factors Act 1889 was to extend the protection, given already in the case of mercantile agents in possession, accorded to *bona fide* purchasers relying on the semblance of ownership or authority reflected by other cases of possession. Like other *nemo dat* exceptions, the seller in possession rule cannot systematically be rationalized in terms of authority or ownership because it may be a matter of pure accident that the *bona fide* purchaser turns out to have been dealing with a seller in possession; the purchaser may have no idea of the seller's identity, so that the latter's power under section 24 may be better explained as stemming from status rather than appearances. But if, given the origin of section 24, sense has to be made as much as possible of its appearances pedigree, it is not easy to see why it should be extended beyond cases where the seller is in actual possession of goods or documents of title. In *Pacific Motor Auctions Pty Ltd v Motor Credit (Hire Finance) Ltd*,[453] Lord Pearson said: 'The object of the section is to protect an innocent purchaser who is deceived by the vendor's physical possession of goods or documents and who is inevitably unaware of legal rights which fetter the apparent power to dispose.' It must also be remembered that actual possession of documents of title is constructive possession of the underlying goods and that the breadth of the definition of documents of title in sale of goods and factors legislation ensures relatively few cases in which constructive possession through a bailee is evidenced without a document of title.

Constructive possession as possession. Be that as it may, section 1(2) of the **5.128** Factors Act states: 'A person shall be deemed to be in possession of goods or of the documents of title to goods, where the goods or documents are in his actual custody or are held by any other person subject to his control or for him on his behalf.' This provision certainly has a bearing on the interpretation of the seller in possession provision in section 8 since it is contained in a part of the Act headed 'Preliminary', which qualifies the balance of the Act and not just the following

---

controls on dealing with book debts and their proceeds as fatal to the existence of a fixed charge over them: *Agnew v Commissioner of Inland Revenue* [2001] UKPC 28; [2001] 2 AC 710; *Re Spectrum Plus Ltd* [2005] UKHL 41; [2005] 2 AC 680.

[452] Ch. 6 below.
[453] [1965] AC 867, 886.

part only, which deals with dispositions by mercantile agents. It would be perverse to deny the same interpretation to section 24 of the Sale of Goods Act just because it is not qualified by section 1(2). Sections 8 of the Factors Act and 24 of the Sale of Goods Act would therefore seem to apply where, for example, a seller bails goods to a bailee even without receiving a delivery warrant or an acceptance of a delivery order. In *City Fur Manufacturing Co. Ltd v Fureenbond (Brokers) London Ltd*,[454] the owner of certain furs stored in a warehouse sold them to the plaintiffs, promising the latter to apply a portion of the price to the outstanding storage charges and to give them a delivery order. Subsequently, the owner pledged the furs with the defendants for the amount of the storage charges, the defendants drawing a cheque for this amount in favour of the warehouseman and taking physical delivery of the furs. Though the owner was not in actual possession of the goods or the documents of title, the court still held that he was a seller in possession and that possession was to be interpreted in the wide, constructive sense allowed for in section 1(2). More difficult is the case of a bailee who has undertaken to a previous owner to surrender the goods to the seller but, though disposed to deliver the goods to or at the request of the seller, has not given a binding commitment to this effect to the seller. Even this case would appear to fall within the words 'on his behalf' in section 1(2), which, if literally interpreted, is not concerned with the question whether the bailee will respond to the seller's demands.

Quality of Seller's Possession

5.129 **Continuity of possession and quality.** Although section 24 applies where the seller 'continues or is in possession'[455] of the contract goods or documents of title, it makes no reference to the capacity in which the seller holds them, and, in particular, does not provide that the seller shall hold them as seller instead of, for example, as bailee. The earlier cases carried over from the law on mercantile agency a capacity restriction argument, despite the merely incidental reference to mercantile agency in section 24,[456] and held that the seller should hold *qua* seller.[457]

---

[454] [1937] 1 All ER 799, distinguished on the facts in *Fairfax Gerrard Holdings Ltd v Capital Bank Plc* [2006] EWHC 3439 (QB); [2007] 1 Lloyd's Rep. 171 at [31], revd on different grounds [2007] EWCA Civ 1226; [2008] 1 Lloyd's Rep. 297.

[455] The court in *Mercantile Credit Ltd v FC Upton & Sons Pty. Ltd* (1974) 48 ALJR 301 held the seller was in sole possession even though the assignee of the buyer's rights had a registered office on the same premises as the seller.

[456] See the respondent's unsuccessful argument in *Pacific Motor Auctions Pty Ltd v Motor Credit (Hire Finance) Ltd*, n. 453 above.

[457] *Mitchell v Jones* (1905) 24 NZLR 932; *Staffs Motor Guarantee Ltd v British Wagon Co. Ltd* [1934] 2 KB 305; *Olds Discount Co. Ltd v Krett* [1940] 2 KB 117; *Eastern Distributions Ltd v Goldring* [1957] 2 QB 600. The issue did not have to be decided in *Union Transport Finance Ltd v Ballardie* [1937] 1 KB 510, where the dealer retained possession of the car but never attorned to the finance company so as to assume the character of bailee.

Thus in *Staffs Motor Guarantee Ltd v British Wagon Co. Ltd*,[458] where a motor vehicle dealer raised finance on the security of a lorry by selling it to a finance company and hiring it back on hire purchase terms, the lorry remaining at all times in the dealer's possession. The lorry was later sold fraudulently by the dealer to a *bona fide* purchaser and the court held that the dealer's possession of the lorry was referable to his status as hire purchase bailee rather than as seller. Consequently, the dealer was unable to pass title to the purchaser. Similarly, in *Ahrens Ltd v George Cohen, Sons & Co. Ltd*,[459] manufacturing sellers produced a number of masters for sound recordings, at the behest of a buyer, and further undertook from time to time to press sound recordings from these masters. The property in the masters passed under the contract to the buyer. Subsequently, the sellers mortgaged their property and assets in favour of a bank and the question arose whether the bank's title overrode that of the buyer under section 24. The court interpreted the mortgage as confined in its sweep to the manufacturers' own assets, but went on to state that, in view of the sellers' manufacturing responsibilities, their continuing possession was not referable to the contract of sale and section 24 therefore did not apply in any event.

Floor plan transactions.   These prior authorities were convincingly set aside by **5.130** the Privy Council in what is now the leading case on section 24, *Pacific Motor Auctions Pty Ltd v Motor Credits (Hire Finance) Ltd*.[460] In that case, a car dealer entered into a finance agreement in the form of a 'floor plan' with the respondent finance company. Under the terms of this agreement, the finance company was to acquire title to the cars in return for paying the dealer 90 per cent of the price the latter paid its supplier for the cars. Title to the cars would be reconveyed to the dealer on payment back of the 90 per cent advance, together with interest, from the proceeds of sale of the cars to the dealer's customers.[461] Until delivery of these cars to the customers in the dealer's name, the cars remained at all material times in the dealer's possession. Because of the dealer's financial troubles, the respondent withdrew its licence to deal in the cars covered by the 'floor plan'. Subsequently, the dealer sold a number of these cars to another dealer, the appellant company. As the appellant was a creditor of the dealer, the appellant's cheque was endorsed by the dealer in favour of the appellant; the appellant and dealer agreed that the cars in question should be sold back to the dealer if and when the dealer discharged its indebtedness to the appellant.

Bailee or seller?   It was the respondent's contention, *inter alia*, that the dealer **5.131** was in possession of the cars covered by the 'floor plan' as bailee rather than as

---

[458] n. 457 above.
[459] (1934) 50 TLR 411.
[460] n. 456 above.
[461] Very similar to mortgage financing.

seller in possession, but this was rejected by the Privy Council. Counsel for the appellant put this point most neatly in asserting that 'possession' should be viewed in the same manner in which the courts approach an estoppel question, that is to say, by looking at outward appearance rather than the inner fact.[462] Indeed, section 24 was regarded by the Privy Council as extending to purchasers the limited protection afforded by the doctrine of estoppel. It was the Privy Council's view that no decided case had squarely raised the question of an attornment to the buyer by the seller in possession as bailee so as to change the status of the seller to that of bailee.[463] Since the purpose of section 24 was 'to protect an innocent purchaser who is deceived by the vendor's physical possession of goods or documents and who is inevitably unaware of legal rights which fetter the apparent power to dispose',[464] it should not be restricted in the way contended for by the respondent.[465] In addition, the early confinement of the seller in possession provision to documents of title[466] suggested a straightforward interpretation of section 24 which did not look to the character of possession, since it was not easy to see how this character could change with regard to documents of title. Furthermore, the provision of the Factors Act presumptively deeming custody of goods or documents to be possession[467] told also against the respondent's contention.

5.132 **Broken possession.** Another problem dealt with in the *Pacific Motor Auctions* case concerned the continuity of the dealer's possession. Section 24 refers to instances where the seller 'continues or is in possession of the goods'. At first glance, the provision would seem to apply whenever the seller acquires possession, demanding only a unity of two things, namely the seller's identity as someone who has previously sold the goods and his possession of the goods or documents of title. This interpretation would therefore permit the application of section 24 regardless of a break in the continuity of the seller's possession; it should not matter, either, if the seller subsequently recovers possession from someone who did not buy the goods from him, such as a buyer further down the title chain or even a thief. Circumstances in which a seller might conceivably resume an interrupted possession include goods being redelivered for warehousing to a seller by a finance company repossessing them from a defaulting instalment purchaser.[468] Again, a cash or finance buyer of a car may take it for repairs or servicing into the garage

---

[462] n. 453 above, 876.

[463] *Ibid.* 885.

[464] *Ibid.* 886.

[465] See also *Worcester Works Finance Ltd v Cooden Engineering Co. Ltd* [1972] 1 QB 210; *Mercantile Credits Ltd v FC Upton & Sons Pty Ltd*, n. 455 above. The Privy Council in *Pacific Motor Auctions*, n. 453 above, 888–9, also concluded that the respondent's contention failed *in limine* since the seller retained possession of the car *qua* seller.

[466] S. 3 of the 1877 Act.

[467] S. 1(2).

[468] *Olds Discount Co. Ltd v Krett*, n. 457 above.

side of the seller's business. While it may no longer be relevant to ask in what capacity the seller receives back the goods, the question that is squarely presented is whether the above illustrations come within the mischief of section 24. It is no help in resolving this question that section 24 has exceeded the scope of estoppel principles so as to take on the characteristics of a provision that depends on the status of the person making the second sale, pledge, or other disposition.

Continuity of possession and constructive delivery. In *Mitchell v Jones*,[469] **5.133** a New Zealand court concluded that, when the seller delivered the goods to the buyer, 'the relationship of buyer and seller between them was at an end'.[470] One might respond to this that the buyer would be quick enough to call on the seller *qua* seller if he wished to assert a warranty claim and return the goods for the requisite repairs or adjustment. The Privy Council in *Pacific Motor Auctions* held, nevertheless, that *Mitchell v Jones* was correctly decided on this point. It is not clear whether a delivery for present purposes is confined to a physical delivery or extends to a constructive delivery. The court in *Michael Gerson (Leasing) Ltd v Wilkinson*[471] held that a constructive delivery and redelivery had occurred under a sale and leaseback agreement, where physical possession was never surrendered by the seller. After the constructive redelivery, the seller held the goods in the altered character of lessee. No account was taken in the case of any difficulties presented by *Mitchell v Jones* and *Pacific Motor Auctions*,[472] from which it may be inferred that physical delivery is required for the seller's possession to be broken. In *Mitchell v Jones*, the court further observed that the words 'or is in possession' in section 24 countenanced a case where the seller was not in possession of the goods at the time of the sale but subsequently acquired them.[473] This was said in *Pacific Motor Auctions* to be 'plainly right'[474] and nothing further was said on the subject. Nevertheless, it will be relatively rare for seller and first buyer to agree on the passing of property to goods not yet in the seller's possession; the above interpretation seems therefore somewhat strained. On the other hand, some of the more extreme hypotheses concerning the circumstances in which a seller resumes possession argue a need to limit a literal application of section 24. It is noteworthy that section 24 makes no explicit reference to the first buyer's consent to the seller's possession[475]

---

[469] n. 457 above.

[470] *Ibid.*, 935.

[471] [2001] QB 514.

[472] The case involved successive sale and leaseback agreements concerning the same goods. The court's focus was on the second of these agreements, to determine whether there had occurred a delivery and a redelivery by constructive means. Had the court considered the *first* of these sale and leaseback agreements, the issue presented by *Mitchell v Jones* and by *Pacific Motor Auctions* would have presented itself.

[473] See also *Worcester Works Finance*, n. 465 above; *Bradshaw v Epp* [1937] 4 DLR 746, 752–3.

[474] n. 453 above, 885.

[475] See *Worcester Works Finance*, n. 465 above.

and so, for example, would not appear to require discussion of the authorities dealing with larceny by a trick.

5.134 **Appreciation of risk.** It might well, however, be sensible to permit broken possession to lead to a disposing power under section 24 if this were linked to the idea that certain buyers appreciate more than others the risks of a seller resuming possession. This would apply more to finance companies turning over repossessed goods to a former seller than, for example, to a consumer buyer taking in his car a year later for warranty work or servicing. The one should be aware of the risk while the other might be justifiably ignorant. The claims of a *bona fide* purchaser seem to have some considerable force against the former, and rather less against the latter. In *Pacific Motor Auctions*, the court itself rejected the contention that the seller should be treated as though he were a mercantile agent, but to deny the application of section 24 where a seller resumes possession of repossessed goods is tantamount to requiring the seller to receive them *qua* mercantile agent, as is the case with section 2(1) of the Factors Act.

5.135 **Criticism.** Despite the considerable authority of the Privy Council, it is therefore submitted that, in cases of broken possession, the character of the seller *qua* seller should play a relevant part. Though the line is not easy to draw, it is submitted that a seller should continue to have disposing power when it is by virtue of the original sale relationship that he resumes possession.[476] This would be so when an original seller is obliged under the terms of a recourse or similar arrangement with a finance company to assist in the storage or sale or repossession of goods the subject of an agreement on which there has been a default. It would not be so where a buyer adventitiously takes a car for servicing to the garage from which he bought it. More difficult is the case of a consumer buyer taking a car in for warranty repairs, whether by virtue of his Sale of Goods Act rights or by virtue of an extended express warranty given by the manufacturer. This last instance might sensibly be read out of section 24, but the difficulty of doing so with the buyer whose car needs servicing illustrates the agony of the *nemo dat* rule and its exceptions in tight circumstances. If only because of the ignorance of the risk of the consumer buyer in the former instance, it is submitted that section 24 should be interpreted in his favour; careful law reform seems, however, a better alternative. A final argument in favour of extending section 24 to at least some broken possession cases is that the purpose of the provision could easily be frustrated by an almost symbolic possession taken, for example, by the first buyer, a finance company under a stocking plan of the type in *Pacific Motors*, which sends one of its representatives down from time to time to drive cars around the block.

---

[476] See the similar buyer in possession argument in *Langmead v Thyer Rubber Co. Ltd* [1947] SASR 29.

Delivery and Transfer

Goods and documents.   Another issue raised by section 24 concerns the mean-   **5.136**
ing of 'the delivery or transfer . . . of the goods or documents of title'. At first sight,
it might seem that 'delivery' and 'transfer' both equally refer to 'goods' and 'documents of title'. On this interpretation, bearer documents, for example, might be
delivered and goods might be transferred by the seller in possession under the second transaction. If this were so, a seller in possession might effectively 'transfer'
goods to a second buyer without actually delivering them. The law, however, has
read 'transfer' as exclusively referable to 'documents of title' and 'delivery' as exclusively referable to 'goods'.[477] In consequence, the second buyer must take delivery
if he is to override the title of the first buyer in a case not involving documents of
title.[478] The opposite result would not be impracticable since a second buyer who
does not take delivery would be vulnerable to a third buyer, and so on.

Transfer of documents.   The effect of section 11 of the Factors Act is that docu-   **5.137**
ments of title are transferred by delivery in the case of bearer documents and documents indorsed in blank by a named consignee, or by indorsement to a named
transferee. Where indorsement occurs, the better view is that a transfer would be
completed only when the bill of lading is also delivered to the indorsee.[479] Apart
from this detail, section 11 restates the common law. In the case of delivery of
goods, the question is whether constructive delivery is permitted. Section 1(2)
states that constructive possession is tantamount to actual possession. Although
the provision could be invoked in aid of interpreting section 8 of the Factors
Act,[480] it is of limited value since it does not refer to delivery as such. Prior to the
decision of the Court of Appeal in *Michael Gerson (Leasing) Ltd v Wilkinson*, the
view was that section 24 required the second buyer to take actual possession. In
Nicholson v Harper,[481] the second transaction was a pledge of the goods to a warehouseman who at all times had been in possession of the goods anyway. Even
assuming that he could have attorned to himself as the new bailor so as to effect a
constructive delivery, the court held that section 24 was not satisfied.[482] The same

---

[477] *Nicholson v Harper* [1895] 2 Ch. 415, 418; *Michael Gerson (Leasing) Ltd v Wilkinson* [2001]
QB 514 at [10].

[478] *Kitto v Bilbie, Hobson & Co.* (1895) 72 LT 266 (assignment alone insufficient). See also *Bank
of New South Wales v Palmer* [1970] 2 NSWLR 532; *NZ Securities & Finance Ltd v Wrightcars Ltd*
[1976] 1 NZLR 77.

[479] *Sanders v Maclean* (1883) 11 QBD 327 (Bowen LJ).

[480] And not the almost identical s. 24 of the Sale of Goods Act.

[481] n. 477 above, followed in *New Zealand Securities & Finance Ltd v Wrightcars Ltd*, n. 478
above.

[482] The case has been explained as merely holding that a delivery is required in addition to a sale
etc: *Gamer's Motor Centre (Newcastle) Pty Ltd v Natwest Wholesale Australia Pty Ltd* (1987) 163 CLR
236, 249 (Mason CJ); *Forsyth International (UK) Ltd v Silver Shipping Co. Ltd (The Saetta)* [1994]
1 WLR 1334, 1345.

result was reached in *Bank of New South Wales v Palmer*,[483] where the property in
a boat had passed to the buyer at the relevant stages in its construction before the
boat-builder mortgaged it in favour of a bank. Since physical possession had never
been transferred to the bank, the court ruled in favour of the buyer. Nor would a seizure of the goods have helped the bank's cause, since delivery is defined in the Sale of
Goods Act as 'the voluntary transfer of possession from one person to another'.[484]
A delayed voluntary transfer of the goods to the bank ought to enable it to override
the interest of the first buyer, for section 24 requires delivery to take place 'under' the
sale, pledge, or other disposition, and not necessarily at the same time.

5.138 **Constructive delivery.** The above section 24 cases, however, were undermined
by a number of decisions under section 25(1) recognizing that delivery could
occur by constructive means.[485] Since in this respect no distinction could ration-
ally be drawn between sections 24 and 25(1), the section 24 cases discussed could
not safely be treated as authoritative on the modern approach to the issue of constructive delivery. Although the *Nicholson* case is not referred to in the judgments,
and the *Bank of New South Wales* case is not referred to at all, the decision in
Michael Gerson (Leasing) Ltd v Wilkinson has put it beyond doubt that constructive delivery is delivery for the purpose of section 24. The case concerned an
owner of equipment who had entered into a sale and leaseback agreement with the
first financier and, whilst still in possession of the equipment, had entered into the
same type of arrangement with a second financier. As against the first financier,
the original owner was a seller in possession[486] and, as regards the second financier,
it had delivered the goods to it under the second sale and leaseback. The issue of
delivery to the second financier was treated as anterior to the issue of delivery back
to the original owner under the sale and leaseback.[487] It was the court's conclusion
that the character of a seller's possession could change as a result of his acknowledgment that he remained in possession of the goods for another who had
the right to possess those goods as owner.[488] There had thus been a 'delivery to the
buyer [the second financier] followed by an immediate redelivery to the seller [the
original owner] as bailee'. [489] Christopher Clarke LJ discussed at some length
the question whether the original owner had received possession of the equipment
under the second leg of the sale and leaseback transaction with the second

---

[483] n. 478 above.
[484] See also *Forsyth International (UK) Ltd v Silver Shipping Co. Ltd (The Saetta)*, n. 482 above.
[485] See discussion below.
[486] The first financier did not exercise a sufficient quality and extent of control for the original owner to have mere custody of the equipment: *Michael Gerson (Leasing) Ltd v Wilkinson*, n. 477 above, at [13]–[15].
[487] *Ibid.*, at [21].
[488] The court relied upon *Marvin v Wallace* (1856) 25 LJQB 369.
[489] *Ibid.*, at [28]. The court also declined to be constrained in its holding by the definition of possession in concrete terms in s. 1(2) of the Factors Act 1889: *ibid.*, at [33].

financier,[490] but there is no reason to suppose that this matter impinged in any direct way upon the title dispute between the first and second financiers.[491] The second financier defeated the first at the moment it received constructive delivery of the equipment pursuant to the first leg of the sale and leaseback transaction. The immediate redelivery, again constructive, to the original owner did not vitiate the second financier's superior title.

Documents of title problem.   The above conclusion, that delivery may occur by   **5.139** constructive means, is helpful in dealing with a problem concerning the transfer of documents of title. Suppose that a seller in possession of goods issues a document of title, for example a delivery warrant, to a second buyer. The goods themselves are not physically delivered; nor is a document of title transferred. Although 'transfer' has been given a loose interpretation, so as to be satisfied where a buyer in possession of a delivery order issued a fresh delivery order to the sub-buyer,[492] it could not confidently be predicted that the case mentioned above of the seller issuing a delivery warrant would be treated as a case of transfer. It would therefore be better to find that the seller accepting the status of bailee has constructively delivered the goods.

The 1995 Property Reforms

Undivided shares.   This conclusion leads in to a series of problems arising under   **5.140** the Sale of Goods Act as amended by the Sale of Goods (Amendment) Act 1995.[493] Suppose that a seller in possession of a bulk has succeeded in passing to a number of prepaying buyers an undivided share in the contract bulk in such a way as to account for the whole bulk. Subsequently, that seller wrongfully sells a portion of the bulk to a later buyer. This gives rise to a number of difficulties. First, if the seller were to issue a document of title to that later buyer so as to effect a constructive delivery, the principle of deemed consent to removals from the bulk brought in by the 1995 reforms seems not to extend to such cases of 'over-sales'.[494] The Law Commission was of the view, however, that the later buyer would acquire property rights with the assistance of section 24.[495] Yet it has to be demonstrated that a seller who has succeeded in transferring an undivided interest to earlier buyers has 'sold' goods according to section 24. The definition of 'goods' may have been extended

---

[490] *Ibid.*, at [29]–[36].

[491] Cf Pill LJ, *ibid.*, at [90].

[492] *DF Mount Ltd v Jay & Jay (Provisions) Ltd* [1960] 1 QB 159, discussed in Ch. 11 below.

[493] Discussed in Ch. 3 above. References to this Act below will be to the provisions that it introduces into the Sale of Goods Act 1979.

[494] Law Com. No. 215, para. 4.18. Although the deemed consent applies to 'any delivery' to 'any other owner in common of the bulk' (s. 20B(1)(a)), it appears to be confined to owners who acquire rights under s. 20A, a passing of property rather than a transfer of title provision.

[495] *Ibid.* See R. Bradgate and F. White [1994] *LMCLQ* 315, 321, for criticism of the Law Commission's assumption that problems of this nature can be dealt with routinely under s. 24.

to include an undivided share in goods[496] but nothing has been done to change the definition of 'sale' in the Sale of Goods Act, which requires the transfer of the general property.[497] It would be anomalous if the buyer obtaining an undivided share were less vulnerable to section 24 than a buyer of ascertained goods who has left the seller in possession. Indirect support comes from section 2(2), which provides that there can be a contract of sale between one co-owner and another, and deals in the same section with contracts of sale that become sales.[498] It is submitted therefore that the outright transfer of an undivided share should be seen as the transfer of the general property in that undivided share so as to render applicable section 24. A later buyer receiving the goods themselves rather than a document of title would be in the same position but would not have to deal with issues of constructive delivery and the transfer of documents.

5.141   **Later buyer.**   A second group of problems arises out of the rights that a later buyer, obtaining a document of title rather than the goods themselves, acquires at the expense of the earlier co-owning buyers. The Law Commission seems to take the view that the later buyer simply joins earlier buyers as a rateable owner of the bulk in the following way.[499] Assuming two earlier buyers have each acquired an entitlement to 30,000 tonnes from a 60,000 tonne bulk, before the seller unlawfully sells 30,000 tonnes in the same bulk to a later buyer, then all three buyers would each have a 20,000-tonne entitlement in the bulk. Now, this offends a principle of title transfer law, which is that losses caused by a rogue are not simply divided between owner and innocent third party.[500] Section 24, which cannot just be impressionistically combined with the 1995 Act as the Law Commission would want, grants rights to the later buyer at the expense of earlier buyers. Consequently, the later buyer should have a 30,000-tonne entitlement and the earlier buyers, whose shares will have commensurately abated, 15,000 tonnes each.[501]

5.142   **Shrinkage in the bulk.**   The next issue concerns later shrinkage in the bulk. Unless and until that later buyer's goods have been separated from the bulk, it is submitted that the later buyer's overriding interest amounts to an undivided share of the bulk and is therefore liable to be abated in the usual rateable way. But is that later buyer also vulnerable to removals from the bulk by those co-owners whose shares were earlier reduced by the unlawful sale? Could one of the earlier buyers recover from the bulk his full 30,000 tonnes before the unlawful sale later comes to light, at the expense not only of his co-owner at the time but also of the later

---

[496]   S. 61(1).
[497]   S. 2(4)–(6).
[498]   S. 2(4).
[499]   Law Com. No. 215, para. 4.18.
[500]   See discussion in the text accompanying nn. 202–3 above.
[501]   If it looks perverse to give the later buyer greater rights than the earlier ones, this is consistent with general principles of title transfer dealt with in this chapter.

buyer? If this were allowed, the effect of the section 24 transaction would be reversed as regards that earlier buyer. The rule of consent to removals from the bulk applies in respect of buyers who obtain an undivided share in the bulk 'by virtue of section 20A'.[502] On one view of the matter, the later buyer's rights arise by virtue of section 24 of the Sale of Goods Act, a title transfer provision, together with antecedent case law authority by which the non-ascertainmn of goods is no bar to the acquisition of rights by third parties under the transfer of title provisions of the Sale of Goods Act.[503] They do not arise by virtue of section 20A, a passing of property provision. A different, and it is submitted preferable, view is that, while the effect of section 24 is that the sale to the later buyer is deemed to have been authorized by the original buyers, the section is not sufficient in explaining why the later buyer becomes a co-owner of the bulk. Section 20A is needed for this purpose.[504] Although an undivided share in goods is goods for the purpose of the Sale of Goods Act,[505] the subject matter of the oversale is not an undivided share, but rather a quantity of goods.[506] This interpretation is favoured also for pragmatic reasons. If the later buyer's rights are not liable to be defeated by removals from the bulk, this would give rise to difficult accounting exercises where multiple dealings occur in a bulk, and would be at odds with the evident policy in the 1995 reforms of avoiding complex accounting exercises of this nature.

Sub-buyers. There also has to be considered the position of the sub-buyer to **5.143** whom, for example, a co-owning buyer has transferred a delivery warrant issued by the seller. This case is covered by section 20B(1)(b), which provides that the other co-owners are deemed to consent to 'any dealing with or removal or disposal of goods in the bulk' by a co-owning buyer 'in so far as the goods fall within that co-owning owner's undivided share in the bulk'. If shrinkage has already occurred in the bulk before the transfer of the warrant, then the buyer's share will have been reduced and the other co-owning buyers' consent will be limited to that reduced share. There does not appear to be a *nemo dat* exception protecting the sub-buyer from shrinkage. As regards the other co-owning buyers, the buyer is not a seller in possession under section 24 or a buyer in possession under section 25(1). But if the original seller retains a share in the undivided bulk, then the transaction entered into by the buyer could, pursuant to section 25(1), give the sub-buyer protection against shrinkage at the original seller's expense.

---

[502] S. 20B(1).

[503] *Ant Jurgens Margarine-Fabrieken v Louis Dreyfus & Co.* [1914] 3 KB 40; *Capital and Counties Bank Ltd v Warriner* (1896) 12 TLR 216. Discussed in the text accompanying nn. 568–9 below.

[504] For a different view, see *Benjamin's Sale of Goods* (7th edn, by A. G. Guest, Sweet & Maxwell, 2006), para. 5–126; Gullifer [1999] *LMCLQ* 93.

[505] S. 61(1) ('goods').

[506] A more difficult case is where the subject matter of the oversale is an undivided share, as opposed to a quantity of goods because the buyer would not need s. 20A to acquire an undivided share.

5.144 Notice and good faith. A final point concerning the 1995 reforms is that the deemed consent of co-owning buyers to removals from the bulk under section 20B(1)(a) appears not to be qualified by notice or good faith requirements. If this is correct, then an unusual exception to the rule of *nemo dat* has been created. A buyer who learns of a shrinkage in the bulk, perhaps of an unlawful sale of an undivided share to a later buyer, has a positive incentive to race to the warehouse and claim his full contractual share.[507] It is more than possible that this apparent departure from basic principle will be trimmed down by restrictive interpretation. It is more than possible, too, that the 1995 reforms will give rise to real problems in the years ahead. It was passed with the laudable intention of solving a problem that was a real impediment to international trade in commodities, but an *ad hoc* reform of this nature, bolted on to the Sale of Goods Act, is no substitute for a root-and-branch review of the whole law of passing of property and title transfer.

Dispositions

5.145 Meaning. The transaction entered into by the seller in possession must be a 'sale, pledge or other disposition' if it is to override the first buyer's title to the goods. 'Sale' has the meaning ordinarily given to it in the Sale of Goods Act and cannot therefore extend to an agreement to sell,[508] such as a conditional sale where instalments remain outstanding. *A fortiori*, a hire purchase agreement is not caught by 'sale', since the bailee never undertakes that he will exercise the option to purchase.[509] When the hire purchase and the conditional sale agreements are fully executed so that a sale is consummated,[510] it still could not be said that the delivery of the goods took place 'under a sale' since in fact it occurred with a view to a future agreed or potential sale. But it is a different question whether transactions like these are covered by 'disposition'.

5.146 Pledge. 'Pledge' in s. 25(1) has the meaning ordinarily given to it in personal property law.[511] Delivery under an agreement to pledge would therefore not qualify, though, like an executory sale, it is appropriate to consider whether it is a 'disposition'. One problem concerning the meaning of 'disposition' is whether it catches an outright gift. On the face of it section 24 does not require the disponee to have furnished any consideration but, given the almost grudging nature of the legislative response to the rigours imposed by the *nemo dat* rule, it would be curiously generous to gratuitous disponees to allow them to take the goods clear of the first buyer's title. In the Factors Act, as was observed above, section 5 requires the

---

[507] Cf *Barber v Meyerstein* (1870) LR 4 HL 317.
[508] S. 2(4), (5).
[509] *Lee v Butler* [1893] 2 QB 318; *Helby v Matthews* [1895] AC 471; *Belsize Motor Supply Co. v Cox* [1914] 1 KB 244.
[510] S. 2(6).
[511] Bridge, n. 11 above, 175–8.

presence of consideration for the 'validity of a sale, pledge, or other disposition'. This clearly bears upon section 2(1) of the Factors Act since that provision and section 5 are contained in a part of the Act headed 'Dispositions by Mercantile Agents'. It has been stated that this part of the Act should be read independently of those sections in the United Kingdom Act headed 'Dispositions by Buyers and Sellers of Goods'.[512] This view is more troublesome in the case of section 24, since section 25, as we shall see, has been interpreted as requiring the incorporation by reference of the provisions relating to mercantile agents. It is submitted that, regardless of whether section 5 of the Factors Act may be relied upon to assist in the interpretation of section 24 of the Sale of Goods Act,[513] an *eiusdem generis* reading of 'sale, pledge or other disposition' should require consideration to be present for a disposition, as it clearly has to be in the case of sale and pledge because of their very nature.[514]

Disposition. The meaning of 'disposition' was considered at some length in **5.147** *Worcester Works Finance Ltd v Cooden Engineering Co. Ltd.*[515] The respondents owned a car which they sold to Griffiths, who paid for it with a cheque that was dishonoured on each of the three occasions the respondents presented it to the bank. Meanwhile, Griffiths used the car to set up a sham hire purchase transaction with the innocent appellants and a bailee, his confederate Millerick, who signed a delivery receipt but never took delivery of the car from Griffiths. The sham transaction involved a purported sale of the goods to the appellants. Later, the respondents repossessed the car, which was still in Griffiths' possession, apparently with his consent.[516] Griffiths kept up in Millerick's name the payment of the instalments to the appellants, and then stopped payments, leaving the appellants and respondents to dispute title to the car. The Court of Appeal held that there had been a 'disposition' by Griffiths, the seller in possession *qua* the appellants, back to the respondents, the original sellers. Lord Denning thought that 'disposition' was 'a very wide word' capable of extending 'to all acts by which a new interest (legal or equitable) in the property is effectually created'.[517] This is plainly too wide, for it would allow a subsequent equitable interest to override a prior legal interest,[518] hardly the result that any court should strive for when legislation does

---

[512] *Inglis v Robertson* [1898] AC 616, 629–30 (Lord Herschell).

[513] See *Worcester Works Finance Ltd v Cooden Engineering Co. Ltd* [1972] 1 QB 210, 220 (Megaw LJ: the provisions of factors and sale of goods legislation to be read 'for many purposes . . . as one code').

[514] *Contra* A. D. Preston (1972) 88 LQR 239, 243, relying upon *Kitto v Bilbie, Hobson & Co.* (1895) 72 LT 266.

[515] n. 513 above.

[516] *Ibid.* 219.

[517] *Ibid.* 218, quoting *Carter v Carter* [1896] 1 Ch. 62, 67.

[518] Preston, n. 514 above, 244. But see *P4 Ltd v Unite Integrated Solutions Plc* [2006] EWHC 2640 (TCC) at [115], approving the approach adopted in *Worcester Works*.

not compel it. Megaw LJ asserted that a disposition had occurred in the present case, for what was required was 'some transfer of an interest in property, in the technical sense of the word "property" as contrasted with mere possession'.[519] Similarly, Phillimore LJ said that 'there must be some disposal of the goods which involved transfer of property'.[520]

5.148 Repossession and unilateral avoidance. The fortunate respondents in *Worcester Works* had the unwitting presence of mind to avoid two possible courses of action, either of which might have proved fatal to their claim under section 24. They might simply have repossessed without the knowledge, leave, or cooperation of Griffiths; there could not then have been a 'disposition' by Griffiths in the absence of some conscious act on his part.[521] The respondents might also have purported unilaterally to avoid the contract of sale, because of the fraud of Griffiths, after the resale by Griffiths to the appellants.[522] This would have been ineffective under section 23 of the Sale of Goods Act, because his voidable title would already have been transmitted to the appellants. But it might have undermined any later disposition by Griffiths under section 24, because the purported avoidance would have destroyed whatever residual title to the goods Griffiths might have had. How could Griffiths have transferred any property in the goods, to someone claiming their ownership, over and above possession of them in that event? Whatever puzzling difficulties might be posed in relation to the meaning of disposition in section 24, it is submitted that the word should catch delivery under an executory conditional sale or hire purchase agreement,[523] which compels or permits the eventual purchase of the goods. The buyer or bailee, having paid a deposit, acquires an interest in the goods transcending mere possession that is hard to rationalize in terms of legal and equitable interests but is recognized in various important

---

[519] n. 514 above, 220 (Megaw LJ). In a buyer-in-possession case, however, it was held that delivery to an auctioneer for the purpose of sale was a 'disposition': *Shenstone & Co. v Hilton* [1894] 2 QB 52. This is plainly wrong and inconsistent with authorities decided under s. 2 of the Factors Act: *Waddington and Sons v Neale and Sons* (1907) 96 LT 786; *Roache v Australian Mercantile Land & Finance Co. Ltd* (1996) 67 SR(NSW) 54, 59 (something in the nature of a sale). See also the buyer in possession case of *Smith v Campbell* (1911) 17 WLR 49 (Can.) (not delivery for storage to warehouse).

[520] n. 514 above, 219.

[521] Or even a 'delivery': see s. 61(1) and *Forsyth International (UK) Ltd v Silver Shipping Co. Ltd (The Saetta)*, n. 482 above.

[522] At first blush, an avoidance of the contract of sale before the resale by Griffiths to the appellants would have been equally ineffective, for Griffiths would still have had the disposing power of a buyer in possession under s. 25(1) so long as he remained in actual possession. But Griffiths never in fact delivered the car to the appellants, and therefore a recovery of the goods by the respondents before such a delivery would have been effective. Had the appellants beaten the respondents to the goods in Griffiths's hands, and had obtained delivery from him, their title would then have been perfected under s. 25(1).

[523] See *Union Transport Finance Ltd v Ballardie* [1937] 1 KB 510.

ways.[524] The argument in favour of the second purchaser is even more clearly made, at least for conditional sales, by the extended language in section 8 of the Factors Act, which protects such a purchaser taking 'under *any agreement* for sale, pledge, or other disposition (emphasis added)'.

Effect of Section 24

Interpretation difficulties. Once the seller delivers goods under a sale, pledge, or other disposition, this transaction 'has the same effect as if the person making the delivery or transfer were expressly authorised by the owner of the goods to make the same'. In the case of delivery of goods, the argument has been advanced that section 24 amounts to rather less than an overriding of the first buyer's title for all that it does is to sanction the delivery by the seller in possession, and would therefore only protect the second buyer against a conversion action based on the receipt of (rather than the later refusal to deliver up) the goods.[525] Support for this view is said to lie in 3 of the Factors Act 1877, the forerunner of sections 8 of the Factors Act 1889 and 24 of the Sale of Goods Act. Section 3 only applied to transactions involving delivery of the goods or transfer of documents where the seller had been left in possession of the documents of title.[526] Moreover, it provided that such delivery or transfer 'shall be as valid and effectual as if such a vendor or person were an agent or person entrusted with the goods or documents', a formula similar to the one that is present in section 25 (the buyer in possession exception) but not in section 24 of the Sale of Goods Act. Thus the argument is pressed that this evidences a legislative will to give inferior protection to persons taking delivery of goods from sellers left in possession of just the goods.[527]

5.149

Effect of cases. The cases decided under section 24 are squarely against this view,[528] which, moreover, understates the difficulty of attaining precision in the drafting of legislation in this area. It is hard to see, too, why the legislature should ever have seen fit to confer such minimal protection on buyers from sellers in possession of goods. Moreover, the same heterodoxical argument could be made in the case of transfer of documents of title, since their transfer will not necessarily pass the general property in the underlying goods. It depends on the intention of the transferor,[529] and a conservative reading of section 24 would not be satisfied with the provision's failure to state the deemed intention of the owner. In consequence, the argument makes internal linguistic sense but does not speak at all to

5.150

---

[524] Ch. 11 below.
[525] L. A. Rutherford and I. A. Todd [1979] *CLJ* 346.
[526] Note, not possession of the goods alone.
[527] n. 525 above.
[528] See, e.g., *Pacific Motor Auctions Pty Ltd v Motor Credit (Hire Finance) Ltd* [1965] AC 867.
[529] *Sewell v Burdick* (1884) 10 App. Cas. 74.

the evolution of the *nemo dat* exceptions and does not come to terms with commercial reality.

5.151 **'Owner'.**   The reference to the 'owner' in section 24 could be useful in solving one acute difficulty. Suppose a seller continues in possession of goods and, prior to his transfer to the second buyer, the first buyer assigns his interest in the contract goods to a sub-buyer. Does the title of the second buyer under section 24 override that of the sub-buyer? Another possibility is that the first buyer has granted a security over his future property in favour of a finance company, and this security attaches at the moment the property passes to the first buyer under the contract of sale. A decision in favour of the sub-buyer, it is submitted, would unduly shrink the protection given to those dealing with sellers in possession and would fail to meet the mischief of the section. The original seller continues in possession at all material times and the transfer to the second buyer is deemed by section 24 to occur with the consent, not of the first buyer, but of the 'owner'. There seems every reason to interpret this as the first buyer or the sub-buyer, as the case may be.[530] Where the sub-buyer is a finance company claiming an interest under a future property clause, there is the added reason that its interest, springing on attachment, is only an equitable one,[531] and therefore vulnerable to *bona fide* purchasers of the legal estate, who will not therefore need to invoke section 24.

Good Faith and Notice

5.152 **Meaning.**   Section 24 requires that the second buyer act in good faith and without notice, which has the same meaning here[532] as under section 2(1) of the Factors Act. There is, however, no requirement that the seller in possession act in the ordinary course of business; the behaviour of the seller in *Pacific Motor Auctions*[533] in indorsing back the second buyer's cheque is a graphic illustration of this.

The Buyer in Possession

5.153 **Introduction.**   Like the seller in possession section, the buyer in possession provision originated in the Factors Act 1877. The same difficulties arise with respect to parallel provisions in factors and sale-of-goods legislation and to the influence of the former legislation in interpreting the latter, though they are diminished significantly by the explicit incorporation of the mercantile agency standard in section 25(1). Case law decided before 1877 established that a buyer in possession

---

[530] A similar problem under s. 25(1) is discussed in the text accompanying nn. 560 *et seq.* below.

[531] *Holroyd v Marshall* (1862) 10 HLC 191; *Tailby v Official Receiver* (1888) 13 App. Cas. 523.

[532] *Worcester Works Finance Ltd*, n. 513 above.

[533] n. 528 above.

could not without more ado be treated as a mercantile agent.[534] The present provision is section 25(1) of the Sale of Goods Act:

> Where a person having bought or agreed to buy goods obtains, with the consent of the seller, possession of the goods or documents of title to the goods, the delivery or transfer by that person, or by a mercantile agent acting for him, of the goods or documents of title, under a sale, pledge, or other disposition thereof, to any person receiving the same in good faith and without notice of any lien or other right of the original seller in respect of the goods, has the same effect as if the person making the delivery or transfer were a mercantile agent in possession of the goods or documents of title with the consent of the owner.

A number of themes, such as the meaning of 'transfer' and 'disposition', are common to section 25(1) and will not be repeated. Notice and good faith have been considered in connection with section 2(1) of the Factors Act. A preliminary question is whether section 25[535] extends beyond sale of goods to catch work and materials contracts. Unlike other provisions of the Sale of Goods Act that operate as rules of presumed intention, section 25(1), in common with other statutory exceptions to the *nemo dat* rule, does not codify contractual practice or pre-Act case law. There is authority which seems to exclude it from work and materials contracts,[536] although a plausible argument could be made that the materials under such a transaction are bought or agreed to be bought. Certainly, the mischief of section 25(1) could accommodate its extension to such transactions.[537] If the objection were taken that sections 24–25(1) of the Sale of Goods Act may only apply to sale of goods contracts as therein defined, the same cannot be said of their near-identical counterparts, sections 8 to 9 of the Factors Act.

'Bought or Agreed to Buy'

Interpretation of 'bought'.   The first difficulty in section 25(1) concerns the **5.154** meaning of 'bought or agreed to buy' goods. If the buyer has bought the goods so that the general property has vested in him, it is not clear why he should need to be empowered by section 25(1) to transmit title to a second buyer; he should be able to do that on normal title principles. Inserting a reference to 'bought' also raises the troublesome possibility that a second purchaser, apprised of a seller's complaint against the first buyer and therefore affected by notice of it, may be defeated in a title action brought by the seller, even though title would have otherwise passed

---

[534] *Jenkyns v Usborne* (1844) 7 M & G 678; *M'Ewan v Smith* (1849) 2 HLC 309; *Cole v North Western Bank* (1875) LR 10 CP 354.

[535] And s. 24, too, although the problem is more likely to arise under s. 25(1).

[536] *Dawber Williamson Roofing Ltd v Humberside County Council* (1979) 14 Build. LR 70, 77. Cf *Close Asset Finance Ltd v Care Graphics Machinery Ltd* [2000] CCLR 43.

[537] The contracts in the building cases of *Archivent Sales & Developments Ltd v Strathclyde Regional Council* (1984) 27 Build. LR 98 and *W Hanson (Harrow) Ltd v Rapid Civil Engineering Ltd* (1987) 38 Build. LR 106 were sale of goods contracts.

down the chain according to normal principles. Nevertheless, some limited sense can be made of this provision. If there were any lingering belief that a seller terminating a contract for non-payment by the buyer in possession could revest the property in himself,[538] section 25(1) would come to the assistance of those dealing with the buyer in possession. Furthermore, section 25(1) might need to be understood in terms of the unpaid seller's lien.[539] Although at common law a possessory lien endures only as long as the lienholder retains possession, there is authority for the view that a temporary release of the goods on the agreed terms that the lien shall persist does not destroy a lien.[540] If this were so, it would serve to justify the ability of the buyer in possession to transmit a clear title to a second purchaser taking 'without notice of any lien' attaching to the goods in which the buyer has the general property.[541] Another instance in which the word 'bought' can be said to have a meaning concerns contracts of sale, under which the property has passed to the buyer, that are avoided for the buyer's fraud or misrepresentation. Section 23 of the Sale of Goods Act does not permit the transfer of a voidable title after the seller has publicized an intention to avoid the contract. In contrast, as will be seen below, the power of a buyer to transmit a voidable title under section 25(1) survives even a publicized avoidance of the contract by the seller.

5.155 **Interpretation of 'agreed to buy'.** The words 'agreed to buy' in section 25(1) catch the case of a conditional sale.[542] Section 25(1) also applies where the passing of property through a proffered bill of exchange is under section 19(3) conditional upon the buyer's acceptance of the bill.[543] Receipt on sale or return on approval terms is excluded, since the recipient has not agreed to buy and holds the goods as a bailee to whom an offer of sale has been addressed.[544] Hire purchase is also excluded since the bailee does not agree to buy and may not exercise a unilateral option to purchase.[545] The fact that the option to purchase may be exercised for a

---

[538] He cannot: *RV Ward Ltd v Bignall* [1967] 1 QB 534.

[539] J. C. Smith (1963) 7 *JSPTL* 225.

[540] *Albemarle Supply Co. Ltd v Hind* [1928] 1 KB 307. See also the trust receipt authorities (pledge surviving release of bill of lading).

[541] Conversely, the buyer to whom the property has passed in goods that are subject to a seller's lien, and who unlawfully removes them from the seller's possession, so that the lien remains intact (see Ch. 11 below), will not be able to transfer title clear of this lien: the seller will not have consented to the buyer's possession.

[542] *Lee v Butler* [1893] 2 QB 318; *General Motors Acceptance Corpn v Hubbard* (1978) 87 DLR (3d) 39. Cf *Kozak v Ford Motor Credit Co.* (1971) 18 DLR (3d) 735. Note that s. 25(2) excludes consumer conditional sales (as defined in s. 25(2)(b) and s. 8 of the Consumer Credit Act 1974) from the scope of s. 25(1).

[543] *Cahn v Pockett's Bristol Channel Steam Packet Co. Ltd* [1899] 1 QB 643; see also *Marten v Whale* [1917] 2 KB 480.

[544] *Percy Edwards Ltd v Vaughan* (1910) 26 TLR 545.

[545] *Helby v Matthews* [1895] AC 471.

nominal sum does not vitiate the character of the agreement as hire purchase.[546]
The distinction between a conditional sale contract and a hire purchase contract
was at issue in *Forthright Finance Ltd v Carlyle Finance Ltd*.[547] The interesting feature of the relevant agreement in that case, placing it between orthodox drafts of
hire purchase and conditional sale contracts, was that it required the 'hirer' of the
goods to pay all of the instalments making up the price of the car. The hirer thereupon would be deemed to have exercised a hire purchaser's option so as to acquire
title to the car 'unless the hirer has told the owner before that time that such is not
the case'. Since the 'hirer' had to pay all of the instalments, the agreement was held
to be in both substance and form a conditional sale agreement. The seller's attempt
to protect itself from acquisitions by subsequent trade or finance purchasers was
dismissed as 'specious'. An agreement to buy can therefore exist under section
25(1) even if the buyer has an option to put the goods back on the seller. In principle, this should be so whether the buyer with such an option is or is not paid for
the goods upon resale to the original seller.

Consent of the Seller

Type of consent.   The buyer in possession must receive the goods or documents   **5.156**
of title with the 'consent' of the seller. Larceny by a trick and its effect on consent
arise in the same way as they do for mercantile agents and section 2(1) of the
Factors Act, and the section 25(1) authorities go the same way.[548] In principle, the
authorities on section 25(1) can, and should, take the same broad line as those
under section 24 dealing with the question whether the buyer should be in possession of the goods *qua* buyer. In the nature of things, this issue is likely to arise
less often in section 25(1), but it did arise in *Langmead v Thyer Rubber Co. Ltd*.[549]
In that case, the parties, after bargaining about the price of a car with or without a
new coat of paint applied by the seller, agreed that the buyer should be allowed to
take the car away to have it painted. The seller had refused to accept the buyer's
cheque in payment and it seems that the parties agreed to a presently binding contract of sale defeasible in the event of the buyer being unable to pay, in which event
he was to be reimbursed by the seller for the cost of repainting the car. After the
buyer had taken the car away, he sold it to a dealer, who purchased it in good faith.
The South Australian court held that the dealer was protected by section 25(1) on

---

[546] *Ibid.* For a bold but unsuccessful attempt to overturn over a century of established law on
the meaning of hire purchase, see *Close Asset Finance Ltd v Care Graphics Machinery Ltd* [2000]
CCLR 43.
[547] [1997] 4 All ER 90.
[548] *Du Jardin v Beadman Bros* [1952] 2 QB 712; *Reed v Motors Ltd* [1926] SASR 128. It should
not matter that the contract is illegal (but see *Belvoir Finance Co. Ltd v Harold G Cole & Co. Ltd*
[1969] 1 WLR 1877). It is also immaterial that the contract is unenforceable for want of compliance
with the Consumer Credit Act 1974: *R v Modupe, The Times*, 27 Feb. 1991.
[549] [1947] SASR 29.

the ground that there had been some degree of causal connection between the buyer's possession and the contract of sale.[550] Thus, one of the judges doubted that section 25(1) would apply to possession given for a 'special and temporary purpose which cannot be related to the contractual intention'.[551] This is similar to the argument made above that section 24 should be applied to certain instances of broken possession by the seller.

Mercantile Agency and Buyer in Possession

5.157   **Acting as mercantile agent.**   Undoubtedly the most difficult issue arising out of section 25(1) concerns the comparison of the sale, pledge, or other disposition to that which would have been made by a mercantile agent in the same situation. The question is whether the buyer has to act in the way that a mercantile agent would have acted, so as to be empowered to transmit a good title to the second buyer, or whether it is sufficient that the buyer should act as a buyer in possession might act, in which case the law gives the same effect to the transaction of the buyer in possession as it gives to a transaction duly accomplished by a mercantile agent in possession.[552] The former view was taken by the Court of Appeal in *Newtons of Wembley Ltd v Williams*,[553] where a dealer sold a car to a rogue, who paid for it with a cheque that was later dishonoured. Property was not to pass until the cheque had been cleared, but the dealer allowed the rogue to take the car away. The rogue sold the car in a London street market to a second buyer, who in turn sold it to a third buyer, the present defendant. Before the rogue sold the car to the second buyer, the dealer had taken steps to avoid the contract,[554] so that the rogue was no longer empowered to pass his voidable title under section 23 of the Sale of Goods Act.

5.158   **Meaning of ordinary course.**   According to the court, the transaction between the rogue and the second buyer had to take place in the ordinary course of business of a mercantile agent if the second buyer, and through him the third buyer, were to be protected by section 25(1). The position was admittedly obscure, but in the opinion of the court no other solution was possible. Sellers LJ emphasized the need to avoid giving an expansive reading to section 25(1) since it abrogated in

---

[550]   *Ibid.*, 33–4, 41.

[551]   *Ibid.* (Napier CJ, citing the case of the seller who allows the buyer to borrow his car in order to fetch a mechanic to the buyer's car, which has just broken down).

[552]   See *Gamer's Motor Centre Pty Ltd v Natwest Wholesale Australia Pty Ltd* (1987) 163 CLR 236, 259; *Langmead v Thyer Rubber Co. Ltd*, n. 476 above, 39, where Reed J describes s. 25(1) as an 'as if provision' and so selects the second alternative. This view was also favoured in *Forsyth International (UK) Ltd v Silver Shipping Co. Ltd (The Saetta)*, n. 482 above, 1351, but the court was bound by the contrary decision in the *Newton's of Wembley* case, discussed in the text accompanying nn. 553 *et seq.* below.

[553]   [1965] 1 QB 560; see also *Kozak v Ford Motor Credit Co.*, n. 542 above.

[554]   *Car and Universal Finance Co. Ltd v Caldwell* [1965] 1 QB 525.

part the *nemo dat* rule which protects ownership.[555] Yet, it should not be forgotten that, as a result of the interpretation of section 2(1) of the Factors Act, the test of the ordinary course of business of a mercantile agent is not at all demanding; it merely requires a general observance of business forms.[556] In consequence, the sale in the London street market was to be regarded as made in the ordinary course of business of a mercantile agent, since, though private sellers went there, it was also a place resorted to by dealers. It is only this laxity of practice that makes the court's invocation of section 2(1) either sensible in determining the scope of section 25(1) or plausible in terms of statutory construction. Had the sale by the buyer in possession taken place away from trade premises, and the sale by the second to the third buyer occurred on trade premises, the result would have been quite different, for the demands of section 25(1) are not met by behaviour *qua* a mercantile agent occurring further down the chain.

Protecting the innocent purchaser. But it would be a mistake to take the deci- **5.159** sion in *Newtons of Wembley* completely at face value, for by invoking the mercantile agent test the court saved the day for the second and third buyers. An avoidance of the contract under section 23 of the Sale of Goods Act would have required that same behaviour by the dealer to have been treated as a determination of its consent to the buyer retaining possession of the car. Bringing in the mercantile agent, however, served also to introduce section 2(2) of the Factors Act,[557] by which the dealer's initial consent was deemed to continue until the first of alternative events occurred, namely the repossession of the goods by the dealer or the receipt of notice by the second buyer of the revocation of consent. Neither of these events had occurred in *Newtons of Wembley* by the relevant date.[558] Far from being unfavourable to second buyers, *Newtons of Wembley* in fact gives their interests a boost at the expense of owners.

'Seller' and 'Owner' the Same Person

Interpretation difficulty. A rather odd problem of interpretation that has **5.160** emerged under section 25(1)[559] has been the subject of decision first in Canadian and New Zealand courts[560] and more recently in the House of Lords.[561] Section 25(1), having referred to the buyer obtaining possession with the consent of the

---

[555] n. 553 above, 574.

[556] *Oppenheimer v Attenborough & Son* [1908] 1 KB 221.

[557] Reversing *Fuentes v Montis* (1868) LR 3 CP 831.

[558] A Canadian court refused to follow *Newtons of Wembley* where there had been no publicized avoidance of the contract by the seller: *General Motors Acceptance Corpn Ltd v Hubbard*, n. 542 above.

[559] It could also arise under s. 24.

[560] *Brandon v Leckie* (1972) 29 DLR (3d) 633; *Elwyn v O'Regan* [1971] NZLR 1124; A. Zysblatt (1974) 9 *UBC LR* 186.

[561] *National Employers Mutual General Insurance Association Ltd v Jones* [1990] 1 AC 24.

'seller', then makes the transaction entered into by the buyer turn upon the conduct of a hypothetical mercantile agent in possession with the consent of the 'owner'. Suppose that A, an owner, entrusts goods to B, not a mercantile agent, in circumstances that do not meet the requirements of apparent authority or ownership. B unlawfully sells the goods to C, who in turn resells them to D. Under ordinary *nemo dat* principles, C would be defeated in a title dispute with A. But an argument has been made that C is in possession with the consent of his seller, B, and that C's transaction with D is supported by the deemed consent of the owner, A, to C's possession of the goods. The argument in effect requires a separation of the persons of seller and owner in section 25(1) and, while linguistically ingenious, is quite at odds with *nemo dat* principles and with the way the law has developed in this area. The only *nemo dat* exception that is not concerned with the history of the first flawed transaction in a title chain was the now-repealed market overt rule, and the decisions rejecting the above argument are perfectly sound. Any other result would leave the *nemo dat* rule in shreds and reduce the owner's protection to a conversion action against the rogue and the first innocent purchaser in the chain.

5.161 **Authority.** In *National Employers Mutual General Insurance Association Ltd v Jones*,[562] there was a lengthy title chain reducible to the above A–B–C–D model, with a thief occupying the position of B. The owner succeeded by a majority in the Court of Appeal.[563] In the House of Lords, Lord Goff delivered the judgment of the court in favour of the owner, and demonstrated, through a review of the emergence of the exceptions to the *nemo dat* rule, especially the factors legislation, that the language of section 25(1) could not be given a literal meaning. The seller and buyer in possession exceptions were added to that of the mercantile agent because sellers and buyers in possession could not be treated as mercantile agents,[564] and were not meant to usher in a change in policy of a fundamental kind.[565] One might add that Part III of the Hire Purchase Act 1964[566] would make little sense at all if the argument of the second buyer in *Jones* had been upheld.

---

[562] n. 561 above.

[563] [1987] 3 All ER 385. Croom Johnson LJ, 399, asserted that s. 25(1) presupposed 'a valid transaction by or on behalf of the true owner at some stage'. May LJ, 396, was of the view that the general property should pass or purportedly pass from B to C which, since B was a thief, it could not. With respect, a thief surrendering the totality of his rights to a buyer is just as much transferring the general property as a true owner selling his goods. The title that the thief transfers, however, is a weak one, but that is a different matter.

[564] See the need for a mercantile agent to be in possession *qua* mercantile agent, discussed in the text accompanying nn. 335 *et seq.* above.

[565] n. 561 above, 58–60, 62.

[566] Discussed in the text accompanying nn. 598 *et seq.* below.

Lien and Stoppage in Transit

Dual provisions. Besides parallel buyer and seller in possession provisions in   **5.162**
sale of goods and factors legislation, the same duplication occurs with provisons
concerning the loss of the seller's lien and his right of stoppage *in transitu*.[567] This
provision allows the above rights to be defeated once the buyer in possession of a
document of title lawfully transfers it to a holder providing consideration. It
therefore covers some common ground with section 25(1) of the Sale of Goods
Act. The difficulties generated by these provisions will be dealt with in the next
chapter, but two points may usefully be dealt with here. First, in relation to a document of title, whether it takes the form of a warrant issued by a warehouseman,
or an order addressed by a seller to a warehouseman, there is a problem of compat-
ibility between sections 25(1) and 47(2) of the Sale of Goods Act, on the one
hand, and section 16 of the same Act, on the other. The question is whether the
seller's rights may be defeated by a transfer of a document of title even though the
goods that are subject to the document have not been separated from bulk and
have not therefore been ascertained so as to permit the property to pass. Existing
authority holds that the seller's rights can be defeated,[568] but is hard to justify on
anything other than estoppel grounds. With the passing of the Sale of Goods
(Amendment) Act 1995, further support for these decisions comes from the seller
having an undivided interest by way of tenancy in common in a defined bulk of
goods.[569] A sale of an undivided share in goods is now a sale of goods for the purposes of the Sale of Goods Act,[570] including sections 24 and 25(1).[571]

'Transfer'. The second point, which may be taken solely as a section 25(1)   **5.163**
point, concerns whether a buyer in possession of a bill of lading can be said to
'transfer' a delivery order that he issues under it in order to deal with a parcel of the
underlying cargo, when he delivers the order to the sub-buyer. It would be unduly
technical to deny protection to the second buyer on these facts. Indeed, section
47, depriving the seller of his lien where a document has been 'transferred' to a
buyer in possession, has been applied to a seller issuing a delivery order to that
buyer.[572] Similarly, a transfer has been held to occur when the seller issues a delivery order to a bailee who, on receipt of it, gives a delivery warrant to the buyer who
then transfers that warrant to the sub-buyer.[573]

---

[567] S. 47 of the Sale of Goods Act and s. 10 of the Factors Act.
[568] *Ant Jurgens Margarine-Fabrieken v Louis Dreyfus & Co.* [1914] 3 KB 40; *Capital and Counties Bank Ltd v Warriner* (1896) 12 TLR 216. But see A. Nicol (1979) 42 *MLR* 129.
[569] See Ch. 3 above.
[570] S. 2(c) of the 1995 Act amending the definition of 'goods' in s. 61(1) of the Sale of Goods Act 1979.
[571] *Quaere* for the purposes of the Factors Act 1889?
[572] *Ant Jurgens Margarine-Fabrieken v Louis Dreyfus* & *Co.* n. 568 above.
[573] *Capital and Counties Bank Ltd v Warriner*, n. 568 above.

Delivery by Buyer in Possession

5.164 **Constructive delivery.**   The transaction entered into by the buyer in possession must involve either a transfer of documents of title or a delivery of goods. In recent years, it has become clear that such delivery can occur by constructive means.[574] In *Four Point Garage Ltd v Carter*,[575] the sellers, pursuant to directions given by the buyer, delivered a car directly to the sub-buyer in the mistaken belief that the sub-buyer was merely leasing it from the buyer. The sub-buyer paid the buyer and the buyer defaulted on payment to the sellers. It was the sellers' contention that section 25(1) did not apply since the buyer had not delivered the goods, but the court had little difficulty in seeing that the arrangement merely abbreviated delivery to the buyer and redelivery to the sub-buyer. When the sellers responded to the buyer's directions, there occurred a constructive delivery to the buyer coupled with a redelivery by the sellers, acting as the buyer's agent, to the sub-buyer.[576] The result is firmly within the mischief of section 25(1). If a sub-buyer is likely to be misled by the appearance of agency or ownership in a buyer given possession, the likelihood is all the greater if the seller actively assists the buyer in performing the latter's obligations under the sub-sale contract.

5.165 **Floor plan.**   Constructive delivery was also recognized as effective in transferring title in *Gamer's Motor Centre (Newcastle) Pty Ltd v Natwest Wholesale Australia Pty Ltd,*[577] which concerned a 'floor plan' for the financing of a dealer's inventory of second-hand cars similar to the plan in *Pacific Motor Auctions*.[578] Cars in the dealer's inventory were sold to the respondent finance company and bailed back to the dealer without ever leaving the dealer's possession. At issue was the question whether the dealer had delivered the cars to the finance company for the purpose of section 25(1), for the dealer did not have an unfettered title to the vehicles in question but had acquired them from the appellant seller under an agreement to sell. In the New South Wales Court of Appeal,[579] the dissenting judge maintained the actual delivery was required if the bank was to override the interest of the respondent seller under section 25.[580] The seller-in-possession authorities took this view of identical language in section 24 and the word 'receiving', present in

---

[574] Symbolic means should also be effective: *Forsyth International (UK) Ltd v Silver Shipping Ltd (The Saetta)*, n. 482 above, 1346 (citing a passage on the meaning of delivery in M. Chalmers, *The Sale of Goods Act, 1893, Including the Factors Acts, 1889 & 1890* (5th edn, Butterworths, London, 1902)).

[575] [1985] 3 All ER 12; see also *Archivent Sales & Development Ltd v Strathclyde Regional Council*, 1985 SLT 154.

[576] See also *E & S Ruben Ltd v Faire Bros & Co. Ltd* [1949] 1 KB 254; *Hardy Wine Co. Ltd v Tasman Liquor Traders Pty Ltd* [2006] SASC 168.

[577] (1987) 163 CLR 236.

[578] [1965] AC 867.

[579] [1985] NSWLR 475.

[580] *Ibid.*, 479–82 (Kirby P).

both subsections, pointed to actual and not constructive delivery.[581] Moreover, the policy of the subsection was to draw title inferences from an actual change in possession manifest to the world at large. The majority, however, was more concerned to point to the way that delivery in sales law was generally taken to connote both actual and constructive delivery,[582] an approach subsequently adopted by the majority of a divided High Court. They noted that 'received' in section 25 could be usefully contrasted with 'actually received' in section 5 of the Sale of Goods Act, the Statute of Frauds provision. Furthermore, they could not see why the *bona fide* purchaser should have to obtain possession of the goods that was demonstrable to the world at large. As McHugh JA put it: 'The problem arises because the original buyer is in possession not because of what the sub-buyer does.'[583] In other words, any failure of the second buyer under section 25 to take actual delivery can only prejudicially affect subsequent, and not prior, buyers, and a second buyer who does not insist on actual delivery takes a risk as regards third buyers, and so on.

Constructive delivery and undivided shares.   An extended form of constructive   **5.166**
delivery has been created by the Sale of Goods (Amendment) Act 1995. The definition of 'delivery' in section 61(1) of the Sale of Goods Act 1979 has been amended to include contractual appropriations of goods that serve to pass the property in the goods to the buyer under section 20A or section 20B.[584] This means that a buyer in possession of goods or of documents of title to goods has the power to give a good title in an undivided share of bulk goods to a pre-paying sub-buyer, even without the removal of the goods, or the transfer of a document of title, or the attornment of the bailee to the sub-buyer. It is not clear why this sub-buyer should succeed under section 25(1) when any other sub-buyer would have to show a delivery or constructive delivery of the goods or a transfer of a document of title.

Voluntary.   Even a constructive delivery, however, must be a voluntary one. This   **5.167**
point underpins the decision in *Forsyth International (UK) Ltd v Silver Shipping Ltd*,[585] where a tanker had been chartered under a Shelltime 4 charterparty. In time charterparties, possession of the vessel remains at all times with the shipowners, whose servant, the master, is required to respond to the charterers' orders. Upon redelivery of the vessel, the charterers commonly leave it with the same quantity of bunkers as it had on delivery at the commencement of the charter period. In the present case, this was achieved by a sale of existing bunkers to the charterers with provision for a sale back of bunkers on board the vessel when the ship was redelivered.

---

[581] See also *Bank of New South Wales v Palmer* [1970] 2 NSWLR 532.
[582] n. 579 above, 487 *et seq.*
[583] *Ibid.*, 493.
[584] S. 2(b) of the 1995 Act.
[585] [1994] 1 WLR 1332.

The plaintiffs contracted to sell bunkers to the charterers and had them delivered to the ship. When the shipowners terminated the charterparty contract for non-payment of hire, payment had not yet been made for these bunkers. The shipowners claimed that the buyer in possession, the charterers, had delivered these bunkers to the sub-buyer, the shipowners, under the sale back in the charterparty. This claim was unsuccessful. Although the court was prepared to accept that there could be a constructive delivery under a section 25(1) transaction,[586] it held that the delivery that occurred in the present case did not satisfy the delivery test in section 61(1) of 'a voluntary transfer of possession'. The buyer did not acquiesce in the withdrawal of the ship,[587] which occurred when the shipowners unilaterally exercised their right to terminate the charterparty for breach of contract.

5.168   **Criticism.**   Now this decision presents two difficulties. First, the decision, on its own terms, would have had to go the other way if the charterparty had run its course without the commission of a discharging breach of contract by the charterer. It seems odd that the seller's rights should depend upon whether the charterparty was discharged by breach or by performance. In exercising their right to withdraw the ship and terminate the contract, the shipowners were acting in accordance with rights voluntarily agreed under the contract, even if the bunkers the actual subject of the sale back would not necessarily have been the bunkers left in the vessel had the charterparty run its full course. Secondly, the court held, quite correctly, that the shipowners, who never surrendered possession of the vessel to the charterers, were therefore also in possession of the bunkers.[588] More controversially, however, it also held that the charterers had the right to immediate possession since the shipowners were contractually bound, through the master, to obey the charterers' orders for the employment of the vessel (an activity necessitating the consumption of bunkers). Even if this right to immediate possession were rephrased in terms of constructive possession,[589] it is not easy to see why a charterer has any more of a right to the possession of bunker fuels than a passenger in a London taxicab has of the contents of its fuel tank. The significance of this point is that the court looked for a delivery of the bunkers in terms of the voluntary surrender of this right to immediate possession. If the shipowners had had at all material times possession, unlimited by any such right of the charterers', then delivery would already have occurred and the decision could not have gone against them on the ground that it did. Even if a right to immediate possession is

---

[586] It was not critical of the decisions in *Four Point Garage*, n. 575 above, and *Gamer's*, n. 577 above.

[587] Unlike the rogue in *Worcester Works Finance Ltd v Cooden Engineering Co. Ltd* [1972] 1 QB 210, who 'cheerfully hand[ed] over the key'.

[588] Following *The Span Terza (No. 2)* [1984] 1 WLR 27.

[589] The right to immediate possession is the right to demand actual possession at any time, which hardly fits the present case.

conceded to the charterers, it is arguable that the possession of the shipowners means that delivery was made when the bunkers were put on board.

Agreement to sell by buyer in possession. Section 25(1) requires the second **5.169** buyer to take delivery of the goods 'under any sale, pledge or other disposition thereof'. Although not a decision on section 25(1), *Shaw v Commissioner of Police of the Metropolis*[590] supports the view that an agreement to sell will not suffice for present purposes.[591] It was held in that case that the rogue and the innocent purchaser did not intend the property to pass to the latter until his bank draft had been honoured. Even allowing for any court's deep reluctance to find such parties intending the property to pass before payment, it is difficult to see how an unpalatable result could be avoided if the property was plainly intended to pass and the purchaser had not yet paid the absconding rogue. A further point concerns additional language in section 9 of the Factors Act, which treats as authorized by the owner a delivery of goods 'under *any agreement for* sale, pledge, or other disposition thereof' (emphasis added). This language would have been broad enough to catch the events in *Shaw* if the contract between owner and rogue had been characterized as one of sale rather than agency. It was interpreted in *Re Highway Foods International Ltd*,[592] where both sale and resale contracts contained a retention of title clause and payment had been made under neither contract. The goods, a quantity of meat, were then returned by the sub-buyer to the seller to permit safety checks to be made, and seller and sub-buyer concluded a new contract for a price identical to the one the sub-buyer had earlier agreed to pay the buyer. Receivers acting for the buyer argued that title to the goods had already passed to the sub-buyer under section 9 so that the seller had no right to repossess them and sell them on fresh terms directly to the sub-buyer. It was not clear in the buyer's case how the assertion that the sub-buyer had obtained title was compatible with the buyer's own retention-of-title clause.[593] The buyer failed because, although the sub-buyer

---

[590] [1987] 3 All ER 405, discussed in the text accompanying nn. 225–6 above.

[591] See also *W. Hanson (Harrow) Ltd v Rapid Civil Engineering Ltd* (1987) 37 Build. LR 106; *P4 Ltd v Unite Integrated Foods Ltd* [2006] BLR 150. Nevertheless, it was held at a later stage in the *P4* proceedings that the delivery by a sub-contractor of materials on to a site amounted to a 'disposition' in favour of the contractor occupying the site since the sub-contractor had given up the right to remove those materials from the site: [2006] EWHC 2640 (TCC) at [120]: '[O]nce the unfixed materials and goods are delivered then the sub-contractor cannot remove them except to use in the works, subject to the consent of the contractor to the removal of these materials and goods. The sub-contractor therefore gives up most of the characteristics of ownership of the goods or materials, pending payment. This in my judgment amounts to a sufficient transfer of an interest, legal or equitable, in property of those goods and materials to amount to a "disposition".' The third-party effect of the disposition in favour of the contractor is, however, by no means clear. The property in the materials was agreed between contractor and sub-contractor to pass only upon payment by the contractor.

[592] [1995] BCC 271.

[593] The practical issue at the heart of this case was whether the buyer had a claim to the moneys placed on deposit by the sub-buyer pending resolution of the title dispute between the seller and buyer.

acquired authorized and thus lawful possession under section 9, this was short of the title needed to override the title of the seller. A further and smaller quantity of meat had been processed to such a degree that it lost its original identity. Although the issue would have benefited from a fuller discussion, it seems that title to this meat passed upon its transformation by the sub-buyer by virtue of the rule of law that the operator becomes the owner of new products[594] without any need to invoke sections 9 or 25(1).

Consumer Conditional Sales

5.170 **Special treatment.** It is ironic that consumer conditional sales are removed from section 25(1) because of their kinship with hire purchase transactions, given that one of the reasons for the emergence of hire purchase was the desire to avoid the seller-in-possession exception to the rule of *nemo dat*.[595] Instead of extending section 25(1) to protect those deriving title from hire purchase bailees, section 25(1) was cut down to remove its protection from those deriving title from consumer conditional buyers.[596] Most consumer cases, however, will involve motor vehicles, and special legislation, applicable to both hire purchase and conditional sale transactions, has to some extent reproduced the protection given to innocent purchasers by section 25(1) of the Sale of Goods Act.[597]

Part III of the Hire Purchase Act 1964

5.171 **Scope.** Part III of the Hire Purchase Act 1964[598] applies to motor vehicles[599] that are the subject of either conditional sale[600] or hire purchase agreements.[601] It does not apply to sale or return agreements, security bills of sale,[602] or to financial

---

[594] See Ch. 3 above.

[595] *Helby v Matthews* [1893] AC 471.

[596] This was effective with the implementation of the 1979 Act but it was foreshadowed by provisions of the Consumer Credit Act 1974 (s. 192(4) and Sch. 4, para. 4) that never came into force.

[597] Hire purchase and conditional sale contracts are defined in identical terms in the Consumer Credit Act 1974, s. 189, and in Part III of the Hire Purchase Act 1964, s. 29(1), as amended by the Consumer Credit Act, Sch. 4, para. 22. Oddly enough, non-consumer conditional sales may be the subject of both a s. 25(1) and a Part III transaction.

[598] As amended by the Consumer Credit Act 1974, Sch. 4, para. 22.

[599] S. 29(1): 'a mechanically propelled vehicle intended or adapted for use on roads to which the public has access'. This could include farm vehicles, although they are by no means exclusively or mainly (words absent from s. 29(1)) used on public roads.

[600] See *Dodds v Yorkshire Bank Finance* [1992] CCLR 92.

[601] References hereafter to bailees will include both conditional buyers and hire purchase bailees. Part III refers to them compendiously as 'the debtor'. Part III does not apply where the agreement in question is vitiated by a fundamental mistake of identity so that no agreement can be said to have been concluded between the bailee and the owner of the vehicle: *Shogun Finance Ltd v Hudson* [2003] UKHL 62; [2004] 1 AC 919, discussed above.

[602] A point not lost on a South Wales car dealer eager to avoid losing title under Part III: see the *Independent*, 29 Sept. 1989.

leases, despite the fact that the latter two perform the same economic function as hire purchase and conditional sale agreements. Nor would it apply to a case where a dealer permits a prospective hire purchase bailee to take away a car before the bailee's hire purchase proposal is turned down by the finance company,[603] though it will apply where an agreement is concluded informally prior to the finance company's written acceptance and the vehicle is disposed of by the bailee before that written acceptance is made.[604] As a purely pragmatic response to the fact that title problems usually erupt in the case of second-hand cars rather than refrigerators, Part III does not sit easily in any attempt to erect a comprehensive theory of *nemo dat* and its exceptions. The statutory techniques of protecting innocent purchasers are also different from those displayed in the Factors Act and Sale of Goods Act. The limited coverage of Part III makes it a matter of happy accident for those *bona fide* purchasers who, in a subsequent dispute with a finance company owner, discover that they dealt with a bailee rather than a financial lessee.

Deeming provision. A disposition made by a bailee[605] to a private purchaser **5.172** acting in good faith and without notice is deemed to have been made with the owner's title vested in the bailee immediately before the disposition.[606] Curiously, the Act does not begin by deeming that the purchaser acquires a good title from the bailee or that the bailee acts as the authorized agent of the finance company owner.[607] This way of phrasing the matter would protect the purchaser from any possibility of liability in conversion arising from the act of dealing with the bailee. More significantly, it would also mean that the purchaser acquires the motor vehicle on whatever title terms have been agreed with the bailee. In accordance with normal principle, private purchasers who have acquired a good title under Part III will be able to transmit that title clear of the finance company's interest, regardless of the *bona fides* or notice of purchasers who deal with them. The Act defines a private purchaser in negative terms as one who does not carry on the business of a trade or finance purchaser at the time of the disposition.[608] A trade or finance

---

603 The position in *Central Newbury Car Auctions Ltd v Unity Finance Ltd* [1957] 1 QB 371.

604 *Hitchens v General Guarantee Corpn* [2001] EWCA Civ 359; see also *Carlyle Finance Ltd v Pallas Industrial Finance* [1999] 1 All ER (Comm.) 659.

605 In *Keeble v Combined Lease Finance plc* [1996] CCLR 63, the question was whether, in the case of a car bailed to two partners each jointly and severally liable to the finance company, a good title could be passed under the Act by only one of them to a *bona fide* private purchaser. The court held that 'the debtor' in section 27(1) meant 'the persons, or either of them, to whom the vehicle is bailed'. Consequently, the finance company's technical argument failed and the private purchaser acquired good title under the Act.

606 S. 27(2). If the owner's title is defective, the protection given to private purchasers is commensurately reduced: s. 29(5).

607 *Quaere* the liability of that bailee under the contract of sale to his purchaser? Could it be said that the bailee has the right to sell under s. 12(1) of the Sale of Goods Act? See discussion of s. 12(1) above.

608 S. 29(2).

purchaser is defined as one carrying on a business that consists wholly or partly of buying motor vehicles for the purpose of resale or supply on hire purchase or conditional sale terms.[609] The mischief of the legislation is plain enough: trade or finance purchasers have the opportunity to consult registers of hire purchase and conditional sale agreements,[610] whereas private purchasers do not. In *Stevenson v Beverley Bentinck Ltd*,[611] the plaintiff was a tool inspector who, in his spare time, purchased and renovated vehicles prior to reselling them.[612] He bought for his personal use a car that turned out to be the subject of a hire purchase agreement and the question was whether he could claim the protection of section 27(2). It was held that he could not, since carrying on the business of a trade or finance purchaser was a matter of status rather than of the capacity in which the purchaser was acting at the time of the disposition. The plaintiff carried on a business, even if it was only a part-time one.[613] The private purchaser issue also arose in *GE Capital Bank Ltd v Rushton*,[614] where a car dealer was in possession of motor vehicles supplied on title retention terms by the claimant bank. In need of finance, the dealer obtained a loan from a property company, to which he granted a debenture repayable on demand. When the lender called in the debenture, an agreement was reached that an associate of the lender would purchase any unsold stock remaining on the dealer's premises at the end of the month. The vehicles later sold and delivered to the associate included vehicles belonging to the claimant bank; the relevant portion of the price was paid over to the lender. The question was whether the associate was a private purchaser when he was not an established car dealer at the time of the sale. Taking the view that the purpose of Part III was to give protection to those who did not buy in the course of trade, the Court of Appeal withheld protection from the associate because he had by his own admission purchased the vehicles as a business venture with a view to selling them at a profit.[615] The definition of a trade or finance purchaser in Part III was 'intended to direct attention not

---

[609] *Ibid.* Again, note the absence of any reference to financial leasing. A finance company whose business in respect of motor vehicles consisted exclusively of financial leases would by definition be a private purchaser (hardly a sensible result), unless its practice of selling vehicles at discounted prices at the end of the term, whether to the lessee or otherwise, made a difference.

[610] Notably the information services provided by Experian. A trade or finance purchaser, unable to obtain good title under Part III, may however, provided the agreement is a non-consumer conditional sale, and not a consumer conditional sale or a hire purchase agreement, obtain good title under s. 25 of the Sale of Goods Act: see *Forthright Finance Ltd v Carlyle Finance Ltd* [1997] 4 All ER 90.

[611] [1976] 1 WLR 483.

[612] The court counted 37 transactions in the preceding 18 months. Sometimes the plaintiff acted for a principal.

[613] Cf. the matter of dealing as a consumer under the Unfair Contract Terms Act 1977, discussed in Ch. 9 below.

[614] [2005] EWCA Civ 1556; [2006] 1 WLR 899.

[615] The details of the arrangements between the lender and the associate are not disclosed in the case.

merely to the business of the purchaser immediately prior to and at the time of the disposition but also to the purpose for which the vehicle is bought'.[616]

Operation of legislation. Should a trade or finance purchaser acquire the vehi-   **5.173** cle from the bailee, then title will pass to a private purchaser dealing with the trade or finance purchaser, provided that that private purchaser acted in good faith and without notice.[617] The same result will follow if there is more than one trade or finance purchaser between bailee and the first private purchaser.[618] The technique is to deem that, for the purpose of the disposition to the first private purchaser, title was vested in the bailee immediately before the disposition to the first trade or finance purchaser. This limited deeming provision will therefore leave at risk of liability in conversion any number of trade or finance purchasers in the chain between the bailee and the first private purchaser.[619] The first private purchaser will have a protected statutory title, but not the previous trade or finance purchaser or purchasers. A reading of the above provisions shows that a statutory title passes only if the first private purchaser has acted in good faith and without notice. If the first private purchaser falls short of this standard, then it does not matter how much good faith is mustered among any number of subsequent private purchasers, for they are all damned. If this does not seem an attractive result, it should be recalled that purchasers dealing with mercantile agents or buyers and sellers in possession cannot pass a good title to good faith disponees if they themselves fail to comply with the standard of good faith and absence of notice. Nevertheless, odd results might flow from this limitation in Part III. Suppose, for example, that on a matrimonial break-up a spouse, with or without the consent of the finance company owner, assumes the burden of paying instalments, but unlawfully disposes of the vehicle before all of the instalments have been paid. The arrangement between the two spouses would probably pass the test of a disposition[620] but,

---

[616] Above n. 614, at [39]. The court considered a wide range of authorities, including those on moneylenders legislation, but referred in particular to the non-moneylending cases of *Stevenson v Rogers* [1999] QB 1028 and *Davies v Sumner* [1984] 1 WLR 1301. The emphasis laid in those cases on the integrality of a purchase to the buyer's business, as well as on the regularity of purchases by a buyer, was evidently of little assistance in the present case of a purchaser who was starting a business. It is questionable how much assistance can be gained when interpreting a statutory provision by looking at similar language in different statutes serving different purposes. For the similar question whether a person can be a mercantile agent on the first occasion when he so acts, see *Heyman v Flewker* (1863) 13 CBNS 519, 527.

[617] S. 27(3).

[618] *Ibid.*

[619] This is confirmed by s. 27(6) which also, for the avoidance of doubt, states that the bailee is not exonerated from any civil or criminal liability by virtue of the provisions of Part III. S. 27(6) applies also to the liability of trade or finance purchasers. It has been held that its effect is to keep alive the contractual liability of a conditional seller under an express term that the seller was the owner of the goods at the contract date: *Barber v NWS Bank plc*, n. 4 above.

[620] In s. 29(1). The first spouse's transfer of the option should be a sale of goods since there is an intention to divest himself of the whole of his interest in the vehicle. In addition, agreeing to make payment to a third party would not detract from the agreement being classified as one of sale.

since the spouse agreeing to make the payments clearly has notice of the outstanding hire purchase agreement, it follows that no title could be transmitted under Part III to a subsequent purchaser.

5.174 **Time of absence of notice.** Section 27(4) makes as obscurely as it can an important point about the time when a private purchaser's good faith and absence of notice are to be considered. Where the disposition made to the first private purchaser is a hire purchase agreement, it appears that that private purchaser[621] will acquire a good title if he acted in good faith at the time the vehicle was first acquired on bailment terms. The bailee should thus be at liberty to keep up the hire purchase agreement and exercise an effective option to purchase at the end of the term, even though by that time he has notice of the original owner's title. This provision is not extended to conditional buyers. The reason would appear to be that hire purchase was singled out because of the double disposition factor, namely, the initial acquisition on hire purchase terms and the subsequent sale implemented by the exercise of the option to purchase. Section 27(4) ensures that the bailee is not disqualified as a result of the second disposition. In a conditional sale, there is only the one disposition, made when the goods were acquired on sale terms, since the passing of property is an automatic affair once all the instalments have been paid. Part III makes it plain that a disposition includes a conditional sale agreement and not the acquisition of title under a conditional sale agreement.[622] A conditional buyer's protection will not therefore be lost as a result of discovering the existence of the original owner after the conclusion of the conditional sale contract.[623]

5.175 **Nature of notice.** Subject to section 29(4), the question of a bailee's good faith should be determined in the same way as it is for other areas of title transfer. The absence of notice of a pre-existing hire purchase or conditional sale contract, however, also invites consideration of section 29(3), which refers to the absence of 'actual notice that the vehicle is *or was* the subject of any such agreement' (emphasis added). Section 29(3) was considered in *Barker v Bell*,[624] where a private purchaser was falsely informed by the bailee that all of the payments had been made. The Court of Appeal held that the purchaser acquired a good title under Part III. The use of the past tense in section 29(3) appeared to deny such a title since the purchaser certainly knew that the vehicle had been the subject of a hire purchase agreement. But this language could sensibly be confined to the case where a hire purchase agreement was automatically terminated according to its own terms at the moment

---

[621] As well as anyone to whom he transfers his option to purchase: s. 27(4)(b) ('a person claiming under him').

[622] S. 29(1). See also s. 29(3): 'a person becomes a purchaser . . . if, and at the time when, a disposition of the vehicle is made to him'.

[623] S. 29(1) would appear to protect the buyer even before delivery of the goods or before any portion of the price has been paid.

[624] [1971] 1 WLR 983.

of the unlawful disposition by the bailee. Hence, 'a purchaser is only affected by notice if he has actual notice that the car is on hire-purchase'.[625]

Presumptions. In his forensic tasks, the private purchaser who claims a good title, or any subsequent purchaser claiming through him, is aided by an impressive series of presumptions:[626] that the disposition to the first private purchaser was made directly by the bailee;[627] that if there was no such direct disposition, then the bailee disposed of the goods directly to a different private purchaser, who acted in good faith, and that the present private purchaser can trace his title back to that other private purchaser;[628] and that, if it should be proved that the bailee disposed of the goods directly to a trade or finance purchaser, then the first private purchaser who came along acted in good faith and the present private purchaser can trace his title back to that other private purchaser.[629]

5.176

Other legislation. Finally, section 27(5) states that the provisions of the section apply notwithstanding section 21 of the Sale of Goods Act,[630] and without prejudice to the Factors Act 1889 and any other enactment authorizing the apparent owner to dispose of goods as though he were the true owner. They therefore leave unimpaired, for example, the buyer in possession exception in section 25 of the Sale of Goods Act.[631] This means, in the case of a non-consumer conditional sale, that persons dealing, or in a chain originating, with the conditional buyer have the choice of seeking title protection under Part III[632] or section 25[633] of the Sale of Goods Act. The benefits of Part III are that a purchaser can claim protection even though payment has not been made in full or delivery taken before notice of the owner's claim arises. A trade or finance purchaser appearing on the scene before the first private purchaser, on the other hand, would take the section 25 route. A purchaser whose disposition is governed by both sets of provisions does not have to satisfy both. They are facultative provisions which state when a purchaser acquires a good title: they do not each say that a purchaser will acquire good title only if he satisfies section 25 or Part III as the case may be.

5.177

Other Powers of Sale

Validity and title. Section 21(2)(b) contains a saving provision that the *nemo dat* rule, as formulated in section 21(1), does not affect 'the validity of any

5.178

---

[625] *Ibid.*, 986.
[626] These are rebuttable: see *Soneco Ltd v Barcross Finance Ltd* [1978] RTR 444.
[627] S. 28(1),(2).
[628] S. 28(3).
[629] S. 28(4).
[630] They therefore override the rule of *nemo dat quod non habet*.
[631] Also s. 8 of the Factors Act.
[632] Which is not confined to consumer transactions.
[633] Which still applies to non-consumer conditional sales.

contract of sale under any special common law or statutory power of sale or under the order of a court of competent jurisdiction'. The purpose of this provision is tolerably plain as being to preserve the effectiveness of certain titles, conferred under special and statutory powers of sale, but the drafting is quite curious in saving the validity of the 'contract of sale' rather than the title or the 'sale' itself. The contract of sale of goods belonging to another[634] is not an illegal contract at common law or otherwise invalid. Indeed, it generally supports a breach of contract action based on section 12 of the Sale of Goods Act if the seller has not acquired the right to sell at the time when the property is to pass to the buyer. In the event of the exercise of a power of sale, whether at common law or under statute, the question of the purchaser's title is not settled by section 21(2)(b) but by the relevant common law or statutory rules dealing with the power of sale. The aim of section 21(2)(b), however, appears to be to put it beyond doubt that the enactment in section 21(1) of the *nemo dat* rule does not repeal certain common law and statutory powers of title transfer outside the Factors and Sale of Goods Acts. The provision should also reinforce the immunity of sellers from a section 12 action in those cases where an effective title is transferred pursuant to the exercise of the power of sale.

5.179 **Common law powers of sale.** Common law powers of sale include those of pledgees,[635] mortgagees,[636] and agents of necessity.[637] Under statute, bailees may dispose of uncollected goods[638] and confer 'a good title to the purchaser as against the bailor'[639] but not as against the owner.[640] Another example is the unpaid seller who, upon reselling after exercising a right of lien or stoppage in transit, is able to confer a good title on the new buyer as against the original buyer.[641] Other common statutory examples include sales by innkeepers,[642] pawnbrokers,[643] sheriffs,[644]

---

[634] e.g., *Varley v Whipp* [1900] 1 QB 513.

[635] *Halliday v Holgate* (1868) LR 2 Ex. 299; *Burdick v Sewell* (1884) 13 QBD 159, 174.

[636] *Deverges v Sandeman, Clark & Co. Ltd* [1902] 1 Ch. 579; *Stubbs v Slater* [1910] 1–Ch. 632; *Re Morritt* (1886) 18 QBD 222 (power regulated by the Bills of Sale Act 1878 (Amendment) Act 1882, ss. 7, 13).

[637] *Great Northern Railway Co. Ltd v Swaffield* (1874) LR 9 Ex. 132, 138; *Sims & Co. Ltd v Midland Railway Co. Ltd* [1913] 1 KB 103.

[638] Torts (Interference with Goods) Act 1977, ss. 12–13.

[639] *Ibid.*, ss. 12(6), 13(2).

[640] *Ibid.*, s. 12(4).

[641] S. 48(2). Although the modern orthodoxy is to treat title as revesting in the unpaid seller upon contractual termination, this was not always so: see Ch. 10 below.

[642] Innkeepers Act 1878, s. 1.

[643] Consumer Credit Act 1974, s. 121.

[644] Insolvency Act 1986, ss. 183, 184(2), 346; *Curtis v Maloney* [1951] 1 KB 736; *Dyal Singh v Kenyan Insurance Co.* [1954] AC 287; Courts Act 2003, Sch. 7, para. 11; County Courts Act 1984, s. 98. Special provision used to be made for executing sheriffs in s. 26 of the Sale of Goods Act 1893, not consolidated in the Sale of Goods Act 1979 and repealed in 1982.

tax collectors,[645] liquidators,[646] company administrators,[647] administrative receivers,[648] distraining landlords,[649] and receivers of wrecks[650] and of salved property.[651]

Implied intention to confer good title.   Where a power of sale exists, clarity   **5.180** requires that, in addition to the seller's personal immunity, a good title should flow to the purchaser, but this, regrettably, is frequently left to inference. It seems hardly sensible to confer a power, and thus an immunity, on the seller, the effect of which is to procure the commission of the tort of conversion by the purchaser. The issue was discussed in *Bulbruin Ltd v Romanyszyn*,[652] in connection with a local authority's powers to dispose of abandoned vehicles.[653] The Court of Appeal, on a close reading of the relevant provisions, discerned an intention to give the purchaser a good title against the original owner.[654] Furthermore, there is little point in giving a seller a power to sell, and thus immunity against the owner, if that seller can be sued under section 12 of the Sale of Goods Act by a buyer who does not obtain good title against the owner.[655] Yet this position is clearly contemplated in the case of bailees exercising powers of sale,[656] and the seller can presumably, by entering into a limited title sale, protect himself against a breach of contract action by the disappointed buyer.

---

[645] Taxes Management Act 1970, s. 61.

[646] *Ibid.*, s. 234(3), (4).

[647] *Ibid.*, s. 234(3),(4) and Sch. B1, paras 70–2.

[648] *Ibid.*, ss. 43, 234(3), (4). The statutory power to sell the assets of a company in administrative receivership (Insolvency Act 1986, s. 42(1) and Sch. 1, para. 2) or in administration (*ibid.*, Sch. B1, para. 60 and Sch. 1, para. 2), and the powers of a trustee-in-bankruptcy (*ibid.*, s. 314 and Sch. 5, para. 9) and liquidator (*ibid.*, ss. 165(2), 167(1) and Sch. 4, para. 6) to sell assets of the insolvent do not amount to a power of sale of assets owned by someone else.

[649] Distress for Rent Act 1689, s. 1; Insolvency Act 1986, s. 347. When the relevant provisions of the Tribunals, Courts and Enforcement Act 2007 are brought into effect, the common law right to distrain for arrears of rent will be abolished and there will be a new statutory procedure for taking control of goods: see s. 71 and Sch. 12.

[650] Merchant Shipping Act 1995, s. 227.

[651] *Ibid.*, ss. 240, 243(2), 244(2) (sale without prejudice to title of third party).

[652] [1994] RTR 273. For the protection of buyers purchasing goods subject to execution, see County Courts Act 1984, s. 98; Courts Act 2003, Sch. 7, para. 11.

[653] Road Traffic Regulation Act 1984, ss. 99, 101, and Removal and Disposal of Vehicles Regulations 1986, SI 1986 No. 183, reg. 15(1).

[654] It also pointed to cases where it was 'clear' that title passes on sale, namely, sales by distraining landlords (Distress for Rent Act 1689), by innkeepers (Innkeepers Act 1870), and by tax collectors (Taxes Management Act 1970); see also Tribunals, Courts and Enforcement Act 2007, Sch. 12, para. 51 (not yet in force).

[655] *Bulbruin Ltd v Romanyszyn*, n. 652 above, 278.

[656] Torts (Interference with Goods) Act 1977, s. 12(4), (6).

6

DELIVERY, ACCEPTANCE, AND PAYMENT

Introduction. The seller is required to deliver the goods to the buyer[1] at the **6.01** time and in the mode and quantity required by the contract. The buyer is bound to accept and pay for the goods,[2] the presumption being that delivery and payment are mutual and concurrent conditions.[3]

The Seller's Duty to Deliver

Meaning of Delivery and Acceptance

Delivery. In common speech, delivery suggests the active transportation of the **6.02** goods to the buyer. That is not the meaning it has in sale of goods law, presumptive or otherwise.[4] According to section 61(1), "'delivery" means voluntary transfer of

---

[1] S. 27.

[2] *Ibid.*

[3] S. 28.

[4] *Gamer's Motor Centre (Newcastle) Pty Ltd v Natwest Wholesale Australia Pty Ltd* (1987) 163 CLR 236 at [12]. For a rejection of the view that a seller under a duty to supply and deliver supplies the goods at its own premises and delivers them to the buyer's, see *MBM Fabri-Clad Ltd v Eisen-und Huttenwerke Thale AG* [2000] CLC 373 (German seller under obligation to deliver in England).

possession from one person to another'.[5] In the law of personal property, posses-sion is the relationship between a person and a chattel based upon both the fact and intention of excluding all others from effective control of the chattel.[6] The scope of the control needed for this purpose depends upon the size, shape, and location of the chattel.[7] When the seller transfers possession of goods to the buyer, this entails yielding effective control over them to the buyer coupled with the abandonment by the seller of an intention to exercise effective control and the simultaneous assertion of such an intention by the buyer. It is not enough for the seller to tender the goods to the buyer; the latter must also receive them.[8] Where delivery is to be made at the buyer's premises, it will be effective if the seller without negligence hands over the goods to someone apparently having authority to receive them.[9]

6.03 Constructive delivery. Besides a physical tender and receipt of the goods, possession may be transferred to effectuate delivery in various ways.[10] It is possible for a seller to deliver the goods without surrendering possession. This will occur where the seller assumes the character of bailee holding the goods on behalf of the buyer.[11] Delivery may occur symbolically, where a portion of the goods is handed over as representative of the whole,[12] or constructively, where the buyer is given

---

   [5] For a discussion of 'purported' delivery where the wrong goods were received by the buyer along with the right delivery note, with destructive consequences, see *Albright & Wilson UK Ltd v Biachem Ltd* [2002] UKHL 36; [2002] 2 All ER (Comm.) 753, reversing in part [2001] EWCA Civ 301; [2001] 1 All ER (Comm.) 537. The meaning of delivery is extended, in certain cases, where the buyer acquires an undivided interest in goods, pursuant to s. 61(1) of the Sale of Goods Act 1979 as amended by s. 2(b) of the Sale of Goods (Amendment) Act 1995, to include an appropriation of goods to the contract that results in the passing of property to the buyer. See the notes to ss. 20A(5) and 20B(1) of the draft bill contained in Law Commission, *Sale of Goods Forming Part of a Bulk* (Law Com. No. 215), 39.
   [6] F. Pollock and R. Wright, *An Essay on Possession in the Common Law* (Clarendon Press, 1888); Harris, 'The Concept of Possession in English Law', in A. G. Guest (ed.), *Oxford Essays in Jurisprudence* (Oxford, 1961); M. Bridge, *Personal Property Law* (3rd edn, Clarendon Law, 2002), Ch. 2.
   [7] *The Tubantia* [1924] P 78; *Young v Hitchens* (1844) 6 QB 606.
   [8] See *Caradoc Nurseries Ltd v Marsh* (1959) 19 DLR (2d) 491.
   [9] *Galbraith and Grant Ltd v Block* [1922] 2 KB 155; *Computer 2000 Distribution Ltd v ICM Computer Solutions Plc* [2004] EWCA Civ 1634.
   [10] *Gamer's Motor Centre (Newcastle) Pty Ltd v Natwest Wholesale Australia Pty Ltd*, n. 4 above at [15] (Mason CJ): '[T]he seller's obligation under s.[27] of the Act cannot always be sensibly discharged by actual delivery. A commodity or chattel incapable of actual physical delivery, except perhaps at great inconvenience and cost, such as a yacht (see Bank of New South Wales v. Palmer (1970) 2 NSWR 532), must be capable of constructive or symbolic delivery falling short of actual delivery.'
   [11] *Castle v Sworder* (1861) 6 H & N 828; *Elmore v Stone* (1809) 1 Taunt, 458; *Marvin v Wallis* (1856) 6 E & B 726; *Mills v Charlesworth* (1890) 25 QBD 421, 425; *Dublin City Distillery Ltd v Doherty* [1914] AC 823, 844; *Gamer's Motor Centre (Newcastle) Pty Ltd v Natwest Wholesale Australia Pty Ltd*, n. 4 above at [19]–[21].
   [12] *Dixon v Yates* (1833) 5 B & Ad. 313; *Kemp v Falk* (1882) 7 App. Cas. 573, *per* Lord Blackburn.

the only effective means[13] of access to the goods, such as a warehouse key.[14] Another constructive delivery takes place where the seller transfers to the buyer an on- board bill of lading, which is a common law document of title,[15] for in such a case the bailee in possession is bound to deliver the goods to the holder of the document even before attorning to the holder.[16] The transfer of a document that meets the wider definition of a document of title under the Factors Act 1889 and the Sale of Goods Act[17] would not be a constructive delivery of the goods. In such a case, constructive delivery would occur only when the bailee attorns to the buyer, for the bailee would not be under an obligation to the buyer to deliver until doing so.[18]

Delivery and shipping terms. According to section 32(1), delivery *prima facie* **6.04** occurs where goods are handed over by the seller to an independent carrier[19] for the purpose of transmission to the buyer.[20] The reason for this is that the carrier is presumptively the buyer's agent.[21] The *prima facie* rule in section 32(1) applies even if the carrier is not nominated by the buyer; it is not uncommon for an f.o.b. seller, whose duty to deliver consists of placing the goods free on board a ship, to negotiate a contract of carriage as agent for the buyer.[22] Since the rule in

---

[13] For the requirement of exclusive access, see *Dublin City Distillery Ltd v Doherty*, n. 11 above, 843–4.

[14] *Ellis v Hunt* (1789) 3 TR 464; *Wrightson v McArthur and Hutchinsons (1919) Ltd* [1921] 2 KB 807, where the court preferred to conclude that there had been a true delivery rather than a constructive delivery.

[15] *Lickbarrow v Mason* (1794) 5 TR 683. But note the wider definition in certain local Acts: e.g. the Port of London Act 1968, s. 183.

[16] M. Bridge, *International Sale of Goods[:] Law and Practice* (2nd edn, Oup, 2007), 406–8.

[17] Ch. 5 above.

[18] S. 29(4); *Laurie and Morewood v Dudin and Sons* [1926] 1 KB 223; *Farina v Home* (1846) 16 M & W 119; *Dublin City Distillery Ltd v Doherty*, n. 11 above, 847–8; *Lackington v Atherton* (1844) 7 Man. & Gr. 360; *M'Ewan v Smith* (1849) 2 HLC 309; *Wardar's (Import & Export) Co. Ltd v W Norwood & Sons Ltd* [1968] 2 QB 663. Cf. *Salter v Woollams* (1841) 2 Man. & Gr. 650; *Poulton & Son v Anglo-American Oil Co.* (1911) 27 TLR 216.

[19] Not an employee: *Galbraith and Grant Ltd v Block*, n. 9 above; *Caradoc Nurseries Ltd v Marsh*, n. 8 above.

[20] Sale of Goods Act, s. 32(1); *Wait v Baker* (1848) 2 Ex. 1; *Badische Anilin und Soda Fabrik v Basle Chemical Works* [1898] AC 200; *Dutton v Solomonson* (1803) 3 B & P 582; *Dunlop v Lambert* (1839) 6 Cl. & Fin. 600, 620–1; *Calcutta & Burmah Steam Navigation Co. Ltd v De Mattos* (1863) 31 LJ QB 322, 328; *Ex p. Pearson* (1868) 3 Ch. App 443.

[21] *Wait v Baker*, n. 20 above.

[22] See s. 32(2); *Cork Distilleries Co. v Great Southern and Western Railway Co.* (1874) LR 7 HL 266, 277; *Pyrene Co. Ltd v Scindia Navigation Ltd* [1954] 2 QB 402, 423; *Albacruz (Cargo Owners) v Albazero (Cargo Owners) (The Albazero)* [1977] AC 774, 785–6, 841–2. The issue is complicated by the question of who has standing to sue the carrier for damage done in transit: Ch. 4 above; *The Albazero*, above; *Leigh and Sillavan Ltd v Aliakmon Shipping Ltd* [1986] AC 785. If the seller were able to sue, it would be because he was still the owner of the goods or (less likely) bore the risk, and thus could be said to contract with the carrier as principal: *The Albazero*, above, 844–5. For a description of the seller's dealings with the carrier in f.o.b. contracts, see *Pyrene Co. Ltd v Scindia Navigation Ltd*, above.

section 32(1) is a *prima facie* one, it should be displaced where goods are deliverable under a non-negotiable waybill to a named consignee but the seller consigning the goods has reserved, under the contract of carriage, the right to alter delivery instructions.[23] Section 32(1) is also ousted in those cases where delivery to the carrier is not intended by the seller to be delivery to the buyer. This will be so where the seller retains the right of disposal under section 19,[24] where delivery will take place constructively on the exchange of documents between seller and buyer.[25] The rule in section 32(1) will therefore be displaced for c.i.f. (cost, insurance, and freight) sales. Indeed, the goods may already be afloat before the contract of sale is concluded or before a particular cargo is appropriated to the contract, so that it is impossible to treat the carrier retrospectively as the agent for the buyer.[26] In c.i.f. contracts, the seller's delivery obligation is commuted into an obligation to transfer shipping documents[27] and the buyer obtains the benefit of the contract of affreightment on the documentary exchange.[28] The section 32(1) rule will also be displaced in *ex* ship contracts, where delivery is effected when the goods are discharged from the ship.[29] As a result of changes introduced by a European Directive,[30] section 32(1) 'must be ignored' where the buyer deals as a consumer;[31] delivery to the carrier is not delivery to the consumer, even where the seller is 'authorised or required to send' the goods to the buyer.[32] This change was made in aid of changing the risk rule in such cases so that risk would be transferred to the consumer only when the consumer actually received the goods.[33]

---

[23] The seller has a freedom to intervene in the performance of the contract of carriage that is significantly greater than the freedom that exists where the seller exercises the right of stoppage in transit under s. 44 of the Sale of Goods Act.

[24] *Wait v Baker*, n. 20 above, 8. *Quaere* the buyer as named consignee in the bill of lading retained by the seller until payment? See *Moakes v Nicholson* (1865) 19 CB(NS) 290 (no delivery). See also *The Albazero*, n. 22 above, 800–1, 809–12; *Scottish & Newcastle International Ltd v Othon Ghalanos Ltd* [2008] UKHL 11; [2008] 1 Lloyd's Rep. 462 at [20] (Lord Rodger) ('at least arguable' that retention of bill of lading as security for payment displaces in c.i.f. and f.o.b. contracts the prima facie rule in s. 32(1)).

[25] *E Clemens Horst Co. v Biddell Bros* [1912] AC 18, 22–3.

[26] *Keighley, Maxsted & Co. v Durant* [1901] AC 240.

[27] See *Manbre Saccharine Co. Ltd v Corn Products Co. Ltd* [1919] 1 KB 198, 202; *Comptoir d'Achat et du Boerenbond Belge SA v Luis de Ridder Lda (The Julia)* [1949] AC 293, 312; discussed in the text accompanying nn. 261 *et seq.* below.

[28] This can be accomplished under the Carriage of Goods by Sea Act 1992, s. 2(1), by means of a wider range of documents than the negotiable bill of lading, to which the Bills of Lading Act 1855 limited the potentiality of assignment of the contract of affreightment; see Bridge, n. 16 above, 387–91.

[29] Cf *Beaver Specialty Ltd v Donald H Bain Ltd* [1974] SCR 903.

[30] Directive 1999/44/EC of the European Parliament and of the Council of 25 May 1999 on certain aspects of sale of consumer goods and associated guarantees, OJ No. L171, 7.7.99, p. 12.

[31] For the meaning of dealing as a consumer, see s. 61(5A), discussed in Ch. 9 below.

[32] S. 32(4); *Independiente Ltd v Music Trading On-Line (HK) Ltd* [2007] EWHC 533 (Ch); [2007] FSR 21. Similarly, s. 32(2) is also overridden by s. 32(4).

[33] See Ch. 4 above.

Acceptance. The meaning of acceptance across sale of goods law is highly **6.05**
ambiguous.[34] It can mean, for example, the event that precludes rejection of the
goods for breach of condition, which may occur some considerable time after the
seller has delivered the goods.[35] In this chapter, acceptance means the cooperative
acts that the buyer must perform in order to enable the seller to make delivery as
above defined. It therefore means taking delivery. The seller cannot deliver unless
the buyer voluntarily receives the goods since delivery calls for the consensual
transfer of possession.[36] In section 37(1), the Sale of Goods Act makes express
provision for the liability of a buyer who, in response to the seller's request when
that seller is ready and willing to deliver,[37] fails within a reasonable time of this
request to take delivery. Where delivery is agreed on a precise date, the buyer's
reasonable time may be expected to be almost instantaneous. The same may be
said where the buyer has selected the date within an agreed or open-ended delivery
range, or even of any case where the buyer has received a prior intimation of a
coming delivery, as where the seller notifies the buyer that delivery will take place
on a future date in those cases where it is the seller who chooses the date. The
nature of the goods, however, may permit a more generous allocation of time.[38]
Apart from any right the seller may have to terminate the contract, the defaulting
buyer is liable under section 37(1) to the seller for 'any loss occasioned by his
neglect or refusal to take delivery, and also for a reasonable charge for the care
and custody of the goods'. The first of these two items could have been left to the
special damages rule in section 54, though the latter goes beyond that provision.
In a case where section 37(1) might have applied by the court but was not, a delinquent buyer was required to pay, not for any loss suffered by the seller, but for the
benefit of occupying space on the seller's premises.[39] The decision of the court
was therefore in line with the second of the two methods of assessing damages
provided for in section 37(1).

---

[34] See Ch. 10 below.
[35] *Ibid.*, s. 35.
[36] S. 61(1) ('delivery').
[37] An interesting question is whether a seller is ready and willing to deliver when exercising under
s. 41 an unpaid seller's lien or right of retention. It is submitted that a seller is ready and willing to
deliver under a cash on delivery transaction (s. 28) even when awaiting payment by the buyer and
declining to deliver to a buyer who is not ready and willing to pay. Readiness and willingness, in
other words, should be measured by the terms of the contract of sale.
[38] See *Penarth Dock Engineering Co. v Pounds* [1963] 1 Lloyd's Rep. 359 (floating dock), where
s. 37(1) was not cited. The buyer had expressly undertaken to remove the goods as speedily as
practicable.
[39] *Penarth Dock Engineering Co. v Pounds*, n. 38 above. Applying wayleave and related cases
(*Whitwham v Westminster Brymbo Coal and Coak Co.* [1896] 2 Ch. 538; *Strand Electric and
Engineering Co. Ltd v Brisford Entertainments Ltd* [1952] 2 QB 246, 253–4), the court stated that
'the test of the measure of damages is not what the plaintiffs have lost, but what benefit the defendant
obtained by having the use of the berth': *ibid.*, 362.

6.06 **Acceptance and constructive delivery.**   Where delivery occurs constructively by means of a bill of lading, the transfer of that document, effective to give the buyer constructive possession of the goods, will not occur until the buyer voluntarily takes delivery of the bill.[40] In cases where constructive delivery depends upon the presentation of a delivery order, and the contract expressly or impliedly provides for the buyer to present this document to the bailee, the buyer's duty of acceptance requires that he receive this document and that he present it to the bailee in order to procure the necessary attornment. The seller's delivery duty will be accomplished when the bailee attorns to the buyer, giving the buyer direct rights against that bailee[41] and not at the point when the seller gives the buyer a documentary introduction to the bailee. A delivery order directed to the bailee does not of itself impose any obligation on the bailee towards the buyer,[42] though the position may be different if under the contract of bailment the buyer acquires direct rights of enforcement against the bailee pursuant to the Contracts (Rights of Third Parties) Act 1999.[43] The seller will be responsible for non-delivery if the bailee, whether or not in breach of the contract of bailment, refuses to surrender the goods to the buyer.[44] Armed with the delivery order, the buyer has the documentary means of completing delivery on behalf of the seller by presenting the order for attornment by the bailee. If the buyer neglects to procure the bailee's attornment, the seller's delivery may not be complete. The seller, however, will have displayed readiness and willingness to deliver and the buyer who fails to accept the goods by procuring the bailee's attornment will be precluded from claiming non-delivery.[45] Where, however, the seller's delivery duty is complete with the aid of a delivery order, this may not always be synchronous with the completion of the buyer's duty of acceptance. A buyer who obtains the bailee's attornment and does not either take possession of the goods or arrange for their storage in his own name will not have accepted the goods as required by section 27.

6.07 **Other acts of buyer.**   In numerous cases, a seller will be unable to make delivery until the buyer performs a preliminary act. For example, a seller may require a statement of the buyer's specifications[46] or, if needing to obtain an export licence before shipping the goods, may require from the buyer information concerning

---

[40] *Aegean Sea Traders Corpn v Repsol Petroleo SA (The Aegean Sea)* [1998] 2 Lloyd's Rep. 39.

[41] *Sterns Ltd v Vickers Ltd* [1923] 1 KB 78, 83.

[42] *Colin & Shields v W Weddel & Co. Ltd* [1952] 2 All ER 337, 343.

[43] As might occur under s. 2 if the contract of bailment identifies the existence of buyers as a class of purported contractual beneficiaries and requires the bailee to surrender the goods to a member of that class upon the seller's direction.

[44] It is uncertain whether the seller will be absolved from liability on the ground that the buyer might invoke a right of action directly against the bailee under the 1999 Act. The better view is that the buyer should have alternative rights of action against the seller (non-delivery) and the bailee.

[45] See *Alghussein Establishment v Eton College* [1988] 1 WLR 587.

[46] *Kidston and Co. v Monceau Ironworks Co.* (1902) 7 Com. Cas. 82.

the ultimate destination of the goods.[47] A contract for delivery 'as required' by the buyer[48] or at buyer's call[49] will bind the buyer to give delivery instructions to the seller. An f.o.b. buyer is under a presumptive duty to nominate a ship so that the seller can effect delivery on board.[50]

Place of Delivery and Acceptance

General rules. The principal rules concerning the place of delivery are laid **6.08** down in section 29 of the Act. Sub-section (1) begins by stating that it depends upon the express and implied provisions of the contract whether the seller has to send the goods to the buyer or the buyer has to come and take possession of them. In the absence of any contractual indication to this effect,[51] the presumptive rule in sub-section (2), in all cases bar one, is that delivery occurs at the seller's place of business (or residence if there is no place of business). The buyer will have an implied licence to enter the seller's premises to receive the goods, which, if growing crops, may need to be severed.[52] Sub-section (2) also states the exceptional case to which the above presumptive rule does not apply. Where the contract is for specific goods, the location of the goods, if known to the parties at the contract date, is presumptively the place of delivery.[53] In the great majority of cases involving specific goods, however, the goods are likely to be on the seller's premises. Further, if the seller knows the whereabouts of the goods and the buyer does not, it is quite possible that the delivery rule will be excluded between the parties and that special transport arrangements will be made.[54]

Constructive delivery and place. The rules in section 29(2) are ill-suited to **6.09** constructive delivery. Where there is an attornment by a bailee, delivery will occur as and where the attornment takes place.[55] In the case of shipping documents, as used in c.i.f. contracts for example, it has been said that, in the absence of proven trade usage or an express or implied term based upon prior business dealings, it is doubtful that the seller has to tender documents at the buyer's premises.[56] On the

---

[47] *Kyprianou v Cyprus Textiles Ltd* [1958] 2 Lloyd's Rep. 60.
[48] *Jones v Gibbons* (1853) 8 Ex. 920.
[49] *Tradax-Export SA v Italgrani di Francesco Ambrosia* [1986] 1 Lloyd's Rep. 112; *Bunge v Tradax England* [1975] 2 Lloyd's Rep. 235.
[50] *Cargill UK Ltd v Continental UK Ltd* [1989] 2 Lloyd's Rep. 290; *Richco International v Bunge* [1991] 2 Lloyd's Rep. 92; *Colley v Overseas Exporters* [1921] 3 KB 302
[51] An Australian court interpreted expansively the buyer's request 'please supply us' as requiring delivery at the buyer's premises: *Wiskin v Terdich Bros Pty Ltd* [1928] VLR 387.
[52] *James Jones & Sons Ltd v Earl of Tankerville* [1909] 2 Ch. 440, 442.
[53] *Salter v Woollams*, n. 18 above.
[54] See *Varley v Whipp* [1900] 1 QB 513.
[55] This should be the place of receipt by the buyer.
[56] *Stein, Forbes & Co. v County Tailoring Co.* (1916) 88 LJ KB 448 (Atkin J). But see *Johnson v Taylor Bros and Co. Ltd* [1920] AC 144, 156.

other hand, in *Johnson v Taylor Bros and Co. Ltd*,[57] where the c.i.f. buyer had to show a breach of contract committed within the jurisdiction in order to effect service abroad, it was held 'without hesitation' that the failure to tender documents to the English buyer, concerning goods shipped in Sweden, had taken place in England.[58] The case involved a requirements contract between a Swedish manufacturer of pig iron and an English industrialist purchasing the iron in order to manufacture axles. The buyer clearly needed the bill of lading to receive the goods from the carrier in England. Where commodities are sold, and the buyer is a trader who has no such physical use for the goods, or where the goods are not sold on credit, the same conclusion is not so compelling. According to Brandon J in *The Albazero*, shipping documents 'would normally be sent to the seller's agent for presentation to the buyer, or delivered to a banker against a confirmed credit, leaving the banker to forward them to his agent at the place of payment for collection of the price'.[59] The place of delivery would therefore be wherever the seller's agent has to present the documents to obtain payment. It is unlikely to be important in practical terms at what precise point in the inter-bank system the documents are exchanged against payment.

6.10   **Shipping terms and place.**   The method of delivery, often designated by the use of shipping terms, frequently indicates the place of delivery. A sale *ex* factory or works accords with the main presumptive rule in section 29(2). Under an f.a.s. contract, the seller is required to lay the goods free alongside the ship[60] after they have been cleared by customs.[61] Where the sale is on *ex* ship terms,[62] delivery will take place once the goods have been landed at the port of discharge. In the absence of contractual provision, the actual location within the port will depend upon what is usual or customary in that port.[63] An f.o.b. sale requires the seller to place the goods on board a ship.[64] Where there is a choice or range of ports, it is presumptively the buyer who chooses, which accords with the buyer's presumptive

---

[57] n. 56 above.
[58] The court relied upon Kennedy LJ in *Biddell Bros v E Clemens Horst Co.* [1911] 1 KB 934, 962. See also *The Albazero*, n. 22 above, 800 (Brandon J), 810 (Roskill LJ).
[59] n. 22 above, 800.
[60] *Nippon Yusen Kaisha v Ramjiban Serowgee* [1938] AC 429.
[61] *AV Pound & Co. Ltd v MW Hardy & Co. Inc.* [1956] AC 588.
[62] DES in the language of Incoterms 2000.
[63] *Yangtse Insurance Association v Lukmanjee* [1918] AC 585.
[64] *Pyrene Co. Ltd v Scindia Navigation Ltd*, n. 22 above. A c.i.f. contract substitutes, for physical delivery to the buyer, a duty to ship the goods and a duty to enter into a reasonable contract of carriage and to procure insurance on terms usual in the trade, before delivering documents representing those functions to the buyer. The seller will bear the cost of shipment and the cost of making the documents available to the buyer. For further details on c.i.f. and f.o.b. contracts, see Bridge, n. 16 above, Chs 3–4.

duty to select the ship,[65] but sometimes the choice is explicitly given to the seller.[66] Under the contract the seller may have the choice of different berths in the port.[67] The f.o.b. shipment term binds both parties. The seller may not unilaterally alter the port[68] and the buyer may not unilaterally require delivery on shore before shipment if unable to nominate a ship, even if the buyer's claim on its face alleviates the seller's burden.[69]

Expenses.   Certain incidental matters may arise in connection with delivery   **6.11** under an f.o.b. contract. According to section 29(6), the expenses of and incidental to putting the goods in a deliverable state are presumptively borne by the seller.[70] Hence the f.o.b. seller bears the cost of putting the goods on board.[71] Although entry into the contract of affreightment with the carrier is the responsibility of the buyer under the so-called 'classic' f.o.b. contract,[72] it is common for this responsibility to be placed upon the seller,[73] who will carry it out as agent for the buyer.[74]

Place of acceptance.   The Sale of Goods Act says nothing about the place of   **6.12** acceptance. Given the consensual character of delivery,[75] acceptance for the purpose of section 27 is the reflection of the seller's duty under the same provision if actual possession of the goods is transferred or of a document of title relating to those goods. The place of acceptance will therefore be the same place as the place

---

[65] *David T Boyd & Co. Ltd v Louis Louca* [1973] 1 Lloyd's Rep. 209. In the case of an f.o.t. (free on truck) contract, the seller has been recognized as having the right to choose among a range of points of shipment, since it is the seller who has to make the transport arrangements with the railway company: *Bulk Trading Corpn Ltd v Zenziper Grains and Feedstuffs* [2001] 1 Lloyd's Rep. 357. The same should also apply to those f.o.b. contracts where it is the seller who makes the transport arrangements.

[66] *Gill & Duffus v Soc. pour l'Exportation des Sucres* [1985] 1 Lloyd's Rep. 621.

[67] *Miserocchi v Agricultores Federados Argentinos* [1982] 1 Lloyd's Rep. 202.

[68] *Petrotrade Inc. v Stinnes Handels GmbH* [1995] 1 Lloyd's Rep. 142.

[69] *Maine Shipping Co. v Sutcliffe* (1918) 87 LJ KB 382. Cf *Cohen & Co. v Ockerby & Co. Ltd* (1917) 24 CLR 288, 299.

[70] See also Incoterms 2000, FOB Rules, para. A6 (costs to ship's rail borne by seller).

[71] *Attorney-General v Leopold Walford (London) Ltd* (1923) 14 Ll. LR 359.

[72] *Pyrene Co. Ltd v Scindia Navigation Ltd*, n. 22 above, 402. See the criticism in *HD Bain v Field & Co. (Fruit Merchants)* (1920) 3 Ll. LR 26, affd. (1920) 5 Ll. LR 16. A buyer will often employ the services of a freight-forwarding agent.

[73] *Pyrene Co. Ltd v Scindia Navigation Ltd*, n. 64 above.

[74] See s. 32(2); *Cork Distilleries Co. v Great Southern and Western Railway Co.* (1874) LR 7 HL 266, 277; *Pyrene Co. Ltd v Scindia Navigation Ltd*, n. 22 above, 423; *The Albazero*, n. 22 above, 785–6 (Brandon J), 841–2 (Lord Diplock). S. 32(2) does not apply where the buyer deals as a consumer: s. 32(4). A seller authorized or required to send the goods to the buyer will therefore deal with the carrier as principal and not agent, though the provision does not say so in so many words. Literally interpreted, s. 32(4)'s provision that the rule in s. 32(2) 'must be ignored' invites a reading of s. 32(2) so that the seller is *not* under an obligation to enter into a reasonable contract of carriage on behalf of the buyer, but this reading would make no sense. The true meaning of s. 32(4) is that the seller is not acting on behalf of the buyer.

[75] S. 61(1).

of delivery. In other cases involving bailees, it was stated above that the seller might have complied with his delivery duty before the buyer has accepted the goods. This points to the buyer's acceptance taking place where the buyer presents any necessary document to the seller for collection of the goods or for their continuing storage. Other cases might be posited too, typically involving carriage, where the seller has done all that can be done to effect delivery to the buyer but the buyer needs to act so as to take the goods off the carrier's hands. As a broad rule, it might be proposed that the buyer has not accepted the goods where to leave them in the hands of the bailee would generate costs imposed by the bailee on the seller under the bailment contract.[76]

Time of Delivery and Acceptance

6.13   **General.**   If the contract mentions a precise delivery date, the seller will be bound to deliver and the buyer to accept on that date, which will not be interpreted as a mere target date to be met only if the seller has goods to hand.[77] Nor will the contract be interpreted as permitting delivery on a prior date[78] in the absence of a contrary usage.[79] On the day of delivery itself, a demand or tender of delivery may be rendered ineffectual under section 29(5) unless made at a reasonable hour.[80]

6.14   **No delivery date.**   Should the contract contain no fixed or determinable delivery date, section 29(3) provides that a seller who has to send the goods to the buyer must do so within a reasonable time.[81] A similar implied term would certainly apply to other types of delivery. A reasonable time, as a question of fact,[82] will be

---

[76]   Cf s. 37(1) of the Sale of Goods Act.

[77]   *Raineri v Miles* [1981] AC 1050 (sale of land). But a seller may undertake only 'best endeavours' to deliver by a stated date: *Hartwell's of Oxford Ltd v British Motor Trade Association Ltd* [1951] Ch. 50; *Monkland v Jack Barclay Ltd* [1951] 2 KB 252.

[78]   *Bowes v Shand* (1877) 2 App. Cas. 455.

[79]   *Imperial Grain & Milling Co. v Slobinsky Bros* (1922) 69 DLR 258.

[80]   *Startup v Macdonald* (1843) 6 Man. & Gr. 593.

[81]   In cases covered by the Consumer Protection (Distance Selling) Regulations 2000, SI 2000 No. 2334 (Ch. 1 above), where the contract is concluded by 'distance communication' (see the indicative list in Sch. 1)), the period of performance is 30 days unless the parties otherwise agree (reg. 19(1)). The period starts on the day after the consumer's order is sent to the supplier (*ibid.*). A supplier unable to perform within this period must notify the consumer and reimburse any money already paid (reg. 19(2)) as soon as possible and no later than 30 days running from the day after the 30-day performance period (reg. 19(4)). No provision is made for a contrary agreement and, indeed, contracting-out is prohibited in the case of provisions designed for the consumer's protection (reg. 25). Although the contract is 'treated as if it had not been made', the supplier is still open to a claim for damages for non-delivery for breach of the contract of sale (reg. 19(5)). Where the contract permits it and the requisite information is supplied beforehand, the supplier may substitute instead goods of equivalent price and quality (reg. 19(7)). Implicitly, the goods must be equivalent too: a supplier could hardly substitute goods of a different type.

[82]   S. 59; *Hick v Raymond & Reid* [1893] AC 22, 29 (Lord Herschell).

influenced by the nature of the goods so that a shorter period should apply to perishable goods[83] or to fashion items than to durable goods. It may also prevent the seller from making premature delivery, as in the case of seasonal goods where to the seller's knowledge the buyer has no storage facilities.[84] Account should be taken of the position of the parties at the contract date in determining a reasonable time,[85] but this should not preclude a reference to post-contractual circumstances, too, when these, outside the seller's control, delay delivery.[86] In certain contracts, however, the seller may assume responsibility for delays attributable to a third party, as in one case where a carrier's negligent navigation delayed the transfer of cottonseed, shipped in Karachi, from the carrier's vessel to the buyer's craft in Hull.[87] Where in one case a c.i.f seller was entitled to substitute a vessel if the named ship was unavailable, this right of substitution could only be exercised once the named ship remained unavailable after the post-contract reasonable period had expired.[88]

Ready and willing. Whatever the date of delivery, the presumptive rule in section 28 is that the seller must be ready and willing to deliver and the buyer ready and willing to accept and pay for the goods.[89] These main obligations of the parties, therefore, are mutual and concurrent conditions and take place at the same time.[90] It is not so clear, however, that section 28 mandates exact simultaneity,[91] which would be hard to achieve in practice, especially where delivery and payment occur in different places. The Act sensibly leaves the exact protocol of performance to the particular circumstances of the contract, to be worked out sensibly by the parties on the spot. Any doubt about the precise timing of performance may, however, be exercised in favour of the seller since section 41(1)

6.15

---

83 Market usage may require an untimed delivery to be 'immediate', interpreted as 72 hours in a case dealing with the sale of potatoes: *FC Bradley & Sons v Colonial Continental Trading Co.* (1964) 108 SJ 599.

84 *Dauphin Consumers Cooperative Ltd v Puchalski* (1984) 26 Man. R (2d) 179 (Can.) (fertilizer).

85 *Ellis v Thompson* (1838) 3 M & W 445, 456–7.

86 *Monkland v Jack Barclay Ltd* [1951] 2 KB 252; *Hick v Raymond & Reid* [1893] AC 22 (strike).

87 *Re AH Cravers & Co. and ED Sassoon & Co.* (1911) 17 Com. Cas. 59.

88 *Thomas Borthwick (Glasgow) Ltd v Bunge & Co. Ltd* [1969] 1 Lloyd's Rep. 17.

89 The wording is grounded in the old pleading rules. A buyer, for example, averring nondelivery by the seller would have to show that he was ready and willing to take delivery and pay for the goods at the time of the refusal or failure to deliver: *Morton v Lamb* (1797) 7 TR 125; *Rawson v Johnson* (1801) 1 East 203.

90 *Forrestt and Son Ltd v Aramayo* (1900) 83 LT 335, 338.

91 See Serjeant Williams's notes to *Pordage v Cole* (1669) 1 Wms Saund 319, 320–5: 'Where two acts are to be done at the same time, as, where A covenants to convey an estate to B on such a day, and in consideration thereof B covenants to pay a sum of money on the same day, neither can maintain an action without shewing performance or an offer to perform his part, though it is not certain which of them is obliged to do the first act: and this particularly applies to all cases of sale.' The exact timing of performance is more of a problem with sale of land than sale of goods transactions.

allows the seller to retain possession of the goods until payment or tender of the price where the goods have been sold without any stipulation as to credit, which is the case where section 28 applies.[92]

Express Delivery Terms

6.16 **General.** Express terms concerning the time of delivery that do not provide an exact date sometimes have to be construed. No general rule can be advanced to meet the wide variety of expressions that are not specific as to date, but the abiding sense of judicial intereptation in these matters is one of commercial common sense and expediency, rather than punctiliousness.[93] Hence, to deliver 'as soon as possible' means to do so at the earliest date within a reasonable range. Bramwell LJ once said: 'To do a thing as soon as possible means to do it within a reasonable time with an undertaking to do it in the shortest possible time.'[94] The buyer's expectations in this respect might have to take a reasonable account of the seller's obligations to other buyers,[95] which does not mean that a seller may divert scarce goods from a buyer, who has ordered them on forward delivery terms, to later buyers prepared to pay higher spot prices.[96] Other express terms include 'immediately', which does not mean 'the very next instant of time after the demand'.[97] A seller in possession of goods should therefore have time to gather the goods and make delivery arrangements expeditiously and without delay.

6.17 **Length of delivery period.** Problems of interpretation sometimes arise where a delivery period is stipulated. In *Coddington v Paleologo*,[98] the contract called for 900 lengths of cloth, which the buyer intended to bleach for resale, 'delivering on April 17, complete 8 May'. A falling market prompted the question whether, under this severable contract, the seller had to deliver at least some of the goods on 17 April itself, or whether it was sufficient that the cloth be delivered in instalments within the delivery range. The seller argued that the date of commencement was fixed in his interest, while the date of completion was fixed in the buyer's interest. With the Court of Exchequer equally divided, the lower court prevailed

---

[92] Cf sale of land, where the resolution of doubt might go in favour of the buyer: see *Bankart v Bowers* (1866) LR 1 CP 484, 489.

[93] Imprecise expressions such as 'prompt', 'as soon as possible' and 'immediately' are to be disregarded for the purpose of documentary letters of credit and the Rules in UCP 600: Art. 3.

[94] *Hydraulic Engineering Co. v McHaffie* (1878) 4 QBD 670, 673. See also *Attwood v Emery* (1856) 26 LJ CP 73; *Cote v Briggs* [1953] 4 DLR 527; *Société Italo-Belge pour le Commerce et l'Industrie v Palm and Vegetable Oils (Malaysia) Sdn Bhd (The Post Chaser)* [1981] 2 Lloyd's Rep. 695.

[95] *Bonner-Worth Co. v Geddes Bros* (1921) 50 OLR 257, 263 (Can.).

[96] *Madden v McCallum* [1923] 3 DLR 41.

[97] *Moore v Shelley* (1883) 8 App. Cas. 285, 293 (security); see also *Toms v Wilson* (1862) 4 B & S 455.

[98] (1867) LR 2 Ex. 193.

in its holding that the seller did not have to commence delivery on the first day.[99] The alternative view would have been difficult to justify in view of the failure of the contract to stipulate the size of the first instalment.[100]

Requirements contracts. A number of contracts oblige the seller to supply goods **6.18** 'as required' by the buyer. The precise effect of these words cannot be understood without construing the whole contract. One question is whether the seller is bound to supply goods whenever the buyer makes a demand, or may at any time before the buyer makes a demand withdraw what amounts to a standing offer to supply goods as and when the buyer accepts that offer by making a demand. Another question, assuming the seller is bound to supply under the terms of a contract of uncertain quantity and is not merely making a standing offer, relates to the quantity of goods that the buyer may demand from the seller, a related question going to what exactly constitutes the buyer's requirements. As to the first question, the seller may only have made a standing offer,[101] which in accordance with ordinary contract principle may be withdrawn at any time unless the buyer pays for it to be kept open, as would be the case with an option. As long as the seller's offer remains open, the buyer may accept by placing an order.[102] If the seller is not making a standing offer but is bound to comply with the buyer's orders under a contract of uncertain quantity, the contract is unlikely to be struck down for lack of certainty,[103] since executory uncertainty can be clarified by executed demands. As for the quantity of goods that the buyer may call for under such a contract, the minimum quantity may be defined in such a way as not to permit the buyer to resort to a third-party source for the goods, the buyer having promised the seller exclusivity.[104] As for the maximum quantity, it will again depend upon the construction of the contract whether the buyer's need are measured against the buyer's consumptive appetite or whether they are measured against a variety of buyer uses from consumption to resale.[105] Where a contract calls for delivery of a stated quantity, the term 'as required' should not mean that the buyer's duty of acceptance is conditional upon actually needing the goods for personal use or consumption.[106]

---

[99] For the buyer, Martin B said: 'I think it better that a shabby defence should prevail, than a loose construction be put upon a mercantile contact, the inevitable consequence of which is uncertainty, litigation and expense': *ibid.* 198.

[100] *Ibid.* 199 (Pigott B).

[101] *Great Northern Railway Co. v Witham* (1873) LR 9 CP 16.

[102] *Percival v London County Council Asylum Committee* (1918) 87 LJKB 677.

[103] See Ch. 1 above.

[104] See *Tancred, Arrol & Co. v Steel Co. of Scotland Ltd* (1890) 15 App. Cas. 125; *Percival v London County Council Asylum Committee*, n. 102 above.

[105] Cf the assignment case of *Tolhurst v Associated Portland Cement Manufacturers (1900) Ltd* [1903] AC 414, for facts showing that a buyer's entitlement might be measured by what it can personally consume.

[106] *Wingold v William Looser & Co. Ltd* [1951] 1 DLR 429; see generally M. Howard (1973) 19 *McGill LJ* 224.

6.19 **Size of requirements instalments.**   The issue of the size of instalments emerged as a side issue in a case involving non-conforming goods, *Jackson v Rotax Motor and Cycle Co.*,[107] where the sellers, French manufacturers, were to supply more than 600 motor horns 'as required'. The court held that the contract was not entire but instead contemplated delivery on severable instalment terms,[108] so that acceptance of earlier instalments would not prejudice the right to reject later non-conforming instalments. Each delivery was to be treated as a separate contract.[109] Suppose, however, that the buyer demanded delivery in one instalment. It is by no means clear that, in contracts of this type, this should be disallowed, and certainly no clearer how many or how few[110] requests for delivery the buyers should make under the contract and in what amounts. Such a contract might be construed as an entire one that confers on a buyer the option to have delivery instead in separate instalments. Were attention to be drawn to the seller's prejudice in having to deliver at once all of the agreed goods, one response is that this might suit some sellers; another is that the concept of a reasonable time to meet the buyer's demand is flexible enough to accommodate periods of different length depending upon the quantity of goods demanded. In the case of a buyer purchasing raw materials for the manufacture of goods, a reasonable construction of the agreement might be that it contemplates approximately even quantities at even intervals. A further problem with flexible delivery arrangements of this kind concerns the extent to which, especially if delivery occurs over a prolonged period, the buyer should be allowed to frame his demands according to the movement of the market in volatile trading conditions.[111] The construction of 'as required' contracts will depend upon all the circumstances, including the volume of contract goods and the relationship of this figure to the seller's storage or productive capacity and to the buyer's consumption or resale needs as apparent to both parties at the contract date.

6.20 **Response to buyer's requirements.**   In those cases where the seller must act in accordance with the buyer's demands, the next question concerns how quickly the seller must respond to the buyer's order. Given the cooperative climate of delivery on 'as required' terms, the buyer's demand must be made in such a way as to afford the seller a reasonable opportunity to provide the goods. A sensible approach, if the contract fails to state a delivery range, would be to require the buyer to make his demand within a reasonable time[112] and the seller to respond to the demand within a reasonable time,[113] with the reasonableness of each party's action assessed

---

[107] [1910] 2 KB 937. See also *Tarling v O'Riordan* (1878) 2 LR Ir. 82.
[108] *Jackson*, n. 107 above, Cozens-Hardy MR, 944.
[109] *Ibid.*, Farwell LJ, 948; Kennedy LJ, 949.
[110] Farwell LJ thought the buyer was entitled to call for delivery of a single horn: *ibid.*, 948.
[111] This will have implications for damages assessments for non-delivery; see Ch. 10 below.
[112] *Wingold v William Looser & Co. Ltd*, n. 106 above.
[113] Cf *Tai Hing Cotton Mill Ltd v Kamsing Knitting Factory* [1979] AC 91.

in the light of his knowledge of the circumstances of the other. Particular circumstances may require a more immediate response from the seller, especially where there is a delivery range. In *Cie Commerciale Sucres et Denrées v Czarnikow Ltd (The Naxos)*,[114] the House of Lords held that the term, 'the seller shall have the sugar ready to be delivered' when the ship presented itself for loading, in a contract for the sale of 12,000 tonnes of sugar f.o.b. Dunkirk, meant that 'the seller shall have the sugar called forward available for loading without delay or interruption as soon as the vessel is ready to load the cargo in question.' According to Sir Michael Kerr in the court below:

> '[R]eady to be delivered' . . . does not mean that [the sugar] must be physically stacked on the quay when the vessel comes alongside. It means that it must then be available for loading without delay or interruption in the event that the vessel is able to start loading at once and to continue to load without interruption.[115]

In congested port conditions, it is undesirable and expensive to keep a ship tied up waiting for cargo. A buyer chartering a ship to lift a cargo would also run the risk of having to pay the shipowner substantial sums in demurrage payments during this period.

Abandonment

General. Particular difficulties arise with 'as required' delivery terms in instal- **6.21** ment contracts. Sometimes, such contracts have been satisfied only in part, with the balance of delivery being overlooked until the buyer recovers his memory on a rising market. On the face of it, it seems unfair to permit a buyer to make a demand out of time binding on the seller. Nevertheless, if the contract has not yet been terminated for the buyer's breach, assuming the buyer to be in breach and the breach to be a discharging breach,[116] which may not be the case, the seller is in difficulties. Indeed, the rule has been laid down that the seller, prior to terminating for a failure to state requirements, must first give the buyer notice to state those requirements within a reasonable time,[117] which has some kinship with making time of the essence. Section 37(1) imposes a damages liability on a buyer who fails within a reasonable time to take delivery of the goods in response to a request of the seller, but sub-section (2) makes it plain that the remedy in sub-section (1) is without prejudice to any right the seller might otherwise have to terminate the contract for breach.

Abandonment by inactivity. The seller's difficulties have been surmounted by **6.22** inferring a mutual intention of both parties to abandon the contract, so far as it

---

[114] [1990] 1 WLR 1337.
[115] [1989] 2 Lloyd's Rep. 462, 468.
[116] Ch. 10 below.
[117] *Jones v Gibbons* (1853) 8 Ex. 920.

relates to undelivered instalments, in the wake of a protracted or 'inordinate' delay. In *Pearl Mill Co. Ltd v Ivy Tannery Co. Ltd*,[118] the contract was for 50 dozen roller skins 'as required'. Between November 1913 and September 1914, twenty dozen skins were delivered, but thereafter the buyers (as well as the sellers) appeared to forget about the order until the buyers demanded delivery of the remaining skins in July 1917. Between September 1914 and July 1917, the buyers turned down various proposals by the sellers to supply skins on the same terms under a new contract, gave an order to another supplier in July 1915 for 50 dozen skins and informed the sellers that all of their 1916 requirements had been met. It was held that the contract, so far as it related to the undelivered balance of 30 dozen skins, had been abandoned, as each party was entitled to infer this from the other's inactivity.[119] Although the result suppresses opportunistic behaviour by the buyer, the basis of abandonment requires further elaboration.

6.23 **Basis of abandonment.** The best starting point is that the buyer is under a duty to request delivery within a reasonable time; a failure to do so may amount to a repudiatory breach that may be accepted by the seller without communication.[120] Other approaches are to rationalize abandonment as a contract to abandon the balance of an agreement,[121] based upon mutual uncommunicated promises by the parties; or as the outcome of an implied term in the contract that a delivery lapse if not called for within a reasonable time,[122] or as based upon a representation or an estoppel that becomes binding upon the inactive buyer when the seller relies upon it or alters his position.[123] However abandonment is rationalized, it must be based on evidence supporting the clear intention of one party to abandon the contract and an assent of the other party to that abandonment.[124] The difficulty with a contract to abandon is that it is impossible to see how a contract can be concluded by silent offer and silent acceptance.[125] Offer and acceptance by conduct remains a possibility, although hard as a matter of interpretation to infer from

---

[118] [1919] 1 KB 78.

[119] McCardie J adds further that the buyers were estopped from demanding more deliveries: n. 118 above, 83–4.

[120] See *Andre et Cie SA v Marine Transocean Ltd (The Splendid Sun)* [1981] QB 694, 704 (Denning MR); *Allied Marine Transport v Vale do Rio Doce Navegacao SA (The Leonidas D)* [1985] 1 WLR 925, 928. In the latter case, Robert Goff LJ, 939, thought this the explanation of the *Pearl Mill* case, but it is difficult to see support for this view in the judgments in that case.

[121] *Moore v Crofton* (1846) 3 Jon. & L 438, 445: 'Abandonment of a contract . . . is a contract in itself.'

[122] See *The Leonidas D*, n. 120 above; *Food Corpn of India v Antclizo Shipping Corpn* [1988] 1 WLR 603.

[123] See *Collin v Duke of Westminster* [1985] QB 581, 595 (Oliver LJ); *Paal Wilson & Co. A/S v Partenreederei Hannah Blumenthal (The Hannah Blumenthal)* [1983] AC 854, 914 (Lord Brandon), 915–7 (Lord Diplock).

[124] *Thai-Europe Tapioca Service Ltd v Seine Navigation Co. Inc.* [1989] 2 Lloyd's Rep. 506.

[125] See *The Leonidas D*, n. 120 above, 936–7 (Robert Goff LJ.). Cf *Tankreederei Ahrenkeil GmbH v Frahuil SA (The Multitank Holsatia)* [1988] 2 Lloyd's Rep. 486, 513–14.

mutual inactivity.[126] A similar difficulty of interpretation impedes the inference of a binding estoppel.[127] What is clear is that a contract will not be treated as frustrated simply by mutual inactivity.[128]

Delivery, Acceptance, and Time of the Essence

General. A more prominent difficulty arising from the time of delivery is whether **6.24** timely delivery is of the essence of the contract. Because of the interlocking character of the seller's delivery and the buyer's acceptance duties, it is convenient to treat them together. A minor obstacle to this approach is section 27, which recites 'the *duty* . . . of the buyer to accept and pay for [the goods]'.[129] Notwithstanding this provision, it is better to treat the buyer as having separate primary duties of acceptance and payment, for it should not be assumed that the two duties will always be treated with the same degree of strictness. The Act separates acceptance and payment, in section 28 when making payment of the price and delivery mutual and concurrent conditions, and in section 10, which states that stipulations concerning payment are presumptively not of the essence of the contract. Nevertheless, a buyer on cash terms who declines to pay while expressing a willingness to accept delivery will be open to an action for damages for non-acceptance. His duty is to accept according to the terms of the contract,[130] and these do not allow for credit.[131]

Importance of timely performance. The basic rules of timely performance[132] **6.25** are, first, that the time of payment is presumptively not of the essence of the contract,[133] and, secondly, that it depends upon the construction of the contract whether any other term is of the essence.[134] Now, this section[135] makes no explicit mention of the doctrine of conditions and warranties, so dominant elsewhere in the Sale of Goods Act.[136] It also fails to lend support to intermediate stipulations or to failure of consideration and, by dividing time obligations into those that are and are not of the essence of the contract, produces a binary classification of its own on lines similar to condition and warranty. As for the words 'of the essence of

---

[126] *Food Corpn of India v Antclizo Shipping Corpn*, n. 122 above; *Gebr. van Weelde Scheepvaartkantor BV v Cia Naviera Sea Orient SA* [1987] 2 Lloyd's Rep. 223.

[127] See *The Hannah Blumenthal*, n. 123 above, 924 (Lord Brightman).

[128] *Ibid.*

[129] Emphasis added.

[130] S. 27.

[131] Similarly, a buyer to whom a bailee attorns (thereby effecting delivery by the seller) will be liable for non-acceptance if refusing to pay.

[132] See also ss. 37(1) and 48(3).

[133] S. 10(1).

[134] S. 10(2).

[135] Said by Mc Cardie J to give 'a very slender notion of the existing law': *Hartley v Hymans* [1920] 3 KB 475, 483.

[136] Ch. 10 below.

the contract', these seem to have originated in conveyancing practice and to have been transplanted into the common law of sale in imitation of equity's treatment of sale of land contracts;[137] in equity, time is presumptively not of the essence of the contract.[138] In drafting the Sale of Goods Act 1893, Chalmers for the most part faithfully followed the antecedent common law. It had in recent memory been firmly laid down by the House of Lords that the time of delivery in mercantile contracts, which comprised the great majority of reported cases before 1893, was of the essence of the contract.[139] On the face of it, section 10 is therefore strangely reticent in leaving the time of performance of non-payment obligations as an open question of contractual construction, unless this can be attributed to uncertainty surrounding the role to be played by equitable ideas of timely performance. The cases decided since sale was first codified have generally held that timely delivery and acceptance are of the essence of the contract in commercial cases.[140] They have usually failed to say why this should be so. Even where the issue is dealt with in some detail, discussion is confined to the particular type of contract before the court without canvassing the issue of timely performance in sale of goods law as a whole.[141] In the words of McCardie J in *Hartley v Hymans*: 'Now the common law and the law merchant did not make the question whether time was of the essence depend on the terms of the contract, unless indeed those terms were express on the point. It looked rather to the nature of the contract and the character of the goods dealt with.'[142]

6.26 **Intermediate stipulations.** Where time is held not to be of the essence, a problem arises concerning the suitability of introducing intermediate stipulations analysis to permit discharge when the breach goes to the root of the contract. Speaking of an f.o.b. buyer's duty to give notice of readiness to load, Lord Wilberforce stated that the intermediate stipulation analysis of Diplock LJ in *Hongkong Fir Shipping Co. Ltd v Kawasaki Kisen Kaisha Ltd*[143] is inappropriate, for there is only one kind of breach possible, namely to be late.[144] His lordship

---

[137] See *Martindale v Smith* (1841) 1 QB 389. In *United Scientific Holdings Ltd v Burnley Borough Council* [1978] AC 904, 925–6, Lord Diplock spoke of the common law's tendency, in the 19th century, to adopt a more rational scheme for classifying contractual obligations, thereby pre-empting equitable intervention.

[138] *Stickney v Keeble* [1915] AC 386; *United Scientific Holdings*, n. 137 above; *Seton v Slade* (1802) 7 Ves. Jun. 265.

[139] *Bowes v Shand* (1877) 2 App. Cas. 455. See also *Reuter, Hufeland & Co. v Sala & Co.* (1879) 4 CPD 239; *Coddington v Paleologo* (1867) LR 2 Ex. 193.

[140] e.g., *Hartley v Hymans* [1920] 3 KB 475.

[141] e.g., *Bunge Corpn v Tradax Export SA* [1981] 1 WLR 711; *Peter Turnbull & Co. Ltd v Mundus Trading Co. Pty Ltd* (1954) 90 CLR 235; *Toepfer v Lenersan-Poortman NV* [1980] 1 Lloyd's Rep. 143.

[142] n. 136 above, 483–4.

[143] [1962] 2 QB 26.

[144] *Bunge Corpn v Tradax SA*, n. 141 above, 715.

appeared to mean, however, that a time provision should be examined to see whether it is expressly or impliedly a condition before attention is turned to the question of its breach going to the root of the contract. It cannot be the law that, if a time provision fails to meet the test of a condition, there can never arise from the circumstances of its breach a right to terminate, for otherwise a party might be compelled to wait in a state of perpetual suspense for performance that will or might never arrive. That party must be entitled to assume eventually that late performance has become non-performance. A number of decisions on timely delivery are consistent in result with this approach and Lord Wilberforce's words are best understood as underlining the critical importance of time in f.o.b. shipments such that all relevant terms ought to be classified as conditions.

Timely Delivery

Delivery and time of the essence.   The leading case on the seller's duty of timely   **6.27** delivery is *Bowes v Shand*,[145] where a seller shipped the greater part of a quantity of Madras rice in February when the contract called for shipment 'during the months of March and/or April'. The buyer refused to accept the shipping documents since these included February bills of lading, and the House of Lords held that the seller's action for non-acceptance failed. The seller had not complied with all necessary conditions precedent since the time of shipment was part of the contractual description of the goods.[146] *Bowes v Shand* reveals a predisposition to solving problems of termination by contractual construction. This allows standard-form commodities contracts to be treated alike; the loss of flexibility in individual cases is compensated by certainty across the range of such transactions and amongst the various connected contracts in string trading conditions.[147] Apart from the observation that technical excuses may be used to escape from a bad bargain,[148] there is absent from the case any examination of the parties' behaviour in terms of the allocation of the risk of market rise and fall. It is difficult to see the seller's early shipment,[149] a venial transgression that had no effect on the quality of the rice at the port of discharge, as an attempt to speculate in the rice market at the buyer's expense. Further, the buyer's behaviour, apparently not associated with any grievance concerning the quality of the goods, is hard to explain except in terms of a determination to use any available excuse to avoid a falling market. Nor is there any discussion in the case of the hardship a seller might suffer by bringing goods at great expense from a distant location, only to have them rejected by the buyer.

---

[145] n. 139 above. See S. Stoljar (1955) 71 *LQR* 527, 533–7.

[146] Lord Blackburn. See also *Kwei Tek Chao v British Traders and Shippers Ltd* [1954] 2 QB 459, 480–1; *Finagrain SA Geneva v P. Kruse Hamburg* [1976] 2 Lloyd's Rep. 508, 540–1.

[147] *Bunge Corpn v Tradax SA*, n. 141 above.

[148] Lord Hatherley, n. 139 above, 476.

[149] Much of the report is taken up with the meaning of 'shipped', interpreted as loaded on board rather than leaving port.

The expense of carriage is one that the seller will bear in any event,[150] but the resale of the goods in distress circumstances or in thin trading conditions could mean that the loss suffered by the seller exceeds the market decline that a buyer accepting the goods would have experienced. The approach in *Bowes v Shand* might be admirably suited to ensuring predictability and certainty in a conventional commodities agreement, but it could well cause hardship in other sales contracts.

6.28 **Buyer's pre-delivery obligation.** The consistently strict attitude to time in commodities contracts and the desire to offer certainty to future contracting parties are revealed in *Bunge Corpn v Tradax SA*.[151] The f.o.b. sellers were required to ship 5,000 tonnes of soya meal in June at a Gulf of Mexico port of their own choice. It was the buyers' prior duty to nominate an effective ship and to give the sellers 15 days' notice of readiness to load. The buyers were intermediate parties in a string of connected contracts for June soya meal and therefore had to await a notice from the ultimate buyers before passing it on to their own sellers. Delays in the transmission of the notice at various points in the string meant that the buyers were four days late in passing this notice on to their own sellers.[152] The sellers therefore repudiated the contract[153] and sued for damages on a declining market.[154] The entitlement of the sellers to do this depended upon the status of the buyers' duty as a contractual condition, for the sellers did not argue that the buyers' breach in the circumstances went to the root of the contract. In both the Court of Appeal and the House of Lords, the buyers' duty was held to be a condition,[155] though both courts conceded that there was a role in sale of goods law for intermediate stipulations analysis.

6.29 **Reasons for time being of the essence.** *Bunge* reasserts the line taken in *Bowes v Shand* that the status of a contract term is a question of construction and therefore one of law; trade opinion might well be influential in this inquiry but it would not bind a court of construction.[156] The courts relied upon explicit policy arguments not discussed a hundred years before in *Bowes v Shand*. Commercial certainty was advanced by treating the buyer's pre-delivery obligation as a condition, since it

---

[150] The cost of freight would be reflected in the market price (albeit a falling one) commanded by the goods when sold in the importing country.

[151] N. 141 above; see M. Bridge (1983) 28 *McGill LJ* 867.

[152] For the circumstances of the delay, see the judgment of Parker J at [1981] 2 All ER 513.

[153] Rather this particular shipment, treated as a separate contract from the balance of the 15,000-tonnes contract.

[154] The report gives no reason for the sellers' behaviour. They may have been faced with difficulties of transport and storage (assuming they were the shippers) in managing their many contracts; they may have been imposing commercial discipline on the buyers; or they may have been taking a principled stand on the general importance of timely performance in commodities trading conditions.

[155] See also *Peter Turnbull & Co. Ltd v Mundus Trading Co. Pty Ltd*, n. 141 above.

[156] [1981] 2 All ER 513, 532 (Megaw LJ); [1981] 1 WLR 711, 730 (Lord Roskill).

preceded the seller's obligation to deliver, which was an established condition.[157] Treating the buyers' duty as a condition freed the sellers from having to make difficult judgements of the degree of prejudice emerging from evolving facts,[158] and avoided the risk of their prematurely, and thus unlawfully, repudiating the contract. Strict termination rights would also spare courts the task of dealing with difficult issues of damages assessment and would tend to avoid protracted trials and the cumbersome procedure of a seller issuing notice making time of the essence of the contract.[159] It was also emphasized that a strict rule of construction would facilitate the administration by commodities traders of complex arrays of continuing contracts and would bring about consistency of result for each contract in a sales string.[160] Furthermore, the rule could not be criticized as unduly pro-seller since one of the characteristics of the commodities trade is that the identities of seller and buyer are interchangeable.[161] The point was also made that any decision treating the buyers' duty as less than a contractual condition would be an 'arrogant and unjustifiable' interference with the parties' own assessment that 15 days' notice was reasonable, presumably because it would give the buyers more time to perform.[162] The flaw in this argument is that, even if the term were not a condition, the buyers would still be in breach for giving only eleven days' notice, and it is difficult to see any interference where the parties have refrained from expressly designating a term as a condition.[163]

Certainty. Finally, the courts involved in the *Bunge* litigation were keen to **6.30** promote certainty, not merely in the relations of the buyers and sellers *inter se*, but in commodities trading as a whole. The contracts here are invariably standard form and amount in substance to a form of private legislation assented to by those in the trade; it is the form that is being interpreted rather than the particular contract, as shown by the policy arguments relied upon and the deference to antecedent commercial practice and established trade opinion. The demands of certainty also require that the parties' clear designation of a term should be respected, hence the impatience shown for arguments tending to undermine the autonomy

---

157 [1981] 1 WLR 711, 729 (Lord Roskill); *PT Berlian Laju Tanker TBK v Nuse Shipping Ltd* [2008] EWHC 1330 (Comm) at [66]; *Mansel Oil Ltd v Troon Storage Tankers SA* [2008] EWHC 1269 (Comm) at [62]. Cf *Kidston & Co. v Monceau Ironworks Co.*, n. 46 above (discussed below).

158 n. 156 above, 536 (Megaw LJ); see J. A. Weir [1976] CLJ 33.

159 n. 157 above, 545–6 (Lord Lowry).

160 *Ibid.*

161 *Ibid.*

162 n. 156 above, 532 (Megaw LJ).

163 In *Tarrabochia v Hickie* (1856) 1 H & N 183, 188, Bramwell B said: 'No doubt it is competent for the parties, if they think fit, to declare in express terms that any matter shall be a condition precedent, but when they have not so expressed themselves, it is necessary for those who construe the instrument to see whether they intended to do it. Since, however, they could have done it, those who construe the instrument should be chary in doing for them that which they might, but have not done for themselves.'

of the parties[164] by requiring a particular breach to go in fact to the root of the contract before termination is allowed.[165]

6.31 Other obligations.   Similar obligations concerning the time of performance in commodities contracts have been treated as contractual conditions.[166] Consistently with the line taken in voyage charter cases,[167] the 'expected ready to load' clause in sale of goods has always been regarded as a contractual condition.[168] Obligations relating to the timely tender of shipping documents have also been treated as being of the essence of the contract.[169] It has been held, however, that the duty of the c.i.f. seller seeking to invoke a prohibition clause when exports are prevented or impaired by governmental action is not an implied condition but rather an intermediate stipulation.[170] But the buyer's performance in such a case is not affected by the receipt of a timely notice from the seller. In addition, there are exceptional cases where the time of performance in international commodity sales has been held not to be of the essence of the contract,[171] and the adoption of charterparty clauses in sale contracts has led to a similar outcome where damages have been seen as an adequate remedy for the breach of that same clause in charterparty contracts.[172]

6.32 Particular contracts.   While these commodities decisions bear out with great force the proposition that time is normally of the essence, the strictness they reveal should not unthinkingly be extended to all other mercantile contracts. Suppose a

---

  164 See *Bettini v Gye* (1876) 1 QBD 183.
  165 See the treatment in *Bunge*, n. 141 above, at 714–9, 724–7 and 730, of the judgment of Diplock LJ in *Hongkong Fir Shipping Co. Ltd v Kawasaki Kisen Kasha* [1962] 2 QB 26.
  166 *Graves v Legg* (1857) 2 H & N 210; *Bowes v Shand*, n. 78 above; *Reuter, Hufeland & Co. v Sala & Co.*, n. 139 above; *Cie Continentale d'Importation v Handelsvertretung der Union* (1928) 44 TLR 297; *Bremer Handelsgesellschaft mbH v J H Rayner & Co. Ltd* [1979] 2 Lloyd's Rep. 216; *Toepfer v Lenersan-Poortman NV* [1980] 1 Lloyd's Rep. 143; *Société Italo-Belge pour le Commerce et l'Industrie v Palm and Vegetable Oils (Malaysia) Sdn Bhd (The Post Chaser)*, n. 94 above; *Bergerco USA v Vegoil Ltd* [1984] 1 Lloyd's Rep. 440; *Tradax Export SA v Italgrani di Francesco Ambrosio* [1983] 2 Lloyd's Rep. 109; *Scandinavian Trading Co. A/B v Zodiac Petroleum SA* [1981] 1 Lloyd's Rep. 81; *Gill & Dufus SA v Soc. pour l'Exportation des Sucres SA* [1986] 1 Lloyd's Rep. 322; *Cie Commerciale Sucres et Denrées v Czarnikow Ltd* [1990] 1 WLR 1337. Cf *Phibro Energy AG v Nissho Iwai Corpn (The Honam Jade)* [1991] 1 Lloyd's Rep. 38.
  167 *Behn v Burness* (1863) 3 B & S 751; *Maredelanto Cia Naviera SA v Bergbau-Handels GmbH (The Mihalis Angelos)* [1971] 1 QB 64.
  168 *The Mihalis Angelos*, n. 167 above; *Finnish Govt v H. Ford & Co.* (1921) 6 Ll. LR 188.
  169 *Toepfer v Lenersan-Poortman NV*, n. 166 above.
  170 *Bremer Handelsgesellschaft mbH v Vanden-Avenne Izegem PVBA* [1978] 2 Lloyd's Rep. 109; *Bunge SA v Kruse* [1979] 1 Lloyd's Rep. 209. This notice has been said not to be 'part of the machinery of performance': *Société Italo-Belge pour le Commerce et l'Industrie v Palm and Vegetable Oils (Malaysia) Sdn Bhd (The Post Chaser)*, n. 94 above, 699.
  171 *Phibro Energy AG v Nissho Iwai Corpn (The Honam Jade)*, n. 166 above (seller's duty of timely acceptance of buyer's nomination of ship).
  172 *ERG Raffinerie Méditerranée SpA v Chevron USA Inc. (The Luxmar)* [2007] EWCA Civ 494; [2007] 2 All E.R. (Comm.) 248.

seller has to gather raw materials and over an extended period erect a machine to the buyer's personal specifications. Where buyer and seller are committed to a cooperative enterprise of this kind, where various communications are likely to pass between them before delivery, a punctilious concern for time backed up by draconian termination rights is unlikely to be set out expressly in the contract. All sorts of unpredictable factors may affect the seller's ability to perform on time under a complex contract of this type, and the buyer's concerns can be met by a negotiated liquidated damages or price reduction clause. An application of the *Bunge* reasoning to such a contract would be out of place, especially since no ready market would exist for a custom-built machine unwanted by the buyer, and since a defaulting seller would therefore be excessively prejudiced by termination of the contract[173] and vulnerable to oppressive renegotiation on the part of the buyer. A court, it is submitted, should be unwilling to construe or recognize an implied or express intention to permit termination for late delivery where a buyer of this sort has not suffered a substantial detriment.[174]

Contrary intention. In other cases, the contract may point away from time **6.33** being of the essence, as it did where a cancellation clause permitted termination after a stated period of delay, thereby negativing time being of the essence of the agreed delivery date.[175] The failure of a contract to state a delivery date, so that a reasonable time has to be implied,[176] makes it unlikely that time will be regarded as of the essence.[177] Instead, the length of a reasonable time is likely to flow into the assessment of a frustrating delay as account is taken of the attainment by the buyer of his contractual purpose. The existence of a breach and its severity would thus be conflated. A different conclusion might, however, follow if the parties explicitly stipulate for performance within a reasonable time, especially if a reasonable time is expressed to run from a stated date.[178] Time will not normally be of the essence of a contract for the delivery of consumer goods.[179] On the other

---

[173] See the old inequality of damages argument in *Duke of St Albans v Shore* (1789) 1 H Bl. 270.

[174] See *Paton & Sons v Payne & Co.* (1897) 35 SLR 112 (printing machine).

[175] *Steel Co. of Canada v Dominion Radiator Co. Ltd* (1919) 48 DLR 350.

[176] S. 29(3).

[177] *D.T.R. Nominees Pty Ltd v Mona Homes Pty Ltd* (1978) 138 CLR 423, 430.

[178] In *McDougall v Aeromarine of Emsworth Ltd* [1958] 3 All ER 431, 439, Diplock J thought such an obligation a condition. Cf *DTR Nominees Pty Ltd v Mona Homes Pty Ltd*, n. 177 above, 430 (Stephen, Mason, and Jacobs JJ): '[W]e fail to see how a stipulation calling for action to be taken expeditiously of itself constitutes an essential term.' In *Société Italo-Belge pour le Commerce et l'Industrie v Palm and Vegetable Oils (Malaysia) Sdn Bhd (The Post Chaser)*, n. 94 above, 699, Robert Goff J was of the view that an obligation to nominate a ship 'as soon as possible after vessel's sailing' was a condition.

[179] *Allen v Danforth Motors Ltd* (1957) 12 DLR (2d) 572. For a case where time was not of the essence of a contract for the delivery of machinery for the use of the commercial buyer, see *Paton & Sons v Payne & Co.*, n. 174 above.

hand, special factors may point to the time of delivery as essential, as they did in one case where a ring had to be supplied in time for a silver wedding celebration.[180] Furthermore, if the delivery date is far advanced so as to give the seller ample time to perform by the agreed date, time is more likely to be regarded as of the essence, especially if the buyer announces well in advance that he needs the goods for a particular purpose at that time.[181] By stating a paramount need, the buyer has notified the seller that delayed performance will substantially deprive him of the benefit of the bargain as effectively as if time had expressly been declared to be of the essence of the contract. In cases like the last two, the same result will flow whether time is classified as a condition or as an intermediate stipulation.

6.34 **Making time of the essence.** Supposing that time is not of the essence of the contract, the next question is whether it can become so by subsequent events. It was an equitable innovation that time, initially at large, could by notice later be made of the essence of the contract.[182] The process, explicable in sale of land agreements where it was difficult to make title, is hardly fitted to commercial contracts,[183] especially those involving goods. Where a notice may be given, there is no need to wait until an undue or improper delay has occurred; the notice may be served as soon as the time for performance has expired.[184] Under existing common law principles, a buyer or seller should not be able to serve a notice making time of the essence if the effect of so doing would produce a unilateral variation of the contract.[185] In the case of a sale of goods contract, therefore, the significance of serving a notice is probably best seen as crystallizing the period of delay that will produce a breach going to the root of the contract.[186]

Timely Acceptance

6.35 **Introduction.** Since a seller cannot deliver unless a buyer actually or constructively accepts the goods, the buyer's duty to accept the goods on time should be treated with the same degree of strictness or leniency, as the case may be, as the

---

[180] *Alteen's Jewellers Ltd v Cann* (1980) 40 NSR 504 (Can.).
[181] See *Charles Rickards Ltd v Oppenhaim* [1950] 1 KB 616.
[182] *United Scientific Holdings Ltd v Burnley Borough Council* [1978] AC 904, 928; *Cornwall v Henson* [1900] 2 Ch. 298. For the import of making time of the essence of sale of goods agreements, see *Lambert v Slack* [1924] 2 DLR 166, 170; *Portaria Shipping Co. v Gulf Pacific Navigation Co. Ltd* [1981] 2 Lloyd's Rep. 180, 185; *Charles Rickards Ltd v Oppenhaim*, n. 181 above.
[183] *British and Commonwealth Holdings Plc v Quadrex Holdings Inc.* [1989] QB 842, 856 *et seq.*
[184] *Behzadi v Shaftesbury Hotels Ltd* [1991] 2 All ER 477, disapproving on this point *British and Commonwealth Holdings Plc v Quadrex Holdings Inc.*, n. 183 above.
[185] *Behzadi v Shaftesbury Hotels Ltd*, n. 184 above, 496; *Astea (UK) Ltd v Time Publishing Group Ltd* [2003] EWHC 725 (TCC) at [147]–[148].
[186] A form of making time of the essence also appears in the United Nations Convention for the International Sale of Goods (Vienna, 1980). The buyer or seller can fix an additional reasonable time for performance and may declare the contract avoided if performance does not occur by that date: Arts 47, 49(1)(b), 63, 64(1)(b).

seller's duty to deliver. The same reasoning does not apply to duties of the buyer that are anterior to the seller's duty to deliver, though the courts are loth to deny the status of condition to a duty that interlocks with a duty of the seller that is a condition.[187]

Time of the essence of acceptance. The rather thin case law on acceptance by the buyer shows that it cannot easily be determined whether time will be of the essence. The approach of the courts is sometimes based upon a construction of the contract, but sometimes, consistently with intermediate stipulations analysis, takes account of the consequences of breach. This latter approach is evident in one case where the buyer was one working day late after declining, for religious reasons, to collect goods from the auctioneer's premises on a Saturday. The seller was not entitled to terminate.[188] Time was also held not to be of the essence in *Kidston & Co. v Monceau Ironworks Co.*,[189] where the buyers were late in furnishing specifications for a quantity of iron to be manufactured by the sellers. The buyers' duty had to be performed before the sellers could ship the goods in May or June as required by the contract, but the court emphasized that the buyers' failure to provide the specifications due at the beginning of May did not impede the sellers' ability to organize their production schedule and arrange for shipment within the contract period. Assuming timely performance by the buyers, the sellers' duty to deliver would probably have been treated as of the essence of the contract, and yet the buyers' anterior duty was dealt with in a way consistent with modern intermediate stipulations analysis. This is at odds with *Bunge,*[190] where the buyers' duty to give notice of readiness to load was treated as necessarily a condition because the sellers' ensuing duty of delivery was a condition.[191] But *Bunge* was a commodities case where commercial certainty was advanced by consistent treatment of the standard form throughout the trade and down the contractual string. The contract in *Kidston*, though a commonplace one, was by no means of such a standard type and it did not take place in volatile market conditions. Furthermore, though the point is not raised in *Kidston*, it is not illogical to treat a buyer's duty to give timely specifications as an intermediate stipulation and, to the extent of the buyer's default, allow the seller to use this as a defence if used for his own forced failure to deliver on time. The buyer's breach could operate so as to suspend or retard the seller's duty of timely delivery where the buyer's delinquency eats into the time reasonably available to the seller to perform.

6.36

---

[187] *Bunge Corpn v Tradax SA*, n. 141 above.
[188] *Woolfe v Horne* (1877) 2 QBD 355.
[189] n. 46 above.
[190] n. 141 above.
[191] See also *PT Berlian Laju Tanker TBK v Nuse Shipping Ltd* [2008] EWHC 1330 (Comm) at [66]; *Mansel Oil Ltd v Troon Storage Tankers SA* [2008] EWHC 1269 (Comm) at [62].

6.37 **Spot transaction.** Time was, however, treated as of the essence in a 'spot' transaction for the sale of ten bales of Hessian bags, cash payment against a delivery
order on or before 19 September. The sellers were responsible for storage and
insurance up to that date and the clearly expeditious character of the c.o.d transaction supported the court's conclusion that time was of the essence of the buyers'
duty to take delivery.[192] According to Sankey J: '[T]he whole object of the contract
was to make a bargain that should be completed by the buyers at least by September
19.'[193] Time was also held to be of the essence in a case involving the sale of
potatoes to be shipped by canal before Christmas, emphasis being laid upon the
perishable nature of the goods.[194]

Equitable Ideas

6.38 **Fusion of law and equity.** Any treatment of the strictness of timely delivery and
acceptance would be incomplete if it failed to take account of attempts made over
the years to introduce equitable ideas to counter the strictness of the common
law's approach to timely performance. The fusion in 1873 of the courts of equity
and common law, with the consequent administration of principles of equity and
common law in the same judicial system, led to the enactment of a rule[195] modified in 1925[196] to read as follows: 'Stipulations in a contract, as to time or otherwise, which according to rules of equity are not deemed to be or to have become
of the essence of the contract, are also to be construed and have effect in law in
accordance with the same rules.' In *Reuter, Hufeland & Co. v Sala & Co.*,[197] a case
of a c.i.f. contract for the sale of 25 tons of Penang pepper, one of the issues
concerned the sellers' duty to tender properly dated bills of lading, which was held
to a condition of the contract. Cotton LJ said:

> It was argued that the rules of equity are now to be regarded in all courts, and that
> equity enforced contracts though the time fixed therein for completion had passed.
> This was in cases of contracts such as purchases and sales of land, where, unless a
> contrary intention could be collected from the contract, the Court presumed that
> time was not an essential condition. To apply this to mercantile contracts would be
> dangerous and unreasonable . . . [T]he decisions in equity, on which reliance is
> placed, do not apply.[198]

The same view was stated in *Stickney v Keeble*,[199] where it was asserted that the
equitable view on time was a component of the doctrine of specific performance

---

192 *Thames Sack and Bag Co. Ltd v Knowles & Co. Ltd* (1918) 88 LJ KB 585.
193 *Ibid.*, 587.
194 *Sharp v Christmas* (1892) 8 TLR 687.
195 Supreme Court of Judicature Act 1873, s. 25(7).
196 Law of Property Act 1925, s. 41.
197 (1879) 4 CPD 239.
198 *Ibid.*, 249.
199 [1915] AC 386.

and applied only to the type of contract falling within the jurisdiction to grant that remedy. A provision like section 41 of the Law of Property Act should not therefore be understood as allowing the infiltration of equitable ideas throughout the whole law of contract but should be confined to the types of contract, linked to the doctrine of specific performance, that preoccupied equity before fusion. Since equity's concern with sale of goods contracts was minimal, and specific performance rarely granted, it would follow that section 41 should have little, if any, impact upon the law of sale of goods. Some uncertainty stems from the House of Lords decision in *United Scientific Holdings Ltd v Burnley Borough Council*,[200] which concerned a rent review clause in a long-term lease of commercial premises. Opinions were expressed that equity should not be frozen in its pre-fusion boundaries but should be free to expand or retract as the case may be.[201] If such a resurgent equity were to be allowed into commercial sale of goods agreements, it would be destructive of the certainty and forward-planning valued so highly by the House of Lords in *Bunge Corpn v Tradax SA*.[202] Concessions were, however, made in *United Scientific Holdings* that the time of delivery remained of the essence in commercial sale of goods agreements. It cannot be said that the position will never change, but the entitlement of parties to designate a term as a contractual condition,[203] and the general rule that time of delivery is of the essence of commercial sales contracts, have both survived attempts made to undermine them by praying in aid equitable principles.

The Seller's Duty to Deliver the Agreed Quantity

General. The Sale of Goods Act is strict in the duty it lays on the seller in section **6.39** 30 to deliver the agreed quantity, for the buyer is entitled to reject the goods if the seller tenders more,[204] or fewer,[205] goods than the agreed amount. These provisions are all subject to any trade usage, special agreement, or course of dealing between the parties.[206] Section 30 does not state explicitly that it is a breach of contract for the seller to deliver the wrong quantity of goods. It is therefore unclear whether the seller may cure the defective delivery within the delivery period.[207] A surplus or shortfall will often be evident at the point of delivery. If the buyer rejects the seller's tender, there is a case for saying that the seller may re-tender. The difficulty here is that the buyer may accept, for example, a short tender and then sue

---

[200] n. 182 above.
[201] *Ibid.*, 924–8 (Lord Diplock); 940–7 (Lord Simon); 957–8 (Lord Fraser).
[202] n. 141 above.
[203] *Bunge Corpn v Tradax SA*, n. 141 above, clearly shows this to have survived *United Scientific Holdings*.
[204] S. 30(2).
[205] S. 30(1).
[206] S. 30(5).
[207] See Ch. 10 below.

for damages[208] without, it seems, having to apprise the seller first of the short tender (if the seller does not already know). No confident statement may therefore be made about the seller's right or lack of right to cure. The buyer's right to reject the wrong quantity has been modified in a different way in modern times. In non-consumer cases, the buyer no longer has the right to reject goods, since changes to the Sale of Goods Act introduced by the Sale and Supply of Goods Act 1994, where the excess or shortfall is so slight that rejection would be unreasonable.[209] No guidance is given as to what is a slight excess or shortage. The burden of showing a slight departure from the agreed quantity and the unreasonableness of the buyer's behaviour rests upon the seller.[210]

Entire or Severable?

6.40 **Construction.** Some contracts raise difficult questions of construction as to whether severable (or instalment) delivery is permitted. For example, a contract calling for delivery 'as required' might, as seen above, be interpreted in various ways. Commodities contracts present difficulties too, largely because of the mismatch between the language of the standard form and the expectations generated by a particular contractual adventure, but also because of the modern practice of bulk shipments. In *Cobec Brazilian Trading and Warehousing Corpn v Alfred C Toepfer*,[211] a c. & f. contract for the sale of 25,000 tonnes of Argentinian soya beans incorporated the terms of the FOSFA 22 form, which contained the usual provision that each shipment, if more than one were made, should be regarded as a separate contract. Of the 25,000 tonnes, it was agreed that about 19,000 tonnes should be discharged in Santander and about 6,000 tonnes in Seville. The contract called for shipment between 25 June and 10 July. More than 18,000 tonnes were shipped before 10 July; the rest were shipped on 14 July and the ship sailed on the following day. The buyers were held entitled to reject the entire shipment. The contract created an indivisible duty to ship by 10 July, and did not call for delivery in two instalments for Santander and for Seville. Had this been the case, the timely bills could have been applied to the Santander goods and the buyers could have been required to accept them. Separate bills of lading had been issued, a factor favouring divisibility, but other factors tilted the balance in favour of indivisibility. The loading schedule and storage plan of the vessel revealed that, on the sellers' construction, the so-called Santander cargo, despite having to be discharged earlier, was overstowed by the Seville cargo. The FOSFA 22 form was designed to cover a broad range of contractual expectations and a reference to the

---

[208] See below.
[209] S. 30(2A). See the discussion of the companion provision, s. 15A, in Ch. 10 below. See below for discussion of unreasonableness.
[210] S. 30(2B).
[211] [1982] 1 Lloyd's Rep. 528, affirmed [1983] 2 Lloyd's Rep. 386.

possibility of separate shipments did not create such a right on the present occasion.

Election to sever. The *Cobec* case shows why sellers should be keen to argue for **6.41** the severability of the contract. If the contract falls to be disposed of under the repudiatory breach regime of section 31(2), or the common law equivalent, so that the buyer is entitled to terminate only if the breach goes to the root of the contract, this is more tolerant of the seller's quantitative and temporal failings than is section 30(1). In *Reuter, Hufeland & Co. v Sala & Co.*,[212] the contract was for the sale of 25 tons of Penang pepper 'October and/or November shipment . . . per sailing vessel or vessels . . . [t]he name of the vessel or vessels . . . to be declared . . . within sixty days from date of bill of lading'. The seller appropriated to the contract three parcels of pepper shipped on the same vessel. The bill of lading for one of these parcels (five tons) was dated outside the shipment period in December. The buyers asserted they could reject all the bills of lading, even the two representing the 20 tons shipped in time. The Court of Appeal nevertheless held that the seller's delivery obligation was indivisible. Thesiger LJ interpreted the contract as conferring on the seller an election to make divisible or indivisible delivery[213] which, by appropriating three parcels on the same vessel, the sellers had irrevocably exercised in favour of indivisibility so as to fall foul of section 30(1). The same view appears to have been taken by the other majority judge, Cotton LJ, who stated that the severability option could only have been exercised by shipment on board more than one vessel.[214]

Instalments and Quantity

Quantity and section 30. Even if a contract allows for instalment delivery, the **6.42** conjunction of sections 30 and 31 prompts the question whether a seller may call upon the buyer to accept any instalments at all if it is plain that the seller will be unable to tender the whole of the contractually agreed amount by the end of the delivery period, because, for example, the right to tender one or more instalments has lapsed. Section 31(2) refers to 'defective' deliveries by the seller, which might imply that matters of quantity are dealt with by section 30. There is furthermore a mirror problem, that of the buyer who in similar circumstances has failed to accept delivery. While there is an argument that section 30(1) could apply to the seller's short delivery, it is not in its terms capable of applying to the non-accepting buyer. It would obviously be unreasonable to treat these two cases with differing degrees of severity. In addition, the language of section 31(2) is more apt to cover

---

212 n. 139 above.
213 *Ibid.*, 246–7.
214 *Ibid.*, 250–1.

the defaulting buyer.[215] In *Regent OHG Aisenstadt und Barig v Francesco of Jermyn Street Ltd*,[216] the court had to deal with the conflict between sections 30(1) and 31(2) and with the need to subordinate one to the other in instalment contracts.[217] It also observed that the latter provision was more consistent with the modern emphasis in contractual termination on intermediate stipulation analysis, and that 'the business sense of a contract of sale requires the more flexible provisions of s. 31(2) to be applied in preference to those of s. 30(1)'.[218] The contract was for the sale of 62 men's suits and 48 jackets for delivery in instalments at the sellers' discretion over a three-month period. The buyers unlawfully repudiated the contract before the sellers, in accordance with their plan to dispatch the goods in five consignments, tendered the first three of these to the buyers, who refused them all. The sellers then informed the buyers that, owing to a shortage of cloth, they would be unable to tender one of the suits they had planned to ship in the fourth consignment; this was confirmed by the invoice sent with that consignment. The buyers refused this consignment as well as the fifth, which confirmed the overall shortfall of one suit. Sued for damages for non-acceptance, the buyers' technical defence was that the sellers' failure to tender the missing suit vitiated all the tenders under section 30(1). Although the defence would have been sound if the contract had been indivisible,[219] the court held that the contract was for delivery by instalments. Hence the issue was governed by section 31(2)[220] and the breach did not go to the root of the contract.

6.43 First instalment. In another chapter,[221] a number of instalment delivery cases are discussed that reveal a stricter attitude to breaches occurring on the delivery of the first instalment.[222] This differentiation between instalment breaches does not readily accord with the repudiatory breach test laid down in section 31(2), first enacted after these cases were decided. Moreover, to the extent that these cases suggest in matters of quantity a preference for the stricter standard of section 30(1) when the contract is still at the executory stage, they are also hard to reconcile with the *Regent* case and so are unlikely to represent the modern law.

6.44 Rejecting individual instalments. A final point emerging from *Regent* concerns a buyer's right to reject individual instalments even though the contract as a whole may not be terminated because the breach does not go to the root of the contract.

---

[215] '[T]he buyer neglects or refuses to take delivery of or pay for one or more instalments.'

[216] [1981] 3 All ER 327.

[217] *Ibid.*, 334.

[218] *Ibid.*

[219] *Ibid.*, 334. Section 30(2A) (see below) was not then in force.

[220] Although a divisible contract, it is not properly speaking governed by s. 31(2), which applies to delivery by 'stated' instalments, but rather by an identical common law principle.

[221] See Ch. 10.

[222] *Viz.*, *Simpson v Crippen* (1872) LR 8 QB 14; *Honck v Muller* (1881) 7 QBD 92.

Although there is little authority, it seems to be the law that the rejection of an individual instalment is governed by the principles of termination of indivisible contracts,[223] at least if the breach concerns quality or time. There seems no reason to exclude the same approach for quantitative lapses. In cases where the instalments are stated in precise quantities and the timetabling rigid, this will no doubt result in the lapse of the buyer's obligations regarding the goods covered by the rejected instalment.[224] But a seller with the latitude given by the contract in *Regent* could organize his tenders in such a way as to minimize the damage that would be caused by the rejection of an instalment and defer the deficiency until all the clothing bar the missing suit has been tendered and accepted.

Indivisible (or Entire) Contracts and Short Delivery

Short delivery.   Where the contract is indivisible, section 30(1) is given free rein.   **6.45** The buyer is entitled to reject the short delivery but, if accepting it,[225] must pay at the contract rate.[226] If the buyer has already paid in full and desires to retain the goods delivered, the buyer may recover the excess price[227] and may sue for damages for short delivery.[228] As for the nature of the quantitative standard in section 30(1), the cases show that even a minor lapse will not be excused,[229] even if the seller has no intention of pursuing the buyer for that part of the price referable to the missing goods. There is no room for the application of a substantial compliance doctrine[230] which would allow the seller to claim the price subject to a damages counterclaim, or simply sue for damages for non-acceptance.[231] In some contracts, the quantity stated is merely a conditional or benchmark figure, the seller undertaking to supply up to a certain amount or no more than a certain amount according to availability. A delivery short of this figure does not infringe section 30(1).[232] In allowing a buyer to reject a short delivery, section 30(1) should be read in conjunction with section 31(1), which states that in the absence of a

---

223 This is now recognized by implication in s. 35A(2). It is also reinforced in international sale contracts containing an express clause that each shipment is to be treated as a separate contract.

224 See also the discussion of *Pearl Mill Co. Ltd v Ivy Tannery Co. Ltd* [1919] 1 KB 78.

225 For a waiver of the buyer's right to the missing quantity, see the discussion of waiver below.

226 S. 30(1) thus codifies *Oxendale v Wetherell* (1829) 9 B&C 386.

227 See below.

228 *Colonial Insurance Co. of New Zealand v Adelaide Marine Insurance Co.* (1886) 12 App. Cas. 128, 139; *Household Machines Ltd v Cosmos Exporters Ltd* [1947] KB 217; *European Grain & Shipping Ltd v Peter Cremer* [1983] 2 Lloyd's Rep. 211, 216.

229 *Harland and Wolff Ltd v J Burstall & Co.* (1901) 84 LT 324 (470 instead of 500 loads of timber); *Regent OHG Aisenstadt und Barig v Francesco of Jermyn Street Ltd*, n. 218 above, 334 (if the contract had been indivisible, the absence of one suit from a tender of 62 suits and 48 jackets would have been fatal).

230 See *H Dakin & Co. Ltd v Lee* [1916] 1 KB 566; *Hoenig v Isaacs* [1952] 2 All ER 176.

231 *Arcos Ltd v EA Ronaasen & Son* [1933] AC 470.

232 *Goldsborough Mort & Co. Ltd v Carter* (1914) 19 CLR 429; *Symes v Hutley* (1860) 2 LT 509; *Arbuthnot v Streckeisen* (1866) 35 LJCP 305.

contrary agreement a buyer is not bound to accept delivery by instalments. If the parties have not agreed to severable delivery, the seller may not deliver some of the goods on account.[233]

6.46 **Illustrative case.** Section 30(1) is illustrated by *Behrend & Co. v Produce Brokers Co.*,[234] a case concerning two contracts for the sale of 176 and 400 tons of cotton seed on *ex* ship London terms, delivery to occur on discharge into the buyers' craft alongside the ship. Because of the way the goods had been stowed, the carrier was able to discharge only 15 tons of one contractual parcel and 22 tons of the other. The remaining quantities were stowed under other cargo that had first to be discharged in Hull before the vessel returned to London two weeks later to discharge the balance of the contract goods. Prior to the vessel's return, the buyers notified the sellers that they would not accept the balance of the goods. They were held entitled to do this; it mattered not that the problem was caused by the way the carrier stowed the cargo. Had the contract been on f.o.b. instead of *ex* ship terms, delivery would have occurred as the goods were received on board and the buyers would have borne the risk of the carrier's stowage plan.[235]

6.47 **Microscopic and slight shortfall.** If the carrier in *Behrend* had discharged the whole of its cargo in one continuous process, it should not have mattered if the buyers' goods had come out in irregular intervals punctuated by goods destined for other consignees. In a similar spirit, the courts will tolerate microscopic (but not minor)[236] deviations from the contractual amount falling within the maxim *de minimis non curat lex*,[237] though there is a dearth of authority showing the successful application of this maxim in cases of short as opposed to long delivery.[238] It is uncertain what the new section 30(2A) adds to the *de minimis* maxim; it prevents the rejection of a short tender by a non-consumer buyer where the shortfall is slight and rejection would be unreasonable. It must add something since, unlike the *de minimis* maxim, it does not apply to consumer buyers, but it is unlikely to stretch any appreciable distance beyond the *de minimis* limits. In particular, it cannot be said with confidence that the reasonableness of the buyer's behaviour

---

[233] *Reuter, Hufeland & Co. v Sala & Co.*, n. 139 above.

[234] [1920] 3 KB 530. See also *Oxendale v Wetherell*, n. 226 above; *Morgan v Gath* (1865) 3 H & C 748.

[235] Similarly, if the goods are sold on c.i.f. terms and the seller delivers the correct amount to the carrier, the buyer will not be able to reject the goods for bad stowage—established by implication in *Berger & Co. Inc. v Gill and Duffus SA* [1984] AC 382.

[236] n. 229 above.

[237] *Margaronis Navigation Agency Ltd v Henry W Peabody & Co. Ltd* [1965] 2 QB 430 (obligation to load full and complete cargo under charterparty: 12,588.2 tons instead of 12,600 tons).

[238] The resistance of the *de minimis* maxim in matters of description may be seen in cases such as *Arcos Ltd v EA Ronaasen & Son* [1933] AC 470; *Rapalli v KL Take Ltd* [1958] 2 Lloyd's Rep. 469; *Wilensko Slaski Towarzystwo Drewno v Fenwick & Co. (West Hartlepool) Ltd* [1938] 3 All ER 429.

depends upon whether the seller is willing to impose no charge for an excess.[239] There is an argument that a seller who refuses to give a price rebate for a short delivery will be unable to complain that, though the shortfall is slight, the buyer's conduct in rejecting the goods is unreasonable. But the buyer's right to reject is lost, not when the quantitative difference is slight *and* it would be unreasonable to reject, but when it is so slight *that* it would be unreasonable to reject. In other words, the unreasonableness of the buyer's action is measured by the quantitative shortcoming and not by other aspects of the seller's conduct.

New contract. Section 30(1) also provides that a buyer accepting the lesser   **6.48** quantity tendered must pay for them at the contract rate,[240] though it will be open to the parties to agree a fair value instead, a suitable approach where the shortfall upsets unit price calculations. If the buyer accepts the shortfall, it seems correct to regard this as entry into a new contract[241] for the following reasons. First, even before the introduction of the new right of partial rejection,[242] a buyer accepting a shortfall under an entire contract was surely entitled to refuse a tender of the balance by the seller at a later date. Secondly, where a portion of the agreed goods is removed by the buyer from a contractual parcel of whose quantitative deficiency he is justifiably ignorant, the buyer will be bound to pay only for the goods actually removed. He will not be bound to bear the risk of shrinkage in the diminished parcel occurring after delivery.[243] Thirdly, a buyer who accepts a shortfall having already paid is entitled to sue for the balance of the price as on a failure of consideration,[244] which is difficult to explain where the buyer has obtained a benefit under the original contract. But the result is acceptable if the buyer's partial recovery of the price paid is seen as a recovery in full of the price paid under the original contract subject to a set-off of the lesser price owed to the seller for the goods accepted under the new contract. The new contract will not as such expunge the original one. The mere acceptance of a shortfall under a new contract should not

---

239 If there is a shortfall, s. 30(1) already reduces the price by requiring the buyer to pay at the contract rate. Where the buyer freely elects to accept more goods, payment is to be made at the contract rate: s. 30(3).

240 *Shipton v Casson* (1826) 5 B & C 378 (action by buyer and set-off by seller of value of delivered goods).

241 Whether implied in fact or on a restitutionary basis. The new contract should not prejudice the buyer's right to damages in respect of the deficiency: cf *Gabriel Wade & English Ltd v Arcos Ltd* (1929) 34 LL LR 306.

242 Cf s. 35A.

243 See *Barrow, Lane & Ballard Ltd v Phillip Phillips & Co. Ltd* [1929] 1 KB 574.

244 *Behrend & Co. Ltd v Produce Brokers Co*, n. 234 above; *Ebrahim Dawood Ltd v Health Ltd* [1961] 2 Lloyd's Rep. 512; *Biggerstaff v Rowatt's Wharf Ltd* [1896] 2 Ch. 93, 100 (total failure of consideration as to goods not delivered). On the need to show a total failure of consideration before recovering money, see, however, *Pan Ocean Shipping Co. Ltd v Creditcorp Ltd (The Trident Beauty)* [1994] 1 WLR 161, 164–5 (Lord Goff); H. Beale (1996) 112 *LQR* 205, 208.

estop the buyer from claiming damages for non-delivery under the original contract.[245]

Long Delivery

6.49 **Introduction.** In the case of long delivery, section 30(2) permits the buyer to reject or accept the whole of the goods or accept just the contract quantity.[246] If the buyer accepts the whole delivery, he must pay for the goods at the contract rate. It is unlikely that a buyer accepting a long delivery will have suffered loss with a consequent right to damages.[247] Where section 30(2) departs from section 30(1) is in the buyer's right to remove from the delivery the excess quantity; in the case of a short tender, the buyer may not accept some goods and reject the rest. The difference is easily defensible since, in the case of long delivery, the buyer is merely appropriating the agreed amount to the contract; no such justification could be made for a buyer abstracting a lesser amount from a short delivery.[248]

6.50 **Microscopic and slight excess.** As in the case of short delivery, the *de minimis* maxim has a part to play. In *Shipton, Anderson & Co. v Weil Bros & Co.*,[249] the seller, whose delivery obligation had a minimum to maximum range, exceeded the maximum of 4,950 tons by a margin of 55 lbs. or 0.0005 per cent, which was held to be *de minimis*. Further, section 30(2A) prevents a non-consumer buyer from rejecting the goods where the excess of goods is slight and rejection would be unreasonable. As in the case of short delivery, it is unclear what this provision adds to the *de minimis* maxim, but it should go some little way beyond the *de minimis* maxim. The limitations of its wording are more apparent in the case of long delivery than they are for short delivery. For example, suppose a seller delivers on credit three tons instead of the contractually agreed quantity of two tons. The seller undertakes to remove at its own expense the excess and to charge the buyer for only two tons. The effect of the seller's breach in delivering an excess quantity of goods may well in such circumstances be slight or even non-existent, but section

---

[245] See *Household Machines Ltd v Cosmos Exporters Ltd*, n. 228 above (loss of profits on resale and indemnities owed to sub-buyers).

[246] See *Cunliffe v Harrison* (1851) 6 Ex. 903 (15 hogsheads of claret instead of 10), *per* Parke B, 906: '[T]he person to whom they are sent cannot tell which are the ten that are to be his; and it is no answer to the objection to say, that he may choose which ten he likes, for that would be to force a new contract upon him.' Against this, it might be argued that the inconvenience suffered by the buyer in selecting the contract quantity would be minimal, especially since the buyer's duties in respect of rejected goods are so modest (see s. 36). See also *Tamvaco v Lucas* (1859) 1 E & E 581; *Payne & Routh v Lillico & Sons* (1920) 36 TLR 569 (exceeding the 2% allowance).

[247] Cf. short delivery, discussed above. See also *Gabriel Wade & English Ltd v Arcos Ltd*, n. 241 above, 309, where the court held that the buyer accepting a long delivery had entered into a new contract and could not claim damages for breach of the original contract.

[248] This is not a case of partial acceptance, the subject of the new s. 35A (see Ch. 10 below), which applies in the case of title, quality, fitness, and description, and not quantity.

[249] [1912] 1 KB 574.

30(2A) does not require the *breach* to have slight consequences; it is the *excess* that has to be slight and a one-ton excess in the example given cannot be said to be a slight excess. Similarly, it cannot be said with confidence that the reasonableness of the buyer's behaviour depends upon whether the seller is willing to impose no charge for an excess.[250] Section 15A has no application to these two cases because the breach does not concern the implied terms in sections 13–15. The quantity of goods delivered should not be treated as part of the description of the goods under section 13.[251]

Estimated Quantities

Words of estimation.   A matter common to both sub-sections (1) and (2) of **6.51** section 30 concerns the use of words estimating the amount of a specific batch of goods whose exact quantity is unknown. It is settled that, in such cases, the failure to deliver the amount corresponding to the estimate will not infringe section 30 and consequently the buyer must accept delivery. The words, however, must be truly words of estimate and the parties must have agreed that the buyer shall take the whole batch. In *Re Harrison and Micks, Lambert & Co.*,[252] the contract was for the remainder of a cargo of wheat 'more or less about 5400 quarters'. The word 'about' in the contract signified a range of plus or minus 5 per cent and the remainder of the cargo amounted to 5,974 quarters, which fell outside the 5 per cent range. Nevertheless, the effect of adding the words 'more or less' was to convert the contract quantity into words of estimate so that, as agreed, the buyers had to accept the whole of the remainder of the cargo.[253] Words of estimate, however, may not always be effective in giving the seller latitude. In *Kreuger v Blanck*,[254] the sale of a 'cargo' of lathwood, 'in all about sixty cubic fathoms', could not be fulfilled by the seller setting aside that quantity out of a larger quantity of eighty-three cubic fathoms constituting the cargo of the ship. The subject matter of the contract was the entire cargo and eighty-three tons was not 'about' sixty tons.

Unascertained and future goods.   Words of estimate may also qualify the seller's **6.52** delivery duty in respect of unascertained and future goods. Where sellers agreed

---

250 No corresponding problem arises in the case of a shortfall. If there is a shortfall, s. 30(1) already reduces the price by requiring the buyer to pay at the contract rate. Where the buyer freely elects to accept more goods, payment is to be made at the contract rate: s. 30(3).

251 See Ch. 7.

252 [1917] 1 KB 755.

253 See also *Levi Guano Co. Ltd v Berk & Co.* [1886] 2 TLR 898; *Borrowman v Drayton* (1876) 2 Ex D 15; *McLay & Co. v Perry & Co.* (1881) 44 LT 152; *Macdonald v Longbottom* (1860) 1 E & E 987; *McConnel v Murphy* (1873) LR 5 PC 203. A seller might, however, warrant that all due care has been taken in giving the estimate: see *Esso Petroleum Co. Ltd v Mardon* [1976] QB 801. Rescission for misrepresentation is also a possibility: *Re Harrison and Micks, Lambert & Co.*, n. 252 above, 761 (Atkin J).

254 (1870) LR 5 Ex 179, 186, noting problems that otherwise might arise out of insurance, the carrier's lien and the mixture of the buyer's goods with goods of a different quality.

to supply the whole of the buyers' steel requirements for the construction of the Forth Bridge, estimated at '30,000 tons more or less', the buyer could not turn to an alternative source of supply for steel in excess of the 30,000 tons.[255] A less tolerant view is likely to be taken of quantifying words such as 'about' and 'more or less' where the seller does not need to make an estimate, being in a position to state the quantity of future goods with some precision and unreasonably falling short or long. In the Canadian case of *Canada Law Book Co. v Boston Book Co.*,[256] a contract for the exclusive distribution rights in Canada of the English Reports Reprint (150 volumes more or less 'of about' 1,500 pages each) did not permit the tender of about 190 volumes, most of which fell short of the 1,500 page mark. It was known in advance what was to be reprinted and the work that had to be done could be calculated within narrow limits; hence, only a slight increase over 150 volumes could be tolerated. There will be even less reason to interpret in a slack fashion words such as 'about' and 'more or less' where the contract is an ordinary one for the sale of unascertained goods from no unusually restricted source.

The Seller's Documentary Delivery Obligations

6.53 **General.** In international sales,[257] the seller is commonly under a duty to supply documents to the buyer. In the case, of an f.o.b. contract, the seller may[258] have to tender a bill of lading in addition to performing the physical duty of shipment. The seller may also have other duties to perform, such as supplying a certificate of origin of the goods[259] and, if arranging shipment, giving notice of it to the buyer.[260] Where the contract is entered into on c.i.f. (cost, insurance, and freight) terms, the seller's physical duty to deliver is displaced by documentary obligations, for the contract is properly characterized as a documentary sale.[261] The seller has to enter into or procure proper contracts of affreightment and insurance in respect of goods shipped that, in terms of description, quantity, and quality of the goods, conform to the c.i.f. contract, and transfer to the buyer the benefit of these contracts. The carrier is not the agent of the buyer in taking delivery of the goods on shipment,[262] and it is not a necessary part of the c.i.f. contract that the goods

---

[255] *Tancred, Arrol & Co. v Steel Co. of Scotland Ltd* (1890) 15 App. Cas. 125.

[256] (1922) 64 SCR 182.

[257] See generally Bridge, n. 16 above.

[258] It will depend upon the type of f.o.b. contract: see *Pyrene Co. Ltd v Scindia Navigation Ltd*, n. 22 above.

[259] A common express term in f.o.b. contracts.

[260] *Wimble Sons & Co. v Rosenberg & Sons* [1913] 3 KB 743.

[261] See *Manbre Saccharine Co. Ltd v Corn Products Co. Ltd*, n. 27 above, 202; *Comptoir d'Achat et du Boerenbond Belge SA v Luis de Ridder Lda*, n. 27 above, 312.

[262] See the text accompanying nn. 19 *et seq.* above.

actually be discharged at the named port of destination.[263] The c.i.f. buyer is presumptively[264] under a duty to pay against a tender of shipping documents,[265] which will include a bill of lading (or other transport document), an insurance document, and an invoice.[266]

Trade terms. Trade terms such as c.i.f., c. & f.[267] and f.o.b. are shorthand descrip- **6.54** tions of particular delivery obligations. It is a characteristic of such contracts that the obligations of the parties, particularly as they relate to documents and time, are usually strict.[268] The meaning and significance of trade terms are largely to be gathered from commercial custom and usage as amplified by judicial inter- pretation from time to time.[269] In this regard, the standard terms (Incoterms) issued by the International Chamber of Commerce and revised from time to time[270] are most useful in guiding contractual draftsmanship and in assisting contractual interpretation, especially where the contracting parties are not particularly adept in handling export sales. They are by no means so deeply rooted in international trade practice as to constitute binding custom or usage that need not be expressly incorporated in a contract.[271] Indeed, they are rarely to be found applying to international commodity sales governed by English law. Delivery terms may be found in various gradations stretching from the seller's to the buyer's premises. Commercial ingenuity sometimes prompts their emer- gence in hybrid forms.[272] The parties' own designation of the contract may not

---

263 *Congimex Cia Geral de Comercio SARL v Tradax Export SA* [1983] 1 Lloyd's Rep. 250. It is enough that the contract of affreightment requires the carrier to take them there. The contract may contain additional terms requiring discharge in the named port or country of destination: see, e.g., *Lindon Tricotagefabrik v White & Meacham* [1975] 1 Lloyd's Rep. 384.

264 See s. 28.

265 *E Clemens Horst & Co. v Biddell Bros* [1911] 1 KB 934 (Kennedy LJ).

266 The precise documents and their variants and additions will be discussed in the text accom- panying nn. 286 *et seq.* below.

267 This differs from a c.i.f. contract only in that the buyer remains responsible for insurance: *Norsk Bjergningskompagni A/S v Owners of the Steamship Pantanassa* [1970] 1 All ER 848.

268 See *SIAT di del Ferro v Tradax Overseas SA* [1980] 1 Lloyd's Rep. 53 (attempted use of 'Tradax documents clause' to dilute seller's documentary responsibilities); *Bunge Corpn v Tradax SA*, n. 141 above; *Toepfer v Lenersan-Poortman NV*, n. 141 above.

269 Usage settled by prior decisions need not be the subject of fresh evidence: *Brandao v Barnett* (1846) 12 Cl. & Fin. 786 (Lord Campbell). But the meaning of certain provisions may change over time: *C Groom Ltd v Barber* [1915] 1 KB 316.

270 Last issued in 2000.

271 The ICC-sponsored Uniform Customs and Practice for Documentary Credits 2007 (UCP 600) are much more widely used and will apply unless excluded by the parties.

272 e.g., *The Parchim* [1918] AC 157; *Comptoir d'Achat et du Boerenbond Belge SA v Luis de Ridder Lda*, n. 27 above. In *The Albazero*, n. 22 above, 809, Roskill LJ drew attention to the care needed in interpreting certain contracts where letters such as c.i.f. and f.o.b. are mistakenly understood by contracting parties. See also Ontario Law Reform Commission, *Report on Sale of Goods* (1979), ii, 347. Incoterms 2000 advises the 'greatest caution' when adding further obligations to the known obligations of the c.i.f. seller: Introduction, para. 9(3).

accurately reflect its contents, so that the contract is recharacterized as a different type of contract.[273]

C.i.f. Contracts

6.55 **Introduction.** The c.i.f. contract is in frequent use in international sales. Its use may have declined in certain areas of international trade in recent times but it remains very popular indeed in the international commodities markets. The contract developed in the middle years of the nineteenth century but it was not until the period around the First World War that a series of important cases laid down its principal features. Some of these cases arose out of the war itself; the Second World War was responsible for a flurry of later activity.

6.56 **Seller's duties.** The duties of a c.i.f. seller[274] have been stated authoritatively on a number of occasions.[275] First, the seller must enter into a reasonable contract of affreightment[276] with a carrier[277] requiring the carrier to carry the goods to the named port of discharge. Secondly, the seller must take out insurance on the terms current in the trade[278] unless the contract otherwise provides. Thirdly, goods answering to the contract must actually be shipped, and from the named port of shipment if one is named. Fourthly, the seller must make out an invoice for the goods. Fifthly, the seller must tender to the buyer the invoice, the insurance policy, and the bill of lading.[279] Where the buyer pays by means of a documentary letter of credit, the documents that the seller, as beneficiary of the letter of credit, must tender to the bank in order to enforce the bank's promise to pay will be spelt out in the letter of credit.[280] The documentary duties of the seller under the c.i.f. contract will be restated in these documentary requirements in the letter of credit. Cases on the strictness of documentary compliance under letters of credit and

---

[273] See, e.g., *Scottish & Newcastle International Ltd v Othon Ghalanos Ltd*, n. 24 above (f.o.b contract wrongly described as c. & f.).

[274] It is assumed in the following discussion that the seller is the shipper. Frequently, however, the seller is an intermediate party in a sales string to whom the goods have been sold on c.i.f. terms by a previous seller.

[275] *Ireland v Livingstone* (1872) LR 5 HL 395; *Biddell Bros v E Clemens Horst Co.* [1914] 1 KB 214 (Hamilton J); *Johnson v Taylor Bros & Co. Ltd* [1920] AC 144 (Lord Atkinson); *Ross T Smyth & Co. Ltd v Bailey Son & Co.* [1940] 3 All ER 60 (Lord Wright).

[276] Sale of Goods Act 1979, s. 32(2).

[277] Or the seller may charter a ship.

[278] *C Groom Ltd v Barber*, n. 269 above.

[279] Modern contracts frequently provide for different forms of insurance and transport documents.

[280] Where the terms of the documentary credit depart from the contract of sale, the presentation of documents to the bank under the credit may give rise to a variation of the contract of sale or a waiver of the buyer's documentary rights thereunder: *Ficom SA v Sociedad Cadex Lda* [1980] 2 Lloyd's Rep. 118.

c.i.f. contracts are therefore, to a large extent, interchangeable.[281] Whether or not the buyer pays under a letter of credit, the documentary tender by the seller will commonly occur through the agency of a bank and must take place on the agreed date[282] or, if no date is agreed, with all reasonable dispatch.[283] There is no need in c.i.f. contracts for the documents to reach the buyer before the ship arrives at the port of discharge[284] but the parties may establish a timetable that requires documentary tender and payment before the arrival of the ship.[285]

Invoice. A c.i.f. tender therefore involves principally an invoice, an insurance **6.57** policy, and a bill of lading. The content of the invoice will obviously depend upon the express terms of the contract but, assuming the contract to be silent, it is as a matter of custom and usage sufficient if the invoice is reasonably referable to the consignment appropriated to the contract. Certainly, the practice of shipment in bulk under indivisible bills of lading, with separation only on discharge,[286] is common enough for the invoice not to have to identify the very goods appropriated to the contract. One purpose of the invoice is to permit the buyer to ascertain which portion of the price refers to the cost of the goods themselves and which to the freight and insurance. It is the seller who absorbs the risk of a rise and fall in freight rates and insurance premiums between the contract date and performance.[287] When Blackburn J described the practice in *Ireland v Livingstone*,[288] the buyer would pay the cost of freight on discharge and this item would be credited to him against the overall c.i.f. price in the invoice; nowadays, it is common for the freight to be paid in advance by the seller.[289]

---

281 Attempts have been made to lessen the standard of documentary compliance under letters of credit. Under UCP 600, Art 14(d): 'Data in a document, when read in context with the credit, the document itself and international standard banking practice, need not be identical to, but must not conflict with, data in that document, any other stipulated document or the credit.'

282 *Toepfer v Lenersan-Poortman NV*, n. 141 above.

283 *Johnson v Taylor Bros & Co. Ltd*, n. 275 above; *C Sharpe & Co. Ltd v Nosawa* [1917] 2 KB 814 (where the date when the goods should have arrived was taken as the basis for calculating damages).

284 *Sanders Bros v Maclean & Co.* (1883) 11 QBD 327. The UCP 600 rules impose time requirements on the presentation of documents but do not link them to the arrival of the goods at the port of discharge: Arts 6 and 29.

285 *Toepfer v Lenersan-Poortman NV*, n. 141 above.

286 See, e.g., *Re Wait* [1927] 1 Ch. 606; *Karlhamns Oljefabriker v Eastport Navigation Corpn (The Elafi)* [1982] 1 All ER 208.

287 *Ireland v Livingstone*, n. 275 above, 407; *Blyth & Co. v Richards, Turpin & Co.* (1916) 114 LT 753.

288 *Ibid.*

289 For a discussion of 'freight prepaid' and 'freight collect' bills, see *Soproma SpA v Marine and Animal By-Products Corpn* [1966] 1 Lloyd's Rep. 367; *Norsk Bjergningskompagni A/S v Owners of the Steamship Pantanassa*, n. 267 above. In a 'freight collect' case, the buyer deducts the cost of freight from the c.i.f. price.

Insurance Documents

6.58 **Insurance policy.** The seller's duty regarding insurance documents has caused some difficulties in practice. The classic view is that the seller must tender the policy of insurance itself and not a mere certificate of insurance. In *Diamond Alkali Export Corpn v Fl. Bourgeois*,[290] a quantity of soda ash was shipped from an American port and the seller, in accordance with a growing American practice, tendered a certificate of insurance which in its own words 'represents and takes the place of the policy and conveys all the rights of the signed policy holder . . . as fully as if the property was covered by a special policy direct to the holder of this certificate'. Unable to see a prior course of dealing between the parties or an established trade usage to justify a tender of the certificate, McCardie J held the tender was bad. It was plain in the learned judge's view that the certificate had been issued under a floating policy and the awkwardness of analysing the buyer's position as assignee under the master policy was reason enough to maintain the orthodox position that a tender of the policy was necessary.[291] The proliferation of floating policies and the acceptability of certificates under modern standard-form contracts[292] has probably changed the law in this area. Standard-form contracts allow for the tender of certificates.[293] But it is an axiom of c.i.f. sales that, besides acquiring direct rights against the insurer, the buyer should be aware from the document tendered what are the terms of insurance in order to determine whether these accord with the cover that the c.i.f seller should procure.[294]

6.59 **Absence of insurance.** Where tender of a certificate is allowed or the need for a policy is waived, the c.i.f. seller warrants to the buyer that statements in it are true.[295] The seller is also bound to maintain insurance for the whole of the transit. In *Orient Co. Ltd v Brekke & Howlid*,[296] the contract was for 20 cases of French walnuts c.i.f. Hull. Payment was to be made 30 days after delivery of the documents. These, when tendered, did not include a policy of insurance, for the seller

---

[290] [1923] 3 KB 443.

[291] *A fortiori* a broker's cover note will not be a satisfactory document: *Wilson, Holgate & Co. v Belgian Grain & Produce Co.* [1920] 2 KB 1, 7. A certificate has also been held to be a bad tender under a documentary letter of credit calling for 'an approved policy': *Donald H Scott & Co. v Barclays Bank Ltd* [1923] 2 KB 1.

[292] See also Incoterms 2000, para. A.3(b) (CIF) ('insurance policy or other evidence of contract cover').

[293] e.g., GAFTA 100, cl 11(b).

[294] See *Donald H Scott & Co. v Barclays Bank Ltd*, n. 291 above, 15 (Scrutton LJ); *Malmberg v Evans* (1924) 30 Com. Cas. 107. A certificate could, if properly framed, meet this standard, a point left open: *Donald H. Scott, ibid.*, 17 (Atkin LJ); see also *Promos v European Grain* [1979] 1 Lloyd's Rep. 375 (certificate).

[295] *AC Harper & Co. Ltd v Mackechnie & Co.* [1925] 2 KB 423; see also *Comptoir d'Achat et du Boerenbond Belge SA v Luis de Ridder Lda*, n. 27 above.

[296] [1913] 1 KB 532. See also *AC Harper & Co. Ltd v Mackechnie & Co*, n. 295 above; *Lindon Tricotagefabrik v White & Meacham* [1975] 1 Lloyd's Rep. 384.

had not insured the goods at all. When the seller sued for the price, the court held that it was a condition of the buyer's duty to pay that an insurance policy be tendered. It did not avail the seller to show that the goods had arrived safely. The report does not show whether they had arrived before the documentary tender, but it should not have mattered either way since a c.i.f. seller may not unilaterally vary the contract and deliver landed goods. Similarly, it should not have made a difference if the seller had reduced the price to take account of the savings on insurance.

Bill of Lading

Functions of bill of lading. Of the three principal shipping documents, by far **6.60** the greatest volume of litigation has concerned the bill of lading, which performs three principal functions. First, it is evidence of the contract of carriage;[297] secondly, it is a receipt for the goods issued by the carrier;[298] and thirdly, it is a document of title. The former two functions, concerning as they do the contractual and bailment responsibilities of the carrier, may be left to texts dealing with carriage.[299] The third function concerns the transferability to the buyer of the seller's rights against the carrier and will be considered further here.

Negotiable document. The significance of a bill of lading in negotiable form[300] **6.61** is that its transfer from seller to buyer effects a constructive delivery of the goods. Subject to the carrier's lien for unpaid freight, the buyer may demand the goods at discharge without the carrier's attornment to the buyer as the new bailor. Whether the buyer is named from the outset as the consignee, which will not happen in string sales, or has the bill of lading indorsed and delivered to him, he will need to present it to the carrier to demand the goods, for the carrier is both bound and entitled to surrender the goods only to the holder of the bill.[301] Apart from constructive delivery, the bill of lading is also commonly used to effect the passing of the property in the goods to the buyer. The transfer of the bill need not have that consequence; it depends upon the accompanying intention.[302] The passing of the

---

[297] *The Ardennes* [1951] 1 KB 55; *Sewell v Burdick* (1884) 10 App. Cas. 74.

[298] It also affords evidence, sometimes conclusive, of the condition of the goods on shipment: see *J Aron & Co. Inc. v Comptoir Wegimont* [1921] 3 KB 435; Hague–Visby Rules, Art. III.

[299] e.g., G. H. Treitel and F. M. B. Reynolds, *Carver on Bills of Lading* (2nd edn, Sweet & Maxwell, 2005); N. Gaskell, R. Asariotis, and Y. Baatz, *Bills of Lading: Law and Contracts* (LLP, 2000).

[300] The following discussion does not apply to waybills, where the function of the document, which need not be presented by the buyer, is to identify the person to whom the carrier is to deliver the goods.

[301] *The Stettin* (1889) 14 PD 142; *Sze Hai Tong Bank v Rambler Cycle Co.* [1959] AC 576. But see *SA Sucre Export v Northern River Shipping Ltd (The Sormovskiy 3068)* [1994] 2 Lloyd's Rep. 266, 272 (lost bill of lading).

[302] *Sewell v Burdick*, n. 297 above; *Leigh and Sillavan Ltd v Aliakmon Shipping Ltd*, n. 22 above. The transfer of the bill, even with an intention to pass the property, will not have that effect

property in association with the bill was, before the Carriage of Goods by Sea Act 1992, of critical importance in determining whether the buyer could sue the carrier upon the contract of affreightment. The constructive delivery of the goods did not alone produce this result.[303] According to the now-repealed section 1 of the Bills of Lading Act 1855, the property in the goods had to pass 'upon or by reason of [the] consignment [of the goods to the buyer] or endorsement' of the bill of lading, in the name of the buyer, which meant that the indorsement of the bill had to play an essential causal part in the passing of property.[304] Since the Carriage of Goods by Sea Act 1992, the passing of property is no longer relevant in determining whether the buyer acquires rights against the carrier. A buyer now acquires rights as the lawful holder of a bill of lading, whether of the 'on-board' or 'received for shipment' kind; as the person to whom delivery is to be made under a ship's delivery order; and as the person to whom the carrier is to make delivery under a sea waybill.[305]

6.62 **Type of bill of lading.** The next question concerns the c.i.f. seller's contractual duty to tender a bill of lading to the buyer. The starting point is the contract.[306] Modern commodities contracts[307] permit either an on-board bill of lading or a negotiable ship's delivery order. The virtue of the former document, as opposed to a received-for-shipment document, is that the holder of the bill of lading receives the assurance that the goods are locked up in the 'floating warehouse' and covered by the agreed insurance. A ship's delivery order, if addressed by the carrier to the buyer at destination, will give the buyer holding it the right to demand the goods from the carrier without further attornment. In the absence of such contractual provision, it remains a vexed question what type of transport document the seller must tender to the buyer. It is certainly the case that the seller must tender a document of title. There may no longer be a need for such a document to confer on the buyer direct contractual rights against the carrier,[308] but the buyer will still need a document that entitles him to delivery without attornment, and a document of title is also useful as a pledge for raising finance from a bank.[309]

---

if the goods remain unascertained in the hold: s. 16. It may now serve to pass an undivided share in an ascertained bulk under changes to the Sale of Goods Act brought in by the Sale of Goods (Amendment) Act 1995 (Ch. 5 above). Nor will the transfer of the bill of lading be effective if the property in the goods has already been transferred to a third party: *The Future Express* [1992] 2 Lloyd's Rep. 79, affirmed [1993] 2 Lloyd's Rep. 542.

[303] *Thompson v Dominy* (1845) 14 M & W 403.
[304] *The Delfini* [1990] 1 Lloyd's Rep. 202 (Mustill LJ).
[305] 1992 Act, ss. 1, 2(1). For the incurring of liabilities to the carrier, see s. 3.
[306] If the contract calls for a bill of lading, a delivery order obviously will not do: *Forbes v Pelling* (1921) 9 Ll. LR 202.
[307] e.g., GAFTA 100, cl 11(b).
[308] Carriage of Goods by Sea Act 1992, s. 2(1).
[309] *Sewell v Burdick*, n. 297 above; *The Albazero*, n. 22 above (Brandon J); *Ross T Smyth & Co. Ltd v Bailey Son & Co.* [1940] 3 All ER 60; *The Future Express*, n. 302 above; M. Bridge [1993] *JBL* 379–83.

On-board bill. According to McCardie J, after a careful review of the earlier   **6.63**
authorities in *Diamond Alkali Export Corpn v Fl. Bourgeois*,[310] only the on-board
bill of lading in negotiable form fell within the mercantile custom, proved in
Lickbarrow v Mason,[311] as satisfying the definition of a document of title at common law. It was noteworthy that the Bills of Lading Act 1855 recited this very
custom in the preamble.[312] The c.i.f. seller therefore had to tender such a bill and
not a received-for shipment bill. A contrary view, that a received-for shipment bill
of lading was a document of title, had earlier been expressed by the Privy Council
in *The Marlborough Hill*.[313] The court referred to the practice, different from bulk
shipments, of small parcels being taken in hand by the carrier and shipped only in
the event of a final stowage plan for the cargo as a whole.[314] That case, however,
concerned admiralty jurisdiction to entertain claims by holders of bills of lading
against a carrier for damage to goods. Despite the headnote, it does not hold that
a received-for shipment bill of lading is a bill of lading for the purpose of the Bills
of Lading Act 1855.[315] Moreover, no effort was made to prove a mercantile custom to this effect.[316] A document of title can be found to be such by virtue of local
custom, but it has been emphasized that the proof required is rigorous and that
stamping the document 'non-negotiable' defeats the custom.[317] The role of custom cannot be supplanted by contractual language in determining the status of a
document of title: the status of a document as one of title has an impact upon the
liabilities of third parties such as carriers.[318] In *Ishag v Allied Bank International*,[319]
the court held that a document referring to goods 'intended to be shipped' was a
document of title since it was tantamount to the received-for shipment bill found
to be a document of title in *The Marlborough Hill*, but *Ishag* does not mention
on-board bills or the *Diamond Alkali* case.

Received-for shipment bill. It is submitted that a received-for shipment bill of   **6.64**
lading is not a document of title at common law. No custom to such effect has ever
been proved. As common as the practice may be to issue such bills, it is always
possible for the carrier later to annotate a received-for shipment bill of lading to

---

[310] n. 290 above.
[311] (1794) 5 TR 683.
[312] *Diamond Alkali Export Corpn v Fl. Bourgeois*, n. 290 above, 450.
[313] [1921] 1 AC 444.
[314] *Ibid.*, 451.
[315] Strictly speaking, it was never necessary for s. 1 of the 1855 Act to operate to transfer rights
and duties that a bill of lading be a document of title. The property in goods covered by a bill of lading could pass without transferring the bill: *The Future Express*, n. 302 above.
[316] Cf *Ishag v Allied Bank International* [1981] 1 Lloyd's Rep. 92, 97–8, where a custom was said
to have been proved.
[317] *Kum v Wah Tat Bank Ltd* [1971] 1 Lloyd's Rep. 439, 442 *et seq* (mate's receipt).
[318] *The Future Express*, n. 302 above, 95.
[319] n. 316 above.

show that the goods are now on board,[320] so as to convert it into an on-board bill.[321] Furthermore, a c.i.f. seller is in breach if the goods are never shipped[322] and it is axiomatic that a buyer in documentary sales should be able to see from the documents tendered, and before making payment, that the seller has duly performed the contract. A received-for shipment bill gives no such assurance. Finally, the chaos caused in matters of title transfer by the circulation at the same time of sets of received-for shipment bills and on-board bills, dealing with the same goods,[323] favours the taking of a restrictive view of a document of title.

6.65 **Negotiability and transferability.** The bill of lading tendered by the c.i.f. seller must be a 'negotiable' one,[324] which means that it may be transferred from one holder to another so as to affect rights in the underlying goods.[325] To say that a bill of lading is negotiable does not mean that the rights of a duly qualified holder override any defect in the title to the goods of the transferor; it is not negotiable in the sense that a bill of exchange is negotiable. Accordingly, for example, a pledgee to whom a bill of lading is transferred cannot, by transferring it to a new holder, confer on that new holder the general property in the goods. The issue and negotiation of a bill of lading will not heal any defects in the title to the goods of the original shipper.[326] To be negotiable, a bill of lading must be made out to a named consignee 'or order', or simply to bearer. It will then be negotiated, in the former case by indorsement and delivery to a named indorsee and, in the latter case, by manual delivery. A holder who is the named indorsee can convert the bill of lading into a bearer bill by the simple expedient of signing it in blank. The main purpose behind the requirement that the bill of lading be negotiable is to permit dealings in goods through the documentary medium: '[T]he object and result of a c.i.f. contract is to enable sellers and buyers to deal with cargoes or parcels afloat and to transfer them freely from hand to hand by giving constructive possession of the goods which are being dealt with.'[327]

---

[320] See Incoterms 1980 para. A. 7 (CIF).

[321] See *Westpac Banking Corpn v South Carolina National Bank* [1986] 1 Lloyd's Rep. 311 for the proposition that such a bill is a good on board (or shipped) bill.

[322] *Hindley & Co. Ltd v East India Produce Co. Ltd* [1973] 2 Lloyd's Rep. 515.

[323] See *Ishag v Allied Bank International*, n. 316 above.

[324] *Lickbarrow v Mason*, n. 311 above (coining the expression 'negotiable'); *Diamond Alkali Export Corpn v Fl. Bourgeois*, n. 290 above; *CP Henderson & Co. v Comptoir d'Escompte de Paris* (1873) LR 5 PC 253; *Soproma SpA v Marine and Animal By-Products Corpn* [1966] 1 Lloyd's Rep. 367.

[325] *Diamond Alkali Export Corpn v Fl. Bourgeois*, n. 290 above; *Gurney v Behrend* (1854) 3 E & B 622; *Thompson v Dominy* (1845) 14 M & W 403.

[326] In some cases, the holder of a bill of lading will be able, under one of the exceptions to the rule of *nemo dat quod non habet*, to transfer a greater title than his own; see Ch. 5 above.

[327] *Comptoir d'Achat et du Boerenbond Belge SA v Luis de Ridder Lda*, n. 27 above, *per* Lord Porter, 311–12.

Bills of Lading in Sets

Originals. Bills of lading are commonly issued in sets of three (sometimes four) **6.66** originals, a practice explained by the uncertainties of shipping in the days of sail.[328] Over a century ago, Lord Blackburn said:

> I have never been able to learn why merchants and shipowners continue the practice of working out a bill of lading in parts. I should have thought that, at least since the introduction of quick and regular communication by steamers, and still more since the establishment of the electric telegraph, every purpose would be answered by making one bill of lading only which should be the sole document of title, and taking as many copies, certified by the master to be true copies, as is thought to be convenient.[329]

He nevertheless accurately predicted that the practice would continue since 'merchants dislike to depart from an old custom for fear that the novelty may produce some unforeseen effect'.[330] It is not uncommon nowadays, however, for two or even one original bill to be issued.[331] Frequently, though not in the commodities trade, the carriage of goods takes place under a non-negotiable sea waybill, which has no pretensions to being a document of title and whose purpose is but to identify the person to whom delivery must be made by the carrier. It is not produced by the consignee as a precondition of surrender of the cargo. Furthermore, the introduction of electronic 'documentation' will lead to the redundancy of the traditional bill of lading, though negotiability may be retained by electronic means.[332]

Order of presentation. Where bills of lading are issued in a set, the various orig- **6.67** inals are identified as 'first', 'second', or 'third', as the case may be.[333] Each one of these bills may be negotiated and each will recite the formula 'the one of which bills being accomplished the others to stand void' or something to similar effect.[334] The meaning of this formula is discussed in cases dealing with the risk of fraud presented by the practice of issuing multiple bills of lading. In *Barber v Meyerstein*,[335] the consignee of goods indorsed the first two bills of lading from a set of three in

---

[328] Where the practice is still employed, the various originals will be sent by different routes, with the first coming by the fastest route (nowadays by air but formerly by fast passenger steamer: D. Sassoon, *C.I.F. and F.O.B. Contracts* (4th edn, Sweet & Maxwell, 1995), para. 257. The practice is trenchantly criticized in R. Goode, *Proprietary Rights and Insolvency in Sales Transactions* (2nd edn, Sweet & Maxwell, 1989), 77–8.

[329] *Glyn Mills, Currie & Co. v East and West India Dock Co.* (1882) 7 App. Cas. 591, 605; see also *Sanders Bros. v Maclean & Co.* (1883) 11 QBD 327, 341–2.

[330] *Ibid.*

[331] Sassoon, n. 328 above, para. 257.

[332] The implications of such a change affect the contract of carriage more than the contract of sale and so are outside the scope of this book.

[333] *Glyn Mills, Currie & Co. v East and West India Dock Co.*, n. 329 above.

[334] *Ibid.*; *Barber v Meyerstein* (1870) LR 4 HL 317.

[335] n. 335 above.

favour of the plaintiff pledgee and subsequently by fraud obtained advances from the defendant broker on the security of the third bill of lading. The goods in question had been landed at a river wharf before either of the above transactions took place. The defendant argued, on the basis of the above-quoted language in the bill of lading, that, despite the landing of the goods, the first two bills had not been 'accomplished' when the third bill was negotiated, since the freight had not yet been paid. In consequence, according to the defendant, 'it simply becomes a matter of expedition and race between the several parties who have taken those different assignments of the bill of lading'[336] with the prize going to the third party himself as the first to obtain actual possession of the goods. The conclusion of the House of Lords, however, was that the first assignee for value of one or more of the bills of lading obtained priority over the other assignees.[337] As Lord Westbury put it:

> There can be no doubt . . . that the first person who for value[338] gets the transfer of a bill of lading, though it be only one of a set of three bills, acquires the property; and all subsequent dealings with the other two bills must in law be subordinate to that first one, and for this reason, because the property is in the person who first gets a transfer of the bill of lading.[339]

6.68 **Tender of incomplete set.** The practice of issuing bills of lading arose in a more directly contractual context in *Sanders Bros v Maclean & Co.*,[340] where the seller tendered to the buyer two bills of lading from a set of three and demanded payment; the third bill had been retained by the original shipper who, however, did not use it in any way. When the seller sued for damages for non-acceptance, the court held that the buyer was not justified in rejecting the seller's tender. As Brett MR put it, it would be 'contrary to practice and the known principles of mercantile law with regard to bills of lading' if the buyer were to be allowed to reject an

---

336 n. 334 above, 326 (Lord Hatherley).

337 See also *Glyn Mills, Currie & Co. v East and West India Dock Co.*, n. 329 above, *per* Lord Blackburn, 604: '[T]he very object of making a bill of lading in parts would be baffled unless the delivery of one part of the bill of lading, duly assigned, had the same effect as delivery of all the parts would have had.' *Sanders Bros v Maclean & Co.*, n. 329 above, also notes that the carrier is not liable, for the stipulation in the bill of lading ('the one of which bills being accomplished the others to stand void') exists to permit the master to surrender the goods on the presentment of the first document. If the master has notice of the existence of more than one claimant, then he should interplead, for delivery would otherwise take place at his peril: *Glyn Mills, Currie & Co.*, *ibid.*, 613.

338 A gratuitous transfer will therefore not serve to pass a general or special property. See also *Leask v Scott* (1877) 2 QBD 376 (past consideration and defeat of unpaid seller's right of stoppage in transit) (cf *Rodger v Comptoir d'Escompte de Paris* (1869) LR 2 PC 393).

339 n. 334 above, 336. A special property arising from a pledge will not exhaust the whole of the indorser's property, and a second indorsee will therefore obtain the residue of that property. *Barber v Meyerstein* was decided before the enactment in 1877 of the seller in possession exception to the rule of *nemo dat quod non habet*, now contained in s. 24 of the Sale of Goods Act 1979. The impact of that provision in the case of multiple bills is discussed in Ch. 5 above.

340 n. 329 above.

instrument which 'would pass the property and give the right to possession'[341] merely because the whole set of three was not tendered. Likewise, Bowen LJ asserted that such a strict tender requirement would run counter to mercantile usage, which was concerned far more with the risk of insolvency than with the risk of fraud:

> The only possible object of requiring the presentation of the third original must be to prevent the chance, more or less remote, of fraud on the part of the shipper or some previous owner of the goods. But the practice of merchants, it is never superfluous to remark, is not based upon the supposition of possible frauds. The object of mercantile usages is to prevent the risk of insolvency, not of fraud; and any one who attempts to follow and understand the law merchant will soon find himself lost if he begins by assuming that merchants conduct their business on the basis of attempting to insure themselves against fraudulent dealing. The contrary is the case. Credit, not distrust, is the basis of commercial dealings; mercantile genius consists principally in knowing whom to trust and with whom to deal, and commercial intercourse and communication is no more based on the supposition of fraud than it is on the supposition of forgery.[342]

Contractual requirement. A contract may, however, expressly call for a full set **6.69** of bills of lading, which is the case with modern commodities forms[343] and with Incoterms.[344] If such is the case, then a seller may not tender an incomplete set coupled with a letter of indemnity.[345] If the bill of lading is not available for tender when the ship arrives, commodities forms will require the seller also to provide the buyer with an indemnity for the carrier so that the carrier will surrender the goods.[346]

Contents of Bill of Lading

Evidencing the contract of affreightment. A number of issues arise out of the **6.70** contents of the bill of lading. The bill must evidence that the seller has procured or adopted a proper contract of affreightment with the carrier.[347] More particularly, the buyer should be able to determine that the goods are being carried to the right destination and that the terms of the contract of affreightment accord with the seller's c.i.f. responsibilities. In *SIAT di del Ferro v Tradax Overseas SA*,[348]

---

[341] n. 329 above, 335.

[342] n. 329 above, 343.

[343] e.g., GAFTA 100, cl. 11(b) (which permits an alternative tender of ship's delivery orders, needed where the contract goods are shipped as part of a larger bulk).

[344] Incoterms 2000, para. A8 (CIF).

[345] *Donald H. Scott & Co. Ltd v Barclays Bank Ltd* [1923] 2 KB 1, 11 (Bankes LJ) and 16 (Scrutton LJ) (a documentary credit case but the principle is the same). UCC Art. 2–323(2) enacts a presumptive rule that only one original need be tendered for overseas sales and, even if the contract requires a full set, permits a seller to tender an incomplete set coupled with a letter of indemnity.

[346] e.g., GAFTA 100, cl. 11(c).

[347] *Soon Hua Seng Co. Ltd v Glencore Grain Ltd* [1996] 1 Lloyd's Rep. 398.

[348] n. 268 above; see also *Lecky & Co. Ltd v Ogilvy, Gilanders & Co.* (1897) 3 Com. Cas. 29.

certain bills of lading for a bulk cargo of soya been meal c.i.f. Venice stated the destination 'as per charterparty' and others as 'Ancona/Ravenna'. The tender was bad: the first bills were insufficiently informative and the latter evidenced that the sellers had not fulfilled their c.i.f. responsibilities. In *Finska Cellulosa Föreningen v Westfield Paper Co.*,[349] the bill of lading contained the following clause: 'All conditions and exceptions as per charterparty dated [blank].' Responding to the question whether the seller had to tender the original of the charterparty, the court answered no: it was not on the list of documents that the c.i.f. seller had to tender to the buyer. It seems, however, that from previous dealings the buyer was acquainted with the standard form of charterparty used. The real issue in a case of this kind is whether the buyer is given or has access to sufficient information about the contract of affreightment. The need to inform is one of the reasons for the traditional rule that a c.i.f. seller must tender the policy of insurance. The terms of the contract of affreightment cannot be divined from the clause quoted above.[350] It is submitted that the c.i.f. seller should as a general rule have to give the buyer access to the terms of the contract of affreightment if these are not set out in full in the bill of lading. This might be done by supplying a copy of the charterparty or by referring the buyer to a well-known charterparty form.[351] If the bill of lading is tendered to the buyer under a contract not involving the assignment of rights and liabilities under the contract of affreightment, as where the goods are sold landed in the country of destination,[352] there is no reason why the buyer, who needs the bill to collect the goods, should be informed of the terms of the contract of affreightment.

6.71 **Clean bill.**   The bill of lading must be 'clean',[353] which means that it must not qualify the goods or the packing as other than in good order and condition on receipt by the carrier.[354] The abiding principle is that the buyer is entitled to documents that can be disposed of in trade without disponees being put off by questions raised about the goods on the face of the documents. Where a bill of lading is 'claused', that is, annotated to show that the goods are not in good order and condition, the documents may be rejected even if the underlying defect in the goods is not so serious as to justify a rejection of the goods themselves.[355] There is

---

[349] [1940] 4 All ER 473.

[350] Incoterms 1990, para. A8, required a copy of the charterparty if the bill of lading contained a reference to a charterparty. This requirement is absent from Incoterms 2000, which do not impose a duty on the seller to inform the buyer of the terms of carriage.

[351] See *Burstall v Grimsdale* (1906) 11 Com. Cas. 280.

[352] See *Holland Colombo Trading Soc. v Alawdeen* [1954] 2 Lloyd's Rep. 45.

[353] *Cremer v General Carriers SA* [1974] 1 WLR 341; *British Imex Industries Ltd v Midland Bank Ltd* [1958] 1 QB 542. It is usually in such letters of credit cases that the issue arises. Incoterms 1980 explicitly required 'clean' bills of lading and documents: Foreword, para. 9; para. A.7 (FOB); para. A.6 (CFR); para. A.7 (CIF). This explicit requirement was dropped in the Incoterms 1990 and is also absent in Incoterms 2000.

[354] *British Imex Industries Ltd v Midland Bank Ltd* [1958] 1 QB 542, 551.

[355] *Cehave NV v Bremer Handelsgesellschaft mbH* [1976] QB 44.

an exception to the requirement of a clean bill; it concerns a bill that is claused to show that damage has occurred to the goods after the risk has been transferred to the buyer.[356] If the buyer were able to reject the documents, this would subvert the allocation of risk between the parties. In *M Golodetz & Co. Inc. v Czarnikow-Rionda Co. Inc.*,[357] sugar was in the process of being loaded under a c. & f. contract when a fire broke out on board ship, destroying 200 tons that had already been loaded. The standard-form bill of lading attested to the good order and condition of the sugar, but a typed addition dealt with the condition of the sugar after the fire. It was held that this addition did not vitiate the requirement that the bill of lading be clean since it referred to the condition of the sugar after shipment, when the risk had passed to the buyer.[358]

Bills of Lading and Letters of Credit

Bills of lading and banks.   If payment is to be made pursuant to a documentary **6.72** letter of credit, the seller must comply with the documentary requirements of the letter if he wishes to enforce payment according to its terms. Further, to the extent that the letter of credit restates or supersedes the c.i.f. documentary obligations of the seller, then compliance with its requirements is tantamount to the performance by the seller of his documentary duties under the contract of sale. In commercial matters generally, a strict standard of contractual performance is expected for the sake of certainty and confidence as to one's legal position in fast-moving markets, but the strictness of the compliance standard for letters of credit is additionally supported by the further reason that bankers are not as well informed as buyers of the underlying business. They cannot inquire into the concrete transaction and will need to know for sure that they are properly making payment according to the terms of the letter of credit, which payment will then be recoverable from the buyer.[359] Referring to shipping documents generally, Lord Sumner once said:

> These documents have to be handled by banks, they have to be taken up or rejected promptly and without any opportunity for prolonged inquiry, they have to be such

---

[356] In c.i.f. contracts, risk is transferred as from shipment: *Comptoir d'Achat et du Boerenbond Belge SA v Luis de Ridder Lda*, n. 27 above.

[357] [1980] 1 WLR 495.

[358] See *Comptoir d'Achat et du Boerenbond Belge SA v Luis de Ridder Lda*, n. 27 above, and Ch. 4 above.

[359] *JH Rayner & Co. Ltd v Hambro's Bank Ltd* [1943] 1 KB 37. At common law, the terms of the contract between the bank and the applicant for the credit (the buyer) require strict scrutiny of the shipping documents by the bank: *Midland Bank Ltd v Seymour* [1955] 2 Lloyd's Rep. 147. The UCP Rules were formerly more lenient in requiring the bank to exercise 'reasonable care' in applying the standard of 'international banking practice' to determine whether the documents conform (UCP 500, Art. 13a), but UCP 600, Art. 14, contains no reference to reasonable care. Since the bank's function is essentially a clerical one, it is doubtful that the deletion of reasonable care has made a difference to what can be expected of the bank.

as can be re-tendered to sub-purchasers,[360] and it is essential that they should so conform to the accustomed shipping documents as to be reasonably and readily fit to pass current in commerce.[361]

6.73 Standard of compliance. The standard of compliance is both exacting and exact;[362] there is no room to apply the maxim *de minimis non curat lex*.[363] A letter of credit calling for bills of lading to be marked 'freight prepaid' need not be honoured if the seller tenders bills marked 'freight collect'.[364] Another example is *JH Rayner & Co. Ltd v Hambro's Bank Ltd*,[365] where a letter of credit requirement that the goods be 'Coromandel groundnuts' was not met by the tender of a bill of lading referring to 'machine shelled groundnut kernels'; it did not matter that it was well understood in the trade that the latter expression meant Coromandel groundnuts, since the bank could not be expected to possess an informed understanding of the trade.

6.74 Relaxation. Some relaxation of the strictness of the above standard is evident in *Soproma SpA v Marine and Animal By-Products Corpn*,[366] where the letter of credit specified shipping documents for 'CHILEAN FISH FULLMEAL, 70% Protein'. The bill of lading, however, referred to 'Chilean Fishmeal' while the commercial invoices described the shipment as 'CHILEAN FISH FULLMEAL 70% protein'. Further slight deviations were to be found in certificates of quality and analysis; the former mentioned a protein count of '67% minimum' and the latter 'protein 69.7%'. McNair J held that the description of the goods in the invoices was accurate and the bare statement in the bill of lading was adequate (despite the conflated reference to fishmeal instead of fish full meal) but that the discrepancies in protein count in both quality and analysis certificates rendered them invalid. This ruling was in accordance with an earlier version of the UCP Rules, which read: 'The description of the goods in the Commercial Invoice must correspond with the description in the credit. Wherever the goods are described in the remaining documents, description in general terms will be acceptable.' The present version, Article 14(e) of UCP 600, now reads: 'In documents other than the commercial invoice, the description of the goods . . . may be in general terms not conflicting

---

[360] Which underlines the strictness of compliance between buyer and seller.
[361] *Hansson v Hamel and Horley Ltd* [1922] 2 AC 36, 46.
[362] *English, Scottish and Australasian Bank Ltd* (1922) 13 Ll. LR 21; *Equitable Trust Co. of New York v Dawson Partners Ltd* (1927) 27 Ll. LR 49, 52; *Seaconsar Far East Ltd v Bank Markhazi Jomhouri* [1993] 1 Lloyd's Rep. 236; *Banque de l'Indochine SA v JH Rayner (Mincing Lane) Ltd* [1983] QB 711.
[363] *Soproma SpA v Marine and Animal By-Products Corpn* [1966] 1 Lloyd's Rep. 367. For some relaxation of the standard where the credit is governed by UCP 600, see Art. 14(d).
[364] *Ibid.*
[365] n. 359 above.
[366] n. 363 above.

with their description in the credit.'[367] This rule is in substance the same as the earlier one and, moreover, is likely to reflect the position that English law would adopt[368] if the UCP Rules were not incorporated in the credit,[369] given that Article 14(e) is in harmony with a tendency to relax punctilious standards in unimportant details.[370] Where the UCP Rules apply, the seller is given a quantitative leeway of 5 per cent more or less, which, more generous than the position under section 30 of the Sale of Goods Act, will be recorded in the invoice.[371]

Time Obligations and Shipping Documents

Forwarding documents. Once the goods have been delivered to the carrier and shipping documents issued, it is the seller's duty to forward them with all reasonable dispatch to the buyer or the buyer's bank for the documentary exchange.[372] It has long been settled that there is no necessary requirement that the documents reach the buyer before the arrival of the ship in the port of discharge.[373] In modern conditions, a combination of speedy shipping and slow postal services has made this a common event. It is, of course, open to the parties to agree expressly or by implication that the documents must arrive before the arrival of the ship, as happened in one case[374] where payment was due on arrival of the ship or twenty days after the bill of lading date, whichever was earlier. Since nothing had displaced the rule that payment was to occur against a tender of documents, the seller was in breach for not tendering the documents when the twenty days had elapsed and the ship had not yet arrived. Timely performance is a strict condition, breach of which entitles the buyer to terminate the contract.[375]

6.75

Issued on shipment. The seller must also tender a bill of lading that has been issued on shipment. This does not mean that the bill of lading must be signed contemporaneously with the goods being put on board,[376] since it is common practice for the bills to be signed after loading has been completed and indeed

6.76

---

[367] This rule was not incorporated in the letter of credit in *JH Rayner & Co. Ltd v Hambro's Bank Ltd*, n. 359 above.

[368] Whether dealing with the letter of credit or the c.i.f. contract itself.

[369] But see *Moralice (London) Ltd v ED & F Man* [1954] 2 Lloyd's Rep. 526 for a standard of exact compliance in the invoice,

[370] e.g., *Bremer Handelsgesellschaft mbH v Toepfer* [1980] 2 Lloyd's Rep. 43.

[371] UCP 600, Art. 30(b).

[372] *Johnson v Taylor Bros & Co. Ltd* [1920] AC 144; *C Sharpe & Co. Ltd v Nosawa* [1917] 2 KB 814 (where the date when the documents should have arrived was taken as the basis for calculating damages, on which point see also *Aruna Mills Ltd v Gobindram* [1968] 1 QB 655).

[373] *Sanders Bros v Maclean & Co.* (1883) 11 QBD 327.

[374] *Toepfer v Lenersan-Poortman NV*, n. 141 above.

[375] *Ibid.*

[376] *Westpac Banking Corpn v South Carolina National Bank* [1986] 1 Lloyd's Rep. 311, 316.

after the ship has sailed; a reasonable margin of tolerance is permitted.[377] Nevertheless, it has been held that a bill issued 'thirteen days after the original shipment, at another port in another country many hundreds of miles away, is not duly procured "on shipment."[378] A bill of lading was also held to be irregular in another case where it was issued seven weeks after the loading, between which dates the ship visited other ports before returning to the loading port.[379]

6.77 **Accurate dating.** Besides attesting to timely shipment of the goods, the bill of lading must be dated accurately as of the time when the goods are actually loaded.[380] If the contract gives the seller the option of tendering a received-for shipment bill, or indifferently states the goods are received or shipped and then recites a date that does not discriminate between the two, then the buyer may not complain if the bill is dated from the receipt.[381]

Continuous Documentary Coverage

6.78 **Transhipment.** The reason for the requirement that the bill of lading be issued promptly on or after shipment is that the buyer on c.i.f. or similar terms is entitled to continuous documentary coverage.[382] This has emerged as a particular problem in transhipment cases where prior parts of the carriage process may have occurred before the part for which the seller tenders a bill of lading. Transhipment also raises problems concerning responsibility to the transferee buyer, where more than one carrier is employed. In *Landauer & Co. v Craven & Speeding Bros*,[383] a c.i.f. contract for the sale of 400 bales of hemp called for shipment from Hong Kong or from a Philippines port by steamer or steamers direct or indirect to London, with the bill of lading dated between 1 October and 31 December. The contract therefore permitted transhipment. The sellers elected to ship from Manila and obtained a bill of lading dated 28 December. The ship, however, was going no further than Hong Kong, so the sellers forwarded the bill of lading to their Hong Kong agent with instructions to find London shipping space forthwith. The agent was unable to enter into a contract of affreightment until long after the ship had left Manila, and the goods were transhipped from Hong Kong under fresh bills of lading dated

---

[377] *Hansson v Hamel and Horley Ltd*, n. 361 above, 47 (Lord Sumner). This is particularly likely in transhipment cases.

[378] *Ibid.*

[379] *Foreman and Ellams Ltd v Blackburn* [1928] 2 KB 60.

[380] Hence, even if the shipment occurs within the shipment period, the seller will be in breach if the bill of lading is falsely dated. This point was not contested by the seller on appeal in *Procter & Gamble Corpn v Becher* [1988] 2 Lloyd's Rep. 88.

[381] *Weis v Produce Brokers' Co.* (1920) 7 Ll. LR 211; *United Baltic Corpn v Burgett & Newsam* (1921) 8 Ll. LR 190.

[382] *Hansson v Hamel and Horley Ltd*, n. 361 above; *Holland Colombo Trading Soc. v Alawdeen* [1954] 2 Lloyd's Rep. 45.

[383] [1912] 2 KB 95.

25 March. The second bill of lading for the Hong Kong to London leg was tendered to the buyers, the first bill not having arrived in London, and the buyers accepted the documents under protest. It was the normal course of business for goods shipped at Manila to be transhipped at Hong Kong, but nevertheless shipped under a through bill of lading covering the entire voyage. Scrutton J held that the documentary tender was bad for two reasons. First, when the goods were originally shipped, a contract for the second leg of the voyage had not been entered into. Consequently, the second leg of the voyage was out of time. Secondly, the sellers' tender did not include the first bill of lading, and thus the buyers were not put in possession of any document that permitted them to launch an action against the first carrier should this have become necessary.

The bill of lading and the first carrier.   The second ground for the decision in   **6.79** *Landauer* was confirmed by the House of Lords in *Hansson v Hamel and Horley Ltd*,[384] which concerned a quantity of guano sold c.i.f. Yokohama and shipped at Braatvag, a Norwegian port. The Japanese carrier did not call at Braatvag so it was necessary to tranship at Hamburg. When the goods were transhipped on to the Japanese ship at Hamburg, the bills of lading were signed on 5 May and stipulated that the goods had been shipped in good order and condition from Braatvag on 22 April. In the judgment of the House of Lords, these bills were not true through bills since, though speaking to the condition of the goods in Braatvag, they gave the buyers no contractual recourse against the first carrier. Moreover, the Japanese carrier did not accept responsibility for the goods prior to their arrival in Hamburg. As Lord Sumner put it: 'When documents are to be taken up the buyer is entitled to documents which substantially confer protective rights throughout. He is not buying a litigation.'[385] Had the ship foundered off the Norwegian coast, the buyers would have had no rights against the Japanese carrier, since no contract with that carrier would ever have been forthcoming.[386] In Lord Sumner's view, the sellers should either have tendered a bill of lading authorizing transhipment and signed by the Japanese carrier's agent at Braatvag, or should have forwarded the goods on their own account to Hamburg and shipped them from that port to Yokohama.[387] It is submitted that the tender of two bills of lading, one issued by the local carrier for the Braatvag to Hamburg leg and the other by the Japanese carrier for the Hamburg to Yokohama leg, would not have been good. Having two carriers blaming each other in the event of damage to the goods would be tantamount to 'buying a litigation'.

---

[384] [1922] 2 AC 36.
[385] *Ibid.*, 46.
[386] *Ibid.*, 47.
[387] *Ibid.*, 49.

6.80 **Availability of claims against the carrier.** These cases show that it is possible to effect a documentary exchange in transhipment cases if the correct procedures are used. The buyer is entitled above all to continuous documentary coverage and does not get it if the carrier disclaims all responsibility before[388] or after[389] the point of transhipment, but is not deprived of it merely because the bill of lading gives the carrier a liberty to tranship on such terms and this liberty is not in fact exercised.[390] Continuous documentary coverage requires the continuance of a claim against the carrier. *Colin & Shields v W Weddel & Co. Ltd*[391] concerned the tender of a delivery order instead of a bill of lading. The contract called for discharge[392] in Liverpool but the goods were shipped on a vessel bound for Manchester that did not call in at Liverpool. The sellers were in breach on the ground that there was no bill of lading evidencing a proper contract of affreightment of the goods to Liverpool. Furthermore, they were also in breach in that the delivery order they tendered was not properly drawn. The goods had been transhipped at Manchester on a barge and the order tendered by the sellers was addressed, not to the carrier, but to a master porter at one of the berths in the Liverpool docks. Unlike a bill of lading, this document was wholly ineffectual in giving the buyers recourse against the carrier. What is ordinarily needed is a document drawn on the carrier in which the carrier attorns to the buyer.[393] In this case, the contract expressly demanded that the delivery order 'be countersigned by a banker, shipbroker, captain or mate if so required' and that the buyers were to be 'put in the same position as if they had been in possession of' a bill of lading. On neither account, had the sellers made a good tender.

Delivery Orders

6.81 **Ship's delivery orders.** The above discussion recounts the documentary obligations of a c.i.f. seller and, where relevant, those of c. & f. and f.o.b. sellers where a documentary exchange is envisaged. The common practice of shipping commodities in bulk has led to an increasing number of cases in which the seller pursuant to the contract tenders a ship's delivery order drawn on and accepted by the ship instead of a bill of lading.[394] Such delivery orders will not permit symbolic dealings with the general property in the goods as would a bill of lading for they are

---

[388] *Hansson v Hamel and Horley Ltd*, n. 361 above.

[389] *Holland Colombo Trading Soc. v Alawdeen*, n. 382 above, 53 (a non-c.i.f. contract requiring a documentary tender).

[390] *Soproma SpA v Marine and Animal By-Products Corpn* [1966] 1 Lloyd's Rep. 367.

[391] [1952] 2 All ER 237.

[392] It was not a pure c.i.f. contract.

[393] See also *Waren Import Gesellschaft Krohn & Co. v International Graanhandel Thegra NV* [1975] 1 Lloyd's Rep. 146.

[394] See *Re Wait* [1927] 1 Ch. 606; *Comptoir d'Achat et du Boerenbond Belge SA v Luis de Ridder Lda*, n. 27 above; *Colin & Shields v W Weddel & Co. Ltd*, n. 391 above; *Cremer v General Carriers SA*, n. 353. If it is not drawn on the person in possession of the goods, the documentary tender will

not documents of title.[395] Increasingly, international sales contracts (outside the area of commodities) will permit the tender of a received for shipment bill of lading instead of an on-board bill.[396] Furthermore, the accelerating practice in certain trade sectors of substituting, for negotiable bills of lading, non-negotiable documents such as waybills, freight receipts, and multimodal transport documents combining terrestrial and maritime transport[397] impedes symbolic dealings with the goods in transit[398] and has ramifications for the carrier's liability and insurance coverage. It is probably too early to assess the implications, for the well-worked out positions of buyer and seller under a documentary sale, of the issuance of shipping documents by electronic means.[399]

Import and Export Licences

Principal questions. International sales frequently require the issue of a licence **6.82** if goods are to be exported and imported. Two fundamental questions are raised at this point. First, which party is responsible for applying for the licence? Secondly, is the applicant under an obligation to use due diligence in applying for a licence or is the burden a stricter one?[400] In deciding who has the duty to apply for a

---

be invalid: *Waren Import Gesellschaft Krohn & Co. v International Graanhandel Thegra NV*, n. 393 above.

[395] *Margarine Union GmbH v Cambay Prince Steamship Co.* [1969] 1 QB 219; *Comptoir d'Achat et du Boerenbond Belge SA v Luis de Ridder Lda*, n. 27 above. Nor is a mate's receipt a document of title, though its holder is *prima facie* entitled to the issue of a bill of lading: *Nippon Yusen Kaisha v Ramjiban Serowgee* [1938] AC 429. The issue of mate's receipts is not now a common practice since forwarding agents frequently arrange for shipping space with loading brokers: Sassoon, *C.I.F. and F.O.B. Contracts* (4th edn, Sweet & Maxwell, 1995), para. 133; *Heskell v Continental Express Ltd* [1950] 1 All ER 1033.

[396] See Incoterms 1990, Introduction, para. 16 (nowadays goods are usually delivered by seller to carrier before shipment on board takes place).

[397] See Incoterms 1990, Introduction, para. 19. For a useful description of modern documentary practice superseding the ocean bill of lading, see Goode, n. 328 above, 78–84.

[398] Commonly such documents are used because there is no intention of dealing with the goods in transit.

[399] See the passing reference to EDI procedures in Incoterms 2000, Introduction, para. 2. On electronic systems generally, see D Faber, 'Electronic Bills of Lading' [1996] *Lloyd's MCLQ* 232–44; R. M. Goode (ed.), *Electronic Banking* [:] *The Legal Implications* (Institute of Bankers, 1985), Ch. 10: 'The Electronic Transfer and Presentation of Shipping Documents' (A. Urbach), ch. 11: 'International Trade Data Interchange Systems' (B. Wheble); P. Todd, *Modern Bills of Lading* (2nd edn., Blackwell, 1990), Ch. 17; B. Kozolchyk, 'Evolution and Present State of the Ocean Bill of Lading from a Banking Law Perspective' (1992) 23 *J of Maritime Law and Commerce* 161, 196–245; K. Gronfors, *Cargo Key Receipt and Transport Document Replacement* (Gothenburg Maritime Law Association, 1982); C. Reed, *Electronic Finance Law* (1991), Ch. 8: 'International Trade Transactions and Electronic Data Interchange'; Toh See Kiat, *Paperless International Trade: Law of Telematic Data Interchange* (Butterworths Asia, 1992), Ch. 5: 'Paperless International Trade'.

[400] A related issue to the strictness of the duty is its relationship to an express force majeure or prohibition of export clause. A seller may be under a strict duty yet be protected by such a clause in some cases when unable to obtain a licence: see, e.g., *Pagnan SpA v Tradax Ocean Transportation SA* [1987] 2 Lloyd's Rep. 342.

licence it is convenient to distinguish between export and import licences. Furthermore, one must distinguish the various contracts, which fall into two principal groupings: there are f.o.b. and similar contracts, such as the f.a.s. (free alongside) contract, where the seller's delivery obligations are accomplished at the port of loading, and there are c.i.f. and similar contracts, such as the c. & f. contract, where the goods will have left the loading port before the seller's documentary obligations are performed and, in some cases, before the contract is concluded.

6.83 **F.o.b. contracts.** The starting point is that the identity of the applicant is a question of contractual construction. This is not evident, however, if one looks at Incoterms, which state that the seller must '[o]btain at his own risk and expense any export licence or other official authorization'.[401] In the case of f.a.s. delivery, it was formerly the case that the buyer applied for the export licence; the seller's duty was only to '[r]ender the buyer, at the latter's request, risk and expense, every assistance in obtaining any export licence'.[402] In the present version of Incoterms, it is the seller who is responsible for the export licence, in just the same way as an f.o.b. seller.[403] In neither f.o.b. nor f.a.s., can the clear-cut Incoterms approach be said to represent the English case law in those cases where Incoterms are not incorporated in the contract. In *HO Brandt & Co. v HN Morris & Co. Ltd*,[404] a contract was concluded in time of war between two Manchester merchants for the sale of a quantity of aniline oil f.o.b. Manchester in circumstances showing that the goods were destined for an American recipient. During most of the shipment period, an export licence system, introduced after the contract date and sensitive to the destination of the goods, was in force. The court held that responsibility for the licence rested on the buyers.[405] Scrutton LJ put it in terms of the f.o.b. buyer's duty to provide an effective (in this instance, a legal) ship,[406] an overstatement of the position. But the result in the case can be supported on the ground that the sellers were no better placed than the buyers to apply for a licence and, furthermore, the buyers knew the identity of the American recipient. There will be cases where it makes more sense to put the duty to apply on the seller, for example, where the seller resides in the country of export and the buyer does not. Such a case-by-case approach may lack the simplicity (or dogmatism) of Incoterms, which give a clear guide to merchants, but it is commendably flexible.

---

[401] Incoterms 2000, para. A2 (FOB). The seller is bound to pay for export costs incurred before the goods pass the ship's rail: *ibid.*, para. A6.
[402] Incoterms 1990, para. A2 (FAS).
[403] Incoterms 2000, para. A2 (FAS).
[404] [1917] 2 KB 784.
[405] *Ibid.*, 795 and 798.
[406] *Ibid.*

No general rule.   The most important feature of the House of Lords decision in   **6.84**
AV Pound & Co. Ltd v MW Hardy & Co. Inc.[407] lies in its conclusion that there is
no general rule governing the duty to apply for a licence, the matter being one of
contractual construction. A contract was made in England between English sellers and the English branch office of an American company for the sale of a quantity of Portuguese turpentine on f.a.s. Lisbon terms. The sellers knew that the
turpentine was destined for an East German port but, since they (and the buyers
for that matter too) were not registered with the Portuguese authorities, they
could not apply for an export licence. But the sellers' supplier, whose identity was
kept carefully concealed from the buyers,[408] did apply for a licence to export the
turpentine to East Germany, which was refused. The goods had to clear Portuguese
customs before they could be laid up alongside the ship. The sellers contended
that the buyers were bound to give fresh delivery instructions while the buyers,
initially, counterclaimed damages for non-delivery. The House of Lords concluded that the buyers in the present case were under no duty to apply for the
licence; the abandonment of the buyers' counterclaim meant that they did not
examine the nature of the duty that rested upon the sellers.[409] The court's refusal
to lay down general or unnecessary rules was most clearly stated by Lord
Somervell:

> I think this is an area in which it is impossible to lay down general rules. There might
> be a licence system based not on destination but on the proportion of a manufactur-
> er's product to be sent out of the country. In such a case the facts necessary to be
> stated would be known to the producer and not to the buyer. It would seem obvious
> that in such a case it would be for the seller to apply. There may well be cases in which
> each party must be ready and willing to co-operate. If, in the present case, the sellers
> had written to the buyers; told them of the licensing system; told them of the suppli-
> ers' names and asked them to give the name of the destination and the ship, there
> might well have been an obligation on the buyers to do these things . . . There can be
> no general rule.[410]

Cooperative behaviour.   This passage usefully emphasizes that applying for a   **6.85**
licence often calls for cooperative behaviour between seller and buyer, which
could be implied in contracts as a matter of business efficacy. Problems of the kind
in this case cannot be resolved by easy assertions that in f.o.b. contracts it is the
buyer's duty to nominate an effective ship, for it could just as easily be said in
opposition that f.o.b. and f.a.s. sellers are under a duty to deliver 'effective goods',
that is, goods that may be lawfully carried to their destination.[411] As for import
licences, their acquisition is collateral to the performance of such contracts and

---

[407] [1956] AC 588.
[408] *Ibid.*, 604.
[409] [1956] AC 612–13.
[410] *Ibid.*, 611.
[411] *Ibid.*, 607–8.

concern the factual expectations of the buyer. When Incoterms put the duty on the buyer,[412] they are providing the importing buyer with a checklist of things to do rather than laying down the legal characteristics of f.o.b. and f.a.s. contracts.

6.86 **C.i.f. contracts.** In the case of c.i.f. contracts, Incoterms squarely put on the seller the duty to apply for an export licence[413] and on the buyer the duty to apply for an import licence.[414] Nevertheless, although the general approach of the *Pound* case is just as applicable here too, the case law does not depart radically from Incoterms, subject to the following discussion. It is not easy to contemplate a case where the c.i.f. buyer has the duty to apply for an export licence, especially since the goods may be afloat before they are appropriated to the contract. As regards import licences, in *Mitchell Cotts & Co. v Hairco Ltd*,[415] the c.i.f. London buyer of Sudanese goat hair was bound under the contract to pay for the goods after they had been landed in England. The English buyers, already in possession of the shipping documents, had not applied for an import licence and the customs authorities confiscated the cargo when it arrived. The Sudanese sellers successfully sued for the price of the goods. This c.i.f. contract clearly contemplated the landing of the goods in England, but it should not be assumed that c.i.f. contracts will always require the goods to be landed in the country of the destination port. In *Congimex Cia Geral de Comercio SARL v Tradax Export SA*[416] the buyer of c.i.f. Lisbon soya bean meal, denied an import licence by the Portuguese authorities, claimed that the contract had been frustrated. It was held, nevertheless, that the goods did not have to be landed in Portugal for the contract to be performed; they could be transhipped or oncarried by the same ship to a French destination.[417]

6.87 **Other contracts.** Where the contract is on *ex* ship or *ex* quay terms, it seems as a matter of construction likely that the seller will bear the burden of applying for both export and import licences (though the buyer may have cooperative duties to perform). Yet Incoterms puts the duty on the buyer in the case of an *ex* ship contract[418] and on the buyer in the case of *ex* quay terms.[419]

6.88 **Strictness of duty.** The question of how strict is the duty to apply for a licence is again one of contractual construction.[420] The applicant may guarantee or be

---

412 Para. B2 (FAS); para. B2 (FOB).
413 Incoterms 2000, para. A2 (CIF); *ibid.*, para. A2 (CFR (i.e., c.& f.)).
414 Incoterms 2000, para. B2 (CIF); *ibid.*, para. B2 (CFR).
415 [1943] 2 All ER 552.
416 [1983] 1 Lloyd's Rep. 250.
417 Lisbon is an unlikely port for traffic of this kind. But it is common to ship bulk commodities to ARA ports (Amsterdam/Rotterdam/Antwerp) and then to tranship parcels to further destinations.
418 Incoterms 2000, para. B2 (DES (i.e., *ex* ship)).
419 Incoterms 2000, para. A2 (DEQ (i.e., *ex* quay)).
420 For a difficult case, see *Czarnikow Ltd v Centrala Handlu Zagranicnego Rolimpex* [1979] AC 351. The language of Incoterms ('obtain') is too terse to reveal an intention to impose a stricter

strictly liable for its procurement, or undertake only to use due diligence. In the absence of contrary indications in the contract, the test of business efficacy for the implication of contractual terms supplies a duty of due diligence.[421] A seller faced with a supervening export prohibition or quota restriction may be liable for the lack of due diligence where it cannot demonstrate that with energy it could have avoided the difficulty[422] or where its difficulties are self-imposed.[423] In applying for a licence, the applicant is entitled to any necessary cooperation from the other contracting party.[424]

Undertaking stricter duty.   There are cases where the applicant has impliedly **6.89** undertaken a stricter responsibility. In *Peter Cassidy Seed* v *Osuustukkukauppa*,[425] the Finnish sellers of a quantity of Finnish ant eggs assured the buyer that the procurement of an export licence was a mere formality, despite having no grounds for making such a statement. In the circumstances they were held to have guaranteed the licence. In *Pagnan SpA* v *Tradax Ocean Transportation SA*,[426] the contract was for the sale of Thai tapioca pellets to Italian buyers. No export market for this commodity existed apart from an artificial one subsidized by the EC for limited imports into the EC. The contract stated that the seller 'would provide for [an] export certificate', which was a precondition to the grant of import permission by the EC. There was at all material times a quota export system between Thailand and the EC. Since export certificates for the shipment period had already been allocated in full before the present shipment, the Thai authorities refused one to the sellers. The sellers were held to have undertaken an absolute duty to procure a certificate. They had a more substantial business presence in Thailand than the buyers and were better able to assess the risk of failure to obtain a certificate. Moreover, the goods were no use at all to the buyer if they could not be imported into the EC. Nevertheless, the sellers' absolute duty only went so far as 'oversight, error, mishap, bureaucratic inefficiency or delay, and probably also if the certificate was not provided for simply because the Thai authorities failed to issue it'. The sellers were therefore not liable where the grant of certificates was 'entirely abrogated or suspended by governmental decree', which had occurred in the present case.

---

standard than one of due diligence; an English court interpreting a contract incorporating Incoterms would be likely to require due diligence.

[421] *Re Anglo-Russian Merchant Traders Ltd* [1917] 2 KB 79; *Coloniale Import-Export v Loumidis* [1978] 2 Lloyd's Rep. 60; *Brauer & Co. v James Clark Ltd* [1952] 2 All ER 497; *Peter Cassidy Seed v Osuustukkukauppa* [1957] 1 WLR 273.

[422] *Agroexport State Enterprise v Cie Européenne de Céréales* [1974] 1 Lloyd's Rep. 499.

[423] *KC Sethia Ltd v Partabmull Rameshwar* [1950] 1 All ER 51.

[424] *Kyprianou v Cyprus Textiles Ltd* [1958] 2 Lloyd's Rep. 60.

[425] n. 421 above.

[426] n. 400 above.

The Buyer's Duty to Pay

6.90 **General.** A contract of sale involves the payment by the buyer of 'a money consideration, called the price'[427] and section 27 of the Sale of Goods Act recites the buyer's duty to pay the price. Nothing in the Act, however, deals with the form in which this money consideration has to be paid and there are no rules concerning the place of payment that correspond to the delivery rules in section 29. The contract may state the form of payment. International sales often specify 'net cash against shipping documents' or call for the acceptance by the buyer of a draft bill of exchange which the seller may then discount before its maturity. Where the contract is silent, the common law rule is that payment must be made in legal tender; that is, in coin or bank notes.[428]

6.91 **Payment by cheque.** Despite the legal tender rule, payment is commonly made by cheque. At the very least, this practice establishes that legal tender is commonly waived by sellers; it may also show that in certain trades payment by cheque has become a customarily acceptable form of payment.[429] Where the buyer does pay by cheque, and this is accepted by the seller, payment is treated in the absence of a contrary intention as having been made conditionally[430] on the cheque not being subsequently dishonoured by the bank on which it is drawn. In some cases, the seller will announce in advance that payment can be made by means falling outside the legal tender rule. This is commonly seen in cases where the symbol of a credit card is displayed. Payment by credit card is regarded as absolute payment, the merchant having no recourse against the cardholder in the event of default by the credit card company.[431] This is to be contrasted with the ordinary case of payment by cheque, as well as with payment pursuant to a documentary letter of credit, where the buyer's duty to pay is suspended and not substituted by the bank's promise to pay.[432]

---

[427] S. 2 of the Sale of Goods Act; see Ch. 2 above.

[428] *Gordon v Strange* (1847) 1 Ex. 477; see Ch. 2 above.

[429] Canadian reform proposals (never implemented), in recognition of this, would have allowed payment 'when made by any means and in any manner current in the ordinary course of business': Ontario, Draft Sale of Goods Bill 1979, s. 7.2; Uniform Sale of Goods Act 1981, s. 76(2). The seller's residual entitlement to legal tender is nevertheless retained by his right to insist on legal tender provided he gives the buyer an extension that is 'reasonably necessary to procure it': *ibid.*

[430] Sale of Goods Act, s. 38(1)(b); *Currie v Misa* (1875) LR 10 Ex. 153, affirmed (1876) 1 App. Cas. 554; *Re Romer and Haslam* [1893] 2 QB 286; *Gunn v Bolckow, Vaughan & Co.* (1875) LR 10 Ch. App. 491; *Bolt and Nut Co. (Tipton) Ltd v Rowlands Nicholls & Co. Ltd* [1964] 2 QB 10. It should make no difference that the cheque is supported by a bank guarantee card: *Re Charge Card Services Ltd* [1987] Ch. 150 (Millett J).

[431] *Re Charge Card Services Ltd* [1989] Ch. 497; see Ch. 2 above.

[432] *WJ Alan & Co. v El Nasr Export and Import Co.* [1972] 2 QB 189; *Maran Road Saw Mill v Austin Taylor & Co. Ltd* [1975] 1 Lloyd's Rep. 156; *ED & F Man Ltd v Nigerian Sweets & Confectionery Co. Ltd* [1977] 2 Lloyd's Rep. 50.

Place of payment.   Unless the contrast specifies otherwise, the rule is that the   **6.92**
debtor should seek out the creditor.[433] Consequently, unless the parties otherwise
agree,[434] in the case of sale and other contracts money payable must be paid at the
payee's place of business.[435] This complements the presumptive rule that delivery
takes place at the seller's place of business. Where delivery is to occur at some other
place, and the presumptive rule that delivery and payment are mutual and concurrent[436] is not displaced, this may give rise to an implied intention that payment
is to occur at the stipulated place of delivery.

Documentary sales.   In documentary sales, where the parties are physically sep-   **6.93**
arate and the duration of the transit makes it practical and economical to deal in
the goods through their documentary expression, it is common for both place and
means of payment to depart from the general rule. The separation of buyer and
seller creates two major problems for the seller. First of all, once the seller has
delivered the goods to the carrier and until payment is received, his capital is tied
up in the cargo and does not produce income. Secondly, unless the seller takes
preventive measures, after abandoning control of the goods he courts the risk of
non-payment by the buyer. This event may arise for various reasons, but notably
because of the buyer's insolvency. The key to the resolution of these problems is
for the seller to control the goods until payment through the medium of the shipping documents.[437] The liquidity problem is resolved in part by the ability of the
seller, pending the documentary exchange, to pledge the bill of lading with the
bank so as to raise bridging finance.[438] But unless the buyer pays cash or its equivalent on the documentary exchange, the seller will find himself extending credit to
the buyer and he may not wish to do that. Furthermore, the seller may also run the
risk of non-payment by the buyer and to avoid this may wish to retain a property
interest in the goods and their proceeds[439] or to obtain a guarantee of payment by
the buyer from a third party whose credit is solid. The virtue of the latter step is
that it covers the risk of a seller incurring expenses in preparing for performance
before the buyer repudiates or otherwise fails to perform the contract.

---

[433] *Drexel v Drexel* [1916] 1 Ch. 251, 259–60; *Fowler v Midland Electric Corpn Ltd* [1917] 1
Ch. 656; *The Eider* [1891] P 119, 131. There is an exception where the contract is governed by
English law and the payee is abroad: *Korner v Witkowitzer* [1950] 2 KB 128, 159.

[434] *Comber v Leyland* [1898] AC 524; *Thorn v City Rice Mills* (1889) 40 Ch. D 357.

[435] *Rein v Stein* [1892] 1 QB 753, 758; *Robey & Co. v Snaefell Mining Co. Ltd* (1887) 20 QBD
152; *Bremer Öltransport GmbH v Drewry* [1933] 1 KB 753, 765–6; *Thompson v Palmer* [1893]
2 QB 80, 84; *Charles Duval & Co. Ltd v Gans* [1904] 2 KB 685, 692.

[436] S. 28.

[437] Some protection is afforded the seller in the case of buyer insolvency by the right of stoppage
in transit, but it is a right rarely exercised in modern conditions: see Ch. 11 below.

[438] *Sewell v Burdick*, n. 297 above; *The Albazero*, n. 22 above (Brandon J); *Ross T Smyth & Co. Ltd
v Bailey Son & Co.* [1940] 3 All ER 60; *The Future Express*, n. 302 above.

[439] See Ch. 3 above.

Documentary Letters of Credit

6.94 **Documents on acceptance.** One method of securing most of the seller's objectives, not so commonly employed nowadays but in frequent use in the nineteenth century,[440] is for the parties to proceed on a 'documents on acceptance' basis. The seller ships the goods and draws on the buyer for the price. This draft,[441] which may be payable on sight or at an interval,[442] can be discounted by the seller with a bank, which receives also the shipping documents and presents the draft to the buyer for acceptance.[443] When the buyer accepts the draft, the shipping documents are released to him. Although the bill of lading itself is a useful medium for reserving the right of disposal, the seller's bank may not wish to become involved with a buyer of unknown credit and may well prefer to have dealings with another bank standing behind the buyer. Moreover, the buyer's acceptance of the draft is in itself no guarantee that the buyer will ultimately honour the draft when it is presented for payment. The seller remains vulnerable to a recourse action by his bank if such dishonour by the buyer occurs.

6.95 **Documentary letters of credit: general.** The drawbacks to the documents on acceptance approach are resolved by the system of bankers' documentary letters of credit.[444] A typical example of the working of the system is the following.[445] The buyer (the applicant) persuades a bank, usually in his own country, to issue a letter of credit in favour of a named beneficiary, the seller. This issuing bank corresponds with an advising (or corresponding) bank, usually in the seller's country, which advises the seller of the credit and acts as the issuing bank's agent in effecting payment under the letter of credit. In this paying capacity, it is often referred to as the nominated bank. The advising bank may add its own promise to that of the issuing bank, in which event it acts as a confirming bank. Once assured of the promise of payment according to the tenor of the letter of credit, the seller then ships the goods and forwards the requested shipping documents to the advising bank. Payment may take various forms, including the payment of cash, at sight or on a deferred basis, or the acceptance of a draft, or the reimbursement of another

---

[440] The practice is dealt with in s. 19(3) of the Sale of Goods Act. For a description, see *Guaranty Trust Co. of New York v Hannay & Co.* [1918] 2 KB 623, 659–60 (Scrutton LJ).

[441] It is common to prepare more than one draft ('the first of exchange', 'the second of exchange', etc.) to accompany the separate bills of lading sent by different routes to the buyer.

[442] Or 'usance'.

[443] The seller's bank may act as a 'remitting bank' and send the documents to a 'presenting bank' near the buyer.

[444] They are sometimes referred to as documentary credits or commercial credits. See generally H. C. Gutteridge and M. Megrah, *The Law of Bankers' Commercial Credits* (7th edn, Europa, 1984); E. P. Ellinger, *Documentary Letters of Credit* (University of Singapore Press, 1970); R. Jack, A. Malek, and D. Quest, *Documentary Credits* (3rd edn, Butterworths LexisNexis, 2000); Bridge, n. 16 above, Ch. 6.

[445] See *WJ Alan & Co. v El Nasr Export and Import Co.* [1972] 2 QB 189 (Denning MR).

bank that has negotiated the shipping documents. When it receives the shipping documents, the issuing bank turns them over to the buyer, who subsequently presents the bill of lading to the carrier when the goods are ready for collection. A continuing security in the form of a trust receipt may be taken by the issuing bank, pending repayment of the moneys forwarded to the seller, over the goods and their proceeds.[446] The terms of the contract between the buyer and the issuing bank will govern the reimbursement of the latter.

Types of credit. A number of distinctions may be made between different types   **6.96** of credit. First of all, they may be confirmed or unconfirmed; in the former case, the advising bank adds its own undertaking to the seller that payment will be made. Credits may also be revocable or irrevocable. If the credit is revocable, the seller cannot prepare the goods for shipment with the assurance that payment will be made on the documentary tender.[447] A revocable credit may be cancelled at any time without liability on the part of the bank.[448] A distinction also exists between transferable and non-transferable credits.[449] In the former case, the benefit of a letter of credit may be transferred by the named beneficiary through intermediate sellers to the head seller in a sales string.[450]

Binding contract. Once the letter of credit has been opened, a binding contract   **6.97** between the seller and the issuing bank is constituted[451] in which, it seems plain, technical difficulties posed by the doctrine of consideration[452] will not be permitted to impede commercial expediency.[453] If the letter of credit is irrevocable, then, in the absence of fraud, the obligation of the issuing bank to pay is absolute and may not be qualified by the state of the underlying contract of sale.[454] Although

---

[446] *North Western Bank Ltd v Poynter, Son and Macdonalds* [1895] AC 56 (a continuing pledge despite the release of the documents); *Re David Allester Ltd* [1922] 2 Ch. 211; *Lloyds Bank Ltd v Bank of America National Trust and Savings Asscn* [1938] 2 KB 146.

[447] UCP 600 provides that a '[a] credit is irrevocable even if there is no indication to that effect' (Art. 3). Similarly, departing from previous editions of the UCP Rules, the 1993 edition (UCP 500) stipulated that a credit was irrevocable unless otherwise stated: Art. 6c. On the former Art. 7(1)(c) in the 1983 edn, see E. P. Ellinger [1984] *LMCLQ* 578.

[448] This was stated explicitly in UCP 500, Art. 8a. UCP 600 is silent on the matter, but it does not prohibit the issue of revocable letters of credit.

[449] UCP 600, Art. 38.

[450] See *WJ Alan & Co. v El Nasr Export and Import Co.*, n. 445 above; *Ian Stach Co. Ltd v Baker Bosley Ltd* [1958] 2 QB 130.

[451] *Urquart, Lindsay & Co. Ltd v Eastern Bank Ltd* [1922] 1 KB 318; *Hamzeh Malas & Sons v British Imex Industries Ltd* [1958] 2 QB 127.

[452] The seller may not yet have performed the act requested in the letter of credit by shipping the goods.

[453] Clarke [1974] *CLJ* 260.

[454] *Offshore International SA v Banco Central SA* [1977] 1 WLR 399, 401 ('absolute obligation to pay irrespective of any dispute' in the underlying contract); *United City Merchants (Investments) Ltd v Royal Bank of Canada* [1983] 1 AC 168, 183 ('an assured right to be paid'); *Trendtex Trading Corpn v Central Bank of Nigeria* [1977] QB 529, 552 ('completely separate from the contract of sale').

buyer and seller are perfectly free to stipulate that the seller shall look to a third party for payment without recourse against the buyer,[455] this interpretation will not in the absence of express language be drawn to meet the rare case of an issuing bank defaulting on a letter of credit.[456] One consequence of this concerns a buyer who takes physical delivery of goods before the documents are rejected by the bank for non-conformity. The buyer's conduct may amount to a waiver of the seller's physical breach so that the buyer may not shelter, as the bank itself does, behind the documentary non-conformity and has to make payment directly to the seller.[457]

Time and Payment

6.98   **Time of payment.**   The first question that arises under this heading concerns the time of payment. Where payment is made directly to the seller in bank notes or coin or by means of a credit card, then the time of payment presents no difficulty. Since payment by credit card constitutes absolute and not conditional payment,[458] the taking of the credit card details accompanied by a signature or pin number identifies the time of payment. Where the seller accepts a cheque in payment, the status of the cheque as conditional payment[459] means that payment is presumed to have been made at the time the seller receives the cheque. The time of payment becomes more of an issue when the buyer is required to make payment by a due date and by other means. When the buyer makes a payment into the seller's account at a bank, the precise moment of payment is difficult to capture because payment is not so much an event as a process that lies within the range separating the bank's receipt of a payment instruction and the customer's facility to draw on the account without incurring interest charges.[460] It has been said tentatively that the acceptance by a bank of a payment order[461] directing that a customer's account with the bank be credited is the equivalent of a cash payment to the bank with the same direction, since payment orders are generally accepted as cash in the payment world.[462] Payment is received by the bank in its own right but subject to

---

[455] *Harrison v Luke* (1845) 14 M & W 139; *Re Charge Card Services Ltd*, n. 431 above.

[456] *WJ Alan & Co. v El Nasr Export and Import Co.*, n. 445 above, 210 (Denning MR), disapproving *Soproma SpA v Marine and Animal By-Products Corpn* [1966] 1 Lloyd's Rep. 367, 385–6.

[457] *Saffron v Société Minière Cafrika* (1958) 100 CLR 231; *Uzinterimpex JSC v Standard Bank Plc* [2008] EWCA Civ 819 at [28]–[29].

[458] *Re Charge Card Services Ltd*, n. 431 above.

[459] n. 430 above,

[460] See generally B. Geva, *Bank Collections and Payment Transactions* (OUP, 2001), 270 *et seq.*

[461] Not the mere receipt of an order: *Tenax Steamship Ltd v The Brimnes (Owners) (The Brimnes)* [1973] 1 WLR 386, 400 (Brandon J); [1975] QB 929, 965 (Megaw LJ).

[462] *Mardorf Peach & Co. Ltd v Attica Sea Carriers Corpn of Liberia Ltd (The Laconia)* [1977] AC 850, 880 (Lord Salmon): 'There has been a great deal of argument as to whether payment . . . by a payment order just before the bank closed . . . would have amounted to a good payment under the [contract]. The point does not however arise for decision and I prefer to express no concluded view

a direction to the bank to incur a corresponding indebtedness to the customer for whose benefit the payment is being made.[463] Until the customer's account is credited, an argument exists that payment is conditional in the way that payment by cheque is conditional until the cheque is cleared and the payee's account credited. On this view, the buyer would pay when the seller's bank accepts the payment instruction. The adoption of this view would render unimportant for sale purposes the determination of the exact time an account is credited[464] and the need to resort to the practice of bankers in this respect.[465] On the other hand, the more traditional view is that payment occurs when the amount is actually placed in the customer's account.[466] It has been cogently stressed that a payment instruction does not have the negotiable character of a cheque and therefore cannot be equated to a cheque.[467] Moreover, if the contract of sale calls for payment in 'cash', then it should follow that payment occurs only when the customer may draw on his account for the relevant amount without paying interest charges,[468] for otherwise the buyer would receive payment in an amount less than the contract price if making an earlier drawing. In determining the time that payment takes place, the choice lies between the bank's decision to credit the customer's account and the actual crediting of the account so that the customer does not have to pay interest when making a withdrawal, and the use of the word 'cash' in the contract of sale should not make a difference. Overall, the authorities do not provide a clear answer. On balance, for the purpose of payment under a contract of sale, payment is made, it is submitted, when the buyer may draw on his account without having to pay interest.

---

about it. As at present advised however I am inclined to think that . . . there is no real difference between a payment in dollar bills and a payment by payment orders which in the banking world are generally regarded and accepted as cash.' See also *Tenax Steamship Ltd v The Brimnes (Owners) (The Brimnes)*, n. 461 above, 948 (Edmund Davies LJ) ('the tendering of the commercial equivalent of cash'). At first instance in the same case, above, Brandon J at 402 concludes that payment occurs at the time the bank decides to credit the customer's account; see further *Momm v Barclays Bank International Ltd* [1977] QB 790.

[463] See *Foley v Hill* (1848) 2 HLC 28; King (1982) 45 *MLR* 369.

[464] On which see *Momm v Barclays Bank International Ltd*, n. 462 above (in-house bank transfer).

[465] *Afovos Shipping Co v Pagnan & F.lli* [1983] 1 WLR 195, 204 (Lord Roskill) (payment a matter of banking practice rather than a matter of law).

[466] *Eyles v Ellis* (1827) 4 Bing 112, 113. See also *The Laconia*, n. 462 above, 884 (Lord Fraser) ('payment would not have taken place until the bank acted on the request in the payment order and credited the . . . account').

[467] *Tenax Steamship Ltd v The Brimnes (Owners) (The Brimnes)*, n. 461 above, 963 (Megaw LJ): 'Whatever mode or process is used, "payment" is not achieved until the process has reached the stage at which the creditor has received cash or that which he is prepared to treat as the equivalent of cash or has a credit available on which, in the normal course of business or banking practice, he can draw, if he wishes, in the form of cash.'

[468] *Awilco of Oslo A/S v Fulvia SpA di Navigazione of Cagliari (The Chikuma)* [1981] AC 314. See also *Tayeb v HSBC Bank Plc* [2005] EWHC 1529 (Comm); [2004] 4 All ER 1024.

6.99 **Timely payment.** The second question under this heading concerns the importance of timely payment. Given its importance, there is surprisingly little authority dealing with timely payment by the buyer. One reason is that payment is commonly conditioned by the seller's delivery and that uncertainty in the contractual timetable is played out through cases dealing with timely delivery. Section 10(1) of the Sale of Goods Act firmly states that the time of payment is presumptively not of the essence of the contract, thereby legislating the result in *Martindale v Smith*.[469] In that case, the seller contracted to sell to the buyer six stacks of oats on terms giving the buyer liberty to let the oats stand on the seller's land until the middle of August but requiring payment by 16 July. The contract thus separated the buyer's duties of acceptance and payment. The seller repudiated the contract when the buyer defaulted in making timely payment, having warned the buyer in early July that this would happen. The seller subsequently refused two later tenders of the price and declined to allow the buyer to remove the stacks in mid-August.

6.100 **Unlawful repudiation.** The seller's repudiation of the contract was held unlawful on two grounds. First, it seems, the goods being specific and the property having passed to the buyer at the contract date, any contractual right of the seller to refuse later payment and retain the goods involved a rescission of the contract that was no longer possible.[470] The other reason was expressed by the court in these terms: 'In a sale of chattels, time is not of the essence of the contract, unless it is made so by express agreement, than which nothing can be more easy, by introducing conventional words into the bargain.'[471] This reasoning appears to be derived from the practice of the Court of Chancery, where the presumption that time is not of the essence was commonly countered by the insertion in the agreement of sale of a time of the essence clause.[472] The practice of certain conveyancers in adopting clauses of this type did not make its way into the much less formal world of sale of goods agreements.

6.101 **Displacing the presumption.** Despite the language of *Martindale v Smith* and section 10(1), it is relatively easy in practice to displace the presumption, especially where payment and acceptance are concurrent.[473] Where goods are delivered on credit, it is less likely that the presumption in section 10(1) will be displaced. [474] Where the buyer has an option that has to be exercised and

---

[469] (1841) 1 QB 389.
[470] See M. Bridge (1983) 28 *McGill LJ* 867, 917–18.
[471] n. 469 above, 395.
[472] Sanctioned by *Seton v Slade* (1802) 7 Ves. Jun. 265.
[473] See *Mooney v Lipka* [1926] 4 DLR 647.
[474] S. 10(1) was applied to timely payment in *Lidl UK GmbH v Hertford Foods Ltd* [2001] EWCA Civ 938 at [40].

followed by payment on a certain date, the accepted position that compliance with the terms of an option is strictly required[475] will colour the strictness of the duty to pay on time and be more than a match for any presumption in section 10(1).[476] Moreover, a contract calling for part-payment of the price by way of deposit 'as security for the correct fulfilment of this contract' will be interpreted as making time of the essence.[477] The reason given in this case for regarding timely payment as of the essence was that the seller needed the security of a for-feitable deposit in hand before proceeding with further contractual perform-ance.[478] Unless the market in secondhand ships were as volatile as the market in freight rates, it would make more sense, instead of permitting the outright termi-nation of the contract, to allow the seller to suspend further performance of the contract until the deposit is paid.[479] Declining to treat timely payment as a con-tractual condition is not tantamount to affording the buyer an infinitely elastic time in which to pay, for eventually the failure to pay will go to the root of the contract.[480] Similarly, though a series of delays in making instalments may not be repuditory merely because of their repeated character,[481] their cumulative effect in some cases will be serious enough to merit termination.[482] Treating timely payment as of the essence in some cases is in tune with the general trend of asserting in commercial matters the importance of timely performance.[483] In international documentary sales, the seller's delivery duty is normally conditional upon performance by the buyer of his payment duty and *vice versa*.[484] The failure by the buyer to pay in these circumstances will be treated as a breach of condi-tion.[485] Similarly, the failure of the buyer to pay in the place stipulated in the contract will be a condition.[486] It is also established that, if payment is to be made by a letter of credit, the letter of credit must conform strictly to the contract

---

[475] *Holwell Securities Ltd v Hughes* [1974] 1 WLR 155.
[476] Cf *Hare v Nicol* [1966] 2 QB 130 (speculative shares and fluctuating markets).
[477] *Portaria Shipping Co. Ltd v Gulf Pacific Navigation Co. Ltd* [1981] 2 Lloyd's Rep. 180 (sale of ship).
[478] *Ibid.*
[479] On the question of suspension, see the discussion of s. 28, below.
[480] *Decro-Wall International SA v Practitioners in Marketing Ltd* [1971] 1 WLR 361; *Lambert v Slack* [1926] 2 DLR 166, 170.
[481] *Decro-Wall*, n. 480 above; see also *Engineered Medical Systems v Bregas AB* [2003] EWHC 3287 (Comm).
[482] *Alan Auld Associates Ltd v Rick Pollard Associates* [2008] EWCA Civ 655.
[483] *Bunge Corpn v Tradax Export SA*, n. 141 above.
[484] See *Shepherd v Harrison* (1871) LR 5 HL 116, 132; *Dix v Granger* (1922) 10 Ll. LR 496; *Cohen & Co. v Ockerby & Co. Ltd* (1917) 24 CLR 288.
[485] *Berger & Co. Inc. v Gill and Duffus SA*, n. 235 above, 391 (Lord Diplock); *Nichimen Corpn v Gatoil Overseas Inc.* [1987] 2 Lloyd's Rep. 46.
[486] *PT Berlian Laju Tanker TBK v Nuse Shipping Ltd* [2008] EWHC 1330 (Comm) at [66].

of sale,[487] and that a failure to provide such a letter of credit is also a discharging breach of contract.[488]

Opening Letters of Credit

6.102 **Unstated date of opening:** c.i.f. Letters of credit act as an assurance to the seller that he can make preparations for the performance of the contract.[489] Where the contract fails to stipulate the date on which or the time within which the credit must be opened, this raises problems of interpretation that are difficult to resolve. Starting with c.i.f. contracts, in *Pavia & Co. SpA v Thurmann-Nielsen*,[490] a contract concluded on 20 January for the c.i.f. Genoa sale of Brazilian groundnuts called for payment by confirmed, irrevocable credit, and permitted the sellers to ship half of the goods between 1 February and 30 April and the remaining half between 1 March and 31 May. The sellers contended that the credit should have been made available throughout the shipment period (that is, from 1 February onwards) or, alternatively, as soon as possible, or within a reasonable time, from the beginning of the shipment period. In the judgment of the Court of Appeal, the first of these two contentions was accurate. As Denning LJ expressed it:

> In the absence of express stipulation, I think the credit must be made available to the seller at the beginning of the shipment period. The reason is because the seller is entitled, before he ships the goods to be assured that, on shipment, he will be paid. . . . [W]henever he does ship the goods, he must be able to draw on the credit. He may ship on the very first day of the shipment period.[491]

Since it is the c.i.f. seller who controls the timetable, and should therefore be able to make preparations to ship on the first day of the shipment period secure in the knowledge that he will be paid, Denning LJ's own observations show that the date of opening the credit should be even earlier than the first shipment date. The buyer should have to furnish the credit within a reasonable time before the commencement of the shipment period or, more exactly, by such a date as would afford the seller the chance to ship on the first date if the seller so chose. The pre-shipment period will obviously have to be squeezed, however, to afford the buyer time to open the credit where the contract, as was the case in *Pavia* itself, is concluded close to the commencement of the shipment period.

6.103 **Before the shipment period.** The conclusion of the court in *Pavia* may have been influenced by the limited way in which the sellers put their case. In *Sinaison-Teicher*

---

[487] *Enrico Furst & Co. v WE Fisher Ltd* [1960] 2 Lloyd's Rep. 340 (confirming bank's credit had to be irrevocable too); *Wahbe Tamari & Sons Ltd v Colprogeca Sociedade Geral de Fibras Lda* [1969] 2 Lloyd's Rep. 18 (credit not confirmed where bank retained right of recourse against seller).

[488] *Ibid.* But a non-conforming letter of credit may be cured in time: *Kronman & Co. v Steinberger* (1922) 10 Ll. LR 39.

[489] *United City Merchants (Investments) Ltd v Royal Bank of Canada* [1983] 1 AC 168, 183.

[490] [1952] 2 QB 84.

[491] *Ibid.*, 88.

Inter-American Grain Corpn v Oilcakes and Oilseed Trading Co. Ltd,[492] a case involving not a letter of credit but a functionally similar bank guarantee, a c.i.f. Antwerp/Hamburg contract for the sale of Canadian grain concluded on 11 August called for October/November shipment and for payment in London net cash against shipping documents. On 10 September, the sellers repudiated the contract, not having received the guarantee by that date, and refused to relent when, later that day, a guarantee of payment was issued. The Court of Appeal confirmed the ruling of an arbitration appeal committee that the buyers had to provide the guarantee within a reasonable time before the commencement of the shipment period and had in fact done so. The court pointed out that the buyers were engaged in a 'switch transaction', buying in dollars and reselling in sterling, a procedure that in those days of exchange control required the consent of the Bank of England. The buyers' position was known to the sellers and governed the application of the reasonable time test. In applying the test, a court should take care that a reasonable time before shipment does not become a reasonable time after the conclusion of the contract.

F.o.b. contracts.   In the case of f.o.b. contracts, it has been held that, where the **6.104** goods are to be shipped on a certain date, the credit should be made available a reasonable time before this date,[493] an unexceptionable holding. Where the f.o.b. contract provides for a shipment period, however, the conclusion is not so obvious. It is generally the buyer's duty to nominate an effective ship[494] and therefore the buyer who in such cases controls the shipping timetable, in contrast with c.i.f. contracts, where it is the seller who controls the timetable. This would suggest a duty on the buyer to open a credit when the ship is named, since in the absence of a stated period of notice the buyer must notify the seller of the ship in such time as to give the seller a reasonable time to get the cargo to the shipment port. Nevertheless, a different view was taken in *Ian Stach Co. Ltd v Baker Bosley Ltd*.[495] That case concerned an f.o.b. contract for the sale of ship plates, shipment to occur August/September. Both contracting parties were in the middle of a sales string and the buyers never did succeed in opening a credit within the shipment period. In a damages action by the sellers, the court held that it was the buyers' duty to open the credit by 1 August at the latest. Striving to avoid uncertainty, Diplock J had this to say:

> It seems to me that, particularly in a trade of this kind, where, as is known to all parties participating, that there may well be a string of contracts all of which are financed

---

[492] [1954] 1 WLR 1394.
[493] *Plasticmoda SpA v Davidson's (Manchester) Ltd* [1952] 1 Lloyd's Rep. 527.
[494] *Ibid.*
[495] [1958] 2 QB 130. If the credit has to be opened 'immediately', the buyer may not wait until the beginning of the shipment period: *State Trading Corpn of India Ltd v Cie Française d'Importation et de Distribution* [1983] 2 Lloyd's Rep. 679.

by, and can only be financed by, the credit opened by the ultimate user which goes down the string, getting less and less until it comes to the ultimate supplier, the business sense of the arrangement requires that by the time the shipping period starts each of the sellers should receive the assurance from the banker that if he performs his part of the contract he will receive payment. That seems to me at least to have the advantage of providing a definite date by which the parties know that they have to fulfil the obligation of opening a credit.[496]

6.105 **Criticism.** The best way to dissipate uncertainty is to have a definite date in the contract for the opening of the credit and a seller, aware of supply conditions back up the string, may be faulted for not insisting upon this. Furthermore, the above rule gives an illusory air of certainty if it were to be confined to certain string contracts, not operating as a general rule for all f.o.b. contracts. In other f.o.b. cases, where there is only one buyer, or even a string of buyers without provision being made for a transferable letter of credit, it is not easy to see why the buyer should have to open a credit on the first day of the shipment period. Moreover, the first day of that period would not be sufficient notice if the buyer proposed shipment on that same day.[497] There are, moreover, positive disadvantages in adopting Diplock J's approach, even in the case of string contracts where the letter of credit is a transferable one. A parallel case is the nomination of a ship in f.o.b. string trading conditions. The nomination will have to come from the end buyer, and each buyer will have to give his seller timely notice of the ship for every contract in the string. Obviously, the longer the string, the more likely it is that the first buyer will not give the head seller enough notice of the arrival of the ship.[498] The problem becomes, not so much one of timely notice, but rather one of timely relay of a notice originating with the end buyer. The same could be said for relying advice of a transferable credit in the perhaps rare case[499] of the same credit being used at all stages in the string. The head seller should certainly have reasonable notice of the opening of a credit in order to prepare for shipment. The end buyer should also give sufficient notice of the credit to enable it to be relayed with proper dispatch up a sales string to reach the head seller in time for shipment to be prepared. The difficulty is that the end buyer may not realize there is a sales string or, if asked to open a transferable credit extendable to multiple beneficiaries, may not realize the length of the sales string. The approach favoured by Diplock J

---

[496] Above, n.143. See also the earlier case of *'Baltimex' Baltic Import & Export Co. Ltd v Metallo Chemical Refining Co. Ltd* [1955] 2 Lloyd's Rep. 438. The approach taken by Diplock J was also followed in *State Trading Corpn of India Ltd v Cie Francaise d'Importation et de Distribution* [1983] 1 Lloyd's Rep. 679, 680, but in this case it was the f.o.b. *seller* who controlled the shipping timetable.

[497] If a reasonable time before the commencement of the shipment period were to be required, Diplock J's certainty would be lost.

[498] As shown in *Bunge Corpn v Tradax Export SA*, n. 141 above.

[499] According to UCP 600, Art. 38(b), (d), a transferable credit can be made available in whole or in part to a second beneficiary but cannot be transferred at the request of the second beneficiary to a subsequent beneficiary.

has the drawback of being fashioned for an apparently unusual case. In many sales strings, different (back-to-back) credits may be opened by different buyers; the length of the sales string should therefore have no effect upon the notice that an individual buyer should give. It is submitted that a preferable approach to the one favoured by Diplock J is for the buyer to give the seller notice of the credit a reasonable time before shipment. If the buyer realizes there is a string, whether or not advised of the length of the string, the extent of the buyer's knowledge that the notice has to be passed on can be factored into the length of a reasonable time.

Payment and Examination

Examination.   In a later chapter,[500] consideration will be given to the place of   **6.106** examination as it affected the buyer's right to reject non-conforming goods. Examination also poses the question whether the buyer may decline to pay the price until he has exercised his right to examine the goods.[501] In the case of c.i.f. contracts, it is clearly settled that the buyer is under a duty to pay the price on the documentary transfer and may not defer this duty until the goods have been landed and examined.[502] Though the place of shipment may once in f.o.b. contracts have been *prima facie* the place where the buyer should examine,[503] this rule has frequently been displaced in the interest of preserving the buyer's right of rejection,[504] so that now there may be no presumptive rule at all, the place of examination depending upon the construction of the particular contract.[505]

Examination postponed.   Postponing examination, however, will not necessar-   **6.107** ily mean that the buyer's duty to pay the price is correspondingly deferred.[506] Where an f.o.b. contract calls for payment against documents, examination to take place at the port of discharge, the buyer will be bound to pay when the documents are tendered and may not claim to delay this duty.[507] It should not matter that the goods have arrived in port before the documentary exchange because the bill of lading will still be necessary for access to the goods. Support for this

---

[500] See Ch. 10 below.

[501] Ss. 28 and 34(2) of the Sale of Goods Act.

[502] *Polenghi Bros. v Dried Milk Co. Ltd* (1904) 10 Com. Cas. 42; *E Clemens Horst & Co. v Biddell Bros* [1911] 1 KB 934 (Kennedy LJ); *Berger & Co. Inc. v Gill and Duffus SA*, n. 235 above.

[503] *Perkins v Bell* [1893] 1 QB 193.

[504] *Molling & Co. v Dean & Sons Ltd* (1901) 18 TLR 217; *AJ Frank & Sons Ltd v Northern Peat Co.* [1963] 2 OR 415 (Can.); *Hammer and Barrow v Coca-Cola* [1962] NZLR 723. See now s. 35(6)(b) of the Sale of Goods Act (as amended in 1994).

[505] *JW Schofield & Sons v Rownson, Drew and Clydesdale Ltd* (1922) 10 Ll. LR 480, 482.

[506] Sassoon, *C.I.F. and F.O.B. Contracts*, n. 328 above, paras 626–7, *pace* S. Williston, *The Law Governing Sales of Goods at Common Law and under the Uniform Sales Act* (rev. edn, Baker Voorhis, 1948), para. 448a.

[507] *Morrison v Morrow* (1916) 36 OLR 400 (Can.).

position comes from section 28 of the Sale of Goods Act, which presumptively requires payment on delivery. Delivery to the carrier is presumptively delivery to the buyer under an f.o.b. contract[508] so that the duty to pay would arise at that point unless it were deferred until documents were presented by the seller.[509] If the contract permits the buyer to examine at the port of shipment, the exercise of this right would spare the buyer the trouble of pursuing a defaulting seller to recover the price. In other cases, where the carriage of goods is required but payment is to take place after the goods arrive at their destination,[510] it will depend upon the construction of the contract when exactly payment must be made, but it is likely that the buyer will first have the right to examine the goods.

6.108   **Payment before examination.**   Where the buyer is bound by the contract to pay before examining the goods, attempts are sometimes made to free the buyer from this duty, especially where payment is to be effected through a documentary letter of credit. In such cases, the question is not merely whether the buyer may resist payment but whether an issuing or confirming bank may be restrained from honouring its promise to pay the seller. The very reliability of the binding letter of credit may encourage dubious sales practices and put the buyer in the position of having to sue a remote foreign seller in an unfriendly forum. The bank's obligation to the buyer is to pay against a transfer of documents that on their face are conforming;[511] it would inhibit the free flow of international documentary transactions if the bank were required or permitted to penetrate the documents and look to the condition of the underlying goods.[512] For a similar reason, although the buyer has a reasonable time to reject non-conforming documents, the bank is not permitted to give the buyer time to scrutinize the documents.[513] Nevertheless, the possibility of going behind the documents emerges in a number of cases where the seller, the beneficiary of credit, has been guilty of fraud.

---

[508] S. 32(1); *Wimble Sons & Co. v Rosenberg & Sons*, n. 260 above; *Wait v Baker*, n. 20 above; *Badische Anilin und Soda Fabrik v Basle Chemical Works* [1898] AC 200; *Dutton v Solomonson* (1803) 3 B & P 582; *Dunlop v Lambert* (1839) 6 Cl. & Fin. 600, 620–1; *Calcutta & Burmah Steam Navigation Co. Ltd v De Mattos* (1863) 32 LJ QB 322, 328; *Ex p. Pearson* (1868) 3 Ch. App 443.

[509] In an f.o.b. contract, these would consist principally of bill of lading and invoice. Where the bill of lading never comes into the seller's hands (see *Pyrene Co. Ltd v Scindia Navigation Ltd*, n. 22 above) the contract is likely to require payment against the invoice and a mate's receipt. See *FE Napier v Dexter's Ltd* (1926) 26 Ll. LR 62.

[510] S. 28 thus being displaced.

[511] *Urquart, Lindsay & Co. Ltd v Eastern Bank Ltd* [1922] 1 KB 318, 323; *Westpac Banking Corpn v South Carolina National Bank* [1986] 1 Lloyd's Rep. 311.

[512] UCP 600, Art. 5: all parties to credit operations deal in documents and not in goods and services.

[513] *Bankers Trust Co. v State Bank of India* [1991] 2 Lloyd's Rep. 443.

Payment under Letters of Credit

Documentary compliance.   Where payment is to be made by letter of credit, the   **6.109**
seller's right to be paid depends upon the tender of documents that conform to the
stated requirements on the letter of credit.[514] The documents must be tendered
within the period stipulated in the letter of credit.[515] The strict standard of compliance of the documents with the conditions laid down in the credit was noted
above in relation to bills of lading. Where the credit incorporates UCP 600, documentary conformity is measured by international standard banking practice,[516]
which tolerates minor conformity in the documents. Documents are nevertheless
non-compliant if they do not have the characteristics called for by the UCP rules[517]
or if they contain material omissions.[518] So too are bills of lading dated outside the
stipulated period.[519] A commercial invoice describing the goods as 'in new condition' instead of 'new' sounds alarm bells and is non-compliant.[520] Where a letter
of credit called for bills of lading for about 1400 tons 'Coromandel groundnuts',
the bills were rightly rejected when they referred to 'machine-shelled groundnut
kernels' and had a marginal reference to 'C.R.S.', a trade abbreviation for 'Coros'
or 'Coromandels'.[521] Banks are not expected to have specialist knowledge of the
underlying trade and it is in the nature of documentary compliance that the letter
of credit contract is autonomous of the underlying contract.[522] Banks examine
only the documents to see if the beneficiary is entitled to payment.[523] They have a

---

[514] See further Bridge, n. 16 above, Ch. 6.

[515] UCP 600, Art. 6(d)(i).

[516] According to Article 14(d): 'Data in a document, when read in context with the credit, the
document itself and international standard banking practice, need not be identical to, but must
not conflict with, data in that document, or any other stipulated document or the credit.' This is
somewhat more tolerant than the common law standard (see *Kredietbank Antwerp v Midland Bank
Plc* [1999] 1 Lloyd's Rep. 219), which is likely now to be less strictly observed precisely because of
the change in practice evidenced by the UCP Rules. See *Equitable Trust Co. of New York v Dawson
Partners Ltd* (1927) 27 Ll LR 49, 52. (Lord Sumner): 'There is no room for documents which are
almost the same, or which will do just as well. Business could not proceed securely on any other
lines.'

[517] See UCP 600, Arts 19–28.

[518] *Skandinaviska Kreditaktiebolaget v Barclays Bank* (1925) 22 Ll LR 523.

[519] *Credit Agricole Indosuez v Generale Bank* [2000] 1 Lloyd's Rep. 123.

[520] *Bank Melli Iran v Barclays Bank (Dominion Colonial and Overseas)* [1951] 2 Lloyd's
Rep. 367.

[521] *Rayner (JH) & Co Ltd v Hambro's Bank Ltd* [1943] 1 KB 37.

[522] UCP 600, Art. 4(a).

[523] UCP 600, Art. 5. See *O'Meara (Maurice) Co v National Park Bank*, 146 NE 636 (1925)
at 639: 'The bank . . . was under no obligation to ascertain, either by a personal examination or
otherwise, whether the [goods] conformed to the contract between the buyer and the seller. The
bank was concerned only in the drafts and the documents accompanying them. . . If the drafts,
when presented, were accompanied by proper documents then it was absolutely bound to make the
payment under the letter of credit . . .' See also *Urquart Lindsay & Co v Eastern Bank Ltd* [1922]
1 KB 318, 323.

'maximum of five banking days' to determine whether a presentation is compliant.[524] The stated maximum may in time become the conventional period, though banks in developed commercial centres may need less time in the normal run of case.

6.110 **Copies and originals.** Article 17(a) of UCP 600 calls for at least one original of each document required. Article 17(b) imposes on banks a duty against documents that appear to be original: 'A bank shall treat as an original any document bearing an apparently original signature, mark, stamp, or label of the issuer of the document, unless the document itself indicates that it is not an original.'[525] This places on the bank the burden of showing that a document is not original, which will be hard to discharge given the sophistication of modern copying methods. Moreover, if a document 'states' that it is an original, the bank must accept it.[526] The bank must also accept as an original a document that is 'written, typed, perforated or stamped by the document issuer's hand'[527] or that appears to be on the issuer's 'original stationery'.[528]

6.111 **Fraud.** The autonomy principle mentioned above means that a buyer's complaint about the goods is just as ineffectual to defeat payment under the letter of credit as it is to provide a defence to a claim brought against the buyer as maker of a promissory note or acceptor of a bill of exchange. The letter of credit can therefore serve as a vehicle for the fraudulent exploitation of buyers behind a screen of impeccable documents. The buyer pays and, on examining the goods, finds himself to be the victim of a fraudulent deception. Though hard to establish in practice, fraud on the part of the seller presenting the documents[529] is an important exception to the autonomy principle and a defence to the payment obligation under the letter of credit.[530] Fraud here has its ordinary common law meaning,[531] which is the making of representations by word or conduct without believing

---

[524] UCP 600, Art. 14.

[525] For the difficulties that arose under earlier versions of the UCP Rules, see *Glencore International AG v Bank of China* [1996] 1 Lloyd's Rep. 135; *Kredietbank Antwerp v Midland Bank Plc* [1999] 1 Lloyd's Rep. 219; *Crédit Industriel v China Merchants Bank* [2002] 2 All ER (Comm.) 427.

[526] UCP 600, Art. 17(c)(iii).

[527] UCP 600, Art. 17(c)(i).

[528] UCP 600, Art. 17(c)(ii).

[529] But not the fraud of a third party for whom the buyer is not responsible: *United City Merchants (Investments) Ltd v Royal Bank of Canada* [1983] 1 AC 169.

[530] *Discount Records Ltd v Barclays Bank Ltd* [1975] 1 Lloyd's Rep. 444; *United City Merchants (Investments) Ltd v Royal Bank of Canada*, n. 529 above; *Owen (Edward) Engineering Ltd v Barclays Bank International Ltd* [1978] QB 159; *Harbottle v National Westminster Bank Ltd* [1978] QB 146; *United Trading Corpn SA v Allied Arab Bank Ltd* [1985] 2 Lloyd's Rep. 554 note; *Et. Esefka International Anstalt v Central Bank of Nigeria* [1979] 1 Lloyd's Rep. 445; *Turkiye Is Bankasi AS v Bank of China* [1998] CLC 182; *Wahda Bank v Arab Bank plc* [1998] CLC 689.

[531] *GKN Contractors Ltd v Lloyds Bank plc* (1985) 30 Build LR 48.

them to be true.[532] Lord Diplock has said that the necessary fraud had to embrace 'expressly or by implication, material representations of fact that to [the seller's] knowledge are untrue'.[533] Fraud can be found in the forging of documents or in the making of deliberately untrue statements in documents.[534] Lord Diplock has stressed the public policy basis for suppressing fraud in terms of the maxim *ex turpi causa non oritur actio* or fraud unravels all.[535] Fraud, with its tendency to contaminate transactions and financial systems, cannot therefore be treated only as a matter of private right. The law has an interest in suppressing fraud.[536] Nevertheless, viewed in terms of contract law, the absence of fraud by the applicant may be seen as resting on an implied term in the contract between an issuing bank and an applicant, and in the contracts between issuing bank and beneficiary, and confirming bank and beneficiary.[537]

Injunctive and other relief.   The buyer applicant may apply for an injunction to   **6.112** prevent payment if the bank does not comply with a request to stop payment. The application may seek to restrain the bank from making payment or it may seek to enjoin the seller from claiming under the letter of credit.[538] If the bank has already paid the beneficiary, the buyer will avoid reimbursing the bank only if the latter was 'clearly aware' of the fraud at the time of payment or if fraud was the only reasonable inference to be drawn at the time.[539] It is very difficult and rare for a buyer to succeed in proving fraud at this stage of the proceedings.[540] The mere allegation

---

532   (1889) 14 App. Cas. 337.

533   *United City Merchants (Investments) Ltd v Royal Bank of Canada*, n. 529 above, 183; see also *KBC Bank v Industrial Steels (UK) Ltd* [2001] 1 Lloyd's Rep. 370, 374.

534   *Sztejn v Schroder (Henry J) Banking Corp*, 31 NYS 2d 631 (1941) (approved in the performance bond case of *Owen (Edward) Engineering Ltd v Barclays Bank International Ltd* [1978] QB 159); see *Standard Chartered Bank v Pakistan National Shipping Corp (No 1)* [1998] 1 Lloyd's Rep. 684 (antedating the bill of lading).

535   *United City Merchants (Investments) Ltd v Royal Bank of Canada*, n. 529 above, 184.

536   *Bolivinter Oil SA v Chase Manhattan Bank NA* [1984] 1 Lloyd's Rep. 251, 254. See also the applicant's argument in *Czarnikow-Rionda Sugar Trading Inc. v Standard Bank London Ltd* [1999] 2 Lloyd's Rep. 187, 197.

537   See *Czarnikow-Rionda Sugar Trading Inc. v Standard Bank London Ltd*, n. 536 above. It is not just the applicant buyer, however, who is at risk of fraud. A bank may also suffer loss to the extent that any security it has acquired over shipping documents is of diminished value. See *Solo Industries UK Ltd v Canara Bank* [2001] 1 WLR 1800 (collusive scheme between applicant and beneficiary to defraud the bank by means of imaginary shipments).

538   For statements that the fraud rule is the same in both cases, see *Group Josi Re v Walbrook Insurance Co Ltd* [1996] 1 Lloyd's Rep. 345, 361 (Staughton LJ); *Bolivinter Oil SA v Chase Manhattan Bank NA*, n. 536 above, 256 (Donaldson MR).

539   See *United Trading Corpn SA v Allied Arab Bank Ltd*, n. 530 above, 560; *GKN Contractors Ltd v Lloyds Bank Ltd* (1985) 30 Build LR 48; *Turkiye Is Bankasi AS v Bank of China* [1998] CLC 182; *Wahda Bank v Arab Bank plc*, n. 530 above; *Kvaerner John Brown Ltd v Midland Bank plc* [1998] CLC 446.

540   *Tukan Timber Ltd v Barclays Bank plc* [1987] 1 Lloyd's Rep. 171, 174. See Phillips J in *Deutsche Ruckversicherung AG v Walbrook Insurance Co. Ltd* [1995] 1 WLR 1017, 1030, noting that no application for an injunction on the ground of fraud had ever been upheld in *inter partes* proceedings,

of fraud is not sufficient.[541] Fraud is far from being established just because the conduct of the seller is 'suspicious' and suggests 'the possibility of sharp practice'.[542] A rigorous standard of proof is required, the court being satisfied only with 'clear' evidence[543] of a high standard[544] of which the bank has notice,[545] but it is overstating the case to say that the evidence must exclude any possibility of an innocent explanation.[546] Ackner LJ has called for 'strong corroborative evidence of the allegation, usually in the form of contemporary documents, particularly those emanating from the buyer' so that the buyer has to show that it is seriously arguable that 'the only realistic inference to draw is that of fraud'.[547] In very many cases, moreover, the buyer will not discover the fraud in time to seek the prevention of payment. Even if the buyer is able to act in time, the normal equitable requirement that the balance of convenience should be in favour of granting an injunction is difficult to satisfy. As the matter was put by Kerr J in *Harbottle (RD) (Mercantile) Ltd v National Westminster Bank Ltd*,[548] the applicant has an 'insuperable difficulty': if the bank pays and debits the applicant's bank account, it either did so pursuant to the contract with the applicant, in which case the applicant cannot complain of payment, or it did so in breach of contract, in which case the bank is good for a damages action brought by the applicant.

---

but note the grant of an injunction in *Themehelp Ltd v West* [1996] QB 84 and the refusal of the court to discharge a pre-trial injunction in *Kvaerner John Brown Ltd v Midland Bank plc*, n. 539 above. See the criticism of these cases by Rix J in *Czarnikow-Rionda Sugar Trading Inc. v Standard Bank London Ltd*, n. 536 above.

[541] *Bolivinter Oil SA v Chase Manhattan Bank SA*, n. 536 above, 257; *Discount Records Ltd v Barclays Bank*, n. 530 above.

[542] *Owen (Edward) Engineering Ltd v Barclays Bank*, n. 530 above (Geoffrey Lane LJ).

[543] *Ibid.; Owen (Edward) Engineering Ltd v Barclays Bank*, n. 530 above; *Tukan Timber Ltd v Barclays Bank Plc*, n. 540 above; *Bank of Nova Scotia v Angelica-Whitewear Ltd* (1987) 36 DLR (4th) 161.

[544] *Rafsanjan Producers Co-operative Co. v Bank Leumi (UK) Plc* [1992] 1 Lloyd's Rep. 513.

[545] *Owen (Edward) Engineering Ltd v Barclays Bank*, n. 530 above.

[546] *United Trading Corpn SA v Allied Arab Bank Ltd*, n. 530 above.

[547] *United Trading Corpn SA v Allied Arab Bank Ltd*, n. 530 above, 561. In addition, the seller should be given the chance to answer the allegation: *ibid.* Further support for the heavy nature of the onus on the buyer comes from *Rafsanjan Pistachio Producers Co-Operative v Bank Leumi plc*, n. 544 above; *Discount Records Ltd v Barclays Bank Ltd* [1975] 1 WLR 315; *Bolivinter Oil SA v Chase Manhattan Bank NA* [1984] 1 Lloyd's Rep. 251 (evidence must be 'clear' both as to the fact of fraud and as to the bank's knowledge of it); *Society of Lloyd's v Canadian Imperial Bank of Commerce* [1993] 2 Lloyd's Rep. 579 (fraud must be proven and notice of it to a reasonable banker is not enough). But in *Banque Saudi Fransi v Lear Siegler Services Inc.* [2006] EWCA Civ 1130; [2007] 2 Lloyd's Rep. 47, there is some evidence of an emerging laxer approach to fraud than the standard of 'obvious fraud'. Instead, the test was the usual one for summary judgment under CPR 24.2: there had to be a 'real prospect' of establishing fraud at trial.

[548] [1978] QB 146, 155. See also *United Trading Corpn v Allied Arab Bank Ltd*, n. 530 above, 566–6; *Tukan Timber Ltd v Barclays Bank Ltd*, n. 540 above; *Czarnikow-Rionda Sugar Trading Inc. v Standard Bank London Ltd*, n. 536 above, 190.

The balance of convenience is therefore 'hopelessly weighted' against an applicant seeking to enjoin payment.[549]

Bank resisting payment. If the bank itself resists payment under the letter of credit, the question is whether the bank, like the beneficiary seeking to enjoin payment, must have 'clear evidence' of fraud to resist the beneficiary's demand for payment. A further question is what evidence of fraud must be led by the bank to resist an application by the beneficiary to strike out the bank's fraud defence to payment and an application for summary judgment in favour of the beneficiary. The requirement of clear fraud appears to stem from Lord Diplock's speech in *United City Merchants* but that speech has been cogently shown to make no such demand which, in any case, would be unworkable.[550] The Court of Appeal has laid down in fraud cases the normal test for a defence to summary judgment, namely, that the defendant bank show that there is a 'real prospect' that fraud will be established at trial.[551] In *Balfour Beatty Civil Engineering v Technical & General Guarantee Co Ltd*,[552] the court considered at length the case of the bank, lacking the necessary evidence, which refuses payment to the beneficiary in the expectation that the necessary evidence will be gathered by the time the matter is brought by the beneficiary to court. According to the court, a bank with a clear case that emerges between the making of the demand and the summary judgment stage of the proceedings has a counterclaim to the beneficiary's claim for payment under the credit. A counterclaim would not ordinarily prevent summary judgment from being given in respect of the claim under the credit, but it might be strong enough to generate its own summary judgment. In that case, the two judgments would cancel each other out. If the evidence of beneficiary fraud is not quite so strong but nevertheless powerful, there might ensue a stay of execution on the beneficiary's summary judgment until the issue of fraud is resolved.

6.113

Other possible exceptions to payment. Various other exceptions to the bank's duty to pay against documents have been mooted in the past, including the presence of false statements in the documents, forgery, and documentary nullity. In *United City Merchants (Investments) Ltd v Royal Bank of Canada*,[553] the House of Lords rejected the argument that the presence of even material misstatements[554]

6.114

---

[549] This is so despite the law's keen interest in suppressing fraud and despite the lower forensic standard for establishing the existence of fraud in interlocutory proceedings: *Czarnikow-Rionda Sugar Trading Inc. v Standard Bank London Ltd*, n. 536 above, 202.

[550] *Mahonia Ltd v JP Morgan Chase Bank (No 1)* [2003] EWHC 1927 (Comm); [2003] 2 Lloyd's Rep. 911, 921–2 (Colman J).

[551] *Banque Saudi Fransi v Lear Siegler Services Inc.*, n. 547 above.

[552] (1999) 68 Con LR 180; *Mahonia Ltd v JP Morgan Chase Bank (No 1)*, n. 550 above; see also *Safa Ltd v Banque du Caire* [2000] EWCA Civ 221; [2000] 2 Lloyd's Rep. 600.

[553] n. 529 above, 184.

[554] *Ibid.*

in the documents operated as a defence to payment.[555] The position of a bank resisting payment, or of an applicant seeking to prevent it, was not improved by the presence in one or more documents of false statements rendering them forgeries. In the Court of Appeal in *United City Merchants (Investments) Ltd v Royal Bank of Canada*, Stephenson LJ defined a forgery as a document that told a lie about itself.[556] The bill of lading in that case was certainly forged, in that it was falsely dated, but this fact in the judgment of the House of Lords did not of itself prevent payment to a beneficiary who was not the forger or the forger's principal. The fact that a document contains a false statement, even a false statement of material fact, such as the date of shipment in a bill of lading, does not make it a nullity.[557] A falsely dated bill of lading still performs the functions of a receipt and a document of title to the goods, as well as providing evidence of the terms of the contract of carriage. A bill of lading issued by someone other than the carrier or the carrier's actual or apparent agent might be a nullity since it imposes no binding obligations on the carrier.[558] A bill of lading attesting to an imaginary shipment will certainly be a nullity since it recites something that never in fact took place.[559] The fact that a document has been forged does not make it a nullity,[560] though documentary nullities will certainly contain false statements and may also be forged. Although the matter of a nullity defence to payment was left open by the House of Lords in *United City Merchants*, the Court of Appeal in *Montrod Ltd v Grundkotter Fleischvertriebs-GmbH*[561] firmly ruled against a nullity defence. According to Potter LJ, a general nullity exception was not 'susceptible of precision, involves making undesirable inroads into the principles of autonomy and negotiability universally recognized in relation to letter of credit transactions'.[562]

---

[555] Nevertheless, there is support for the view that a beneficiary who, though not privy to any fraud, becomes aware it before presenting the documents, is disentitled from receiving payment. See Lord Diplock in *United City Merchants (Investments) Ltd v Royal Bank of* Canada, n. 529 above, 183; *Group Josi Re v Walbrook Insurance Co Ltd* [1996] 1 Lloyd's Rep. 345 (Staughton LJ). This position is difficult to justify. Beneficiaries do not warrant the accuracy of the documents they present.

[556] [1981] 3 All ER 142, 159. A bill of lading would be forged if it were falsely dated or signed with a false signature (whether the forged signature of the master or the true signature of someone claiming in the bill to be the master).

[557] See Devlin J in *Kwei Tek Chao v British Traders and Shippers* [1954] 2 QB 459, 475; *Lombard Finance Ltd v Brookplain Trading Ltd* [1991] 1 WLR 271, 277.

[558] *Montrod Ltd v Grundkotter Fleischvertriebs-GmbH* [2001] EWCA Civ 1954; [2002] 1 WLR 1975 would indicate that such a document is a nullity.

[559] Cf *Hindley v East India Produce* [1973] 2 Lloyd's Rep. 515. See also *Rafsanjan Pistachio Producers Co-operative v Bank Leumi plc*, n. 544 above, 540 (invoice a 'complete concoction, and . . . not a commercial invoice at all, since it does not reflect a transaction which actually took place').

[560] Cf also the distinction drawn between bills of lading that could not refer to any cargo, because the goods were never shipped, and bills of lading not issued in accordance with a charter party because they were antedated, made by Morison J in *Transpacific Discovery SA v Cargill International SA (The Elpa)* [2001] 2 Lloyd's Rep. 596 (Inter-Club Agreement between insurers).

[561] n. 558 above.

[562] *Ibid.*, at [58].

There is ample cause for caution in defining what constitutes a nullity; even impaired documents may perform some functions. Nevertheless, a strong case exists for developing a nullity defence to payment as long as nullity is defined in restrictive terms so as to comprise sham pieces of paper, as opposed to unauthorized documents and documents containing misstatements.[563] An inspection certificate signed by the wrong person may still in appropriate cases be called an inspection certificate, but a bill of lading reciting a non-existent shipment is no less a mere scrap of paper than a bill of lading issued by a non-existent shipping line. A 'bill of lading' of this sort evidences or embodies none of the obligations in a genuine bill of lading. The bank's undertaking to pay against a bill of lading must be an undertaking to pay against something that can be described as a genuine bill of lading, embodying at least one of the functions associated with a bill of lading properly so-called. Moreover, the bank might be entitled and bound not to pay under the terms of the UCP Rules themselves, since payment is required against 'stipulated documents'.[564] A piece of paper entitled 'bill of lading' but performing none of the functions performed by bills of lading cannot be a stipulated document.

Illegality. Recently, illegality[565] has emerged as an independent ground for preventing payment under a letter of credit. The illegality may present itself either in the relevant letter of credit contract or in the underlying transaction. So far as it affects the latter then, illegality as an impediment to payment constitutes an exception to the autonomy principle. *Mahonia Ltd v JP Morgan Chase Bank (No. 1)*[566] concerned letters of credit issued under a series of swaps transactions designed in breach of United States law to disguise a loan that should have appeared in the claimant company's accounts. The court concluded that the claimant could not enforce the letter of credit against the defendant bank. English law had long recognized that contracts involving the commission of illegal acts in foreign friendly countries should not be enforced.[567] A distinction was to be drawn, however, between conduct directly prohibited by legislation and conduct that was collateral to an act that was directly prohibited.[568] Letters of credit that were

6.115

---

[563] The Singapore courts have recognized the nullity exception to payment in *Beam Technologies v Standard Chartered Bank* [2003] 1 SLR 597.

[564] UCP 600, Arts 7–8.

[565] To be distinguished from unenforceability under legislation implementing international conventions: *United City Merchants (Investments) Ltd v Royal Bank of Canada*, n. 529 above (Bretton Woods Agreement).

[566] n. 550 above. The question of illegality had earlier been raised in *Group Josi Re v Walbrook Insurance Co Ltd*, n. 555 above. Staughton LJ was firmly of the view that a letter of credit could be tainted by an illegal underlying transaction, citing the case of illegal shipments of arms to Iraq.

[567] *Foster v Driscoll* [1929] 1 KB 470; *Regazzoni v Sethia (KC) (1944) Ltd* [1958] AC 301.

[568] Adopting a distinction made by Clark J at trial in *Group Josi Re v Walbrook Insurance Co Ltd*, n. 555 above, 353-4.

merely a 'facility' to assist performance in a manner that itself was not specifically made illegal were enforceable. Exceptionally, nevertheless, they would not be enforced in flagrant cases of illegal underlying transactions, such as illegal arms sales and the sale of heroin. Somewhat unsatisfactorily, the scope of the illegality exception where conduct is not directly prohibited amounts to a matter of degree, dependent on the extent to which a latter of credit is tainted by the underlying transaction. The present case was 'appropriately serious' for there to be a strongly arguable case that the letter of credit ought not to be enforced against the bank,[569] which should be given leave to defend its actions when the beneficiary sought summary judgment.[570]

Concurrence of Payment and Delivery

6.116 **General.**   A final difficulty arising from the buyer's payment duty is presented by section 28 of the Sale of Goods Act,[571] which states that, unless otherwise agreed,[572] delivery and payment are concurrent conditions. Why, if time of payment is presumptively not of the essence of contracts of sale,[573] and time of delivery is presumptively of the essence of commercial contracts[574] and an open question of construction in other cases,[575] is it possible to say that the duties of payment and delivery are concurrent, which is a clear statement of their equality? One critic has asked: 'Why . . . should the buyer be entitled to repudiate the bargain when the seller is unpunctual, but not the seller when the buyer is at fault?'[576]

6.117 **Differential development.**   One way to resolve the conflict is to assert that the law governing the seller's duty to deliver and the buyer's duty to pay did not develop evenly and the Act captured the law at a time of lop-sided development. Consequently, taking the view that the strictness of the buyer's duty is understated, the conclusion is that the buyer's duty to pay is of the essence whenever the seller's duty is of the essence.[577] This view prefers section 28 in the event of conflict with section 10(1). Another approach would be to modulate the language of section 10(1) by accepting that, while the time of payment may be presumptively not of the essence of all contracts, yet it is presumptively of the essence for that subclass known as commercial sales agreements. The difficulty with this view is that the law was originally codified on the back of commercial contracts. One writer

---

[569] n. 550 above, 926–8.

[570] The evidentiary position was discussed in the case with reference to the position in cases of fraud, discussed above.

[571] Stating the pre-Act common law: *Morton v Lamb* (1797) 7 TR 125.

[572] As it frequently is in commercial sales where 30-day credit and more is commonplace.

[573] Sale of Goods, s. 10(1).

[574] *Bunge Corpn v Tradax Export SA*, n. 141 above.

[575] S. 10(2).

[576] S. Stoljar (1955) 71 *LQR* 527, 538.

[577] See *Mooney v Lipka*, n. 473 above.

has stated that the seller's right under section 48(3) to resell the goods if the buyer does not pay within a reasonable time blunts the impact of section 10(1) and helps to reduce the conflict between it and section 28 to minor proportions.[578]

Separation of buyer's duties.   Another approach is to separate the buyer's duties   **6.118** of payment and acceptance and stress the absence of any reference to the latter in section 10(1); the buyer's duty of acceptance and the seller's duty of delivery could then be equalized. Sales practice allows the separation of the buyer's two duties. If a buyer is allowed to take delivery before payment, this effectuates the parties' intention that the buyer is to have credit. In such a case, it may be quite proper to conclude that the delinquent buyer's breach is not of a term that is of the essence of the contract; The seller has already surrendered his lien[579] and the difference between, for example, an agreed thirty days' credit and the thirty-one or more days taken by the buyer may not be essential. But if the terms of the contract require payment on delivery, the laying of emphasis upon the buyer's failure to take delivery in the manner required by the contract, that is, accompanied by payment,[580] brings out the critical point that it is the intention of the parties that the buyer is to receive no credit. As practically sensible as this approach is, it is hobbled by the failure of section 28 to make any reference to the buyer's duty of acceptance: it is the duty to pay that is said to be correlative with the seller's duty to deliver.

Order of performance.   The most elegant solution to this difficulty, and it is   **6.119** submitted the best one, is to accept that sections 10(1) and 28 both accurately reflect the law but to assert that a critical distinction exists between the order of performance of contractual obligations and the termination of contracts. Section 28 deals with the former and section 10(1) with the latter. A buyer unable or failing to pay where payment and delivery are concurrent could not call upon the seller to deliver since he has failed to perform a condition precedent to delivery, but this would not necessarily mean that the seller might terminate the contract on the day payment failed to materialize. If time of payment were not of the essence, the seller would in effect be entitled to suspend his own delivery obligation, citing in defence the buyer's non-payment, but would only be allowed to terminate the contract when the buyer's breach over time went to the root of the contract. Where the default is on the seller's side and time is of the essence of the seller's performance, the buyer would not have to wait but could terminate immediately upon the seller's breach. This solution accommodates the differing failure of consideration and dependent promises principles[581] and the contrasting cases

---

[578] P. S. Atiyah, *The Sale of Goods* (11th edn, by J. N. Adams, Longman, 2005), 309–10.
[579] S. 43(1).
[580] S. 27.
[581] Ch. 10 below.

of *Hongkong Fir Shipping Co. Ltd v Kawasaki Kisen Kaisha Ltd*[582] and *Bunge Corpn v Tradax Export SA*.[583] Further support for this solution lies in the case where a seller wrongfully claims a price in excess of that agreed but, having taken a mistaken view of its rights under the contract, cannot be said by the act of demanding a higher price alone to have repudiated the contract. In such a case,[584] it cannot be said that the seller is ready and willing to perform. Consequently, the buyer should be dispensed from having to accept the goods and pay for them so long as the seller remains unready and unwilling, but would be entitled to terminate the contract only if the seller rejected a tender of the correct price.

Waiver of Delivery and Payment Obligations

6.120 **Meaning of waiver.** Few words in contract law can be surrounded by so much terminological confusion as 'waiver'. First of all, it can refer to cases where a party (the waivor) excuses another (the waivee) from performing an obligation in full or in the manner or by the date required by the contract. In this sense, waiver operates to prevent the waivor from refusing modified performance from the waivee and from terminating the contract because the modified performance departs from the original contract standard; it also precludes a damages action for breach of contract brought by the waivor. Even here, waiver needs to be distinguished from rescission, variation, and promissory estoppel which, in pursuit of the same goals, have developed along different lines, largely because of difficulties posed by the old writing requirement for sale of goods and by the doctrine of consideration.[585] Secondly, waiver is used more loosely to connote an election between inconsistent rights, such that, the waivor having chosen one right, he is thereafter prevented from changing his mind and pursuing the other. If the waivor equivocates, however, his decision may be made for him by the law.[586] Waiver in this second sense is dealt with explicitly in section 11(2) of the Sale of Goods Act, which states that the buyer, faced with a breach of condition by the seller, 'may elect to elect the breach of condition as a breach of warranty and not as a ground for treating the contract as repudiated'. Section 35 then puts such a waiver in the context of the buyer accepting the goods so as to lose the right to reject them and terminate the contract.[587] In this case, however, the buyer's right to damages for breach of contract is not extinguished.

---

[582] [1962] 2 QB 26.
[583] n. 141 above.
[584] *Vaswani v Italian Motors (Sales and Services) Ltd* [1996] 1 WLR 270.
[585] S. Stoljar (1957) 35 *Can. Bar Rev.* 485; G. H. Treitel, *The Law of Contract* (12th edn, by E. Peel, Sweet & Maxwell, 2007), 204–7.
[586] *The Kanchenjunga* [1990] 1 Lloyd's Rep. 391, 398 (Lord Goff).
[587] *Ibid.*

Election.   It has been proposed that the above two meanings should be distin-   **6.121**
guished by referring to the first as 'total waiver' and the second as 'waiver in the
sense of election'.[588] Both types of waiver demand a clear[589] representation by
words or conduct emanating from the waivor,[590] but there are differences. Total
waiver requires prejudicial reliance by the waivee on the representation, or such
other alteration of position as would make it unfair or inequitable for the waivor
to retract the representation.[591] Election waiver, however, imposes no such requirement[592] and is best seen as promoting the interests of certainty and constancy in
contractual dealings: having approbated, the waivor may not reprobate.[593] In the
case of total waiver, the requirement of a clear representation does not necessitate
that the waivor knew the consequences of what he was doing or was aware of the
legal significance of the step he was taking.[594] But since election waiver is based,
not upon the reasonable interpretation by the waivee of the waivor's conduct, but
rather upon the choice by the waivor between inconsistent rights, this choice
needs to be an informed one.[595] How informed the choice must be is a difficult
question: at one end of the spectrum is the view that the waivor must know the
facts supporting his right to choose without being aware of the legal significance
of his choice,[596] or even that there is a right to choose,[597] while at the other end
knowledge of the legal right to choose between inconsistent rights is necessary.[598]
As pure as the latter approach may be, it does condone ignorance of the law.

---

[588] Treitel, n. 585 above at 909.

[589] *Bunge SA v Cie Européenne de Céréales* [1982] 2 Lloyd's Rep. 306; *Société Italo-Belge pour le Commerce et l'Industrie v Palm and Vegetable Oils (Malaysia) Sdn Bhd (The Post Chaser)*, n. 94 above.

[590] Other examples are: *Finagrain SA Geneva v P Kruse Hamburg* [1976] 2 Lloyd's Rep. 508; *Edm. JM Mertens & Co. PVBA v Veevoder Import Export Vimex BV* [1979] 2 Lloyd's Rep. 372; *Peter Cremer v Granaria BV* [1981] 2 Lloyd's Rep. 583; *Bunge SA v Schleswig-Holsteinische Hauptgenossenschaft GmbH* [1978] 1 Lloyd's Rep. 480; *Bremer Handels GmbH v Bunge Corpn* [1983] 1 Lloyd's Rep. 476; *Bremer Handels GmbH v Deutsche-Conti Handels GmbH* [1983] 2 Lloyd's Rep. 45; *Bremer Handels GmbH v Raiffeisen EG* [1982] 1 Lloyd's Rep. 599; *Cobec Brazilian Trading and Warehousing Corpn v Alfred C. Toepfer* [1983] 2 Lloyd's Rep. 386.

[591] *Société Italo-Belge pour le Commerce et l'Industrie v Palm and Vegetable Oils (Malaysia) Sdn. Bhd.*, n. 94 above.

[592] *Peyman v Lanjani* [1985] Ch. 457.

[593] *Scarf v Jardine* [1882] 7 App. Cas. 345; *Craine v Colonial Mutual Fire Insurance Co.* (1920) 28 CLR 305, 326–7; *Clough v LNWR Co.* (1871) LR 7 Ex. 26; *China National Foreign Trade Corpn v Evlogia Shipping* [1979] 1 WLR 1018; *Peyman v Lanjani*, n. 592 above.

[594] *Peyman v Lanjani*, n. 592 above, 189; *Panchaud Frères SA v Ets. General Grain Co.* [1970] 1 Lloyd's Rep. 53; *The Kanchenjunga*, n. 586 above, 398–9.

[595] *Peyman v Lanjani*, n. 592 above. This case shows that election may fail for want of knowledge but that the same conduct may give rise to a binding estoppel. Since the facts may support election and total waiver in close proximity, the confusion between the two waivers is hardly surprising: *Bremer Handels GmbH v C. Mackprang Jr.* [1979] 1 Lloyds's Rep. 221.

[596] *Cerealgamani v Toepfer* [1981] 1 Lloyd's Rep. 337.

[597] *Kammins Ballroom Co. Ltd v Zenith Investments Ltd* [1971] AC 850, 863 (Lord Diplock).

[598] *Peyman v Lanjani*, n. 592 above, 188. This view received a cool reception from Lord Goff in *The Kanchenjunga*, n. 586 above, 398–9. *Peyman* asserts also that the elector need not know that his choice is irrevocable (at 180) or understand the legal consequences of his choice.

Moreover, if applied relentlessly in practice, it is doubtful that there could ever be a binding election. In the case where election is most likely to be of practical significance, namely, where the buyer wishes to reject the goods and terminate the contract, the acceptance rules of section 35 of the Sale of Goods Act create a special regime of election that excludes the issue of knowledge.

6.122 **Distinguishing waiver and election.** The factual difficulty of separating these two principal meanings of waiver is borne out by an examination of *Panoutsos v Raymond Hadley Corpn of New York*.[599] A divisible contract for the sale of 4,000 tons of flour provided that the buyer should pay for each shipment by means of a confirmed credit. The seller made a number of shipments before declining to make more on the ground that the credit opened by the buyer at the beginning of the shipment period was not a confirmed credit. The question was whether the seller, having taken no objection to the unconfirmed credit in the past, could cancel the contract without notice in respect of outstanding shipments. The answer was that the seller could not, but that his conduct in drawing knowingly on an unconfirmed credit would not prevent him from giving for the future reasonable notice that a confirmed credit be opened.

6.123 **Difficulty of drawing distinction.** As regards past shipments, the conduct of the seller in shipping the goods might be seen as an election to affirm the contract, reserving any entitlement to claim damages; but each such act of condonation might also be seen as a representation by way of total waiver to the buyer that he could continue to make the unconfirmed credit available for future shipments. What makes it hard to separate the two waivers is that breaches of contract of this kind may not yield a provable damages claim, so that one distinguishing feature of the two waivers[600] is empirically absent. In addition, the divisibility of the contract means that any election by the seller relates only to the particular shipment, a state of affairs which, again empirically, is hard to distinguish from the freedom given to a total waivor in contracts involving continual or protracted performance to retract the waiver upon reasonable notice to the waivee. By stating that the seller could reinstate the need for a confirmed credit upon reasonable notice to the buyer, the court would seem to have applied a version of total waiver.[601] But this does not mean that the history of the transaction to date could not be explained in terms of election waiver; indeed, the seller's action in making the *first* shipment against the

---

[599] [1917] 1 KB 767. This may account for a judicial failure from time to time to distinguish the two types of waiver: see, e.g., *Harthley v Hymans* [1920] 3 KB 75.

[600] *Ets. Soules & Cie v International Trade Development Co.* [1979] 1 Lloyd's Rep. 122, 133, affirmed on this point [1980] 1 Lloyd's Rep. 129.

[601] By way of contrast, a court's conclusion that the acceptance of non-conforming performance in the past under a divisible contract is no representation that similar performance will be accepted in the future seems more in line with election waiver. See, e.g., *Jackson v Rotax Motor and Cycle Co.* [1910] 2 KB 937; *Finagrain SA Geneva v P Kruse Hamburg*, n. 590 above.

unconfirmed credit, no prior material representation having been made to the buyer, could only be explained as election waiver in relation to that shipment.

A difficult case.   The need to distinguish the two types of waiver is also evident   **6.124**
in *Panchaud Frères SA v Ets. General Grain Co.*,[602] which concerned a contract for
the sale of 5,500 tonnes of Brazilian yellow maize c.i.f. Antwerp, shipment June/
July. The sellers tendered a bill of lading relating to one shipment for 200 tonnes
dated 31 July but an accompanying certificate clearly showed that shipment had
occurred around 10 to 12 August.[603] When the documents were tendered, the
buyers paid without objection and, raising the issue of late shipment some two
years after the dispute with the sellers arose, were held to have lost the right to
reject the goods on that ground. Lord Denning explained the result in terms of
total waiver or, as he preferred to call it, estoppel by conduct,[604] since the seller had
been led to believe that strict rejection rights for late shipment would not be
enforced.[605] Yet he confused the picture by introducing as an example of such an
estoppel the acceptance rules in section 35 of the Sale of Goods Act. These have
nothing to do with total waiver;[606] they amount to a statutorily modified version
of election waiver that leaves intact the buyer's right to claim damages, a right that
would disappear in the case of total waiver and its cognates, such as estoppel by
conduct and promissory estoppel. Winn LJ also thought in terms of total waiver,
though he preferred to reword it as a requirement of fair conduct between the parties.[607] Yet he too introduced confusion with election waiver by going on to say
that '[t]here may be an inchoate doctrine stemming from the manifest convenience of consistency in pragmatic affairs, negativing any liberty to blow hot and
cold in commercial conduct'.[608] Given the above lack of clarity in the law, it was

---

[602]   n. 594 above. It was applied in *Bunge GmbH v Alfred C Toepfer* [1978] 1 Lloyd's Rep. 506,
approved in *Glencore Grain Rotterdam BV v Liberco* [1997] 4 All ER 514, 527 distinguished on more
or less identical facts in *V Berg & Son Ltd v Vanden-Avenne Izegem PVBA* [1977] 1 Lloyd's Rep. 499
and criticized in *Procter & Gamble Phillipine Manufacturing Corpn v Peter Cremer GmbH & Co.
(The Manila)* [1988] 3 All ER 843, 853 ('no distinctive principle of law can be distilled from the
Panchaud case, which . . . is so often cited as an authority of the last resort'), where the court declined
to overturn an arbitral finding that the buyers had not waived their right to reject the goods.

[603]   In any conflict of dates between the two documents, the date in the certificate is to be preferred because an independent inspector has no reason to falsify the date, whereas bills of lading are
notoriously dated on that most elastic of dates, the last of the month.

[604]   See also *Intertradex SA v Lesieur Tourteaux SARL* [1978] 2 Lloyd's Rep. 509.

[605]   n. 594 above, 57.

[606]   See *BP Exploration Co. (Libya) Ltd v Hunt* [1979] 1 WLR 783, 810–12 (Robert Goff LJ).

[607]   n. 594 above, 59. For the view that the *Panchaud* principle should be applied with 'robust-
ness' and that grain traders are not 'fragile characters wilting under the ups and downs of international trade', see *V Berg & Son Ltd v Vanden-Avenne Izegem PVBA*, n. 602 above, 505 (Lawton LJ).

[608]   n. 595 above, 59. In *BP Exploration Co. (Libya) Ltd v Hunt*, n. 606 above, 810–12, Robert
Goff LJ is under no doubt that the root of *Panchaud Frères* is election waiver: 'The decision stems
from the need for finality in commercial transactions. . . . [It] does not depend in any way on the
representee having relied upon any representation by the buyer.'

no great surprise that the claim was made by a seller in a subsequent case[609] that the buyers' taking up of manifestly non-conforming documents amounted also to a representation that they would not pursue a damages claim against the seller; the court, however, found no sufficiently clear representation to this effect.[610] The problem is compounded by the fusion of total waiver, exercised in the past by common law courts in respect of the manner and time of payment and delivery, but not the substance of those obligations, and promissory estoppel,[611] which has been applied to alter with permanent effect the substance of contractual obligations. Since promissory estoppel is capable of having such permanent characteristics, it becomes all the more important not to confuse it with election waiver.

6.125 **Effect of waiving delivery date.** As stated above, total waiver has been preoccupied in the past with the modalities as opposed to the substance of contractual performance. For example, in *Hartley v Hymans*[612] a contract for the sale of 11,000 pounds of cotton yarn required delivery at the rate of 1,100 pounds a week. The buyers could have terminated for the various delays of the sellers in making deliveries, but their demand for better deliveries induced the sellers to believe that the contract was still on foot. Without giving the sellers notice that outstanding deliveries should be made within a reasonable time, the buyers peremptorily repudiated the contract. McCardie J held that the conduct of the buyers in pressing the sellers for further deliveries implied a new agreement that these deliveries could be made in an extended, reasonable period to be defined by the buyers. But the buyers never did define this further period and were liable in damages for non-acceptance when not honouring their undertaking to accept the outstanding deliveries. The effect of waiving the agreed date is that any condition in the contract that the goods be delivered on the agreed date is deemed never to have existed.[613] A waiver may be effective, moreover, even where it occurs after the contractual delivery period has expired.[614]

---

609 *Ets. Soules & Cie v International Trade Development Co.* [1980] 1 Lloyd's Rep. 129.

610 See too *Cook Industries Inc. v Meuneries Liégeoises SA* [1981] 1 Lloyd's Rep. 359; *Bunge SA v Cie Européenne de Céréales*, n. 589 above; *Bremer Handels GmbH v Finagrain Cie Commerciale Agricole et Financière SA* [1981] 2 Lloyd's Rep. 259. See also Robert Goff LJ in *Ets. Soules & Cie*, n. 609 above, 133: 'Now there is no question of the buyers being deprived of their right to claim damages by any application of the doctrine of election. The sellers recognize that what they must do is to invoke the principle of equitable estoppel.'

611 *Charles Rickards Ltd v Oppenhaim*, n. 181 above.

612 [1920] 3 KB 475.

613 See *Alexander v Gardner* (1835) 1 Bing NC 671 (where the buyer accepted shipping documents evidencing a late shipment and the goods were lost in a shipwreck), approved in *Hartley v Hymans*, n. 612 above, 486. When s. 4 of the Sale of Goods Act 1893 (as well as its predecessor, s. 4 of the Statute of Frauds 1677) was in force, a verbal agreement to accept delivery out of time could not be enforced for want of writing: *Plevins v Downing* (1876) 1 CPD 220.

614 *Tyers v Rosedale and Ferryhill Iron Co.* (1875) LR 10 Ex 195; *Hartley v Hymans*, n. 612 above, 487, disapproving *Corn Products Co. v Fry* [1917] WN 224.

Reviving time of the essence after waiver. A waiver of the due delivery date   **6.126**
arose in *Charles Rickards Ltd v Oppenhaim,*[615] where a contract for the sale of a
coach-built car required delivery at the latest within seven months. When the car
was not delivered on time, the buyer continued to press for delivery; he had thus
elected not to terminate and had represented to the seller that he would accept a
late delivery. After further delays, the buyer informed the seller that he would not
accept the car after a stated future date, which the seller was again unable to meet.
The seller argued that the buyer's waiver of the original delivery date, which was
of the essence of the contract, meant that time was now at large. Delivery thereafter had to be made within a reasonable time, a formula that should take account
of the seller's material and labour difficulties. The court, however, found for the
buyer who was entitled by a proper notice to make time of the essence again.[616] In
this sense, the buyer's waiver was revocable on reasonable notice, but a seller irrevocably relying upon a buyer's waiver, such as the seller shipping through Rotterdam
instead of Ostend, should fear no such change of mind by the buyer.

Waiver and place of delivery. The place of delivery was the subject of a waiver   **6.127**
in a case[617] where the goods were to be shipped through Ostend but the sellers
rerouted them through Rotterdam.[618] The buyer made no objection when the
sellers announced this was to happen. The ship carrying the rerouted goods was
stranded and the goods lost. Since the buyer by his conduct had waived the sellers'
obligation to ship *via* Ostend, it meant that the risk had passed to the buyer, who
therefore was liable to pay the price.

---

[615] n. 181 above.
[616] No notice would be required if a specific extension period is given and lapses: *Nichimen
Corpn v Gatoil Overseas Inc.* [1987] 2 Lloyd's Rep. 46.
[617] *Leather-Cloth Co. v Hieronimus* (1875) LR 10 QB 140.
[618] In fact Ostend had been initially chosen over Rotterdam only because the latter had earlier
been ice-bound.

7

THE IMPLIED TERMS OF DESCRIPTION, FITNESS, AND QUALITY

Introduction. This chapter deals with terms concerning the description, **7.01** fitness, and quality of the contract goods that are implied by statute into the contract[1] unless the parties have excluded them within the limits permitted by

---

[1] In so far as certain statutory changes made to the original Act of 1893 affect the substance of the terms, note should be taken of the implementation dates of these changes: see Sale of Goods Act 1979, Sch. 1 for the position before and after the Supply of Goods (Implied Terms) Act 1973. (References hereinafter to the law before and after 1973 are to the passing of this Act.) See also the Sale and Supply of Goods Act 1994 for the position after 2 Jan. 1995.

the law.[2] An examination of the general law of contract shows that it is not easy to pin down the nature of implied contractual terms. Expressed as a simple dichotomy, they come in two different versions: first, terms agreed in fact by the parties that are either so obvious that they do not need to be stated[3] or that the parties have not troubled to record in writing;[4] and secondly, those terms implied by law into contracts to give them a minimum of business efficacy,[5] doubtless in accordance with the paramount intention of the parties to create a workable contractual agreement.[6] One explanation of certain implied terms is that initially they express the actual agreement of contracting parties but that, under the weight of case law and inherited assumptions, they become over time automatic accessories of particular contract types.[7] The final stages in the development of an implied term may then be seen in its incorporation in a statute that codifies the common law and in subsequent attempts by common law and statutory means to prevent its exclusion. It is arguable that this has been the history of implied terms, the subject of this chapter. Nevertheless, there is a powerful and compelling contrary argument that the nineteenth-century cases laid down in an interventionist way these implied terms from the outset as rules of law.[8]

7.02 **Additional implied terms.** Whatever may be the origin of the implied terms, section 14(1) of the Sale of Goods Act states that no other implied terms of fitness and quality exist in a contract of sale[9] apart from those laid down in section 14,[10] thereby declaring that section 14 is a complete code of implied fitness and quality. This provision, it is submitted, ought not to be read as ousting a term that can genuinely be implied in fact,[11] though one should not underestimate the flexibility and range of the statutory implied terms. The statutory scheme of implied

---

[2] On exclusion and similar clauses, see Ch. 9 below.

[3] *Shirlaw v Southern Foundries* (1926) Ltd [1939] 2 KB 206; *Trollope and Colls Ltd v North West Regional Hospital Board* [1973] 1 WLR 601.

[4] *Liverpool City Council v Irwin* [1977] AC 239.

[5] *The Moorcock* (1889) 14 PD 64; *Lister v Romford Ice Co. Ltd* [1957] AC 555.

[6] Cf Lord Tomlin in *Hillas & Co. Ltd v Arcos* [1932] All ER 494, 499: '[T]he problem for a court of construction must always be so to balance matters that, without violation of essential principle, the dealings of men may so far as possible be treated as effective, and that the law may not incur the reproach of being the destroyer of bargains.'

[7] Cf Lord Radcliffe in *Lister v Romford Ice Co. Ltd*, n. 5 above, 591–2: '[T]he common law is a body of law which develops in process of time in response to the developments of society in which it rules. Its movement may not be perceptible at any distinct point of time, nor can we always see how it gets from one point to another; but I do not think that, for all that, we need abandon the conviction of Galileo that somehow, by some means, there is a movement.'

[8] See B. Nicholas, 'Fault and Breach of Contract', in J. Beatson and D. Friedmann (eds), *Good Faith and Fault in Contract Law* (OUP, London, 1995). Support for this view comes from the language of the judgment of Best CJ in *Jones v Bright* (1829) 5 Bing. 533.

[9] See *McDonald v Empire Garage (Blackburn) Ltd*, *The Times*, 8 October 1975.

[10] And s. 15 for sales by sample.

[11] S. 62(2) permits the incorporation of supplementary common law.

terms may be seen as a device that preempts much litigation about quality and fitness, setting a standard against which the parties can define their contractual rights and duties. Section 14(1) may also have a dampening effect on the inference of duties in tort between the seller and buyer.[12]

Caveat emptor.   The implied terms provide buyers with a healthy measure of   **7.03** protection against defective, disappointing, and substandard goods.[13] The existence of these very effective implied terms is less widely known among the population at large than it should be and there exist commonplace misunderstandings that manufacturers are liable for defective goods, and that buyers may freely return goods to retail sellers for no other reason than a change of mind. At frequent intervals there surfaces the maxim *caveat emptor*. It lingers in section 14(1) but its pedigree and meaning are both obscure. Translated literally, it exhorts buyers to beware, and buyers exhibit proper caution who examine goods carefully before they purchase them or secure from the seller an express warranty. As a general bar to recovery, *caveat emptor* belongs to a primitive economy of specific goods and concrete transactions. Even at its height, it never condoned fraud and other unscrupulous practices; if it has a meaning today, the maxim does not instruct buyers that they contract at their own risk but that they should take sensible precautions. It may also serve as a reminder that sellers have no duty of disclosure, either at common law or under the Sale of Goods Act.[14] *Caveat emptor* has been severely criticized for its spurious Roman pretensions and its incompatibility with mediaeval and religious notions of sellers' obligations for the quality of their wares. It has been described as a nineteenth-century invention that 'sharpened wits, taught self-reliance, [and] made a man—an economic man—out of the buyer'.[15] The lingering presence of *caveat emptor* in section 14(1) is rendered largely insignificant by the extensive protection afforded to buyers by the implied terms in that section, as well as by guarantees and product liability provisions.[16]

Correspondence with Contractual Description

General.   According to section 13(1) of the Sale of Goods Act,[17] it is an implied   **7.04** term of the contract that the goods shall correspond with their description where the contract is for the sale of goods by description. This term has the status

---

12 See *Medivance Instruments Ltd v Gaslane Pipework Services Ltd* [2002] EWCA Civ 500 at [15].
13 As for express guarantees and warranties, see Ch. 8 below.
14 See *Stewart v Perth and Kinross Council* [2004] UKHL 16 at [18] (Lord Hope).
15 W. H. Hamilton, 'The Ancient Maxim Caveat Emptor' (1928) 40 *Yale LJ* 1133, 1186.
16 Ch. 8 below.
17 As modified by the Sale and Supply of Goods Act 1994, Sch. 2.

of a condition. This provision prompts two principal questions.[18] First, when does a sale of goods agreement take place by description, and secondly, which words used constitute that description? An answer to the first question in the affirmative does not as such identify the relevant words of description.[19] The words of section 13(1) afford no help in answering either question but some assistance is given in answering the first question by section 13(3), which states that exposing goods for sale or hire does not prevent a sale of goods from being a sale by description. As for the second question, section 13(2) makes it clear that, in the case of a sale by sample, the compliance of the goods with the sample does not dispense with the need to comply also with the description.[20]

Description and Satisfactory Quality

7.05 **Buying by description.** A long-standing difficulty with the description condition has been its relationship over the years with the merchantable (now satisfactory) quality condition. Formerly,[21] in order for the merchantable quality condition to apply, the goods had to be 'bought by description from a seller who deals in goods of that description'; section 13 therefore operated as a gateway into the merchantable quality condition in section 14(2). The tendency in some older authorities to assert that a sale of specific goods is not a sale by description[22] is a clear example of *caveat emptor* thinking and such authorities should therefore be treated with caution. Denying the application of section 13 served to exclude merchantable quality and meant that a buyer, unless able to rely upon the fitness for purpose condition, had to protect himself either by a careful pre-examination of the goods or by bargaining with the seller for an express warranty. The enactment of the Sale of Goods Act in 1893 changed the law by providing that the opportunity to examine goods did not as such rule out merchantable quality;[23] rather, it was excluded only by an actual examination and then to the extent only of 'defects which such examination ought to have revealed'.[24] Now, since goods available for pre-contractual examination had to be specific goods or part of a specific bulk, this meant that the merchantable quality condition could, despite

---

[18] There is a confusing tendency in the cases to conflate them; see, e.g., *Harlingdon and Leinster Enterprises Ltd v Christopher Hull Fine Art Ltd* [1991] 1 QB 564 (Nourse LJ).
[19] See *Rosengrans Tann Ltd v Ayres* [2001] EWCA Civ 997 at [27].
[20] See *Wallis, Son & Wells v Pratt & Haynes* [1911] AC 394, 399. For the pre-statutory position, see *Nichol v Godts* (1854) 10 Ex. 191; *Azémar v Casella* (1867) LR 2 CP 431; *Josling v Kingsford* (1863) 13 CBNS 447.
[21] Before 1973.
[22] Discussed in the text accompanying nn. 30 *et seq.* below.
[23] Cf *Jones v Just* (1868) LR 3 QB 197, where examination precluded protection even against latent, undiscoverable defects. The law was otherwise in the case of latent misdescription: *Josling v Kingsford*, n. 20 above.
[24] S. 14(2) of the 1893 Act.

the *caveat emptor* maxim, apply to specific goods;[25] it meant also that the sales of some specific goods at least had to be sales by description.

Quality and description.   The intimate connection between description and merchantable quality is also revealed by the difficulty of distinguishing them in the early cases. For example, in *Gardiner v Gray*,[26] Lord Ellenborough said of a contract for the sale of twelve bags of waste silk: **7.06**

> [T]he purchaser has a right to expect a saleable article answering the description in the contract. Without any particular warranty, this is an implied term in every such contract. Where there is no opportunity to inspect the commodity, the maxim *caveat emptor* does not apply. He cannot without a warranty insist that it shall be of any particular quality or fineness, but the intention of both parties must be taken to be, that it shall be saleable in the market under the denomination mentioned in the contract between them. The purchaser cannot be supposed to buy goods to lay them on a dunghill.

Later cases, however, showed there was more to merchantable quality than saleability under the contract description. Goods might satisfy the contract description and yet be unmerchantable;[27] it was never likely that goods could be of merchantable quality without complying with their description.

Significance of examination.   Lord Ellenborough's words are useful in positing a distinction, not between specific and unascertained goods as such, but between goods that could and goods that could not have been examined before the contract. As will be seen, this has had an impact not just on the presence of the description condition but also on its range in a given case. The early existence of a description requirement in at least some specific goods cases is also apparent in the way that description can apply to a sale by sample[28] for, in effect, the buyer is being offered an implicit assurance that he will receive the specific goods, or that the goods supplied will come from the specific bulk, from which the sample is drawn. Yet the belief, once entertained, that specific goods are sold as such and not by description has given rise to difficulties lingering on to the present day.   **7.07**

Sale by Description

Goods exposed for sale.   As stated above, section 13(1) is of no help in showing when a sale takes place by description. The issue here is not how far the range of description goes in a given case but whether there is any description at all. The presence of at least some descriptive language is needed before section 13(1) can apply to a particular contract; the range of the description then determines   **7.08**

---

25 *Taylor v Combined Buyers Ltd* [1924] NZLR 627, 635.
26 (1815) 4 Camp. 144, 145. See also *Wieler v Schilizzi* (1856) 17 CB 619; *Mody v Gregson* (1868) LR 4 Ex. 49.
27 *Jones v Just*, n. 23 above, and cases discussed below.
28 Referred to in the text accompanying n. 20 above.

whether section 13(1) has been infringed. Section 13(3)[29] provides: 'A sale of goods is not prevented from being a sale by description by reason only that, being exposed for sale or hire, they are selected by the buyer.' Because this provision again does not cover the range of description, its enactment was probably unnecessary since, at the same time, the merchantable quality condition was amended so as to remove any need for the sale to take place by description. Be that as it may, this provision removed any lingering doubt that the selection of goods by a buyer from a shelf in a retail store prevented a sale from taking place by description;[30] it did not, however, assert that such a sale necessarily did take place by description, or that all sales were in one degree or another sales by description.

7.09 Unascertained goods.   Where the contract is for unascertained goods, it is beyond controversy that the sale must be by description since the buyer must have some means of knowing whether the goods tendered by the seller are the goods called for by the contract. More difficult in such a case is the range of the description and, in particular, the difference between words that identify goods and those that denote the quality of goods.[31] Specific goods, on the other hand, have been identified and agreed upon at the contract date. Where the buyer has seen the goods,[32] he may not need words from the seller to recognize them when they are delivered at a later date, but does this mean that such a sale does not take place by description?

7.10 Specific goods.   In *Taylor v Combined Buyers Ltd*, Salmond J said:

> In the case of specific articles . . . it is possible to sell them without any description at all. The article sold may conceivably be identified merely by its presence and sold *tale quale* without any description of its nature whatever, the buyer taking the chance, for example, as to whether the article submitted to him is a diamond or a piece of glass. In practice, however, even specific articles are generally sold by description in some sense. They are sold as being of some specified or disclosed nature. An animal is sold as a horse, or as a cow. A precious stone is sold as being a diamond or a ruby.[33]

In other words, specific goods are, apart from exceptional cases, sold by description.[34] In *Grant v Australian Knitting Mills Ltd*, Lord Wright made it clear that the sale of items in a retail store took place by description:[35]

> It may be pointed out that there is a sale by description even though the buyer is buying something displayed before him on the counter: a thing is sold by description,

---

[29] Dating from 1973, with minor changes made in 1979.

[30] See *Wren v Holt* [1903] 1 KB 610, 615.

[31] Discussed in the text accompanying nn. 43 *et seq.* below.

[32] In some cases of specific goods, the buyer will not have seen them, e.g., *Varley v Whipp* [1900] 1 QB 513.

[33] N. 25 above, 633–4. See also *ibid.*, 635–6: '[T]he mere fact that a sale is a sale of a specific chattel is not conclusive to show that it is not a sale by description.'

[34] [1936] AC 85, 100.

[35] A proposition more tentatively expressed in the later s. 13(3).

though it is specific, so long as it is not sold merely as the specific thing but as a thing corresponding to a description, e.g., woollen undergarments, a hot-water bottle, a second-hand reaping machine, to select a few obvious examples.[36]

To make sense of it all, it should be understood that words of description need not take a written or oral form; they can be circumstantial. It is not for nothing that section 13 deals with the *implied* condition of correspondence with description. Beyond the proposition that a seller may employ words of description and yet not give an express warranty, a nineteenth-century truth that seems outmoded in modern times, the language of section 13(1) also underlines that description is coloured by place and conduct. To revert to Salmond J's example in *Taylor v Combined Buyers Ltd*,[37] a buyer may take the chance of an item proffered being either diamond or glass, but it would be a most unusual contract. Expensive jewellery stores sell gems, not pieces of glass, and the price demanded of the buyer will be the price commanded by a gem and not a piece of glass. In such circumstances, even if the word diamond is not used, the sale of an item got up to look like a diamond and priced like a diamond will be a sale by description of a diamond; the quality of the diamond, however, will be a different matter. Similarly, if a customer picks up in a supermarket a banana that turns out to be made of wax, it will not avail the seller to argue that the customer bought the specific article *tale quale*, taking the chance of it being real or waxen. The contract would be for the sale of a banana.

Rudimentary description.   Since description and merchantable quality have **7.11** now been separated by legislative means, and since the seller's liability under section 13(1) depends upon the range of the contractual description, the way seems clear for asserting that all sales are sales by description, albeit in varying degrees. If a buyer and seller agree on 'that thing' out of two similar-looking items, the seller may deliver only the item that he and the buyer have identified by words and gesture. Likewise, the identification of 'that thing' when gesture can refer only to one item would not allow the seller to deliver a quite different item. In all sale of goods contracts, the seller is bound to deliver the agreed goods; even in the most barebones contract, this delivery obligation has to be attachable to some goods and, to the extent that it is so attached, expresses a description requirement, even one so rudimentary as merely to restate the delivery duty in section 27.[38] It is entirely possible that a sale of goods, not known to be diamond or glass, might

---

[36] See also *Thornett v Fehr & Beers* [1919] 1 KB 486, 488–9; *David Jones Ltd v Willis* (1934) 52 CLR 110; *Godley v Perry* [1960] 1 WLR 9; *Beale v Taylor* [1967] 1 WLR 1193; *Morelli v Fitch and Gibbons* [1928] 2 KB 636; *Yelland v National Cafe* (1955) 16 WWR 529 (Can.). Cf. Vaughan Williams LJ in *Wren v Holt*, n. 30 above. Opinion was divided in *Wallis v Russell* [1902] 2 IR 585.

[37] N. 25 above.

[38] Consistent with this approach is the sale by sample case of *Mody v Gregson* (1868) LR 4 Ex. 49.

take place as a sale of 'that thing'[39] but even such limited words are descriptive. Nevertheless, as stated above, the context of the sale may extend the range of the description beyond this modest content. The contract may allocate the risk of the item being either diamond or glass to the buyer, but where the context points to diamond the seller may fall foul of the various rules governing exclusion clauses, including those in the Unfair Contract Terms Act 1977.[40] The line between defining an obligation and excluding it can be a very difficult one to draw, especially the closer one gets to the rudimentary descriptive core of an item. It should not be forgotten that a contract may give the seller the right to tender peas or beans;[41] but the description would still be 'peas or beans' and the seller could not tender cabbages.

Words of Description

7.12 **Summary of modern law.** In the modern law, the most important issue is the range of the contractual description, the chief difficulty being the separation of words of description and of quality. Another important theme, bulking increasingly large nowadays, is the relationship of description to the law governing express warranties and misrepresentations.[42] The issue of the range of description has arisen in a number of practical settings, such as the application of an exclusion clause,[43] the scope of the merchantable quality condition,[44] the acceptance rules in sections 11 and 35,[45] and the extent of a private seller's liability under section 13(1).[46]

7.13 **Development.** To understand the modern law, it is first necessary to consider the development of description through some of the earlier cases.[47] Those decided prior to *Varley v Whipp*[48] fail to reveal a clear distinction between specific and unascertained goods; what seems to have been critical was whether the buyer had the opportunity to examine the goods before the contract was concluded. A number of unascertained goods cases at that time required the seller to deliver

---

[39] *Wood v Boynton* (1885) 25 NW 42 (US).

[40] See Ch. 9 below.

[41] See the extrajudicial example given by Lord Devlin [1966] *CLJ* 192, 212 (a contract for peas, beans, or something else satisfied by delivery of peas, beans, or something *eiusdem generis*).

[42] For the relationship with express warranties, see text accompanying nn. 118 *et seq.* below.

[43] See, e.g. *Nichol v Godts* (1854) 10 Ex. 191; *Azémar v Casella* (1867) LR 2 CP 431; *Josling v Kingsford* (1863) 13 CB(NS) 447; *Shepherd v Kain* (1821) 5 B & Ald. 240 ('copper-fastened vessel' taken 'with all faults'). See too *Viger Bros v Sanderson Bros* [1901] 1 KB 508.

[44] Discussed below.

[45] *Varley v Whipp*, n. 32 above.

[46] *Beale v Taylor*, n. 36 above. A private seller incurs no liability under s. 14.

[47] See S. Stoljar (1952) 15 *MLR* 425; M. Bridge, 'Description and the Sale of Goods: *The Diana Prosperity*' in C. Mitchell and P. Mitchell (eds), *Landmark Cases in the Law of Contract* (Hart Publishing, 2008).

[48] N. 32 above.

goods that conformed to the identity of those agreed upon at the contract date, as opposed to any collateral attributes they might have been represented as having. Thus goods failed to conform to their contractual description when they were in one case 'Western Madras' cotton, an inferior type, instead of the 'Long-staple Salem' cotton called for by the contract;[49] likewise, in another case the goods were 'scarlet cuttings' with an adulterative addition of serge, so that the goods did not conform to the market understanding of 'scarlet cuttings'.[50] In these cases, the buyer's entitlement to reject the goods was a separate matter from any liability that the seller might have incurred in damages for the breach of warranty.[51] To give rise to an implied condition liberating the buyer from having to take the goods, the non-conformity had to be sufficiently serious for the goods delivered to be not the goods that were ordered.[52] It was precisely because some goods were sold without a warranty that the buyer seeking relief and the recovery of a price that had been paid had to show that an implied condition justified his rejection of the goods.[53] Compliance with description on the part of the seller was a condition precedent to the buyer's liability to take up the goods and pay for them.[54]

Description and non-delivery.   In *Chanter v Hopkins*,[55] the seller installed in the   **7.14** buyer's brewery a 'Chanter's smoke-consuming furnace' that failed to do the job for which it was required. The case turned primarily upon whether the seller was liable for the machine's failure, but it raises two points of interest for the purposes of description. First, the machine was treated by the court as more akin to specific than to ascertained goods, since the subject matter of the contract was a 'defined and well-known machine' of which the seller was known to hold the patent, clearly an assumption that the attributes of mass-produced articles do not vary in the way that they do for natural commodities. Secondly, Abinger CB made it plain in a well-known passage that a failure by the seller to comply with the contractual description meant that he had not delivered the contract goods at all, rather than that he had delivered non-conforming goods:

> A warranty is an express or implied statement of something which a party undertakes shall be part of a contract, and though part of the contract, collateral to the express object of it. But in many of the cases, the circumstance of a party selling a particular

---

[49] *Azémar v Casella*, n. 20 above.

[50] *Bridge v Wain* (1816) 1 Stark. 504.

[51] See *Bannerman v White* (1861) 10 CB(NS) 844; *Barr v Gibson* (1838) 3 M&W 391, 399; *Dawson v Collis* (1851) 10 CB 523, 530 (bill of exchange). See also *Gompertz v Denton* (1832) 1 C & M 207 (condition in the contract authorizing the return of goods).

[52] *Chanter v Hopkins* (1838) 4 M & W 399, discussed below; *Azémar v Casella*, n. 20 above; *Bridge v Wain*, n. 50 above. See also the bills of exchange cases of *Young v Cole* (1837) 3 Bing (NC) 724 and *Jones v Ryde* (1814) 5 Taunt 488.

[53] *Wieler v Schilizzi*, n. 26 above; *Gompertz v Bartlett* (1853) 2 E & B 849 (bill of exchange).

[54] *Wallis, Son and Wells v Pratt & Haynes* [1910] 2 KB 1003, 1018 (Farwell LJ)

[55] n. 52 above.

thing by its proper description has been called a warranty, and the breach of such a contract a breach of warranty; but it would be better to distinguish such cases as a non-compliance with a contract which a party has engaged to fulfil; as if a man offers to buy peas of another and he sends him beans, he does not perform his contract; but that is not a warranty; there is no warranty that he should sell him peas, the contract is to sell peas, and if he sells him anything else in their stead, it is a non-performance of it.[56]

This passage has had a substantial impact on the law governing exclusion clauses, as well as on the pre-1967 law concerning the buyer's right to reject specific goods where the seller was in breach of his description obligation.[57] It is consistent, too, with a narrow range being given to description, to which end a better example than a contract to supply peas instead of beans could hardly have been chosen.

7.15 **Specific goods unseen.** In a number of nineteenth-century cases, the description condition was held not to have been satisfied in the case of specific goods unseen by the buyer prior to the contract. Thus the seller on c.i.f. terms of a specific cargo afloat, described as 'Calcutta linseed, *tale quale*', was held to be in breach of contract when the cargo turned out to be heavily adulterated with rape and mustard seed.[58] Similarly, a seller by sample of 'foreign refined rape oil' that was adulterated with hemp oil was unable to sue the buyer for damages for non-acceptance since the goods were not those called for by the contract.[59] In the case of a sale of a specific ship that, unknown to the parties, had gone aground in the Gulf of St Lawrence at the contract date, the question was whether the goods could still be described as a 'ship'; inclement weather and the remoteness of the location greatly reduced the chances of getting the ship off the rock that would have existed closer to England.[60] Even in the case of specific goods examined before the contract, the description obligation could still be infringed where the examination did not and could not have discovered a latent misdescription, as where the substantial admixture of Epsom salts could not be detected by the naked eye in a quantity of oxalic acid.[61]

7.16 **Essence or identity.** Deficient as the above cases were in any philosophical discussion of the distinction between essence and attributes, they are generally quite consistent with description being limited to the essential nature or identity

---

[56] (1838) 4 M & W 404.

[57] *Varley v Whipp*, n. 32 above.

[58] *Wieler v Schilizzi*, n. 26 above. The cargo was only about 85% pure, instead of the 97–98% which the commodity was capable of attaining.

[59] *Nichol v Godts*, n. 20 above.

[60] *Barr v Gibson* (1838) 3 M & W 390. The case was sent for retrial since the court refused to admit in the definition of a 'ship' any geographical diversity.

[61] *Josling v Kingsford*, n. 20 above.

of the contract goods.[62] An expansion of the range of description is, however, evident in *Bowes v Shand*,[63] where it was invoked to justify a strict approach to timely shipment of an agreed quantity of unascertained goods and is apparent too in *Varley v Whipp*.[64] The latter contract was for the sale of 'a second-hand self-binder reaping machine . . . new the previous year, and only . . . used to cut fifty or sixty acres'. The seller delivered the reaper free on rail and the buyer returned it to the seller after some unsatisfactory correspondence. At no time prior to the contract had the buyer seen the machine;[65] indeed, it was owned by a third party until bought by the seller after he had entered into a binding contract with the buyer.[66] The machine turned out to be an old, heavily used, mended machine. The Divisional Court found a breach of section 13. Bucknill J was clearly of the view that all of the above-quoted words went to description;[67] Channell J gave no ruling as such but cited as examples of a breach an agreement to supply the 4-year-old horse in the last stall of a stable, which contained instead a cow or a horse of a different age.[68] Channell J also went on to say that there would be a breach of a 'collateral warranty'[69] if a horse stated to be sound proved not to be so. If these examples are a sure guide, both judges would probably agree that the words 'second-hand self-binder reaping machine . . . new the previous year' went to description; there might have been disagreement over the words 'at Upton' and there could well have been disagreement over the words 'only . . . used to cut fifty or sixty acres'.[70]

Incidental quality. The drawing of the line between description and incidental quality was explored further by Bailhache J in *T & J Harrison v Knowles & Foster*,[71] where the judge was at pains to say that his observations were confined to 'the sale   **7.17**

---

[62] Perhaps surprisingly, there appears at this stage of development no explicit link with the authorities on common law mistake, such as *Kennedy v Australia, New Zealand and Panama Royal Mail Co.* (1867) LR 2 QB 580, restated in *Bell v Lever Bros Ltd* [1932] AC 161.

[63] (1877) 2 App. Cas. 455. The effects of this are still to be seen: *Coastal (Bermuda) Petroleum Ltd v VTT Vulcan Petroleum SA (The Marine Star)* [1994] CLC 1019 (date of shipment); *Petrograde Inc. v Stinnes Handels GmbH* [1995] 1 Lloyd's Rep. 142 (port of shipment).

[64] n. 32 above.

[65] But it was still a contract for specific goods.

[66] The goods were future goods (s. 5(1)) as well as specific goods.

[67] n. 32 above, 517.

[68] *Ibid.*, 516. Somewhat elliptically, he locates his discussion of description in the passage dealing with the passing of property.

[69] n. 32 above, 516, showing the influence of Abinger CB in *Chanter v Hopkins*, n. 52 above.

[70] The case has been criticized in the Commonwealth: *Taylor v Combined Buyers Ltd* [1924] NZLR 627, 643 (Salmond J: 'difficult and unsatisfactory'); *New Hamburg Manufacturing Co. v Webb* (1911) 23 OLR 44, 54 (Can.) (Riddell J: 'going to the very verge (some will say going beyond)').

[71] [1917] 2 KB 606, affirmed other grounds [1918] 1 KB 608.

of an existing specific chattel'.[72] The contract concerned two sister ships[73] stated by the seller to have a dead-weight capacity of 460 tons. After taking delivery of the ships, the buyer's examination of one of them showed that its deadweight capacity came to only 360 tons. This made the ships useless for the purpose the buyers had in mind, namely, plying for cargo between West African rivers and the ocean, a purpose they had not disclosed to the sellers. In discussing whether the words about the ships' capacity went to contractual description or collateral warranty, Bailhache put the matter in terms of the difference between condition and warranty,[74] the merit of which is that it aligns the law of description and of express warranty and limits the divergence of the general law of contract and the special law of sale. Concluding that the words of capacity amounted to a warranty, Bailhache J made it clear that 'the absence of such quality or the possession of it to a smaller extent [did not make] the thing sold different in kind from the thing described in the contract'.[75] The difference between the two tonnage figures was 'essentially one of degree and not of kind'.[76]

Specific and Unascertained Goods

7.18 **Range of description: unascertained goods.** The decisions in *Varley* and *T & J Harrison* were carefully considered by Salmond J in *Taylor v Combined Buyers Ltd*[77] when proposing a sharp division between the range of description for both specific and for unascertained goods. In the case of unascertained goods, he asserted:

> The description defines the contractual obligation of the vendor. He has promised to deliver under his contract goods of a certain number, quality, kind, state, quantity, condition, or other attributes. If he subsequently delivers goods which in any respect whatever fail to conform to this contractual description of them he has broken his contract, and the buyer is not bound to accept the goods. The statutory implied condition of correspondence with the description means in the case of unascertained goods that a buyer is not bound to accept in performance of the contract a delivery of goods different in any respect whatever from this which the vendor promised to supply him.[78]

---

[72] *Ibid.*, 610. It was not clear that the buyers saw the goods before the contract but quite probable that they did not.

[73] One of which was later named 'The Mafia'.

[74] See also *Abel v Hannay* (1956) 19 WWR 453 (Can.); *Hart-Parr Co. v Wells* (1918) 40 DLR 169.

[75] n. 71 above, 610.

[76] *Ibid.*

[77] n. 25 above.

[78] *Ibid.*, 636, citing only *Bowes v Shand* (1877) 2 App. Cas. 455. For a similar approach by Canadian authorities on unascertained goods, see *Burlington Canning Co. v Campbell* (1908) 7 WLR 544; *Alabastine Co. of Paris Ltd v Canadian Producer Co. Ltd* (1914) 30 OLR 394; *Hart-Parr Co. v Wells* (1918) 40 DLR 169; *Renewo Products Ltd v Macdonald & Wilson Ltd* [1938] 3 WWR 418.

Range of description: specific goods. For specific goods, however, Salmond J   **7.19**
thought the position different in at least two respects. First, drawing on common
law decisions concerning agreements that are invalid because of the shared
mistake of the parties, description went, not to the obligation of the seller to
deliver conforming goods, but to the very 'validity'[79] of the contract.[80] This points
to the seller not being liable in damages for failing to comply with his description
obligation, an unlikely construction to put on any contract of sale[81] unless the
seller were liable for non-delivery under section 27. Secondly, as regards the range
of description, statements made about specific goods might be mere representations inducing the contract, or mere warranties sounding in damages if breached,
or conditions of the validity of the contract.[82] A buyer refusing a tender of the
goods would have to show that the descriptive words had been incorporated in the
contract at the level of a condition.[83] To do this, the buyer would have to demonstrate that the words went to the 'kind, class, or species to which the article
belongs'[84] or, alternatively put, to 'the essential or specific nature of the article
sold';[85] words carefully excluded by this analysis were those of 'degree', 'quality',
and 'unessential attributes'.[86]

Unseen goods. The above distinction, however, is not consistent with the broad   **7.20**
range given to description in the case of specific goods unseen by the buyer in
Varley v Whipp,[87] where the outcome is that such goods are assimilated for present
purposes to unascertained goods.[88]

The Modern Law

Specific goods in modern times. Be that as it may, it remains to be seen whether   **7.21**
more recent authorities have maintained the distinction between specific and
unascertained goods, and whether the broad range of description in the latter case
has been trimmed. Because the difficulties in the modern law have mainly
concerned unascertained goods, specific goods will be considered first. In their
case, Salmond J's approach appears still to be valid. The description condition was

---

79 But later he refers to this as a 'condition of the contract': n. 25 above, 638.
80 *Ibid.*, 636–7.
81 But perhaps a lingering expression of *caveat emptor* reasoning.
82 n. 25 above, 637.
83 *Ibid.*, 638.
84 *Ibid.*, 639.
85 *Ibid.*
86 *Ibid.*, 640. For Canadian cases on specific goods taking a similar line, see *Twaites v Morrison*
(1918) 43 DLR 73; *New Hamburg Mfg. Co. v Webb*, n. 70 above; *Bailey v Croft* [1932] 1 WWR 106.
87 n. 32 above.
88 For Canadian cases that do the same thing, see *Bannerman v Barlow* (1908) 7 WLR 859 (facts
'almost identical' to those in *Varley v Whipp*); *Runnymede Iron & Steel Ltd v Rossen Engineering &*
Construction Co. [1962] SCR 26.

infringed where a 'breeding bull' turned out to be infertile[89] and where semen from a particular Simmental bull was ordered, but that from a Brown Swiss bull delivered instead.[90] Similarly, the authenticity of tablecloths and napkins as formerly owned by Charles I went to description in section 13.[91] It is a difficult question of degree whether statements concerning the age of goods go to their identity; the degree of divergence from the stated age appears to have a bearing on this. Thus the seller was in breach of section 13(1) in delivering a tower crane, described as 'like new' and just over 2 years old, but which turned out to be 10 years old, as well as defective.[92] Similarly, the section was infringed where a car sold as a 1972 model turned out to have a 1969 or 1970 engine,[93] and where a car sold as a 1200 cc model built in 1961 proved to be composed of two parts, one of which was older, and to contain a smaller engine.[94] The age of motor vehicles has also been argued as a matter of express warranty.[95] A buyer able to establish an express warranty but unable or unwilling to reject the goods may not wish to press an additional claim under section 13(1).

7.22 **Unascertained goods in modern times.**   Where the goods are unascertained, the broad view of description stated in *Taylor v Combined Buyers Ltd*[96] was applied in a number of cases and indeed held the stage until modern times. The leading case in this area is *Arcos Ltd v EA Ronaasen and Son,*[97] where the seller agreed to supply a quantity of whitewood and redwood staves to be shipped in the summer of 1930 from Archangel. The contract provided that the wood had to comply with precise measurements of length, breadth, and thickness, but nearly all of the wood strayed in some small measure from these dimensions, though not in a way injurious to the buyers' purpose of making staves for cement barrels.[98] The buyers' rejection of the goods was dictated by nothing more than a desire to repurchase on a falling market but the House of Lords held nevertheless that they were entitled to do so because of the sellers' breach of section 13(1). In so holding, the court made it

---

[89] *Elder Smith Goldsborough Mort Ltd v McBride* [1976] 2 NSWLR 631; see also *Cotter v Luckie* [1918] NZLR 811 ('stud bull').

[90] *Steele v Maurer* (1976) 73 DLR (3d) 85 (really, unascertained goods from a specific bulk), reversed other grounds (1977) 79 DLR (3d) 764.

[91] *Nicholson and Venn v Smith-Marriott* (1947) 177 LT 189.

[92] *Tower Equipment Rental Ltd v Joint Venture Equipment Sales Ltd* (1975) 9 OR (2d) 453 (Can.).

[93] *Carr v G & B Auto Mart* [1978] 5 WWR 361 (Can.).

[94] *Beale v Taylor*, n. 36 above.

[95] *Oscar Chess Ltd v Williams* [1957] 1 WLR 325, the buyer failing since the seller's lack of expertise made the statement one of opinion only.

[96] n. 25 above.

[97] [1933] AC 470.

[98] e.g., of the 28-inch staves, 85.3% were between 1/2 and 9/16 inches thick instead of the 1/2 inch required by the contract; the percentage was 75.3% in the case of 17-inch staves. There was evidence that exposure to rain had affected the thickness of the staves.

plain both that physical measurement was a matter of description[99] and that compliance with description meant exact and not approximate compliance, the latter having to be bargained for by a seller who wanted it. As Lord Atkin put it: 'A ton does not mean about a ton, or a yard about a yard. Still less when you descend to minute measurements does 1/2 inch mean about 1/2 inch. If a seller wants a margin he must and in my experience does stipulate for it.'[100] He did nevertheless concede that trade usage might give a special meaning to particular figures;[101] moreover, descriptive words may acquire a special meaning by usage.[102] A dramatic example of the strictness of description is afforded by *Re Moore & Co. and Landauer & Co.*,[103] where the seller delivered Australian tinned peaches differing from the contractual specification only in that some tins were packed in cases of twenty-four instead of the thirty tins required by the contract. Though suffering no injury at all and seeking only to escape from a bad bargain, the buyer was allowed to reject the goods.[104]

Restricting description.   In *Ashington Piggeries Ltd v Christopher Hill Ltd*,[105] a   **7.23**
major decision covering the whole of sections 13 to 14 of the Sale of Goods Act, the range of description for unascertained goods was clearly cut down. The case concerned the supply under two connected contracts of Norwegian herring meal containing a poisonous additive.[106] In one contract, herring meal was one of the ingredients in mink feed compounded by the sellers according to a recipe provided by the buyers, and the question was whether the mink feed could properly be described as including herring meal when that herring meal contained the poisonous additive. The sellers obtained the herring meal from Norwegian suppliers under the terms of a contract calling for 'NORWEGIAN HERRING MEAL fair average quality of the season, expected to analyse not less than 70% protein, not more than 12% fat and not more than 4% salt'. In the case of this latter contract, the question was how many of the quoted words went to the description of the herring meal and, again, whether the presence of the poisonous additive entailed a breach by the suppliers of their section 13(1) obligation.

Essential nature.   In both contracts, the House of Lords found there had   **7.24**
not been a breach of section 13(1). Dealing with the first contract for the sale of

---

[99] See also *Ebrahim Dawood Ltd v Heath Ltd* [1961] 2 Lloyd's Rep. 512.

[100] n. 97 above, 479. For an example of an allowance being stipulated for by words like 'about', see *Vigers Bros. v Sanderson Bros.* [1901] 1 KB 508; see Ch. 6 above.

[101] n. 97 above, 479.

[102] *Steels & Busks Ltd v Bleecker Bik & Co. Ltd* [1956] 1 Lloyd's Rep. 228 ('pale crepe rubber'); *Peter Darlington and Partners Ltd v Gosho Co. Ltd* [1964] 1 Lloyd's Rep. 149 ('pure' canary seed); *Grenfell v EB Myrowitz Ltd* [1936] 2 All ER 1313 ('safety glass').

[103] [1921] 2 KB 119.

[104] Including the conforming portion of goods: s. 30(3).

[105] [1972] AC 441.

[106] Dimethylnitrosamine, a by-product of the curing process.

compounded mink feed, Lord Wilberforce clearly framed description in terms of the essential nature of the goods to be supplied:

> Whether in a given case a substance in or upon which there has been produced by chemical interaction some additional substance can properly be described or . . . identified . . . as the original substance qualified by the addition of a past participle such as contaminated or oxidised, or as the original substance plus, or intermixed with, an additional substance, may, if pressed to analysis, be a question of an Aristotelian character. Where does a substance with a quality pass into an aggregate of substances? . . . The test of description, at least where commodities are concerned, is intended to be a broader, more common sense, test of a mercantile character. The question whether that is what the buyer bargained for has to be answered according to such tests as the men in the market would apply, leaving more delicate questions of condition, or quality, to be determined under other clauses of the contract or sections of the Act.[107]

A distinction was therefore drawn between description and quality.[108] As regards the second contract, Lord Guest was consistent with this approach when rejecting the argument that the words 'fair average quality' and the expected analysis of the goods constituted part of the description for, in his view, 'description implies a specification where the goods can be identified by the buyer'.[109]

7.25 **Identification and identity.** *Ashington Piggeries* therefore removed the collateral attributes of unascertained goods from the range of description.[110] In stressing the role played by identification, however, the case does not reveal whether the range of description is now the same for both specific and unascertained goods, or whether identification and identity (or essence) amount to the same thing. This latter question is dealt with in detail in *Reardon Smith Line Ltd v Yngvar Hansen-Tangen*,[111] a time charterparty case governed by principles akin to sale. The dispute arose from an attempt to finance the building of a number of supertankers by a Japanese ship-building company and to control the market in charter hire.

---

[107] n. 105 above, 489. See also Lord Diplock, 503–4: '[U]ltimately the test is whether the buyer could fairly and reasonably refuse to accept the physical goods proffered to him on the ground that their failure to correspond with that part of what was said about them in the contract makes them goods of a different kind from those he had agreed to buy. The key to section 13 is identification.'

[108] Cf. *Alfred C Toepfer v Continental Grain Co.* [1974] 1 Lloyd's Rep. 11, 13 (Lord Denning MR): 'The "description" of goods often includes a statement of their quality. Thus "new-laid eggs" contains both quality and description all in one. "Quality" is often part of the description. In this very case the word "hard" is a word both of quality and of description.' Sometimes words of quality may be used to identify the goods: *Baker v Fowkes* (1874) 35 UCQB 302 (Can.: sale of the seller's 'new' hearse as opposed to his 'old' hearse).

[109] n. 105 above, 475; see also *Total International Ltd v Addax BV* [1996] 2 Lloyd's Rep. 333.

[110] The presence of additives, therefore, is unlikely as such to entail a breach of s. 13; cf. *Pinnock Bros v Lewis and Peat Ltd* [1923] 1 KB 690 (castor seed mixed in with copra cake).

[111] [1976] 1 WLR 989; see also *Bakker v Bowness Auto Parts Co. Ltd* (1975) 68 DLR (3d) 173. For a discussion of the background to the litigation in the *Reardon Smith* case, see Bridge, n. 47 above.

The attempt consisted of creating strings of future time charters and sub-charters entered into in respect of each vessel before it was built. The charter market declined and intermediate charterers in the present case wished to avoid the contract. The contract called for the supply of a 'Newbuilding motor tank vessel called Yard No. 354 at Osaka Zosen'. Because Osaka Zosen (that is, Osaka Shipbuilding) was unable to build a tanker of the required size in its yard, it arranged for a new yard to be built 300 miles away in Oshima.[112] In the books of this new yard, the tanker was numbered 004, though referred to as 354 in the Osaka books.

Absence of breach.   On the analogy of section 13(1) of the Sale of Goods Act, **7.26** the charterers contended that the number of the vessel and the building of it in Oshima amounted to a breach of the obligation to tender a vessel answering the contract description. Rejecting the charterers' contention, the House of Lords seems to have decided that no breach of contract had occurred, though this remains unclear, since any breach of contract that might have occurred caused no loss.[113] As Lord Wilberforce put it, the disputed words in the present case were only 'simple substitutes for a name',[114] helping to identify the same subject matter for each of the contracts in the contractual string of charters and sub-charters. On this basis, the vessel tendered might have been capable of being described in both Oshima and Osaka terms.

Identification and identity distinguished.   Apart from this and assuming that **7.27** there was a breach of contract, the House of Lords ruled that sale of goods authorities should not be extended to contracts of the present nature and that the disputed words in the contract were never intended to be a matter of fundamental obligation but only a means of identifying the vessel. A conflict thereby emerged with *Ashington Piggeries,* resolved by Lord Wilberforce in these terms:

> It is one thing to say of given words that their purpose is to state (identify) an essential part of the description of the goods. It is another to say that they provide one party with a specific indication (identification) of the goods so that he can find them and if he wishes sub-dispose of them. The [charterers] wish to say of words which 'identify' the goods in the second sense, that they describe them in the first.[115]

Although the language is not entirely clear, Lord Wilberforce seems to imply that description goes to the essence or identity of goods in the case of unascertained as well as specific goods. In support of this, he makes it clear that some description

---

[112] It also took a 50% interest in the company incorporated for this purpose.
[113] The case is as much of an authority on contractual interpretation as it is on description.
[114] n. 111 above, 998.
[115] n. 111 above, 999.

decisions stand in need of reappraisal because of their 'excessively technical'[116] aspect. Nevertheless, in another passage, he throws the matter into some doubt when he says:

> Even if a strict and technical view must be taken as regards the description of unascertained future goods (e.g., commodities) as to which each detail of the description must be assumed to be vital, it may be, and in my opinion is, right to treat other contracts of sale of goods in a similar manner to other contracts generally so as to ask whether a particular item in a description constitutes a substantial ingredient of the 'identity' of the thing sold, and only if it does to treat it as a condition.[117]

7.28 **Description and general contract law.** His lordship was explicitly concerned to see that the law on description kept in step with the law on express warranties and intermediate stipulations as expounded in *Hongkong Fir Shipping Co. Ltd v Kawasaki Kisen Kaisha Ltd*[118] and *Cehave NV v Bremer Handelsgesellschaft mbH*.[119] This explains what appears to be a two-tiered approach to the construction of descriptive words—a strict approach to words that relate to the 'identity' of the thing sold and fall within section 13, and a flexible approach to other descriptive words outside the core of identity and therefore to be treated as express contractual terms, so that the right to terminate would depend upon whether the breach went to the root of the contract.[120] As for non-core words that merely 'identify' goods, Lord Wilberforce was of the opinion that they could be 'construed much more liberally than they would have to be construed if they were providing essential elements of the description'.[121] Since *Reardon Smith* itself concerned unascertained future goods, Lord Wilberforce's words concerning the need for strictness should properly be understood as relating to transactions in fast-moving, stratified, and volatile markets such as the world of commodities. In such contracts, words relating to the grading and geographical origin and type of goods, such as 'No 1 Oregon winter wheat' would still be regarded as descriptive and interpreted strictly.[122] Nothing in *Reardon Smith*, however, would suggest that

---

[116] *Ibid.*, 998. He cites *Re Moore & Co. and Landauer & Co.*, n. 103 above, but, interestingly, not *Arcos Ltd v EA Ronaasen and Son*, n. 97 above.

[117] n. 111 above, 998. See *Alfred C Toepfer v Continental Grain Co.*, n. 108 above ('hard' wheat a matter of description); *Toepfer v Warinco AG* [1978] 2 Lloyd's Rep. 569 ('fine-ground' soya bean meal).

[118] [1962] 2 QB 26.

[119] [1976] QB 44.

[120] See *Hopkins v Hitchcock* (1863) 14 CB(NS) 65. The contract called for the supply of 'S & H' stamped iron, Snowdon & Hopkins being the manufacturers. When Snowdon retired from the partnership, Hopkins had the iron stamped 'H & Co'. The sellers were held entitled to stamp the iron in the latter way since the words were concerned with iron of a particular quality rather than iron of a particular brand.

[121] n. 111 above, 999.

[122] See *Berger and Co. Inc. v Gill & Duffus SA* [1982] AC 382, 394 (Lord Diplock); *Tradax Export SA v European Grain & Shipping Ltd* [1983] 2 Lloyd's Rep. 100 ('maximum 7.5% fibre'); *Toepfer v Warinco AG* [1978] 2 Lloyd's Rep. 569. For a broad view of description, see also *Coastal (Bermuda)*

even in such cases words like 'fair average quality' should be treated as part of the description of goods.

Meaning of identity.   The range of description for specific and unascertained **7.29** goods alike has stabilized around the identity of the goods. But the identity of goods is not a constant thing and will vary from case to case. It will also depend very much on the type of goods and the circumstances in which they are bought and sold.[123] Where commodities are sold under a wide array of labels, it may be expected that identity has a fuller meaning than it has in the case of a sale of a specific horse. This allows the special treatment of commodities cases without departing from an identity-based core of description. Similarly, goods unseen by the buyer may have a more extensive identity than goods seen.[124] It therefore seems that the range of description could be extended by the terms of the contract itself.[125] Nevertheless, a better approach, it is submitted, is not to vary or expand the meaning of identity when dealing with goods in particular markets, but to maintain that same meaning and treat words going beyond identity, if important enough, as express contractual conditions. This would serve further to align the special law of sale with the general law of contract.

Description and Reliance

Expertise and reliance.   Another attempt to align the law on description with **7.30** the law on express warranties is present in *Harlingdon and Leinster Enterprises Ltd v Christopher Hull Fine Art Ltd*.[126] One dealer sold to another a painting stated unequivocally by the seller to be the work of a German expressionist artist, Gabriele Münter. The seller relied upon an attribution in an earlier auction catalogue; he was not at all expert in German expressionist art, whereas the buyer was. It was found as a fact at trial that the buyer did not rely upon the seller's statement but upon his own examination of the painting, which turned out to be a forgery. By a majority, the Court of Appeal held the seller was not liable under section 13(1).

Petroleum Ltd v VTT Vulcan Petroleum SA (The Marine Star) [1994] CLC 1019 (date of shipment); *Petrograde Inc. v Stinnes Handels GmbH* [1995] 1 Lloyd's Rep. 142 (port of shipment). Cf *Tradax Internacional SA v Goldschmidt SA* [1977] 2 Lloyd's Rep. 604, where it was common ground between the parties that the maximum stated percentage in a cargo of white Syrian barley did not go to description.

123 See *Wallis, Son & Wells v Pratt & Haynes* [1911] AC 394, 399 ('giant sainfoin [is] a thing as distinct in agricultural knowledge from common English sainfoin as in ordinary commerce a silver watch would be distinct from a gold watch').

124 See *Berger and Co. Inc. v Gill & Duffus SA*, n. 122 above (the sample example).

125 But see *Montagu L Meyer Ltd v Kivisto* (1929) 142 LT 480, where timber had to be 'properly seasoned for shipment' and to be measured as appropriate 'for such description of goods'. The court appears to have held that the parties did not mean description in the technical sense; the goods were the goods 'specified' in the contract.

126 [1991] 1 QB 564; M. Bridge [1990] *LMCLQ* 455.

Of the majority judges, Nourse LJ thought the sale had not taken place by description.[127] Furthermore, for section 13(1) to be breached the seller's statement should have passed the test of a contractual condition, which it failed to do because of the buyer's lack of reliance. The other majority judge, Slade LJ, saw description as depending upon a common contractual intention that the disputed statement be a term of the contract.[128] Reliance was not a necessary requirement of section 13(1) liability but its absence in the present case was enough to disqualify the statement from constituting part of the description. The dissenting judge, Stuart-Smith LJ, saw no role for reliance at all.

7.31 **Innovative character of reliance.** The introduction of reliance into description in *Harlingdon and Leinster* is innovative.[129] Reliance is a feature of fitness for purpose under section 14(3), where the buyer must rely upon the seller's skill and judgment for the seller to be liable. But reliance in this sense, as opposed to the buyer's reliance on the painting being by Gabriele Münter, which assists in defining the core of description and the basis of the bargain and was certainly present in the case,[130] has in the past been foreign to section 13(1). Nevertheless, there is high authority for the view that the authorship of a painting is not part of the identity of specific goods for the purpose of common mistake.[131] If the identity of goods in section 13(1) is defined in similar strict terms, which accords with the trend of modern authorities on description, then the decision in *Harlingdon and Leinster* is defensible on this ground. Whichever ground best supports the outcome in *Harlingdon and Leinster*, if the case is successful in integrating description into the law governing express warranties, there seems little point in retaining description and section 13(1) as a separate head of liability.[132]

---

[127] But even if the attribution to Gabriele Münter was not part of the description, this should not mean that the sale did not take place by description. If canvas and rubber boots do not have to be 'waders' for the purpose of s. 13(1) (see *Joseph Travers & Sons Ltd v Longel Ltd* (1948) 44 TLR 150), they should still be made of canvas and rubber if that is the basis upon which they are sold.

[128] For the view that it is a preliminary question whether words are part of the contract in the first place before they can be classified as words of description or not, see *Rosengrans Tann Ltd v Ayres* [2001] EWCA Civ 997 at [28].

[129] The case is also important for the role it implies for reliance in the law of express warranty: see Ch. 8 below.

[130] Cf *Joseph Travers & Sons Ltd v Longel Ltd*, n. 127 above, where the parties introduced the word 'waders' as a convenient way of labelling war surplus goods for which there was no defined market. The buyer did not set out to obtain goods that passed the market test of 'waders'.

[131] *Bell v Lever Bros* [1932] AC 161 (Lord Atkin); *Leaf v International Galleries* [1950] 2 KB 86 (Denning LJ).

[132] Description was removed from the Canadian Uniform Sale of Goods Act 1981 (not yet in force in any Canadian province), though it remained present in the Ontario Draft Sale of Goods Bill 1979 (s. 5.11) that paved the way for the Uniform Act.

Satisfactory Quality

Evolution of satisfactory quality. According to the current text of section 14(2) **7.32**
of the Sale of Goods Act, there is an implied term that, where the seller
sells goods in the course of a business, the goods supplied shall be of satisfactory
quality. Unlike section 13(1), this implied term applies only to business and not
to private sellers. Since the enactment of the Sale and Supply of Goods Act 1994,
amending in this respect the Sale of Goods Act 1979, section 14(2) is framed as
a 'term', but the new section 14(6) explicitly makes that term a condition. The
condition of satisfactory quality was known before the 1994 Act as merchantable
quality. Apart from the change of name, a number of alterations were made in that
Act to the definition of merchantable quality. The very existence of a definition,
now to be found in section 14(2A)(2B) but formerly contained in the old section
14(6) of the Sale of Goods Act, dates, not from the original Act of 1893,[133] but
from 1973. Different judicial views have been taken of the desirability or not of
examining authorities decided before merchantable quality was defined in 1973.[134]
The specific debate about merchantable quality resembles the more general debate
whether authorities decided before 1893 should be considered when interpreting
a statute codifying the law of sale.[135] Over time, courts routinely went behind the
statutory provisions to consider the pre-1893 authorities. Since the definition of
merchantable quality enacted in 1973 was in no sense a true definition, but rather
an instruction to take account of variable criteria whose relative importance would
depend upon the facts of individual cases, it was always somewhat sanguine to
believe that its meaning in a given case could be determined without referring
to the authorities that preceded it. Nevertheless, a word of caution is necessary.
So far as the definition might have altered the law or have altered the balance of
the various elements in merchantable quality, it was advisable to consider the
pre-1973 authorities with a degree of care. The change from merchantable quality
to satisfactory quality, as will be seen, is largely a terminological change designed
to reflect the altered emphasis of the law that took effect over a lengthy period, but
in at least one respect it has altered the law.[136]

---

[133] In *Jones v Just*, n. 23 above, Blackburn J did not feel it necessary to direct the Liverpool jury
on the meaning of merchantability: see Roskill LJ in *Cehave NV v Bremer Handelsgesellschaft mbH*,
n. 119 above.

[134] In favour: *M/S Aswan Engineering Establishment Co. v Lupdine Ltd* [1987] 1 WLR 1. Against:
Rogers v Parish Motors (Scarborough) Ltd [1987] 2 All ER 232 (Mustill LJ); *Marimpex Mineralöls
Handels GmbH v Louis Dreyfus et Cie GmbH* [1995] 1 Lloyd's Rep. 167, 179.

[135] See Ch. 1 above.

[136] In 'appropriate cases', the goods must be fit for all common purposes: discussed below.

7.33 **Authorities on merchantable quality.** The terminological aspect of the change to satisfactory quality positively invites a consideration of the authorities that preceded and prompted it, but the substantive change in the law underlines to an even greater degree the need to consider with care those authorities decided before the 1994 changes came into effect. Because the definition of satisfactory quality is of the same type as that of merchantable quality, the arguments in favour of consulting earlier authorities still hold, especially since it is quite rare for the implied terms of the Sale of Goods Act to attract the same degree of attention in the higher courts that they did at an earlier stage in the development of the law. It is, however, understandable that courts might weary of listening to a concatenation of old authorities and insist upon some selectivity. In any event, the relevance of older authorities to the meaning of satisfactory quality will be decided, not upon any *a priori* consideration of their relevance, but upon whether they are in fact taken up and used in contemporary cases. In the light of these considerations and of the somewhat complex legislative history of satisfactory quality, the best starting point is to examine the development of merchantable quality before 1973, and then consider merchantable quality in the light of the statutory definition introduced in that year before turning to the new definition of satisfactory quality and any changes that it might have made.[137] The principal features of satisfactory quality will be dealt with in this way before attention is turned to certain of its particular applications. Before this is done, however, it is necessary to consider in further detail the types of seller bound by the satisfactory quality standard in section 14(2).

Sale in the Course of a Business

7.34 **Nature of business sale.** The requirement in section 14(2) that the seller sell the goods 'in the course of a business' dates from 1973. Before that date, it was necessary to show that the goods were 'bought by description from a seller who deals in goods of that description (whether he be the manufacturer or not)'. Two propositions were embraced in this formula. First, a private seller would in no circumstances be liable under section 14(2). Secondly, a business seller would be liable only in restricted circumstances, bounded by the technicalities of the description doctrine.[138] It has been observed already that, in order to enter section 14(2), the buyer had to go through the gateway of section 13 by showing that the goods had been bought by description. The next question was what was meant by the seller dealing in goods of that description. Even before the law was changed in 1973, this limitation on the scope of the implied term had in effect been lifted.

---

[137] See M. Bridge [1995] *JBL* 398.

[138] The first of these propositions will be considered further under fitness for purpose below.

Lord Wilberforce observed in *Ashington Piggeries Ltd v Christopher Hill Ltd*[139] that it meant only that the seller had to be a dealer in the kinds of goods supplied, and not in goods of the particular description supplied under the contract.[140] Consequently, the character of the seller required to invoke the merchantable quality term was the same as that needed for the fitness for purpose term which, prior to 1973, applied when 'the goods are of a description which it is in the course of the seller's business to supply'.[141] In the same case, Lord Wilberforce went further when he made it plain that the seller could be liable even if this was the first time that the seller had supplied goods of that kind.[142] The mink feed in *Ashington Piggeries* was, it was assumed, sold with Norwegian herring meal as an ingredient for the first time.[143] Lord Wilberforce's words that the implied term in section 14(2) governs 'persons in the way of business, as distinct from private persons'[144] are equivalent to the present wording introduced in 1973 that the seller sell the goods 'in the course of a business'.

Equipment sales. An issue that does present a problem concerns the business **7.35** seller who is not a dealer as such but who from time to time, perhaps at irregular and protracted intervals, disposes of second-hand items of unwanted capital equipment.[145] This raises the question why liability should be visited on business sellers but not on private sellers.[146] It also compels a comparison with a similar formula in the Trade Descriptions Act 1968,[147] a regulatory statute, which in section 1(1) applied to '[a]ny person who, in the course of a trade or business . . . supplies . . . any goods'. In *Davies v Sumner*,[148] the House of Lords, referring to the long title of the 1968 Act,[149] held that the formula 'in the context of an Act having consumer protection as its primary purpose conveys the concept of some degree

---

[139] n. 105 above, 494–5.

[140] *Ibid.*, 494: '[W]hat the Act had in mind was something quite simple and rational: to limit the implied conditions of fitness and quality to persons in the way of business, as distinct from private persons.' See also *Spencer Trading Co. Ltd v Devon* [1947] 1 All ER 284 (flypaper contained for first time artificial additives instead of natural ingredients).

[141] Lord Wilberforce dealt with this aspect of both implied terms indifferently. See also *Farmer v Canada Packers Ltd* (1956) 6 DLR (2d) 63, 73 (where both terms were held to apply simply where a sale took place in the course of a business); *Buckley v Lever Bros. Ltd* [1953] OR 704 (Can.).

[142] n. 105 above, 494 (if the seller is 'willing to accept orders').

[143] *Ibid.*

[144] *Ibid.*

[145] The Ontario Law Reform Commission was opposed to liability in this case: see *Report on Sale of Goods*, i, 209.

[146] Discussed with fitness for purpose below.

[147] Now repealed by the Consumer Protection from Unfair Trading Regulations 2008, SI 2008 No. 1277. The Regulations came into force on 26 May 2008.

[148] [1984] 1 WLR 1301; see also *Havering London Borough v Stevenson* [1970] 1 WLR 1375.

[149] 'An Act . . . prohibiting certain misdescriptions of goods, services, accommodation and facilities provided in the course of trade'.

of regularity'.[150] The defendant was a courier disposing of a vehicle, by way of trade-in with a car dealer, which he used almost exclusively for transporting film and televisual material. The courier fell outside the 1968 Act because he had not built up a practice of disposing of cars. Further, the car was not something he exploited as stock-in-trade. For the purposes of a somewhat different statute, the Unfair Contract Terms Act 1977,[151] the Court of Appeal in *R & B Customs Brokers Ltd v United Dominions Trust Ltd*[152] followed the approach of the House of Lords and held that a *buyer* did not purchase in the course of a business[153] where the car purchased was incidental to the buyer's business activity and no pattern of regularity in the purchase of cars had developed to make it integral to the buyer's business. If the approach in these cases had been followed in section 14(2), it would have required a gloss to be put on the plain language of section 14(2) which, as stated above, enacted in clearer terms a position that was entrenched shortly before the 1973 changes by *Ashington Piggeries Ltd v Christopher Hill Ltd.*[154] In *Stevenson v Rogers,*[155] the question was whether a fisherman selling his boat did so in the ordinary course of business for the purpose of section 14(2) of the Sale of Goods Act. After a thorough review of the authorities and the legislative history of the provision, the Court of Appeal concluded that the words of the statute should be given 'their wide face value'. A simple comparison of the current provision and the original 1893 provision was enough to show the intention of Parliament to open up the scope of liability under section 14(2). Moreover, if the words of the statute were to be impliedly limited, such limitation would be difficult to define.[156] In further support of the decision, it could be said that no good reason existed for limiting the scope of the section 14(2) wording in the Sale of Goods Act, a statute whose purposes differ from the Trade Descriptions Act 1968 and the Unfair Contract Terms Act 1977.[157] A later case involving the sale of the business

---

[150] n. 148 above, 1305.

[151] See Ch. 9 below.

[152] [1988] 1 WLR 321.

[153] So as to deal as a consumer for the purpose of the 1977 Act, s. 12.

[154] n. 105 above.

[155] [1999] QB 1028; see also *Feldaroll Foundry Plc v Hermes Leasing (London) Ltd* [2004] EWCA Civ 747 at [15].

[156] Above, 1039.

[157] Certain Canadian cases put a gloss upon the requirements of the section by requiring that the sale be in the ordinary course of the seller's business. This runs counter to imposing liability where the seller deals in goods of the contract type for the first time (discussed above) and is contrary to English law. So the application of the section was ousted when one farmer sold seed to another as a personal favour (*Buckle v Morrison* [1924] 3 WWR 702) and where a municipality sold grain on credit to an impecunious farmer as a sort of outdoor relief (*Lilldal v Rurat Municipality of Meota no 468* [1920] 2 WWR 336). See also *Rahtjen v Stern GMC Trucks (1969) Ltd* (1976) 66 DLR (3d) 566 (no liability where second-hand car dealer supplied trailer on one-off basis). Cf. *Connop v Canadian Car Division Hawker Siddeley Canada Ltd* (1978) 24 OR (2d) 593 (Can.) (manufacturer of insulated lorries and subway carriages liable when defective insulating material was installed as a favour in the buyer's yacht).

itself raised the question whether the business assets were being sold in the course of the seller's business. The court ruled that it was at least arguable that the sale of business assets took place in the course of a business when they had previously been sold by the business.[158] Speaking of equipment rather than stock-in-trade, Potter LJ in *Stevenson v Rogers* remarked that it would be 'a most curious result that the sale by a seller of the very asset without which he could not carry on his business, with the intention of purchasing a replacement for the purpose of continuing that business, should not be regarded as a sale made in the course of a business'.[159]

'Business'.   It was not until 1973 that the Sale of Goods Act (as amended)   **7.36** gave a definition of business. According to section 61(1), '"business" includes a profession and the activities of any government department . . . or local or public authority'. It is submitted that this definition should be given a broad reading so as to embrace all non-private bodies, such as universities and charities like the National Trust. Private individuals who are not traders operating from business premises or adopting business patterns of behaviour may yet sell in the course of a business if they deal with sufficient regularity and with a view to profit.[160] It is submitted that, in the case of doubt, the application of section 14(2) should go in favour of the buyer to the extent that the buyer is denied information that tends to limit the liability of the seller. The burden should not be put on the buyer of inquiring how and for what purpose the university library is disposing of unwanted books or the National Trust is organizing the sale of outdoor clothing. The same idea is evident in section 14(5), which provides that a sale through an agent acting in the course of a business will be deemed to be in the course of a business of the principal seller, unless either the buyer does know that the seller is not acting in the course of a business or reasonable efforts have been made to bring this to the attention of the buyer.[161]

Development of Merchantable Quality

Merchantable quality and description.   Merchantable quality, the predecessor   **7.37** of satisfactory quality, developed in close companionship with the concept of description and it was difficult to see any distinction between them. In a nutshell, goods were regarded in the nineteenth century as of merchantable quality if saleable under the contract description. This was not the same as requiring

---

[158] *Browning v Brachers* [2004] EWHC 16 (QB) at [47]. The sale of a business has been held to take place in the ordinary course of business for the purpose of a floating charge: *Re Borax Co.* [1901] 1 Ch 326; see also *Ashborder BV v Green Gas Power Ltd* [2005] 1 BCLC 623.

[159] n. 155 above at 1042.

[160] Cf *Stevenson v Beverley Bentinck Ltd* [1976] 1 WLR 483.

[161] See *Boyter v Thomson* [1995] 2 AC 628.

the goods to be free from latent defects, for merchantable quality was based upon the market. All manner of goods may be sold in the market and, depending upon their condition and quality, will be priced accordingly. The history of merchantable quality shows that buyers seeking a guarantee against the presence of latent defects must secure an express warranty. Difficulties posed in modern times by the meaning of merchantable quality and the terminological shift from merchantable to satisfactory quality evidence a shift in the law. The prevailing policy is to impose strict liability for defective manufactured goods, in other words, to provide a warranty against latent defects.

7.38 **Example.** A convenient starting point in the case law is *Parkinson v Lee*,[162] where the contract was for the sale of five pockets of hops that, unknown to the parties, who were both dealers, had been fraudulently watered by the grower. The watering was not evident from samples previously examined by the buyer or from the bulk of the hops at the time of contracting. The Court of King's Bench held that the seller should not in the absence of fraud be liable for latent defects, unless the buyer secured an express warranty, at least where both parties were equally acquainted with the bargained-for commodity.[163]

7.39 **Opportunity to examine.** The significance of the buyer's opportunity to examine the goods, as ineffectual as it was to discover the latent defect in *Parkinson v Lee*, emerged more clearly in *Gardiner v Gray*,[164] where the contract was for the sale of twelve bags of waste silk. A specimen of the silk was produced at the time of the contract for the purpose only of allowing the buyer to form a reasonable judgment of the unseen goods, but the seller gave no warranty that the specimen provided was equal to the delivered goods. The silk subsequently delivered proved to be much inferior to the sample and could not even be described as waste silk. The court was adamant that the buyer was not entitled to a particular fineness or quality of goods, but was entitled to goods that answered the description of waste silk.

7.40 **Fitness for purpose.** A refinement of the understanding of merchantable quality laid down in *Gardiner v Gray*[165] came in *Jones v Bright*,[166] where Best CJ introduced the notion that goods were merchantable if fit for any of the purposes for which such goods were normally required. Referring to the contractual description of goods, it followed that if the goods so described could be used for more than one purpose, and were in fact usable for at least one purpose, they were of merchantable quality. A buyer with a particular purpose in mind would have to

---

[162] (1802) 2 East 314.
[163] *Ibid.*, 322; a position well-established for the sale of horses.
[164] (1815) 4 Camp. 144.
[165] Above.
[166] (1829) 5 Bing. 333.

communicate this to the seller to secure an implied obligation of fitness for particular purpose. The next important case in defining merchantable quality[167] was *James Drummond and Sons v EH Van Ingen & Co.*,[168] where cloth merchants purchased from cloth manufacturers a quantity of worsted coatings equal in quality and weight to samples previously supplied. As the sellers knew, it was the buyers' intention to resell the cloth ('corkscrew twills') to clothiers or tailors. The cloth suffered from the defect of slippage between the warp and the weft, so that it lacked the cohesion necessary to prevent undue wear. This fault was not apparent on any reasonable examination of the samples supplied, which were likewise affected. The cloth was therefore not fit for any of the purposes for which goods of that same general class had been previously used in the trade. The sellers were held to be in breach of the merchantable quality obligation. The decision of the House of Lords was certainly influenced by the presence of a defect in the goods: it was not a mere characteristic[169] to be expected in a cheaper kind of twill. Furthermore, cloth of the contract type was not ordinarily used in the making of inferior clothing,[170] though it is quite possible that such a market could have been found had it been sold under a description connoting the defect. In short, the standard of merchantable quality was in this case clearly influenced by the notions of defectiveness and ordinary trade user. The cloth was not of merchantable quality merely because it could have been put to profitable use at the right price.

Summary of pre-Act position.   The *Drummond* case shows that, on the eve of   **7.41** the first codification of sale in 1893, *Parkinson v Lee*[171] was still good law in holding that a merchantable quality obligation did not arise when the buyer had the opportunity to discover the fault in the goods before the contract. As we shall see, the law in this respect was changed in 1893. *Drummond* also served notice that merchantable quality could not be understood solely in terms of description and saleability; one had to look too at ordinary purpose and defectiveness, and quite possibly too at price. The Act of 1893 did not define merchantable quality, though it did provide that the quality of the goods included their state or condition. The consequence of this was that a number of judicial attempts were made to clarify merchantable quality in a series of important cases.

---

[167] The landmark case of *Jones v Just*, n. 23 above, contains a masterful summary of antecedent developments.

[168] (1887) 12 App. Cas. 284.

[169] *Ibid.*, 292.

[170] This distinguishes the case from *Jones v Padgett* (1890) 24 QBD 650.

[171] n. 162 above.

Judicial Definitions of Merchantable Quality

7.42 **Aspects of merchantable quality.** Before merchantable quality received its first full statutory definition in 1973, it was analysed at length in a number of important case. In *Bristol Tramways Carriage Co. Ltd v Fiat Motors Ltd*,[172] Farwell LJ defined merchantable quality 'as meaning that the article is of such quality and in such condition that a reasonable man acting reasonably would after a full examination accept it under the circumstances of the case in performance of his offer to buy that article whether he buys for his own use or to sell again'.[173] This test involves a radical departure from the classical criteria of description and saleability. For a descriptive standard of what is commercially passable between buyers and sellers in the particular market, it focuses on the reasonable response of the buyer to the seller's tender. Whereas the market (or merchantability) approach was concerned with the minimum standard of saleability that could still pass muster under the contract description, the *Bristol Tramways* test set in train a movement towards treating merchantable quality as imposing a minimum quality standard. It can therefore be regarded as the source of the change from merchantable to satisfactory quality. Although the test has come in for criticism,[174] it is consistent with the modern law's preoccupation with the goods after they have come into the buyer's hands and with modern attempts to define merchantable or satisfactory quality by statutory means. In particular, the test draws attention to those buyers who do not themselves deal with the goods in trade but instead use and consume them over an extended period.

7.43 **Relevance of market place.** The *Bristol Tramways* test was criticized by Salmond J in *Taylor v Combined Buyers*[175] for its circularity of reasoning: a reasonable buyer will accept the goods when bound to accept them and is bound to accept them when he will accept them. This judgment asserts uncompromisingly that merchantable quality is not concerned with a disembodied quality standard defined without reference to the contract or the market place:

> [T]he term merchantable does not mean of good, fair, or average quality. Goods may be of inferior or even of bad quality but yet fulfil the legal requirement of merchantable quality. For goods may be in the market in any grade, good, bad, or indifferent, and yet all equally merchantable. On a sale of goods there is no implied condition that they are of any particular grade or standard. If the buyer wishes to guard himself in this respect he must expressly bargain for the particular grade or standard that he requires. If he does not do so, *caveat emptor*; and he must accept the goods, however

---

[172] [1910] 2 KB 831.
[173] *Ibid.*, 841.
[174] See, e.g., Lord Reid in *Henry Kendall & Sons v William Lillico & Sons Ltd* [1969] 2 AC 31, 78–9.
[175] n. 25 above, 646.

inferior in quality, so long as they conform to the description under which they are sold and are of merchantable quality.

Although the case itself concerned manufactured goods, Salmond J's observations belong to a world of horse and agricultural produce sales. Merchantable quality caused trouble in modern conditions because it did not accommodate goods mass-produced to an attainable standard of perfection. Even the cheapest of new cars should not be scratched or suffer from other minor faults that can be banished from the manufacturing process. Agricultural produce, on the other hand, may, in the right kind of market, be sold in a damaged condition, and its characteristics will depend upon climate and other variables in the growing year.[176] This degree of seasonal relativity is not to be found, or at least should not be found, in the case of manufactured goods. The descriptive possibilities for new consumer goods are much narrower than for natural commodities, so that it is easier in the former than in the latter case to infer a breach of section 14(2). Merchantable quality, and its successor, satisfactory quality, is a subtle and varying standard whose application is clearly influenced by the type of damage caused by defective goods, as well as the nature of the goods.

An alternative definition. Although Salmond J asserted the importance of **7.44** description, he was adamant that the conditions of merchantable quality and description were separate;[177] for example, beef and bread might still be describable as beef and bread, though unfit for consumption and therefore unmerchantable.[178] Moreover, saleability was no synonym for merchantable quality since few things cannot be disposed of at the right price.[179] In the view of Salmond J, a suitably modified definition of merchantable quality would run as follows:

> [G]oods sold by description are merchantable in the legal sense when they are of such quality as to be saleable under that description to a buyer who has full and accurate knowledge of that quality, and who is buying for the ordinary and normal purposes for which goods are bought under that description in the market.[180]

The reference to ordinary purposes incorporates the *Drummond*[181] approach, though that case was not referred to in Salmond J's judgment; the reference to the buyer's knowledge of the actual quality of the goods goes unexplained in the judgment but presumably refers to the notion of acceptable quality laid down in

---

[176] It is common in international sales for merchantable quality to be superseded by an express term in the contract that the goods shall be of fair average quality of the season's shipments or something similar.
[177] n. 25 above, 644.
[178] *Ibid.*
[179] *Ibid.*
[180] *Ibid.*, 645.
[181] n. 168 above.

Bristol Tramways.[182] Above all, *Taylor v Combined Buyers Ltd* illustrates that merchantable quality could not be defined in the abstract but had to be understood in the context of the specific contract, in particular, of the description given thereunder to the goods.[183] Besides its failure to come to terms with mass-produced goods, *Taylor* also failed to take account of mass-produced contracts whose every characteristic was the same in all cases.

7.45 **Price.** The significance of the price paid for the goods, hinted at in the *Drummond* case, was emphasized by Dixon J in *Australian Knitting Mills Ltd v Grant* when he stated:

> [The goods] should be in such an actual state that a buyer fully acquainted with the facts and, therefore, knowing what hidden defects exist and not being limited to their apparent condition would buy them without abatement of the price obtainable for such goods if in reasonable sound order and condition and without special terms.[184]

In effect, the notion of price is here substituted for the ordinary use of goods. Instead of the ordinary use supplementing the contractual description so as to identify the market range in which the parties are dealing, price is called upon to perform that function. The above test refers simply to 'a buyer', who may be any buyer; it is indifferent to the various uses to which goods might be put within the market range. The goods supplied might not be fit for all such uses, and, more particularly, not for the use planned by the actual buyer. Even a reasonable buyer might react differently from the informed buyer depending upon the use that that buyer had in mind for the goods. To capture the idea that goods are merchantable if, despite defects disqualifying them from one of these uses they can yet be sold at the same price for another use, Lord Reid later proposed the substitution in the above test of 'some buyers' for 'a buyer'.[185]

7.46 **Another test.** Another oft-quoted definition is that of Lord Wright in *Cammell Laird & Co. Ltd v Manganese Bronze and Brass Co. Ltd*,[186] where he stated that, for them to be unmerchantable, goods 'in the form in which they are tendered' should be 'of no use for any purpose for which such goods would ordinarily be used and hence . . . not saleable under that description'. As Lord Reid has observed, the words 'such goods' must refer to an ideal tender of the goods conforming to the contractual description, rather than to the disputed actual tender;[187] it makes little sense to define a breach of contract by internal reference to itself rather than to the

---

[182] n. 172 above.
[183] n. 25 above, 646–7.
[184] (1933) 50 CLR 387, 413.
[185] *Henry Kendall & Sons v William Lillico & Sons Ltd*, n. 174 above, 79.
[186] [1934] AC 402, 430.
[187] *Henry Kendall & Sons v William Lillico & Sons Ltd*, n. 174 above, 77.

contract standard. Lord Wright's test is essentially a compound of *Jones v Bright*,[188] *Gardiner v Gray*,[189] and *James Drummond and Sons v EH Van Ingen & Co.*;[190] it adds nothing new to the discussion.

Reassessment of elements of merchantable quality. The various elements of **7.47** merchantable quality laid out above—description, fitness for purpose, acceptance, saleability, and price—were assessed by Lord Reid in *Henry Kendall & Sons v William Lillico & Sons Ltd*,[191] who laid particular emphasis on commercial saleability. In that case, Brazilian groundnut extract, because of a toxic additive, had poisoned a large number of pheasants. Lord Reid posed the question whether, notwithstanding this, it was commercially saleable according to the terms on which it was sold. In his view, merchantable quality was not to be judged solely by reference to market behaviour at the time of the contract of sale. On close examination, the explanation for his lordship's willingness to extend the date of the inquiry stems from the stitching of protection against latent defects to the classical merchantable quality element of saleability under the contractual description.

Alternative use. Saleability, in Lord Reid's view, could not mean simply that **7.48** other buyers might have bought the disputed goods on the same terms as the actual buyer, for otherwise there would be no protection against latent defects.[192] In considering whether there was an alternative use for the disputed goods, recognized by the market under the same contractual description at the contract date, it was necessary to impute to a hypothetical alternative buyer knowledge of the toxicity of these goods and then to ask whether that buyer would have accepted the goods under the contractual description.[193] Nevertheless, this alternative buyer should not react in the same way that the market itself did in the immediate aftermath of the discovery that Brazilian groundnut extract was toxic, when the extract was 'virtually unsaleable'; rather, the buyer was to react as the market did when it settled down upon discovering that the extract could still be used, although in a more circumspect and limited manner than had previously been the case.[194] Any other approach, in Lord Reid's view, was artificial;[195] moreover, there was evidence in the present case of how the market settled down. This evidence, rather surprisingly, showed that similarly toxic Indian groundnut extract was accepted by trade buyers for compounding into cattle feed. They protested when they

---

[188] (1829) 5 Bing. 333.
[189] n. 164 above.
[190] n. 168 above.
[191] n. 174 above.
[192] *Ibid.*, 75.
[193] *Ibid.*, 75–6.
[194] *Ibid.*, 75.
[195] *Ibid.*

discovered the toxicity and requested price rebates but did not press the matter in the face of their sellers' intransigence.[196]

7.49 **Merchantable quality and fitness for purpose.** Lord Reid therefore concluded that the goods were of merchantable quality since they were saleable under the contractual description to buyers who had in mind, not the purpose of compounding poultry or pheasant feed, but that of compounding cattle feed.[197] The condition of merchantable quality cut out at the point where fitness for purpose picked up; a buyer seeking coverage for the former purpose would therefore have to notify it to the seller in accordance with section 14(3). It is note worthy that Lord Reid was guided more by the notion of acceptability of the goods than by their initial saleability. The fact that some buyers might grudgingly retain goods, however, does not mean that they would have bought them on the same terms, or accepted the seller's tender of them, had they known of the defect. Lord Pearce, dissenting, maintained that the behaviour of these alternative buyers, admittedly based on a hypothetical market in which the defect was deemed to be known, had to occur in a market that could plausibly have existed at the date of the actual supply.[198] He did not believe that a buyer could have been found without a price abatement and drove his point home with the example of goods infected by a deadly poison, a simple antidote to which is discovered two years after the date of supply. Although the goods might well be saleable two years down the road, they would be unsaleable at the contract date.[199] It is submitted that Lord Pearce's approach is more in tune with saleability as it has long been understood. One might also ask how Lord Reid would have dealt with the case of a buyer of goods for animal feed who finds that the goods supplied have perished in the interval between the discovery that they are toxic and the discovery that they may, however, be fed to cattle.

7.50 **Criticism.** In one sense, *Henry Kendall & Sons v William Lillico & Sons Ltd*[200] is in line with merchantable quality authorities in maintaining that the existence of a defect in the goods does not necessarily make them unmerchantable. But it is submitted that it takes a wrong turning by looking at the way certain buyers might have behaved upon discovering a defect in the goods after delivery, rather than at the way they would have behaved on entering into the contract in the first place or at the point of tender. This shift of focus would seem to be due to the ambiguity of acceptance, implicity understood in the present case in the special sense given

---

[196] *Ibid.*, 76, 79.
[197] *Ibid.*
[198] *Ibid.*, 119.
[199] *Ibid.* Sympathy was expressed for Lord Pearce's view by Lloyd LJ in *M/S Aswan Engineering Establishment Co. Ltd v Lupdine Ltd* [1987] 1 WLR 1, 15.
[200] n. 174 above.

to it by section 35, in connection with the right of rejection, rather than in the sense that it has in section 27, which concerns the buyer's duty to accept the seller's tender of the goods.[201] The real question is whether the seller should have sold, not whether the buyer ought to have accepted (in the sense of not rejecting after delivery). Although a greater preoccupation with protection against latent defects looks to the fate of the goods in the buyer's hands, and should therefore expand the buyer's protection under section 14(2), it paradoxically abridged the buyer's protection in the present case. *Henry Kendall & Sons* is criticized here, not because it held that goods fit for an ordinary purpose within the contract description and price range are of merchantable quality though unfit for another purpose;[202] rather, it is criticized because of its failure to appreciate that markets evolve and that market behaviour should be assessed at the critical time when the goods were supplied and not at some later date with the benefit of hindsight.[203]

A special case. A final authority to consider on the evolving meaning of **7.51** merchantable quality before it was given a statutory is *Cehave NV v Bremer Handelsgesellschaft mbH*.[204] The facts were unusual.[205] The buyers' behaviour in repurchasing at a distress sale overheated but usable citrus pulp pellets that they had previously rejected showed in the opinion of the court that they should not fairly have rejected those goods and should have been content with damages. About one-fifth of the market value of the goods had been lost by the overheating and, unlike *Henry Kendall & Sons*,[206] the condition of the cargo was apparent on its receipt by the buyers. There was no evidence that some buyers would have accepted the goods without an abatement of the price; indeed, there was trade evidence of the appropriate price discount for goods in that condition. Permitting the buyer to reject the goods might seem harsh but, on the face of it, an application of the merchantable quality standard should have led to that result. The problem with cases like *Cehave* lies not with the meaning of merchantable quality but with its status as a condition in all cases, which ultimately the Law Commission decided not to overturn.[207] The status of the term as a condition is responsible for difficult

---

[201] See Ch. 6 above.

[202] This has been the law since *Jones v Bright*, n. 166 above; *James Drummond and Sons v EH Van Ingen & Co.*, n. 168 above. More recently, see also *Canada Atlantic Grain Export Co. v Eilers* (1929) 35 Ll. LR 206, 213 (Lord Wright); *M/S Aswan Engineering Establishment Co. Ltd v Lupdine Ltd*, n. 199 above. In this respect, the law appears to have been changed by the Sale and Supply of Goods Act 1994, discussed in the text accompanying nn. 233 *et seq.* below.

[203] The issue here is related to the issue of *when* the seller breaches the satisfactory quality standard, discussed below.

[204] n. 119 above.

[205] See Ch. 10 below.

[206] n. 174 above.

[207] Report on *Sale and Supply of Goods* (Law Com. No. 160, 1987) at para. 4.25, with which contrast its Consultative Document (WP No. 85, 1983) at paras 2.30–31 and 5.4, where it provisionally concluded that the statutory implied terms in ss. 13–14 should cease to be conditions.

questions about whether goods may be of satisfactory quality though suffering from cosmetic or functional defects.[208]

7.52 **Other terms of the contract.** Lord Denning rehearsed the various elements of merchantable quality but interestingly introduced another—the remaining terms of the contract.[209] Merchantable quality was seen in terms of whether, to a commercial man, the buyers should be permitted to reject the goods and whether that commercial man would be guided by an express price abatement clause in the contract, even if it did not apply to the subject matter of the present dispute. This was an unusual approach to adopt for the following reasons. Clause 5 of the standard form agreement[210] gave a price allowance for goods adulterated by sand, silica, or castor seed, but made no mention of overheating damage. It might have been better if it had done so, but Lord Denning's approach is open to the criticism that it repairs the deficiency of the form by distorting the interpretation of merchantable quality. If there had not also existed in the contract an express term that the goods had to be shipped in good condition, the above interpretation of merchantable quality would have left the buyers without a remedy at all, even though the damage to the goods eliminated one-fifth of their commercial value. It is hard to imagine that a reasonable seller apprised of the condition of the goods would not have sold them without a qualifying word such as 'overheated' or 'damaged'.[211] There is, however, merit in Lord Denning's view that merchantable quality should be assessed in its contractual context. Account could be taken of trade usages and expectations as well as the express terms of the contract, but it is submitted that Lord Denning's approach goes too far. The attitude of a court to minor defects in new manufactured goods might properly be angled to take account of contractual terms setting out a seller's responsibility for dealing with teething problems, or of the seller's evident willingness to correct minor faults or the effectiveness of the manufacturer's warranty programme.[212] Nevertheless, the Court of Appeal in *Rogers v Parish Motors (Scarborough) Ltd*,[213] perhaps influenced by the history of manufacturers' warranties in seeking to curtail rights under the contractual of sale, was loth to allow recourse to them in aid of defining the standard of merchantable quality. Moreover, the repudiation of cure as a brake on rejection by

---

[208] See discussion below.

[209] n. 119 above, 63.

[210] Form 100 of the Cattle Food Trade Association, now GAFTA 100.

[211] The judgments of Ormerod and Roskill LJJ appear to overlook the significance of words of description in the contract. The former is concerned to uphold an arbitral finding and the latter appears to equate fitness for purpose and merchantable quality.

[212] This can be inferred from *Bernstein v Pamson Motors (Golders Green) Ltd* [1987] 2 All ER 220.

[213] [1987] 2 All ER 232; see also *Lamarra v Capital Bank Plc* [2006] CSIH 49; 2007 SC 95 at [62].

the Law Commission[214] will not make it easy to invoke the availability of cure by a willing seller as an aid to interpreting merchantable (now satisfactory) quality.

The 1973 Definition of Merchantable Quality

First statutory definition.   The first statutory definition of merchantable   **7.53** quality, as introduced in 1973[215] and incorporated in section 14(6) of the Sale of Goods Act 1979, read as follows:

> Goods of any kind are of merchantable quality . . . if they are as fit for the purpose or purposes for which goods of that kind are commonly bought as it is reasonable to expect having regard to any description applied to them, the price (if relevant) and all the other relevant circumstances.

On the face of it, this definition was too bland to solve difficult problems,[216] although routine cases might have been disposed of without too minute a parsing of the statutory language. It is a commonplace that judicial passages should not be interpreted with the rigour accorded to a statutory text since they are expounded in a limited factual context and need to be adapted to changing circumstances.[217] The above treatment of merchantable quality is a standard, rather than a hard and fast definition. It demands imaginative judicial interpretation, since quality is relative, elusive, and dependent upon the type of goods and market. The danger of restrictive canons of interpretation cramping a statutory standard like that set out above is evident in the way the definition has been criticized.[218] This criticism takes the 1973 definition to task because fitness for purpose bulks too large, thereby suggesting that cosmetic and æsthetic aspects of the goods are less important than whether they do the job assigned to them. Similarly, it is argued that to see fitness through reasonable expectations allows account to be taken of actual manufacturing standards, which may be tolerant of minor defects, rather than attainable excellence. This narrow interpretation of the definition of merchantable quality is a by-product of rendering into a statutory form something that perhaps had best been left to judicial exposition. One way to counter the drift to a form of interpretation that destroys the spirit of a broad-textured idea is to maintain contact with the underlying case law. Unfortunately, it could not be assumed that the 1973 definition was designed merely to codify the earlier cases, and it was predictably asserted that the 'intricacies' of the earlier decisions should

---

[214] See Ch. 10 below.

[215] By the Supply of Goods (Implied Terms) Act, s. 3.

[216] But Lord Denning thought it the best definition to date in *Cehave NV v Bremer Handelsgesellschaft mbH*, n. 119 above, 62.

[217] See *Cammell Laird & Co. Ltd v Manganese Bronze and Brass Co. Ltd*, n. 186 above, 429 (Lord Wright); *Henry Kendall & Sons v William Lillico & Sons Ltd*, n. 174 above, 75 (Lord Reid); *BS Brown & Son Ltd v Craiks Ltd* [1970] 1 All ER 823.

[218] See Law Com. WP No. 85, n. 207 above, paras 2.10–12.

be looked at only in exceptional cases.[219] Opinions may differ about whether the 1973 definition was 'clear and free from technicality'[220] or so vague as to be meaningless, and as stated earlier there is much to be said for the practice of turning to the cases for enlightenment,[221] provided this is not done as a matter of mechanical routine in straightforward cases.

7.54 **Reasonable fitness and reasonable acceptance.** A similar criticism of the 1973 definition[222] was that reasonable fitness was not the same as the reasonable acceptance test first propounded by Farwell LJ in *Bristol Tramways Carriage Co. Ltd v Fiat Motors Ltd.*[223] A reasonable buyer might jib at minor defects that would pass the reasonable fitness test. It was indeed a shortcoming of the 1973 definition that it omitted a reference to reasonable acceptance, and it was possible to see a pointed omission in the case of a criterion well established in the case law. In its working paper preceding the enactment of the Supply of Goods (Implied Terms) Act 1973, the Law Commission put out for consultation the following definition:

> 'Merchantable quality' means that the goods tendered in performance of the contract shall be of such type and quality and in such condition that, having regard to all the circumstances, including the price and description under which the goods are sold, a buyer, with full knowledge of the quality and characteristics of the goods including knowledge of any defects, would, acting reasonably, accept the goods in performance of the contract.[224]

An explicit reference to fitness for purpose might usefully have been added, although it is arguably implicit in the notion of acceptance. This definition, however, was criticized as too complex and as circular, since the test of whether a buyer should accept the goods[225] depended upon whether a reasonable buyer would have accepted them. Any definition of merchantable quality is bound to be complex: the concept is a complex one. It is also true that there is an element of circularity in the acceptance test[226] but it is not serious: the reasonable buyer and the actual buyer are not one and the same person.

7.55 **Protean character of merchantable quality.** It remains true, however, that merchantable quality was too difficult and protean for its various applications to be encompassed with ease by a statutory definition. The same can be said today

---

[219] *Rogers v Parish Motors (Scarborough) Ltd*, n. 213 above, 235 (Mustill LJ); see also *Marimpex Mineralöl Handels GmbH v Louis Dreyfus et Cie GmbH*, n. 134 above.

[220] n. 213 above (Mustill LJ).

[221] See Lloyd LJ in *M/S Aswan Engineering Establishment Co. v Lupdine Ltd*, n. 199 above, 6.

[222] See Ontario Law Reform Commission, *Report on Sale of Goods*, i, pp. 212–13.

[223] n. 172 above.

[224] Working Paper (No 18, 1968), *Provisional Proposals Relating to Amendments to Ss. 12–15 of the Sale of Goods Act 1893 and Contracting Out of the Conditions and Warranties Implied by those Sections*, para. 23.

[225] That is, not reject them for breach of the merchantable quality condition.

[226] See *Taylor v Combined Buyers Ltd*, n. 25 above, 646.

about satisfactory quality. Merchantable quality in section 14(2) applied to natural commodities, such as grain,[227] and to complex manufactured goods; it also applied to new and to used goods, and to goods purchased for resale, as well as to goods purchased for private consumption. Farwell LJ once observed that '[t]he phrase "merchantable quality" seems more appropriate to a retail purchaser buying from a wholesale firm than to private buyers, and to natural products, such as grain, wool, or flour, than to a complicated machine, but it is clear that it extends to both'.[228] Continuing discomfort with the statutory definition of merchantable quality led to a restructuring and a renaming of the implied term in the Sale and Supply of Goods Act 1994.[229] The name chosen in the Act was 'satisfactory quality' instead of the Law Commission's recommended 'acceptable quality'. The Law Commission was not attracted by neutral adjectives like 'proper' and 'suitable'[230] and thought that 'acceptable' with its reference to the reasonable buyer would encourage out-of-court settlement.

Satisfactory Quality

Introduction

New definition.   The definition of satisfactory quality enacted in 1994 reads as **7.56** follows:

> (2A) [G]oods are of satisfactory quality if they meet the standard that a reasonable person would regard as satisfactory, taking account of any description of the goods, the price (if relevant) and all the other relevant circumstances.
> (2B) [T]he quality of goods includes their state and condition and the following (among others) are in appropriate cases aspects of the quality of goods—
> > (a) fitness for all the purposes for which goods of the kind in question are commonly supplied,
> > (b) appearance and finish,
> > (c) freedom from minor defects,
> > (d) safety, and
> > (e) durability.

To this definition has been added certain provisions,[231] transposed from the **7.57** Directive on certain aspects of the law of consumer sales and associated guarantees,[232] that require account to be taken in consumer sales, when assessing satisfactory quality, of any 'public statements' made about specific characteristics of the goods in advertising the goods or labelling them. In non-consumer cases, it is also

---

227 See *Wallis v Russell* [1902] 2 IR 585 (dressed crab).
228 *Bristol Tramways Carriage Co. Ltd v Fiat Motors Ltd*, n. 172 above, 840.
229 See M. Bridge [1995] *JBL* 398.
230 Law Com. No. 160, para. 3.18.
231 S. 14(2D)–(2F), inserted by SI 2002 No. 3045, reg. 3.
232 Directive 1999/44/EC of the European Parliament and of the Council of 25 May 1999, OJ No. L171, 7.7.99, p. 12.

made clear that a public statement might be a relevant circumstance under section 14(2A). The new section 14(2A) departs from the old definition of merchantable quality in more than just the name; it substitutes in the main part of the definition the response of the reasonable person[233] for the fitness for purpose of the goods. The new definition is just as circular as the Law Commission's tentative 1968 definition of merchantable quality: goods are of satisfactory quality if a reasonable person would regard them as satisfactory. Fitness for purpose now appears in a supplementary provision, the new section 14(2B), alongside a number of newly explicit references to various practical aspects of satisfactory quality; this statutory technique can only be beneficial in giving some guidance to the meaning of the implied term. To supplement the above references to statutory definitions of quality, a treatment of the various aspects of satisfactory quality as stated in the legislation is in order. There is no practical gain in drawing a hierarchical distinction between matters mentioned in section 14(2A)—namely, reasonable person, description, price, and other relevant circumstances[234]—and matters mentioned in section 14(2B)—namely, fitness for purpose, appearance and finish, freedom from minor defects, safety, and durability (to which should now be added public statements in consumer sales). This is because the matters mentioned in section 14(2B) are all relevant circumstances for the purpose of section 14(2A).[235] Secondly, there is no reason to suppose that 'the price (if relevant)' in section 14(2A), should be regarded as more important than 'fitness for all [common] purposes' in 'appropriate cases' in section 14(2B).

7.58 **Average or basic quality?**   The old rule of *caveat emptor* retains a vestigial hold on the law concerning satisfactory quality, so far as goods supplied may be of varying quality. In certain instruments, attempts have been made to impose on sellers a default obligation to supply goods of average quality.[236] This is not the

---

[233] The test has been said to be an objective one based on someone who is in the buyer's position and has his knowledge, and not on someone who is a stranger without any knowledge of the background of the transaction: *Bramhill v Edwards* [2004] EWCA Civ 403; [2004] 2 Lloyd's Rep. 653 at [39] (Auld LJ); *Egan v Motor Services (Bath) Ltd* [2007] EWCA Civ 1002; [2008] 1 All ER 1156 at [47]. Cf *Lamarra v Capital Bank Plc* [2006] CSIH 49; 2007 SC 95 at [73] (hire purchase: not the reasonableness of a contracting party that is the relevant criterion) and at [76] (but the test is an objective one).

[234] Such circumstances must relate to the quality of the goods (and thus exclude reference to a manufacturer's guarantee): *Lamarra v Capital Bank Plc*, n. 233 above at [62]. Circumstances must be disregarded if they relate to matters (in this case, technical drawings) not incorporated in the contracts: *Rosengrans Tann Ltd v Ayres* [2001] EWCA Civ 997 at [30]. The description of a vehicle in an inspection report, however, is a relevant circumstance: *Stewart v Perth and Kinross Council* [2004] UKHL 16 at [17]. So too is the conformity of the goods to an industry standard: *Britvic Soft Drinks Ltd v Messer UK Ltd* [2002] 1 Lloyd's Rep. 20 at [77] (BS4105).

[235] *Lamarra v Capital Bank Plc*, n. 233 above at [69].

[236] Principles of European Contract Law, Art. 6:108 (at least average performance if the contract silent); Unidroit Principles of International Commercial Contracts, Art. 5.1.6 ('not less than average').

case with English law. Whereas those instruments would place upon the seller the burden of defining responsibility by reference to a quality range, English law places the burden on buyers of demanding something higher than the bottom end of the range of satisfactoriness, either by means of express warranty or by means of technical specifications in the contract. Subject to the goods now having to fit all ordinary purposes in appropriate cases, the implied term of satisfactory quality, like its predecessor, is concerned only with the minimum level of quality that is saleable under the contract description. In one case,[237] the buyers of a quantity of beetroot canned in vinegar failed in their merchantable quality claim when they could establish only that its shelf life of one year would have been longer if the beetroot had been canned in brine. The same result should be reached today in the case of satisfactory quality. Emphasis has rightly been placed on unsatisfactory goods being sub-standard goods,[238] but this is not the same as below average. A buyer seeking a higher standard should seek an express warranty or make use of the fitness for purpose term in section 14(3).[239] In consumer cases, the introduction of a new criterion of satisfactory quality, based on public statements in advertisements and promotional literature, may serve to elevate the satisfactory quality standard and in some cases spare consumer buyers the need to specify any particular purpose to attract the seller's liability under section 14(3).

Fitness for Purpose

All common purposes.   Cases like *James Drummond and Sons v EH Van Ingen &* **7.59** *Co.*[240] and *Henry Kendall & Sons v William Lillico & Sons Ltd*[241] established that multipurpose goods were of merchantable quality if fit for at least one purpose in the range of ordinary purposes;[242] a buyer seeking added protection therefore had to communicate his particular purpose to the seller to invoke the separate implied term of reasonable fitness. If the purpose of a non-communicating buyer were not satisfied by the goods, it was always a difficult matter to determine whether there were other existing purposes in the range of ordinary purposes, not to mention where the burden of persuasion lay in establishing the range of ordinary purposes. An expensive car could not be said to be of merchantable quality just because it could be sold quite satisfactorily as scrap, for the price and description of the

---

237 *Geo. Wills & Co. Ltd v Daniels Pty Ltd* (1957) 98 CLR 77.

238 *Jewson Ltd v Boyhan* [2003] EWCA Civ 1030; [2004] 1 Lloyd's Rep. 505 at [77] (Sedley LJ); *Balmoral Group Ltd v Borealis (UK) Ltd* [2006] EWHC 1900 (Comm); [2006] 2 Lloyd's Rep. 629 at [140].

239 *Jewson Ltd v Boyhan*, n. 238 above at [46]–[47] (Clarke LJ); *Balmoral Group Ltd v Borealis (UK) Ltd*, n. 238 above at [140]. In the former case, electric boilers worked satisfactorily as boilers but had a low energy rating.

240 n. 168 above.

241 n. 174 above.

242 Even if the buyer's purpose, not served by the goods, was the most common purpose: *FE Hookway & Co. Ltd v Alfred Isaacs & Sons* [1954] 1 Lloyd's Rep. 491.

goods would exclude scrap from the range of ordinary purposes. In *Jones v Padgett*[243] a quantity of indigo cloth was sold to a woollen merchant who also carried on business as a tailor. The buyer intended to have the cloth made up for servants' liveries in his tailoring business, but did not inform the seller that this was his purpose or indeed that he intended to deal with the cloth as tailor rather than merchant. Because of a latent defect, the cloth could not be used for making liveries but there was nothing to show that it could not be used for other ordinary purposes. Consequently, the seller was not liable for breach of the merchantable quality term. The later decision in *Henry Kendall & Sons v William Lillico & Sons Ltd*[244] endorsed the outcome of *Jones v Padgett* but went further in applying the reasoning to dangerous goods.[245]

7.60 **All purposes.** The enactment of the first statutory definition of merchantable quality in 1973 posed the question whether the seller's immunity if the goods were fit for one ordinary purpose had survived. It was argued in *M/S Aswan Engineering Establishment Co. v Lupdine Ltd*[246] that the law had changed because now the goods had to be 'as fit for the purpose or purposes', meaning all the purposes 'for which goods of that kind are commonly bought as it is reasonable to expect'. In that case, sellers of liquid waterproof compound were held liable to the buyers because the plastic containers, when stacked, collapsed in conditions of intense heat and pressure when exposed for a lengthy period to the Kuwait sun. The sellers in turn sought to pass on this liability to the manufacturing sellers of the containers, who conceded that the containers had been described in the contract as heavy duty pails for export shipment.[247] If the containers were perfectly suitable for export to Europe, as appeared to be the case, the question was whether the manufacturing sellers could be held liable for the different purpose of export to Kuwait, which was not a purpose disclosed to them at the contract date. The Court of Appeal held that the manufacturing sellers were not in breach of section 14(2). Although he would have wished to look at the work of the Law Commission,[248] which was denied him by counsel for both sides, Lloyd LJ[249] concluded that, if Parliament had wished to change the law in the radical way advocated by the claimants, an explicit reference to all purposes would have been made.

---

[243] n. 170 above.

[244] n. 174 above.

[245] See discussion above and the grounds of Lord Pearce's dissent.

[246] n. 134 above.

[247] *Ibid.*, 25.

[248] The Law Commission has stated that the 1973 definition of merchantable quality did not change the view taken in *Henry Kendall & Sons v William Lillico & Sons Ltd*, n. 174 above, that goods need only be fit for one of their ordinary purposes: Law Com. No. 160, para. 3.32.

[249] With whom Fox LJ agreed. Nicholls LJ delivered a concurring judgment, observing that it would be unreasonable to impose liability when the containers were perfectly adequate for the job in all but the most unusual conditions.

Moreover, if the claimants had been right, the distinction between merchantable quality and fitness for purpose would have been largely obliterated.[250]

Defining purpose or purposes.   A point left unsettled by the *Aswan* case was   **7.61** how a purpose or purposes is to be defined. The court treated export to Kuwait and to Europe as separate purposes, but it is arguable that there is but one purpose, packaging sealant for export. If this were so, then the focus would shift to whether the containers were reasonably fit for that one purpose as a whole.[251] If Kuwait and Europe are separate purposes, then why should not further differentiation occur so that different countries in Europe are distinguished, perhaps in different seasons, each with its own peculiar climactic conditions? The need to consider this thorny issue has been obviated by the new definition of satisfactory quality, which includes 'in appropriate cases . . . fitness for all the purposes for which goods of the kind in question are commonly supplied'.[252] The Law Commission clearly recommended a change that departed from well-established law, asserting that the buyer was entitled to expect that the goods would be fit for all ordinary purposes as defined by the description and the price paid.[253] The burden would therefore be on the seller to limit the description of the goods in order to keep his liability in check.[254] If indeed the old law has been turned on its head, this involves the rejection of the principle that a buyer seeking a guarantee of quality has to bargain for an express warranty and dilutes the requirements of section 14(3). It is regrettable that the Law Commission did not explore the matter more fully and, in particular, consider whether the change would be as appropriate for commercial as for consumer transactions. There are signs in its 1987 Report that the general law of sale of goods is being increasingly moulded by the imperatives of consumer protection, and the time may come when separate commercial and consumer statutes are needed.

'Appropriate cases'.   Be that as it may, despite the Law Commission's wish for a   **7.62** clear definition that would serve useful practical purposes, some considerable uncertainty remains with the new definition of satisfactory quality. In particular, what are 'appropriate cases' for making the seller liable in respect of all ordinary purposes?[255] It is arguable that the result in the *Aswan* case should stand, given the

---

[250] n. 134 above, 15.

[251] Discussed with s. 14(3) below.

[252] S. 14(2B)(a).

[253] Law Com. No. 160, para. 3.35.

[254] *Quaere* might this be open to challenge as an attempt to exclude liability notwithstanding the controls in the Unfair Contract Terms Act 1977?

[255] Note the silence on this issue of *Balmoral Group Ltd v Borealis (UK) Ltd*, n. 238 above (see [141]), where the court held that section 14(2) had not been infringed (material supplied was suitable for rotomoulding generally, but not for the particular purpose of constructing above-ground static tanks to be used for storing oil over long periods).

extremity of the conditions in which the containers collapsed. Furthermore, it is difficult to see why the seller in *Jones v Padgett*[256] should be liable to a woollen broker who does not tell him that he proposes to use cloth for liveries or even that he intends to deal with it as a tailor. It may not be appropriate to permit a buyer to reject unwanted goods for breach of section 14(2) just because they are not fit for an ordinary purpose for which the buyer had no intention to use them. The argument is even stronger if the buyer has positively informed the seller that his purpose is a different one. In addition to this difficulty, one may predict that the battleground will shift from enumerating ordinary purposes to determining the difference between ordinary and special purposes. This will encourage some degree of metaphysical discussion. When does a single ordinary purpose split to become two ordinary purposes? How ordinary must a purpose be in order not to be a special one? The use of the containers in *Aswan*, in extreme conditions of temperature and pressure, is quite arguably special rather than ordinary.

Price

7.63 **Ordinary purpose and price.** The impact of the new definition of satisfactory quality has to be considered in the light of the relationship between ordinary purpose and price, discussed in *B. S. Brown & Son Ltd v Craiks Ltd*.[257] The quality of the goods in appropriate cases will include fitness for all purposes, and the satisfactoriness of the quality will require account to be taken of the price paid where this is relevant. In *Brown*, a quantity of 'Fibro Plain Cloth' was sold according to detailed technical specifications[258] which did not disclose the precise purpose of the buyers. The agreed price was 36¼ pence a yard and the buyers, unknown to the sellers, intended to use the cloth for making dresses. At trial,[259] it was found that the price was low for dress fabrics but at the top end for industrial fabrics, without being unreasonably high. On appeal,[260] it was further stated that the sellers' equipment and staff were geared to the production of the coarse and cheap cloth used for industrial fabrics and that the sellers would never have accepted the order if informed that the buyers intended to make dresses. The irregularity of the weaving in the fabric meant that it was not fit for the making of dresses.

7.64 **Price as substitute for disclosure.** The prudent course would have been for the buyers to disclose to the sellers that they intended to make dresses. In essence, they were substituting an untenable merchantable quality claim for a fitness claim

---

[256] n. 170 above. See also *Colyer Watson Pty Ltd v Riverstone Meat Co. Pty Ltd* (1944) 46 SR (NSW) 32 (pickled pelts suitable for making leather goods though not for processing into high-grade leather).

[257] n. 217 above.

[258] '"49" No. 1717 Fibro 22×22, 2/9s, 2/8s; all viscose yarns, 4½ denier, 6 "staple"'.

[259] 1969 SLT 107, 109.

[260] 1969 SLT 357.

barred by the lack of disclosure. Their argument was that the price paid took the cloth out of the range of industrial wear and limited its ordinary purpose to dress manufacturing. The buyers were unsuccessful because of the above finding of fact at trial, that the price paid was still within the range for industrial fabric. But *Brown* is significant in that the House of Lords did accept that the price, even in the absence of helpful descriptive language, might define the range of ordinary purposes for the application of the merchantable quality standard. There was, however, some disagreement about the amount of price movement needed to affect the application of the implied term in this way. The sellers had resold some of the cloth at 30 pence a yard and, assuming the new buyers' purpose to be the making of industrial fabric, Lord Guest believed that the difference between this price and the price in the disputed contract (36 pence) would have to be 'substantial' for the aggrieved buyers' claim to be well-founded; moreover, the resale price would have to be in the nature of a 'throw away price'.[261] Lord Reid, on the other hand, was of the view that the contract price would have to have been 'substantially higher' than the price paid for the purchase of industrial fabric if the buyers were to succeed.[262] There was no disagreement, however, over the conclusion that the buyers fell well short of making their case that the price paid excluded the ordinary use of industrial fabric. Whichever view is adopted, it seems that Dixon J's view on price abatement, expressed in *Australian Knitting Mills Ltd v Grant*,[263] would have to be moderated in a case of this kind.

Defects

Relevant defects.   Where goods suffer from more than minor defects,[264] it is   **7.65** very likely that they will not be of satisfactory quality if they are sold as new and are not sold under an intelligible description that brings home to the mind of the buyer that they are defective.[265] Some degree of tolerance of defects may also be associated with the price charged for the goods, to the extent that price differences in the market place are associated with different qualities and degrees

---

[261] n. 217 above, 828. This part of the judgment is somewhat unclear. Presumably Lord Guest does not mean, by 'throw away', a nominal price but rather a price that, in comparison with the original contract price, is greatly reduced.

[262] *Ibid.*, 825.

[263] (1933) 50 CLR 387, 413.

[264] Discussed below.

[265] See, e.g., *Stalham Engineering Co. Ltd v Horner* [1999] EWCA Civ 1289. It is submitted that the Brazilian groundnut extract in *Henry Kendall & Sons v William Lillico & Sons Ltd*, n. 174 above, should be regarded as unsatisfactory under the present definition. But see *Egan v Motor Services (Bath) Ltd*, n. 233 above, where the court, perhaps surprisingly, concluded at [32] that the trial judge was entitled to find that a car was not defective when the steering pulled it to the left on being driven at certain speeds.

of perfection.[266] The case of viscose fabric sold with an irregularity in the weave, *B. S. Brown & Son Ltd v Craiks Ltd*,[267] stands in a long line of cases holding that the presence of a defect in goods is not sufficient of itself to render them unmerchantable (or unsatisfactory). *B. S. Brown & Sons* also invites consideration of what constitutes a defect. A defect may be regarded as something more than an irregularity or imperfection not preventing the goods from serving perfectly well the purpose for which they are bought. To that extent, it may be distinguished from appearance and finish.[268] Subject to this point, modern manufactured goods are marketed and sold against a background of high expectations and quality control procedures. This undoubtedly has influenced the standard to be expected from the application of section 14(2). Nevertheless, it is a common experience in the case of complex goods, particularly cars, that they suffer from initial problems. Conflicting views have been expressed whether account should be taken of this and of a manufacturer's warranty programme in moderating the quality standard,[269] but the established view is that it should not.[270] This would rule out an application of Lord Denning's opinion in *Cehave NV v Bremer Handelsgesellschaft mbH*[271] that the quality term might be considered in the light of the remaining terms of the contract, for example, any provision made for the return of the goods for adjustment and repair under the terms of a warranty programme.

7.66   **Examples of defects.**   As stated above, the presence of defects in the goods will normally be sufficient for them to be of unsatisfactory quality. Routine cases of defect call for little discussion in the case law. Thus, to take a few examples, goods suffering from the following defects were held to be non-conforming: random and unpredictable failures in the computer hard drives;[272] the inability of a press to operate as a vacuum transfer press but only as a hydraulic press;[273] an overweight keel on a yacht;[274] a disease in a herd of goats;[275] and problems with the transmission on an expensive motor vehicle.[276] The cost of rectifying a defect is no

---

[266] For words of caution that a breach of s.14(2) may not necessarily be inferred from the presence of defects, see *Stewart v Perth and Kinross Council*, n. 234 above at [18] (Lord Steyn).

[267] n. 217 above.

[268] The line between defect and appearance may be difficult to draw: see the distinction between lifting roof tiles and curling roof tiles in *Cembritt Blunn Ltd v Apex Roofing Services LLP* [2007] EWHC 111 (Ch).

[269] See discussion in the text accompanying nn. 288 *et seq.* below.

[270] *Rogers v Parish Motors (Scarborough) Ltd*, n. 213 above; *Lamarra v Capital Bank Plc*, n. 213 above at [62]; *Mitchell v BJ Marine Ltd* [2005] NIQB 72 at [30].

[271] n. 119 above.

[272] *Amstrad Plc v Seagate Technology Inc.* (1998) 86 BLR 34.

[273] *Peakman v Express Circuits Ltd* [1998] EWCA Civ 135.

[274] *Clegg v Andersson* [2003] EWCA Civ 320; [2003] 2 Lloyd's Rep. 32.

[275] *Browning v Brachers*, n. 158 above at [49] ('very difficult to argue' otherwise).

[276] *Lamarra v Capital Bank Plc*, n. 213 above (hire purchase: other defects too). See also *ibid.* at [62]; *Rogers v Parish Motors (Scarborough) Ltd*, n. 213 above.

reliable indicator of whether goods are of satisfactory quality,[277] not least because the absence of a breach of section 14(2) by the seller would leave the buyer of defective goods in some cases without a remedy altogether.[278]

Public safety standards.   The question of what constitutes a defect has to be   **7.67** considered in the light of safety standards issued by public bodies, which bears both upon satisfactory quality and, to a slightly lesser degree, fitness for purpose.[279] The presence of certain additives in goods in a highly sensitive market place, especially where the manufacturing buyer has a brand image to protect and real fears about the deleterious effect of adverse press coverage, has the effect of imposing a particularly strict form of liability under section 14(2).[280] Where in one case a public authority, the Food Standards Authority, adopted a 'zero tolerance policy' to a certain dye used in colouring foodstuffs, the subject matter of the present contract, so that the offending dye was liable to be posted on its website or goods made with it recalled, a finding that the goods were not of satisfactory quality was made with little discussion.[281] Nevertheless, simply because a relevant industry standard has not yet regulated the presence or quantity of a particular ingredient in goods does not mean that the goods are of satisfactory quality despite containing a harmful ingredient.[282] Generally, however, compliance with an industry standard will provide the seller with 'strong assistance' under section 14(2).[283]

Appearance and Finish and Minor Defects

Manufactured quality.   The ability of manufacturers to achieve something like   **7.68** technical perfection with modern manufacturing processes has been noted. Suppose, however, that the goods supplied suffer from a minor blemish or fault, perhaps one that can be corrected quickly and inexpensively. In its report on *Sale and Supply of Goods*,[284] the Law Commission expressed concern that the concentration of the merchantable quality definition upon fitness for purpose might encourage the view that manufacturing blemishes should be condoned if the

---

[277] *Clegg v Andersson*, n. 274 above at [47].

[278] But the court in *Clegg v Andersson, ibid.* at [49], did imply that goods might be of satisfactory quality if 'minimal remedial work' was needed to put right a defect. See also *Mitchell v BJ Marine Ltd*, n. 270 above at [38] (more than minimal repairs needed) which, however, points out that a buyer may be without a remedy if a breach of s. 14(2) is held not to exist because defects are minor in character: *ibid.* It is submitted that the use of s. 15A to curtail rejection is a better way to deal with the issue of minor defects; see also *Lamarra v Capital Bank Plc*, n. 213 above at [61] (no statutory recognition of 'remediable breach of contract').

[279] Discussed below.

[280] See *Britvic Soft Drinks Ltd v Messer UK Ltd*, n. 234 above at [92].

[281] *Hazlewood Grocery Ltd v Lion Foods Ltd* [2007] EWHC 1887 (QB) at [194]–[195].

[282] *Britvic Soft Drinks Ltd v Messer UK Ltd*, n. 234 above at [78].

[283] See *Medivance Instruments Ltd v Gaslane Pipework Services Ltd*, n. 12 above at [38].

[284] Law Com. No. 160, 1987.

goods work well enough.[285] There is no good reason why the aesthetic appearance of goods and their freedom from annoying minor defects should not, as well as their function, be seen as part of the buyer's purpose, but there is some little evidence for the Law Commission's concerns.[286] The Law Commission's preoccupation with this problem, together with the concern expressed throughout its Report with consumer protection and the ensuing reference in section 14(2B)(b)(c) to 'appearance and finish' and 'freedom from minor defects', would suggest that the standard of satisfactory quality will be a demanding one in its application to new goods.[287] A variety of considerations militate in favour of this view—the absence of any other remedy if minor defects are condoned under section 14(2),[288] the irrelevance of a manufacturer's guarantee to the satisfactory quality standard,[289] and the applicability of that standard as of the date of delivery and not as of some subsequent date.[290] This is not to say that the appearance and finish of a car at the bottom end of the price range should be comparable to that of a luxury car. Goods sold to resemble natural materials, but at a fraction of the cost of those materials, may be of satisfactory quality even if their appearance is somewhat inferior.[291] A difficult case mentioned by the Law Commission[292] is that of the sale of earthenware, where minor imperfections cannot be banished from the manufacturing process.[293] Account should be taken of this in the application of section 14(2B), but the existence of a separate market in 'seconds' will prevent any dilution of the standard for earthenware and similar products not sold under the description of 'seconds'.

7.69 **Strictness of quality standard.** There already exists authority predating any statutory definition of the quality standard showing the strictness of the implied term in section 14(2). In *International Business Machines Co. v Shcherban*,[294] a computing scale sold for $295 was shipped by post to a buyer. The buyer rejected it because a small piece of glass protecting the dial, costing 30 cents to replace, had been broken. Applying the reasonable acceptance test in *Bristol Tramways Carriage*

---

[285] *Ibid.*, paras. 2.11 *et seq.*
[286] See *Millars of Falkirk Ltd v Turpie* 1976 SLT (Notes) 66. Cf *Lamarra v Capital Bank Plc*, n. 213 above at [67]–[68]. The enactment of section 15A, discussed in Ch. 10 below, should lessen any need to find an absence of breach in cases of minor defects.
[287] Cf *Egan v Motor Services (Bath) Ltd*, n. 233 above at [47]. Second-hand goods are, of course, a different matter when it comes to minor defects.
[288] See discussion above.
[289] See discussion above.
[290] See discussion below.
[291] *Cembritt Blunn Ltd v Apex Roofing Services LLP*, n. 268 above at [123] (fibre roof tiles one-fifth of the cost of natural slate).
[292] Law Com. No. 160, para. 3.40.
[293] See the discussion of whether benzene could be eradicated from the manufactured of bottled carbon dioxide in *Britvic Soft Drinks Ltd v Messer UK Ltd*, n. 234 above.
[294] [1925] 1 WWR 405; see also *Winsley Bros v Woodfield Importing Co.* [1929] NZLR 480.

Co. Ltd v Fiat Motors Ltd,[295] the court held the scale to be unmerchantable. The maxim *de minimis non curat lex* did not apply: the buyer could not be made to accept damaged goods, even if the damage was slight.[296] If the result appears harsh, this was the seller's second attempt to make a conforming tender. The buyer had already shipped back to Toronto a defective machine. Moreover, there was no assurance of a swift repair, since the buyer lived in a small town some distance from the seller's provincial office in Saskatoon.

Example. A similar approach is evident in *Jackson v Rotax Motor & Cycle Co.*,[297] **7.70** where a Paris manufacturer sold to an English buyer a large number of motor horns, many of which had become dented or scratched because of inadequate packing. It seemed, according to the referee, that the horns could have been made merchantable at slight cost; he was prepared to make an allowance of £35 on the purchase price of £450. Yet the price allowance does not seem slight, there was no indication of who was to make the horns merchantable, and the sellers were some considerable distance away. The buyers were in the market for unmarked horns, not marked horns plus a price allowance. Moreover, the status of merchantable quality as a condition should not have permitted a result whereby the buyers had to keep the horns but were granted an allowance. Reversing the referee and the court below, the Court of Appeal was surely correct in holding that the horns were unmerchantable.

Durability

Significance. Durability is a feature of satisfactory quality that has attracted **7.71** specific mention in section 14(2B). It might have been tidier for it to be regarded as an aspect of fitness for purpose. The merchantable quality standard—and there is nothing to suggest that satisfactory quality is different[298]—spoke to the character and condition of the goods at the moment of delivery.[299] Fitness for purpose, on the other hand, invites an inquiry into the fate of the goods in the buyer's hands as they are applied to the buyer's purpose,[300] which will be a protracted one for the consumer buyer. Be that as it may, the Law Commission recommended the

---

[295] n. 172 above.
[296] For a different result where a missing minor part prevented a second-hand engine from working, see *Robinson v Burgeson* [1918] 2 WWR 879 (Can.).
[297] [1910] 2 KB 937.
[298] See *Cembritt Blunn Ltd v Apex Roofing Services LLP*, n. 268 above at [124].
[299] See *Bernstein v Pamson Motors (Golders Green) Ltd* [1987] 2 All ER 220, 226; *Lee v York Coach and Marine* [1977] RTR 35; *Henry Kendall & Sons v William Lillico & Sons Ltd*, n. 174 above, 118; *Lamarra v Capital Bank Plc*, n. 213 above at [61]. See also Law Com. No. 160, paras 3.53–4 (date of supply). The relevant date was said in *R & B Customs Brokers Ltd v United Dominions Trust Ltd*, n. 152 above, 326, to be the date of the contract, but delivery had already occurred before the contract date. Fitness for purpose cases will be discussed below.
[300] *Lambert v Lewis* [1982] AC 225, 276 (Lord Diplock: 'the goods will continue to be fit . . . for a reasonable time after delivery').

reference to durability in the definition of satisfactory quality after rejecting proposals to lay down specific periods of durability and to incorporate industry codes of practice.[301] Durability will depend very much on the particular facts and, as a factor of fading strength, will become increasingly difficult to handle with the passage of time. The longer the buyer retains the goods, the more scope there is for argument that the goods have lasted long enough; the more the buyer's own treatment of the goods will bulk large; and the more difficult the buyer will find it to trace the breakdown of the goods to their condition at the date of delivery.

7.72 **Presumption in consumer cases.** The position of consumer buyers is eased under section 48A(3) by the creation of a presumption that goods shown to be non-conforming within six months of the delivery date shall be deemed to be non-conforming at the delivery date. Under section 48A(4), the presumption of non-conformity at the delivery date thus created may be rebutted by the seller. The same provision has a particular application to perishable goods or goods with a limited commercial life, in that it also exonerates the seller if the seller is able to show that the nature of the goods or of the non-conformity is incompatible with the presumption.

Safety

7.73 **Dangerous goods.** The fact that the goods may safely be used does not mean that they are of satisfactory quality.[302] But if the goods are dangerously defective, especially where they pose a risk of personal injury to human consumers, it is almost axiomatic that they will be held unsatisfactory.[303] A breach of section 14(2) was established without undue difficulty in cases where beer contained too much arsenic,[304] a loaf of bread contained particles of glass,[305] chocolate milk contained shards of glass,[306] a consignment of proprietary fuel contained an explosive fragment,[307] and a stone in a bun was discovered dentally by the buyer.[308] The courts in the relevant cases did not ask themselves whether a buyer apprised of the adulterant in the goods and able to remove it would still have bought the goods without a price abatement. Goods that pose a degree of danger in their ordinary

---

[301] Law Com. No. 160, para. 3.49–50; see also Ontario Law Reform Commission, *Report on Sale of Goods*, i, 215–16.

[302] *Clegg v Andersson*, n. 274 above at [40].

[303] See *Bernstein v Pamson Motors (Golders Green) Ltd*, n. 299 above, 226: '[I]t would be only in the most exceptional case (of which for the moment I cannot imagine an example) that a new car which on delivery was incapable of being driven in safety could ever be classed as being of merchantable quality.'

[304] *Wren v Holt* [1903] 1 KB 610.

[305] *Arendale v Canada Bread Co. Ltd* [1941] 2 DLR 41.

[306] *Shandloff v City Dairy Ltd* [1936] OR 579 (Can.).

[307] *Wilson v Rickett Cockerell & Co. Ltd* [1954] 1 QB 598.

[308] *Chaproniere v Mason* (1905) 21 TLR 633.

use and that are supplied without safety devices, even if these were not required by
law when they were first manufactured, are likely on that account to be of unsatisfactory quality in light of the specific mention of safety in the current definition.[309] It has, nevertheless, been held that goods whose use could be prevented
under regulations concerning road vehicles were of satisfactory quality when
the vehicles inspectorate turned a blind eye to the relevant infraction.[310] Goods
may also be unsatisfactory if one component poses the threat of damage to other
components of the goods.[311]

Unsafe for any purpose.   Where goods are produced for animal consumption, a   **7.74**
breach of section 14(2) follows almost as a matter of course if the defect renders
the goods unsafe to use at any price or for any purpose. Hence, animal bones
improperly cooked by the seller, and so retaining bacteria that killed animals
consuming feed made with the bones, were held to be unmerchantable.[312] The
same result followed in a case where antarctic whale meat was infected with an
undiscoverable botulin toxin.[313] But decisions like *Henry Kendall & Sons v William
Lillico & Sons Ltd*[314] show that the mere presence of a defect causing extensive
consequential damage will not establish a breach of section 14(2) if the goods
could have been purchased on the same terms and applied without causing harm
to another ordinary purpose.[315]

Public Statements

Seller's liability for statements of others.   According to section 14(2D) of the   **7.75**
Sale of Goods Act,[316] the circumstances in section 14(2A) relevant to the question
of satisfactory quality include in cases where the buyer deals as a consumer[317] any
public statements on the specific characteristics of the goods made about them by
the creditor, the producer or his representative, particularly in advertising or on
labelling. Sellers are nevertheless protected from liability if they could not reasonably have been aware of the public statement at the time of the statement, or the

---

309   *SW Tubes Ltd v Owen Stuart Ltd* [2002] EWCA Civ 854.
310   *Bramhill v Edwards*, n. 233 above (sale of wide motor-home imported from US). The fact
that the vehicle was uninsurable did not mean that it was of unsatisfactory quality.
311   *Clegg v Andersson*, n. 274 above.
312   *Feed-Rite Mills (1962) Ltd v East-West Packers Ltd* (1975) 65 DLR (3d) 175.
313   *Farmer v Canada Packers Ltd* [1956] OR 657 (Can.).
314   n. 174 above.
315   In *Ashington Piggeries Ltd v Christopher Hill Ltd*, n. 105 above, the sellers were unable to
demonstrate that the goods could safely have been fed to animals other than mink. The 1994
changes would anyway render such efforts unavailing.
316   Inserted by the Sale and Supply of Goods to Consumers Regulations 2002, SI 2002
No. 3045. Similar provisions are inserted in the Supply of Goods (Implied Terms) Act 1973 and the
Supply of Goods and Services Act 1982.
317   As stated above, in non-consumer cases it is always open to the buyer to show that a public
statement was a relevant circumstance under s. 14(2A): see s. 14(2F).

statement has been withdrawn or corrected in public, or the decision to acquire the goods could not have been influenced by the statement.[318] The forensic difficulties facing the seller in proving that the buyer's decision to acquire the goods could not have been affected by the public statement ought not to be underestimated.

Second-hand Goods

7.76 **Second-hand goods and reduced expectations.** The same strict standard of freedom from minor defects cannot be expected for second-hand goods. There is surprisingly little case law on the subject,[319] and the issue has not troubled the Law Commission, which may explain the absence of any explicit reference to second-hand goods in the definition of satisfactory quality. The standard required of the seller depends upon what the reasonable person may expect, in the light of the description and the price, the latter surely being especially relevant in the sale of second-hand goods. Specific disclosures made by the seller about the condition of the goods should be considered under the heading of 'other relevant circumstances' in section 14(2A); such statements assist in defining satisfactory quality in a given case and ought not to be treated as exclusion clauses ousting or limiting the seller's liability under section 14(2). Cars, whether of the same or different ages, are expected to be of variable quality. They may have different mileage figures, which should be reflected in the price. They may have been well or ill-used by previous owners. They may be sold as needing mechanical attention. These variables will affect the extent to which the seller may dispose of defective goods without attracting liability under section 14(2). Unless qualifying language is used, a second-hand car must at least be roadworthy and capable of being safely driven.[320] Lord Denning once said in a second-hand goods case that the standard of liability for merchantable quality was less strict than for fitness for purpose,[321] and the seller's obligations in respect of second-hand goods will be discussed in more detail under that head.

Resale

7.77 **Responsibility for resaleability.** The existence of defects in the goods may pose a particular difficulty when it bears upon the buyer's prospects of reselling the goods. Two cases may be contrasted. First, in *Niblett v Confectioners' Materials*

---

[318] S. 14(E).

[319] *Bartlett v Sidney Marcus Ltd* [1965] 1 WLR 1013; *Lee v York Coach and Marine* [1977] RTR 35; *Shine v General Guarantee* [1988] 1 All ER 911; *Business Applications Specialists Ltd v Nationwide Credit Corpn Ltd* [1988] RTR 332.

[320] See *Lee v York Coach and Marine*, n. 319 above, 42.

[321] *Bartlett v Sidney Marcus Ltd*, n. 319 above, 1016. The liability of the seller in *Crowther v Shannon Motors Ltd* [1975] 1 WLR 30 was dealt with solely in terms of fitness for purpose.

Co. Ltd[322] the buyers were supplied with a substantial quantity of condensed milk infringing a well-known trade mark. The goods could only be released from the customs shed upon an undertaking by the buyers to destroy the labels, which meant that they could be sold only at a distress price. No buyer aware of the defect in the goods would have bought them on terms similar to those on which they were bought by the actual buyers;[323] the buyers were left with a law suit or a costly embarrassment. On the other hand, in *Sumner Permain & Co. Ltd v Webb & Co. Ltd*,[324] the decision went in favour of the sellers, who had sold to English buyers on f.o.b. an English port terms a quantity of 'Webb's Indian Tonic'. This tonic contained salicylic acid, an illegal ingredient in the domestic Argentinian market, to which the sellers knew the goods were bound. There was no liability in respect of the fitness for purpose term,[325] since the buyers rather than the sellers knew the Argentinian market. Moreover, for the purpose of section 14(2), there was nothing to show that the tonic might not have been sold in other export markets or in the domestic market. It was therefore perfectly possible that other buyers, knowing of the salicylic acid, would have bought the tonic on the same terms as the actual buyers. The court made it plain that the buyers were not entitled to a guarantee that the goods could be resold in all circumstances, a perfectly sensible result. If the tonic had not been saleable in England, but saleable in a number of other export markets, then its sale on export terms should also have resulted in no liability. Conversely, if it had not been saleable in England and had not been sold on export terms, liability should have issued on the ground that no other ordinary purpose existed for the goods in the light of the contractual terms.

Impact of new definition. The definition of satisfactory quality, with its crite- **7.78**
rion in section 14(2B) of 'fitness for all the purposes for which goods of the kind in question are commonly supplied', could well reverse the outcome of cases like *Sumner Permain*. This would hardly be a sensible reform and it may be that any possible excesses in the statutory changes will be toned down by the qualifying statement that fitness for all purposes will be demanded only in appropriate cases,[326] as well as by a restricted reading of what constitutes an ordinary purpose. If goods can be exported to scores of countries, but the buyer chooses one unfamiliar to the seller, the purpose would appear sufficiently special to require the buyer to satisfy the demands of the fitness for purpose term.

[322] [1921] 3 KB 387.
[323] *Ibid.*
[324] [1922] 1 KB 55.
[325] *Ibid.* 57 note.
[326] S. 14(2B).

Examination

7.79 **Pre-contract examination.** It was stated earlier that case law preceding the first codification of sale in 1893 retained *caveat emptor* to the extent that no warranty of merchantable quality existed for goods that the buyer could have examined before the contract of sale.[327] In that year, the law was changed when the Act provided that the merchantable quality condition was excepted in respect of examination only 'if the buyer has examined the goods' and 'as regards defects that such examination ought to have revealed'. This exception was plainly confined to specific goods, or at least a specific bulk. The examination was one conducted before the contract of sale;[328] it was not the post-contract examination upon which hinged the buyer's right to reject the goods and terminate the contract. This point emerged more explicitly when the provision was amended in the 1979 Act to provide that the section 14(2) condition was excepted 'if the buyer examines the goods before the contract is made, as regards defects which that examination ought to reveal'.[329] This stance is continued in the present section 14(2C)(b), which excepts liability for 'any matter making the quality of goods unsatisfactory . . . where the buyer examines the goods before the contract is made, which that examination ought to reveal'.

7.80 **Nature of examination.** It seems on the face of it strange that a feckless buyer who conducts no examination at all, even if the chance to examine has been offered, should be better off than a more prudent buyer whose examination is negligently conducted.[330] It may be, nevertheless, that a buyer may decide not to examine in order to avoid limiting the seller's responsibilities under section 14(2). The above contradiction emerged in a pointed manner in *Thornett & Fehr v Beers & Son*,[331] where the representatives of the buyer, in a hurry because of their lateness for the appointment, conducted a cursory examination of the outside of barrels of vegetable glue. They did not open up the barrels to discover the evident defect in the glue. The court held that the examination exception applied. There had in fact been an examination which, if conducted properly, would have revealed the defect.[332] It did not matter that no examination of just the outside of the barrels would have disclosed the defect. The decision has attracted criticism but is

---

[327] See *Jones v Just*, n. 23 above, 202–3 (first and fifth propositions)—even as regards latent defects, at least where the seller was not the manufacturer or the grower.

[328] *Taylor v Combined Buyers Ltd* [1924] NZLR 627, 635.

[329] S. 14(2)(b).

[330] The provision was criticized as too generous to buyers by the Law Reform Commission of New South Wales in *Working Paper on The Sale of Goods: Warranties, Remedies, Frustration and Other Matters* (1975), paras 8.59 *et seq.*

[331] [1919] 1 KB 486.

[332] See also *Bramhill v Edwards* n. 233 above (internal dimensions of motor-home should have alerted buyer to its external dimensions). Cf *Frank v Grosvenor Motor Auctions Pty Ltd* [1960] VR 607.

defensible in that the sellers' careful arrangements for an examination, to which the buyers agreed, indicated a clear intention to avoid liability for any evident defects; the buyers were 'willing to take the risk, the price being so low'.[333] Since 1973, the word 'that' has taken the place of 'such' in the phrase 'such examination'. It has been cautiously suggested that this change might have overturned the *Thornett* decision,[334] but this argument relies upon a degree of finesse not usually dislayed in the armoury of the modern Parliamentary draftsman. The change of wording would, however, give the courts an opportunity to wipe the slate clean if they wished. The examination conducted by the buyer must amount to more than a sighting or even a touching of the goods;[335] a threshold should be crossed before the examination exception begins to operate.

Reasonable examination. The type of examination that the buyer does **7.81** conduct need only be a reasonable one; the seller's liability is not excepted because a latent defect in the goods could have been detected by an exhaustive examination. Merely drawing back the elastic was a reasonable examination for a retailer to conduct when purchasing a consignment of plastic catapults; it was not sufficient to reveal a flaw in the plastic.[336] Likewise, the consumer buyer's examination of beer was not capable of detecting an excess of arsenic[337] and the buyer of a yacht that he had seen at a trade show could not be expected to retain the services of a consulting chemist to discover the latent fault that subsequently produced 'blistering' of the hull.[338]

Conditional sale difficulty. A difficult issue arising out of the time of the exami- **7.82** nation occurred in *R. & B. Customs Brokers Ltd v United Dominions Trust Ltd*,[339] where prospective buyers on conditional sale terms were allowed the use of a car before their proposal was accepted by the finance company sellers. They discovered a leak in the roof of the car before they signed the agreement. Because of the buyers' continuing reliance on the skill or judgment of the sellers' agent, the dealer,[340] the Court of Appeal was spared the need to reach a conclusion on the question whether the buyers were prevented from invoking section 14(2) when their pre-contractual use of the car revealed its leaking roof. It is difficult to see why the examination exception should not apply to the advantage of the seller in

333 *Ibid.*, 489.
334 *Benjamin's Sale of Goods* (7th edn, by A. G. Guest, Sweet & Maxwell, 2006), para. 11–042.
335 The best explanation for the view that the buyer of a car who merely sits in it prior to the contract of sale yet retains the benefit of s. 14(2): see *Frank v Grosvenor Motors Ltd* [1960] VR 607, 609.
336 *Godley v Perry* [1960] 1 WLR 9, 15.
337 *Wren v Holt*, n. 304 above, 616, expressed wrongly in terms of an opportunity to examine.
338 *Canadian Yacht Sales v MacDonald* [1977] 2 Lloyd's Rep. 298 (Can.); see also *John Macdonald & Co. Ltd v Princess Manufacturing Co. Ltd* [1926] SCR 472 (Can.) ('reasonable inspection').
339 n. 152 above.
340 So that the sellers were liable under s. 14(3).

such a case, though sellers would presumably waive their rights under the exception if they or their agents undertook that the defect would be corrected.

7.83 **Notifying buyer of defects.** The examination exception was expanded in 1973 so as to provide that the seller was not responsible 'as regards defects specifically drawn to the buyer's attention before the contract was made'. The current text (section 14(2C)(a)) substitutes for the expression 'as regards defects' the words 'any matter making the quality of goods unsatisfactory', which is not a change of any substance. The requirement that the defect or matter be referred to specifically is designed to prevent sellers from excluding their liability under section 14(2) in the guise of a blanket statement designed to take advantage of the exception in section 14(2C)(a). It should be noted that the defect need not be one pointed out by the seller.

Reasonable Fitness for Purpose

7.84 **General.** Section 14(3) of the Sale of Goods Act states, in brief, that the goods supplied by a seller in the course of a business must be reasonably fit for any particular purpose of the buyer when this is expressly or impliedly made known to the seller and the buyer relies upon the seller's skill or judgment.[341] In the 1893 Act, the fitness term preceded merchantable quality as section 14(1) in the body of the Act, and in the years thereafter, for reasons discussed below, it proved a more effective source of protection for the disappointed buyer than the merchantable quality term. Reforms of the latter, starting in 1973, have rid it of some difficult aspects, yet it is questionable whether the requirement of satisfactory quality will be any easier to apply than its predecessor, merchantable quality, which lost ground to fitness for purpose because of the latter's greater ease of application. Lord Reid once said that the judicial tendency to limit the scope of merchantable quality had been balanced by a countervailing tendency to give an expansive reading to fitness for purpose.[342] Fitness for purpose was of general application, capable of embracing all sales, whether or not descriptive words were used or the

---

[341] According to s. 14(3):
  Where the seller sells goods in the course of a business and the buyer, expressly or by implication, makes known—
  (a) to the seller, or
  (b) where the purchase price or part of it is payable by instalments and the goods were previously sold by a credit-broker to the seller, to that credit-broker,
  any particular purpose for which the goods are being bought, there is an implied condition that the goods supplied under the contract are reasonably fit for that purpose, whether or not that is a purpose for which such goods are commonly supplied, except where the circumstances show that the buyer does not rely, or that it is unreasonable for him to rely, on the skill or judgment of the seller or credit-broker.

[342] *Henry Kendall & Sons v William Lillico & Sons Ltd*, n. 174 above, 79.

goods were specific. Before 1973, merchantable quality, on the other hand, was confined to sales by description, which would largely have excluded sales of specific goods as the law was understood in 1893. The technical limits of description on section 14(2) had been eased even before 1973, but fitness for purpose developed apace as it was applied to commonplace as well as esoteric purposes and as the trade name proviso[343] became largely redundant fifty years before its formal abolition in 1973. Fitness for purpose occupies a crucial strategic position. A given set of facts will frequently permit multiple claims to branch off into express warranty, fitness for purpose, negligence (failure to warn) and negligent misstatement, and misrepresentation.

Fitness and express warranty.   The implied term of fitness for purpose has over   **7.85** the years diminished the impact in sale of goods law of the express warranty decision of the House of Lords in *Heilbut, Symons & Co. v Buckleton*,[344] which imposed the limiting requirement that a statement had to be made with contractual intention to constitute an express warranty. Although it is easier in modern times to infer an express warranty,[345] a buyer's ability to seek recourse under the fitness term when impliedly or expressly disclosing his purpose to the seller has ensured that there is only a relatively small number of reported decisions on express warranty in sale of goods law.[346]

Development of Fitness for Purpose

Judicial intervention.   The cases preceding the 1893 Act did not always draw a   **7.86** consistent distinction between the fitness for purpose and merchantable quality terms.[347] A discernible fitness for purpose strand emerges in *Jones v Bright*,[348] where sheets of copper sold for sheathing a barque became perforated in use, lasting for one four-month trip instead of the normal four years. Despite the selection of the (apparently) specific goods by the buyer, the seller was liable in an action on the case in damages. The judgment of Best CJ is important for two reasons. First, it separates merchantable quality from fitness, the former requiring the goods to be fit for some purpose and the latter for a particular purpose when sold for that purpose.[349] Secondly, in a way wholly distant from the spirit of *laissez faire* and

---

[343] See discussion in the text accompanying nn. 483 *et seq.* below.

[344] [1913] AC 30.

[345] See Ch. 8 below.

[346] The doctrine of privity of contract is responsible for a number of cases, since express warranty bridges the gap separating the buyer from a manufacturer or from a dealer whose contract of sale is with a finance company.

[347] See *Jones v Just*, n. 23 above; *Shepherd v Pybus* (1842) 3 Man. & Gr. 868; *James Drummond and Sons v E. H. Van Ingen & Co.*, n. 168 above.

[348] (1829) 5 Bing. 533. See also *Gray v Cox* (1825) 4 B & C 108; *Bluett v Osborne* (1816) 1 Stark. 384.

[349] A distinction set aside by the 1994 changes to satisfactory quality discussed above.

caveat emptor, it candidly asserts that it is the business of the courts to promote quality control in the manufacture of goods since they should 'make it the interest of manufacturers and those who sell, to furnish the best article that can be supplied'.[350] Furthermore, 'the case is of great importance . . . because it will teach manufacturers that they must not aim at underselling each other by producing goods of inferior quality, and that the law will protect purchasers who are necessarily ignorant of the commodity sold'.[351]

7.87 **Manufacturers and other sellers.** The fitness for purpose obligation was extended in *Brown v Edgington*[352] to a non-manufacturing seller who supplied a hoisting rope that snapped to a buyer who requested it for raising pipes of wine from a cellar. The court declined to distinguish between manufacturers and those who undertook to get articles made. The seller had told the buyer that the rope would be specially made and had left the impression with the buyer that he would be making it.

7.88 **Standard goods.** The development of this head of liability was stemmed by the Court of Exchequer in *Chanter v Hopkins*[353] where the buyer purchased a furnace from the seller, the patentee of 'Chanter's smoke-consuming furnace'. Although the furnace was useless when installed in the buyer's brewery, the court held the seller not liable for the breach of an implied fitness warranty, since the buyer had purchased 'a defined and well-known machine'. There was nothing, like the undertaking[354] in *Brown v Edgington* flowing from the supply of custom-built goods for the buyer's purpose, to indicate that the seller had accepted responsibility for the furnace to work in the buyer's brewery. The furnace had well-known properties and was just like any other object of its kind. Consequently, the buyer should trust his own judgment.

7.89 **Seller's undertaking.** The idea of an undertaking was taken further in *Shepherd v Pybus*,[355] when the buyer purchased a barge lying at the seller's wharf in order to carry cement. The barge leaked in a way that would not have been discoverable on inspection and the Court of Common Pleas ordered a new trial on the ground that the jury's verdict in favour of the buyer had to be supported by more than just the seller's knowledge of the buyer's special purpose. The buyer also had to give a 'distinct notice . . . or declaration'[356] so as, it would seem, to engage an implied undertaking issuing from the seller that the barge would be fit for that special purpose.

---

[350] n. 348 above, 543.
[351] *Ibid.*, 546.
[352] (1841) 2 Man. & Gr. 279.
[353] n. 52 above.
[354] By this date, the liability of sellers had migrated from case to special *assumpsit*.
[355] n. 347 above.
[356] *Ibid.* 881.

Had the barge been purchased only for general use as a barge, it seems that an implied disclosure by the buyer would have been adequate.[357]

Pre-Act position.   It was subsequently confirmed that the *caveat emptor* rule **7.90** continued to govern sales of specific goods.[358] The Sale of Goods Act 1893, in an earlier draft, would have ruled out a fitness for purpose term where the buyer had the opportunity to examine the goods. The fitness term would thus have been excluded in most cases of specific goods. But the only significance of pre-contractual examination in the modern law is that it may tend against reliance on the seller's skill or judgement. Shortly before the first codification of sale, it was firmly laid down in *Randell v Newson*[359] that the liability of the seller was strict in that there was no exception based upon latent, undiscoverable defects. On the eve of the 1893 Act, it was possible to see the broad outline of the fitness for purpose term.[360] It applied to intermediate as well as to manufacturing sellers; the more general the purpose, the more likely the seller's undertaking would be inferred; liability was more likely to attach to custom-built than to mass-produced items; the seller was strictly liable, even if his skill or judgement could never have revealed a latent defect; and finally, inspection would tend against liability except that, it seems, a buyer would not be expected to find undiscoverable latent defects, just as the seller would be liable despite an inability to find them.

Sale in the Course of a Business

Equipment sales.   As with the satisfactory quality term, the fitness term applies **7.91** only if the seller sells goods in the course of a business. It may therefore apply even if the seller is disposing of unwanted equipment, as opposed to stock-in-trade, and even if there is no regular pattern of sales activity.[361] The development of fitness for purpose liability had nothing to do with status: sellers were adjudged liable not because they were in business, but because they had a skill or judgement that was denied to the buyer. The most obvious example of such skill was the seller who was the manufacturer of the goods and so knew of their properties or was in a position to guard against the emergence of defects in the manufacturing process.[362] Further examples of skill or judgement concerned wholesalers or retailers who selected goods for distribution to buyers.[363] The law developed so as to

---

[357] This would involve a departure from *Chanter v Hopkins*, n. 353 above.

[358] *Emmerton v Mathews* (1862) 7 H & N 586 (buyer a meat retailer purchasing from a market trader); see also *Turner v Mucklow* (1862) 6 LT 690.

[359] (1877) 2 QBD 102.

[360] The original s. 14(1) was described as a 'crystallization of the common law' in *Randall v Sawyer-Massey Co.* (1918) 43 OLR 602, 607 (Can.).

[361] In this respect, the s. 14(2) discussion above applies here.

[362] See, e.g., *Jones v Bright*, n. 348 above.

[363] See, e.g., *Preist v Last* [1903] 2 KB 148.

visit liability on such sellers even if they could not by taking all due care have avoided injury to the buyer. To the extent that their liability became strict, it made sense to say that business sellers as a class were susceptible to liability under section 14(3). The reference in the pre-1973 fitness term to the business seller being liable, whether he was the manufacturer or not, was designed to show that wholesalers and retailers could be liable; it did not mean that liability was confined to manufactured products and excluded natural products. Nevertheless, counsel for the buyer in *Jones v Bright*[364] argued a difference between the two: the reason for this suggested distinction was to establish that the *caveat emptor* immunities of a horse seller should not be extended to a copper manufacturer, since it was only in the former case that 'the seller has no more means than the buyer of guarding against or knowing intrinsic or hidden defects'.[365] Once liability extended beyond manufacturing sellers, the distinction between manufactured and natural products had to collapse.

7.92 **Private sellers.** Since private sellers do not sell new goods, it is hardly surprising that the extension of liability beyond manufacturers did not reach as far as them, given the uncertain nature in the nineteenth century of the liability of all sellers of natural products. The mass production of consumer goods is a post-1893 phenomenon, likewise the disposal of second-hand consumer durables. The private seller of a second-hand car knows a great deal about its history and characteristics, so to this extent there is no shortage of skill or judgement. The immunity of private sellers, however, may be defended on a different ground. Unlike the civil law,[366] the common law of sale has declined to sever the two issues of contractual termination and liability in damages.[367] Unless insurance against consequential losses became popular, it would be hard to justify imposing a damages liability on private sellers with no ability to spread the loss or write it off for tax purposes.[368] To permit a buyer to return goods to a private seller or to recover a price abatement would incur no such reproach, but there is no sanction for this in the Sale of Goods Act or the common law of contract.

---

[364] n. 348 above.

[365] *Ibid.* 536. According to K. Llewellyn, 'Of Warranty of Quality and Society' (1936) 36 *Col LR* 699, 711: 'Warranty, 1780–1850, divides conveniently in England, and indeed in several of the United States, into horse and non-horse.'

[366] See, e.g., the French Code civil, Arts 1641, 1644–5.

[367] The Ontario Law Reform Commission, *Report on Sale of Goods* (1979), i, 209, notes a 'persuasive argument' in favour of allowing a price reduction action (Cf. CISG (the Vienna Convention on International Sale of Goods 1980), Art. 50) against a private seller but stops short of a recommendation.

[368] The Ontario Law Reform Commission was not persuaded that the express warranty damages liability of a private seller should be restricted by statute: i, 140–41. But the Uniform Act sponsored by the Uniform Law Conference of Canada would allow in such cases a reduction in damages (s. 114).

Transferring liability. A further reason for drawing a distinction between **7.93** business and private sellers is this. The modern law of fitness for purpose shows a degree of strictness in its application to retailers and wholesalers that is clearly actuated by a desire, where goods are defective, to move liability up the chain to the source of the defect, namely the manufacturer or producer.[369] Private sellers, who usually dispose of second-hand goods, are not in the same position as business sellers to remit liability, since the second-hand goods they sell are not the new goods that were sold to them.

Strict Liability

Hybrid liability. Liability under section 14(3) is strict but strangely hybrid in **7.94** nature. The seller's duty is an absolute one, to see to it not that the goods are absolutely fit for the buyer's purpose, but that they are reasonably fit. This gives the subsection a measure of flexibility that can in certain instances dilute the seller's responsibility. It permits a distinction to be made between new and second-hand goods, the buyer's reasonable expectations being lower for the latter. It permits also a distinction to be made between unsuitability and defectiveness, and between defects that are irritants and defects that are dangerous. Section 14(3) does not as such demand that the goods be defective,[370] though goods that are defective are the more likely to be held unfit for purpose. Paradoxically, even though reasonable fitness gives rise to a dilution of liability in some cases, the very flexibility of fitness and its emancipation from defectiveness allows, as will be seen, a very strict form of product liability in other cases.

Defect not discoverable. Although section 14(3) is brought into play by the **7.95** buyer's reliance on the seller's skill or judgement, liability may exist even if no degree of skill or judgement on the part of the seller could have detected a hidden defect, such as a flaw in a carriage pole[371] or typhoid germs in milk.[372] A retail seller who sells sealed goods that are impossible to examine without breaking the seal is no less liable under section 14(3).[373] Yet the seller must be given a chance to exercise skill or judgement; hence the buyer must state his purpose

---

[369] See, e.g., *Ashington Piggeries Ltd v Christopher Hill Ltd*, n. 105 above; *Henry Kendall & Sons v William Lillico & Sons Ltd*, n. 174 above; *Young & Marten Ltd v McManus Childs Ltd* [1969] 1 AC 454 (Lord Upjohn: 'the ultimate culprit, the manufacturer').

[370] See, e.g., *Macfarlane v Taylor* (1868) LR 1 HL (Sc. & D) 245 (whisky for the West African market, coloured with logwood to resemble rum, produced alarming red secretions in its consumers). If the buyer is misled as to the character of the goods supplied, this should in an appropriate case give rise to a finding of unfitness: see *Albright & Wilson UK Ltd v Biachem Ltd* [2002] UKHL 37; [2002] 2 All ER (Comm.) 753 (liability of carrier when delivering the correct goods but with the wrong delivery note, thus misleading the buyer with destructive consequences).

[371] *Randell v Newson*, n. 359 above.

[372] *Frost v Aylesbury Dairy Co. Ltd* [1905] 1 KB 608.

[373] *Bigge v Parkinson* (1862) 7 H & N 955.

expressly or impliedly.[374] Lord Reid has remarked upon the relationship between strict liability and skill or judgement:

> If the law were always logical one would suppose that a buyer, who has obtained a right to rely on the seller's skill or judgment, would only obtain thereby an assurance that proper skill and judgment had been exercised, and would only be entitled to a remedy if a defect in goods was due to failure to exercise such skill and judgment. But the law has always gone further than this. By getting the seller to use his skill and judgment the buyer gets under [section 14(3)] an assurance that the goods will be reasonably fit for his purpose and that covers not only defects that the seller ought to have detected but also defects which are latent in the sense that even the utmost skill and judgment on the part of the seller would not have detected them.[375]

As strict as liability is, the impact of it cannot be fully understood without regard to the degree of disclosure that the buyer must make and to the definition of 'particular purpose'. Initially, fitness for purpose evolved to satisfy special or esoteric purposes that the buyer had in mind. Thus the question in *Jones v Bright*[376] was whether sheets of copper, which might have been used for any one of a number of different purposes, were impliedly warranted as fit for the special purpose of sheathing a vessel. But doubts about the extent of liability for merchantable quality led to the application of section 14(3) in cases where the goods had only one purpose and a common one at that. Thus in *Priest v Last*,[377] the seller of a rubber hot water bottle was liable in damages under section 14(3) when it burst and injured the buyer's wife.

Disclosure and Purpose

7.96 **Degree of disclosure.** The expansion of section 14(3) from esoteric to commonplace purposes obviously had an impact upon the degree of disclosure a buyer had to make to invoke the seller's responsibility.[378] An esoteric purpose will clearly have to be brought home to the seller for most practical purposes by explicit notification,[379] unless, for example, the buyer's identity and activities make that purpose a notorious one.[380] The burden of disclosure is very much on the buyer in

---

[374] This explains the partial dissent of Lord Diplock in *Ashington Piggeries Ltd v Christopher Hill Ltd*, n. 105 above.

[375] *Henry Kendall & Sons v William Lillico & Sons Ltd*, n. 174 above, 84.

[376] (1829) 5 Bing. 533.

[377] n. 363 above. See also *Grant v Australian Knitting Mills Ltd*, n. 35 above; *Frost v Aylesbury Dairy Co. Ltd*, n. 372 above.

[378] S. 14(3) allows disclosure to be made to a credit-broker, defined in s. 61(1), where the price or part of it is payable on instalment terms.

[379] For a good example, see *Jewson Ltd v Boyhan* [2003] EWCA Civ 1030; [2004] 1 Lloyd's Rep. 505, where the buyer, purchasing boilers for installation in new flats, failed to say anything to the seller about the character of the flats in which the boilers were being installed.

[380] See *Hamilton v Papakura District Council* [2002] UKPC 9 (failure to inform seller that water needed to grow delicate cherry tomatoes). Lords Hutton and Rodger, dissenting, thought that the

such cases.[381] A commonplace purpose, on the other hand, need not be expressly communicated to the seller,[382] who is likely to assume that that is the buyer's purpose anyway unless informed to the contrary. Thus the buyer in *Priest v Last*[383] did not have to say that the water bottle was needed to warm the bed, nor the doctor in *Grant v Australian Knitting Mills*[384] that the woollen undergarments were designed to be worn under external clothing. As a matter of fact, as opposed to law, any evidentiary need for the buyer explicitly to inform the seller will be directly proportional to the speciality of purpose for which the goods are needed. The expansion of section 14(3) into commonplace purposes benefited the consumer buyers of finished, single-purpose goods; it did nothing for the trade buyer of goods, who might use them for any one of a number of different purposes.[385]

Commonplace and esoteric purposes. Once it became established that a seller could incur liability under section 14(3) in respect of commonplace purposes, difficult taxonomic questions were later posed concerning the relationship between commonplace purposes liability and esoteric purposes liability. In particular, what was the commonplace (or even *a* commonplace) purpose of certain goods, and when was that purpose so far from the norm that it had to be treated as a special purpose? As the subsequent cases showed, determining the range of a purpose and deciding at what point one purpose was separated from another was more than a philosophical inquiry but rather was vital in defining the extent of a seller's liability. A further question concerned goods that proved to be unfit for an undisclosed esoteric purpose, but that would also have proved unfit if applied to the commonplace purpose served by the goods.   **7.97**

Leading cases. The above questions are best answered through a review of two House of Lords decisions. In the first of these, *Henry Kendall & Sons v William Lillico & Sons Ltd*,[386] a quantity of Brazilian groundnut extract had been sold by   **7.98**

---

ordering of a large quantity of water was sufficient disclosure of the buyer's needs for it in his greenhouses. The fitness of goods for an esoteric purpose may be brought in by the remoteness of damage rule so far as goods have to be fit for a general purpose and that esoteric purpose is a branch of the general purpose rather than a different kind of purpose: *Ashington Piggeries Ltd v Christopher Hill Ltd*, n. 105 above, discussed below.

381 See *Slater v Finning Ltd* [1997] AC 473, 486 (Lord Steyn).

382 *Priest v Last*, n. 363 above; *Hamilton v Papakura District Council*, n. 380 above. No difficulty is posed by the parol evidence rule in the workings of fitness for purpose liability: *Bristol Tramways Carriage Co. Ltd v Fiat Motors Ltd*, n. 172 above; *Cammell Laird & Co. Ltd v Manganese Bronze and Brass Co. Ltd*, n. 186 above.

383 n. 363 above.

384 n. 377 above.

385 But it did lay the foundation of the developments in *Ashington Piggeries Ltd v Christopher Hill Ltd*, n. 105 above, discussed below.

386 n. 174 above.

one dealer in animal feedstuffs (Kendall) to another (Grimsdale); at the next stage in the distribution chain, the extract was compounded by Grimsdale's buyer into poultry feed and it was then sold to a game farm. When fed to the game farm's breeding pheasants, the feed killed a large number of them because the groundnut extract was contaminated by aflatoxin, the poisonous product of a mould caused by a fungus growing on the groundnuts. At the time of the contract, Kendall knew that the extract that it was selling to Grimsdale would be resold to compounders of animal feed; it did not know whether the extract would ultimately be compounded into cattle feed or poultry feed. In a general sense, the groundnut extract was unfit because it was toxic in varying degrees to cattle and poultry. Furthermore, Kendall could hardly complain of Grimsdale's failure to warn it that the extract would be compounded into poultry feed since its own ignorance of the toxicity of the goods and the varying vulnerability of cattle and poultry meant that the sale would have gone through in any event. Kendall was therefore not deprived of any opportunity to exercise its skill or judgement by the absence of information from Grimsdale and so was held liable in damages under section 14(3).

7.99 **Market conditions.** The House of Lords was at pains, nevertheless, to show that its decision was confined to market conditions prevailing at the date of the contract.[387] It later became known that even toxic groundnut extract could be fed to cattle, though in modest proportions smaller than those used in compounding poultry feed in the instant case. The extract remained unfit, however, for poultry, even if used in modest proportions.[388] Thus in the animal feed market, after it became known that Brazilian groundnut extract was contaminated by aflatoxin, and was therefore lethal to poultry and safe for cattle only if used in small quantities, no market at all existed for the goods in the compounding of poultry feed, while a market continued to exist for cattle feed. In order for a seller to be liable under subsequent contracts for harm done to poultry, a basic question raised in *Henry Kendall & Sons* was whether that seller might merely be informed that the extract was needed for animal feed or whether the buyer had to make it known that it was destined for poultry. Lord Reid doubted that liability should exist in the former case,[389] which is consistent with the tenor of the case as a whole. The resale of the goods for compounding into animal feed would no longer be sufficient to engage a seller's responsibility for all types of animal feed. The buyer would have to be more explicit.

---

[387] n. 174 above at 116, *per* Lord Pearce ('according to current standards'); *ibid.*, at 84, *per* Lord Reid.

[388] *Ibid.*, 117 (no need for compounder to use 'abnormally small' proportions to remove lethal effect).

[389] *Ibid.*, 84.

Market behaviour and purpose.   The major lesson to be learned from *Henry* **7.100**
Kendall & Sons is that 'particular purpose' is not a static idea but is to be understood by reference to informed market activity. Goods may pass muster under
section 14(3), even though defective, provided there is an attainable purpose to
which they can be applied. Increasing knowledge of the properties of goods will
therefore modify the market over time and thus the application of section 14(3).
For example, while groundnut extract contaminated by aflatoxin might suitably
be fed to cattle, a subsequent discovery that beef cattle fed in this way could not be
slaughtered for human consumption because of the carcinogenic quality of the
meat would change the picture again. If a market still existed for cattle other than
beef cattle, then a buyer purchasing goods for beef cattle should have to inform
the seller of this to engage the seller's liability under section 14(3) for harm done
to beef cattle.

Liability and the seller's knowledge.   The inference from *Henry Kendall & Sons*, **7.101**
that a buyer of groundnut extract, purchasing for resale to compounders of animal
feed, would in future have to inform the seller if the feed were ultimately to be fed
to poultry, has to be modified to take account of the House of Lords decision in
Ashington Piggeries Ltd v Christopher Hill Ltd.[390] In that case, Norwegian producers sold a quantity of herring meal to English compounders of animal feed; the
Norwegian producers were not informed of the ultimate destination of the goods.
In fact, the meal was used in compounding mink feed according to an original
recipe supplied by the sub-buyers, English mink breeders. The herring meal was
contaminated by the presence of dimethylnitrosamine (DMNA), a by-product of
the preserving process adopted by the Norwegian producers, and a large number
of the sub-buyers' mink died. A successful fitness for purpose claim was brought
by the sub-buyers against the buyer, who now claimed over against the sellers, the
Norwegian producers. As the complex evidence showed, it was not known at any
relevant time that the method of preservation used could bring about DMNA
poisoning. Mink were specially vulnerable to this toxic additive, which attacked
the liver, but it was never shown how, if at all, the contaminated herring meal
might be fed to other animals. When the herring meal was supplied by the
Norwegian producers, they knew that herring meal had been fed in the past to
Norwegian mink, a practice that at that date had not emerged in England; they
also knew of the mysterious deaths in recent years of Norwegian mink but were
unaware of any connection between this and herring meal.

General unfitness.   The Norwegian producers were held liable in damages **7.102**
under section 14(3) although they did not know—and it was unlikely that they
actually contemplated—that the herring meal would eventually be fed to mink.

---

[390] n. 105 above.

It was enough for the buyers to establish that herring meal was generally unfit for compounding into animal feed[391] and that, in accordance with the contractual remoteness of damage rule, had the Norwegian producers contemplated the matter at the contract date, they would have realized it was not unlikely that the herring meal would be fed to mink. *Ashington Piggeries* involves an expansion of section 14(3) liability, as expounded in *Henry Kendall & Sons*, in that it boosts the evidentiary position of the buyer. To establish general unsuitability, a buyer need not show that goods of the same type have actually injured animals other than mink in the range covered by animal feed in general, nor even that, if fed to any of those animals, such as pigs, chickens, cattle, and sheep, the herring meal would cause injury. Rather, the presence of toxicity would raise an evidentiary inference of unfitness across the range.[392] The burden would then fall on the seller to show that the contaminated meal could be fed to other animals in the range,[393] so that the special vulnerability of mink would be seen as an idiosyncracy peculiar to them and falling within the buyer's area of responsibility.[394] Obviously, it would be at least as hard for the seller to prove this as for the buyer to prove the opposite.

7.103 **Remoteness of damage.** Interesting, too, is the court's use of the remoteness of damage rule. The heart of the buyer's case is that the seller commits a breach of contract when the buyer receives, before putting to use, goods that in general terms are unfit across the broad range of the buyer's purpose (selling to an animal feed compounder). It therefore follows that any actual loss incurred by a seller in respect of herring meal compounded into mink feed, in excess of what would have been incurred if the meal had found its way into sheep or cattle feed, is recoverable subject to the remoteness rule.[395] This rule seems to have been quite leniently applied in favour of buyers in *Ashington Piggeries*.[396] The Norwegian producers were held liable in an amount that could well have exceeded any sums they might

---

[391] n. 105 above, at 492–3, 497–8 (Lord Wilberforce).

[392] *Ibid., per* Lord Wilberforce at 492: '[N]ot only mink have livers.'

[393] *Quaere* how many species? In principle, one ought to suffice. Another point is that such species should be safely fed the herring meal compounded in sensible, rather than microscopic, proportions: see Lord Pearce in *Henry Kendall & Sons v William Lillico & Sons Ltd*, n. 174 above, 117.

[394] The subject of divided responsibility is considered below.

[395] This rule in principle requires the type of loss rather than its quantum to be within the reasonable contemplation of the parties at the contract date: *Wroth v Tyler* [1974] Ch. 30. Notwithstanding principle, however, the courts *de facto* seem to require some degree of foresight of quantum when a claim is made for lost profits: *Victoria Laundry (Windsor) Ltd v Newman Industries Ltd* [1949] 2 KB 528 and *Horne v Midland Railway Co.* (1873) LR 8 CP 131 (refusal to award damages for especially lucrative profits); see further Ch. 12 below.

[396] From the Norwegian producers' point of view, the chances of the herring meal being fed to mink must have been quite slender. Cf. *Koufos v C Czarnikow Ltd (The Heron II)* [1969] 1 AC 350. This remoteness point lies at the heart of the dissent in *Hamilton v Papakura District Council*, n. 380 above. Lords Hutton and Rodger, at [58]–[59], considered that it was not unlikely that water supplied for general crop cultivation would be applied to the growth of cherry tomatoes.

have had to pay if the herring meal had been fed to any other animal species. In the light of the facts as they emerged in the case, a subsequent seller of herring meal might well be chary, even if a preserving process not posing the risk of DMNA poisoning is used, in view of the particular vulnerability of mink, of supplying such goods to a buyer who intends either to use them for mink feed or to sell them to a sub-buyer with such a use in mind. That seller might wish to recommend a less risky ingredient or decline to sell to a buyer with such a sensitive use in mind. The very success of the buyers in their action against the Norwegian producers might bring about market conditions in which the trade would view a general disclosure of animal feed compounding or selling to feed compounders as insufficient to cover loss caused to mink.

Dissent.   A similar point to the above emerges in the vigorous dissent of Lord   **7.104** Diplock in *Ashington Piggeries* on the matter of the Norwegian producers' liability.[397] The core of this speech is that a buyer who acquaints the seller merely with a broadly defined purpose, not all the sub-categories of which are best suited by goods possessing identical characteristics, fails to give the seller a proper opportunity to exercise skill or judgement. Lord Diplock would therefore have read the words 'particular purpose' in section 14(3) more restrictively than the majority of the court and would have dispensed with the remoteness of damage approach by requiring knowledge, not foresight, of the sub-category that the buyer had in mind. It was possible that the Norwegian producers might, if given the chance, have recommended against the purchase of herring meal for mink feed for reasons quite unconnected with DMNA poisoning, for example its high fat content.[398]

Product liability implications.   There is much substance in Lord Diplock's dis-   **7.105** sent. Since liability is strict and independent of any knowledge of latent defects, it might be thought that sellers should be given a fair chance to minimize their liability.[399] On the other hand, the decision against the Norwegian producers is consistent with the modern trend for the implied terms in section 14 to operate as guarantees against latent defects, applied in such a way as to push liability up the distribution chain to the point where the defect was created. Lord Diplock's approach could not readily be applied in the case of a buyer purchasing feedstuffs on a general basis, who might at the time of the contract not know the identity and particular purpose of the sub-buyer. The decision of the majority in *Ashington Piggeries* against the Norwegian producers appears to have settled the law, sanctioning a form of strict product liability implemented by means of linked

---

[397] n. 105 above, 509–13.
[398] *Ibid.*, 510–11.
[399] To this effect, see *Hamilton v Papakura District Council*, n. 380 above at [25], though the court stressed that it was a decision on the facts of the case.

indemnity actions connecting the last buyer to the manufacturer or producer of defective goods.[400]

7.106 Buyer's incentive to disclose. In *Henry Kendall & Sons*, Lord Pearce observed that the more circumscribed the purpose of the buyer, the narrower the range of goods from which the seller might select in fulfilment of the contract.[401] This would appear to encourage buyers to inform sellers as closely as possible of their needs, not merely for the obvious reason that this encourages sellers to deliver goods that best correspond to buyer' needs, but also because buyers are thus bargaining for stricter seller liability.[402] Yet, if Lord Diplock's criticism in *Ashington Piggeries* is accurate, the decision, in some cases at least, does not encourage buyers to describe in detail the destination of the goods. *Ashington Piggeries*, however, does not abridge the right of sellers to exclude or limit their liability under section 14(3) to the extent that this is permitted by law[403] or to require of their buyers a clear statement of purpose.

Hypersensitive Buyers

7.107 Informing the seller. The decision in *Ashingon Piggeries* has implications for the position of the hypersensitive buyer. Goods supplied have to be reasonably fit for the buyer's purpose; they do not have to satisfy the scrutiny of a hypercritical buyer. Another way of putting this is to say that a buyer, apparently purchasing goods to perform the same task for which they would be required by any other buyer, should inform the seller of any special sensitivity on his part if the seller's liability under section 14(3) is to be engaged. The best example of this is *Griffiths v Peter Conway Ltd*,[404] where a woman bought a Harris Tweed coat, fit for wear by ordinary individuals, without informing the sellers that she had abnormally sensitive skin. She contracted dermatitis and failed in her action against the seller.[405] The plaintiff, like the mink in *Ashington Piggeries*, was more sensitive than other consumers of the goods. Nevertheless, Harris Tweed, unlike the effect of

---

[400] See Ch. 8 below.

[401] n. 174 above, 115; see also *Bristol Tramways Carriage Co. Ltd v Fiat Motors Ltd*, n. 172 above.

[402] See also the remoteness of damage authorities echoing the same theme: e.g., *Diamond v Campbell-Jones* [1961] Ch. 22; *British Columbia and Vancouver's Island Spar, Lumber and Sawmill Co. Ltd v Nettleship* (1868) LR 3 CP 499; *Horne v Midland Railway Co.*, n. 395 above.

[403] See the discussion of exclusion clauses in Ch. 8 below. The ability of a future defendant to exclude liability may be seen as a corrective to the (sometimes) generous application of the remoteness of damage rule in favour of the claimant.

[404] [1939] 1 All ER 685. See also *Slater v Finning Ltd* [1997] AC 473, where a camshaft supplied for a ship was unsuitable because of the idiosyncracies of the particular ship, not known at the relevant time to either seller or buyer.

[405] A similar result was reached in *Ingham v Emes* [1955] 2 All ER 740. Cases of this kind raise problems of contributory negligence, which is not as such offset against strict liability. See M. G. Bridge (1982) 6 *Can. Bus. LJ* 184 and Ch. 12 below.

contaminated herring meal on other animals, does not harm other human beings. Suppose, however, that the coat sold had been made of such a coarse fabric that it would have made any wearer, or a substantial number of wearers, uncomfortable. It would be strange if this made a difference to the outcome of the plaintiff's case, especially if any other Harris Tweed coat would have induced in her the same physical reaction to the fabric. On one reading of *Ashington Piggeries*, the coarse fabric would be generally unsuitable for human wear, and it might be in the reasonable contemplation of the seller that some sensitive wearers would be not unlikely to react especially severely because of that unsuitability. This reading, surely too broad, could be checked if the notion of unsuitability across the range, coupled with acute unsuitability within a narrow part of that range,[406] were confined to cases where the goods generally cause physical harm and not mere discomfort across the range.[407] Confining *Ashington Piggeries* in this way would conform to the idea of reasonable fitness in section 14(3).[408]

Reasonable Fitness

A flexible standard.   The idea that goods need only be reasonably fit under   **7.108**
section 14(3) appears in a number of forms. A vivid illustration is given by Lord Pearce in *Henry Kendall & Sons*[409] in the context of broad fitness requirements presented by the buyer. Supposing a car were sold in England for general touring purposes, section 14(3) would not be breached merely because the car was not 'well adapted for . . . a heat wave'. It seems that what Lord Pearce had in mind was discomfort, because of poor air circulation for instance, and possibly starting and stalling problems. Persistent rainfall being more common in this country, Lord Pearce was disposed to believe that a car was unfit if it did not cope adequately with rain.[410] But it was not just a question of the frequency with which problems arose when goods were applied to a single but versatile purpose; account should also be taken of the quality of harm ensuing, so that goods could be unfit even if they only rarely 'developed some lethal or dangerous trick'.[411]

Minor defects.   Lord Pearce's views encourage the belief that goods may still be   **7.109**
reasonably fit for the buyer's purpose even when suffering from a minor defect.[412]

---

[406] Or, though it is more likely in a case of poisonous contaminants, an evidentiary inference thereof.
[407] For a decision on the facts that uncomfortable clothes are not unfit, see *Gordon Campbell Ltd v Metro Transit Operating Co.* (1983) 23 BLR 177 (Can.).
[408] The idea of divided responsibility, discussed in the text accompanying nn. 469 *et seq.* below, also supports this.
[409] n. 174 above, 115.
[410] *Ibid.*
[411] *Ibid.* An example would be the engine cutting out in a heat wave when the car is in motion.
[412] The slight breach rule in s. 15A (discussed in Ch. 10) gives courts greater latitude to find that liability arises from minor defects: see *Filobake Ltd v Rondo Ltd* [2004] EWHA 695 (TCC).

The stringency of section 14(3), which operates as a contractual condition, might encourage courts to find the absence of a breach of section 14(3) in the case of complex manufactured goods. The difficulty with this position is that it would compel a buyer of new goods to put up with defects or repair them at his own expense; it also fails to take account of the common, even universal, practice of selling expensive consumer goods with an express manufacturer's guarantee, so that the dealer, acting for the manufacturer, cures the defective part,[413] or replaces it or the goods themselves. The absence of case law could be due in no small part to this practice. The controls now in existence preventing rejection and termination for slight breach[414] should encourage courts to find a breach in the case of non-consumer goods where goods suffer from minor defects, though they might baulk at the same conclusion in consumer cases. An intellectually satisfying way of dealing with the small defect problem is to say that the buyer of complex goods is buying more than just the goods, for he is acquiring also an after-sales service and a guarantee. Goods may therefore be reasonably fit for the buyer's purpose if minor problems can and will be put right with little inconvenience to the buyer and in such a way that the buyer cannot legitimately doubt their future reliability. This use of cure to pre-empt a breach of section 14(3) is not, however, easy to reconcile with the Law Commission's rejection of cure.[415] Moreover, the idea that the buyer acquires not just the goods but also a guarantee package was rejected by the Court of Appeal in a merchantable quality case.[416] The position therefore remains uncertain.

7.110 Sensitive markets. A further aspect of reasonable fitness concerns foods and related items sold in markets displaying an increasing concern with additives and contaminants that might be dangerous to health. The foods in question might not be resaleable or usable in the manufacturing process by the buyer in the event of widespread public fears or an intervention by a government agency. It is evident that the notion of reasonable fitness has been adapted on the facts of particular cases so as to impose a high level of liability under section 14(3).[417] Standards imposed by public bodies and based on the principle that certain additives can be eliminated from the manufacturing process are likely to be taken as the measure of whether goods of this type are reasonably fit for the buyer's purpose.[418]

---

[413] See the discussion of cure in Ch. 10 below.

[414] Discussed in Ch. 10 below.

[415] Law Com. No. 160, paras 4.13 *et seq.* Ch. 5 above.

[416] *Rogers v Parish Motors (Scarborough) Ltd*, n. 213 above. But support for the idea may be inferred from *Bernstein v Pamson Motors (Golders Green) Ltd* [1987] 2 All ER 220.

[417] See *Hazlewood Grocery Ltd v Lion Foods Ltd*, n. 281 above.

[418] *Britvic Soft Drinks Ltd v Messer UK Ltd*, n. 234 above at [74] *et seq.* The finding of liability on the grounds that the goods were not reasonably fit or of satisfactory quality was not challenged on appeal: [2002] 2 Lloyd's Rep. 368.

Liability can therefore arise even if the foods are not injurious to health.[419] The relevance of standards has also emerged in connection with the supply of manufactured goods. The Court of Appeal in *Medivance Instruments Ltd v Gaslane Pipework Services Ltd* took the position that safety standards are more directly relevant to merchantable quality, but that they play a part too under section 14(3).[420] Safety standards are relevant in so far as compliance with them tends towards the seller being absolved from liability under section 14(3), whereas a departure from them tends towards liability. It is in the former case in particular that care must be taken when considering safety standards. The buyer's communication of purpose to the seller and the seller's correlative undertaking of responsibility may in some cases exceed the demands of the safety standards.

Improvable goods. Pitching the seller's fitness liability at the level of what is rea-   **7.111** sonable inhibits the development of liability so that a seller is held to account on the ground that the goods could have been better. In *Medivance Instruments Ltd v Gaslane Pipework Services Ltd*, a fan heater was supplied without a thermostatic device or guard to prevent fires, though there was a warning that materials should not be placed near the heat grill and there was clear evidence that the buyer had heeded that warning in the past and instructed its workforce of the dangers. In the circumstances, the goods were reasonably fit for their purpose. Mere improvability should not lead to a finding of liability, for 'it would place an intolerable burden on suppliers of goods, and therefore would represent a serious interference with normal commerce, if a claim brought under section 14 succeeded every time it could be shown that the article concerned could have been safer, more merchantable or more fit for its purpose than it actually was'.[421] The position might be different, however, if improvements to goods of the type supplied were 'common practice, easy and cheap to achieve, and had obvious benefits'.[422] In a similar vein, section 14(3) places a duty on the seller to respond to the buyer's purpose. It does not as such put the burden on the seller of providing information or educating the buyer. Although the giving of a warning may curtail a seller's liability under section 14(3), it should not be supposed that a seller is conventionally under a duty to cooperate with the buyer so as to define and refine the buyer's purpose, or else incur liability for a failure to warn or inform.[423]

---

[419] *Ibid.*, at [92].

[420] *Medivance Instruments Ltd v Gaslane Pipework Services Ltd*, n. 12 above at [34]. The facts of the case predated the alteration of merchantable quality to satisfactory quality.

[421] n. 420 above at [22].

[422] *Ibid.*

[423] *UCB Invoice Discounting Ltd v Creative Services Inc.* [1998] EWCA Civ 1724 at [13]–[14].

Second-hand Goods

7.112 **Diminished standard of liability.** The notion of reasonable fitness helps to explain the diluted application of section 14(3) to second-hand goods. Just as the satisfactory quality term in section 14(2) must take account of varying goods and standards in the market,[424] so section 14(3) bears the mark of differential application as it embraces new and second-hand goods alike. It would be quite unreasonable for the buyer of second-hand goods to receive the same implied guarantee of fitness as the buyer of new goods, but entirely appropriate that the former buyer have some fitness rights. As a working rule, it may be said that the reasonable fitness standard will be graded according to what is reasonable in the circumstances; it will therefore take account of the age of and price paid for the goods, and of descriptive language used concerning the goods. If a car is sold as a car, and not as a broken-down vehicle fit only for scrap and the salvage of spare parts, then, no matter how old it is or how little the buyer paid for it, the buyer should receive a car that is fit to be driven in safety on the road and that will give fair warning before it has to be taken into a garage for necessary repairs (however expensive these may be). But if the buyer is advised at the time of the contract that certain repairs or changes will need to be carried out to render the car roadworthy, the buyer will not be able to complain of a breach of section 14(3) just because these matters have to be taken in hand. By the use of qualifying or descriptive language, the seller is not excluding liability under section 14(3), which would attract the provisions of the Unfair Contract Terms Act 1977,[425] but is rather defining the circumstances in which the differential standard is to be applied. Whether the goods are reasonably fit for the buyer's purpose involves questions of fact and degree, and the seller is thus filling out the factual background.

7.113 **Lesser or minimum standard?** The question of the fitness of second-hand goods arose in *Bartlett v Sidney Marcus Ltd*,[426] where a Jaguar car was sold in 1964 for £950. At the time of the contract, the sellers mentioned an oil pressure problem concerning the clutch that could be rectified, depending upon the nature of the problem, either by bleeding the clutch or (more expensively) by repairing a leak between the principal and slave cylinders. The buyer was offered a choice of taking the car with the problem or paying an extra £25 to have the problem rectified by the sellers. The buyer took the car with the problem[427] but felt aggrieved when two weeks later the clutch and oil pressure began to cause trouble, and two

---

[424] See discussion in the text accompanying nn. 175 *et seq.* above.

[425] Discussed Ch. 9 below.

[426] [1965] 1 WLR 1013. The report fails to state the age of the car, important in applying the differential standard. See also the s. 14(2) cases, n. 319 above.

[427] The memorandum of sale, though not mentioning the possibility that repair might be required, did say: 'Clutch to be bled. At client's expense.'

weeks after that he was told by a garage that the clutch needed to be replaced for £45. The Court of Appeal held that the seller was not in breach of section 14(3). In the words of Lord Denning MR, a second-hand car was reasonably fit for purpose if 'in a roadworthy condition, fit to be driven along the road in safety, even though not as perfect as a new car'.[428] As plain as it is that section 14(3) was not breached in *Bartlett*, Lord Denning's words come perilously close to a minimal and uniform standard for all second-hand cars,[429] whereas the standard should vary according to age and price. The buyer in *Bartlett* paid a considerable sum for the car, which was at the upper end of the second-hand car market, and should therefore, for example, have felt rightly aggrieved if the engine had needed to be replaced after six months or even a year.

Durability

Purpose use and breach date. This survey of second-hand goods shows just **7.114** how much the issue of durability is integral to the reasonable fitness standard. We saw earlier that durability has been treated in the past as an aspect of merchantable quality and indeed is now to be seen as a factor mentioned explicitly in the statutory definition of satisfactory quality. Satisfactory quality speaks to the condition of goods at the date of delivery[430] or sale,[431] whereas fitness for purpose invites an inquiry into the subsequent history of the goods as they are applied to the buyer's purpose,[432] which may be a protracted one in the case of a consuming buyer. This makes fitness for purpose a more natural carrier for durability.[433] In principle, section 14(3) ought, forensically speaking, to be more helpful to a buyer, who should not be compelled, if the goods break down after delivery, to show a causal link between the breakdown and their condition on delivery. Satisfactory quality, at least in its former identity as merchantable quality, was strictly concerned with the saleability of goods as between seller and buyer, and the moment of sale was the obvious time to assess the matter of saleability. On the other hand, goods are not fit for the buyer's purpose if they are fit only at the moment of sale, because it is not the buyer's purpose to have them only fit at

---

[428] n. 426 above, 1017.

[429] *A fortiori*, Salmon LJ, *ibid*. Another example of a second-hand car is *Crowther v Shannon Motor Co.* [1975] 1 WLR 30.

[430] *Bernstein v Pamson Motors (Golders Green) Ltd*, n. 416 above, 226.

[431] Which commonly takes place on delivery.

[432] *Lambert v Lewis* [1982] AC 225, 276.

[433] Cf. Law Com. No. 160, paras 3.47 *et seq*; Ontario Law Reform Commission, *Report on Sale of Goods* (1979), i, 214–15, which does not consider assigning durability to s. 14(3). For the position of consumer buyers able to rely upon the presumption of non-conformity at the delivery date when the goods break down within six months of delivery, see s. 48A(3) and the circumstances in which this presumption may be rebutted under s. 48A(4): discussed above in the text following n. 301.

that time. Whatever the principle of the matter, nevertheless, Lord Denning MR in *Crowther v Shannon Motor Co.*[434] asserted that the relevant date for assessing the fitness of goods is the time of sale and not the date of the subsequent breakdown of the goods, although he conceded that the breakdown could be evidence of the condition of the goods at the date of the sale. In practical terms, the issue is reduced to who has the burden of explaining whether the breakdown is due to the seller's breach of section 14(3) or to the buyer's mistreatment of the goods. Perhaps, a flexible evidentiary approach is best, which increases the burden on the buyer to lead evidence the longer the goods are in the buyer's possession.[435]

7.115 **Carriage of goods.** One element of the durability of goods is their fitness to withstand carriage. In an earlier chapter,[436] the seller's liability for entering into an unreasonable contract of carriage was discussed, as well as the reconciliation of the presumptive rule that the buyer bears the risk of deterioration to the goods once these have been delivered to the carrier, on the one hand, and the implied conditions of satisfactory quality and fitness, on the other. The conclusion there reached was that goods would not be reasonably fit on shipment unless they were capable of withstanding the rigours of a normal journey. If they were, their subsequent fate would be a matter for the doctrine of risk. If the journey were an exceptionally long or arduous one, a court would probably require cogent evidence of an implied undertaking by the seller to be answerable under section 14(3) for their durability in such a case. Another way of putting it is that it would have to be reasonable for the buyer to rely upon the seller's skill or judgement in the particular circumstances.

7.116 **Repairs and spare parts.** Another issue arising out of the durability of manufactured goods is the continuing availability of repair facilities and spare parts. If goods priced for a lengthy life become unusable because, for example, they have been superseded by a later model and vital parts cannot be had, a buyer may rightly feel aggrieved. The argument was advanced earlier, in connection with the minor defects problem, that the sale of such goods could be seen as an integrated whole embracing repair facilities, express warranties, and implied obligations. For a seller to be made liable under existing law for a failure to supply spare parts or an after-sales service, an argument would have to be developed along these lines. A seller might be required to guarantee that these facilities would be reasonably available somewhere, not necessarily at the seller's establishment. As the law stands, it seems unlikely that a seller should incur general liability under section 14 in respect of these matters. To place on retail sellers responsibility for a manufacturer's production policies seems unduly onerous. Furthermore, to require sellers to

---

[434] n. 429 above, 33.
[435] See *Phillips v Chrysler Corpn of Canada Ltd* [1962] OR 375 (Can.).
[436] See Ch. 6 above.

maintain substantial stocks of parts would be costly. Yet there could be exceptional cases of liability. For example, a seller failing to disclose the imminent obsolescence of goods needing routine supplementary parts that will thereafter become unobtainable—a special type of bag for a vacuum cleaner, for example—may well incur liability under section 14(3).

Law reform.   The Law Commission was firmly of the view that the law should **7.117** not be changed to require sellers to guarantee the availability of spare parts and repair facilities and noted the absence of any support for such a proposal.[437] It also favoured leaving the matter to manufacturers' codes of practice devised under the auspices of the Office of Fair Trading.[438] Indeed, it is the commitment of the law to privity of contract that conceals the point that it is obviously the manufacturer who should bear any responsibility that exists for repairs and spare parts. It is possible that a manufacturer could incur warranty liability to consumer buyers on the basis of advertising or the content of express guarantees.[439] Finally, it should, nevertheless, be noted that the liability of the seller in respect of spare parts and repair facilities is a feature of certain Canadian consumer product legislation[440] and has long been part of special legislation dealing with the sale of farm implements,[441] explicable in the latter case by the fragility of distribution networks in a large country with remote farm settlements.

Reliance

Exclusive or partial reliance?   It is not sufficient for the buyer to establish **7.118** disclosure of purpose and the lack of fitness of the goods. The buyer must also rely on the seller's skill or judgement.[442] The matter of reliance raises a number of issues. First of all, actual reliance is a question of fact 'to be answered by examining all that was said and done with regard to the proposed transaction on either side

---

[437] Law Com. No. 160, para. 3.66.

[438] *Ibid.*

[439] See Ch. 8 below.

[440] The Consumer Products Warranties Act, RSS, ch. C-30 (Saskatchewan), s. 11.8. The Ontario Law Reform Commission recommended a duty, in the case of new goods, to make spare parts and repair facilities available for a reasonable period: *Report on Sale of Goods* (1979), i, 216.

[441] See M. Bridge, *Sale of Goods* (Butterworths, Toronto, 1988), 520–3.

[442] This can give rise to difficulties, especially in building cases, in certain three-party cases, where A has a contract with B and requires B to purchase goods from C in order to perform the A–B contract. In such cases, A may not rely upon B and so will not have an action against B under s. 14(3) or the equivalent labour and materials provision: see, e.g., *University of Warwick v Sir Robert McAlpine* (1989) 42 BLR 1. Whether A will have an action against C on a collateral express warranty depends upon whether C warranted the goods to A (see Chap. 8 below). The difficulties of A acquiring rights under the B–C contract by reference to the Contracts (Rights of Third Parties) Act 1990 have already been noted (*ibid.*).

from its first inception to the conclusion of the agreement'.[443] The buyer need not rely exclusively on the seller in order for the seller to be liable. A buyer might, for example, rely to some extent on his own skill or judgement or upon the reputation of the manufacturer.[444] In a way not dissimilar to the issue of partial inducement in actionable misrepresentation,[445] partial reliance by the buyer will be sufficient to engage the seller's responsibility under section 14(3).[446] It has been authoritatively stated that reliance need not be 'exclusive'.[447] Lord Reid has observed that it will be rare for a buyer not to rely at least in part on a manufacturing seller.[448] Lord Sumner has also stated that reliance amounting to a 'substantial and effective inducement' to the buyer's entry into the contract will suffice.[449] Under the Sale of Goods Act 1893, the burden of proof of reliance was on the buyer. It was often established as a matter of inference.[450] The wording of the present section 14(3) appears to create a presumption of reliance since liability is negatived 'where the circumstances show that the buyer does not rely, or that it is unreasonable for him to rely, on the skill or judgment of the seller'.[451] A higher court, disinclined to interfere with a finding of actual reliance, may be more willing to intervene on the question of whether the buyer's reliance was reasonable.

7.119 **Examination and reliance.** Reliance may be inferred in appropriate cases under the present wording of section 14(3).[452] There is no provision equivalent to section 14(2C)(b), which excludes liability for unsatisfactory goods as regards matters that an examination conducted by the buyer ought to have revealed. Where the buyer examines the goods, however, the circumstances of an examination may also negative reliance on the seller for the purpose of section 14(3). Furthermore, a warning given by the seller in respect of the goods might to some

---

[443] *Medway Oil & Storage Co. Ltd v Silica Gel Corpn* (1928) 33 Com. Cas. 195, 196, *per* Lord Sumner. See also *Preload Co. of Canada Ltd v City of Regina* [1959] SCR 801 (Can.); *Laminated Structures & Holdings Ltd v Eastern Woodworkers Ltd* [1962] SCR 160 (Can.).

[444] See the discussion of trade names below.

[445] See Ch. 8 below.

[446] *UCB Invoice Discounting Ltd v Creative Services Inc.*, n. 423 above at [18].

[447] *Cammell Laird & Co. Ltd v Manganese Bronze and Brass Co. Ltd*, n. 186 above, 427 (Lord Wright).

[448] *Henry Kendall & Sons v William Lillico & Sons Ltd*, n. 174 above, 82–3.

[449] *Medway Oil & Storage Co. Ltd v Silica Gel Corpn*, n. 443 above; *McNeil v Village Locksmith Ltd* (1981) 35 OR (2d) 59 (Can.).

[450] This is laid down in numerous cases. See in particular *Grant v Australian Knitting Mills Ltd*, n. 34 above, 99, *per* Lord Wright; *Manchester Liners Ltd v Rea* [1922] 2 AC 74, 81 (Viscount Dunedin); *Ashford Shire Council v Dependable Motors Pty Ltd* [1961] AC 336, 351 (Lord Reid).

[451] For the proposition that section 14(3) in its present form reversed the burden of proof by requiring the seller to show absence of reliance, see *UCB Invoice Discounting Ltd v Creative Services Inc.*, n. 423 above at [16]; *Balmoral Group Ltd v Borealis (UK) Ltd*, n. 238 above at [142]. Similarly, the buyer's disclosure of reliance need no longer show, as it did under the former s. 14(1), that the buyer was relying upon the seller: *UCB Invoice Discounting v Creative Services Inc.*

[452] *M/S Aswan Engineering Establishment Co. v Lupdine Ltd*, n. 246 above, 17, *per* Lloyd LJ.

extent serve the same purpose that examination does for satisfactory quality in limiting or excluding the seller's liability under section 14(3), though it could not be decisive of the matter.[453]

Seller's response to buyer's disclosure.   A more difficult question relates to the   **7.120** seller's response to the buyer's disclosure of purpose. The 1893 Act required the disclosure to be such that the seller 'realised or ought to have realised that the buyer was relying on his skill or judgment'. This wording brought out the important theme that the seller impliedly undertook to hold himself responsible if the buyer's purpose was not satisfied.[454] In the words of Lord Wright in *Cammell Laird & Co. Ltd v Manganese Bronze and Brass Co. Ltd*: '[T]he buyer must bring home to the mind of the seller that he is relying on him in such a way that the seller can be said to have contracted on that footing. The reliance is to be the basis of a contractual obligation.'[455] Although the relevant words are no longer to be found in the text of section 14(3), it is submitted that this approach is still a useful basis for finding the presence (or absence) of reliance by the buyer.

Pre-contract discussions.   It follows from the above that mere tentative discus   **7.121** sions between buyer and seller, grounded in no particular expertise of, or profession of expertise by, the seller, should not produce the requisite reliance of the buyer. This limitation is to be understood as confined to special purposes, rather than to the general purpose that forms the basis of liability for faulty goods; the latter needs no explicit disclosure at all.[456] Goods may be free from defect and yet not suit the buyer's purpose at all; alternatively, they may suffer from a latent fault not shared by otherwise identical goods produced by the same manufacturing process. This distinction should be understood when considering *M/S Aswan Engineering Establishment Co. v Lupdine Ltd*.[457] In that case, the buyers sought pails strong enough to be used for waterproofing compound sent overseas. They selected a certain type of pail from a catalogue and obtained a sample from the manufacturing sellers before putting in an order. The pails proved unequal to the task of withstanding extreme conditions of temperature and pressure, not disclosed to the sellers, so the buyers' claim under section 14(3) failed on that ground. Although Lloyd LJ[458] also concluded on the above facts that reliance by the buyer was absent, it is submitted that the following distinction needs to be drawn. The buyers' behaviour may have shown an absence of reliance in respect of

---

[453] *Medivance Instruments Ltd v Gaslane Pipework Services Ltd*, n. 12 above at [45].

[454] *James Drummond and Sons v EH Van Ingen & Co. Ltd*, n. 168 above (Lord Macnaghten); *Manchester Liners Ltd v Rea*, n. 450 above (Lord Buckmaster); *Cammell Laird & Co. Ltd v Manganese Bronze and Brass Co. Ltd*, n. 186 above (Lord Wright).

[455] *Ibid*. See also *Hamilton v Papakura District Council*, n. 380 above.

[456] See *Priest v Last* [1903] 2 KB 148.

[457] n. 246 above.

[458] *Ibid.*, 17. Fox LJ concurred.

the type of pail, but they certainly would have relied upon the sellers not to select defective pails from stock.[459] In another respect, Lloyd LJ's remarks may have been perhaps too robust, taking insufficient account of the possibility that reliance may be partial, which is recognized by Nicholls LJ in the same case.[460]

7.122   Extravagant purposes.   Viewing the reliance issue against the backdrop of the seller's undertaking shows that the buyer may not engage the seller's responsibility by an extravagantly stated purpose. Even before the present text of section 14(3) explicitly required reasonable reliance, this requirement was most probably the law. A mere statement by the buyer that he expects to be perfectly satisfied, or that the goods will never display in their working life even the smallest difficulties, should not render the seller liable in the absence of supporting factors including the nature of the market, the precision that the manufacturing process is capable of achieving, and the price paid. To obtain such an undertaking on the part of the seller would probably require an express assumption of responsibility. A case that seems to go very close to the margin of the realistic and fair range of the seller's skill or judgement, quite possibly requiring reconsideration in the light of the amended text of section 14(3), is *Manchester Liners Ltd v Rea*.[461]

7.123   Example.   The buyers, Manchester shipowners, ordered from the sellers, Liverpool coal merchants, 500 tons of South Wales bunker coal, stating the coal was needed for their ship, the *Manchester Importer*. Both parties knew that, in the post-war regulated market, access to South Wales bunker coal was limited to supplies currently on the high seas. These supplies were reduced by a railway strike that prevented more coal from being shipped. The coal supplied to the buyers came from a vessel at sea that had been diverted to Manchester. This coal turned out to be unsuitable as bunker fuel in the buyers' ship, but it might have been suitable for other ships. The buyers knew the coal was to come from the diverted ship but they had not agreed to take that coal, however fit or unfit it proved for the *Manchester Importer*. The sellers were held liable under section 14(3) since 'it must . . . be assumed that the [sellers] knew the nature of her furnaces and the character of the coal she used, for it was this coal that [they] contracted to supply'.[462]

7.124   Goods in short supply.   The *Manchester Importer* may well have been an ordinary type of Manchester vessel handled by an ordinary and competent

---

[459] See *Marshall v Ryan Motors Ltd* [1922] 1 WWR 364 (Can.); *Grant v Australian Knitting Mills Ltd*, n. 34 above, 99. Similarly, a buyer may rely upon a seller to supply boilers suitable for installation in flats but not rely upon the seller in respect of intrinsic aspects of the boilers, such as whether they gave a lower or higher home energy rating (the effect of a lower one relying upon peak rate electricity consumption being to discourage the purchase of flats in which the boilers were installed): *Jewson Ltd v Boyhan* [2003] EWCA Civ 1030; [2004] 1 Lloyd's Rep. 505.

[460] *Ibid.*, 27. See discussion above of buyer's reliance upon persons other than the seller.

[461] n. 450 above.

[462] *Ibid.*, 79 (Lord Buckmaster).

Manchester crew,[463] but it is close to the line to say that the mere disclosure of a narrow purpose may amount to sufficient evidence of reliance on the seller's skill or judgement,[464] especially where the potentially suitable goods are in very short supply. Nevertheless, the sellers, as coal merchants, must have known or ought to have known that the bunker fuel on the diverted vessel might not have suited the buyers' vessel, and yet did nothing to disclaim responsibility in such an event. In *Teheran-Europe Co. Ltd v ST Belton (Tractors) Ltd*,[465] the buyers, an Iranian company, bought air compressors from English sellers through an English intermediary. The sellers knew that the goods were destined for resale in Iran.[466] When it transpired that under Iranian law the goods could not be resold as 'new and unused', the court gave short shrift to the buyers' argument that the sellers were liable, for the buyers knew all and the sellers nothing about the Iranian market.

Product liability considerations.   Where the seller is no more expert than the   **7.125**
buyer, it might be thought that there exists no disparity of skill or judgement between buyer and seller to justify liability under section 14(3). This fails to take account of the product liability policy that those responsible for defects in goods should ultimately be made liable by means of the indemnity chain. In *Henry Kendall & Sons v William Lillico & Sons Ltd*,[467] the toxic Brazilian groundnut extract had been supplied towards the head of the distribution chain by one dealer to another, both members of the London Cattle Food Traders' Association, and interchangeable as buyer and seller in their mutual dealings. Lord Reid was prepared to conclude that a normal sale of goods from a familiar source between these parties would not attract liability (surely questionable if it is the particular goods and not their product type that are defective). Nevertheless, he held with three colleagues[468] that, since these goods came from a new source, the sellers were exercising skill or judgement in putting them on the market, thus vouching that goods of this type were generally fit.

Partial Reliance

Types of partial reliance.   As stated above, partial reliance ought to be sufficient   **7.126**
to make the seller liable. Nevertheless, it is important to distinguish the different ways in which partial reliance arises.[469] First, the buyer may rely upon the seller in

---

463 *Ibid.*, 88 (Lord Atkinson).

464 *Ibid.*, 89 (Lord Dunedin).

465 [1968] 2 QB 545. See also *Corbett Construction Ltd v Simplot Chemical Co. Ltd* [1971] 2 WWR 332, where the sellers, informed by the buyers that they intended to use ammonium nitrate pellets in blasting operations, informed the buyers that they did not manufacture 'explosive fertilizer'.

466 *Ibid.*, 554 (Denning MR).

467 n. 174 above. The facts are stated in the text accompanying nn. 191 *et seq.*

468 Lord Guest dissenting.

469 *UCB Invoice Discounting Ltd v Creative Services Inc.*, n. 423 above at [18].

respect of the whole of the goods, but rely also upon himself or a third party. As stated above, such partial reliance is sufficient for the seller to be responsible for the fitness of the goods supplied. Secondly, the buyer may rely upon the seller only in respect of certain aspects of the goods or of the manufacturing process. This latter case of partial reliance is met in those cases where seller and buyer apportion responsibility according to a division of skill or judgement. A third possible case of partial reliance is that of the buyer who relies upon the seller for the goods to be suited for their common purpose but not on the seller for suitability for a particular purpose not sufficiently communicated to the seller.[470] It is not particularly helpful to analyse the issue presented here in terms of partial reliance; rather, it is a case where the buyer did not rely upon the seller for a particular purpose. The second type of partial reliance arose in *Cammell Laird & Co. Ltd v Manganese Bronze and Brass Co. Ltd*,[471] where a shipbuilder ordered a ship's propeller from a sub-contractor and gave detailed specifications of the power, pitch, diameter, materials, and finishing. Certain details of the thickness of the blades were left to the sub-contractor and, because the propeller proved excessively noisy for reasons linked to the sub-contractor's area of responsibility, liability in damages was imposed pursuant to section 14(3). Similarly, in *Ashington Piggeries Ltd v Christopher Hill Ltd*,[472] the sellers of mink feed were held liable because one of the ingredients they supplied was toxic; if injury to the mink had been caused by the recipe supplied by the buyers, there would have been no liability under section 14(3).

7.127 **Apportioning responsibility.** The apportionment of responsibility also arises where products have to be treated in a particular way by the buyer prior to their use. Hence damages will not be awarded to a buyer who fails to take the elementary precaution of cooking meats long enough to kill parasites naturally or notoriously present in it.[473] Unless put on notice of the buyer's unfamiliarity with what is needed, the seller is entitled to expect the buyer to take elementary precautions.[474] Apportioned responsibility is also relevant to those cases of hypersensitive or allergic buyers. The decision against the buyer in *Griffiths v Peter Conway Ltd*,[475] at some risk because of the reasoning in *Ashington Piggeries*, may still be justified on the ground that the buyer retained responsibility for her personal needs since she had failed to enlarge the sellers' responsibility by putting them on notice that she expected something more than a coat that would not cause

---

[470] See *Jewson Ltd v Boyhan*, n. 238 above at [53]–[60](Clarke LJ).
[471] [1934] AC 402.
[472] [1972] AC 441. See also *Venus Electric Ltd v Brevel Products Ltd* (1978) 85 DLR (3d) 282; *Hunter Engineering Co. Inc. v Syncrude Canada Ltd* [1989] 1 SCR 426 (Can.).
[473] *Heil v Hedges* [1951] 1 TLR 512; *Yachetti v John Duff & Sons Ltd* [1942] OR 682 (Can.).
[474] *Heil v Hedges*, n. 473 above.
[475] n. 404 above.

dermatitis in the general population. The same could be said of *Ingham v Emes*,[476] where a customer in a hair salon did not disclose that she had on a previous occasion reacted adversely to a proprietary hair dye. And yet this same decision raises questions of contributory negligence on the part of the buyer, as well as of the scope of a duty of care in negligence on the part of sellers to warn buyers that they might be hypersensitive or that they should take care to ensure that they are not.[477] In addition, the circumstances in which the skin sensitivity test was applied in *Ingham v Emes* raise doubts about the correctness of the decision. Although the plaintiff knew of her past adverse reaction to the hair dye, instructions on the bottle read out to her contained a statement by the manufacturer that the skin test, which was administered to her, would reveal any predisposition to skin trouble. This should, at least, have raised a serious question as to whether the range of the seller's skill or judgement was thereby being enlarged.

Negligent Buyers

Contributory negligence. The question of the buyer's reasonable reliance also **7.128** prompts consideration of a buyer's contributory negligence. An apportionment of liability cannot be made between a seller's strict liability under section 14(3) and a buyer's negligence, for the seller's behaviour cannot be treated as a tort for purposes of apportionment under the Law Reform (Contributory Negligence) Act 1945.[478] The matter has to be treated in all-or-nothing terms. In *Lambert v Lewis*,[479] a buyer was negligent in continuing to use a defective towing hitch, which caused a serious road accident. There does not appear to have been a finding of fact that the buyer knew of the damage,[480] though the buyer failed to take any steps to maintain or inspect the hitch. The Court of Appeal found the sellers liable, since the buyer's conduct was not so unreasonable as to break the chain of causation between the sellers' breach (of the fitness and merchantable quality terms) and the accident. The result did not depend upon whether the defect in the hitch was patent or latent at that time.[481] But the House of Lords, treating the buyer as aware of the defect,[482] reversed the judgment below. The buyer was entitled to invoke the

---

[476] [1955] 2 All ER 740.
[477] The manufacturer may well have such a tortious duty: *O'Fallon v Inecto Rapid (Canada) Ltd* [1940] 4 DLR 276.
[478] See G. H. Treitel, *The Law of Contract* (12th edn, by E. Peel, Sweet & Maxwell, 2007), 1064–9; *Forsikringsaktieselskapet Vesta v Butcher* [1989] AC 852, 856 (CA); *Barclays Bank plc v Fairclough Building Ltd* [1995] QB 214. Cf. M. Bridge (1982) 6 *Can. Bus. LJ* 184; Law Commission, *Contributory Negligence as a Defence in Contract* (Law Com. No. 219, 1993).
[479] [1982] AC 225.
[480] But the trial judge refers to it as 'plainly' and 'manifestly' damaged: [1979] RTR 61, 87.
[481] [1980] 2 WLR 299, 317. For a similar approach, see *Mowbray v Merryweather* [1895] 2 QB 640.
[482] n. 479 above.

fitness term only until it became 'apparent' that the hitch was broken. To make the sellers liable after that time would be tantamount to the finding that the sellers undertook—which plainly they did not—that the buyer could safely use an obviously damaged hitch on a highway. This approach is not dissimilar to treating any continuing reliance by the buyer after that time as unreasonable.

Trade Name

7.129 **Buyer's reliance.** A final point concerning reliance deserves mention. Prior to the Supply of Goods (Implied Terms) Act 1973, the seller's fitness liability did not extend to 'the sale of a specified[483] article under its patent or other trade name'. It embodied the decision of the Court of Exchequer in *Chanter v Hopkins*,[484] where a manufacturer sold the buyer one of his proprietary furnaces. The buyer's action failed since, by purchasing an established product whose properties were well-known and no different from any other example of the genre, the buyer was not calling upon the skill or judgement of the seller to respond to his specific need that the furnace work in his brewery. This reasoning does not appear to support a universal exception of liability where goods are ordered under a trade name, and in particular does not embrace defective examples of goods within the genre where the buyer trusts the seller to select a sound example of the genre.[485] No one can better be relied upon to make such a selection than a seller who is also the manufacturer. Lord Wright once said that the fitness for purpose section laid down a 'canon of construction' rather than 'peremptory law'.[486] This approach to the old section probably best explains the leading case of *Baldry v Marshall*,[487] concerning the sale of a Bugatti car for touring purposes, where the court held that the seller could not escape from liability where there had in fact been reliance by the buyer. This decision substantially undermined the seller's dispensation from liability in trade name, cases, even before it was repealed in 1973.[488]

Negligence and the Seller

7.130 **Seller's instructions.** A final matter to consider under section 14(3) is the relationship between the seller's strict liability for unfit goods and negligence. The seller's duty under section 14(3) has been applied, not just to the goods sold, but also to ancillary packages or containers supplied with the goods, whether

---

[483] Not specific. This provision was capable of applying to contracts for unascertained goods.
[484] n. 52 above.
[485] See discussion of reliance in the text accompanying nn. 456 *et seq.* above.
[486] *Cammell Laird & Co. Ltd v Manganese Bronze and Brass Co. Ltd*, n. 186 above, 429.
[487] [1925] 1 KB 260. See *Bristol Tramways Carriage Co. Ltd v Fiat Motors Ltd*, n. 172 above.
[488] But see *Daniels v White* [1938] 4 All ER 258; *Wilson v Rickett Cockerell & Co. Ltd* [1954] 1 QB 598.

returnable or not.[489] A more difficult question emerges in the case of goods that can only properly be put to use if the buyer acts in accordance with the seller's instructions. The existence of a contract between seller and buyer does not prevent the seller from owing a duty in the tort of negligence to warn the buyer of dangers associated with the goods;[490] tortious and contractual duties can coexist. The difficulty about any duty on the seller's part to advise or warn is whether it should sound at the level of negligence or is so much a component of the goods themselves as to attract strict liability under section 14(3). It is also questionable whether goods can be separated from instructions if they can be used only in accordance with instructions.[491] These issues have been canvassed in a few cases.

Negligence or strict liability? In *Lem v Barotto Sports Ltd*,[492] the buyer, experienced with guns, bought a machine for the reloading of spent casings. If operated according to the manufacturer's instructions, the machine would produce shells of factory-made quality. The buyer, injured when the machine was charged with too much powder and shot, complained that the instructions failed to stress the importance of compliance. The court treated the matter as one concerning the duty to warn, and not fitness liability; in the circumstances the warning and instructions had been adequate. A decison like this prevents a buyer from subverting the principles of the tort of negligence, especially the rule of apportionment where the claimant has been guilty of contributory negligence, by artificially extending the boundary of the fitness term. It should not be assumed, however, that a warning only ever goes to negligence liability. In *Vacwell Engineering Co. Ltd v BDH Chemicals Ltd*,[493] an explosion fatally injured the buyers' employee. It was caused by water coming into contact with the contents (boron tribromide) of cracked ampoules, caused when the employee washed off warning labels adverting to the risk of vapours but not of explosions. The trial judge found both a breach of the fitness term and negligence on the part of the sellers. In his view, there was no contributory negligence on the part of the buyers or their deceased employee. On appeal, the Court of Appeal noted with approval the terms of a settlement based upon the negligence of the sellers and a 20 per cent deduction against a damages award to be later assessed.[494] The case therefore appears to support attempts to rein in section 14(3) when otherwise it would subvert contributory negligence.

7.131

---

[489] *Gedding v Marsh* [1920] 1 KB 668; *Marleau v People's Gas Supply Co.* [1940] SCR 708 (Can.). See also *Wilson v Rickett Cockerell & Co. Ltd*, n. 488 above (exploding substance in fuel), rejecting the conclusion in *Duke v Wilson* 1921 SC 362 (detonator in coal) that the fitness of goods is a question apart from the presence of a severable additive.

[490] *Clarke v Army & Navy Co-operative Society Ltd* [1903] 1 KB 155.

[491] Cf the discussion of computer software as 'goods' in Ch. 2 above.

[492] (1976) 69 DLR (3d) 276.

[493] [1969] 3 All ER 1681.

[494] [1970] 3 All ER 553.

7.132 **Warning adequate.** Nevertheless, a manufacturer's instructions were dealt with under section 14(3) in *Wormell v RHM Agriculture (East) Ltd.*[495] A farmer bought a herbicide to kill wild oats threatening his winter wheat crop. Poor weather delayed the spraying of the crop, but the farmer decided to risk a late application, despite the warning in the manufacturer's instructions that this might damage the crop. The instructions failed to warn,[496] however, that a late application might prove wholly inefficacious. This proved to be the case and the sellers were held liable under section 14(3) at trial on the ground that the instructions were as much an integral part of the goods as the packaging. But the decision was overturned on appeal because the warning was deemed adequate in the circumstances.[497]

7.133 **Convergence of liability standards.** Too much should not be made of the difference between fitness and negligence. In the case of aberrant products coming off the assembly line, the tort of negligence is often applied in a way hard to distinguish from strict liability.[498] Furthermore, the presence of reasonableness in the definition of fitness encourages an accommodation between the two heads of liability. Even in a case like *Lem v Barotto Sports Ltd,*[499] harmony between these two heads can be arrived at by maintaining that a buyer minded to use a product in a negligent manner may only rely upon the seller's skill or judgement if this is brought to the attention of the seller and elicits a clear (and unlikely) undertaking by the seller.[500] Intractable problems are likely to remain, nevertheless, in the case of goods that amount to reified information, such as computer software. In such a case, the inquiry is likely to be pushed back one stage to pose the question whether the agreement is truly one of sale of goods at all or whether the seller is really dispensing mass-produced advice.[501] Obviously, in the case of software as of a book, a distinction is there to be drawn between packaging[502] and contents. Unless it is desired to extend strict liability into the giving of advice, which could have profound implications for publishers and booksellers, the sound conclusion in such cases would be to subject the seller of books and software only to negligence liability in respect of contents. It is, after all, only in modern times that the negligent giver of advice has been subject to liability at all.[503]

---

[495] [1986] 1 WLR 336. See also *Medivance Instruments Ltd v Gaslane Pipework Services Ltd*, n. 12 above at [47].

[496] And therefore the sellers too. The court also declined to find that the buyer had relied upon the manufacturer's skill or judgment rather than the sellers'.

[497] [1987] 1 WLR 1091.

[498] See Ch. 8 above.

[499] n. 492 above.

[500] Cf. *Lambert v Lewis* [1982] AC 225.

[501] See Ch. 2 above; cf *Lee v Griffin* (1861) 1 B & S 27.

[502] Does the binding of the book come away? Are there blank pages?

[503] *Hedley, Byrne & Co. Ltd v Heller & Partners Ltd* [1964] AC 465.

Terms Implied in a Sale by Sample

Description and sample.   It was noted above that under section 13(2) a seller   **7.134**
had to comply with the requirements of the description condition even if the
goods were sold by sample as well as by description. The governing provision on
sales by sample is section 15, which was the subject of a number of consequential
amendments under the Sale and Supply of Goods Act 1994.[504] Although little
turns nowadays on the distinction between sales by sample and ordinary sales,[505]
a sale by sample should be defined. There is no statutory definition and the
starting point is the classic statement of Lord Macnaghten in *James Drummond
and Sons v EH Van Ingen & Co. Ltd*: 'The office of a sample is to present to the eye
the real meaning and intention of the parties with regard to the subject-matter of
the contract, which, owing to the imperfections of language, it may be difficult or
impossible to express in words.'[506] The proffering of a sample therefore amounts
to a non-verbal demonstration of the goods that the buyer may expect to receive;
it mutely describes them.[507] It is not every time that a sample is displayed that the
contract takes place under section 15. The seller must expressly or impliedly
undertake[508] that the bulk will relate to the sample in the way provided for in
section 15. Consequently, a sale by sample takes place where there is an express or
implied term of the contract to that effect.[509] Lord Ellenborough concluded in
Gardiner v Gray that the sale did not take place by sample because the 'sample was
not produced as a warranty that the bulk correspond with it but to enable the
purchaser to form a reasonable judgment of the commodity'.[510] It is inherently
more likely that a sale by sample will be inferred where the seller already has the
bulk in stock than, for example, where he is a manufacturer proffering specimens
of the goods. A sale by sample, however, may arise when later dealings are
conducted on the basis of a sample provided for an earlier contract.[511] In modern

---

[504]   e.g., the buyer's right to compare the bulk with the sample has now been written into s. 34,
the main text dealing with examination.

[505]   J. R. Murdoch (1981) 44 *MLR* 388.

[506]   n. 168 above.

[507]   S. Williston, *The Law Governing Sales of Goods at Common Law and under the Uniform Sales
Act* (rev. edn, Baker Voorhis, 1948), para. 250. The meaning of s. 13(2) is therefore that the description of goods may be found in both the sample and in accompanying language. *Quaere* an inconsistency between the sample and the descriptive language?

[508]   Sometimes a sale by sample will be implied by trade usage: *Syers v Jonas* (1848) 2 Ex. 111
(tobacco trade).

[509]   S. 15(1).

[510]   (1815) 4 Camp. 144, 145. A provision to this effect in the Sale of Goods Bill of 1892 was
deleted. See also *Re Faulckners Ltd* (1917) 38 DLR 84 (not a sale by sample but a 'sale from samples');
East Asiatic Co. Inc. v Canadian Rice Mills Ltd (No. 1) [1939] 3 WWR 180. Cf *Dawson v Collis*
(1851) 10 CB 523.

[511]   *RW Green Ltd v Cade Bros Farms* [1978] 1 Lloyd's Rep. 602.

commodities trading, goods are more likely to be sold according to grades based upon analysis and protein content, and laid down by inspection agencies, than by sample. The detailed cloth specification in *BS Brown & Son Ltd v Craiks Ltd*[512] obviated the need to display a sample, for the sample binds as to the bulk only in respect of the normal trade examination, which is usually a visual or rudimentarily tactile one.[513] It is possible to find a hybrid transaction that is located between a sale by grade and a sale by sample. This was the case where shellac had to be supplied in accordance with a sample kept in London and not physically produced before the contract.[514] Devlin J concluded[515] that principles 'analogous' to those in section 15 should be applied, an approach diminishing the importance of the section and the concept of a sale by sample.

7.135 **Correspondence with quality of sample.** Once the sale is by sample, the bulk must correspond with the sample in quality.[516] This is a question of fact, easier to resolve than the test of satisfactory quality; there is little case law directly on the issue of compliance. Compliance with sample sometimes arises collaterally to other issues. Thus in *Champanhac & Co. Ltd v Waller & Co. Ltd*,[517] a quantity of surplus government balloons had been sold with 'all faults and imperfections', a phrase apt to exclude merchantable quality[518] but not the seller's separate duty to tender a bulk consistent in quality with the sample.

7.136 **Additional qualities.** Compliance with sample has emerged in a more direct way where the buyer is demanding, over and above description and merchantable quality obligations, that the bulk contain enhancing qualities present in the sample but not detectable on an ordinary examination. Lord Macnaghten once said that:

> The sample speaks for itself. But it cannot be treated as saying more than such a sample would tell a merchant of the class to which the buyer belongs, using due care and diligence, and appealing to it in the ordinary way and with the knowledge possessed by merchants of that class at the time. No doubt the sample might be made to say a great deal more. Pulled to pieces and examined by unusual tests which curiosity and suspicion might suggest, it would doubtless reveal every secret of its construction. But that is not the way business is done in this country.[519]

---

[512] n. 217 above.

[513] Discussed in the text accompanying nn. 520 *et seq*. below.

[514] *FE Hookway & Co. Ltd v Alfred Isaacs & Sons* [1954] 1 Lloyd's Rep. 491. A sample may also be used to clarify descriptive language: *RW Cameron & Co. v L Slutskin Pty Ltd* (1923) 32 CLR 81.

[515] In the *Hookway* case, n. 514 above.

[516] S. 15(2)(a). See *Russell v Nicolopulo* (1860) 8 CB(NS) 362; *Carter v Crick* (1859) 4H & N 412; *E and S Ruben Ltd v Faire Brothers Ltd* [1949] 1 KB 254 (ease of buyer correcting fault no defence).

[517] [1948] 2 All ER 724; see also *Parker v Palmer* (1821) 4 B & Ald. 387.

[518] Now satisfactory quality in s. 15(2)(c).

[519] *James Drummond and Sons v EH Van Ingen & Co. Ltd*, n. 168 above, 297.

In *FE Hookway & Co. Ltd v Alfred Isaacs & Sons*,[520] the buyer of shellac for the manufacture of gramophone records was aggrieved when the shellac turned out to be unfit for this purpose (not disclosed to the seller) since it lacked the 'flow' possessed by the standard sample in London. Recovery was denied in that case because the flow of the shellac delivered could only be discovered on an analysis exceeding the standard of the ordinary trade examination of the sample. Similarly, in *Steels & Busks Ltd v Bleecker Bik & Co.*,[521] a quantity of pale crepe rubber was supplied that, because of a preservative added in the course of its manufacture, stained materials with which it came into contact. The preservative was not present in the sample but, because its absence from the bulk could only have been verified by an extraordinary examination, the seller was not in breach of section 15(2)(a). A seller may undertake expressly to reproduce in the bulk qualities not detectable in the sample by ordinary trade methods, as where a sample of guano was offered along with a detailed chemical analysis of the ammonium content.[522]

Examination of sample.   The requirement that the goods supplied be of satis-   **7.137** factory quality is no different from the obligation of the seller in other types of sale contract, with this difference. Whereas, in the latter case, the seller's satisfactory quality obligation does not extend to defects that an *actual* examination of the goods before the contact should have revealed, the satisfactory quality obligation in a sale by sample is excluded in respect of defects that are 'apparent on reasonable examination of the sample', regardless of whether such examination was in fact carried out. This suggests that sales by sample cannot be collapsed into the general law of sales, but one should not make too much of this difference. A buyer by sample will by definition usually have the sample to hand before the contract[523] and will in the great majority of cases have carried out an actual examination. Moreover, the proffering of the sample may be seen as merely one instance in which the satisfactory quality obligations of the seller might be modified in relation to examination.[524]

Nature of examination.   As regards the nature of the buyer's examination,   **7.138** the buyer of shoes destined for the French army in the Franco-Prussian War could not be expected to rip open the shoes, which was the only way of discovering the unmerchantable presence of paper in the soles.[525] Likewise, an ordinary

---

[520] n. 514 above.

[521] [1956] 1 Lloyd's Rep. 228.

[522] *Towerson v Aspatria Agricultural Co-operative Society Ltd* (1872) 27 LT 276.

[523] But not in a sample case like *FE Hookway & Co. Ltd v Alfred Isaacs & Sons*, n. 514 above. Why should there be an examination difference in such a case?

[524] See *Thornett & Fehr v Beers & Son* [1919] 1 KB 486.

[525] *Heilbutt v Hickson* (1872) LR 7 CP 438. See also *Godley v Perry* [1960] 1 WLR 9, where drawing back the elastic of a plastic catapult was held a sufficient examination by a retailer. The same examination sufficed between importer and wholesaler who had done business together before.

examination of shirtings would not have revealed the presence of china clay added only to bring the cloth up to contract weight;[526] the tender of an unhelpfully small sample of Brazilian coffee beans was insufficient to show that the bulk of the coffee was unsound;[527] and the examination of a sample of flax seeds would not reveal the presence of 'exceedingly small' wild mustard seeds.[528] The examination of the sample for defects under section 15(2)(c) therefore accords with the examination of the sample under section 15(2)(a) for qualities that should be present in both sample and bulk.

7.139 Criticism. It is hard to justify the continuing existence of a separate sale by sample.[529] The rules concerning such sales are petrified incidents in the evolution of modern law of sale. Sale by sample rules should not be allowed to impede the natural development of the law. Fitness for purpose had not evolved into its modern form by the time the sale by sample rules crystallized, and perhaps in consequence fitness for purpose is not listed as one of the seller's obligations in section 15(2). But this should not prevent the owing of a fitness obligation by the seller under section 14(3).

Other Implied Terms

7.140 'Usage'. Section 14(4) provides for the annexation by 'usage' of implied terms of quality or fitness. These are not designated as conditions or warranties.[530] This trade usage provision, of little importance in the modern law because of the extensive scope of the implied terms of fitness and satisfactory quality in sections 14(2) and (3),[531] was more important in the nineteenth century, when the other implied terms were in an evolutionary state and where trade usage was something of a last resort for those challenging the rigours of *caveat emptor*. In *Jones v Bowden*,[532] it was the custom in auction sales of drugs to describe them as sea-damaged if this had occurred. A seller who repacked a quantity of pimentos damaged at sea without noting this in the broker's catalogue was therefore liable in damages to the buyer.

7.141 Manufacturers. Section 14(1) proscribes the implication of fitness and quality terms other than those set out in the remainder of the section. There is, however,

---

526 *Mody v Gregson* (1868) LR 4 Ex. 49.
527 *Jurgenson v FE Hookway & Co. Ltd* [1951] 2 Lloyd's Rep. 129.
528 *Carlstadt Development Co. v Alberta Pacific Elevator Co.* (1912) 4 AR 366 (Can.).
529 In UCC Art. 2, the compliance of the bulk with a sample is relegated to an instance of express warranty: Art. 2–313(1)(c).
530 S. 14(6).
531 But see *Steele v Maurer* (1976) 73 DLR (3d) 85; *Banks v Biensch* (1977) 5 AR 83 (Can.).
532 (1813) 4 Taunt. 847.

well-established authority that manufacturers selling goods, of the type they manufacture themselves, undertake that these goods are of their own manufacture.[533]
This term concerns description rather than quality, and therefore should not be
caught by the proscription in section 14(1).[534]

Terms in Transactions Similar to Sale

Kinship of sale and related contracts. Even before the passing of the Supply of   **7.142**
Goods and Services Act 1982, there was a developed judicial trend to treat
contracts akin to sales as though they were sales for the purpose of implying terms
of quality and fitness.[535] The contracts in question include work and materials,
barter, and chattel leases. To take work and materials as one example, according to
Lord Upjohn,[536] it would be 'most unsatisfactory, illogical, and indeed a severe
blow to any idea of a coherent system of law' not to subject the supply of roofing
tiles by a sub-contractor under a work and materials contract to implied terms like
those in the Sale of Goods Act.[537] Similarly, a veterinary surgeon was held strictly
liable for a latent defect in serum used to inoculate the plaintiff's cattle.[538]

Modern codification. The 1982 Act[539] now lays down the implied terms in   **7.143**
contracts 'for the transfer of goods', defined in section 1(1) as contracts under
which the property in goods is transferred or agreed to be transferred. A number
of such transactions are excepted from the Act.[540] They include transactions for
which pre-existing statute provides implied terms,[541] security agreements, under
which the security will be redeemed once the loan advanced is repaid, and transactions under seal not otherwise supported by consideration. For practical purposes,

---

[533] *Johnson v Raylton, Dickson & Co.* (1881) 7 QBD 438; *Randall v Sawyer-Massey & Co.* (1918)
43 OLR 602 (Can.).

[534] For other cases falling outside s. 14(1), see *Scaliaris v E Ofverberg & Co.* (1921) 37 TLR 307;
Harris & Sons v Plymouth Varnish & Colour Co. Ltd (1933) 49 TLR 521.

[535] See, e.g., *Young & Marten Ltd v McManus Childs Ltd* [1969] 1 AC 454; *Samuels v Davis*
[1943] 1 KB 526; *Dodds v Wilson* [1946] 2 All ER 691; *GH Myers & Co. v Brent Cross Service Co.*
[1934] 1 KB 46.

[536] In *Young & Marten Ltd v McManus Childs Ltd*, n. 535 above, 473.

[537] See also *Rotherham Metropolitan Borough Council v Frank Haslam Milan & Co. Ltd* [1996] CLC
1378; *AG Canada v Eastern Woodworkers Ltd* [1962] SCR 160 (Can.); *Helicopter Sales (Australia)
Pty Ltd v Motor Works Pty Ltd* (1974) 132 CLR 1; *Gloucestershire CC v Richardson* [1969] 1 AC 480;
Waston v Buckley, Osbourne, Garrett & Co. Ltd [1940] 1 All ER 174; *Star Express Manufacturing Co.
Pty Ltd v VG McGrath Pty Ltd* [1959] VR 443.

[538] *Dodds v Wilson*, n. 535 above.

[539] See Law Commission, *Law of Contract[:] Implied Terms in Contracts for the Supply of Goods*
(Law Com. No. 95, 1979).

[540] S. 1(2).

[541] e.g., hire purchase (see below).

section 1(1) therefore concerns work and materials and barter agreements.[542] To the extent that they are supplied pursuant to contract,[543] goods supplied under manufacturers' and similar promotional schemes should also be caught by the provision.[544] The implied terms in question concern title[545] as well as description, fitness for purpose, satisfactory quality, and equality to sample. Apart from necessary minor modifications, these are identical to the terms laid down for sale of goods agreements. The drafting technique used to attain this result, however, is in one respect indirect in its operation. In Schedule 2 to the Sale and Supply of Goods Act 1994, the definition of satisfactory quality in paragraph 6 is the former definition of merchantable quality with 'satisfactory' substituted for 'merchantable'. But in paragraph 10, fitness for all common purposes, together with safety, durability, freedom from minor defects, and appearance and finish are brought into the definition of 'quality'. The result is a definition for transfer contracts of satisfactory quality that tracks the definition for sale of goods.

7.144 **Services and work and materials.** The provision of services does not prevent a work and materials contract from being a contract transferring goods under the 1982 Act.[546] Further, the standard of liability for services (or work) is the negligence standard of section 13,[547] not the strict liability standard for the goods themselves. In such cases, there may exist two standards of liability under the contract. The Act gives no guidance on the separation of work and materials; the preceding case law appears still to be valid. It shows the distinction to be no easy one to draw. Where work is clearly ancillary to the supply of goods, for example, the garage fitting a new part to the buyer's car, liability should be strict for the goods and fault-based for the labour. It may be difficult, however, to determine whether an accident is caused by defective parts or ineffective work and a court may not be astute enough to determine that it was the latter. Strict liability and fault-based liability will yield the same result in many cases.

7.145 **Fault and strict liability.** A case that blurs the distinction between fault and strict liability is *Stewart v Reavell's Garage*,[548] where a garage relining the brakes of a Bentley used a liner that was unsuitable for the car's brake drums. The welded, instead of seamless, liner used came away from the brake drums, causing the car to crash. Strict liability clearly existed in that the brake liner was unfit for the buyer's purpose, but the issues were clouded by a statement of the supplier's obligation as

---

[542] Barter agreements can in many cases be rationalized as back-to-back sales: see Ch. 2 above. A provision in the 1892 Bill would have applied the Act to barter agreements.
[543] See *Esso Petroleum Ltd v Commissioners of Customs and Excise* [1976] 1 All ER 117.
[544] See *Buckley v Lever Bros Ltd* [1953] OR 704 (Can.).
[545] See Ch. 5 above.
[546] S. 1(3).
[547] See also *Kimber v William Willett Ltd* [1947] 1 All ER 61.
[548] [1952] 2 QB 545.

being 'to provide good workmanship, materials of good quality and a braking system reasonably fit for its purpose'.[549] To require the whole system to be fit for the buyer's purpose appears to challenge basic principle, for it would subject to strict liability a supplier who incompetently attached the correct type of liner to the brake drums.

New product. Less controversial instances of strict liability exist where work **7.146** and materials are integrated in the manufacture of a new product distinguishable from its materials.[550] The manufacturer of custom-built goods for a buyer should be treated as a seller under the Sale of Goods Act, but even where such a contract has been treated as work, and materials liability for the goods supplied has been strict. In *Samuels v Davis*,[551] dentures made by a dentist were required to be fit for the patient's purpose. But fault should be the standard for the fitting of the completed denture to the patient's mouth, though difficult factual distinctions might have to be made if the dentist had to make a number of trial fittings and adjustments.

Design. The principle applied in *Samuels v Davis* has been taken a step further **7.147** to support strict liability against a firm of engineers providing only a design and no materials of any kind. In *Greaves & Co. (Contractors) Ltd v Baynham Meikle and Partners*,[552] building contractors had been held liable to the owner of a warehouse when the floor cracked under the movements of fork lift trucks. The contractors in turn claimed over against the defendants, structural engineers, who had designed the warehouse. Conceding that professionals normally owe a duty of reasonable care and skill, the court nevertheless concluded on the particular facts, but without explaining why, that the engineers had undertaken to design a warehouse fit for its purpose. Some light can be thrown on the case if we consider the hypothetical case of a buyer entrusting the design of a complex machine to a designer acting in concert with a manufacturer. Suppose the machine is unfit for the buyer's purpose because of the design, executed with due care and skill, and not because of the materials or their assembly. The buyer would be without a remedy: the designer would not be at fault and the buyer would not have relied upon the manufacturer's skill and judgement in respect of the design. If the functions of designer and manufacturer had been united in the same person, however, then liability for the fitness of the machine supplied would have been strict.

---

[549] *Ibid.*, 551 (Sellers J).

[550] A case of *specificatio*.

[551] [1943] 1 KB 526.

[552] [1975] 3 All ER 99. See the extensive discussion of this case in *Platform Funding Ltd v Bank of Scotland Plc* [2008] EWCA Civ 930, which also contains a valuable discussion about the circumstances in which a professional might incur contractual responsibility above and beyond the exercise of due care. See in particular the example of the photographer who takes a picture of the wrong person at [19] and [51].

The above division of function should not be troublesome in practice, because a court might well infer negligence in the design. Should such a finding not be possible, a potential line of development, perhaps difficult to reconcile with the fault standard for services laid down in section 13 the 1982 Act, would be the ready inference of implied strict liability undertakings for design functions closely allied to manufacture.

7.148 **Hire purchase.** Hire purchase contracts are not within the 1982 Act. After a dubious authority applying the implied terms provisions of the Sale of Goods Act to hire purchase contracts,[553] the problem was largely resolved by case law developments.[554] In addition, for contracts within the statutory financial limits, there were implied terms in the Hire Purchase Act 1938 and subsequent hire purchase legislation. Since the Supply of Goods (Implied Terms) Act 1973, all hire purchase contracts contain these implied terms. For practical purposes, the title,[555] description, fitness, satisfactory quality, and equality to sample[556] terms are the same as those for sale of goods agreements. They come into effect when goods are 'bailed', that is supplied.

7.149 **Hire.** Contracts of hire (or leasing) attract separate treatment, not only from hire purchase but also from proprietary transfer contracts in the Supply of Goods and Services Act 1982. The scope of implied terms of description, satisfactory quality, fitness for purpose, and equality to sample[557] is the same as for proprietary transfer contracts under the 1982 Act.[558]

---

[553] *Felston Tile Co. Ltd v Winget Ltd* [1936] 3 All ER 473.

[554] e.g., *Karsales (Harrow) Ltd v Wallis* [1956] 2 All ER 866; *Astley Industrial Trust Ltd v Grimley* [1963] 2 All ER 33; *Yeoman Credit Ltd v Apps* [1962] 2 QB 508.

[555] For additional common law developments, see Ch. 5 above.

[556] Are hire purchase goods really supplied by sample or is the draftsman being tidy?

[557] 1982 Act, ss. 8–10.

[558] Discussed in the text accompanying nn. 539 *et seq.* above. For a discussion of the evolving common law concerning contracts of hire, see Bridge, n. 441 above, 528–32.

8

OTHER LIABILITIES OF THE SELLER AND LIABILITIES OF THIRD PARTIES

Introduction.   This chapter deals with liabilities concerning the supply of non-   **8.01**
conforming goods that fall outside the Sale of Goods Act. The liabilities may be
those of the seller for innocent misrepresentation or breach of express warranty, or
they may be those of a third party to the contract of sale, such as a producer.[1] The
importance of the statutory implied terms is such that the liabilities of the seller
dealt with here are, in comparison, of secondary importance. Express warranty,
for example, has played a relatively minor role in sale of goods, compared to other
areas of law, because of the statutory implied terms. Third parties may be liable to
a buyer on the basis of a collateral warranty, or in the tort of negligence or under
statute laying down strict product liability.

Other Liabilities of the Seller

Statements.   The present chapter is concerned with the liability of sellers arising   **8.02**
out of statements made prior to or at the time of the contract. Liability in such
cases might arise in the form of express warranty, innocent misrepresentation, or

---

[1] Where the Consumer Protection Act 1987 applies, the term (usefully) employed is 'producer'
rather than 'manufacturer', since the former includes the latter and includes also those who originate
a product by means of mineral extraction or agricultural processing. In this chapter, 'producer' will
be used instead of 'manufacturer', unless the particular context requires the latter word.

the tort of deceit. The plethora of rules and remedies arising out of false and misleading statements, made in and around the conclusion of a contract, has been cogently criticized as 'an area of law in which the courts have significantly failed to create a coherent body of rules to deal with what is basically a simple situation'.[2] This state of affairs has not been improved by a statutory overlay, the Misrepresentation Act 1967, on the efforts of the courts.

Development of Express Warranty

8.03 **Exclusion from Sale of Goods Act.** In common with innocent misrepresentation and deceit, express warranty is not included in the Sale of Goods Act and in consequence is not defined therein.[3] The Act does define 'warranty',[4] but only in its special sense to mean a term of the contract whose breach sounds only in damages.[5] This definition does not signify a term of the contract, as opposed to a mere representation that induces the contract, which is the meaning given to 'warranty' in this chapter. In its development, express warranty has been intimately connected to the implied terms of description, fitness, and satisfactory quality.[6] Even in recent times, the need to resort to express warranty has been lessened by the expansion of the statutory implied terms. So-called public statements made by a seller when advertising or labelling goods are now to be treated as aspects of satisfactory quality under section 14(2D).[7] An understanding of the meaning of express warranty in the modern law and of the importance of the role it plays is dependent upon a survey of its evolution prior to the House of Lords decision of 1913 that established the shape of the modern law.[8]

8.04 **Warranty and deceit.** Though plainly an aspect of contract in the modern law, warranty emerged from the action on the case for deceit. Thus in *Chandelor v Lopus*[9] the buyer was unsuccessful in his action on the case for the seller's affirmation that he was selling a bezar stone. To succeed, the buyer would have had to

---

[2] D. Greig (1971) 87 *LQR* 179, 211.

[3] See, however, Williston's definition in the American Uniform Sales Act 1906, s. 12: 'Any affirmation of fact or any promise by the seller relating to the goods is an express warranty if the natural tendency of such affirmation or promise is to induce the buyer to purchase the goods, and if the buyer purchases the goods relying thereon. No affirmation of the value of the goods, nor any statement purporting to be a statement of the seller's opinion only shall be construed as a warranty.'

[4] A word with numerous senses. See *Chalmers' Sale of Goods Act 1979 Including the Factors Acts 1889 & 1890* (18th edn, by M. Mark, Butterworths, 1981), App. II, for the history and examples of warranty.

[5] If the term is a condition, any breach permits the injured party to terminate the contract: see Ch. 10 below.

[6] See Ch. 7 above.

[7] As added by the Sale and Supply of Goods to Consumers Regulations 2002, SI 2002 No. 3045.

[8] *Heilbut, Symons & Co. Ltd v Buckleton* [1913] AC 30.

[9] (1603) Cro. Jac. 4.

establish either knowledge by the seller that the affirmation was false or the warranting of the stone as a bezar stone. In the latter case, the deceptiveness of the warranty would lie in its disarming the buyer from making further inquiry.[10] It seems that it was necessary for the formal language of warranty to be uttered,[11] and it was certainly necessary as a pleading matter that the plaintiff recite explicitly in his declaration the giving of the warranty.[12]

False affirmation.   Subsequently, however, an action on the case was allowed for   **8.05** the false affirmation that two oxen belonged to the seller; it was no defence that the buyer failed to declare that the seller warranted his ownership or knew of a third party's superior title.[13] Where this case differed from earlier authorities was that the buyer had no means of discovering the falsity of the seller's statement. Liability for affirmation of ownership was later said to lie in all cases where the seller was in possession of the goods.[14]

Dearth of case law.   Somewhat surprisingly, there is a dearth of eighteenth-cen-   **8.06** tury warranty cases, particularly noticeable in matters of quality. Consequently, no rule of liability had emerged for bare affirmations inducing reasonable reliance by the time that warranty migrated from the action on the case to special assumpsit. From its first reported instance in assumpsit in 1778,[15] warranty became increasingly pleaded in this way until it became compulsory to do so in 1841.[16] The consequence of this was that warranty came to be seen as a contractual promise and as requiring consideration from the promisee to be enforceable.[17] Consideration was all the more necessary at a time when warranty was seen as a collateral matter, not integrated into the principal contract to which it was annexed. This contractualization of warranty may also explain why courts became more willing to depart from matters of fact and find warranty in statements of opinion; it certainly explains the assimilation by warranty of statements of intention. Because the action on the case required the defendant's statement to be one of fact, a jury in one old case[18] was directed that the attribution of paintings to Claude and Teniers could only be a matter of opinion since the artists had been dead for 100 years and the paintings could not be traced back to an authentic

---

10 *Williamson v Allison* (1802) 2 East 446, 451.
11 *Chandelor v Lopus*, n. 9 above. See S. Williston, *The Law Governing Sales of Goods at Common Law and under the Uniform Sales Act* (rev. edn, Baker Voorhis, New York, 1948), paras 183, 195.
12 Williston, n. 11 above, para. 195.
13 *Crosse v Gardner* (1688) Carth. 90, 3 Mod. 261 (*sub. nom. Cross v Garret*).
14 *Medina v Stoughton* (1699) 1 Salk. 210, 1 Ld. Raym. 593.
15 *Stuart v Wilkins* (1778) 1 Dougl. 18.
16 *Brown v Edgington* (1841) 2 Man. & Gr. 279.
17 *Roscorla v Thomas* (1842) 3 QB 234. Cf. *Butterfield v Burroughs* (1706) 1 Salk. 211. This movement untimately produced a veritable jungle of collateral terms, collateral contracts, the Statute of Frauds 1679, and the parol evidence rule.
18 *Jendwine v Slade* (1797) 2 Esp. 572.

source. The buyer was expected to exercise his own judgement. The court may, however, have been influenced by the sharp conflict of expert evidence. In a later case,[19] the trial judge was held not to have misdirected the jury when allowing it to decide (as it did) that the attribution of a painting to Canaletto, who had died in more recent memory, was a warranty.

8.07 Later developments. Later developments included the tightening up of the requirement of fraud in the action for deceit,[20] which thereafter could not accommodate the overflow from the increasing contractualization of warranty. Equity gave relief in some cases where factual misrepresentations induced the making of a contract,[21] but the remedy was rescission and not damages, and rescission was denied if the contract was too far advanced in performance. The characterization of warranty as contractual led in time to the House of Lords decision in *Heilbut, Symons & Co. v Buckleton*,[22] which firmly established that an affirmation amounted to a warranty only when made with contractual intention. Intention would be gauged by the perceptions of the objective bystander[23] or the reasonable co-contractant. The court found some dubious support for contractual intention in pre-assumpsit authority,[24] best explained as showing intention to be useful in distinguishing statements of fact and opinion, not statements of fact and contractual undertakings.[25]

8.08 Innocent misrepresentation and negligent misstatement. The legacy of this course of development was that statements were treated as warranties only with difficulty when not made in close contemporaneity with the contract,[26] or when made informally and not included in a later written document.[27] The refusal to contemplate damages for a mere representation falling short of warranty, evidenced also by the tightened definition of fraud, meant that innocent misrepresentation bore an increasing burden.[28] It still laboured under the limitations on rescission and could not, until its statutory reform in 1967, provide a remedy in damages.[29] Meanwhile, liability in tort for negligent misstatements opened up in

---

[19] *Power v Barham* (1835) 7 C & P 356, affirmed (1836) 4 Ad. & E 473.

[20] *Derry v Peek* (1889) 14 App. Cas. 337. But the movement dates from about 1850: Greig, n. 2 above. See the criticisms of S. Williston (1911) 24 *Harv LR* 415.

[21] Discussed in the text accompanying nn. 76 ff. below.

[22] N. 8 above, criticized by S. Williston (1913) 27 *Harv LR* 1.

[23] *Dick Bentley Productions Ltd v Harold Smith (Motors) Ltd* [1965] 1 WLR 623.

[24] *Pasley v Freeman* (1789) 3 TR 51.

[25] D. Greig, n. 2 above, 182.

[26] But see *Schawel v Reade* [1913] 2 IR 64.

[27] This used to pose difficulties with the parol evidence rule.

[28] It was extended to cases where the contract had been executed: *Leaf v International Galleries* [1950] 2 KB 86; *Redgrave v Hurd* (1881) 20 Ch. D 1; *MacKenzie v Royal Bank of Canada* [1934] AC 468; *Solle v Butcher* [1950] 1 KB 671; *Lever Bros v Bell* [1931] 1 KB 557, 588; *Senanayake v King* [1966] AC 63.

[29] Discussed in the text accompanying nn. 119 ff. below.

the 1960s[30] at the same time as the warranty test of contractual intention began to be liberalized in practice. Furthermore, the development of the implied description and fitness for purpose conditions[31] owes something to the barriers placed in the way of treating sellers' statements as express warranties.[32]

Modern Law of Express Warranty

An evidence-based test. A contractual intention to warrant is inferred from the **8.09** 'totality of the evidence' surrounding the making of a statement; there are no 'secondary principles' that are 'universally true'.[33] Despite occasional observations that the matter is one of fact for a jury to decide,[34] and although the existence of a warranty turns upon a careful scrutiny of all the evidence, the presence of an intention to warrant, like any other question of contractual intention, is ultimately one of law in this sense: there will have to be a sufficiency of evidence to justify any finding of a warranty.[35] The importance of infinitely variable fact, however, means that no single test of warranty suffices[36] and that the *indicia* of intention may work in different combinations from case to case. Furthermore, abiding by such a test may conceal over the years *de facto* changes in the law. The test for a warranty laid down in *Heilbut, Symons* has remained unchanged, apart from a tendency in modern times to take account of reliance,[37] but without any doubt a modern court is more ready to infer a warranty than its counterpart of eighty years ago.[38] In addition, the approach adopted in modern times for shrinking the core of descriptive words under section 13 has meant that language, which might formerly have been embraced by the implied condition of correspondence

---

[30] *Hedley Byrne & Co. Ltd v Heller & Partners Ltd* [1964] AC 465; see *Clerk and Lindsell on Torts* (19th edn, by A. M. Dugdale, Sweet & Maxwell, 2006), 443–65.

[31] See Ch. 7 above.

[32] Description is treated as part of express warranty in UCC, Art. 2–313(1)(b) (*aliter* Uniform Sales Act 1906, s. 14.).

[33] *Heilbut, Symons & Co. Ltd v Buckleton*, n. 8 above, 50; see also *Howard Marine & Dredging Co. Ltd v A Ogden & Sons (Excavations) Ltd* [1978] QB 574, 595.

[34] e.g., *De Wynter v Fulton* (1915) 7 WWR 1361; *Miller v Cannon Hill Estates Ltd* [1931] 2 KB 113. The modern practice of a judge sitting without a jury shows the futility of trying to separate fact and law in this area. *Heilbut Symons* should leave no doubt about judicial determination to control the inference of warranty, complementing the takeover of former jury questions concerning the classification of contractual terms and the remoteness of damage.

[35] Indeed, Denning LJ in *Oscar Chess Ltd v Williams* [1957] 1 WLR 370, 375, is adamant that the inference of a warranty from the totality of the evidence is a question of law.

[36] *Heilbut Symons*, n. 33 above.

[37] *Lambert v Lewis* [1982] AC 225. Note also the implications for express warranty of the Court of Appeal decision in *Harlingdon and Leinster Enterprises Ltd v Christopher Hull Fine Art Ltd* [1991] 1 QB 564, which introduced reliance into contractual description in the cause of aligning description and express warranty: see Ch. 7 above.

[38] *Howard Marine & Dredging Co. Ltd v A Ogden & Sons (Excavations) Ltd*, n. 33 above, 590–1.

with description, is now more likely to be regarded as going to express warranty.[39] Nevertheless, the law has not moved so far that it can be said that any pre-contractual statement intended to be acted on and in fact acted on gives rise to a warranty. The continuing requirement of an intention to warrant prevents this step from being taken.[40] This is a particularly important point for contracts that are concluded after lengthy negotiations, a sale of business assets for example, where the formal document signed at the conclusion of the process will usually contain a clause stating that the document constitutes the entire agreement of the parties,[41] sometimes going on to add that no warranties are given except as recited in the document.[42] Clauses of this kind perform a legitimate function and are especially valuable where negotiations have been complex and have involved discussions with a number of the seller's employees and agents.[43]

8.10 **Commendation and warranty.** In principle, the law still maintains that mere language of commendation or puffery does not constitute warranty, but attitudes have changed. While statements that a reaper was 'a very good second hand' model which will 'cut . . . grain crop[s] efficiently'[44] may have been mere puffery a century ago, identifying puffery in the consumerist conditions of today is practically impossible when a car dealer can be liable for describing a car as a 'good little bus' on which he would stake his life,[45] and a grain dealer for asserting that his goods will fatten poultry at least as well as his competitors' products.[46] Even if a statement is one of opinion, this is no longer conclusive against the claimant[47] if the court finds an implied assertion of underlying fact.[48] In *Esso Petroleum Co. Ltd v*

---

[39] See *Reardon Smith Line Ltd v Yngvar Hansen-Tangen* [1976] 1 WLR 989. This case also displays a tendency to gauge the accuracy of language used by reference to the factual matrix of the contract, which might point to satisfaction with approximate rather than literal truth.

[40] See *Independent Broadcasting Authority v EMI Electronics Ltd* (1980) 14 BLR 1. See also the critical reference of Lightman J in *Inntrepreneur Pub Co. (GL) v East Crown Ltd* [2000] 2 Lloyd's Rep. 611 at [11] to dicta of Lord Denning MR in *J Evans & Son (Portsmouth) Ltd v Andrea Merzario Ltd* [1976] 1 WLR 1078, 1081 (where an inducing intention was treated as tantamount to the giving of a warranty once the statement was acted upon) and in *Dick Bentley Productions Ltd v Harold Smith (Motors) Ltd*, n. 23 above, 627 (where the same circumstances were treated as raising only a prima facie case of warranty). There is no single test of warranty, since the existence of a warranty depends upon all of the evidence: see below.

[41] *Inntrepreneur Pub Co. (GL) v East Crown Ltd*, n. 40 above.

[42] *Deepak v Imperial Chemical Industries plc* [1999] 1 Lloyd's Rep. 387.

[43] *Inntrepreneur Pub Co. (GL) v East Crown Ltd*, n. 40 above at [7]; *Cheverny Consulting Ltd v Whitehead Mann Ltd* [2005] EWHC 2431 (Ch) at [101]; see Ch. 9 below.

[44] *Chalmers v Harding* (1868) 17 LT 571. Cf *Osborne v Hart* (1871) 23 LT 851 ('superior old port').

[45] *Andrews v Hopkinson* [1957] 1 QB 229; *Uhle v Kroeker* [1927] 3 WWR 636.

[46] *Quaker Oats Co. v Kitzul* (1965) 53 DLR (2d) 630.

[47] But for cases where the plaintiff failed for this reason, see *Oscar Chess Ltd v Williams*, n. 35 above; *Savage and Sons Pty Ltd v Blakney* (1970) 119 CLR 435 (see also trial judgment at [1973] VLR 385); *Uhle v Kroeker*, n. 45 above (assurance that seed flax would plough).

[48] *Esso Petroleum Co. Ltd v Mardon* [1976] QB 801. Cf *Hummingbird Motors Ltd v Hobbs* [1986] RTR 276 (where the trade seller had no knowledge of the history of a car and stated that

Mardon,[49] a statement about the through-put potential of a filling station was held not to guarantee a particular volume of trade: it did, however, impliedly warrant that care had been taken in predicting the volume of business. Damages were therefore awarded to put the tenant of the filling station back in the position he occupied before the contract;[50] he did not receive an expectation award based upon the accuracy of the prediction. *Esso Petroleum* clearly shows the recent inroad of tort into pre-contractual relationships.

Negotiations. In a review of the cases decided since *Heilbut, Symons* suggests **8.11** various 'criteria of value' for discovering an intention to warrant. Perhaps the most important of these is the making of a statement 'during and as part of the negotiations for a contract'.[51] The closer the statement to the conclusion of a contract, the more likely it is to be a warranty,[52] and the further from the conclusion of the contract, the less so.[53] But even a statement made some weeks before the contract, if sufficiently powerful, may be a warranty,[54] while a statement made on the eve of a contract might not be.[55]

Importance of statement. The manifest importance to the recipient of a state- **8.12** ment is influential in the inference of a warranty,[56] as where a buyer let it be known that he would not even bid for a heifer unless assured that it was not in calf.[57] Between parties of equal bargaining power, their failure to incorporate an

---

an odometer reading was true to the best of his knowledge and belief). The same technique can sometimes convert a statement of opinion into an actionable misrepresentation if the unstated premise of the opinion is that it is based on fact: *Smith v Land and House Property Corpn* (1884) 28 Ch D 7; *Brown v Raphael* [1958] Ch 656. In certain cases, the statement of opinion may give rise to a fraudulent misrepresentation of existing fact if the opinion is not genuinely held, for 'the state of a man's mind is as much a fact as the state of his digestion': *Edgington v Fitzmaurice* (1885) 29 Ch. D 459, 482.

49 N. 48 above.

50 For similar reasoning, see *Perry v Sidney Phillips & Son* [1982] 1 WLR 1297.

51 *Hudson-Mettagami Exploration Mining Co. Ltd v Wettlaufer Bros Ltd* (1928) 62 OLR 387 (Can.). See also *Dick Bentley Productions Ltd v Harold Smith (Motors) Ltd*, n. 23 above; *Murray v Sperry Rand Corpn* (1979) 23 OR (2d) 456.

52 *Couchman v Hill* [1947] KB 554; *Harling v Eddy* [1951] 2 KB 739.

53 *Howard Marine & Dredging Co. Ltd v A Ogden & Sons (Excavations) Ltd*, n. 33 above (three months before delivery of the goods).

54 *Schawel v Reade* [1913] 2 IR 64; *Miller v Cannon Hill Estates Ltd* [1931] 2 KB 113 (five weeks).

55 *Hopkins v Tanqueray* (1854) 15 CB 130 (a case that would probably not be decided the same way today but is still referred to at intervals).

56 *Otto v Bolton* [1936] 2 KB 46 (seller aware of importance of statement to buyer and of its inducing effect). Cf *Oscar Chess Ltd v Williams*, n. 35 above, where the 'vital importance' of the stated age of a car in its logbook persuaded Morris LJ, dissenting, that the statement should be a warranty. Denning LJ regarded the trial judge as having been misled by the importance of the statement into leaping directly into the issue of whether it was a condition or warranty (in the sense of a lesser term) without first determining properly whether it was a term of the contract at all (*ibid.*, 374).

57 *Couchman v Hill*, n. 52 above; *Bannerman v White* (1861) 10 CN (NS) 844. Cf *Oscar Chess Ltd v Williams*, n. 35 above (consumer 'seller' in trade-in with dealer).

assurance in a later written contract will tell against a warranty.[58] Where the maker of a statement assumes responsibility for the accuracy of it, a court is likely to infer a warranty. Thus a seller's assurance that a horse was sound, which dissuaded the buyer from continuing with his examination, was held to be a warranty even though made some weeks before the contract of sale.[59] Conversely, if the seller makes it plain that the buyer should obtain independent corroboration of the truth of his statement, he is negativing any intention to be bound.[60] Expressed in the language of tort, it would not be reasonable for this buyer to rely upon the seller. The reliance factor becomes particularly important when the statement is made by an earlier seller in the distribution chain, such as a producer,[61] for the buyer must show that he entered the main contract of sale on the faith of that statement.[62] Although such reliance should readily be found if the statement is made in persuasive promotional literature,[63] it has been unconvincingly said that a buyer might rely instead upon a producer's reputation as opposed to promotional utterances.[64]

8.13 **Skill and knowledge.** One of the most cogent *indicia* of warranty is the balance of skill, knowledge, and experience between the maker of the statement and its recipient.[65] In encouraging analysis along the lines of reasonable reliance, which brings out the tortious origins of warranty, this accords with the parallel development of liability in tort for negligent misstatement. An attempt was made in *De Lassalle v Guildford* to lay down the test for warranty as follows:[66]

> [A] decisive test is whether the vendor assumes to assert a fact of which the buyer is ignorant, or merely states an opinion or judgment upon a matter of which the vendor has no special knowledge, and on which the buyer may also be expected to have an opinion and to exercise his judgment.

In *Heilbut, Symons*,[67] this statement was disapproved for substituting a definitive test for a broad test based upon all the evidence and administered by the jury.

---

[58] *Howard Marine & Dredging Co. Ltd v A Ogden & Sons (Excavations) Ltd*, n. 33 above; *Routledge v McKay* [1954] 1 All ER 855. Cf. *Birch v Paramount Estates Ltd* (1956) 167 EG 396.

[59] *Schawel v Reade*, n. 54 above.

[60] *Ecay v Godfrey* (1947) 80 Ll. LR 286; likewise, if an independent survey is normally expected (*Howard Marine & Dredging Co. Ltd v A Ogden & Sons (Excavations) Ltd*, n. 33 above), a powerful reason for the resilience of *caveat emptor* reasoning in sale of land contracts (see M. G. Bridge (1986) 20 *UBC LR* 53).

[61] A term used generically herein instead of manufacturer.

[62] *Lambert v Lewis*, n. 37 above; *Murray v Sperry Rand Corpn*, n. 51 above; *Wells (Merstham) Ltd v Buckland Sand & Silica Co. Ltd* [1965] 2 QB 170; *Shanklin Pier v Detel Products Ltd* [1951] 2 KB 854.

[63] *Murray v Sperry Rand Corpn*, n. 51 above.

[64] *Lambert v Lewis*, n. 37 above, 94, *per* Stocker J at trial.

[65] Discussed immediately below.

[66] [1910] 2 KB 215, 221.

[67] [1913] AC 30.

The absence of juries in modern civil trials has done away with the need for circumspect directions to be made to them and has encouraged harder-edged judicial statements. Decisions of the past fifty years are consistent with the test in *De Lassalle* if the change of substituting 'very persuasive' for 'decisive' is made.

Opinion.   In *Oscar Chess Ltd v Williams*,[68] a private seller trading in a car adopted   **8.14**
the statement of its age in the registration document. Since he plainly had no means of verifying the statement, while the trade buyer had, the court held it was one of opinion only. The result was that the private seller was able to retain the excess price that had been paid for the vehicle. In contrast, a different result was reached in *Dick Bentley Productions Ltd v Harold Smith (Motors) Ltd*,[69] where the trade seller of a car incorrectly told the private buyer that it had been driven only 20,000 miles after being fitted with a replacement engine and gearbox. The court saw no reason for overturning the evidentiary presumption that a statement made to induce entry into a contract was a warranty.[70] Unlike the private seller in *Oscar Chess*, the trade seller in *Dick Bentley* had the means of discovering the truth and his statement lacked all reasonable foundation. Negligence of the maker of a statement and reasonable reliance by the other party have become motive forces in the inference of warranty,[71] though a breach of warranty may yet occur where all due care has been taken.[72] To the extent that negligence and warranty are in the process of fusion, or are so in a given case, it must be asked whether the law should protect the contractual expectation interest or indemnify on a tortious basis. The difference in practice between the two approaches, however, ought not to be overstated.

Summary.   The following five-step approach to the inference of warranty was   **8.15**
provided by Lightman J in *Inntrepreneur Pub Co. (GL) v East Crown Ltd*:[73]

(1) a pre-contractual statement will only be treated as having contractual effect if the evidence shows that parties intended this to be the case. Intention is a question of fact to be decided by looking at the totality of the evidence;

(2) the test is the ordinary objective test for the formation of a contract: what is relevant is not the subjective thought of one party but what a reasonable outside observer would infer from all the circumstances;

---

[68] n. 35 above.
[69] n. 23 above.
[70] Though a factor in favour of warranty, it was perhaps novel to put it in terms of an evidentiary presumption.
[71] See also *McRae v Commonwealth Disposals Commission* (1950) 84 CLR 377 (Aust. HC).
[72] But cf *Harlingdon and Leinster Enterprises Ltd v Christopher Hull Fine Art Ltd* [1991] 1 QB 564.
[73] n. 40 above at [10]. The approach has been adopted in a number of cases, e.g., *Marako Ltd v C. Mendès SA* 2001 WL 1903412; *Kellogg Brown & Root Inc. v Concordia Maritime AG* [2006] EWHC 3358 (Comm); *Business Environment Bow Lane v Deanwater Estates Ltd* [2007] EWCA Civ 622; [2007] L & TR 26; *ING Lease (UK) Ltd v Harwood* [2007] EWHC 2292 (QB).

(3) in deciding the question of intention, one important consideration will be whether the statement is followed by further negotiations and a written contract not containing any term corresponding to the statement. In such a case, it will be harder to infer that the statement was intended to have contractual effect because the prima facie assumption will be that the written contract includes all the terms the parties wanted to be binding between them;

(4) a further important factor will be the lapse of time between the statement and the making of the formal contract. The longer the interval, the greater the presumption must be that the parties did not intend the statement to have contractual effect in relation to a subsequent deal;

(5) a representation of fact is much more likely intended to have contractual effect than a statement of future fact or a future forecast.

Deceit

8.16 **Constructive fraud.** Though once invoked more freely than it is nowadays,[74] it was settled over a century ago that common law fraud, conduct of the most reprehensible kind, was not akin to carelessness and did not assume a constructive form. Courts are intolerant of slack and unfounded allegations of fraud[75] and treat such behaviour as professionally improper to be penalized in costs.[76] Furthermore, the more serious the allegation of fraud, the higher the degree of probability required to establish it.[77] Equity, however, traditionally viewed fraud more expansively, as a species of conduct where one party unconscientiously takes advantage of another, but this more expansive notion of fraud has not survived. Established grounds of intervention exist in cases such as equitable misrepresentation, undue influence and economic duress. The modern trend, however, is for the law not to intervene to soften the harsher features of a one-sided bargain,[78] though there is a group of cases that give some tenuous support for those who advocate a broader species of equitable intervention on the ground of inequality of bargaining power.[79]

---

[74] See as the evidence of this the Statute of Frauds (Amendment) Act 1828 (Lord Tenterden's Act), 9 Geo. 4, cap. 14.

[75] Salmon LJ, *Some Thoughts on the Tradition of the English Bar*, Middle Temple, 25 June 1964: 'To make an allegation of fraud . . . without proper material is an abuse of the process of the Court as a potent form of blackmail.'

[76] For the court's powers and discretion as to costs, see Supreme Court Act 1981, s. 51, and CPR Part 44.

[77] *Hornal v Neuberger Products Ltd* [1957] 1 QB 247, 258; *Petromec Inc v Petroleo Brasiliero SA Petrobas* [2006] EWHC 1443 (Comm); [2007] 1 Lloyd's Rep. 29 at [90].

[78] *Bridge v Campbell Discount Co. Ltd* [1962] AC 600, 626; *Union Eagle Ltd v Golden Achievement Ltd* [1997] AC 514, 519; *Irvani v Irvani* [2000] 1 Lloyd's Rep. 412.

[79] See, e.g., *Earl of Aylesford v Morris* (1873) 8 Ch. App. 484; *Nocton v Lord Ashburton* [1914] AC 932, 953–5; *Lloyds Bank Ltd v Bundy* [1975] QB 326 (Lord Denning MR); *Hart v O'Connor* [1985] AC 1000, 1017–18 (Lord Brightman); *Alec Lobb (Garages) Ltd v Total Oil (Great Britain) Ltd* [1985] 1 WLR 173, 183. Canadian cases have given this general head of intervention a longer

Definition of fraud.   Fraud was defined in *Derry v Peak*[80] by Lord Herschell as   **8.17**
making a false representation '(1) knowingly, or (2) without belief in its truth, or
(3) recklessly, careless whether it be true or false'. The lowest common denomina-
tor of fraud is thus the making of a statement, which happens to be false, without
believing it to be true. This state of mind can exist where the maker of the statement knows it may be untrue but deliberately fails to make the necessary enquiries
to determine whether this is the case.[81] The presence of a motive for making a false
statement adds force to a claim that it was made with the necessary knowledge of
its falsity.[82] Although there must be an intention to deceive,[83] as well as an actual
inducing effect on the victim,[84] the motive of the maker of the statement, including any intention or not to injure the other person, is irrelevant.[85] To that extent,
the dishonesty that arises where a fraudulent statement is made is not the dishonesty of the criminal law.[86] Thus confined, fraud has played little part in the development of contract and sales law. It has been stated that, for a fraudulent
misrepresentation to be operative, it must be a material misrepresentation, in the
sense that it would have had an inducing effect on a reasonable person,[87] but
the better view is that no such requirement exists.[88] If fraud is pleaded successfully,
the claimant benefits from having the rescission bars applied more leniently.[89]
Fraud also gives rise to damages in the tort of deceit, the claimant recovering for

life: *Morrison v Coast Finance Ltd* (1965) 55 DLR (2d) 710; *Knupp v Bell* (1968) 67 DLR (2d) 256;
Harry v Kreutziger (1978) 95 DLR (3d) 231; *JFB v MAB* (2001) 203 DLR (4th) 738.

80   (1889) 14 App. Cas. 337, 374.

81   *Manifest Shipping Co. Ltd v Uni-Polaris Insurance Co. Ltd (The Star Sea)* [2003] 1 AC 469;
Petromec Inc. v Petroleo Brasiliero SA Petrobas, n. 77 above at [94].

82   *Derry v Peek*, n. 80 above, 374; *Gallaher International Ltd v Tlais Enterprises Ltd* [2008] EWHC
804 (Comm) at [1170].

83   *Tackey v McBain* [1912] AC 186. There must therefore be an inducing intention for liability
in deceit to arise as well as, according to *Gross v Hillman Ltd* [1970] 1 Ch 445 and *Goose v Wilson
Sandford & Co. (No. 2)* [2001] Lloyd's Rep. P.N. 189, an intention that the victim understand the
statement in the sense in which it is false.

84   Relying upon *Attwood v Small* (1838) 6 Cl. & Fin 232, Lord Wensleydale in *Smith v Kay*
(1859) 7 HLC 750 was of the view that the contract had to be the cause of the fraud, though not
necessarily the only cause, if it were to be set aside, but cf *Barton v Armstrong* [1976] AC 104 (for
duress and fraud, entry into the contract need only be *a* cause of the conduct).

85   *Ibid*; *Standard Chartered Bank v Pakistan National Shipping Corpn* [1995] 2 Lloyd's Rep. 365,
375; *Gallaher International Ltd v Tlais Enterprises Ltd*, n. 82 above at [1171]. Liability can arise even
if the maker of the statement believes his actions to be justified: *Brown Jenkinson & Co. Ltd v Percy
Dalton (London) Ltd* [1957] 2 QB 621.

86   *Standard Chartered Bank v Pakistan National Shipping Corpn (No 2)* [2000] 1 Lloyd's Rep. 218
at [27] reversed on other grounds at [2002] UKHL 43.

87   *Downs v Chappell* [1997] 1 WLR 426 (Hobhouse LJ).

88   See *Smith v Kay*, n. 84 above, 770 (Lord Cranworth); *Rafsanjan Pistachio Producers Co-operative
v Bank Leumi (UK) plc* [1992] 1 Lloyd's Rep. 514, 542. Materiality is not listed as a requirement in
Bradford Third Equitable Benefit Building Society v Borders [1941] 2 All ER 205, 211.

89   *Erlanger v New Sombrero Phosphate Co.* (1878) 3 App. Cas. 1218; *Spence v Crawford* [1939]
3 All ER 271; *Hughes v Clewley* [1996] 1 Lloyd's Rep. 35, 63.

losses flowing directly from the fraud.[90] Although put back in the pre-contractual position,[91] the claimant is in principle entitled to the benefit of alternative opportunities forgone when contracting with the defendant. In certain cases, the difference between a contractual expectation award, as would be available for a breach of contract, and an indemnification for tortious injury, may therefore not be great.[92]

Innocent Misrepresentation

8.18 Innocent and negligent misrepresentation. Prior to the Misrepresentation Act 1967, misrepresentations were divided into those that were fraudulent and those that were not, the latter being referred to as innocent misrepresentations. The 1967 Act introduced the category of negligent misrepresentation and gave some encouragement to the use of the expression 'innocent misrepresention' to mean a non-negligent misrepresentation. The older meaning of innocent misrepresentation as non-fraudulent misrepresentation will, however, be retained in this work. Unless otherwise stated below, innocent misrepresentation is herein treated as synonymous with equitable misrepresentation.[93]

8.19 Reasons for innocent misrepresentation. Innocent misrepresentation developed in equity to redress the rigours of the common law embodied in the strictness of its definition of fraud and in the early reluctance to infer warranty. There was also a common law rule of misrepresentation, but relief was granted only in a very limited range of cases: a fundamental mistake amounting to an operative mistake had to have occurred,[94] so that the only role of the misrepresentation itself was as the agent of the mistake induced in the mind of the recipient of the misrepresentation. The judgment of Jessel MR in *Redgrave v Hurd* is credited with establishing the modern law of innocent misrepresentation as concurrent in scope with its more restrictive counterpart, so as to deprive common law misrepresentation of any practical significance. From contracts habitually within the jurisdiction of courts of equity, such as agreements for the sale of land, innocent misrepresentation spread to common law contracts for the sale of goods.[95] Furthermore, though the point was disputed in Australasian authority,[96] it has never been seriously

---

[90] *Doyle v Olby (Ironmongers) Ltd* [1969] 2 QB 158, 167; *East v Maurer* [1991] 1 WLR 461; *Archer v Brown* [1985] QB 401 (including losses occurring after the rescission of the contract).
[91] *Hughes v Clewley*, n. 89 above, 62–3.
[92] See *East v Maurer*, n. 90 above.
[93] See generally M. Bridge (2004) 57 *Current Legal Problems* 277.
[94] *Kennedy v Panama, New Zealand and Australia Royal Mail Co.* (1867) LR 2 QB 580, 587 (Blackburn J): '[W]here there has been an innocent misrepresentation or misapprehension, it does not authorize a rescission, unless it is such as to shew that there is a complete difference in substance between what was supposed to be and what was taken, so as to constitute a failure of consideration'.
[95] See also Ch. 10 below.
[96] *Riddiford v Warren* (1901) 20 NZLR 572; *Watt v Westhoven* [1933] VLR 458.

doubted in English law that the doctrine of innocent misrepresentation can apply to a sale of goods contract notwithstanding the failure of the Sale of Goods Act expressly to provide for its preservation in such cases.

Definition of actionable misrepresentation. In equity, for a misrepresentation **8.20** to give rise to a right to rescind the contract there has to be a false statement of material[97] fact that induces, at least in part,[98] entry into the contract.[99] As with warranty, fact is capable of embracing opinion statements if they contain an implied assertion that care has been taken in formulating them.[100] It can also embrace statements of future intention so that a misrepresentation is made if the maker of a statement has no present intention of acting in accordance with his declared intention.[101] A statement is material in so far as it would have influenced a reasonable person in the position of the one to whom the statement was made.[102] It may be relied upon even if an inquiry would have revealed its falsity.[103] Once it is shown that a misrepresentation was material and that at a later date the claimant entered the contract, it is wrong to say, as Jessel MR did,[104] that reliance can be taken to have followed as a matter of law from materiality.[105] Nevertheless, a court may fairly infer from those facts alone that the claimant did in fact rely upon the misrepresentation.[106] This is not quite the same as saying that the burden is on the defendant to show a lack of reliance[107] since a judge as finder of fact is not bound to find reliance in those circumstances. Furthermore, one way for a claimant to show materiality is probably to demonstrate that he in fact did reasonably rely

---

[97] *Redgrave v Hurd* (1881) 20 Ch D 1; *Pan Atlantic Insurance Co. Ltd v Pine Top Insurance Co. Ltd* [1995] 1 AC 501.

[98] *Edgington v Fitzmaurice* (1885) 29 Ch D 459, 481 (Cotton LJ). Some doubt is, however, expressed about the sufficiency of partial inducement in the case of innocent misrepresentation: *Standard Chartered Bank v Pakistan National Shipping Corpn (No. 2)* [2002] UKHL 43; [2003] 1 AC 959 at [17].

[99] *Redgrave v Hurd*, n. 97 above; *Pan Atlantic Insurance Co. Ltd v Pine Top Insurance Co. Ltd*, n. 97 above.

[100] *Smith v Land and House Property Corpn* (1884) 28 Ch. D 7.

[101] *Edgington v Fitzmaurice*, n. 98 above, 482.

[102] *Smith v Chadwick* (1882) 20 Ch. D 27, affirmed (1884) 9 App. Cas. 187. Other inducing factors may influence the judgement of the person to whom the misrepresentation is made: *Edgington v Fitzmaurice*, n. 98 above.

[103] *Redgrave v Hurd*, n. 97 above. An ineffectual verification of the misrepresentation may, however, show an absence of reliance on the statement: *Attwood v Small* (1838) 6 Cl. & F 232.

[104] *Redgrave v Hurd*, n. 97 above, 21.

[105] *Pan Atlantic Insurance Co. Ltd v Pine Top Insurance Co. Ltd*, n. 97 above, 570; *Smith v Chadwick*, n. 102 above, 196.

[106] *Smith v Chadwick*, n. 102 above, 196–7 (Lord Blackburn). The case concerned fraudulent misrepresentation.

[107] See *Arkwright v Newbold* (1881) 17 Ch. D 201, where all three members of the Court of Appeal stated that the plaintiff had the burden of proving that a fraudulent misrepresentation induced entry into the contract. Cf G. H. Treitel, *The Law of Contract* (12th edn, by E. Peel, Sweet & Maxwell, 2007), 343.

upon the statement,[108] though it should not be assumed that materiality flows from reliance.[109]

8.21 Rescission. Before the enactment of the Misrepresentation Act 1967, the only remedy for an innocent misrepresentation was not damages but rescission *ab initio*, which bears a superficial resemblance to the common law remedy of contractual discharge or termination, granted where there has been a breach of a condition or of a lesser term going to the root of the contract.[110] Rescission *ab initio* is a drastic remedy that survives the incorporation of a misrepresentation as a term in the contract.[111] This duality of a statement as both an inducing misrepresentation and as a contractual term creates significant difficulties in coordinating the remedies available for each.[112] In particular, the right to rescind, a self-executing remedy,[113] may be lost in circumstances where a right to reject goods and terminate the contract for breach may yet endure. The right to rescind is lost in four separate cases: first, where the claimant affirms the contract;[114] or secondly, delays too long in rescinding;[115] or where, thirdly, the subject matter of the contract cannot be restored in its original state;[116] or, fourthly, third-party purchasers have acquired in the interim property rights in the subject matter.[117] Prior to the Misrepresentation Act 1967, there was no right to damages for innocent misrepresentation. Consequently, the loss of the right to rescind left without a remedy a claimant unable to demonstrate fraud, the incorporation of the statement as a term of the contract or the inducement of an operative mistake by the statement.

8.22 Reasons for equitable intervention. Innocent misrepresentation is far more liberal in its grant of rescission rights than is the common law when allowing contractual release in the event of an operative mistake[118] or a discharging breach of contract.[119] This imbalance lies at the heart of the difficulty of reconciling

[108] Pleading precedents, for example *Atkin's Court Forms* (2nd edn, Butterworths, 1984) (Title: 'Misrepresentation and Fraud'), set out actual reliance in statements of claim.
[109] Cf *Museprime Properties Ltd v Adhill Properties Ltd* [1990] 2 EGLR 196.
[110] Ch. 10 below.
[111] Misrepresentation Act 1967, s. 1(a). For the position in Commonwealth countries, see Bridge, n. 60 above.
[112] For restrictions imposed upon the right to rescind for innocent misrepresentation where the right to reject for breach of contract has been lost under s. 35 of the Sale of Goods Act, see *Leaf v International Galleries* [1950] 2 KB 86 and Ch. 10 below.
[113] *Abram Steamship Co. v Westville Shipping Co. Ltd* [1923] AC 773; *Reese River Silver Mining Co. v Smith* (1869) LR 4 HL 64, 73.
[114] *United Shoe Machinery Co. of Canada v Brunet* [1909] AC 330.
[115] *Leaf v International Galleries Ltd*, n. 112 above.
[116] *Clarke v Dickson* (1858) E B & E 148, 155.
[117] *Clough v North Western Railway Co.* (1871) LR 7 Ex. 26, 35; *Car & Universal Finance Co. Ltd v Caldwell* [1965] 1 QB 525.
[118] *Kennedy v Panama, New Zealand and Australia Royal Mail Co.*, n. 94 above; *Bell v Lever Bros* [1932] AC 161.
[119] Ch. 10 below.

innocent misrepresentation with the governing principles of sale of goods law.[120]
The justification for equitable intervention in this area, as stated by Jessel MR in
Redgrave v Hurd, rested on two grounds: first, that the maker of a statement is 'not
to be allowed to get a benefit from a statement which he now admits to be false';
and secondly, that it amounts to 'moral fraud' to insist on retaining a beneficial
contract knowing that it was 'obtained . . . by a statement which [the maker] now
knows to be false'. The first statement is more of an assertion than a ground or reason, while the latter sits uncomfortably alongside the retrenchment of fraud in
Derry v Peek.[121] The expansive character of equitable intervention in this area may
be due at least in some measure to the fact that equitable intervention has always
had two tasks to perform: first, the setting aside of agreements in appropriate
cases; and secondly, the refusal of specific performance on discretionary grounds.
An expansive view of equitable grounds of relief might be more appropriate in
the latter case than in the former.[122] However that may be, equitable intervention
on the ground of moral fraud is not readily reconciled with innocent misrepresentation operating as a vice of consent.[123] It has been argued that it is 'essential' for
a misrepresentation to be operative that it be made with an inducing intention.[124]
Such a requirement would bolster the moral fraud pretensions of innocent
misrepresentation, but, in the absence of clear authority other than textbooks,

---

[120] Bridge, n. 60 above.
[121] n. 80 above, where Lord Herschell nevertheless recognized that a contract induced by an
honest and blameless misrepresentation 'cannot stand': *ibid.*, 359.
[122] According to Lindley LJ in *Re Terry and White's Contract* (1886) 32 Ch D 14, 29, 'it is well
known that a less serious misleading is sufficient to enable a purchaser to resist specific performance
than is sufficient to enable him to resist the contract'. Apart from the statutory discretion in s. 2(2)
of the Misrepresentation Act 1967 to declare a contract subsisting, it is not clear that this represents
the law today.
[123] But see R. Meagher, W. Gummow, and J. Lehane, *Equity: Doctrine and Remedies* (4th edn,
LexisNexis 2002), para 13–070, explaining misrepresentation both as a vice inherent in the formation of the contract' and as 'not . . . resting on the reality of consent' but rather on 'the inequity of
allowing a defendant to retain a benefit'. For the view that misrepresentation 'looks like an external
vice' which 'causes or induces a mistake', see S. Stoljar, *Mistake and Misrepresentation: A Study in
Contractual Principles* (Sweet & Maxwell, 1968).
[124] R. Meagher, W. Gummow, and J. Lehane, n. 123 above, para. 13–030, citing *Nautamix
BV v Jenkins of Retford Ltd* [1975] FSR 385, 39–8, which, however, was a case of fraudulent misrepresentation. A similar view is expressed in W. Northcote (ed.), *Fry on Specific Performance* (6th
edn, Stevens, 1921), citing *Attwood v Small*, n. 84 above, 444 (Lord Brougham), a case of fraud,
and *Smith v Kay*, n. 84 above, 755, which gives no clear support. See also G. Spencer Bower and
A. Turner, *The Law of Actionable Misrepresentation* (3rd edn, Butterworths, 1974), at para. 117
(though proof goes by the board in the majority of cases (*ibid.*, §118)). Lord Hoffmann mentions
without comment a statement made in the court below about the need for an inducing intention
in *Standard Chartered Bank v Pakistan National Shipping Corpn (No. 2)* [2002] UKHL 43; [2003]
1 AC 959 at [14]. An inducing intention has been said to be necessary for an action for damages
under s.2(1) of the Misrepresentation Act 1967, because of the fiction of fraud in that provision
and the requirement of an inducing intention for fraud: *Banque Keyser Ullmann SA v Skandia (UK)
Insurance Co. Ltd* [1990] 1 QB 665, 790.

it cannot with confidence be said to be the law[125] and, if it were, would come close to eradicating the distinction between innocent misrepresentation and express warranty. It would, moreover, render unnecessary any reason to resort to the notion of materiality: inducing intention, if it ever was required outside cases of fraud, seems to have been absorbed in materiality.

8.23 **Drastic nature of rescission.** The test of innocent misrepresentation is easier to satisfy than the test for express warranty, and even when the latter is established the remedy may well be damages without contractual termination rights. For this reason, it is difficult in some cases to justify the drastic remedy of rescission when the common law remedy may be a lesser one or even non-existent. Such criticism has been deflected by the argument that the common law is preoccupied with crystallizing the bargain struck between the parties, whereas equity is concerned to suppress a broad range of unconscientious conduct encapsulated in the notion of equitable fraud. Consequently, common law and equitable concerns are not in *pari materia*.[126] As expressed in innocent misrepresentation, equitable fraud, not to be confused with common law fraud,[127] deems it unconscientious for the maker of a statement to insist on retaining the benefits of a contract once apprised that his innocent but false statement induced the other party's entry into the contract.[128] In the time-honoured tradition of equitable entitlement, equity does not deny the maker's common law rights but binds his conscience not to exercise them. Given the drastic consequences that can flow from rescission after a relatively venial misrepresentation with only a partial inducing effect, this argument, nevertheless, lacks conviction.

8.24 **Controlling rescission.** There is, however, in modern times the statutory discretion to declare a contract subsisting under section 2(2) of the Misrepresentation Act 1967, but there is insufficient evidence of its application in court to determine whether it has eradicated the anomalous distinction between express warranty and misrepresentation in the matter of putting an end to the contract. The court's discretion may be exercised whether the party to whom the misrepresentation has been made[129] has already rescinded the contract without the help of the court or is seeking assistance to effect a return of the parties to the pre-contractual position: the provision awards the discretion 'if it is claimed, in any proceedings arising out

---

[125] *Chitty on Contracts* (29th edn, by H. Beale, Sweet & Maxwell, 2004), para. 6–029. See Bridge, n. 93 above, 285–7.

[126] R. Meagher, W. Gummow, and J. Lehane, n. 124 above, para. 13–070 (termination for breach and rescission *ab initio* 'are quite distinct and operate at opposite ends of the scale').

[127] *Derry v Peek*, n. 80 above; *Le Lievre v Gould* [1893] 1 QB 491, 498 (denial by Esher MR of the very existence of equitable fraud).

[128] *Redgrave v Hurd*, n. 97 above.

[129] It does not apply to non-disclosure cases: *Banque Keyser Ullmann SA v Skandia (UK) Insurance Ltd* [1990] 1 QB 665.

of the contract, that the contract ought to be or has been rescinded'. It may seem that this discretion cannot be activated if a contract is executory and the victim of the misrepresentation declines to perform it, but the other party could put a claim for rescission into the mouth of a victim by seeking a declaration that the contract was subsisting.[130] The court may declare the contract subsisting or revived when awarding damages instead[131] to the victim of the misrepresentation. Presumably, it might enforce the contract by an award of specific performance if in other respects the case was an appropriate one for that remedy: there is nothing in section 2(2) to enlarge that jurisdiction. The burden of persuading the court to exercise its discretion in favour of damages is on the party seeking to avoid rescission.[132]

Discretionary or self-executing remedy?   The discretion in section 2(2) raises   **8.25** the further question whether rescission *ab initio* is a discretionary remedy or a self-executing remedy. There is modern authority for the view that rescission is a self-executing remedy,[133] though against this is the considerable authority of Lord Wright that rescission is a discretionary remedy.[134] The existence of a judicial discretion is not to be reconciled with rescission as a self-executing remedy, for a court in exercising a discretion is not the obedient servant of a contracting party electing to rescind. As so often is the case, however, the issue is confused by a failure to separate fraudulent and innocent misrepresentation. In the case of rescission at common law for fraud, the focus has consistently been on the victim's election to affirm or disaffirm the contract,[135] which has not been the case with rescission *ab initio* for innocent misrepresentation.[136] Yet there is a case against self-executing rescission for innocent misrepresentation. So far as the rescission bars are not examples of a wholly calcified discretion, then the continuing development of

---

[130] The court is most likely to decline to exercise its discretion, however, where the contract remains executory.

[131] The award of damages is discussed below.

[132] *British & Commonwealth Holdings Plc v Quadrex Holdings Plc* [1995] CLC 1169, 1199–1200.

[133] *Abram Steamship Co Ltd v Westville Shipping Co Ltd* [1923] AC 773; *TSB Bank plc v Camfield* [1995] 1 All ER 951; *Alati v Kruger* (1955) 94 CLR 216. On self-execution, see J. O'Sullivan [2000] *CLJ* 509.

[134] In *Spence v Crawford* [1939] 3 All ER 271, 288.

[135] See *Clough v London and North Western Railway Co.* (1871) LR 7 Ex. 26, 35.

[136] In *Reese Silver Mining Co. v Smith* (1869) LR 4 HL 64, an attempt was made to reconcile rescission as the act of the affected party with the retrospective character of rescission. The court in that case ordered the removal of a rescinding shareholder's name from the register of company members with backdated effect, so that it preceded a winding-up order made against the company. Against that case, presenting rescission as the act of the affected party, even though it is the court that directs the revesting in that party of property transferred under an executed contract, does not look quite so artificial, though artificial it remains.

a judicial discretion with respect to them is inconsistent with rescission as the act of the affected party.[137]

8.26 **Resolution.** In its report on *Innocent Misrepresentation*, the Law Reform Committee assumed that rescission was a remedy granted by the court.[138] Similarly, although the Misrepresentation Act 1967 does not take a firm stand on whether rescission is a self-executing remedy—section 2(2) refers to proceedings where it is claimed that the contract has been or ought to be rescinded[139]—its subjection of all cases of rescission to a judicial discretion to affirm the contract is incompatible with self-executing rescission. Given its universal scope, section 2(2) cannot be treated as episodic statutory intervention leaving no mark on the underlying common law. Nor does it avail to try to separate rescission and the consequences of rescission, for that would merely equate rescission with the election to seek rescission. The election to seek rescission would therefore resemble the election to seek specific performance of a contract which, in Lord Wilberforce's words, is 'merely electing for a course which may or may not lead to the implementation of the contract'.[140]

Misrepresentation and Insolvency

8.27 **Important issue.** But for one very important point, the question whether rescission *ab initio* is a self-executing remedy is not of great practical significance, given the existence of the bars to rescission which, amongst other things, protect third parties with intervening rights in the subject matter of the contract. Although it is surprising that the issue has not given rise to great practical inconvenience, the revesting of the property in the subject matter of the contract in the victim of the misrepresentation has significant insolvency implications, is a matter that demands careful examination, that, properly considered, goes to the very heart of the self-execution issue.

8.28 **Revesting of property.** Innocent misrepresentation poses a particular difficulty when the property in goods or money is transferred to the maker of a misrepresentation who later becomes insolvent.[141] Should the transferor have the first call on the assets of the transferee ahead of the latter's other creditors? If the transferor had

---

[137] The extirpation of the equitable doctrine of common mistake in *Great Peace Shipping Ltd v Tsavliris Salvage (International) Ltd* [2002] EWCA Civ 1407; [2003] QB 679 has as its by-product the surrender of the flexible equitable approach to rescission demonstrated nowhere better than in *Solle v Butcher* [1950] 1 KB 671. The Court of Appeal in *Great Peace*, however, was not opposed to flexibility in the avoidance of contracts for common mistake and thought indeed that legislation might be needed to restore it.

[138] See its Tenth Report on *Innocent Misrepresentation* (Cmnd 1782), para. 11.

[139] Not 'ought to have been rescinded'.

[140] *Johnson v Agnew* [1980] AC 367, 398.

[141] See S. Worthington [2002] *Restitution L Rev* 28.

merely common law rights of termination, then his only claim would be for the usual meagre insolvency dividend, since the property in goods delivered to the buyer will not revest in the seller after termination.[142] But if rescission *ab initio* were to be applied literally, the transferor would recover the subject matter of the contract if it remained identifiable. The incorporation of a misrepresentation as a term of the contract should not prevent the transferor from invoking his right to rescind.[143] Yet equitable fraud in the unjust retention of the fruits of a misrepresentation, however useful in reconciling discord in the past between common law and equity, seems a rather fragile principle to justify preferring the transferor in the transferee's insolvency, especially if the inducement was only a partial one. Moreover, if misrepresentation does not function fully as a vice of consent, but is concerned to suppress unconscientious conduct,[144] then there seems no justification for proprietary purposes in distinguishing between it and a wilful breach of contract. Equity acts *in personam* when reallocating rights in a bilateral relationship, but insolvency distribution is above all a collective procedure that calls for a multilateral assessment of inconsistent rights. There is a need to control the proliferation of proprietary rights that have a disruptive effect in insolvency proceedings.[145]

Trustees-in-bankruptcy and third parties.   There is little evidence of transferors **8.29** in the past asserting the right to rescind and recover property on an insolvency. One of the normal rescission bars is the acquisition by third parties of rights in the subject matter prior to rescission. Yet, although the estate of a bankrupt vests in the trustee in bankruptcy,[146] trustees in bankruptcy are not third parties, for they stand in the shoes of the insolvent transferee and their consciences are burdened accordingly.[147]

Company liquidation.   Company liquidators differ from trustees in the follow- **8.30** ing respect. The property of the company does not automatically vest in them, though provision is made in the Insolvency Act for the liquidator in a compulsory winding-up to apply for a vesting order.[148] Upon a winding-up, a trust of sorts

---

142 *RV Ward Ltd v Bignall* [1967] 1 QB 534.

143 Misrepresentation Act 1967, s. 1(a).

144 See discussion above.

145 For a general recognition of this need, see *Westdeutsche Landesbank Girozentrale v Islington London Borough Council* [1996] AC 669 (Lord Browne-Wilkinson).

146 Insolvency Act, s. 306.

147 *McEntire v Crossley Bros* [1895] AC 457, 461; *Madell v Thomas* [1891] 2 QB 230, 238; *Re Eastgate* [1905] 1 KB 465; Spencer Bower and Turner, *The Law of Actionable Misrepresentation* (3rd edn, Butterworths, 1974), para. 278.

148 S. 145. Rarely exercised: R. Pennington, *Company Law* (5th edn, Butterworths, 1985), 913–4. In any winding-up, the liquidator is empowered to deal with the property of the company and does not need a vesting order to do so: Insolvency Act 1986, Sch. 4 para. 6.

settles upon the property of the company for the benefit of its creditors,[149] though the beneficial interest is held in suspense pending the ascertainment of the various claims against the company.[150] It cannot therefore be said that the creditors are third parties acquiring an interest in the property before the rescission.[151] The two processes of bankruptcy and winding-up closely resemble each other and amount to 'a statutory execution for the benefit of all creditors'.[152] All of this suggests that no distinction should exist between bankruptcy and liquidation for the purpose of rescission *ab initio*. There is nevertheless firm authority[153] that a contract for the allotment of shares may not be rescinded after the commencement of the winding-up, except where, before the start of the winding-up, the allottee has renounced the contract and has taken steps towards having his name removed from the company register. The reason is that other shareholders and creditors may have entered into dealings with the company on the faith of the allottee's name being upon the register.[154] This reasoning does not extend to a supplier of goods seeking the rescission of a contract for misrepresentation, and the recovery of goods supplied, after the commencement of a winding-up.

8.31 **Revesting and money.**   There is authority for the recovery of goods by rescission upon a bankruptcy in the case of common law fraud,[155] and it is difficult to see why any distinction should be drawn for present purposes between fraudulent and innocent misrepresentation, since both render the contract voidable.[156] The Privy Council, however, in *Re Goldcorp Exchange Ltd*[157] gave short shrift to a misrepresentation claim[158] for the recovery of money.[159] In so far as particular funds

---

[149] *Re Oriental Inland Steam Co.* (1874) LR 9 Ch. App. 557; *Ayerst v C & K Construction Ltd* [1976] AC 167; *Re MC Bacon Ltd* [1991] Ch. 127. But trust applies only as an analogy in the process of distribution: *Commissioner of Taxation v Linter Textiles Australia Ltd* [2005] HCA 20; (2005) 220 CLR 592 at [25]–[49]. See also *Re Calgary and Edmonton Land Co. Ltd* [1975] 1 WLR 355, 379 (Megarry J): 'It is one thing to say that there is a trust or fiduciary duty, and another to say that the members [of the company] are beneficiaries under a trust.'

[150] *Pritchard v MH Builders (Wilmslow) Ltd* [1969] 2 All ER 670; *Ayerst v C & K Construction Ltd*, n. 149 above.

[151] Still less third-party purchasers, for they will have provided no further consideration.

[152] *Oakes v Turquand* (1867) LR 2 HL 325. Execution creditors are not purchasers for value: Spencer Bower and Turner, n. 147 above.

[153] *Oakes v Turquand*, n. 152 above; *Re Scottish Petroleum* (1883) 13 Ch. D 413. See D. L. McConnell and J. G. Monroe, *Kerr on the Law of Fraud and Mistake* (7th edn, Sweet & Maxwell, 1952), 514–17.

[154] And of the amount of uncalled capital.

[155] *Re Eastgate*, n. 147 above; *Tilley v Bowman Ltd* [1910] 1 KB 745.

[156] *Clough v London and North Western Railway Co.* (1871) LR 7 Ex. 26, 34.

[157] [1995] 1 AC 74.

[158] It is not made clear whether the misrepresentation was innocent or fraudulent: '[T]he misrepresentations . . . were presumably that (in fact) the company intended to carry out the collateral promise to establish a separate stock and also that (in law) if this promise was performed the customer would obtain a title to the bullion': *ibid.*, 220.

[159] Such restitution claims for the recovery of money are treated as personal claims: Lord Goff and G. Jones, *The Law of Restitution* (7th edn, Sweet & Maxwell, 2007), 102–3.

could not be identified *in specie*, then the claim in that case for the recovery of the same sum could only be treated as unsecured. The Privy Council, however, appeared to go further and say that money always vests outright in the transferee and that the transferor, upon a later rescission, has only an *in personam* claim for the repayment of an equivalent sum.[160] This would make the transferor just another unsecured creditor. Furthermore, if goods or money were transferred and the transferee had already given a creditor a floating charge over after-acquired assets, then the assets would be encumbered by the charge at the moment of their acquisition by the transferee and the chargee's interest would prevail once the charge crystallized.[161] The intervention of the third-party creditor's rights would therefore suffice to bar a later attempt to rescind.

Revesting and insolvency. There yet remains the possibility that the recovery of **8.32** goods might be permitted after an innocent or fraudulent misrepresentation despite the insolvency of the transferee, which was not ruled out by the Privy Council. The existing law of misrepresentation appears not to debar such a claim, despite the weakness of the distinction between the claimant and other creditors of the insolvent. It is questionable whether the law should be prepared to sanction such *in rem* claims that shrink the size of an insolvent's distributable estate. Although the claim may defeat the transferee's unsecured creditors, its effect upon secured creditors demands further consideration. Since the matter goes to equity's auxiliary jurisdiction, it would seem that, once the transferor declares the contract rescinded, the equitable property in the goods will revest in the transferor and the transferee will later be required by the court to reconvey the legal property in the goods to the transferor.[162] The transferor should certainly defeat a floating charge crystallizing after the declaration of rescission[163] but should lose to a purchaser of the legal estate taking without notice before the court orders the reconveyance in law of the goods.[164] If the charge has already crystallized, however, then the fixed interest of the chargee ought to defeat the later fixed interest of the transferor.[165]

Subsisting contract. A final point is whether the transferor might be faced with **8.33** a claim by the transferee's trustee or liquidator, defending or taking proceedings in the name of the transferee, that the contract be declared subsisting under section 2(2) of the 1967 Act. The result would be that the transferor would have a claim for damages that could not be collected from the insolvent transferee's estate. It is questionable whether a court would apply this provision, framed in terms of the

---

[160] *Ibid.*
[161] *Ibid.*
[162] *Quaere* when does this occur in the case of fraud?
[163] See *Re Castell & Brown Ltd* [1898] 1 Ch. 315.
[164] See *Pilcher v Rawlins* (1871) LR 7 Ch. App. 259, 269; *Macmillan Inc. v Bishopsgate Trust (No. 3)* [1995] 1 WLR 978, 999–1001.
[165] *Qui prior est tempore, potior est jure.*

interests of the immediate contracting parties, so as to embrace the interests of third-party creditors.

Effect of Misrepresentation Act 1967

8.34 **Limited effect of Act.** The law on innocent misrepresentation was heavily amended by the Misrepresentation Act 1967, which is by no means a codification of the law on the subject. The Act does not define an actionable misrepresentation, nor does it state what rescission *ab initio* is or, subject to what follows, when it is available. Apart from the discretion to award damages in lieu of rescission under section 2(2) of the Misrepresentation Act, the Act, whilst refraining from dealing directly with rescission *ab initio*, intersects with it in two other places. First, the Act provides that the mere incorporation of the misrepresentation in the contract as a term does not deprive the victim of the right to rescind the contract for misrepresentation.[166] A false statement, in other words, can do double duty as both an inducing misrepresentation *dehors* the contract and as a component of that induced contract.[167] Secondly, the right to rescind a contract for misrepresentation is not barred by the mere fact of the execution of that contract.[168]

8.35 **Continuing effect of inducing misrepresentation.** The survival under section 1(a) of an inducing misrepresentation that also becomes a term of the contract generates a number of practical difficulties. Two points stand out here. First, any contractual term that has a double existence as an inducing misrepresentation as well is liable to upset an agreed risk allocation under the contract.[169] If the breach of the term is a breach sounding only in damages, this will be because the parties did not intend it to be a promissory condition whose every breach gives rise to a right to terminate the contract. Section 1(a) therefore runs counter to the modern tendency to confine express promissory conditions to well-trodden areas of commercial contracts involving time and documents.[170] Secondly, the survival of an inducing misrepresentation can only mean that the Act treats misrepresentation as a vice of consent, the weakness of which approach has been examined already. If misrepresentation were treated instead as a species of fault, there is no reason why it should not be compromised by the terms of the contract like other risks, so as to remove the right of rescission where no right to terminate the contract for breach is available. The destructive effects of section 1(a) are admittedly liable to

---

[166] S. 1(a).

[167] In recommending a provision to this effect in its Tenth Report on *Innocent Misrepresentation* (Cmnd 1782), the Law Reform Committee linked it (in paras 14–6) with another recommendation designed to preserve the right of a buyer of specific goods to reject the goods for a breach of condition despite the property in the goods having passed to the buyer (see Ch. 3 above). In both case, the Committee was conscious of going beyond its terms of reference.

[168] S. 1(b).

[169] See the discussion of entire agreement and related clauses in Ch. 9.

[170] See, e.g., *Cehave NV v Bremer Handelsgesellschaft GmbH* [1976] AC 44 and Ch. 10 below.

be cancelled out by the judicial discretion to declare the contract subsisting in section 2(2), but this only prompts the question why section 1(a) was introduced in the first place. Furthermore, the continuing duality of an inducing misrepresentation and a term of the contract threatens to undermine a rational step taken over half a century ago to prevent rescission for misrepresentation when the right to reject goods for breach of contract had been lost under section 35 of the Sale of Goods Act.[171] Section 1(a) states that, where a misrepresentation becomes a term of the contract, the right to rescind the contract, if otherwise available, shall remain available.

Execution bar.   The second area of statutory intervention lies in the rule that the **8.36** right to rescind survives the execution of the contract. Had the execution bar—whose extent and existence were somewhat debatable—been of general application, and had it survived the Misrepresentation Act, then the issue of whether rescission is a self-executing remedy would hardly have arisen and there would also have been scarcely any need for the judicial discretion to declare the discretion subsisting in section 2(2).[172] It is this discretion—the third area of statutory intervention—where the Act most importantly touches upon the right to rescind.

Damages

Damages and ensuing contract.   The Act introduced a damages remedy for a **8.37** negligent misrepresentation[173] and, as seen above, conferred a discretion on the court to award damages in lieu of rescission in those cases where rescission would be too harsh a remedy.[174] These remedies are available only in the case of a contract entered into consequent upon the making of a misrepresentation, and only against the other party to the contract and not against his agent.[175] In the ensuing case law, difficulties emerged as to the measure of damages in both these cases and as to whether damages might be awarded in the latter case despite the loss of the right to rescind in the circumstances set out above.

Damages actions.   If the legislative aim was ever to achieve an harmonious fit **8.38** between the previous common law and the Misrepresentation Act 1967, the aim was not successfully accomplished. So far as it sanctions damages awards under section 2, the Act sits very badly within the scheme of rules governing damages

---

171 *Leaf v International Galleries*, n. 28 above, discussed in Ch. 10 below.

172 See the connection made between the abolition of the execution bar and a statutory power to declare the contract subsisting in the Tenth Report of the Law Reform Committee on *Innocent Misrepresentation* (Cmnd 1782), para. 11.

173 S. 2(1).

174 S. 2(2).

175 *Resolute Maritime Inc. v Nippon Kaiji Kyokai (The Skolas)* [1983] 1 WLR 857; *MCI WorldCom International Ltd v Primus Telecommunications Ltd* [2003] EWHC 2182 (Comm); [2004] 1 All ER (Comm.) 138 at [59].

awards in tort and contract. Two damages actions were created by the Act, of which the action in section 2(1) is much the more important. It provides:

> Where a person has entered into a contract after a misrepresentation has been made to him by another person thereto and as a result thereof he has suffered loss, then, if the person making the misrepresentation would be liable to damages in respect thereof had the misrepresentation been made fraudulently, that person shall be so liable notwithstanding that the representation was not made fraudulently, unless he proves that he had reasonable ground to believe and did believe up to the time the contract was made that the facts represented were true.

Section 2(1) is in the nature of a statutory tort. From its enactment, it has been bedevilled by its mysterious reference to fraud. The reader is called upon first to imagine that fraud has been committed in the uttering of the misrepresentation before unimagining it. It is not unlike entering a building through a revolving door and going round the full 360 degrees. A reference to the law as it stood in the early 1960s, before the Misrepresentation Act and the decision of the House of Lords in *Hedley Byrne & Co. Ltd v Heller & Partners Ltd*,[176] reveals the gnomic statement of the period, 'No damages for misrepresentation in the absence of fraud'. Taking that statement as the point of departure, section 2(1) could in its confused way be read as a powerful rhetorical statement that fraud has no part to play in the grant of damages thereunder.[177]

8.39 **Damages under section 2(1).** The first cases under section 2(1) ruled that the measure of damages was the tort measure as opposed to the contract measure.[178] Going further, the Court of Appeal, instead of allowing the two references to fraud in section 2(1) to cancel each other out, has on two subsequent occasions stated that the measure of damages for fraud is the proper measure under section 2(1).[179] That measure is a stringent, even a punitive, one, because it would permit recovery for all losses directly flowing from the misrepresentation.[180]

---

[176] [1964] AC 465.

[177] The reference to fraud, however, did spare the draftsman of the Act the task of defining a misrepresentation. For the view that fraud was the 'natural point of reference for the proposed new remedy of damages', see J. Cartwright, *Misrepresentation, Mistake and Non-Disclosure* (2nd edn, Sweet & Maxwell, 2007), para. 717, noting that the Tenth Report of the Law Reform Committee on *Innocent Misrepresentation* (Cmnd 1782, 1962) pre-dated the decision of the House of Lords in *Hedley Byrne & Co. Ltd v Heller & Partners Ltd*, n. 176 above. This view is borne out by para. 17 of the Report but the Committee's recommendation of a damages remedy did not itself refer to fraud.

[178] *Sharneyford Supplies Ltd v Edge* [1985] 3 WLR 1, 15–16; *F & B Entertainments Ltd v Leisure Enterprises Ltd* (1976) 240 EG 455, 460–1; *André et Cie SA v Ets Michel Blanc et Fils* [1977] 2 Lloyd's Rep. 166, 181; *Naughton v O'Callaghan* [1990] 3 All ER 191. For the contractual approach, see *Watts v Spence* [1976] Ch. 165; *Jarvis v Swans Tours Ltd* [1973] 1 QB 233, 237.

[179] *Royscot Trust Ltd v Rogerson* [1991] 2 QB 297; *William Sindall Plc v Cambridgeshire County Council* [1994] 1 WLR 1016. See R. Hooley (1991) 107 *LQR* 547.

[180] *Doyle v Olby (Ironmongers) Ltd* [1969] 2 QB 158; see also *Clef Aquitaine SARL v Laporte Materials (Barrow) Ltd* [2001] QB 488 (recovery of damages for loss of more profitable venture).

Writing extrajudicially,[181] Lord Hoffmann has drawn a distinction between damages awards that compensate for all adverse consequences of a claimant entering into a contract, and damages awards that compensate just for the consequences of entering into a contract on a false basis. Take the case of a sale involving shares in a dot.com company just before the speculative bubble burst some years ago. On a declining share market, the former approach would impose on the maker of the statement the full cost of the decline. The seller would be liable for all losses flowing directly from entering into the contract, and not only for those losses that are reasonably foreseeable.[182] Neither seller nor buyer of the shares in this case foresaw the catastrophic fall in the value of dot.com shares.

Damages and scope of duty.   It would be no great oversimplification to say that   **8.40** the second type of damages award—where compensation is made for entering into the contract on a false basis—would limit liability to the financial difference between the price actually paid for the shares and the price that would have been paid had the truth been known. The choice, in Lord Hoffmann's view, is not a matter of factual causation but of the scope of the relevant duty that is being imposed. This does not necessarily make the law any simpler: it means that difficulties of factual causation give way to assumptions about the scope of duty. The general interest of deterring fraud, in Lord Hoffmann's view, argues in favour of the more stringent approach.[183] In consequence, the victim of fraud who would have purchased the shares in any event, whether at a lesser price or even at the same price, is able under the fraud rule to reverse the risk of market decline and put it back on the seller. In financial terms, it is as though the buyer of the shares had been able to terminate the contract for a discharging breach, for the reversal of market risk is one of the consequences of termination of contract.

Criticism.   However much the rule of damages assessment in cases of fraud   **8.41** might be a salutary one, section 2(1) damages can be awarded against a defendant who is not fraudulent and who has not been proven to have acted negligently. For this reason, despite the matter being settled at the level of the Court of Appeal, it would be desirable for the House of Lords, if the occasion were to present itself, to make it plain that fraud has no practical part to play in the assessment of damages under section 2(1). There is no good reason why innocent misrepresentation, treated in section 2(1) as a species of fault rather than vice of consent, should be

---

[181] 'Common Sense and Causing Loss': a lecture to the Chancery Bar Association (15 June 1999).

[182] *Smith New Court Securities Ltd v Scrimgeour Vickers Ltd* [1997] AC 254.

[183] The less stringent approach of calculating damages for the consequences of having acted on a false basis has been taken in actions against negligent valuers. See *Banque Bruxelles Lambert SA v Eagle Star Insurance Co.* [1997] AC 191; see also *Nykredit Mortgage Bank v Edward Erdman Group (No. 2)* [1997] 1 WLR 1627; *Platform Home Loans v Oysten Shipways* [2000] 2 AC 190.

allowed to reallocate basic contractual risk when it does not amount to a promissory condition of the contract giving rise to termination rights.

8.42 **Damages 'in lieu' of rescission.** Section 2(2) of the 1967 Act permits a court to award damages 'in lieu' of rescission. Two major problems arise under this provision. First, the substitution of damages for rescission poses the question whether this may be done if rescission is no longer available. Before turning to the cases, the merits of a case where such an award might be made should be considered. First of all, a claim is unlikely to be made in those cases where any damages may be claimed instead under section 2(1).[184] This is recognized in section 2(3), which makes provision for offsetting any damages recovered under section 2(2) against any larger sum to be awarded under section 2(1). A party who has lost the right to rescind and who can claim damages under section 2(1) has no reason to claim instead under section 2(2). In consequence, if section 2(2) can yield a claim for damages without a right to rescission being surrendered, then it will operate for the benefit only of those parties who are prevented from claiming under section 2(1). This group of claimants consists of those whose defendants have been able to discharge the presumptive negligence imposed by section 2(1). Furthermore, since section 2(2) cannot give rise to damages exceeding the measure for a breach of contract,[185] it follows that the question of recovery without surrendering a right to rescind is of interest only to those claimants who are the victims of misrepresentations that were manifestly not negligently made and that did not become terms of the contract. Such claimants do not constitute a meritorious group. In addition, given the opaqueness of calculating the measure of damages under both section 2(1) and section 2(2),[186] it has to be asked why Parliament should have wanted to manufacture two damages remedies when in the interest of economy one would have sufficed, and why it was appropriate to create a statutory tort of strict liability in section 2(2)[187] alongside another statutory tort of semi-strict liability[188] in section 2(1).

8.43 **Differing views.** In two relatively recent cases, diametrically opposed views have been taken by first instance judges about the extent of the discretion in section 2(2). In one case,[189] as a result of the rule in *Pepper v Hart*[190] being invoked, the judge

---

[184] See *William Sindall Plc v Cambridgeshire County Council* [1994] 1 WLR 1016 (Hoffmann LJ).
[185] *Ibid.*
[186] See below.
[187] Note, however, that this is in the nature of a *sui generis* claim that is neither contractual nor tortious: see Treitel, n. 107 above, 350–2. It is nevertheless unsatisfactory and a reproach to the rational structure of English law to introduce a new category into the classification of private law called, for want of a better name, 'Unclassifiable Statute'.
[188] Semi-strict because of the presumption of negligence.
[189] *Thomas Witter Ltd v TBP Industries Ltd* [1996] 2 All ER 573 (Jacob J).
[190] [1993] AC 593.

turned to Hansard and found the Solicitor-General, in debate, asserting that a claim for damages could be advanced under what was then clause 2(2) of the Misrepresentation Bill even though the right to rescind had been lost. In the later case,[191] the judge discounted the Solicitor-General's extempore response in the middle of an all-night debate. He considered that no power to award damages lay where the right to rescind had been lost, since section 2(2) gave a 'discretionary power to hold the contract to be subsisting and to award damages where it would otherwise be obliged to grant rescission or to hold that the contract had been rescinded by the representee'. For reasons given above, it is submitted that this is correct. Furthermore, it is submitted, damages 'in lieu of' rescission is too clear to admit of the ambiguity necessary to call *Pepper v Hart* into play. If a contract cannot be rescinded, damages cannot be substituted for something that does not exist. Finally, there seems no point in asking the tribunal, in the exercise of its discretion, to compare the position of the maker of the misrepresentation, if the contract were rescinded, with the position of the other party, if the contract were upheld, in those cases where there is no right to rescind being traded against damages. If the right to rescind is not being surrendered, the discretionary guidelines given to the court are largely meaningless.

Measure of damages under section 2(2). The method of assessing damages **8.44** under section 2(2)[192] is less clearly settled. If the starting point were the position that a right to rescission is being taken away, then damages could be seen as the fair price to be paid for deprivation of that right. That would provide a frame of reference and accord with the view that section 2(2) confers a power to award damages 'in a wholly new situation'[193] under the terms of a broad discretion. Since section 2(2) is concerned with cases of innocent, non-negligent misrepresentation—and for practical purposes one that does not become a term of the contract—then an apprehension that rescission rights are too easily granted under the present law[194] could lead to the conclusion that damages granted on an equitable basis might be less than adequate to indemnify the victim of the misrepresentation against loss, however that might be defined. Following this approach, damages could serve a purpose broadly similar to those provisions in the Law Reform (Frustrated Contracts)

---

[191] *Government of Zanzibar v British Aerospace (Lancaster House) Ltd* (HH Judge Jack QC) [2000] 1 WLR 2333; see also *Atlantic Lines and Navigation Co. Inc. v Hallam Ltd (The Lucy)* [1983] 1 Lloyd's Rep. 188 (Mustill J).

[192] There are other damages issues too, such as the relevant rule of remoteness.

[193] *William Sindall Plc v Cambridgeshire County Council* [1994] 1 WLR 1016, 1037 (Hoffmann LJ). See also *MCI WorldCom International Ltd v Primus Telecommunications Ltd* [2003] EWHC 2182 (Comm); [2004] 1 All ER (Comm.) 138 at [72]–[77].

[194] See the Tenth Report of the Law Reform Committee on *Innocent Misrepresentation* (Cmnd 1782), para 11: 'Unless the court's power to grant rescission is made more elastic than it is at present, the court will not be able to take account of the relative importance or unimportance of the facts which have been represented.'

Act 1943 which provide for a financial adjustment between the parties in the event of frustration of contract. Section 2(2) does not contain causal language: nothing in it connects loss caused by the misrepresentation to the damages award. It states merely that a tribunal 'may declare the contract subsisting and award damages in lieu of rescission'. This wording does not even make it clear whether, if the contract is declared to be subsisting, damages *must* be awarded. It has nevertheless been stated by Hoffmann LJ that damages should not exceed those available as on a breach of warranty, in circumstances where the implication was that they might be less.[195] Furthermore, Hoffmann LJ has made it plain that the purpose of damages is not to compensate for the loss of the right to rescind. Rather, '[d]amages under section 2(2) are ... damages for the misrepresentation as such'.[196]

8.45 Relevant factors. Section 2(2) refers the tribunal, in the exercise of its discretion to declare the contract subsisting, to 'hav[e] regard to the nature of the misrepresentation and the loss that would be caused by it if the contract were upheld, as well as to the loss that rescission would cause to the other party'. It might be asked whether these factors are also relevant to the calculation of damages. The first factor is the 'nature' of the representation. At first sight, this might be thought to refer to the existence of fault on the part of the maker of the statement, but fraudulent misrepresentations are excluded from section 2(2) and the availability of a larger sum of damages for presumed negligence under section 2(1) that simulates the economic effect of rescission deprives section 2(2) of any significance in such cases. This factor has been interpreted as going to the relative importance of the misrepresentation,[197] which seems to give no assistance at all in the calculation of damages. Similarly, the other two factors appear unhelpful. The loss caused by the misrepresentation if the contract were to be upheld points to the case for allowing rescission and not to the calculation of damages in lieu. The loss that rescission would cause to the maker of the statement tells us nothing about the price that that person ought to pay for retaining the contract, since it does not compare with the loss caused by the misrepresentation to the victim of the misrepresentation.

8.46 Comparison with breach of contract. Lord Hoffmann, in a case involving the transfer of land, stated that damages in lieu should be a sum 'compensating the plaintiff for the loss he has suffered on account of the property not having been what it was represented to be', a sum that could not exceed an award for breach of warranty.[198] This approach does in fact look exactly like treating a mere misrepresentation as a term of the contract and awarding damages for its breach, and it looks too like a conventional assessment under section 2(2). If breach of

---

[195] In *William Sindall Plc v Cambridgeshire County Council*, n. 193 above.
[196] *Ibid.*, 1037.
[197] *Ibid.*, 1036.
[198] *Ibid.*, 1038 (Hoffmann LJ).

contract damages had been appropriate, then one might have expected some reference to contract in section 2(2). A better approach would be to approach section 2(2) with no preconceptions but to examine the particular circumstances, without classifying section 2(2) as sanctioning a contract measure or a tort measure or some other kind of measure. A tribunal may declare a contract subsisting where the claimant who claims to have rescinded the contract might have elected instead to claim damages for breach of contract or damages for negligent misrepresentation. In the former of these cases, the court should be at liberty[199] to award contractual damages, and in the latter damages in accordance with section 2(1), which as the law currently stands would bring in the fraud rule. Where the misrepresentation is both non-negligent and non-contractual, damages should be at large, guided by the court's discretionary decision to avoid the hardship that would accrue to the maker of the statement if rescission were to be allowed.[200] In financial terms, the party seeking rescission might be no worse off for being confined to damages, while the other party might be spared losses consequent upon a rescission. If the accent were therefore placed upon the avoidance of disproportionate loss, the court should be at liberty to adjust the award according to the particular circumstances. It might, for example, be appropriate to make a restitutionary award if the maker of the false statement has been unjustly enriched as a result of it. Or the award might take account of the better terms that the other party might have negotiated but for the misrepresentation, in which case it would be in the nature of an adjustment of the contract price. Whichever approach is adopted under section 2(2), care should be taken to avoid double compensation where a claim to rescind has been combined with a claim for damages under section 2(1).[201] Section 2(3) provides that any damages awarded under section 2(2) should be taken into account in those cases where section 2(1) damages are claimed. This suggests a statutory expectation that the damages recoverable under section 2(2) will be lower than those recoverable under section 2(1).

Negligent Misstatement in Tort Law

Assumption of responsibility.   The landmark decision of the House of Lords in   **8.47** *Hedley Byrne & Co. Ltd v Heller & Partners*[202] recognized the existence of liability in tort for negligent misstatements causing economic loss. In the years following

---

[199] Subject to any pleading difficulties that might arise.

[200] The decision to exercise the discretion may be taken precisely because the misrepresentation causes no loss: *Bank Negara Indonesia 1946 v Taylor* [1995] CLC 255.

[201] *MCI WorldCom International Ltd v Primus Telecommunications Ltd* [2003] EWHC 2182 (Comm); [2004] 1 All ER (Comm.) 138 at [at 76] ('the appropriate remedies, where rescission can be ordered, cannot be viewed in isolation').

[202] n. 176 above. Reference should be made to the standard texts on tort law for a fuller treatment of this subject. For a helpful survey of the development of this area of law, see *BP Plc v AON Ltd* [2007] EWHC 1056 (Comm).

the decision, the scope of liability for economic loss caused by negligent acts and omissions expanded[203] and then contracted,[204] but the particular case of economic loss caused by negligent misstatement and advice survived and became refined. The keynote of *Hedley Byrne* liability lay in Lord Devlin's expression, gathered from an earlier House of Lords decision on fiduciary relations,[205] that liability should arise in cases that were 'equivalent to contract'[206] where a 'special relationship' between the parties arose. The idea of equivalence to contract captured the essential idea that liability did not arise as a matter of imposed duty and proximity, but rather because one party possessed of a special skill or knowledge assumed responsibility for statements made to another, and that other relied upon the those statements.[207] The twin notions of assumed responsibility and reliance, limiting as they do the range of possible claimants, render it unnecessary to have resort to any further filter that it be 'fair, just and reasonable'[208] for liability to be imposed on the defendant.[209] The need for assumption of responsibility and reliance in the case of negligent misstatement has not been strictly adhered to in some subsequent cases,[210] and liability under this heading has been permitted to spill out of statements and into the supply of services,[211] but liability in tort for negligent misstatement has survived as a separate head and has not lost its separate identity within the greater tort of negligence.[212]

8.48 **Reduced importance of negligent misstatement.** The presumptive case of negligence that arises in section 2(1) of the Misrepresentation Act 1967 largely deprives of any significance the possibility that a seller might also be liable in tort for pre-contractual negligent misstatements. As stated above, liability in tort for negligent misstatement depends upon the establishment of a 'special relationship' between the maker and the recipient of the misstatement involving an assumption of responsibility by the maker. There are no appreciable advantages in laying a claim in negligent misstatement when section 2(1) is available, for example, in the assessment of damages. Nevertheless, section 2(1) is only available in the case of negligent misrepresentation inducing entry into a contract; no such limitation governs negligent misstatement, which can therefore embrace cases of bad advice

---

[203] e.g., *Anns v Merton London Borough Council* [1978] AC 728; *Junior Books Ltd v Veitchi Co. Ltd* [1982] 1 AC 520.

[204] e.g., *Murphy v Brentwood District Council* [1991] 1 AC 398.

[205] *Nocton v Ashburton* [1914] AC 932.

[206] n. 202 above, 522 (Lord Devlin).

[207] See especially Lords Devlin and Morris in *Hedley Byrne*, n. 176 above.

[208] *Caparo plc v Dickman* [1990] 2 AC 605, 617–18 (Lord Bridge).

[209] *Henderson v Merrett Syndicates Ltd* [1995] 2 AC 145, 180–1 (Lord Goff).

[210] *Smith v Eric S Bush* [1990] 1 AC 831; *White v Jones* [1995] 2 AC 207.

[211] *Henderson v Merrett Syndicates Ltd*, n. 209 above.

[212] On the question whether the test of assumption of responsibility should apply to all cases of economic loss, see *Customs and Excise Commissioners v Barclays Bank Plc* [2006] UKHL 28; [2007] 1 AC 181.

concerning goods after a contract of sale has been concluded, in circumstances too where the implied terms of quality and fitness in section 14 of the Sale of Goods Act are not engaged. In determining the scope of negligent misstatement where there is a contract or a chain of contracts, it is important to understand that liability principles will not be permitted to undermine any contractual relationship between the maker and the recipient of the statement. In addition, where a contract is negotiated with a corporate entity through an agent, who is employed or otherwise, it is unlikely that the agent will assume personal responsibility within the limits of the *Hedley Byrne* principle, over and above the contract concluded between his principal and a third party.[213] Furthermore, where there is a chain of contracts designed to contain rights and duties in a series of bilateral relationships, liability in tort will not lightly be recognized between non-contiguous parties in this chain, for fear that it will have a disruptive effect on the allocation of risk and responsibility in each contractual link in the chain.[214] This latter consideration, however, is more likely to be recognized in chains of contracts in the building industry than in chains of contracts concerning the distribution of goods. Where goods are distributed down a chain, however, the opportunities for inferring that an express warranty has been given by a producer, for example, to the ultimate purchaser are likely to render it unnecessary to resort to negligent misstatement to find a remedy.

Criminal Offences

Compensation orders. Prior to the enactment of the Consumer Protection **8.49** from Unfair Trading Regulations 2008,[215] the Trade Descriptions Act 1968 and the Consumer Protection Act 1987 dealt with abuses connected with the distribution of goods and misleading price indications. The relevant provisions of these statutes were repealed by the 2008 Regulations,[216] which substituted a different set of offences.[217] The Consumer Protection Act continues to possess a number of

---

[213] See *Williams v Natural Life Health Foods* [1988] 1 WLR 830; *Trevor Ivory Ltd v Anderson* [1992] 2 NZLR 517. Cf *Standard Chartered Bank v Pakistan National Shipping Corpn* [2003] 1 AC 959 (fraud).

[214] *Henderson v Merrett Syndicates Ltd*, n. 209 above, 195–6. See also *Simaan Contracting Co. v Pilkington Ltd (No. 2)* [1988] 1 QB 758, 781.

[215] SI 2008 No. 277. The Regulations came into force on 26 May 2008. They transpose Directive 2005/29/EC of the European Parliament and the Council on unfair business-to-consumer commercial practices in the internal market (OJ No L 149, 11.6.2005).

[216] See Sch. 4. Oddly, in the case of the Trade Descriptions Act, the provisions laying down the relevant offences have been repealed but the definitions of the conduct (ss. 2–4: trade description, false trade description, and applying a trade description to goods) giving rise to the offences have not.

[217] Despite the extensive literature and case law on the Trade Descriptions Act, it cannot usefully be consulted with a view to interpreting and applying the Consumer Protection from Unfair Trading Regulations 2008. As broad as these Regulations are, and as likely as they are to embrace all activities that amounted to false trade descriptions, as well as some that did not because of restricted wording in the Act, the scheme and concepts of the Regulations are so different from what has gone before that a fresh start is required.

provisions dealing with the issue of regulations concerning consumer safety and with offences related to consumer safety.[218] For present civil purposes, such criminal legislation is relevant in so far as the courts are empowered under the Powers of Criminal Courts (Sentencing) Act 2000 to make compensation orders in favour of those suffering 'personal injury, loss or damage' as a result of a criminal offence.[219] This formula appears to exclude claims by those who have suffered economic loss as a result of paying an inflated price for goods, for example, when buying a car with a false odometer reading, a practice that was a fruitful source of prosecutions under the Trade Descriptions Act. Nevertheless, compensation orders have been made in respect of disappointing holidays,[220] though it is improbable that an award based on disappointment with a sub-standard holiday would be made if a defendant seriously contested the propriety of a compensation order.[221] It is unlikely that the tort of breach of statutory duty could be invoked to provide a civil remedy under the 2008 Regulations. A legislative intention to treat the prohibitions therein as actionable in the tort of breach of statutory duty appears to be impliedly negatived by regulation 29, which, following in this respect the Trade Descriptions Act,[222] states that the commission of an offence does not render a contract void or unenforceable.[223] Furthermore, the Directive that prompted the Regulations is clear that Member States are required only to lay down penalties[224] and that contract law, including its rules on the validity, formation, and effect of a contract, are not affected by the Directive.[225]

Unfair Trading

8.50 **Unfair commercial practices.** The Consumer Protection from Unfair Trading Regulations 2008[226] are directed at 'unfair commercial practices' in business-to-consumer transactions. After a general definition, the Regulations make specific reference to three groupings of unfair commercial practices: misleading

---

[218] In Part II (ss. 10–19). Given the civil content of the Act in Part I, these provisions ought not to give rise to a civil compensation award. See also the General Product Safety Regulations 1994, SI 1994 No. 2328, and the Food Safety Act 1990 (for various offences concerning the sale of food not of the nature, substance or quality demanded, and the false description or presentation of food (ss. 14–15)).

[219] S. 130. The amount awarded is such as the court considers 'appropriate' (s.130(4)), except that there is a £5,000 cap on awards in magistrates' courts (s. 131).

[220] *R v Thomson Holidays Ltd* [1974] QB 592.

[221] See, e.g., *R v Broughton* (1986) 8 Cr. App. R (S) 379; *R v Holden* [1985] Crim. LR 397; see also the Criminal Law Revision Committee, *Theft and Related Offences* (Eighth Report 1966, Cmnd 2977), 76–9 (restitution and compensation).

[222] S. 35.

[223] It is unlikely that, in the absence of a provision in the statute sanctioning a breach of statutory duty action, one will be implied in a statute laying down penalties for prohibited behaviour: see, e.g., *Square v Model Farms Dairies (Bournemouth) Ltd* [1939] 2 KB 365.

[224] Art. 13.

[225] Art. 3.2.

[226] n. 215 above.

actions; misleading omissions; and aggressive commercial practices. Schedule 1 contains a list of thirty-one commercial practices that are considered in all circumstances unfair. This list covers all three groupings and nothing in the list is distributed to any specific one of those groupings. The existence of the list does not, of course, rule out the treatment of other commercial practices as unfair in particular circumstances. It is unlikely, however, that a court would seek to lay down a binding ruling that a commercial practice not on the list should for the future always be treated as an unfair commercial practice. With just two exceptions in Schedule 1,[227] engaging in unfair commercial practices gives rise to an offence.

Definition of unfairness. Regulation 3 prohibits unfair commercial practices. **8.51** The general definition provides that a commercial practice is unfair if it contravenes the 'requirements of professional diligence' and 'materially distorts or is likely to materially distort the economic behaviour of the average consumer[228] with regard to the product'. Professional diligence is defined as the 'standard of special skill and care' that a trader[229] can reasonably be expected to exercise towards consumers, which is commensurate with either 'honest market practice in the trader's field of activity' or 'the general principle of good faith in the trader's field of activity'.[230] It is not clear what the word 'special' adds to professional diligence. Given the purpose of the Regulations and the required mental element for the commission of an offence with regard to this Regulation, it seems also that the words 'care and skill' send a false signal. The suppression of unfair commercial practices is not really a matter of requiring diligence at all but of imposing standards of proper conduct. The keynotes are 'honesty' and 'good faith', the latter of which is undefined. In the Directive, honest market practice and good faith are grammatically linked with 'and/or',[231] whereas in the Regulations the relationship between the two is disjunctive. The provision in the Directive does not therefore suggest that an expansive reading be given to good faith in the Regulations. Given also the criminal rather than civil purpose of the Regulations, it is submitted that 'good faith' ought to be interpreted as more akin to honesty than to fair dealing; the techniques of the European draftsman do not, as they might in the case of the Westminster draftsman, compel the inference that good faith must mean

---

[227] Reg. 12: see paras 11 (undeclared and paid for promotional material in the media) and 28 (exhorting children to buy products or bully parents or other adults to buy the products).

[228] A consumer is defined as 'any individual who in relation to a commercial practice is acting for purposes which are outside his business': reg. 2(1). A business is defined as including a 'trade, craft or profession'. A member of the criminal bar purchasing law books out of academic interest may therefore be a consumer; a legal academic may not be.

[229] Defined as meaning 'any person who in relation to a commercial practice is acting for purposes relating to his business, and anyone acting in the name of or on behalf of the trader': reg. 2(1).

[230] Reg. 2(1).

[231] Art. 2(h).

something other than honesty. The second element of unfair commercial practices is the distortion of consumer decision-making. The word 'economic' seems to be of little assistance: any decision of the consumer, whether and on what terms to buy a product, seems an economic one.[232] It is also unlikely that any court will be burdened by extensive evidence on the actual reactions of 'average' consumers to a practice. It is far more probable that a court will form its own impressions of 'likely' reactions of consumers in general: indeed, the word 'likely' seems designed to ease the evidential burden in making prosecutions and to permit the court to draw its own inferences.

8.52 **Schedule 1.** In practice, it is likely that a court will not dwell upon the above general definition of an unfair commercial practice but rather go directly to the list contained in Schedule 1 and then the three groupings if necessary. The first of these groupings is misleading actions,[233] defined in alternative ways. According to the first alternative,[234] a misleading action is one that contains false information relating to:

(a) the existence or nature of the product;

(b) the main characteristics of the product . . .;[235]

(c) the extent of the trader's commitments;

(d) the motives for the commercial practice;

(e) the nature of the sales process;

(f) any statement or symbol relating to direct or indirect sponsorship or approval of the trader or the product;

(g) the price or manner in which the price is calculated;

(h) the existence of a specific price advantage;

(i) the need for a service, part, replacement or repair;

(j) the nature, attributes and rights of the trader . . .;[236]

(k) the consumer's rights or the risks he may face.

The provision of false information is not sufficient. To constitute a misleading action under the first alternative, it must also cause or be likely to cause the

---

[232] This is borne out by the way misleading actions are defined: see below.

[233] Reg. 5.

[234] Reg. 5(2).

[235] Reg. 5(5) contains a formidable and purportedly comprehensive list of the main characteristics of the product, viz, availability, benefits, risks, execution (*sic*), composition, accessories, after-sales assistance, complaints handling, method and date of manufacture and of provision, delivery, usage (*sic*), quantity, specification, geographical or commercial origin, expected results, and test results, and related matters.

[236] Reg. 5(6) states that 'nature, attribution and rights' includes the trader's identity, assets, qualifications, status, approval, affiliations or connections, ownership of industrial, commercial, or intellectual property rights, and awards and distinctions.

average consumer to take a transactional decision he would not otherwise have taken.

Misleading action. The other definition of misleading action[237] takes two **8.53** forms. The first form occurs where the marketing of a product creates confusion with any products, trade marks, trade names or other distinguishing marks of a competitor. The second form occurs with the failure of a trader to comply with a commitment, expressed in firm and not aspirational terms, contained in a code of conduct,[238] where the commitment causes or is likely to cause the average consumer to take a transactional decision he would not otherwise have taken, having regard to the factual content and all features and circumstances of the commitment.

Misleading omissions. The second grouping of unfair commercial practices **8.54** consists of misleading omissions. These are defined as consisting in their 'factual context' of the omission or hiding of material information, or the presentation of it in an 'unclear, unintelligible, ambiguous or untimely'[239] manner, or the failure of the commercial practice 'to identify its commercial intent' where this is not apparent from the context. The factual context[240] comprises the time, space, and other limitations of the medium used to convey the practice, alternative means available to the trader to overcome limitations of space and time, and all the features and circumstances of commercial practice. Information is material so far as the average consumer needs it for an informed decision or if it is required as a matter of Community obligation.[241] More particularly, if the commercial practice amounts to an invitation to purchase, information is also material, if not already apparent from the context, so far as it concerns the main characteristics of the product that might be appropriately conveyed in the medium used for the invitation to purchase, the identity of the trader, the geographical address of the trader, the price or means of calculating it (where it cannot reasonably be calculated in advance), freight, delivery, and postal charges (where relevant), or having to pay such charges (where they cannot reasonably be calculated in advance), arrangements for payment, delivery, performance, and handling complaints (where these

---

[237] Reg. 5(3). Though presented as a single definition, there are in fact two.

[238] Defined as 'an agreement or set of rules (which is not imposed by legal or administrative requirements) which defines the behaviour of traders who undertake to be bound by it in relation to one or more commercial practices or business sectors': reg. 2(1).

[239] There is a particular risk of untimely information in some trades, e.g., the funeral trade.

[240] As opposed perhaps to the philosophical, historical, and literary contexts of the commercial practice.

[241] Reg. 6(3).

depart from professional diligence),[242] and the existence of a right of withdrawal or cancellation (where relevant).[243]

8.55 **Aggressive commercial practices.** The third grouping of unfair commercial practices consists of aggressive commercial practices.[244] These are defined as consisting in their 'factual context', taking account of all features and circumstances, of practices that significantly impair (or are likely significantly to impair) the consumer's freedom of choice by means of harassment, coercion,[245] or undue influence[246] so that the consumer makes a transactional decision that he would not otherwise have made.[247] In determining whether there has been harassment, coercion, or undue influence in a commercial practice, account is to be taken of the timing, location, nature, or persistence of the practice, the use of threatening or abusive language, the exploitation by the trader of circumstances that impair the particular consumer's judgement, any onerous or disproportionate barrier raised by the trader to the exercise by the consumer of rights under the contract, including rights of termination, and any threat to take legal action that cannot lawfully be taken.[248]

8.56 **Examples of unfair commercial practices.** The following examples of unfair commercial practices, drawn from the list of thirty-one incontrovertibly unfair commercial practices, relate particularly to contracts of sale: inviting offers to purchase products at a specified price when the trader knows that the products cannot or will not be supplied at that price,[249] falsely stating that a product will be available at all or on specified terms for only a limited time and thus impairing the consumer's informed choice,[250] stating or giving the impression that a product can be legally sold when this is not the case,[251] presenting the consumer's legal rights as though they came from the trader,[252] presenting a product as the make of a particular manufacturer when this is not the case,[253] claiming that the trader is closing down or moving when this is not the case,[254] falsely claiming that a product can cure 'illnesses, dysfunction or malformations',[255] giving inaccurate information

---

[242] It is not clear what this means.
[243] Reg. 6(4).
[244] Reg. 7.
[245] This includes the use of physical force: reg. 7(3)(a).
[246] This means 'exploiting a position of power', even without the use or threat of physical force, so as to apply pressure that limits a consumer's ability to make an informed decision: reg. 7(3)(b).
[247] Reg. 7(1).
[248] Reg. 7(2).
[249] Sch. 1 paras 5–6.
[250] Sch. 1 para. 7.
[251] Sch. 1 para. 9.
[252] Sch. 1 para. 10.
[253] Sch. 1 para. 13.
[254] Sch. 1 para. 15.
[255] Sch. 1 para. 17. There is no definition of 'malformations'.

about market conditions,[256] describing a product as 'free' when the consumer has to pay more than the delivery cost,[257] creating the impression that the consumer cannot leave the premises until a contract is formed,[258] making excessive solicitations by remote media,[259] exhorting in advertisements children to buy products,[260] demanding payment for unsolicited goods,[261] and informing the consumer that the trader's job is at risk if the consumer does not make a purchase.[262]

Mental element.   The requisite mental element, in relation to unfair commercial practices in general in Regulation 3, needed for the commission of a criminal offence by traders is that they have knowingly or recklessly[263] engaged in a commercial practice which contravenes the requirements of professional diligence, and which distorts or is likely to distort in a material way the economic behaviour of the average consumer.[264] The reference to professional diligence prompts a reference back to honest market practice and good faith.[265] In substance, the trader must know that he is, or not care whether he is, acting dishonestly. Engaging in misleading omissions and aggressive commercial practices amount to criminal offences;[266] no further mental element is required. The same applies to misleading actions, with the exception of commitments made in a code of practice[267] and, with two exceptions,[268] to those commercial practices listed in Schedule 1.   **8.57**

Defences.   There are two defences available to a trader who would otherwise commit an offence. These defences are available to the trader in those cases where he would otherwise commit an offence because of the act or default of another.[269] The first, the due diligence defence, is where the trader is able to show that the offence is due to a mistake, reliance on information supplied by another, the act or default of another,[270] an accident or another cause beyond his control.[271]   **8.58**

---

256 Sch. 1 para 18.
257 Sch. 1 para 20.
258 Sch. 1 para 24.
259 Sch. 1 para 26.
260 Sch. 1 para 28.
261 Sch. 1 para 29.
262 Sch. 1 para 30.
263 A trader is reckless who pays no regard to whether a practice contravenes professional diligence: reg. 8(2).
264 Reg. 8(1).
265 Reg. 2(1).
266 Regs. 10-11.
267 Reg. 9.
268 Mentioned above.
269 Reg. 16. This other person need not have been a trader or have committed a commercial practice. An example would arise on the sale of a car previously traded in by a private party who dishonestly rolled back the odometer reading.
270 This refers back to reg. 16, n. 269 above.
271 Reg. 17.

The second defence is available to publishers who innocently publish advertise-ments in the ordinary course of business.[272]

Liabilities of Third Parties

8.59 General.   Under this heading, we may group a number of parties in the distribu-tion chain, such as producers,[273] importers, and wholesalers, who are not privy to the final contract between the consumer buyer of new goods and his immediate seller.[274] Landmark decisions on the implied terms of satisfactory quality and fit-ness for purpose have been actuated by the judicial policy of pushing responsibil-ity for defective goods back up the distribution chain to the responsible source.[275] This will be the producer or, if the producer is abroad and unamenable to suit, the importer. Nevertheless, the proper claimant in each case is the immediate buyer, though related actions by each buyer in the distribution chain, which ranges from the producer to the consumer buyer, may be conjoined or consolidated in one set of proceedings. Apart from actions on the implied terms in the Sale of Goods Act, a remote seller, such as the producer, may incur liability on an express warranty or guarantee forming part of a contract collateral to the contract of sale. In addition, there may be liability in the tort of negligence for personal injury and property damage, and liability under the Consumer Protection Act 1987. At times there have also been mooted proposals to make the producer liable directly to the con-sumer buyer in respect of the implied term of satisfactory quality in the Sale of Goods Act,[276] but this seems no longer to be an active issue.

The Indemnity Chain

8.60 Privity of contract.   To understand the difficulties facing a buyer in mounting a claim for defective goods against a party other than the immediate seller, the start-ing point is the doctrine of privity of contract whereby only parties to the contract may derive rights and liabilities from it.[277] In products liability jargon, 'vertical privity' prevents a buyer from suing on a warranty[278] in a contract further up the

---

272 Reg. 18.

273 A term used here to include manufacturers.

274 W. L. Prosser (1960) 69 *Yale LJ* 1099; *ibid.* (1966) 50 *Minn LR* 791; C. J. Miller and R. S. Goldberg, *Product Liability* (2nd edn, OUP, 2004; Law Commission, *Liability for Defective Products* (Law Com. No. 82, 1977); Ontario Law Reform Commission, *Report on Products Liability* (1979): J. Stapleton, *Product Liability* (Butterworths, London, 1994); G. G. Howells, *Comparative Product Liability* (Dartmouth, Aldershot, 1993).

275 *Ashington Piggeries Ltd v Christopher Hill Ltd* [1972] AC 441; *Young & Marten Ltd v McManus Childs Ltd* [1969] 1 AC 454.

276 Cf *Medivance Instruments Ltd v Gaslane Pipework Services Ltd* [2002] EWCA Civ 500 at [17].

277 *Dunlop Pneumatic Tyre Co. Ltd v Selfridge & Co. Ltd* [1915] AC 847, 853.

278 For simplicity, 'warranty' will be used to embrace express and implied warranties and conditions.

chain, between, for example, the wholesaler and retailer. 'Horizontal privity' prevents persons altogether outside the distribution chain, such as a non-purchasing user of the goods[279] or an outsider injured by goods under the control of the buyer or a user, from moving laterally into the buyer's shoes to launch against his seller a warranty action. Were outsiders able to overcome the horizontal privity obstacle, they would still have to deal with vertical privity in pursuing sellers further up the chain. The privity doctrine is closely associated with the rule that consideration must move from the promisee,[280] and emerged when distribution chains were rudimentary, and a contract formed directly between producer and consumer buyer not at all uncommon.[281] The later development of lengthier distribution chains, before the tort of negligence had expanded to give consumer buyers and users some recourse against producers, served to insulate producers from consumer grievances and stimulated the growth of strict warranty liability against retail sellers, even when those sellers had resold packaged goods they could not have examined.[282]

Breaks in the indemnity chain.   Strict though the liability of the immediate   **8.61**
seller is, and sympathetic as courts are to the pushing of liability up the distribution chain, this process of indemnification, based upon a system of third-party notices,[283] can break down for a number of reasons at some point in the chain.[284] There might, for example, be an intervening bankruptcy,[285] or an exemption clause in one of the contracts may bring liability to a halt, or the disclosure of one of the buyer's purposes may not be precise enough to allow indemnification,[286] or one of the buyers may have difficulty identifying his seller,[287] or a limitation period may toll so as to arrest the process of indemnification.[288]

Negligence

Types of negligence.   Where a buyer suffers personal injury or property   **8.62**
damage, a claim in negligence may be launched directly against the producer.[289]

---

279 A borrower or donee.
280 *Price v Easton* (1833) 4 B & Ad. 433; *Tweddle v Atkinson* (1861) 1 B & S 393; *Coulls v Bagot's Executor and Trustee Co. Ltd* (1967) 119 CLR 460; B. Coote [1978] *CLJ* 301.
281 Sutton (1969) 7 *Alta LR* 130, 173.
282 See, e.g., *Bigge v Parkinson* (1862) 7 H & N 955.
283 *Young & Marten*, n. 275 above.
284 S. Schwartz (1979) 11 *Ottawa LR* 583.
285 *Muirhead v Industrial Tank Specialties Ltd* [1986] QB 507.
286 But see attempts to minimize this difficulty in *Ashington Piggeries*, n. 275 above.
287 *Lambert v Lewis*, n. 37 above.
288 *Young & Marten*, n. 275 above.
289 *George v Skivington* (1869) LR 5 Ex. 1; *Donoghue v Stevenson* [1932] AC 562; *Grant v Australian Knitting Mills Ltd* [1936] AC 85.

In the case of design faults, it may be difficult to establish negligence in fact[290] but aberrant products fresh from the assembly line so loudly bespeak negligence, once fault by the buyer and anyone else between him and the producer has been eliminated, that one may as well speak of an evidentiary presumption of negligence, of whatever strength, on the part of the producer.[291] Some goods are not so much defective as suitable for use only if the producer issues an adequate warning or instructions about their proper use: a failure to issue such a warning will be treated as negligence.[292] Similarly, an immediate seller may also incur liability in negligence for a failure to warn or instruct, the existence of a contract of sale being no bar to such a tort action.[293] A difficult question is whether comparisons might be drawn between a producer's liability in negligence and a seller's liability in respect of the quality and fitness of the goods supplied. In one case involving goods that damaged the buyer's property, the court was prepared to assume for the purposes of the case that a producer was liable in negligence if the goods were not of merchantable quality or were unfit for purpose.[294] To adopt this approach in general, however, would court the risk of transforming liability in negligence into a form of strict product liability, which is already catered for to a substantial degree in the Consumer Protection Act 1987.[295] Even if this were a step that courts might be prepared to take, the reference to fitness ought to be to the general purpose or purposes of the goods and not to any special purpose communicated to the immediate seller, at least if that special purpose were not also communicated to the producer.

8.63 Economic loss.   With respect to economic loss caused by defective goods, exemplified by loss of profits attributable to inefficiency in the goods, the cost of repairing them, or an inherent loss of value, the courts have generally held fast against an extension of negligence liability.[296] But some exceptions have emerged. Recovery is likely to be permitted where the buyer expends money on the goods in order to avert the risk of physical loss posed by a defect.[297] In addition, where the buyer suffers physical loss, recovery will be allowed in respect of economic loss consequent

---

290 *Wyngrove's Curator Bonis v Scottish Omnibuses Ltd*, 1966 SC (HL) 47; *Davie v New Merton Board Mills Ltd* [1959] AC 604.

291 *Grant v Australian Knitting Mills Ltd*, n. 289 above. But see *Daniels v White & Sons Ltd* [1938] 4 All ER 258.

292 *Lambert v Lastoplex Chemicals Co. Ltd* [1972] SCR 569 (Can.); *Buchan v Ortho (Pharmaceutical) Canada Ltd* (1986) 25 DLR (4th) 658.

293 *Clarke v Army and Navy Co-operative Society Ltd* [1903] 1 KB 155.

294 *Medivance Instruments Ltd v Gaslane Pipework Services Ltd*, n. 276 above at [17].

295 Discussed below.

296 *Young & Marten*, n. 275 above; *Rivtow Marine Ltd v Washington Iron Works* [1974] SCR 1189 (Can.); *Dutton v Bognor Regis UDC* [1972] 1 QB 372 (Stamp LJ). Cf *Junior Books Ltd v Veitchi Co. Ltd* [1982] 1 AC 520.

297 *D & F Estates v Church of England Commissioners* [1989] AC 177. In the case of complex products, a difficult question is whether damage caused by a component to the rest of the product is physical or economic loss. See the views of Lords Bridge and Oliver: *ibid.*

upon that physical loss.[298] The House of Lords decision in *Junior Books Ltd v Veitchi Co Ltd*,[299] marooned by recent decisions of the same court drawing back the tide of economic loss liability in negligence, allowed a privity-vaulting factory owner to recover directly from a flooring sub-contractor the cost of prematurely having to replace a defective floor. No explanation was given for why the factory owner chose not to sue the main contractor.[300] In *Lambert v Lewis*,[301] the House of Lords stated its willingness to allow the retail seller of a defective towing hitch to recover the damages liability it owed to the buyer, not from the wholesaler, who could not be identified, but directly from the producer. Since the retail seller was held not liable, however, the claim did not in the end have to be pressed. It is by no means certain that a court would now be so sympathetic to the buyer.

Policy. It would be wrong to see in the above developments an opening up of **8.64** liability for economic loss that would make deep inroads into the privity of contract doctrine. The retrenchment of liability for economic loss[302] has occurred hand in hand with the direction that claimants should protect themselves from loss by contract and seek recourse against their contractual partners.[303] This accords with buyers pursuing their sellers rather than producers. One obvious objection to extending the liability in negligence of the producer is that it outflanks a producer's attempt to limit or exclude contractual liability by a clause to that effect in the contract with the immediate buyer. After initially being attracted to the idea,[304] the House of Lords later preferred to deny recovery altogether than to mould the content of any negligence duty, sounding in economic loss and owed, for example, by a producer to a consumer buyer, to fit the contractual duty of the producer at the top of the distribution chain.[305] Since producers can be reached by way of the indemnity process, it seems a somewhat technical defence to allow them to invoke privity when they are not sheltering behind a wall of limited or excluded liability contained in the immediate purchase contract.

---

[298] See *Muirhead*, n. 285 above, where on the facts the distinction between recoverable and irrecoverable losses is not clearly drawn. Profits from the sale of lobsters killed in a tank as a result of a defective pump should be allowed, but not profits that would have been made if further lobsters had been put into a properly functioning tank.

[299] n. 296 above; D. Cohen (1984) 18 *UBC LR* 289.

[300] The building industry is, however, particularly prone to the risk of insolvency.

[301] n. 287 above.

[302] e.g. *Candlewood Navigation Corpn. Ltd v Mitsui OSK Lines Ltd* [1985] 2 All ER 935; *Leigh and Sillavan Ltd v Aliakmon Shipping Co. Ltd* [1986] AC 785; *Muirhead v Industrial Tank Specialities Ltd*, n. 285 above; *Murphy v Brentwood District Council* [1991] AC 398 (overruling *Anns v Merton London Borough Council* [1978] AC 728).

[303] *Leigh and Sillavan Ltd v Aliakmon Shipping Co. Ltd*, n. 302 above.

[304] *Junior Books v Veitchi Co. Ltd*, n. 296 above.

[305] See *Leigh and Sillavan Ltd v Aliakmon Shipping Co. Ltd*, n. 302 above.

Express Warranty and Guarantee

8.65 **Promoting sales.** If producers choose to promote their products and stimulate sales at the retail level so as to feed commercial activity further down the distribution chain, a strong case can be made for making them liable to the consumer buyer. Unlike their American counterparts, English courts have not been prepared to give such buyers extended implied warranty rights against producers. Nevertheless, there is the possibility of express warranty liability arising out of advertising[306] and of rights promised in producers' guarantees addressed to the consumer buyer.

8.66 **Collateral contract.** Although it has been established for over 100 years that a producer reaching out to a consumer can incur liability on a collateral contract,[307] reported instances of such liability are rare and tend not to involve mass advertising.[308] Where a statement is made by a third party to a consumer contract of sale,[309] the tortious characteristics of warranty are heightened. Suppose that A, a producer, makes a statement to B, a consumer buyer, who then purchases goods from C, a retail seller. According to collateral contract analysis, for A to be liable, A should bargain for B's entry into the contract with C, and B should do so in a way suggestive of accepting an offer of liability from A if the statement turns out to be incorrect. Courts are rarely so pedantic as to observe the niceties of these legal steps in actual decision-making. What appears to count is B's reliance upon the statement.[310] Judicial scepticism about the consumer buyer's reliance was shown in the lower courts in *Lambert v Lewis*, where a retailer sued a manufacturer on a statement that its towing hitch needed no maintenance and was foolproof. The Court of Appeal showed a surprising reluctance to infer a contractual intention on the part of a manufacturer in respect of the contents of its sales literature.[311] The trial judge[312] showed a corresponding readiness to believe that the retailer relied upon the manufacturer's reputation rather than its statements, as though any neat separation could be made between the two.

---

[306] Distinct from the liability of the immediate seller for breach of the implied term of satisfactory quality, so far as the latter is defined to take account of public statements made by a producer: s.14(2D).

[307] *Carlill v Carbolic Smoke Ball Co.* [1893] 1 QB 256. On collateral contracts generally, see K. W. Wedderburn (1959) *CLJ* 58.

[308] *Shanklin Pier v Detel Products Ltd*, n. 62 above; *Wells (Merstham) Ltd v Buckland Sand & Silica Co. Ltd* [1965] 2 QB 170.

[309] Car dealers may be liable for warranty statements that are collateral to a finance contract such as hire purchase: *Andrews v Hopkinson* [1957] 1 QB 229; *Webster v Higgin* [1948] 2 All ER 127.

[310] *Lambert v Lewis*, n. 37 above; *Wells (Merstham) Ltd v Buckland Sand & Silica Co. Ltd*, n. 308 above.

[311] *Lambert v Lewis*, n. 37 above, 262.

[312] [1979] RTR 61, 94.

Manufacturers' guarantees as collateral contracts. Whether the looser **8.67** approach to analysing the steps in a collateral contract is adopted, or a rigorous analysis preferred, many producers' guarantees fall outside a collateral contract since they come too late to affect the consumer buyer's decision to enter into the contract with the retail seller. A good example of this is the guarantee that is to be found inside the packaged goods once purchased.[313]

Reasons for collateral contract liability. The inference of warranty on the part **8.68** of a third party such as a producer is commonly a device that serves to prevent the doctrine of privity of contract from diluting contractual responsibility.[314] Statements from a producer may appease a buyer who then desists from securing a corresponding warranty from the retail seller or from displaying his reliance upon the skill and judgement of that seller. The collateral contract breaks down the insulation of the producer from that retail contract. It may be the case, however, that in special circumstances contracts are structured in such a way as to reflect the parties' common intention that the maker of a statement, not party to a contract of supply, is not to incur any responsibility for the subject matter of the main contract.[315] Apart from this case, though Lord Moulton said over eighty years ago that the incidence of collateral contracts was rare,[316] his words do not accurately record the modern tolerance of collateral warranties. With the disappearance of the parol evidence rule,[317] it is somewhat incongruous to speak of two contracts between the same parties arising out of the same contractual adventure, as opposed to the one contract that is a blend of writing and informal collateral warranty.[318] Nevertheless, Lord Moulton's words may still retain some vitality. In *Lambert v Lewis*,[319] the Court of Appeal indicated that the requirement of contractual intention was harder to satisfy where the alleged collateral warranty came from a third party to the supply contract.[320]

---

[313] Though it would be forensically difficult to establish, a buyer of goods on repeated occasions might be able to establish a warranty on the basis of previous transactions, provided the warranty statement is contained in the packaging on the instant occasion.

[314] See *Shanklin Pier v Detel Products Ltd*, n. 62 above; *Wells (Merstham) Ltd v Buckland Sand & Silica Co. Ltd*, n. 308 above.

[315] *Fuji Seal Europe Ltd v Catalytic Combustion Corpn* [2005] EWHC 1659 (TCC) at [149]–[158]. This is more likely to happen in complex cases involving detailed technical specifications.

[316] *Heilbut, Symons & Co. v Buckleton* n. 8 above, 47.

[317] Law Commission, *Law of Contract [:] The Parol Evidence Rule* (No. 154, 1986, Cmnd 9700). Older authorities supporting the rule are *Morgan v Griffith* (1871) LR 6 Ex. 70; *Erskine v Adeane* (1873) LR 8 Ch. App. 756; *Henderson v Arthur* [1907] 1 KB 10. But see now *City and Westminster Properties (1934) Ltd v Mudd* [1959] Ch. 129; *Brikom Investments Ltd v Carr* [1979] QB 467.

[318] See *J Evans & Son (Portsmouth) Ltd v Andrea Merzario Ltd* [1976] 1 WLR 1078.

[319] n. 37 above.

[320] *Ibid.*, 262. The third party was the producer and the supply contract was between wholesaler and retailer.

8.69 **Proposals to extend producer liability.** Doubts as to the legal liability of a producer on a guarantee were inconclusively addressed by the Department of Trade and Industry in a consultative paper issued in the early 1990s,[321] which canvassed the possibility of making guarantees civilly enforceable by statutory means. The Department at the time also sought guidance on the appropriate measure of damages (whether it be tort or contract), whilst ruling out prescriptive measures to determine the scope and duration of any guarantee that a producer might choose to give. A further question asked at the time was whether the retailer should be jointly and severally liable with the producer on the latter's guarantees. This initiative seems to have been overtaken for practical purposes by an EC initiative which culminated in the Directive dealing with certain aspects of sale of goods and associated guarantees.[322] The process started with a European Commission green paper[323] which, exploring the possibility of a unified European approach, sought reactions to a range of solutions to the problem of 'commercial' guarantees. These possible solutions extended from compulsory to voluntary schemes of regulation,[324] and from the enforcement of guarantees only in the country where they are given to their portability throughout the countries of the European Union. The relevant provision in the Directive, Article 6, stated that: guarantees were to be binding to the extent of their own terms and of associated advertising; guarantees should make it clear that they did not detract from additional rights given by legislation to buyers of consumer goods; and guarantees should, in plain and intelligible language, set out their duration and territorial scope, and the claims procedure to be followed.

8.70 **2002 Regulations.** The Directive was transposed in the form of Sale and Supply of Goods to Consumers Regulations 2002:[325]

(1) Where goods are sold or otherwise supplied to a consumer which are offered with a consumer guarantee, the consumer guarantee takes effect at the time the goods are delivered as a contractual obligation. (2) The guarantor shall ensure that the guarantee sets out in plain and intelligible language the contents of the guarantee and the essential particulars necessary for making claims under the guarantee, notably the duration and territorial scope of the guarantee as well as the name and address of the guarantor.[326]

---

[321] *Consumer Guarantees*, February 1992.
[322] Directive 1999/44/EC of the European Parliament and of the Council of 25 May 1999 (OJ No. L171, 7.7.99, p. 12).
[323] *Green Paper on Guarantees for Consumer Goods and After-Sales Services*, COM(93)509, 15 Nov 1993.
[324] Dealing with the legal enforceability of commercial guarantees, the circumstances governing their presentation, advertising that mentions them, their relationship with 'legal' guarantees arising under the sale contract etc.
[325] SI 2002 No. 3045, reg.15.
[326] Reg. 15 also provides for the guarantee to be in English, if the goods are offered in the United Kingdom, and to be made available in writing or in another durable medium. If the

This provision, regulation 15, does not depend for its implementation upon collateral contract analysis. In particular, the guarantee becomes binding upon delivery of the goods and not upon entry into the main contract of supply. In addition, the provision does not require that a guarantee be given: it merely prescribes the conditions that govern when associated guarantees are provided. When it was first enacted, regulation 15 did not transpose the requirement in the Directive that the guarantee should make it clear that it did not detract from legislative rights.[327] Guarantees have in the past notoriously been used as a vehicle for conveying an exclusion of liability other than in terms of the guarantee itself. Nevertheless, it has been an offence since the 1970s for a guarantee dealing with the fitness, description, or quality of goods to suggest that it supersedes the buyer's statutory implied term rights, and also an offence for the consumer not to be informed that his statutory rights are unaffected.[328] The offence may be committed both by sellers and by those, such as producers, who supply goods that are intended or expected to be the subject of a consumer transaction.[329] In 2008, however, the missing portion of the Directive was enacted when a positive duty was laid down, not merely to avoid misleading the consumer, but to inform the consumer that a guarantee does not derogate from statutory rights concerning the goods.[330] In more general terms, misleading practices in consumer transactions are prohibited.[331] These practices might influence a consumer to take a transactional decision that he might not otherwise have taken. The language is broad enough to include a decision not to pursue rights and remedies outside the guarantee.

Guarantees as exemption clauses.   A final point arising from producers' guaran-   **8.71**
tees concerns their use as a medium for clauses exempting the producer from liability at common law for negligence. There are stringent statutory controls of clauses excluding or limiting liability in consumer transactions. Apart from any difficulty the producer might have at common law in inferring consent to the

---

contents and availability of the guarantee are not in compliance with reg. 15, the consumer may apply for an injunction, which the court may grant on such terms as it thinks fit. The requirement in the Directive that sellers be made liable on associated guarantees given by others was transposed in the form of the added s. 14(2D) of the Sale of Goods Act (an identical provision is in legislation dealing with other supply contracts).

327 Art. 6(2): 'The guarantee shall–state that the consumer has legal rights under applicable national legislation governing the sale of consumer goods and make clear that these rights are not affected by the guarantee'.

328 Consumer Transactions (Restrictions on Statements) Order 1976, SI 1976 No. 1813, as am. by SI 1978 No. 127, reg. 5 (made under the Fair Trading Act 1973).

329 *Ibid.*

330 Consumer Protection from Unfair Trading Regulations 2008, SI 2008 No. 1277, Sch. 2 para. 97, inserting a new para. (2A) into reg. 15 of the Sale and Supply of Goods to Consumers Regulations 2002, n. 325 above.

331 *Ibid.*, reg.5.

exemption from a consumer's acceptance of the guarantee, the Unfair Contract Terms Act 1977 denies legal effect to such exemptions.[332]

Product Liability and Extended Warranty

8.72 **Extended warranty or strict product liability?**   In the common law world, many attempts have been made in the courts and legislatures to confer rights against distributors outside the consumer sale contract. These distributors are usually producers and importers, and those whom it is sought to benefit are consumer users and buyers and other persons injured by defective goods. The avenues of recourse to the outside distributor include strict liability in tort and extended warranty rights. An extended warranty liability would arise if the consumer buyer, for example, were given the benefit of a contractual warranty in the contract between, for example, the producer and wholesaler. A theoretical alternative to this type of extended warranty would be the imposition of the warranty liability of the retail seller, under the consumer sale, on parties such as the producer further up the distribution chain. The fountain head of these initiatives in tort and extended warranty is the United States.

8.73 **Extending producer liability in the US.**   In that country, liability has attached to producers and distributors of defective products for the injuries of a victim not privy to any contract with them on two bases: extended warranty and strict product liability. In the case of extended warranty,[333] the liability of producers to ultimate product users has been justified on the ground that the producer, of an automobile for instance, puts the product 'in the stream of trade and promotes its purchase by the public',[334] and it is reasonably to be contemplated that the injured user may not be the buyer.[335] It was observed in one case, where the consumer buyer of a carpet sued the producer directly, that the intermediate seller was 'simply a way station, a conduit on [the carpet's] trip from manufacturer to consumer'.[336] Furthermore, it was said that the indemnification process based upon privity encouraged circuity[337] of actions and placed an improper burden on the consumer buyer, where the dealer, for one reason or another, was not amenable to suit.[338]

---

[332] S. 5. The Unfair Contract Terms Act 1977, together with the Unfair Terms in Consumer Contracts Regulations 1999, SI 1999 No. 2083, is dealt with in detail in Ch. 9 below.

[333] *Henningsen v Bloomfield Motors Inc.* (1960) 161 A 2d 69; *Spence v Three Rivers Builders & Masonry Supply Inc.* (1958) 90 NW 2d 873.

[334] *Henningsen*, n. 333 above, 84 (overcoming vertical privity).

[335] *Ibid.*, 99–100 (overcoming horizontal privity).

[336] *Santor v Karagheuzian Inc.* (1965) 207 A 2d 305, 309. This cannot be true of all products and all industries.

[337] Multiplicity?

[338] *Santor v Karagheuzian Inc.*, n. 336 above.

Devices to extend liability.   The implied warranty owed by a producer to his   **8.74**
immediate buyer has been extended down the distribution chain by various
devices, including the idea that it runs with products like a covenant runs
with land; that it extends, by way of exception to privity, to anyone who can be
identified as a third-party beneficiary; that public policy demands the producer's
liability; and that warranties are effectively writ large in producers' advertising.[339]
In a number of American jurisdictions, this liability has extended to cases where
the buyer's loss is economic in the sense that there is no physical or personal injury,
but just a buyer's disappointment that the product is as a result of defects not
worth the price paid for it.[340] Article 2 of the Uniform Commercial Code contains
three optional provisions on extended warranty liability for adoption by individual
states,[341] only one of which is open to the reasonable interpretation that it covers
economic loss.

Tort

US position.   A number of states, reflecting a view promoted by section 402A   **8.75**
of the Restatement Second on Torts, favour making the producer of defective
products strictly liable in tort for distributing hazardous products. One advantage
of this approach is that it more readily than warranty accommodates victims, such
as users and outsiders, standing outside the distribution chain and, furthermore,
is not radically divergent in effect from the way that the tort of negligence is often
applied in the case of aberrant products.[342] Although strict liability in tort does
not seem the obvious way to accommodate an economic loss claim for a disappointing bargain, a number of courts have permitted this.[343] The California
courts, on the other hand, have strongly taken the position that contract law, not
tort law, is the proper vehicle for vindicating bargain claims.[344] There is much to
commend this view, though its conceptual purity strikes an odd note in a body of
law dominated by pragmatic considerations.

---

[339] *Santor v Karagheuzian Inc.*, n. 336 above. See also *Nobility Homes of Texas Inc. v Shivers* (1977)
557 SW 2d 77, which articulates the fear of intermediate 'collapsible corporations' in the distribution chain.

[340] e.g. *Santor v Karagheuzian Inc.*, n. 336 above; *Nobility Homes of Texas Inc. v Shivers*, n. 339
above; *Morrow v New Moon Homes Inc.* (1976) 548 P 2d 279. *Contra*, see, e.g., *State of Oregon v
Campbell* (1968) 448 P 2d 215; *John R Dudley Construction Inc. v Drott Manufacturing Co.* (1979)
412 NYS 2d 512: *Williams v General Motors Corpn* (1973) 198 SE 2d 766.

[341] UCC Art. 2–318.

[342] See *Grant v Australian Knitting Mills Ltd*, n. 289 above.

[343] The alternative holding in *Santor v Karagheuzian Inc.*, n. 336 above. See also *Mead Corpn v
Allendale Mutual Insurance Co.* (1979) 465 F Supp. 355.

[344] *Seely v White Motor Co.* (1965) 403 P 2d 145.

Reform

8.76 **Canadian proposals.** A number of Canadian jurisdictions have consumer legislation that incorporates extended warranty rights.[345] Extended warranty liability for personal injury and property damage was recommended in 1972 by the Ontario Law Reform Commission.[346] The Commission's 1979 report on *Sale of Goods*,[347] never enacted, favoured extended warranty protection for buyers. Although this proposal was largely actuated by economic loss claims, including inherent loss of value, it was wide enough to extend also to personal injury and property damage.

8.77 **Arguments for producers' economic loss liability.** Despite being unpersuaded by them, the Ontario Law Reform Commission rehearsed the various arguments justifying the exclusion of liability for economic loss to remote buyers as follows.[348] First, there is not the same case for deterrence in economic loss vindication as there is for physical loss. Secondly, it would be anomalous to grant recovery in economic loss against a producer for breach of a strict warranty when the tort of negligence is ungenerous in compensating such loss. Thirdly, commercial buyers at least ought to be able to protect their interests by private bargain. And fourthly, economic loss liability would increase a producer's enterprise risks and make it difficult to plan future costs and secure insurance cover. Dismissing these arguments, the Commission was persuaded by other reasons for extending economic loss liability, namely, that producers reach out to the consuming public and the line between express and implied warranties is commonly thin; that it is often a matter of mere chance whether a defective product causes physical or economic injury; that the producer's economic loss liability is a known risk since it is already borne in respect of the immediate buyer; that an intervening bankruptcy in the distribution chain might exclude a deserving warranty claimant; and that extended warranty recourse might cut out wasteful indemnity actions. A modified version of the proposed provision was adopted as uniform law but has never been enacted.[349]

8.78 **UK consultation.** In 1992, the Department of Trade and Industry in the UK, in a consultative paper,[350] launched a tentative proposal that producers (and where

---

[345] Notably Saskatchewan and New Brunswick. See M. Bridge, *Sale of Goods* (Butterworths, Toronto, 1988), 540–2. There is also farm implement legislation of long standing that makes interesting inroads into the doctrine of privity: *ibid.* 539–40.

[346] *Report on Consumer Warranties and Guarantees in the Sale of Goods.*

[347] See also the *Report on Products Liability* (1979).

[348] *Report on Sale of Goods* (1979), i, 245–7.

[349] Uniform Sale of Goods Act 1981, s. 50. See Alberta Institute of Law Research and Reform, *The Uniform Sale of Goods Act* (Report No. 38, 1982), 125–6; Manitoba Law Reform Commission, *Uniform Sale of Goods Act* (Report No. 57, 1983).

[350] *Consumer Guarantees*, Feb. 1992, 8–9.

relevant importers) should be liable along with the retail seller for the satisfactory quality of the goods. The proposal was a vague one. It seemed not to extend to the fitness-for-purpose implied term in the consumer sale contract. What was clearer, however, was that the producer would be bound by the retail sale contract; the proposal was not that the consumer buyer would derive rights from the sale contract to which the producer was a party. It was therefore a case of extended liability rather than extended warranty. The consultative paper advised that caution might be needed in that the producer would not normally control the price of the goods paid by the consumer buyer or the description of the goods by the retail seller, both important elements in the present statutory definition of satisfactory quality. It seemed also that the producer was not to be allowed to shelter behind any exclusion clauses in its contract of sale with the wholesaler or retailer, as the case may be. The proposal was unclear on whether the liability of producer and retailer would be joint and several. Nor was the proposal informative about the mechanics of rejection of the goods and contractual termination.

Contracts (Rights of Third Parties) Act 1999.   At one time in the course of its **8.79** passage through Parliament, the Contracts (Rights of Third Parties) Act 1999 might have been used as a vehicle for third parties to take advantage of warranty rights in contracts to which they were not privy. It allows contracting parties to grant third parties direct rights of enforcement of the contract and also contains machinery that restricts the freedom of the contracting parties to take away those rights.[351]

Express identification of third party.   Section 1 of the Act creates enforcement **8.80** rights for third parties. A third party is defined as someone who is 'not a party to the contract'.[352] To acquire direct enforcement rights, the third party need not be named in the contract. It is enough that the third party is expressly identified by name or as a member of a class or as answering to a particular description, even if the third party is not in existence at the contract date.[353] But the third party must be expressly identified by one of these three means (name, description, or class). Third parties are able under section 1 to enforce, not the contract as such, but one or more terms of the contract. Apart from the example given in the Act of exemption clauses, the Act does not define a term of the contract, though the notion of enforcing terms seems to presuppose that they are promises if they are not exemption clauses.

---

[351] For a fuller treatment, see M. Bridge, (2001) 5 *Edinburgh Law Review* 85–102.
[352] S. 1(1). The Act does not define 'party to the contract' but this will be clear enough in most cases.
[353] S. 1(3).

8.81 **Direct enforcement by third party.** Where the contract does not expressly provide that a third party may enforce a term in his own name, the third party may
do so only if the following two conditions are fulfilled: first, the contract term
'purports' to confer a benefit on the third party, and secondly, there is nothing to
rebut the statutory presumption that, as a beneficiary, the third party may enforce
the term.[354] The Act does not define the meaning of 'purports' but it is apparent
from the Law Commission Report that the word signifies the intention of the
contracting parties that the third party shall obtain a benefit.[355] It is not clear how
strong the intention must be or whether it can be said to exist at all if there is
another and more dominant intention. It may be, too, that the contracting parties
approach the matter with different states of mind. One may positively wish to
confer a benefit; the other may wish merely to do something compliant with the
other's wishes. The most likely way of purporting to confer a benefit is for the term
to state expressly that a benefit is being conferred on the third party without making mention of enforcement. Nevertheless, a contract term may also purport to
confer a benefit by implication. In lengthy contractual documents, for example, a
third party may be expressly named, described, or identified in the contract but
not in the contract term itself. The original Law Commission draft Bill referred to
third-party beneficiaries enforcing a contract in which they were expressly named,
described, or identified.[356] So did the Bill when it was introduced in the House of
Lords. When the Bill was amended to provide that the third-party beneficiary
might enforce the term, instead of the contract, there was no corresponding
change to require the third party to be named, described, or identified in the
term.

8.82 **Implied terms problem.** This alteration to the Bill has in fact cut down the
rights of third parties in sale of goods contracts. Suppose that goods are bought
from a seller as a wedding present and turn out to be defective, thus bringing
about a breach of the statutory implied terms of satisfactory quality and fitness for
purpose in section 14 of the Sale of Goods Act. In the Law Commission's view, the
store has promised to confer a benefit on the donees,[357] but the difficulty lies in
identifying the relevant term or terms of the contract. If an express warranty can
be found, then the third party may upon a proper construction of the warranty
obtain rights of direct enforcement. But the Contracts (Rights of Third Parties)
Act does not amend the implied terms in the Sale of Goods Act. In no sense are
these varied or modified in individual contracts of sale to meet the case of the third-
party donee. They do not expressly or impliedly confer a benefit on third parties.

---

[354] Ss. 1(1)(b), (2).
[355] Paras 7.18(ii), 7.25.
[356] Cl. 1(1)(b).
[357] Para. 7.41 (Illustration 14).

Direct enforcement depends, as seen above, on the term and not the contract benefiting the third party.

Irrevocability of third party's right. The beneficiary's right of direct enforce- **8.83** ment, once granted, may not in designated circumstances be taken away by the contracting parties. The circumstances are: first, the third party has relied upon the promise and the promisor is actually aware of this;[358] secondly, the third party has actually relied upon the promise and the promisor, without knowing this, could reasonably have foreseen such reliance;[359] and thirdly, the third party by words or conduct has communicated his assent to the term to the promisor.[360] The Act does not state what is meant by reliance, though it must be more than mere knowledge by the third party. Whether the third party must alter his position or go further still and rely to his detriment is unclear from a reading only of the Act. The Law Commission, however, was clear that the reliance need not be prejudicial,[361] when stating somewhat dogmatically that under simple reliance it is easier to justify the award of expectation damages for non-performance. There is no discretionary element in the enforcement of the third party's rights in the Act, which gives some further support for the view that detriment is not needed. Furthermore, the absence of detriment is in harmony with a third party's ability to acquire irrevocable rights upon communicating his assent to the promisor. Contracting parties who feel concern over the extent to which the third party is able to take away their freedom of action are free to stipulate in the contract for a right to vary or rescind the contract without the 'consent'[362] of the third party or for the third party's rights to become irrevocable in a way other than provided in the Act.

European green paper. A similar proposal to that made by the Department **8.84** of Trade and Industry was found in a green paper issued shortly afterwards by the European Commission.[363] This document mentioned the illogicality of having a consumer buyer seek recourse only against a retailer, who had no influence on the production process. The Commission was also struck by the 'counter-intuitive' nature of a producer's liability for physical injury to the person and property of individuals[364] and immunity from claims that the product was

---

[358] S. 2(1)(b).

[359] S. 2(1)(c).

[360] S. 2(1)(a), (2)(a).

[361] Para. 9.19.

[362] Note the careful way the Act in s. 2 distinguishes between consent and assent.

[363] *Green Paper on Guarantees for Consumer Goods and After-Sales Services*, n. 323 above, 86–8. See S. Weatherill (1994) 110 *LQR* 545. An earlier attempt to legislate in this area by introducing the subject inappropriately into the Directive on Unfair Terms in Consumer Contracts was checked by the Council of Ministers.

[364] See EEC Directive 85/374 [1985] OJ L210/29 and the Consumer Protection Act 1987.

economically disappointing. The liability proposed, a joint one with the seller of defective goods, was to be of a 'quasi-subsidiary' nature, in that the producer would be brought in only if it were impossible or onerous to sue the seller. Moreover, the contract of sale would not as such be terminated *qua* the producer, who could nevertheless be called upon to cure the seller's defective performance and to answer for the buyer's 'direct losses'. This proposal did not prosper. The eventual Directive on Consumer Sales Guarantees[365] retreated from the model of consumer access to the producer and reinforced the consumer's conventional rights against the immediate seller. There remained in the Directive, nevertheless, some relic of the earlier proposal in the form of Article 4, which was never transposed in English law:

> Where the final seller is liable to the consumer because of a lack of conformity resulting from an act or omission by the producer, a previous seller in the same chain of contracts or any other intermediary, the final seller shall be entitled to pursue remedies against the person or persons liable in the distribution chain. The person or persons liable against whom the final seller may pursue remedies, together with the relevant actions and conditions of exercise, shall be determined by national law.

It was no cause for surprise that no steps were taken to implement this provision in English law; it does not seem to direct Member States to take any action at all, except possibly to see to it that someone would be held liable to the final seller.[366] The European Commission's original version of Article 4 revealed a more ambitious purpose:

> Where the final seller is liable to the consumer because of a lack of conformity resulting from an act of commission or omission by the producer, a previous seller in the same chain of contracts or any other intermediary, the final seller shall be entitled to pursue remedies against the responsible person, under the conditions laid down by national law.

Had this version survived, the role of national law would have been limited to the circumstances in which the final seller might exercise rights against the person responsible; the rights themselves, however, would have been mandated by the Directive.

The Consumer Protection Act 1987

8.85 **Strict liability in tort.** Pursuant to a European Directive on Product Liability, the Consumer Protection Act was passed in 1987.[367] The origin of the Directive lay in the need to standardize the liability of producers so as to bring about level

---

[365] Directive 1999/44/EEC.

[366] See M. Bridge, 'Article 4 and the Right of Redress' in M. Bianca and S. Grundmann (eds), *EU sales directive[:]Commentary* (Intersentia, 2002), 179–210.

[367] 85/374/EEC [1985] OJ L210/29. See J. Stapleton, 'Three Problems with the New Product Liability' in P. Cane and J. Stapleton (eds), *Essays for Patrick Atiyah* (Oxford, 1991); *ibid., Product*

competitive conditions within the Member States of the European Community, though there are other influencing considerations, such as the perceived incongruity of buyers and non-buyers having different legal rights, and of a consumer having recourse only against a retail seller when defects in the goods are the responsibility of the producer. The Consumer Protection Act transposing the Directive lays down a form of strict tortious liability on producers to those injured by defective products. Although the Directive does not have direct effect, it has been consulted, in accordance with section 1(1) of the Act, in aid of interpreting the Act.[368] A complaint had previously been made by the Commission against the UK government for a defective transposition of the Directive. Though dismissed, it was done so in the expectation that cases later to be decided under the Act would implement the Directive with the aid of section 1(1), which provides that '[t]his Part shall have effect for the purpose of making such provision as is necessary in order to comply with the product liability Directive and shall be construed accordingly'.[369]

Products and goods. Liability under the Act arises in respect of a 'product', **8.86** which includes goods (as well as their components and raw materials) and electricity.[370] 'Goods' are then defined to include 'substances', which themselves include liquids, vapours and gases, and crops and fixtures.[371] Overall, products for the purposes of the 1987 Act are broader than the Sale of Goods Act definition of goods.[372] Section 2 of the Act makes liable the 'producer',[373] who is defined as the producer or the person who won, abstracted, or processed the product. The extension beyond manufacturers is clearly needed to bring in those producing minerals and forms of energy.

'Producer'. The word 'producer' also includes importers and those who attach **8.87** their own brands to a product,[374] such as a supermarket chain. It excludes the suppliers of game and agricultural produce that have not yet undergone an industrial process,[375] as well as those who do not supply in the course of a business.[376]

Liability (Butterworths, 1994); C J. Miller and R. S. Goldberg, *Product Liability* (2nd edn, Oxford, 2004).

[368] *A v National Blood Authority (No. 2)* [2001] 3 All ER 289; G. Howells and M. Mildred (2002) 65 *MLR* 95; R. S. Goldberg (2002) 10 *Med LR* 165. The parties and the court indeed went directly to the terms of the Directive in the proceedings.

[369] *Ibid.*, at [2].

[370] S. 1(2).

[371] S. 45(1). See *AB v South West Water Services Ltd* [1993] QB 507 (water).

[372] See Ch. 2 above.

[373] S. 2(2)(a). A producer can be a retailer adding hot water to a teabag: *B v McDonald's Restaurants Ltd* [2002] EWHC 490 at [74].

[374] S. 2(2)(b)(c).

[375] S. 2(4).

[376] S. 4(1)(c).

There is also a provision designed to ensure that intermediate sellers cooperate in passing on the names of producers where a request is made within a reasonable time by injured persons who cannot practicably identify the producers themselves.[377] Those sellers are themselves deemed to be producers if they do not, or even cannot, supply the information sought or the names of their immediate sellers (to whom the injured person might then make a further enquiry). Those sellers need not directly have supplied the product to the claimant.[378]

8.88 **Producer's liability.** A producer's liability is strict and does not depend upon fault[379] or foreseeability of harm.[380] It exists where 'any damage is caused wholly or partly by a defect in a product'.[381] A 'defect' exists if 'the safety of the product is not such as persons generally are entitled to expect'.[382] The language of section 3(1) thus contains the germ of a state-of-the-art (or development risks) defence, recited in express terms in the following section. Its wording also permits account to be taken of the essential and unavoidable character of certain types of goods.[383] Cigarettes are inherently dangerous to health; guns are designed to be handled with great care by the user. The danger they pose, whilst it cannot be eliminated, can however be reduced by means of warnings, instructions, safety features, and the like. The burden of proof is on the claimant to show that the product is defective.[384]

8.89 **Expectations.** In determining what persons generally are entitled to expect, the Directive, expressed in simpler language than the Act, makes specific mention in

---

[377] S. 2(3).

[378] This follows from the language of s. 2(3).

[379] *A v National Blood Authority (No. 2)*, n. 368 above at [31], citing Newdick at (1987) 103 *LQR* 288 and [1988] *CLJ* 455.

[380] *Abouzaid v Mothercare (UK) Ltd* (Unreported, 21 December 2000) at [38]. Nevertheless, the Act permits the defence of contributory negligence to be raised by the defendant producer against the claimant's strict liability claim: s. 6(4).

[381] S. 2(1). For a failure to prove cause, see *Loveday v Renton The Times*, 31 Mar. 1988 (pertussis vaccine).

[382] S. 3(1). See C. Newdick [1988] *CLJ* 455. The language of s. 3(1) is hortative: what counts is what persons are entitled to expect, not what in fact they do expect, whether this is higher or lower than entitlement. It is a matter of 'objectively assessed legitimate expectation': *A v National Blood Authority (No. 2)*, n. 368 above at [31]. It has also been said that the 'product is to be judged by the expectations of the public at large, as determined by the Court': *Abouzaid v Mothercare (UK) Ltd*, n. 380 above at [25].

[383] 'A harmful characteristic in a product, which has led to injury or damage, may or may not be a defect as so defined . . .': *A v National Blood Authority (No. 2)*, n. 368 above at [31]. No complaint may be made about certain types of product with harmful characteristics by their very nature or intended use—'knives, guns and poison . . . alcohol, tobacco, perhaps foie gras': *ibid*. In addition: 'Drugs with harmful side-effects may fall within this category . . . the known dangerous characteristics need not be the desired one—eg carcinogenicity in tobacco' (*ibid.*).

[384] This was common ground in *A v National Blood Authority (No. 2)*, n. 368 above at [31], [46]. Although the Act is silent on this matter, the Directive in Art. 4 is very clear: 'The injured person shall be required to prove the damage, the defect and the causal relationship between defect and damage'.

Article 6 of three factors: the 'presentation of the product;'[385] the 'use to which it could reasonably be expected to be put';[386] and the 'time when the product was put into circulation'.[387] These factors, however, are not exclusive.[388] The issue of a danger that cannot be eliminated, in combination with what persons were entitled to expect, presented itself in *A v National Blood Authority* in relation to the Hepatitis C virus in transfused blood, where it was held that blood infected by the virus was defective because of a legitimate expectation in members of the public that it would be free of the virus. The blood was a non-standard product that deviated from the norm, which was uncontaminated blood, and there had been no warnings or adverse publicity to lower the legitimate expectations of the public;[389] the knowledge of the medical profession that the virus could not be eliminated could not therefore be taken into consideration in determining whether the blood was defective.[390]

Better products.   Article 6 goes on to state that a product is not defective solely   **8.90** because a better product is later put into circulation.[391] It does not identify whether it is the defendant or some other person who circulates the better product, but the better view, since it leads into another provision giving a state-of-the-art defence, is that it refers to persons in general. This provision again echoes the state-of-the-art defence in the following section, having the particular effect that legitimate expectations are to be judged at the time the product is put into circulation and are not to be elevated with the aid of hindsight.

State of the art.   In section 4(1)(e), it is a defence if the defendant is able to show   **8.91** that 'the state of scientific and technical knowledge at the relevant time' was such

---

385   The corresponding language of s. 3(2)(a) of the Act is 'the manner in which, and purposes for which, the product has been marketed, its get-up, the use of any mark in relation to the product and any instructions for, or warnings with respect to, doing or refraining form doing anything with or in relation to the product'.

386   Section 3(2)(b) states 'what might reasonably be expected to be done with or in relation to the product'.

387   Section 3(2)(c) states 'the time when the product was supplied by its producer to another'. The expression 'put into circulation' is used more than once in the Directive, where it is not defined, but it is not used in the Act.

388   *A v National Blood Authority (No. 2)*, n. 368 above at [34].

389   The legitimate expectations of tea drinkers were met by a safety system of training employees to cap the drinks in *B v McDonald's Restaurants Ltd*, n. 373 above at [77].

390   *A v National Blood Authority (No. 2)*, n. 368 above, at [80]. The court reached its conclusions on the basis of a number of agreed points, e.g., that liability was strict and that the burden of proof of defect was on the claimant, but it also conducted a very wide-ranging survey of the academic literature and of the decisions of other national courts on the transposed Directive. Cf *Richardson v LRC Products Ltd* [2000] PIQR 164, 170–1, where the conclusion reached, that a fractured condom was not defective under the Act given the existence of 'inexplicable failures' with condoms from time to time, must be doubted.

391   The Act states in s. 3(2) that 'nothing in this section shall require a defect to be inferred from the fact alone that the safety of a product which is supplied after that time is greater than the safety of the product in question'.

that 'a producer of products of the same description as the product in question might be expected to have discovered the defect if it had existed in his products while they were under his control'.[392] This appears to come close to a passport to exemption from liability for those, such as drug companies, who manufacture innovative products. Yet liability under the Act is quite different from negligence, in that the burden of raising the defence, which does not look easy to discharge, rests upon the producer.[393] In *Richardson v LRC Products Ltd*, the trial judge said: 'This provision is, to my mind, not apt to protect a defendant in the case of a defect of a known character, merely because there is no test which is apt to reveal its existence in every case.'[394] In addition, according to Pill LJ in *Abouzaid v Mothercare (UK) Ltd*: 'Knowledge of previous accidents is not an ingredient necessary to a finding that a defect, within the meaning of the section, is present. Different considerations apply to negligence at common law where foreseeability of injury, as defined in the authorities, is a necessary ingredient.'[395] Furthermore, reference has been made to the 'very restricted conditions, whereby a producer who has taken all possible precautions (certainly all legitimately expectable precautions, if the terms of Article 6, as construed by [counsel for the defendants], are to be cross-referred) *remains* liable unless that producer can show that "*the state of scientific and technical knowledge* [anywhere and anyone's in the world, provided reasonably accessible] *was not such as to enable the existence of the defect to be discovered*".'[396] Section 4(1)(e), so far as applicable, does provide some relief from the stringency of section 3: the latter will not save from liability a producer where the risks are unknown, but section 4(1)(e) may do.[397] Section 4(1)(e), however, does not provide protection to the producer where there is knowledge of a defect.[398] The notion of 'defect' is not on the face of the Act differentially interpreted according to whether the injury caused by the product arises out of defective design, defective manufacture, or defective instructions or warnings accompanying the product. The state-of-the-art defence, however, is peculiarly apt in matters of design.

8.92 **Additional defences.** Section 4 contains additional defences. The first of these defences is that the defect is 'attributable to compliance with any requirement imposed by or under any enactment or with any Community obligation'.[399]

---

[392] It is arguable that the defence is more broadly drawn than Art. 7(e) of the Directive—'the state of scientific and technical knowledge at the time when [the producer] put the product into circulation was not such as to enable the existence of the defect to be discovered'.
[393] The burden is on the defendant: *Abouzaid v Mothercare (UK) Ltd*, n. 380 above at [10].
[394] n. 390 above, 171.
[395] n. 380 above at [29].
[396] *A v National Blood Authority (No. 2)*, n. 368 above at [64] (original emphasis).
[397] *Ibid.*, at [78].
[398] *A v National Blood Authority (No. 2)*, n. 368 above at [84].
[399] S. 4(1)(a).

The second defence is that the defendant did not in fact 'supply the product to another',[400] and so did not put the product in circulation. The third defence is that the supply of the product did not take place in the course of the defendant's business[401] and that, if the defendant did produce, brand, or import the product into a member State from a non-member State, it was not with a view to profit.[402] The fourth defence is that the defect did not exist in the product 'at the relevant time'.[403] The relevant time is when the goods were put into circulation by a producer, brander, or importer supplying the goods to another;[404] alternatively, if the defendant is an intermediate seller and deemed producer, because the producer is not or cannot be identified, the time when the producer last supplied the product.[405] In the case of electricity, this is supplied at the time it is generated.[406] If a product is contaminated at some stage in its journey between the producer and the claimant, the defect in the form of the contaminant will not have been present at the relevant time, but if the producer has neglected to use an effective product security device, the failure to do so may amount to a defect, which will be present at the relevant time. The fifth defence is that the defect was in a 'subsequent product' in which the 'product in question' had been comprised in the allegedly defective product, and was 'wholly attributable to the design of the subsequent product or to compliance by the producer of the product in question with instructions given by the producer of the subsequent product'. The expression 'wholly attributable' should ensure that this defence will rarely be successfully raised.

Damage. The damage for which a producer may be liable is 'death or personal injury or any loss of or damage to any property (including land)'.[407] It can include a claim for loss of future earnings.[408] If a claim is made for damage to property, this has to be property of a description ordinarily intended for private use, occupation or consumption, and intended by the person suffering loss or damage for his own private use, occupation, or consumption.[409] In *A v National Blood Authority*,[410]   **8.93**

---

[400] S. 4(1)(b).
[401] In s. 45(1), 'business' is defined as including 'a trade or profession and the activities of a professional or trade association or of a local authority or other public authority'.
[402] S. 4(1)(c).
[403] S. 4(1)(d).
[404] S. 4(2)(a).
[405] S. 4(2)(b). If the draftsman had tried to make the meaning of this more obscure, whilst continuing with the English language and obeying its rules of syntax, it is doubtful that he would have been successful. S. 4(2)(b) *seems* to refer back to deemed producers in s. 2(3). It may be thought rather difficult for a deemed producer defendant to identify the time when a producer, brander, or importer last supplied the product in those cases where the deemed producer is not able to identify the producer.
[406] S. 4(2).
[407] S. 5(1).
[408] *Abouzaid v Mothercare (UK) Ltd*, n. 380 above.
[409] S. 5(3). The provision does not state that the claimant should own the property.
[410] n. 368 above.

the defendants, drawing upon authority measuring damages according to the nature of the duty imposed,[411] argued that their liability should be limited to the adverse consequences flowing from a failure to screen the infected blood, which would have yielded a measure based on the loss of a chance.[412] The court, however, preferred the claimant's argument that the 'damage to be compensated to the claimant is the damage caused by a defect in a product, and not by any conduct, wrongful or otherwise, or breach of duty'.[413] This might include the cost of future treatment for the claimants,[414] as well as loss relating to social handicap, employment stigma, and the costs and availability of financial services and insurance coverage.[415] The damage for which a producer is liable does not, however, include damage done by the product to itself,[416] in reality a form of economic loss. The claim in such a case is that value for money is not received when a product does not last as long as it ought to have done. To prevent trivial claims from being advanced, the Act does not rely only upon the usual cost deterrent to small-scale litigation: it disallows the award of damages in property cases where the amount recoverable would not exceed £275.[417]

8.94 **Claimants.** Rather surprisingly, the Act does not explicitly state who may bring an action against the producer. It must necessarily be someone who suffers injury as defined by the Act, an injury caused by a defect in the product. Section 7 refers in general terms, for the purpose of preventing the disclaimer of a producer's liability under the Act by notice or contractual clause, to 'a person who has suffered damage'. There is no reason to exclude anyone who suffers the relevant injury,[418] for example, a motorist injured as a result of the defective steering on another motorist's car. There would appear to be no need that the claimant be a retail buyer or a member of the buyer's family.

8.95 **Limitations.** A claim brought under the Act must be brought within three years from the later of date on which the cause of action accrued and the date of the claimant's knowledge.[419] Otherwise, the period is ten years.[420]

---

[411] *Banque Bruxelles Lambert SA v Eagle Star Insurance Co.* [1997] AC 191.

[412] n. 380 above at [177]. They would or might have suffered from hepatitis B in any event.

[413] *Ibid.,* at [178].

[414] *Ibid.,* at [217]–[219].

[415] *Ibid.,* [219]–[225]. Compensation may also be given to carers providing gratuitous services to claimants: *ibid.,* at [226]–[231].

[416] S. 5(2).

[417] S. 5(4).

[418] In *Abouzaid v Mothercare (UK) Ltd,* n. 380 above, it was a 12-year-old child helping his mother.

[419] Limitation Act 1980, s. 11A(4), which does not say to what the knowledge relates.

[420] *Ibid.,* s. 11A(3), which extinguishes the right of action.

Issuers of Credit Cards

Credit.   The provision of credit to accommodate a buyer, who cannot or does   **8.96**
not wish to pay on cash-on-delivery terms, multiples the number of sale of goods
transactions concluded. Credit may be given by the seller to the buyer, the seller's
own cash flow needs being accommodated by a financier, such as a bank advancing credit to the seller and taking a mix of fixed and floating charges over the seller's
assets. Alternatively, credit may be advanced by a third party to the buyer. There
are numerous ways in which this may be done. The buyer may have a simple overdraft facility that permits funds to be drawn down without any reference to the
bank of the purpose of the buyer's transaction. Alternatively, the buyer may enter
into a financing agreement directly with the third party, who supplies the goods to
the buyer on hire purchase, conditional sale, or finance lease terms, after purchasing the goods from the seller. The financier in such a case will be responsible for
the description, quality, and fitness of the goods under legislation whose identity
turns upon the nature of the supply agreement.[421] Instead of itself being the supplier of goods to the buyer, however, the financier may come in later by taking an
assignment of the contractual rights of the retail supplier of the goods under the
terms of a block discounting arrangement.[422] That supplier will already have supplied those goods, usually on hire purchase or conditional sale terms. When it acts
as an assignee in this way, the financier does not assume primary responsibility for
the matters of description, quality, and fitness, but takes the supplier's right to
payment subject to the usual defences and set-off entitlements that an account
debtor can raise against an assignor.[423] There is no question here of any ancillary
liability on the part of the financier, giving rise in appropriate cases to a damages
claim by the buyer against the financier. But a credit card issuer does incur ancillary liability when a buyer acquires goods under a contract of sale with the aid of a
credit card issued by a third party. The principal difference between the credit card
issuer and the assignee financier is that, in the former case, the cardholder is perfectly aware of the role of the card issuer in facilitating entry into the supply transaction; in the latter case, though the availability of block discounting arrangements
encourages the supplier to provide goods on credit terms, it will normally be on
terms by which the supplier continues to collect payments on behalf of the financier from a buyer or hirer who has no knowledge of the assignment.

---

[421] Sale of Goods Act 1979, ss. 13–15 (conditional sale); Supply of Goods (Implied Terms) Act
1973, ss. 9–10 (hire purchase); Supply of Goods and Service Act 1982, ss. 3–4 (finance lease).
[422] See R. Goode, *Commercial Law* (3rd edn, Penguin 2004), Ch. 27.
[423] Law of Property Act 1925, s. 136; *Government of Newfoundland v Newfoundland Railway Co.*
(1888) 13 App. Cas. 199; *Young v Kitchin* (1878) 3 Ex D 127. In regulated consumer credit agreements,
the financier cannot improve its position by having the supplier procure the acceptance of a bill of
exchange from, or the making of a promissory note by, a consumer, before taking a subsequent transfer
of that negotiable instrument as a holder in due course: Consumer Credit Act 1974, ss. 123, 125.

8.97 **Reasons for card issuer liability.** The case for liability on the part of the credit card issuer is that, whilst it may not directly supply the goods, yet it is a 'connected lender' who assists in the supply of goods.[424] The Crowther Committee on Consumer Credit[425] noted that

> there is in fact a close business between an issuer and the suppliers who have agreed to accept that issuer's credit cards. The issuer, through the provision of the credit card, swells the turnover of the supplier, and for conferring this benefit usually receives by way of discount an agreed percentage of the invoice price of the goods or services supplied. Moreover, a cardholder dealing with a reputable issuer has every reason to assume that the issuer will list only reputable suppliers.[426]

The Committee recommended that the credit card issuer should be answerable for the supplier's non-performance, noting that the issuer would have the practical ability to exercise an indemnity claim against the supplier by way of set-off. The issuer was in a better position than the cardholder to obtain satisfaction from the supplier.[427]

8.98 **Issuers and supplier liability.** Credit card issuers are made liable for breaches of contract by suppliers in section 75(1) of the Consumer Credit Act 1974. Section 75(1) does not impose liability on credit card issuers *eo nomine*, but makes them liable because the debtor has entered into a particular type of 'debtor-creditor-supplier' agreement, namely, 'a restricted-use credit agreement which falls within section 11(1)(b)[428] and is made by the creditor under pre-existing arrangements, or in contemplation of future arrangements, between himself and the supplier'.[429] The pre-existing arrangements are those by which the supplier undertakes to accept the credit card in payment[430] and the credit is provided on a

---

[424] An assignee financier is not a lender. It does not advance credit to the buyer of the goods; that is done by the supplier.

[425] Cmnd 4596, 1971. For a survey of the American position on connected lender liability around this time, see M. Bridge (1977) 28 *NILQ* 382, 411–27.

[426] Para. 6.12.9. The weakness of this reasoning lies in its assumption that liability is incurred by unreputable suppliers, whereas perfectly respectable suppliers incur liability under ss. 13–14 of the Sale of Goods Act and related legislation and the credit card issuer's liability that followed on from the recommendations of the Crowther Committee is a joint and several primary liability, and not a secondary liability to be called in only if and when the supplier refuses or otherwise fails to give the cardholder satisfaction.

[427] Cmnd 4596, 1971, para. 6.12.10.

[428] Because it finances a transaction between a debtor and a supplier who is not the creditor.

[429] S. 75 refers back to debtor-creditor-supplier agreements falling under either s. 12(b) or (c). The type that arises where a credit card is used is the section 12(b) type (restricted use). The agreement must be one that is not exempted from the Act, which means that the debtor must be an individual and the credit supplied, if the individual is acting for business purposes, must not exceed £25,000 (ss. 8 and 16B of the Consumer Credit Act 1974). For consumers, the £25,000 upper limit was removed with effect from 6 April 2008. There is also a provision (s. 16A, which came into effect on 6 April 2008) allowing for regulations to be made to exempt high net worth debtors (which is unlikely on its terms to apply to a case involving credit cards).

[430] Consumer Credit Act 1987, s. 187.

restricted-use basis[431] because, though the restriction is hardly a narrow one, the card can be used only with suppliers who have agreed to honour it.[432] The liability imposed on the card issuer by section 75(1) is a 'like claim' to the one the card-holder has against the supplier. Instead of the card issuer's ancillary liability being a secondary one, the card issuer is jointly and severally liable with the supplier.[433] Consequently, the claim against the card issuer is not limited to the amount owed to the card issuer as a result of the transaction and the cardholder may have a substantial damages claim against the card issuer going beyond a mere defence to non-payment of the amount owed to the card issuer under the individual transaction. Moreover, the card issuer cannot contract out of its liability to the cardholder.[434] The card issuer, nevertheless, has an indemnity claim against the supplier under section 75(2), except where the indemnity is excluded by agree-ment between them.

Use of cards overseas.   Section 75(1) has attracted surprisingly little attention in   **8.99** the reported cases. The very imposition of liability on credit card issuers seems to carry the idea of connected lender liability to its very limits, especially when the credit card is used, as so often it is, as a convenient and near-universal substitute for cash,[435] whose users would find any process of careful vetting of suppliers to determine their reputable character as an inconvenient impediment to the cash features of the card.[436] Invoking the liability of the card issuer is not the first response of a buyer who has acquired defective goods, when there is an available seller or a producer who has given a guarantee. Recourse against the card issuer, nevertheless, is the resort of a cardholder for whom action against an insolvent seller is not a practical matter, or who faces the difficult prospect of overseas litiga-tion under an unknown applicable law against an uncooperative seller. In *Office of*

---

431   *Ibid.*, s. 11(1)(b).

432   See *Office of Fair Trading v Lloyds Bank plc* [2006] EWCA Civ 268 at [56]–[60].

433   In addition, any negotiations conducted between the supplier and the cardholder prior to the conclusion of the supply contract are deemed under s. 56(1)(c) to be conducted by the supplier on behalf of the card issuer where the debtor-creditor-supplier agreement is of the type where joint and several liability between creditor and supplier is imposed under s.75. The effect of s. 56(1)(c) is that the card issuer will incur primary liability. It should mean, for example, that the card issuer may incur liability in damages under s. 2(1) of the Misrepresentation Act 1967, though beyond that it is difficult to appreciate the reach of the provision. It seems unlikely that the cardholder using the card to acquire a car under a contract of sale could reject the car *qua* the card issuer and claim the return of the price, or that damages in lieu of rescission could be awarded against the card issuer under s.2(2).

434   Consumer Credit Act, s. 173(1).

435   S. 75 does not apply when debit cards are used: no credit is extended to cardholders in such cases.

436   A particular feature of liability in cases where goods or services are supplied abroad is that the card issuer in the United Kingdom will not have selected the supplier; that will have been done by an independent card issuer in the country concerned. The United Kingdom card issuer is nevertheless liable for breaches of contract by this supplier under s. 75.

Fair Trading v Lloyds TSB Bank plc,[437] the question was whether section 75(1) applied where the card was used abroad to acquire goods and services under agreements governed by a foreign law. It was not a matter of extraterritorial effect or not, since in this case the appellant conceded that section 75(1) applied only to credit card issuers carrying on business in the United Kingdom.[438] The House of Lords came down in favour of the appellant for reasons clearly presented by Lord Hope.

> The simple and unqualified statement of the right that is expressed in section 75(1) is consistent with the policy that lies behind the Act, informed by recommendations by the Crowther Committee. Its long title states that the new system which it lays down is 'for the protection of consumers'. That policy applies to debtors and creditors within the territorial reach of the Act generally. Transactions of that kind are to the commercial advantage of the supplier and the creditor. The creditor is in a better position than the debtor, in a question with a foreign supplier, to obtain redress. It is not to be assumed that the creditor will always get his money back. But, if he does not, the loss must lie with him as he has the broader back. He is in a better position, if redress is not readily obtainable, to spread the cost. He is in a better position to argue for sanctions against a supplier who is not reliable. For his part, the debtor is entitled to assume that he can trust suppliers who are authorised to accept his credit card.

In reaching this conclusion, the House of Lords ruled that section 75(1) was not impliedly limited by the territorial limits on section 75(2), which could not be invoked to allow the United Kingdom card issuer to proceed against a foreign supplier. It was perfectly possible to disconnect the matter of the card issuer's joint and several liability under section 75(1) and its right to an indemnity under section 75(2). Furthermore, the fact that certain provisions of the Consumer Credit Act were difficult to implement in respect of foreign suppliers, notably those dealing with the right of cancellation,[439] was not an argument for limiting the unqualified language of section 75(1).

8.100 **Recruitment of merchants.** Another aspect of section 75 was at issue in the *Lloyds Bank* litigation. It concerned the question whether pre-existing arrangements exist between the card issuer and the supplier where the supplier is recruited by a so-called merchant acquirer, not to a scheme operated by that card issuer, but rather to an operating network of credit card issuers, namely, Visa or Master Card. This results in a four- rather than a three-party arrangement and particularly facilitates the use of a credit card overseas. In the Court of Appeal,[440] the card issuer

---

[437] [2007] UKHL 48.

[438] The card issuer, however, would for reasons of extra-territoriality be unable to claim an indemnity from the foreign supplier under s. 75(2): *Office of Fair Trading v Lloyds Bank TSB plc*, n. 437 above, at [11] and [35].

[439] Ss. 67–71.

[440] [2006] EWCA Civ 268 at [55] and [61]–[66].

was unsuccessful in arguing that pre-existing arrangements did not exist in four-party cases, where the particular card issuer was not the person who recruited the particular supplier into the network. The court's conclusion was driven by the need for consumer protection and by the broad language of the Consumer Credit Act. The House of Lords refused leave to appeal on this point.

Means of redress.   A final point on the credit card issuer's liability concerns the   **8.101** means by which the cardholder might obtain redress. If the cardholder has not yet made payment in respect of the transaction, then the cardholder ought to be able to exercise a right of equitable set-off when a claim for payment is made by the credit card issuer.[441] If payment for that transaction has already been made, equitable set-off ought not to be available as against payments due from the cardholder in respect of other transactions. The necessary degree of transactional connectedness between the cardholder's claim against the card issuer and the card issuer's claim for reimbursement of sums advanced to the cardholder does not exist. Since the cardholder's claim will be for damages, then no right of common law (or statutory) set-off will exist in either case.[442]

---

[441] See *Bim Kemi v Blackburn Chemicals Ltd* [2001] EWCA Civ 457; [2001] 2 Lloyd's Rep. 92; *Smith v Muscat* [2003] EWCA Civ 962; [2003] 1 WLR 2853.
[442] *Crawford v Sterling* (1802) 2 Esp 407, 409 ('in moneys numbered').

9

UNFAIR CONTRACT TERMS

Common Law	9.01
Statute	9.19

Common Law

Introduction. This chapter deals with the exclusion or limitation of duties owed **9.01** by a seller to a buyer under or in connection with a contract of sale. The duties in question may be those imposed by the implied terms of title, description, fitness for purpose, satisfactory quality, and correspondence to sample,[1] as well as by the contract itself in relation to matters such as the amount and time of delivery. There are also duties imposed on the seller by operation of law, principally the duty of care in negligence, where the necessary degree of proximity is brought about between seller and buyer as a result of their entry into a contract of sale. A seller's attempt to exclude or limit its liability is subject to various controls existing at common law or under statute. In reviewing clauses, these controls have to be separately applied and the dividing line between them ought not to be blurred.[2] The common law controls will be discussed first before attention is turned to statutory controls.

Definition of exemption clause. Since special rules apply to clauses excluding **9.02** or limiting liability (exemption clauses),[3] these clauses must first be defined. Even before any statutory definitions fall to be considered, it is necessary to have an

---

[1] Ss. 12–15 of the Sale of Goods Act.

[2] *Watford Electronics Ltd v Sanderson CFL Ltd* [2001] EWCA Civ 317; [2001] All ER (Comm.) 696.

[3] Fine distinctions can be drawn that separate exclusion, exemption, and exception clauses. For the purpose of this text, the expression 'exemption clause' will be used to signify a clause that either excludes liability (exclusion clause) or limits liability (limitation clause), by either defining the procedure to be followed in making a claim or the time in which a claim should be made or the maximum amount recoverable for any one claim.

understanding of the type of clause that merits the particular attention of a court applying common law principles. It should not be assumed that the same definition that might suffice for common law purposes will be the same as the definition or definitions needed for statutory purposes. Moreover, it is not possible to define exemption clauses for common law purposes with the type of precision to be found in a statute and, in any case, common law controls tend to be on a sliding scale of intervention according to the pretensions of particular contractual clauses.[4] The starting point is to determine what liability would arise but for the particular clause under the contract or at law.[5] This was the approach applied by Scrutton LJ in a case concerning the construction of an exclusion clause.[6] It is not without relevance for the matter of incorporation. Although the distinction usually drawn in such cases is between contractual and non-contractual language in documents and notices, particularly exigent clauses, even before the Unfair Contract Terms Act 1977, had to comply with demanding standards of incorporation.[7] Scrutton LJ's approach is apt to deal with clauses that exclude liability and clauses that limit liability, but it may also have an application to some clauses that define liability.[8] In a real sense, all terms excluding and limiting liability define liability, in the sense that they are an integral part of the contractual undertaking of the party to whose performance they refer and are not mere defensive shields coming into play only at the stage when legal proceedings have commenced.[9] Furthermore, the definition of liability for present purposes needs to be teased out in order to identify the target clauses. A clause in a contract of sale providing for delivery within fifteen days defines the seller's duty. So far as the fifteen days is a reasonable time, the clause makes express what would otherwise pass for implied. Clauses of this kind should therefore not be treated as akin to clauses excluding the seller's duty to

---

[4] *Photo Production Ltd v Securicor Transport Ltd* [1980] AC 827, 850: 'Since the presumption is that the parties by entering into the contract intended to accept the implied obligations exclusion clauses are to be construed strictly and the degree of strictness appropriate to be applied to their construction may properly depend upon the extent to which they involve departure from the implied obligations' (Lord Diplock).

[5] A duty of care in negligence may indifferently arise also as an implied term of the contract.

[6] *Rutter v Palmer* [1922] 2 KB 87, 92.

[7] *Menselssohn v Normand* [1970] 1 QB 177; *Thornton v Shoe Lane Parking* [1971] 2 QB 163.

[8] There are other types of exemption clause that in effect exclude or limit liability, though not in so many words, e.g., clauses that purportedly acknowledge the receipt of conforming goods (see *Lowe v Lombank Ltd* [1960] 1 WLR 696 (hire)). Associated with exclusion and limitation clauses, in the judicial and statutory treatment afforded to them, are other clauses that alter the balance of the contractual bargain, such as indemnity clauses; see *Gillespie Bros & Co. Ltd v Roy Bowles Transport Ltd* [1973] QB 400.

[9] B. Coote, *Exception Clauses* (1970) ('Instead of being shields to claims based on breach of accrued rights, exception clauses substantively delimit the rights themselves': p.17); *Photo Production Ltd v Securicor Transport Ltd,* n. 4 above (Lord Diplock). It is submitted that a covenant not to sue, intended to take effect before any legal proceedings and indeed to pre-empt them, should be regarded for present purposes as an exemption clause: the issue was discussed but not resolved in *Macquarie International Investments Ltd v Glencore (UK) Ltd* [2008] EWHC 1716 (Comm) at [17].

deliver within a reasonable time. Suppose instead that the clause requires the seller only to deliver goods 'as seen' or the buyer to accept the goods 'with all faults'. The clause may not be expressed so as to exclude the seller's duties under section 14 of the Sale of Goods Act, but it purports to have the same practical effect and therefore should be treated in the same way as a clause that expressly excludes liability.[10] The dividing line between clauses that genuinely define liability and clauses that covertly exclude liability may depend upon context and the reasonable expectations of the parties. A clause permitting the seller to deliver either peas or beans may genuinely reflect the substance of the bargain, but if the seller and buyer have negotiated a contract for the sale of peas and the seller's standard terms permit it to deliver beans instead, then the clause functions as an exemption clause.

Force majeure **clauses.**   A question of some difficulty is whether *force majeure*   **9.03** and similar[11] clauses qualify for treatment as exemption clauses. As a matter of first impression, since it is their function to give protection against the consequences of non-performance, they should be so treated. A clause that excuses a seller who is unable to transport goods because of a dock strike, for example, in circumstances where frustration of contract could not be claimed at common law, excuses the strict liability otherwise borne by the seller. Nevertheless, a clause that gives the seller a moratorium, in the case of a temporary inability to perform, redefines performance in a way that is not so readily tantamount to contractual exemption.[12] Given the range of *force majeure* clauses, it should come as no surprise to find that their treatment as exemption clauses or not is far from clear-cut.[13] *Force majeure* clauses that are broad enough to encompass negligence will be subjected to a *contra proferentem* reading so as to confine them to cases where the liability of the excused party is strict and to prevent them from extending to negligence.[14] Since common law tests of incorporation and interpretation apply on a sliding scale according to the nature and extent of the exemption clause, it seems that the

---

[10] Coote, above, distinguishes between exception clauses that qualify primary or secondary contractual rights and clauses 'whose effect . . . is upon the accrual of particular primary rights': p. 9. The former category would include exclusion and limitation clauses.

[11] For example, prohibition clauses in standard commodity contracts that provide the shipper with a defensive shield in the case of government intervention prohibiting or restricting export.

[12] See the analysis of the former type of clause as an exemption clause in *Cero Navigation Corpn v Jean Lion & Cie (The Solon)* [2000] 1 Lloyd's Rep. 292, 299. See also *Trade and Transport Inc. v Iino Kainu Kaisha Ltd (The Angelia)* [1973] 1 WLR 210, 231, declining to apply the doctrine of fundamental breach in a case where a clause excused a party for a failure to perform in circumstances beyond his control.

[13] Lord Tucker does not give a clear response in *Fairclough Dodd & Jones Ltd v JH Vantol Ltd* [1956] 1 WLR 136, 143–4 when distinguishing between clauses excusing and clauses redefining performance.

[14] *J Lauritzen AS v Wijsmuller BV (The Super Servant Two)* [1990] 1 Lloyd's Rep. 1, 7, 12.

question whether *force majeure* clauses are exemption clauses for common law purposes is not a question of great practical significance.

9.04 **Incorporation.** At common law, exemption clauses are controlled principally by the tests of incorporation and construction.[15] Incorporation is concerned with whether an exclusion clause has been included in a contract and is (apart from the signed documents rule) a question of fact. The cases fall into two categories. The first is where a document is signed by the party and the second is where an informal or semi-formal contract is to be supplemented by the contents of a notice or ancillary document. The rule concerning signed documents is sometimes expressed as a rule of law, in that it follows ineluctably from the signature that the signing party consents to be bound by the terms of the signed document. The leading case of *L'Estrange v Graucob Ltd*[16] concerned the instalment sale of a cigarette vending machine. The contract was printed on brown paper and contained, in 'regrettably small print but quite legible', a clause that excluded the seller's fitness for purpose liability. The Divisional Court held that, in the absence of fraud or misrepresentation,[17] the buyer was bound by the terms of the document and it was 'wholly immaterial' whether she had read them or not.[18] A distinction was drawn between a case like the present, where a document was signed, and the so-called 'ticket cases', where the person seeking the benefit of the clause had to prove that the other party was aware, or ought to have been aware, that the ticket contained terms and conditions. So stated, the rule of consent to the content of signed documents may be seen as depending upon the fact of signature as necessarily signifying awareness of the existence of terms and conditions in the signed document, or as necessarily signifying the signing party's assent to whatever is in the document, whether or not read or understood. It is hardly satisfactory to assert as a matter of law and without further ado that signature equals consent to whatever is in the signed document.[19] Indeed, Scrutton LJ went on to add the gloss that the

---

[15] See G. H. Treitel, *The Law of Contract* (12th edn, by E. Peel, Sweet & Maxwell, London, 2007), 240–61.

[16] [1934] 2 KB 394.

[17] For misrepresentation, see *Curtis v Chemical Cleaning and Dyeing Co.* [1951] 1 KB 805. A clause may also be overridden by the assurance or undertaking of an agent or employee of the party relying on the clause, acting within the scope of an actual or apparent authority: *Mendelssohn v Normand Ltd* [1970] 1 QB 177. See also *Couchman v Hill* [1947] KB 554; *Harling v Eddy* [1951] 2 KB 739; *Gallaher Ltd v British Road Services Ltd* [1974] 2 Lloyd's Rep. 440; *Overbrooke Estates Ltd v Glencombe Properties Ltd* [1974] 1 WLR 1335; *J Evans & Son (Portsmouth) Ltd v Merzario* [1976] 1 WLR 1078.

[18] N. 16 above, 403 (Scrutton LJ). Maugham LJ added the (necessary) case of *non est factum*: *ibid*, 406.

[19] Cf *McCutcheon v David MacBrayne Ltd* [1964] 1 WLR 125, 134, where Lord Devlin thought that the signing party was bound by the terms of the document 'because they are in the contract'. See also *Parker v London and South Eastern Railway Co.* (1877) 2 CPD 416, 421 (Mellish LJ); *The Luna* [1920] P 22 (where a Dutch sea captain who spoke no English was bound by the terms of a document that he plainly could not have read or understood); *Bahamas Oil Refining Co. v Kristiansands*

buyer in *L'Estrange v Graucob Ltd* 'cannot be heard to say' that she was not bound by unread contractual terms.[20]

Signature and estoppel.   These words of Scrutton LJ amount to a reference   **9.05**
to estoppel and hark back to older authority, notably, *Harris v Great Western Railway Co*.[21] In this case, Blackburn J said that a person who signs a document 'represents to the other side that he has made himself acquainted with the contents of that writing and assents to them, and so induces the other side to act upon that representation by entering into the contract with him, and is consequently precluded from denying that he did not make himself acquainted with those terms'.[22] Of all doctrines, estoppel is particularly sensitive to what in fact is said and what in fact is done. The practical question is how exactly, in the particular circumstances, did the non-signing party understand the conduct of the other party in signing the document. In many cases, it would be plain to the former that the signing party did not read the document. Nevertheless, the act of signature might reasonably be understood as meaning that the signing party is insensitive to the actual contents and is prepared to submit to whatever is in the document. A more likely explanation of that conduct in most cases, it is submitted, is that the signing party is prepared, in the eyes of a reasonable co-contractant, to assent to the contents of the document on the assumption that it does not contain anything oppressive or out of the ordinary.[23] The test is not easy to formulate but the expression 'onerous and unusual', which has acquired some currency in non-signature cases,[24] captures reasonably well the type of clause whose presence in a signed document requires the non-signing party, as a practical matter, to take active steps to secure the signing party's consent to all the terms of the signed document. Passivity and muteness when proffering a document for signature should not be a universal passport to the signing party's contractual obligation. It may be due to the important role played by railway companies in this area of the law that the test for contractual incorporation has in the past been satisfied by a standard that treats those who rely upon the terms of standard form contracts as legislators rather than private

Tank Rederie A/S (The Polyduke) [1978] 1 Lloyd's Rep. 211 (where the court appears to have rejected any requirement that the document be clearly intended to have contractual effect).

[20] N. 16 above, 404.

[21] (1876) 1 QBD 515.

[22] *Ibid.*, 530; see J. Spencer [1973] CLJ 104.

[23] See the willingness of the court to depart in an 'extreme case' ('onerous and unusual') from the signed documents rule in *Ocean Chemical Transport Inc. v Exnor Craggs Ltd* [2000] 1 Lloyd's Rep. 446, 454.

[24] *Tilden Rent-A-Car Co. v Clendenning* (1978) 83 DLR (3rd) 400 (Can); *Nutting v Baldwin* [1995] 1 WLR 201, 211; *Sumukan Ltd v Commonwealth Secretariat* [2007] EWCA Civ 243; [2007] 2 Lloyd's Rep. 287 ('onerous or unusual'). See also *Interfoto Picture Library Ltd v Stiletto Visual Programmes Ltd* [1989] QB 433 ('particularly onerous', 'unreasonable and extortionate'); *O'Brien v MGN Ltd* [2001] EWCA Civ 1279; [2002] CLC 33 ('onerous or outlandish').

contracting parties. In modern times, a railway company's byelaws should not be equated with its terms of contracting and the same may be said with appropriate adaptations for other major companies dealing with the public at large. The signed documents rule is ripe for reappraisal to bring it into line with fundamental principles of estoppel and contractual consent. Its continuing survival owes something to the existence of modern legislation controlling the excesses of exemption clauses by other means, thus postponing a reappraisal of the rule.

9.06 **Test for incorporation.** Where there is no signed document, it is possible for ancillary documents and notices to be incorporated into a contract of sale. Although such cases are unlikely to have a direct application to sale of goods contracts, because of the different circumstances in which a sale of goods contract is likely to be concluded in comparison, for example, with a contract of carriage, it is useful to summarize these ticket cases before turning to cases with a more direct application to sale of goods, namely, the incorporation of terms from previous dealings between the same parties. The classical test laid down for the incorporation of terms in non-signature cases is in *Parker v South Eastern Railway Co*,[25] where Mellish LJ states the need for 'evidence independently of the agreement itself to prove' assent, available broadly in two instances. The first is where one party delivers to another paper containing writing, and the recipient knows that the writing contains conditions intended to have contractual effect. In that case, the act of receiving and keeping the paper is an assent to those conditions. In the second case, assent is also to be inferred where the recipient knows that the paper contains writing, though not that it contains conditions, provided that the delivery of the paper, so that the recipient might discern writing on it, is sufficient notice of the conditions in the paper. The test of incorporation does not turn upon any duty of the recipient to read or become aware of the conditions.[26]

9.07 **Recipient's knowledge.** The incorporation of conditions in an unsigned contract has more often been found in the second of Mellish LJ's two instances, and it is here too that incorporation has more often failed. This has been for three principal reasons. The first reason is where the conditions are contained on a piece of paper, such as a receipt, that the recipient has no reason to suppose will contain contractual conditions.[27] This may in some cases be because there is no sufficient reference on the front of the paper to the presence of conditions on the back.[28] The second is

---

[25] (1877) 2 CPD 416.

[26] *Ibid.*, 422; see also *Hood v Anchor Line (Henderson Brothers) Ltd* [1918] AC 837.

[27] *Chapelton v Barry Urban District Council* [1940] 1 KB 532.

[28] *Henderson v Stevenson* (1875) LR 2 Sc & Div 270; *Sugar v London Midland & Scottish Railway Co.* [1941] 1 All ER 172 (date stamp obliterated reference to back of ticket); see also *Poseidon Freight Forwarding Co. Ltd v Davies Turner Southern Ltd* [1996] 2 Lloyd's Rep. 388.

where the contract has already been concluded so that the paper (or notice) comes too late, where the absence of laborious argument that the contract has been subsequently varied is noticeably absent from the cases.[29] The third reason, latterly coming to prominence, signals a movement away from notice of conditions to notice of the particular condition or exclusion,[30] and thus from away notice itself to instruction. The more that a clause is 'wide and destructive of rights', the greater the need to bring it to the attention of the party to be bound by it 'in the most explicit way'.[31] Older authority recognizing incorporation by reference, where a notice states the availability of conditions, which might be consulted on payment of a fee and the expenditure of time and trouble, is unlikely to be followed today.[32] In any case, it would be open to challenge under the relevant legislation. Incorporation by reference, however, is otherwise permissible[33] and may occur where a contracting party is fully aware that the other party always does business on its own standard terms and is indifferent to that other party's terms because of his own standard practice of taking out insurance.[34] Nevertheless, in accordance with the increasing emphasis placed on consensus in modern times, the receipt of conditions by someone incapable of reading or understanding the conditions to the co-contractant's knowledge is unlikely to be sufficient to incorporate the terms in the contract.[35]

Course of dealing. Incorporation of contractual conditions may occur as a **9.08** result of an established course of dealing between the parties, even though it cannot be said that the requisite steps to give notice of the clause have been otherwise taken on the instant occasion. The course of dealing must be a consistent one[36] but the number of previous transactions may depend upon the sophistication of

---

[29] *Olley v Marlborough Court Ltd* [1949] 1 KB 532

[30] See especially Lord Denning MR in *J Spurling Ltd v Bradshaw* [1956] 1 WLR 461, 466; *Thornton v Shoe Lane Parking Ltd*, n. 7 above.

[31] *Thornton v Shoe Lane Parking Ltd*, n. 7 above, 170.

[32] See, e.g., *Thompson v London Midland & Scottish Railway Co.* [1930] 1 KB 31. The terms must be available to consult: *Jayaar Impex Ltd v Toaken Group Ltd* [1996] 2 Lloyd's Rep. 437.

[33] *McCutcheon v David MacBrayne Ltd*, n. 19 above (Lord Devlin); *Smith v South Wales Switchgear Co. Ltd* [1978] 1 WLR 165; *Circle Freight International Ltd v Medeast Gulf Freights Ltd* [1988] 2 Lloyd's Rep. 427; *O'Brien v MGN Ltd*, n. 24 above; *Sumukan Ltd v Commonwealth Secretariat* [2007] EWCA Civ 243; [2007] 2 Lloyd's Rep. 287.

[34] *Laceys Footwear (Wholesale) Ltd v Bowler International Freight Ltd* [1997] 2 Lloyd's Rep. 369, 378. Cf *Jayaar Impex Ltd v Toaken Group Ltd*, n. 32 above, 445.

[35] *Geier v Kujara Weston & Warne Bros Transport* [1970] 1 Lloyd's Rep. 364; see also *Richardson Spence & Co. v Rowntree* [1894] AC 217.

[36] *McCutcheon v David MacBrayne Ltd*, n. 19 above; *SIAT di Dal Ferro v Tradax Overseas SA* [1980] 1 Lloyd's Rep. 53; *George Mitchell (Chesterhall) Ltd v Finney Lock Seeds Ltd* [1984] QB 284, 295; *Metaalhandel JA Magnus BV v Ardfields Transport Ltd* [1988] 1 Lloyd's Rep. 197. See *Hardwick Game Farm v Suffolk Agricultural Poultry Producers Asscn* [1969] 2 AC 31 (CA) (three or four dealings a month over the previous three years); *Circle Freight International Ltd v Medeast Gulf Freights Ltd*, n. 33 above (eleven invoices); *Photolibrary Group Ltd v Burda Senator Verlag GmbH* [2008] EWHC 1343 (QB) at [60] ('very substantial course of dealing' and terms not 'particularly onerous or unusual').

the party to be bound. The previous dealings must establish knowledge of and consent to the terms on the present occasion,[37] notwithstanding their present absence.[38] A smaller number of previous dealings should suffice between commercial parties[39] than in a consumer transaction.[40] Incorporation may also take place between commercial parties in accordance with trade custom, where each party knows that business is done on terms current in the trade and knows the substance of those terms.[41]

9.09 *Contra proferentem* **interpretation.** Even if a clause passes the factual incorporation test, it may yet fail to exclude or limit a claim if its language is not apt for this purpose. In contrast with incorporation, the meaning of written clauses is a question of law. In scrutinizing the language of clauses,[42] the courts have long applied a *contra proferentem* rule of construction. According to this rule, exemption clauses will be construed in such a way that any ambiguity or omission in the clause will be resolved against the person proffering it (the *proferens*) for his protection. Examples of clauses omitting vital words are easy enough to supply. For example, a seller giving 'no warranty express or implied' does not thereby exclude a condition;[43] the sale of goods 'with all faults' will not absolve the seller from the obligation to supply goods corresponding to the contractual description;[44] a contractual provision that no warranty 'is given' will not exclude liability for an express

---

[37] See *Johnson Matthey Bankers Ltd v State Trading Corpn of India* [1984] 1 Lloyd's Rep. 427, 434 ('what each party by his words and conduct would have led the other party as a reasonable man to believe that he was accepting'); *Circle Freight International Ltd v Medeast Gulf Freights Ltd*, n. 33 above, 433. But the consent may be of the passive kind that flows from a party's indifference to the content of the relevant conditions: *J Spurling Ltd v Bradshaw* [1956] 1 WLR 461; *Britain & Overseas Trading (Bristles) Ltd v Brooks Wharf & Bull Wharf* [1967] 2 Lloyd's Rep. 51.

[38] *McCutcheon v David MacBrayne Ltd*, n. 19 above, 134 (Lord Devlin).

[39] *Chevron International Oil Co. Ltd v A/S Sea Team (The TS Havprins)* [1983] 2 Lloyd's Rep. 356 (three transactions in five years, but the agents ordering the bunker fuel had acted also for numerous other principals).

[40] *Hollier v Rambler Motors (AMC) Ltd* [1972] 2 QB 71 (three or four occasions over a five-year period).

[41] *British Crane Hire Corpn Ltd v Ipswich Plant Hire Ltd* [1975] 2 QB 303 (the party to be bound indeed used similar terms when itself supplying equipment for hire).

[42] A question of law, like all issues of interpretation of written contracts; see, e.g., *Bunge Corpn v Tradax SA* [1981] 1 WLR 711.

[43] *Wallis Son & Wells v Pratt & Haynes* [1911] AC 394; *Henry Kendall & Sons v William Lillico & Sons* [1969] AC 231.

[44] *Shepherd v Kain* (1821) 5 B & Ald. 240. Similarly a clause preventing rejection in respect of goods 'herein specified': *Montagu L Meyer Ltd v Kivisto* (1929) 35 Ll L R 265 (discoloured wood remained 'unsorted redwood'); *White Sea Timber Trust Ltd v WW North Ltd* (1932) 44 Ll L R 390 ('herein specified' went to description generally and not just to the contractual specification). See also *Vigers Bros v Sanderson Bros* [1901] 1 KB 608; *NV Bunge v Cie Noga d'Importation et d'Exportation (The Bow Cedar)* [1980] 2 Lloyd's Rep. 601; *WN Lindsay & Co Ltd v European Grain and Shipping Agency Ltd* [1963] 1 Lloyd's Rep. 437. Cf *Huyton SA v Distribuidora Internacional de Productos Agricolas SA* [2002] EWHC 2088 (Comm).

warranty already given;[45] a clause excluding liability for breach of implied terms does not exclude liability for breach of express terms;[46] a clause referring to 'goods delivered' does not protect the seller when he is sued by the buyer for non-delivery of goods;[47] a clause guaranteeing documentary performance of a c.i.f. contract is not effective to permit the seller to convert a documentary delivery obligation into an obligation to deliver the goods instead;[48] and a clause certifying the quality of goods does not extend to packing requirements.[49]

Modern contractual interpretation.   The practice of drafting clauses of ever **9.10** wider scope, with general language encapsulating a wide variety of events, exposes the limitations of this kind of judicial control. It remains to be seen, nevertheless, how far the technique of *contra proferentem* interpretation can be taken. In dealing with this question, the modern approach to the construction of contracts, with its reference to the factual matrix surrounding the conclusion of the contract and its willingness to go beyond the primary meaning of words even where there is no patent ambiguity in the language of the contract,[50] has untested implications for the construction of exemption clauses.[51] The modern approach to interpretation, so far as it departs from the literal interpretation of language, holds out the possibility of construction techniques that are more supple and sensitive to different contractual circumstances than has been displayed in the past.

Weight of *contra proferentem* rule.   The principle behind the *contra proferentem* **9.11** rule of interpretation is that rights and duties that would otherwise arise under or in connection with a contract may not lightly be displaced. It is implicit in this principle that parties are not recognized as contracting on a blank sheet of paper and that implied rights and duties liable to be displaced by the language of the

---

[45] *Webster v Higgin* [1948] 2 All ER 127.

[46] *Andrews Bros (Bournemouth) Ltd. v Singer and Co. Ltd* [1934] 1 KB 17.

[47] *Beck & Co. v Szymanowski* [1924] AC 43.

[48] *SIAT di Dal Ferro v Tradax Overseas SA*, n. 36 above.

[49] *Kollerich & Cie SA v State Trading Corpn of India* [1979] 2 Lloyd's Rep. 442. A clause providing that a certificate is final in matters of quality will not apply to the condition of the goods: *Cremer v General Carriers SA* [1974] 1 WLR 341.

[50] See, e.g., *Investors Compensation Scheme v West Bromwich Building Society Ltd* [1998] 1 WLR 896; *Charter Reinsurance Co. v Fagan* [1997] AC 331; *Mannai Investment Co. Ltd v Eagle StarLife Assurance Co. Ltd* [1997] AC 749.

[51] In *Bank of Credit and Commerce International SA v Ali* [2001] UKHL 8; [2002] 1 AC 251 at [62], Lord Hoffmann nevertheless said that 'the disappearance of artificial rules for the construction of exemption clauses seems to me in accordance with the general trend in matters of construction, which has been to try to assimilate judicial techniques of construction to those which would be used by a reasonable speaker of the language in the interpretation of any serious utterance in ordinary life'.

contract have an imposed rather than a default character.[52] The guiding approach to the application of the rule is that a contracting party seeking to alter what would otherwise be the governing rights and duties bears the burden of demonstrating that the language used is effective and clear in its aims.[53] It is estimating the weight of this burden, however, that constitutes the real issue in appraising the modern scope of the *contra proferentem* rule. Prior to the introduction of the Unfair Contract Terms Act 1977, exemption clauses were controlled by various means, including the doctrine of fundamental breach[54] and an application of the *contra proferentem* rule that has been candidly recognized at the highest judicial level as ascribing a 'strained interpretation' or a 'tortured meaning'[55] to such clauses. More recently, the House of Lords has signalled a desire to return to more straightforward canons of construction, at least where the parties are of equal bargaining power.[56] Lord Wilberforce has also cautioned that 'one must not strive to create ambiguities by strained construction' and one should instead give words their 'natural, plain meaning'.[57] The allocation of risk is a respectable commercial ambition.[58] The danger with the previous approach was that it was capable of striking down freely agreed clauses supported by sensible business reasons, such as the allocation of a particular risk to the least-cost insurer, who is more likely to be the one taking out indemnity insurance rather than liability insurance. Yet it cannot be said with any confidence that the language of exemption clauses will be read in the same way as the language of other contractual clauses. For one thing, it is recognized that limitation clauses should not be subject to the same strict

---

[52] Lord Fraser has mentioned 'the inherent improbability that . . . [a] party . . . intended to release the proferens from a liability that would otherwise fall upon him': *Ailsa Craig Shipping Co. Ltd v Malvern Fishing Co. Ltd (The Strathallan)* [1983] 1 WLR 964, 970.

[53] In *Pera Shipping Corpn v Petroship SA (The Pera)* [1985] 2 Lloyd's Rep. 103, 108, Griffiths LJ refers to 'the fundamental rule that a contractual clause intended to cut down the rights which a party to a contract would otherwise enjoy, must be expressed in clear and unambiguous language'.

[54] Discussed below.

[55] *George Mitchell (Chesterhall) Ltd v Finney Lock Seeds Ltd* [1983] 2 AC 803, 810 (Lord Diplock). See in particular the approach adopted in the Court of Appeal in that case: [1983] QB 284.

[56] *Photo Production Ltd v Securicor Transport Ltd*, n. 4 above. See also *Tradigrain SA v Intertek Testing Services (ITS) Canada Ltd*: [2007] EWCA Civ 154; [2007] 1 CLC 188 at [46]:

> It is certainly true that English law has traditionally taken a restrictive approach to the construction of exemption clauses and clauses limiting liability for breaches of contract and other wrongful acts. However, in recent years it has been increasingly willing to recognise that parties to commercial contracts are entitled to apportion the risk of loss as they see fit and that provisions which limit or exclude liability must be construed in the same way as other terms: see, for example, *Photo Production Ltd v Securicor Transport Ltd* [1980] AC 827.

[57] *Ailsa Craig Shipping Co. Ltd v Malvern Fishing Co. Ltd (The Strathallan)*, n. 52 above, 966. Cf Lord Fraser at 969 ('special conditions. . .must be strictly construed against the proferens').

[58] See *Tradigrain SA v Intertek Testing Services (ITS) (Canada) Ltd*, n. 56 above at[46].

standards of interpretation as exclusion clauses.[59] Even after moderating this statement to take account of different degrees of limitation, it is significant that the statement recognizes a difference between exclusion and limitation clauses, from which it must follow that there is a difference between them both and other contractual clauses when it comes to construction. The most likely assessment of the standing of the *contra proferentem* rule today is that, despite modern legislation, it is still applicable[60] and significant but that certain excesses in its application in the past will not be repeated.

Excluding liability for negligence. The treatment of liability in negligence is **9.12** particularly illustrative of the *contra proferentem* rule. The classic approach, of Lord Morton in the Privy Council in *Canada Steamship Lines Ltd v R*,[61] consists of three rules.[62] First, effect must be given to an express exemption from liability in negligence. Secondly, 'if the only liability of the person pleading the exemption is a liability for negligence, the clause will more readily operate to exempt him'.[63] It is not necessary that the word 'negligence' be used explicitly; general language if clear enough will suffice.[64] Thirdly, if the clause contains only general language of exemption, the existence of a head of liability other than negligence is 'fatal' to the application of the clause to cases of negligence 'even if the words used are prima

---

[59] *Ailsa Craig*, n. 52 above, 970 (Lord Fraser), referring to the 'specially exacting standards which are applied to exclusion and indemnity clauses'. The contract in *Ailsa Craig* was concluded six years before the 1977 Act came into force but there is nothing in Lord Fraser's judgment to indicate that a different approach should be adopted after the Act. See also *George Mitchell (Chesterhall) Ltd v Finney Lock Seeds Ltd*, n. 55 above, 814; *EE Caledonia Ltd v Orbit Valve Europe* [1994] 1 WLR 1515, 1521. The standard applicable to clauses indemnifying the *proferens* against the consequences of his own negligence appears to be higher still: *Canada Steamship Lines Ltd v R* [1952] AC 192; *Smith v South Wales Switchgear Ltd* [1978] 1 WLR 165, 168.

[60] See, e.g., Lord Hoffmann in *Homburg Houtimport BV v Agrosin Private Ltd (The Starsin)* [2003] UKHL 12, [2004] 1 AC 715: 'If a party, otherwise liable, is to exclude or limit his liability or to rely on an exemption, he must do so in clear words. Unclear words do not suffice...Any ambiguity or lack of clarity must be resolved against that party.' Lord Hoffmann's leading role in the modern approach to contractual construction gives his words added force.

[61] N. 59 above, 208.

[62] *HIH Casualty and General Insurance Ltd v Chase Manhattan Bank* [2003] UKHL 6; [2003] 2 Lloyd's Rep. 61 at [11] (Lord Bingham) and [116] (Lord Scott). Lord Hoffmann at [63] emphasized that *Canada Steamship* dated from a time when there was no legislation in place to control exemption clauses. See also *Trident Turboprop Dublin Ltd v First Flight Couriers Ltd* [2008] EWHC 1686 (Comm) at [41] ('The principles set out by Lord Morton in the *Canada Steamship* case are a guide, not a code'); *Macquarie International Investments Ltd v Glencore (UK) Ltd* [2008] EWHC 1716 (Comm) at [17] *et seq.*

[63] *Rutter v Palmer*, n. 6 above (Scrutton LJ).

[64] *Canada Steamship Lines Ltd v R*, n. 59 above; *Hollier v Rambler Motors (AMC) Ltd* [1972] 2 QB 71; *Gillespie Bros & Co. Ltd v Roy Bowles Transport Ltd* [1973] QB 400, 419; *Gallaher Ltd v British Road Services Ltd* [1974] 2 Lloyd's Rep. 440 ('under the preceding Conditions'); *Lamport & Holt Lines Ltd v Coubro & Scrutton (M&I) Ltd (The Raphael)* [1982] 2 Lloyd's Rep. 42 ('any act or omission').

facie wide enough to to cover negligence'.[65] In this third instance, Lord Greene MR in *Alderslade v Hendon Laundry Ltd* had this to say:[66]

> Where the head of damage in respect of which limitation of liability is sought to be imposed by such a clause is one which rests on negligence and nothing else, the clause must be construed as extending to that head of damage, because it would otherwise lack subject-matter. Where, on the other hand, the head of damage may be based on some other ground than that of negligence, the general principle is that the clause must be confined in its application to loss occurring through that other cause to the exclusion of loss arising through negligence. The reason is that if a contracting party wishes in such a case to limit his liability in respect of negligence, he must do so in clear terms in the absence of which the clause is construed as relating to a liability not based on negligence.

To sum up the second and third rules, general words of exclusion, not explicitly mentioning negligence but capable of extending to it, will apply to negligence-based liability if negligence is the only plausible head of liability.[67] The presence of another head of liability that is not 'fanciful or remote'[68] will attract the coverage of the clause and leave liability in negligence exposed. For negligence also to be covered in accordance with the third rule, the word itself or some synonym must be mentioned; a word of emphasis, such as 'whatsoever', will not suffice.[69] Given the

---

[65] *Canada Steamship Lines Ltd v R*, n. 59 above, 208. See also *Toomey v Eagle Star Insurance Co Ltd (No. 2)* [1995] 2 Lloyd's Rep. 88, where a clause in a reinsurance contract that it was not 'cancellable or voidable' was held to extend only to innocent material representation (and innocent material non-disclosure) and not also negligent material misrepresentation (and negligent material non-disclosure). It might, however, be considered that there is only material misrepresentation and material non-disclosure, and the existence of negligence or not goes only to the different ways in which the misrepresentation or non-disclosure might arise. The line taken in *Toomey* was disapproved by Lords Hoffmann (and Rix LJ in the court below) in *HIH Casualty and General Insurance Ltd v Chase Manhattan Bank*, n. 62 above at [65]–[67]. The rule does not apply to differentiate between different types of negligence (e.g., liability in the tort of negligence and liability for breach of a contractual duty to take care): *Deepak Fertilisers and Petrochemicals Corpn v ICI Chemicals & Polymers Ltd* [1999] 1 Lloyd's Rep. 387.

[66] [1945] 1 KB 189, 192.

[67] In *Hollier v Rambler Motors (AMC) Ltd*, n. 64 above, the plausible alternative, strict liability for fire damage to customers' cars, existed only in the minds of uninformed members of the public, where it had been placed by Salmon LJ. His lordship was of the view that customers of a garage would be 'surprised and horrified' to learn that the garage could be relieved from the consequences of its own negligence because of the general words in the contractual condition. The more likely reality is that their surprise and horror would be due to the garage being able to protect itself at all if the right words were used. On negligence and fire, see also *Dorset CC v Southern Felt Roofing Co* (1990) 48 BLR 96.

[68] *Canada Steamship Lines Ltd v R*, n. 65 above, 208 (Lord Morton); *Hair and Skin Trading Co. Ltd v Norman Airfreight Carriers Ltd* [1974] 1 Lloyd's Rep. 442; *Lamport & Holt Lines Ltd v Coubro & Scrutton (M&I) Ltd (The Raphael)*, n. 64 above.

[69] *Smith v South Wales Switchgear Ltd* [1978] 1 WLR 165, 173, distinguishing *Gillespie Bros & Co. Ltd v Roy Bowles Transport Ltd* [1973] QB 400. Cf the brief statement of Pill LJ in *Brown v Drake International Ltd* [2004] EWCA Civ 1629 at [21], which is surely open to question: 'The expression "however caused" gives the clearest indication that negligence and breach of statutory duty are included.'

presence of strict liability in the Sale of Goods Act, this third rule has a particular application to sale of goods and related contracts, which are subject to statutory strict liability. So, in *White v John Warwick & Co. Ltd*,[70] a contract for the hire of a cycle provided that 'nothing in this agreement shall render the owner liable for any personal injuries'. The defective saddle injured the hirer and the owner was held liable for breach of its duty to take care in supplying a safe cycle. A stricter form of liability, arising from the breach of an implied duty to supply a cycle fit for its purpose, was covered by the clause and therefore ousted negligence from it. There are limits to the above judicial controls over the abuse of contractual power associated with exemption clauses. Familiarity with these controls simply encourages the drafting of exclusions or limitations of all liability, whether for breach of warranty or condition, express or implied, in negligence or otherwise.

'Consequential damage'.   A further example of the continuing operation of the   **9.13** *contra proferentem* rule is the treatment of clauses that exclude or limit liability for 'consequential damage'. This is an expression that has a fairly clear commercial meaning. In the case of defective goods, a merchant would understand consequential loss to include further losses caused by those goods that are not inherent in their defective state, such as loss of business, profits, and reputation, damage caused by those goods to the property of the merchant, and personal injuries.[71] The term, however, has been given a rather esoteric and narrower interpretation so as to connote damage falling within the second limb of the rule in *Hadley v Baxendale*[72] and recoverable therefore in the case where the contract breaker has special knowledge or has been the recipient of a pre-contractual disclosure by the other party. A better label for damage under this second limb, however, might be 'particular' or 'special' damage, since the *consequential* character of damage is more a matter of factual causation than of foreseeability. In *Croudace Construction Ltd v Cawoods Concrete Products Ltd*,[73] a case dealing with the late delivery of masonry blocks needed on a construction site, the distinction drawn between 'direct' and 'consequential' damage, for the purpose of interpreting a clause excluding liability for the latter, was that direct damage included losses that began to 'clock up at once', such as the cost of plant and an idle workforce. In *British Sugar Plc v NEI Power Projects Ltd*,[74] a case involving the supply of defective electrical equipment which brought to a halt a production process, a claim to have consequential loss

---

[70] [1953] 1 WLR 1285. See also *Shell Chemicals UK Ltd v P&O Roadtanks Ltd* [1995] 1 Lloyd's Rep. 297 (conversion and negligence); *EE Caledonia Ltd v Orbit Valve Europe*, n. 59 above; *Mediterranean Freight Services Ltd v BP Oil International Ltd (The Fiona)* [1994] 2 Lloyd's Rep. 506; *Casson v Ostley PJ Ltd* [2001] EWCA Civ 1013; [2003] BLR 147.

[71] See also *Mondel v Steel* (1841) 8 M & W 858.

[72] (1856) 9 Ex 341.

[73] [1978] 2 Lloyd's Rep. 55.

[74] (1998) 87 BLR 42. See also *Millar's Machinery Co Ltd v David Way & Son* (1935) 40 Com Cas 204; *Saint Line Ltd v Richardsons Westgarth & Co. Ltd* [1940] 2 KB 99; *BHP Petroleum Ltd v British*

include loss of profits was rejected for the same reason, despite an attempt to inject business understanding into the interpretation of a limitation clause. Where, in *Deepak Fertilisers and Petrochemicals Corpn v ICI Chemicals & Polymers Ltd*,[75] the parties had concluded a technology transfer agreement so that the claimant might build an ethanol plant, the trial judge sought to distinguish between direct loss, the cost of getting the plant right, and consequential loss, the losses flowing from getting the plant wrong. The distinction, however, was rejected on appeal, where the court concluded that direct loss included, not just the cost of reconstructing the plant, but also the overhead and profits lost during the period of delay while this was done. Since 'direct' and 'consequential' authoritatively stand in antinomy to each other, and since the language of directness is the language of the first limb of the rule in *Hadley v Baxendale* as recited in the Sale of Goods Act,[76] it seems to follow from this line of authorities that 'consequential' losses come within the second limb, even though the word itself is not used in that second limb. The result, given the special and restricted circumstances in which second limb losses might be recovered, is that a clause excluding or limiting consequential losses has only a limited effect on liability.[77] In particular, it cannot be treated as a synonym for loss of profits, since a conventional claim for loss of profits will come within the first limb of the rule in *Hadley v Baxendale*.[78]

9.14 Entire agreement and related clauses.   In contracts involving complex and protracted negotiations, which is unlikely to be the case with most sale of goods transactions, there is a deal of common sense in seeking to confine the rights and duties of the parties to the (often very lengthy) contents of the final written instrument. The parties' positions may have shifted during the negotiation process, there is much to be said for the purchaser (in particular) carrying out a a thorough pre-contract investigation ('due diligence'), and an accurate calculation of commercial risk is facilitated if the final instrument contains the sum of rights and duties. A clause, or more than one clause, will seek to advance these desiderata in two principal ways: first, by providing that the final instrument constitutes the 'entire agreement' of the parties, so as to preclude the addition to the contract of

---

Steel Plc [1999] 2 Lloyd's Rep. 583; *Hotel Services Ltd v Hilton International Hotels (UK) Ltd* [2000] 1 All ER (Comm.) 750.

[75] n. 65 above.

[76] Ss. 50(2), 51(2) and 53(2) ('directly and naturally') (though of these only the word 'naturally' is used by Alderson B in stating the first limb of the rule).

[77] Note, however, that Lord Hoffmann's wish to reserve the question whether the above line of cases is correct: *Caledonia North Sea Ltd v British Telecommunications Plc* [2002] UKHL 4; [2002] 1 Lloyd's Rep. 553 at [99]–[100]. Se also E. Peel 'Whither Contra Proferentem', in A. Burrows and E. Peel, *Contract Terms* (OUP, 2007).

[78] See *Victoria Laundry (Windsor) Ltd v Newman Industries Ltd* [1949] 2 QB 528, drawing a distinction between ordinary laundry profits (first limb) and the profits from specially lucrative dyeing contracts (second limb).

any prior informal or formal undertakings not embodied in the final instrument; and secondly, by providing that no previous representation has had an inducing effect on a party for the purpose of actionable misrepresentation. In this latter case, the technique often adopted is for one party to acknowledge that it has not entered into the contract in reliance on any statements that are not contained in the final instrument. In the words of Lightman J in *Inntrepreneur Pub Co. (GL) v East Crown Ltd*:

> 'The purpose of an entire agreement clause is to preclude a party to a written agreement from threshing through the undergrowth and finding in the course of negotiations some (chance) remark or statement (often long forgotten or difficult to recall or explain) on which to found a claim such as the present to the existence of a collateral warranty. The entire agreement clause obviates the occasion for any such search and the peril to the contracting parties posed by the need which may arise in its absence to conduct such a search.[79]

It has not proved straightforward, nevertheless, to have effect given to these entire agreement clauses. The clause in *Thomas Witter Ltd v TBP Industries Ltd* provided as follows:

> This Agreement sets forth the entire agreement and understanding between the parties or any of them in connection with the Business and the sale and purchase described herein. In particular, but without prejudice to the generality of the foregoing, the Purchaser acknowledges that it has not been induced to enter this Agreement by any representation or warranty other than the statements contained or referred to in Schedule 6.

The clause was raised against a purchaser claiming damages for misrepresentation under section 2(1) of the Misrepresentation Act 1967, but it failed on various grounds to protect the vendor of a business. First, if the clause were designed to protect the vendor against those misrepresentations that achieved the status of contractual terms, it was ineffective. Section 1(a) of the 1967 Act preserved the dual identity of a statement as a warranty and an inducing misrepresentation. The judge seemed to say that section 1(a), which states that a contract may be rescinded for misrepresentation notwithstanding the misrepresentation becoming a term of the contract, prevents an entire agreement clause of this type from taking effect: 'I think that where a man has been sold a pup, even if it is a warranted pup, there is nothing, unless the contract expressly says so, [to prevent] the man also treating it as a misrepresented pup, if that was indeed the case.'

Non-reliance and evidential estoppel.   Secondly, as a matter of interpretation,   **9.15**
this 'mealy-mouthed' clause did not exclude liability for misrepresentation.[80]

---

[79] [2000] 2 Lloyd's Rep. 611 at [7].
[80] Contrast the treatment of a similar clause in *Deepak v Imperial Chemical Industries plc* [1998] 2 Lloyd's Rep. 139, affirmed [1999] 1 Lloyd's Rep. 387.

The judge was also doubtful that the purchaser's acknowledgment of non-reliance could negative any reliance that in fact existed.[81] There is substance in this: either the clause states the facts accurately or it does not. If in fact the purchaser was induced to enter the contract, language of this sort cannot deny the fact. As a standard provision, it is not easy to see that it even has much evidential value in demonstrating non-reliance. In *EA Grimstead & Son Ltd v McGarrigan*,[82] the court had to consider a clause similar in terms to the second sentence of the above clause in *Thomas Witter*. In its view, the clause was capable of operating as an evidential estoppel.[83] Nevertheless, the court was of the view that a vendor making representations that it intended the purchaser to act upon could not rely upon a clause that to its knowledge did not represent the true position.[84] Later cases have proved more sympathetic to entire agreement clauses than *Thomas Witter*,[85] but there remains the possibility that clauses of this nature will not be permitted to perform their legitimate risk allocation function. An agreement between the parties that no pre-contractual representations have been *made*, however, has been upheld as effective.[86] In some cases, however, the parties might have entered into a genuine collateral contract designed not to be caught by an entire agreement clause in the main contract.[87]

9.16 **Fraud.** Before attention is turned to the Unfair Contract Terms Act 1977 and related legislation, an account should be taken of other common law controls over exemption clauses. First of all, it is at least very likely that liability for fraud may not be excluded.[88] Lord Bingham has expressed this proposition with some degree

---

[81] [1996] 2 All ER 573, 597.

[82] 1999 WL 852482.

[83] *Ibid.*, 29: 'The acknowledgements in the present case are not acknowledgements as to what representations were made to the purchaser; they are acknowledgements as to what acknowledgements the purchaser relied upon.' The court referred to *Lowe v Lombank Ltd* [1960] 1 WLR 196 for the requirements of the estoppel.

[84] *Ibid.*, 30.

[85] See *Watford Electronics Ltd v Sanderson CFL Ltd*, n. 2 above [39]–[40] and *Inntrepreneur Pub Co. (GL) v East Crown Ltd*, n. 79 above at [8], displaying a more sympathetic approach towards such clauses and declining to treat them as exclusions of liability for the purpose of s. 3 of the Misrepresentation Act 1967. See also *Exxonmobil Sales and Supply Corpn v Texaco Ltd (The Helene Knutsen)* [2003] 2 Lloyd's Rep. 686 at [24]; *Ravennavi SPA v New Century Shipbuilding Co. Ltd* [2006] 2 Lloyd's Rep. 280 at [32]; *Peekay Intermark Ltd v Australia and New Zealand Banking Group Ltd* [2006] EWCA Civ 386; [2006] 2 Lloyd's Rep. 511 at [57].

[86] *Trident Turboprop Dublin Ltd v First Flight Couriers Ltd* [2008] EWHC 1686 (Comm) at [36].

[87] *Ryanair Ltd v SR Technics Ireland Ltd* [2007] EWHC 3089 (QB) at [142]. There may also be difficulties of interpretation where a prior agreement is of a different type to the later agreement with the entire agreement clause and it cannot be determined from the clause alone whether the prior agreement is superseded by the later agreement: *Satyam Computer Services Ltd v Unpaid Systems Ltd* [2008] EWCA Civ 487 at [56].

[88] See *S Pearson & Son Ltd v Dublin Corpn* [1907] AC 351; *HIH Casualty and General Insurance Ltd v Chase Manhattan Bank*, n. 62 above; *Frans Maas (UK) Ltd v Samsung Electronics (UK) Ltd*

of caution;[89] this may be due to a possible distinction being drawn between a person's own fraud and that of his servants or agents,[90] though such a distinction would require some adjustment in the case of company principals to separate those who are part of the directing mind and will of the company and those through whom the company otherwise acts. Assuming nevertheless that liability for fraud may not be excluded at all, it should follow that it may not be limited either, for otherwise any outright prohibition on exclusion could easily be circumvented. It may also be impossible to exclude or limit liability for breach of a fiduciary duty,[91] though there are degrees of fiduciary duty.[92] At times, there has been some degree of support for the avoidance of unfair or unreasonable exemption clauses,[93] but the better view now is that legislation plays the controlling role in this area, leaving no room for any common law rule to apply.

Fundamental breach. Any attempt to prohibit exemption clauses at common **9.17** law on the ground of unfairness or unreasonableness is redolent of the doctrine of fundamental breach of contract. As judicially expounded, this doctrine took on legislative functions in the control of exemption clauses and, shortly after the passing of the 1977 Act, was laid to rest by the House of Lords.[94] A series of decisions prior to the decision of the House of Lords in *Suisse Atlantique Societe d'Armement Maritime SA v NV Rotterdamsche Kolen Centrale*[95] laid down, or was understood to lay down, a rule of law that an exemption clause could not as a matter of substantive law give protection in the case of a fundamental breach of contract or a breach of a fundamental term of the contract.[96] It was never entirely clear what was a fundamental breach but it could not be said with full confidence to have

---

[2004] EWHC (Comm) 1502; [2004] 2 Lloyd's Rep. 251 at [154]. See also the extraordinary case of *Thomas Witter Ltd v TBP Industries Ltd*, n. 81 above, 598, where the court, applying the very opposite of the *contra proferentem* rule of interpretation, interpreted a clause in general language as extending to fraud before striking it down as an impermissible exclusion ('If it excludes liability for one kind of misrepresentation it does so for all'). Cf *Regus (UK) Ltd v Epcot Solutions Ltd* [2008] EWCA Civ 361 at [34] (reference to a general clause that would not 'naturally be construed as purporting to exclude liability for fraud').

[89] See *HIH Casualty*, n. 62 above, at [16], noting the difficulty of interpreting the *Pearson* decision (on which see also Lord Hoffmann at [80]), above. In *HIH Casualty*, Lord Hobhouse was content at [121]–[122] to accept a rule of public policy preventing the exclusion of liability for fcccccraud.

[90] See *HIH Casualty*, n. 62 above, at [76] (Lord Hoffmann).

[91] *Gluckstein v Barnes* [1900] AC 240.

[92] Even so, a fiduciary duty is unlikely to arise in the case of a contract of sale, unless the contract is concluded between a company and one or more of its directors.

[93] *Levison v Patent Steam Carpet Cleaning Co. Ltd* [1978] QB 69, 79 (clause unreasonable in itself or in its application); *Laceys Footwear (Wholesale) Ltd v Bowler International Freight Ltd* [1997] 2 Lloyd's Rep. 369, 385 (unfairness).

[94] In *Photo Production Ltd v Securicor Transport Ltd*, n. 4 above.

[95] [1967] 1 AC 361.

[96] See, e.g., *Karsales (Harrow) Ltd v Wallis* [1956] 1 WLR 936; *Yeoman Credit Ltd v Apps* [1962] 2 QB 508; *Charterhouse Credit Co. Ltd v Tolly* [1963] 2 QB 683.

been limited to those breaches that went to the root of the contract.[97] As for the breach of a fundamental term, again it was not clear whether the category was broader than promissory conditions, or was limited to promissory conditions, or was confined further to promissory conditions of the most essential character, such as those dealing with description and the seller's title.[98] The distinction between fundamental breach and breach of fundamental term was often elided and the expression 'fundamental breach' used in a wider sense to embrace both categories. The *Suisse Atlantique* case laid down the rule, or was widely believed to have laid down the rule, that whether a fundamental breach of contract in the wide sense was covered by an exemption clause depended on the construction of the contract. It was perhaps unsurprising, given the severity of the breach and the destructive impact of the clause on contractual rights, that the difference in practice between applying the rule of fundamental breach as a matter of substantive law and as matter of construction was not always readily apparent, though a judicial unwillingness to engage closely with the language of the clause was revealing.[99] What was more surprising was a reading of *Suisse Atlantique* that confined its support of a rule of construction to those cases where the contract was affirmed after a fundamental breach of contract, leaving a rule of substantive law applicable in those cases where the contract had been terminated. The reason for the difference was that the termination of the contract served also to bring an end to the exemption clause.[100] In setting its stamp finally upon treating the fundamental breach rule as one of construction, the House of Lords in *Photo Production Ltd v Securicor Transport Ltd*[101] also repudiated the view that the effect of termination was to eradicate exemption clauses.[102] Like other clauses of a secondary kind, they

---

[97] See Ch. 10 below. Cf *Suisse Atlantique Societe d'Armement Maritime SA v NV Rotterdamsche Kolen Centrale* [1967] 1 AC 361, 431 (Lord Wilberforce); *Wathes (Western) Ltd v Austins Menswear Ltd* [1976] 1 Lloyd's Rep. 14, 19 (Megaw LJ), applying the test of deprivation of substantially the whole benefit as laid down in *Hongkong Fir Shipping Co. Ltd v Kawasaki Kisen Kaisha* [1962] 2 QB 26. See this latter case on the questions whether the fundamental character of the breach should be judged as of the time of its occurrence or at the date of the contract, and whether this depended on the affirmation or termination of the contract.

[98] In *Smeaton Hanscomb & Co. Ltd v Sassoon I Setty Son & Co.* [1953] 1 WLR 1468, Devlin J defined a fundamental term as 'something which underlies the whole contract so that, if it is not complied with, the performance becomes something totally different from that which the contract contemplates'. The reference to performance blurs the line that Devlin J was keen to retain between fundamental breach and breach of a fundamental term.

[99] See, e.g., *Wathes (Western) Ltd v Austins Menswear Ltd*, n. 97 above, 25 (Sir John Pennycuick).

[100] See, e.g., *Harbutts 'Plasticine' Ltd v Wayne Tank Co. Ltd* [1970] 1 QB 447; *Kenyon Son and Craven Ltd v Baxter Hoare & Co. Ltd* [1971] 1 WLR 519; *Levison v Patent Steam Cleaning Co. Ltd* [1978] QB 69.

[101] n. 4 above; see also *Heyman v Darwins Ltd* [1942] AC 356 (Lord Porter).

[102] A statutory version of the rule of construction is found in s. 9(1) of the Unfair Contract Terms Act 1977, which provides that a clause compliant with the reasonableness standard will be given effect notwithstanding termination of the contract.

survived termination and continued to define the contracting parties' rights and duties. In so far as fundamental breach became just another rule of construction, it lost in effect its existence as a rule at all and was submerged in a broader rule of, or rather approach to, construction, that the more destructive a clause is of contractual rights, the heavier the burden of persuasion on the *proferens* to show that the clause was indeed intended to apply to the instant case.

Other rules of construction.   Even as the doctrine of fundamental breach **9.18** flourished, there remained in existence rules of construction that allowed for protection to the *proferens* only so far as he was performing the contract in its essential respects, that is to say, within the four corners of the contract[103] or in accordance with the 'main object and intent of the contract', [104] which permitted a clause to be struck down for its repugnancy to one or more other provisions of the contract.[105] It is this approach, it is submitted, that, despite the abolition of the doctrine of fundamental breach, accommodates Lord Wilberforce's assertion that contracting parties cannot have contemplated that a clause should have so wide an effect as to reduce the contract to a declaration of intent.[106] Again, on the basis of this same approach, a clause will be construed against total contractual non-performance and the performance of something completely different from the requirements of the contract.[107] This approach best explains too the continuing strict approach to deviation, which should no longer be explained in terms of a substantive rule of law.[108] Similarly, though the deliberate character of a breach was apparently to be disregarded in the classification of a breach as fundamental,[109] it is a matter of significance in the construction of exemption clauses.[110]

---

[103] *Gibaud v Great Eastern Railway Co.* [1921] 2 KB 426.

[104] e.g., *Glynn Margetson & Co.* [1893] AC 351 (confining a liberty clause that gave a shipowner a very broad and express entitlement to call in at any port in the Mediterranean, on the coast of Africa, and Great Britain and Ireland, to ports on the way from Malaga to Liverpool); *Sze Hai Tong Bank v Rambler Cycle Co. Ltd* [1959] AC 576 (failure of a carrier to perform its basic obligation of delivery to the holder of a bill of lading); *Mitsubishi Corpn v Eastwind Transport Ltd (The Irbenskiy Proliv)* [2004] EWHC 2924 (Comm); [2005] 1 Lloyd's Rep. 383.

[105] *Daiwoo Heavy Industries Ltd v Klipriver Shipping Ltd (The Kapitan Petko Voivoda)* [2002] EWHC 1306; [2002] 2 All ER (Comm.) 560 (Langley J at [23]).

[106] *Suisse Atlantique Societe d'Armement Maritime SA v NV Rotterdamsche Kolen Centrale* [1967] 1 AC 361, 432; *Tor Line AB v Alltrans Group of Canada Ltd* [1984] 1 WLR 48, 58–9.

[107] *George Mitchell (Chesterhall) Ltd v Finney Lock Seeds Ltd*, n. 55 above.

[108] See, e.g., *Daiwoo Heavy Industries Ltd v Klipriver Shipping Ltd (The Kapitan Petko Voivoda)*, n. 105 above; *Kenya Railways v Antares Co Pte Ltd (The Antares) (No. 1)* [1987] 1 Lloyd's Rep. 424, 430.

[109] *Suisse Atlantique Societe d'Armement Maritime SA v NV Rotterdamsche Kolen Centrale*, n. 106 above.

[110] *Sze Hai Tong Bank v Rambler Cycle Co. Ltd*, n. 104 above.

Statute

The Unfair Contract Terms Act 1977

9.19 Introduction. The control of exemption clauses by the Unfair Contract Terms Act 1977 does not as such detract from the existence and exercise of common law controls on exemption clauses, though its enactment presented the opportunity to abandon the doctrine of fundamental breach and some of the more far-fetched interpretations of clauses. The Act builds upon and consolidates provisions in earlier legislation, the Supply of Goods (Implied Terms) Act 1973,[111] and adds new provisions.[112] It also amends the Misrepresentation Act 1967. The structure of the 1977 Act is complex and unsystematic. So far as the Act applies to sale of goods, it is capable of applying in different degrees to private sales, consumer sales, and business sales. Despite its title, the Act is not a statute that deals comprehensively with 'unfair terms': it has nothing to say, for example, about penalty clauses, forfeiture clauses, acceleration clauses, and price escalation clauses, or about clauses that exact an oppressively high price for goods or services.[113] The Act instead deals with exclusion clauses, limitation clauses, and indemnity clauses,[114] as well as with clauses that perform the same role by defining performance.[115] Besides clauses excluding and restricting liability, an exclusion clause under the Act includes clauses making liability or enforcement subject to restrictive or onerous conditions.[116] Falling within this category are clauses denying the right of set-off that might otherwise arise[117] and clauses that subject claims to a shorter limitation period than that provided by statute.[118] This category will also include clauses that require claims to be notified within a stated time or period, so long as the period is a restrictive or onerous one.[119] An example might be a clause requiring notification of faults within an unreasonably short period after delivery. A clause imposing an

---

[111] Provisions of this Act, now consolidated in the 1977 Act, placed controls on the exclusion of the implied terms in ss.12–15 of the Sale of Goods Act 1893 (as it then was).

[112] The 1977 Act responded to the Law Commission's *Second Report on Exemption Clauses* (Law Com. No. 69, 1975).

[113] *Interfoto Picture Library Ltd v Stiletto Visual Programmes Ltd* [1989] QB 433.

[114] It also deals with non-contractual notices excluding tortious liability.

[115] S. 3(2)(b).

[116] S. 13(a).

[117] *Stewart Gill Ltd v Horatio Myer & Co. Ltd* [1992] QB 600; *Schenkers Ltd v Overland Shoes Ltd* [1998] 1 Lloyd's Rep 498.

[118] *BHP Petroleum Ltd v British Steel Plc* [1999] 2 Lloyd's Rep. 583, 592. Such a clause may be reasonable, however, especially where the defendant is an intermediate party subject to a limitation period in making a claim over: *Granville Oil & Chemicals Ltd v Davis Turner & Co. Ltd* [2003] EWCA Civ 570; [2003] 2 Lloyd's Rep. 356 at [22]–[23].

[119] *Bacardi-Martini Beverages Ltd v Thomas Hardy Packaging Ltd* [2002] 1 Lloyd's Rep. 62 at [37] (notice of defect within five days even for latent defects).

onerous procedure for making a claim should also be treated as an exemption clause within the meaning of the Act.

Negligence. Whether the attempt is made in a contract term or in a notice, lia- **9.20** bility for negligence may not be excluded or restricted[120] in the case of death or personal injury.[121] In the case of 'other loss or damage', the exclusion or restriction has to pass the test of reasonableness.[122] Nor is agreement to, or awareness of, a clause or notice to be taken as amounting to a voluntary acceptance of risk.[123] So far as these provisions apply to contract, they apply to all contracts, whether of a private, consumer, or business character. The language of the Act is unrestricted.

Dealing as a consumer. Section 3 of the 1977 Act introduces a standard of rea- **9.21** sonableness for specified contract terms, without regard to the type or head of lia- bility, in two quite different cases. The first is where one of the contracting parties deals as a consumer. The notion of dealing as a consumer is not straightforward and in fact comprises three elements. Applying the notion to a contract of sale involving a consumer buyer, first, the buyer does not contract in the course of a business or hold himself out as doing so. Secondly, the seller does contract in the course of a business. Business is defined as including 'a profession and the activi- ties of any government department or local or public authority'.[124] Inclusive defi- nitions are short on certainty; a lengthy list of examples might have provided some measure of predictability, but this definition does little to suggest the outer bound- aries of business. Nevertheless, the reference to professions and government is indicative that a broad sense of business lies behind the concept of dealing as a consumer. For example, there is little reason to doubt that a charity engaging in commercial activity in furtherance of its aims is acting in the course of a business when selling goods. The reference to government in the definition ensures that business cannot be defined according to the profit motive, but rather means some- thing that itself is recurrent and systematic or in aid of something else that is recur- rent and systematic. Thirdly, provided the buyer is not an individual,[125] there is an additional requirement. In the case of non-individual buyers, the goods[126] must be of a type ordinarily supplied for private use or consumption.[127] If ordinarily

---

[120] Discussed below.

[121] S.2(1).

[122] S.3(2). Reasonableness is discussed below.

[123] S.3(3).

[124] S. 14, which suggests a broad view should be taken of the activities of universities, whether ancient, old or new.

[125] This proviso was added by SI 2002 No. 3045, reg.14.

[126] The meaning of which is the same as in the Sale of Goods Act: s. 14.

[127] S. 12(1). The character of the goods is relevant for sale, hire purchase, and miscellaneous con- tracts under which the property in goods passes: s. 12(1)(c). The concept of dealing as a consumer is relevant also for exemption clauses dealing with the implied terms of description, quality, and fitness in the Sale of Goods Act and related statutes. These terms cannot be excluded or restricted where

they are so supplied, the fact that they might also be supplied for business use should not prevent them from completing the definition of dealing as a consumer. Auctions and similar types of sale are excluded from the definition of dealing as a consumer to the following extent. First, a buyer who is an individual does not deal as a consumer when purchasing second-hand goods at a public auction where individuals may attend in person. This should mean that an individual who uses an agent to conduct the bidding or who bids over the telephone or in some other way removed from the auction room is not dealing as a consumer. Secondly, a buyer who is not an individual does not deal as a consumer when buying goods by auction or competitive tender.[128] The reasons why the definition of dealing as a consumer are as complex as this are not easy to see. The burden is also on those claiming that someone does not deal as a consumer to show this.[129] Thus, as the case may be, a seller would bear the burden of showing that the buyer purchased the goods in the course of a business, or that he himself was not contracting in the course of a business or that, so far as the requirement is applicable, the goods were not of a type ordinarily supplied for private use or consumption.

9.22 **Course of a business.** The question whether the buyer was purchasing in the course of a business arose in *R & B Customs Brokers Co. Ltd v United Dominions Trust Ltd*.[130] The buyer was a private company in business as a shipping broker and a car was bought on conditional sale terms for the personal and business use of two directors. The court concluded that the buyer did not make the contract in the course of a business and drew a distinction between purchases integral to and purchases incidental to a buyer's business. In the latter case, though not in the former, there would have to be a sufficient degree of regularity in the type of transaction for it to be said that the buyer was acting in the course of a business. The buyer in this case did not purchase vehicles sufficiently regularly[131] for this transaction to have been conducted in the course of its business. In reaching this conclusion, the court relied upon a House of Lords decision, *Davies v Sumner*,[132] arising out of a similarly worded provision in the Trade Descriptions Act 1968.[133] In that case, the question was whether the *seller* was acting in the course of a business; it was not whether the buyer was *not* acting in the course of a business.

---

the buyer is dealing as a consumer: s. 6(2). Where the buyer is not dealing as a consumer because the seller is not acting in the course of a business, an exemption clause is subject to a statutory standard of reasonableness. Consequently, a private seller may exclude the description condition, subject to reasonableness, regardless of the identity and purpose of the buyer.

[128] S. 12(2) (added by SI 2002 No. 3045, reg.14).

[129] S. 12(3).

[130] [1988] 1 All ER 847. The case was followed in *Feldaroll Foundry Plc v Hermes Leasing Plc* [2004] EWCA Civ 747.

[131] This was only the second or third vehicle acquired on credit terms.

[132] [1984] 1 WLR 1301 (HL).

[133] S. 1(1) of the Trade Descriptions Act 1968 ('in the course of a trade or business').

The seller was a self-employed courier acting for a television company who had traded in his car with a false odometer reading after driving it for more than 100,000 miles. In concluding that the lack of regularity of the courier in disposing of his car meant that he was not acting in the course of a trade or business, the House of Lords distinguished an earlier case,[134] where a car hire company disposed of its fleet at two-year intervals and was acting in the course of a trade or business. The distinction can be justified on the ground that criminal legislation might appropriately distinguish between expert and non-expert sellers, using the notion of regularity as a test in doing so. This does not mean that the same approach in construing undefined statutory language should be adopted for the purpose of all statutes with identical or similar wording.[135] Moreover, the reliance of the court in *R & B Customs Brokers Co. Ltd* on a case involving the seller, and on a notion of regularity devised to determine the incidence of criminal liability, does not assist in seeking the purpose of the protection given to consumers in the Unfair Contract Terms Act 1977. Admittedly, the test of dealing as a consumer does not as such serve as a bright line to identify cases where the buyer needs protection and cases where the buyer does not, since both categories of buyer obtain protection under the Act, albeit in varying degrees.[136] But it is there for a purpose and that purpose, it is submitted, may have been to capture those cases where businesses are acting as consumers and where the principle of strict seller liability for non-conforming goods under the Sale of Goods Act should rule without exclusion or restriction, regardless of the type of consumer buyer. A small business purchasing paper or even office equipment, for example, might for this reason stake a claim to protection under section 3 of the Unfair Contract Terms Act[137] despite the regularity of its purchases. If that business is in the financial sector, for instance, and if its office purchases are carried out by relatively junior staff with no authority to negotiate over the seller's terms, the relationship of that business to the seller is not significantly different from that of any other member of the public.

Mixed use.   In *R & B Customs Brokers Co. Ltd*, Dillon LJ considered also another   **9.23** aspect of dealing as a consumer that had not been argued in the case. First of all, he assumed that an individual buyer purchasing goods for a mixture of personal and business reasons would be regarded as dealing as a consumer, which is surely correct. He then considered that it would be anomalous to reach a different

---

134 *Havering London Borough v Stevenson* [1970] 1 WLR 1377.

135 The seller disposing of equipment surplus to his business requirements at irregular and infrequent intervals does act in the course of a business for the purpose of s. 14 of the Sale of Goods Act: see *Stevenson v Rogers* [1999] QB 1028, declining to follow the *R&B Customs Brokers* interpretation of 'the course of a business' in a different statutory provision, and Ch. 7 above.

136 See Dillon LJ, n. 130 above, 853 ('two classes of innocent contracting parties . . . for whom differing degrees of protection against unfair contract terms are afforded').

137 As well as to the fuller protection under s. 6(2) given to those dealing as a consumer.

conclusion just because the purchase was made by the company itself for its directors, who themselves would use it for combined personal and business reasons. In other words, he would have avoided classifying, as a business purpose only, the company's purpose in letting its directors have the use of the car for mixed personal and business purposes. Dillon LJ would have been prepared to pierce the corporate veil to avoid an 'anomalous' distinction between these two cases.[138] It is not self-evident that the corporate veil should be pierced in this way.

9.24   **Dealing on another's standard terms.**   Section 3 of the Unfair Contract Terms Act also applies the standard of reasonableness to exemption clauses where one party deals on the other's written standard terms of business. Contracts between businesses, whether corporate or non-corporate, are therefore within the reach of the section. As expressed, section 3 should not apply to standard terms promulgated by bipartisan trading associations representing both sellers and buyers, for the reason that these terms are not the terms of 'one party'.[139] The provision should apply, nevertheless, in the case of terms promulgated by associations representing only sellers if a seller adopts the provisions as its own.[140] It may be that in neither case will there be bargaining over particular standard terms, but in the case of bipartisan terms the interests of both parties to the contract will at least have been consulted in an even-handed way during the drawing up of the standard form. An issue concerning the application of section 3 might also arise, in the case where business assets are sold, where the terms derive from the standard precedents of major law firms. It might be said in such a case that the terms of its agents are the terms, for example, of the seller of those assets, even though the buyer's solicitors will be proffering their own standard terms. In such cases, the negotiations will centre on a few key provisions where the parties are at variance, the remaining terms being more or less identical. So far as there is true negotiation over the disputed clause or clauses, the argument in favour of applying section 3 is weakened.

---

[138] See Dillon LJ, n. 130 above, 855.

[139] Cf the more general language used in *Hadley Design Associates Ltd v Lord Mayor and Citizens of the City of Westminster* [2003] EWHC 1617 (TCC); [2004] TCLR 1 at [78] (written terms 'intended to be adopted more or less automatically in all transactions of a particular type without any significant opportunity for negotiation'). In *Granville Oil & Chemicals Ltd v Davis Turner & Co. Ltd*, n. 118 above at [9], the court went on to apply the standard of reasonableness even after noting that the standard terms were negotiated between a freight forwarders' association and a committee of customers.

[140] See *Frans Maas (UK) Ltd v Samsung Electronics (UK) Ltd* [2004] EWHC (Comm) 1502; [2004] 2 Lloyd's Rep. 251; *Granville Oil & Chemicals Ltd v Davis Turner & Co Ltd*, n. 118 above (both cases on freight forwarders' terms, where s. 3 was assumed to be applicable). Cf *British Fermentation Products Ltd v Compair Reavell Ltd* [1999] 2 All ER (Comm.) 389, where the judge, after a careful review of the work of the Law Commission, concluded that a company of mechanical engineers, using Institute of Mechanical Engineers standard terms, did not do business on its own written standard terms since, for that to be the case, those terms should 'invariably or at least usually be used by the party in question', which had neither been alleged nor proved by the other party to the contract.

Section 3 nevertheless is predicated upon one party doing business 'on the basis' of the other's standard terms. Even if particular terms are negotiated, the former party, when negotiating, is doing business and the latter's standard terms serve as the basis of that negotiation.[141] The safer conclusion, therefore, is that section 3 is engaged but that the criterion of reasonableness is more likely to be satisfied by the presence of bargaining and give-and-take.[142] Arguments in favour of not imposing the standard of reasonableness in section 3 tend also to uphold clauses as reasonable if the standard is imposed.

Different performance.   Section 3 governs clauses that exclude or restrict liabil- **9.25** ity, and thus both exclusion and limitation clauses. In addition, it governs clauses supporting a claim 'to render a contractual performance substantially different from that which was reasonably expected' or 'to render no performance at all'. Section 3 is broad enough to deal with clauses that covertly exclude or limit liability by defining performance in a discretionary way. The latter formulation would thus apply to clauses reducing the contract to a declaration of intent by reserving a discretion to the seller not to perform at all.[143] Beyond that, its protective scope is obscure. A literal application of the rule would have it strike down clauses containing promissory conditions that allow a party to terminate the contract for a breach of contract that produces slight or no injurious effects, but the history of the legislation and its antecedent case law gives no support to the interpretation of the section in this way.[144] As for the meaning of 'render[ing] a contractual performance substantially different' from that expected, it should be applicable to a clause permitting the seller to substitute a different type of goods in the event of the agreed goods becoming unavailable.

Indemnity clauses.   Where one party deals as a consumer, the standard of rea- **9.26** sonableness is extended in section 4 of the Unfair Contract Terms Act to all contract terms providing an indemnity to the person who is not dealing as a consumer against liability for negligence or breach of contract. The liability in question may be towards the person dealing as a consumer, in which case the indemnity clause operates in a covert way to exclude liability, or it may be towards a third party.[145] The latter type of indemnity is unlikely to arise in a sale of goods contract.

Statutory implied terms.   In section 6, the Unfair Contract Terms Act controls **9.27** clauses excluding or restricting liability for breach of the implied terms as to title,

---

[141] See *St Albans City and District Council v International Computers Ltd* [1996] 4 All ER 481.

[142] See *Watford Electronics Ltd v Sanderson CFL Ltd*, n. 2 above.

[143] Cf Treitel, n. 15 above, 275, for the view that the provision might not apply if the contractual term grants a 'totally free discretion' and thus imposes no obligation at all.

[144] Cf also *Ilanchelian v Esso Petroleum Co. Ltd*, Unreported, 28 September 1998, discussed in Ch. 10 below.

[145] S. 4(2).

description, satisfactory quality, fitness for purpose, and correspondence to sample. The seller's obligations under section 12 of the Sale of Goods Act may not be excluded or restricted at all, regardless of the character of the sale as a consumer or non-consumer transaction.[146] As stated in an earlier chapter, this prohibition requires a difficult distinction to be drawn between limited title sales and sales with a prohibited exemption clause.[147] As for the implied terms of description, satisfactory quality, fitness for purpose, and correspondence to sample, these may not be excluded or restricted at all where the buyer deals as a consumer; in other cases, clauses excusing or restricting liability are subjected to a standard of reasonableness.[148] This provision is not likely to be interpreted narrowly. A car dealer's attempt to sell goods 'as seen and inspected' was stated to be an invalid attempt to cut down the scope of his description duty in *Hughes v Hall*.[149] A clause in the contract requiring a consumer buyer to elect in favour of accepting unsatisfactory or unfit goods with a price allowance, rather than rejecting them and recovering the price, should also be seen as 'restricting' liability and hence as ineffectual.[150] The test of dealing as a consumer is the same as for section 3[151] but the extension beyond clauses excluding or restricting liability to clauses that render performance different from that expected is for no apparent reason not repeated in section 6.

9.28 **Criteria of reasonableness.** Where the buyer does not deal as a consumer and where negligence is not sought to be excluded, the criteria of reasonableness are to be found in Schedule 2.[152] Where applicable, the requirement of reasonableness

---

[146] S. 6(1) (sale of goods and hire purchase: seller's right to sell, freedom from encumbrances and quiet possession). For the equivalent provision for other contracts where possession or ownership is transferred, see s. 7(3A), but see also s. 7(4) and the application of reasonableness to certain cases.

[147] See Ch. 5 above.

[148] S. 6(2), (3) (which makes also corresponding provision for hire purchase contracts). S. 7(2), (3) makes corresponding provision for other types of contract where possession or ownership is transferred.

[149] [1981] RTR 430 (a decision under the Consumer Transactions (Restrictions on Statements) Order 1976, SI 1976, No. 1813, as am. by SI 1978 No. 127). Cf *Cavendish-Woodhouse Ltd v Manley* (1984) 82 LGR 376 (decided under the same Order), where the Divisional Court concluded that a similar expression ('bought as seen') meant only that the consumer had seen the goods. The point of a clause having no higher aspiration than that is hard to see.

[150] There is this difficulty with the stated proposition. In the very similar case of a buyer signing a delivery note containing small print expressing satisfaction with the goods, the Law Commission proposed additional legislation (in Law Com. No. 160, *Sale and Supply of Goods*) whose effect is to provide that the buyer is deemed not to have accepted the goods prior to an opportunity to examine them. This legislation became s. 35(2), (3) of the Sale of Goods Act as amended by the Sale and Supply of Goods Act 1994.

[151] Indeed, *R & B Customs Brokers Co. Ltd v United Dominions Trust Ltd*, n. 130 above was decided under s. 6.

[152] The criteria are also used outside the instances prescribed in Sch. 2, for example, under s. 3: see *Singer (UK) Ltd v Tees and Hartlepool Port Authority* [1988] 2 Lloyd's Rep. 164, 169; *Flamar Interocean Ltd v Denmac Ltd (The Flamar Pride and the Flamar Progress)* [1990] 1 Lloyd's Rep. 434, 438-39; *Stewart Gill Ltd v Horatio Myer & Co. Ltd*, n. 117 above, 608; *Granville Oil & Chemicals Ltd v Davis Turner & Co. Ltd*, n. 118 above at [5].

continues to apply even where the party affected by an exemption clause affirms the contract upon the other's discharging breach.[153] The criteria in Schedule 2 include the strength of the parties' bargaining power[154] and the buyer's ability to acquire the goods elsewhere, the existence of an inducement to the buyer to accept the exclusion clause,[155] whether the buyer should have known of the term,[156] the reasonableness of complying with a condition that would have suspended the exclusion clause,[157] and the manufacture, process or adaptation of goods to the buyer's special order.[158] Obviously, since these are guidelines, they are only illustrative and other sensible criteria should not be excluded.[159] For example, it might make perfect commercial sense for the parties to agree that defects be put right under the terms of the manufacturer's (satisfactory) guarantee scheme. The reasonableness of a clause might also depend upon its cumulative effect with other clauses in the contract.[160] A clause may be found to be reasonable if it is common use in the trade concerned and can be said to reflect the customs of that trade.[161] Other relevant criteria not specifically mentioned in the Act include whether the parties did in fact negotiate over the terms of the exemption clause,[162] a contracting party's awareness and understanding of an exemption clause,[163] and whether the terms are taken from a third party's standard form in a way that demonstrates

---

[153] S. 9(2). S. 9(1) provides that a reasonable exemption clause remains effective despite termination of the contract, thus preventing the revival within the scheme of the Act of the doctrine of fundamental breach of contract. Oddly, the provision includes the case of a contract 'terminated . . . by breach' as well as by party's election to treat the contract as terminated. This is probably a reference to the heterodoxical view of Lord Denning MR in *Harbutts 'Plasticine' Ltd v Wayne Tank Co. Ltd* [1970] 1 QB 447 that a fundamental breach of contract could automatically terminate a contract.

[154] See *Marplace (Number 512) Ltd v Chaffe Street* [2006] EWHC 1919 (Ch) at [484] ('sophisticated and wealthy consumer'). The ability of the smaller party to drive a hard bargain is a relevant consideration: *Bacardi-Martini Beverages Ltd v Thomas Hardy Packaging Ltd*, n. 119 above at [34]. For a distinction between cases where there is equal bargaining on price but not on terms, see *Balmoral Group Ltd v Borealis UK Ltd* [2006] 2 Lloyd's Rep. 629 at [409].

[155] A lower price would be such an inducement.

[156] *AEG (UK) Ltd v Logic Resource Ltd* [1996] CLC 265; see also the above discussion of incorporation.

[157] This would include, e.g., a requirement that defects be notified to the seller within a given time.

[158] The court in *Sterling Hydraulics Ltd v Dichomatic Ltd* [2006] EWHC 2004 (QB) at [31] had difficulty seeing the relevance of this criterion, and the arguments advanced seemed to go more to substantive liability than to the reasonableness of an exemption clause. The line between these two matters is not easy to draw. A seller may not have detailed knowledge of the buyer's needs in 'a low value high volume contract': *ibid.*, [29].

[159] S. 11(2) declares them to be of 'particular' relevance.

[160] *AEG (UK) Ltd v Logic Resource Ltd*, n. 156 above.

[161] *Schenkers Ltd v Overland Shoes Ltd* [1998] 1 Lloyd's Rep 498, 507.

[162] *Watford Electronics Ltd v Sanderson CFL Ltd*, n. 2 above.

[163] *Britvic Soft Drinks Ltd v Messer UK Ltd* [2002] 2 Lloyd's Rep. 368 at [21] ('actual extent and quality of the knowledge of a party').

that they are not being imposed by one party on the other.[164] The court in *Watford Electronics Ltd v Sanderson CFL Ltd*[165] was particularly influenced by the fact that the two contracting parties, of equal bargaining power, were represented by experienced negotiators, and that there were negotiations on price (where the claimant licensee of software successfully exacted concessions) as well as on the restriction of liability (where the claimant was less successful, obtaining only the addition of a best efforts clause). It was able therefore to conclude summarily that a limitation clause was reasonable because, in dealing with direct losses, it gave the claimant the same recovery as it would have got from the presumptive measure of damages for breach of warranty of quality in the Sale of Goods Act 1979 (measured by the ceiling of the warranted value of the goods supplied).[166] It has also been held material in a finding that a clause was unreasonable that it might relate to damage occurring in a way that the parties might not have foreseen, for example, the introduction of an extraneous contaminant into the manufacturing process,[167] though it might be thought that this is precisely the case where a *proferens* might reasonably hope to be protected from liability. If the liabilities excluded are very wide, a *proferens* is unlikely to be able to show that a clause excluding liability is reasonable.[168] The unreasonableness of a clause may turn upon the contract being concluded in rapid circumstances, where there is no real opportunity to weigh its contents and to arrange for insurance cover.[169] Again, an exclusion of liability is likely to be unreasonable if the burden of carrying liability on an insurance policy is very much less than the catastrophic loss that would be borne by the other party, especially if the liability relates to an elementary standard of care and skill that does not bear down heavily on a professional person.[170]

9.29 **Monetary limitation.** As for monetary limitation clauses, section 11(4) adds the further criteria, to which particular regard should be had, of the resources of the *proferens* available to meet any liability if it should arise and the extent to which it was open to him to cover himself by insurance.[171] These criteria are not restricted

---

[164] *RW Green Ltd v Cade Bros Farms Ltd* [1978] 1 Lloyd's Rep. 602.

[165] n. 162 above.

[166] It should be emphasized that, in some cases, loss of profits will fall within the first limb of the rule in *Hadley v Baxendale* (see, n. 72 above) so that the same conclusion cannot readily be reached where the buyer is claiming normal loss of profits (which were not as such being claimed in the *Watford* case).

[167] *Bacardi-Martini Beverages Ltd v Thomas Hardy Packaging Ltd* [2002] 1 Lloyd's Rep. 62, affirmed [2002] EWCA Civ 549; [2002] 2 Lloyd's Rep. 379 at [25]–[26].

[168] *Bacardi-Martini Beverages Ltd v Thomas Hardy Packaging Ltd*, n. 167 above at [37].

[169] *Phillips Products Ltd v Hyland* [1987] 1 WLR 659.

[170] *Smith v Eric S Bush* [1990] 1 AC 831, 858-59.

[171] See *Salvage Association v CAP Financial Services Ltd* [1995] FSR 654 (where also it would have been 'prohibitively expensive' for the claimants to insure in respect of the software system supplied under the contract). The lower premiums for indemnity than for liability insurance may also be a relevant consideration: *Singer (UK) Ltd v Tees and Hartlepool Port Authority*, n. 152 above, 169.

to the field of application marked out for Schedule 2 but apply in all cases where liability is restricted. Where Schedule 2 does apply, the criteria therein are also applicable to monetary limitation clauses. It is not clear why the size of the money sum does not receive mention[172] and why these factors are not also made specifically relevant in the case of other types of clause.[173]

Burden of persuasion.   The relevant burden is to show that a clause is reasonable **9.30** and not to show that it is unreasonable; it therefore rests on the *proferens*.[174] The assessment of an exemption clause as reasonable depends upon general criteria applied to fluid fact. This is a recipe for unpredictability in the assessment of exemption clauses, which is not helped by the judicial direction calling for restraint when the conclusions of trial judges come under review in a higher court. According to Lord Bridge in *George Mitchell (Chesterhall) Ltd v Finney Lock Seeds Ltd*, the trial judge is acting in a manner akin to the exercise of a discretion and, for his decision to be reversed, must have 'proceeded upon some erroneous principle or was plainly and obviously wrong'.[175] In *Watford Electronics Ltd v Sanderson CFL Ltd*,[176] the Court of Appeal reversed a trial judge's finding that a clause was not reasonable. The judge had found to be irrelevant the use of a similar clause in the claimant licensee's own standard trading terms, when in fact these demonstrated the claimant's awareness of the commercial considerations in favour of restricting liability and of the way in which such clauses affect the price which a licensor of software is prepared to accept.[177] The court in *Watford* therefore displayed a willingness to overturn a finding of unreasonableness (the same should also hold true of the opposite finding) in cases where a relevant criterion is dismissed as irrelevant. Similarly, a finding of unreasonableness can be reversed where the trial judge proceeds on the assumption that exemption clauses are unreasonable if they deprive the claimant of any remedy;[178] the trial judge's approach is

---

Nevertheless, it has been said that s. 11(4) looks at the resources and insurance prospects of the *proferens* and not of the other party: *Britvic Soft Drinks Ltd v Messer UK Ltd*, n. 163 above at [154]. The fact that litigation is in effect between two insurance companies is not a relevant consideration: *ibid*. It is also the *availability* of insurance, at the contract date, rather than the actual insurance position that is the relevant consideration: see *Flamar Interocean Ltd v Denmac Ltd (The Flamar Pride and the Flamar Progress)*, n. 152 above, 439 (and the authorities there cited).

[172] A monetary limitation clause is more likely to be upheld as reasonable if the amount is a substantial one: *Britvic Soft Drinks Ltd v Messer UK Ltd*, n. 163 above at [154]; see also *Bacardi-Martini Beverages Ltd v Thomas Hardy Packaging Ltd*, n. 167 above.

[173] Even though s. 11(4) is not applicable in terms to exclusion clauses, the criteria laid down there are relevant in the case of such clauses: *Flamar Interocean Ltd v Denmac Ltd (The Flamar Pride and the Flamar Progress)*, n. 152 above, 438–9.

[174] S. 11(5); *Overseas Medical Supplies Ltd v Orient Transport Services Ltd* [1999] 2 Lloyd's Rep. 273; see also *SAM business Systems Ltd v Hedley and Co.* [2002] EWHC 2733 (TCC) at [64].

[175] n. 55 above, 816.

[176] n. 2 above.

[177] See also *Balmoral Group Ltd v Borealis UK Ltd*, n. 154 above.

[178] *Regus (UK) Ltd v Epcot Solutions Ltd* [2008] EWCA Civ 361 at [37].

wrong in principle and is tantamount to treating exclusion clauses as *per se* unreasonable. Once a higher court is able, however, to reverse the trial judge, it can then freely substitute its own application of the reasonableness standard. It is not clear whether the court in *Watford* would have been quite as willing to reverse a trial judge whose finding made no overt reference to a relevant criterion, though a failure to mention the statutory criteria could well be different. Section 11(2) states that 'regard shall be had in particular to the matters mentioned in Schedule 2'. This is mandatory and a trial judge who does not manifestly pay regard to a criterion laid down by statute runs the risk of a successful appeal. This same consideration would not apply as such to the criteria in Schedule 2, where these are relevant rather than mandatory. It is less clear whether a trial judge's finding should also be free from reversal by a higher court if the judge declines to weigh the relevant criteria when of the view that some types of liability ought not to be excluded at all.[179]

9.31 **Effect of the Act on exemption clauses.** The Unfair Contract Terms Act does not give the clearest guidance about its effect on a clause that fails to meet the standards laid down by the Act and in particular does not declare offending terms to be void.[180] Furthermore, no clear answer is given to the question whether the term may remain effective to the extent that it does not go beyond the limits laid down in the Act. Starting with the words of the statute, the statutory technique is to focus on a party and say that that party 'cannot' exclude or limit liability, or render unexpected performance, in certain cases;[181] to focus on the other party and say that party 'cannot' be made to indemnify;[182] and to focus on a type of liability and say that it 'cannot' be excluded.[183] This technique seems more apt for criminal and regulatory legislation than for legislation dealing with private law rights and duties. The Act continues in a similar vein: for non-consumers, certain liabilities 'can' be excluded or restricted 'in so far as the term satisfies the requirement of reasonableness';[184] and under secondary contracts, a party 'is not bound'

---

[179] But see *Britvic Soft Drinks Ltd v Messer UK Ltd* [2002] 1 Lloyd's Rep. 20 at [151] ('In my judgment it is wholly unreasonable for the supplier of a bulk commodity such as CO_2 for a food application to seek to exclude liability for the commodity not being of satisfactory quality or being unfit for its purpose where that has come about as a result of a breakdown in the manufacturing process allowing the inadvertent introduction of a redundant carcinogen'). For the supporting view of the Court of Appeal in the same case, see [2002] 2 Lloyd's Rep. 368 at [24]–[26]. In a less dogmatic way, it has been said that 'all things being equal' it should be the seller who bears responsibility for latent defects in goods: see *Balmoral Group Ltd v Borealis UK Ltd*, n. 54 above at [422].
[180] See generally Treitel, n. 15 above, 278-80.
[181] See ss. 2(1), (2), 3(2).
[182] See s. 4(1)).
[183] See ss. 6(1),(2), 7(2), (3A), (4)).
[184] See ss. 6(3), 7(3)).

by the relevant contract term. Despite this variety of expression in the Act, at no time is any provision made to bear directly on the term itself.[185]

Wording of the Act. As a matter of first impression, a contract term offending for example, section 2(1) by excluding liability for personal injury should survive to the extent that it lawfully excludes or restricts another form of liability. In the case of 'other loss or damage',[186] the formulation of section 2(2) substantially means that such loss or damage *can* be excluded so far as it is done reasonably. So, a reading of the section that, where a term excludes liability for negligence in respect of all types of harm, the whole term is struck down for non-compliance with section 2(1), would be inconsistent with section 2(2). The support given by section 2(2) to a straightforward reading of section 2(1) is not available in a case where a clause extends to a type of liability not specifically dealt with by the Act, for example, a seller's liability for late delivery. In this case, a straightforward reading of section 2(1) is still to be preferred, so as to conclude that the whole term is not struck down. In addition, there is no statutory definition of a 'term' and no necessary reason to deny that a given set of words assembled in a paragraph could be construed as consisting of more than one term. If the words can be grammatically severed, there are compelling reasons for allowing the remnants of a term to survive even if the rest of the term is struck down by section 2(1). Although this solution is supported by a case decided on similar legislation pre-dating the Act,[187] it is opposed by authority decided under the Act.[188] If the latter is correct, the danger arises that a term will be read excessively broadly and the whole term rendered ineffectual.[189] It is therefore submitted that the former approach allowing severance is preferable in principle.[190] Moreover, to say that a term as a whole has to be reasonable under the Act[191] begs the question what is a term. It should not be assumed that a term is just a clause under another name. If the above submission is acceptable, it might apply that even the two or more terms contained in the same sentence or paragraph were distinguishable but nevertheless incapable of clean grammatical severance. The Court of Appeal has recently exercised severance in the case of a clause whose component parts could have been separately numbered

9.32

---

[185] Cf the Unfair Terms in Consumer Contracts Regulations 1999, where the focus is on the term, which 'shall not be binding on a consumer' (reg. 8).

[186] S. 2(2), viz other than death and personal injury).

[187] *RW Green Ltd v Cade Bros Farms Ltd*, n. 164 above.

[188] *Stewart Gill Ltd v Horatio Myer & Co. Ltd*, n. 117 above. Note, however, the doubts of Mance LJ in *Bacardi-Martini Beverages Ltd v Thomas Hardy Packaging Ltd*, n. 119 above at [26] and see now *Regus (UK) Ltd v Epcot Solutions Ltd*, n. 178 above at [46].

[189] For a striking example of this, see *Thomas Witter Ltd v TBP Industries Ltd*, n. 88 above, 597, decided under s. 3 of the Misrepresentation Act 1967. This very danger was pointed out in *Skipskredittforeningen v Emperor Navigation* [1998] 1 Lloyd's Rep. 67, 75.

[190] Cf s. 3 of the Misrepresentation Act 1967, where a term, though rendered 'of no effect', is saved 'in so far as it satisfies the requirement of reasonableness'.

[191] *Stewart Gill Ltd v Horatio Myer & Co. Ltd*, n. 117 above.

but were not.[192] A court should not, however, be set the task of rewriting the contract for the *proferens*. A clause providing that liability is excluded or restricted to the extent that it is reasonable to do so under the Act should be ineffective. Similarly, a court will not read down an exclusion clause by converting it into a limitation clause.[193]

9.33 **Manufacturers' guarantees.** Section 5 of the Unfair Contract Terms Act makes provision for exemption clauses in connection with manufacturers' guarantees.[194] In particular, 'the negligence of a person concerned in the manufacture or distribution of goods' may not be excluded or restricted by a contract term or notice contained in or referring to a guarantee, where goods ordinarily supplied for private use or consumption turn out to be defective when in consumer use. This formula is broad enough to include manufacturers, producers, importers and all sellers prior to the immediate seller, as well as (since section 5 uses the passive voice) their employees and agents.[195] The immediate seller would appear to be excluded since section 5(3) provides that the 'section does not apply as between the parties to a contract under or in pursuance of which possession or ownership of the goods passed'.[196] Unlike negligence liability in section 2 for loss other than personal injury and death, clauses excluding or restricting liability under section 5 are not saved if they are reasonable. This oddly means that a retail seller might be able to exclude or restrict liability for negligence to the extent of reasonableness when giving a warning or instructions relating to the use of the goods[197] when other parties in the distribution chain cannot. Although the retail seller might be able to do this, the manufacturer cannot do this for the retail seller by virtue of the guarantee. This is because section 10 provides that a person is 'not bound' by any 'contract term' (an expression that should include a term in a manufacturer's guarantee)

---

[192] *Regus (UK) Ltd v Epcot Solutions Ltd*, n. 178 above at [46].

[193] *George Mitchell (Chesterhall) Ltd v Finney Lock Seeds Ltd*, n. 55 above, 816.

[194] An offence is committed by manufacturers, *inter alia*, if guarantees dealing with the fitness, description or quality of goods suggest that they supersede the buyer's statutory implied term rights, or fail to inform the consumer that those rights are unaffected by the guarantee: Consumer Transactions (Restrictions on Statements) Order 1976 SI 1976 No. 1813, as am. by SI 1978 No. 127, reg. 5 (made under the Fair Trading Act 1973).

[195] For employees and agents, this prevents their taking advantage of the Contracts (Rights of Third Parties) Act 1999, s. 2.

[196] These words could be clearer and are very similar to those used in s. 7 for identifying a group of contracts other than sale and hire purchase. It is submitted, however, that they should not be given such a narrow reading since there is no reason for distinguishing different types of transfer contract for present purposes.

[197] It is likely, however, in such a case that the strict liability of the seller under s. 14 of the Sale of Goods Act would be engaged, with the consequence that liability under that section might not be excluded at all as against a person dealing as a consumer (s. 6(2) of the Unfair Contract Terms Act).

that prejudices or takes away[198] rights arising under 'another contract' so far as those rights relate to 'another's liability'.[199] Under section 5, goods are treated as being in consumer use whenever they are not used exclusively in the course of a business.[200] A guarantee for present purposes is 'anything in writing . . . if it contains or purports to contain some promise or assurance (however worded or presented) that defects will be made good by complete or partial replacement, or by repair, monetary compensation or otherwise'.[201]

Consumer Protection Act. The Consumer Protection Act 1987 contains a **9.34** separate provision providing that the liability under the Act of a manufacturer or other producer of a product to a person suffering damage caused wholly or partly by a product defect, or to a dependant or relative of such a person, may not be excluded by a contractual term, notice or other provision.[202] This provision does not apply to liability arising under a manufacturer's guarantee.

Misrepresentation. Section 3 of the Misrepresentation Act 1967[203] subjects all **9.35** clauses excluding or restricting liability or the availability of remedies to the standard of reasonableness laid down in the Unfair Contract Terms Act.[204] It is not clear why consumer and non-consumer contracts should in this one respect be treated alike, but the 1967 Act is not the only measure to have been consolidated in the Unfair Contract Terms Act without an attempt being made to produce rational uniformity throughout the Act.[205] The test of reasonableness has been rendered the same as the test laid down by section 11(1) of the Unfair Contract Terms Act, enacted ten years later, which is that the term must have been fair and reasonable to include in the contract in the light of what was known or contemplated by the parties to the contract at that time. Previously, it was reliance upon the clause that had to be reasonable, which would have spared certain widely drawn exemption clauses from being struck down. Whereas, in its application to breaches of contract, an exemption clause will look to what will happen in the future, the

---

[198] It would have been better of the Act had contained more consistent terminology. Other provisions refer to clauses excluding or restricting liability, and it cannot be known whether the change in terminology has any particular significance.

[199] This is a very clumsily worded provision, the side-note to which is entitled 'Evasion by means of secondary contract'. It is not entirely clear whether the reference to 'another's liability' is necessarily the liability of a third party to the contract that creates an evasion of liability, but the liability of a third party is certainly included in that provision.

[200] S. 5(2)(a).

[201] S. 5(2)(b).

[202] S. 7; see Ch. 8 above.

[203] As amended by the Unfair Contract Terms Act 1977.

[204] The general standard in s. 11(1) as opposed to Sch. 2.

[205] There are no stated limits on the application of s. 3. In particular, ss. 26–27 (discussed above) have no application to cases of misrepresentation.

clause looks to what has already happened in its application to misrepresentation. Nothing, however, appears to turn upon this distinction. The burden of proof relating to reasonableness is the same for misrepresentation as it is for other matters falling under section 11(1), namely, that it is for the *proferens* to show that the clause is reasonable.[206] Section 3 has not been confined to clauses excluding or restricting liability or the availability of remedies, but extends to clauses that seek to define liability in the first place by disclaiming responsibility for the accuracy of information supplied.[207] As stated above, section 3 will not apply to entire agreement clauses when they provide that one party has not been induced to rely upon the other's pre-contractual representations.[208]

The Unfair Terms in Consumer Contracts Regulations 1999

9.36 The European Directive. The Unfair Terms in Consumer Contracts Regulations 1999 transposed a European Directive dealing with unfair terms in consumer contracts after the matter was put out for consultation by the Department of Trade and Industry.[209] The first set of Regulations[210] were replaced some years later by the current version. The 1999 Regulations have no specific application to sale of goods contracts, though the Directive itself in its recitals states a need to assist the sale of goods and services by stimulating competition and to provide effective consumer protection by rendering European sales law uniform, pointing also to consumers' ignorance of sales law in other member states of the European Union.[211] At present, the Regulations and the Unfair Contract Terms Act operate in parallel, so that some exemption clauses will have to comply with both instruments. Compliance only with one instrument will not prevent the other instrument from striking down the clause. The techniques used in combating exemption and similar clauses, however, are not the same in the two instruments. The Act, unlike the Regulations, also applies to non-consumer contracts, but the Law Commission has recommended that the two instruments be fused in such a way that the protection given by the Regulations is extended to small businesses.

---

[206] For the pre-1977 version of s. 3, the burden was reversed.

[207] *Cremdean Properties Ltd v Nash* [1977] 1 EGLR 58.

[208] See above.

[209] Implementation of the EC Directive on Unfair Terms in Consumer Contracts (93/13/EEC) [1993] OJ L95/29.

[210] The Unfair Terms in Consumer Contracts Regulations SI 1994 No. 3159, effective 1 July 1995. See generally N. M. Padfield (1995) 10 *JIBL* 175; H. Beale, 'Legislative Control of Fairness: The Directive on Unfair Terms in Consumer Contracts', in J. Beatson and D. Friedmann (eds), *Good Faith and Fault in Contract Law* (OUP, 1995).

[211] Recitals (2), (3) (5), (7), (10), and (11).

Scope. The Regulations are applicable to contracts[212] concluded between **9.37**
a 'seller or supplier' and a 'consumer'. A seller or supplier is defined as 'any natural
or legal person who . . . is acting for purposes relating to his trade, business or
profession, whether publicly owned or privately owned'. The words 'relating to'
suggest that a broad interpretation be given to the meaning of 'seller or supplier'
and that the difficulties posed by English legislation concerning the meaning of
'course of a business' and similar expressions will not be repeated under the
Regulations. Consequently, a sale of unwanted used equipment to a consumer
will come within the Regulations, even if the seller does not regularly sell used
equipment. A consumer is defined as 'any natural person who . . . is acting for purposes which are outside his trade, business, or profession'.[213] This formulation is
narrow in that it excludes small companies purchasing goods or services for consumer purposes and is open to the interpretation that the purpose of the purchase
is altogether outside matters of trade, business, or profession. If this were so, then
a purchaser with mixed personal and business purposes would not be protected
under the Regulations. Although the Regulations define 'seller or supplier', they
do not define 'sale or supply', but they do make it apparent outside the interpretation regulation[214] that the Regulations apply to goods and services.[215] The meaning of 'goods' should not be assumed to be the same as it is under the Sale of Goods
Act since the Regulations are a harmonization measure transposing a Directive
designed to be implemented in numerous States with different legal systems and
languages. Consequently, apart from the question whether the supply of software
amounts to the supply of services, it should be treated as the sale or supply of
goods under the Regulations, notwithstanding any doubts about its coverage
under the Sale of Goods Act.[216] Again, the supply of electricity should be treated
as caught by the Regulations, even if electricity is neither a service nor goods under

---

[212] Although the Regulations do not contain a list of excluded contracts, the Directive itself
lists certain contracts that 'must be excluded from this Directive': above n. 209, recital (10):
'contracts relating to employment, contracts relating to succession rights, contracts relating to
rights under family law and contracts relating to the incorporation and organisation of companies or partnership agreements'. Despite the failure to include this provision in the Regulations,
it is likely that they would be interpreted as excluding these contracts In *R (on the application
of Khatun) v Newham LBC* [2005] EWCA Civ 55; [2005] QB 37 at [56], the parties did not
dispute that the scope of the Regulations should be determined by the scope of the Directive
('uncontentious').

[213] A consumer may be a consumer despite the transaction having a very high value: *Standard
Bank of London Ltd v Apostolakis* [2000] CLC 933.

[214] Reg. 3.

[215] Reg. 6.

[216] Cf. *St Albans City and District Council v International Computers Ltd* [1996] 4 All ER 481.

the Sale of Goods Act.[217] A 'purposive'[218] approach in the cause of providing 'a high level of protection'[219] is the keynote of the interpretation and application of the Regulations.

9.38 **Unfair terms and individual negotiation.** The Regulations apply to those terms of regulated contracts that are 'unfair'. Unfairness in the Regulations has both a procedural and a substantive aspect.[220] The procedural aspect is that the terms have not been individually negotiated: the burden of showing that they have been rests on the seller or supplier.[221] The substantive aspect is that, contrary to good faith, the contractual term in question causes a 'significant imbalance' in the parties' contractual rights and obligations to the detriment of the consumer. It is not precisely clear what individual negotiation means, but the Regulations do state that individual negotiation is absent where a term has been drafted 'in advance' and the consumer has not been able to influence the substance of that term.[222] All terms are drafted in advance of a contract, even if they are drawn up shortly before agreement, so the temporal point of reference must be before any invitation to treat or commencement of discussions takes place. Where a seller or supplier adopts a take-it-or-leave-it stance with a consumer, this will not be negotiation, no matter how many times that stance is taken. A consumer who objects to the content of an exemption clause, which is unlikely, and who is placated with concessions elsewhere in the contract, which is also unlikely, will still not have negotiated the term in question. If the consumer's attention is drawn to a particular clause in the contract and his consent actively sought, this again is not a matter of negotiation but of actual agreement. The same holds, *a fortiori*, for those cases where the consumer simply signs a document. Negotiation is a matter of give and take and of jockeying for position, which is likely to take place only in the rarest of consumer transactions, in view of the matters that are absent from the scope of unfair terms.[223] Exemption clauses are rarely questioned, let alone negotiated, and

---

217 Complaints under the Regulations may be considered by a qualifying body, the list of which in Sch. 1 includes the Gas and Electricity Markets Authority and the Director General of Electricity Supply for Northern Ireland. In *R (on the application of Khatun) v Newham LBC* n. 212 above, the court went so far as to hold the Regulations applicable to the grant of an interest in land, on the basis that the equivalent expression in the French, Italian, Spanish, and Portuguese versions of the Directive, all equally authoritative with the English version, included land (at [78]). On this point, see also *Starmark Enterprises Ltd v CPL Distribution Ltd* [2002] Ch 306; *Freiburger Kommunalbauten GmbH Baugesellschaft & Co. KG v Hofstetter* Case C-237/02, [2004] CMLR 13 (opinion of Advocate General). This indicates that 'goods' should be given a very broad meaning.
218 It was agreed by the parties in *R (on the application of Khatun) v Newham LBC*, n. 212 above, at [57], that the Regulations should be interpreted 'purposively'.
219 Art. 95(3) of the Treaty of Amsterdam, replacing the former Art. 100a(3).
220 Reg. 5(1).
221 Reg. 5(4).
222 Reg. 5(2).
223 Where plain language is used, the price of goods and services is not a relevant consideration.

a question posed to the seller or supplier about the meaning of a clause will not be taken to be negotiation. A further provision in the Regulations is that the individual negotiation of a term or of aspects of that term does not prevent the Regulations from applying to the balance of the contract if it is a pre-formulated standard contract. It is not clear what this means. If it means only that there may be more than one term open to challenge, and that the individual negotiation of one term does not provide an exemption from the Regulations for any other term, then it states the obvious. It is perplexing, however, that there is a reference to pre-formulated standard forms instead of to the absence of individual negotiation where this is the case.[224] A further issue arises in respect of the source of the disputed term. The Regulations do not require it to be the seller or supplier's term; there is no reason why the term should not be drawn from the standard form of a third party, which is a point that seems to be a little clearer in the Directive with the greater emphasis placed there upon pre-formulated standard forms.[225] In one case concerning a building contract,[226] the consumer was the one who suggested the use of a JCT form. The court left open the point, which had not been argued, whether the Regulations should apply when the consumer had had the opportunity to influence the content of the disputed terms but had not taken it up.[227] In sum, the procedural aspect of unfairness, therefore, presents a very low barrier for the consumer to surmount.

Significant imbalance.   The substantive aspect of unfairness relates to the exist-   **9.39**
ence of a significant imbalance in the parties' contractual rights and obligations, contrary to good faith.[228] The Regulations, therefore, are not aimed at terms or notices granting exemption from liability in tort, though the freedom of a claimant to frame an action based upon negligence on an implied term of the contract deprives this point of most of its significance. The reference to good faith is not clear. One possible meaning is that a significant imbalance is not *per se* tantamount to unfairness and that an additional element of bad faith must exist. Another interpretation reduces good faith to a rhetorical statement about the conduct of someone who introduces unfairness into a contract: the demonstration

---

224   There is a clearer link between individual negotiation and pre-formulation in Art. 3(2) of the Directive, which nevertheless remains just as unclear on this point.

225   Art. 3.

226   *Bryen & Langley Ltd v Boston* [2005] EWCA Civ 973; [2005] BLR 508 at [46].

227   Even though the consumer was given the benefit of the doubt on this point, he fell at the good faith hurdle when the substantive aspect of unfairness was considered: *ibid.*

228   See *Director General of Fair Trading v First National Bank Plc* [2001] UKHL 52; [2002] 1 AC 481, where, applying the very similar 1994 Regulations, the House of Lords found not to be unfair a term requiring interest on an unpaid sum to accrue at the contract rate until a judgment debt in the creditor's favour for unpaid sums had been discharged; *Munkenbeck & Marshall v Harold* [2005] EWHC 356 (TCC), where a court find 'unusual and onerous' terms requiring an owner to indemnify an architect for his legal costs and to pay interest of 8% over the base rate on unpaid invoices, when these had not been drawn to the owner's attention.

of a significant imbalance can only be accounted for by bad faith on the part of the seller or supplier. The choice between the two, or of some intermediate position between the two, is not an easy one. On the one hand, since the primary purpose of the Regulations is consumer protection, the latter view has much to commend it in requiring only that a significant imbalance be shown. A consumer disadvantaged by a significant imbalance, moreover, is unlikely to be further disadvantaged because the seller or supplier acted in bad faith as well. The Directive gives some guidance in this matter. It directs, in the matter of good faith, that particular regard be had to the strength of bargaining position of the parties, the existence of an inducement to the consumer to agree to the term, and whether the goods were sold or supplied to the special order of the consumer.[229] These criteria are drawn from Schedule 2 to the Unfair Contract Terms Act. Their presence in the Directive in this way lends considerable comfort to those common lawyers who would say that good faith is just another name for reasonableness.[230] In this way, the Directive also provides an objective standard of good faith that makes it an additional but by no means onerous supplement to significant imbalance. The Regulations also make provision for establishing the absence of good faith, but make no reference to the criteria laid down in the Directive. Instead, they refer to the nature of the goods or services, the circumstances surrounding the conclusion of the contract, and the remaining terms of the contract or the terms of a connected contract.[231] This formula is very vague and, given the wording of the Directive, less helpful than a cross-reference to reasonableness under the Unfair Contract Terms Act would have been.

9.40   **Excluded criteria.**   Subject to one exception, the Regulations draw back from examining the core of the contractual bargain in determining the assessment of a term as in conformity with good faith and with the absence of a significant imbalance. Regulation 6(2), concerned with significant imbalance, though it does not say so expressly, provides that the assessment of a term for fairness shall pay no regard to the 'definition of the main subject matter of the contract' and 'the adequacy of the price or remuneration' in relation to the goods or services supplied.[232] The Regulations, following the Directive in this regard, draw back from the heavy

---

229   Recital (16).

230   But in *Director General of Fair Trading v First National Bank Plc*, n. 228 above, at [17], Lord Bingham refers to good faith as not having an 'artificial or technical concept' but as connoting 'good standards of commercial morality and practice', requiring 'fair and open dealing' and requiring a seller or supplier not to exploit a consumer's vulnerability. On good faith, see also *Office of Fair Trading v Abbey National Plc* [2008] EWHC 875 (Comm) at [437] *et seq.*

231   Reg. 6(1).

232   These are separate assessments from the exemption from fairness: *Office of Fair Trading v Abbey National Plc*, n. 230 above at [341]. Reg. 6(2) is confined to express terms of the contract: *Office of Fair Trading v Abbey National Plc*, *ibid.* at [102]. For the meaning of 'price or remuneration', see *Office of Fair Trading v Abbey National Plc*, *ibid.* at [384] *et seq.*

task of reviewing all contracts for fairness and require some sort of a distinction to be drawn between a significant imbalance in contractual rights and obligations and a significant imbalance in reciprocal contractual benefits, though even here it might be said that contractual rights are not balanced if the price paid by a consumer is greatly in excess of the value of goods supplied. Although the reference to price seems reasonably clear, less clear is the reference to the subject matter of the contract. This may refer to cases allowing, for example, a seller to draw from a range of goods that include goods not of the highest quality; if it does, the formula is just another way of expressing the presence of an excessive price or of excessive remuneration. Although the assessment process is not directed to price and definition of the subject matter, terms dealing with these matters are clearly of relevance in determining whether *other* terms are unfair.[233] Moreover, there is, as stated above, one exceptional case where price and definition terms are directly assessed. In the absence of 'plain, intelligible language', the exceptions in Regulation 6(2) do not apply and the core of the bargain can be assessed for unfairness. The introduction of this exception clearly frames the purpose of the Regulations as not to police the fairness of bargains but rather to correct market failures.

Assessing unfairness. The conclusion reached above was that the absence of **9.41** good faith is an additional requirement for assessing a term as unfair. The burden of establishing this would appear to rest on the claimant. The burden of showing that terms have been individually negotiated is expressly placed on the *proferens*,[234] but no such express provision is made in respect of good faith. Support for this view is to be found in the matter of establishing a substantive imbalance: the claimant's case is assisted by an indicative list in Schedule 2 of clauses that are unfair. It should be the case that there is to be a rebuttable presumption that a term found on the list is unfair, for otherwise the list would be of little value. The strength of that presumption, however, might vary from one indicative term to another. Support for the view that a presumption of unfairness arises comes from the use of pejorative language in describing some of the terms in the indicative list in Schedule 2, since the term itself is criticized rather than highlighted as the type of term that might in particular circumstances be unfair.[235] The implication arising from the indicative list is that the claimant carries the burden of establishing unfairness when a disputed term is not on that list, even though the list is stated not to be exhaustive.[236] In addition to rights that arise where a term is unfair, the consumer is also aided by the *contra proferentem* rule of construction.

233 Recital (19) of the Directive.
234 Reg. 5(4).
235 e.g., 'unreasonably', 'inappropriately', 'without a valid reason', and 'unduly restricting'.
236 It is not clear whether case law could add further terms to the list so as to raise for the future a presumption in favour of the consumer.

Regulation 7(2) provides that, where there is 'doubt' about the meaning of a written term, the interpretation most favourable to the consumer will prevail.[237]

9.42   **The indicative list.**   The list in Schedule 2 includes terms that go beyond the range of exemption and related clauses that are the subject of the Unfair Contract Terms Act and is suggestive of contractual abuses that might not have been evident in all States, including the United Kingdom, transposing the Directive. Schedule 2 includes terms: making a contract binding on the consumer when the other party has an unfettered discretion to perform;[238] allowing the seller or supplier to 'dissolve' the contract on a discretionary basis when the same entitlement is not given to the consumer;[239] obliging the consumer to fulfil all of his obligations where the seller or supplier does not perform his obligations;[240] enabling the seller or supplier to terminate a contract of indefinite duration without giving reasonable notice;[241] extending a fixed-term contract when the consumer fails to observe an unreasonably early deadline to prevent automatic contract renewal;[242] allowing the seller or supplier unilaterally to alter terms of the contract without a valid reason, which would have to be stated in the contract;[243] in a similar vein, allowing the seller or supplier to alter the characteristics of the goods or services without a valid reason;[244] giving the seller or supplier the exclusive right to determine whether goods or services are in conformity with the contract or to interpret terms of the contract;[245] limiting the seller or supplier's obligation to respect commitments given by his agents or making those

---

[237] Reg. 7(2) itself provides one exception to this, namely, where the Director General of Unfair Trading is seeking an injunction to prevent the continued use of an unfair term. The rule in reg. 7(2) is not limited to terms that have not been individually negotiated: *Office of Fair Trading v Abbey National Plc*, n. 230 above.

[238] Para. 1(c).

[239] Para. 1(f).

[240] Para. 1(o).

[241] Para. 1(g). Oddly, the term seems not to be regarded as unfair when in fact the seller or supplier has serious grounds to terminate the contract. This wording shifts the focus from the term to the conditions of its exercise. In addition, the 'serious grounds' are not easy to discern. There is no reason why they should be confined to breach of contract by the consumer. They might exist, for example, where a business is restructured and a sale of business assets occurs. The scope of para. 1(g) is restricted in the case where financial services are supplied: para. 2(a). Moreover, para. 1(g) does not apply to securities and similar instruments whose price fluctuates according to an exchange or index and does not apply to foreign exchange and related transactions: para. 2(c).

[242] Para. 1(h). Moreover, para. 1(h) does not apply to securities and similar instruments whose price fluctuates according to an exchange or index and does not apply to foreign exchange and related transactions: para. 2(c).

[243] Para. 1(j). Para. 1(j) is restricted in its application to cases where a supplier of financial services arises the interest rate and to cases where a seller or supplier alters unilaterally the terms of a contract of unlimited duration: see para. 2(b). Moreover, para. 1(j) does not apply to securities and similar instruments whose price fluctuates according to an exchange or index and does not apply to foreign exchange and related transactions: para. 2(c).

[244] Para. 1(k).

[245] Para. 1(m).

commitments subject to a particular formality;[246] without the consumer's consent, allowing the seller or supplier to transfer obligations under the contract where this might reduce the consumer's guarantees;[247] and excluding or restricting the consumer's right of legal action by requiring arbitration, unduly restricting the range of relevant evidence and altering the burden of proof.[248] Some of the indicatively unfair terms relate to the consumer having to make a payment or forfeit a payment. These comprise terms: permitting the seller or supplier to retain sums paid by the consumer when the latter decides not to conclude or perform the contract, when no equivalent provision bears down on the seller or supplier;[249] requiring a non-performing consumer to pay a disproportionately high sum in compensation;[250] and permitting a seller or supplier to fix the price at the date of delivery or raise the price after the contract date without allowing the consumer to cancel the contract.[251] Finally, Schedule 2 contains terms that are closely related to terms that are regulated by the Unfair Contract Terms Act. It includes terms: excluding or limiting a seller or supplier's liability for the consumer's death or personal injury;[252] inappropriately excluding or limiting liability for the total or partial non-performance or inadequate performance of the contract by the seller or supplier or excluding a right of set-off;[253] and irrevocably binding the consumer to contract terms that the consumer could not have become acquainted with prior to the contract.[254]

Effect of unfairness. The Regulations provide that an unfair term shall not be **9.43** binding on the consumer and that the contract shall continue to be binding if capable of continuing without the unfair term. In the case of exemption clauses, as integral as they may be to the bargain,[255] it ought to be the case that the contract

---

[246] Para. 1(n). This could apply where an agent's usual authority is restricted by small print in a contractual document.

[247] Para. 1(p).

[248] Para. 1(q). It is unlikely that any arbitration term could be demonstrated to be fair when it keep the consumer out of the Small Claims Court.

[249] Para. 1(d). It may be that a seller or supplier, able to demonstrate loss caused by the consumer's unlawful repudiation of a contract, may this demonstrate that the term is not in fact unfair. The attempt to find equivalence in the matter of forfeiting deposits and other prepayments is odd, because it is not in the nature of contracts for the sale or supply of goods or services that the seller or supplier should pay a deposit or make any other prepayment.

[250] Para. 1(e). This provision has clear affinities with the rule against penalty clauses in English law but it does not displace that rule; *Office of Fair Trading v Abbey National Plc*, n. 230 above at [331].

[251] Para. 1(l). But this provision is without prejudice to lawful price indexation clauses that explicitly describe the method of indexation: para 2(d).

[252] Para. 1(a). Cf. s. 2 of the Unfair Contract Terms Act.

[253] Para. 1(b).

[254] Para. 1(i). Apart from the contents of signed documents, these terms could be excluded from the contract by the rules on incorporation in English law.

[255] See above.

is capable of continuance despite their excision. The Regulations do not make any allowance for the possibility that, in the absence of such a clause, a different price for the goods or services might have been agreed. The notion of capability of continuance does not extend to considerations of this sort. For other types of unfair term, the effect of their removal on the contract must be calculated on an individual basis.[256] A particular mention ought to be made of those cases where the absence of plain, intelligible language in the contract permits a court to strike down a clause defining the basis of the bargain, for example, a price clause.[257] No power is given to the court to rewrite the contract so it must be concluded that the contract cannot continue and that it must be unwound.

9.44 **'Plain, intelligible language'.** As stated above, the absence of 'plain, intelligible language' in the seller or supplier's terms lays open the core terms of a contract to assessment for unfairness. In addition, there is a further provision of the Regulations, particularly relevant when the Regulations are sought to be enforced by a public body,[258] that without reference to the fairness or otherwise of contract terms, calls for them to be expressed in 'plain, intelligible language'.[259] According to Andrew Smith J: 'The question of plain intelligible language is . . . directed to whether the contractual terms put forward by the seller or supplier are sufficiently clear to enable the typical consumer to have a proper understanding of them for sensible and practical purposes.'[260] The regulatory scope for rewriting standard form contracts in the consumer sector is therefore a large one.

9.45 **Enforcement of the Regulations.** There is a dual system of enforcement of the 1999 Regulations. In addition to enforcement as between an individual claimant and the *proferens*, enforcement is also a matter for public bodies.[261] The Director General of Fair Trading is required to consider any complaint of unfairness referred to him, and unless it is frivolous or vexatious or a qualifying body[262] notifies the Director that it will take responsibility for dealing with the complaint.[263] The Director is required to give reasons for his decision to apply or not to apply for an injunction[264] against a person making use of an unfair term.[265] In arriving at his decision, the Director may have regard to undertakings given to him related to

---

[256] See the terms listed above.
[257] Reg. 6(2).
[258] See below.
[259] Reg. 7(1). See *Office of Fair Trading v Abbey National Plc*, n. 230 above.
[260] *Office of Fair Trading v Abbey National Plc*, n. 230 above at [119].
[261] Lord Steyn in *Director General of Fair Trading v First National Bank Ltd* [2001] UKHL 52; [2002] 1 AC 481 at [33] referred to this arrangement as 'a dual system of ex casu challenges and pre-emptive or collective challenges by appropriate bodies'.
[262] The list of qualifying bodies is in Sch. 1.
[263] Reg. 10(1).
[264] Provision is made for this under reg. 12(1).
[265] Reg. 10(2).

the continued use of the unfair term.[266] A qualifying body notifying the Director of its intention to deal with the complaint is bound to go on to consider that complaint.[267] It then falls under the same obligations as the Director in relation to the giving of reasons and the acceptance of undertakings.[268] If a qualifying body decides to apply for an injunction, it must give the Director fourteen days' notice (or such shorter period as agreed with the Director) before making the application.[269] The court has a free discretion in the grant of any injunction and the injunction need not be confined to the exact language of the unfair term but can extend to terms of like effect.[270] In carrying out their investigations and in reviewing compliance with the terms of an injunction or undertaking, the Director and qualifying bodies are given statutory powers to obtain certain documents and information.[271] The qualifying body is under a duty to report to the Director about the undertakings given to it before legal proceedings or in court and about the outcome of its application for an injunction.[272] Finally, the Director has extensive powers to publish details of undertakings and injunctions and a duty to inform the complainant of the outcome of the complaint.[273]

---

[266] Reg. 10(3).
[267] Reg. 11(1).
[268] Reg. 11(2).
[269] Reg. 12(2).
[270] Reg. 12(3), (4),
[271] Reg. 13.
[272] Reg. 14.
[273] Reg. 15.

10

TERMINATION OF THE CONTRACT FOR BREACH

Introduction

10.01

General.   This chapter deals with the right of one contracting party to terminate the contract as a result of the other party's breach. The right to terminate for breach[1] can arise in two types of case.[2] First, the factual consequences of breaching a contractual term may be so serious that the injured party is entitled to terminate. The requisite degree of seriousness is expressed in a number of ways. It may be said that the injured party is deprived of the bargained-for consideration or of the

---

[1] Sometimes called discharge for breach. Cancellation is not uncommon in the US; avoidance is used in the Vienna Convention on the International Sale of Goods 1980.

[2] The contract may also establish its own termination protocol, for example, by allowing one party to terminate when the other has not responded to a notice requiring rectification of a 'material breach'.

substance of the contract,[3] or that the breach goes to the root of the contract or is a frustrating breach. For reasons that will emerge, sale of goods contracts are relatively unlikely to be terminated in this way. Secondly, a term of the contract may be regarded by statute, the express intention of the parties or the implied intention that arises from established commercial practice[4] as being so important that any breach of that term, regardless of its consequences, severe or slight, gives rise to the right to terminate. A term of this importance is known as a condition of the contract. The word 'condition' is notoriously ambiguous but in this context connotes a contractual obligation that envelopes an event. The contractual obligation may be express, such as a seller's promise to deliver by or on a stipulated date, or it may be implied, such as the seller's duty to supply goods of satisfactory quality. It is again the event, namely, the consequences of the breach, that gives the injured party the right to terminate. Nevertheless, there is no question in this case of weighing the gravity of the factual consequences of the breach. Where the contractual term is designated a condition, all consequences of the breach are deemed to be sufficiently serious to justify termination.

10.02 **Loss of termination right.**   The right to terminate a contract may be lost when the contract is affirmed. Affirmation occurs when the injured party elects to keep the contract on foot instead of terminating it. To a major extent, the common law rules on affirmation and election are superseded by special statutory rules in the case of a breach committed by the seller.[5] Under section 35, the right to terminate is lost when the goods have been accepted in one of the three ways laid down in that section. In some cases, there may be a breach of condition by the seller in circumstances where the seller also makes an actionable misrepresentation. Although termination is sometimes called, though rarely nowadays, rescission for breach, the latter expression must be distinguished from rescission *ab initio*, which applies, for example, in cases of actionable misrepresentation.[6] Rescission *ab initio* involves placing the parties in the position they occupied before entry into the contract,

---

[3] Substance and substantiality are not the same thing: a deprivation of the substance of the contract is more serious than a substantial deprivation of contractual benefit.

[4] *Maredelanto Cia Naviera SA v Bergbau-Handel GmbH (The Mihalis Angelos)* [1971] 1 QB 164.

[5] Where the common law rules remain applicable, as they do to breaches by the buyer and to breaches by the seller where the goods are not delivered, the conduct of one party in the face of a repudiation by the other, whether present or anticipatory, will also have to be considered in determining whether that repudiation has been accepted. No particular form is required for an acceptance of a repudiation as long as the party terminating the contract clearly and unequivocally demonstrates this to the party in breach: *Vitol SA v Norelf Ltd (The Santa Clara)* [1996] AC 800, 810–11; *South Caribbean Trading Ltd v Trafigura Beheer NV* [2004] EWHC 2676 (Comm); [2005] 1 Lloyd's Rep. 618 at [129]. Cf *State Trading Corpn of India v M Golodetz Ltd* [1989] 2 Lloyd's Rep. 277, 286 (silence or inactivity not enough), criticized in *Vitol SA* above, 812. As for the question of a binding election between affirmation and termination, see Ch. 6 above.

[6] *Johnson v Agnew* [1980] AC 367, 392–3; *Shevill v Builders Licensing Board* (1989) 149 CLR 620, 627.

whereas termination brings the contract to a premature end without unwinding it. Nevertheless, termination and rescission *ab initio* by the buyer in a simple sale of goods transaction both have the factual outcome of returning the goods to the seller. Case law developments have therefore sought to align the section 35 rules on acceptance with the somewhat differently expressed rules dealing with the loss of the right to rescind *ab initio*.[7]

Prospective effect of termination.   Termination operates prospectively: the **10.03** injured party is released from further performance and the breaching party's unperformed primary obligations are commuted into secondary obligations to pay damages.[8] Rights that have been unconditionally acquired prior to termination are not as a result of termination divested.[9] Certain contractual provisions, such as arbitration agreements and exclusion and limitation clauses, survive termination.[10] An important feature of termination, when the existence of the right has prompted litigation, is that it frees the injured party from a market risk imposed by the contract. For example, when the market price for goods declines after the contract, a buyer will often be keen to take advantage of termination rights consequent upon late delivery or the delivery of non-conforming goods. This will permit the acquisition of cheaper substitute goods on a declining market from a different source. A buyer terminating a contract because the goods, for example, are not reasonably fit for purpose is thereby able to recapture a lost market opportunity when acquiring substitute goods at a saving that is due to market decline after the date of the first contract.[11] In contrast, the buyer affirming the contract, retaining goods and suing for damages has to absorb the fall in their market value.[12] The long-standing position of English law is that the motive behind the exercise of termination rights, particularly the desire to use technical rights to escape from a losing contract, does not qualify or exclude those rights.[13] This must now be moderated in the light of section 15A, added by the Sale and Supply of Goods Act 1994, which in certain instances prevents an unreasonable termination where the breach of an implied condition in the Sale of Goods Act produces only slight consequences.

---

[7] *Leaf v International Galleries* [1950] 2 KB 86.

[8] *Photo Production Ltd v Securicor Transport Ltd* [1980] AC 827.

[9] *McDonald v Dennys Lascelles Ltd* (1933) 48 CLR 457 (Dixon J). For the position regarding the recovery of money on a failure of consideration, see Ch. 11 below.

[10] *Ibid.*

[11] Contrast this with damages, where the object is to put the plaintiff in the position he would have occupied if the contract had been performed: *Wertheim v Chicoutimi Pulp Co.* [1911] AC 301; *Procter & Gamble Philippine Mfg Corpn v Kurt A Becher GmbH & Co.* [1988] 2 Lloyd's Rep. 21; see Ch 12 below.

[12] But cf the odd case of *Naughton v O'Callaghan* [1990] 3 All ER 191, discussed in Ch. 12 below.

[13] *Bowes v Shand* (1877) 2 App Cas 455; *Cargill UK Ltd v Continental UK Ltd* [1989] 2 Lloyd's Rep. 290.

Discharge: Conditions, Warranties, and Intermediate Stipulations[14]

10.04 **Policy issues.** In cases where the right to terminate is not explicitly provided for by Parliament or in the contract, it is especially necessary to draw a consistent and predictable line between cases where termination rights do and do not lie for a breach of contract.[15] Numerous factors might be considered in marking out this line. A firm commitment to the binding force of contract might stress the importance of contractual undertakings and use the goad of extensive termination rights to encourage the performance of contractual promises, as penalty clauses might do if they were lawful. A commitment to the consumer interest would see in extensive termination rights an effective lever for redressing the imbalance between a business seller and a consumer buyer.[16] Extensive termination rights might also be supported on the grounds that it is futile to imprison parties in a continuing embittered relationship, and that freeing them to seek their opportunities elsewhere might avoid economic waste and put their abilities and resources to more productive use. Arguments, like the need to avoid economic waste may sometimes go both ways. A desire to avoid economic waste would also be consistent with a bias against termination for short-term relationships where future cooperation is not in prospect, because, for example, the buyer may be better placed than the seller to avoid economic waste in using defective goods. Other countervailing considerations pit the conviction, that the needs of certainty and forward-planning favour strict and predictable law, against the belief that the merits of the parties can only fairly be considered in view of the consequences of the breach. This latter approach could take account of considerations of hardship, and would, for example, permit a distinction between the tardy manufacturer of machinery designed for the buyer's unique specifications and the tardy supplier of commodities, for which a market can always be found. An argument against strict termination rights is that they permit the assertion of technical claims by a party when the market has swung against him, thus undermining the broad allocation of market risk agreed upon at the outset of the contract.

---

[14] M. Bridge, 'Discharge for Breach of the Contract of Sale of Goods' (1983) 28 *McGill LJ* 867; J. Carter, *Breach of Contract* (2nd edn, Law Book Co.,1991); New South Wales Law Reform Commission, *Working Paper on the Sale of Goods (Warranties, Remedies, Frustration and Other Matters)* 1975; R. Bradgate, 'Rejection and Termination in Contracts for the Sale of Goods', in J. Birds, R. Bradgate, and J. Villiers, *Termination of Contracts* (Wiley Chancery, 1995).

[15] Ontario Law Reform Commission, *Report on Sale of Goods* (1979), i, 145–50; Alberta Institute of Law Research and Reform, *The Uniform Sale of Goods Act* (Report no. 38, 1982), 140–57.

[16] Law Commission, *Sale and Supply of Goods* (Law Com. No. 160, 1987).

Party autonomy.   A clear commitment to freedom of contract in English law means   **10.05**
that the parties are at liberty to stipulate that a contractual term is a condition, so that
any breach gives rise to termination rights.[17] In the words of Blackburn J in *Bettini
v Gye*: 'Parties may think some matter, apparently of very little importance, essential; and if they sufficiently express an intention to make the literal fulfilment of
such a thing a condition precedent, it will be one . . .'.[18] This proposition has been
repeated by the Court of Appeal in modern times, the court adding the corollary
that the party terminating the contract for breach is also entitled to recover damages for future non-performance by the party in breach.[19] The effect of the parties
designating a term as a condition is that any breach of that term has to be seen as
going to the root of the contract.[20] As clear as the commitment to party autonomy
is in principle, courts will nevertheless lean against construing a contractual term
as a condition if the consequences of such a construction are considered to be
unreasonable.[21] The more a result is apparently unreasonable, the more the expression of intent must be made crystal clear.

Unfair contract terms.   Contractual termination rights have been challenged   **10.06**
unsuccessfully under the Unfair Contract Terms Act 1977. Where one party deals
on another's standard terms of business, section 3(2)(b)(ii) states that the latter
cannot by reference to any contract term 'claim to be entitled . . . in respect of the
whole or any part of his contractual obligation, to render no performance at all . . .'
The 1977 Act is primarily directed to the regulation of contractual terms that

---

[17] The availability of relief against forfeiture (see Ch. 11 below), including the statutory version
that applies to conditional sale contracts (Consumer Credit Act 1974, s. 90), may serve as an impediment to the exercise of contractual termination rights. The 1974 Act also imposes limits on the
right to terminate a regulated agreement, by providing for the service of default notices (ss. 87–89),
and for the making of orders to give the consumer additional time to perform (ss. 129–30).

[18] (1876) 1 QBD 183, 187.

[19] *Lombard North Central plc v Butterworth* [1987] QB 527, 536 ('axiomatic': Mustill LJ). It had
previously been asserted in a series of hire purchase cases that the breaching hirer would not have to
pay damages if the finance company invoked an express right to terminate in circumstances where
the hirer was not shown to have committed a repudiatory breach: see *Financings Ltd v Baldock*
[1963] 2 QB 104.

[20] *Lombard North Central plc v Butterworth*, n. 19 above, 546 (Nicholls LJ).

[21] See *Schuler (L) AG v Wickman Machine Tool Sales Ltd* [1974] AC 235, where the House of
Lords declined to interpret the word 'condition' in the contract in its technical legal sense. The
contractual provision did not explicitly set out the consequences of breach. See also *Rice v Great
Yarmouth Borough Council*, The Times, 26 July 2000, where the Court of Appeal held that a clause
entitling the local authority to terminate the contract, 'if the contractor commits a breach of any
of its obligations under the Contract . . .', did not mean what it plainly said, since the contract
neglected to identify any of these obligations as conditions. It should follow that a clause designating a term as a condition, and also going on to say that the promisee is entitled to terminate for
any breach of that term, would compel the judicial conclusion that the term was indeed a condition.
Nevertheless, an omnibus clause providing that all obligations of a particular contracting party are
conditions might still attract the hostile interpretation of a court as evidenced in *Rice*. See *Antaios Co.
SA v Salen AB (The Antaios)* [1985] AC 191, 200–1, 205; *Crowther v Brownsword* [1999] EWCA Civ
1921 at [23].

exclude or restrict liability or that grant an indemnity, but the eclectic character of the legislation opens the way to affording it a broader scope. Section 3(2)(b)(ii), if literally interpreted, has the potential of being stretched beyond the exclusion or restriction of liability so as to control termination rights. In *Ilanchelian v Esso Petroleum Co Ltd*,[22] Rimer J summarily rejected a very similar argument that a petroleum company could not terminate a licensing agreement for the licensee's failure to pay moneys owed as this would result in its rendering contractual performance 'substantially different from that which was reasonably expected of' it.[23] Termination clauses are nevertheless open to challenge under the Unfair Terms in Consumer Contract Regulations 1999. The Regulations indicatively treat as unfair those clauses permitting the termination of contracts of indeterminate duration in the absence of serious grounds for doing so.[24] If the Law Commission's proposal to combine the Act and the Regulations[25] bears fruit, this could lead to future statutory challenges to termination clauses going beyond consumer cases.

10.07 **Penalty clauses.**   Hire purchase and related cases show the interplay between termination clauses in a contract and the rule against penalties. In *Lombard North Central Plc v Butterworth*, the rule against penalties was held not to apply to the designation of contractual terms as conditions.[26] The court expressed concern, nevertheless, that the rule against penalties, in its application to a minimum payments clause in a hire purchase agreement, could be easily avoided by a clause giving rise to the recovery of general (or loss of bargain) damages after a breach of condition.[27] In the earlier Court of Appeal decision in *Financings Ltd v Baldock*,[28] one reason why the court refused to allow damages for losses arising out of the termination of the contract by the finance company was that the right of termination could be exercised upon the occurrence of various events, some of which were not breaches of contract.[29] The termination clause was not designated in so many words as a condition of the contract. The finance company was also unable to

---

[22] Unreported, 28 September 1998.

[23] S. 3(2)(b)(i) of the Unfair Contract Terms Act 1977.

[24] SI 1999 No. 2083. Para. 1(g) of Sch. 2 contains, in an indicative and non-exhaustive list of unfair terms, clauses 'enabling the seller or supplier to terminate a contract of indeterminate duration without reasonable notice except where there are serious grounds for doing so'. This provision does not fit the case of clauses permitting termination for breach of a conventional or instalment sale of goods contract, but the significant point is that the Regulations can be applied to the exercise of termination rights and that the list of clauses in Sch. 2 is only an indicative one. The general scope of application of the Regulations is discussed in Ch. 9 above.

[25] *Unfair Terms in Contracts* (Law Com. No. 292, 2005).

[26] *Lombard North Central Plc v Butterworth*, n. 19 above, 535 (Mustill LJ's eighth proposition).

[27] See especially Nicholls LJ, above (n. 20) at 546, noting that the difference between a clause granting a power to terminate for non-payment of an instalment and a clause allowing termination because non-payment of an instalment was regarded as a breach of condition was 'one of drafting form, and wholly without substance'.

[28] [1963] 2 QB 104.

[29] *Ibid.*, 118 (Diplock LJ).

establish the existence of a repudiatory breach by the hirer that would independently have established a right to terminate for breach with an entitlement to loss of bargain damages. Although *Lombard North Central* endorses the right of contracting parties to designate contractual terms as promissory conditions, it does not do so in the forthright terms that might have been expected for a proposition of such contractual orthodoxy.[30] The equivocal attitude of the courts over the decades to the transaction of hire purchase[31] had previously created a rift between hire purchase law and general contract law. This rift has now been closed by *Lombard North Central*, albeit with some judicial misgivings. If hirers of goods are deserving of protection, this is better done by special legislation[32] than by distorting contractual principle.

Breach of Contract Principles Before the Codification of Sale

Debt, covenants and assumpsit. The right to terminate a contract for breach in **10.08** the modern law stems from a variety of sources. An exploration of its emergence assists in understanding the configuration of modern rights to terminate. Prior to the rise of *assumpsit* in the sixteenth century, what we would now call contractual actions were enforced by the writs of debt and covenant.[33] Neither debt nor covenant focused on the mutuality of promises in a consensual transaction. Debt transcended the modern range of contract in dealing with the liability to pay a liquidated sum of one who had obtained a *quid pro quo*;[34] covenant dealt with the unilateral obligation to perform a promise made under seal. The emergence of *assumpsit* brought with it the idea that mutual and executory promises are binding because each is consideration for the other.[35] Only later did this interdependence

---

[30] Note that Mustill LJ considered that the 'real controversy' in the case concerned whether the rule against penalties applied to the designation of contractual terms as conditions: n. 19 above, 535. The real point of the case, however, is that the sovereign right of contracting parties to designate terms as conditions applies just as much to hire purchase contracts as to other types of contract.

[31] Hire purchase, *inter alia*, protects the finance company from being classed as a moneylender and from having to comply with bills of sale legislation.

[32] e.g., Consumer Credit Act 1974, ss. 100 and 129 (liability of hirer on termination; time orders).

[33] See A. W. B. Simpson, *A History of the Common Law of Contract [:] The Rise of Assumpsit* (OUP, 1975); S. F. C. Milsom, *Historical Foundations of the Common Law* (2nd edn, Butterworths, 1981); C. H. Fifoot, *History and Sources of the Common Law [:] Tort and Contract* (Stevens, London, 1949); T. Plucknett, *A Concise History of the Common Law* (5th edn, Butterworths, London, 1956); J. H. Baker, *An Introduction to English Legal History* (3rd edn, Butterworths, 1990); S. Stoljar, *A History of Contract at Common Law* (Australian National University Press, Canberra, 1975). For the view that the importance of the penal bond in the development of contract law has been understated, see A. W. B. Simpson (1966) 81 *LQR* 392.

[34] See *United Australia Ltd v Barclays Bank Ltd* [1941] AC 1, 26 (Lord Atkin).

[35] See *Norwood v Norwood and Read* (1558) 1 Plowd. 180, 182 ('every contract executory is an *assumpsit* in itself'); *Slade's Case* (1602) Co. Rep. 92(b).

also assist in defining the right of termination for breach.[36] To this extent, the dependency of contractual promises upon each other determined the order in which they were to be performed. Hence the failure by one party to perform a promise might have the consequence that the promise of the other party did not spring. A different principle, failure of consideration, reigned where a contract had been imperfectly executed by one party and the other sought termination. The challenge facing the legal system was to accommodate these two principles of dependent promises and failure of consideration within a unitary doctrine of termination for breach.

10.09 **The dependency principle.**   *Kingston v Preston*[37] contains the classical exposition of the dependency principle. It swept aside the formalist approach of earlier authority and ruled that the order of performance turned upon 'the evident sense and meaning of the parties'.[38] In that case, despite the absence of a formal connection between a vendor's promise to transfer his business and the purchaser's promise to give security for future payments, the court ruled that the purchaser had to perform first, for otherwise the vendor would be robbed of a major inducement to contract. Lord Mansfield divided contractual promises into three categories:[39] first, independent promises, where a party's failure to perform sounds only in damages and does not release the other from performing his promise; secondly, dependent promises, where a party's promise is dependent upon prior performance of his promise by the other; and thirdly, concurrent dependent promises, where each party's performance is dependent upon prior performance by the other. The evident circularity in the last category was broken by allowing the plaintiff to aver readiness and willingness to perform as a condition precedent to suing the defendant for his failure to perform.[40]

10.10 **Failure of consideration.**   If the above dependency rules were uncompromisingly applied, a party unable to complete performance, and thus unable to aver performance of all conditions precedent to the other's duty to perform, would leave the other in possession of the fruits of incomplete performance. To avoid such enrichment, the other was required to perform and bring a cross action for damages for defective performance.[41] This is shown by the great case of *Boone v Eyre*,[42] where the vendor of a plantation and the slaves upon it received from the

---

[36] This was not immediately obvious. See *Nichols v Raynbred* (1615) Hob. 88, where Nichols could sue Raynbred on his promise to pay without averring that he was ready and willing to deliver the agreed cow. Raynbred's remedy for breach was a cross action.

[37] (1773), unreported but recounted in *Jones v Barkley* (1781) 2 Dougl. 684, 689–91.

[38] *Ibid.*, 691.

[39] *Ibid.*, 690–1. See C. Morison, *Rescission of Contracts* (Stevens, 1916), 61–9, who points out that Lord Mansfield was speaking of *covenants*, that is, promises under seal. If his words were meant to be so confined, the later cases seem not to have restricted them in this way.

[40] See *Jones v Barkley*, n. 37 above; Sale of Goods Act, s. 28.

[41] See Serjeant Williams's famous notes to *Pordage v Cole* (1669) 1 Wms Saund 319, 320.

[42] (1777) 1 H Bl 273; see also *Campbell v Jones* (1796) 6 TR 570.

purchaser the agreed sum of £500 but was denied the agreed annuity of £160. The purchaser pleaded that the vendor was not lawfully possessed of the slaves. In the court's view, the vendor's breach went only to a part of the consideration bargained for by the purchaser and could be compensated in damages. Judgment for the purchaser would have allowed him to retain the plantation at an under-value.[43]

Inequality of damages. The result in *Boone v Eyre* was explained in *Duke of St Albans v Shore*[44] in terms of the inequality of damages, namely, that to deprive the vendor of his annuity would inflict upon him a loss out of all proportion to the loss suffered by the purchaser when the contract was breached.[45] In *Duke of St Albans* itself, the purchaser was entitled to refuse to complete the purchase of a farm upon discovery that the vendor had cut down a large number of trees. The vendor could not recover in his debt action 'unless [he] has done all that it was incumbent on him to do'.[46] Assuming the breach to be no more serious than the breach of the vendor in *Boone*, there was a vital distinction between the two cases. The purchaser had obtained no benefits under the contract in *Duke of St Albans* when declining to proceed further with performance. The related ideas of inequality of damages and the receipt of a valuable benefit pointed to a critical distinction between executory and partly executed contracts.[47] **10.11**

Unitary termination rules. The stage was now set for bringing together valuable benefit, inequality of damages, dependency of promises, and failure of consideration within a unitary system of termination rules, which occurred during the nineteenth century. Contractual termination was treated as a question of law and therefore outside the province of the jury, a development contemporaneously affecting also the remoteness of damages rules.[48] The intention of the parties, as manifested in the contract itself, was the paramount principle governing termination.[49] This intention might be that each and every breach should permit termination.[50] In the absence of such an express intention, a jury considering the hypothetical range of consequences flowing from the breach of a particular term would state **10.12**

---

[43] Serjeant Williams attached importance to the fact that the contract had been performed in part: n. 41 above. The seller could not have recovered the value of the plantation on the common count of *quantum valebat* since this would have been inconsistent with the terms of an open (that is, unrescinded) contract: see *Cutter v Powell* (1795) 6 TR 320.

[44] (1789) 1 H Bl 270.

[45] *Ibid.*, 279. For a modern decision actuated by this principle and applying it through the medium of damages assessment, see *Jacob & Youngs Inc. v Kent* (1921) 129 NE 889 (NY).

[46] n. 44 above.

[47] See *Ellen v Topp* (1851) 6 Ex. 424 (but not trivial benefit: *ibid.* 442); *Graves v Legg* (1854) 9 Ex. 710, affirmed (1857) 2 H & N 210; *Hoare v Rennie* (1859) 5 H & N 19; *Simpson v Crippen* (1872) LR 8 QB 14; *Honck v Muller* (1881) 7 QBD 92.

[48] *Hadley v Baxendale* (1854) 9 Ex. 341; J. Danzig (1975) 4 *J Leg. Stud.* 249.

[49] Bridge, n. 14, above 881–4, discussing *Bettini v Gye*, n. 18 above; *Poussard v Spiers* (1876) 1 QBD 410; *Bentsen v Taylor, Sons & Co. (No. 2)* [1893] 2 QB 274.

[50] *Bettini v Gye*, n. 18 above, 187.

the effect of any breach on 'the substance and foundation of the adventure'.[51] The judge would then decide whether the range of consequences was so serious that any breach of the term should permit termination.[52] Because of the close identification of the term and its consequences, the practice developed of labelling as conditions[53] those terms whose every breach gave rise to termination rights, instead of as warranties coupled with a condition precedent.[54] Terms that did not give rise to termination rights were known simply as warranties,[55] a confusing usage since all inducing statements made with contractual intention were also known as warranties.[56] Some of these latter terms might be important enough to pass the above test of a promissory condition.

10.13 Effects of new rules. This new terminology supplanted the language of mutual and dependent promises and encouraged certainty by cataloguing the status of specific terms of commercial contracts such as sale and charterparties. But it also promoted rigidity by disregarding the effects produced by specific breaches of contract,[57] thus eclipsing or concealing the failure of consideration principle. The Sale of Goods Act is imbued with the language of conditions and warranties to a degree that impedes the search for a flexible solution to problems. Not entirely suppressed, however, the failure of consideration principle has been transformed into various rules controlling in some measure the extensive termination rights granted by the Act.

Statutory Termination Rules before the Sale and Supply of Goods Act 1994

10.14 Conditions and warranties. Chalmers claimed the Sale of Goods Act 1893 'endeavoured to reproduce as exactly as possible the existing law'.[58] The terminology of conditions and warranties, expounded in key cases leading up to the 1893 Act, is therefore writ large in the Act and in its successor, unchanged in this respect, the Act of 1979. A significant, though partial, reform is contained in the Sale and Supply of Goods Act 1994. Apart from this last development, a superficial reading

---

[51] *Bentsen v Taylor, Sons & Co. (No. 2)*, n. 49 above.

[52] A question of construction, and therefore subject to review by a higher court.

[53] A stern critic of this technique was S. Williston. The use of 'condition' in this way seems to date from *Glaholm v Hays* (1841) 2 Man. & Gr. 257. See also J. Montrose [1964] *CLJ* 60, 75–82; F. M. B. Reynolds (1963) 79 *LQR* 534, 534–40. This practice remains the clearest way of conveying the parties' meaning (but see *Wickman Machine Tool Sales Ltd v L Schuler AG* [1974] AC 235). On the need for clear language, see *Bowes v Chalyer* (1923) 32 CLR 159, 182.

[54] See Diplock LJ in *Hongkong Fir Shipping Co. Ltd v Kawasaki Kisen Kaisha* [1962] 2 QB 26, 71.

[55] For statements of the binary distinction between conditions and warranties, see *Bentsen v Taylor, Sons & Co. (No. 2)*, n. 49 above; *Wallis, Son & Wells v Pratt & Haynes* [1910] 2 KB 1003; *Tramways Advertising Pty Ltd v Luna Park (NSW) Ltd* (1938) 38 SR (NSW) 632, 641–2 (Jordan CJ).

[56] See Ch. 8 above.

[57] *Hongkong Fir Shipping Co. Ltd v Kawasaki Kisen Kaisha*, n. 54 above.

[58] Introduction to the 1st edition of M. Chalmers, *The Sale of Goods Act, 1893* (Butterworths, 1894) and reprinted in subsequent editions.

of the Sale of Goods Act might encourage the view that termination rights can by a process of construction be predicted in all cases at the outset of the contract.

Provisions of the Act. The starting point is section 11(3):   **10.15**

> Whether a stipulation in a contract of sale is a condition, the breach of which may give rise to a right to treat the contract as repudiated, or a warranty, the breach of which may give rise to a claim for damages but not to a right to reject the goods and treat the contract as repudiated, depends in each case on the construction of the contract; and a stipulation may be a condition, though called a warranty in the contract.

Section 11(3) does not explicitly state that all stipulations in contracts of sale are either conditions or warranties, but that is the implication. It denies, moreover, that a breach of warranty could ever give rise to termination. Furthermore, until the Sale and Supply of Goods Act 1994, the Sale of Goods Act did not in the list of events preventing the buyer from rejecting the goods and terminating the contract[59] list minor or trivial injury. The comprehensive pretensions of section 11(3) are bolstered by the binary technique of the draftsman in section 61(1) in defining only 'warranty', leaving 'condition' to be understood as any stipulation that is not a warranty. Since a warranty is 'collateral to the main purpose of [the] contract', a condition must therefore not be collateral, that is, central to the main purpose. The conclusion that slight breaches of condition never disallow termination, while serious breaches of warranty never permit it, seems ineluctable in interpreting the 1979 Act before the 1994 amendments.

Treatment of implied terms.   The above binary view is reinforced by the way   **10.16** that the Sale of Goods Act classifies the various implied terms. Thus the seller's duties regarding his right to sell, description, satisfactory quality,[60] fitness for purpose and correspondence with sample are stated to be conditions.[61] On the other hand, the seller's duties regarding the buyer's quiet possession and the freedom of the goods from encumbrances are classed as warranties.[62] This binary approach treats termination entitlement as a matter of *a priori* construction of the contract. In the language of the old law, it is as if termination depended exclusively upon the dependent promises rules. What therefore became of failure of consideration and cognate ideas, such as the receipt of benefit, inequality of damages and partial execution? There are a number of responses to this.

Failure of consideration.   First, failure of consideration is preserved in effect by   **10.17** section 31(2) of the Act, which deals with severable instalment contracts, where

---

[59] Ss. 11(2), 35.
[60] As merchantable quality has become with effect from the 1994 Act.
[61] Ss. 12(1) and 13–15.
[62] S. 12(2).

discharge from the outstanding portion of a partly executed contract turns 'on the terms of the contract and the circumstances of the breach'. This involves a consideration of the factual circumstances of the breach. Secondly, failure of consideration is free to invade duties of the buyer and the seller, notably those concerning the time, manner, and content of delivery and payment and acceptance duties, which are not designated by the Act as conditions or warranties. Duties of delivery and acceptance in section 27 escape classification as conditions or warranties. In addition, according to section 10:

(1) Unless a different intention appears from the terms of the contract, stipulations as to time of payment are not of the essence of a contract of sale.

(2) Whether any other stipulation as to time is or is not of the essence of the contract depends upon the terms of the contract.

This permits courts to be flexible and look to the consequences of breach. Moreover, even (for example) if timely payment by the buyer were construed as not being of the essence of the contract, a failure to pay would over time become non-payment rather than late payment[63] and the seller would be able to terminate. The seller cannot be expected to abide by the contract until the crack of doom because timely payment is not of the essence of the contract. Thirdly, the Act does not expressly provide that the doctrine of conditions and warranties applies also to express terms of the contract.[64]

10.18 **Execution and benefit.** Fourthly, the Sale of Goods Act contains a number of provisions attesting to the importance of execution and benefit in defining termination entitlement. The implied terms of quiet possession and freedom from encumbrances,[65] which connote interference after the event with the beneficial enjoyment of goods, are designated as warranties that never give rise to termination rights. The receipt of a benefit was also implicit in the now-repealed provision that, if the property in specific goods passed at the date of the contract, the buyer could not reject the goods for breach of condition.[66] The quasi-contractual origins of this provision show it to have been fed by the inability of a buyer, who had obtained even the abstract property in goods, to rescind the contract *ab initio*, at that time a necessary precondition to an action for the recovery of money on a failure of consideration.[67]

---

[63] Williston stressed that it was 'desirable to distinguish between a breach of promise to do a thing and a breach of promise as to the time when it shall be done': S. Williston and G. Thompson, *A Treatise on the Law of Contracts* (rev. edn, Baker Voorhis, 1936), iii, para. 845.

[64] But s. 11(3) could be so interpreted; discussed further below.

[65] S. 12(2).

[66] S. 11(1)(c) of the Sale of Goods Act 1893 in combination with s. 18, Rule 1.

[67] *Cutter v Powell* (1795) 6 TR 320; *Weston v Downes* (1778) 1 Dougl. 23; *Towers v Barrett* (1786) 1 TR 133; *Hunt v Silk* (1804) 5 East 449; *Street v Blay* (1831) 5 B & Ad. 456. For a fuller explanation see M. Bridge (1986) 20 *UBC LR* 53. On the notions of execution and benefit undermining strict terms, see *Behn v Burness* (1863) 3 B & S 751, 755–6. *Graves v Legg* (1854) 9 Ex. 710 asserts that

Acceptance rules.   Fifthly, the acceptance rules in section 35 clearly recognize   **10.19**
the distinction between executory and executed contracts for the purpose of termination. Though there is no explicit link to section 35, section 11(2), which
states that a buyer may waive a breach of condition by the seller and elect instead
to treat it as a breach of warranty, is the inspiration behind the later provision.
Section 11(4) echoes section 11(2) in stating that acceptance means that a breach
of condition by the seller can only be treated as a breach of warranty. The circumstances in section 35 in which the buyer accepts the goods are threefold: when the
buyer intimates an acceptance to the seller, when after delivery the buyer performs
an act inconsistent with the ownership of the seller, and when the buyer retains the
goods beyond a reasonable time even though not intimating acceptance. All three
cases are consistent with an election to retain the goods and sue for damages, but
the third, probably the most common in practice, is also consistent with execution
and benefit analysis.

Extending time for acceptance.   It may be argued that the reason the Act treats   **10.20**
so many of the implied terms as conditions is that initially a very short time was
contemplated between delivery and acceptance, during which the buyer would be
unlikely to derive a practical benefit from the contract. Canadian cases in particular have stretched the meaning of a reasonable time in extending the buyer's right
of rejection.[68] It is noticeable that, in so doing, the courts have often stressed that
the breach of an implied condition binding the seller in the circumstances amounts
to a fundamental breach or otherwise produces grave effects. Such a buyer is
unlikely to derive a net benefit from the contract.[69] The result is not dissimilar to
the two-tier approach to rejection in Article 2 of the US Uniform Commercial Code,
consisting of successive rights of rejection and revocation of acceptance,[70] the latter
lying in stated cases where the value of the goods to the buyer is substantially
impaired. Under the current legislation, it is unlikely that an English court would
follow this approach.

Conditions and section 35.   Section 35 does not mount a head-on assault on   **10.21**
the doctrine of conditions and warranties but undermines it covertly. A term that
for remedial purposes must be treated as a warranty is still essentially a condition.[71]

---

the difference for termination purposes between executory and executed contracts did not affect the
initial characterization of a term as a condition precedent, with which cf. *Ellen v Topp* (1851) 6 Ex.
424 (construction of contracts 'varied by matter *ex post facto*'). This last proposition was criticized in
Wallis, Son & Wells v Pratt & Haynes [1911] AC 394, 400, tacitly disapproving of Farwell LJ in the
court below at [1910] 2 KB 1003, 1018.

   68 Discussed at n. 151 and the text accompanying n. 197 below.
   69 See also *Rowland v Divall* [1923] 2 KB 500, discussed in Ch. 5 above.
   70 UCC Arts. 2–602, 608.
   71 See *Wallis, Son & Wells v Pratt & Haynes* [1910] 2 KB 1003, *per* Fletcher Moulton LJ (dissenting),
whose judgment was adopted as a model statement of the law by the House of Lords, n. 67 above.

The corollary to the proposition, once a condition always a condition, is the proposition, once a warranty always a warranty. The Sale of Goods Act contains no overt concession to the failure of consideration principle by allowing termination for factually serious breaches of warranty. This is not too surprising, since the Act is so strict in classifying the important implied terms as conditions, thus obviating a need to invoke failure of consideration.

Slight Breach and Section 15A

10.22 **Restricting termination rights.** A new section 15A, inserted in the Sale of Goods Act by section 4 of the Sale and Supply of Goods Act 1994,[72] limits the right of the buyer in non-consumer sales to terminate for breach of the implied description, quality, and fitness conditions in sections 13–15 in the following terms:

> (1) Where in the case of a contract of sale—
>   (a) the buyer would, apart from this subsection, have the right to reject goods by reason of the breach on the part of the seller of a term implied by section 13, 14 or 15 . . ., but
>   (b) the breach is so slight that it would be unreasonable for him to reject them,
>   then if the buyer does not deal as a consumer, the breach is not to be treated as a breach of condition but may be treated as a breach of warranty.[73]

10.23 **Burden of persuasion.** Subsection (3) goes on to place on the seller the burden of persuasion of showing that the terms of sub-section (1) have been met, which in practice will not be easy to discharge. There is also a provision curtailing the buyer's rights under section 30 where the seller delivers too many or too few goods and the shortfall or excess is so slight that it would be unreasonable for the buyer to reject the goods.[74]

10.24 **Slight breach and cure.** Section 15A was recommended by the Law Commission in its report on *Sale and Supply of Goods*.[75] It was conceived as an alternative to the introduction of the principle of curing a defective delivery in commercial cases.[76] The reasons given by the Law Commission for a reform of the Sale of Goods Act with perceived minor practical consequences were as follows. In taking advantage of rejection and termination rights for slight breaches of condition, the buyer was sometimes able to put on the seller a disproportionate loss. This is a version of the

---

[72] See M. Bridge [1995] *JBL* 398.

[73] Similar provisions were introduced into the Supply of Goods (Implied Terms) Act 1973 for hire purchase agreements (s. 11A) and into the Supply of Goods and Services Act 1982 for other contracts of proprietary transfer (s. 5A) and for hire contracts (s. 10A).

[74] S. 30(2A).

[75] Law Com. No. 160, 1987.

[76] *Ibid.*, paras 4.16–21.

inequality of damages argument.[77] The buyer in so doing might reverse the effect of a market risk that under the contract had gone against him,[78] one of the consequences of a lawful termination. The introduction of a control like that in section 15A would therefore, in this one specific case, prevent action being taken by the buyer in bad faith,[79] although the Law Commission took care to say that the buyer's motive in terminating a contract was not a matter for review.[80] These two positions are not easily reconciled. So as probably not to upset the commodities markets, the new provision is considered not to overrule those authorities that state that the time of delivery in commercial contracts is normally of the essence of the contract,[81] although an advantageous termination to recapture a lost market movement is likely to be particularly in evidence in such cases. It is noticeable too from the text of section 15A that it does nothing to undermine the strictness of section 12(1) and the seller's right to sell.[82] If for example a small amount is left outstanding under a financed conditional sale, and the finance company demands that sum from a sub-buyer, the latter will be able to invoke the full rigour of section 12(1) against the intermediate seller.

Minor defects.   An argument supporting section 15A is that it would avoid any   **10.25** judicial tendency to weaken the implied conditions of fitness and quality in the Act to deal with cases where the deficiencies in the goods are minor.[83] The new provision certainly accords with standard form contracts for the sale of commodities that confine the buyer's remedies to a price allowance for damaged goods. In many such cases, the buyer is the party better able to make economic use of

---

[77] *Ibid.*, para. 4.1.

[78] Para. 4.5.

[79] Para. 4.18.

[80] Para. 4.19.

[81] Para. 4.24. But note that timely delivery is historically explained in terms of description: *Bowes v Shand*, n. 13 above; *Kwei Tek Chao v British Traders and Shippers Ltd* [1954] 2 QB 459, 480–1. So, too, in more recent times has been the condition that an f.o.b. seller deliver goods at the nominated port of shipment: *Petrograde Inc. v Stinnes Handels GmbH* [1995] 1 Lloyd's Rep. 142. Do these cases apply s. 13 or concern express conditions inspired by the content of s. 13? Could a stipulation be both an express condition and part of the s. 13 description condition, and if so, could a buyer freely elect in favour of the former to avoid the application of s. 15A? In the litigious world of commodities trading, these questions are likely one day to be asked. The systemic certainties of these terms being treated as conditions are at some risk of being undermined by s. 15A. It is likely, nevertheless, that s 15A will be checked in its application to time provisions, not least because it can apply only to time breaches committed by the seller and not to time breaches committed by the buyer. A buyer seeking to terminate for a time breach, moreover, need not plead s. 13 at all, thus checking s. 15A *in limine*. For the view that s 15A may affect the enforcement of the rule that the time of delivery is of the essence of commercial contracts, see however E. McKendrick (ed.), *Sale of Goods* (LLP, 2000), 611–12 ('section 15A would appear to be in play').

[82] See Ch. 5 above.

[83] The Law Commission mentions *Millars of Falkirk v Turpie* 1976 SLT 66 but might also have referred to the unconvincing conclusion on merchantable quality of the Court of Appeal in *Cehave NV v Bremer Handelsgesellschaft mbH* [1976] QB 44.

sub-standard goods. An additional benefit of section 15A might be the avoidance of strained interpretations of the meaning of description in section 13 of the Act.[84] It is possible too that the threat of the section may persuade a buyer to permit a seller to cure a defect or other non-conformity in the goods supplied, which would go some little way to redress the Law Commission's recommendation that the seller not be given a statutory right to cure.

10.26 **Unreasonable conduct.** The provision in section 15A applies only where the consequences of the breach are so slight that it would be unreasonable for the buyer to reject the goods. An example of its application is the supply of goods with a defective component that can easily be replaced.[85] It is an arguable point whether section 15A would come into play to prevent a buyer from using a right to reject as a lever to force an uncooperative seller to put right an irritating minor defect when only that seller has the power to do so.[86] It is submitted that section 15A should be read in favour of the buyer, but the buyer's case would be stronger if the section had required a slight breach *and* unreasonable conduct on the part of the buyer. Section 15A should not prevent rejection where the breach cannot be described as slight but the buyer is unreasonable in, for example, turning down an offer of cure. The slight breach limitation on termination is a long way from the test of a discharging breach laid down in *Hongkong Fir Shipping Co. Ltd v Kawasaki Kisen Kaisha*,[87] which few claimants would be able to satisfy in practice, and falls considerably short of the test for a material breach required by Scots law.[88] The Law Commission is surely right to conclude that it will therefore be of infrequent application[89] but perhaps has not estimated sufficiently the disruptive possibilities in a structural reform like this one.

10.27 **Exclusion.** The parties are permitted expressly or impliedly to oust section 15A.[90] Nothing in the text of the new provision states that this will be subject to the controls laid down for exclusion clauses in the Unfair Contract Terms Act 1977.[91] It would not be easy anyway to see how the 1977 Act could apply to an implied exclusion. As for an express exclusion, the 1977 Act was not amended to take account of section 15A but, in section 3(2), does contain a provision that might be thought to embrace a buyer's written standard terms excluding section 15A.

---

[84] See Ch. 7 above.

[85] *Filobake Ltd v Rondo Ltd* [2004] EWHC 695 (TCC) at [121] (belt and tensioning device in baking equipment); *Truk (UK) Ltd v Tokmakidis GmbH* [2000] 1 Lloyd's Rep. 543.

[86] See *International Business Machines Co. v Shcherban* [1925] 1 WWR 405, discussed in Ch. 7 above.

[87] n. 57 above.

[88] S. 11(5).

[89] n. 75 above, para. 4.21.

[90] S. 15A(2).

[91] See Ch. 9 above.

But there is an insuperable difficulty in thus applying section 3. Section 15A constrains the buyer's rights under section 11 of the Sale of Goods Act, and a clause excluding section 15A would be one that lifts an impediment to the exercise of the buyer's statutory rights. Section 3(2) of the 1977 Act is designed to prevent a party from excluding or restricting liability when in breach of contract or claiming to render no performance or a performance substantially different from that which was reasonably expected. This is a long way from dealing with a clause ousting section 15A and the limits it places on the exercise of the buyer's statutory rights under section 11 of the Sale of Goods Act. Any argument that the clause restricts the buyer's liability to pay the purchase price for the goods appears strained.

Non-consumer cases.   Lastly, just as the decision not to pursue the seller's right   **10.28** to cure a defective tender in consumer cases gave leverage to the consumer buyer in dealings with the seller, so too would the retention of the present strict law serve the same purpose. Hence section 15A is confined to non-consumer cases, namely, those cases that do not pass the test of a consumer transaction in the 1977 Act.[92] It may seem hard on retailers to leave them exposed to strict termination rights exercised by consumer buyers, yet be disabled by section 15A from terminating the contract *qua* their own suppliers. But this is a particular example of the general problem sellers face when their conditions of sale differ from those on which they acquired the goods.[93] It should also be remembered that the loss felt by their consumer buyers may not be the same as the loss they seek to pass on to their suppliers. Moreover, they may already have lost the right to reject the goods under section 35. Finally, if they have been exposed to the termination of their own sales contracts, it may be that their own attempts to terminate would not fall foul of section 15A.

Termination Developments in Modern Contract Law

Complex undertakings.   Any conviction that the doctrine of conditions and   **10.29** warranties, as codified in the Sale of Goods Act, was of general application to all contracts and their terms, was jolted by *Hongkong Fir Shipping Co. Ltd v Kawasaki Kisen Kaisha*.[94] A quality obligation in a time charter, namely the owner's duty to provide a seaworthy ship, was neither a condition, whose every breach would permit the charterer to terminate, nor a warranty, whose breach could only ever give rise to a damages claim. Rather, in the judgment of Diplock LJ, it belonged to a large group of intermediate terms permitting termination only if the injured party

---

[92] n. 75 above, para. 4.8. For the definition of consumer transactions, see Ch. 9 above.
[93] n. 75 above, para. 4.26.
[94] n. 87 above; see C. Mitchell and P. Mitchell (eds), *Landmark Cases in the Law of Contract* (Hart Publishing, 2008), Ch. 9 (D. Nolan).

were deprived of substantially the whole of the contracted-for benefit. Alternative language of long standing would refer to a failure of consideration, a frustrating breach, and a breach going to the root of the contract.[95] At the heart of the case lies the idea that it is not so much the status of the term breached that governs the existence of termination rights, but rather the impact of the events flowing from the breach on the injured party's bargain.[96] Indeed, the judgment of Diplock LJ for a time put in doubt the parties' freedom to define all future outcomes of a breach as going to the root of the contract by designating it as a condition.[97] According to Diplock LJ, certain complex undertakings, like the owner's duty to provide a seaworthy ship, cannot be classified simply as conditions or warranties, since the range of outcomes produced by a breach can run from the trivial to the serious, from a rusty nail on the deck to broken down engines.[98] Whilst Diplock LJ conceived of intermediate terms as a *tertium quid* in additional to conditions and warranties, Upjohn LJ in the same case displayed greater fidelity to the foundations of termination. The essential test for termination was whether the breach of any contractual term went to the root of the contract. By way of exception, however, all breaches of certain terms were considered to go to the root of the contract if they were classified as conditions, either by the legislature or by the contracting parties, whether expressly or by necessary implication.[99] Upjohn LJ's approach, nevertheless, would need to be modified to accommodate those few legislative cases of statutory implied warranties, where statute limits the remedy for breach to damages.

10.30 **Terms as conditions.** Upjohn LJ made it clear that it was a matter of interpreting the contract to determine whether a term was a condition[100] though not

---

[95] There is little to choose between the various formulations, but the preferred approach in this text is for root (or radical breach) language (see *Davidson v Gwynne* (1810) 12 East 381).

[96] n. 87 above, 68–9. Cf *Peter Lind and Co. v Constable Hart and Co.* [1979] 2 Lloyd's Rep. 248, 253.

[97] Nothing in Diplock LJ's judgment supports the view that the parties may *a priori* define any breach of a contractual term as having this effect. Cf Blackburn J in *Bettini v Gye*, n. 18 above, 187, and see the criticism of Diplock LJ's judgment by Megaw LJ in *Bunge Corpn v Tradax Export SA* [1981] 2 All ER 513, 536–7.

[98] n. 87 above, 69–71.

[99] n. 87 above, 64. See also *Bentsen v Taylor Sons & Co. (No. 2)* [1893] 2 QB 274, 281 (Bowen LJ); *Bunge Corpn v Tradax SA* [1971] 1 WLR 711, 717 (Lord Scarman). A two-tier approach to termination rights is also shown in *Cehave NV v Bremer Handelsgesellschaft mbH* [1976] QB 44, discussed below, and in the judgment of Kirby J in *Koompahtoo Local Aboriginal Land Council v Sanpine Pty Ltd* [2007] HCA 61 at [107]–[109], with which contrast the approach of the majority in the same case.

[100] For an interesting approach to intention in determining whether a term is a condition, see *Tramways Advertising Pty Ltd v Luna Park (NSW) Ltd* (1938) 38 SR (NSW) 632, 641–2, where Jordan CJ posed the question whether the innocent party would have entered into the contract unless assured of a strict or substantial performance of the promise. If the promisee expected strict performance, then anything less than literal performance would permit termination. If substantial performance was expected, then a substantial breach would ordinarily justify termination. The latter

designated so by legislation,[101] an approach sanctioned in the same terms by section 11(3) of the Sale of Goods Act. Nevertheless, in a significant number of cases, terms have been treated as conditions, or time provisions have been treated as being of the essence of the contract, having regard more to the type of contract than to any detailed interpretation of it. In the words of Fletcher Moulton LJ: 'There are some [obligations] which go so directly to the substance of the contract or, in other words, are so essential to its very nature that their non-performance may fairly be considered by the other party as a substantial failure to perform the contract at all. On the other hand there are other obligations which, though they must be performed, are not so vital that a failure to perform them goes to the substance of the contract.'[102] The range of possible consequences flowing from the breach of a particular term affecting 'the substance and foundation of the adventure' might be so serious that the term should be regarded in law as a condition.[103] McCardie J in *Hartley v Hymans* stated that '[i]n ordinary commercial contracts for the sale of goods the rule clearly is that time is prima facie of the essence with regard to delivery'.[104] In a similar vein, Lord Diplock spoke of some terms being contractual conditions by 'implication of law'.[105] It is not clear why any implication of law should be needed as a matter of business necessity if the parties themselves have neither expressly nor impliedly designated a term as a condition, but it is not likely that the implication of law approach will, in practice, yield differences in outcome from an approach supposedly or actually based upon implied intention.[106] If an explanation is needed for the absence of reference in some cases to intention, it would seem to lie in the construction of written contracts being treated as a matter of law. Any possible intention of the present parties to a well-known type of contract is therefore overshadowed by past practice.

Commercial usage. *The Mihalis Angelos*,[107] a case concerning an 'expected ready to load' clause in a voyage charter, displays a reaction against the emphasis placed **10.31**

---

proposition is clearly suspect. For criticism of this approach, see *DTR Nominees Pty Ltd v Mona Homes Pty Ltd* (1978) 138 CLR 423, 436 (Murphy J); *Koompahtoo Local Aboriginal Land Council v Sanpine Pty Ltd*, n. 99 above at [100]–[101].

101 To similar effect, see *Koompahtoo Local Aboriginal Land Council v Sanpine Pty Ltd*, n. 99 above.

102 *Wallis, Son & Wells v Pratt & Haynes* [1910] 2 KB 1003, 1012.

103 *Bentsen v Taylor, Sons & Co. (No. 2)*, n. 99 above.

104 [1920] 3 KB 475, 484. See also Lord Lowry's reference to 'a practical expedient founded on and dictated by the experience of businessmen': *Bunge Corpn v Tradax SA*, n. 99 above, 719.

105 *Photo Production Ltd v Securicor Transport Ltd*, n. 8 above, 849. See also Bramwell B's reference to contractual terms being conditions even if the parties have not themselves made them so: *Tarrabochia v Hickie* (1856) 1 H&N 183, 188.

106 Both approaches are used by Lords Scarman and Lowry in *Bunge Corpn v Tradax SA*, n. 99 above, 717, 719.

107 *Maredelanto Cia Naviera SA v Bergbau Handels GmbH* [1971] 1 QB 164; see D. Greig (1973) 89 *LQR* 93.

in *Hongkong Fir* on defining termination rights by reference to events. The ship-owner was in breach by failing honestly and reasonably to believe that the ship would be ready to load in Hanoi by the stated date. In concluding that the clause was a condition, the court laid particular emphasis on long-standing commercial authority and usage,[108] a clear concession to the importance of commercial certainty.[109] The decision was not based upon intention but rather upon a settled view of the importance of time in commercial cases.

10.32   *Hongkong Fir* **and sale of goods.**   The above cases do not draw a clear line between conditions and intermediate stipulations for clauses other than the ones under review. Nor do they relate the autonomy of the parties in grading contractual terms to the role of the court in quantifying the severity of a breach. Neither case, moreover, has anything to say about the reconciliation of their divergent approaches within the statutory framework of sale of goods agreements.[110] In *Cehave NV v Bremer Handelsgesellschaft mbH*,[111] the *Hongkong Fir* approach was imported into the law of sale of goods. The contract called for the shipment 'in good condition' of a quantity of citrus pulp pellets for compounding into cattle feed.[112] A substantial portion of the shipment had suffered from overheating. The buyers, having paid against shipping documents, rejected the goods and sought the return of the price. In a falling market at the port of discharge, they repurchased the goods, through an agent at a judicial sale, for a price significantly below their value as damaged goods.[113] Besides throwing the market risk back on the sellers, the buyers therefore benefited from the distress sale. Later, by carefully eking out the goods, they used them all in compounding feed. By their own actions, they showed that damages would have been a perfectly adequate remedy for the breach.[114]

---

[108] T. Scrutton, *Scrutton on Charterparties and Bills of Lading* (10th edn, Sweet & Maxwell, London, 1921) (an edition for which Scrutton retained responsibility); *Finnish Govt v H Ford & Co. Ltd* (1921) 6 L1 LR 188; *Samuel Sanday & Co. v Keighley Maxsted & Co.* (1922) 27 Com. Cas. 296.

[109] n. 107 above, 199 and 207, where Edmund Davies and Megaw LJJ approved the language of Williams J in *Behn v Burness* (1863) 3 B & S 751, 759, asserting that the time of a ship's arrival was of prime importance to a charterer 'considering winds, markets and dependent contracts'.

[110] But treating *Hongkong Fir* as though it concerned the sale of goods, the 'seller's' obligation to tender a conforming ship might well have been a condition but the 'buyer's' right of rejection might have been lost by acceptance under s. 35.

[111] *The Hansa Nord* [1976] QB 44. See also *Total International Ltd v Addax BV* [1996] 2 Lloyd's Rep. 333.

[112] Cl. 7 of the form 200 of the now-defunct Cattle Food Trade Association.

[113] The contract price was £100,000, the market price at delivery for sound goods was £86,000, and a reasonable price allowance for the damage would have been £20,000. In 'an astonishing sequence of events', n. 111 above, 55–6 (Denning MR), the buyers' agents paid £33,720 for the goods at the judicial sale and turned them over at that price to the buyers.

[114] Indeed, if the decision of the Court of Appeal in *Bence Graphics International Ltd v Fasson UK Ltd* [1998] QB 87 is correct (see the criticism below in Ch. 12), they would thereby have shown that they were entitled only to nominal damages.

Express terms and the Act.   In finding for the sellers, the court in *Cehave* had to   **10.33**
confront the obstacle of the statutory doctrine of conditions and warranties. A
rather striking aspect of the case was that, despite the serious damage to the goods,
the sellers were held not to be in breach of the merchantable quality condition.[115]
This difficulty out of the way, the court unanimously concluded that the express
shipment term was not a contractual condition.[116] Consequently, the buyers were
entitled to terminate only if the breach went to the root of the contract, which
plainly it did not. For the binary system of conditions and warranties laid down in
the Sale of Goods Act, the court in accommodating express terms substituted a
different binary system.[117] This system would still admit the possibility of contractual conditions, established as such by statute, party choice, and commercial
usage, though no court would liberally add to the known stock of conditions.[118]
In addition, there would be the residuum of contractual terms, namely warranties, the normal remedy for whose breach would be damages but which would
afford 'back-up'[119] termination rights if the breach went to the root of the contract. Besides its discordance with the language of the Act, in particular section
11(3), which implies that the doctrine of conditions and warranties extends to *all*
contractual stipulations, and not just implied terms, this view does not accommodate statutory implied warranties, which in no circumstances permit termination for breach.[120] But this is a minor difficulty. The approach in *Cehave* may not
be one of unimpeachable fidelity to the language of the Act, but the court's decision represents a determined effort to avoid a rift between sale of goods law and a
constantly changing general contract law.[121]

International commodity contracts.   *Cehave* was not the last swing of the   **10.34**
pendulum. A later House of Lords decision, *Bunge Corp v Tradax Export SA*,[122]
pointed the way to strict termination rights in the case of time of performance of
primary obligations in international commodities contracts, a line that for the
most part was confirmed in subsequent decisions.[123] The contract was for the

---

[115] Ch. 7 above; see M. G. Bridge (1983) 28 *McGill LJ* 867, 898–9.

[116] No case law existed to show that it was.

[117] n. 111 above, 73 (Roskill LJ) and 84 (Ormerod LJ). Lord Denning, *ibid.* 61, however,
saw contractual terms as falling into three categories: conditions, warranties, and intermediate
stipulations.

[118] N. 111 above, 70–1 (Roskill LJ).

[119] A phrase of Ormerod LJ: n. 111 above, 83.

[120] Ss. 11(3), 61(1); see Bridge, n. 14 above, 898–9.

[121] n. 111 above, 60, 72–3, 82–3; see also the description case of *Harlingdon and Leinster
Enterprises Ltd v Christopher Hull Fine Art Ltd* [1991] 1 QB 564.

[122] n. 99 above, affirming the decision of the Court of Appeal, n. 97 above, which had reversed
Parker J.

[123] *Toepfer v Lenersan-Poortman NV* [1980] 1 Lloyd's Rep. 143; *Cie Commerciale Sucres et Denrées
v Czarnikow Ltd (The Naxos)* [1990] 1 WLR 1337; *Gill & Duffus v Soc. pour l'Exportation des Sucres*
[1985] 1 Lloyd's Rep. 621. *Aliter, Phibro Energy AG v Nissho Iwai Corpn (The Honam Jade)* [1991]

f.o.b. bulk shipment of soya bean meal from an American Gulf of Mexico port, under which the buyers were to give the sellers fifteen days' notice of expected readiness to load. When the buyers were four days late in giving the notice, the sellers terminated the contract and sued for damages on a falling market.[124] The buyer's breach did not go to the root of the contract so the seller had to establish that the buyer's duty was a condition. At all levels it was held to be a condition, largely because of the need to promote certainty in the forward-planning and contractual management aspects of the international commodities trade and to simplify dispute settlement. Difficult issues of damages entitlement, protracted trials, and complex time of the essence clauses could all be avoided by treating time obligations as conditions.[125] Lord Wilberforce went as far as to deny any role to intermediate stipulations in dealing with time obligations in commercial contracts since 'there is only one kind of breach possible, namely to be late'.[126] Yet the prejudice of a party receiving late performance frequently mounts from day to day, so as eventually to deprive him of substantially the benefit for which he bargained. A further reason for the outcome was that the seller's subsequent duty of timely shipment was a condition, so the buyer's anterior duty to give notice had to be one too.[127]

10.35 **Predicting termination rights.** *Bunge Corpn v Tradax SA* makes it possible to predict termination rights with some degree of precision. First, the decision accepted in principle intermediate stipulations whilst denying their application to time provisions in commercial contracts. The autonomy of the parties in grading a contractual term as a condition if they so wished—a freedom put in some doubt by *Hongkong Fir*—was also underwritten.[128] In consequence, the approach to termination rights is a two-fold one: first, the construction of the contract to see if

1 Lloyd's Rep. 38. A less strict approach is taken to incidental obligations: *Bremer Handelsgesellschaft mbH v Vanden Avenne-Izegem SA* [1978] 2 Lloyd's Rep. 109; *State Trading Corpn v Golodetz* [1988] 2 Lloyd's Rep. 182.

   124 It is not clear why the sellers defied conventional wisdom.
   125 See Lord Lowry, n. 99 above, 718–20. This speed and consistency of result is of course a by-product of making termination rights a pure matter of construction and therefore of law. See the deference paid to the views of arbitrators and trade boards at the same time as the sovereignty of the courts is asserted: n. 97 above, 532 (Megaw LJ) and n. 99 above, 730 (Lord Roskill). See also Lord Radcliffe's discussion of the respective roles of arbitrator and judge in the frustration case of *Davis Contractors Ltd v Fareham UDC* [1956] AC 696, 730.
   126 n. 99 above, 715; see also Megaw LJ, n. 97 above, 534.
   127 In the House of Lords, n. 99 above, 729 (Lord Roskill); in the Court of Appeal, n. 97 above, 532 and 540 (Megaw and Browne LJJ). This does not logically follow: see Ch. 6 above. More generally, the seller's own ability to perform depended upon prior performance by the buyer: n. 99 above, at 716 (Lord Wilberforce) and 718 (Lord Scarman).
   128 n. 97 above, 536–7 (Megaw LJ) and n. 99 above, 725–6 (Lord Roskill). See also the judgments in the *Hongkong Fir* case of Sellers and Upjohn LJJ: [1962] 2 QB 26, 60 and 63. The right of parties to designate a term as a condition was upheld in *Lombard North Central Plc v Butterworth* [1987] QB 527.

the term breached was a condition; and secondly, failing this, the appraisal of the effects of the breach to see if it went to the root of the contract.[129] As a summary of the antecedent law, *Bunge* suggests a basic distinction between quality and time obligations.[130] The former are particularly apt for an intermediate stipulations approach, though the implied conditions of quality, fitness, and description are put beyond the reach of this by the Sale of Goods Act. If they give rise to a slight breach, the new section 15A can prevent unreasonable termination, but this is quite a long way from the intermediate stipulations approach.

Time obligations.　In the case of commodities contracts at least, time obliga-　**10.36** tions would usually be conditions even if not expressed to be such. Since less importance is attached to time in consumer contracts than in the commodities markets, it might be preferable to permit termination of such contracts only when the consequences of breach assume serious proportions.[131] Nevertheless, even here it is questionable whether the restrictive *Hongkong Fir* test should be applied to consumer buyers in its full rigour. For different reasons, time provisions in contracts for the sale of non-market items, such as complex machinery, commonly designed or tailored to the buyer's particular specifications, should not as a matter of course be construed impliedly as conditions.[132] The prejudice suffered on termination by the defaulting seller might be out of all proportion to the injury suffered on breach by the buyer. Furthermore, the opportunities for delay in such contracts are manifold and not always easily countered; sellers may, for example, rely upon the arrival of parts from their suppliers. The contracts themselves commonly involve a protracted process of negotiation, giving the buyer an opportunity to insert an express condition, and contain liquidated damages clauses for delay, thereby suggesting that termination should not arise for every breach.

Termination protocol.　As a result of *Bunge*, a clear protocol is visible for ascer-　**10.37** taining the existence of termination rights. The first question to ask is whether the term in question is a condition. If it is, there is no need to consider the consequences of its breach. If the term is not a condition, the next question is whether its breach goes to the root of the contract. The practical application of the law therefore inverts the logic of termination rights, which starts from the premise that termination is permitted if a breach goes to the root of the contract.

Express termination clauses.　It is common in contracts of a continuing charac-　**10.38** ter for contracting parties to make express provision for contractual termination

---

129　See also Denning MR in *Cehave*, n. 111 above.

130　n. 97 above, 534 (Megaw LJ) and n. 99 above, 715 (Lord Wilberforce).

131　*Allen v Danforth Motors Ltd* (1957) 12 DLR (2d) 572. Cf *Charles Rickards Ltd v Oppenhaim* [1950] 1 KB 616, where the buyer, who had throughout made it clear that he needed the car for a continental trip, waited patiently for the agreed distant delivery date.

132　*Fairbanks Soap Co. v Sheppard* [1953] 1 SCR 314.

without reference to the terminology of conditions, repudiation, and breaches going to the root of the contract. A common type of clause permits termination where a 'material breach' is committed, usually after a stipulated time that allows the party in breach to 'remedy' it. Express clauses sometimes provide on their face for the contract to be terminated automatically, as might, for example, be the case where a breach is irremediable. The principal questions raised concern the meaning of a material breach, the relationship of contractual remedies for material breach to termination rights arising at law, whether a breach is remediable, and whether a contract may be terminated automatically on breach if the parties so provide.

10.39 **Material breach.** The concept of a material breach is not a term of art in English law;[133] it takes its meaning as a matter of construction from the particular contract. In *Dalkia Utilities Services plc v Celtech International Ltd*,[134] a case concerning the provision of energy services, it was common ground between the parties that a breach did not have to be repudiatory for it to be material for the purpose of an express payment clause in the contract. The court appears to have accepted this because otherwise the material breach clause would add nothing to the common law position. One reason for such a conclusion is that the presence of a procedure in the clause for remedying breaches may show an intention to apply the clause to more than just repudiatory breaches.[135] Nevertheless, a universal meaning should not be ascribed to material breach clauses that pays no heed to their particular contractual context. It is quite possible, however, for the parties to intend that a clause of this nature not depart from the common law. The language of materiality may be chosen, for example, because its meaning is clearer to business parties than is the language of repudiation. As for what constitutes the relevant criteria for determining materiality, according to Christopher Clarke J: 'In assessing the materiality of any breach it is relevant to consider not only of what the breach consists but also the circumstances in which the breach arises, including any explanation given or apparent as to why it has occurred.'[136] The failure by the energy taker to pay in the present case was not due to some oversight but rather to its precarious financial position. Consequently, the breach was material even though it was by no means repudiatory.[137] The amounts unpaid were only a small part of the total amounts payable over a fifteen-year period, but they represented payments due in the current quarter and 8.5 per cent of all amounts for the remainder of the initial period of the agreement. In such cases, the provision of

---

[133] Scots law is a different matter.
[134] [2006] EWHC 63 (Comm); [2001] 1 Lloyd's Rep. 599.
[135] See also *National Power plc v United Gas Co. Ltd* [1998] All ER (D) 321.
[136] Above, at [102]; see also *Glolite Ltd v Jasper Conran Ltd*, The Times, 28 January 1998.
[137] *Decro-Wall International SA v Practitioners in Marketing Ltd* [1971] 1 WLR 361; *Shevill v Builders Licensing Board* (1989) 149 CLR 620, 630.

credit, as might happen where goods are at intervals supplied with payment due later, plays an important part in characterizing non-payment as material.[138] In different circumstances, the reference to material breach may evidence the intention of parties that a contract not be terminated in the event of a breach of condition with slight or venial consequences.[139]

Express terms and other termination rights. A further issue arising from **10.40** material breach concerns the effect of a contractual provision, for dealing with material breaches, on termination rights that would otherwise arise by operation of law, whether because the breach in question is repudiatory or because there is a parallel breach of a statutory condition. Subject to unfair contract terms legislation, it is open to the parties to contract out of termination rights. The mere provision of express contractual rights of termination, however, will not of itself serve to exclude those common law rights. The two regimes may coexist and common law rights of termination are not waived because the injured party invokes a right to terminate under a material breach or similar clause.[140] If, however, a contractual provision is invoked and it gives the non-performing party a time within which to rectify non-performance, it ought to follow that the injured party is indeed waiving a right to terminate so long as that period of grace has not expired.

Irremediable breach. The expressions material breach and irremediable breach **10.41** have been said to be overlapping expressions.[141] They do overlap in the sense that a material breach may be subjected successfully to a remedial process. As for what constitutes the remedying of a breach, a degree of common sense has to be applied. In one sense, the clock cannot be wound back in order to enable what was not done to be done, or what was not done on time to be done on time. Commercial representatives cannot retrospectively conduct periodical site visits and security guards cannot retrospectively patrol guarded premises, though goods not delivered can be delivered. Yet, so far as the effect of delinquency can be repaired for the future, a clause requiring a breach to be remedied within a stipulated period ought to be satisfied.[142]

---

138 See *Fortman Holdings Ltd v Modem Holdings Ltd* [2001] EWCA Civ 1235 (loan notes unpaid on sale of entire share capital of a company where purchaser 'enjoyed an unrestricted right to the benefits of the sale agreement').

139 Cf *Fitzroy House Epworth House (No. 1) Ltd v Financial Times* [2006] 1 WLR 2207.

140 *Dalkia Utilities Services plc v Celtech International Ltd*, n. 134 above at [143]; *Stocznia Gdanska SA v Latvian Shipping Co.* [2002] EWCA Civ 889; [2002] 2 Lloyd's Rep. 436 at [88]. See also *Stocznia Gdynia SA v Gearbulk Holdings Ltd* [2008] EWHC 944 (Comm) at [35] *et seq.*

141 *Phoenix Media Ltd v Cobweb Information Ltd* (Unreported, 16 May 2000) at [59].

142 See *Phoenix Media Ltd v Cobweb Information Ltd*, n. 141 above at [72]: 'In one sense, irremediability of a breach is impossible. The example that is frequently given is this: if there is an obligation on a tenant to paint in the fifth year of the term and he fails to do so, that is irremediable because, even if he paints thereafter, he has not painted in the fifth year of the term. Yet failing to

10.42 **Automatic termination.** The last issue here is whether contracting parties may provide that a contract be terminated automatically upon the commission of stipulated breaches of contract. It is clear that courts lean against the construction of a contract favouring automatic termination,[143] sometimes employing a rule that notice of termination should be given if termination is to be effective. This implies that termination itself is elective if it shall not take place unless a party chooses to give the notice. In principle, nevertheless, there is no reason why a contract may not provide for automatic termination if the expression of intention is clear enough.

The Buyer's Rights of Examination and Rejection

General

10.43 **Rejection and termination.** A buyer exercising a right to terminate the contract may thereby reject a non-conforming tender of goods by the seller and refuse to accept tenders that would, but for the termination, have fallen due at a future date. Although termination entails rejection, it does not logically follow that a buyer entitled to reject goods is thereby entitled to or does terminate the contract.[144] When the principle of cure is examined below, the significance of this gap between rejection and termination will become apparent.

10.44 **The Act.** The Sale of Goods Act is not explicit in its treatment of termination and rejection and their effect upon the rights and duties of the parties. There is no definition at all of termination or of any of its synonyms such as discharge, rescission for breach, or cancellation. Sometimes, the Act refers to the entitlement of a party to treat the contract as repudiated for the other's breach,[145] but it does not say what in practical terms that means. The precise meaning of rejection is not defined in the Act,[146] but the cases require a clear intention on the buyer's part to throw the goods back on the seller,[147] and a statement to that effect will carry no weight if the

---

paint in the fifth year of the term is clearly remediable. To my mind, therefore, irremediability has to be interpreted in a common sense way.'

[143] See *Artpower Ltd v Bespoke Couture Ltd* [2006] EWCA Civ 1696; *Total Gas Marketing Ltd v Arco British Ltd* [1998] 2 Lloyd's Rep. 209. The notion of automatic termination is also associated with the decision in *Harbutt's 'Plasticine' Ltd v Wayne Tank and Pump Co. Ltd* [1970] 1 QB 447, overruled in *Photo Production Ltd v Securicor Transport Ltd*, n. 8 above.

[144] But see *Kwei Tek Chao v British Traders and Shippers Ltd*, n. 81 above, 480, where Devlin J treats rejection as tantamount to termination.

[145] Ss. 11(3), (4), 31(2), and 61(1) ('warranty'). For a discussion of the various meanings of repudiation, see *Koompahtoo Local Aboriginal Land Council v Sanpine Pty Ltd*, n. 100 above.

[146] The parties themselves may prescribe the permitted method of rejection: *Cockshutt v Mills* (1905) 7 Terr. LR 392 (Can.).

[147] *Couston, Thomson & Co. v Chapman* (1868) LR 2 HL 250 (Sc.): 'clear and distinct notification of the breaking off of the contract'; see also *Grimoldby v Wells* (1875) LR 10 CP 391. See also *SAM Business Systems Ltd v Hedley and Co.* [2002] EWHC 2733 (TCC) at [141]–[142].

buyer's actions are not consistent with the statement.[148] The buyer's rejection of the goods will not be vitiated by his failure to take active steps to return them to the seller, since it is sufficient that he intimate to the seller that he is not accepting the goods,[149] leaving the seller to take any necessary steps to recover them. Although the Act does not define rejection, it does recite the circumstances in which the right is lost by the buyer's acceptance of the goods[150] and refers to one instance of rejection, the refusal to accept a tender of non-conforming goods, when providing that the buyer is under no obligation to return the goods to the seller.[151] Additional remedies for consumer buyers and transposed in the form of supplementary provisions in the Sale of Goods Act give rise to some difficulty in determining their coexistence with the right of rejection under the Sale of Goods Act.[152]

Coordination of rejection and termination.   The link between termination and **10.45** rejection is left obscure by the Sale of Goods Act. Certainly, where the seller is in breach of a statutory implied warranty, the buyer may neither reject the goods nor treat the contract as repudiated.[153] Where there is a breach of condition, the Act says merely that it 'may give rise' to a right to treat the contract as repudiated.[154] In the case of non-conforming goods, the Act also fails to say precisely when a breach of condition occurs, whether on the appropriation of the goods to the contract, on tender or delivery of them to the buyer, or when their unsatisfactory or unfit quality comes to light. Nor does the Act state explicitly for late delivery whether the breach of condition occurs on the expiry of the delivery date or period or in the event of a frustrating delay.[155] In classifying certain implied terms as conditions, the Act does not relate them explicitly to rejection. It also expressly recites rejection rights where the seller is long or short on delivery, but again fails to state the consequences of this as a matter of termination.[156]

Submission.   Any conclusions advanced on the subject of rejection and termi- **10.46** nation must necessarily be tentative. On one view, a breach of condition (other than a slight breach under section 15A), or the commission of any other discharging breach, allows the buyer to terminate the contract, apart from the possible right of

---

[148] *Graanhandel T Link BV v European Grain & Shipping Ltd* [1989] 2 Lloyd's Rep. 531 (persisting with a sale of rejected goods for the account of the sellers despite the sellers' refusal to give buyers authority to sell on their behalf). See also *Morton v Chapman* (1843) 11 M & W 534; *Vargas Pena Apezteguia v Peter Cremer GmbH* [1987] 1 Lloyd's Rep. 394. Cf *Tradax Export SA v European Grain & Shipping Ltd* [1983] 2 Lloyd's Rep. 100.
[149] S. 36.
[150] S. 35.
[151] S. 36.
[152] Part 5A of the Act. These provisions are discussed below.
[153] Ss. 11(3) and 61(1).
[154] S. 11(3).
[155] See the discussion of cure below.
[156] S. 30.

a seller to cure a defective tender. The opposite view would have it that all terminating breaches by the seller may ultimately be reduced to one of two forms: either, the seller fails to deliver conforming goods on time,[157] in those cases where time is of the essence of the contract, or within the limits of a frustrating delay, where the buyer has to show a breach that goes to the root of the contract; or the seller, by his conduct in tendering or delivering non-conforming goods, thereby repudiates the contract by either renouncing his obligations or by demonstrating a manifest inability to perform them. The advantage of the former view is that it provides some measure of commercial certainty. The latter view, nevertheless, has a thread of supporting authority. In *Heisler v Anglo-Dal Ltd*,[158] Somervell LJ referred to the well-known rule that a party terminating a contract is entitled to do so where good grounds for termination exist, even though he may have cited the wrong reason for terminating the contract.[159] Nevertheless, he went on to say that this rule was subject to a proviso: 'If the point not taken is one which if taken could have been put right, the principle will not apply.'[160] This latter view also has the merit of being better adapted to deal with severable instalment contracts.[161] So far as it is advanced in cases where a buyer rejects a non-conforming tender, and never takes delivery, it also accords with authority that supports a seller's right to cure a non-conforming tender (as opposed to a non-conforming delivery).[162] For these reasons, it is submitted that a court should not assume that the lawful rejection of goods by the buyer necessarily amounts to termination of the contract and that the seller has a chance to put matters right within the limits of the second view stated above.

Examination

10.47 **Right of examination.** The buyer's right of examination is to be found in section 34,[163] which reads:

> Unless otherwise agreed, when the seller tenders delivery of goods to the buyer, he is bound on request to afford the buyer a reasonable opportunity of examining the goods for the purpose of ascertaining whether they are in conformity with the contract and, in the case of a contract for sale by sample, of comparing the bulk with the sample.

---

[157] See Lord Devlin [1966] *CLJ* 192, 203.

[158] [1954] 1 WLR 1273, 1278.

[159] Discussed below.

[160] See also *South Caribbean Trading Ltd v Trafigura Beheer BV* [2004] EWHC 2676 (Comm); [2005] 1 Lloyd's Rep. 128 at [133]. This dictum was also cited with apparent approval by Andrew Smith J in *Cenargo Ltd v Empresa Nacional Bazan de Construcciones Navales Militares SA* [2002] EWCA Civ 524; [2002] CLC 1151 at [61], though he went on to say that it did not 'impose a general obligation upon a buyer to draw deficiencies to the seller's attention before taking delivery'. In this case, an appeal was allowed in part and on different grounds: *ibid*.

[161] See the text accompanying nn. 334 *et seq*. below.

[162] See discussion of cure below.

[163] As modified by the Sale and Supply of Goods Act 1994, s. 2(2).

This section is the former section 34(2) with the addition to its main provision of a specific example of its application to sales by sample.[164] The former sub-section (1) has, for the sake of clarity, been reworked into the body of section 35, which deals with the loss of a buyer's right of rejection consequent upon acceptance of the goods. The amendment to section 34 is the latest step in an attempt to devise a protocol clearly showing that the examination rule takes precedence over the acceptance rules.[165] It does so by inhibiting the operation of the section 35 rules on acceptance where the buyer has not had a reasonable opportunity to examine the goods. The amended section 34 evidences the conflict that has emerged over the years between the two sections as the commercial and legal practice of examination has changed.

Place of examination.   The existence of a reasonable opportunity to examine   **10.48**
the goods is determined in part by the place where the buyer should conduct the examination. The case law reveals a gradual change from examination at the seller's premises to examination at the buyer's premises. In the nineteenth-century cases, the buyer's assent to an unconditional appropriation of the goods by the seller and his examination of the goods were one and the same act. It was not as such the passing of property in unascertained goods that prevented the buyer from rejecting them but rather the buyer's approval of goods after examination or his waiver[166] of this right to examine. The equivalent rule for specific goods, most of which would have been examined or available for examination before the contract, prevented rejection after the passing of property and was based upon the idea of a notional delivery to the buyer at the contract date.[167] For local deliveries in particular, the place of examination was the seller's premises, which remains the presumptive place of delivery[168] and therefore the place where the buyer presumptively makes payment.[169] A buyer satisfied with his examination of goods unconditionally appropriated by the seller would thereupon intimate to the seller that he was accepting them[170] and make payment. In such a case, the buyer's right of rejection would therefore be evanescent and commonly lost altogether if the buyer waived the right to examine or conducted a brief examination at the point of delivery.[171]

Carriage.   The link between the seller's premises and examination was necessar-   **10.49**
ily broken where buyer and seller were separated by a distance and the services of

---

164 Drawn from the former text of s. 15.
165 See the earlier difficulties posed by *Hardy & Co. (London) v Hillerns & Fowler* [1923] 2 KB 490.
166 See the waiver principle in s. 11(2).
167 *Dixon v Yates* (1833) 5 B & Ad. 313; see Ch. 3 above.
168 S. 29(2).
169 S. 28 and Ch. 6 above.
170 The first heading of acceptance in s. 35.
171 *John Hallam Ltd v Bainton* (1919) 45 OLR 483 (Can.).

a carrier were employed to transport the goods to the buyer. What seems to have been a rule that the place of examination was the seller's premises was relaxed as it became established that the buyer could examine on the arrival of the goods.[172] The carrier might have been able to provide a deemed assent to the seller's unconditional appropriation but not to examine and accept the goods on the buyer's behalf. In some cases, the link between assent and examination was not easily sundered: these cases went so far as to hold that a buyer examining the goods away from the seller's premises had not given prior assent to the seller's unconditional appropriation of non-conforming goods to the contract.[173] The passing of property would not nowadays pose an obstacle to the buyer's examination and rejection of the goods. A right of examination is necessarily postponed in the case of goods sold whilst in transit.[174] Postponement is also appropriate for goods that cannot adequately be inspected until they have reached their destination.[175] Where buyer and seller contemplate that the goods will be examined by a distant sub-buyer, it may also be their intention to postpone examination by or on behalf of the buyer to that place and time.[176] Although the shift of the place of examination once excited fears in some cases that certain buyers might unscrupulously exploit the distance of the seller in extracting concessions,[177] the point is not usually taken nowadays that the place of delivery is the place of examination.[178] Complex manufactured goods may not practicably be examined at the point of

---

[172] *Bragg v Villanova* (1923) 40 TLR 154; *Thames Canning Co. v Eckhardt* (1915) 34 OLR 72 (Can.); *Tower Equipment Rental Ltd v Joint Venture Equipment Sales* (1975) 9 OR (2d) 453 (Can.).

[173] *Ollett v Jordan* [1918] 2 KB 41. In *Hardy & Co. v Hillerns & Fowler*, n. 165 above, 499 Atkin LJ states that the property in c.i.f. goods does not pass upon the documentary transfer until the buyer has had an opportunity to examine the goods. See also *Perkins v Bell* [1893] 1 QB 190, 198: rejection right surrendered on passing of property upon delivery.

[174] A buyer cannot practicably examine goods that have not yet been appropriated to the contract. The right of inspection in c.i.f. contracts is deferred since the buyer's duty is to pay against conforming documents (*Polenghi Bros v Dried Milk Co. Ltd* (1904) 92 LT 64; *E Clemens Horst Co. v Biddell Bros* [1912] AC 18). Lord Mance in *Scottish & Newcastle International Ltd v Othon Galanos Ltd* [2008] UKHL 11; [2008] 1 Lloyd's Rep. 462 said at [31] that examination after arrival of the goods at their destination 'is a commonplace of international sales'. An exception is where a third party, as is the common practice, examines the goods at the point of shipment and issues an inspection certificate that becomes part of the documentary package tendered to the buyer.

[175] *Winnipeg Fish Co. v Whitman Fish Co.* (1909) 41 SCR 453 (frozen fish that first had to thaw).

[176] *Molling & Co. v Dean & Son Ltd* (1901) 18 TLR 217; *AJ Frank & Sons Ltd v Northern Peat Co.* [1963] 2 OR 415 (Can.). Where goods cannot practicably be examined at the point of delivery, the right of examination will be deferred: *Heilbutt v Hickson* (1872) LR 7 CP 438; *Grimoldby v Wells* (1875) LR 10 CP 391.

[177] *Szymanowski and Co. v Beck and Co.* [1923] 1 KB 457, 467 ('rejection . . . as a lever to extort a reduction in the price'); *Re Faulckners Ltd* (1917) 38 DLR 84.

[178] e.g., *Bernstein v Pamson Motors (Golders Green) Ltd* [1987] 2 All ER 220. See, however, *Long v Lloyd* [1958] 2 All ER 402, 406, where the court, dealing with the sale of a second-hand lorry, stated that apart from special circumstances the buyer should examine upon delivery. This now appears anachronistic.

delivery, so, for example, the tolling of a reasonable time for the buyer's acceptance of the goods under section 35 should run from the time the buyer has a reasonable opportunity to examine the goods on his own premises. For consumer buyers, the issue of the place of examination, where goods are dispatched to them by means of a carrier, has been resolved indirectly by deeming delivery not to take place when the goods are delivered to the carrier.[179]

Nature of examination   Section 34 does not define what amounts to an exami-   **10.50** nation of the goods. At one extreme, it could be a brief and superficial inspection of the outward aspect of the goods; at the other, it could be a prolonged and beneficial use of the goods in service. The range embraces goods as diverse as natural commodities and manufactured items, but the section 34 case law does not overtly reveal any difference in the understanding of examination for the purpose of dealing with these two types of goods. What is clear is that the law has not surrendered to the possibility that examination could extend to the latter of the above extremes. One objection to such a concession is that it would bring the buyer's right of examination into even more conflict with the acceptance bars to rejection in section 35.[180] The right of examination has, nevertheless, been extended to the hidden characteristics of goods, even when this has entailed some degree of destructive testing.[181] Postponing examination and extending its scope, however, is responsible for the battle for precedence in modern times between sections 34 and 35, resolved firmly in favour of the former.

Failure to allow examination.   Section 34 provides that the seller is bound on   **10.51** request to afford the buyer a reasonable opportunity to examine the goods but it makes no mention of the sanction for non-compliance. Certainly, a refusal to permit the buyer to examine may be seen as destroying the lawfulness of the seller's tender so that the seller may not complain if the buyer refuses to accept and pay for the goods.[182] It has been said that a refusal to allow examination is a discharging breach.[183] This may be justified on the ground that the seller's conduct amounts to a repudiation or prevents due delivery in circumstances where time is of the essence of the contract.

Waiving right of examination.   Apart from consumer transactions, a buyer   **10.52** may waive, or under the terms of the contract surrender, the right of examination.

---

[179] S. 32(4), as added by the Sale and Supply of Goods to Consumers Regulations 2002, SI 2002 No. 3045, reg. 4.

[180] Notably the retention of the goods beyond a reasonable time and the performance of an act inconsistent with the ownership of the seller. *Bernstein*, n. 178 above: a reasonable time is not the time needed to discover a hidden defect in the goods.

[181] *Heilbutt v Hickson*, n. 176 above; *Toulmin v Hedley* (1845) 2 Car. & K 157; *Winnipeg Fish Co v Whitman Fish Co.*, n. 175 above; *Reevie v White Co. Ltd* [1929] 4 DLR 296.

[182] *Isherwood v Whitmore* (1843) 11 M & W 347.

[183] *Lorymer v Smith* (1822) 1 B & C 1.

The latter is commonly done in international commodity sales where disinterested inspection agencies issue certificates that are final and binding on the parties.[184] This system meets the concerns of a seller about having to dispose of rejected goods in a distant place. To a degree, that seller, if already paid by the buyer against shipping documents, has the tactical upper hand since it is up to the buyer to reject the goods and take steps to recover the price.[185] Under section 35(2),[186] the buyer is not bound by an acceptance of the goods, taking the form of an intimation of acceptance or the performance of an act inconsistent with the ownership of the seller, where the buyer has not had a chance to examine the goods. Although the buyer's examination rights for the purpose of section 35 may be waived or surrendered,[187] this is not allowed if the buyer is a consumer.[188] In non-consumer sales, a waiver, not amounting to a variation of the contract, of the right to examine should not be caught by the Unfair Contract Terms Act. The only relevant provision, section 3, applicable to a buyer doing business on the seller's written standard terms, governs the use of contract terms. A post-contract waiver of rights in a delivery note, for example, is not a contract term. Section 3 could extend to a surrender of the right to examine in the contract itself, but the difficult and technical argument would have to be made that the seller is excluding a liability to return the purchase price as a consequence of the rejection of the goods.[189]

Acceptance

10.53 **General.** Section 11(4) provides that the buyer of goods under a non-severable contract[190] loses the right of rejection, and thus may not treat the contract as repudiated, after acceptance of the goods or a part of them.[191] This provision is made expressly subject to section 35A which permits such a buyer, if there is no express

---

[184] See, e.g., *Alfred C Toepfer v Continental Grain Co.* [1974] 1 Lloyd's Rep. 11; *Berger & Co. Inc. v Gill & Duffus SA* [1984] AC 382. Questions may arise whether such a provision is confined to defects of quality: *N V Bunge v Cie Noga d'Importation et d'Exportation SA* [1980] 2 Lloyd's Rep. 601 (admixture of soya oil and groundnut oil).

[185] The buyer has no lien for the recovery of the price: see *JL Lyons & Co. v May and Baker Ltd* [1923] 1 KB 685; *Kwei Tek Chao v British Traders & Shippers Ltd*, n. 81 above.

[186] Sale and Supply of Goods Act 1994, s. 2(1).

[187] As implied by s. 35(3) for non-consumer cases.

[188] The definition of a consumer sale is taken from the Unfair Contract Terms Act 1977, Ch. 9 above.

[189] What if the buyer has not yet paid?

[190] On entire and severable contracts see Ch. 6 above.

[191] This provision does not apply to consumer conditional sale contracts, which for this purpose are treated as hire purchase contracts: Supply of Goods (Implied Terms) Act 1973, s. 14 (see below). A buyer is a consumer who deals as a consumer for the purpose of Part I of the Unfair Contract Terms Act 1977: *ibid.*

or implied contrary intention,[192] to reject non-conforming goods while accepting all those goods that are unaffected by the seller's breach.[193] The breach has to be serious enough that the buyer could have rejected the goods in their entirety, since section 35A does not manufacture a right of rejection where none existed before. If, for example, the seller were to sell a job lot, described as goods of varying quality and condition, the buyer would not be entitled to isolate in that lot those goods that fall below the average standard and reject them, when the goods as a whole comply with the conditions of description, fitness, and quality in sections 13–14. A more difficult question concerns the buyer who, under section 15A, would be unreasonable in rejecting goods for a slight breach of one or more of these implied terms.[194] Could the buyer reject a portion of the goods and retain all the rest? It might appear reasonable for the buyer to do this but section 35A requires that the buyer first have a right to reject the goods and section 15A deprives the buyer of the right of rejection.[195] The answer would therefore seem to be no.

Wrong goods.   It was stated above that rejection of the goods might not necessarily lead to termination of the contract. The question now is whether the rules on acceptance in section 35 must necessarily be applied if the buyer seeks to terminate after delivery has been made. It has been held that the rules on acceptance do not apply where the seller delivers the wrong goods.[196] The court in the same case also rejected the argument that the rules on acceptance in section 35 would apply even where the goods were so seriously defective that the seller was guilty of total non-performance of the contract.[197] If the contract goods are specific goods, the delivery of the wrong goods might be seen as amounting to an offer to enter into a new contract of sale with the buyer, though the circumstances might not display any clear intention about what is to happen to the old contract. By analogy with sale or return and sale on approval transactions,[198] the rules on acceptance of the offer of sale could be applied to determine whether and when a new contract comes into existence. It is noticeable that the three ways in which an offer to sell

10.54

---

[192] S. 35A(4). The difficulties stated above in applying the provisions of the Unfair Contract Terms Act to implied exclusions of s. 15 apply here too. S. 35A contains no equivalent to s. 35(3), which in consumer cases preserves the buyer's right to examine notwithstanding waiver or contrary agreement.

[193] S. 35A(1)(b). This does not take away the right of a buyer in receipt of an excess tender to accept only that quantity required by the contract: s. 30(2).

[194] The question also arises where the buyer is prevented from rejecting goods for slight deficiencies or surpluses: s. 30(2A).

[195] S. 15A: 'Where . . . the buyer would, apart from this subsection, have the right to reject goods . . .'.

[196] *Broadcrest CD Ltd v Ruddock* 2000 WL 1881420 at [45] (referring to the seller's intention to pass title to the machines identified by serial number in the invoice and not to the machines actually delivered, which belonged to someone else).

[197] *Ibid.*, at [44] and [47].

[198] Discussed above.

may be accepted in section 18 Rule 4 correspond quite closely to the three ways in which a buyer's acceptance of the goods precludes rejection in section 35,[199] though the language is somewhat different.[200] Therefore, it might prove inconsequential if the operation of section 35 was excluded in the case of the wrong goods. For unascertained goods, identifying the goods delivered as the wrong goods is not so straightforward, though the modern approach to confine description in section 13 to matters of identity[201] might make it possible to equate a breach of section 13 with the delivery of the wrong goods. The case of seriously defective goods whose delivery amounts to total non-performance does not as such make a case for disapplying section 35. Nevertheless, it is precisely in such a case that a buyer might be able to assert a total failure of consideration, which has been relied on in section 12 cases to justify a claim for the recovery of the price paid even though the buyer has not complied with section 35 in terminating the contract[202] or has not even sought to terminate the contract at all.[203] It will, nevertheless, be a rare case where there is a complete absence of benefit accruing to the buyer and it is precisely in such a rare case that a buyer is likely to exercise rights of rejection and termination with some alacrity. In sum, the slender authority supporting the disapplication of section 35 cannot with great confidence be followed, but it is unlikely that the issue will ever have any great practical relevance.

Partial Rejection

10.55 **Extent of partial rejection.** The right of partial rejection, created whenever there has been a breach of condition, express or implied, or other breach going to the root of the contract, is an enlargement of the previous right of partial rejection given to the buyer for a breach of the seller's description obligation.[204] Section 30(4), stating this latter right, has now been repealed[205] because of its absorption by the more extensive provision in section 35A. Partial acceptance will often make good commercial sense and can be seen at work already in the cases where the

---

199 Discussed below.

200 Cf 'signifies his approval or acceptance' (s. 18 Rule 4) and 'intimates to the seller that he has accepted' (s. 35); 'retains the goods without giving notice of rejection etc' (s. 18 Rule 4) and 'after the lapse of a reasonable time [the buyer] retains the goods' (s. 35)); '[the buyer] does any . . . act adopting the transaction' (s. 18 Rule 4) and '[the buyer] does any act . . .which is inconsistent with the ownership of the seller' (s. 35)). Note also the way the Court of Appeal has applied s. 35 when determining whether acceptance has taken place by passage of time under s. 18, Rule 4 in *Atari Corpn (UK) Ltd v Electronic Boutique Stores Ltd* [1998] QB 539.

201 Discussed in Ch. 7 above.

202 *Rowland v Divall,* n. 69 above and Ch. 5 above.

203 Cf *Warman v Southern Counties Car Finance Corpn* [1949] 2 KB 576 (hire purchase).

204 *W Barker Jnr & Co. Ltd v ET Agius Ltd* (1927) 33 Com. Cas. 120; Law Com. No. 120, paras 6.6 *et seq.*

205 Sale and Supply of Goods Act 1994, s. 3(3).

parties have voluntarily agreed upon it.[206] It can often be the solution that mini-
mizes the losses caused by the tender of non-conforming goods. The buyer exercising the new right of partial rejection must retain all conforming goods but may
also, if he wishes, retain some of the non-conforming goods.[207] In the exercise of
these rights, the buyer may not break up a commercial unit of goods; an acceptance of any of the goods in a unit is a deemed acceptance of all the goods in that
unit.[208] Although the new provision does not say so, the buyer should pay for the
goods retained at the contract rate, which is the rule laid down for short delivery
by section 30(1). Similarly, if the buyer has already paid, so much of the contract
price as corresponds to the rejected goods should be recoverable as on a failure of
consideration.[209]

Meaning of Acceptance

Methods of acceptance.   Section 35 lays down three ways in which the buyer, by   **10.56**
accepting the goods, loses the right of rejection. It should not be forgotten that an
injured party may also in more general terms lose the right to reject the goods
under section 11(2) by electing to treat a breach of condition as a breach of warranty. Nevertheless, the requirements of an election are so stringent[210] that it is
difficult to conceive of such a case that does not also fall within the heads of
acceptance, especially the first, in section 35. These three acceptance heads are:
first, an intimation to the seller that the buyer is accepting the goods; secondly, the
performance after delivery of an act inconsistent with the seller's ownership; and
thirdly, the retention of the goods after the lapse of a reasonable time.

Meanings of acceptance.   Before these different modes of acceptance are con-   **10.57**
sidered, it is useful to consider two matters: the diverse meanings of acceptance in
sales law and the common law foundation of the statutory notion of acceptance
in section 35. In modern sales law, acceptance has at least three meanings. First, as
one of the exceptions to the written evidence requirement, which is still to be
found in some jurisdictions with an Act based upon the imperial Sale of Goods

---

[206] *Manifatture Tessile Laniera Wooltex v JB Ashley Ltd* [1979] 2 Lloyd's Rep. 28; *Molling v Dean*
(1901) 18 TLR 217 (seller stamped the names of different sub-buyers on a consignment of 40,000
books). It is also common in the international commodity sale forms. A significant number of
Canadian cases have in the past permitted partial acceptance despite the Act or (for pre-Act cases)
the entire contracts rule. See M. Bridge, *Sale of Goods* (Butterworths, Toronto, 1988), 297–8.
[207] S. 35A(1)(b). Law Com. No. 160, para. 6.11.
[208] S. 35(7). Law Com. No. 160, paras 6.12–13. Examples given are individual volumes in a set
of encyclopaedias and one of a pair of shoes.
[209] Partial recovery claims are not uncontroversial but are sanctioned by a number of authorities:
see *Devaux v Connolly* (1849) 8 CB 640; *Biggerstaff v Rowatt's Wharf Ltd* [1896] 2 Ch. 93, 100, 105;
Behrend & Co. Ltd v Produce Brokers Co. Ltd [1920] 3 KB 530, 535; *Ebrahim Dawood Ltd v Heath
Ltd* [1961] 2 Lloyd's Rep. 512.
[210] *Peyman v Lanjani* [1985] Ch. 457.

Act 1893, it is behaviour, sometimes prior to the receipt of goods,[211] that acknowledges the existence of a contract of sale.[212] This meaning of acceptance should be distinguished from the second meaning, the acceptance that forecloses rejection rights under sections 11(4) and 35.[213] The third meaning emerges from section 27, which speaks of the buyer's duty to accept and pay for the goods, the correlative of the seller's duty of delivery. This duty of the buyer is needed to allow the seller to effect delivery. This form of acceptance occurs upon the transfer of possession of the goods, actual or constructive, to the buyer. The buyer must receive the seller's tender, which may occur in various ways, for example, through the agency of a carrier under section 32(1). These three meanings reveal the explosion of the idea of acceptance as it has been pressed to perform different functions. The old written evidence acceptance might well precede the section 27 acceptance, which will almost always precede the section 35 acceptance. It is the section 27 meaning that is the essential meaning of acceptance; the others represent departures from this norm.[214] Acceptance as an exception to the written evidence requirement was accelerated to provide alternative unwritten evidence, while acceptance under section 35 was delayed, and continues further to be delayed, in order to accommodate to some degree the buyer prejudiced by hidden faults in complex manufactured goods.

10.58 **Election and acceptance.**   The delaying of acceptance in section 35 has not been accomplished uniformly throughout the cases.[215] So much uncertainty surrounds the length of the acceptance period in section 35 that a buyer can rarely be advised with full confidence that rejection is or is not still an available remedy. Though it will not dissipate the uncertainty, an exploration of the common law underpinning of section 35 would at least rationalize it. Section 11(2) provides that a buyer may elect to treat a breach of condition as a breach of warranty. When this provision is harnessed to acceptance in sections 11(4) and 35, acceptance may be seen as a statutory variant of election,[216] the idea being that the buyer's section 35 conduct evinces an objective intention to pursue only a damages remedy. In a similar vein, it has been said that a buyer may be estopped from rejecting the goods,[217] though modern acceptance cases do not ask whether the seller has relied to his detriment or altered his position as a result of the buyer's behaviour. Election and estoppel are not to be confounded, since the former turns on a manifest choice of

---

[211] *Morton v Tibbett* (1850) 15 QB 428; *Cusack v Robinson* (1861) 1 B & S 299.

[212] S. 5(3) of the 1893 Act.

[213] *Abbot & Co. v Wolsey* [1895] 2 QB 97.

[214] S. 35 is expressed not in terms of acceptance but rather of *deemed* acceptance.

[215] Until recent years, it could be said to have been more pronounced in Canada than in England, but recent English (and Scottish) cases indicate a more lenient attitude nowadays to the passage of time under s. 35.

[216] See *The Kanchenjunga* [1990] 1 Lloyd's Rep. 391.

[217] *Heilbut v Hickson* (1872) LR 7 CP 438, 451.

remedies by the buyer and the latter on reliance by the seller.[218] Whichever principle is brought in to support the notion of acceptance in section 35, it can justify an extension of the acceptance period when the seller requests an opportunity to correct faults in the goods or takes his time when responding to the buyer's complaints. Can such a seller fairly assert an irrevocable choice of remedies by the buyer or claim to have been put off balance by the buyer's behaviour? Section 35(6)(a) states that the buyer will not be deemed to have accepted the goods merely because 'he asks for, or agrees to, their repair by or under an arrangement with the seller'. The effect of this provision on the length of the acceptance period will be discussed below.

Extended rejection rights. An alternative route to the relaxation of section 35 is to be found in section 11(4), which points to an implied or express term permitting rejection of the goods after acceptance.[219] Another possibility, not evident on the face of section 35, is that a buyer who has derived no benefit from the goods should be entitled to reject them.[220] This is one possible explanation for the Canadian cases, mentioned above, invoking the doctrine of fundamental breach to allow a belated rejection of the goods.[221] This particular approach has yet to commend itself to English courts. A related idea, expressed in negative terms, that the buyer may not reject goods if they cannot be restored to the state they were in at the contract date, was rejected by the Law Commission for inclusion in section 35.[222] It would have strengthened further the post-contract bargaining position of retailers, and there was no evidence of difficulties in practice making a case for such a reform. This last point is explicable at least in part by the brevity of the acceptance period. **10.59**

Intimation of Acceptance

Meaning of 'intimation'. The first head of acceptance in section 35 is the buyer's intimation of acceptance to the seller. It was stated above that the origin of this head of acceptance lay in the practice of buyers, examining goods at the seller's premises, acceding to the seller's delivery of them under the contract, which would account for the rather vague word 'intimation'. This head of acceptance is not **10.60**

---

218 Discussed in Ch. 6 above.

219 *Rowland v Divall*, n. 69 above, 507; *O'Flaherty v McKinlay* [1953] 2 DLR 514; *Bannerman v White* (1861) 10 CB(NS) 844; *Head v Tattersall* (1872) LR 7 Ex. 7.

220 See *Behn v Burness* (1863) 3 B & S 751; *Poulton v Lattimore* (1829) 9 B & C 259 (useless seed).

221 *Lightburn v Belmont Sales Ltd* (1969) 69 WWR 734; *Beldessi v Island Equipment Ltd* (1973) 41 DLR (3d) 147; *Grafco Enterprises Ltd v Schofield* [1983] 4 WWR 135. Some Canadian cases have demanded grave consequences attendant upon a breach the longer the buyer has possession of the goods before rejection: *Lightburn v Belmont Sales Ltd, ibid.; Barber v Inland Truck Sales Ltd* (1970) 11 DLR (3d) 469; *Gibbons v Trapp Motors Ltd* (1970) 9 DLR (3d) 742.

222 Law Com. No. 160, para. 5.40. But note that this is one of the grounds for losing the right to rescind for misrepresentation.

often applied[223] but the Law Commission was concerned lest it be invoked by sellers procuring the buyer's signature to a delivery note containing an acceptance statement.[224] As seen above, the problem was resolved in the Sale and Supply of Goods Act 1994 by providing that an intimation of acceptance would not be deemed an acceptance under section 35 before the buyer had had a reasonable opportunity to examine the goods.[225] Furthermore, consumer buyers could not waive their rights under this provision.[226]

10.61 **Conditional statements.** It is not easy in practice for a seller to show that the buyer has lost the right of rejection under this head. Apart from the case of the buyer with full knowledge of defects in the goods who states that he will retain them, a buyer's other actions and statements are too easily interpreted as conditional upon the buyer's current information proving to be accurate. An intimation of acceptance has to be informed and unequivocal.[227] As for actions and statements that might be relied upon as intimations of acceptance, section 35(6)(a) first of all puts it beyond any doubt that a buyer asking for or agreeing to a repair by the seller does not thereby intimate an acceptance of the goods. A demand that the seller do something or the goods will be rejected may lead to the loss of rejection rights, not because it amounts to an intimation of acceptance but on the ground that that the buyer has left it too long to reject.[228] Letters of complaint will not readily be construed as intimating acceptance, even if they are insufficiently clear to be a rejection.[229] In *Clegg v Andersson*,[230] a variety of statements on the buyer's part were held at trial to be an intimation of acceptance. They comprised a statement by the buyer after a short voyage that he liked the yacht, despite its overweight keel, a statement to the seller that it was his (the buyer's) decision whether remedial work should be done on the yacht, and a statement that he intended to move the yacht to Portugal in a few months' time. These statements were all held by the Court of Appeal to fall short of intimations of acceptance: they were conditional on the information to be provided by the seller being satisfactory. For the same reason, the Court of Appeal also reversed the trial judge when

---

[223] But see *Staiman Steel Ltd v Franki Canada Ltd* (1985) 53 OR (2d) 93. The Ontario court was unable to discover another case decided under this head. Intimation of acceptance was discussed at length in *Clegg v Andersson* [2003] EWCA Civ 320; [2003] 2 Lloyd's Rep. 32, but the court held on the facts that the buyer had not accepted the goods.

[224] Law Com. No. 160, para. 5.20. Signing a delivery note can be an acceptance under s. 35: *Albright & Wilson UK Ltd v Biachem Ltd* [2001] EWCA Civ 301; [2001] 2 All ER (Comm.) 537 at [25].

[225] S. 35(2); see *Mitchell v BJ Marine Ltd* [2005] NIQB 72.

[226] S. 35(3). An exclusion of non-consumer buyers' rights would be subject to the Unfair Contract Terms Act 1977: see Law Com. No. 160, para. 5.24.

[227] *Clegg v Andersson*, n. 223 above.

[228] *Lee v York Coach and Marine* [1977] RTR 35.

[229] *Varley v Whipp* [1900] 1 QB 513.

[230] n. 223 above.

holding that leaving personal possessions on the yacht was not an intimation of acceptance.

Acts Inconsistent with the Seller's Ownership

Meaning of inconsistent act. The second head of acceptance in section 35 is the **10.62** performance by the buyer of an act inconsistent with the seller's ownership, perhaps the most difficult head of acceptance to understand.[231] Once it was settled that the buyer's right of rejection was no longer encompassed by examination at the point of delivery, this head was bound to cause problems of interpretation and degree. For example, although the buyer of goods for personal consumption may reject them even after some degree of beneficial use,[232] the degree of wear and tear might reach a point where the buyer's inability to return the goods in substantially the same condition as when they were delivered amounts to the performance of an inconsistent act.[233] A handling of the goods short of this point may be seen as authorized by the seller and therefore as consistent with the seller's ownership.[234] The use of goods pending attempts to repair them may also provide the buyer with appreciable benefits, yet not amount to an inconsistent act.[235] Various prudential actions of the buyer performed on the goods will not be regarded as inconsistent with seller's ownership.[236] A refusal to agree to repairs proposed by the buyer will also not amount to acceptance if the buyer is seeking further information about defects in the goods.[237] Rejection has been allowed where a portion of the goods have been destroyed by a method of testing that was the only way to reveal hidden flaws.[238] Sometimes, however, the goods may be so worthless that the distinction between resisting payment or demanding the return of the price, on the one hand, and claiming damages for breach of warranty of quality, on the other, is barely worth drawing.[239]

---

[231] See Law Com. No. 160, para. 5.33.

[232] See *Mitchell v BJ Marine Ltd*, n. 225 above at [48].

[233] Law Commission, *Sale and Supply of Goods*, Consultative Document No. 58 (1983), 45.

[234] But see *Armaghdown Motors Ltd v Gray Motors Ltd* [1963] NZLR 5 (registration of vehicle in buyer's name an inconsistent act: surely wrong).

[235] See *Fiat Auto Financial Services v Connelly* 2007 S.L.T. (Sh Ct) 111 (use of taxi for 40,000 miles over a nine-month period).

[236] See *Clegg v Andersson*, n. 223 above, where the buyer's actions in insuring a yacht and taking steps to register it in his name were done in fulfilment of an obligation under the loan agreement financing his purchase.

[237] *Ibid.*

[238] *Heilbut v Hickson*, n. 217 above (Brett J; cf other judgments); *Winnipeg Fish Co. v Whitman Fish Co.*, n. 175 above (testing by consumption). Excessive destructive testing might amount to an inconsistent act: *Harnor v Groves* (1855) 15 CB 667; *Heilbut v Hickson*, above. Likewise the incorporation of goods in other goods or in a building: *Charles Henshaw & Sons Ltd v Antlerport* [1995] CLC 1312 (Ct. of Session).

[239] n. 150 above and accompanying text. There is high authority in Canada that a seller, faced with a damages claim, has the burden of proving the residual value of the goods which will be considered worthless in the absence of such proof: *Massey Harris Co. v Skelding* [1934] SCR 431; *Ford*

10.63 **Transfer of rights to third party.** Subject to the conduct of a prior examination, the transfer by the buyer of proprietary rights to a third party has been treated as an inconsistent act. This was so in one case where the buyer granted a security bill of sale over the goods.[240] If, however, the goods supplied fall within a pre-existing security over future property granted by the buyer, this should not be regarded as an inconsistent act. That security attaches automatically to the goods and not as a result of any further voluntary act on the part of the buyer.[241] The revesting in the seller of the property in the goods should normally override equitable interests in those goods acquired in the meantime by a third party. If the recovery of the goods by the seller from the buyer is not prejudiced, the courts tend to resist the finding of an inconsistent act.[242] The resale of the goods by the buyer is precisely the kind of inconsistent act contemplated by section 35,[243] but a number of difficulties, the subject of statutory intervention on two occasions, have arisen where goods have been delivered to a sub-buyer before the buyer has examined them.

10.64 **Inconsistent act and examination.** At the centre of the debate lies the Court of Appeal decision in *E Hardy & Co. (London) Ltd v Hillerns & Fowler*,[244] which involved the sale of Argentinian wheat on c.i.f. London terms. On outturn in England, the buyers broke bulk and consigned parcels to a number of sub-buyers before suspicions that the goods were non-conforming were confirmed by their sub-buyers. They then sought to reject the goods and the question was whether the act of reselling and forwarding the goods was inconsistent with the seller's ownership. There was a finding of fact that, at the time they performed these acts, the buyers had not had sufficient time to examine the goods. The buyers would obviously not have wished to incur the added expense of warehousing the goods before conducting an examination of them. As the Act then stood, there was nothing in sections 34 and 35 to establish which of them took precedence. The court concluded that sections 34 and 35 were independent of each other and the buyers had lost the right to reject under section 35.

10.65 **Seller delivering to sub-buyer.** In *Hardy*, the seller took no part in the delivery to the sub-buyers. In an earlier case,[245] books were packed by the seller for an

---

Motor Co. v Haley [1967] SCR 437; *Evanchuk Transport Ltd v Canadian Trailmobile Ltd* (1971) 21 DLR (3d) 246. *Sed quaere?*

[240] *Meta's Ltd v Diamond* [1930] 3 DLR 886 (plumbing supplies); Cf *Truk (UK) Ltd v Tokmakidis GmbH,* n. 85 above.

[241] *Tailby v Official Receiver* (1888) 13 App. Cas. 523.

[242] *Fisher, Reeves & Co. Ltd v Armour & Co. Ltd* [1920] 3 KB 614, 624, Scrutton LJ (making tentative plans to resell the goods); *J & S Robertson (Australia) Pty. Ltd v Martin* (1955) 94 CLR 30 (claiming from the insurer).

[243] *Parker v Palmer* (1821) 4 B & Ald. 387 (buyer put defective goods up for auction and bought them in himself); *Morton v Chapman,* n. 148 above; Cf *Truk (UK) Ltd v Tokmakidis GmbH,* n. 85 above.

[244] [1923] 2 KB 490. See also *Parker v Palmer,* n. 243 above; *Benaim v Debono* [1924] AC 514.

[245] *Molling v Dean* (1901) 18 TLR 217.

ocean voyage and marked with the American sub-buyer's name. The sub-buyer rejected the books and the buyer shipped them back to England before rejecting them. The rejection was held to be effective. The United States was the agreed place of examination and the buyer recovered the two-way carriage costs to the sub-buyer since they were within the reasonable contemplation of buyer and seller. [246] Nevertheless, the restrictive rule in *Hardy* was extended in *E & S Ruben Ltd v Faire Bros. & Co. Ltd*[247] where, as interpreted by the court, the delivery of rubber sheeting was made at the seller's premises before the seller, as agent for the buyer, shipped the goods to the sub-buyer. It was held that the buyer could not reject the goods when these were rejected by the sub-buyer since the act of dispatching them to the latter's premises was inconsistent with the seller's ownership. On similar facts, *Ruben* was distinguished in the New Zealand case of *Hammer and Barrow v Coca Cola Export Corpn.*[248] where a quantity of yo-yos were delivered by the seller to a Christchurch carrier destined, as the seller knew, for an Auckland sub-buyer. Because Auckland was held to be the place of examination, the carriage of the goods was not an inconsistent act and the buyer could still reject the goods. Similarly, in the Canadian case of *AJ Frank & Sons Ltd v Northern Peat Co.*,[249] the Ontario seller consigned a quantity of rail to the Ontario buyer's order in a Quebec town. When the Quebec sub-buyer rejected the goods, the buyer recovered possession of them and rejected them, lawfully in the view of the court since the Quebec town was the place of examination.[250]

Relationship of examination to acceptance. When section 35 of the Sale of Goods   **10.66** Act was amended in 1967,[251] subsection (1) was declared subject to section 34. This was designed to reverse the result in *Hardy*,[252] though it still remained open to sellers to claim that a buyer not availing himself of an opportunity to examine the goods had waived his right to do so, thus accepting the goods. In the post-1994 sub-section (2), the buyer is 'not deemed to have accepted' the goods by the performance of an inconsistent act under sub-section (1)[253] until he has had a reasonable opportunity to examine them for conformity. The point is also made explicitly in the new sub-section (6)(b) that the delivery of the goods to another

---

[246] This case was criticized in *Hardy*, n. 244 above.

[247] [1949] 1 KB 254; L. C. B. Gower (1949) 12 *MLR* 368.

[248] [1962] NZLR 723.

[249] [1963] 2 OR 415.

[250] See also *Winnipeg Fish Co. v Whitman Fish Co.*, n. 175 above: frozen fish could only be inspected when it had thawed out at the sub-buyer's premises.

[251] By the Misrepresentation Act 1967, s. 4(2).

[252] Despite the criticism that the *Hardy* case has attracted over the years, the result—that defective goods should not be thrown back on a c.i.f. seller but should be the subject of a price allowance—is expressly required by the principal commodities trading forms, e.g., GAFTA 100, cl. 5.

[253] S. 35(1) refers to an act after delivery to the buyer. This must also include delivery by the seller directly to the sub-buyer, or the inconsistent act rule would have no application at all in such cases.

under a sub-sale or other disposition is not a deemed acceptance. Presumably, since the Act, as it always has done, says 'not deemed to have accepted', instead of 'deemed not to have accepted', there may be cases where the seller can draw on additional behaviour of the buyer to show the performance of an inconsistent act. The new provisions go on to state that a consumer buyer may not waive his rights under sub-section (2), thereby implicitly recognizing that a non-consumer buyer may. The unanswered question is why a buyer, who voluntarily chooses to dispatch goods without delay to a sub-buyer, can be said not to have had an opportunity to examine them, at least in those cases where the seller is unaware of the resale plans.

10.67 **Place of rejection.** The relaxation of the inconsistent act rule in section 35 prompts the question where rejection should take place. Section 36 states that the buyer refusing to accept the goods after delivery need only intimate to the seller that he is refusing them and need not return them to the seller. This pitches the behaviour of the buyer at a standard lower than is commonly met in commercial life. The section does not refer to, and may not have been designed to deal with, a delivery under a sub-sale. A seller having to recover the goods from an inaccessible place or an uncooperative sub-buyer could suffer considerable hardship. It might have been better if the changes to section 35 had dispensed with the inconsistent act doctrine[254] so as to allow rejection where the buyer was able to place the goods at the disposal of the seller. Any expenses incurred by the buyer in making arrangements to recover the goods could, within the bounds of the remoteness rule, be compensated in damages.

10.68 **Reversionary ownership and inconsistent act.** The final difficulty raised by the inconsistent act doctrine, untouched by the 1994 amendments, is how can a buyer to whom the property in the goods has passed perform an act inconsistent with the seller's ownership? This has been the subject of inquiry in the case of documentary sales on c.i.f. terms. It is settled law that the c.i.f. buyer normally acquires the property in the goods when paying against the exchange of shipping documents. A view once entertained, however, was that the property did not pass on the documentary exchange but later, when the buyer had an opportunity to examine the goods.[255] The better, but uncomfortably circular, view is that the inconsistent act refers to the reversionary entitlement of the seller that would have sprung at the moment of rejection but for the inconsistent act.[256] An outmoded view has

---

[254] As was initially proposed at the consultative stage for consumer sales by the Law Commission: n. 163 above (paras. 4.85–88) but later rejected in the Report (Law Com. No. 160, para. 5.37).

[255] In the *Hardy* case: n. 244 above, 499 (Atkin LJ). Not the position that the paying buyer would want to put forward if the seller became insolvent in the meantime.

[256] *Ibid.*, 496 (Bankes LJ). See also *Kwei Tek Chao v British Traders & Shippers Ltd*, n. 81 above, 487; *Clegg v Andersson* [2003] EWCA Civ 320; [2003] 2 Lloyd's Rep. 32.

it that a discharging breach of contract prevents the property from passing in the first place.[257]

Shipping documents.   One last point presented by the *Hardy* case concerns sub-   **10.69**
sales performed by an exchange of shipping documents. Dealings with the documents, as they are passed down a c.i.f. sales string, will not be treated as inconsistent acts that take away any right to reject the goods themselves once they are landed.[258]

Lapse of Time

General.   The third acceptance head in section 35 is the lapse of a reasonable   **10.70**
time. Whether a reasonable time has elapsed is a question of fact.[259] The fact-based character of this head of acceptance has rendered it the most difficult of the heads to apply in practice,[260] though the paucity of reported disputes[261] helped to persuade the Law Commission not to recommend statutory change, and in particular not to introduce fixed periods for different classes of goods.[262] It has been said that a buyer's interest in rejecting goods, instead of suing for damages for diminished value, is stronger where goods are bought for consumption rather than resale.[263] A reselling buyer will often be able to find a market even for defective goods, though care may be needed in settling the terms of such a resale if the buyer's reputation is not to be injured. Neither the Sale of Goods Act, nor the cases decided under it, however, give explicit recognition to this distinction.

Difficulty of rejecting.   The lack of English case law requires some explanation.   **10.71**
A buyer, particularly one who is a consumer, requires a degree of nerve to exercise rejection rights. First of all, the uncertainty of the rejection period makes it difficult to give advice on the subject. Further, if the buyer has paid for the goods, they will have to be put out of commission if the rejection is to pass the test of unequivocality. Although rejected goods need not be returned to the seller,[264] the buyer of

---

[257] Expressed in *Ollett v Jordan* [1918] 2 KB 41. See now the *Hardy* case, n. 244 above, 499 (alternative view of Atkin LJ); *McDougall v Aeromarine of Emsworth Ltd* [1958] 1 WLR 1126; *Kwei Tek Chao v British Traders & Shippers Ltd*, n. 81 above, 487–8; *Colonial Insurance Co. of New Zealand v Adelaide Marine Insurance Co.* (1886) 12 App. Cas. 128, 140.

[258] *Kwei Tek Chao*, n. 81 above; the *Hardy* case, n. 244 above, 499 (Atkin LJ).

[259] S. 59.

[260] Law Com. No. 160, para. 2.48: '[N]o limit on the number of factors which the court is entitled to take into account.'

[261] In England; there have been quite a lot in Canada.

[262] Law Com. No. 160, para. 5.19. Creating a fixed period or periods would be open to the same criticisms as creating fixed durability periods under s. 14.

[263] J. Honnold (1949) 97 *U Penn LR* 457, 469. Also, as the trading forms for agricultural commodities recognize, where such goods are used in a buyer's manufacturing process.

[264] S. 36. It is not clear what duty, if any, is owed by the buyer to the seller in respect to the custody and care of rejected goods. Should the buyer incur reasonable expenses in looking after the goods, these should be recoverable as consequential damages under s. 54.

a defective car, for example, is likely to wait a long time for the seller to come and collect it and may not have the resources to provide for alternative transport in the meantime. All the while, the car will be depreciating and suffering from neglect. Returning the car and keys to the seller may prove to be tactically more effective. If payment is outstanding, the buyer faces a problem common to all contracting parties exercising uncertain termination rights. If the buyer has inadvertently accepted the goods, a repudiation of the contract will turn out to be unlawful and the buyer will be open to an action by the seller.

10.72 **Factors in assessing reasonable time.** Various factors may be considered in determining the lapse of a reasonable time but the time needed to discover a latent defect is not one of them,[265] although the speedy discovery of a defect may abridge the time given to the buyer.[266] Furthermore, as stated above, it is not likely that the notion of examination can be stretched to cover beneficial use in service and take advantage of the subordination of the acceptance rules to the buyer's right of examination. But the complexity of the goods may have some bearing upon the length of the period: it has been said that the buyer of a bicycle would have to reject sooner than the buyer of a nuclear submarine.[267] The nature of the fault may be material, especially if the buyer monitors it for a short while before determining that it is serious enough to warrant decisive action.[268] The obviousness or not of a defect in the goods would also appear to be a material factor.[269] It has also been said that the period should not be extended in favour of the buyer, since it is commercially desirable for the seller to close his ledger.[270] Nevertheless, a seller facing a damages claim for breach of contract is in no position to close his ledger on the transaction. The intensity of use of the goods by the buyer is likely to be relevant: here, the lapse of time shades into the performance of an inconsistent act. Where the rejection of the goods would amount to a grave business decision against a seller disputing liability, and might imperil future relations with the seller, a buyer may be entitled to take some time to consider his position carefully.[271] Canadian cases have permitted the rejection of goods many months after delivery on the ground that their continued use in service by the buyer is causing significant business

---

[265] e.g., *Bernstein v Pamson Motors (Golders Green) Ltd* [1987] 2 All ER 220; see also *Laurelgates Ltd v Lombard North Central Ltd* (1983) 133 NLJ 720.

[266] *Couston, Thomson & Co. v Chapman* (1872) LR 2 HL 250.

[267] *Bernstein v Pamson Motors (Golders Green) Ltd*, n. 265 above. This is difficult to reconcile with the court's view that the period is not computed by the time taken to discover a defect. For the view that the complexity of the intended function of goods defines the time for rejection, see *Charles Henshaw & Sons Ltd v Antlerport* [1995] CLC 1312 (Ct of Session).

[268] See *Baynham v North West Securities Ltd*, 7 Dec. 1982, discussed in *Bernstein*, n. 265 above, 227.

[269] *Jones v Gallagher* [2004] EWCA Civ 10; [2005] 1 Lloyd's Rep. 377.

[270] *Bernstein v Pamson Motors (Golders Green) Ltd*, n. 265 above.

[271] *Manifatture Tessile Laniera Wooltex v JB Ashley Ltd* [1979] 2 Lloyd's Rep. 28; *Fisher, Reeves and Co. Ltd v Armour and Co. Ltd* [1920] 3 KB 614 at 624 (Scrutton LJ).

losses,[272] but English courts are unlikely to be so generous to a buyer who can mitigate business losses by acquiring substitute goods from another source.

Length of period. The computation of a reasonable time is an elastic affair but   **10.73**
the period, in a case not complicated by communications passing back and forward between seller and buyer, is unlikely to extend beyond a few weeks and may
be shorter. In *Bernstein v Pamson Motors (Golders Green) Ltd*,[273] the plaintiff's new
car broke down 'on its first proper trip' on a motorway less than four weeks after
he had acquired it. In that time, it had been driven for only 140 miles. The fault
was a minor one and easily, though expensively, put right, but the defendant sellers were in breach of the merchantable quality condition.[274] Nevertheless, the
plaintiff informed the defendants the day after the breakdown that he was rejecting the car and refused to collect it from the defendants' garage, where it was later
repaired under the manufacturer's guarantee and made 'effectively as good as new'.
The buyer had waited too long.[275] It is questionable, however, that the court would
have been so strict if the buyer had correctly believed that the fault in the car
threatened future problems. The gravity of the fault may also be a factor affecting
the length of the acceptance period.

Inconsistent case. An appeal in the *Bernstein* case was compromised. In *Rogers*   **10.74**
v Parish (Scarborough) Ltd,[276] the buyer of a car, itself the replacement for an
unsatisfactory model returned after a few weeks, was rejected by the buyer six
months after the delivery of the original vehicle and after it had been driven without satisfaction for 5,500 miles. During that time, there had occurred a series of
inspections and attempted repairs. The defendants attempted on appeal to argue
that the buyer was too late to reject but, since the matter had not been taken in
the pleadings and in the court below, and hence critical findings of fact about the
course of dealings had not been made, the Court of Appeal refused to allow the
matter to be raised.

---

272 *Public Utilities Commission of Waterloo v Burroughs Business Machines* (1974) 6 OR (2d) 257;
Burroughs Business Machines Ltd v Feed-Rite Mills (1962) Ltd (1973) 42 DLR (3d) 303, affirmed
[1976] 1 SCR *v* (computer systems).
273 n. 265 above. General words of caution were uttered about the *Bernstein* case in *Clegg v
Andersson*, n. 223 above at [63] by Morritt V-C ('In my view it does not represent the law now')
where the court noted that section 35 had been made the subject of statutory changes since it was
decided. These changes, however, would seem not to affect the factual basis of the *Bernstein* case.
The court's words in *Clegg* may nevertheless serve as a warning that findings of fact (for example,
three weeks is too long) should not be elevated into rules of law.
274 A piece of sealant had entered the lubrication system and interrupted the flow of oil to the
camshaft.
275 See *Long v Lloyd*, n. 178 above, a misrepresentation case where the right to rescind was lost
after less than a week, the court following the acceptance rules in s. 35. A modern court would not
take such a strict view.
276 [1987] 2 All ER 232. See also *Truk (UK) Ltd v Tokmakidis GmbH*, n. 85 above.

10.75 **Agreeing to repairs.** It is a matter of speculation, therefore, how much the various interventions by the seller in *Rogers v Parish (Scarborough) Ltd* might have extended the acceptance period.[277] Enacted subsequently to that case, section 35(6)(a) provides that the buyer in these circumstances does not by agreeing to or requesting repairs accept the goods.[278] As expressed, the provision makes it clear that the buyer is not performing an inconsistent act when requesting or agreeing to repairs.[279] Nevertheless, section 35(6)(a) is also capable of affecting or suspending the passage of a reasonable time, though it leaves a number of questions unanswered. Its lack of explicitness on the running of time means that no guidance can be given on whether time elapsing before a repair arrangement is reached may be cumulated with time running from the breakdown of such an arrangement. Section 35(6)(a) also leaves unanswered the question whether prolonged and intensive use as the buyer awaits action by the seller might still be an acceptance.

10.76 **Suspending the passage of time.** Section 35(6)(a) was considered by the Court of Appeal in *Clegg v Andersson*,[280] which held that the period referred to therein included the time needed to carry out repairs, which itself included the time for ascertaining what had to be done to repair the goods. The failure of the seller to supply the necessary information over a period of seven months or so seems to have been treated as suspending the passage of a reasonable time. In addition, the passage of a reasonable time under section 35 commencing thereafter was held not to have occurred when the buyer wrote a letter of rejection three weeks after receiving the information.

10.77 **No conclusive test.** It may be reasonable that time should stand still while the seller's efforts are continuing.[281] Nevertheless, the Law Commission initially recommended a provision that the acceptance period be extended in these circumstances but in its final report prudently drew back from a complex provision.[282] Furthermore, Buxton LJ in *Jones v Gallagher*[283] was at pains to show that the

---

[277] It has long been accepted that the conduct of the seller, for example, persuading the buyer to extend a trial of the goods, affects the length of a reasonable time: *Heilbutt v Hickson*, n. 176 above, 452.

[278] Cf *Long v Lloyd*, n. 178 above. See *J & H Ritchie Ltd v Lloyd* [2007] UKHL 9; [2007] 1 WLR 670, discussed below. A case predating s. 35(6)(a) and treating the acceptance period as prolonged by repairs is *Peakman v Express Circuits Ltd* [1998] EWCA Civ 135.

[279] The orientation of s. 35(6)(a) towards the inconsistent act rule is confirmed by s. 35(6)(b), which states that the buyer is not deemed to have accepted the goods by delivering the goods under a sub-sale or other disposition.

[280] n. 223 above.

[281] *Fiat Auto Financial Services v Connelly*, n. 235 above. But cf *Lee v York Coach and Marine* [1977] RTR 35 on the position before the Sale and Supply of Goods Act 1994.

[282] Law Com. No. 160, para. 5.42.

[283] [2004] EWCA Civ 10, [2005] 1 Lloyd's Rep. 377 at [33]–[35]. The court in that case applied both the Supply of Goods and Services Act 1982 and the Sale of Goods Act 1979, though the contract looks like one of work and materials.

approach in *Clegg v Andersson* was dependent upon its particular facts. He observed that requesting or agreeing to repairs was only part of the 'factual assessment that is placed on the court' under section 35, and the approach adopted in *Clegg v Andersson*[284] in respect of the buyer's request for information was not apt in a case involving goods whose defects were 'apparent and easily ascertained'. Nevertheless, Thomas LJ, the other member of the court in *Jones v Gallagher*, was of the view that time allowed by the buyer for repairs was not to count against the buyer, who had requested repairs.[285] These two views are not easily reconciled. Whilst it is clear that acceptance depends upon the particular facts of a case, which means that careful findings at trial are unlikely to be disturbed on appeal, the passage of time should be suspended if the buyer has been assured by the seller that a repair will be forthcoming, or if the buyer has requested a repair and it is or remains reasonable to expect that the seller will accede to that request. At some point, however, the seller's unresponsive or ineffectual efforts should alert the buyer that steps need to be taken quite soon if the goods are to be rejected. In cases where Part 5A of the Sale of Goods Act applies,[286] with its particular regime of remedies for consumer buyers, a buyer who has required a seller to repair or replace goods may not reject the goods and terminate the contract so long as a reasonable time for repair or replacement has not elapsed.[287] This provision suggests that the acceptance period ought to be suspended so long as the buyer's hands are tied. In aid of avoiding further complications in this already complex area of law, it would be desirable to adopt this same approach of suspension to cases that do not involve section 35. Nevertheless, even if time is suspended whilst repair is considered or attempted, it may be expected that the buyer will know enough about the goods and their problems at the end of the repair period to be expected to act with dispatch in rejecting the goods thereafter.

Complaints. Where communications between seller and buyer, or from buyer to seller, make no reference to repairs but consist of complaints about the quality of the goods, the issue is one of the passage of a reasonable time under section 35. Although section 35(6)(a) is not relevant on such facts, it may nevertheless be inferred that its enactment either has prompted or evidences a more relaxed approach to the passage of a reasonable time under section 35 than is evident in prior cases. **10.78**

Other Contracts and Affirmation

Hire, hire purchase, and consumer conditional sales. The above rules in section 35 apply to sale of goods agreements with the exception of consumer **10.79**

---

[284] Specifically in the judgment of Hale LJ.
[285] Ibid at [23]. See also *Fiat Auto Financial Services v Connelly*, n. 235 above.
[286] Discussed below.
[287] S. 48D.

conditional sale contracts. Section 14 of the Supply of Goods (Implied Terms) Act 1973 requires the latter agreements to be treated in the same way for present purposes as hire purchase contracts. The right to reject goods under a hire purchase contract, in common with other contracts for the transfer of a proprietary interest in goods[288] and with hire contracts,[289] turns upon the common law doctrine of affirmation.[290] A contract is affirmed by an injured party who elects to keep it on foot.[291] If election is to be understood in the way advanced by the Court of Appeal in *Peyman v Lanjani*,[292] as existing only if the elector is aware, not only of the fact of a serious breach but also of the choice of remedies available,[293] then few hire purchase agreements would ever be affirmed. As much as this laxity may accord with the imperative of consumer protection, it has little to commend it for non-consumer contracts involving the supply of goods. There is some evidence of leniency in respect of a hire purchase bailee's right to reject goods. In *Yeoman Credit Ltd v Apps*,[294] the bailee paid hire for three months despite the presence of serious defects in a car and retained possession for a further two months before the finance company repossesed the car with the bailee's consent. Holroyd Pearce LJ, attracted by the analogy of a simple hire contract, was of the view that the 'continuing repudiation' by the finance company meant that the right to reject remained alive throughout the period. This continuous breach reasoning was, however, rejected by the Court of Appeal in *UCB Leasing Ltd v Holtom*.[295] A different approach, also favourable to the hire purchase bailee, is evident in *Farnworth Finance Facilities Ltd v Attryde*,[296] where the bailee of a motor cycle was held not to have affirmed the contract by electing to retain it. He had used the cycle for five or six weeks after its return from the manufacturer, where it had been sent for repairs. The effect of election is that a bailee who has not discovered defects in goods may still reject them despite a lapse of time that would be fatal to a buyer under section 35 of the Sale of Goods Act.

---

[288] Supply of Goods and Services Act 1982; see Ch. 7 above.

[289] See *Guarantee Trust of Jersey Ltd v Gardner* (1973) 117 SJ 564.

[290] See Law Com. No. 160, paras 2.50 *et seq.*

[291] For affirmation generally, see G. H. Treitel, *The Law of Contract* (12th edn, by E. Peel, Sweet & Maxwell, 2007), 908–14.

[292] [1985] Ch. 457.

[293] See Ch. 6 above.

[294] [1962] 2 QB 508.

[295] [1987] RTR 362.

[296] [1970] 2 All ER 774. See also *Laurelgates Ltd v Lombard North Central Finance* (1983) 133 NLJ 720 (10 months and a number of repairs); *Jackson v Chrysler Acceptances Ltd* [1978] RTR 474, 480–1.

Instalment Contracts

Entire and severable contracts.   The Sale of Goods Act lays down special rules   **10.80**
for the termination of instalment contracts, their point of departure being the
distinction between entire and severable contracts, which is of less significance in
sales law than in certain other branches of contract law. The typical problem to
which this distinction speaks concerns an act whose performance in full is a condition precedent to payment by the other contracting party. For this reason, a builder
who is to be paid only when the building has been completed cannot demand
payment under the contract until this has been done.[297] If, for example, the builder
cannot finish because of lack of funds, there is a risk of the site owner being
enriched at the expense of the builder.

Substantial performance.   Various attempts have been made over the years to   **10.81**
dull the sharp edge of this rule by creating exceptions. The retention of the land,
with its incomplete building, by the owner gives no comfort to the builder: the
owner enjoying his land will not be seen as impliedly undertaking to pay for the
incomplete work.[298] But it has been established that substantially completing
the building permits the builder to claim the price under the contract, subject to
the owner's counterclaim for damages for the cost of completing the work to
standard.[299] No appreciable need has been felt for such a substantial performance
rule in sales law. Goods are movable; buildings are not. A buyer retaining a defective or short tender of goods accepts them and therefore will have to pay for them.
Nevertheless, there will be some cases where the rigour of entire contracts analysis
could produce hardship, an example being the seller manufacturing machinery to
the buyer's specifications and installing it in the buyer's premises over time.[300] The
prejudice of a seller who finds goods of this nature thrown back on his hands could
be substantial, and the acceptance rules in the Act would do nothing to lessen it.[301]
In appropriate cases, the doctrine of substantial performance could be invoked to
require the buyer in fact to retain the machinery and claim damages from the
seller.[302] Restitutionary analysis might also be appropriate where the buyer has
consumed or dispersed a portion of the contract goods before discovering his right

---

[297] *Sumpter v Hedges* [1898] 1 QB 673.

[298] *Ibid.*

[299] *H Dakin & Co. Ltd v Lee* [1918] 1 KB 566; *Hoenig v Isaacs* [1952] 2 All ER 176.

[300] *Appleby v Myers* (1867) LR 2 CP 651; *Fairbanks Soap Co. v Sheppard* [1953] 1 SCR 314
(Can.).

[301] Cf *Carter v Scargill* (1875) LR 10 QB 564 (benefit and incomplete performance in the sale of
a business).

[302] But see *Appleby v Myers*, n. 300 above (no enduring benefit); *Fairbanks Soap, ibid.*
(abandonment).

to avoid the contract under section 6 because the goods in their entirety did not exist at the contract date.[303]

10.82 Stage payments. Builders may take steps under the contract to protect themselves from the consequences of incomplete performance. The contract may, and commonly does, provide that instalments of the price are payable once the building arrives at designated stages of completion. This renders the contract severable: the designated stages are made conditions precedent to the payment of the stated instalments of the price. A similar application of the principle of severability is at work in section 31 of the Sale of Goods Act which departs from the doctrine of conditions and warranties in laying down a separate rule for terminating instalment contracts.[304] Even before the enactment of the new section 35A and the rule of partial acceptance, the buyer's acceptance of one or more instalments did not prejudice his right to reject the remainder if he could later establish a right to terminate the contract.[305]

Termination of Instalment Contracts

10.83 Terminating the outstanding balance. Section 31 does not expressly deal with the rejection of individual instalments, a matter for common law principles and section 35A(2), but it does deal with the termination of the contract as it affects the outstanding balance of performance. According to section 31(2), where the seller makes 'defective deliveries in respect of one or more instalments', it depends upon the terms of the contract and the circumstances of the case whether the breach is a repudiation of the whole contract or a severable breach giving rise to 'a claim for compensation but not to a right to treat the whole contract as repudiated'. The section applies the same rule where the buyer does not take delivery or pay for the goods.

10.84 Stated instalments. The language of section 31(2) raises a number of points. First, it applies only to goods 'delivered by stated instalments, which are to be separately paid for'. Although the Act does not translate instalment contracts into the language of entire and severable contracts, these are certainly severable contracts. In addition, certain contracts for instalment deliveries excluded by section 31(2), for example, because the size of each instalment is not 'stated' or because the intervals

---

[303] See *Barrow, Lane & Ballard Ltd v Phillip Phillips & Co.* [1929] 1 KB 574 (buyer voluntarily paid for goods consumed before apprised of short tender).

[304] The distinction laid down by the Act between instalment and non-instalment transactions does not repeal the common law distinction between entire and severable contracts. There may be severable contracts that are not instalment transactions (e.g. *Longbottom v Bass, Walker & Co.* [1922] WN 245) and entire contracts under which the goods are deliverable in instalments (e.g., *Boyd v Sullivan* (1888) 15 OR 492 (Can.)). See Ontario Law Reform Commission, *Report on Sale of Goods* (1979), ii, 541–54.

[305] Sale of Goods Act, ss. 11(4), 31(2).

and amounts of payment do not match the instalments,[306] would be severable contracts, except where payment comes in one lump sum.[307] Severable contracts falling outside section 31(2) would be governed by equivalent common law principles brought in through section 62(2).[308]

Breaches by seller and buyer. The second point rising from section 31(2) is that **10.85** it applies to breaches of both seller and buyer, though in practice it is more often the delivery obligations of buyer and seller, rather than the payment obligation of the buyer,[309] to which the subsection is applied. This versatility explains why the provision speaks of 'compensation' rather than damages: a seller unable to treat the buyer's breach as a repudiation will have a lesser remedy that may include an action for the price of instalments delivered.[310]

Repudiation. Thirdly, the injured party's termination rights are dressed up in **10.86** the language of repudiation, which is the present disavowal of,[311] or declared or manifest inability to carry out,[312] future obligations in a manner sufficiently serious to permit the injured party to anticipate future non-performance by terminating the contract.[313] Trivial breaches will not by mere repetition or the threat of repetition thereby become repudiatory.[314] A genuine disagreement about the interpretation of a contract will not be a repudiation just because it is ill-founded.[315] But a repudiation was found where the buyer demanded credit before accepting future deliveries, when the contract required payment on delivery,[316] and in

---

[306] See *Jackson v Rotax Motor & Cycle Co.* [1910] 2 KB 937; *Regent OHG Aisenstadt und Barig v Francesco of Jermyn Street* [1981] 3 All ER 327 (where the court, erroneously it is submitted, applied s. 31(2)).

[307] n. 304 above. The new rule of partial rejection in s. 35A would avoid any hardship caused by the buyer under an entire contract accepting a portion of the goods before defects in the remainder come to light.

[308] So the result in *Regent OHG Aisenstadt*, n. 306 above, should remain the same.

[309] But see, e.g., *Mersey Steel and Iron Co. v Naylor Benzon & Co.* (1884) 9 App. Cas. 434; *Bloomer v Bernstein* (1874) LR 9 CP 588; *Decro-Wall International SA v Practitioners in Marketing Ltd* [1971] 1 WLR 361.

[310] See *Workman, Clark & Co. Ltd v Lloyd Brazileño* [1908] 1 KB 968, 978–9. (The seller's entitlement to the first instalment of the price having fallen due, the seller was entitled to recover this without reference to the resale of the goods to a third party.)

[311] See the buyer's language in *Taylor v Oakes, Roncoroni and Co.* (1922) 127 LT 267.

[312] *Foran v Wight* (1989) 64 ALJR 1, 9, 17; *British and Beningtons Ltd v North Western Cachar Tea Co. Ltd* [1923] AC 48; *Rawson v Hobbs* (1961) 107 CLR 466; *Universal Cargo Carriers Ltd v Citati* [1957] 2 QB 401; *Anchor Line Ltd v Keith Rowell Ltd* [1980] 2 Lloyd's Rep. 351.

[313] See, e.g., *Withers v Reynolds* (1831) 2 B & Ad. 882; *Geddes Bros v American Red Cross* [1921] 1 WWR 185.

[314] *Freeth v Burr* (1874) LR 9 CP 208; *Decro-Wall*, n. 309 above; *Shevill v Builders Licensing Board* (1989) 149 CLR 620, 630.

[315] *Woodar Investment Development Ltd v Wimpey Construction UK Ltd* [1980] 1 WLR 277; *Sweet & Maxwell Ltd v Universal News Service Ltd* [1964] 2 QB 699.

[316] *Withers v Reynolds*, n. 313 above.

another case where the buyer demanded a price allowance for past deliveries before accepting future deliveries.[317]

10.87 **Misinterpretation of contract.** Correct as it is to say that an ill-founded interpretation is not as such repudiatory, and that a refusal to perform must be clear and absolute,[318] the impact of a declared misinterpretation on the future performance of the contract must be considered. For example, if the buyer makes it clear that he will not accept a tender from the seller in a way that conforms to the seller's (correct) interpretation of the contract, the seller will be entitled to terminate: the buyer may not impose unilaterally even a minor variation of contract on the seller and the seller is entitled to assume the refusal of his tender when the time comes.[319] Again, if it is the seller who is insistent that he will tender in a way departing from the contract standard, it will depend upon whether at the delivery date the buyer could have rejected the seller's tender. A breach of contract is not the more potent for being anticipatory.[320]

10.88 **Likelihood of future breach.** Section 31(2), by employing the concept of repudiation, predicts the future of the contract in the light of the breaching party's past and present performance. It therefore says nothing about the rejection of delivery instalments already accepted, which according to severable contracts analysis must be retained by the buyer. Where there is a general refusal or renunciation, the injured party is entitled to assume the worst.[321] If, however, the repudiation has to be inferred from the present defective performance of a party not expressing a wish to renounce the contract in full, a difficult inquiry is launched which must take account, *inter alia*, of the chances of the breach being repeated in future.[322] Consequently, in *Maple Flock Co. Ltd v Universal Furniture Products (Wembley) Ltd*,[323] where the breach affected only one instalment out of about sixty-five and occurred a quarter of the way through the delivery schedule, and was moreover a freak occurrence unlikely to be repeated, the court held that the buyer could not

---

[317] *McCowan v McKay* (1901) 13 Man. LR 590 (Can.).

[318] See *Chilean Nitrate Sales Corpn v Marine Transport Co. Ltd (The Hermosa)* [1982] 1 Lloyd's Rep. 570, 572–3.

[319] See *Warinco AG v Samor SpA* [1979] 1 Lloyd's Rep. 450. For the buyer who refuses to pay for past deliveries over which the seller has surrendered his lien, see *Yeast v Knight & Watson* [1919] 2 WWR 467 (not a repudiation). The buyer was seeking to suspend payment until the second delivery was made and was rightly suspicious of the seller's intention to deliver.

[320] See *Afovos Shipping Co. SA v R Pagnan & Fgli* [1983] 1 WLR 195, 203, where Lord Diplock's requirement that the breach in future deprive the innocent party of substantially the whole benefit of the contract should be read as including also any threatened breach of a condition. See on this point *Foran v Wight*, n. 312 above, 5 (Mason CJ), 14 (Brennan J). See also *Federal Commerce & Navigation Co. Ltd v Molena Alpha Inc* [1979] AC 757, 779 (Lord Wilberforce).

[321] *Freeth v Burr*, n. 314 above; *Mersey Steel and Iron Co. v Naylor Benzon & Co.*, n. 309 above.

[322] *Dickinson v Fanshaw* (1892) 8 TLR 271; *Maple Flock Co. Ltd v Universal Furniture Products (Wembley) Ltd* [1934] 1 KB 148.

[323] Above.

treat the seller's breach in delivering contaminated rag flock as a repudiation of the remainder of the contract.

Impact of past and present breaches.   Although section 31(2) employs the for-   **10.89** ward-looking concept of repudiation, the injured party's termination rights are not in practice estimated without account being taken of the impact of past and present breaches.[324] So in one case calling for the delivery of 1,100 pieces of timber where the seller tendered a non-conforming first instalment of 750 pieces, the court, though basing its judgment on the inference of future breaches from the tender of this defective instalment, could not but have been influenced by the preponderant volume of that instalment.[325] Moreover, the leading modern case, *Maple Flock Co. Ltd v Universal Furniture Products (Wembley) Ltd*, though looking at the chances of repeated breaches, also took into account the quantitative ratio of the present breach to the contract as a whole. In some cases, the court may have to consider the combined effect of a breach and an external event, for which the party in breach is not responsible and therefore not liable in damages, in determining whether the overall event is serious enough to permit termination.[326]

Early breach.   Another difficulty emerging from section 31(2) concerns the tim-   **10.90** ing of the breach and raises the question whether an early failure to perform, particularly in respect of the first instalment, is more serious than a later failure. In *Hoare v Rennie*,[327] a contract called for 667 tons of Swedish iron to be delivered between June and September in four approximately equal instalments. The seller tendered twenty-one tons in June, whereupon the buyer repudiated the contract. The Court of Exchequer held the buyer's repudiation to be justified since the contract had begun 'at the outset . . . with a breach'. Since the buyer had received no benefit, there was no difficulty in putting the parties back in *statu quo ante*.[328] This decision was trenchantly criticized in *Simpson v Crippen*,[329] where 6–8,000 tons of

---

[324] *Berliner Gramophone Co. v Phinney and Co. Ltd* (1921) 57 DLR 596, 601–2 ('often "the last straw" which causes trouble'). Cf *Nitrate Corpn of Chile Ltd v Pansuiza Cia de Navigacion SA* [1980] 1 Lloyd's Rep. 638, 653, affirmed *sub nom Chilean Nitrate Sales Corpn v Marine Transport Co. Ltd*, n. 318 above. Acceptance of defective instalments in the past is no waiver of the buyer's rejection rights concerning the same defect in future instalments: *Bremer Handelsgesellschaft mbH v Deutsche Conti Handelsgesellschaft mbH* [1981] 2 Lloyd's Rep. 112. Even if such instalments may no longer be rejected, it is submitted they may still be weighed at a later date in assessing the impact of the seller's breach under s. 31(2). The more advanced in performance a contract is that has been satisfactorily performed in the past, the harder it will be to terminate the balance of the contract under s. 31(2): see *Cornwall v Henson* [1900] 2 Ch. 298.

[325] *Millars' Karri & Jarrah Co. v Weddel, Turner & Co.* (1908) 11 LT 128. See also *Maple Flock Co. Ltd v Universal Furniture Products (Wembley) Ltd*, n. 322 above, 158 (serious single breach may be enough).

[326] *Nitrate Corpn of Chile Ltd v Pansuiza Cia De Navigacion SA*, n. 324 above, 649.

[327] (1859) 5 H & N 19.

[328] Prospective termination is a modern notion.

[329] (1872) LR 8 QB 14.

coal were to be delivered over a year in approximately equal monthly instalments. The buyer having sent for delivery of only 158 tons in the first month, the seller repudiated the contract at the start of the second month. The court held that the buyer's breach in taking less than the agreed quantity went only to a part of the consideration bargained for and the seller's repudiation was therefore unlawful.

10.91 **First instalment.**   The court in *Honck v Muller*[330] had difficulty in reconciling these two cases. In that case, the buyer failed to take delivery of the first instalment of 2,000 tons of pig iron deliverable in three monthly instalments. Bramwell LJ stated the vital significance of a default on the first instalment and a repudiation by the injured party before any deliveries were made since a 'contract . . . part performed . . . cannot be undone'.[331] Now the facts of *Honck v Muller*, where the breach went to a third of the contractual quantity, could justify its divergence from *Simpson v Crippen*, where the breach affected less than one-twelfth of the agreed amount, if both were to be subject to a simple repudiatory breach test. Moreover, on the facts of *Honck v Muller*, a buyer who defaults on the first instalment may default also on the second and third; a buyer who accepts delivery of the first instalment but defaults on the second may default again only in respect of the third instalment. This factual difference apart, no reason in law justifies distinguishing between the first and subsequent instalments.

Rejecting Particular Instalments

10.92 **Rejecting instalments and termination.**   As noted above, section 31(2) does not state whether, for example, a buyer may reject a defective instalment of goods in circumstances where he may not terminate the contract as a whole. It has been said that a 'contract for the sale of goods by instalments is a single contract, not a complex of as many contracts as there are instalments under it'.[332] Although this may seem to deny severable rejection rights, there is considerable case law support for the buyer's right to reject non-conforming instalments, even if the buyer has lost the right to terminate the contract or has not yet acquired it.[333] Since section 31(2)

---

[330] (1881) 7 QBD 92.

[331] *Ibid.*, 98–9. See also Baggallay LJ, 101–2. In *Coddington v Paleologo* (1867) LR 2 Ex. 193, the first instalment was for an unstated amount, but the decision went off on a point of interpretation.

[332] *Maple Flock Co. Ltd v Universal Furniture Products (Wembley) Ltd*, n. 322 above, 154. This is so even if the contract contains a clause providing that each delivery is a separate contract: *Panoutsos v Raymond Hadley Corpn of New York* [1917] 2 KB 473; *Ross T Smyth & Co. Ltd v TD Bailey Son & Co.* [1940] 3 All ER 60; *J Rosenthal & Sons v Esmail* [1965] 1 WLR 1117; *Robert A Munro and Co. Ltd v Meyer* [1930] 2 KB 312, 332; *Re Grainex Canada Ltd* (1987) 34 DLR (4th) 646.

[333] See *Molling & Co. v Dean & Son Ltd* (1901) 18 TLR 217; *Jackson v Rotax Motor & Cycle Co.* [1910] 2 KB 937; *Sierichs v Hughes* (1918) 42 OLR 608 (Can.); *Regent OHG Alsenstadt und Barig v Francesco of Jermyn Street* [1981] 3 All ER 327. *Quaere* may a buyer treat the timely delivery of an instalment as of the essence in respect of that instalment when the balance of the contract may not be terminated because the effects of the breach are not sufficiently severe?

does not on its terms apply to the rejection of individual instalments, it would seem that rejection would depend upon the application of the normal principles relating to conditions, warranties, and intermediate stipulations. A breach of the satisfactory quality term in section 14(2) in respect of an instalment should therefore permit the rejection of the instalment, subject to a claim by the seller that the buyer should not be allowed to reject if the consequences of the breach are slight and rejection would be unreasonable.[334] The existence of severable rejection rights is implicit in section 35A(2), which permits the buyer to accept only a part of a non-conforming instalment and reject the rest. In certain cases, where the contractual timetable has been disturbed and deliveries have not been made at the agreed times, courts have been prepared to conclude that the contract has lapsed *pro tanto* by a process of mutual abandonment.[335] The seller may not make a subsequent late tender and is not thereby released from liability in damages.[336] As we shall see when we look at cure, a distinction may be drawn between rejection and termination, which supports severable rejection rights while the contract remains on foot.

Additional Rights and Remedies for Consumer Buyers

Origin and Scope

General.   In Part 5A, the Sale of Goods Act contains a number of provisions, **10.93** brought into force in 2003, dealing with additional 'rights' for consumer buyers. Part 5A was inserted by secondary legislation made under the European Communities Act 1972,[337] transposing a European Directive dealing with certain aspects of sale of consumer goods and associated guarantees.[338] Part 5A does to some extent expand a consumer buyer's rights, but is less explicit than the Directive in so far as the requirements of the Directive are considered to be met already by the implied terms of description, quality, and fitness in the rest of the Sale of Goods Act. The major impact of the Directive is on the range of remedies available to a consumer buyer in respect of rights already recognized under the

---

[334] S. 15A.

[335] On abandonment generally, see Ch. 6, above. Where a party requests a delivery not to be made, an application of waiver or variation principles might support the mutual intention that delivery be postponed, with the consequence that it does not lapse: *Tyers v Rosedale and Ferryhill Co. Ltd* (1875) LR 10 Ex. 195. Some of the above difficulties stem from an approach to anticipatory repudiation treating it as an offer to rescind on terms: see *Geddes Bros v American Red Cross* [1921] 1 WWR 185; P. M. Nienabr [1962] CLJ 213; F. Dawson [1981] *CLJ* 83.

[336] F. Dawson [1981] *CLJ* 83; see also *De Oleaga v West Cumberland Iron & Steel Co. Ltd* (1879) 4 QBD 472.

[337] The Sale and Supply of Goods to Consumers Regulations 2002, SI 2002 No. 3045 (in force 31 March 2003).

[338] Directive 1999/44/EC of the European Parliament and of the Council of 25 May 1999, OJ No. L171, 7.7.99, p. 12. See generally L. Miller [2007] *JBL* 378.

Sale of Goods Act and general contract law. This section of the book will focus on the remedies in Part 5A to the extent that they create or affect the exercise of a right to terminate the contract. The remaining aspects of Part 5A are dealt with elsewhere.

10.94 **Policy.** The policy behind the Directive, as stated in its recitals, is to enable consumers confidently to cross national boundaries and play their part in completing the internal market.[339] In addition, because competition between sellers in different States was being distorted by the disparate character of different national laws dealing with the sale of consumer goods, it was considered that a measure of harmonization was needed to redress this. Doubts, nevertheless, have been expressed about the likelihood of the Directive succeeding in sending forth consumers, whether physically or electronically, in sufficient numbers into States where they do not reside to build up the internal market.[340] Furthermore, it is certainly questionable how far distortions of competition can be redressed by a measure that seeks only to approximate national legislation, whilst allowing States to adopt or maintain more stringent measures of consumer protection.

10.95 **Remedial structure.** There is much in Part 5A that is unfamiliar to an English lawyer. Some of its provisions can be seen as rooted in the UN Convention on the International Sale of Goods 1980.[341] The choice facing the English legislator was either to weave the Directive into the fabric of existing English law, a matter of daunting difficulty, or to transpose its major parts in bulk alongside existing provisions, leaving it to practitioners and courts to navigate a course between the old and the new. Not surprisingly, perhaps, the latter course was adopted with regard to the remedies. Part 5A does at one point seek to establish a protocol governing the relationship between old and new remedies, but by and large the issue has been left to be resolved judicially at some future date. A further choice that might have been made, but was not, would have been to assimilate consumer and commercial remedies, as already is the case elsewhere in the Sale of Goods Act. The failure to do so has the benefit of not introducing into commercial sales a range of remedies that are of uncertain scope and difficult to understand. But this benefit comes at the cost of great remedial complexity.

10.96 **Dealing as a consumer.** Part 5A applies in cases where the buyer deals as consumer,[342] which is an expression that antedates Part 5A of the Sale of Goods Act and which has the same meaning as it has in Part 1 of the Unfair Contract Terms

---

[339] See recitals (4)–(5).

[340] R. Cranston [1995] *Consumer Law Journal* 110 (noting that the obstacles to cross-border purchasing are 'social and technical, rather than legal'); H. Beale and G. Howells (1997) 12 *Journal of Contract Law* 21, 22–24.

[341] For example, price reduction and requiring performance.

[342] S. 48(1)(a). In Scotland, if there is a consumer contract and the buyer is a consumer: *ibid.*

Act 1977.[343] For sale of goods contracts, the expression means that the buyer does not make the contract in the course of a business[344] and does not hold himself out as doing so, and that the seller does make the contract in the course of a business.[345] The additional requirement in the 1977 Act, that the goods must be of a type ordinarily supplied for private use or consumption,[346] does not extend to Part 5A cases where the party not making the contract in the course of a business is an individual.[347] The burden is on the seller to show that the buyer does not deal as a consumer.[348] This means that the seller will discharge the burden when showing either that the buyer does make the contract in the course of a business (or holds himself out as doing so) or that the seller himself does not make the contract in the course of a business. It is questionable whether there was any need to introduce the complexities of the Unfair Contract Terms Act into the already complex remedial structure of Part 5A. The Regulations transposing the Directive have a simple definition of 'consumer',[349] relevant for a provision they contain on consumer guarantees.[350]

Non-conformity.   Part 5A introduces a concept, non-conformity, that does not   **10.97** have a lengthy history in English law.[351] The remedies in Part 5A are applicable if 'the goods do not conform to the contract of sale at the time of delivery'. Section 48A states that a seller delivers non-conforming goods when in breach of the statutory implied conditions of description, fitness and quality in sections 13–15 of the Act.[352] The question here is whether this amounts to a comprehensive or merely illustrative definition of non-conformity.[353] The Directive defines conformity rather than non-conformity and refers to description, quality, fitness, and performance. Since the purpose of the Regulations introducing Part 5A was accurately to transpose the provisions of the Directive, some assistance may be sought from the Directive, which states a positive duty to deliver conforming goods.

---

343 S. 61(5A).

344 Defined in s. 14 of the Unfair Contract Terms Act 1977 as including 'a profession and the activities of any government department or local or public authority'.

345 Unfair Contract Terms Act 1977, s. 12(1). There is an exception for certain auction sales in s. 12(2) (as substituted by reg.14(3) of the Sale and Supply of Goods to Consumers Regulations 2002, SI 2002 No. 3045).

346 S. 12(1)(c).

347 S. 12(1A) (as added by reg.14(2) of the Sale and Supply of Goods to Consumers Regulations 2002, SI 2002 No. 3045).

348 *Ibid.*

349 SI 2002 No. 3045, reg. 2: '"consumer" means any natural person who . . . is acting for purposes which are outside his trade, business or profession'.

350 *Ibid*, reg.15.

351 It is to be found in s. 3 of the Sale and Supply of Goods Act 1994.

352 Despite the reference to s. 15, it is most unlikely that a consumer buyer will enter into a contract of sale by sample.

353 S.48A(3) also introduces a presumption of non-conformity of limited duration; see also Ch. 7 above.

It seems not to have been intended, however, that the Directive should be applied to cases of non-delivery: apart from rescission, no other remedy is relevant to the case of non-delivery. The linchpin of the remedial structure of Part 5A is the buyer's right (subject to exceptions) to require the seller to repair or replace the contract goods. Neither repair nor replacement is appropriate to the case of undelivered goods. From this it follows that Part 5A should not apply to cases of short and long delivery under section 30 of the Act. It would be wholly artificial to assert a buyer's right to require, for example, that a delivery of eighty widgets be replaced by a delivery of a hundred widgets. Furthermore, if timely delivery is not of the essence of a consumer contract, it would not be possible to navigate through the remedies of Part 5A to reach the remedy of rescission since there would first have to be a buyer's requirement that the goods be repaired or replaced.

10.98 **Express warranties.** A more difficult case is that of the seller in breach of an express term that is not a condition of the contract. Referring to the Directive again, it should not be supposed that 'description', in a measure designed for transposition across the EU, has the technical meaning given to it under section 13 of the Sale of Goods Act. Rather, it should be given a non-technical interpretation extending to the condition[354] and any other attributes of the goods.[355] The lack of a statutory definition of description in the Sale of Goods Act is of some assistance here. The result is that Part 5A can apply to cases where the breach of an express intermediate contractual term does not go to the root of the contract. At least one of the remedies in Part 5A, price reduction, is a suitable remedy for the breach of such an express term of the contract. The other remedies, however, are capable of operating adversely to the modern trend in English law to limit the cases where a contract may be terminated for a breach of its express terms.

Rescission

10.99 **The remedies.** Part 5A lays down four so-called rights, in reality remedies, where the goods delivered are non-conforming. These are repair, replacement, price reduction, and rescission. Repair and replacement amount to a form of specific performance, and price reduction, though not as such a damages remedy but rather a rewriting of the contract by way of self-help, bears some resemblance to damages. Only rescission calls for detailed examination here. The effect of the other three on rescission, and on rejection and termination outside Part 5A, will also be considered, but their particular features will be dealt with elsewhere.[356]

---

[354] Cf *Cehave NV v Bremer Handelsgesellschaft mbH*, n. 111 above.

[355] Recital (7) of the Directive states the imperative requirement that goods should conform to their 'specification'.

[356] For repair and replacement, and for price reduction, see Ch. 11 below.

Meaning of rescission.   Rescission is not defined in either Part 5A or in the   **10.100**
Directive. In one respect, Part 5A goes further than the Directive when allowing
partial rescission as regards those goods delivered that are non-conforming. This
aligns rescission in Part 5A with the right of partial rejection in section 35A of the
Sale of Goods Act. Although the Directive would disallow rescission where 'the
lack of conformity is minor',[357] this limitation on the availability of the remedy
was not introduced in Part 5A.[358] This is consistent with the confinement of the
slight breach rule in section 15A to non-consumer contracts. As for rescission
itself, it ought not to be given the meaning that it has acquired in modern times in
English law, rescission *ab initio*. Part 5A does not preclude a claim for damages
and indeed, going beyond the Directive, permits the court to make an order 'on
such terms and conditions as to damages . . . as it thinks just'.[359] It therefore
assumes that the right to damages for breach of contract remains extant, subject to
any modification called for in the exercise of the court's discretion. One way to
explain rescission, therefore, would be to describe it as the procedure of rejecting
the goods and recovering the price. For partial rescission, this would entail a partial recovery of the price, with the precise amount dependent upon whether a
court would adopt a unit pricing or some other method of valuation.

Accounting for the use of the goods.   Where the buyer claims the right to   **10.101**
rescind, the court has the power to order that a deduction be made from any price
reimbursed to the buyer to take account of any use of the goods by the buyer.[360]
Oddly, there is no express power to order that a non-paying buyer pay part of
the price for the use of the goods, or that the seller pay interest on the price that is
later reimbursed. The court's broad discretion under section 48E(6), 'to make an
order . . . on such terms and conditions as to damages, payment of the price and
otherwise as it thinks just', is broad enough in terms to deal with both claims.
Nevertheless, the court's power exists only in 'proceedings in which a remedy is
sought by virtue of this Part'. This formula puts the buyer in charge of proceedings
since the seller is not in a position to claim any remedy in Part 5A. A non-paying
buyer would not need the assistance of the court to reject goods and terminate a
contract of sale under sections 11 and 35. This prompts the question whether
rescission under Part 5A is self-executing or whether a buyer may rescind only
with the assistance of the court. Since in other provisions of the Act and in general
contract law the right to terminate a contract is self-executing, as is the right to

---

[357] Art. 3(6).
[358] But see the general discretion that might justify price reduction instead of rescission in
s. 48E(3), (4).
[359] S. 48E(6).
[360] S. 48E(5).

rescind *ab initio*,[361] and since nothing in the Directive points to the need for court intervention, the remedy should be treated as self-executing under Part 5A.[362] It would follow from this that a buyer who has not paid is in no position to be compelled to pay part of the price for using the goods.

10.102 **Rescission and avoidance.** As described above, rescission under Part 5A resembles avoidance of the contract under the UN Convention on the International Sale of Goods 1980. Avoidance in the Convention entails the prospective termination of the contract,[363] followed by a type of reverse sale of the goods by the buyer back to the seller. This is without prejudice to a claim for damages for breach of contract.[364] The Convention, however, creates correlative restitutionary duties on the seller to pay interest on the price paid and on the buyer to account for any benefits obtained from the goods. Whereas the seller has to pay interest regardless of what he has done with the purchase price received,[365] the buyer need only account for benefits actually derived from the goods.[366] In a contract avoided shortly after performance, these restitutionary duties may have only a limited effect on the unwinding of the contract, but the right of avoidance may lie under the Convention despite the passage of a substantial time from the delivery of the goods.[367]

10.103 **Time.** This leads into the next question, whether the buyer under Part 5A has in any circumstances a similarly lengthy period in which to decide upon exercising his rights and, where relevant, rescind the contract of sale. There is nothing in Part 5A to indicate that the buyer's remedies are time-limited. In some legal systems, and under the UN Convention for the International Sale of Goods,[368] rights of contractual avoidance are indirectly time-limited by a requirement that the buyer within a stated or reasonable period give notice of defects affecting the goods. The Directive was permissive in respect of such limitations,[369] but there is no similar

---

[361] *Abram Steamship Co. Ltd v Westville Shipping Co. Ltd* [1923] AC 773; *TSB Bank plc v Camfield* [1995] 1 All ER 951; *Alati v Kruger* (1955) 94 CLR 216. Cf *Spence v Crawford* [1939] 3 All ER 271, 288 (Lord Wright); see M. Bridge (2004) 57 *CLP* 277, 290–2.

[362] The wording of s. 48E(3)(a) also points in this direction.

[363] Art. 81(1).

[364] Under Art. 74.

[365] Art. 84(1).

[366] Art. 84(2).

[367] The right of avoidance must be exercised within a reasonable time after a party knew or ought to have known of the breach (Arts 49(2)(b)(i) and 64(2)(b)(i)), which is more generous than the time provision in s. 35 of the Sale of Goods Act. There is a requirement that the buyer should be able to make *restitutio in integrum* of the goods (Art. 82(1)), which is not recognized in those terms in the Sale of Goods Act as a drag on rejection and termination, but this requirement is circumscribed by exceptions, the effect of which is to allow avoidance even where the buyer is unable to return the goods or a part of them (Art. 82(2)).

[368] Arts 39 and 44.

[369] Art. 5(2) (two months).

limitation in the English law of sale and, understandably, none was imported into Part 5A. Section 35 of the Sale of Goods Act expresses a modified doctrine of election, rooted in the idea of affirmation, which can be inferred from inactivity over time. Part 5A does not as such recognize or deny the applicability of affirmation and election to a consumer contract of sale.

Exclusion. In addition, Part 5A does not itself prevent the parties from agreeing to a modification or exclusion of the remedies in Part 5A. Article 7(1) of the Directive, on the other hand, makes it clear that an agreement or term directly or indirectly waiving or excluding rights arising under the Directive shall not be binding on the buyer.[370] The Unfair Contract Terms Act 1977 prevents agreements of this sort from being made and enforced. It treats as an exemption clause a clause 'excluding or restricting any right or remedy in respect' of a liability.[371] It would therefore render void attempts to modify or exclude the remedies conferred by Part 5A in respect of breaches of sections 13–15 of the Sale of Goods Act[372] and would subject to a standard of reasonableness exemption clauses affecting the Part 5A remedies for breach of express terms.[373] None of this, however, applies to the loss of remedies by operation of law. It is submitted that, in English law, it is open to a court to find by way of affirmation that certain rights arising under Part 5A are no longer available to a consumer buyer. It may, however, be a rare case that amounts to such an affirmation. The lack of awareness of most consumer buyers of their rights suggests that the conditions for a binding election of remedies[374] will rarely be present. Again, election would be difficult in some cases to infer from action, for how, for example, could it be known whether the conduct of a consumer buyer means that he is rejecting the goods and terminating the contract, which are not formalistic in their exercise, or rescinding the contract? Moreover, even if affirmation is inferred from the buyer's inactivity over a lengthy period, this is by no means the same thing as applying section 35 and the rules on acceptance to the Part 5A remedies.

10.104

Choice of Remedies

New and old remedies. A related question is whether a consumer buyer, faced with a choice of remedies between Part 5A and those otherwise arising under the Sale of Goods Act, can make a binding election between the two sets of remedies or at all times remains free to change the remedies track. Section 48D provides

10.105

---

[370] The Directive nevertheless recognizes that the parties may vary the remedy when settling a dispute: recital (12).

[371] Unfair Contract Terms Act, s. 13.

[372] *Ibid.*, s. 6(2)(a).

[373] *Ibid.*, s. 3. The Directive may therefore not have been accurately transposed in respect of express terms of the contract.

[374] See Ch. 6 above.

that a buyer, once he has required the seller to repair or replace the goods, may not reject the goods and terminate the contract until a reasonable time has passed. By implication from this limited provision, the buyer should be free to revert to the right of rejection and termination if the seller fails to repair or replace within a reasonable time, instead of moving on to rescind the contract or reduce the price, which would be the next step if the buyer decided to stay on the Part 5A remedies track.[375] In any case, it is submitted, this area of law is already so complex that any further complication of it, to the mystification of consumer buyers, ought to be avoided. Conversely, a consumer buyer who has attempted unsuccessfully to reject the goods should be free to revert to the Part 5A remedies track, even if it leads ultimately to rescission.

10.106 **Part 5A remedies.**   It remains to be considered when the buyer may resort to rescission, as opposed to the other three remedies, under Part 5A. In the first place, the buyer may not proceed directly to rescind the contract under Part 5A but must either require the seller to replace or repair the goods, which the seller fails to do in a reasonable time, or be prevented from requiring the seller to do so, on the ground that this would be impossible or disproportionately costly in relation to the cost of rescission.[376] The latter state of affairs is more likely to arise in the case of repair than replacement. The choice faced by the buyer between price reduction and rescission in section 48C is subject to the court's discretion in section 48E, where the buyer requires the seller to give effect to either price reduction or rescission.[377] It is not clear what is the overall meaning of section 48E. First of all, it needs to be emphasized that, apart from the case of rescission[378] the court's discretion comes into play only where 'proceedings' are brought seeking a remedy or seeking effect to be given to a remedy.[379] Secondly, a buyer who has not yet paid, but who takes a view on how much the price should be reduced, may not appear to be requiring the seller to give effect to the price reduction remedy, but it should be observed that price reduction entitles the buyer only 'to require the seller to reduce the purchase price' and not to reduce the price himself.[380] The seller's and the buyer's views of an appropriate price reduction are likely to be different.

---

[375] S. 48C(2)(b).

[376] Ss. 48B(3), (4) and 48C. The choice between repair and replacement is made by the buyer but that choice is limited in two respects: the buyer may not require repair as long as a requirement of replacement is still pending (and *vice versa*) (s. 48C); and the buyer may not require repair if this is disproportionately expensive in comparison with replacement (and *vice versa*) (ss. 48B(3)(b) and 48B(4). The choice between repair and replacement is also governed in more general terms by what the court considers just in s. 48E. Repair or replacement, as a type of specific performance, is discussed in Ch. 11 below.

[377] S. 48E(3)(b).

[378] Except where the buyer 'has claims' to rescind: s. 48E(3)(a).

[379] S. 48E(1).

[380] S. 48B(2)(b)(i).

Thirdly, if the buyer has not yet paid and wishes to rescind, the buyer is not as such requiring the seller to give effect to rescission if the buyer need only make the goods available to the seller to collect,[381] as opposed to having the seller take delivery of the goods. Nevertheless, in the case of rescission, the court's discretion is engaged merely by the buyer having claimed the right to rescind.[382] Fourthly, the court's discretion to award rescission instead of price reduction or *vice versa* is an open-ended one, dependent upon what is 'appropriate' and just.[383] There is no general provision in the Directive authorizing such a discretion to be exercised; there is, however, a specific provision stating that the buyer is not entitled to rescission where the non-conformity is minor.[384] That rule does not appear on its face to be a discretionary one, yet it does not say that the buyer is disentitled from obtaining rescission. On this view, a court might therefore allow rescission on a discretionary basis even if the non-conformity is minor. So far as a court exercises its discretion against rescission and in favour of price reduction, in a case where the breach of an intermediate stipulation is more than 'minor' yet less than a breach going to the root of the contract, it is strongly arguable that this would be at variance with the Directive.

Innocent Misrepresentation and Rescission

General.   In an earlier chapter,[385] it was noted that English courts accord a place **10.107** in sales law to innocent misrepresentation, although it is not dealt with in the Sale of Goods Act, and section 62(2), when incorporating the rules of common law, makes no mention of the rules of equity. Although some Commonwealth cases[386] have denied the availability of rescission once the contract has been executed, section 1(b) of the Misrepresentation Act 1967 put it beyond doubt that execution[387] was no bar to rescission. Section 1(b) therefore confirmed the antecedent case law, which permitted rescission notwithstanding execution.[388] This section will deal

---

[381] By analogy with s. 36 of the Act.

[382] S. 48E(3)(a).

[383] S. 48E(6).

[384] Art. 3(6).

[385] See Ch. 1 above.

[386] See Bridge, n. 67 above.

[387] Not the passing of property but the fact that 'the contract has been performed'. Canadian cases also equate execution with delivery of the goods: Bridge, n. 67 above.

[388] *T & H Harrison v Knowles and Foster* [1918] 1 KB 608; *Leaf v International Galleries*, n. 7 above; *Long v Lloyd*, n. 178 above All ER 402; *Goldsmith v Roger* [1962] 2 Lloyd's Rep. 249; *Aliter Armstrong v Jackson* [1917] 2 KB 822. Note how, in the above cases concerning specific goods, rescission for misrepresentation gave an opportunity for buyers to return them when the rules on breach, prior to the enactment of s. 4 of the Misrepresentation Act, deprived such buyers altogether of the right of rejection if the property had passed at the contract date (which remains the presumptive rule).

only with the relationship between rescission for misrepresentation and rejection and termination for breach of contract.[389] The actionability of an innocent misrepresentation, including the measure of damages available in such cases, is dealt with above.[390]

Rescission and Rejection

10.108 **Misrepresentation and term.** Section 1(a) of the Misrepresentation Act removes another possible bar to rescission by providing that the fact of a misrepresentation becoming a term of the contract does not prevent rescission for innocent misrepresentation. Unlike the abolition of the execution bar to rescission, this provision has left difficulties in its wake. Rescission *ab initio* and termination are different remedies: one is retrospective and the other prospective, but they both involve the return of the goods to the buyer. A buyer able to return the goods and resist payment of or recover the price, and who has no interest in pressing a damages claim,[391] will be indifferent to whether this process is accomplished by a retrospective dismantling or a prospective truncation of the contract.[392] Nevertheless, the rules on rescission for misrepresentation are not identical to acceptance as defined in section 35. The right to rescind is lost when one of the rescission bars intrudes, namely, the acquisition of third-party rights in the subject matter of the contract, or the affirmation of the contract by the party to whom the misrepresentation is made, or the lapse of a reasonable time, or the alteration of the subject matter making impossible a true *restitutio in integrum*.[393] Consequently, the question that needs to be addressed is whether an attempt should be made to subordinate the rescission rules to the rules on rejection and termination. This will require an understanding of the role accorded to equitable remedies when invoked to supplement the common law as well as an analysis of section 1(a) of the Misrepresentation Act.

10.109 **Reason for equitable intervention.** Equity developed to redress the rigours of the common law.[394] Rescission for innocent misrepresention emerged in its present general form,[395] unconfined to those contracts falling within the province

---

389 Other aspects of misrepresentation are dealt with above in Ch. 8.

390 See Ch. 8 above.

391 e.g., because the market is falling.

392 For cautionary remarks about the ambiguity of rescission, see *Mersey Steel and Iron Co. v Naylor Benzon & Co.* (1882) 9 QBD 648, 671.

393 See Ch. 8 above.

394 Supporting the loss of rescission rights, see P. S. Atiyah (1959) 22 *MLR* 76. The Law Reform Committee has drawn attention to the sometimes drastic nature of rescission when compared to the veniality of some representations: Tenth Report of the English Law Reform Committee on *Innocent Misrepresentation* (Cmnd 1782, 1962), para. 11. See Misrepresentation Act 1967, s. 2(2), for the discretion to award damages instead of rescission; see also J. Unger (1963) 26 *MLR* 292, 293.

395 *Redgrave v Hurd* (1882) 20 Ch. D 1.

of equity in the years preceding the fusion of the courts of equity and common law, at a time when common law fraud was undergoing a rigorous definition,[396] and the inference of warranties from pre-contractual representations was substantially restricted to prevent the award of damages for a mere representation.[397] Fraud may still be defined in restrictive terms, but rights based upon express warranty have so far expanded in modern times that it is difficult to see a continuing need for equity to correct the common law. In addition, since 1967, damages have been available for negligent misrepresentation. It could also be argued that the continuance of broad rescission rights is at odds with the *Hongkong Fir*[398] exhortation to look for serious consequences flowing from a breach rather than at the executory classification of a term as a condition or warranty. Subject to section 2(2) of the Misrepresentation Act, a contract may be rescinded for a misrepresentation that only in part induces entry into a contract. A reassessment of the role accorded to rescission for innocent misrepresentation is consistent with the adoption of a dynamic approach to equity. Equity should not be staked to its pre-fusion boundaries but should as required expand or retract.[399] All of this makes a case that rescission for innocent misrepresentation should not be permitted once the misrepresentation becomes a term of the contract, but that is the very opposite of what is provided by section 1(a). Consequently, if the case made above, that the role of innocent misrepresentation in sales law should be controlled, is sufficiently compelling, such control will have to be exercised in either of two ways. First, the discretion given to courts in section 2(2) of the Misrepresentation Act, to award damages in lieu of rescission, might be widely exercised. Secondly, the rules governing the loss of the right to rescind might be aligned with the acceptance rules in section 35.

Controlling rescission.   The first of these approaches ought to be uncontroversial once the case is successfully made that rescission is unduly generous to the claimant compared to the relief afforded by breach of contract principles. The criticism that rescission for misrepresentation can too easily undo a contract that could not be terminated for breach is not satisfactorily answered by asserting that the common law 'is dealing with discharge by acceptance of repudiation, equity with a vice inherent in the formation of a contract'.[400] Section 2(2) empowers a court to declare a contract subsisting (or revive one that has been rescinded by a self-executing act of rescission) if this is equitable considering the nature of, and the harm caused by, the misrepresentation and the loss caused by rescinding   **10.110**

---

[396] *Derry v Peek* (1889) 14 App. Cas. 337.

[397] *Heilbut, Symons & Co. v Buckleton* [1913] AC 30; see Ch. 8 above.

[398] n. 87 above.

[399] See *United Scientific Holdings Ltd v Burnley Borough Council* [1978] AC 904.

[400] R. P. Meagher, W. M. C. Gummow, and J. R. F. Lehane, *Equity[:]Doctrines and Remedies* (3rd edn, Law Book Co., 1992), para. 1314.

the contract. The second approach imports the difficulty of knowing how far it can be pressed: should it be confined to cases where the buyer has a right to reject goods for breach of condition, or should it also play a part where the misrepresentation is incorporated in the contract as a mere warranty or intermediate stipulation whose breach does not give rise to a right to terminate the contract?

10.111 **Lapse of time.** The lapse of time needed for rescission to be denied is longer than the reasonable period stipulated for an acceptance in section 35, despite the taking of a more relaxed approach to the passage of time in recent years. The buyer in *Bernstein v Pamson Motors (Golders Green) Ltd*,[401] could not readily be accused of the type of delay that in equity is treated as laches, namely delay that amounts to acquiescence or induces detrimental reliance by the seller.[402] The passage of a shorter period of time is nevertheless taken account of indirectly by the bar preventing rescission where *restitutio in integrum* cannot be made, which has no counterpart in section 35. In many cases, time will have lapsed under section 35 when it is still possible for *restitutio in integrum* to be made. The potentiality for rescission to outlast rejection and termination can also be seen in the absence of a bar to rescission for acts inconsistent with the ownership of the seller.[403] It must therefore be asked whether the right to rescind for misrepresentation should be allowed to survive the loss of the right to reject under section 35.

Aligning Rescission and Rejection Rights

10.112 **Reconciling rescission and rejection.** In *Leaf v International Galleries*,[404] the plaintiff bought a picture entitled 'Salisbury Cathedral' from the sellers, who represented it as the work of Constable. Five years later, the plaintiff, intending to sell the picture, discovered it was not a Constable. He returned it and asked for the price to be reimbursed. At trial, the plaintiff's modest demand seems to have been treated as an action for the recovery of the price consequent upon rescinding the contract for innocent misrepresentation, the plaintiff having resisted the judge's invitation to claim damages for breach of warranty. Rescission, denied at trial because the contract had been executed, was refused for different reasons in the Court of Appeal. According to Denning LJ, the right to rescind for misrepresentation should have been refused when the right to reject for breach of condition have been lost; the statement in question was a condition and the right

---

[401] n. 178 above.

[402] *Erlanger v New Sombrero Phosphate Co.* (1878) 3 App. Cas. 1218, 1279 ('due diligence' in the light of 'notice or knowledge'). See further Meagher, Gummow, and Lehane, n. 400 above, Ch. 36.

[403] It is technically possible that the right to rescind might be lost before the buyer accepts the goods: *restitutio in integrum* is not one of the heads of acceptance in s. 35. No court is likely to cut down the s. 35 period for this reason.

[404] n. 7 above; L. C. B. Gower (1950) 13 *MLR* 362.

to reject had lapsed.[405] Jenkins LJ appeared to reverse the trial judge's finding that rescission was not barred by laches,[406] while Evershed MR, observing that undoing transactions late in the day would undermine finality in business matters, agreed with Denning LJ that rescission should not lie when acceptance precludes rejection.[407]

Criticism. *Leaf* gives less than a full explanation why rescission should be subordinated to the termination rules of the Sale of Goods Act, though it contains statements that misrepresentation is 'less potent' than a breach of condition[408] and that the availability of a common law damages remedy lessens the need to resort to equitable remedies.[409] Nothing was said to the effect that the Act established a comprehensive remedial structure that could only be upset by the erruption of innocent misrepresentation.[410]

10.113

Primacy of common law breach. The decision in *Leaf* is squarely based upon the primacy of common law breach of contract over innocent misrepresentation. Yet it is at risk of being overturned as a result of section 1(a) of the Misrepresentation Act, whose effect is that the incorporation of a misrepresentation as a term of the contract does not take away the right to rescind if rescission would have been available but for such incorporation. Although this provision was enacted to deal with the case of a misrepresentation that becomes a warranty, it is equally capable of embracing the circumstances of *Leaf*. This would be most undesirable.

10.114

Implications of *Leaf*. Prior to section 1(a), there was significant support for the view that the incorporation of a misrepresentation as a mere warranty took away the right to rescind.[411] In favour of subsuming the misrepresentation in the term is the idea that breach of contract generates the superior right[412] and that it dispenses with the need to resort to equity for rescission. Section 1(a) would not, however, prevent a court from exercising its discretion to declare the contract subsisting under section 2(2). A more difficult question is whether the approach adopted in *Leaf* to cap rescission rights could be employed to similar effect in the

10.115

---

405 *Ibid.*, 90. This same approach was adopted in *Long v Lloyd*, n. 178 above.

406 *Ibid.*, 92.

407 *Ibid.*, 94–5.

408 *Ibid.*, 90–1.

409 *Ibid.*, 95.

410 Cf the refusal to recognize non-consensual equitable property rights, given the presence of a comprehensive set of rules on the passing of property, in *Re Wait* [1927] 1 Ch 606.

411 Supporting the loss of rescission rights are *Pennsylvania Shipping Co. v Cie Nationale de Navigation* [1936] 2 All ER 1167; *Zien v Field* (1963) 43 WWR 577. Asserting the opposite view are *Cie Nationale des Chemins de Fer Paris-Orléans v Leeston Shipping Co.* (1919) 2 L1. LR 235; *Academy of Health and Fitness Pty Ltd v Power* [1973] VR 254.

412 In one case, incorporation as a warranty was not fatal to rescission because the recovery of damages would have been of little practical value to the plaintiff: *Academy of Health and Fitness Pty Ltd v Power*, n. 411 above.

case of a warranty (or intermediate stipulation) whose breach does not give rise to a right to terminate the contract and therefore does not bring into play the acceptance heads in section 35. If rejection rights are non-existent, it would be decidedly odd if a buyer were able to rescind in the case of a subsequent warranty when he would not have been able to do so if the misrepresentation had become a condition of the contract. One solution to this would be to cap rescission if, had the misrepresentation become a condition, the right to reject would have been lost under section 35. But this in its turn would highlight the oddity of rescission being available in the case of misrepresentation, not significant enough to become a term of the contract at all, when it would have been denied had the misrepresentation become a term. These difficulties point to the superior solution that it would be better to extirpate rescission for innocent misrepresentation altogether from sales law.[413] This would come close to the conclusion in the New Zealand case of *Riddiford v Warren*[414] that innocent misrepresentation has no place in sales law, but on the above view there would remain the right to damages for negligent misrepresentation under section 2(1) of the Misrepresentation Act. In a climate hostile to changes in sales law that might somehow deprive consumers of a present advantage,[415] it is unlikely that this solution would ever receive legislative support. It is unlikely too that, judicially interpreted, section 2(2) would be conventionally applied to prevent rescission where, recognizing or deeming the existence of a breach of contract, no right to terminate would arise.

Rejection and Documentary Sales

10.116 **General.** A c.i.f. contract is a documentary sale in that the seller's normal duty to deliver goods is substituted by a duty to ship or cause them to be shipped and a duty to tender certain documents evidencing that carriage and insurance contracts have been entered into on appropriate terms.[416] In transit, the goods are represented by a transport document, classically a bill of lading,[417] which is their documentary expression until the transit comes to an end. The orthodox view is that the buyer has separate rights of rejection and termination arising out of documentary breaches and breaches concerning the quality and timely shipment of the goods,[418] but the true position is a little more complex than this. The rejection of

---

[413] See the alternative solution of Gower, n. 404 above, where he would deem all misrepresentations to be contractual conditions so as to prevent rescission where rejection was no longer available.

[414] (1901) 20 NZLR 572.

[415] A strong theme in Law Com. No. 160.

[416] The seller's documentary duties are considered in Ch. 6 above.

[417] *Sanders v Maclean & Co.* (1883) 11 QBD 327, 341.

[418] *Kwei Tek Chao v British Traders and Shippers Ltd*, n. 81 above.

documents will entail the rejection of the goods, since the c.i.f. seller may not uni-laterally alter the contract and tender the goods physically on shore.[419] Likewise, the rejection of the goods will require the buyer to place any documents already received at the disposal of the seller.

Documentary and Physical Breach

Dual breaches.   A seller may commit separate documentary and physical   **10.117** breaches arising out of the same facts. In *James Finlay & Co. Ltd v NV Kwik Hoo Tong Handel Maatschappij*,[420] where goods were shipped out of time under a bill of lading falsely dated, the seller was guilty both of late shipment and of breaching an implied contractual duty that the bill of lading be correctly dated. Devlin J in *Kwei Tek Chao v British Traders and Shippers Ltd*,[421] another case of late shipment and false dating of the bill of lading, stated that the right to reject non-conforming documents is distinct from the right to reject non-conforming goods. The former arises on tender and the latter only when the goods are landed and found after examination not to conform to the contract.[422] The acceptance of a falsely dated bill of lading will therefore not prevent the buyer from rejecting the goods for late shipment.[423]

Separate rights of rejection.   If the goods are landed and it transpires that the   **10.118** seller has committed breaches of the fitness, quality, or description conditions,[424] the buyer will not be prevented from rejecting the goods by dint of an earlier acceptance of the documents. Furthermore, the buyer's right to reject the goods will not be barred under section 35 by dealings with the documents inconsistent with the seller's ownership, such as pledging the documents or even delivering them to a sub-buyer in a sales string.[425] The application of section 35 here would

---

[419] *Orient Co. Ltd v Brekke & Howlid* [1913] 1 KB 532.

[420] [1929] 1 KB 400. See also *Hindley & Co. Ltd v East India Produce Co. Ltd* [1973] 2 Lloyd's Rep. 515. Cf *Johnson v Taylor Bros. & Co. Ltd* [1920] AC 144, where the court declined to allow a writ to be served out of the jurisdiction when the failure to tender documents in England stemmed from a failure to ship them in Sweden.

[421] n. 81 above.

[422] It is more correct to say that the right to reject the goods arises after the buyer has acquired the documents. According to Lord Diplock in *Berger & Co. Inc. v Gill & Duffus SA*, n. 184 above, the c.i.f. buyer's right to reject the goods arises after they are unconditionally appropriated to the contract. This would occur once the seller's reservation of the right of disposal is released on the buyer paying against the documents.

[423] Subject to the buyer's waiver of late shipment (*Panchaud Frères v Ets. General Grain Co.* [1970] 1 Lloyd's Rep. 53), which is not to be inferred lightly (*Procter and Gamble Phillipines v Peter Cremer* [1988] 3 All ER 843). Where the bill of lading is falsely dated but shipment is timely, the buyer does not have a separate right of rejection of the goods (*Procter & Gamble Philippine Mfg Corpn v Kurt A Becher GmbH & Co.* [1988] 2 Lloyd's Rep. 21).

[424] In the standard trading forms, fitness and quality discrepancies are usually the subject of a price allowance.

[425] *Kwei Tek Chao v British Traders and Shippers Ltd*, n. 81 above.

be most inconvenient and would bar the exercise of rights of rejection of the goods in sales strings. In *Kwei Tek Chao*, Devlin J stated that the buyer acquired on the documentary exchange a conditional property in the goods that would be resolved by condition subsequent on a later, lawful rejection of the goods.[426] A pledge or resale of the documents amounts only to a dealing in this conditional property and does not touch the seller's conditional reversion; only an interference with the latter would deprive the buyer of a later entitlement to reject the goods.[427] The appeal to commercial convenience is more persuasive than the appeal to legal logic.

10.119 **Payment and commercial risk.** In a c.i.f. contract, the buyer's duty to pay against documents before examining the goods[428] in a real sense allocates to the buyer the commercial risk of having to pursue the seller to recover the price once the goods are proved to be defective. The free flow of shipping documents in c.i.f. transactions requires that the buyer not be permitted to go behind documents regular on their face so as to exercise prematurely a right of rejection of the goods. Attempts by buyers to do precisely this have produced difficulties, as demonstrated in the following cases.

10.120 **A difficult case.** In *Braithwaite v Foreign Hardwood Co.*,[429] the contract was for the sale of about 100 tons of Honduras rosewood to be delivered in instalments and paid for against bills of lading. The dispute centred on a shipment of 63 tons, whose documents the buyers rejected for reasons that later proved groundless. Later, the buyers discovered that a portion of the shipment fell short of the cargo standard,[430] by which time the seller had accepted the buyers' repudiation and resold the cargo to a third party. In the seller's action for damages for non-acceptance, the question was whether the buyers' refusal of the documents could be justified by their later discovery. The trial judge made an allowance against the seller's damages for the qualitative shortcomings of the shipment, which was accepted (rather grudgingly) by the majority of the Court of Appeal.[431] By repudiating the contract, the buyers were regarded as having waived the seller's future obligation that the goods conform.[432]

---

[426] *Berger & Co. Inc. v Gill & Duffus SA*, n. 184 above, 395 ('trite law').

[427] n. 81 above, 485–8.

[428] *E Clemens Horst Co. v Biddell Bros*, n. 174 above; discussed in Ch. 6 above.

[429] [1905] 2 KB 543.

[430] Probably to a minor extent.

[431] n. 429 above, 552 ('damages [assessed] from the point of view of common sense rather than strict law').

[432] *Ripley v M'Lure* (1849) 4 Ex. 34. See also *Cort v Ambergate, Nottingham, and Boston etc. Railway Co.* (1851) 17 QB 127 (contract-breaker unable to enter plea traversing other party's averment of readiness and willingness to perform).

Problems. A number of questions are prompted by *Braithwaite*.[433] First, does **10.121**
the decision undermine the orthodox proposition that an injured party has the
right to terminate a contract even if he is unaware of his legal entitlement to do so,
or even cites a different (and ill-founded) reason for doing so?[434] Secondly, supposing that the buyers would have been entitled to reject the shipment on arrival
(which was perhaps unlikely), did this mean that they were entitled to reject a
prior tender of shipping documents regular on their face? Thirdly, if the buyers
had no such right to reject conforming documents, what effect did their repudiation, and the seller's later acceptance of it, have on the seller's future duty concerning the quality of the goods? Fourthly, if the seller's duty in respect of the goods
were waived by the buyers' earlier repudiation, how far did this waiver go and,
in particular, was it relevant in assessing the seller's damages for the buyer's
non-acceptance of the documents?[435] Finally, what bearing does the case and its
ensuing treatment have on the proposition that the integrity of documentary
transactions should be safeguarded for reasons of commercial convenience?

Distinguishing *Braithwaite*. *Braithwaite* clearly troubled the trial judge and **10.122**
Court of Appeal in *Taylor v Oakes, Roncoroni & Co*.[436] A number of instalments of
rabbit skins had been taken by the buyers before they repudiated the contract in
the light of the sub-buyer's refusal to take further skins, prompted by adverse market conditions. The seller claimed damages for non-acceptance, whereupon the
buyers discovered a breach of description in respect of skins already delivered.
Nevertheless, the seller's breach was held to be severable and so the buyers were not
entitled to terminate the balance of the contract. Two points of interest emerge
from the case. First of all, the buyers unsuccessfully argued that account should be
taken of the seller's likely ability to comply with the contract in future. The buyer's
repudiatory breach, once accepted by the sellers, rendered irrelevant, even (it seems)
for the purpose of calculating the sellers' damages, any consideration of the sellers'

---

[433] In support of the decision, see *Continental Contractors Ltd v Medway Oil and Storage Co. Ltd*
(1925) 23 Ll. LR 124, reversed on other grounds (1926) 25 Ll. LR 298. Doubt was cast on it by
Lord Summer in *British and Beningtons Ltd v North Western Cachar Tea Co. Ltd* [1923] AC 48, 70.
It clearly bothered the court in *Taylor v Oakes, Roncoroni & Co.* (1922) 127 LT 267 and was left
open by Lord Pearson in *J. Rosenthal & Sons Ltd v Esmail*, n. 332 above. See also *Fercometal SRL v
Mediterranean Shipping Co. SA* [1989] 1 AC 788; *Foran v Wight* (1989) 64 ALJR 1.

[434] Among the many authorities, see *Boston Deep Sea Fishing & Ice Co. v Ansell* (1889) 39 Ch. D
339; *British and Beningtons Ltd v North Western Cachar Tea Co. Ltd*, above; *Arcos Ltd v EA Ronaasen
& Son* [1933] AC 470; *Glencore Grain Rotterdam NV v Lebanese Organisation for International
Commerce* [1997] 2 Lloyd's Rep. 380; *Stocznia Gdanska SA v Latvian Shipping Co.* [2002] EWCA
Civ 889; [2002] 2 Lloyd's Rep. 436 at [32]; *South Caribbean Trading Ltd v Trafigura Beheer BV*
[2004] EWHC 2676; [2005] 1 Lloyd's Rep. 128 at [133]. But see *Heisler v Anglo-Dal Ltd* [1954] 1
WLR 1273, 1278.

[435] A premature rejection of the shipment does not as such prejudice a seller who cannot in time
appropriate a substitute shipment to the contract.

[436] n. 433 above This seems to have been a c.i.f. contract or a close equivalent.

readiness and willingness to perform in future. Secondly, the various judges in *Taylor* were concerned to distinguish *Braithwaite* so as to maintain the right to terminate a contract in those cases where the injured party failed to state a reason for so doing. Two judges in *Taylor*[437] asserted that in *Braithwaite* no actual tender of the shipping documents had taken place.[438] Instead, the seller had merely declared his intention to tender those shipping documents and had accepted the buyers' repudiation before doing so. The reason for this distinction was the belief that the buyers in *Braithwaite* could lawfully have rejected even conforming documents, provided they betokened a non-conforming cargo that could be rejected, even if the buyers were unaware of the non-conformity in the cargo when rejecting the documents. Although the reasoning is incomplete, one may surmise that the two judges in *Taylor* saw the act of tendering the documents as appropriating the cargo they represented, triggering a discharging breach regarding the goods themselves. Since no such tender occurred, no discharging breach ever took place. But the true explanation of *Braithwaite* may be more simple. It seems to have concerned a c.i.f. contract, though the report fails to say so. If that is correct, the seller could not be in breach with respect to the cargo before the buyer actually accepted the shipping documents.

10.123 **Explanation.** Another point stemming from *Braithwaite* concerns one possible interpretation of this obscure case, that the seller had not accepted the buyers' repudiation. It is orthodox law that a party, faced with a repudiation by the other, may elect either to accept the repudiation and bring the contract to an end, or to affirm the contract. In the latter case, the affirming party keeps the contract alive for all purposes, including the raising of subsequent defences by the party who had previously repudiated the contract.[439] Furthermore, the affirming party remains liable to fulfil the contract for his own part, and thus runs the risk that the contract will be terminated against him for his own future non-performance.[440] There is no third choice available to the party faced with a repudiation, namely, 'to affirm the contract and yet be absolved from tendering further performance unless and until [the repudiating party] gives notice that he is once again able and willing to perform'.[441]

---

[437] n. 433, above, 269 (Greer J at trial), 271 (Bankes LJ). Scrutton and Atkin LJJ (at 271, 272) left the point open.

[438] Relying upon equivocal language of Collins MR at [1905] 2 KB 543, 549 (the seller was 'ready to hand over' the bill of lading). See also *Esmail v J Rosenthal & Sons Ltd* [1964] 2 Lloyd's Rep. 447, 466 (Salmon LJ); *Fercometal SARL v Mediterranean Shipping Co. SA*, n. 433 above, 804–5.

[439] *Avery v Bowden* (1855) 5 E & B 714.

[440] *Fercometal SARL v Mediterranean Shipping Co. SA*, n. 433 above (charterer invoked cancellation clause because ship not ready to load); *Segap Garages Ltd v Gap Oil (Great Britain) Ltd, The Times*, 24 Oct. 1988.

[441] *Fercometal SARL*, n. 433 above, 805. Cf. *Foran v Wight*, n. 433 above, 5 (Mason CJ), 16 (Brennan J). The Australian High Court is more open to a right of contractual suspension, but the

Readiness and willingness. On the *Taylor* proposition that the seller's future **10.124** ability to perform becomes irrelevant once he accepts the buyer's repudiation, it has been persuasively argued that an unlawful repudiation by one party, while freeing the other from having to show a readiness and willingness to perform at the future date when his performance would fall due, does not, however, dispense the latter 'from having to show at the time of the repudiation he was disposed and able to complete the contract had it not been renounced' by the other party.[442] By this reasoning, a seller who would have gone on to commit a discharging breach of contract should not be able to reap a windfall from the buyer's premature repudiation and sue the buyer for breach. It has been cogently asserted that a party who lacks the capacity to perform, at a time when the other wilfully repudiates the contract, himself commits an anticipatory repudiation.[443]

Damages and Prospective Physical Breach

Future incapacity. There is an alternative approach to the incapable seller, par- **10.125** ticularly useful perhaps if there is uncertainty concerning the degree of proof of his future incapacity. It is submitted that account might be taken when assessing damages of how the seller would probably have performed at the future date.[444] This approach would dispense the seller from having to show a prior disposition and willingness to perform as a condition for bringing suit against the buyer, but would take account of his performance potential in settling damages, since the buyer should be held liable only for such losses as he actually causes.[445] This approach could extend also to inevitable future non-performance. In *The Mihalis Angelos*,[446] where the charterers prematurely terminated a charter to which they would certainly have been entitled and would have wished to terminate at a later date, nominal damages only were awarded the shipowners.

Discounting damages. The above line of reasoning and the documen- **10.126** tary integrity of c.i.f. transactions came together in *Berger & Co. Inc. v Gill &*

---

court in *Fercometal*, whilst rejecting any third choice, came close to recognizing it so far as the repudiating party by his conduct was estopped from claiming performance from the other party. See also *Stocznia Gdanska SA v Latvian Shipping Co.* [2002] EWCA Civ 889; [2002] 2 Lloyd's Rep. 436 at [87] (the innocent party has time to make up his mind).

[442] F. Dawson (1980) 96 *LQR* 239, relying upon the language of Lord Campbell CJ in *Cort v Ambergate, Nottingham, and Boston etc Rly Co.*, n. 432 above, 144.

[443] *Foran v Wight*, n. 433 above, 9 (Mason CJ), 17 (Brennan J), relying upon *British and Beningtons Ltd v North Western Cachar Tea Co. Ltd*, n. 433 above; *Rawson v Hobbs* (1961) 107 CLR 466; *Universal Cargo Carriers Corpn v Citati* [1957] 2 QB 401.

[444] See the inconclusive discussion in *Bunge Corpn v Vegetable Vitamin Foods (Private) Ltd* [1985] 1 Lloyd's Rep. 613.

[445] *Quinn v Burch Bros (Builders) Ltd* [1966] 2 QB 370; *Cia Financiera Soliada SA v Hamoor Tanker Corpn Inc. (The Borag)* [1981] 1 WLR 274.

[446] *Maredelanto Cia Naviera SA v Bergbau-Handel GmbH* [1971] 1 QB 164.

Duffus SA.[447] The contract was for 500 tonnes of Argentinian bolita beans c.i.f. Le Havre and provided that an inspector's certificate of quality on discharge was to be final. The sellers' documentary tender did not include this certificate, so the buyers declined to pay, and eventually the sellers accepted the buyers' repudiation as terminating the contract. The House of Lords held that the quality certificate procured on discharge was not one of the documents that the seller had to tender in order to demand payment of the buyer. Consequently, the buyers' conduct was wrongful[448] and the sellers were entitled to damages for non-acceptance. This result is quite consistent with the long-standing rule that a c.i.f. buyer does not have the right to examine the goods on discharge before making payment.[449] It transpired that the certificate evidenced that the goods came up to the contractual standard, but their Lordships considered what the position would have been if the goods were non-conforming. In their view, consistently with the result in *Braithwaite,*[450] account should be taken of the possibility that the buyers would have gone on to recover damages representing any deficiency in the goods coming to light once they were landed. The court's willingness to discount the sellers' damages, even though the sellers' physical duties in respect of the goods had not yet fallen due and now, as a result of the termination of the contract never would, is consistent with general contract principle. The purpose of a damages award is to put the plaintiff in the position he would have occupied if the defendant had performed the contract. Assuming, then, that the buyers had paid the sellers in *Berger,* the sellers would thereupon be in breach if the goods were non-conforming and open to a damages action by the buyers. If, for example, the buyers had then been able to reject the goods, and in the estimation of the court would have done so, the sellers' damages for the buyers' earlier breach should be discounted in the light of that possibility. This could, in certain cases, produce a nominal damages award, which for all practical purposes would lift from the c.i.f. buyer the commercial risk of having to pay before seeing the goods.

Cure and Termination

10.127 **Right to cure?**   Earlier in this chapter, the lack of explicit statutory connection between the buyer's right to reject and right to terminate was discussed. Suppose the seller delivers goods that the buyer is entitled to reject. The question that arises

---

[447] n. 184 above. See also *Golden Strait Corpn v Nippon Yusen Kubishika Kaisha (The Golden Victory)* [2005] EWCA Civ 1190; [2006] 1 WLR 533, affirmed [2007] UKHL 12; [2007] 2 AC 353, discussed in Ch. 12 below.

[448] The House firmly disapproved of contrary judgments in the Australian High Court in *Henry Dean & Sons (Sydney) Ltd v O'Day Pty Ltd* (1927) 39 CLR 330 (Knox CJ and Higgins J).

[449] *E Clemens Horst Co. v Biddell Bros,* n. 174 above.

[450] Curiously ignored in the arguments and the judgment.

is whether the buyer may *ipso facto* terminate the contract or the seller make amends by redelivering conforming goods. A variation of this question concerns the position where the seller's tender is refused by the buyer and thus no delivery takes place. If the seller is entitled to make amends by redelivering or retendering the goods, then this comes at the expense of the buyer's right to terminate the contract, usually for a breach of condition. Whether the seller should have this right is commonly expressed in terms of the seller's right (or not) to cure.[451] Sometimes the question is asked whether the buyer should have a right to demand cure. A form of this exists, as seen above, in Part 5A of the Sale of Goods Act, so far as a consumer buyer exercises the right to demand repair or replacement of non-conforming goods. Whereas a seller exercising a so-called right to cure would be attempting to avoid termination by the buyer, or at least to reduce the level of a damages award for breach of contract, a buyer seeking cure would be demanding a type of specific performance of the contract.[452] Since this chapter is concerned with termination and related matters, it will hereafter focus on cure by the seller.

No formal recognition of cure.   The Sale of Goods Act does not formally recog-   **10.128**
nize a seller's right to cure. It does not necessarily follow, however, that no room for cure can be found in the Act.[453] Nevertheless, a number of difficult questions have to be answered before it can be said in a particular case that there is a right to cure. The first question is whether the delivery date or period has expired, and if so, whether the time of delivery is of the essence of the contract. If there is time for a cure to be effected, it must then be determined whether a choice exists between substituting different goods and delivering the original goods in a repaired or modified condition, and whether that choice is to be made by the seller or by the buyer. The existence of this choice in turn may depend upon whether the goods are specific goods. Alternatively, if the goods are unascertained, it may be necessary to look at the description of the goods and the process of appropriating goods to the contract. If cure is to be allowed, a further issue is whether it should lie wherever the breach is serious enough on the facts to justify termination, or whether it should be confined to cases where the buyer is seeking to terminate the contract for a technical breach of condition. This position could arise where the seller has committed a breach of an express term of the contract or the buyer has lost the right to reject the goods for a breach of condition under section 35. A final

---

[451] The expression derives from Art. 2–508 of the American Uniform Commercial Code. See R. J. Adhar [1990] *LMCLQ* 364; Apps [1994] *LMCLQ* 525; R. M. Goode, *Commercial Law* (3rd edn, Penguin, 2004), 342–5.

[452] One possibility concerning a buyer's right to cure is whether it should be given so that, if it is not provided, a non-discharging breach by the seller can be converted into a discharging breach: see below.

[453] But see *Lamarra v Capital Bank Plc* [2006] CSIH 49; 2007 SC 95 at [61] (no right to remedy a breach of contract).

question is whether the prospect of cure prevents a breach of condition or a breach going to the root of the contract ever from occurring. There is an analogy here with the supply of consumer goods together with a manufacturer's warranty. If it is arguable in such a case that the buyer's expectations may reasonably be defined in terms of the entire package purchased by the consumer, which includes the manufacturer's warranty and the after-sales service,[454] then the prospect of cure could be regarded as an integral part of the seller's performance.

10.129 **Law reform proposals.** In 1983, the Law Commission noted that 'there is great uncertainty . . . as to the existence or extent of the seller's right to repair or replace defective goods'.[455] The Commission put forward for consultation a number or remedial regimes incorporating the notion of cure in consumer sales.[456] In its 1987 Report, however, the Commission rejected the statutory introduction in consumer sales of a seller's right to cure, because it gave leverage to sellers against buyers and posed complex practical problems of implementation.[457] For non-consumer sales, the Commission's provisional recommendation for consultation purposes was that cure should not be introduced: the circumstances of such sales were complex and cure would in many cases be impracticable.[458] Its rejection of cure in consumer cases fortified the Commission in its provisional recommendations.[459] It should be noted, however, that the new rules on termination for slight breach in sections 15A and 30(2A) deal with one problem that the introduction of cure was designed to counter, namely, abusive termination for trivial breaches. Furthermore, the stance of the Law Commission does not affect the present existence of a doctrine of cure in so far as it may be garnered from various corners of sales law. The Commission did not conduct a survey of the area. In addition, there is always the possibility that the contracting parties themselves may agree upon a cure. An agreement of this kind, it will be shown, raises its own difficulties.[460]

Tender and Cure

10.130 **Non-conforming tender.** Before the authorities are discussed, a general assessment of the existing position is in order. Suppose the seller tenders goods, originally unascertained, that are not of satisfactory quality. The buyer may refuse them on tender. This will prevent the passing of property in them if the presumptive rule in section 18, Rule 5, operates. Or the buyer may take delivery and reject them within the section 35 acceptance period. If the buyer refuses the seller's

---

454 But see Ch. 7 above.
455 Consultative Document No. 58, para. 2.38.
456 *Ibid.*, paras. 4.36 *et seq.*
457 Law Com. No. 160, paras. 4.13 *et seq.*
458 Above, paras. 4.52 *et seq.*
459 n. 457 above, paras 4.16 *et seq.*
460 See *J & H Ritchie Ltd v Lloyd* [2007] UKHL 9; [2007] 1 WLR 670.

tender, and there is further time to perform, denying the seller the right to make a tender of substitute goods would be tantamount to saying that defective tenders are *per se* repudiatory breaches, regardless of whether in the particular circumstances the buyer justifiably loses faith in the seller's ability to produce a conforming tender. The Sale of Goods Act does not say *when* the seller commits a breach of condition concerning the quality or fitness of goods. In the case of unascertained goods, the modern view appears to be crystallizing around breach occurring at the time of delivery, presumptively the time when property passes if the seller does not reserve the right of disposal.[461] Although technically specific goods might be seen as a different case, whether because the property may have passed or the seller is unable to switch to conforming goods because of the uniqueness of the specific goods, it would be undesirable to have the timing of a breach differing between contracts for specific and for unascertained goods. A seller of unascertained goods might thus have time to make a second *tender* if goods answering the contract description[462] are available. This second tender will have to be of substitute goods: repaired goods would probably fall foul of any description in the contract requiring them to be new.[463] The second tender[464] would have to be made within the delivery period where time is of the essence.[465] Where time is not of the essence, there seems no reason to prevent a late cure if it occurs before the delay assumes frustrating proportions.[466]

Non-conforming delivery.   If the buyer has taken delivery, the question of cure   **10.131** becomes more difficult. The seller will be in breach and the existence of any cure entitlement has two formidable obstacles to surmount. First, if the seller is to be prevented from exercising a right to terminate the contract for breach of condition under section 11(3), it may be necessary to find an implied term, stemming from business efficacy,[467] to that effect. This seems very unlikely. A slightly more promising approach is to observe that a breach of condition *may* under section 11(3)

---

[461] See Ch. 7 above, note 299; *Viskase Ltd v Paul Kiefel GmbH* [1999] 1 WLR 1305, 1321–2 (Morritt LJ, explaining a passage in Lord Diplock's judgment in *Lambert v Lewis* [1982] AC 225, 276–7); *MBM Fabri-Clad Ltd v Eisen-und Huttenwerke Thale AG* [2000] CLC 373; *VAI Industries (UK) Ltd v Bostock & Bramley* [2003] EWCA Civ 1069 at [16] and [23]. The same approach is supported by Part 5A so far as it applies to goods that are non-conforming at the time of delivery: s. 48A(1)(b) and necessarily applies where the seller delivers a lesser or greater quantity of goods under s. 30.

[462] Discussed Ch. 7 above.

[463] See *Annand & Thompson Pty Ltd v Trade Practices Commission* (1979) 40 FLR 165.

[464] If this too is defective, the seller may in the circumstances have committed a repudiatory breach.

[465] A general entitlement for the seller to cure would in effect convert all breaches into time breaches. The buyer would terminate because the seller had failed to deliver conforming goods on time.

[466] See Lord Devlin [1966] *CLJ* 192, 203.

[467] *The Moorcock* (1889) 14 PD 64.

give rise to a right to reject goods and treat the contract as repudiated. The difficulty here is that section 11(3) appears to link the buyer's rejection of the goods seamlessly to treating the contract as repudiated, thus leaving no room for the implication of some step, control, or constraint between those two actions of the buyer. Secondly, the act of appropriating goods to a contract with the consent of the buyer may fix a description on them so that the seller may not unilaterally recall and substitute them.[468]

10.132   **Different cases.**   In the case of specific goods, their uniqueness will prevent a seller from substituting them. The carrying out of any repairs will pose the same descriptive difficulties as were observed above for unascertained goods. For both specific and unascertained goods, the obligations of the seller discussed concerned the fitness and quality of the goods. But there may be other seller's duties, whose breach permits the buyer to terminate, that afford greater scope to cure. For example, the strict duties concerning the contract quantity in section 30 are not expressed as contractual conditions. In consequence, section 11(3) does not come into play. Various duties relating to the delivery of the goods in export sales may, as we shall see, allow some scope for cure.

10.133   **A supporting case.**   The case most commonly cited in favour of cure is *Borrowman Phillips & Co. v Free & Hollis*.[469] The c.i.f. sellers of a quantity of corn declared their intention to tender a cargo aboard the *Charles Platt* but the buyers declared they would not accept it because the sellers did not have the shipping documents to hand. Subsequently, the sellers offered a cargo aboard the *Maria D* for which they had a correctly dated bill of lading. The buyers also refused this offer on the ground that the sellers could not substitute the first cargo, and were sued successfully by the sellers for damages for non-acceptance. Reversing the trial judge on this point, the Court of Appeal ruled that the sellers had not irrevocably appropriated the cargo of the *Charles Platt*. The judgments are not as clear as they might be, but it seems that the sellers had merely offered to tender a cargo, and the offer never became binding because it was not accepted by the buyers. It is not clear from the judgments as a whole whether this was because the sellers' initial offer was tentative or whether it could only have become binding if it had been accepted by the buyer. The latter seems likely, so the case is similar to that, discussed above, of the buyer rejecting a tender of the goods. A number of authorities would allow

---

[468] This is seen most clearly in the export sale cases. Supposing a c.i.f. contract calling for goods shipped at a Gulf of Mexico port in August, the seller's later notice of appropriation, accepted by the buyer and naming a particular ship under a bill of lading of a given date, prevents the seller from substituting cargoes, unless the seller has bargained for the right to do so. See M. Bridge, *International Sale of Goods[:]Law and Practice* (2nd edn, OUP, 2007), 138–55.

[469] (1878) 4 QBD 500.

the seller in this case to make a second tender.[470] Because of the uncertainty generated by the first defective tender, the seller may have to move expeditiously to
make a second tender prior to the expiry of a delivery period.[471]

Modern treatment. The *Borrowman* case was decided before the development   **10.134**
of the modern practice of issuing notices of appropriation before the tendering of
the documents. Such a notice was rejected by the buyers in *Getreide Import
Gesellschaft mbH v Itoh & Co. (America) Inc.*[472] but, since it was thereby rendered
ineffectual, the sellers were able to give a later, valid notice.[473] A similar approach
is evident in f.o.b. contracts where the buyer is required to nominate a ship a stipulated number of days in advance of its expected arrival. This is tantamount to
offering to tender the nominated ship so that, if the seller turns down the original
advance notice because it is too short, and another ship can be nominated to arrive
within the shipment period, the seller will be bound to accept it.[474] A buyer nomi-
nating a ship close to the end of the shipment period may find, if the original ship
unexpectedly cannot arrive within that period, that there is insufficient time to
give the seller the requisite number of days' advance notice. A separate advance
notice is required of the substitute ship; the buyer cannot build upon the original
advance notice. For example, suppose a buyer nominates the *m.v. Chalmers* for an
August shipment, and gives on 16 August the stipulated ten days' notice of its
expected arrival on 26 August. The ship founders on 23 August before arriving at
the loading port. The buyer has run out of time to give ten days' notice of the
arrival of the substitute vessel, the *m.v Blackburn*, so that it will arrive in time for
an August shipment.[475]

---

[470] *The Kanchenjunga* [1990] 1 Lloyd's Rep. 391, 399 (Lord Goff); *Ashmore & Son v CS Cox &
Co.* [1899] 1 QB 436, 440–1; *EE & Brian Smith (1928) Ltd v Wheatsheaf Mills Ltd* [1939] 1 KB
302, 314; *McDougall v Aeromarine of Emsworth Ltd* [1958] 3 All ER 431; *Empresa Exportadora de
Azucar v Industria Azucarera Nacional SA (The Playa Larga)* [1983] 2 Lloyd's Rep. 171, 186; *SIAT di
del Ferro v Tradax Overseas SA* [1980] 1 Lloyd's Rep. 53, 62–3 (shipping documents, where a buyer's
rejection rights operate only at the tender stage).

[471] Cf *Ashmore & Son v CS Cox & Co.* n. 470 above, 440–1.

[472] [1979] 1 Lloyd's Rep. 592.

[473] *Quaere* the buyer who accepts a notice in the expectation that the seller will not be able to
subsequently make a proper tender? Is this a waiver? Cf. the odd case of *Waren Import Gesellschaft v
Alfred C Toepfer* [1975] 1 Lloyd's Rep. 322 (buyer not entitled to reject notice formally valid on its
face but pointing to future non-performance).

[474] See *Bremer Handelsgesellschaft mbH v JH Rayner & Co. Ltd* [1979] AC 216. In *Agricultores
Federados Argentinos Soc. Lda v Ampro SA* [1965] 2 Lloyd's Rep. 157, the buyer was not bound to
nominate in advance, so the seller could not take objection to the retraction of a voluntary nomination and the substitution of another ship expected to arrive within the shipment period.

[475] See *Cargill UK Ltd v Continental UK Ltd* [1989] 2 Lloyd's Rep. 290; H. Bennett [1990] *LMCLQ*
466. A number of modern sales forms give the buyer some latitude in these circumstances.

10.135 **Tender and delivery distinguished.** The above authorities support cure only to the limited extent of correcting a defective tender, not a defective delivery.[476] This limited view was taken in early editions of *Benjamin*: 'But an appropriation and tender of goods, not in accordance with the contract, and in consequence rejected by the purchaser, is revocable, and the seller may afterwards, within the contract time, appropriate and tender other goods which are according to the contract.'[477] English law therefore cannot be seen as permitting the cure of a non-conforming delivery by the seller against an unwilling buyer, for otherwise breaches of condition taking the form of the delivery of unfit goods, for example, would have to be reassessed against the standard of a repudiatory breach. The question would become whether the seller was unwilling or unable to put right the non-conforming delivery. Although the Law Commission decided against statutory reform, cure, whether taking the form of substitute goods or repaired or adjusted goods, is common enough in countless unlitigated examples of contracting parties settling their differences.

10.136 **Other jurisdictions.** A broad statement of cure has been proposed for adoption in the various provinces of Canada.[478] Taking its cue from Article 2 of the American Uniform Commercial Code,[479] this would allow cure of any 'type' that is 'reasonable in the circumstances', if supplied within a reasonable time 'whether before or after the time for performance has expired'. This is subject to the cure not causing 'unreasonable prejudice or inconvenience' to the buyer. This is an expansive formula whose meaning would take shape in litigation. An extensive cure provision is enacted in the United Nations Convention on Contracts for the International Sale of Goods 1980. Article 48[480] allows the seller to cure after the delivery date if this can be done 'without unreasonable delay and without causing the buyer unreasonable inconvenience or uncertainty of reimbursement by the seller of expenses advanced by the buyer'. This provision does not specify the form of cure.[481] Article 48 exists in a system that generally eschews strict termination

---

[476] Note how UCC 2–508, the cure provision, refers to the buyer's rejection of a 'tender or delivery'. The difference between tender and delivery is referred to in *Albright & Wilson UK Ltd v Biachem Ltd* [2001] EWCA Civ 301; [2001] 2 All ER (Comm.) 537 at [29] and [37], reversed in part on different grounds [2002] UKHL 37; [2002] 2 All ER (Comm.) 753.

[477] 6th edn, 402. See how this statement was pushed beyond its limits in *Scythes & Co. v Dods Knitting Co.* (1922) 52 OLR 475 (Can.). The appropriation referred to here would appear to be the seller's, the buyer's rejection of which prevents it from becoming consensual with the consequences dealt with above.

[478] Uniform Sale of Goods Act 1981, s. 73. See also Ontario Law Reform Commission, *Report on Sale of Goods*, (1979), ii, 444–67; Alberta Institute of Law Research and Reform, *The Uniform Sale of Goods Act* (Report no. 38, 1982), 184–97.

[479] Art. 2–508.

[480] Art. 37 deals with cases where the goods are delivered before the delivery date.

[481] Art. 37 refers to the delivery of missing goods, parts and substitute goods, and also to 'remedy[ing] any lack of conformity in the goods delivered'.

(or avoidance) rights,[482] whose approach to time breaches is not easy to discern. In particular, the relationship of cure to fundamental breach is not spelt out; it is also not easy to see how a time breach can be 'cured'.[483]

Agreements to Cure

Informal agreement and rejection.   In *J & H Ritchie Ltd v Lloyd*,[484] a combina-   **10.137** tion seed drill and power harrow was delivered to the buyer. When the machine was put into service, the harrow's drive chain started to vibrate. The parties agreed that the harrow should be taken away by the sellers 'with a view to investigation and, if possible, repair',[485] and the buyer was lent a second-hand harrow in order to complete the season's sowing. The sellers discovered that two missing bearings in the harrow were the cause of the vibrations and repaired the harrow to 'factory gate specification'.[486] The sellers notified the buyer that the harrow was ready but the buyer refused to take delivery when the sellers, though pressed by the buyer for the engineer's report, declined to explain the nature of the defect or the steps taken to repair the harrow. The buyer rejected the machine and demanded the return of the purchase price. Succeeding at trial, the buyer lost two successive appeals in Scotland before appealing again to the House of Lords. The House of Lords unanimously reversed the decision of the Inner House of the Court of Session and held that the buyer's rejection of the machine was justified. Although the buyer had discovered the nature of the defect by informal means prior to rejecting the goods, he was for good reason concerned that the missing bearings might have damaged the harrow and that, if he put the machine in store until the following season, he might find that the manufacturer's guarantee had expired by the time he discovered any further damage.

Limited assistance of Act.   The Sale of Goods Act provides little assistance in the   **10.138** resolution of this matter. There is, of course, section 35(6)(a), which provides that a buyer agreeing to the repair of the goods does not by virtue of such arrangement accept them. But this provision, expressed in negative terms, does not make clear how a repair arrangement or contract amounts to a waiver or modification of a buyer's right of rejection. Of the four members of the House of Lords delivering judgments,[487] Lord Hope was of the view that there was in the contract of sale

---

[482] See Art. 25 (fundamental breach).

[483] The Convention also recognizes a buyer's right to demand cure as a type of 'requiring performance' (or specific performance, in the terminology of English law). But this right cannot be exercised against an unwilling seller in circumstances falling short of a fundamental breach of contract by the seller: Art. 46(2).

[484] [2007] UKHL 9; [2007] 1 WLR 670, reversing 2005 S.L.T. 64. See K.Low [2007] 123 *LQR* 536; K. Loi [2007] *JBL* 807; M. Bridge [2007] *JBL* 814.

[485] [2007] UKHL 9 at [5].

[486] 2005 S.L.T. 64 at [36].

[487] Lord Scott concurred with all four judgments.

'an implied term to fill the gap in the statutory code'[488] that the buyer should be informed of the nature of the defect. It would seem that the term arose at the time when the repair arrangement was agreed, by way of modification of the already concluded contract of sale. The other three members of the court preferred to see the sellers' duty to the buyer rest in a collateral repair contract. It was Lord Rodger's opinion that, as long as the sellers duly performed their obligations under this contract, which was 'some kind of innominate contract', the buyer was prevented from terminating the contract of sale.[489] He was also of the view that the repaired harrow was tendered under the collateral repair contract and that the seller materially breached[490] that contract, so as to allow the buyer to terminate it and revive his right to terminate the contract of sale.[491] Lord Brown agreed that the repaired harrow was tendered under the contract of repair[492] and that the sellers had lost the right to compel the buyer to take delivery for the second time under the contract of sale.[493] For Lord Mance, the sellers were in material breach of the contract of repair and had thus 'lost the opportunity to persuade the buyer to accept the goods'.[494] It is, however, the judgment of Lord Rodger that best explains the connection between the contract of sale and the repair arrangement or contract and thus the justification for the outcome of the case.

---

[488] n. 485 at [15].

[489] *Ibid.* at [34]. The buyer might be seen as having a duty under the collateral contract not to terminate the main contract of sale. Alternatively, the buyer was estopped from terminating the contract, in both cases as long as the sellers carried out the repair arrangement.

[490] The Scots doctrine of material breach has no counterpart in English law. In following the reasoning and result in this case, an English court would in practical terms be compelled to rule that there was a breach of an implied condition in the repair contract. The seller's duty to inform, it is submitted, would be classified as a condition because of its close connection with the buyer's right to terminate the contract of sale itself for breach of condition.

[491] [2007] UKHL 9; [2007] 1 WLR 670 at [38]–[39].

[492] *Ibid.*, at [43].

[493] *Ibid.*, at [45].

[494] But surely the sellers were bargaining for more than the right to persuade the buyer to accept the machine when they agreed to the repair arrangement.

11

THE REMEDIES OF THE SELLER
AND THE BUYER I

Introduction. This chapter and the next chapter are concerned with the reme- **11.01** dies of seller and buyer. The present chapter will deal with remedies other than damages, leaving the last chapter of this work to deal with damages. In both chapters, alongside the particular treatment of sale of goods remedies, the general law of contractual remedies will be considered to the extent that it is necessary for an understanding of its particular application to the law of sale. So far only as it is incidentally necessary, the first of these chapters will also discuss remedies that might lie in tort, such as damages for trespass or conversion.[1] The seller has a number of real remedies that can be exercised against the contract goods. These are listed in the Sale of Goods Act as the unpaid seller's lien, or right to withhold delivery where the property has not yet passed, the right of stoppage in transit, and the right of resale.[2] The seller may also sue in debt for the price of the goods if the appropriate conditions are met; unlike the buyer's claim to specific performance, the subject of a discretionary award, the seller's claim is granted as of right in those cases where the seller meets the requirements of the Act. In commercial cases, the seller is likely also to have a claim for interest against a delinquent buyer. A buyer who has paid the price for goods that the seller does not deliver, or that are delivered

---

[1] For a fuller treatment, see the standard tort texts and M. Bridge, *Personal Property Law* (3rd edn, Clarendon Law, 2002), Ch. 3.
[2] S. 39(1).

and rightly rejected, will wish to recover the price as on a total failure of consideration. Specific performance is also available in exceptional cases, usually to a buyer
in lieu of damages for non-delivery. Additional remedies have been made available
to consumer buyers further to the EC Directive on certain aspects of the sale of
consumer goods and associated guarantees.[3]

The Seller's Real Remedies

11.02 **General.**   A lien or right of retention, as the case may be, may be asserted by an
unpaid seller.[4] The seller's other real remedies, namely, stoppage in transit and
resale, are triggered respectively by insolvency[5] and discharging breach, where the
failure of the buyer to pay is usually the dominant reason for the exercise of the
remedy. Before examining any of these remedies in detail, it is convenient to begin
with a definition of 'unpaid seller' and 'insolvency'.

'Unpaid Seller'

11.03 **Definition.**   As defined by section 38(1) of the Sale of Goods Act, an 'unpaid
seller' is one who either has not been paid in full,[6] or who has accepted conditional
payment by bill of exchange or other negotiable instrument, and the condition
has been defeated by the dishonour of the instrument or otherwise. Payment in
full poses a particular difficulty for severable instalment contracts and will be
referred to below. In an earlier chapter, it was established that payment by negotiable instrument will normally constitute conditional payment.[7] The significance
of this is that a lien lost on conditional payment will revive if the condition is
not met.[8]

11.04 **'Seller'.**   For the purpose of section 38 and the following sections, a 'seller' is
defined to include certain agents occupying the position of seller, such as an agent
who is the indorsee of a bill of lading.[9] If, therefore, a principal consigns goods to
a buyer and indorses the bill of lading in his agent's favour, the agent, in his dealings with the buyer, will be able to exercise the real rights of the seller.[10] The other

---

    3 Directive 1999/44/EC of the European Parliament and of the Council of 25 May 1999, OJ
No. L171, 7.7.99, p. 12, transposed by the Sale and Supply of Goods to Consumers Regulations
2002, SI 2002 No. 3045 (in force 31 March 2003).
    4 S. 38(1).
    5 See s. 39(1)(b).
    6 See *Feise v Wray* (1802) 3 East 93.
    7 See Ch. 6 above. It may exceptionally amount to absolute payment: see Ch. 2 above.
    8 *Valpy v Oakeley* (1851) 16 QB 941; *Griffiths v Perry* (1859) 1 E & E 680 (right akin to stoppage
in transit).
    9 S. 38(2).
    10 *Morison v Gray* (1824) 2 Bing. 260.

example given in section 38 is the 'consignor or agent who has himself paid (or is directly responsible for) the price'. A commission agent purchasing goods on behalf of a principal and paying for them himself will therefore be able, in relation to a principal who fails to repay him, to exercise the rights of an unpaid seller.[11] It is well settled that a buyer rejecting goods has no real rights that he may exercise so as to secure repayment of the price paid.[12]

Insolvency

Definition. The buyer's insolvency is an event that activates the seller's right of **11.05** stoppage in transit. It may also persuade the seller to exercise a lien or right of retention to guard against non-payment. Section 61(4) of the Sale of Goods Act[13] gives the following definition of insolvency: 'A person shall be deemed to be insolvent within the meaning of this Act if he has either ceased to pay his debts in the ordinary course of business or he cannot pay his debts as they become due.' Provisions in insolvency legislation may render some assistance in interpreting section 61(4). The central feature of the relevant sections is the debtor's inability to pay.[14] A corporate debtor is deemed unable to pay its debts if it fails to pay a debt of at least £750 within three weeks of a written statutory demand being served at the company's registered office.[15] The statutory demand can thus be used also to deal with the debtor who can pay but refuses to do so. For both corporate insolvency and bankruptcy, the failure to satisfy a judgment wholly or in part also amounts to an inability to pay one's debts.[16] The buyer's own statement that he is unable to pay his debts as they fall due will be treated as conclusive evidence of insolvency for present purposes,[17] but the circumstances of a particular case may be more equivocal. In *Re Phoenix Bessemer Steel Co.*,[18] it was held that the buyer had not made a declaration of insolvency when it invited its principal creditors to 'a private meeting of two or three . . . friends'. The buyer was a limited company with a large amount of property and fixed plant and with a very considerable amount of uncalled capital. For about three months after the meeting it carried on

---

[11] *Van Casteel v Booker* (1848) 2 Ex. 691; *Feise v Wray*, n. 6 above. See the explanation of this in *Ireland v Livingstone* (1872) LR 5 HL 395, 408–9 (Blackburn J) and in *Cassaboglou v Gibb* (1883) 11 QBD 797, 803–4 (Brett MR), 806–7 (Fry LJ).

[12] *J L Lyons & Co. v May and Baker Ltd* [1923] 1 KB 685; *Kwei Tek Chao v British Traders and Shippers Ltd* [1954] 2 QB 459.

[13] As amended by s. 235 and Sch. 10, Part III, of the Insolvency Act 1985.

[14] Insolvency Act 1986, s. 123. For a discussion of this statutory test of insolvency, see *Re Cheyne Finance Plc* [2007] EWHC 2462 (Ch); [2008] BCC 182. Added to this in the case of individual insolvency (bankruptcy) is the lack of reasonable prospect of being able to pay: *ibid.*, s. 267(2)(c).

[15] *Ibid.*, s. 123. No minimum amount is prescribed in s. 268 for bankruptcy.

[16] *Ibid.*, ss. 123(1)(b), 268(1)(b).

[17] See *Ex p. Chalmers* (1873) 8 Ch. App. 289 (declaration at creditors' meeting).

[18] (1876) 4 Ch. D 108.

business as a solvent concern, meeting its debts as they fell due. The court there-fore held that the buyer was not insolvent.

11.06   **Effect of buyer insolvency on contracts.**   The effect of the buyer's insolvency on outstanding contracts must next be considered.[19] First of all, insolvency will not alone amount to an anticipatory breach entitling the seller to terminate the con-tract.[20] It has been said that the circumstances must show an intention or an ina-bility to perform.[21] A manifest inability to perform with all the goodwill in the world may still amount to an anticipatory repudiation.[22] A seller who has difficul-ties showing a repudiation by the buyer may try an alternative route. A contract still to be performed at least in part may be abandoned by mutual agreement of the parties.[23] In *Morgan v Bain*,[24] deliveries under an instalment contract were due to start two weeks after the buyers filed a liquidation petition. The contract was not mentioned at the creditors' meeting and the buyers did nothing until, six weeks after the date performance had fallen due, they obtained fresh capital and offered cash for the agreed goods on a rising market. The buyers' inaction follow-ing upon a declaration of insolvency amounted to a presumptive intention to abandon the contract[25] and the failure of the sellers to deliver at the agreed time constituted evidence of an intention to accept the buyers' offer of abandonment.[26] Apart from repudiation and abandonment, it is open to parties to provide that the contract will be determined in the event of the insolvency of one of them.[27] It is common for commodity contracts[28] to provide that unperformed contracts will be closed out at the market rate then prevailing. This means that the contract is transformed into one for financial differences and a party pays or receives a settle-ment according to how the market at that date (and not the estimated delivery date) stands in relation to the contract price. It used to be common for contracts to be 'invoiced back', so that, if the non-insolvent party made a gain as a result of

---

[19]   See F. Oditah (1992) 108 *LQR* 459, 494–6.

[20]   *Ex p. Chalmers*, n. 17 above; *Mess v Duffus* (1901) 6 Com. Cas. 165; *Griffiths v Perry* (1859) 1 E & E 680, 688; *Jenning's Trustee v King* [1952] 2 All ER 608; *Re Grainex Canada Ltd* (1987) 34 DLR (4th) 646.

[21]   *Mess v Duffus*, n. 20 above.

[22]   *Foran v Wight* (1989) 64 ALJR 1, 9, 17; *British and Beningtons Ltd v North Western Cachar Tea Co. Ltd* [1923] AC 48; *Rawson v Hobbs* (1961) 107 CLR 466; *Universal Cargo Carriers Corpn v Citati* [1957] 2 QB 401; *Anchor Line Ltd v Keith Rowell Ltd* [1980] 2 Lloyd's Rep. 351; see also *Ex p. Stapleton* (1879) 10 Ch. D 586, 589.

[23]   The difficulty of showing rescission by mutual abandonment should not be underestimated: see Ch. 6 above.

[24]   (1874) LR 10 CP 15.

[25]   *Ibid*. 26 (Brett J, relying upon *Ex p. Chalmers*, n. 17 above); see also *Lawrence v Knowles* (1839) 5 Bing. NC 399.

[26]   *Morgan v Bain*, n. 24 above, 28.

[27]   F. Oditah, n. 19 above.

[28]   GAFTA (Grain and Feed Trade Association) and FOSFA (Federation of Oils, Seeds and Fats Associations) contracts contain such provisions.

a substitute transaction, that gain had to be accounted for to the other party's liquidator. In *Shipton Anderson & Co. (1927) Ltd v Micks Lambert & Co.*,[29] the insolvency clause did not automatically close out the transaction. The buyer took care not to elect to invoke it and was thereby spared having to account under the provision for the gain made when purchasing the goods for a lesser sum on a falling market.

Disclaimer and modification. If the contract has not been terminated by **11.07** mutual abandonment or consequent upon the buyer's repudiation, its fate rests with the trustee-in-bankruptcy or company liquidator who has a statutory power to disclaim onerous property (which includes contracts).[30] In a real sense, once the buyer becomes insolvent, the contract is thereupon frozen so that the question whether the contract is to proceed to performance is left to be decided by the trustee or liquidator. In view of the doctrines of repudiation and abandonment, a trustee or liquidator had better decide promptly in favour of continuance.[31] Even if the contract continues, it will not necessarily do so upon the same terms. Contracts that have extended credit to the buyer or have given the buyer the option of paying cash or on deferred payment terms can be enforced only by a trustee or liquidator prepared to pay cash.[32] In *Ex p. Chalmers*, the sellers were held entitled to demand cash to cover not only the undelivered instalment itself, but also the previous instalment for which payment had not yet been made. This is tantamount to reviving a lost lien in the case of that previous instalment and is hard to justify except as an exercise in practical justice.[33] The above rules relating to the role of the trustee or liquidator apply whether or not the property in the contract goods has passed to the buyer; in other words, they apply where the seller exercises his lien or right to withhold delivery, as well as where the goods are stopped in transit.[34]

The Unpaid Seller's Lien

Lien and right of retention. A lien at common law is a passive right of retention **11.08** that may be exercised by the members of certain professions or callings against the

---

[29] [1936] 2 All ER 1032.

[30] Insolvency Act 1986, ss. 178, 315. For the general powers of a company administrator, see *ibid.*, Schs. 1 and B1, paras 59 *et seq*.

[31] *Morgan v Bain*, n. 24 above; *Ex p. Stapleton*, n. 22 above; *Ex p. Chalmers*, n. 17 above; *Re Grainex Canada Ltd*, n. 20 above.

[32] *Ex p. Chalmers*, n. 20 above; *Re Grainex Canada Ltd*, n. 20 above; *Morgan v Bain*, n. 24 above.

[33] For further discussion, see below.

[34] It has also been asserted that the rights of a trustee-in-bankruptcy may be exercised by a sub-buyer: *Ex p. Stapleton*, n. 22 above, *sed quaere*? This has been explained as turning on the equitable interest (in all sales?) acquired by the sub-buyer in the contract goods: *Kemp v Falk* (1882) 7 App. Cas. 573, 578. This is hard to justify in the light of *Re Wait* [1927] 1 Ch. 606, discussed in Ch. 3 above.

owner where the lienee acquires possession[35] of goods with the actual or apparent consent[36] of the owner. An unpaid seller has a lien when the property has passed to the buyer but a right of retention if the property has not yet passed.[37] In the latter case, although the permissible conduct of the seller in relation to the goods is otherwise identical, the seller is not exercising any right against the owner, for the seller is the owner.

11.09 **Scope of seller's lien.**   A common law lien does not come with powers of enjoyment and sale, but the unpaid seller has a statutory right of resale.[38] The seller's lien, like other special liens at common law, is coextensive only with the debt. It follows that the lien over the goods is just for the price and not for any sums incurred in storing or maintaining the goods.[39] Expenses exclusively referable to the exercise of a lien by the lienee may not be recovered at all from the lienor,[40] still less be secured by a lien over the goods on which the expenses were incurred. The seller who stores goods may not claim another lien over them as warehouseman, for the reason that at common law a warehouseman does not have a lien for storage charges.[41] The seller's enjoyment of a lien over goods the property in which has passed to the buyer has two significant features for defining his liability: first, it acts as a defence to any action that a buyer might wish to take for the seller's failure to perform his contractual delivery obligation,[42] and secondly, it denies the buyer out of possession that right to the immediate possession of the goods that is necessary to maintain an action in conversion.[43] So long as the lien persists, the seller is entitled to resist performance for his part, and eventually, if payment is not forthcoming, will be able to move to the resale of the goods.[44] The seller exercising a lien has sufficient possession to maintain an action in conversion against a wrongdoer.[45]

---

[35] In some cases, e.g. the innkeeper and the guest's luggage, the lienee exercises control rather than possession before taking effective action: *Lord's Trustee v Great Eastern Railway Co. Ltd* [1908] 2 KB 54 (Fletcher Moulton LJ).

[36] *Bowmaker Ltd v Wycombe Motors Ltd* [1946] KB 505; *Tappenden v Artus* [1964] 2 QB 185.

[37] The seller's right will be hereafter referred to as a lien unless it needs to be differentiated from the right of retention. In actuality, the right of retention language was added for the purpose of enactment in Scotland.

[38] *Thames Ironworks Co. v Patent Derrick Co.* (1860) 1 J & H 93; *Cowell v Simpson* (1809) 16 Ves. Jun. 275 (difference between passive lien and vendor's lien).

[39] *Somes v British Empire Shipping Co.* (1859) 28 LJQB 220; *China Pacific SA v Food Corpn of India (The Winson)* [1982] AC 939, 962–3; *T Comedy (UK) Ltd v Easy Managed Transport Ltd* [2007] EWHC 611 (Comm); [2007] 2 Lloyd's Rep. 397.

[40] *China-Pacific SA v Food Corpn of India* [1982] AC 939, 962. See N. E. Palmer, *Bailment* (2nd edn, Sweet & Maxwell, 1991), 943 *et seq.*

[41] Palmer, *ibid.*, 872 ('extremely doubtful'); *Hatton v Car Maintenance Co. Ltd* [1915] 1 Ch. 621.

[42] Ss. 27 and 51 of the Act must therefore be read subject to s. 39.

[43] *Lord v Price* (1874) LR 9 Ex. 54; *McGregor v Whalen* (1914) 31 OLR 543, 555 (Can.).

[44] S. 48.

[45] *Nippon Yusen Kaisha v Ramjiban Serowgee* [1938] AC 429.

There is no reason to deny this in cases where the wrongdoer is a buyer to whom the property has passed.

Unlawful exercise of lien.   Should the lien be unlawfully exercised by the seller,   **11.10**
or the goods unlawfully disposed of,[46] it follows that the seller's defences fall and he becomes vulnerable to an action on the contract for damages for non-delivery, or in conversion.[47] If the buyer has not paid, such a seller will be able to set off the buyer's liability for the price in a tort action brought by the buyer.[48] Damages will therefore be nominal unless there has been a market rise; the remedial outcome will thus be the same as if the buyer had sued in contract for damages for non-delivery.[49]

Lien and presumptive performance.   In addition to the buyer's insolvency, sec-   **11.11**
tion 41(1) expresses the seller's lien (or right of retention) as arising and subsisting until the price is tendered when the goods have been sold without any stipulation as to credit, or where the goods have been sold on credit but the term of credit has expired. The first of these two cases,[50] a sale not concluded on credit terms, contemplates the presumptive interpretation of contractual performance contained in section 28 of the Sale of Goods Act, by which delivery and payment are mutual and concurrent conditions. Where this rule applies and the buyer is late in tendering payment, the seller has a contractual right to refrain from delivering the goods. If the property has not passed to the buyer, this right of retention cannot truly be regarded as a 'right against the goods'.[51] The right becomes a proprietary right by way of lien when the property in the goods has passed to the buyer. This will be so when the goods are specific and the presumptive rule in section 18, Rule 1, serves to pass the property at the contract date. A lien will also arise in the case of goods initially unascertained if they have been by agreement unconditionally appropriated to the contract under section 18, Rule 5.[52] It is increasingly unlikely that the rule for specific goods in section 18, Rule 1, will be applied nowadays. Furthermore, the unconditional appropriation of goods initially unascertained will usually occur when the seller surrenders possession on delivery. Unpaid sellers have also in modern times developed a keen appreciation of the wisdom of inserting retention of title clauses in their standard trading terms. Consequently, the exercise of

---

[46] Or the seller unlawfully refuses the buyer's tender of the price: *Martindale v Smith* (1841) 1 QB 389. But if the seller has to sue the buyer for the price, his lien will last until judgment for the price is satisfied: s. 43(2), codifying *Scrivener v Great Northern Railway Co.* (1871) 19 WR 388.

[47] *Mulliner v Florence* (1878) 3 QBD 484, 491; *McGregor v Whalen*, n. 43 above.

[48] *Miles v Gorton* (1834) 2 C & M 504; *Chinery v Viall* (1860) 5 H & N 288; *McGregor v Whalen*, n. 43 above. If the buyer is insolvent, the seller may exercise this right of set off against the buyer's insolvency representative: Insolvency Act 1986, s. 323; Insolvency Rules, rr. 2.85 and 4.90.

[49] *Valpy v Oakeley* (1851) 16 QB 941.

[50] *Bloxam v Sanders* (1825) 4 B & C 941; *Miles v Gorton*, n. 48 above.

[51] Part V of the Sale of Goods Act is entitled 'Rights of Unpaid Seller Against the Goods'.

[52] Or the property has passed pursuant to an intention under s. 17.

the seller's lien will be a significantly rarer event than the exercise of a contractual right of retention.

Credit

11.12   **Meaning of credit.**   The second of the two cases of the seller's lien, which turns on the expiry of the credit granted to the buyer, is harder to explain, for the reason that credit is normally granted in the form of allowing the buyer delivery before payment with the period of credit running from delivery. In this case, the grant of credit is tied up with the surrender of possession by the seller and therefore the loss of his lien.[53] In s. 41(1)(b), however, credit appears rather to signify the disconnection of payment and delivery, where the buyer is entitled to call for delivery before payment but is bound to pay within a stated period.[54] Credit would thus mean the seller's agreement not to demand payment as soon as the contract is concluded, even though the goods are specific or ascertained and in a deliverable state, and the buyer is entitled to demand the goods at any time.[55] If the buyer fails for whatever reason to take delivery of the goods before the last date for payment, the lien waived[56] by the seller when granting credit is revived and with it the seller's contractual right under section 28 not to deliver before payment. Some sellers who have granted credit in this way may be fortuitously still in possession of the goods when the buyer becomes insolvent.[57] Even though the period of credit has not expired, they will be able to exercise a lien under section 41(1)(c).

11.13   **Seller as bailee.**   Section 41(2) provides that the seller's lien is not lost merely because the seller attorns to the buyer as bailee or agent.[58] But an unpaid seller granting credit to the buyer, who stores goods for the buyer after an attornment, may exercise a lien after the expiry of the credit period.[59] Case law decided before the Act under section 17 of the Statute of Frauds held that a buyer could be in actual receipt of goods for the purpose of the section if the seller attorned to him as bailee, on the ground that the seller's lien would in such circumstances be lost.[60] It was later held, however, that the insolvency of the buyer would allow the lien to

---

[53]   This may be regarded as a waiver of the seller's lien under s. 43(1)(c).

[54]   *Bunney v Poyntz* (1833) 4 B & Ad 568; *New v Swain* (1828) Dan. & Ll. 193.

[55]   In *Dixon v Yates* (1833) 5 B & Ad. 313, 340, Parke B explained the passing of property in specific goods at the contract date as turning upon a deemed delivery of them to the buyer. This idea gives some assistance in understanding the sense in which credit is used in s. 41(1)(b).

[56]   See s. 43(1)(c); *Poulton and Son v Anglo-American Oil Co. Ltd* (1911) 27 TLR 216, affirmed on other grounds (1911) 27 TLR 216.

[57]   *Ex p. Chalmers*, n. 17 above.

[58]   But the facts may show a waiver of the lien under s. 43(1)(c).

[59]   S. 41(1)(b).

[60]   *Cusack v Robinson* (1861) 1 B & S 299 (Blackburn J). See also *Marvin v Wallace* (1856) 25 LJQB 369; *Michael Gerson (Leasing) Ltd v Wilkinson* [2001] QB 514 at [21]–[28].

revive where goods were being held by the seller in the capacity of warehouseman.[61] At one stage in its drafting history, section 41(2) was confined to insolvency to reflect the above development but now permits the survival of the lien on the more extended basis stated above.

Loss of Lien

General.   According to section 43(1), the seller's lien is lost in the following   **11.14** three cases: first, when the goods are delivered to a carrier or other bailee for the purpose of transmission to the buyer and the right of disposal has not been reserved; secondly, when the buyer or an agent lawfully obtains possession of the goods; and thirdly, when the seller waives his lien.[62]

Delivery to carrier.   The first of these cases is but a particular example of the sec-   **11.15** ond, for the carrier is *prima facie* the agent of the buyer,[63] so that delivery and the transfer of possession for general sales purposes occur on surrender of the goods to the carrier.[64] This is subject to the seller's right of stoppage in transit which, when validly exercised, revives the seller's lien. If the seller has retained the right of disposal, this negatives delivery to the buyer once the goods are surrendered to the carrier[65] and so, consistently with this, the seller continues to exercise his right to withhold delivery constructively through the shipping documents.[66] In some cases, the waiver of the lien is of finite duration;[67] whether it is capable of being permanent will be determined in accordance with the standard rules on waiver and promissory estoppel.

Buyer in possession.   The transfer of possession by the seller to the buyer or his   **11.16** agent under section 43(1)(b) will not normally be a difficult matter, but occasional problems are presented in drawing inferences from the fact of control over the goods.[68] In one case, timber in the possession of a wharfinger was measured, stamped, and treated by the buyer in accordance with the contract of sale, to such an extent that the court held that possession had been lost by the seller.[69] The case may be better explained as involving an attornment[70] by the wharfinger, for an

---

[61] *Gunn v Bolckow Vaughan & Co.* (1875) LR 10 Ch. App. 491; *Grice v Richardson* (1877) 3 App. Cas. 319.

[62] These instances are in addition to tender, unlawful disposal, and execution of judgment.

[63] See Ch. 6 above.

[64] S. 32(1).

[65] See Ch. 3 above.

[66] By reserving the right of disposal, the seller prevents the property from passing.

[67] Where a period of credit is extended to the buyer.

[68] See *Wrightson v McArthur and Hutchinson's (1919) Ltd* [1921] 2 KB 807.

[69] *Cooper v Bill* (1865) 3 H & C 722; see also *McGregor v Whalen* (1914) 31 OLR 543, 555 (Can.).

[70] Attornment is discussed in Ch. 6 above.

attornment by a bailee to the buyer will destroy the seller's lien.[71] A mere instruction from the seller to the bailee to hold the goods for the buyer will not amount to the constructive change of possession that is produced by an attornment.[72]

11.17 Lawful possession. The possession acquired by the buyer under section 43(1)(b) must be a lawful one; a wrongful taking of the goods by the buyer will not destroy the lien.[73] It follows that such a buyer, though having bought the goods, will not have obtained possession of the goods with the consent of the seller for the purpose of section 25(1). Although the property in the goods has passed to the buyer, the title transferred by the buyer to the sub-buyer will therefore be encumbered with the seller's lien.[74] Section 47(1) provides that the seller's lien[75] is not affected by a sub-sale negotiated by the buyer unless the seller assents to it, which is not the case in this instance.[76]

11.18 Waiver. As stated earlier, an assent to a sub-sale may be regarded as an instance of the waiver principle contained in section 43(1)(c). The seller's assent will not be inferred from mere notice of the sub-sale; it has to amount to a renunciation of his rights over the goods and to show the seller's intention for the sub-contract to be performed without regard to the terms of the head contract.[77] The passive receipt by the seller of a delivery order from the sub-buyer, even when coupled with the past practice of delivery pursuant to such orders once the immediate buyer paid for the goods, has been held not be an assent.[78] But in *D. F. Mount Ltd v Jay & Jay (Provisions) Ltd*,[79] the sellers agreed to sell on a falling market a quantity of tinned peaches from a larger bulk lying in their name in a warehouse. It was agreed between sellers and buyers that the price should come from the moneys received by the buyers from their sub-buyers. The sellers issued a delivery order in favour of the buyers, and the buyers in turn issued a delivery order in favour of the sub-buyers. In the sub-sale contract, it was provided that the sub-buyers should resell the goods back to the buyers a week later at a small profit. At that time, the sub-buyers duly gave a delivery order in favour of the buyers, receiving from the buyers a cheque in payment that was later dishonoured. They cancelled the delivery order in favour of the buyers and then claimed the goods. The sellers, meanwhile, had not been paid and they too claimed the goods. The warehouseman interpleaded

---

[71] *Pooley v Great Eastern Railway Co.* (1876) 34 LT 537.
[72] *Poulton and Son v Anglo-American Oil Co.*, n. 56 above.
[73] *Wallace v Woodgate* (1824) 1 C & P 575.
[74] See Ch. 5 above.
[75] And the right of stoppage in transit.
[76] There seems no reason to confine this to a case where the goods at all material times are in the seller's possession.
[77] *Mordaunt Bros v British Oil and Cake Mills Ltd* [1910] 2 KB 502.
[78] *Ibid.* Note that the requirement of an assent may be easier to infer in a case of specific goods.
[79] [1960] 1 QB 159.

between the rival claimants, sellers, and sub-buyers. The court held that the sellers had assented to the sub-sale by assuming the risk of the buyers' dishonesty. Besides the sellers' knowledge that the price would come from the sub-sale price, the sellers were aware that the buyers had to issue a delivery order to the sub-buyers in order to secure payment. It did not matter, moreover, that the goods in question had at no material time been ascertained from bulk;[80] the sellers' right to withhold delivery[81] was abated as regards the bulk to the extent of the contract quantity.

Transfer of document of title. Section 47(2) of the Sale of Goods Act also provides that the seller's lien[82] is defeated when a document of title[83] lawfully transferred[84] to the buyer is in turn transferred on for valuable consideration to a sub-buyer or pledgee acting in good faith. In *DF Mount Ltd v Jay & Jay (Provisions) Ltd*,[85] it was held that the requirement of transfer was satisfied even though the seller had issued a delivery order in favour of the buyer, who in turn issued a fresh delivery order in favour of the sub-buyer.[86] It would have been unduly technical to read the requirement of transfer as including only cases where the same document changes hands twice. A delivery order has also been held to be a document of title under section 47(2) when it is issued against a carrier in respect of part of a bulk shipment, the whole of which is represented by a bill of lading.[87] Like the seller's assent to the sub-sale, this rule is also capable of explanation in terms of waiver.   **11.19**

Part delivery. Waiver may be seen too in section 42, which states that a seller who delivers part of the agreed goods may nevertheless exercise a lien on the remainder of the goods unless the circumstances show an agreement to waive the lien. The principal provision of section 42 comes from case law ruling that part-delivery does not amount to a constructive delivery of the whole.[88] But circumstances may show that part-delivery is truly intended by the parties to represent the whole.[89] Nevertheless, it is *prima facie* not to be regarded as delivery of the whole.[90]   **11.20**

---

[80] A conclusion easier to reach now that the Sale of Goods (Amendment) Act 1995 has been passed, conferring rights by way of tenancy in common in a defined bulk.

[81] Not a lien: the property had not passed.

[82] And right of stoppage in transit.

[83] Defined by s. 1(4) of the Factors Act 1889 and s. 61(1) of the Sale of Goods Act in more expensive terms than at common law: see Ch. 5 above.

[84] If the document is transferred by way of pledge, the owner's rights are defeated only up to the amount of the pledge: *Sewell v Burdick* (1884) 10 App. Cas. 74; see Ch. 5 above.

[85] n. 79 above.

[86] See also *Ant Jurgens Margarine Fabrieken v Louis Dreyfus & Co.* [1914] 3 KB 40. Cf *Farmeloe v Bain* (1876) 1 CPD 445.

[87] *Ant Jurgens*, n. 86 above.

[88] *Miles v Gorton* (1834) 2 C & M 504; *Dixon v Yates* (1833) 5 B & Ad. 313 (seller refused to give delivery receipt for all the goods); see also *Bunney v Poyntz* (1833) 4 B & Ad. 568.

[89] *Kemp v Falk* (1882) 7 App. Cas. 573 (Lord Blackburn).

[90] *Ex p. Cooper* (1879) 11 Ch. D 68, 73.

11.21 **Revival of lien.**   It is clear that a lien temporarily or conditionally waived, for example, where a period of credit is extended to the buyer or a negotiable instrument is accepted in payment, may revive where the term expires or the instrument is dishonoured.[91] Less clear, however, is the issue whether a lien that has been released unconditionally and irrevocably may revive at a future date. In one old case, it was held that goods returned to a seller solely for the purpose of packing could not be made the subject of an unpaid seller's lien.[92] This could be explained as based on the absence of an intention of buyer and seller that the seller was to have a lien entitlement, and on the seller's repossession of the goods in the capacity of someone other than a seller.[93] As between buyer and seller alone, there seems no reason why the parties might not agree to the revival of an abandoned lien, provided possession is duly resumed by the seller.[94] This view was upheld in one New Zealand case where the goods, a quantity of logs, were at all times present on the seller's land, where a construction project was in progress.[95] But the court went on to say that the seller's lien thus revived was the original lien and not a new lien, with the consequence that it defeated an intervening mechanic's lien pressed by a third party.[96] It is submitted that a lien might still be a valid lien if taken *de novo*, which avoids the unfairness of permitting it to defeat an intervening security. A later New Zealand case refused to accept the proposition that an abandoned lien could be revived by repossession.[97] On this point, the case appears to go too far, but the result is supportable, because the goods had been returned to the seller only for the purpose of repair, and not so as to permit the seller to reassert the lost lien.

11.22 **Priority.**   A reading of the Sale of Goods Act and of the antecedent common law supports a strong argument that the seller's lien is superior to any security interest of the buyer's creditors. If the lien can be asserted against purchasers from the buyer, then *a fortiori* it can be asserted against those with a security interest over the buyer's assets, for the buyer's property in the goods is already encumbered to the extent of the lien.

11.23 **Instalment contracts.**   Severable instalment contracts have presented some difficulties in respect of the scope of the seller's lien. In principle, a seller who delivers an instalment on credit terms loses his lien over that instalment, and it does not revive on non-payment. Furthermore, provided the buyer has not committed a

---

[91] *Poulton and Son v Anglo-American Oil Co. Ltd* (1910) 27 TLR 38.

[92] *Valpy v Gibson* (1847) 4 CB 837.

[93] Cf *Pacific Motor Auctions Pty Ltd v Motor Credits (Hire Finance) Ltd* [1965] AC 867 and s. 24 of the Sale of Goods Act, discussed in Ch. 5 above.

[94] See *Harris v Tong* (1930) 65 OLR 133, 144 (Can.).

[95] *Bines v Sankey* [1958] NZLR 886.

[96] *Ibid.*, 898.

[97] *United Plastics Ltd v Reliance Electric (NZ) Ltd* [1977] 2 NZLR 125 (where the *Bines* case was not cited in the judgment).

discharging breach by failing to pay, the seller may not demand that cash be received against delivery of the next instalment, for the contract, still on foot, provides for the grant of credit to the buyer.[98] The situation is different, however, where the buyer becomes insolvent, and it is only the intervention of the buyer's insolvency representative that prevents the seller from invoking a repudiation of the contract based on the buyer's manifest inability to pay. In such cases, it has been held that the trustee must pay cash for future instalments, and may not demand future instalments even on such terms if he does not also pay for outstanding instalments.[99] Since the trustee does not have to adopt the contract, it has been said that he should take the contract as a whole and not merely the beneficial portion, for it would otherwise be unfair to require the seller to prove in bankruptcy.[100] A final point concerns the buyer's insolvency, which does not justify the seller in refusing to deliver an instalment for which payment actually has been made.[101]

The Right of Stoppage in Transit

General. This is an extraordinary right given to the seller,[102] in the event of the **11.24** buyer's insolvency, to resume possession of the goods[103] and thereby reassert his lien, notwithstanding that the property in the goods has passed to the buyer and that constructive delivery of the goods to the buyer has already been made on the delivery of the goods to the carrier.[104] It may be asserted at any time before the transit of the goods to their agreed destination has been completed.[105]

Passing of property. The right of stoppage in transit strictly only applies where **11.25** the property in the goods has passed to the buyer, for if it has not, the seller may instead fall back on his ownership of the goods on the buyer's insolvency.[106] Nevertheless, stoppage decisions and principles may usefully be looked at even if

---

[98] *Steinberger v Atkinson and Co. Ltd* (1914) 31 TLR 110; *Snagproof Ltd v Brody* [1922] 3 WWR 432, 437.

[99] *Ex p. Chalmers*, n. 17 above; *Re Grainex Canada Ltd*, n. 20 above, 671.

[100] *Re Grainex Canada Ltd*, n. 20 above, 671.

[101] *Merchant Banking Co. of London v Phoenix Bessemer Steel Co.* (1877) 5 Ch. D 205.

[102] Or someone in the position of the seller: s. 38(2). See also *The Tigress* (1863) 32 LJ Adm. 97; *Bird v Brown* (1850) 4 Ex. 786. Even before the enactment of s. 20A of the Sale of Goods Act in 1995, a seller could stop in transit even if, for want of ascertainment, the goods had never vested in him: *Jenkyns v Usborne* (1844) 7 M & G 678.

[103] The right of stoppage will extend to the proceeds of sale once a prior-ranking pledge has been satisfied: *Kemp v Falk* (1882) 7 App. Cas. 573. But it does not extend to insurance moneys received after the destruction of or damage done to goods: *Berndtson v Strang* (1886) LR 3 Ch. App. 588, reversing in part (1867) LR 4 Eq. 481. It will extend to the proceeds of sale if there has been a sub-sale; *Ex p. Golding Davis* (1880) 13 Ch. D 628.

[104] The general entitlement is set out in s. 44.

[105] S. 45.

[106] See *Gibson v Carruthers* (1841) 8 M & W 321; *Bolton v Lancashire and Yorkshire Railway Co.* (1866) LR 1 CP 431.

the property has not passed, especially in so far as they deal with the rights and duties of seller and carrier *inter se*. Support for this approach comes from section 39(2) of the Sale of Goods Act, which confers on a seller in whom the property in the goods is still vested 'a right of withholding delivery similar to and co-extensive with the rights of lien and stoppage in transit where the property has passed to the buyer'. A seller invoking section 39(2) and claiming rights akin to stoppage will therefore be at least as well placed as a seller invoking stoppage, properly so-called, in resuming possession of the goods. Evidence of the relative unimportance of the distinction between the two cases comes from the extension of stoppage to the case where goods have been rejected by the buyer,[107] so that the property in them revests in the seller.

11.26 **Rarity of stoppage.** Reported cases on the subject of stoppage have been exceedingly rare in the last century, and this is not merely attributable to the fact that the law on the subject has been settled. The right of stoppage in transit is predicated upon the lengthy transit of goods that have been shipped on credit terms in which, typically, the seller exchanges the shipping documents against a draft upon the buyer, which the buyer accepts. In times of rapid transit,[108] the ability of a seller to issue a stop notice is correspondingly abridged. More importantly, the practice in international sales of sellers reserving the right of disposal after shipment, surrendering this right on the documentary exchange only against payment under a banker's credit, guarantees them the continuing property in the goods and a reliable and solvent paymaster. In either event, such sellers will not need the additional right of stoppage in transit conferred by the Sale of Goods Act.

11.27 **Origin of stoppage right.** Ninety years ago, Scrutton J spoke of the right of stoppage as 'a custom ... which had grown up with no special reference or congruity to the English law' creating 'considerable difficulty in fitting in this international usage and national law'.[109] Not the least difficult aspect of the ill-fitting right of stoppage in transit is the way that it allows a seller, even when the carriage contract is concluded between the carrier and the buyer, to give binding directions to the carrier. The sale of goods contract being largely the preserve of common lawyers, there has been a tendency to dub the right of stoppage as an equitable right.[110] Some resemblance between this right and equitable rights emerges in the rule that the right of stoppage is curtailed as soon as the bill of lading is transferred

---

[107] S. 45(4), codifying *Bolton v Lancashire and Yorkshire Railway Co*, n. 106 above.

[108] S. 45(1) of the 1893 Act was confined to land and water transit; these limitations are absent from the 1979 Act. Statutory comprehensiveness? Or may air carriers look forward to dealing with stop notices?

[109] *Booth Steamship Co. Ltd v Cargo Fleet Iron Co. Ltd* [1916] 2 KB 579, 597.

[110] *Kemp v Falk*, n. 103 above; *Ex p. Golding Davis*, n. 103 above; *Nippon Yusen Kaisha v Ramjiban Serowgee* [1938] AC 429.

to a *bona fide* purchaser for value.[111] In reality, however, the right of stoppage was taken from the law merchant in the late seventeenth century[112] and for a long time was exercised under the bankruptcy jurisdiction of the Lord Chancellor.[113] It is therefore based upon international commercial custom, though recognized by law and equity[114] and now by statute.

Justification for Right of Stoppage

Seller's preference.   A more difficult inquiry concerns the justification for giving   **11.28** the seller a preferential right on the buyer's insolvency, for the seller has already parted with the property in and possession of the goods. More than 200 years ago, it was asserted that the seller's goods should not be applied to the payment of the insolvent buyer's debts,[115] but since the property has passed, it can hardly be said that these are still the seller's goods. Moreover, if this explanation still retains its force, it is difficult to see why it should not continue to give the seller a bankruptcy preference while the goods remain in an identifiable form in the buyer's possession. As it is, the seller's preference trades on the technicality of the rule that delivery to the carrier is constructive delivery to the buyer and, for the purpose of the extraordinary right of stoppage, deems that delivery does not in fact occur before the transit is over.

Buyer's defeasible possession.   A slightly different explanation of the right of   **11.29** stoppage was given in *Bloxam v Sanders*,[116] where it was said that the buyer's right to possession of goods, the property in which has passed to him, is defeasible on his insolvency; but nothing is said about why the buyer's property and possession should be defeasible in transit cases. A Canadian judge once referred to the 'persuasive equity' of the stoppage rule, which restored goods to the unpaid seller instead of distributing them among the buyer's creditors.[117] Stoppage in transit has also been explained as introduced for the benefit of trade,[118] which presumably means that sellers are encouraged to surrender goods to a carrier when they know that the goods can be stopped on the buyer's insolvency. The response to this is that sellers can more effectively protect themselves by retaining the right of disposal and stipulating for payment under a documentary letter of credit.

---

111   S. 47(2), discussed above in the text accompanying nn. 82 *et seq.* above.
112   *Wiseman v Vandeputt* (1690) 2 Vern. 203.
113   *Gibson v Carruthers*, n. 106 above; *Booth Steamship*, n. 109 above.
114   *Kendall v Marshall, Stevens & Co.* (1883) 11 QBD 356, 364. Stoppage was adopted at common law in *Lickbarrow v Mason* (1793) 4 Bro. Parl. Cas. 57, 6 East 22 note, reinstating (1787) 2 TR 63, itself revd. by (1790) 1 H Bl. 357. In equity, the right of stoppage was enforced by a bill: *Schotsmans v Lancashire and Yorkshire Railway Co.* (1867) LR 2 Ch. App. 332.
115   *D'Aquila v Lambert* (1761) 1 Amb. 399, approved in *Booth Steamship*, n. 109 above, 580.
116   (1825) 4 B & C 941.
117   *Wiley v Smith* (1876) 1 OAR 179, 217 (Can.).
118   *Bohtlingk v Inglis* (1803) 3 East 381; *Berndtson v Strang*, n. 103 above, 490.

Failing this, a seller might contract on retention of title terms. Stoppage in transit therefore seems difficult to reconcile with modern patterns of selling activity. Its continued existence, it is submitted, is best explained by inertia and by the conviction that the buyer's creditors, secured and unsecured, should be denied access to goods that the buyer has never paid for and that have not come into his actual, visible possession.

Duration of Transit

11.30 **End of transit.**   Section 45 deals with the duration of the transit and contains two principal rules for determining the duration of the transit. Sub-section (1) provides that the transit is over when the carrier or other bailee[119] charged with transmitting the goods to the buyer actually delivers them to the buyer or his agent.[120] This rule clearly demonstrates that, for the purpose of stoppage in transit, delivery is essentially based on actual rather than constructive possession by the buyer.[121] The buyer is therefore not in actual possession while the goods are in the hands of the carrier, even if the carrier is appointed by the buyer,[122] for the carrier's agency to accept delivery on behalf of the buyer, in circumstances whereby the property in the goods vests in the buyer, is not sufficient to defeat the right of stoppage.[123] Indeed, it has been said that the 'essential feature of a stoppage *in transitu . . .* is, that the goods at the time should be in the possession of a middleman'.[124]

11.31 **Bailee's attornment to buyer.**   Section 45(1) must, however, be read subject to the other principal rule in the section, which is to be found in sub-section(3):

> If after the arrival of the goods at the appointed destination the carrier or other bailee or custodier acknowledges to the buyer or his agent that he holds the goods on his behalf and continues in possession of them as bailee or custodier for the buyer or his agent, the transit is at an end, and it is immaterial that a further destination for the goods may have been indicated by the buyer.

Sub-section (3) places pragmatic limits upon a right of stoppage that might otherwise endure for months or even years if the buyer delays in removing the goods from storage at the port of discharge.[125] It recognizes that some buyers may never take actual delivery of the goods but may, instead, choose to deal with them

---

[119] *Smith v Goss* (1808) 1 Camp. 282 (wharfinger).
[120] *Dixon v Baldwin* (1804) 5 East 175. Or the buyer's insolvency representative: *Ellis v Hunt* (1789) 3 TR 464.
[121] *Gibson v Carruthers*, n. 106 above; *Berndtson v Strang*, n. 103 above; *Bohtlingk v Inglis*, n. 118 above; *Heninekey v Earle* (1858) 4 E & B 427; *Ex p. Rosevear China Co.* (1879) 11 Ch. D 560.
[122] *Ibid.*
[123] *Bethell & Co. v Clark & Co.* (1888) 20 QBD 615, 617, 619.
[124] *Schotsmans v Lancashire and Yorkshire Railway Co*, n. 114 above, 338.
[125] *Wiley v Smith*, n. 117 above.

through the medium of warehouse receipts, delivery orders, and the like. In what may be the interests of simplicity, it seems also to formulate a broad rule that the seller is not entitled to trace the goods through too many middlemen involved in the transit of the goods. Because it is sometimes difficult to decide which of the two subsections, sub-section (1) or (3), accounts for a decision, the various instances of the loss of stoppage rights under the two provisions will be considered together.

Part-delivery. Actual receipt of the goods will obviously defeat the seller's right **11.32** of stoppage in transit, but a partial delivery and receipt will do so in principle only in respect of the part delivered.[126] It is possible, however, for the part to be a symbolic delivery of the whole, but the burden of establishing this will rest on the buyer's insolvency representative or on whoever else seeks to overcome the seller's right.[127] The burden might well be discharged if the part delivered were a component of a manufactured machine.[128]

Constructive possession of buyer. It is clear that constructive possession at the **11.33** port of discharge, in such a way that the buyer may remove the goods whenever he wishes, defeats the seller's right of stoppage. Thus a buyer who initially refused to accept goods, but then subsequently accepted the key to the warehouse in which they were stored, thereby curtailed the seller's right of stoppage.[129] This would not be the case, however, where a buyer who has declined to accept goods mistakenly takes possession of them, whether personally or through an agent.[130]

Buyer's ship. It is also clear that delivery of the goods on board a ship that is **11.34** owned by the buyer will prevent the seller from stopping the goods.[131] The same result should follow where the buyer has chartered the ship by demise,[132] for in such cases the buyer obtains possession of the ship itself. If a buyer merely travels as a passenger on board the ship, this will, of course, not be sufficient to reduce the goods into his possession.[133] It has on a number of occasions been held that the right of stoppage persists even though it is the buyer who has booked space on

---

[126] S. 45(7); *Whitehead v Anderson* (1842) 9 M & W 518; *Griffith v Perry* (1859) 1 E & E 680; *Ex p. Cooper* (1879) 11 Ch. D 68.

[127] *Ex p. Cooper*, n. 126 above.

[128] *Ibid.*

[129] *Heinekey v Earle*, n. 121 above. See also *Whitehead v Anderson*, n. 126 above (entry on board ship by buyer's assignee in bankruptcy, who touched the goods, did not break transit).

[130] *Bolton v Lancashire and Yorkshire Railway Co.*, n. 106 above.

[131] *Van Casteel v Booker* (1848) 2 Ex. 691; *Schotsmans v Lancashire and Yorkshire Railway Co.*, n. 114 above; *Berndtson v Strang*, n. 103 above, 489.

[132] S. 45(5) states that it depends upon the circumstances whether the master on a chartered ship has goods in his possession as carrier or as agent for the buyer.

[133] *Lyons v Hoffnung* (1890) 15 App. Cas. 391.

the ship[134] or has chartered it for a particular voyage.[135] Furthermore, the transfer to the buyer of the bill of lading will not in itself defeat the seller's right of stoppage.[136] Yet it has been said that the right of stoppage is defeated if the goods are delivered on board a ship that is destined for a 'roving voyage'.[137] The reason for this limitation is hard to see, unless it is based on the need to confine the right of stoppage to relatively narrow temporal limits. Certainly, the right of stoppage persists even though goods are loaded on a ship whose actual destination is unknown to the seller,[138] so this factor probably does not explain the 'roving voyage' limitation.

11.35 **Compound transit.** Certain difficulties are presented in cases of compound transit where, for example, goods are first shipped by road or rail and later transhipped for an ocean voyage. If the seller ships the goods by an inland carrier to a forwarding agent acting for the buyer at the port of overseas shipment and awaiting instructions from the buyer, the transit comes to an end as soon as the goods come into the hands of the forwarding agent;[139] it makes no difference that the seller knows the ultimate destination. If, however, the goods come into the hands of the ocean carrier in pursuance of an arrangement to that effect between seller and buyer, it is clear that the seller's right of stoppage survives delivery of the goods by the inland to the ocean carrier.[140] It is a question of construction of the contract of sale[141] and of the subsequent conduct of the parties whether such an extended shipment is thus contemplated. Lord Esher once said:

> [W]here the transit is a transit which has been caused either by the terms of the contract or by the directions of the purchaser to the vendor, the right of stoppage in transitu exists: but, if the goods are not in the hands of the carrier by means either of the terms of the contract or of the directions of the purchaser to the vendor, but are in transitu afterwards in consequence of fresh directions given by the purchaser for a new transit, then such transit is no part of the original transit, and the right to stop is gone. So also, if the purchaser gives orders that the goods shall be sent to a particular place, these to be kept till he gives fresh orders as to their destination to a new carrier, the original transit is at an end when they have reached that place.[142]

---

[134] e.g., *Bethell & Co. v Clark & Co.*, n. 123 above; *Ex p. Golding Davis* (1880) 13 Ch. D 628.

[135] *Bohtlingk v Inglis*, n. 118 above; *Berndston v Strang*, n. 103 above; *Ex p. Rosevear China Co.*, n. 121 above; *Kemp v Falk* (1882) 7 App. Cas. 573.

[136] e.g., *Schotsmans v Lancashire and Yorkshire Railway Co.*, n. 114 above; *Lyons v Hoffnung*, n. 133 above; *The Tigress* (1863) 32 LJ Adm 97.

[137] *Berndtson v Strang*, n. 103 above, 490.

[138] *Ex p. Rosevear China Co.*, n. 121 above. A seller in a hurry can read a shipping register.

[139] *Valpy v Gibson* (1847) 4 CB 837. See also *Ex p. Miles* (1885) 15 QBD 39; *Kendall v Marshall Stevens & Co.* (1883) 11 QBD 356; *Jobson v Eppenheim* (1905) 21 TLR 468.

[140] *Bethell & Co. v Clark & Co.*, n. 123 above; *Kemp v Ismay, Imrie & Co.* (1909) 100 LT 996; *Reddall v Union Castle Mail Steamship Co. Ltd* (1914) 84 LJKB 360.

[141] *Ex p. Watson* (1877) 5 Ch. D 35.

[142] *Bethell & Co. v Clark & Co.*, n. 123 above, 617.

Thus, where a London merchant bought goods from an English manufacturer 150 miles away, and after the contract requested the manufacturer to consign the goods 'to the *Darling Downs*, to Melbourne, loading in the East India Docks', it was held that the transit did not end before the ship reached Melbourne.[143] If, however, the second carrier specially attorns to the buyer, the situation is the same as if the goods had come into the hands of a forwarding agent, and the transit is deemed at an end.[144]

Application of rules. As seen earlier, section 45(3) deems the transit to have **11.36** ended when the goods arrive at their appointed destination and the carrier or other bailee attorns to the buyer. The application of this rule has not always been straightforward, but the cases support the following propositions. First of all, when the goods have arrived at their destination and the carrier continues to hold them *qua* carrier, the transit will be considered as still continuing.[145] Merely informing the buyer that the goods are ready for collection,[146] or that they will be given up when practical arrangements can be made to that effect,[147] will not in itself amount to an attornment. The rule of attornment is thus applied with some rigour so as to demand distinct evidence of a true undertaking by the carrier to hold the goods for the buyer, and even an acceptance by the buyer in response to the carrier's undertaking,[148] which may be inferred from the lapse of a reasonable time.[149] By declining to take delivery of the goods, the buyer may prolong the transit to the advantage of the seller.[150] The right of stoppage tends to be construed generously in favour of the seller.[151] If, on arrival at the discharge port, the carrier warehouses the goods on the buyer's instructions, the transit thereupon comes to an end.[152]

Freight. Regardless of attornment, the transit will be treated as coming to an **11.37** end where the buyer pays or tenders the freight, for any subsequent refusal by the carrier to deliver once his lien has thus been lifted will be wrongful.[153] It depends upon the circumstances whether an unpaid carrier with a lien over the goods continues to hold them *qua* carrier[154] or *qua* warehouseman.[155] The right of stoppage

---

[143] *Ibid.*

[144] *Reddall v Union Castle Mail Steamship Co. Ltd*, n. 140 above.

[145] *Bolton v Lancashire and Yorkshire Railway Co.*, n. 106 above; *Ex p. Barrow* (1877) 6 Ch. D 783 (goods held by carrier's agent).

[146] *Mechan & Sons v North Eastern Railway Co.* 1911 SC 1348.

[147] *Coventry v Gladstone* (1868) LR 6 Eq. 44.

[148] *Bolton v Lancashire and Yorkshire Railway Co.*, n. 106 above.

[149] *Taylor v Great Eastern Railway Co.* (1901) 17 TLR 394.

[150] *Ex p. Cooper* (1879) 11 Ch. D 68, 73. See also *James v Griffin* (1837) 2 M & W 623 (buyer asked agent to take delivery on behalf of the seller).

[151] *Bethell & Co. v Clark & Co.*, n. 123 above, 617.

[152] *Johann Plischke und Sohne GmbH v Allison Bros Ltd* [1936] 2 All ER 1009.

[153] S. 45(6); *Bird v Brown* (1850) 4 Ex. 786.

[154] *Crawshay v Eades* (1823) 1 B & C 181.

[155] *Kemp v Falk* (1882) 7 App. Cas. 573, 584.

will, however, persist, despite a warehousing of the goods by the carrier, if the goods are warehoused in the name of the seller,[156] or even in the name of a bank that has financed the contract of sale.[157]

11.38 **Unlawful seizure from carrier.** Section 45(2) provides that the transit is at end if the buyer or an agent obtains delivery of the goods before they have arrived at their appointed destination.[158] It is not clear what the position would be if the buyer were to seize the goods unlawfully in defiance of the carrier's lien but it is likely that, though this would be a wrong committed against the carrier, it would be effective against the seller.[159] A related matter concerns seizure of the goods in transit by the buyer's insolvency representative or by a sheriff executing a judgment. This should be regarded as terminating the transit.[160]

11.39 **Rescission of contract.** Notwithstanding the termination of the transit, or the seller's failure to issue a timely stop notice, the buyer and seller may consensually rescind the contract of sale so as to revest the property in the seller, provided this is done before the buyer's insolvency.[161] Similarly, a buyer who rejects the contract goods thereby revests the property in the seller and revives a right akin[162] to the right of stoppage.[163] This will be the case even if the seller refuses to take back the goods.[164]

Effect of Stoppage

11.40 **Resumption of possession.** The mere exercise of a right of stoppage does not as such rescind the contract of sale.[165] Insolvency, as discussed above, does not of itself amount to an anticipatory repudiation of the contract. Rather, a seller who stops the goods[166] is to be treated as having resumed possession of the goods,[167] thereby reasserting the lien he surrendered on delivering the goods to the carrier.

---

[156] *Lewis v Mason* (1875) 36 UCQB 590 (Can.).
[157] *Re Alcock Ingram & Co. Ltd* [1924] 1 DLR 388.
[158] *Whitehead v Anderson* (1842) 9 M & W 518; *London and North Western Railway Co. v Bartlett* (1861) 7 H & N 400; *Reddall v Union Castle Mail Steamship Co. Ltd*, n. 140 above. But not just because the buyer demands the goods while they are in transit: *Jackson v Nichol* (1839) 5 Bing. NC 50.
[159] *Whitehead v Anderson*, n. 158 above, 534.
[160] *Ellis v Hunt*, n. 120 above; *Oppenheim v Russell* (1802) 3 B & P 42.
[161] And does not amount to a preference: Insolvency Act 1986, ss. 239, 340.
[162] S. 39(2).
[163] S. 45(4); *Bolton v Lancashire and Yorkshire Railway Co.*, n. 106 above.
[164] *Ibid.*
[165] S. 48(1); *Schotsmans v Lancashire and Yorkshire Railway Co.*, n. 114 above; *Kemp v Falk*, n. 155 above; *Booth Steamship Co. Ltd v Cargo Fleet Iron Co. Ltd*, n. 109 above. The question was still thought a doubtful one in *Phelps Stokes & Co. v Comber* (1885) 29 Ch. D 813, 821.
[166] Whether he receives possession or directs the carrier to hold to his order: s. 46(1); *Booth Steamship*, n. 109 above. The carrier's duty is to be found in s. 46(4). See also *Continental Grain Co. v Islamic Republic of Iran Shipping Lines* [1983] 2 Lloyd's Rep. 620.
[167] S. 44.

In that position, the seller may proceed to a termination of the contract and a resale of the goods in the event of the buyer's insolvency representative disclaiming the contract of sale as onerous property or otherwise failing to perform the contract.

Transit and transfer of document of title. According to section 47(2), the seller's right of stoppage in transit is defeated in the event of a document of title[168] being lawfully transferred to a *bona fide* purchaser for the value. In the case of a transfer occurring under a sale, the seller's right is defeated altogether,[169] while it is postponed subject to the interest of the pledgee where the transfer occurs under a pledge.[170] The section is applicable even if the buyer has made a sub-sale prior to receiving the bill of lading.[171] Even if the transfer takes place under a sub-sale, it has been held that the transit continues so long as the sub-buyer has not actually paid for the goods.[172] Since the seller's right of stoppage is curtailed in the interests of *bona fide* purchasers and not of the buyer's creditors, this result seems correct in principle[173] provided the stop notice otherwise arrives in time. A seller may also stop the goods to the prejudice of a sub-buyer who has paid for them and to whom the property has passed, if there has not been a transfer of the document of title.[174]   **11.41**

Stop notice. The seller's stop notice[175] must make plain his intention to resume possession of the goods.[176] It must also identify with sufficient certainty the contract goods: a notice was held not to be sufficient when it failed to indicate to a warehouseman which particular items despatched to a consignee, out of a much larger number held by the warehouseman in the name of the consignee, were subject to the notice.[177] Section 46(2) provides that the 'notice may be given either to the person in actual possession of the goods or to his principal'.[178]   **11.42**

---

[168] In the expanded statutory sense of s. 61(1) of the Sale of Goods Act and s. 1(4) of the Factors Act 1889, overruling in this respect *Lackington v Atherton* (1844) 7 M & G 360, where the transfer of a delivery order (not a common law document of title) did not defeat the right of stoppage.

[169] S. 47(2)(a); *Leask v Scott* (1877) 2 QBD 376; *Cahn v Pockett's Bristol Channel Steam Packet Co. Ltd* [1899] 1 QB 643.

[170] S. 47(2)(b); *Kemp v Falk*, n. 155 above.

[171] *Cahn v Pockett's Bristol Channel Steam Packet Co. Ltd*, n. 169 above.

[172] *Ex p. Golding Davis* (1880) 13 Ch. D 628. See also *Ex p. Falk* (1880) 14 Ch. D 446.

[173] See, however, *Kemp v Falk*, n. 155 above.

[174] The sub-buyer falls outside the protective language of s. 47. See also *Kemp v Falk*, n. 155 above, from which this may be inferred. *Quaere* the constructive possession of the buyer in possession under s. 25(1)? It would surely strain that provision if a constructive delivery to the sub-buyer could be founded upon the constructive delivery to the buyer that occurred with the start of the transit.

[175] The seller may effectively recover possession without issuing a notice: s. 46(1).

[176] *Phelps Stokes & Co. v Comber*, n. 165 above, 821–2.

[177] *Clementson v Grand Trunk Railway Co.* (1877) 42 UCQB 263 (Can.).

[178] *Whitehead v Anderson* (1842) 9 M & W 518.

Consequently, a notice reaching the ship's master will be sufficient; likewise one to the offices of the carrier, provided it gives the carrier sufficient time to communicate diligently with the master.[179] It is unlikely that a notice issued to the consignee would be adequate.[180]

11.43 **Seller's right to immediate possession.** Once a valid stop notice has been issued to the carrier,[181] the seller is to be regarded as having the right to immediate possession of the goods and can therefore maintain an action in conversion if the carrier declines to surrender the goods or hold them to the seller's order, or persists in delivering the goods to the consignee.[182] If the notice is given to the carrier, the carrier must forward it with reasonable diligence to the master of the ship.[183] The seller, however, is under an obligation to pay the carrier's freight both up to the point of stoppage[184] and to the redelivery point,[185] and the carrier has a lien on the cargo for the freight.[186] The carrier has only a special lien for the freight and may not claim under the contract of carriage in respect of any general lien for the whole amount of the indebtedness of the buyer under a running account.[187] Whether the relationship between carrier and seller is contractual or quasicontractual[188] is probably of little account, for the above rights and duties are clearly established as a matter of customary mercantile law.

The Right of Resale

11.44 **Anachronistic provisions.** The modern understanding of section 48 of the Sale of Goods Act, which deals with the seller's right of resale, is probably further from the intention of the draftsman than is the case with any other section of the Act. To anyone approaching it with the values and principles of contract law in the late twentieth century, section 48 is a mystery. To make sense of the section, it has to be first interpreted in the light of the case law on which it was founded before the modern revisionist view is discussed. The principal difficulties in

---

[179] S. 46(3); *Kemp v Falk*, n. 155 above.

[180] See *Phelps Stokes & Co. v Comber*, n. 165 above, 822 (opinion declined).

[181] The carrier is under no duty to determine if the seller's demand is justified: *The Tigress* (1863) 32 LJ Adm. 97, 101.

[182] *Litt v Cowley* (1816) 7 Taunt. 169; *Thompson v Traill* (1826) 6 B & C 36; *Booth Steamship Co. Ltd v Cargo Fleet Iron Co. Ltd*, n. 109 above; *The Tigress*, n. 181 above.

[183] *Kemp v Falk*, n. 155 above, 585–6.

[184] *Booth Steamship*, n. 109 above. *Quaere* the seller who is not party to the contract of carriage with the carrier? It is submitted that the seller should pay, for otherwise the seller condemns the carrier to pursue a freight claim against an insolvent buyer and without the benefit of a lien.

[185] S. 46(4).

[186] *Booth Steamship Co. Ltd v Cargo Fleet Iron Co. Ltd*, n. 109 above.

[187] *Booth Steamship*, n. 109 above; *Oppenheim v Russell*, n. 160 above; *United States Steel Products Co. v Great Western Railway Co.* [1916] 1 AC 689.

[188] See *The Tigress*, n. 181 above; *Booth Steamship*, n. 109 above.

section 48 lie in sub-sections (3) and (4) and in the relationship between the two provisions:

> (3) Where the goods are of a perishable nature, or where the unpaid seller gives notice to the buyer of his intention to re-sell, and the buyer does not within a reasonable time pay or tender the price, the unpaid seller may re-sell the goods and recover from the original buyer damages for any loss occasioned by his breach of contract.
> (4) Where the seller expressly reserves the right of resale in case the buyer should make default, and on the buyer making default re-sells the goods, the original contract of sale is rescinded but without prejudice to any claim the seller may have for damages.

Development of Resale Right

Explanation. The first point to note about these provisions is that, while **11.45** founded upon a breach of contract by the buyer, they do not expressly demand that the buyer commit a discharging breach of contract. Sub-section (3) refers to the buyer's failure to pay, and sub-section (4) to the more general case of default. As the law was established in *Martindale v Smith*,[189] the buyer's duty of timely payment was not of the essence of the contract, so the absence of any reference to discharge in section 48 is quite understandable. The next point to make is that sub-section (3) was based on case law ruling that the seller could recover from the buyer a loss occasioned by the resale, even if the seller's behaviour was wrongful.[190] This will be explained in due course. The seller's claim, as encapsulated in sub-section (3), consisted in essence of the deficiency between the initial contract price and the resale price. This could be recovered by the seller in the form of an action on the contract for damages for non-acceptance,[191] or possibly in the form of an action for the original contract price,[192] in which latter case it seems to have been assumed that the seller could not reap a windfall by failing to give credit to the buyer for the resale price and for any deposit paid by the buyer.[193] The difference between these two forms of action seems to have been one of pleading only.[194]

Open contract. In order for the above deficiency claim to be made, the contract **11.46** had to remain 'open', that is to say, unrescinded.[195] An action for damages could

---

[189] (1841) 1 QB 389.

[190] *Page v Cowasjee Eduljee* (1866) LR 1 PC 127.

[191] *Maclean v Dunn* (1828) 4 Bing. 722.

[192] Tentative support for this is in *Acebal v Levy* (1834) 10 Bing. 376. See also *Page v Cowasjee Eduljee*, n. 190 above, 145–6. The property would have had to pass for this approach to be adopted: s. 49(1). Cf *Maclean v Dunn*, above, 728 (tentative view that the seller could not sue for the price after resale).

[193] *Acebal v Levy*, n. 192 above. Cf. *Lamond v Davall* (1847) 9 QB 1030.

[194] *Acebal v Levy*, n. 192 above, 384. But note the difficulties in *R. V. Ward Ltd v Bignall* [1967] 1 QB 534.

[195] *Maclean v Dunn*, n. 191 above, 728 (the resale did not rescind); *Greaves v Ashlin* (1813) 3 Camp. 426.

not be maintained on a rescinded contract, for the understanding was that rescission operated retrospectively so as to destroy contractual entitlement *ab initio*. Nor could the seller frame an action for the price in the counts of goods bargained and sold or goods sold and delivered, for the passing of property to the buyer was essential for such an action to succeed, and rescission *ab initio* also destroyed the conveyance of the general property in the goods to the buyer. In consequence, the property in the goods was still vested in the buyer at the moment the seller resold the goods and the seller exercised rights midway between those of a lienee and those of an owner;[196] he was to be treated as though he were a pledgee with a right of sale in the event of the pledgor's failure to redeem the pledge. Hence, section 48(3) could be seen as conferring a power of sale that complemented the unpaid seller's lien provided for elsewhere in the Act.[197]

11.47 **Recovering deficiency.** In order for the seller to recover his deficiency, authority existed to the effect that it was not necessary for the resale to be preceded by notice to the buyer of the seller's intention to resell;[198] the specific reference to the perishables in section 48(3) was merely an illustrative case of resale[199] where urgent circumstances dispensed with any need for notice.[200] But notice of resale could be explained in various ways, for example, as the best evidence of the seller's intention not to rescind the contract *ab initio*,[201] or as necessary to make time of the essence of the contract so as to render the resale lawful,[202] or as akin to the procedure to be employed by a pledgee in effecting a lawful[203] sale of the pledged goods.[204] Provided the resale were conducted lawfully, even a buyer to whom the property had passed could not complain, for his failure to perform the contract

---

[196] Lord Blackburn, *A Treatise on the Effect of the Contract of Sale on the Legal Rights of Property and Possession in Goods, Wares and Merchandise* (2nd edn. by J. C. Graham, 1885), 445–6; *Sawyer v. Pringle* (1891) 28 OAR 218, 226, 231 (Can.); *McPherson v United States Fidelity and Guarantee Co.* (1915) 33 OLR 524, 538 (Can.).

[197] *McCowan v Bowes* [1923] 3 DLR 756, 766.

[198] *Maclean v Dunn*, n. 191 above; *Fitt v Cassanet* (1842) 4 M & G 898; *McCowan v Bowes*, n. 197 above, 762–3. A failure to notify where time was not of the essence would make the resale wrongful with the consequences noted below: *Page v Cowasjee Eduljee*, n. 190 above.

[199] In *Maclean v Dunn*, n. 191 above, 91, 728, Best CJ said that price volatility made all goods perishables, the rise and fall of the market making a general resale rule expedient.

[200] Cf agency of necessity: *Pragen v Blatspiel, Stamp and Heacock Ltd* [1924] 1 KB 566.

[201] *Page v Cowasjee Eduljee*, n. 190 above.

[202] *Ibid.*, 245. On making time of the essence, see *Cornwall v Henson* [1900] 2 Ch. 298 (land); *Lambert v Slack* [1926] 2 DLR 166, 170.

[203] *Page v Cowasjee Eduljee*, n. 190 above; *Sawyer v Pringle*, n. 196 above; *McPherson v United States Fidelity and Guarantee Co.*, n. 196 above. These cases establish that an unlawful sale may be tortious without rescinding the contract of sale.

[204] *Halliday v Holgate* (1868) LR 3 Ex. 399. This is probably the best explanation of *Ex p. Stapleton* (1879) 10 Ch. D 586.

meant that he lacked the immediate right to possession necessary to maintain an action in conversion.[205]

Unlawful action by seller.   Suppose, however, that the seller failed to conduct   **11.48**
the sale in a lawful manner, assuming that this required a notice to be first issued to the buyer,[206] or even that the seller unlawfully repossessed the goods prior to resale.[207] The effect of this was that the buyer obtained the right to immediate possession and hence title to sue in conversion. But the buyer who had not paid would not recover the full value of the goods;[208] investing the buyer with such an action merely made doubly certain that a seller suing for a deficiency could not reap a windfall, for it prevented a seller from recovering the price without giving credit for the resale price and for any deposit received from the buyer.[209]

Resale and second buyer.   The cases underlying section 48(3) seem all to have   **11.49**
been decided on the basis of property having passed to and remaining in the buyer,[210] so that section 48(2) became necessary for the protection of the second buyer on the resale. It provides that such a buyer obtains a good title as against the original buyer if the resale occurs after the seller exercises his lien or his right of stoppage in transit. No reference is made to the seller's power of withholding delivery, the counterpart of the unpaid seller's lien where the property has not passed. Furthermore, the index of the seller's real rights in section 39(2), which applies where the property has not passed, does not mention resale; mention of it is, however, made in the index in section 39(1), which applies where the property has passed. In consequence, the seller's power to transmit title where the property remains vested in him is but a feature of the general law of title transfer.[211] Where the property has passed, section 48(2) comes into play to protect the second buyer. Unlike section 24, it imposes no requirements of continuity of possession, good faith, and delivery, which omission buttresses the argument that the seller is exercising a right of resale[212] akin to that of a pledgee.[213]

[205] *Lord v Price* (1874) LR 9 Ex. 54; *Milgate v Kebble* (1841) 3 M & G 100.
[206] *Page v Cowasjee Eduljee*, n. 190 above, 145.
[207] *Ibid.*
[208] See *Chinery v Viall* (1860) 5 H & N 288.
[209] *Page v Cowasjee Eduljee*, n. 190 above; *Stephens v Wilkinson* (1831) 2 B & Ad. 320 (trespass). For the observation that it is curious that a seller repossessing the goods may elect to keep, and not resell, them and also forfeit the buyer's deposit, see *Gallagher v Shilcock* [1949] 2 KB 765.
[210] This seems also to have been true to *Maclean v Dunn*, n. 191 above, though the court makes nothing of it. See *Page v Cowasjee Eduljee*, n. 190 above (though there had been no formal registration of the change of ownership under the relevant shipping legislation).
[211] *Wait v Baker* (1848) 2 Ex. 1; *RV Ward Ltd v Bignall*, n. 194 above.
[212] The modern understanding of resale, treating it as the outcome of a contractual termination revesting the property in the seller, empties s. 48(2) of content.
[213] See s. 21(2)(b) of the Sale of Goods Act 1979.

11.50 **Effect of resale on prior sale.** Section 48(4) still requires explanation. It is based on the decision in *Lamond v Davall*,[214] which proved hard to assimilate into the remainder of the case law and whose legacy was therefore a separate statutory provision. In *Lamond v Davall*, the contract contained an express right of resale[215] and deficiency entitlement if the buyer failed to pay for the subject matter (shares) by a certain date. The court held that the right of resale rendered conditional a sale that, without it, would have been absolute. By invoking the right and reselling the goods, which occurred at a loss, the seller thereby nullified the earlier sale. It followed that the seller could not claim the price on either of the relevant common counts.[216] Besides, the court assumed that allowing the seller to sue for the price would allow him to retain the resale price as a windfall,[217] which was unfair; moreover, the seller might find it inconvenient to be treated as the buyer's agent for resale purposes. But the seller was allowed to maintain an action for damages for the deficiency and the cost of resale. Although section 48(4), supposedly codifying *Lamond v Davall*, speaks of resale under an express power as rescinding the contract, nothing is said in that case about the contract being rescinded *ab initio*. Rescinding the contract *ab initio* would make it difficult to explain the continuing existence of a damages entitlement under an express provision of that contract as the law then stood. The separate existence of sub-section (4) unduly complicates an already difficult area of law; the decision in *Lamond v Davall* could have been folded into sub-section (3).[218]

Modern Rationalization

11.51 **Modern orthodoxy.** Such was the separate evolution of sub-sections (3) and (4) of section 48. Codifying statutes summarize the case law thrown up by the accidents of litigation and do not, unless the product of a severely rational mind, make allowances for gaps in the system to which litigation has not yet responded. The modern contractual orthodoxy of prospective discharge for breach destroyed the

---

214 (1847) 9 QB 1030.

215 The absence of such a clause was said in *Maclean v Dunn*, n. 191 above, not to negative an implied right of resale; the practice of inserting such clauses in East India Company contracts was done *ex abundante cautela*: *ibid.*, 728–9.

216 Goods bargained and sold and goods sold and delivered.

217 Cf *Acebal v Levy*, n. 192 above.

218 The result in the case is quite consistent with *Maclean v Dunn*, n. 191 above, where the court did not have to consider the locus of property. Williston was not happy with s. 48 and the results of this are in the Uniform Sales Act 1906, s. 60. It differs from s. 48 in the following principal respects: (a) it explicitly allows resale in the additional case where the buyer's failure to pay goes on beyond a reasonable time; (b) it states that notice of the resale is not necessary for its validity, though it may be material in determining whether the buyer's delay is unreasonable; (c) it imposes on the seller a duty of reasonable care and judgement in resale (a matter not broached in the English case law); (d) it makes it plain that the seller does not hold any surplus for the buyer; and (e) it makes no mention of rescission and collapses the distinction between the presence and absence of resale clauses. Rescission itself is dealt with in s. 61.

foundation of section 48(3) and (4) and, in *RV Ward Ltd v Bignall*,[219] created the opportunity for statutory revision. That case concerned a claim rising out of an entire contract for the sale of two cars. When the buyer refused to take delivery, the sellers wrote a letter asserting that the property had passed to the buyer, that the buyer was liable to pay the price, and that, furthermore, the sellers would dispose of the cars for the best price they could command and look to the buyer for the deficiency if he failed to pay by a stated date. The deficiency claim was expressed by the sellers as a claim for damages. By the time of the trial, only one of the cars had been sold. The court therefore awarded a large sum as deficiency damages, which included a rateable portion of the sale price for the unsold car, and did not make an order for the disposal of the unsold car. However, applying the principles underlying the pre-codification cases, the judgment was quite consistent with a conclusion that the contract of sale had never been rescinded, that the property in the unsold car remained vested in the buyer, that the sellers had merely exercised a statutory right of sale annexed to their unpaid seller's lien, and that the unsold car would be released to its owner, the buyer, once the judgment debt was paid in full.[220]

Seller acting as owner. But this was not at all the way that the sellers' claim was **11.52** rationalized by the Court of Appeal, whose approach was based on the premise that the resale was conducted by the seller *qua* owner, rather than *qua* creditor with a possessory security and right of sale, and that any revesting of the property in the sellers[221] had to occur on the basis of a contract that had been discharged for the buyer's breach.[222] As Diplock LJ put it: 'Any act which puts it out of his power to perform thereafter his primary obligations under the contract, if it is an act which he is entitled to do without notice to the party in default, must amount to an election to rescind the contract.'[223] Contractual termination operated prospectively[224] but nevertheless effected a divesting of the buyer's property in the goods. This latter proposition, the mechanics of which were not explained, was regarded as self-evident.[225] The particular virtue of treating the resale as consequent upon the termination of the contract was that it protected the seller from the unnecessary complication of an action by the buyer in conversion or for damages in contract

---

[219] n. 194 above.

[220] But see the difficulty the court had in following the argument through the pleadings.

[221] The court concluded that the passing of property rule in s. 18, Rule 1, had been impliedly ousted by the parties but went on to deal with the case on the assumption it applied.

[222] Hence the overruling of *Gallagher v Shilcock*, n. 209 above.

[223] n. 194 above, 548. Note that Diplock LJ brings s. 48(1) into his analysis as showing that the exercise of a lien or a right of stoppage in transit would not necessarily amount to contractual termination.

[224] This approach would extend also to s. 48(4). For the gradual triumph of prospective termination in sale of land cases, see, e.g., *Harold Wood Brick Ltd v Ferris* [1935] WN 21; *Johnson v Agnew* [1980] AC 367 (overruling *Capital and Suburban Properties Ltd v Swycher* [1976] Ch. 319 and *Horsler v Zorro* [1975] Ch. 302).

[225] *Ibid.* 550 ('of course, well-established'). No cases were cited.

for non-delivery of the goods.[226] This was achieved by interpreting section 48(3) as providing that time was of the essence for all sales of perishables, hence the absence of a need to serve notice on the buyer, as well as for any sale where the seller chose to make it so by serving notice on the buyer.[227] The lack of a reference to rescission in section 48(3), when it was mentioned in section 48(4), was explained away as displaying an intention that the exercise of an express contractual right of resale under the latter provision was not to be treated as an act performed by the seller as agent for the buyer.[228]

11.53 **Modern approach to contract termination.**   *RV Ward Ltd v Bignall* imposes the modern view of contractual termination on statutory provisions that were actuated by a different philosophy. Despite the confident tone of Diplock LJ's judgment, the decision represents unconvincing legal history, but it does have three compelling merits. First, it avoids the confusion that would inevitably spring up if the section were applied without a thorough understanding of the outmoded principles on which it was based. Secondly, a seller terminating the contract for the buyer's discharging breach will be able to recover damages in the normal way.[229] The seller will be seeking to recover any shortfall between the original contract price and the price recoverable on a resale. If the market rule for the assessment of damages operates, the seller will in effect have to mitigate his damages by securing the best available resale price. If the resale price itself defines the damages claim, the mitigation rule is introduced in a more overt way. The role of mitigation, though not excluded by the pre-codification cases, was not sanctioned by them either. Thirdly, by introducing contractual discharge, the case avoids the troublesome possibility of the buyer activating the seller's obligation to deliver by tendering the price after the resale. It does, however, leave unexplained quite why, and how, the revesting of property in the seller occurs on prospective contractual discharge.

11.54 **Resolutive condition.**   As a matter of technique, this would clearly have to be done on the basis of an implied resolutive condition, or condition subsequent.[230] If the buyer becomes insolvent before the condition is sprung, this should not of itself prejudice the seller, since the buyer's insolvency representative stands in the buyer's shoes and takes subject to the proprietary claims maintainable against the buyer.[231] So, in a case like *RV Ward Ltd v Bignall*, where the seller remains in

---

[226] n. 194 above, 550.

[227] *Ibid.*, 550.

[228] *Ibid.*, 543, 551

[229] See discussion of damages for non-acceptance in Ch. 12 below.

[230] See *Automatic Fire Sprinklers Pty Ltd v Watson* (1946) 72 CLR 435, 463–4; *Commission Car Sales (Hastings) Ltd v Saul* [1957] NZLR 144. See also *Albright & Wilson UK Ltd v Biachem Ltd* [2001] EWCA Civ 301; [2001] 2 All ER (Comm.) 537 at [28], rejecting the proposition that the property in goods rejected by a buyer revests in the seller by virtue of s. 36 of the Sale of Goods Act.

[231] See Ch. 8 above.

possession, he would be protected against a solvent or an insolvent buyer alike by virtue of his statutory lien and right of resale. These rights would not, however, avail the seller after he delivers the goods to the buyer or delivers them to a carrier and loses his right of stoppage in transit. The silence of the Sale of Goods Act beyond the point when stoppage in transit might be exercised testifies to a statutory intention that the unpaid seller has no further real rights.[232] Applying the modern orthodox approach in *RV Ward Ltd v Bignall*, the parties can be treated as impliedly providing for a revesting of the property in the goods in the seller within the same limits of the draftsman's intention. The Sale of Goods Act contains no provisions dealing with the exercise of an express contractual right of repossession, or with the consequences of terminating a contract under which the property remains in the seller but possession is transferred to the buyer, or with the case where the contract expressly springs a revesting of title in the seller. It is clear that a seller surrenders all real rights to the goods when both property and possession are transferred to the buyer. Nevertheless, the effect of *RV Ward Ltd v Bignall*, which turns the revesting of property in the seller into a matter of implied contractual intention, is to make it difficult to explain why this should not also happen to a seller who has lost both property and possession. If the contract were to contain a provision allowing the seller, in the event of the buyer's breach, to repossess the goods after property and possession have passed to the buyer, or stipulating for a revesting of the property in the seller in that event, such provisions would be treated as registrable bills of sale or charges under the relevant legislation.[233]

Examples or list? One drawback to the interpretation of section 48(3) adopted   **11.55**
by the courts is that it gives no explanation why the sub-section provides only two examples, if they are indeed meant to be examples rather than a *numerus clausus*, of a discharging breach by the buyer. The buyer's failure to accept and pay for the goods may well go to the root of the contract, even in the case of non-perishable goods where the seller has failed to make time of the essence. Again, the buyer's manifest inability to pay may amount to a repudiation of his contractual obligations.[234] Another example is where the contract itself makes time of the essence without requiring the service of notice on the buyer. Section 48(3) cannot therefore, for practical purposes, be seen as an index of the seller's rights to terminate for breach by the buyer, since the general law supports his right to terminate in other instances too.

Nemo dat **exception.** Another point emerging from *RV Ward Ltd v Bignall* con-   **11.56**
cerns the status of section 48(2) as a *nemo dat* exception. It was noted above that

---

[232] Hence a seizure of the goods by the seller will amount to a conversion: *Page v Cowasjee Eduljee*, n. 190 above.

[233] Bills of Sale Acts 1878–91.

[234] But see the discussion of insolvency in the text accompanying nn. 13 *et seq.* above.

the provision was not needed where the property in the goods had never vested in the buyer, for the seller had the power to transmit title in accordance with ordinary property principles. When the property has revested in the seller after a valid termination of the contract, again the seller's power to transmit title is to be justified by ordinary principle rather than by any dispensing power in section 48(2). But the seller may have resold after exercising his lien or right of stoppage in transit, without having complied satisfied section 48(3) in those cases where this provision is needed to effect a valid termination of the contract. The seller, for example, may have failed to issue a notice making time of the essence or may have issued an inadequate notice.[235] Section 48(2), not preconditioned on a valid termination, would empower the seller nevertheless to transmit title to the second buyer. This, of course, leaves unexplained why the seller's power in this instance, which does not depend upon delivery or the buyer's good faith or unbroken possession,[236] should be broader than his section 24 power. The old view that the seller acts rather as a pledgee with a right of sale provides at least a rational explanation of this difference.

Reservation of Title Clauses

11.57 **Surplus.** A final issue arising out of resale concerns reservation of title clauses where the seller repossesses the goods after the buyer defaults on payment of the agreed price. The issue was discussed at some length in *Clough Mill Ltd v Martin*,[237] where Robert Goff LJ considered the case of a contract that remained subsisting notwithstanding the seller's resale of the contract goods for which the buyer had not paid. He did not say how or why the contract might have remained on foot after repossession and resale, and did not refer to section 48 or to *RV Ward Ltd v Bignall*. It is perfectly possible for a resale to be conducted pursuant to an agreement after the breach by buyer and seller, so the case is no authority on the impact of resale on the contract of sale.

11.58 **Significance of termination.** A distinction was drawn by Robert Goff LJ between contracts that had not and contracts that had been terminated before the resale. This was done in order to demonstrate an implied term in the contract in the former case that the seller should account to the buyer for any surplus received from the resale over and above the amount owed by the buyer. This comes close to treating the seller as a pledgee or mortgagee exercising a power of sale over goods belonging to the buyer. The likelihood of any surplus being realized is greater in the case of all moneys clauses than in the case of a clause reserving title only until

---

[235] This assumes that the seller is otherwise entitled to terminate: see discussion in the text accompanying nn. 219 *et seq*. above.
[236] Stoppage in transit effects a resumption of broken possession.
[237] [1985] 1 WLR 111.

payment is made for the contract goods. A surplus would also be perfectly possible if sellers were ever able effectively to reserve title to new goods manufactured by the buyer from materials supplied by the seller together with the buyer's labour and possibly materials supplied by other sellers.[238] In the case of a contract that had been terminated, Robert Goff LJ could see no basis for an implied term surviving termination requiring the seller to account for a surplus.[239] It is difficult to see why termination should produce starkly different results in the two cases, and Robert Goff LJ did refer to the buyer in the case of termination having an action for the recovery of money on a failure of consideration.[240] But a buyer recovering money in such an action would be denied any appreciation in the value of the chattel; a seller having to account for a surplus would be required to surrender any appreciation as part of that surplus.

Enforcing the Primary Obligations of the Parties

General. This section of the chapter is primarily concerned with those personal actions of buyer and seller that require direct performance by the other party of one or more of his primary obligations under the contract, rather than substituted performance in the form of damages. The seller's action for the price will therefore be dealt with; likewise the availability of specific performance and injunctive relief. The latter remedies are usually associated with actions brought by buyers, but, on appropriate facts, they may be sought by sellers too. The real counterpart to a buyer's action for specific performance is a seller's action for specific performance,[241] requiring the buyer to take delivery of the goods, possibly, for example, to take them on an instalment basis as they roll off the seller's assembly line.[242] When the seller sues the buyer in debt, as he does when he sues for the price, the judgment rendered is that the buyer shall pay a liquidated sum of money; it does not, without more ado, compel the buyer to take delivery of the goods or to compensate a seller who is left with the inconvenience of unwanted goods on his hands.[243] That it may be to the buyer's clear economic advantage to accept   **11.59**

---

238 See Ch. 3 above.

239 *Sed quaere* if termination operates prospectively?

240 Discussed in the text accompanying nn. 362 *et seq.* below.

241 Cf. Lord Denning in *Attica Sea Carriers Corpn v Ferrostaal Poseidon Bulk Reederei GmbH (The Puerto Buitrago)* [1976] 1 Lloyd's Rep. 250, 255 (debt claim as specific performance).

242 A seller may have locked his entire output potential into producing custom-built goods for the buyer's unique needs. Specific performance, or equivalent short-term injunctive relief, may be needed to avert irreparable prejudice.

243 To sue in debt for the price, the seller must aver compliance with all conditions precedent, namely, in the majority of cases, the transfer of the property in the goods together with a readiness and willingness to effect delivery of the goods. For specific performance, the seller need only be ready and willing to perform a contract that is open for future performance.

delivery of goods for which he has been made to pay is quite another matter. In addition to the action for the price and specific relief, this section of the chapter will deal with a variety of matters that relate to the primary obligations of the parties and the reinforcement of performance. These include the award of interest by way of damages, along with currency-related matters. The forfeiture of prepaid moneys in the event of the buyer's default will also be considered. In the process, this section of the chapter will at times cross the line that separates primary performance and secondary performance in the form of damages.

The Action for the Price

11.60 **Availability.** The Sale of Goods Act lays down two instances where the seller may sue for the price, namely, where the property has passed to the buyer, and where the contract clearly characterizes the duty to pay as an obligation independent of the date of performance of the seller's primary obligations. The first of these instances is dealt with by section 49(1): 'Where, under a contract of sale, the property in the goods has passed to the buyer and he wrongfully neglects or refuses to pay for the goods according to the terms of the contract, the seller may maintain an action against him for the price of the goods.'

Passing of Property

11.61 **Eligibility to sue for debt.** The first feature to note is that the above entitlement to maintain a debt action against the buyer is limited to cases where the property has passed and does not include cases where the buyer's obligation to pay simply falls due.[244] As seen in an earlier chapter,[245] the buyer is bound to pay when so required under the contract, and this obligation matures, subject to contrary agreement, when the seller is ready and willing to deliver the goods according to the terms of the contract. Yet it is well established that the mere tender of delivery does not entitle the seller to sue for the price.[246] A further point is that a seller's entitlement to sue for the price depends upon his continuing to be ready and able to deliver the goods to the buyer, so that a seller disposing of the goods must instead mount an action for damages for non-acceptance against a defaulting buyer.[247] Over and above the debt claim, however, there may be an additional damages claim for injury flowing from delayed performance,[248] and this will be subject to the normal remoteness rules.

---

[244] Ss. 27–28.

[245] See Ch. 6 above.

[246] *Colley v Overseas Exporters* [1921] 3 KB 302.

[247] *Maclean v Dunn* (1828) 4 Bing. 722; *Otis Vehicle Rentals Ltd v Cicely Commercials Ltd* [2002] EWCA Civ 1064 at [16].

[248] *Wadsworth v Lydall* [1981] 1 WLR 598; *International Minerals & Chemical Corpn v Karl O Hahn AG* [1986] 1 Lloyd's Rep. 80.

Common counts. The essence of a debt action is that the debtor has actually **11.62** received a *quid pro quo*, an executed consideration,[249] and therefore must account for the debt to his creditor. Before the abolition of the forms of action, the appropriate liquidated money counts were goods bargained and sold and goods sold and delivered, under both of which counts the property had to have passed.[250] These two counts were simplified forms of pleading *indebitatus assumpsit*, which was predicated on a fictitious promise to pay an antecedent debt, and the difficulty of reconciling the buyer's contractual duty to pay with the seller's entitlement to sue in debt may be seen as evidence of the imperfect amalgamation of special *assumpsit* and debt in the modern law of contract.

Merits of debt action. Thus stated, the seller's entitlement to recover the price **11.63** appears to be a technical matter. A disappointing aspect of the case law is that there is no discussion of the merits of permitting sellers to sue in debt rather than for damages. It cannot therefore be said that the present position is explained by a keen judicial or legislative sense of the circumstances where sellers should be afforded the procedural[251] and other advantages of suing in debt.[252] Besides the commercial advantages referred to below, a seller suing in debt for the price will not be constrained by the remoteness of damage rules. Certain speculative losses, hard to prove in a damages action, will lie concealed in a debt claim. In principle, the seller suing for the price will not have to mitigate his damages, since mitigation limits the defendant's secondary obligation to pay damages rather than his primary obligation to pay the price. Debt is not a discretionary remedy[253] and so is not governed by the principles that might apply if the seller were seeking specific performance of the contract. Nevertheless, the Court of Appeal has left open the question whether the right to sue for the price under section 49(2) should be qualified by an equitable discretion.[254] It is not clear whether this position is actuated by particular concerns over section 49(2) or whether the uncertainty thus introduced colours also claims for the price under section 49(1). It is not clear too whether the introduction of an equitable discretion will bring about a fundamental reconsideration of the merits of pursuing a debt claim. This is unlikely.

---

[249] *Martin v Hogan* (1917) 24 CLR 234, 262 (the consideration does not pass until the property passes in sale of goods).

[250] *Atkinson v Bell* (1828) 8 B & C 277; *Colley v Overseas Exporters*, n. 246 above.

[251] For the summary judgment process, see CPR Part 24.

[252] On the distinction between debt and damages claims, see *Jervis v Harris* [1996] Ch 195, 202–3. The rules on remoteness of damage, mitigation and penalties do not apply to debt actions: *ibid*. This makes it easier to obtain summary judgment.

[253] *White & Carter (Councils) Ltd v McGregor* [1962] AC 413, 445 (Lord Hodson).

[254] *Otis Vehicle Rentals Ltd v Cicely Commercials Ltd*, n. 247 above at [17] ('unnecessary to enter upon the difficult territory required to be explored'). Lord Reid's 'legitimate interest' qualification upon the pursuers' debt claim in *White & Carter (Councils) Ltd v McGregor*, n. 253 above, may yet have implications for s. 49(1) and (2).

Equitable discretion may deprive a seller of a right to recover the price where the language of the Sale of Goods Act might otherwise permit it, but it cannot create an entitlement to recover the price if the Act gives the seller no legislative support.

11.64   Responsibility for unwanted goods.   The most important practical issue posed by the debt action is which of the two parties, seller or buyer, should be the one who is left to dispose of unwanted goods.[255] It has also been said to be economically wasteful to force unwanted goods on a buyer,[256] but, if goods may be consumed by the buyer or disposed of in the market without undue difficulty, there should not be any waste. Moreover, if the goods are custom-built for the buyer's needs, greater economic waste is likely to arise if they are left in the seller's hands, good only for their break-up value or for expensive alterations to suit another buyer. It should not be forgotten, moreover, that the buyer is amenable to a price action only if he 'wrongfully' withholds payment,[257] and the merits of a seller who is willing to perform and is faced with a contract-breaking buyer ought not to be overlooked.[258] In some cases, it may be difficult indeed for sellers to prove they have actually incurred a loss because of the buyer's breach.[259] Just as difficulties of assessment can be avoided by securing a deposit to be forfeited on breach, or by inserting in the contract a liquidated damages clause, so the right to sue for the price can obviate an intractable damages inquiry. It is not enough simply to ask which party is better able to dispose of the goods if the above considerations are ignored. For one thing, there may be many cases where a buyer can make grudging use of the contract goods. Not every repudiating buyer will be unable to use raw materials for widget-making because he has quit the widget-making business, or be unable to use the seller's widget-making machines because he has filled his factory with someone else's machines. Furthermore, in many instances involving carriage of the goods to a distant place, requiring the seller to dispose of the goods could be unfairly onerous. Without denying the importance of having the law respond to practical issues, it should never be forgotten that commercial certainty is itself one of those issues. There is a great deal to be said for a rule that states precisely when a seller is entitled to sue for the price, especially if the goods are of volatile value or quickly depreciate, just as a regime of strict rejection of non-conforming goods and contractual termination has its commercial attractions. Whether the

---

[255] Ontario Law Reform Commission, *Report on Sale of Goods* (1979), ii, 416.

[256] *Ibid.*

[257] S. 49(1).

[258] Alberta Institute of Law Research and Reform, *The Uniform Sale of Goods Act* (Report No. 38, 1982), 108.

[259] See the lost volume problem, discussed in Ch. 12 below. A liquidated damages clause may close the indemnity gap between remoteness of damage and factual causation. Diplock LJ said in *Robophone Facilities Ltd v Blank* [1966] 1 WLR 1428, 1448, that it constituted disclosure under the second limb of the rule in *Hadley v Baxendale* (1854) 9 Ex. 341.

relatively precise rule that we currently have is located in the right place, however, is a different matter.

Buyer's cooperation. An important issue arising under section 49(1) of the Sale   **11.65** of Goods Act[260] concerns the seller who is prevented by the buyer, acting in breach of contract, from passing the property in the goods and thus fulfilling the precondition to the price action. The question is whether the precondition can be deemed to be fulfilled in consequence of the buyer's default. The provision was considered at some length in *Colley v Overseas Exporters*,[261] where buyers and sellers were both Sheffield merchants. The contract was for the sale of a quantity of belts on f.o.b. Liverpool terms. It was therefore the sellers' responsibility to get the goods to a ship in Liverpool nominated by the buyers. The ship originally nominated by the buyers was withdrawn by its owners from service, and, despite repeated efforts, the buyers were unable to nominate another ship. Meanwhile, the goods were packed for export and sent by the sellers to Liverpool, where they arrived at the offices of the forwarding agents. At this point, the sellers were faced with an uncertain quantum of future consequential damages,[262] for items such as the cost of consigning goods to a different market, possibly with some repacking, or the cost of keeping the goods in storage until another buyer turned up. The sellers instead took out a specially indorsed writ leading to summary judgment for a liquidated amount, arguing that the buyers' failure to nominate estopped[263] them from denying that the price was due. This argument was rejected by McCardie J, who held that the property would not pass until the goods were put on board[264] and that no principle of law could be invoked to deem that a necessary condition had been fulfilled when in fact it had not been.[265] If the failure of the sellers to

---

[260] For the difficulties in applying this provision to those c.i.f. contracts where the goods are released into the buyer's hands before the documentary exchange, see *Trafigura Beheer BV v BCL Trading GmbH* [2002] EWCA Civ 251 at [31].

[261] n. 246 above. A case difficult to reconcile with an orthodox interpretation of s. 49(1) is *Minister for Supply and Development v Servicemen's Co-operative Joinery Manufacturers Ltd* (1951) 82 CLR 621.

[262] Discussed in Ch. 12 below.

[263] This claim failed *in limine*: n. 246 above, 311: 'Estoppel is a vague word. It is often used to support a submission not capable of precise juristic formulation.'

[264] See Ch. 3 above. If the seller reserves the right of disposal, this is treated as preventing the property from passing. See, e.g., *Stein Forbes & Co. v County Tailoring Co.* (1916) 86 LJKB 448. Atkin J, at 448–9, doubted the unconditional appropriation of goods to the contract where the right of disposal is reserved. Cf. *Napier v Dexters Ltd* (1926) 26 Ll. LR 62, 63–4, where Roche J says that, since the right of disposal is unilateral, the seller may waive it and sue for the price.

[265] Distinguishing *Mackay v Dick* (1881) 6 App. Cas. 251 on the ground that it concerned a resolutive condition (or condition subsequent), namely, the failure of a machine to pass a test, and that the buyer's failure to cooperate meant that no test, and therefore no divesting of the property that had already passed to the buyer, could take place. While a discharging breach classically waives the injured party's readiness and willingness to perform for a damages action, it does not have this effect on a debt action. See *Jones v Barkley* (1781) 2 Dougl. 684; *Laird v Pim* (1846) 7 M & W 474. For a discussion of *Mackay v Dick*, implied obligations of cooperation and the deeming of conditions

comply with all necessary conditions were excused in this case, a seller could sue in debt in all cases where the buyer repudiated,[266] even if the goods were unascertained at the material time.[267] It might also be added that the passing of property is a consensual matter and that the seller cannot put the property on an unwilling buyer.[268]

11.66 'Wrongful' failure to pay.   Although the property may have passed, the buyer may, as stated above, be sued for the price only if his refusal to pay is 'wrongful'. A buyer lawfully rejecting goods, and thereby revesting them in the seller, is not wrongfully refusing to pay.[269] Further, if goods are sold on a 'to arrive' basis and fail to arrive, the seller may not recover the price even if the property has passed.[270] Again, if credit has been extended to the buyer and the period has not yet elapsed, the seller's right to sue for the price will be suspended until the debt falls due. If the seller accepts a bill drawn on a third party as final payment, he may not sue the buyer in debt if that third party defaults.[271] Finally, the meaning of 'wrongfully' should be understood in the context of risk too.[272] If property has passed to the buyer but the risk remains on the seller, it is submitted that the seller will clearly be unable to sue for the price since the concept of risk is to be understood as qualifying the circumstances in which a suit for the price will be allowed.[273] Conversely, where the property remains in the seller but the risk is on the buyer, the seller should be allowed to sue for the price on the theory of all necessary conditions, including the passing of property, being deemed to have been complied with prior to the bringing of the action.[274]

---

to be fulfilled, see *Cie Noga d'Importation et d'Exportation SA v Abacha (No. 3)* [2002] EWCA Civ 1142; [2003] 1 WLR 307 at [94]–[108] (Rix LJ).

[266] A repudiation by one party does not permit the other 'to enforce the contract on the notional footing that he has performed his part of the contract': *Foran v Wight* (1989) 64 ALJR 1, 6 (Mason CJ), citing *Laird v Pim*, n. 265 above.

[267] An f.o.b. seller will commonly reserve the right of disposal, in which case the property will not pass on shipment (see Ch. 3 above) and the seller will not be able to sue for the price. Such a seller, however, will be in a position to claim the price from a bank issuing or confirming a letter of credit as the means of effecting payment.

[268] See Ch. 3 above.

[269] *Vidal v Wm Robinson & Co.* [1952] 1 DLR 1001.

[270] *Calcutta and Burmah Steam Navigation Co. v De Mattos* (1863) 30 LJQB 322.

[271] *Harrison v Luke* (1845) 14 M & W 139.

[272] S. 20.

[273] See Ch. 4 above. On the seller being able to sue for the price where the risk is on the buyer because the property has passed before delivery, see *Habton Farms v Nimmo* [2003] EWCA Civ 68; [2004] QB 1 at [72].

[274] *Alexander v Gardner* (1835) 1 Bing. NC 671; *Castle v Playford* (1872) LR 7 Ex. 98.

Payment on a 'Day Certain'

Separation of delivery and payment.   The other instance where the Sale of   **11.67**
Goods Act explicitly allows an action for the price is to be found in section
49(2):

> Where, under a contract of sale, the price is payable on a day certain irrespective of
> delivery and the buyer wrongfully neglects or refuses to pay such price, the seller may
> maintain an action for the price, although the property in the goods has not passed
> and the goods have not been appropriated to the contract.

The genesis of this provision is Rule 1 of Serjeant Williams's notes to *Pordage v
Cole*.[275] Under section 49(2), in essence, the dependency between the seller's duty
to deliver and the buyer's duty to pay the price, presumptively established by section 28, is severed by the terms of the contract itself. The buyer's duty to pay is
consequently 'irrespective of delivery'[276] and the seller's right to call upon the
buyer to pay the price matures on the date that payment falls due. That date must
be one that is fixed, 'a day certain',[277] for the contract itself would not otherwise
provide a precise standard for determining the maturity of the duty to pay. There
is no need on the face of section 49(2) for a seller to establish that the buyer's duty
to pay is a condition precedent to his own duty to deliver; it is enough that the
duties of payment and delivery are independent of each other. On one view of
section 49(2), the seller need not even show readiness and willingness to deliver
the goods in order to recover the price, for the provision reflects an archaic procedural law under which an aggrieved buyer would have to submit to the price
action and bring a separate cross-action against the seller for non-delivery.[278] The
better view, in modern conditions, is that it would be a defence to the seller's
action for the price if the buyer could establish that the seller is no longer ready
and willing to deliver.[279] Section 49(2) harks back to a time predating the modern
law of breach of contract[280] and, taken with the debt provision in section 49(1),
reveals an antique mixture of debt and seventeenth-century *assumpsit* from a
time predating the statues of set-off.[281] In sum, section 49, taken as a whole, does
not even begin to respond to any of the practical considerations that might be

---

[275] (1669) 1 Wms. Saund. 319 (appointing a day for payment independently of performance by
the payee).

[276] *Muller Maclean & Co. v Leslie and Anderson* [1921] WN 235, decided under s. 49(2), held that
payment against documents was not 'irrespective of delivery' under the terms of that subsection.

[277] *Martin v Hogan* (1917) 24 CLR 234, 261 (a day fixed at the contract date and not left to be
ascertained later).

[278] e.g., *Nichols v Raynbred* (1615) Hob. 88.

[279] *Maclean v Dunn*, n. 191 above; *Otis Vehicle Rentals Ltd v Cicely Commercials Ltd* [2002]
EWCA Civ 1064 at [16].

[280] M. Bridge (1983) 28 *McGill LJ* 867, 873–5.

[281] 2 Geo II c. 22 (1729), s. 13; 8 Geo II c. 24 (1735), ss. 4–5.

examined to discover whether a claimant seller's remedy is more appropriately debt than damages.

11.68 **Application of rule.** An examination of the case law does not throw very much light on the matter. In *Dunlop v Grote*,[282] a contract for the sale of a quantity of iron provided that, if the buyer did call for the iron 'on or before the 30th day of April, 1845, the said iron was to be paid for [on that date]'. The seller was entitled to recover the price once that date arrived because it was a day certain and payment on that date bore no relation to delivery.[283] A number of difficult cases have claims to be included in section 49(2) or possibly in a common law extension to it.[284] In *Workman Clark & Co. v Lloyd Brazileño*,[285] a shipbuilding contract[286] provided that the first instalment fell due once the ship reached a particular stage in its construction; naturally, this was not expressed to occur on a day certain. If the buyers failed to pay at this stage, one of the avenues open to the sellers was the suspension of future work under the contract until payment was made. The court held that the sellers could sue the buyers for a liquidated sum under the summary judgments procedure. Had this been a severable contract for the supply of goods in instalments, the contract could easily have been structured to provide for a debt action under either sub-section (1) or (2) of section 49. The buyers' duty to pay, nevertheless, could without difficulty be reconciled with the language of Serjeant Williams's first rule. *Dunlop v Grote*[287] was only one example of that rule, but it was the one codified in 1893. Another case clearly within the letter of Serjeant Williams's first rule but not the letter of section 49(2) is *Minister for Supply and Development v Servicemen's Co-operative Joinery Manufacturers Ltd*,[288] where a contract for the sale of specific machinery provided that the property was not to pass before delivery[289] but that payment was to be 'net cash before delivery'. Payment, therefore, was irrespective of, indeed antecedent to, delivery, and was not to occur on a day certain. Indeed, it was not easy to say when exactly the buyers had to pay, but the Australian High Court held that the buyers came under a duty to pay within a reasonable time.[290] A failure to pay at that time gave rise to

---

[282] (1845) 2 Car. & K 153.

[283] For a case where, on the construction of a buy-back contract, the buyer's duty to pay was not irrespective of delivery, see *Otis Vehicle Rentals Ltd v Cicely Commercials Ltd* [2002] EWCA Civ 1064.

[284] Under s. 62(2).

[285] [1908] 1 KB 968.

[286] The court did not actually say that it was governed by the Sale of Goods Act.

[287] n. 282 above.

[288] (1951) 82 CLR 621.

[289] Hence s. 49(1) did not apply.

[290] n. 288 above, 642.

a debt, so that the sellers were able to sue for the price without averring that delivery had been made.[291]

Failure to take up shipping documents. In a number of decisions, resistance **11.69** has met the attempts of sellers to sue for the price in documentary sales where the buyer has refused to take up the documents. In *Stein, Forbes & Co. v County Tailoring Co.*,[292] a contract for the sale of a large quantity of dressed sheepskins called for payment 'net cash against documents on arrival of the steamer'. Atkin J held that the seller could not recover the price when the buyer refused the documents. Clearly, the price was not payable on a day certain, and so the case did not fall within section 49(2). Moreover, payment was not to occur irrespective of delivery,[293] and so could not fall within any common law extension of section 49(2) inspired by Serjeant Williams's first rule.

Reform Proposals

Overseas reform. The cases decided under section 49(2) or its common law **11.70** extension, considered as a whole, do not establish a rational and satisfactory line between debt and damages. This matter has not been considered by the Law Commission of this country but it has been reviewed overseas. Although its solution turned upon only one issue—that of who was best able to dispose of unwanted goods—the Ontario Law Reform Commission did look at the substance of the problem. It recommended that an entitlement to recover the price should turn upon the buyer's acceptance of the goods,[294] a test that suffers from being both unduly protracted (and hence unfair to the seller) and unnecessarily vague.[295] The Canadian Uniform Sale of Goods Committee preferred a test that was both easy to administer and established a balance between buyers' and sellers' interests. It preferred delivery as the event permitting a seller to sue for the price.[296] In the majority of cases currently governed by section 49, the same result as to price entitlement would be reached through the medium of the passing of property rules,[297] so the actual legal position would change very little in the event of such a reform.

---

[291] See, however, *Shell-Mex Ltd v Elton Cop Dyeing Co.* (1928) 34 Com. Cas. 39, where the court declined to read the following clause as entitling the seller to recover the price irrespective of delivery: 'Sellers have the right at any time to invoice the buyers the due quantities of oil not taken up and to demand payment of the invoice amounts, and such quantities . . . shall be at buyers' risk and expense.' Wright J, 44, read 'invoice' as 'invoice and deliver'.

[292] (1916) 86 LJKB 448.

[293] See also *Muller, Maclean & Co. v Leslie and Anderson*, n. 276 above; *Martin v Hogan*, n. 277 above.

[294] *Report on Sale of Goods* (1979), ii, 415–18.

[295] Alberta Institute of Law Research and Reform, *The Uniform Sale of Goods Act* (Report No. 38, 1982), 108.

[296] Uniform Sale of Goods Act, s. 106(1)(a), (4).

[297] See Ch. 3 above.

This approach, at least, would be more overtly responsive to the practical issues mentioned above and is therefore to be welcomed.

Interest and Foreign Currency

11.71 **General.** The next question is whether a seller entitled to sue for the price may also recover interest from the buyer for delay in making payment. The same issue presents itself where the buyer rejects the goods and terminates the contract, seeking the return of the price paid. Any entitlement of the seller and buyer that does exist is preserved by section 54, which provides that '[n]othing in this Act affects the right of the buyer and the seller to recover interest . . . in any case where by law interest . . . may be recoverable'. Section 54 therefore does not create any right to interest. Until recently, the common law was unreceptive to claims for interest on unpaid sums in the absence of provision for this in the contract, which necessitated statutory intervention. These statutory provisions, allowing for simple and not compound interest in designated cases, will first be examined before attention is turned to the common law position.

11.72 **Statutory recovery of simple interest.** Since 1982,[298] it has been possible in the High Court[299] to recover simple interest,[300] once proceedings have begun, dating back from the time that the cause of action arose. Where payment of a debt is made late but before the commencement of proceedings, the legislation does not permit the award of interest.[301]According to s. 35A(1) of the Supreme Court Act 1981:

> Subject to rules of court, in proceedings (whenever instituted) before the High Court for the recovery of a debt or damages there may be included in any sum for which judgment is given simple interest, at such rate as the court thinks fit or as rules of

---

[298] S. 35A of the Supreme Court Act 1981 (as added by the Administration of Justice Act 1982 (s. 15 and Sch. 1)). For the recommendations of the Law Commission preceding this statutory change, see *Report on Interest* 1978 (Law Com. No. 88). Preceding legislation, s. 3 of the Law Reform (Miscellaneous Provisons) Act 1934, remains in force for courts of record other than the High Court and County Court. On s. 3, see *Bacon v Cooper (Metals) Ltd* [1982] 1 All ER 397, 402. S. 3 permits interest to be awarded only on sums for which a court is giving judgment and not for the late payment as such of a debt. With certain exceptions, it provides: 'In any proceedings tried in any court of record for the recovery of any debt or damages, the court may, if it thinks fit, order that there shall be included in the sum for which judgment is given interest at such rate as it thinks fit on the whole or any part of the debt or damages for the whole or any part of the period between the date when the cause of action arose and the date of the judgment. . . .'.

[299] For the County Court, see County Courts Act 1984, s. 69. An arbitral tribunal has a discretionary power under s. 49 of the Arbitration Act 1995 to award damages for late payment to the extent that justice requires. Such damages may include a compound interest element and may apply in respect of a period predating the arbitral reference.

[300] Not compound interest: *Westdeutsche Landesbank Girozentrale v Islington LBC* [1996] AC 669.

[301] *IM Properties Plc v Cape & Dalgleish* [1999] QB 297 (interpreting s. 35A in its 'historical context' as related by Lord Brandon in *President of India v La Pintada Cia Navigacion SA* [1985] AC 104, 113, and declining to follow *Westdeutsche Landesbank Girozentrale v Islington LBC*, n. 300 above (where no argument was addressed to the court on the power to award simple interest under s. 35A) so far as it might have stated otherwise).

court may provide, on all or any part of the debt or damages in respect of which judgment is given, or payment is made before judgment, for all or any part of the period between the date when the cause of action arose and—

(a) in the case of any sum paid before judgment, the date of the payment; and

(b) in the case of the sum for which judgment is given, the date of the judgment.

Section 35A(3), which applies only to debt proceedings, further provides for interest assessed in the same way and subject to the same discretion, where the defendant pays the whole of the sum claimed otherwise than pursuant to a judgment of the court. The court has power to award interest on all or any part of the amount claimed, and at different rates for different periods,[302] which gives it therefore a broad discretion.[303] That discretion will be exercised so as to prevent, for example, double recovery. A claimant seller seeking interest on the price due from a buyer should therefore be disallowed interest to the extent the seller continues to derive benefits from the goods while they remain in its possession.[304]

Late payment of commercial debts.   In addition to section 35A, but more limited in its coverage, is the Late Payment of Commercial Debts (Interest) Act 1998, an unnecessarily cumbersome piece of legislation.[305] The recoverability of simple interest is dependent upon a statutory implied term[306] in contracts for the supply of goods or services.[307] Contract terms are void so far as they purport to exclude the right to statutory interest for non-payment of a debt, except where there is a 'substantial contractual remedy for late payment',[308] a form of words that on its face invites litigation to test its limits. The prospect of such a process, however, is diminished by what appears to be a statutory presumption that a 'contractual remedy'[309] is substantial, placing on the claimant the burden of showing that the remedy is not substantial. The Act provides that a remedy is substantial[310] unless it is shown to be insufficient in compensating the supplier or in deterring late

11.73

---

[302] S. 35A(6).

[303] Rules of court are permitted under s. 35A fixing the rate of interest by reference to the rate specified for judgment debts: s. 35A(5). For rules of court dealing with claims for interest, see CPR Part 12 r. 6 (default judgments); CPR Part 16 r. 4(2) (pleading a claim for interest).

[304] See *Janred Properties Ltd v Ente Nazionale Italiano per il Turismo* [1989] 2 All ER 444, 457.

[305] As amended by the Late Payment of Commercial Debts Regulations 2002, SI 2002 No. 1674.

[306] S. 1(1).

[307] S. 2(1). A contract for the supply of goods or services includes a contract for the sale of goods as defined in the Sale of Goods Act: s. 2(2)(a), (7). The Act excludes contracts 'intended to operate by way of mortgage, pledge, charge or other security'. This formula would therefore not exclude conditional sales.

[308] S. 8(1).

[309] Defined as 'a contractual right to interest or any contractual right other than interest': s. 10(1).

[310] The court may look at all the circumstances of the case at the contract date: s. 9(2).

payment, and it would not be fair and reasonable to allow the contractual remedy to oust the right to statutory interest.[311] Fairness and reasonableness turn upon the benefits of commercial certainty, the relative strength of the parties' bargaining power, whether the term was imposed by one party to the detriment of the other, and whether the supplier received an inducement to agree to the term.[312] Where such a substantial remedy exists, it is deemed to exclude the right to statutory interest unless the contract otherwise provides.[313] A variation in the contract of the right to statutory interest must also pass the test of a substantial remedy.[314] So far as the contractual remedy fails to amount to a substantial remedy, it is void[315] and is therefore displaced by the right to statutory interest. Nevertheless, the residual freedom of the parties to vary the statute when dealing with 'the consequences of late payment'[316] points to the absence of statutory controls when the parties are negotiating a settlement, whether formal or informal. This is confirmed by a further provision confirming that the parties are free to agree terms dealing with a debt after it has been created.[317]

11.74 **Qualifying debts.** For statutory interest to be awarded, the debt has to be a 'qualifying debt', which means that it must not already carry interest under another statute or that a right to demand interest existing under any rule of law has been exercised.[318] The power of a court or arbitrator to award interest on a sum claimed otherwise than under the statute does not prevent the award of statutory interest.[319] The availability of interest under section 35A of the Supreme Court Act or under the Arbitration Act does not therefore preclude interest being awarded under the Late Payment of Commercial Debts (Interest) Act 1998. In the case of a right to demand interest under a rule of law, the recent relaxation in the award of interest at common law may cause some difficulty. It is not the award of interest at common law that excludes statutory interest but the demand. It is submitted, nevertheless, that the making of a claim for interest in the particulars of the case[320] does not thereby exclude an award of interest under the 1998 Act as long as the source of entitlement is unstated. Moreover, as regards a claimant who puts his case in the alternative in both common law and statutory terms, it should be said that a 'right to demand interest on a debt' is not being exercised if in the circumstances of the case the amount claimed is too remote. A right to demand

---

[311] S. 9(1).
[312] S. 9(3).
[313] S. 8(2).
[314] S. 8(3) (or the 'overall remedy for late payment', the meaning of which is unclear).
[315] S. 8(4) (unless the overall remedy for late payment is a substantial remedy).
[316] S. 8(5).
[317] S. 7(2)
[318] S. 3.
[319] S. 3(2).
[320] CPR Part 16 r. 4(2).

interest should be interpreted as more than just a right to claim it but should instead be interpreted as a right both to claim and recover it.

Rate and term of interest. The rate of interest for qualifying debts is set by regu- **11.75**
lations made by the Secretary of State,[321] who is guided in the exercise of his rule-making power by the need to protect suppliers whose financial position makes them 'particularly vulnerable' when late payment is made and to deter generally late payment.[322] The rate of interest must be remitted if, by reason of the supplier's conduct before or after the debt is created, the interests of justice require it to be remitted.[323] There is also a requirement to pay an additional fixed sum once interest begins to run.[324] The period for which interest runs starts on the first day after the due date of payment of the debt, as agreed in the contract of supply.[325] If the contract makes no provision for the due date of payment, then interest runs from the first day after the expiry of a thirty-day period beginning with the date the supplier performed his obligation or the date the purchaser is notifed of the amount of the debt, whichever is the later.[326] Interest ceases to run when it would cease to run if it were carried under an express contract term.[327] The meaning of this testing provision is far from clear since it requires a comparison to be made between the statutory implied term and a conjectural express term whose content by definition is non-existent. The most likely possibility is that interest should run in the conventional way until payment of the debt and accrued interest is made, though it would have been easier to say so in so many words. The substantial measure of discretion given to the courts in awarding interest, nevertheless, would seem to lessen the importance of this unclear provision. As with the rate of interest and on similar terms, the court has power to remit the award of interest for the whole or part of the period during which the interest runs.[328] Finally, any contractual provision which 'purports to have the effect of postponing the time at which a qualifying debt would otherwise be created' is subject to the Unfair Contract

---

[321] S. 6(1). The rate is the official dealing rate plus 8%: Late Payment of Commercial Debts (Rate of Interest) (No. 3) Order 2002, SI 2002 No. 1675, art. 4. The official dealing rate is the rate announced from time to time by the Monetary Policy Committee of the Bank of England: *ibid.*, art. 3.

[322] S. 6(2).

[323] S. 6(3), (4).

[324] S. 5A (added by SI 2002 No. 1674). The amount is £40 for a debt of less than £1,000, £70 for debts between £1,000 and £9,999, and £100 for debts in excess of £10,000.

[325] S. 4(2), (3). The date may be fixed or determinable by an event: s. 4(3) (e.g., ten days after the goods are delivered). Special provision is made in s. 11 for the case of obligations to make an 'advance payment', which arise when payment has to be made before the supplier's performance. In such cases, interest begins to run on the day after the supplier has performed because the date of performance is deemed to be the date the debt arising from the advance payment is created.

[326] S. 4(5).

[327] S. 4(7).

[328] S. 5(1), (2), (4).

Terms Act 1977 and is treated as the rendering of a contractual performance different from what was reasonably expected.[329]

11.76 **Common law position.** At common law, the rule was that damages could not be awarded for a failure to pay a sum of money; a claim for interest was seen as tantamount to such a damages claim.[330] This prohibition survived the general application of the remoteness of damage rule to limit recovery in contract cases.[331] Interest was, however, recoverable if the contract made provision for it.[332] Numerous other special instances of interest entitlement existed.[333] In the words of Lord Mance: 'The attitude of English law to interest has been inhibited and undistinguished.'[334] The general prohibition on the recovery of interest as damages for non-payment gave way, in exceptional cases, to awards where a claimant kept out of his money might recover as damages the interest he had to pay a third party in consequence of non-payment.[335] The anomaly to which this development gave rise stemmed from its being seen as corresponding to cases of recovery under the second limb of the rule in *Hadley v Baxendale*,[336] when the general rule of prohibition prevented recovery under the first limb. Consequently, losses generally foreseeable without disclosure and flowing from the non-payment of money did not

---

[329] S. 14, incorporating a reference to s. 3(2) of the Unfair Contract Terms Act 1977. The case of rendering no contractual performance at all in s. 3(2) does not seem to be capable of application in cases of this kind. In addition, s. 3(2) is expanded by s. 14 of the 1998 Act to catch contracts where the parties do *not* do business on the standard terms of one of them.

[330] *London, Chatham and Dover Railway Co. v South Eastern Railway Co.* [1893] AC 429; *Page v Newman* (1829) 9 B & C 378. This position has been confirmed in modern times by the House of Lords: *President of India v La Pintada Cia Navegacion SA* [1985] AC 104.

[331] *Sempra Metals Ltd v Inland Revenue Commissioners* [2007] UKHL 34; [2008] 1 AC 561 at [74]:

> [A]s a general rule a claimant can recover damages for losses caused by a breach of contract or a tort which satisfy the usual remoteness tests. This broad common law principle is subject to an anomalous, that is, unprincipled, exception regarding one particular type of loss arising in respect of one particular type of claim. The exception comprises claims for interest losses by way of damages for breach of a contract to pay a debt. The general common law principle does not apply to such claims. Damages are not recoverable in cases falling within this exception (Lord Nicholls).

[332] *Higgins v Sargent* (1823) 2 B & C 348.

[333] e.g., in Admiralty proceedings (*Tehno-Impex v Gebr. van Weelde Scheepvartkantor BV* [1981] 2 All ER 669) and in equity (*Brown v IRC* [1965] AC 244; *Wallersteiner v Moir (No. 2)* [1975] QB 373; *O'Sullivan v Management Agency & Music Ltd* [1985] QB 429).

[334] *Sempra Metals Ltd v Inland Revenue Commissioners*, n. 331 above at [205].

[335] *Wadsworth v Lydall* [1981] 1 WLR 598 (second limb of the rule in *Hadley v Baxendale*, n. 259 above, discussed below); *Trans Trust SPRL v Danubian Trading Co. Ltd* [1952] 2 QB 297, 306; *President of India*, n. 301 above, at 127. Cf *Cia Financiera Soleada SA v Hamoor Tanker Corpn Inc. (The Borag)* [1981] 1 WLR 274 (cost of high interest charges, arising from a guarantee necessitated by the defendant's breach of contract, on claimant's already overdrawn account not recoverable as damages).

[336] n. 259 above. It was expressed in this way by Lord Brandon in *President of India v La Pintada Cia Navegacion SA*, n. 301 above at 424. For a criticism of this approach, see *Sempra Metals Ltd v Inland Revenue Commissioners*, n. 331 above at [85]–[89] and [215]. For further discussion, see *International Minerals and Chemical Corpn v Karl O. Helm AG* [1986] 1 Lloyd's Rep. 81, 103–4.

give rise to a claim for interest by way of damages when less likely losses, if proper disclosure were made, did.[337] The House of Lords in *Sempra Metals Ltd v Inland Revenue Commissioners*,[338] in a case dealing with a restitutionary action for money paid under a mistake a law,[339] made it unequivocally clear that the old common law prohibition no longer prevented an award of general damages in contract cases under the first limb of the rule in *Hadley v Baxendale*. So far as the old rule survived, it was only those cases where a claim for damages for non-payment of money was 'unparticularised and unproven'.[340] In other cases, subject to the remoteness rule and the rule of mitigation of damages, damages could be awarded that would repair the losses flowing from non-payment. An award could therefore include a compound interest element, whether this derived from the amount that the payee had to borrow to bridge the gap before recovering the moneys owed or the loss of an investment opportunity for moneys not timeously received.[341] Lord Mance had nevertheless words of caution for those who might underestimate the difficulties of satisfying the remoteness rule in a conventional case of non-payment: 'The present case should not therefore be seen as a charter for claims, still less for claims on a compound basis, in respect of interest losses following a breach of contract, where there is no contractual stipulation for its recovery, simply because it can be said that the situation was one where loss of interest might foreseeably, and did in fact, follow on breach.'[342] Despite the common law advantage of compound interest, it cannot be supposed that the statutory provisions discussed above have been overtaken and rendered otiose by the *Sempra Metals* case.

Damages for currency losses.   Since inflation and currency devaluation are **11.77** different sides of the monetary depreciation coin, a claimant may also suffer a

---

[337] For a criticism of the illogicality of claiming interest as special damages when it could not be claimed as general damages at common law, see *President of India v Lips Maritime Corpn* [1985] 2 Lloyd's Rep. 180, 185; *Hungerfords v Walker* (1989) 171 CLR 125, 142; *Sempra Metals Ltd v Inland Revenue Commissioners*, n. 323 above at [6], [87], [165].

[338] n. 331 above.

[339] There were differences as to whether the award of compound interest derived from the common law's restitutionary jurisdiction (Lords Hope, Nicholls and Scott) or equity's equitable jurisdiction (Lords Walker and Mance). More important was the ruling that the claimant's measure of recovery depended upon the benefit retained by the defendant. There were differences among their lordships as to whether the claimant might benefit from a presumption that the claimant's own costs of borrowing gave the measure of the defendant's benefit, which would be displaced to the extent the defendant showed that no such benefit had been received (Lords Hope and Nicholls) or whether the claimant would be put to the proof of demonstrating how much interest the defendant had actually earned over the relevant period (Lords Scott and Mance). Subject to this, a buyer seeking the recovery of the price paid as money had and received may therefore claim compound interest.

[340] n. 331 above at [96] (Lord Nicholls).

[341] n. 331 above at [95] (Lord Nicholls).

[342] n. 331 above at [216].

recoverable currency loss in the event of late payment.[343] Suppose that the currency of payment is US dollars but the claimant conducts its business in euros. The result of late payment of the moneys due where the euro appreciates against the dollar is that the claimant is able to purchase fewer euros than it could have done had payment been timely. A defendant might contemplate that the claimant conducts its business in a currency other than the currency of payment, and it might or might not, more probably the latter, have some intimation of the hedging operations that might be conducted by the claimant to guard itself against currency risk. Even before it was accepted that general damages might be recovered at common law by way of interest for late payment, it had been settled that damages might lie for currency losses caused by late payment[344] and that the restrictions on recovery of interest had no application to currency losses.[345] Furthermore, the distinction between the first and second limb of the rule in *Hadley v Baxendale* was regarded as of no factual significance in currency cases,[346] though a claim for damages would have to be specially pleaded.[347] The failure to consider the distinction between the two limbs of the rule in *Hadley v Baxendale* was due to the court's disregard for matters concerning currency hedging and mitigation of damages. Although a claimant receiving payment in foreign currencies and conducting its operations on an international front might be expected to engage in currency hedges so as to mitigate its damages in the event of default, the complications involved in investigating the position and unravelling the operations of a complex claimant corporation will persuade courts to resist undertaking a mitigation inquiry of this kind.[348] The court will prefer to apply the market rule of damages for non-delivery or non-acceptance of goods by way of analogy so that gains and losses arising from a delay in entering the market by the claimant are equally disregarded and thus charged to the claimant alone.[349]

11.78 **Currency of judgment.** Apart from the question whether damages might be awarded for currency losses arising from a breach of contract, a further question concerned the currency in which judgment might be expressed in favour of

---

[343] *International Minerals and Chemical Corpn v Karl O Helm AG* [1986] 1 Lloyd's Rep. 81; *President of India v Lips Maritime Corpn* [1988] AC 395.

[344] *President of India v Lips Maritime Corpn*, n. 343 above.

[345] *Ibid.*, 424, 429.

[346] *International Minerals and Chemical Corpn v Karl O Helm AG*, n. 343 above at 102.

[347] *Ibid.*, 104.

[348] *International Minerals and Chemical Corpn v Karl O Helm AG*, n. 343 above at 102 ('to try to unravel on a hypothetical basis all the exchange dealings or contracts that a corporate group had made over a period of three years would involve an absurd and maybe impossible investigation'). The defendants, however, did not claim that there had been a failure to mitigate: *ibid.*, 101. A more challenging task for defendants in the case of multiple currency dealings conducted by a claimant would be to show that there has been mitigation in fact.

[349] *Ibid.*, 102.

the claimant.[350] Just as in principle a claimant's damages are calculated in accordance with the position at the date of breach,[351] so the amount owed in a foreign currency was at one time translated into sterling at that same date. If, therefore, sterling devalued against the currency of account between the date when the price should have been paid and the date judgment was given in favour of the seller, the seller would suffer a loss in exchanging the sterling award for the currency of account. This position, based on a philosophy of currency nominalism,[352] was exploded by the emergence of floating exchange rates following upon the collapse of the Bretton Woods agreement and the fixed dollar price for gold. The House of Lords in *Miliangos v George Frank (Textiles) Ltd*[353] ruled that judgment could in future be given in appropriate cases in a foreign currency,[354] a result protecting the Swiss seller in that case entitled under the contract to payment in Swiss francs. This, of course, was the exact equivalent of delaying the date of conversion from the breach date to the judgment date.[355] The governing principle is that judgment should be given in the currency that best expresses the claimant's loss,[356] even if it is not the currency in which payments are made under the contract, provided that currency is the one in which the claimant's loss is felt and the contract itself does not indicate some other currency.[357] In *The Folias*,[358] the claimant charterers were claiming to be indemnified by the shipowner for their liability under a bill of lading contract to cargo receivers whose goods were damaged by the unseaworthiness of the ship. The charterers, whose place of business was in Paris, paid hire under the charterparty in US dollars and had settled with the cargo receivers in Brazilian cruzeiros. But they had purchased those cruzeiros with French francs, and it was within the reasonable contemplation of the shipowner that they should have done so. Consequently, they had suffered their loss in francs and should be indemnified accordingly. This same approach was applied by the House of Lords in *The Texaco Melbourne*,[359] which concerned a carrier's failure under a bill of lading contract to

---

[350] See H. McGregor, *McGregor on Damages* (17th edn, Sweet & Maxwell, 2003), paras 622 *et seq*; *Dicey Morris and Collins on the Conflict of Laws* (14th edn, by L. Collins, Sweet & Maxwell, 2006), Ch. 36.

[351] Discussed in Ch 12 below.

[352] See *Treseder-Griffin v Co-operative Insurance Society* [1956] 2 QB 127, 144: 'Sterling is the constant unit of value by which in the eye of the law everything is measured.'

[353] [1976] AC 443.

[354] For a full discussion of the governing principles and the ensuing case law, see McGregor, n. 350 above.

[355] *Miliangos*, n. 353 above, 501, though, more accurately, the date chosen for conversion was the date the claimant was given leave to execute judgment: *Miliangos*, 468–9.

[356] *Owners of MV Eleftherotria v Owners of the MV Despina R (The Despina R)* [1979] AC 685.

[357] *The Folias* [1979] AC 685, 699 *et seq* (*The Despina R* and *The Folias* were conjoined appeals).

[358] Above.

[359] *Attorney General of the Republic of Ghana v Texaco Overseas Tankships (The Texaco Melbourne)* [1994] 1 Lloyd's Rep. 473; see M. Bridge [1994] *JBL* 155.

deliver a cargo of refined oil and the consignee's contractual action for damages for non-delivery. The damages principles in a carriage case like this are interchangeable with those in sale of goods cases.[360] The Ghanaian owner of a cargo of oil had purchased it as crude in dollars on the world market, the dollars being provided by the Bank of Ghana in return for local currency. The owner had refined the oil in one Ghanaian port and was in the process of having the refined oil transferred to another Ghanaian port when the defendant carrier failed to deliver it. It was the owner's plan to sell the refined oil in the destination port, for Ghanaian currency (as by law it was bound to do). The question was how to compensate the owner for the loss of these sub-sales. By the time of the current proceedings, the Ghanaian currency had declined in value catastrophically against the dollar and it would cost the owner a vastly greater sum to acquire the necessary dollars to find a substitute cargo. The difficult feature of this case is the way that the issue of the currency of damages intersects with the issue of how damages for non-delivery should be assessed. Regarding the latter question, English law has favoured an abstract approach to damages by reference to the market. It is only where there is no alternative market that an alternative measure, such as a sub-sale price, is considered.[361] The court in this case in effect looked at the sub-sales, not to calculate the measure of damages, but in order to arrive at the conclusion that the Ghanaian owner had suffered its loss in Ghanaian currency. One consequence of the court's decision was that the defendant carrier was able to pay a very low sum convertible into Ghanaian currency, given the fate of the latter in the world currency markets in the intervening years.

Instalment Contracts

11.79 **Moneys paid and payable.**   Contracts for the payment of the price in instalments have posed problems concerning the seller's right in respect of instalments of the price that have been paid or have accrued due and payable before the contract is terminated for the buyer's breach. It will be considered below to what extent moneys paid by way of deposit or instalment may be recovered by the contract-breaker. This will involve consideration of the action for money had and received on a failure of consideration and of the seller's right in some cases to forfeit prepaid moneys.

11.80 **Accrued instalments.**   It is well established, in the case of hire[362] and hire purchase[363] contracts, that instalments falling due before the contract is terminated

---

[360] *Williams Brothers v Edward T Agius Ltd* [1914] AC 510; *The Arpad* [1934] P 189, 223; see also *O'Hanlon v Great Western Railway Co.* (1865) 6 B & S 484.

[361] See Ch. 12 below.

[362] See *Robophone Facilities Ltd v Blank*, n. 259 above; *Interoffice Telephones Ltd v Robert Freeman Co. Ltd* [1958] 1 QB 190.

[363] *Brooks v Beirnstein* [1909] 1 KB 98; *Chatterton v Maclean* [1951] 1 All ER 761; *Yeoman Credit Ltd v Waragowski* [1961] 3 All ER 145 (express clause). See also *National Cash Register Co. Ltd v*

for the hirer's breach may be recovered by the supplier by way of debt.[364] This is consistent with the modern orthodoxy that contracts are terminated for breach prospectively without affecting vested entitlements under the contract thus truncated.[365] A claim for outstanding instalments may also be coupled with a damages action for any deficiency incurred by the finance company when disposing of the goods.[366] Earlier cases had drawn a distinction between breaches by the hirer that, in going to the root of the contract, were truly repudiatory and breaches that permitted the finance company merely to exercise a right to withdraw from the agreement. In the former instance, damages for the finance company's deficiency were allowed; in the latter, they were denied on the ground that the loss arose from the finance company's exercise of its right of withdrawal.[367] The question here is whether a hirer's failure to comply with a payments clause, when not going to the root of the contract, necessarily amounts to a breach of condition just because the finance company has an express right of withdrawal for non-payment. The application of conventional contract principles should produce an affirmative answer.[368]

Timely payment of the essence. If controls have to be placed upon the parties' **11.81** autonomy in characterizing terms as conditions in respect of trivial breaches, or if the hirer should be given relief against forfeiture of his interest upon termination, then this should be done without distorting principle. It is settled that a breach of condition will be present (and thus a repudiatory breach need not be demonstrated by the finance company) if timely payment is expressly made of the essence in the contract.[369] The uncertain availability of damages can therefore be avoided

---

Stanley [1921] 3 KB 292 and *Sandford v Dairy Supplies Ltd* [1941] NZLR 141 (duty to pay instalments falling due only after delivery of goods to hirer).

[364] For general authorities supporting the duty to pay sums falling due before termination, see *Hinton v Sparkes* (1868) LR 3 CP 165; *Dewar v Mintoft* [1912] 2 KB 373; *Damon Cia Naviera SA v Hapag-Lloyd International SA* [1983] 2 Lloyd's Rep. 522; *Bank of Boston Connecticut v European Grain and Shipping Ltd (The Dominique)* [1989] AC 1056 (payee in breach).

[365] *Heyman v Darwins Ltd* [1941] AC 356; *McDonald v Dennys Lascelles Ltd* (1933) 48 CLR 457; *Johnson v Agnew* [1980] AC 367; *Photo Production Ltd v Securicor Transport Ltd* [1980] AC 827.

[366] *Lombard North Central Finance Co. Ltd v Butterworth* [1987] QB 52; *Robophone Facilities Ltd v Blank*, n. 259 above; *Interoffice Telephones Ltd v Robert Freeman Co. Ltd*, n. 362 above.

[367] *Financings Ltd v Baldock* [1963] 2 QB 104; *Brady v St Margaret Trust* [1963] 2 QB 494. See also *AMEV–UDC Finance Ltd v Austin* (1986) 68 ALR 185 (Aust. HC); *Shevill v Builders' Licensing Board* (1982) 149 CLR 620 (Aust. HC); *Progressive Mailing Houses Pty Ltd v Tabali* (1985) 157 CLR 17 (Aust. HC).

[368] Cf G. H. Treitel, *The Law of Contract* (12th edn, by E. Peel, 2007), 903–6. The so-called 'condition' in *Wickman Machine Tool Sales Ltd v Schuler AG* [1974] AC 235 was not recognized as such when it surely must have been if the contract had spelt out the manufacturer's right to withdraw from the distributorship on breach of the term by the distributor.

[369] *Lombard North Central Finance Co. Ltd v Butterworth*, n. 366 above. For a case leaving it regrettably unclear how serious must be the hirer's breach for damages to lie after termination, see *Keneric Tractor Sales v Langille* [1987] 2 SCR 440 (Can.), discussed by M. Bridge (1989) 2 *Banking & Finance LR* 344.

by simple drafting. A finance company suffering loss needs an action for damages after termination because it may not both repossess the goods and demand the payment of all future instalments.[370]

11.82 **Payment prior to termination.**   The position with regard to instalments of the purchase price paid or payable under a contract of sale prior to the termination date has not attracted the same quantity of case law. In *Hyundai Heavy Industries Co. Ltd v Papadopoulos*,[371] the House of Lords distinguished shipbuilding contracts from other contracts of sale when holding that termination in the former case did not affect accrued rights to instalments. In particular, moneys payable before that date remained payable and moneys paid could not be recovered as on a failure of consideration by the defaulting buyer. The earlier case of *Dies v British and International Financing and Mining Corporation Ltd*[372] had allowed the buyer to recover a prepaid instalment of the price where the circumstances did not show a contractual intention that this sum be forfeited[373] in the event of termination for his breach. In such cases, payment under the contract is not absolute but conditional on performance.[374] But the peculiar characteristic of a shipbuilding contract, comparable in this respect to a building contract rather than a contract of sale of goods, was that it required the seller to do work or incur expense on the subject matter of the sale. The shipbuilder thus requiring to be put in funds by the buyer was therefore entitled to accrued instalments needed for disbursements on purchasing materials, paying designers and workmen, and paying fees for inspection. The test of failure of consideration depends upon whether the payee has performed any part of the contract, and not upon whether the payer has received a benefit.[375] It is well known that the payment schedule in such contracts marches broadly in step with the pattern of these disbursements. This reasoning may not effectively counter the assertion that a seller seeking protection should expressly bargain for forfeiture, in default of so doing remaining entitled nevertheless to recover disbursements by way of damages from the defaulting buyer, but it does set apart shipbuilding contracts from conventional contracts of sale.

---

[370]   *Laird v Pim* (1841) 7 M & W 474; *McEntire v Crossley Bros. Ltd* [1895] AC 457, 465.

[371]   [1980] 1 WLR 1129. See also *Hyundai Heavy Industries Co. Ltd v Pournaras* [1978] 2 Lloyd's Rep. 502; *Stocznia Gdanska SA v Latvian Shipping Co.* [1998] 1 WLR 574; *Astea (UK) Ltd v Time Publishing Group Ltd* [2003] EWHC 725 (TCC) at [155]–[156].

[372]   [1939] 1 KB 724; see also *Palmer v Temple* (1839) 9 A & E 508.

[373]   Discussed in the text accompanying nn. 383 *et seq.* below.

[374]   *McDonald v Dennys Lascelles Ltd*, n. 365 above; *Palmer v Temple*, n. 372 above; *Dies v British and International Financing and Mining Corporation Ltd*, n. 372 above (described at 744 as the recovery of the buyer's property rather than a failure of consideration action).

[375]   *Stocznia Gdanska SA v Latvian Shipping Co.*, n. 371 above.

Recovery of Money on a Failure of Consideration

It should be realized that the buyer in *Dies* had not taken delivery of the goods. **11.83**
Suppose the contract of sale is concluded on instalment terms and the buyer
obtains the use and enjoyment of the goods before paying in full and acquiring the
general property in them. Conditional contracts of this sort should be treated in
the same way as contracts of hire and hire purchase. The buyer's instalments may
not be payable for the use of the goods as such, but a buyer who has enjoyed the
goods will be in no position to claim that there has been a total failure of consideration to justify the recovery of prepaid moneys. Apart from retaining accrued
instalments, the seller who has suffered a deficiency will be entitled to recover
damages on the same principles as those obtaining in the hire purchase cases. This
is consistent with the modern approach of treating resale as terminating the
contract of sale.[376]

Remoteness and mitigation. The buyer's action to recover money on a failure **11.84**
of consideration, like any other debt action, is in principle not fettered by remoteness and mitigation limitations. It is expressly preserved by section 54 of the Sale
of Goods Act. As stated above, it may be invoked even by a contract-breaking
buyer, subject to any entitlement of the seller to forfeit prepaid moneys. Notice
has already been taken of the peculiarly potent nature of this money action where
the seller is wholly unable to convey a valid title to the buyer.[377] But the action will
also be available in other cases, where the seller fails to deliver or otherwise commits
a discharging breach of contract.[378] In this connection, a failure of consideration
refers, not to the value of the seller's executory promise, but to its value as performed.
The rightful rejection of non-conforming goods will also qualify the buyer for a
price recovery action. Although in principle a buyer may not combine a damages
action on the contract with a claim for money had and received, since the latter
requires first of all the rescission of the contract, the same claim can in substance
be made in the form of a combined damages claim. It is therefore unlikely that a
pleading technicality of this kind could successfully be maintained nowadays.

Seller's right to retain money. The defaulting buyer will not succeed at com- **11.85**
mon law in recovering prepaid money where it is the parties' contractual intention that the seller should keep the money.[379] This intention will be presumed in
the case of deposits,[380] which, in addition to being affected towards payment in

---

[376] *RV Ward Ltd v Bignall*, n. 194 above, overruling on this point *Gallagher v Shilcock*, n. 209
above.
[377] See Ch. 5 below.
[378] *Fitt v Cassanet* (1842) 4 M & G 898.
[379] *Palmer v Temple*, n. 372 above.
[380] *Howe v Smith* (1884) 27 Ch. D 89; *Harrison v Holland and Hannen and Cubitts Ltd* [1922]
1 KB 211.

full, are also designed to serve as earnest money guaranteeing due performance of the contract.[381] As regards instalments, this intention will have to be shown by the seller.[382]

Equitable Relief against Forfeiture

11.86 **Issues.**   Failing common law relief, the next issue is whether equity will afford assistance by way of relief against forfeiture to the defaulting buyer. Four questions arise for consideration. First, is equitable relief confined to transactions, like mortgages, sale of land, and leases, that preoccupied equity in the years preceding fusion?[383] Secondly, is relief restricted to buyers ready and willing to perform at the time they seek relief? Thirdly, does relief take the form of granting specific performance to the buyer or an order requiring the seller to return prepaid moneys? Fourthly, does the buyer have to show a proprietary interest in the goods, the subject matter of the contract?

11.87 **Specific performance and penalties.**   The uncertainty in defining the range of equitable relief against forfeiture lies in pinpointing its position between two equitable doctrines, namely, the doctrine of specific performance and the rule against penalty clauses.[384] The analogy with penalty clauses seems strong when the buyer is simply seeking to recover prepaid money, while specific performance asserts itself when the buyer claims an interest in the contract goods and further time to perform. If specific performance is paramount in the forfeiture doctrine, relief will tend to be confined to contracts of a type amenable to specific performance, which would cramp relief against forfeiture in sale of goods cases. Furthermore, relief would be limited to buyers ready and willing to perform, at least within the further time granted in accordance with equitable views that time is not normally of the essence of the contract.

11.88 **Excess recovery.**   If, however, the rule against penalties inspires relief against forfeiture, the dominant question is whether a seller, forfeiting prepayments or repossessing the goods as the case may be, is calculated at the outset of the contract to secure a benefit in excess of the actual losses suffered under the contract in consequence of the buyer's breach.[385] This could be the case where the payment

---

[381] *Howe v Smith*, n. 380 above; *Soper v Arnold* (1889) 14 App. Cas. 429; *Ockenden v Henley* (1858) 1 EB & E 485; *Hall v Burnell* [1911] 2 Ch 551, 558–9; *Waugh v Pioneer Logging Co.* [1949] SCR 299 (Can.); *PT Berlian Naju Tanker TBK v Nuse Shipping Ltd* [2008] EWHC 1330 (Comm) at [23].

[382] *Mayson v Clouet* [1924] AC 980, disapproving of *Harrison v Holland and Hannen and Cubitts Ltd*, n. 380 above, 213 (Bankes LJ); *McDonald v Dennys Lascelles Ltd*, n. 365 above.

[383] Cf *United Scientific Holdings Ltd v Burnley Borough Council* [1978] AC 904.

[384] See generally Law Commission (Working Paper No. 61, 1975), *Penalty Clauses and Forfeiture of Monies Paid.*

[385] On penalty clauses, see Treitel, n. 368 above, 1074–80.

schedule is planned to stay ahead of any reasonable assessment of the depreciation of the goods in the buyer's hands.[386]

Conditional sale and instalments.   In *Stockloser v Johnson*,[387] the claimant agreed   **11.89**
to buy, on conditional sale terms, quarrying machinery that was subject to hiring agreements with a third party, who paid royalties for the use of the machines. These hiring agreements were assigned to the claimant, whose plans to pay the purchase instalments out of the royalties received were defeated by the reduction of royalty payments caused by poor weather. Upon late payment, the defendant exercised his contractual right to give notice terminating the conditional sale agreements. The conditional sale agreements, besides reserving title in the defendant seller, also permitted the seller on termination to repossess the machinery and forfeit all moneys paid. In the present action, the claimant sought to recover the instalments paid on the ground that their retention amounted to a penalty.

Result.   In the result, the claimant was unsuccessful. The majority view[388] was   **11.90**
that it was not unconscionable for the defendant to forfeit the moneys since the contracts clearly allocated to the claimant the risk of a rise and fall in the level of royalty payments received from the hirer. The minority view[389] would also have denied relief on the ground that, the contract having been terminated, there was no room for relief in the absence of fraud, sharp practice, or unconscionable conduct in the formation of the contract.[390] The majority were of the view that in appropriate circumstances an order could be made directing the repayment of forfeited moneys,[391] thus rejecting the role of specific performance. Denning LJ gives the example of the necklace where 90 per cent of the purchase price has already been paid and the buyer has an 'equity of restitution'.[392] The majority judgments also appear to indicate that retention of the moneys would have to be both penal and unconscionable if recovery were to be ordered. Yet unconscionability is not demanded in the case of penalty clauses, and there seems no good reason to require it where the repayment of forfeited moneys is sought just because the claimant is requesting the assistance of the court to recover moneys vested in

---

[386] Cf *Robophone Facilities Ltd v Blank*, n. 259 above.

[387] [1954] 1 QB 476.

[388] Somervell and Denning LJJ.

[389] Romer LJ.

[390] All vitiating factors giving rise to rescission in equity: see *Galbraith v Mitchenall Estates Ltd* [1965] 2 QB 473, 482. For opposition to the view that courts of equity should 'serve as a general adjuster of men's bargains', see *Bridge v Campbell Discount Co. Ltd* [1962] AC 600, 626 (Lord Radcliffe).

[391] See *Steedman v Drinkle* [1916] AC 275; *Brickles v Snell* [1916] AC 599, 605; *Mussen v Van Diemen's Land Co.* [1938] 2 Ch. 253, 264–6. The majority's interpretation of *Steedman* was criticized by Romer LJ. See also *Galbraith v Mitchenall Estates Ltd*, n. 390 above, 485 (the uncertain state of the law favouring the view of Romer LJ).

[392] n. 387 above, 491.

the defendant. It is noteworthy that clauses permitting the withholding of a portion of the contract price, common in building contracts, are measured by the rule against penalties and not by the principles of relief against forfeiture.[393]

11.91 **Buyer ready and willing.** Romer LJ, in the minority, asserted that relief could only take the form of more time being given, prior to the termination of the contract, to a purchaser ready and willing to perform.[394] In his view, therefore, relief was linked to the doctrine of specific performance though he did not relate it to the type of contracts normally amenable to a specific performance decree. This view appears to have prevailed in subsequent case law.[395] A number of cases have involved applications for further time to perform,[396] where the principle of commercial certainty has been safeguarded against attempts to withdraw contractual termination rights. These cases are therefore unsympathetic to a buyer seeking further time to perform in the face of a seller who has clear rights of termination.

11.92 **Consumer cases.** Consumer cases are a category apart in that statutory provision is made for an extension of time under regulated consumer credit agreements,[397] a category which may include conditional sales and hire purchase,[398] as well as hire agreements.[399] Under section 87(1) of the Consumer Credit Act 1974, a default notice must first be served before a regulated agreement can be terminated or goods repossessed. The notice, in the prescribed form, must specify the breach and, alternatively, the action that has to be taken if the agreement is to be reinstated or the amount of compensation to be paid in respect of the breach.[400] The court has a discretion for the party in breach to be given further time to perform.[401] Further, powers exist to order the repayment of hire purchase instalments after repossession of the goods.[402] A finance company also needs the permission of

---

[393] *Commissioner of Public Works v Hills* [1906] AC 368; *Waugh v Pioneer Logging Co. Ltd* [1949] SCR 299 (Can.); *Gilbert-Ash (Northern) Ltd v Modern Engineering (Bristol) Ltd* [1974] AC 689.

[394] See *Steedman v Drinkle*, n. 391 above; *Re Dagenham (Thames) Dock Co. Ltd* (1873) LR 8 Ch. App. 1022; *Kilmer v B C Orchard Lands Ltd* [1913] AC 319; *Brickles v Snell*, n. 391 above; *Stickney v Keeble* [1915] AC 386.

[395] *Galbraith v Mitchenall Estates Ltd*, n. 390 above. See also the delphic statement in *Starside Properties Ltd v Mustapha* [1974] 1 WLR 816, 824.

[396] See, e.g., *Sport International Bussum BV v Inter-Footwear Ltd* [1984] 1 WLR 776; *Barton Thompson & Co. Ltd v Stapling Machines Co.* [1966] Ch. 499; *BICC Plc v Burndy Corpn* [1985] Ch. 232; *Shiloh Spinners Ltd v Harding* [1973] AC 491; *Afovos Shipping Co. SA v R Pagnan & Flli* [1983] 1 WLR 195; *Scandinavian Trader Tanker Co. AB v Flota Petrola Ecuatoriana* [1983] 2 AC 694; *Mardorf Peach & Co. Ltd v Attica Sea Carriers Corpn* [1977] AC 850; *A/S Awilco v Fulvia SpA di Navigazione* [1981] 1 Lloyd's Rep. 371; *Goker v NWS Bank Plc, The Times*, 23 May 1990.

[397] Consumer Credit Act 1974, s. 8(2).

[398] *Ibid.*, ss. 12–13.

[399] *Ibid.*, s. 15.

[400] *Ibid.*, s. 88.

[401] *Ibid.*, ss. 129 *et seq.*

[402] *Ibid.*, s. 132.

the court when repossessing goods after one-third of the total price of hire purchase or conditional sale goods has been paid.[403]

Excessive deposit. More recently, the majority view in *Stockloser v Johnson*[404] **11.93**
has been accepted in substance if not in form by the Privy Council in *Workers Trust & Merchant Bank Ltd v Dojap Investments Ltd*,[405] where relief against the forfeiture of a 25 per cent 'deposit' in a sale of land agreement was granted on the ground that its retention would amount to a penalty.[406] Such a large payment was not objectively reasonable as earnest money.[407] In declining to recognize that the parties had intended to forfeit prepaid moneys in the first place, the Privy Council did not have to adjudicate between the two views in *Stockloser*.[408] Invoking the penalties rule would leave no room for any unconscionability criterion. It would also exclude any reference to the doctrine of specific performance and thus be of general application, and would survive a clause making time the essence of payment by a buyer. The approach taken in *Workers Trust* would appear to be just as applicable to an instalment payment plan 'frontloaded' to keep the quantum of payments ahead, at least to an unreasonable degree, of any depreciation suffered by the goods. As matters currently stand, a claim for the repayment of money is more likely to hold promise for instalment purchasers than a claim for more time to perform. The difficulties in estimating the role of equitable relief against forfeiture in the recovery of money have been defused by the invocation in *Workers Trust* of the rule against penalties.

Specific Relief

General. Specific performance of the contract of sale[409] is dealt with by **11.94**
section 52(1) of the Sale of Goods Act:

> In any action for breach of contract to deliver specific or ascertained goods the court may, if it thinks fit, on the plaintiff's application, by its judgment or decree direct that the contract be performed specifically, without giving the defendant the option of retaining the goods on payment of damages.

---

[403] *Ibid.*, s. 90.
[404] n. 387 above.
[405] [1993] AC 573.
[406] The court relied upon *Commissioner of Public Works v Hills* [1906] AC 368. But, in a case dealing with repudiation where a seller wrongly invoked a price escalation clause, the Privy Council stated that a 25% deposit on the sale of an expensive car could have been forfeited had the seller demanded the correct sum (and the buyer had not performed): *Vaswani v Italian Motors (Sales and Services) Ltd* [1996] 1 WLR 270, 276.
[407] n. 405 above, 579–80.
[408] n. 387 above.
[409] G. H. Treitel [1966] *JBL* 211; J. Berryman (1985) 17 *Ottawa LR* 295; G. Jones and W. Goodhart, *Specific Performance* (2nd edn, Butterworths, 1996); R. Sharpe, *Injunctions and Specific Performance* (3rd edn, looseleaf, Canada Law Book, 2005). For a theoretical discussion of the efficiency of specific relief, see A. Kronman (1978) 45 *U Chi. LR* 351; A. Schwartz (1979) 89 *Yale LJ* 271.

The section goes on to provide that the application may be made at any time before judgment or decree[410] and that the decree may be unconditional or made on 'such terms and conditions as to damages, payment of the price, and otherwise as seem just to the court'.[411]

Judicial Discretion

11.95 **Statutory extension.** The above provision states in statutory form the equitable discretion associated with the award of specific performance. It dates from a statute of 1856[412] which was designed to encourage the more liberal grant of specific performance so as to bring English law into line with Scots law.[413] It has certainly not had that effect, for no discernible increase in the award of the decree can be traced to section 52. Indeed, it is inherently unlikely that the equitable discretion, exercised on a case-by-case basis, could be applied more generously in favour of buyers just because the court is statutorily reminded that it has a discretion. There would, as a matter of technique, have to be criteria laid down in the statute giving direction as to the way in which the court might exercise the discretion.[414] In any event, far from section 52 actually expanding the grant of specific performance, it has if anything encouraged its contraction, for the failure of the section to speak to cases other than those concerning specific goods and ascertained goods, combined with the belief that the Sale of Goods Act should as far as possible be regarded as a comprehensive code, has led to the conviction that the remedy cannot lie where there is a contract for the sale of unascertained goods not yet ascertained.[415]

11.96 **Injunctive relief.** In reality, however, the Act cannot be treated as a comprehensive code for section 52 does not address itself to injunctive relief, whether in interlocutory or permanent form, that in fact serves the same ends as specific performance.[416] Furthermore, the section deals only with buyers' actions against sellers and not with sellers' actions against buyers. There is an uncodified

---

[410] S. 52(2). This accords with *Johnson v Agnew* [1980] AC 367. But an applicant may in some cases make a binding election in favour of damages before this point is reached: *Ming Leong Devlopment Pte. Ltd v JIP Hong Trading Co. Ltd* [1985] AC 511.

[411] S. 52(3). See *Hart v Herwig* (1873) LR 8 Ch. App. 860, 864 (buyer required to make payment into court).

[412] Mercantile Law Amendment Act 1856, 19 & 20 Vict., cap. 97, s. 2, enacting the recommendations of the Second Report of the Mercantile Law Commissioners 1855.

[413] Treitel, n. 409 above; Berryman, n. 409 above.

[414] Cf the Canadian Uniform Sale of Goods Act, s. 115 (referring to payment and the buyer's proprietary interest).

[415] *Re Wait* [1927] 1 Ch. 606. See *International Finance Corpn v DSNL Offshore Ltd* [2005] EWHC 1844 (Comm); [2007] 2 All ER (Comm.) 305 at [50].

[416] In *Sky Petroleum Ltd v VIP Petroleum Ltd* [1974] 1 WLR 576, Goulding J was aware that an interlocutory injunction amounted to specific performance of a continuing contract for the time being.

discretion to entertain a specific performance claim in the latter case,[417] although it has been observed that the limits laid down in section 52 should be observed.[418] Since this means that a seller of unascertained goods may not apply for specific performance before the goods are ascertained, it is in practical terms a meaningless restriction. Ascertainment is usually effected by sellers rather than buyers and the seller would only have to ascertain and then seek specific performance.

Ascertained goods.   The meaning of 'specific' and 'ascertained' was discussed in   **11.97** earlier chapters. Although the Sale of Goods Act does not state when goods have become 'ascertained', it is established as taking place when they are ear-marked or otherwise identified by the seller as goods he intends to use in fulfilment of the contract.[419] Growing crops and natural products become 'specific or ascertained' once they are severed under a contract of sale.[420] In cases of this nature, it is quite possible that ascertainment occurs at the same time as unconditional appropriation for the purpose of passing the property.[421]

Policy.   A review of the cases shows that the courts have not, in the exercise of   **11.98** their discretion,[422] conceded that it should be moulded by the nature of the question facing them.[423] For example, it cannot be said with any confidence that the judicial discretion will be tilted in one direction, where the seller is insolvent,[424] but in another direction, where the buyer is dependent for his requirements over a long period on the seller. The insolvency difficulties posed when a buyer pays the price before the property in the goods passes were considered in an earlier

---

[417] *Shell-Mex Ltd v Elton Cop Dyeing Co.* (1928) 34 Com. Cas. 39, 46; *Elliott v Pierson* [1948] 1 All ER 939, 942.

[418] *Shell-Mex*, n. 417 above.

[419] *Re Wait*, n. 415 above; *Thames Sack and Bag Co. Ltd v Knowles & Co. Ltd* (1918) 88 LJ KB 585, 588 ('the indivisibility of the goods must in some way be found out').

[420] *James Jones & Sons Ltd v Earl of Tankerville* [1909] 2 Ch. 440, 445. In *Kursell v Timber Operators and Contractors Ltd* [1927] 1 KB 298, the entire cut of a Latvian forest complying with stated dimensions was held not to be 'specific' in connection with property and risk. It is difficult to see too that it was ascertained. Whether in such a case specific performance ought to be awarded, and whether this should depend upon whether buyer or seller severs, are different questions.

[421] S. 52 is applied whether or not the property has passed to the buyer: *James Jones & Sons v Earl of Tankerville*, n. 420 above, 445. Where the seller refuses to deliver goods the property in which has passed to the buyer, and a specific performance claim is or is likely to be unsuccessful, it would seem that the seller would be a seller in possession under s. 24 for the purpose of title transfer. S. 24 does not require the seller to be in possession with the consent of the buyer.

[422] For a good example of the use of discretionary considerations, see *Butler v Countryside Finance Ltd* [1993] 3 NZLR 623.

[423] Treitel, n. 409 above, 211–12.

[424] But see *Swiss Bank Corpn v Lloyds Bank Ltd* [1982] AC 584, 595 (Buckley LJ) and *Eximenco Handels AG v Partredereit Oro Chief* [1983] 2 Lloyd's Rep. 509, 521, to the effect that the seller's insolvency should bear upon the discretion being exercised in the buyer's favour. For the view that insolvency makes no difference, see *Anders Utkilens Rederei A/S v O/Y Louisa Stevedoring Co. A/B* [1985] 3 All ER 669, 674.

chapter[425] and will not be re-examined here. It remains to consider the way in which the equitable discretion is exercised in general terms and how it bears upon particular types of goods. A preliminary point to make is that the award of specific performance is governed by the same considerations as apply where a claimant is seeking the specific delivery of goods,[426] formerly in a detinue action but now when suing in conversion.[427] A buyer to whom the property in specific goods has passed, for example, will be no better off in seeking to recover the goods *in specie* by framing an action in conversion for their recovery instead of in contract for specific performance. The award of specific performance is also granted in a more restrictive fashion than the award of an injunction preventing the defendant from disposing of goods the subject matter of the contract.[428]

Inadequacy of Damages

11.99 **Unique goods.** The foremost consideration in the grant of specific performance is that the remedy is given only where the normal common law remedy of damages is inadequate. This has been described as an 'essential ingredient' in an application for specific performance.[429] In contracts for the sale of goods, this limitation is expressed by the requirement that the goods must be unique or irreplaceable and therefore not to be procured on the market.[430] Nevertheless, the fact that a contract may concern specific goods, so that only these goods and no others, no matter how similar or otherwise identical, may be tendered by the seller in fulfilment of the contract, does not mean that these goods are unique for the purpose of granting specific performance. Specific performance in the sale of goods is very much an exceptional remedy for quite rare circumstances; it is not granted for articles of commerce and trade.[431] Where the article is not to be had upon the open market, it has been said that this demonstrates a *prima facie* case for

---

[425] See Ch. 3 above.

[426] *Whiteley v Hilt* [1918] 2 KB 808; *Cohen v Roche* [1927] 1 KB 269; *Asamera Oil Corpn Ltd v Sea Oil & General Corpn* [1979] 1 SCR 633 (Can.) (undifferentiated treatment of specific performance and specific delivery).

[427] Torts (Interference with Goods) Act 1977, s. 3.

[428] *LauritzenCool AB v Lady Navigation Inc.* [2005] EWCA Civ 579; [2005] 1 WLR 3686 at [15], relying upon *De Mattos v Gibson* (1858) 4 De G & J 276.

[429] *CN Marine Inc. v Stena Line A/B (The Stena Nautica) (No. 2)* [1982] 2 Lloyd's Rep. 336, 342 (Parker J) Cf *ibid.*, 348 (May LJ: specific performance depends upon a general discretion that should not be broken down into 'separate and distinct stages').

[430] *Adderley v Dixon* (1824) 1 Sim. & St. 607, 610. In *Howard E Perry & Co. Ltd v British Railways Board* [1980] 1 WLR 1375, the court ordered, in interlocutory proceedings under s. 4 of the Torts (Interference with Goods) Act 1977, the delivery up of scarce and irreplaceable goods detained by a tortfeasor. See also *Sky Petroleum Ltd v VIP Petroleum Ltd*, n. 416 above, discussed in the text accompanying nn. 382–3 above.

[431] *Buxton v Lister* (1746) 3 Atk. 383; *Cohen v Roche*, n. 426 above; *Dominion Coal Co. Ltd v Dominion Iron and Steel Co. Ltd* [1909] AC 293.

specific performance.[432] This may be putting the matter too favourably for the buyer, for the remedy can be and is denied even where there is no close equivalent available.[433] Since specific performance is a discretionary remedy which will not readily be scrutinized on appeal,[434] a degree of inconsistency in the cases is only to be expected.

Examples.   Specific performance or its equivalent has been ordered in a number   **11.100** of instances dealing with unique chattels, such as two jars of 'unusual beauty, variety and distinction',[435] an Adam door,[436] stone from Old Westminster Bridge[437] and a luxury horsebox needed for summer eventing and horse shows.[438] But in one case concerning the sale of Hepplewhite chairs, specific relief was denied because the buyer was an antique dealer purchasing the chairs for resale and so treating them as ordinary articles of commerce.[439] The availability in some cases of damages awards in contract for emotional and similar losses, which recognizes that contracts may be designed to attain expectancies other than merely financial ones,[440] ought to lead to a willingness to grant specific performance where a chattel has a certain sentimental value. Damages for intangible losses, often quantified on reflexive and instinctual grounds, are much less likely to attain the true contractual expectancy than performance *in specie*. Nevertheless, if the law were as firmly committed to the expectation interest as is sometimes asserted,[441] one would expect a greater judicial willingness to grant specific performance than is the case.

Other cases.   The remedy of specific performance or an equivalent form of relief   **11.101** has also been granted for more mundane objects which are difficult to acquire

---

432   *Eximenco Handels AG*, n. 424 above, 520.

433   e.g. *Cohen v Roche*, n. 426 above. In *CN Marine Inc. v Stena Line A/B (The Stena Nautica) (No. 2)*, n. 429 above, the court reversed the trial judge's award in favour of specific performance, even though the ship had highly individual characteristics. The sellers, whose conduct was 'extraordinary', had chartered the ship for two years and the charterers had incurred substantial expenditure in adapting it for cross-Channel ferry duty.

434   But see *CN Marine*, n. 429 above.

435   *Falcke v Gray* (1859) 4 Drew 651, which suggests that courts should scrutinize the sufficiency of the buyer's consideration, not an inquiry normally undertaken. The contract was unusual in the sense that the parties explicitly agreed that the goods were to be sold at an objectively fair valuation.

436   *Phillips v Lambdin* [1949] 2 KB 33, 41.

437   *Thorn v Commissioners of Works and Public Buildings* (1863) 32 Beav. 490 (the arch stone, spandrill stone, and Bramley stone) The case does not state why the buyer wanted the stone, and nothing suggests it was for its historical or antique value.

438   *George v Ascot Supreme Ltd* [2002] EWHC 1978 (QB) (apparently granted as a matter of course).

439   *Cohen v Roche*, n. 426 above.

440   M. Bridge (1984) 62 *Can. Bar Rev.* 323; D. Harris, A. Ogus, and J. Phillips (1979) 95 *LQR* 581.

441   See *Harvela Investments Ltd v Royal Trust Co. of Canada* [1986] AC 207, 227, for a statement that specific performance when timeously granted promotes the expectation interest in the way that damages does.

because no ready market exists.[442] There has therefore been a tendency to give specific relief in respect of contracts to sell ships.[443] The Australian High Court once
granted specific performance of a contract to sell a taxi cab with its attendant
licence, because such licences were rare and taxi cabs with licences therefore practically unobtainable.[444] In a Canadian case involving the sale of a Cadillac, which
the buyer, an undertaker, initially wished to convert into a hearse, specific performance was allowed because the buyer, despite due diligence, was unable to
obtain another car of this type.[445] It did not appear, however, that the buyer had
to show that no other type of car would have served the same purpose as well as
the Cadillac. A case open to criticism for the way the discretion was exercised is
Société des Industries Métallurgiques SA v Bronx Engineering Co. Ltd,[446] where the
remedy was denied despite the fact that the buyer of a complex machine to be
manufactured by the seller would have to wait a further nine to twelve months for
a substitute machine to be supplied by another seller. Specific performance has
been granted because of the impossible task that would have faced the buyer in proving his loss in damages at trial,[447] but if mere difficulty were sufficient,[448] the remedy should have been granted in the *Bronx Engineering* case[449] and also should lie as
a matter of routine in any long-term delivery contract (which is not the case).[450]

11.102   Mandatory injunctions.   Issues akin to those that arise in specific performance
cases may also arise where a mandatory injunction is sought to ensure the supply
of goods pending trial of the action. An interim injunction was granted in *Sky
Petroleum Ltd v VIP Petroleum Ltd*[451] to prevent future breaches by the seller of a
long-term petrol requirements contract. Because of the impossibility of obtaining
an alternative source of supply in the over-excited oil market prevailing at that
time, there was every reason to believe that the buyer's business might founder
without the seller's oil. The court was in no doubt that the grant of this injunction

---

[442] But the willingness of a court to grant the remedy in such cases may be defeated by the vague-
ness of the description of the goods: *Butler v Countryside Finance Ltd,* n. 422 above.

[443] *Hart v Herwig* (1873) 8 Ch. App. 860 (injunction to prevent German seller from removing
ship from English port); *Behnke v Bede Steam Shipping Co. Ltd* [1927] 1 KB 649 (ship of particular
value to buyer); *Zegluga Polska SA v TR Shipping Ltd* [1996] 1 Lloyd's Rep. 337. See also *De Mattos
v Gibson,* n. 428 above at 299 (charterparty and injunction: 'a chattel of a peculiar value to the
charterer') Cf *CN Marine Inc. v Stena Line A/B (The Stena Nautica) (No. 2),* n. 429 above.

[444] *Dougan v Ley* (1946) 71 CLR 142.

[445] *Simmons & McBride Ltd v Kirkpatrick* [1945] 4 DLR 134.

[446] [1975] 1 Lloyd's Rep. 465.

[447] e.g., *Hart v Herwig,* n. 443 above, 866.

[448] Denied in the injunction case of *Fothergill v Rowland* (1873) LR 17 Eq. 132.

[449] See also *CN Marine Inc. v Stena Line A/B (The Stena Nautica) (No. 2),* n. 429 above at 342
(Parker J: the fact that loss may be difficult to quantify or that it may be too remote to be recoverable
as damages will not of itself justify an award of specific performance).

[450] *Dominion Coal Co. Ltd v Dominion Iron & Steel Co. Ltd,* n. 431 above.

[451] n. 416 above.

was tantamount to an interim decree of specific performance.[452] Moreover, the decree operated with regard to future supplies of oil, that is, goods not yet ascertained and so not within the terms of the statutory discretion in section 52. In *Nottingham Building Society v Eurodynamics Systems Plc*,[453] four governing considerations were identified for the grant of mandatory injunctions. The first was whether a greater injustice would be caused by the grant or the refusal of an injunction, if it transpired that the award turned out to be incorrect having regard to the rights of the parties established at trial. The second consideration was that a court ought to bear in mind that a mandatory injunction requiring positive action to be taken might carry a greater risk of injustice if wrongly made than one prohibiting action. The third consideration was that it was legitimate in mandatory injunction cases for a court to seek a high degree of assurance that the claimant would establish the claimed right at trial, for this requirement would diminish the risk of injustice from granting an injunction. The fourth consideration was that there might nevertheless be some cases where this high degree of assurance was absent, yet the risk of injustice arising from a refusal to grant the injunction would be greater than the risk arising from granting it.

Complex sale agreements. The concern for the vulnerability of the claimant **11.103** expressed in *Sky Petroleum*, helps to explain why some complex sales agreements, assuming the form, for example, of franchise agreements or exclusive distributorship agreements, become the subject of specific relief.[454] The parties to such contracts become heavily integrated into each other's business and damages will often be a very poor substitute for specific relief in view of the loss of good will and the economic dislocation produced on a peremptory breach. These considerations bulked large in *Land Rover Group Ltd v UPF (UK) Ltd*,[455] which concerned the outsourcing of supplies of a chassis, needed in the manufacture of certain motor

---

[452] In a case concerning the grant of an injunction to prevent a vessel from being withdrawn under a time charter, Mance LJ said in *Lauritzen Cool AB v Lady Navigation Inc.* n. 428 above at [10]: 'One can well understand why an injunction restraining a right of withdrawal would be regarded as pregnant with an affirmative order, and as juristically indistinguishable from an order for specific performance. But it is not now suggested that the relief granted by Cooke J was pregnant with any affirmative order. Further, it was, whatever its practical effect, juristically distinct from a decree of specific performance.'

[453] [1993] FSR 468. See also *Films Rover International Ltd v Cannon Film Sales Ltd* [1987] 1 WLR 670; *Zockoll Group Ltd v Mercury Communications Ltd (No. 1)* [1998] FSR 354; *Engineered Medical Systems v Bregas AB* [2003] EWHC 3287 (Comm) at [17].

[454] *Evans Marshall & Co. Ltd v Bertola SA* [1973] 1 WLR 349; *Baxter Motors Ltd v American Motors (Canada) Ltd* (1973) 40 DLR (3d) 450. In *Evans Marshall*, at 380, Sachs LJ referred to 'the creation of certain areas of damage which cannot be taken into monetary account in a common law action for breach of contract: loss of goodwill and trade reputation are examples'. Unlike the remoteness of damage rule, the equitable discretion is not based on the reasonable contemplation of the defendant at the contract date.

[455] [2002] EWHC 3183 (Mercantile Court); [2003] 2 BCLC 222. The court referred to *Sky Petroleum Ltd v VIP Petroleum Ltd*, n. 416 above.

vehicles, to a manufacturing company that later went into receivership. The buyer invested heavily in tools and machinery installed in the seller's premises and the seller in turn invested heavily in dedicating a substantial part of its production to the chassis. The economics of the industry required the existence of a monopoly supplier of the chassis able to deliver the chassises on a 'just in time' basis. When the defendant sellers went into receivership, the receivers sought to alter the terms of supply to the advantage of the sellers. The relationship between the parties was not a joint venture but the court considered it seriously arguable that there were fiduciary duties to act in good faith and not to exploit the economic dependency of the other party to the contract.[456] An injunction to secure continuing supplies of the chassis was granted, on the balance of convenience, and on due account being taken of the fact that the claimants would have to stop vehicle production if they did not secure continuing supplies of the chassis. In view of the status of the receivers as agents of the sellers, and of the danger of undermining the bargaining position of the receivers, the court granted the injunction in the light of the claimants' willingness to meet the costs of the receivership. The court was concerned about the danger of the claimants obtaining an alternative source of supply by the time the case came on for trial, so the date of the trial was expedited. Furthermore, in the opinion of the court, this was a type of contract that was capable of being specifically performed.

Consumer Sales Directive

11.104 **Consumer right to specific performance.** As a result of changes made to the Sale of Goods Act set in train by an EC Directive on certain aspects of the sale of consumer goods and associated guarantees,[457] the position above on the restrictive application of specific performance needs to be reconsidered for consumer sales. The circumstances in which the changes to the Act are operative, as well as the order of application of the various 'rights' given to the consumer buyer, have been considered in an earlier chapter.[458] One of those rights is the right to require the seller to repair or replace non-conforming goods. Under Article 3(2) of the Directive, the consumer buyer is 'entitled to have the goods brought into conformity free of charge by repair or replacement' provided that this is not 'impossible or disproportionate'.[459] The Directive goes on to explain what is meant by 'disproportionate' but it does not define what is meant by 'impossible', apart from stating in the recitals that second-hand goods because of their 'specific nature'

---

[456] The existence of fiduciary duties of mutual trust and confidence was unsuccessfully argued as a reason *not* to grant an injunction in *LauritzenCool AB v Lady Navigation Inc.*, n. 428 above at [33].

[457] 1999/44/EC, transposed by the Sale and Supply of Goods to Consumers Regulations 2002 SI 2002, No3045 (in force 31 March 2003).

[458] Ch. 10 above.

[459] Art. 3(3).

cannot be replaced.[460] Subject to this condition, the consumer buyer would seem to have a free choice between repair and replacement so long as one of these rights in relation to the other is not 'disproportionate'.[461] As envisaged by the Directive, the consumer's right to 'require' the seller to perform either act is not subject to a discretion, and is especially not subject to the type of discretion exercised by a court of equity. The notion of requiring the seller to do something is drawn from the United Nations Convention on the International Sale of Goods 1980,[462] where it is at least coeval with the right to damages for non-performance and thus reflects the importance attached in civil law countries to primary enforcement of the contract at the remedial stage. In the Convention, there is a separate mention of specific performance for the purpose of giving certain countries, typically common law, an opt-out from the remedy of requiring performance.[463] Requiring performance and specific performance are thus clearly linked, though the former is broader than the latter: a price action would fall within the requiring of performance though it would not be treated as a case of specific performance under the Convention. There is no equivalent in the Directive of the indulgence granted to certain countries that limit the award of specific performance in their own domestic law. The question thus raised is what effect does the transposition of the Directive in the Sale of Goods Act have on section 52 of the Act, more particularly the restrictive discretion that has accompanied section 52 down the years.

Enforcing consumer rights. According to section 48A(2)(a), the consumer **11.105** buyer has the 'right' to require the seller to repair or replace the goods within a reasonable time according to stated conditions.[464] The new provisions in the Act do not state the position if the seller fails to act within a reasonable time, but section 60 of the Act already provides that where 'a right, duty or liability is declared by this Act, it may (unless otherwise provided by this Act) be enforced by action'. Damages should thus be available if the seller fails to act within a reasonable time.[465] The enforcement of the consumer buyer's right of repair or replacement is tantamount to specific performance of the contract, though it is not directly described as specific performance in the relevant part of the Act. Nevertheless, section 48E(2) provides that on the buyer's application the court 'may' make an order for specific performance. This is not the same thing as saying that the court

---

[460] Recital (16).

[461] S. 48B(3)(b), discussed below.

[462] Art. 46.

[463] Art. 28: 'If, in accordance with the provisions of this Convention, one party is entitled to require performance of any obligation by the other party, a court is not bound to enter a judgment for specific performance unless the court would do so under its own law in respect of similar contracts of sale not governed by this Convention.'

[464] A reasonable time is computed according to the nature of the goods and the purpose for which they were acquired: s. 48B(5). It is also a question of fact: s. 59.

[465] See also s. 48E(6).

must make the order if the buyer has the right of repair or replacement. A court, for example, may be disinclined to order repair if it involves supervising the defendant seller.[466] On one view, this permissive form of words, coupled with the failure to modify section 52 with reference to the consumer buyer's new rights, may amount to an incorrect transposition of the Directive. It may, however, be possible to avoid this awkward conclusion by treating section 48A(2)(a) as an implied repeal of section 52 to the extent of any inconsistency between the two. Alternatively, it might be argued that a buyer coming to court and seeking repair or replacement is not as such seeking specific performance but is requesting the court to give effect to that right, and that section 48E(2) is merely reminding the court that it can invoke its specific performance powers in aid of the buyer's right. Since, nevertheless, the enforcement of that right will ultimately depend upon those powers, it would be specious to label enforcement as other than specific performance. A dependence upon the implied repeal argument when section 48E(2) itself uses permissive language is unsatisfactory. Much will depend upon whether the court will resort to the language of the Directive, which states that the buyer is 'entitled' to the rights granted,[467] when interpreting the new provisions of the Sale of Goods Act,[468] which is not an ideal solution. A related difficulty arises in connection with section 48E(6), which gives the court a broad discretion in relation to all of the buyer's rights to 'make an order . . . on such terms and conditions as to damages, payment of the price and otherwise as it thinks just'. Care will have to be taken when making an order not to introduce restrictions on the buyer's rights that are not sanctioned by the terms of the Directive itself.

11.106 **Impossibility and disproportionality.** The limits laid down on repair or replacement are those of impossibility and disproportionality. Mention has already been made of second-hand goods as a case of impossibility for the purpose of replacement. Suppose, however, that new goods are supplied and that these are specific goods. Specific goods are unique and therefore, by one measure, they may be said to be impossible to replace. To introduce the restrictive definition of specific goods into a series of provisions that do not take account of the difference between specific and unascertained goods would, it is submitted, depart from a Community understanding of the words of the Directive. The remedy of replacement should be given a reasonably broad meaning and should not be confined by unnecessarily

---

[466] See *Ryan v Mutual Tontine Association* [1893] 1 Ch 116; *Co-operative Insurance Society Ltd v Argyll Stores (Holdings) Ltd* [1998] AC 1. There may not be many sales of goods where the problem of supervising performance will persuade the court not to grant specific performance. In the case of consumer goods and repair, this problem should not be overstated.

[467] Art. 3(2).

[468] See *R (on the application of Khatun) v Newham LBC* [2005] EWCA Civ 55; [2005] QB 37 at [56], referring to the 'uncontentious' argument that the scope of the Unfair Terms in Consumer Contract Regulations 1999 SI 1999, No. 2083, should be determined by the scope of the Directive that they transposed.

introducing the concept of specific goods. Apart from this, the buyer ought not to be able to demand replacement of the original goods with goods of a different description. If a particular model has been superseded and replaced by a model of higher specification priced at a different level, replacement ought not to mean that the seller has to provide that different model at the original price. Moreover, to require replacement at the new price amounts to entry into a new contract of sale; the remedy of replacement is designed to keep the original contract on foot. Disproportionality is a factor too. The buyer may not require replacement where this would be disproportionate to repair.[469] Guidance is given on the meaning of disproportionality in section 48B(4) by reference to the notion of unreasonable costs, which is linked to three factors—the value of the goods had they been conforming, the 'significance' of the lack of conformity, and the effectiveness of any other remedy that does not cause 'significant inconvenience' to the buyer. The heavy depreciation of unwanted goods thrown back on the seller, when compared with the lesser cost of repairing those same goods, ought therefore to militate in favour of repair. The extent of the non-conformity, however, may signify that the seller will have to replace the goods. Goods of relatively low value may be more suitable for replacement than repair. These provisions taken as a whole point to replacement being disproportionate where repair would be effective and relatively inexpensive. If the buyer would have to wait a lengthy period for the goods to be repaired, or have to take a significant period away from the workplace, this would suggest a right to have the goods replaced even if this is more expensive for the seller than repair.[470] The same principles of impossibility and disproportionality apply if the buyer's preference is for repair over replacement. Impossibility here should take the form of physical impossibility, for example, because replacement parts cannot be procured at all. There is a final consideration affecting both repair and replacement. If either price reduction or rescission can be effected without imposing significant inconvenience on the buyer, and if it would be unreasonable for the buyer not to choose one of these remedies given the costs that would be borne by the seller required to repair or replace the goods, then the buyer must go for price reduction or rescission. The free availability of the goods in the market place from another source would not in and of itself suffice to deny the buyer replacement of the goods, to the extent that the buyer's acquisition of the goods elsewhere would be cost-neutral as far as the seller was concerned. The buyer's primary right of replacement in this case would therefore be inconsistent with the approach to specific performance under section 52.

[469] S. 48B(3)(b).
[470] S. 48B(5).

Prohibitory Injunctions

11.107 **Negative covenants.** A question that sometimes arises is whether a prohibitory injunction should issue, restraining the seller from delivering the contract goods to anyone other than the buyer, in circumstances where specific performance would not be available.[471] Such a decree, while not enjoining the seller actually to deliver to the buyer,[472] would in practice amount to the same thing if the seller wished to make any effective use of his assets. Where the contract contains an express negative stipulation to the above effect, the courts have been swayed by the well-known principle in *Doherty v Allman*[473] that an injunction should issue as a matter of course, since the court is merely being requested to sanction something explicitly agreed upon by the parties.[474] Thus, in *Donnell v Bennett*,[475] a manure manufacturer agreed to purchase all the unwanted fish parts produced by a fish processor for a two-year period, and the latter also explicitly undertook not to sell any such goods to other buyers in that same period. Fry J awarded the remedy sought, though with some considerable misgivings, since it did not actually compel the defendant to deliver the goods to the claimant. On the other hand, in *Fothergill v Rowland*,[476] a contract to supply all the coal from a particular colliery seam contained no such express negative covenant. It was admitted by the buyer that specific performance of the contract could not have been obtained, and Jessel MR, despite the revulsion he felt for the defendant's conduct, refused to grant a prohibitory injunction that would have amounted to specific performance by a roundabout method.

11.108 **Distinction between positive and negative covenants.** The distinction between positive and negative covenants may be somewhat elusive in practice for 'every agreement to do a particular thing in one sense involves . . . the negative of doing that which is inconsistent with the thing you are to do'.[477] In the last resort, the distinction between positive and negative has to be pursued as a matter of substance rather than form,[478] and an implied negative covenant may in a proper case

---

[471] See Sharpe, n. 409 above.

[472] *Metropolitan Supply Co. v Ginder* [1901] 2 Ch. 799. See the practical compulsion of the buyer in *Foley v Classique Coaches Ltd* [1934] 2 KB 1; *Servais Bouchard v Prince's-Hall Restaurant Ltd* (1904) 20 TLR 574. A seller may in some cases be enjoined from preventing the buyer from entering land to sever crops: *James Jones & Sons v Tankerville* [1909] 2 Ch. 440.

[473] (1878) 3 App. Cas. 709, 720.

[474] This proves too much for it should support specific performance as the general remedy, subject perhaps to exceptions.

[475] (1883) 22 Ch. D 835. See also *Thomas Borthwick & Sons (Australia) Ltd v South Otago Freezing Co. Ltd* [1978] 1 NZLR 538; *Sanderson Motors (Sales) Pty Ltd v Yorkstar Motors Pty Ltd* [1983] 1 NSWLR 513.

[476] n. 448 above.

[477] *Whitwood Chemical Co. v Hardman* [1891] 2 Ch. 416, 426.

[478] *Manchester Ship Canal Co. v Manchester Racecourse Co.* [1901] 2 Ch. 37.

be discerned in a covenant positively worded.[479] That the law may be less than sat-isfactorily clear in pursuing the negative quality of a covenant is evident in the comparison of an output case, like *Fothergill v Rowland*,[480] where an injunction was denied, with a requirements case, like *Metropolitan Electric Supply Co. Ltd v Ginder*,[481] where an injunction was granted.

Declarations. Like injunctions, declarations are not mentioned in section 52. **11.109** They can serve a valuable function in clarifying the position of the parties, especially in long-term contracts, before disagreements come to a head with a refusal to perform.[482]

[479] *Metropolitan Supply Co. v Ginder* [1901] 2 Ch. 799; *Bower v Bantam Investments Ltd* [1972] 1 WLR 1120.

[480] n. 448 above.

[481] n. 479 above.

[482] See, e.g., *Spettabile Consorzio Veneziano v Northumberland Shipbuilding Co. Ltd* (1919) 121 LT 628, 635; *Louis Dreyfus & Cie v Parnaso Cia Naviera SA* [1960] QB 49; *JH Vantol Ltd v Fairclough, Dodd and Jones* [1955] 1 WLR 642, 648.

12

THE REMEDIES OF THE SELLER
AND THE BUYER II

Introduction.   Where an action for the price is not available or is waived by   **12.01**
the seller, the seller has instead an action against the buyer for damages for non-
acceptance. There is also an action for special or consequential damages in appropriate cases. In the case of the buyer, a right to damages may arise for non-delivery
or for late delivery, or because the goods delivered fail to conform to the standard
set by the express or implied terms of the contract. In addition to the normal
damages due on such an event, the facts of the case may disclose a claim to special
or consequential damages. The various statutory actions for damages contained in
the Sale of Goods Act will be shown as anchored in the law of remoteness of
damage, laid down in a series of cases beginning with *Hadley v Baxendale*,[1] as well
as in the principle of mitigation of damages. The Sale of Goods Act imports
explicitly a reference to the market in the sections dealing with non-delivery and
non-acceptance, and this will be treated as revealing the statutory choice of a
clear-cut rule for the assessment of damages which responds to both remoteness
principles and mitigation.

---

[1] (1854) 9 Ex. 341.

The Secondary Obligation to Pay Damages: Common Issues

Expectation and Reliance Damages

12.02 **Expectation interest and scope of duty.** This section of the chapter deals with damages issues that are common to claims brought by both buyer and seller,[2] though they may arise in a contextually different form in the two instances. The treatment of damages claims in the law of contract conventionally starts from the postulate that damages are awarded to place the claimant in the position he would have occupied had the contract been duly performed by the defendant.[3] This is a contractual application of the principle that the function of damages is to put the injured party in the position he would have been in if the wrong had not been committed.[4] Although the expectation principle has been described as a 'ruling principle',[5] developments in recent years, whose staying power is hard to assess at this relatively early stage, suggest that the principle in some cases will be ousted by another principle as the 'starting point' in approaching the award of damages. According to this latter principle, the scope of the contractual duty assumed by the defendant defines the type or kind of loss for which the defendant might be liable.[6] Only then will it be appropriate to define the expectation of the claimant. In sale of goods cases, this principle is likely to be of rare application. Apart from this consideration, the expectation entitlement, projecting the claimant forward to a post-contract position that the defendant's breach prevented him from attaining, is to be distinguished, at least for the purpose of conceptual analysis, from a reliance entitlement, which would be promoted by returning the claimant to his pre-contract position.[7]

---

[2] *McGregor on Damages* (17th edn, by H. McGregor, 2003); G. H. Treitel, *The Law of Contract* (12th edn, by E. Peel, 2007), Ch. 20; S. M. Waddams, *The Law of Damages* (4th edn, Canada Law Book Co., Toronto, 2004).

[3] *Robinson v Harman* (1848) 1 Ex. 850, 855; *Wertheim v Chicoutimi Pulp Co.* [1911] AC 301, 307; *British Westinghouse Electric and Manufacturing Co. Ltd v Underground Electric Railways Co. of London Ltd* [1912] AC 673, 689.

[4] See *Livingstone v Rawyard's Coal Co.* (1880) 5 App. Cas. 25, 39; *British & Commonwealth Holdings Plc v Quadrex Holdings Plc* [1995] CLC 1169, 1226.

[5] *Wertheim v Chicoutimi Pulp Co.*, n. 3 above at 307.

[6] *Transfield Shipping Inc. v Mercator Shipping Inc. (The Achilleas)* [2008] UKHL 48 at [14]–[23], [30], [69] and [86]–[87] (Lords Hoffmann, Hope, and Walker); *Banque Bruxelles Lambert SA v Eagle Star Insurance Co. Ltd* [1997] AC 191, 211; see also *Mulvenna v Royal Bank of Scotland* [2003] EWCA Civ 1112 at [33].

[7] L. L. Fuller and A. Perdue (1936) 46 *Yale LJ* 52. For the pursuit of the reliance interest where the expectation claim is unprovable, see M. Bridge, 'Expectation Damages and Uncertain Future Losses', in J. Beatson and D. Friedmann (eds), *Good Faith and Fault in Contract Law* (Oxford University Press: 1995).

Expectation and reliance distinguished. As helpful as the distinction between **12.03** expectation and reliance damages might be for intellectual purposes, however, its practical significance stands to be overestimated. Admittedly, a reliance claim is usefully made by claimants who are in no position to prove a speculative expectation entitlement, and whose difficulties of proof are to be attributed to the defendant's breach of contract.[8] In such cases, a financial return of the claimant to his pre-contract position, coupled with an award of interest to compensate him for being kept out of his money,[9] is an acceptable substitute from the vantage-point of justice, even though commercial contracting is inherently more risky than placing investments in a bank deposit account. Awards under this head may include expenses incurred prior to the contract, sunk in the expectation of concluding a binding contract.[10] For reliance expenditure to be recovered, the expenditure must comply with the remoteness of damage rule.[11] The position thus points to a reliance award as a permissible substitute for an unprovable expectation claim.[12] Hence, the claimant is entitled to elect between an expectation claim and a reliance claim.[13] It has, nevertheless, been doubted that a claimant can run both claims in the alternative, not least because it creates forensic difficulties as a result of the burden of proving the expectation resting on the claimant while the burden of proving the contract as a whole is a losing one rests upon the defendant.[14] It has also been doubted how far the claimant's election goes and in particular whether it is confined to cases where the claimant is unable to demonstrate lost profits because of the prophetic character of such an exercise.[15] If, nevertheless, the defendant is able to demonstrate that the contract was financially a losing one for the claimant, the orthodox position is that the expectation award, that might have been made if the claimant had formed his claim in that way, sets the ceiling for any recovery of damages, and so as much of the claimant's reliance claim as exceeds this ceiling is irrecoverable.[16]

---

[8] See, e.g., *Anglia Television Ltd v Reed* [1972] 1 QB 60; *Security Stove & Manufacturing Co. v American Railway Express Co.* (1932) 51 SW 2d 572; *Commonwealth of Australia v Amann Aviation Pty Ltd* (1991) 66 ALJR 123 (noted by G. Treitel (1992) 108 *LQR* 226); Bridge, n. 7 above.

[9] For a discussion of pre-judgment interest, see Waddams, n. 2 above, and McGregor, n. 2 above.

[10] *Anglia Television Ltd v Reed*, n. 8 above; *Lloyd v Stanbury* [1971] 1 WLR 535.

[11] *Ibid.*, 63–4 (referring to pre-contract expenditure, but the principle is of general application).

[12] *Commonwealth of Australia v Amann Aviation Pty Ltd*, n. 8 above.

[13] *Anglia Television Ltd v Reed*, n. 8 at 63–4.

[14] *Filobake Ltd v Rondo Ltd* [2005] EWCA Civ 563 at [64], invoking *Cullinane v British 'Rema' Manufacturing Co.* [1954] 1 QB 292, discussed below.

[15] *Filobake Ltd*, n. 14 above, at [65]. It is not clear how this possible reservation affects the burden of proof of establishing that a contract was a loss-making contract.

[16] *Filobake Ltd*, n. 14 above at [62]; *C. & P. Haulage v Middleton* [1983] 1 WLR 1461; *CCC Films (London) Ltd v Impact Quadrant Films Ltd* [1985] QB 16; *McRae v Commonwealth Disposals Commission* (1951) 84 CLR 377; *Bowlay Logging Ltd v Domtar Ltd* [1978] 4 WWR 105.

12.04 **Lost opportunity.** Apart from this divergence of reliance and expectation, it should be appreciated that an award of reliance damages, in the form of a return of moneys disbursed by the claimant as a result of entering into the contract,[17] will not in itself turn back the clock. If the claimant is truly to be indemnified, he must have restored to him the time or opportunity value of that award. By entering into a contract with the defendant, the claimant may have passed up the opportunity in competitive market conditions of concluding a contract with someone else. An accurate reliance award will compensate the claimant for this lost opportunity, and, in the perhaps unlikely case of perfect market conditions, will yield the same figure as an expectation award.[18] As a *prima facie* rule, the Sale of Goods Act gives a buyer as damages, where the seller fails to deliver, the difference between the contract price and the (higher) market price prevailing at the date fixed for delivery. This could be analysed, in competitive market conditions, as the claimant's lost expectation or, in reliance terms, as the lost opportunity to secure the goods on the same contract terms from another seller who would have delivered.

12.05 **Compensation.** The choice between expectation and reliance damages is in furtherance of the principle that the purpose of the law of damages in contract cases is not to punish or deter but to compensate the claimant. It therefore follows that, as a general rule, the measure of damages for breach of contract is the loss caused to the claimant and not the gain made by the defendant when breaching the contract. The award of gain-based (or restitutionary) damages is therefore not the rule in contract law. Despite the view that the refusal of gain-based damages is desirable because it leads to the allocation of resources to the source that places the highest value on them—which is consistent with the notion of efficient breach of

---

(Cf *Dataliner Ltd v Vehicle Builders and Repairers Assn*, 27 July 1995 (unreported), where the trial judge's ruling that the burden of proof was on the claimant to show that the contract would have been profitable was upheld as the correct approach by the Court of Appeal without consideration of the authorities or the arguments.) It is submitted that a defendant should not be permitted to oppose a restitutionary claim on the ground of a loss-making contract. There is no reason to let the defendant profit from his own breach, or even to retain benefits received from the claimant so as to reduce his own contract losses. The cap placed on the claimant's reliance recovery is at the expense of the possibility that the claimant might in time have turned round a losing contract; it may also permit the defendant to rely upon the terms of the very contract that he is repudiating. The point was left open in *Filobake Ltd v Rondo Ltd*, n. 14 above at [67], where the case was taken of a claim for the return of the price where the goods were useless, so that it was as if no contract had been concluded. The above cap should not be placed on a damages claim where the claimant had speculative, even remote and unprovable, gains to be made: *Security Stove & Manufacturing Co. v American Express Co.*, n. 8 above; *McRae v Commonwealth Disposals Commission*, above; *Commonwealth of Australia Amann Aviation, Pty Ltd* n. 8 above. See also *Wallington v Townsend* [1939] Ch. 558; *Nurse v Barns* (1664) T Raym. 77.

[17] Such an award is more extensive than the indemnity that accompanies rescission *ab initio*: *Whittington v Seale-Hayne* (1900) 82 LT 49; *Newbigging v Adam* (1886) 34 Ch. D 582.

[18] Fuller and Perdue, n. 7 above; Bridge, n. 7 above. See also *East v Maurer* [1991] 2 All ER 733; *V K Mason Construction Ltd v Bank of Nova Scotia* (1985) 16 DLR (4th) 598.

contract—English courts have not been overtly actuated by the same philosophy, though their awards are broadly consistent with it. Problems of this nature are not likely to arise with any great frequency in the law of sale of goods but an outline of the law in this area is nevertheless appropriate. An orthodox application of the rule that a claimant is not entitled to gain-based damages is *Surrey County Council v Bredero Homes Ltd*,[19] where a developer, in breach of a covenant given to the claimant when purchasing land from it, erected in excess of the agreed number of houses. The claimant did not seek an injunction to restrain the building of the houses, but sought instead damages for breach of the covenant. Since it had suffered no loss, it was held entitled to recover only nominal damages. Steyn LJ firmly expressed the view that the damages awarded in *Wrotham Park Estate Co. Ltd v Parkside Homes Ltd*[20] were not compensatory but rather gain-based in nature.[21] In *Wrotham Park*, houses were erected in breach of covenant and the court, in granting equitable damages in lieu of an injunction under Lord Cairns's Act 1858,[22] awarded the claimant a sum representing the price that it might have charged for releasing the defendant from the covenant if it had sought the claimant's permission before developing the land in question, although there was no evidence that the claimant would have agreed to any such bargain. So stated, this approach differs from the award of gain-based damages for breach of contract in two respects. First, the award was not of the profit made by the defendant but rather assumed a bargain beneficial to both parties that divided this profit between them. In fact, the claimant received only 5 per cent of the defendant's anticipated profit, a measure that lends itself to the criticism that the damages award was a mere gesture of admonishment to the defendant. Secondly, the claimant's damages were compensatory in that the claimant was recompensed for being denied the opportunity to bargain with the defendant for release of the covenant. This approach was necessary because it has been authoritatively stated that there is supposedly no difference between the common law approach to damages in such a case and the approach of equity under Lord Cairns's Act 1858.[23] *Wrotham Park* damages may be seen as the price to be paid for a type of compulsory purchase.[24]

---

[19] [1993] 1 WLR 1361.

[20] [1974] 1 WLR 798. See also *Bracewell v Appleby* [1975] Ch 408; *Tito v Waddell (No. 2)* [1977] Ch 106.

[21] n. 19 above at 1369. See also the criticisms of *Wrotham Park* in *Stoke-on-Trent City Council v W & J Wass* [1988] 1 WLR 1406, 1414, 1420. But *Wrotham Park* was followed in *Jaggard v Sawyer* [1995] 1 WLR 269 and its correctness in terms of compensatory damages has now been firmly settled: *WWF–World Wide Fund for Nature v World Wrestling Federation Entertainment Inc.* [2007] EWCA Civ 286; [2008] 1 WLR 445 at [53].

[22] Chancery Amendment Act 1858, 21 and 22 Vict., cap. 97.

[23] See *Johnson v Agnew* [1980] AC 367.

[24] The basis of damages in a *Wrotham Park* type of case were explored at some length in *WWF–World Wide Fund for Nature v World Wrestling Federation Entertainment Inc.* [2006] EWHC 184

12.06 **Gain-based recovery.** Given their artificial quality, *Wrotham Park* damages are barely compatible with the denial of gain-based damages. A major inroad into the latter principle, however, emerged in the case of *Attorney General v Blake*,[25] where a former member of the security services published his memoirs in breach of a confidentiality clause in his contract of employment. The Court of Appeal[26] treated the *Wrotham Park* approach as an exception to the prohibition of gain-based damages and recognized that broader categories of exceptions were appropriate.[27] The first concerned 'skimped performance', where a contractor charged in full for services not rendered in full.[28] For example, if a service provider undertook to have a stated number of personnel on standby in case of the claimant's emergency need, and saved money by diminishing the numbers on standby, the proper measure of damages would be the money saved by the defendant, even if no harm accrued to the claimant because the missing personnel were not needed. This departs from the conventional approach to damages because it cannot be said that the excess payment is caused by the service provider's breach. Rather, that payment precedes the breach. Nevertheless, a conventional approach to damages would deny the claimant's performance interest, by which he would be entitled to receive what he paid for or its monetary equivalent.[29]

12.07 **Performance of prohibited act.** The second exception listed by the Court of Appeal in *Blake* concerned cases where the defendant performed the very act that he had contracted not to do. This category was expressed to be broad enough to cover the present case of the defendant who had published without first obtaining security clearance, as he was contractually bound to do. But its terms are broad enough also to cover the *Wrotham Park* type of case as well as the *Surrey County*

(Ch); [2006] FSR 38, reversed on other grounds, n. 21 above. The court stressed that *Wrotham* damages were compensatory in nature and were not awarded by way of account. They were neither gain-based nor punitive and did not depend upon whether the claimant actually would have released its rights under the covenant. The damages remedy was an exceptional one.

[25] [2001] 1 AC 268. The outcome of the case was that a publisher was ordered not to pay royalties to an author who had committed a serious breach of the Official Secrets Act 1989 when disclosing classified information in his autobiography.

[26] [1998] Ch 439.

[27] Similar to those proposed in a Law Commission consultation paper: *Aggravated, Restitutionary and Exemplary Damages* (1993, No. 132). In its final report (Law Com. No. 247, 1997), the Law Commission stated a preference for leaving the development of restitutionary damages to the courts but recommended that they should be available where exemplary damages might be claimed (paras 1.11-2).

[28] This is compatible with the approach taken in sale of goods cases pre-dating *Bence Graphics International v Fasson* [1998] QB 87, discussed below. Under the earlier law, where a seller of goods delivered sub-standard goods whose market value was less than the contract price, an award of the market difference could be made under s. 53(3), even if the goods were suitable for the buyer's purpose.

[29] D. Friedmann (1995) 111 *LQR* 628; B. Coote [1997] *CLJ* 537; *ibid.*, (2001) 117 *LQR* 81; see discussion below.

Council case (with which it was therefore inconsistent). In fact, it covered all negative obligations and so was too wide.[30] The court did, however, reassert the unavailability of gain-based damages in three stated cases: first, even where the defendant's breach was deliberate and cynical (since contract damages do not play a penal role); secondly, even where there was a clear causal connection between the breach and the defendant's entry into a more profitable alternative contract; and thirdly, even if the defendant, by entering into a new and more profitable contract, put it out of his power to perform the present contract with the claimant.[31] After the Court of Appeal had handed down its decision, the position on gain-based damages could not therefore be regarded as having been put on a stable footing.

Account. The House of Lords[32] was less inclined than the Court of Appeal to sanction the award of gain-based damages, but was prepared in this case to grant a remedy requiring the defendant to account for his gains in breaching the confidentiality clause in his contract, taking its cue from a number of cases involving awards that went beyond the bounds of pure compensation, including *Wrotham Park*. It is not clear from the decision of the court whether this was an existing equitable, or a novel common law, example of account, though any difference between the two might not be important. In any event, the remedy was regarded as an exceptional one required in the interests of justice. Lord Nicholls[33] likened the type of exceptional case needed to the discretion to award specific or injunctive relief: 'In the same way as the plaintiff's interest in performance of a contract may make it just and equitable for a court to make an order for specific performance or grant an injunction, so the plaintiff's interest in performance may make it just and equitable that the defendant should retain no benefit from the breach of contract.'[34] There is a clear indication in this passage of the claimant's performance interest in the contract. In the context of *Wrotham Park*, Lord Nicholls also said that 'it is not easy to see why, as between parties to a contract, a violation of a party's contractual rights should attract a lesser degree of remedy than a violation of his property rights',[35] which has the power to stimulate claims for gain-based damages. Despite Lord Nicholls's insistence that an account is exceptional (the defendant himself was akin to a fiduciary), and his reassurance that the decision would not destroy commercial certainty, together with his acceptance of the cases where the Court of Appeal would not have allowed restitutionary damages, his

12.08

---

[30] As Lord Nicholls stated in the House of Lords: n. 25 above at 286.

[31] Many of these cases in these three categories would fall into the Court of Appeal's second exception anyway.

[32] n. 25 above.

[33] With whom Lords Goff and Browne-Wilkinson concurred. Lord Steyn also concurred but delivered a speech of his own. Lord Hobhouse dissented.

[34] n. 25 above at 285.

[35] n. 25 above at 283.

acknowledgement that the remedy is discretionary and that no fixed rules of recovery can be laid down gives similar encouragement to such claims. His lordship's reference to the claimant's legitimate interest[36] in preventing the defendant from making a profit in breach of contract—which he put forward as a useful guideline—may not prove to be particularly helpful in controlling gain-based claims.

12.09 **Subsequent cases.**   Events subsequent to the *Blake* case suggest that exceptional remedies have the capability over time of becoming quite conventional.[37] More recently, however, an intermediate approach was adopted by the Court of Appeal in *Experience Hendrix LLC v PPX Enterprises*.[38] In that case, the defendant, in breach of a settlement agreement, allegedly entered into licensing agreements permitting the use of master recordings featuring a deceased musician. The court was not prepared to require the defendant to give a full account of the profits made from the masters but, in the absence of proven or rather provable loss accruing to the claimant, ordered the payment of a reasonable sum for the defendant's use of material in breach of the settlement agreement.[39] In *Wrotham Park* terms, the sum was described as the amount that could reasonably have been demanded by the musician's estate for consenting to the licensing of the masters. Peter Gibson LJ summarized the features of the case that made it a suitable one for damages going beyond the normal compensatory range: '(1) [T]here has been a deliberate breach by [the defendant] of its contractual obligations for its own reward, (2) the claimant would have difficulty in establishing financial loss therefrom, and (3) the claimant has a legitimate interest in preventing [the defendant's] profit-making activity carried out in breach of [its] contractual obligations . . .'. The future incidence of gain-based awards cannot therefore be seen as wholly predictable.

Agreed Damages and Penalty Clauses

12.10 **Penalties and liquidated damages.**   It was noted above that the rules on forfeiture relief in the case of prepaid moneys had in modern times been aligned with the rule against penalty clauses. Since it is well settled in modern times that damages are awarded pursuant to an implied secondary obligation of the contract,[40] there can be no objection in principle to the parties themselves agreeing in advance

---

[36] Cf *White & Carter (Councils) Ltd v McGregor* [1962] AC 413 (Lord Reid).

[37] See *Esso Petroleum Co. Ltd v Niad Ltd* (Unreported, 22 November 2001: gains made from breaching a pricing agreement in circumstances where the claimant's loss impossible to quantify recoverable by way of account).

[38] [2003] EWCA Civ 323; [2003] 1 All ER (Comm.) 830.

[39] This is an approach similar to the old wayleave cases in trespass. See, e.g., *Whitwham v Westminster Brimbo Coal and Coke Co.* [1896] 2 Ch. 538; *Watson Laidlaw & Co. Ltd v Cassels & Williamson.* (1914) 31 RPC 104; *Strand Electric and Engineering Co. v Brisford Entertainments Ltd* [1952] 2 QB 26. The authorities are usefully collected in *Stoke-on-Trent City Council v W & J Wass*, n. 21 above.

[40] *Photo Production Ltd v Securicor Transport Ltd* [1980] AC 827.

the measure of recoverable damages. Indeed, it is desirable that they do so to the extent that it simplifies trials by avoiding difficult issues of proof, and even discourages trials altogether. Nevertheless, a liquidated damages clause that strays across the boundary and becomes a penalty may not be enforced by the claimant.[41] In addition, it does not bind the claimant, who is at liberty to ignore it when suing at law for a greater sum of damages than the clause itself would allow.[42] This prohibition on enforcement is not based upon an abuse of power or unconscionable conduct by the claimant,[43] though such conduct may influence the court in characterizing a clause as a penalty or liquidated damages clause. As a result, there is significant evidence of judicial feeling in modern times that the rule against penalties is a somewhat anomalous interference with contractual freedom and should therefore not receive an expansive interpretation.[44] This may be one reason why, instead of an offending clause being void, it has been said to be enforceable to the point where it captures the claimant's loss,[45] which means that the obligee may sue on the clause. If this is correct, it gives the draftsman relatively little incentive to aim accurately for a liquidated damages clause.

The rule against penalties. A penalty clause is often defined as one that provides **12.11** for the payment of money *in terrorem* of the breaching party.[46] This is of little assistance as a diagnostic test. Furthermore, some contracting parties would strive to perform a contract for fear of incurring liability under a liquidated damages clause; other, more robust parties would conduct their affairs without being unduly troubled by the existence of a penalty clause in the contract. Whether a clause amounts to a penalty is a question of construction as of the date of the contract and not the date of the breach. The burden of persuasion that a sum is a clause is a penalty rests upon the party required to make payment under it. The well-known House of Lords decision in *Dunlop Pneumatic Tyre Co. Ltd v New Garage and Motor Co. Ltd*[47] lays down a number of rules of interpretation for determining whether a clause is a penalty.[48] If the clause itself is described as a penalty, this is probably neutral as far as its interpretation is concerned: the clause

---

[41] See below.

[42] *Wall v Rederiaktiebolaget Luggude* [1915] 3 KB 66.

[43] *Jeancharm Ltd v Barnet Football Club Ltd* [2003] EWCA Civ 58. Cf *Elsey v JG Collins Insurance Agencies Ltd* (1978) 83 DLR (3d) 1.

[44] See, for example, *Philips Hong Kong Ltd v Attorney General of Hong Kong* (1993) 61 BLR 64; *Murray v Leisureplay Plc* [2005] EWCA Civ 963 (where particular difficulties with employment contracts are noted); *Alfred MacAlpine Capital Projects Ltd v Tilebox Ltd* [2005] BLR 271 at [48].

[45] *Jobson v Johnson* [1989] 1 WLR 1026, 1040.

[46] *Dunlop Pneumatic Tyre Co. Ltd v New Garage and Motor Co. Ltd* [1915] AC 79. For a useful examination of Lord Dunedin's speech in *Dunlop*, see *Murray v Leisureplay Plc* [2005] EWCA Civ 963.

[47] *Ibid.*

[48] *Firma C-Trade SA v Newcastle Protection and Indemnity Association (The Fanti)* [1989] 1 Lloyd's Rep. 235, 254 (Bingham LJ): 'The principles there laid down have been the subject of remarkably little judicial development.'

might by its name have a deterrent effect, even though it operates as a liquidated damages clause.[49] Nevertheless, for a draftsman to describe a clause as a penalty may be incautious unless the word is thought effectively to deter a breach so that the status of the clause does not become an active matter. Again, a clause described as a liquidated damages clause will not on that account survive scrutiny as a penalty.[50] Finally, the rule against penalties will almost always catch clauses providing for the payment of money, but in exceptional cases will apply also to clauses requiring property (for example, shares) to be made over in the event of breach.[51] It has been held applicable to clauses that require forfeiture of sums paid on breach[52] as well as to clauses that exempt the party invoking them from having to pay moneys to the party in breach.[53]

12.12 Examples of construction. If the sum is payable in the event of a failure to pay a sum of money, and exceeds that sum, then the clause is a penalty.[54] This appears logically unavoidable, yet it fails to take account of the possibility that late payment could be ruinous for a payee exposed in that event to cascading risks. The rule dates from a time when there was no common law liability in damages for failure to pay a sum of money, a rule that in recent times has been made subject to a statutory exceptions and at common law has been diminished to the point where it is an aspect of the rule of remoteness of damage. The rule is therefore ripe for some degree of reappraisal. If a clause provides for payment of a sum that cannot be less than the loss suffered by a breach and in many cases will be more, it will be held to be a penalty. A clear example is the hire purchase case where, regardless of when the hirer's breach occurred, the clause provided for the payment of all outstanding instalments under the contract.[55] On the other hand, if a clause is designed to cover a variety of possible breaches and fixes an amount that falls fairly within the range of loss that could eventuate for each of the breaches, the fact that it provides overcompensation in some cases will not lead to its treatment as a penalty.

---

[49] A clause described as a penalty was held not to be a penalty in *Clydebank Engineering and Shipbuilding Co. Ltd v Yzquierdo y Castaneda* [1905] AC 79.

[50] See *Commissioner of Public Works v Hills* [1906] AC 368, 375: '[I]t is well settled law that the mere form of expression "penalty" or "liquidated damages" does not conclude the matter. Indeed, the form of expression here, "forfeited as and for liquidated damages," if literally taken, may be said to be self-contradictory, the word "forfeited" being peculiarly appropriate to penalty, and not to liquidated damages.'

[51] *Jobson v Johnson*, n. 45 above.

[52] *Workers Trust and Merchant Bank Ltd v Dojap Investments Ltd* [1993] AC 573.

[53] *Commissioner of Public Works v Hills*, n. 50 above (retention fund in railway construction contract); *Gilbert-Ash (Northern) Ltd v Modern Engineering (Bristol) Ltd* [1974] AC 689; *General Trading Co. (Holdings) Ltd v Richmond Corpn Ltd* [2008] EWHC 1479 (Comm). But see the criticism of Bingham LJ in *Firma C-Trade SA v Newcastle Protection and Indemnity Association (The Fanti)*, n. 48 above, 254–5.

[54] *Kemble v Farren* (1829) 6 Bing 141.

[55] *Cooden Engineering Co. Ltd v Stanford* [1953] 1 QB 86.

In *Robophone Facilities Ltd v Blank*,[56] a clause provided that in the event of termination of the agreement for the hirer's breach, the hirer was to pay 50 per cent of all future payments of hire. Depending upon when the contract was terminated for breach, the owner's loss was equivalent to between 47 per cent and 58 per cent of unpaid hire. The clause was therefore not a penalty. Similarly, it is no objection to a clause that damages cannot be assessed in advance with any great accuracy, for it is precisely in such a case that a liquidated damages clause is most useful.[57] A limitation clause, obviously, will not be a penalty since it does not act *in terrorem*, even if in the particular circumstances it gives rise to payment where no loss has in fact occurred.[58] Finally, a clause in a lending agreement will not be a penalty simply because it provides for an increase in the interest rate for payments falling due after the debtor's default.[59] The debtor's default shows that the risk initially assumed by the bank has increased.

Scope of rule. The rule against penalties applies generally to damages and not **12.13** to debt claims.[60] It does not protect the party whose primary obligation to pay a sum of money, whether in a lump sum on a future date or in instalments according to a payments schedule, is modified in the event of breach. Consequently, an acceleration clause that collapses a forward schedule of payments into one currently payable sum does not have to comply with the rule against penalties, even though the payee may benefit as a result of the operation of the clause by virtue of early receipt of the agreed sum.[61] Again, the rule against penalties applies only to clauses providing for payment in the event of a breach. It does not apply where payment is triggered by a non-breach event. Thus, for example, the rule cannot apply to a counter-indemnity clause providing for payment of a sum in the event of the beneficiary of the clause having to pay a third party under the terms of a separate indemnity agreement.[62] Another example is the clause found in standard f.o.b. contracts where, as the price for invoking an option to extend the shipment

---

[56] [1966] 1 WLR 1428.

[57] *Clydebank Engineering and Shipbuilding Co. Ltd v Yzquierdo y Castaneda*, n. 49 above.

[58] *Cellulose Acetate Silk Co. Ltd v Widnes Foundry (1925) Ltd* [1933] AC 20.

[59] *Lordsvale Finance plc v Bank of Zambia* [1996] QB 752.

[60] *Export Credits Guarantee Department v Universal Oil Products Co.* [1983] 2 All ER 205. The exclusion of the rule from debt cases has been criticized as 'simplistic', because the rule has been applied to minimum payments clauses in hire purchase cases: *M & J Polymers Ltd v Imerys Chemicals Ltd* [2008] EWHC 344 (Comm); [2008] 1 Lloyd's Rep. 451 at [41].

[61] *Protector Endowment Loan Co. v Grice* (1880) 5 QBD 592; *Wallingford v Mutual Society* (1880) 5 App. Cas. 685. But it will be a penalty if unearned future interest is accelerated as well: *Oresundsvarvet Aktiebolag v Lemos (The Angelic Star)* [1988] 1 Lloyd's Rep. 122.

[62] *Export Credits Guarantee Department v Universal Oil Products Co.*, n. 60 above. See also *Office of Fair Trading v Abbey National Plc* (No. 2) [2008] EWHC (Comm). The *Abbey National* case also states that a clause may be treated as a penalty when, covering breach and non-breach events, it is invoked on the occasion of a breach: *ibid*, [20]. Moreover, a sum is payable on breach even if there are requirements additional to the breach to be satisfied before the clause may be invoked: *ibid*, [19].

date, the buyer undertakes to pay on a *per diem* basis sums of money representing a percentage of the value of the contract goods.[63] This sum does not equate at all to any added expenses incurred by the seller because of a delay in shipment, but the buyer invoking an extension of the shipment date is not in breach at all. Furthermore, the rule against penalties applies only to the secondary obligation to pay damages, and not to the choice between alternative primary methods of performance. If a seller quotes one price for payment within 30 days and a higher price for later payment, the rule should not apply,[64] though perhaps a different view might be taken if the difference between the alternative payment obligations was so great that the clause might be recharacterized as a colourable attempt to levy a penalty.[65] Subject to this, the danger of widening the scope of the rule against penalties to primary obligations in general is that it might be used to introduce a general measure of unconscionability to commercial contracts in general,[66] despite Lord Radcliffe's injunction that '"[u]nconscionable" must not be taken to be a panacea for adjusting any contract between competent persons when it shows a rough edge to one side or the other'.[67]

Rules Limiting Damages Recovery

Factual Causation

12.14 **Breach occasioning loss.** A claimant's expectation claim, once a breach of contract has been established, has three further hurdles to negotiate. First of all, the claimant must prove in fact that it was the breach of contract, rather than some other event or cause, that produced the loss.[68] The courts have applied a commonsense

---

[63] *Thomas P Gonzales Corpn v FR Waring (International) (Pty) Ltd* [1980] 2 Lloyd's Rep. 60; *Fratelli Moretti SpA v Nidera Handelscompagnie BV* [1981] 2 Lloyd's Rep. 47.

[64] See *Euro London Appointments Ltd v Claessens International Ltd* [2006] EWCA Civ 385; [2006] 2 Lloyd's Rep. 436. Cf *M&J Polymers Ltd v Imerys Chemicals Ltd*, n. 60 above, where the rule was considered in principle applicable to a 'take or pay' clause requiring the buyer to pay for a stated minimum quantity of goods even if not ordering that quantity of goods within the stipulated period. Nevertheless, in the particular case, the clause did not transgress the rule against penalties because it was commercially justifiable and not oppressive and was negotiated between parties of equal bargaining power. The assessment of the clause in this way is not to be reconciled with the approach taken in *Jeancharm Ltd v Barnet Football Club Ltd*, n. 43 above, that the rule against penalties is not based on abuse of power or oppressive conduct.

[65] Cf *Interfoto Picture Library Ltd v Stiletto Visual Programmes Ltd* [1989] QB 443. Chadwick LJ, discussing the *Interfoto* case in *Euro London Appointments Ltd*, above at [28], said: 'I share the view that the clause under consideration in that case must be regarded as vulnerable to attack under the rule against penalties.'

[66] A danger posed by the approach of the court in *M & J Polymers Ltd v Imerys Chemicals Ltd*, n. 60 above.

[67] *Bridge v Campbell Disocunt Co. Ltd* [1962] AC 600, 626.

[68] *Quinn v Burch Bros (Builders) Ltd* [1966] 2 QB 370; *Cia Financiera Soleada SA v Hamoor Tanker Corpn (The Borag)* [1981] 1 WLR 274; see also *Wertheim v Chicoutimi Pulp Co.*, n. 3 above.

approach to factual causation[69] and, driven by absence of apportionment for contributory negligence in contract cases,[70] have drawn a distinction between a breach of contract that causes loss and a breach of contract that merely provides the occasion on which loss or damage occurs.[71] The effect of the defendant's breach may be erased by subsequent conduct of the claimant. In *Beoco Ltd v Alfa Laval Co. Ltd*,[72] the sellers supplied a defective heat exchanger whose replacement, interrupting the buyers' production process, would have entailed a loss of profits. The buyers, however, caused even more disruption to production when their incompetent repair of the exchanger generated an explosion. They were not allowed damages for a notional loss of the profits that would have continued owing to the sellers' breach but for their own intervention.

Scope of factual causation. One explanation of the doctrine of mitigation is **12.15** that the true cause of the claimant's loss is his own failure to take evasive action after the breach,[73] and the same could be said for the denial of damages in certain cases to claimants whose own impecuniosity aggravates any loss attributable to the defendant's breach.[74] Likewise, in cases where a warranty action fails because

[69] See *Monarch Steamship Line Co. Ltd v Karlshamns Oljefabriker (AB)* [1949] AC 196, 228 (Lord Wright): 'Causation is a mental concept, generally based on inference or induction from uniformity of sequence as between two events that there is a causal connexion between them. This is the customary result of an education which starts with our earliest experience [:] the burnt child dreads the fire. I am not entering upon or discussing any theory of causation. Those interested in philosophy will find modern philosophic views on causation explained in Russell's History of Western Philosophy in the chapter on Hume, Book 3, ch. xvii. The common law, however, is not concerned with philosophic speculation, but is only concerned with ordinary everyday life and thoughts and expressions. . .'.
[70] See Ch. 7 above.
[71] *Quinn v Burch Bros (Builders) Ltd*, n. 68 above. As for the question 'How does the court decide whether the breach of duty was the cause of the loss or merely the occasion for the loss?', see *Galoo Ltd v Bright Grahame Murray* [1994] 1 WLR 1360, 1375 ('By the application of the Court's common sense').
[72] [1994] 4 All ER 464, disapproving *Schering Agrochemicals Ltd v Resibel NV SA* (4 June 1991, unreported).
[73] See, e.g., *Payzu Ltd v Saunders* [1919] 2 KB 581; *Sotiros Shipping Inc. v Sameiet Solholt (The Solholt)* [1983] 1 Lloyd's Rep. 605; see discussion below.
[74] *Liesbosch, Dredger v SS Edison* [1933] AC 449; *Freedhof v Pomalift Industries Ltd* (1971) 19 DLR (3d) 153. Cf. *Bacon v Cooper (Metals) Ltd* [1982] 1 All ER 397 (the cost of mitigation, discussed below). Lord Wright's comments on impecuniosity limiting recovery have been disapproved and said to have been 'overtaken by subsequent developments in the law': *Lagden v O'Connor* [2003] UKHL 64; [2004] 1 AC 1067 at [8] (Lord Nicholls). See also Lord Hope at [51] (emphasizing that the tortfeasor must take his victim as he finds him); Lord Scott at [82] and Lord Walker at [102]. In contract cases, impecuniosity issues should normally be resolved through the medium of the remoteness of damage rule and in particular the reasonable contemplation of the defendant in the light of what he knows about the claimant's circumstances at the contract date. See *Trans Trust SPRL v Danubian Trading Co. Ltd* [1952] 2 QB 297, 306. See also *Satef-Huttenes SpA v Paloma Tercera Shipping Co. (The Pegase)* [1981] 1 Lloyd's Rep. 175 (if a defendant should not be taken to know how extensive are the claimant's stocks, still less should he have to know whether run down stocks are due to impecuniosity).

of the claimant's intervening negligence, the denial of damages may be rational-ized in terms of factual causation.[75] There is a paucity of case law directly raising the factual causation problem. This is due in part to the claimant's right, when confronting an unprovable expectation claim, to elect instead in favour of a reliance claim.

12.16 **Loss of chance.** An alternative recourse to a claimant in difficulties is to seek recovery of damages for the loss of a chance. In some cases, this may be preferable to a reliance-based claim for wasted expenditure.[76] Recovery for loss of a chance, however, is not freely allowed just because the claimant cannot prove his expecta-tion loss. The claimant must cross a threshold of probability of success before recovering under this head[77] and, it is submitted, the lost chance must constitute the subject matter of the transaction or at least an integral part of it.[78] This latter qualification rules out such damages in conventional market-based sale of goods cases.[79] Recovery for loss of a chance, nevertheless, may be appropriate in the case of profit-earning chattels. But even in such a case, the price the buyer agrees to pay may already have factored into it the chance of profit so that he cannot demon-strate a genuine loss.[80] In some cases, where the fact though not the amount of lost profits is demonstrable, the court will make an award based on a realistic sense of what might have occurred, without discounting the damages in the way that is done where damages represent a lost chance.[81]

Recognized Head of Loss

12.17 **Intangible losses.** The second hurdle mentioned above is that the loss claimed by the claimant must be of a type or kind recognized by the law. The financial and physical interests of buyer and seller do not pose a problem in this respect, but a long-standing difficulty has been presented by claimants' claims for intangible losses, relating to disappointment, injured feelings, emotional distress,

---

[75] *Lambert v Lewis* [1982] AC 225; *Ingham v Emes* [1955] 2 QB 366.

[76] Discussed above.

[77] See the refusal to award damages in *E Bailey & Co. Ltd v Balholm Securities Ltd* [1973] 2 Lloyd's Rep. 404, where the court refused to award damages for loss of a 'general opportunity to trade' in a futures market, noting the tendency of such markets to go down as well as up.

[78] *Chaplin v Hicks* [1911] 2 KB 786; Bridge, n. 7 above.

[79] See the unusual facts of *North Sea Energy Holdings NV v Petroleum Authority of Thailand* [1999] 1 Lloyd's Rep. 483, where the sellers anticipated making high profits from the supply of oil by a head seller at favourable prices, but there was insufficient evidence that the sellers were vouch-safed a secure long-term supply of oil to fulfil the contract with the defendant buyers. Citing *Allied Maples Group Ltd v Simmons & Simmons* [1995] 1 WLR 1602, the court asserted that the sellers had to show a 'real or substantial chance' that the head seller would have supplied the oil over the contract period and that the sellers also had to establish that they themselves would have taken the necessary action to supply the oil over that period (*ibid.*, 495).

[80] *Sapwell v Bass* [1910] 2 KB 486.

[81] See discussion below.

and similar matters,[82] brought about by a breach of contract. Awards for such losses are usually denied either without regard to whether they pass the test of remoteness of damage or on assertion that they are too remote.[83] But in exceptional cases, the claimant's expectation interest[84] is protected by an award, namely, in those cases where enjoyment[85] or the avoidance of distress[86] are central to the purpose of the contract[87] or are directly related to an allowable claim for physical discomfort or inconvenience.[88] The majority of sale of goods agreements will fall outside these exceptions because goods are usually purchased for commercial or unsentimental reasons. Nevertheless, in *Ruxley Electronics and Constructions Ltd v Forsyth*,[89] a swimming pool was built to afford 'a pleasurable amenity'. When the home owner experienced disappointment because it had not been built to specifications, the trial judge awarded an appreciable sum as damages, which the House of Lords, rejecting an alternative award to rebuild the pool to specification, left in place.[90] The same approach to damages may lie where a yacht builder or coach builder falls short of the contractual standard, but is unlikely where massproduced goods without distinguishing features are the subject matter of the contract.[91]

Scope of duty. In consequence of the House of Lords decision in *Transfield* **12.18** *Shipping Inc. v Mercator Shipping Inc. (The Achilleas)*,[92] it seems now to be settled that the type (or kind) of loss may also be defined by the contractual responsibility assumed by the defendant. Consequently, if a type of loss falls outside the range of the defendant's responsibility, there is no allowable claim to which the rules of remoteness of damage can attach, with the result that recovery will be denied even if the loss satisfies the probability standards of the remoteness of damage rule.

---

82 M. Bridge (1984) 62 *Can. Bar Rev.* 323. There is no similar embargo on physical inconvenience: *Hobbs v London and South Western Railway Co.* (1875) LR 10 QB 111. For discussion of the meaning of *physical* inconvenience, see Lord Scott in *Farley v Skinner* [2002] 2 AC 732, at [85]-[88].

83 See *Hamlin v Great Northern Railway Co.* (1856) 1 H & N 408; *Addis v Gramophone Co.* [1909] AC 488; *Bliss v S E Thames Regional Health Authority* [1987] ICR 700; *Watts v Morrow* [1991] 1 WLR 1421; *Hayes v James & Charles Dodd* [1990] 2 All ER 815; *Cook v Swinfen* [1967] 1 WLR 457. Cf *Perry v Sidney Phillips & Son* [1982] 1 WLR 1297.

84 See D. Harris, A. Ogus, and J. Phillips (1979) 95 *LQR* 581.

85 *Jarvis v Swans Tours* [1973] QB 233; *Jackson v Horizon Holidays Ltd* [1975] 1 WLR 1468.

86 *Heywood v Wellers* [1976] QB 446.

87 e.g., *Jackson v Chrysler Acceptances Ltd* [1978] RTR 474; *Ruxley Electronics and Constructions Ltd v Forsyth* [1996] AC 344.

88 *Watts v Morrow*, n. 83 above at 1445. The correctness of this approach was common ground for the parties in *Farley v Skinner*, n. 82 at [16].

89 n. 87 above and discussed further below.

90 £2,500, which Lord Lloyd thought rather generous in the circumstances: n. 87 above, 374.

91 Unless, for example, the fact that the goods are needed for a special purpose, such as a holiday, is brought to the attention of the seller: *Jackson v Chrysler Acceptances Ltd*, n. 87 above.

92 [2008] UKHL 48.

In *The Achilleas*, time charterers were late in redelivering the vessel, with the result that the vessel was tendered to the next charterer outside the laycan period.[93] The subsequent charterers were entitled to refuse the vessel, but they and the owners reached a compromise by which a lower charter rate was substituted for the rate initially agreed. Between the date the second charter was fixed and the date the ship was delivered to the subsequent charterers, the time charter market had fallen. It was found as a fact by arbitrators that the loss experienced fell within the first limb of the rule in *Hadley v Baxendale*[94] as arising 'naturally, ie according to the usual course of things, from [the] breach of contract itself'.[95] The defendant charterers, however, did not know the date when the subsequent charter was fixed, the charter rate agreed in that charter, or the length of that charter. Reversing the court below, the House of Lords refused the owners' claim for the difference between the initial subsequent charter rate and the varied rate agreed after the vessel had overrun the laycan period (the subsequent charter loss), and confined the owners' damages to the difference between the agreed rate in the first charter and the prevailing market rate for the nine-day period representing the defendants' lateness in redelivering the vessel to the claimant owners (the market loss). The market loss basis for the assessment of damages was the one reflecting the 'general understanding in the shipping market'[96] and the risk accruing to the charterers of late redelivery if the subsequent charter loss basis adopted was unquantifiable.[97] They were two different types of loss and the defendant charterers could not fairly be taken to have accepted responsibility for the subsequent charter loss.[98] The approach thus laid down to the award of damages by a majority of the House of Lords amounts to a preliminary screening of claims[99] before they are submitted to

---

[93] The laycan, or laydays cancelling, clause in a time or voyage charter defines the range within which the owners must deliver the vessel to the charterers. They may not require the charterers to accept delivery before the commencement of the laycan period and the charterers are entitled to cancel the charter if the vessel is tendered after the laycan period has expired.

[94] n. 1 above.

[95] The arbitrators' finding of fact seems to have been reversed by Lord Rodger: n. 92 above at [60], with whom Baroness Hale concurred at [93]. If higher courts are unwilling to overturn findings at trial on the reasonableness of exemption clauses (see Ch. 9 above), still less should they reverse findings of fact of this nature.

[96] n. 92 above at [6] (Lord Hoffmann).

[97] *Ibid.*, at [23] (Lord Hoffmann), [34] (Lord Hope).

[98] *Ibid.*, at [15] (Lord Hoffmann), [30] (Lord Hope), [69] ('common basis on which the parties were contracting), [68]–[69] and [86]–[87] (Lord Walker). Lord Rodger and Baroness Hale did not adopt this approach but concurred with the majority in the result when applying the rule of remoteness of damage: *ibid.*, at [63] and [93].

[99] It is not quite so clear in Lord Walker's speech judged as a whole (see above) that defining the scope of the duty and applying the rule in *Hadley v Baxendale* are separate operations. The approach promoted by Lord Hoffmann in particular will probably apply only to 'particular types of contract arising out of general expectations in certain markets, such as banking and shipping': n. 92 above at [11]. Courts are for understandable reasons particularly sensitive to the need not to upset risk calculations in financial markets, though whether that same sensitivity should apply in the world

the discipline of the remoteness of damage rule and firmly aligns the award of damages with the interpretation of the contract.

Criticism. *The Achilleas* seems by a bare majority to have changed the direc-   **12.19**
tion of the law[100] but only time will determine the extent of that change. Certain aspects of the decision call for comment. First, the decision has not clarified what amounts to different types of loss.[101] There is circularity in treating a different type of loss as one outside the risk for which a contracting party reasonably accepts responsibility, whilst defining the range of responsibility by reference to different types of loss. The difficulty thus created owes much to the need to work with the accepted rule that it is the type and not the extent of loss that has to be contemplated for the purpose of the remoteness rule.[102] Secondly, for the purpose of changing the direction of the law, reliance was placed on certain authorities that were applying in an orthodox way the remoteness of damage rule.[103] Thirdly, as innovative as the approach may be in *The Achilleas*, it is essentially conservative in protecting entrenched commercial understandings, in a way that the House of Lords in *The Heron II*[104] was not, when it overturned a long-established authority limiting a carrier's liability to cargo receivers, for failing to prosecute a voyage with due dispatch, to interest on the invoice value of the cargo during the period of delay.[105] It is not clear from a reading of the case how the understanding of the shipping world was measured. A feature of shipping transactions and commodity sales is that contracts are concluded without the involvement of legal advisers, so that there may be an appreciable difference in some instances between legal understanding and legal misunderstanding. Fourthly, it is not clear upon what evidence the court reached its conclusion that the charterers could not fairly be said to have assumed responsibility for the subsequent charter loss. The interpretation of a written contract is of course a matter of law but the interpretation of this contract rested, not upon the express

---

of shipping is a different matter. This approach is consistent with the approach taken for a lengthy period when dealing with claims for intangible loss. Its innovative quality lies in its application to claims for financial loss, which more than intangible loss lie at the heart of protecting contractual expectations.

[100] It 'adds an interesting but novel dimension to the way in which the question of remoteness of damage in contract is to be considered': *ibid.*, at [93] (Baroness Hale).

[101] Note, however, the example cited by Lord Hoffmann at [22] of *Victoria Laundry (Windsor) Ltd v Newman Industries Ltd* [1949] 2 KB 528, where a distinction was drawn between loss of laundry profits and loss of profits from especially lucrative dyeing contracts.

[102] e.g., *Wroth v Tyler* [1974] Ch 30; *Jackson v Royal Bank of Scotland plc* [2005] UKHL 3; [2005] 1 WLR 377. The tension between type and extent of lost profits is clearly evident in *Satef-Huttenes SpA v Paloma Tercera Shipping Co. (The Pegase)*, n. 74 above.

[103] e.g., *Satef-Huttenes Albertus SpA v Paloma Tercera Shipping Co. SA (The Pegase)*, above; *Monarch Steamship Co. Ltd v Karlhamns Oljefabriker (A/B)* [1949] AC 196.

[104] *Koufos v C Czarnikow Ltd (The Heron II)* [1969] 1 AC 350.

[105] *The Parana* (1877) 2 PD 118.

words of the parties, but upon what might be implied from all the circum-stances. Fifthly, although the notion of remoteness of damage as including a ref-erence to contractual assumptions of responsibility[106] has been deprecated in quite recent times,[107] *The Achilleas* has reinstated its importance and indeed has placed it as a matter to be considered in advance of the remoteness rule itself. Sixthly, if the owners had expressly disclosed the risk of subsequent charter loss to the defendants at the charter date, recovery of subsequent charter loss might have flowed from the ordinary application of the remoteness of damage rule and without any need to have recourse to the preliminary screening process laid down in *The Achilleas*. When the remoteness of damage rule is applied, pre-contractual disclosure under the second limb of the rule in *Hadley v Baxendale* is necessary to recover damages for losses that, in the light of the obli-gor's knowledge, are not sufficiently probable to satisfy the first limb of the rule. This highlights the core of the decision in *The Achilleas*, that it excludes liability for losses that the parties clearly did contemplate as not unlikely to result from a breach of the contract and hence did not need to be made the subject of pre-contractual disclosure. The approach of the majority in *The Achilleas* may be better suited to tort claims, which have to satisfy a lower standard of probability than contract claims. Seventhly, despite the probability of subsequent charter loss, the court reached the conclusion it did despite the fact that certain charters expressly excluded such liability.[108] It might fairly be asked whether the onus should have been on the owners to exclude liability instead of on the charterers to raise expressly the issue of subsequent charter loss. This conclusion may have had something to do with the acquiescence of the owners in the defendant char-terers' decision to order the ship on its last voyage, which resulted in the late redelivery. Nothing in the case, however, suggests that the owners had any right to reject the orders for the last voyage, on the ground that it was too late to be a legitimate last voyage. Even had they expressed their doubts and raised the issue of the charter following on, it is not clear that this would have added to the charterers' contractual responsibility. For the purpose of the second limb of the rule in *Hadley v Baxendale*, such post-contractual disclosure would have come too late. Eighthly, although the relevant authorities are not rehearsed, the result in *The Achilleas* supports the approach taken in sale of goods cases where dam-ages for non-delivery are presumptively assessed by reference to the market pre-vailing at the breach date and not by reference to any sub-sale price previously negotiated by the buyer with a sub-buyer.[109]

---

[106] See *British Columbia etc. Saw Mill Co. v Nettleship* (1868) LR 3 CP 499.
[107] Lord Upjohn in *Koufos v C Czarnikow Ltd (The Heron II)*, n. 104 above at 422. Cf *Robophone Facilities Ltd v Blank*, n. 56 above.
[108] n. 92 above at [26].
[109] See discussion below.

Remoteness of Damage

Limiting the expectancy.   The third hurdle to the claimant's recovery is that of legal   **12.20**
causation, or remoteness of damage. A wholehearted commitment to the expectation
principle would identify compensation with factual causation, but the expectation
principle has been described as 'one of those generous aspirations which the law does
well to put but sparingly into practice'.[110] The same commentator regards the remoteness of damage rule as consonant with the wishes of the business community that a
contracting party should not be the insurer of the other's contractual adventure and
that a fair apportionment of business risk may be attained with the aid of the remoteness rule. It should not be forgotten that many breaches of contract flow from promises whose performance is strict and take place in circumstances where the party in
breach has unavailingly sought with reasonable efforts to avoid this result.

Hadley v Baxendale.   Developments prior to the Court of Exchequer decision   **12.21**
in *Hadley v Baxendale*[111] saw damages awards given over to the discretion of juries
and the acceptability of awards within the tolerance of factual causation. But
Hadley v Baxendale demonstrated that 'it is not always wise to make the defaulting
promisor pay for all the damage which follows as a consequence of his breach'.[112]
An analysis of the case and ensuing damages decisions shows how this was achieved,
but the cases are rather less revealing on the question why this was done by the
courts. In *Hadley v Baxendale* itself, the remoteness rule was expressed by Baron
Alderson in the form of two branches or limbs:

> Where two parties have made a contract which one of them has broken, the damages
> which the other party ought to receive in respect of such breach of contract should
> be such as may fairly and reasonably be considered either arising naturally, i.e. accord-
> ing to the usual course of things, from such breach of contract itself, or such as may
> reasonably be supposed to have been in the contemplation of both parties, at the
> time they made the contract, as the probable result of the breach of it.[113]

As the rule was interpreted over the years,[114] remoteness was a function of two variables, namely, the anticipated[115] probability of the promisee's loss occurring in

---

[110] G. Washington (1931) 47 *LQR* 345, (1932) 48 *LQR* 90, 107.

[111] n. 1 above; J. Danzig (1975) 4 *J Leg. Stud.* 249.

[112] L. L. Fuller and A. Perdue (1936) 6 *Yale LJ* 52, 84. For a useful exposition of the rule and its
subsequent analysis and development, see *Satef-Huttenes SpA v Paloma Tercera Shipping Co. (The
Pegase)*, n. 74 above.

[113] n. 1 above, 354.

[114] See in particular *British Columbia etc. Saw Mill Co. v Nettleship*, n. 106 above; *Re R and H Hall
Ltd and W. H. Pim (Jnr.) and Co.'s Arbitration* (1928) 33 Com. Cas. 324; *Victoria Laundry (Windsor)
Ltd v Newman Industries Ltd*, n. 101 above; *Monarch Steamship Co. Ltd v Karlshamns Oljefabriker
A/B*, n. 103 above; *Koufos v C Czarnikow Ltd (The Heron II)*, n. 104 above.

[115] Namely, what the defendant could have foreseen if he had directed his mind to a
future breach: *Victoria Laundry*, n. 101 above; *H Parsons (Livestock) Ltd v Uttley Ingham & Co. Ltd*
[1978] QB 791.

consequence of the promisor's breach, and the degree of knowledge imputed or specially communicated to the promisor[116] at the date of entry into the contract. Probability was measured in the light of this knowledge.

12.22 **Disclosure.** The rule, as elaborated, therefore created an incentive on promisees to make disclosure by the contract date if they wished promisors to incur a degree of responsibility outside the range of ordinary human contemplation.[117] In response, the promisor might take the opportunity to negotiate contract terms commensurate with this added degree of responsibility or to exclude or limit his liability under the contract. Seen in this way, the increase in liability stemming from disclosure could be justified if the courts permitted arm's-length exclusions of liability and did not invoke unduly rigorous canons of construction in respect of a clause protecting the promisor from the consequences of enhanced disclosure. It was sometimes said that communication of additional information was not in itself enough unless it were also accompanied by an undertaking, implied at least, to bear an added measure of responsibility.[118] This particular gloss may no longer find judicial favour.[119] It may be explained as due to the special contract that a common carrier had to conclude in order to be free of the regime of liability laid down by earlier carriers' legislation for the conduct of what was a common calling.[120] One of the difficulties in assessing the impact of the remoteness rule lies in measuring how much of the inherited law may fairly be said to be special carriers' law rather than general contract law.

12.23 **Imputed knowledge.** In calculating the quantity and the significance of knowledge in a given case, it was sometimes difficult to know where to draw the line between knowledge that should be imputed to the promisor and knowledge that should have been the subject of special disclosure if the promisor's ordinary measure of liability were to be increased. This probably best explains the modern fashion of restating the remoteness rule as a consolidated rule rather than as a rule with separate limbs.[121] Carriers, however, could be expected to know rather less of the

---

[116] It is more accurate to speak of the promisor alone than of promisor and promisee: *Cory v Thames Ironworks and Shipbuilding Co. Ltd* (1868) LR 3 QB 181.

[117] They might not want to. If the buyers in *Cory*, above, had disclosed the exceptionally profitable plans they had for the huge hulk, clearly an embarrassment to the sellers after the default of previous buyers (see *Thames Iron Works Co. v Patent Derrick Co.* (1860) 1J & H 93), the predictable consequence would have been a steep rise in the contract price.

[118] *British Columbia etc. Saw Mill Co. v Nettleship*, n. 106 above; *Horne v Midland Railway Co.* (1873) LR 8 CP 131 (and note the sceptically narrow interpretation of the quite extensive information conveyed in that case); *Robophone Facilities Ltd v Blank*, n. 56 above, 1448.

[119] *The Heron II*, n. 104 above, 442.

[120] See the Carriers Act 1830, 1 Will. 4, cap. 68 (though note this statute was concerned with loss rather than delay).

[121] *Victoria Laundry (Windsor) Ltd v Newman Industries Ltd*, n. 101 above; *The Heron II*, n. 104 above.

consignor's and consignee's businesses[122] than sellers of goods would know of their buyers' businesses. As between sellers, some would be more informed than others of the use that buyers would make of their goods. An engineering company selling a surplus boiler that the buyers were to remove to their own laundry,[123] for example, would know less about the way that boiler would work in the buyers' internal economy than would be known by the sellers of a pulverizing plant, who knew how it was to be installed and how it was to be housed and worked in with ancillary machinery.[124] In principle, the remoteness rule would bear upon the different cases with varying degrees of rigour.[125]

Types of loss.   The application of the remoteness rule was also influenced by the   **12.24** willingness of courts, even as they admitted that the *quantum* of loss need not be contemplated by the promisor,[126] to separate financial loss into different heads or types.[127] The damage suffered, for example, in one case[128] in repurchasing and reshipping lost machinery parts was different in kind from the loss of profits[129] suffered by the consignee in not being able to run a timber mill until the parts were replaced. Where the damage concerned property or the human person, the same willingness to subdivide the loss was absent and this, more than anything, accounts for the harmony in practice of the tort and contract remoteness rules in cases of overlapping liability, even though the rules are assessed in terms of different levels of probability.[130]

Probability.   As for the level of probability in the contract rule, it can probably be   **12.25** said that the amount of judicial ink spilt on the issue has not yielded worthwhile

---

[122] *Horne v Midland Railway Co.*, n. 118 above; *British Columbia etc. Saw Mill Co.*, n. 106 above.

[123] *Victoria Laundry (Windsor) Ltd v Newman Industries Ltd*, n. 101 above.

[124] *Cullinane v British 'Rema' Manufacturing Co. Ltd* [1954] 1 QB 292.

[125] But see *The Heron II*, n. 104 above, where the carrier's liability could not have been any less strict than a seller's would have been in broadly similar circumstances.

[126] e.g., *Wroth v Tyler*, n. 102 above; *Banque Bruxelles Lambert SA v Eagle Star Insurance Co. Ltd* [1995] QB 375, 405; *British and Commonwealth Holdings plc v Quadrex Holdings Inc.* [1995] CA Transcript 333; *Brown v KMR Services Ltd* [1995] 2 Lloyd's Rep. 513, 556–7.

[127] See, e.g., *Cory v Thames Ironworks and Shipbuilding Co. Ltd*, n. 116 above; *Victoria Laundry (Windsor) Ltd v Newman Industries Ltd*, n. 101 above; n. 104 above (separation of market loss and lock-up value claims); *Satef-Huttenes SpA v Paloma Tercera Shipping Co. (The Pegase)*, n. 74 above. For an assertion that not all financial loss claims are of the same kind and that there is a difference between ordinary business profits and very high profits, see *Brown v KMR Services Ltd*, n. 126 above, 542.

[128] *British Columbia etc. Saw Mill Co.*, n. 106 above.

[129] Given the resistance at the time to lost profits claims, this item was expressed as the lost rental value of the mill as a going concern.

[130] *H Parsons (Livestock) Ltd v Uttley Ingham & Co. Ltd*, n. 115 above; n. 104 above (the collapsing ceiling illustration); *Transfield Shipping Inc. v Mercator Shipping Inc. (The Achilleas)*, n. 92 above at [78].

results.[131] Various formulae have been considered, and the choice appears to lie among the following, though none of them would appear to command universal support: the loss is recoverable if, within the reasonable contemplation of the parties at the contract date, it is 'liable'[132] to result, or 'not unlikely'[133] to result, or represents a 'serious possibility'[134] or a 'real danger'.[135] It is clear, however, that the loss consequent upon breach may be considerably less than of even probability,[136] and clear too that probability is not to be regarded in the light of neutral observation, even if such were possible, but is coloured by the dictates of justice in a particular case.[137] This is probably best expressed by Lord du Parcq: circumstances are so infinitely various that, however carefully general rules are framed, they must be construed with some liberality, and not too rigidly applied. It was necessary to lay down principles lest juries should be persuaded to do injustice by imposing an undue, or perhaps inadequate, liability on a defendant. The court must be careful, however, to see that the principles laid down are never so narrowly interpreted as to prevent a jury, or judge of fact, from doing justice between the parties. So to use them would be to misuse them.[138]

12.26 Themes. Although the courts are, perhaps, unduly coy in giving voice to the dictates of justice in particular cases, the decisions appear to yield a number of postulates, not all of which could be applied in harmony in the same case, and a number of which, as a matter of legal fashion, have been pursued with varying degrees of enthusiasm at different stages in their history. A consistent theme in the case law is that the defendant should not be called upon to underwrite a claimant's speculative venture, especially if it is an unsound one; the contractual expectation of the claimant is not that the defendant should become an insurer of his risk.[139]

---

[131] See in particular *Re R and H Hall Ltd and WH Pim (Jnr) & Co.'s Arbitration*, n. 114 above; *Victoria Laundry (Windsor) Ltd v Newman Industries Ltd*, n. 101 above; *Monarch Steamship*, n. 103 above; *The Heron II*, n. 104 above.

[132] *Victoria Laundry (Windsor) Ltd v Newman Industries Ltd*, n. 101 above; *The Heron II*, n. 104 above, 397, 415.

[133] *Re R and H Hall Ltd and WH Pim (Jnr) & Co.'s Arbitration*, n. 114 above, 333–6; *The Heron II*, n. 104 above, 388, 397.

[134] *Monarch Steamship*, n. 103 above, 233; *The Heron II*, n. 104 above, 415, 425.

[135] *Monarch Steamship*, n. 103 above; *The Heron II*, n. 104 above.

[136] *The Heron II*, n. 104 above.

[137] See Lord Denning's attempt to break away from the differences in terminology between contract and tort rules: *H Parsons (Livestock) Ltd v uttley Ingham & Co. Ltd*, n. 115 above. This colouring of probability is likely now to have been superseded by the preliminary screening of types of damages claim flowing from the decision in *Transfield Shipping Inc. v Mercator Shipping Inc. (The Achilleas)*, n. 92 above.

[138] *Monarch Steamship*, n. 103 above, 232, quoted in *The Heron II*, n. 104 above, 397; see also R. Cooke [1978] *CLJ* 288.

[139] *British Columbia etc. Saw Mill Co. v Nettleship*, n. 106 above; *Victoria Laundry (Windsor) Ltd v Newman Industries Ltd*, n. 101 above (very lucrative dyeing contracts); *Munroe Equipment Sales Ltd v Canadian Forest Products Ltd* (1961) 29 DLR (2d) 730.

Similar to this approach is the attitude evinced in some decisions that it would be unjust to impose upon the defendant a ruinous form of liability.[140] This attitude is particularly marked in cases where the defendant's contractual remuneration is out of all proportion to the liability the claimant is seeking to pin on him, a state of affairs especially likely in the case of carriers who act as peripheral conduits rather than as integral elements in the claimant's venture.[141] In the interest of justice, courts will seek to draw the line at the direct financial consequences of a breach, and will not wish to pursue its reverberating and possibly limitless consequences.[142]

Sanction. On the other hand, a court will be disposed to favour the application   **12.27** of the remoteness rule in the interest of the claimant, if otherwise the defendant's breach will go without an effective sanction.[143] If the contractual remuneration is particularly generous[144] or if the terms of the contract and the surrounding circumstances demonstrate a sharply defined undertaking to produce a contractual benefit,[145] then the defendant's damages liability will be accordingly expanded.[146] Another likely impulse concerns deliberate, self-enriching breaches by the defendants. Although the defendant carrier in *The Heron II* undertook to carry the claimant's sugar to Basrah under the terms of a voyage charterparty, it deliberately and unlawfully denied the claimants the exclusive use of the ship, for which they had paid, when it deviated to various ports in performing additional contractual undertakings.[147] Although the deliberate nature of the breach was not remarked upon expressly by the House of Lords, it is difficult to believe this did not impress their lordships, who gave a reading of the remoteness rule that was generous to the claimants.[148] This approach is not truly punitive, for it operates only in the

---

[140] *Victoria Laundry*, n. 101 above ('harsh results'); *Kerr Steamship v Radio Corpn. of America* (1927) 157 NE 140.

[141] *Hadley v Baxendale*, n. 1 above; *British Columbia etc. Saw Mill Co v Nettleship*, n. 106 above; *Victoria Laundry*, n. 101 above; *Horne v Midland Railway Co v Nettleship*, n. 118 above. Cf *The Heron II*, n. 104 above.

[142] *British Columbia etc. Saw Mill Co.v Nettleship*, n. 106 above, 510 (the illustration of the Calcutta barrister); *Freedhof v Pomalift Industries Ltd* (1971) 19 DLR (3d) 153.

[143] *Cory v Thames Ironworks and Shipbuilding Co. Ltd*, n. 116 above. See also the excellent, but unsuccessful, argument of counsel for the carrier in *The Heron II*, n. 104 above.

[144] *Cathcart Inspection Services Ltd v Purolator Courier Ltd* (1982) 39 OR (2d) 656 (Can.).

[145] *Jarvis v Swans Tours Ltd* [1973] QB 233; *Cathcart Inspection Services Ltd v Purolator Courier Ltd*, n. 144 above.

[146] But there is not a special remoteness rule for absolute, as opposed to due care, contractual undertakings: *H. Parsons (Livestock) Ltd v Uttley Ingham & Co. Ltd*, n. 115 above, 811–12.

[147] The defendant's gain as a measure of contract damages was authoritatively rejected in *Surrey County Council v Bredero Homes Ltd* [1993] 1 WLR 1361; P. Birks (1993) 109 *LQR* 518; A. S. Burrows [1993] *LMCLQ* 453. The position now, however, is more attenuated; see text accompanying nn. 19 *et seq*. above.

[148] On deliberate breaches, see also *Re R and H Hall Ltd and WH Pim Inc. and Co.'s Arbitration*, n. 114 above (Lord Blanesburgh).

shortfall between a conventionally applied remoteness rule and the limits of factual causation.[149]

12.28 **One rule or two?** Although the modern fashion is to apply a consolidated rule of remoteness of damage, the lay-out of the relevant sections in the Sale of Goods Act betrays the separate limbs of the rule in *Hadley v Baxendale*.[150] The language of the statutory provisions does not respond exactly to Baron Alderson's famous words in that case, but it is an uncontroversial matter that the Act merely restates the rule.[151] The first limb is to be found in the various sections dealing with damages for non-delivery, non-acceptance, and the delivery of defective goods,[152] while the second limb is to be found in the section dealing with special and consequential damages.[153]

Mitigation of Damages[154]

12.29 **General.** It is a fundamental principle of the law of damages that one injured by the wrong of another may not, if he has the power to take evasive action, remain idle in the face of mounting or threatened prejudice. A contractual claimant who wishes to recover compensatory damages for the loss suffered must bestir himself so that responsibility is not laid at his own door. It is sometimes said that the injured party has a 'duty' to mitigate, but this expression is hardly apt for, if it is a duty at all, it is one that he owes only to himself:[155] he suffers any loss occurring after the time he should have resumed responsibility for his own welfare in the area of the contractual expectancy. This duty to mitigate is accompanied contextually by two other mitigation rules. The first of these is that expenses reasonably incurred in taking steps to minimize the loss may be charged to the account of the contract-breaker. According to the second of these additional rules, any benefits the injured party obtains in taking action that is prompted and occasioned by the breach of contract will, to the extent that it averts a threatened loss, be offset against the liability in damages of the contract breaker. These three mitigation rules, implicitly recognized under the Sale of Goods Act, will now be discussed in turn.

---

[149] See the similar approach to the interpretation of clauses as liquidated damages clauses rather than penalties, according to actual rather than recoverable losses: *Robophone Facilities Ltd v Blank*, n. 56 above, 1447–8.

[150] n. 1 above.

[151] See, e.g., *H Parsons (Livestock) Ltd v Uttley Ingham & Co. Ltd*, n. 115 above, 807; *Bostock & Co. Ltd v Nicholson & Sons Ltd* [1904] 1 KB 725, 735.

[152] Ss. 50–51, 53.

[153] S. 54.

[154] M. Bridge (1989) 105 *LQR* 398.

[155] *Darbishire v Warren* [1963] 1 WLR 1067, 1075; *Sotiros Shipping Inc. v Sameiet Solholt (The Solholt)* [1981] 2 Lloyd's Rep. 574, 580 (Staughton J: duty to mitigate 'a condition attached to the right to claim damages'); *Sealace Shipping Ltd v Oceanvoice Ltd (The Alecos M)* [1991] 1 Lloyd's Rep. 120, 124; *Red Deer College v Michaels* [1976] 2 SCR 324, 330–1 (Can.).

Duty to Mitigate

Causation explanation.   The first of the above mitigation rules, the duty to mit-   **12.30**
igate, is most usually attributed to factual causation, in that a claimant who fails
to stave off an unavoidable loss cannot claim that the loss was caused by the
defendant's breach of contract.[156] As Viscount Haldane put it in *British Westinghouse
Electric and Mfg Co. Ltd v Underground Electric Rys Co. of London Ltd,*[157] the compensatory principle is qualified by a rule 'which imposes on a claimant the duty of
taking all reasonable steps to mitigate the loss consequent on the breach, and
debars him from claiming any part of the damage which is due to his neglect to
take such steps'.[158] This explanation may not be entirely satisfactory since, while
the burden of proof rests upon the claimant to demonstrate that the injury suffered flows from the defendant's breach of contract, it is for the defendant to prove
that losses suffered by the claimant could have been avoided by action taken in
mitigation.[159] Furthermore, it seems rather arbitrary to assert that the claimant's
disputed loss has only one effective cause, namely his own inanition rather than
the preceding breach of contract by the defendant.

Remotness explanation.   Another explanation would be that losses the claimant   **12.31**
could reasonably have avoided cannot be said to be within the reasonable contemplation of the parties at the contract date as liable to result from the defendant's
breach, and thus are too remote.[160] The drawback to this is that mitigation authorities do not usually explore the parties' reasonable contemplation *ex ante*, but rather
look to the reasonableness of the claimant's behaviour in the face of a prospective
or incrementally mounting loss.

Defendant not an insurer.   The statement of mitigation, as a general rule inde-   **12.32**
pendent of remoteness, prompts a search for a different explanation. Probably the
best explanation is that the expectation interest, though a creature of the contract,
is sanctioned by the legal system which, in the interests of justice broadly understood, recoils from unduly prejudicing the defendant by conferring protection to
the full extent of factual causation. Just as the remoteness rule is applied so that, in
ordinary cases, the defendant is not an insurer of contractual adventures, so the

---

[156] For a treatment of the mitigation rules as a matter of causation, see *Koch Marine Inc. v
D'Amica Societa di Navigazione ART (The Elena d'Amico)* [1980] 1 Lloyd's Rep. 75, 88; *Lagden v
O'Connor* [2003] UKHL 64; [2004] 1 AC 1067 at [100] (Lord Walker).

[157] [1912] AC 673.

[158] *Ibid.,* 689. See also *Jamal v Moolla Dawood Sons and Co.* [1916] 1 AC 175, 179; *Koch Marine
Inc. v D'Amica Società Di Navigazione ARL (The Elena d'Amico)* n. 156 above, 88.

[159] *Roper v Johnson* (1873) LR 8 CP 167, 178, 181–2; *James Finlay & Co. v Kwik Hoo Tong
Handel Maatschappij* [1928] 2 KB 604, 614; *Red Deer College v Michaels,* n. 155 above, 331.

[160] *Cia Naviera Maropan SA v Bowater's Lloyd Pulp and Paper Mill Ltd* [1955] 2 QB 68, 93, 98–9;
Radford v De Froberville [1977] 1 WLR 1262, 1272–3; *Perry v Sidney Phillips & Son* [1982] 1 All ER
1005, reversed in part on other grounds [1982] 3 All ER 705; *Wingold Construction Co. Ltd v Kramp*
[1960] SCR 556 (Can.).

mitigation rule instructs claimants that a contractual promise may not absolve them from responsibility for their own welfare, and that they may in the circumstances now be better placed than the defendant to take steps towards the broad goal contemplated by the contract. Such an approach would involve scrutiny of the defendant's behaviour and position, and an inquiry into the means of the claimant and the predicament he was in when the contract was breached.

12.33 **Question of fact.** Mitigation is a question of fact governed by the circumstances of individual cases.[161] The steps the claimant ought to take are defined by prudence and reasonableness.[162] In the words of a Canadian judge, the breach of contract releases to the claimant a capacity to act which 'becomes an asset in [his] hands . . . and he is held to a reasonable employment of it in the course of events flowing from the breach'.[163] It may happen that the reasonable course adopted by the claimant will increase the damages payable by the defendant.[164] If, for reasons of impecuniosity, the claimant is unable to take rapid or effective steps in mitigation, he will not be judged too harshly for this.[165] Where the course of mitigation suggested by the defendant involves complex and risky litigation, the claimant will not be faulted for failing to pursue it.[166] Nor will a claimant buyer be required to impair his commercial reputation by forcing on his sub-buyers non-conforming goods or documents, tendered by the defendant seller.[167] Taking steps to mitigate damages may in some circumstances confer on the claimant a benefit in the form of betterment. In principle, provided the claimant has followed the least-cost approach to mitigation, the claimant ought to be able to recover in full[168] even if thus placed in a better position as a result of the breach. There may be cases, however, where the additional benefit may be quite readily liquidated to the benefit of the claimant, so as to justify an equivalent deduction from the cost of mitigation. For example, if there is no market for the seller's undelivered goods, but the buyer is able to buy a better and more profitable substitute for a higher price, the buyer's larger profit margin ought to be deductible from his claim.

---

[161] See, e.g., *Payzu Ltd v Saunders* [1919] 2 KB 581.

[162] *Karas v Rowlett* [1944] SCR 1, 8.

[163] *Ibid.*

[164] *Lagden v O'Connor*, n. 156 above at [78] (Lord Scott).

[165] *Perry v Sidney Phillips & Son*, n. 160 above; *Clippens Oil Co. Ltd v Edinburgh and District Water Trustees* [1907] AC 291, 303; *Trans Trust SPRL v Danubian Trading Co. Ltd* [1952] 2 QB 297, 306; *Radford v De Froberville*, n. 160 above, 1268; *Dodd Properties Ltd v Canterbury City Council* [1980] 1 WLR 433, 453 (claimant's financial stringency flowing, as a matter of common sense, from defendant's tort); *Bacon v Cooper (Metals) Ltd* [1982] 1 All ER 397; *Lagden v O'Connor*, n. 156 above.

[166] *Pilkington v Wood* [1953] Ch. 770.

[167] *James Finlay & Co. v Kwik Hoo Tong Handel Maatschappij*, n. 159 above. Cf. *Canso Chemicals Ltd v Canadian Westinghouse Ltd* (1974) 10 NSR (2d) 306 (Can.).

[168] *Lagden v O'Connor*, n. 156 above at [34] (Lord Hope); *Harbutt's 'Plasticine' Ltd v Wayne Tank and Pump Co. Ltd* [1970] 1 QB 447.

Extraordinary steps.   A buyer of goods will not be required to take extraordinary   **12.34** steps to buy in equivalent goods on the market. In *Lesters Leather & Skin Co. Ltd v Home and Overseas Brokers Ltd*,[169] a seller failed to deliver a conforming quantity of snake skins that were to be shipped from India c.i.f. a United Kingdom port. The Court of Appeal, held, *inter alia*, that it would be unreasonable to expect the seller to order forward the same goods from India, for this would take eight or nine months; as a commercial venture it would be considerably more onerous than expecting a buyer of Bordeaux wines to mitigate by going to Bordeaux.

Illusory Mitigation

Further dealings with party in breach.   Mitigation has posed particular difficul-   **12.35** ties in sale of goods cases when it involves dealings between the same contracting parties.[170] In *Payzu Ltd v Saunders*,[171] the buyers of a quantity of crêpe de chine to be delivered over a nine-month period on thirty-day credit terms failed to pay promptly for the first instalment. Although this was not a discharging breach, the seller repudiated the contract, and was therefore adjudged herself to be in breach. Nevertheless, the same goods were offered for sale again by the seller at the same price but on net cash terms; the buyers declined the offer and accepted the seller's repudiation as terminating the contract. Since, against a rising market, the buyers were unable to obtain better terms than those offered by the seller, and since the seller was not insisting that the buyers forgo their action for damages for breach of contract,[172] the court held that it was unreasonable for the buyers to turn down the offer. In the words of the trial judge, parties involved in a mercantile dispute should not be permitted 'an unhappy indulgence in far-fetched resentment or an undue sensitiveness to slights or unfortunately worded letters'.[173] Scrutton LJ observed that 'in commercial contracts it is generally reasonable to accept an offer from the party in default'.[174]

Limits of decision.   This approach should be limited to cases where the claimant   **12.36** suffers a loss that could have been avoided by mitigating in this way, and where the claimant does not have to change his plans regarding the use of disposal of the contract goods. A buyer would not therefore be required to accept a tender of defective goods, for this would be tantamount to depriving him of the right of rejection,[175] though a buyer might well be required to take up goods previously rejected because the documents were non-complying or the shipment date was

---

169 [1948] WN 437.
170 Bridge, n. 154 above.
171 n. 161 above.
172 For loss of the credit facility.
173 n. 161 above, 586.
174 *Ibid.*, 589.
175 *Heaven & Kesterton Ltd v Ets. François Albiac & Cie* [1956] 2 Lloyd's Rep. 316. Nor would the buyer have to accept any other offer involving a surrender of rights: *Houndsditch Warehouse Co. Ltd v Waltex Ltd* [1944] KB 579.

wrong.[176] In this latter case, a buyer rejecting documents tendered under a forward contract and now searching for substitute goods on the spot market is unlikely to have good grounds for rejecting the goods, formerly covered by those documents, when of suitable quality.

12.37 **Other cases.** The problem of the relationship between mitigation of damages and contractual termination rights turns up in other cases too. One of these, *Strutt v Whitnell*,[177] is a sale of land case that states a principle germane also to sale of goods. It concerns the sale of a house with a covenant of vacant possession that was infringed because the tenant had acquired statutory protection against ejection. The question was whether the mitigation rule compelled the purchaser to surrender the house to the vendors and recover his money, as opposed to retaining the house and pursuing a claim in damages. In holding that the purchaser could not be faulted for failing to choose the former of two equivalent remedial positions, the court denied the vendors the entitlement to submerge their loss in the diminished capital value of the house instead of suffering it in the form of a damages liability. Had the court ruled otherwise, a litigant might lose completely the right to recover damages if he rejects an offer of settlement that accurately records his injury.[178] *Strutt v Whitnell* therefore demonstrates that the doctrine of mitigation, which sometimes has painful remedial consequences, cannot be used to direct the deployment of assets and their monetary equivalents just between the claimant and the defendant: there will have to be a genuine loss suffered once the combined assets of claimant and defendant are added together before mitigation comes into play.

12.38 **A difficult case.** The above point seems to have been overlooked by the court in *Sotiros Shipping Inc. v Sameiet Solholt (The Solholt)*.[179] A ship was sold for $5 million and rejected because of delivery three days late on a rising market[180] when its value had reached $5.5 million. It was subsequently sold for $5.8 million by the sellers. In the view of the court,[181] the buyers were quite entitled to terminate the contract for late delivery, but should then have offered to repurchase the ship from the sellers at the original contract price and without prejudice to their claim for damages for the three-day delay. Satisfied that the sellers would have agreed to

---

[176] *Heaven & Kesterton Ltd v Ets. François Albiac & Cie*, n. 175 above.

[177] [1975] 1 WLR 870.

[178] *Ibid.* 873.

[179] [1981] 2 Lloyd's Rep. 574, affirmed [1983] 1 Lloyd's Rep. 605.

[180] The reason for the buyers' apparently strange behaviour was not established. One possibility was that they were trying to manoeuvre the sellers into a price reduction.

[181] Following *Payzu Ltd v Saunders*, n. 161 above. Cf *Strutt v Whitnell*, n. 177 above. The criticism of *Strutt v Whitnell* in *The Solholt*, n. 179 above, was noted in *Uzinterimpex JSC v Standard Bank Plc* [2008] EWCA Civ 819 at [60], but the court was at pains to say that an offer made by the vendor of land in that case would not have diminished the purchaser's loss but would have converted it into a different form.

this, the court refused to award damages representing the increased price that the buyers would have had to pay for an equivalent ship. Although troubled by the conclusion that the seller had profited substantially from its own breach, the court was still unable to see the flaw in its decision.

Criticism.   The decision, it is submitted, is for various reasons wrong. First of all, it made the buyers' right of termination an illusory one. The result is exactly the same as if it had been the buyers who had committed the discharging breach and the sellers who had accepted it as terminating the contract. If strict rights of contractual discharge are inappropriate, they should be curtailed directly and not undermined by covert means. Secondly, on the facts, it is difficult to see why the initiative should have come from the buyers and interesting to speculate on how the sellers would have viewed the behaviour and mental state of buyers rejecting a late ship and then asking for it to be delivered after all under a different contract. Thirdly, the doctrine of mitigation should only be applied where the claimant suffers an avoidable loss that he wishes to lay at the door of the defendant to that party's detriment. No such loss occurred in *The Solholt*.[182] The so-called loss of the buyers was merely an alternative expression of the sellers' correlative gain, for in the result the sellers were allowed to keep all the post-contract increase in value of the ship. The buyers' loss only became a loss when they were not permitted to recover as damages the increased value of the ship between the contract date and the due delivery date.   **12.39**

Future events.   Another way of putting this is to say that a buyer's duty to mitigate looks to future events from the point of mitigation, and bears no relation to what has happened in the past. In consequence, the buyers should certainly have recovered the $500,000 increase in value accruing to the due delivery date. As for the subsequent $300,000, accruing up to the date the seller eventually sold the ship, the buyers' failure to take the ship from the sellers might be regarded as a personal speculation concerning the future value of the ship, based on the losing assumption that the value of the ship had peaked[183] and not as a loss caused by the breach of contract.[184] They had the use of their money during that period.[185] If indeed the value of the ship had thereafter declined, the buyers would have made a gain, from witholding their money, to which the sellers would have had no claim.   **12.40**

---

[182] n. 179 above.
[183] See *Jamal v Moolla Dawood Sons and Co.* [1916] 1 AC 175, 179.
[184] *Habton Farms v Nimmo* [2003] EWCA Civ 68; [2004] QB 1 at [64]–[65].
[185] *Quaere* if they had paid in advance? See the discussion on the date of assessment of damages in the text accompanying nn. 244 *et seq.* below.

12.41 **Illusory loss.** This criticism of *The Solholt*[186] prompts a further look at *Payzu Ltd v Saunders*.[187] In that case, on a rising market, the buyers refused to accept the seller's offer of mitigation and so were faced with a higher price for crêpe de chine; correlatively, the seller would presumably have disposed of that same quantity of crêpe de chine at an enhanced market price, higher than the figure in the contract and the offer of mitigation. If the buyers and seller did in fact both enter the same market, the one to buy and the other to sell, then there would not have been a loss at all, for the buyers' increased cost would have matched the seller's increased price. The evidence suggested that there was a shortage of crêpe de chine, so it could not be said that the buyers' failure to mitigate robbed the seller of an additional sale of the commodity.[188] A difficulty with the above treatment of mitigation arises where buyer and seller enter the market at different times, or when either or both fail to enter the market at all. This raises another mitigation issue concerning the date of assessment of damages, discussed below. Subject to that, the mitigation rule operates as a condition on the buyer's right to recover expectation losses in full and ought not to be invoked where the buyer alone truly suffers a loss, and justice does not require that the seller be released from liability.

12.42 **Markets and mitigation.** Another point concerning mitigation may be dealt with here. The Sale of Goods Act provisions for assessing damages for non-acceptance by the buyer and non-delivery by the seller lay down, as *prima facie* rules, that the injured party enter the market at the performance date and resell or buy in, as the case may be.[189] This is sometimes said to embody a mitigation principle,[190] and indeed there are circumstances where it may do so, as where the injured party has the capacity and the need to act promptly on a continuously adverse market. But this state of affairs is likely to arise more frequently in the case of stable rather than volatile commodities. The value of residential land was perceptibly rising at all material times in *Wroth v Tyler*,[191] but the same could not be said for the value of bulk sugar on the Basrah market in *The Heron II*[192] where, despite some evidence of seasonal decline, the House of Lords held that it was a matter of even probability whether the market in sugar would rise or fall at the material date. That being so, if the injured party is required by law to act promptly if the market is to serve as the measure of his loss, it is difficult to justify this in terms of mitigation.

---

[186] n. 179 above.

[187] n. 161 above.

[188] The problem of lost volume is discussed in the text accompanying nn. 421 *et seq.* below.

[189] Ss. 50(3) and 51(3).

[190] See, e.g., *Radford v De Froberville* [1977] 1 WLR 1262, 1285; *Asamera Oil Corpn Ltd v Sea Oil & General Corpn* [1979] 1 SCR 633, 647 (Can.).

[191] n. 102 above.

[192] n. 104 above.

What is important is that a party who delays may equally win or lose by delaying. In reality, he is to be treated as assuming a market risk so that, if he wins, he retains the fruits of his speculation, but if he loses, he may not call in the other party to underwrite that speculation with no hope of reward.[193]

Cost of Mitigation

Heavy expenditure.   A corollary of the duty to mitigate is that the claimant is entitled to recover as damages the expenses incurred in mitigating, for these are attributable to the defendant's breach of contract.[194] Although a claimant placed in a difficult position because of the defendant's breach is not treated too harshly,[195] problems sometimes arise if the claimant's peculiarly vulnerable position necessitates heavy expenditures. Claimants in one case were denied recovery for the heavy interest charges they had to bear on securing a bond to release a ship from arrest.[196] These charges, incurred because the claimants ran their own business within unduly tight financial limits, were treated as the subject of a damages claim that failed to comply with the remoteness rule.[197] But in *Bacon v Cooper (Metals) Ltd*,[198] the claimant had to purchase a new rotor for his fragmentizer when the wrong sort of steel, supplied in breach of contract by the defendants, was fed into the fragmentizer. A second-hand replacement could not be procured. The claimant had no choice but to acquire, on expensive hire purchase terms, a new rotor for the fragmentizer, which was still subject to a hire purchase agreement. The cost of acquiring the replacement rotor was allowed as damages and, moreover, no deduction was made for the 'betterment', or improved position of the claimant, supposedly enjoyed from having a new rotor instead of one that had been used for nearly half of its seven-year life expectancy. Making such a deduction would have been tantamount to forcing the claimant to invest his money in the modernization of his machinery.[199]

12.43

---

[193] *Jamal v Moolla Dawood Sons and Co.*, n. 183 above, 179; *Waddell v Blockley* (1880) 4 QBD 478; *British & Commonwealth Holdings Plc v Quadrex Holdings Plc*, n. 4 above.; *Campbell Mostyn (Provisions) Ltd v Barnett Trading Co. Ltd* [1954] 1 Lloyd's Rep. 65. This is particularly important where an anticipatory repudiation is accepted: *Kaines (UK) Ltd v Österreichische Warengesellschaft mbH* [1993] 2 Lloyd's Rep. 1; M. Bridge [1994] *JBL* 152.

[194] *Banco de Portugal v Waterlow & Sons Ltd* [1932] AC 452; *Wilson v United Counties Bank* [1920] AC 102; *Erie County Natural Gas and Fuel Co. Ltd v Carroll* [1911] AC 105; *Lloyds and Scottish Finance Ltd v Modern Cars and Caravans (Kingston) Ltd* [1966] 1 QB 764.

[195] *Banco de Portugal v Waterlow & Sons Ltd*, n. 194 above, 506.

[196] *Cia Financiera Soleada SA v Hamoor Tanker Corpn. Inc. (The Borag)* [1981] 1 WLR 274.

[197] See also *Liesbosch, Dredger v SS Edison* [1933] AC 449; *Radford v De Froberville*, n. 160 above.

[198] [1982] 1 All ER 397.

[199] Citing *Harbutt's 'Plasticine' Ltd v Wayne Tank and Pump Co. Ltd* [1970] 1 QB 447, 472–3 at 401 of *Bacon*, n. 198 above.

Losses Avoided by Mitigation in Fact

12.44 **Actions arising out of transaction.** Once a claimant takes steps to mitigate damages, it follows that he may not recover for losses avoided. Problems sometimes arise where a claimant acts after a breach of contract and this action in fact has the effect of diminishing his losses, though the duty to mitigate may not have required such action to be taken and it may be difficult to trace a causal link between this action and the breach of contract. The leading case is *British Westinghouse Electric and Mfg Co. Ltd v Underground Electric Rys Co. of London Ltd*,[200] which concerned a contract to sell and erect a number of steam turbines and turbo alternators at various dates between 1904 and 1906. These machines turned out to be non-conforming and defective in design and to consume excessive quantities of coal. Sued for the balance of the price, the buyers abandoned an alternative claim for the actual (to date) plus projected excessive coal consumption by the machines, and claimed instead the cost of excessive coal actually consumed, as well as the cost of replacing the seller's machines and substituting them with a much less expensive and efficient new machine made by a competitor. This substitution actually took place in 1908, before the present action was brought. The arbitrator, with some adjustments, found in favour of the buyers, though he also found that it would have been to the buyers' advantage to replace the sellers' machines, as soon as in fact they did, even if the sellers' machines had been in full conformity with the contract. The award, however, was overturned in the House of Lords for reasons appearing in the following passage from Viscount Haldane's speech:

> [T]he duty of taking all reasonable steps to mitigate the loss . . . does not impose on the claimant an obligation to take any step which a reasonable and prudent man would not ordinarily take in the course of his business. But when in the course of his business he has taken action arising out of the transaction, which action has diminished his loss, the effect in actual diminution of the loss he has suffered may be taken into account even though there was no duty on him to act.[201]

12.45 **Consequences of breach.** In this passage, Viscount Haldane states that the claimant takes action arising out of the 'transaction', whereas in a later passage he states that 'the subsequent transaction, if to be taken into account, must be one arising out of the consequences of the breach'.[202] In *British Westinghouse*, the later substitution could not be said to have arisen from the consequences of the 'breach',

---

[200] [1912] AC 673. The case of the 'lost volume' seller, discussed below in text accompanying notes 421 *et seq.*, also raises issues of mitigation in fact. Where a seller sues a buyer for non-acceptance, the question is whether the seller, in reselling the unwanted goods, is in fact mitigating his damages. The seller does not do so if the loss of profit on the first transaction is not recovered on the resale. See *Charter v Sullivan* [1957] 2 QB 117; *Sony Computer Entertainment UK Ltd v Cinram Logistics UK Ltd* [2008] EWCA Civ 955.

[201] *Ibid.*, 689, citing in support *Staniforth v Lyall* (1830) 7 Bing. 169.

[202] n. 200 above, 690. See also *Habton Farms v Nimmo* [2003] EWCA Civ 68; [2004] QB 1 at [90].

since, as the arbitrator found, it would have happened in any event, breach or no breach. But it did arise out of the transaction[203] in the sense that the buyers' power requirements were to be satisfied by either the sellers' machines or the competitor's machines but not by both; if the buyers were using the competitor's machines, it would only be because they had no further use for the sellers' machines. Another way of putting it is to say that, apart from the excessive coal consumption up to 1908,[204] the buyers had in fact suffered no loss from the sellers' breach of contract. One can only speculate what the result might have been if the buyers had brought their action before substituting the sellers' machines. The sellers might then have been driven with uncertain prospects of success[205] to argue that the buyers had a duty to mitigate in the way they actually did in this case.

Claimant's risk. Assuming that the decision taken in 1908 to replace the sell- **12.46** ers' machines in *British Westinghouse*, besides turning out to be beneficial, was perceptibly risk-free at that time, a real difficulty emerges in cases where the claimant takes a risk that might exacerbate his position. This occurred in a Canadian employment case, *Cockburn v Trusts and Guarantee Co.*,[206] where an employee, dismissed in breach of contract, devoted his time, skill, savings, and credit in purchasing the assets of his former employer, which had gone into liquidation. He then revived the affairs of the company and resold the assets for a figure in excess of the earnings he would have received if his employment contract had not been unlawfully terminated. Because he had made use of his time and skills, which assets would not have been available but for his employer's breach of contract, he was entitled only to nominal damages. It is by no means self-evident that a claimant should take a risk the fruits of which, if the risk is beneficial, should first be applied to reducing the defendant's damages. If the claimant's enterprise in *Cockburn* had failed, he would never have recovered as damages his lost savings or ruined credit. It is submitted that a claimant should not have to surrender to the defendant gains where, if the speculation had been unsuccessful, he would have been unable to charge the defendant with his losses. In *British Westinghouse*, the mitigation principle was repeatedly said by Viscount Haldane to govern only if the later transaction was entered into in the normal course of business.[207] A speculative risk is not something that dismissed salaried employees, or buyers of capital goods, normally undertake.

---

[203] n. 200 above, 691.
[204] The buyers were allowed damages for this.
[205] See *Jewelowski v Propp* [1944] KB 510, 511.
[206] (1917) 55 SCR 264. See also *Lavarack v Woods of Colchester Ltd* [1967] 1 QB 278.
[207] n. 200 above, 689–91. See also *Hill & Sons v Edwin Showell & Sons Ltd* (1918) 87 LJ KB 1106, 1115 ('speculative work not in the ordinary course of business').

12.47 **Commodities trading.** In the normal run of sale of goods contracts, it will be difficult for a defendant seller to show mitigation in fact, taking the form of a substitute purchase, that 'aris[es] out of the consequences of the breach'. A buyer's capacity to act is unlikely to be monopolized by a single contract. But the possibility does arise in cases like *British Westinghouse*, where the buyers' needs were confined to one set of machines. In commodities trading, a factual link between a defendant seller's breach and a buyer's subsequent purchase would seem unlikely; merchants conduct their buying and selling activities across a broad front.[208] Nevertheless, in *R Pagnan & Flli v Corbisa Industrial Agropacuaria Lda*,[209] the buyers lawfully rejected a c.i.f. cargo before purchasing it on a distress basis on shore at the port of discharge. The price was artificially low because the buyers had sequestered the cargo, making it difficult for the sellers to sell to anyone else.[210] Since the later transaction was 'part of a continuous dealing between the same parties in respect of the same goods', and not 'an independent or disconnected transaction',[211] the profit made under it could be offset against the smaller market rise in the goods so that the buyers had suffered no loss in consequence of the sellers' breach.[212] It is unlikely that the same result would have been reached if the buyers had chanced upon another cargo sold by different sellers in distressed circumstances.

Mitigation and Anticipatory Repudiation

12.48 **Basis of anticipatory repudiation.** A number of problems are presented in cases where the claimant has not yet elected to seek relief in damages for the defendant's failure in breach of contract to perform his primary obligations. One such problem arises where the defendant refuses in advance to perform the contract. One somewhat discredited theory, coloured by rescission *ab initio* ideas, is that such an anticipatory repudiation[213] is not a present breach but an offer to rescind on terms.[214] This is consistent with the view that no breach of contract

---

[208] The difficulties of showing a factual connection between the various purchases and sales is dramatically revealed in a series of soya bean cases arising out of the 1973 US export embargo: see M. Bridge, 'The 1973 Mississippi Floods: "Force Majeure" and Prohibition of Export' in E. McKendrick (ed.), *Force Majeure and Frustration of Contract* (2nd edn, LLP, 1995).

[209] [1971] 1 All ER 165.

[210] '[T]he sellers were at a disadvantage which the buyers were able to exploit': *Hussey v Eels* [1990] 2 QB 227, 239.

[211] n. 209 above, 169. Cf. *Hussey v Eels*, above; *Koch Marine Inc. v D'Amica Societa di Navigazione ARL* [1980] 1 Lloyd's Rep. 75.

[212] The court thereby departed from the normal rule, discussed in the text accompanying nn. 235 *et seq.* below, that damages are assessed by reference to the prevailing market price.

[213] J. M. Nienabr [1962] *CLJ* 213; F. Dawson [1981] *CLJ* 83.

[214] *Bradley v H Newsom, Sons & Co.* [1919] AC 16, 52; *Johnstone v Milling* (1886) 16 QBD 460, 473 (contract ceases to exist except for damages); *Hochster v De la Tour* (1853) 2 E & B 678, 685 (consent to ending of contract). Criticized by Nienabr, n. 213 above, 224.

occurs until the repudiation is accepted.[215] There is ample support, however, for a different theory, that a refusal to perform in future is a present breach[216] of an implied term to refrain from impeding the other party's contractual expectations or of fidelity to the contract goal. Suppose a seller declares in advance his refusal to deliver goods at a future date as called for by the contract. The innocent party may elect between accepting the repudiation immediately as determining the contract, or awaiting the date fixed for performance. Depending on which of the above theories is accepted, that party is accepting or declining an offer to rescind, or is affirming the contract or terminating it for the breach of the implied term.

Election to terminate.   No matter which of the above theories is adopted, it is   **12.49** well established that the innocent party is under no compulsion to mitigate damages by electing to terminate the contract. This conclusion is readily supportable if the anticipatory repudiation is not a breach. It is more difficult to justify if a refusal to perform amounts to a present breach, unless the subject of the later damages action is seen as the breach of the primary obligation itself rather than the implied term of fidelity. The inapplicability of mitigation in the face of an anticipatory repudiation is dramatically illustrated by *Tredegar Iron and Coal Co. Ltd v Hawthorn Brothers & Co.*,[217] where an f.o.b. contract called for the supply of coal at a certain price. Unable to nominate an effective ship, the buyers conveyed to the sellers an offer from a third party to buy the same quantity of coal for the domestic market at a price slightly higher than the contract price. The sellers declined to accept this offer and had to sell the coal for less than the contract price shortly after the buyers declined to take delivery at the due date for performance. The sellers were able to recover damages representing the difference between the contract price and the diminished market price. If this result is explicable only according to the technicalities of anticipatory repudiation, it seems extraordinary and argues a case for modifying the substantive law. The result might be less extraordinary, however, if, at the time of the buyers' offer to mitigate, the current market price stands higher than the third party's offer though it later declines, or where the sellers have surplus coal and entertain a legitimate expectation of selling a quantity of coal to that same third party in any event.

---

[215] e.g., *Ripley v M'Lure* (1849) 4 Ex. 345; *Howard v Pickford Tool Co. Ltd* [1951] 1 KB 417, 421 (unaccepted repudiation 'a thing writ in water and of no value to anybody'); *White & Carter (Councils) Ltd v McGregor* [1962] AC 413.

[216] e.g., *Frost v Knight* (1872) LR 7 Ex. 11; *Hochster v De la Tour*, n. 214 above; *Maredelanto Cia Naviera SA v Bergbau-Handels GmbH (The Mihalis Angelos)* [1971] 1 QB 164.

[217] (1902) 18 TLR 716. See also *Lusograin Comercio International de Cereas Lda v Bunge AG* [1986] 2 Lloyd's Rep. 654, where the sellers, declining to accept the buyers' repudiation, were allowed to continue earning the carrying charges to which they were entitled during a shipment extension period.

12.50 Debt. Another case where a claimant is entitled to ignore a repudiation without feeling the need to mitigate is where he is able to press a claim in debt. Debt is in principle far from being a discretionary remedy.[218] For example, a claimant buyer who has prepaid the price, and who wishes to recover it, as on a failure of consideration, upon terminating the contract, need not mitigate in respect of this money claim,[219] though mitigation may in fact bear upon an ancillary damages claim. This amounts to another way of saying that mitigation does not hamper a claimant in exercising termination rights,[220] for the recovery of the pre-paid money is a necessary consequence of termination.

12.51 Qualifying for debt action. A vivid illustration of the irrelevance of mitigation to debt is afforded by *White & Carter (Councils) Ltd v McGregor*,[221] where the repudiation by a garage of a three-year contract for advertising the garage on municipal waste-paper bins accelerated the garage's payment obligation under the contract. The repudiation occurred before the advertising agents had even prepared the advertising plates, but they went ahead, began displaying them, and sued in debt for the three years' payments. The case shows that mitigation does not destroy the right to sue in debt and, furthermore, it does not prevent the innocent party from proceeding unilaterally with performance so as to qualify under the contract for a debt claim, provided that this can be done in compliance with the letter of the contract. Such compliance will be impossible if the cooperation of the other party is needed to perform conditions precedent to the debt entitlement.[222]

12.52 Economic waste. The decision of a bare majority of the House of Lords has been criticized as sanctioning economic waste, but performance in this case was unwanted rather than wasteful; there was nothing to show that the advertising was any the less effective with the general public as a result of the garage's disavowal of it. In the majority, however, Lord Reid qualified his judgment by observing that a claimant would need a 'substantial and legitimate interest'[223] if he were unilaterally

---

[218] But see Lord Denning in *Attica Sea Carriers Corpn. v Ferrostaal Poseidon Bulk Reederei GmbH (The Puerto Buitrago)* [1976] 1 Lloyd's Rep. 250, 255 (debt claim as specific performance, *sed quaere?*).

[219] What about a claimant seeking recovery of the price paid in the form of a damages claim?

[220] *Payzu Ltd v Saunders* [1919] 2 KB 581; *Sotiros Shipping Inc. v Sameiet Solholt (The Solholt)* [1983] 1 Lloyd's Rep. 605; *Heaven & Kesterton Ltd v Ets. François Albiac & Cie* [1956] 2 Lloyd's Rep. 316.

[221] n. 215 above; cf. *Clark v Marsiglia* (1845) 1 Denio 317 (US).

[222] *White & Carter (Councils) Ltd v McGregor*, n. 215 above, 429; *Hounslow London BC v Twickenham Garden Developments Ltd* [1971] Ch. 233; *Finelli v Dee* (1968) 67 DLR (2d) 393; *Clea Shipping Corp. v Bulk Oil International Ltd (No. 2) (The Alaksan Trader)* [1984] 1 All ER 129; *Ocean Marine Navigation Inc. v Koch Carbon Inc. (The Dynamic)* [2003] EWHC 1936 (Comm); [2003] |2 Lloyd's Rep. 693. *Quaere* where the defendant's breach triggers a clause accelerating the duty to pay to a time before work, needing the defendant's cooperation, falls due?

[223] n. 215 above, 431.

to qualify for a debt claim in this way: the burden of showing the absence of this would rest upon the defendant. It is nevertheless difficult to see the ground for this qualification, except a vague and innominate principle of equity.[224] The defenders in *White & Carter* had failed to lead evidence of the absence of such an interest. One might wonder how such an interest could ever be lacking if it was possessed by the advertising agents in this case, the behaviour of whom is hard to explain, unless they faced difficulty in computing a damages claim.[225] In *Clea Shipping Corpn v Bulk Oil International Ltd (The Alaskan Trader) (No. 2)*,[226] Lloyd J declined to interfere with an arbitrator's finding that the owner of a ship had no legitimate interest in refusing to accept the time charterer's repudiation by holding the ship at the disposal of the charterer for the remainder of the charter period. The owner should have taken steps to secure an alternative fixture for the ship. The case clearly recognizes that the normally unfettered right to elect in favour of the continuance of a contract where the other party repudiates is qualified in such a case by 'general equitable principles'.[227]

Impact on sale of goods.   The principle of *White & Carter (Councils) Ltd v McGregor* is of limited significance in sale of goods law. It was seen in an earlier chapter[228] that the cooperation of both parties is needed to pass the property in goods initially unascertained, and that a repudiation by one party is effective in withdrawing his implied assent to the other's unconditional appropriation of the goods to the contract. This combination of assent and unconditional appropriation is required to pass the property in unascertained goods, and the passing of property is the normal case in which a seller is able to sue in debt for the price.[229] Furthermore, as was observed earlier in this chapter, repudiation is not allowed to negative the requirement that conditions precedent be performed before the right to sue in debt arises.[230]   **12.53**

Mitigation and Specific Performance

Right to seek specific relief.   Mitigation has emerged in recent times to qualify a claimant's entitlement to pursue a claim for the specific performance of the contract.   **12.54**

---

[224] *Ibid.*, 430–1: 'some general equitable principle or element of public policy'.

[225] For the problem of lost volume (how many litter bins and advertisers could Clyde bank absorb?), see discussion in the text accompanying nn. 421 *et seq.* below.

[226] n. 222 above.

[227] *Ibid.*, 136. And at 137: '*some* fetter, if only in extreme cases' (emphasis in the original). See also *The Puerto Buitrago*, n. 218 above (redelivery of chartered ship and covenant to repair); *Channel Islands Ferries Ltd v Cenargo Navigation Ltd (The Rozel)* [1994] 2 Lloyd's Rep. 161 (damages for breach of repair covenant).

[228] See Ch. 3 above.

[229] S. 49(1), above.

[230] *Colley v Overseas Exporters* [1921] 3 KB 302, distinguishing *Mackay v Dick* (1881) 6 App. Cas. 251.

Since specific performance is quite a rare remedy in sales law, this development is therefore of limited interest. The claimant house purchaser in *Wroth v Tyler*[231] was able to obtain damages assessed at the judgment date, rather than the breach date, because these were awarded in lieu of specific performance.[232] That a court might in a proper case require a claimant to mitigate, and so award damages assessed at a mitigation date prior to judgment instead of the specific relief it would otherwise be disposed to give, is evident in the Canadian case of *Asamera Oil Corpn Ltd v Sea Oil & General Corpn.*[233] In that case, claimants suing in detinue for the return of shares bailed years ago to the defendant company, or for specific performance of this agreement,[234] were not permitted to press their claim for specific relief through years of delay in litigation and in the face of a volatile market in the shares. They were required after a time, admittedly a considerable time, to purchase an equivalent number of shares on the open market. Specific performance is, after all, a discretionary remedy.

Measuring Losses According to the Market

12.55 **General.** Sections 50 and 51 of the Sale of Goods Act, dealing with the buyer's liability in damages for non-acceptance and the seller's liability in damages for non-delivery, both prescribe in sub-section (3) that the damages due will *prima facie* be the difference between the contract price and the market or current price at the date fixed for acceptance or delivery, as the case may be.[235] There has to be an 'available market' for the goods.[236] Sub-section (3) encapsulates two rules: first, the breach date rule, by which the date for calculating damages is the date that the buyer or seller is in breach of his primary obligation of delivery or acceptance of the goods;[237] and secondly, the rule that the contract price is compared with the

---

[231] n. 102 above.

[232] The decision was supported by the wording of the Chancery Amendment Act 1858 (Lord Cairns's Act), 21 & 22 Vict., cap. 27. See however *Johnson v Agnew*, n. 23 above, where the court preferred a relaxation in the date of assessment of damages at common law to the idea that a difference existed between the equitable and common law approach to damages.

[233] n. 190 above.

[234] The case does not clearly indicate which.

[235] S. 50 (non-acceptance) codifies the decision in *Barrow v Arnaud* (1846) 8 QB 595. If the market price has risen, in the case of a seller's action, or fallen, in the case of a buyer's, the damages will be nominal. See *Erie County Natural Gas and Fuel Co. Ltd v Carroll* [1911] AC 105. On the market rule generally, see M. Bridge, 'The Market Rule of Damages Assessment', in D. Saidov and R. Cunnington (eds), *Contract Damages[:] Domestic and International Perspectives* (Hart Publishing, 2008).

[236] Discussed below.

[237] Where performance takes place over a period, damages will normally be assessed according to the last date allowed for performance: *Roper v Johnson* (1873) LR 8 CP 167; *Brown v Muller* (1872) LR 7 Ex. 319; *Phoeus D Kyprianou Co. v Wm H Pim Jnr & Co. Ltd* [1977] 2 Lloyd's Rep. 570; *Bremer Handelsgesellschaft mbH v Vanden Avenne-Izegem PVBA* [1978] 2 Lloyd's Rep. 109 (the next day in the case of default clauses in commodities forms); *Alfred C Toepfer v Peter Cremer* [1975] 2

prevailing market price, rather than with some other standard. Where the contract allows for a flexible quantity of goods, damages will be assessed at the top end of the scale where it is the claimant who has the quantitative option, and at the bottom where the defendant has the option.[238]

Prima facie rules. Although the two rules in sub-section (3) are contained in a provision stated to be of a *prima facie* nature, they are difficult to displace in practice.[239] They will not be displaced simply because the prospect of a resale or sub-sale satisfies the remoteness of damage test, since the presence of an available market operates as a restraint on recovery.[240] In the absence of an available market, sections 50–51[241] apply the standard of remoteness drawn from the first limb of the rule in *Hadley v Baxendale*[242] and permit the assessment of damages by other means. Such assessment, however, must conform to established principles of factual causation, remoteness of damage, and mitigation of damages.[243]

12.56

Abstract and Concrete Damages Claims

Breach date rule. The breach date rule,[244] as stated earlier in this chapter, is best explained on the ground that an injured party who chooses not to enter the market is speculating for his own benefit or detriment.[245] The rule does not in fact require the claimant to enter the market and, since in abstract terms it permits the

12.57

Lloyd's Rep. 118; *Tai Hing Cotton Mill v Kamsing Knitting Factory* [1979] AC 91; *Intertradex SA v Lesieur-Tourteaux SARL* [1978] 2 Lloyd's Rep. 509, 518–19.

[238] *Cockburn v Alexander* (1846) 6 CB 791; *Toprak Mahsulleri Ofisi v Finagrain Cie Commerciale Agricole et Financière SA* [1979] 2 Lloyd's Rep. 98. An option may be subject to an implied limitation as to the quantities of particular types of contract goods: *Paula Lee Ltd v Robert Zehil & [Co.] Ltd* [1983] 2 All ER 390.

[239] S. 50(3) will, however, be displaced in the case of manufactured goods where the seller's claim for damages for non-acceptance is based on the fact that the buyer's default means that the seller has concluded one sale fewer than he would otherwise have done. See *Re Vic Mill Ltd* [1913] 1 Ch. 465 and the lost volume problem, discussed in the text accompanying nn. 421 *et seq.* below.

[240] *Patrick v Russo-British Grain Export Co. Ltd* [1927] 2 KB 535; *Coastal (Bermuda) Petroleum Ltd v VTT Vulcan Petroleum SA (The Marine Star)* [1994] CLC 1019, 1025. But the market is displaced when in fact it is absent, not when it is absent *and* such absence satisfies the remoteness test: *The Marine Star.*

[241] In sub-s.(2).

[242] n. 1 above. The second limb is conventionally seen as contained in s. 54.

[243] It is common in the absence of a market for sub-sales to be looked at in buyers' actions for non-delivery: *The Arpad* [1934] P 189, 200–2; *Lyon v Fuchs* (1920) 2 Ll. LR 333; *Mott v Muller* (1922) 13 Ll. LR 492; *Patrick v Russo-British Grain Export Co. Ltd*, n. 240 above; *Grébert-Borgnis v J & W Nugent* (1885) 15 QBD 85; *Hydraulic Engineering Co. Ltd v McHaffie, Goslett & Co.* (1878) 4 QBD 670; *J Leavey & Co Ltd v George H Hirst & Co. Ltd* [1944] KB 24; *Richmond Western Wineries Ltd v Simpson* [1940] SCR 1 (Can.). But the subsale must satisfy the remoteness test: *Kwei Tek Chao v British Traders and Shippers Ltd* [1954] 2 QB 459, 492–9; *Coastal International Trading Ltd v Maroil AG* [1988] 1 Lloyd's Rep. 92, 95; *Frank Mott & Co. Ltd v Wm H Muller & Co. (London) Ltd* (1922) 13 Ll L R 492.

[244] S. Waddams (1981) 97 *LQR* 445.

[245] See discussion in the text accompanying nn. 189 *et seq.* above.

claimant's loss to be crystallized as a market position, without a substitute transaction being made, it is in perfect harmony with the speculation principle. Many of the difficulties that arise in the area of damages stem from uncertainty in characterizing the claimant's loss, either as an abstract measure of market disadvantage or as a concrete measure of loss demonstrated by the practical need to enter an adverse market. A claimant in the latter category presses the case for abandoning the philosophy of abstract market disadvantage.

12.58 **Bailment comparison.** One example of this is the prepaying buyer. In early cases,[246] references were made to the liability of a bailee of shares, unlawfully holding over and sued in detinue by the bailor, where damages were assessed at the date of the subsequent proceedings.[247] These bailment authorities were not followed in sales cases where the buyer had not paid at all[248] and where the buyer had paid in part.[249] But the bailment comparison was followed in another case where the buyer had given acceptances at four months that had been discounted and had fallen due.[250] Further support for departing from the breach date rule in favour of assessment at the date of trial, in the case of prepaying buyers, is afforded in other cases.[251] One of these cases points the way to a rationalization of this departure from the breach date rule, namely, that the rule should not apply where a buyer has been deprived of the financial capacity to enter the market, and this possibility is within the reasonable contemplation of the seller at the contract date as liable to result from his breach.[252] This approach comes close to abandoning the abstract approach of English law to damages assessment in favour of a concrete approach.

12.59 **Notional market transaction.** A relaxation of the breach date rule to permit damages to be assessed after the breach date is evident in certain sale of land cases,[253] but it will be an exceptional sale of goods case that calls for such treatment. Suppose that the nature of the goods or of the market is such that an instantaneous market transaction cannot occur. An entry into the market may need to be delayed

---

[246] See *Gainsford v Carroll* (1824) 2 B & C 624; *Startup v Cortazzi* (1835) 2 CM & R 164; *Elliot v Hughes* (1863) 3 F & F 387.

[247] See the discussion of these authorities in *Asamera Oil Corpn Ltd v Sea Oil & General Corpn*, n. 233 above.

[248] *Gainsford v Carroll*, n. 246 above.

[249] *Startup v Cortazzi*, n. 246 above.

[250] *Elliot v Hughes*, n. 246 above.

[251] *Aronson v Mologa Holzindustrie A/G Leningrad* (1927) 32 Com. Cas. 276, 290 (Atkin LJ); *Peebles v Pfeifer* [1918] 2 WWR 877; *Asamera Oil Corpn Ltd v Sea Oil & General Corpn*, n. 233 above.

[252] *Peebles v Pfeifer*, n. 251 above (purchase of grain seed by a farmer). See also *Asamera Oil Corpn Ltd v Sea Oil & General Corpn*, n. 233 above, where a buyer who has not paid is said to have his purchasing power released.

[253] *Wroth v Tyler*, n. 102 above; *Johnson v Agnew*, n. 23 above.

or staggered for reasons concerning shortage, difficulties of communication, or the fear of exciting the market with a large sale or purchase. These difficulties do not detract from the existence of an available market. Nevertheless, the market to be considered remains the one at the breach date and not the later market that the claimant did enter or might have entered.[254] The reason is that the damages assessment under sections 50(3) and 51(3) is based on a 'notional or fictitious sale',[255] which is consistent with English law's preference for an abstract, rather than concrete, approach to these matters. If a prepaying buyer does have the means to enter the market at the breach date, he can always recover as damages the lost investment value of the prepaid sum from the date of actual mitigation.[256]

Waiver. Another clear instance of delayed assessment after the performance date is where there has been an agreed waiver or forbearance; there is no need for a binding variation of the contract. The damages will be assessed at the end of the waiver or forbearance when the claimant is free to go into the market.[257] Assessment will also be delayed where non-conforming goods have been delivered and subsequently rejected by the buyer, who now seeks damages for non-delivery on a rising market.[258] A buyer unlawfully rejecting goods should be treated as refusing to accept them at that date,[259] which should serve as the reference point for damages. **12.60**

Currency difficulties. An interesting case for delaying assessment might also be advanced where the conclusion of the substitute transaction is delayed by currency difficulties. In *Attorney-General of the Republic of Ghana v Texaco Overseas* **12.61**

---

[254] *Garnac Grain Co. Inc. v HMF Faure & Fairclough Ltd* [1968] AC 1130 note, 1138 (description of trial judge's finding); *Shearson Lehman Hutton Inc. v Maclaine Watson & Co. Ltd (No. 2)* [1990] 3 All ER 723, 731. Cf *Petrograde Inc. v Stinnes Handels GmbH* [1995] 1 Lloyd's Rep. 142, 152–53 ('weighted average of the prices that would have been obtained during the . . . period').

[255] *Shearson Lehman Hutton, Inc. v Maclaine Watson & Co. Ltd (No. 2)*, n. 254 above, 731.

[256] *Startup v Cortazzi*, n. 246 above. Alternatively, the court has a broad discretion, where proceedings have begun, to award simple interest on the prepaid sum, for part or all of the period, from the time the cause of action arose to the date of payment or of judgment: Supreme Court Act, s. 35A (added by Administration of Justice Act 1982, s. 15 and Sch. 1); County Courts Act 1984, s. 69. On interest, including interest for late payment of commercial debts, see Ch. 11 above.

[257] *Ogle v Vane* (1868) LR 3 QB 272; *Hickman v Haynes* (1875) LR 10 CP 598; *Blackburn Bobbin Co. Ltd v T W Allen & Sons Ltd* [1918] 1 KB 540; *Toprak Mahsulleri Ofisi v Finagrain Cie Commerciale Agricole et Financière SA* [1979] 2 Lloyd's Rep. 298; *Tyers v Rosedale and Ferryhill Iron Co. Ltd* (1875) LR 10 Ex. 195; *Samuel v Black Lake Asbestos and Chrome Co.* (1921) 62 SCR 472 (Can.); *Petrie v Rae* (1919) 46 OLR 19 (Can.). *Quaere* a unilateral indulgence granted by one party? The market assessment date ought not to be extended, but see *Carbopego-Abastecimento de Combustiveis SA v Amici Export Corpn* [2006] EWHC 72 (Comm); [2006] 1 Lloyd's Rep. 736.

[258] *Kwei Tek Chao v British Traders and Shippers Ltd*, n. 243 above, 492–9 (date buyer discovers breach); *Van Den Hurk v Martens & Co. Ltd* [1920] 1 KB 850 (a s. 53 case) (rejection date, despite delay of goods for months on the French railway system, where buyer could not examine goods before use).

[259] S. 50(3).

Tankships Ltd,[260] the claimants sued, under a bill of lading contract,[261] a carrier who had failed to deliver their oil. An alternative cargo would have had to be purchased from the nearest market in US dollars, but the claimants were prevented by internal difficulties from obtaining the requisite foreign currency and effecting the substitute purchase. In the present proceedings, separated from the non-delivery of the claimants' oil by a catastrophic devaluation of the Ghanainan currency, they sought to recover the value of the cargo in dollars. This relief was refused because the claimants' loss was suffered in the local Ghanaian currency;[262] they had intended to dispose of the oil in Ghana, where oil transactions were conducted in the local currency. This is in accord with principle.[263] But suppose that the claimants had tried a different approach by claiming as a separate item of damages the added currency cost[264] of the substitute cargo arising out of necessary delays in acquiring it. Although the present claimants would have been in great difficulties explaining the very lengthy delay, it is arguable that a claim of this nature ought to succeed if the claimant does move expeditiously and the loss is not too remote.[265] Delaying the reference to the market in goods and compensating for currency loss amount in a case of this kind to the same thing. Oil and currency are both commodities. On the other hand, allowing a claim of this nature runs counter to the governing principle of abstract damages assessment which eschews concrete transactions of resale and subsale.

12.62 **Future contingencies.** There are comparisons to be made between the market damages rule and the general rule relating to the discount of damages for future loss to take account of future contingencies. The issue of discounting damages emerges in its clearest form where the claimant is entitled to an income stream that is now dammed by the acceptance of a repudiatory breach committed by the defendant. In time charter cases, for example, the issue is whether a claimant owner's damages, when the charter is prematurely terminated, should be measured by a simple comparison of the future charter income stream with the market rate prevailing at the date the charter is terminated. To do so, would in effect be to treat the owner's entitlement to that future income stream as a type of capital asset instead of something to be earned by the continuing availability of the ship over

---

[260] *The Texaco Melbourne* [1993] 1 Lloyd's Rep. 471 (M. Bridge [1994] *JBL* 155), affirmed [1994] 1 Lloyd's Rep. 473.

[261] But the case can be treated as a sale of goods for present purposes.

[262] Hence the defendants experienced a very large windfall: their business was conducted in dollars, few of which would now be required to purchase the Ghanaian currency needed to satisfy judgment.

[263] See Ch. 11 above.

[264] *Quaere* could this added cost have been passed on to their purchasers in the local currency so as not to be a loss at all? Or had the steep increase in the price of oil diminished local demand for it?

[265] On the reasonable contemplation of currency movement in modern conditions, see *International Minerals and Chemical Corpn v Karl O. Helm AG* [1986] 1 Lloyd's Rep. 81, 105.

the balance of the charter period. A similar problem could arise in the case of a long-term contract for the supply of goods on an instalment basis. The market damages rule, when applied in its purest form, treats the claimant as having an established right at the breach date and is insensitive to any inquiry based upon an actual loss suffered by the claimant. Departing from this rule, the majority decision of the House of Lords in *The Golden Victory*[266] accepted the need to take account of contingencies affecting the future performance of the contract by the claimant.[267] This was consistent with Lord Blackburn's view that damages should place the claimant in the position he occupied before the breach of contract occurred.[268] The claimant should not be placed in a fictitious pre-breach position, benefiting from a rule that adverse future contingencies should not be considered. The disagreement between the majority and the minority in *The Golden Victory* turned upon the degree of probability that had to exist before account could be taken of a contingency, and also on whether a contingency had to be taken into account in any event if it had come to pass by the time damages came to be assessed. The majority would have taken into account a 'real possibility'[269] so as to discount damages and did take account of the war that had broken out. The minority, influenced by considerations of commercial certainty and forensic efficiency, required more than an 'outside chance' and something that was at least 'likely but not certain'.[270] They would, moreover, not have employed hindsight at all. The event in question was the commencement of a war, more than a year after the charterers had repudiated the contract, that would have permitted the charterer to invoke a cancellation clause and so rid itself of an expensive charter.[271]

---

[266] *Golden Strait Corpn v Nippon Yusen Kubishika Kaisha (The Golden Victory)* [2005] EWCA Civ 1190; [2006] 1 WLR 533, affirmed [2007] UKHL 12; [2007] 2 AC 353, following *Bwllfa and Merthyr Dare Collieries (1891) Ltd v Pontypridd Waterworks Co.* [1903] AC 426. See also *Gill & Duffus SA v Berger & Co.* [1984] AC 382, 392 (Lord Diplock).

[267] See also *Maredelanto Cia Naviera SA v Bergbau-Handel GmbH (The Mihalis Angelos)* [1971] 1 QB 164.

[268] *Livingstone v Rawyards Coal Co.* (1880) 5 App Cas 25.

[269] n. 266 above at [36] (Lord Scott), with whom Lords Brown and Carswell concurred.

[270] *Ibid.*, at [22] (Lord Bingham) with whom Lord Walker concurred. Both Lord Bingham and Lord Walker, at [22] and [45], read the arbitrator's finding of the chance of war, judged as at the breach date, as one of a bare possibility when, it is submitted, the more natural way to read his finding was that war was less than a 50% possibility.

[271] In the Court of Appeal, n. 266 above, see Lord Mance at [23] (charterers would 'probably' have cancelled in the event of war). Lord Mance also said at [24]: "[T]he owners were never entitled to absolute confidence that the charter would run for its full 7 year period. They never had an asset which they could bank or sell on that basis. There is no reason why the transmutation of their claims to performance of this charter into claims for non-performance of the charter should improve their position in this respect.' See also *The Mihalis Angelos*, n. 267 above, 196 (Lord Denning MR: 'all contingencies which might have reduced or extinguished the loss'). A stricter view of the likelihood of future contingencies was taken by Megaw LJ in the same case at 210 ('predestined to happen') See also: *BS&N Ltd (BVI) v Micado Shipping Ltd (Malta) (The Seaflower)* [2000] 2 Lloyd's Rep. 37, 44 ('inevitably'); *North Sea Energy Holdings v Petroleum Authority of Thailand* [1999] 1 Lloyd's Rep.

Apart from these differences, there was common ground among all their lordships that, in a proper case, the market rule of damages, to be assessed once and for all on the breach date, might be set aside. The reason, it is submitted, that the market rule can coexist with the rule for discounting damages for future contingencies is that the latter rule is concerned with future losses that have to be accelerated to the present in order for a once-and-for-all assessment of damages to be made. This justifies a departure from the breach date rule in its market form. The market rule, on the other hand, is concerned with the characterization and measurement of a present loss.[272]

Anticipatory Repudiation

12.63 **Performance date or acceptance?** The date of assessment of damages has proved particularly troublesome in cases of anticipatory repudiation. Taking first an anticipatory repudiation not accepted by the other party, on one view of the law no breach of contract took place at all until it was accepted by the injured party as terminating the contract.[273] Consequently, there was no need to mitigate damages from the moment of repudiation. Suppose, however, that a repudiation is accepted before the performance date. Is the damages reference to the market in sections 50–51 to take place at the due performance date or at the date of the acceptance of the repudiation? And does it make any difference that the claimant brings his damages action before the performance date, so that the future market rate cannot be known?

12.64 **Fixed and movable performance dates.** Sections 50–51 distinguish between contracts providing for a fixed performance date and those that do not. In the former case, it has been held that damages are to be settled by reference to the market price prevailing at the due date of performance.[274] If an action is brought before the due date, a court will make the best surmise that it can of the buyer's loss.[275] As a matter of principle, the same will hold true where the buyer repudiates and the seller brings a damages action for non-acceptance.[276] This approach to damages assessment is quite correct, for the buyer suing for damages

---

483, 496 ('predestined'). See also *Chiemgauer Membran und Zeltbau GmbH v New Millennium Experience Co.* [2002] BPIR 42.

[272] See *The Golden Victory*, n. 266 above, at [35] (Lord Scott): 'In cases . . . where the contract for sale of goods is not simply a contract for a one-off sale, but is a contract for the supply of goods over some specified period, the application of the general rule may not be in the least apt.'

[273] Discussed in the text accompanying nn. 213–16 above.

[274] *Melachrino v Nickoll and Knight* [1920] 1 KB 693; *Millet v Van Heek & Co.* [1921] 2 KB 369; *Garnac Grain Co. Inc. v HMF Faure & Fairclough Ltd*, n. 254 above, 1140; *Lusograin Comercio International de Cereas Lda v Bunge AG* [1986] 2 Lloyd's Rep. 654.

[275] *Melachrino v Nickoll and Knight*, n. 274 above.

[276] *Tai Hing Cotton Mill v Kamsing Knitting Factory* [1979] AC 91, distinguishing, at 103, *Hartley v Hymans* [1920] 3 KB 475 and *Tyers v Rosedale and Ferryhill Iron Co. Ltd*, n. 257 above.

for non-delivery may not claim to be put in a better position after the repudiation than if the contract had been performed, and so may not look to the higher market price prevailing at the date of repudiation.[277] Nevertheless, an important reservation must be entered here. In market conditions, a buyer accepting a repudiation before the due performance date is required to mitigate by 'go[ing] into the market and buy[ing] against the defaulting seller if a reasonable opportunity offers',[278] in which event the act of mitigation will provide the standard for quantifying his damages.[279]

Effect of repurchase.   Should the buyer fail to mitigate, then the date when 12.65 he ought to have acted will be taken as the standard for measuring the market.[280] If the buyer buys in before the performance date and the market later falls, it is submitted that the buyer should have his damages assessed according to the repurchase.[281] Alternatively, the difference between the higher mitigation price and the later market price may be treated as the recoverable costs of mitigation.[282] If the market rises, the seller will be spared the added expense of the market rise. This even-handed approach is to be preferred to an assessment of damages based upon the lowest point in the market between the accepted repudiation and the due performance date, which would require the buyer to take risks for the benefit of the seller and is not the law.[283] There is no reason to suppose that the same principles should not apply where it is the buyer who breaches and the seller who mitigates,[284] though from an evidentiary point of view it may be more difficult to establish a causal link between the contract of sale and a subsequent contract said to be entered into for the purpose of mitigation.[285]

Movable date and damages assessment.   Where the contract fails to state a clear 12.66 date for performance, the last two lines of section 50(3) and of section 51(3) provide that the date for assessing damages is the date the buyer refuses to accept and

---

[277] *Tai Hing Cotton Mill v Kamsing Knitting Factory*, n. 276 above; *Melachrino v Nickoll and Knight*, n. 274 above, 699.

[278] *Melachrino*, n. 274 above.

[279] *Melachrino*, n. 274 above; *Garnac Grain Co. Inc. v HMF Faure & Fairclough Ltd*, n. 254 above; *Kaines (UK) Ltd v Österreichische Warengesellschaft mbH* [1993] 2 Lloyd's Rep. 1.

[280] *Roth and Co. v Tayson, Townsend and Co.* (1895) 73 LT 268; *Kaines (UK) Ltd v Österreichische Warengesellschaft mbH*, n. 279 above.

[281] See *Melachrino*, n. 274 above, 697 (repurchase price sets damages). There is no room for inquiring whether, in market conditions, the buyer's repurchase is reasonable. The market price at any time has factored into it available information about the future and so is *per se* reasonable.

[282] Discussed in the text accompanying nn. 499–504 below.

[283] *Kaines (UK) Ltd v Österreichische Warengesellschaft mbH*, n. 280 above.

[284] *Gebrüder Metelmann GmbH v NBR (London) Ltd* [1984] 1 Lloyd's Rep. 614.

[285] *Gebrüder Metelmann GmbH v NBR (London) Ltd*, n. 284 above. The sellers showed that they had sold on a falling market a quantity of sugar, somewhat larger than the contract quantity, because the buyers' repudiation had left them long. There is no need to appropriate the exact quantity to the repudiated contract.

the seller refuses to deliver. If applied literally, this rule would produce a wholly different rule from the one prevailing where a delivery date is fixed, where the market at the due date of performance serves as the basis of a damages award. Although sense might be made of sub-section (3), in the case of an accepted repudiation, as tacitly embodying the mitigation rule, it appears inconsistent with the principle that an innocent party is not required to accept an anticipatory repudiation and terminate the contract in order to mitigate his damages.[286]

12.67 **Market at due delivery date.** In *Tai Hing Cotton Mill Ltd v Kamsing Knitting Factory*,[287] the buyers brought an action for non-delivery of bales of cotton under a contract that required the sellers to deliver within a reasonable time, agreed for present purposes to be one month, of the buyers giving notice of their requirements. The Privy Council concluded that damages should not be assessed at the date of the refusal to deliver.[288] Instead, it applied a rule, drawn from the general remoteness rule in section 51(2), which was consistent with the *prima facie* rule in section 51(3) as it applied to cases of a fixed delivery date, requiring a reference to the market at the due date of delivery.[289] On a rising market, the sellers had repudiated (on 31 July) but the buyers accepted the repudiation only when they issued a writ (on 28 November). In the intervening month of September, the market price of cotton began to fall steadily down to the date of the trial. The buyers sought to argue that they had bought in the cotton against the sellers when the market was high, but this argument could not be maintained, for the transaction in question took place before the sellers repudiated and therefore before the sellers could be said to be in breach at all.[290] In the opinion of the Board, the damages had to be assessed at one month from the date of acceptance of the repudiation, for the latter date was the last date when the buyers could have called for delivery under the contract; no other date seemed suitable. Although evidence on the point was meagre, the Board was not prepared to accede to the sellers' argument that damages should be nominal, since the buyers had failed to prove the state of the market on 28 December. Instead, a market rate was hypothesized for that date, given the evidence of a steady decline of prices to the date of the trial.

---

[286] Discussed in the text accompanying n. 217 above.

[287] n. 276 above.

[288] Various explanations of the closing lines of sub-s. (3) were attempted by the Board, from an empty vessel to a rule of convenience equating the date of refusal with the due date of delivery in uncertain cases. See also *Millett v Van Heek & Co.*, n. 274 above, 377–8 (Atkin LJ: delivery within a reasonable time is delivery at a fixed date).

[289] Note the way the Board disposed of earlier authority, namely, *Ashmore & Son v CS Cox & Co.* [1899] 1 QB 436 and *Kidston and Co. v Monceau Ironworks Ltd* (1902) 18 TLR 320: *Tai Hing Cotton Mill Ltd v Kamsing Knitting Factory*, n. 276 above, 103.

[290] Cf *Coastal (Bermuda) Petroleum Ltd v VTT Vulcan Petroleum SA (The Marine Star)* [1994] CLC 1019 (no market: substitute cargo already acquired in anticipation of sellers' default).

Concrete Assessment

Market price or transaction price? *Tai Hing* demonstrates a measure of judicial   **12.68**
flexibility in accepting evidence about the state of the market. It has, however,
been questioned whether the market is an altogether appropriate standard for
damages assessment, and that a reference to the actual resale price, in a non-
acceptance case, or the actual repurchase (or cover) price, in a non-delivery case,
might be more appropriate. The obvious advantages of such an approach are that
the assessment of damages is simplified and that clear recognition is given to the
impracticability of the breach date assessment rule in certain instances, though, as
we have seen, shifting the assessment date could meet the latter point.

US approach. Article 2 of the Uniform Commercial Code provides that the   **12.69**
resale price obtained by the seller in a substitute transaction, provided the resale is
conducted in good faith and a commercially reasonable manner, serves as the
standard for assessing damages in a non-acceptance case.[291] Where no resale in fact
takes place, damages are based on the market price prevailing at the breach date
but, if evidence of this market price is not readily available, a reference may be
made instead to the market at a reasonable later date.[292] Likewise, where the seller
fails to deliver, or anticipatorily repudiates his delivery obligation, or the goods are
non-conforming and are rightfully rejected by the buyer, damages are assessed
according to the reasonable repurchase (or cover) price paid by the buyer.[293]
Failing this, the same reference is made to the market as occurs in the case of non-
acceptance by the buyer.[294] Resale and cover prices may constitute evidence of the
market,[295] but, to the extent they diverge from the market, English law in fact
departs from Article 2 just as does English law in theory.

Available Market

Meaning of market. In applying the present market price test, some difficulty   **12.70**
has arisen concerning the meaning of 'available market'[296] in sections 50–51. The
expression was understood in a very tangible way by one of the judges in *Dunkirk
Colliery Co. v Lever*, as meaning a particular place in the nature of a corn or cotton

---

[291] UCC Art. 2–706. The same approach was recommended by the Ontario Law Reform
Commission: *Report on Sale of Goods* 1979, ii, 418–23, 521–8.
[292] UCC Art. 2–708, 723(2).
[293] UCC Art. 2–712.
[294] UCC Art. 2–713, 723(2).
[295] *Maclean v Dunn* (1828) 4 Bing, 722; *Ex p. Stapleton* (1879) 10 Ch. D 586; *Whitaker
Ltd v Bowater Ltd* (1918) 35 TLR 114; *C Sharpe & Co. v Nosawa & Co.* [1917] 2 KB 814, 820
(repurchase price will be market price in well-run commodities market); *Esteve Trading Corpn v
Agropec International (The Golden Rio)* [1990] 2 Lloyd's Rep. 273, 279 ('at best, evidence of the
market price').
[296] A matter of 'mixed law and fact': *Shearson Lehman Hutton Inc. v Maclaine Watson & Co. Ltd
(No. 2)* [1990] 3 All ER 723, 731; see D. Waters (1958) 36 *Can. Bar Rev.* 360.

exchange where buyers and sellers come together.[297] This dictum proved troublesome in *WL Thompson Ltd v Robinson (Gunmakers) Ltd*,[298] which concerned the non-acceptance of a new car, an item not dealt with in such trade circumstances, where the displacement of the *prima facie* market rule was also supported on additional and more justifiable grounds. Upjohn J followed the above approach in *Dunkirk Colliery* with some misgivings and, despite divided judicial opinions in another case dealing with non-delivery,[299] went on to say: 'Had the matter been *res integra* I think I should have found that an "available market" merely means that the situation in the particular trade in the particular area was such that the particular goods could freely be sold.'[300] This statement was later glossed so as to import the additional requirement that the price of goods be settled by the laws of supply and demand.[301] It is submitted that this is a sensible way to read the expression 'available market' in a modern economy and should be followed.

12.71 **Sufficient numbers of buyers and sellers.** It was noted above that an available market existed even if it took time and planning to organize an entry into it.[302] Provided that a sufficiency of buyers and sellers in touch with each other can be assembled, there is a market.[303] And the market is available if the seller, for example, could find at least one immediate buyer prepared to pay a fair price on the day of entry.[304] Mere volatility of price, and hence market movement if the seller's unwanted goods are made available, does not negative the existence of a market.[305] In determining the existence of a market, the nature of the contract goods is important: they can be specialized to the point of insufficient activity to evidence a market.[306]

---

[297] (1878) 9 Ch. D 20, 25.

[298] [1955] Ch. 177.

[299] *Marshall & Co. v Nicoll & Son* 1919 SC 129.

[300] n. 298 above, 187.

[301] *Charter v Sullivan* [1957] 2 QB 117, 128.

[302] *Shearson Lehman Hutton Inc. v Maclaine Watson & Co. Ltd (No. 2)*, n. 296 above.

[303] *ABD (Metals and Waste) Ltd v Anglo Chemical and Ore Co. Ltd* [1955] 2 Lloyd's Rep. 456, 466; *Shearson Lehman Hutton Inc.*, n. 296 above, 728. See also *Borries v Hutchinson* (1865) 18 CB(NS) 445, 460 ('constant demand and supply'); *Heskell v Continental Express Ltd* [1950] 1 All ER 1033, 1056 ('a particular level of trade'); *WL Thompson Ltd v Robinson (Gunmakers) Ltd*, n. 298 above, 187 ('a demand sufficient to absorb readily all the goods that were thrust on it').

[304] *Shearson Lehman Hutton Inc.*, n. 296 above, 730.

[305] *FC Bradley & Sons Ltd v Colonial & Continental Trading Ltd* [1964] 2 Lloyd's Rep. 52, 64 (12,000 boxes of Lebanese potatoes).

[306] *Coastal International Trading Ltd v Maroil AG* [1988] 1 Lloyd's Rep. 92 ('July/August Rumanian bunker C 3.5% straight-run atmospheric'); *Harlow & Jones Ltd v Panex (International) Ltd* [1967] 2 Lloyd's Rep. 509 (an f.o.b. cargo of steel blooms in a Soviet Baltic port); *Zepoli Canada Inc. v Zapata Ugland Drilling Ltd* (1985) 53 Nfld. & PEIR 1 (Can.) (huge quantity of anchor chain); *Butler v Countryside Finance Ltd* [1993] 3 NZLR 623 (second-hand goods). But see *Petrograde Inc. v Stinnes Handels GmbH* [1995] 1 Lloyd's Rep. 142 (market in Germany but not other countries for specialized fuel).

Export sales.   In export sales transactions, difficulties can arise out of matters of   **12.72**
time and place. For example, because of the seller's default under a forward contract for the supply of goods on c.i.f. terms, the buyer may now be looking for
goods of the same description available on spot terms in the country where the
unloading port is situated. In *Lesters Leather & Skin Co. Ltd v Home and Overseas
Brokers Ltd*,[307] where the buyers rightfully rejected a quantity of non-conforming
Indian snake skins sold under a c.i.f. United Kingdom contract, there was no spot
market in Indian snake skins so the court had to award damages by reference to
the buyers' lost profits, namely the profits they would have made by reselling the
individual snake skins or the products thereof.[308] In *Hinde v Liddell*,[309] the buyer
of 2,000 pieces of grey shirtings was unable to obtain them on the market when
the seller defaulted, since they could be obtained only under a forward manufacturing contract. He obtained the same quantity of other shirtings of a superior
quality, for which the price was commensurately higher, and persuaded his sub-
buyer to accept these instead of the grey shirtings. The buyer therefore recovered
the difference between the contract price for grey shirtings and the price he had to
pay for the substitute shirtings, the latter sum representing the value of the contract goods to him.[310] A similar philosophy inspires the view that, in export sales,
the market is determined not just by reference to the type of goods but also their
delivery terms. Thus, in *The Marine Star*,[311] a c.i.f cargo of Russian fuel oil had to
be delivered in the Dutch Antilles in a stated week in August.[312] The sellers' default
left the buyers unable to procure another cargo of Russian fuel oil of the
same description arriving within the same week. Hence there was no available
market.[313]

Related markets.   It may be necessary, in determining market price, for a court   **12.73**
to extrapolate from the market price of a similar commodity or the same commodity in a different time and place.[314] The case of *Ströms Bruks Aktiebolag v
Hutchison*[315] concerned a carrier's failure to lift a c.i.f. cargo of woodpulp to be
shipped from Sweden to Cardiff, but it is analogous to the case of a c.i.f. seller

---

[307] [1948] WN 437.
[308] The claim was a speculative one and so was discounted to a degree.
[309] (1875) LR 10 QB 265. See also *Bridge v Wain* (1816) 1 Stark. 504; *Borries v Hutchinson*,
n. 303 above; *Elbinger Aktiengesellschaft v Armstrong* (1874) LR 9 QB 473, 476–7; *Blackburn Bobbin
Co. v T W Allen & Sons Ltd* [1918] 1 KB 540, 554.
[310] *Ibid.* 270.
[311] n. 290 above.
[312] It is common for an arrival range to be specified in oil contracts, though not the case with dry
commodities.
[313] See also *C Czarnikow Ltd v Bunge & Co. Ltd* [1987] 1 Lloyd's Rep. 202 ('tenderable goods').
[314] See *British & Commonwealth Holdings Plc v Quadrex Holdings Plc*, n. 4 above, 1227–8
('if there is *nearly* an available market, that may provide a just method of calculating the damages'
(emphasis in the original)).
[315] [1905] AC 515.

failing to ship or adopt the shipment of a cargo. Damages were calculated according to the cost of acquiring such goods on the spot market in Cardiff, less the value of the goods in Sweden and the freight and insurance charges, these deductions being the equivalent of the price in sale of goods proceedings. This is consistent with the view that the place of destination of goods sets the standard for damages assessment.[316] In *Esteve Trading Corpn v Agropec International (The Golden Rio)*,[317] a case concerning a bankruptcy clause in a commodities form requiring contracts to be closed out 'at the market price then current for similar goods', the goods (soya beans) had already been shipped from a Brazilian port on f.o.b. Antwerp/Ghent terms when the clause had to be implemented. There was no true market for f.o.b. Antwerp/Ghent soya beans in transit, because, once such goods were shipped, subsequent dealings were conducted on c.i.f. terms. The court's solution was to take the available c.i.f. price and deduct the cost of insurance and freight.

Late Delivery

12.74 **Basis of assessment.** There is no explicit provision in the Sale of Goods Act dealing with late delivery, and there is little authority. Support exists for the view that the buyer's damages should be settled according to the difference in the market rates prevailing at the agreed and actual dates of delivery.[318] Damages should not be assessed according to the buyer's sub-sale price and should not take account of the possibility that the buyer might have protected himself from the consequences of late delivery by making back-to-back arrangements with the sub-buyer.[319] This could only ever be appropriate, however, if the seller contemplates that the buyer has bought the goods for resale. Where the goods are bought for consumption, another measure might be more appropriate, such as the loss of profits[320] because of the delay in delivering a profit-earning chattel, or even consequential damages for the buyer having to let machines stand idle or pay employees who have no work to do,[321] or damage to crops incurred while waiting

---

[316] *Aryeh v Lawrence Kostoris & Son Ltd* [1967] 1 Lloyd's Rep. 63, 71 (f.o.b. and c.i.f.); *C Sharpe & Co. v Nosawa & Co.* [1917] 2 KB 814; *Hasell v Bagot, Shakes & Lewis Ltd* (1911) 13 CLR 374 (*ex* ship Adelaide buyer of Japanese phosphates entitled to buy from Australian importer without going to Japan); *Hendrie v Neelon* (1883) 3 OR 603 (Can.); *Amicale Yarns Inc. v Canadian Worsted Manufacturing Inc.* [1968] 2 OR 59; *Graham v Bigelow* (1912) 3 DLR 404.

[317] n. 295 above.

[318] *The Heron II*, n. 104 above (Lord Pearce); *Addax Ltd v Arcadia Petroleum Ltd* [2000] 1 Lloyd's Rep. 493. This approach was rejected for other reasons in *Wertheim v Chicoutimi Pulp Co.* [1911] AC 301, discussed in the text accompanying nn. 388 *et seq.* below.

[319] *Addax Ltd v Arcadia Petroleum Ltd*, n. 318 above.

[320] *Cory v Thames Ironworks and Shipbuilding Co. Ltd*, n. 116 above; *Victoria Laundry (Windsor) Ltd v Newman Industries Ltd*, n. 101 above; *Hydraulic Engineering Co. Ltd v McHaffie, Goslett & Co.* (1878) 4 QBD 670; *Steam Herring Fleet Ltd v S Richard and Co. Ltd* (1901) 17 TLR 731; *Fletcher v Tayleur* (1855) 17 CB 21.

[321] For the attractions of a liquidated damages clause to avoid problems of proof, see *Clydebank Engineering and Shipbuilding Co. Ltd v Don Jose Ramos Yzquierdo e Castaneda* [1905] AC 6, 11.

for a promised machine.[322] It may even be appropriate to disregard the market altogether and look to the terms of a sub-sale.[323] Where the buyer is at fault in not taking delivery on time, the likely liability will be for consequential damages arising out of an expense such as the seller's increased storage costs.[324]

Residual Damages Claims

Section 54. The sections dealing with late delivery and non-delivery and **12.75** with breach of warranty all contain provisions permitting the award of damages for losses recoverable under the first limb of the rule in *Hadley v Baxendale*.[325] Remaining losses, which may usefully be termed here indirect losses,[326] are recoverable under section 54, a provision common to sellers and buyers that deals with special damages. Although in currency loss and interest cases the conflation of special damages and damages recoverable under the second limb of the rule in *Hadley v Baxendale* has been deprecated,[327] damages of the latter kind may be seen as sanctioned by section 54, which provides that nothing in the Act 'affects the right of the buyer or the seller to recover interest or special damages in a case where by law interest or special damages may be recoverable'. Nothing, however, turns upon whether section 54 is applicable or resort has to be had instead to the rules of the common law under section 62(2). Section 54 is merely a saving provision and does not call for any close scrutiny. Buyers' claims for indirect losses are likely to be more varied in their nature than those of sellers. Sellers are in appropriate cases entitled to recover the cost of storing or warehousing unwanted goods, and of reselling unwanted goods.[328] Satisfying the remoteness rule in such cases will not be unduly difficult; the costs of resale could also be seen as the recoverable costs of mitigation.[329] In one case against a non-accepting buyer, a seller who had concluded a resale on reasonable terms recovered demurrage charges arising out of the delay in delivering the goods.[330]

---

[322] *Smeed v Ford* (1859) 1 E & E 602; see also *Watson v Gray* (1900) 16 TLR 308.

[323] *Wertheim v Chicoutimi Pulp Co.*, n. 318 above.

[324] Discussed immediately below.

[325] n. 1 above.

[326] The more natural expression, consequential losses, may no longer be used since the expression now authoritatively means losses recoverable under the second limb of the rule in *Hadley v Baxendale*: *Croudace Construction Ltd v Cawoods Concrete Products Ltd* [1978] 2 Lloyd's Rep. 55; *British Sugar Plc v NEI Power Projects Ltd* (1987) 87 BLR 42; *Hotel Services Ltd v Hilton International Hotels (UK) Ltd* [2000] 1 All ER (Comm.) 750.

[327] See above.

[328] *Newfoundland Associated Fish Exporters Ltd v Aristomenis Th. Karelas* (1963) 49 MPR 49 (Can.). The buyer's liability for non-acceptance receives particular mention when the time of delivery is at large and the buyer fails to respond to the seller's call for acceptance of delivery: s. 37(1); see *Hal H. Paradise Ltd v Apostolic Trustees of the Friars Minor* (1966) 55 DLR (2d) 671.

[329] Discussed in the text accompanying nn. 194 *et seq.* above.

[330] *Vitol SA v Phibro Energy AG (The Mathraki)* [1990] 2 Lloyd's Rep. 84.

Indemnity Claims

12.76 **Damages and costs.**   Buyers may rely upon section 54 in an indirect loss claim where, in breach of the seller's warranty, goods cause them personal injuries[331] or consequential property damage.[332] Where the buyer is claiming in respect of his personal liability to a sub-buyer, the position is more difficult. Consider the case of the first buyer in a distribution chain who wishes to pass on a liability that he has incurred. The liability is imposed under the last contract in the chain and relates to defective goods. By the time the liability snowball reaches the first buyer, it will consist of two principal items, namely, the damages award recovered by the last buyer and the taxed costs of the various successful claimants in the chain below. To this figure, the first buyer will add another item of loss in his claim over against the head seller—his own solicitor and client costs incurred in defending the claim of his sub-buyer.[333] In certain cases, the damages figure will be represented by the amount of a reasonable settlement.[334]

12.77 **Market loss and physical damage.**   In determining whether a seller's liability may be transmitted back up the chain, a distinction has to be drawn between market loss claims and physical damage claims.[335] For a market loss claim, it seems that the goods must be sold in the various contracts in the chain according to the same warranty and description terms.[336] In the case of physical damage, the

---

[331] e.g., *Randall v Newson* (1877) 2 QBD 102; *Wren v Holt* [1903] 1 KB 610; *Preist v Last* [1903] 2 KB 148; *Chaproniere v Mason* (1905) 21 TLR 633; *Grant v Australian Knitting Mills Ltd* [1936] AC 85; *Godley v Perry* [1960] 1 WLR 9; *Vacwell Engineering Co. Ltd v BDH Chemicals Ltd* [1969] 3 All ER 1681.

[332] e.g., *H Parsons (Livestock) Ltd v Uttley Ingham & Co. Ltd*, n. 115 above; *Henry Kendall & Sons v William Lillico & Son Ltd* [1969] 2 AC 31; *Ashington Piggeries Ltd v Christopher Hill Ltd* [1972] AC 441.

[333] See *Kasler and Cohen v Slavouski* [1928] 1 KB 78.

[334] *Biggin & Co. Ltd v Permanite Ltd* [1951] 2 KB 314. The onus is on the claimant to show the compromise was reasonable: *Seven Seas Properties Ltd v Al-Essa (No. 2)* [1993] 1 WLR 1083, 1089. But not a contractual penalty: *Elbinger Aktiengesellschaft v Armstrong* (1874) LR 9 QB 473. See also *Glencore Grain Ltd v Goldbeam Shipping Inc. (The Mass Glory)* [2002] EWHC 27 (Comm); [2002] 2 Lloyd's Rep. 244 at [63] (seller liable only in respect of so much of the sub-contract as was made known to him further to the second limb of the rule in *Hadley v Baxendale*). The buyer's defence may serve to extinguish the seller's price claim in full if the goods turn out to be worthless, but in so far as the buyer's claim is for special or consequential damages, it cannot be the subject of a defence but must be pleaded as a counterclaim.

[335] *Biggin & Co. Ltd v Permanite Ltd* [1951] 1 KB 422, 433–4, reversed other grounds at [1951] 2 KB 314.

[336] Forcefully expressed by Scrutton LJ in *Dexters Ltd v Hill Crest Oil Co. (Bradford) Ltd* [1926] 1 KB 348, 359. The reason given for this is that the effect of a contractual variation on market value is unpredictable: *Biggin & Co.*, n. 334 above. For examples of transmitted liability, see *Hammond & Co. v Bussey* (1887) 20 QBD 79; *Agius v Great Western Colliery Co.* [1899] 1 QB 413. In both cases, the seller was aware of the final use of the goods (bunker coal). See also *Grébert-Borgnis v J & W Nugent* (1885) 15 QBD 85; *Frank Mott & Co. Ltd v Wm H Muller & Co. (London) Ltd* (1922) 13 Ll. LR 492; *Seven Seas Properties Ltd v Al-Essa (No. 2)*, n. 334 above; *Household Machines Ltd v Cosmos Exporters Ltd* [1947] KB 217 (also an indemnity in respect of sub-sale liabilities).

question is whether the seller ought to have contemplated the loss at the end of the chain, in accordance with the normal remoteness principles;[337] the length of the chain does not matter, provided that the loss is not too remote.[338] The distinction is defensible, in that relatively minor differences in warranty and description are unlikely to have much of a bearing on physical loss claims. Furthermore, if the seller in the chain has a contractual defence, the indemnification process will be severed at that point on the grounds of familiar privity principles.

Severance of causal link. The chain of indemnity may be broken, however, in cer- **12.78**
tain circumstances where an intervening party's negligence severs the causal link between a prior seller's breach of contract and a later buyer's injury.[339] But such a party's failure to notice a defect may not be so causally disruptive as to break the chain.[340] The liability passed back up the chain may be a tort claim or the reasonable cost of defending such a claim.[341] It may also be a criminal penalty,[342] provided that there is no element of fault or negligence on the part of the claimant.[343] Ultimately, the question is whether the seller ought to have contemplated the various losses being passed back,[344] though the stress sometimes placed on a claimant's actual conduct in defending an action[345] might suggest that legal costs should be treated as the costs of mitigation.

Other Claims

Lost profits. In principle, sub-sale profits may not be claimed to the extent that **12.79**
they depart from the market standard,[346] which is one reason why it is accurate to

---

337 *Biggin & Co.*, n. 334 above. See also *Pinnock Bros v Lewis & Peat Ltd* [1923] 1 KB 690; *British Oil and Cake Co. v Burstall & Co.* (1923) 39 TLR 406; *GC Dobell and Co. Ltd v Barber and Garrett* [1931] 1 KB 219.

338 *Ibid.*, 432; *Kasler and Cohen v Slavouski*, n. 333 above. For a further example of liability being passed back up the chain, see *Sidney Bennett Ltd v Kreeger* (1925) 41 TLR 609. Liability may not be transmitted, however, if the physical loss is due to an unusual use that the seller could not have contemplated: *Bostock & Co. Ltd v Nicholson & Sons Ltd*, n. 151 above (with which cf *Ashington Piggeries Ltd*, n. 332 above).

339 *Lambert v Lewis* [1982] AC 225, with which contrast *Mowbray v Merryweather* [1895] 2 QB 640. See M. Bridge (1982) 6 *Can. Bus. LJ* 184. On contributory negligence and the implied term of fitness, see Ch. 7 above.

340 *Hammond & Co. v Bussey*, n. 336 above; *British Oil and Cake Co. Ltd v Burstall & Co.* (1923) 39 TLR 406 ('ominous' dark colour of copra cake).

341 e.g., *Britannia Hygienic Laundry Co. Ltd v John I Thorneycroft and Co. Ltd* (1925) 41 TLR 667.

342 *Proops v WH Chaplin and Co. Ltd* (1920) 37 TLR 112; *Cointat v Myham & Son* [1913] 2 KB 220.

343 *Askey v Golden Wine Co. Ltd* [1948] 2 All ER 35 (buyer guilty of gross negligence): any other result would thwart the aims of the criminal law.

344 See *Hammond & Co. v Bussey*, n. 336 above, 95, for an involved statement of the contemplation chain that the seller hypothetically considers.

345 e.g., *Agius v Great Western Colliery Co.*, n. 336 above.

346 See discussion of the market rule in the text accompanying nn. 235 *et seq.* above, and of sub-sales in the text accompanying nn. 363 *et seq.* below.

say that 'lost profits are seldom recovered as damages'.[347] The absence of a market, however, compels a reference to other means of assessing loss, such as lost profits.[348] Furthermore, damages for lost profits may usually be recovered if the goods are clearly profit-earning chattels in the hands of the buyer.[349] Where damages for lost profits are recoverable, it is appropriate, where the precise quantum cannot be ascertained, to make a realistic prognosis without discounting damages, as would be done if the claim were made for loss of a chance.[350] If the amount claimed is regarded as extravagant, the court is likely to reduce the award by drawing a distinction between different types of profit.[351] In certain cases, a lost profits claim might be allowed, not in respect of the profits directly associated with the contract goods, but because the contract goods so injure the buyer's trade reputation as to blight the possibility of future sales.[352] Damages for loss of clientele arising from the supply of defective goods may in some cases be recoverable without having to satisfy the requirements of the second limb of the rule in *Hadley v Baxendale*.[353] Unless the seller of machines is alerted to the buyer's exclusive or heavy dependency on his machines, it has been doubted that the buyer will be able to recover for losses incurred because the plant stands idle or workers are paid despite having

---

[347] *Satef-Huttenes SpA v Paloma Tercera Shipping Co. (The Pegase)*, n. 74 above, 183.

[348] *Ibid.*; *Montevideo Gas and Drydock Co. Ltd v Clan Line Steamers Ltd* (1921) 6 Ll. LR 539, affirmed (1921) 8 Ll. LR 192 (carriage); see also discussion above.

[349] *Steam Herring Fleet Ltd v S Richard and Co. Ltd* (1901) 17 TLR 731; *Cullinane v British 'Rema' Manufacturing Co. Ltd* [1954] 1 QB 292; *Sunnyside Greenhouses Ltd v Golden West Seeds Ltd* [1972] 4 WWR 420; *RG McLean Ltd v Canadian Vickers Ltd* [1969] 2 OR 249. Cf *Bunting v Tory* (1948) 64 TLR 353 (seller not informed of buyer's profit-making use). The issue of profit-earning chattels is discussed at length in the text accompanying nn. 494 *et seq.* below.

[350] Discussed above. See *Jackson v Royal Bank of Scotland* [2005] 1 WLR 377. This issue has arisen in the past mainly in cases of carriers where the claimant has shipped the goods in order to make a profit from dealing with them at their destination. See *O'Hanlon v Great Western Railway Co.* (1865) 6 B & S 484; *Simpson v London and North Western Railway Co.* (1876) 1 QBD 274.

[351] See *Satef-Huttenes SpA v Paloma Tercera Shipping Co. (The Pegase)*, n. 74 above, where the deviating carrier (the period of delay was by agreement quantified at 65 days) was not aware of the extent to which cargo receivers had depleted their stocks or of the difficulties faced by the cargo receivers in replenishing theirs when they had so little information about the likely arrival of the vessel. The carrier had almost no information about the cargo receivers to whom the bill of lading (it seemed, since the charterers were the sellers of the goods to the receivers) had been transferred. According to Robert Goff J: '[L]ost resale profits at unusually high prices can never be recovered unless the defendant has sufficient knowledge of the resale price at or before the time when the contract was made. . .': *ibid.*, 184. See also *Islamic Republic of Iran Shipping Lines v Ierax Shipping Co. of Panama (The Forum Craftsman)* [1991] 1 Lloyd's Rep. 81.

[352] *GKN Centrax Gears Ltd v Matbro Ltd* [1976] 2 Lloyd's Rep. 555 (defective rear axles and loss of repeat orders from 'dissatisfied and incensed' customers); *Canlin Ltd v Thiokol Fibres Ltd* (1983) 142 DLR (3d) 450 (claimant 'deluged with complaints'). For a stricter and probably now superseded view, see *Simon v Pawson and Leafs* (1932) 28 Com. Cas. 151, 157.

[353] See *Leicester Circuits Ltd v Coates Bros Plc* [2003] EWCA Civ 290 at [63]. Cf *Satef-Huttenes SpA v Paloma Tercera Shipping Co. (The Pegase)*, n. 347 above, 186, where there were no findings of fact sufficient to show that the defendants contemplated the loss of goodwill if goods were delivered late (carriage).

nothing to do,[354] but more recent authority is receptive to a claim based on idle machinery and a workforce that has to stand down as a result of late delivery.[355] If the seller's machine breaks down and the buyer has to reinstall his old discarded machine, the cost of reinstallation has been allowed.[356]

Accelerated capital expenses. Damages have also been given for the accelerated **12.80** capital expense of installing new equipment because the seller's equipment did not last as long as it should have done.[357] A routine type of buyer's special or indirect loss claim will concern wasted freight charges incurred in connection with rejected goods,[358] or the cost incurred in shipping goods back to the seller,[359] or in repacking and shipping goods already sent on to a third party's premises.[360] In a proper case, a buyer may recover for loss of time and out-of-pocket expenses.[361] Special damages have also been awarded to cover the additional transaction costs of acquiring substitute goods from multiple sources.[362]

The Secondary Obligation to Pay Damages: Specific Problems

Introduction. This section of the chapter will deal with a number of problems **12.81** that require detailed treatment. For reasons of convenience, because the profit-earning chattel issue will be discussed here, other issues raised by a seller's breach of warranty regarding the quality of the goods will also be considered.

The Sub-sales Problem

Market as general rule. It was stated earlier that the market was employed as the **12.82** standard for measuring the damages in non-acceptance and non-delivery cases. But the Sale of Goods Act states that the market is a standard that expresses in merely presumptive form the remoteness of damage rule. As seen above, there are cases of a breach causing genuine loss where no available market exists. In such cases, courts have been prepared to look even at sub-contracts to gauge the claimant's loss. A reading of certain decisions, however, might induce the belief that the law

---

[354] *Hydraulic Engineering Co. Ltd v McHaffie, Goslett & Co.* (1878) 4 QBD 670. On appropriate facts, the buyer may recover general damages for disruption, inconvenience and expense: *GKN Centrax Gears Ltd v Matbro Ltd*, n. 352 above.
[355] *Croudace Construction Ltd v Cawoods Concrete Products Ltd*, n. 326 above.
[356] *British American Paint Co. v Fogh* (1915) 24 DLR 61.
[357] *Sunnyside Greenhouses Ltd v Golden West Seeds Ltd*, n. 349 above.
[358] *DM Duncan Machinery Co. Ltd v Canadian National Railways* [1951] OR 578.
[359] *E Brande (London) Ltd v Porter* [1959] 2 Lloyd's Rep. 161.
[360] *Molling v Dean* (1901) 18 TLR 217.
[361] *Lay's Transport Ltd v Meadow Lake Consumers Co-operative Association Ltd* (1982) 20 Sask. R 8 (Can.) (loss of management time and wasted overhead, and company president's time in meeting lawyer).
[362] *Butler v Countryside Finance Ltd*, n. 306 above.

dogmatically refuses ever to look at sub-contracts where a market reference is available. Provided that essential principles of remoteness, causation, and mitigation are kept firmly in view, this pretention should not be accorded unswerving recognition. Some of the following cases demonstrate that an unyielding reference to the market is quite capable of producing under-compensation or over-compensation in a given instance. Recent developments have called into question the law's refusal to look at sub-sales when assessing damages for defective goods,[363] but the refusal to consider sub-sales in non-delivery and non-acceptance cases, as is demonstrated below, remains.

12.83 **Goods sold 'to arrive'.** *Rodocanachi, Sons & Co. v Milburn Bros*[364] concerned an action against carriers for non-delivery of cargo when the ship sank because of its master's negligence. The claimants had already sold the cargo on a 'to arrive' basis[365] at a price below the market price prevailing at the anticipated date of discharge. Despite admitting that they could not have been held liable for the extra loss if the claimants had sold above the market price, the carriers argued that their liability should be measured against the lower sub-contract price. Deciding against the carriers, the Court of Appeal made it plain that damages rules should not be tailored to meet the peculiarities of individual cases, but rather should work approximate justice across the broad range of cases. As Lindley LJ put it: '[T]he rules as to damages can in the nature of things only be approximately just, and . . . they have to be worked out, not by mathematicians, but by juries.'[366] The claimants' sale contract was an 'accidental circumstance' and ought to be disregarded, just as the damages of personal injuries litigants were not to be reduced when insurance moneys or other collateral benefits were released by the accident.[367] Assuming that the carriers would not have been liable if the sub-contract price had stood higher than the market, the decision in this case has a certain symmetry besides the appeal it presents for ease of administration.

12.84 **Charterparty example.** *Rodocanachi* was not applied in a later case involving a charterparty and a sub-charter of the same ship. In *Andrew Weir & Co. v Dobell & Co.*,[368] the owners of a ship chartered it to the claimants for a particular voyage at a freight rate of 21 shillings per ton. The claimants then entered into a sub-charter with the defendants that was coextensive with the head charter, covering the same ship and the same voyage. But the freight rate in the sub-charter was 28½ shillings. The defendants repudiated the sub-charter by refusing to load and the market rate at the breach date was 17 shillings. Now, the claimants did not

---

[363] See discussion below.
[364] (1886) 18 QBD 67.
[365] And thus were not liable to the buyers when the cargo failed to arrive.
[366] n. 364 above, 78.
[367] *Bradburn v Great Western Railway Co.* (1874) LR 10 Ex. 1, the case giving birth to the collateral benefits principle in personal injuries litigation.
[368] [1916] 1 KB 722.

have to put the ship on the market at the prevailing rate since they were able to invoke a cancellation right under the head charter. This crystallized their actual loss at 7½ shillings (28½–21 shillings) rather than 11½ shillings (28½–17 shillings) and the former was held to govern the recoverable damages. As Rowlatt J said: 'It all turns, of course, on the circumstance that the claimants' charterparty was coextensive with that of the defendants, otherwise they could not have dealt with the specific interest thrown on their hands, but only with a different and larger interest at 21s.'[369] The key to the result, therefore, was the integrality of the two contracts, which justified the abandonment of any reference to the market at the breach date.

Application to sale. *Rodocanachi* was extended to the sale of goods in *Williams* **12.85** *Bros v Edward T Agius Ltd*,[370] which concerned the sellers' failure to ship a cargo of coal from a UK port c.i.f. an Italian port at the price of 16¼ shillings per ton. The contract in question required a shipment every two months in 1911, and the dispute concerned the last such shipment in November. The market price of the coal at the end of November stood at 23½ shillings, but on 28 October the buyers had resold the same quantity of coal on identical c.i.f. terms to sub-buyers at 19 shillings.[371] The question was whether the buyers' damages should be assessed by reference to the sub-contract or to the market. The *Rodocanachi* principle was applied so as to award the higher measure of damages based on the market price. Lord Dunedin stressed the merits of a system that ignored the sub-sale price, whether it went up or down:

> The buyer never gets [the goods], and he is entitled to be put in the position in which he would have stood had he got them at the due date. That position is the position of a man who has goods at the market price of the day—and barring special circumstances, the defaulting seller is neither mulct in damages for the extra profit which the buyer would have got owing to a forward resale at over the market price . . . nor can he take benefit of the fact that the buyer has made a forward resale at under the market price.[372]

Causal connection. Lord Dunedin went on to observe that there was no merit **12.86** at all in qualifying liability under the head contract by reference to the sub-contract when the two contracts merely dealt in the same kind of goods.[373] As a matter of causal connection, taking the case of a commodities trader doing business on a

---

[369] *Ibid.*, 725.

[370] [1914] AC 510. See also the Canadian cases of *Freedman v French* (1921) 50 OLR 432 (Can.) and *Merrill v Waddell* (1920) 47 OLR 572 (Can.), where the seller knew of or contemplated the sub-sales.

[371] The umpire found that the buyers had 'appropriated' their Nov. shipment to the sub-sale contract, but the expression was patently used in a very loose way. The cargo cannot have been appropriated in the c.i.f. sense since no cargo was ever shipped.

[372] *Williams Bros v Edward T Agius Ltd*, n. 370 above, 522–3.

[373] *Ibid.*, 523.

wide front, this must be correct, for on what principles could it be asserted that any two contracts, one to buy goods and the other to sell goods, ought to be conjoined? Again, the difficulty of this exercise is emphasized if the contracts concern different quantities or the buyer is disposed to use the goods to fulfil various sub-contracts. The failure of the seller to deliver means that it can never be precisely known what the buyer would have done with the seller's goods.

12.87 **Special clause in sub-contract.** Lord Dunedin also stated that, even if the head contract and the sub-contract concerned the 'identical article', it would be better to allow the rights and liabilities of buyer and seller under both contracts to be separately adjusted.[374] Where the buyer in the head contract secures special advantages under the terms of the sub-contract, a strong argument may be made that the buyer should not be deprived of such advantages. The market approach would preserve the head buyer's advantage and the sub-sale approach would not.[375] A point that arose in the case was whether the head buyer was to be released from liability under the sub-contract if the head seller failed to deliver. This depended on whether the sub-contract was formed on the basis of the bought-and-sold note, containing an exoneration clause, or of the broker's note, which did not contain such a clause. Ultimately, it was decided that the broker's note governed, but the argument for ignoring the sub-contract would have been even stronger if it had contained such a special clause.

12.88 **Example.** The effect of ignoring the sub-contract and allowing the two sets of litigants—seller and buyer, and buyer and sub-buyer—to settle their differences by reference to the market may be demonstrated by the following hypothetical examples. First of all, suppose the seller agrees to sell to the buyer a quantity of widgets at £10 per ton and the buyer in turn appropriates that same consignment of widgets, so that no other widgets may be supplied, to a sub-contract at the enhanced price of £15 per ton. The date of delivery in both contracts is the same,[376] and the market price at the date of delivery has risen to £20 per ton. If the market price rule is followed in both contracts, the sub-buyer recovers from the buyer £5 per ton (£20–£15), while the buyer recovers from the seller £10 per ton (£20–£10). On balance, the buyer retains £5 per ton (£10–£5). Assume, however, that the sub-sale price is taken as the point of reference in calculating the buyer's

---

[374] *Ibid.* Moreover, the umpire's terms of reference allowed him to look only at the head contract and not to consider the overall effect of the liabilities in the distribution chain. Thus the House of Lords declined to take into account a transaction between the sub-buyer and the head seller, by which either the Nov. shipment was sold back to the latter, or the sub-buyer assigned to the latter the benefit of the sub-sale. This contract was concluded on 28 Nov., at a time, presumably, when the sellers knew they could not make the Nov. shipment.

[375] See in the text accompanying nn. 379 *et seq.* below.

[376] If the buyer staggers the delivery dates, this complicates matters but it should be regarded as his own speculation for reasons given in the text accompanying nn. 189–93 above.

damages against the seller. The buyer will still be liable to a market assessment of £5 as regards the sub-buyer, on the assumption that the sub-buyer is not in turn reselling. Under the head contract, the buyer will therefore be limited to recovering £5 per ton, the difference between the two contract prices. But the buyer should also recover, as special or consequential damages,[377] the £5 per ton damages that he has to pay the sub-buyer.[378] On balance, the buyer will be left with a profit of £5 per ton, the same position as that reached under an application of the market rule to the two contracts.

Further example. Suppose, however, that the sale price is £10 per ton but that **12.89** it has risen to £20 per ton under the sub-sale. At the date of performance for both contracts, the market price has fallen back to £15 per ton. The sub-buyer, of course, will not want to sue the buyer and will be relieved to buy in at the lesser price of £15 per ton. If the buyer were allowed to sue the seller on the basis of the sub-sale price, he would recover £10 per ton (£20–£10), but a reference to the market brings in only £5 per ton (£15–£10). In neither case will there be the complicating feature of the buyer's liability to the sub-buyer. On the face of it, the buyer will be under-compensated if the market price is chosen. One response to this is to say that the buyer should be able to go to market and buy in at £15 to fulfil the sub-contract. The profit of £5 made in this way, when added to the £5 per ton damages under the head sale, will give the buyer full compensation. But this cannot be done on the above example, because by appropriating the sale goods to the sub-sale, the buyer has locked himself in and cannot go into the market to buy in goods, even if these are in all other respects identical to the sale goods. Once it is established that the market-price rule leaves the buyer under-compensated, the focus is shifted to the remoteness rule and the question is posed whether the seller should reasonably have contemplated that his own non-performance would deny to a sub-selling buyer the opportunity to go into the market. For an enhanced liability, the seller should have to contemplate both the sub-sale and the impossibility of the buyer going to market. Since it goes to the quantum of damages, the seller need not contemplate the subsale price.

Problem case. A problem of the above sort arose in *Re R and H Hall Ltd and* **12.90** *WH Pim (Jnr) and Co.'s Arbitration.*[379] The case concerned a string of forward sales of Australian wheat. Acting for an undisclosed principal, Pim agreed on 3 November to sell at 51¾ shillings per quarter to Hall, who on 21 November sold the same quantity and type of wheat to Williams at 56¾ shillings. Williams in

---

[377] S. 54.

[378] This should not be difficult, given the interdependency of the two contracts and the fact that the seller's whole argument is that the buyer should be indemnified according to how he stands in relation to the sub-buyers.

[379] n. 114 above.

turn on 25 November agreed to sell the same wheat to Pim again at 59¼ shillings; this time Pim was acting for a different undisclosed principal.[380] All the contracts related to a shipment to be made the following January; it turned out that the market price at the date of delivery[381] had fallen back to 53¾ shillings. Wishing to accommodate as far as possible the apparently divergent interests of their two principals, Pim purchased from Rank on 29 January a cargo on board the SS *Indianic* at sixty shillings. They then appropriated this cargo to the contract with Hall and similar notices were passed down the string. Pim, having started the notices of appropriation, immediately resold the same cargo back to Rank at a price securing the latter a modest profit.

12.91 **Entry into market impossible.** The consequence of all this was that, when Pim failed to deliver to Hall, Hall could not buy in to perform the contract with Williams, and Williams could not buy in to fulfil their contract with Pim. Pim's second principal at the end of the string was therefore able to buy in at the market price, which was lower than its contract price, for Pim had correctly anticipated a fall in the market. Pim sought also to protect the interests of their first principal by arguing that Hall's damages should be assessed according to the market rate prevailing at the date of delivery, rather than the higher sub-contract price. But, of course, Pim had done everything in their power to ensure that Hall could not go to market for the wheat they needed to deliver to Williams. In these circumstances, the House of Lords[382] had little difficulty in ruling that the Hall loss on the Williams contract came within the remoteness rule. The contract between Pim and Hall amply recognized the possibility of a sub-sale of the same goods by the notice of appropriation system. Indeed, the entire system of string c.i.f. contracts is based on a principle of linkage so that no commodities dealer in the string is permitted to speculate unfairly in cargoes at the expense of another dealer in the string.

12.92 **Reception of decision.** The decision in *Re R and H Hall Ltd* was said to have greatly surprised informed commercial and legal opinion.[383] Two members of the Court of Appeal in *James Finlay & Co. v NV Kwik Hoo Tong Handel Maatschappij*[384] seem to have thought it a correct decision and the third,[385] while grudgingly accepting that it might be justified by the application of the remoteness rule to the particular facts, seems to have been more concerned at the failure of the House of

---

[380] See Lord Blanesburgh for an enlightening explanation of Pim's behaviour.

[381] Presumably, this refers to the latest date the documents could lawfully be tendered.

[382] Including Lords Haldane and Dunedin, who had sat in *Williams Bros v Edward T Agius Ltd*, n. 370 above.

[383] '[It] astonished the Temple and surprised St. Mary Axe': *James Finlay & Co. v NV Kwik Hoo Tong Handel Maatschappij* [1929] 1 KB 400, 417.

[384] *Ibid.*, Greer and Sankey LJJ.

[385] Scrutton LJ.

Lords in the later case to reconcile its decision with its own earlier statement in *Williams Bros v Edward T Agius Ltd*.[386] Any system of law that eschews ironclad rules producing the same result in all cases, regardless of the actual loss suffered by the claimant, should find a place for the decision in *Re R and H Hall Ltd*, which underlines the role of remoteness and reminds us that the Sale of Goods Act reference to the market remains a *prima facie* rule.[387]

Late Delivery

Market rule and absence of loss.   The Sale of Goods Act contains no damages **12.93** rules specifically framed to meet the case of late delivery. The problem of market reference presented itself in an acute form in the controversial decision of the Privy Council in *Wertheim v Chicoutimi Pulp Co*.[388] The respondent sellers agreed on 13 March 1900 to sell 3,000 tons of Canadian moist pulpwood to the appellant buyers on f.o.b. Chicoutimi terms. The price was equivalent to twenty-five shillings a ton and the buyer was a German timber merchant; delivery was to take place not later than 1 November 1900. The appellant buyers, meanwhile, had already on 2 March 1900 entered into a contract for the sub-sale of 2,000 tons of pulpwood to a Manchester timber mill, and they had apparently made a number of other sub-sale contracts to account for the whole 3,000 tons due under the head contract. The sub-sale price was sixty-five shillings, and the very large discrepancy between the two prices may be explained only in part by the freight costs of thirteen shillings per ton to transport the timber to the Manchester market. The dearth of evidence in the report concerning the sub-sale contracts and the circumstances in which they were entered into makes it impossible to explain the discrepancy any further.

Delayed performance of sub-contracts.   The sellers failed to deliver the pulp- **12.94** wood on time in Chicoutimi, with the result that delivery had to be held over until the following season. Delivery actually took place in June 1901, the buyers having affirmed the contract, and the buyers were in turn successful in persuading their sub-buyers to accept late delivery when eventually the pulpwood reached Manchester. The market price at the contractual delivery date was seventy shillings; it had fallen to 42½ shillings per ton by the date the pulpwood was actually delivered. The market price was that prevailing in Manchester, so any calculation of the buyers' damages, if the goods were to be bought in, would have to take account of the buyers' freight costs as well as their purchase costs. By this reckoning, the

---

[386] n. 370 above.
[387] General support for *Re R and H Hall Ltd* is to be found in *Kwei Tek Chao v British Traders and Shippers Ltd*, n. 243 above (late shipment).
[388] n. 318 above., sternly criticized by Scrutton LJ in *Slater v Hoyle & Smith* [1920] 2 KB 11, 23–4.

buyers had paid thirty-eight shillings per ton in order to be in a position to resell and deliver the pulpwood in Manchester.

12.95 **Modest damages.** The buyers contended that their damages should be calculated according to the difference between the market prices at the due and actual dates of delivery. On the other hand, the sellers argued that the buyer had suffered no loss since they had been able to persuade the sub-buyers to accept late the agreed pulpwood; a reference to the market would therefore be irrelevant, and nominal damages would be the appropriate remedy. The court below[389] awarded as damages five shillings per ton (the difference between the market price at the due delivery date and the sub-sale price (70–65 shillings)), a figure both modest and utterly irrelevant in any computation of the buyers' loss. This figure was confirmed by the Privy Council as 'the highest rate at which [the buyers' loss] could properly be fixed',[390] a delphic reference, it seems, to the greater propriety of a nominal damages award. The Privy Council, therefore, rejected the buyers' contention that they ought to receive 27½ shillings as the difference between the two market prices (70 shillings–42½ shillings). It should not be forgotten, however, that, in addition to the five shillings actually awarded, the buyers made twenty-seven shillings profit, as the difference between their purchase and resale prices, making in all a profit on the contract of thirty-two shillings.

12.96 **Link between contract and sub-contracts.** An assessment of whether *Wertheim* is correctly decided is in practice impossible, since so little is known of the relationship between the sale contract and the sub-sale contracts. In particular, it cannot be known whether the buyers had actually appropriated the 3,000 tons to the sub-sale contracts, which was unlikely, or whether a shortage of pulpwood on the Manchester market deprived the buyers of a chance to buy in different pulpwood in satisfaction of their sub-sale responsibilities. It is instructive to consider the hypothetical position if the buyers had been in a position to buy in and had actually done so, and had been able to delay this transaction until the market fell to 42½ shillings.[391] The buyers would presumably then have made a profit on the sub-sales of 22½ shillings (65 shillings–42½ shillings) by buying in. To this figure should be added their recoverable losses on the head contract arrived at with the aid of a market assessment, if they were able to persuade a court that this was the proper measure of damages for late delivery in such a case. This figure would consist of 32 shillings (70 shillings–38 shillings), less the actual smaller profit of 4½ shillings realized when the buyers sold or should have sold[392] at the reduced market rate (42½ shillings–38 shillings) making a sum of 27½ shillings.

---

[389] The Court of King's Bench (Appeal Side) of the Province of Quebec.
[390] n. 318 above, 307.
[391] Would the sub-buyers have tolerated this?
[392] Any delay would be a private speculation.

The overall profit of the buyers would thus be fifty shillings per ton (27½ shillings + 22½ shillings).

Speculation. *Wertheim* was approved by Lord Dunedin in *Williams Bros v* **12.97**
Edward T Agius Ltd[393] on the ground that the outcome of events demonstrated
the buyers' actual loss without the need for any judicial speculation. This is certainly correct, it is submitted, if the buyers were locked into the head contract in
their dealings with the sub-buyers. It is harder to resolve the case of the buyer
whose manifest intentions are plainly at all material times to use the seller's goods
in performing the sub-contracts, even though there is no legal compulsion to this
end in the sub-contracts. In such a case, though the question is a difficult one,
there seems to be no good reason for ignoring the sub-sale when it truly demonstrates the buyer's actual loss. If the buyer is not speculating in commodities, he
should not be treated as though he were. Lord Dunedin's statement that there is
no need to speculate on the buyer's loss would cover this case too. But harder still
is the case of the buyer who, taking advantage of the seller's delay, pointedly buys
in to fulfil the sub-sales when otherwise he would not have done.[394] One way of
looking at this is to assert that the buyer should not abuse the seller's breach so as
to enrich himself. Quite the opposite point of view is that the buyer ought to be
able to enter into a particularly beneficial sub-sale, and therefore also to perform
a sub-sale in a way particularly beneficial to himself, without being deprived of the
benefits of this acumen when he later sues the seller. The call is a close one, but if
a buyer actually does buy in and takes a speculative risk in doing so, on familiar
principles[395] he should be allowed to take the benefits and burdens associated with
this activity.[396]

Defective Goods

General. Where non-conforming goods are supplied and accepted by the buyer, **12.98**
who has a damages action for breach of warranty of quality under section 53, there
is a resemblance to late delivery. In both cases, and in contrast with non-delivery
and non-acceptance, the contract remains on foot and the buyer does not seek
damages for substitute goods. Section 53 does not as such mention the market.[397]
It refers instead to the difference in value between what the goods ought to have
been worth if they had answered to the contract and what in fact they were worth

---

[393] n. 370 above.
[394] See the working out of this in the hypothetical example in the previous para.
[395] *Jamal v Moolla Dawood Sons & Co.*, n. 158 above.
[396] Suppose in the above example the sellers failed to deliver at all. The liability should be 70–38
shillings. The buyers would also retain the profit on the sub-sales (65–42½ shillings), making 54½
shillings total profit. The second purchase would clearly be the buyers' private speculation.
[397] But the language of market is used in *Slater v Hoyle & Smith*, n. 388 above, discussed below.

at the time of delivery in consequence of the breach of contract.[398] Although it is not compulsory to do so, a reference is commonly made to market values to determine that value difference.[399] In some instances, however, there will not be a market in non-conforming goods of the contract type, or at least in goods failing to conform in the way of those tendered by the seller.[400]

12.99 **Applying the market rule.** The question whether the market should also be looked at where there are sub-sales has divided the Court of Appeal in two cases set seventy years apart. The first of these is *Slater v Hoyle & Smith*,[401] where the buyers of goods that turned out to be defective were able to persuade their sub-buyers not to exercise their termination rights but to accept non-conforming goods. The case concerned a contract entered into by manufacturing sellers to sell 3,000 pieces of unbleached cloth at 129 shillings per piece. The sellers delivered 1,625 pieces before the buyers refused to accept any more because of the inferior quality of the cloth. The buyers had earlier entered into a contract to sell 2,000 pieces of bleached cloth at a price higher than the one they had paid the manufacturing sellers for the unbleached cloth. In fulfilment of this sub-sale, the buyers delivered, and were paid in full for 691 of the 1,625 pieces, despite the complaints of the sub-buyer. The market price having fallen, the buyers recovered damages representing the difference between the warranty value and actual value of the goods delivered, even though 691 pieces had been resold in a bleached condition without any actual loss. The Court of Appeal observed that the buyers were reselling bleached cloth and therefore could not be said to be dealing in the same article, unbleached cloth, as had been sold by the sellers.[402] Furthermore, the buyers were under no obligation to use the sellers' cloth in fulfilling the sub-sales, and the sellers, moreover, should not be permitted to take advantage of the buyers' good fortune.[403] Similarly, the sellers would not have been responsible for the additional loss if the buyers had had to pay the sub-buyers damages greater than the difference in value.[404] The buyers' behaviour in relation to the sub-buyers may be described as an exercise in business judgement. By retaining and not remitting to their sub-buyers the damages due to them from the sellers, the buyers were taking a business risk with regard to the

---

[398] S. 53(3).
[399] See discussion below.
[400] See *Biggin v Permanite Ltd* [1951] 1 KB 422, 438, reversed in part on other grounds [1952] 2 KB 314.
[401] n. 388 above.
[402] n. 388 above, 15, 17.
[403] *Ibid.*, 18, 23.
[404] But see the possibility of damages for loss of goodwill, discussed below. It is no accident that Scrutton LJ, a member of the Court of Appeal in *Slater*, was opposed to the award of damages for loss of business.

future willingness of the sub-buyers to deal with them after this incident involving sub-standard goods.

Rejecting the market rule. The contrasting Court of Appeal decision is *Bence* **12.100** *Graphics International Ltd v Fasson UK Ltd*,[405] where the Court of Appeal, by a majority, held that certain sub-sale contracts entered into by the buyers should be taken into account when assessing the buyers' damages for breach of warranty of quality. The sellers in *Bence* delivered to the buyers a large quantity of cast vinyl film used by the buyers in manufacturing decals for the container industry. In breach of express and implied terms in the contract, the film failed to survive in a legible state. Consequently, the buyers received extensive complaints from shipping lines which had attached the decals to the containers long-leased to them by the sub-buyers. In awarding the buyers damages amounting to the price paid, the trial judge treated the film as worthless. He noted that, though the buyers had not been sued by sub-buyers of the decals, they remained exposed to such claims and might have suffered a loss of business reputation.[406] The decision was reversed by the Court of Appeal and the buyers' damages limited to the prorated contract price for the small quantity of vinyl remaining in their hands. According to Otton LJ, the *Slater* case, which involved cloth that the buyers bleached and sold on, was to be distinguished from the present case in that here the goods sold on by the buyer (decals) were different from those bought by the buyer (vinyl film).[407] This slender factual distinction, as was noted by the other majority judge, Auld LJ, provides insufficient reason for distinguishing *Slater*. In Otton LJ's view, the sellers had rebutted the presumptive reference to the diminished value of the goods in section 53(3). Damages were to be assessed by reference to the resale of the decals, which was sufficiently contemplated by the parties under the remoteness of damage rule to be taken into consideration in restricting rather than awarding damages. The sellers possessed quite detailed knowledge of the buyers' resale needs. Since the buyers incurred no liability for the decals resold, it followed that they should recover no damages for the film that was used in these sales, though a reference to sub-sales within the contemplation of the parties might in an appropriate case yield a greater measure of damages than the market approach.[408] Auld LJ's judgment went further into the principles of damages recovery but his conclusion was the same as Otton LJ's.[409] He added that the contemplation of sub-sale losses displaced the presumptive value approach in section 53(3).[410] The dissenting

[405] [1998] QB 87.
[406] As quoted aboved, 94–5.
[407] n. 405 above, 98.
[408] *Louis Dreyfus Trading Ltd v Reliance Trading Ltd* [2004] EWCA Civ 525; [2004] 2 Lloyd's Rep. 323.
[409] The learned judge relied heavily on *Wertheim v Chicoutimi Pulp Co.*, n. 318 above.
[410] n. 405 above, 102–7.

judge, Thorpe LJ, was content to fall back on the finding of the trial judge that the sellers had failed to carry the burden of showing the parties' intention to displace the presumptive rule in section 53(3).[411]

12.101 **Merits of market recovery.** In cases like *Slater* and *Bence*, there are opposing approaches to consider. The first, exemplified by *Slater* and those cases adhering to the market rule, is that the systemic integrity of the rule counts for more than the need for accurate compensation in individual cases. The section 53(3) rule is easier to administer than one that demands a close scrutiny of subsequent contracts. Furthermore, it may be seen as easing the forensic burden of a claimant who cannot be sure if and when he might be faced with a claim by sub-buyers and who is unable to prove with the necessary exactitude a loss of business reputation. A loss of value claim for damages provides for such a claimant a rough and ready equivalent to unaccrued and unprovable losses and also expedites litigation. Moreover, at a time when the high cost of legal services and litigation is cause for concern, there is merit in the retention of a market rule that discourages lengthy proceedings and renders it comparatively straightforward to calculate the claimant's damages. In further support of this approach, it is noteworthy that there is no precisely stated rule of factual causation in the Sale of Goods Act. The opposite approach, which was favoured by the majority in *Bence*, is that damages in a case of that type should follow the normal approach to damages assessment and focus on the remoteness rule and the actual loss caused to the present claimant. Factual causation is a vital component of all damages claims, though it does not often emerge in an explicit form in contract cases. The impulse to prevent unjust enrichment, so strong in recent years, may also provide some explanation for the course taken by the court in *Bence*.

12.102 **Criticism.** Nevertheless, it should be asked whether there was in fact a loss caused by the sellers' breach that went uncompensated in *Bence*. The second matter relating to real loss in *Bence* concerns what has come to be regarded as the claimant's performance interest in the contract.[412] Suppose a spaghetti manufacturer contracts to purchase a quantity of number 1 hard durum amber wheat at £200 per ton and the seller instead supplies number 2 wheat. Number 2 wheat has a lower protein content than number 1 wheat and so commands a lower market price of £150 per ton. The buyer consumes the wheat in its manufacturing business by eking out the inferior wheat and mixing it with supplies in store of number 1 wheat.[413] The buyer's customers do not complain. If the decision in *Bence* is

---

[411] n. 405 above, 109. But the displacement of the presumptive rule is not as such a matter of party intention. Cf. Otton LJ, *ibid.*, 101.

[412] See D. Friedmann, (1995) 111 *LQR* 628; C. Webb, (2006) 26 *OJLS* 41; *Alfred MacAlpine Construction Ltd v Panatown Ltd (No. 1)* [2001] 1 AC 518 (HL).

[413] Cf the buyer of the citrus pulp pellets in *Cehave NV v Bremer Handelsgesellschaft mbH* [1976] QB 44 (CA).

correct, the buyer's damages should be nominal. Yet, the seller has delivered to the buyer wheat priced at £200,000 instead of £150,000. By paying too much, the buyer is £50,000 worse off. This ought to be seen as a form of loss caused by the seller's breach. In *Bence* itself, there may not have been a market at all for the defective vinyl film supplied, since it was manufactured as a result of a mistake made by the sellers' own supplier, but there is no reason why the principle should be any different. The buyers in *Bence* paid too much and suffered loss to the extent of the overpayment.[414]

Defending sub-contract claims.   If sub-sales are in principle to be disregarded, **12.103** a problem arises in respect of buyers who are sued by their sub-buyers and suffer loss in the form of costs when unsuccessfully defending the sub-buyers' claim. Within the limits of the second limb of the rule in *Hadley v Baxendale*, courts have allowed recovery of these costs against the seller if the sub-sale was within the contemplation of the parties and the buyer's conduct was reasonable.[415] The award of such consequential damages, it is submitted, is not incompatible with the market rule. This damages claim supplements any claim for direct loss brought under the first limb of the rule in *Hadley v Baxendale*, and the debate about market damages is a debate about the scope of that first limb.

Current position.   The position after *Bence* is not easy to state and its impact on **12.104** the broader application of the market rule is hard to evaluate, especially because only one judge in the majority, Auld LJ, took direct issue with *Slater*.[416] To the extent that *Slater* cannot be distinguished, as a Court of Appeal decision that has not been overruled it has been said to be binding at trial.[417] As a practical matter, *Bence* draws a line between cases of non-delivery and non-acceptance, on the one hand, and defective and late delivery on the other hand,[418] that is, between cases where the contract is terminated and cases where it is not. In the latter cases, whilst a reference to the market remains the presumptive rule, this rule is displaced when sub-sales are within the reasonable contemplation of the parties at the contract date.

---

[414] Waddams cites the example of a buyer receiving defective goods who either gives them away or sells them at an undervalue by way of part gift: n. 2 above, para 1.2580. If the Court of Appeal in *Bence* is correct, this buyer recovers nothing in damages.

[415] *Hammond & Co. v Bussey* (1888) 20 QBD 79 (goods ('steam coal') resold under the same description as in the sale contract) (CA); *Biggin & Co. Ltd v Permanite Ltd* [1951] 1 KB 422; see the discussion of costs recovery above.

[416] In *Bear Stearns Bank Plc v Forum Global Equity Ltd* [2007] EWHC 1576 (Comm) at [204], Andrew Smith J found it difficult to reconcile the two cases, both of which were binding on him. He also stated, at [208], that *Bence* could not be treated as restricting the *prima facie* market rule in cases of non-delivery. Similarly, this was the conclusion to which Langley J felt driven in *Oxus Gold v Templeton Insurance Ltd* [2007] EWHC 770 (Comm) at paras [66]–[83].

[417] *Louis Dreyfus Trading Ltd v Reliance Trading Ltd*, n. 408 above at [20] (breach of warranty of quiet possession).

[418] This was the approach adopted in *Bear Stearns Bank Plc v Forum Global Equity Ltd*, n. 416 above; see also *Oxus Gold Plc v Templeton Insurance Ltd*, n. 416 above at [82].

In practice, much will depend upon the amount of information about sub-sale activity possessed by the seller. General knowledge of the likelihood of a sub-sale should not be enough since 'everyone who sells to a merchant knows that he [buys] for re-sale'.[419] This should mean that *Bence* will be limited to those cases where the seller has detailed knowledge of the sub-sale; the conveying of information to the seller, which would normally serve to increase the damages potentially available, would in a case of this nature have a restrictive impact on the award of damages. There is nevertheless a possibility that the calculation of damages by reference to sub-sales may constitute in practice the norm, given that there was nothing particularly unusual about the sellers' knowledge of sub-sale activities in *Bence*. In addition, however broad or narrow the impact of *Bence* in warranty of quality cases turns out to be, the reasoning behind it could just as easily be applied to non-delivery and non-acceptance. The market rule has been said to work well in general, despite the 'superficial tension' between it and the rule of remoteness of damage.[420] For all of the reasons stated above, it is submitted that *Bence* should be confined to cases of detailed knowledge of sub-sale activities and that, if it and *Slater* are considered by a higher court in a case where they are considered to be in conflict, then *Slater* is to be preferred.

The Lost Volume Problem

12.105 **Nominal or substantial damages?** This problem[421] concerns a difficulty that sometimes arises when a seller sues a buyer for non-acceptance of the contract goods. Suppose that a contract provides for the sale of goods at a certain price and the buyer repudiates his obligations. At all material times, the market is constant and the seller is ultimately able to dispose of the unwanted goods to another buyer at the same price. Taking this resale price as evidence of the market value of the goods at the due date of delivery, the question is whether the seller is entitled only to nominal damages for the buyer's breach, given that there is no difference between the sale and resale prices. An application of section 48(3) of the Sale of Goods Act, the *prima facie* rule that damages are calculated at the difference between the contract and market prices, would produce this result. The same line of reasoning would again produce nominal damages on a rising market and, on a falling market, would produce an award reflecting the market decline since the contract price was negotiated. But the above result ignores the seller's profit margin on his transactions and the concomitant possibility that, in consequence of

---

[419] *Kwei Chek Tao v British Traders & Shippers Ltd*, n. 243 above, 489; *Louis Dreyfus Trading Ltd v Reliance Trading Ltd*, n. 408 above at [23].
[420] *Transfield Shipping Inc. v Mercator Shipping Inc. (The Achilleas)* [2007] EWCA Civ 901; [2007] 1 Lloyd's Rep. 19 at [93], reversed on different grounds at [2008] UKHL 48.
[421] C. J. Goetz and R. E. Scott (1979) 31 *Stan. LR* 323; M. Shanker (1973) 24 *Case WRLR* 697 and 712; R. E. Speidel and K. O. Clay (1972) 57 *Corn. LR* 681.

the buyer's breach, he has made one fewer sale than otherwise he would have done, and thus earned one fewer item of profit.

Supply and Demand

Supply exceeding demand. The problem was dealt with at some length in **12.106** *WL Thompson Ltd v Robinson (Gunmakers) Ltd,* [422] where the following were the facts agreed by the parties or proved. The buyers agreed to purchase a new Vanguard automobile at the manufacturer's fixed list price; under the distribution scheme, the sellers' profit margin was also fixed at a little over £61. The day after the contract was entered into, the buyers repudiated their obligations. As a result of this, the sellers rescinded the contract of sale that they had with their wholesale suppliers,[423] an associated company. The wholesale suppliers took back the car that they had already delivered and did not press a damages claim against the retail sellers.[424] There was no shortage of Vanguard automobiles in the relevant local market and the buyers conceded[425] that the claimant sellers had 'lost a sale in the sense that if another purchaser had come into the claimant's premises there was available for that other purchaser a 'Vanguard' car for immediate delivery[,] so that . . . the plaintiffs . . . had lost their profit'.[426] The claimant sellers claimed as damages their lost profit margin of £61, while the defendant buyers contended that their liability was limited to nominal damages, since the car could have been sold to another customer at the same price or, as actually happened, surrendered to the wholesale suppliers without incurring any damages liability.

Available demand. Upjohn J concluded that the matter should not be resolved **12.107** by applying section 48(3), essentially because he understood, in the light of earlier authority, the expression 'available market' in a physical and technical sense as connoting something in the nature of a commodities exchange.[427] Alternatively, if the expression had to be given a broader meaning, it meant a state of supply and demand 'in the particular trade in the particular area . . . such that the particular goods could be freely sold, and that there was a demand sufficient to absorb readily all the goods that were thrust on it'.[428] In the present case, neither of the above statements described the present circumstances, so he felt able to apply a rule

---

[422] n. 298 above. For earlier recognition of the problem, see *Re Vic Mill Ltd* [1913] 1 Ch. 465; *Mason & Risch Ltd v Christner* (1920) 48 OLR 8, varying (1920) 47 OLR 52, 54 (Can.); *Cameron v Campbell & Worthington Ltd* [1930] SASR 402.

[423] The report does not say whether this contract was concluded before or after the retail contract, but it should not make a difference.

[424] Who therefore did not have a liability to recover from the retail buyer.

[425] The buyer's cooperation is explained by this being a test case with the sellers, win or lose, assuming the costs of the action. Proof is more difficult than principle in this area.

[426] n. 298, above 179.

[427] See discussion in the text accompanying nn. 296 *et seq.* above.

[428] n. 298, above 187.

reflecting the seller's real loss, which was the loss of a sale and its accompanying profit.

12.108 **Demand exceeding supply.** The conditions of supply and demand were quite different in *Charter v Sullivan*,[429] where the buyer defaulted on a contract for the sale of a new Hillman automobile. The market price of retail goods was again fixed by the manufacturer and the seller's evidence, that he could sell all of the Hillman automobiles he could obtain, was held to demonstrate that he had suffered no actual loss.[430] The application of the presumptive rule was therefore displaced; there was an additional reason, that systemic price-fixing negatived the very existence of a market based upon supply and demand. Sellers LJ also observed that the seller, subsequently disposing of the unwanted goods to a new buyer, has the burden of proving that he has suffered a real loss;[431] he would thus have to show why the *prima facie* rule in section 48(3) should not apply. This is consistent with the normal forensic principle in damages matters that the claimant must prove his loss. The seller, in many cases, will also know more about the state of the market than the buyer.

Profit and Supply Price

12.109 **Mitigation.** Where the supply of goods exceeds demand, in the sense that the seller can readily dispose of all the goods he acquires or makes,[432] so that the buyer's default deprives the seller of a sale and thus of a profit, the efforts the seller makes to resell the unwanted goods in the same market are not to be regarded as acts mitigating the loss of that profit. That does not mean, however, that such efforts are irrelevant from the point of view of mitigation. Suppose that a contract of sale concerns goods priced at £1,500 and that £500 represents the seller's profit margin while £1,000 represents the supply price, that is, the cost of the goods to the seller. This supply price cost may be incurred in the form of the price the seller pays to his supplier. Alternatively, if the seller is himself the manufacturer, it will be the cost of raw materials, as well as the labour and other items of expense, incurred in assembling a product that is fit for sale.

---

[429] [1957] 2 QB 117.

[430] But see *Silkstone and Dodsworth Coal and Iron Co. v Joint Stock Coal Co.* (1876) 35 LT 668. The buyer defaulted on a contract to buy coal from a particular mine and the court awarded as damages the whole of the seller's profit margin, even though the coal remained in the mine (whose resources cannot have been infinite) waiting to be brought up for the next buyer. Cf. *Hill & Sons v Edwin Showell & Sons Ltd* (1918) 87 LJ KB 1106 (the buyers defaulting before the sellers manufactured goods, leaving the sellers free to put their limited production facilities to alternative profitable use).

[431] n. 429 above, 134.

[432] *WL Thompson Ltd v Robinson (Gunmakers) Ltd*, n. 298 above.

Seller's supply of goods.   Whichever type of seller is involved, the stock may be   **12.110**
handled in more than one way. Goods may be ordered or manufactured by the
seller on an 'as required' basis, that is, as soon as a binding contract is concluded
with the buyer. Such behaviour is likely where the risks posed by unwanted stock
are severe, in the form of physical perishing, heavy capital expenses, or technological ephemerality, to name a few examples. Another possibility is that a seller will
have on hand a modest stock quota, so that unwanted goods can simply be shunted
on to the next buyer, and the result of the buyer's default is that the seller retains
the last item of this stock in hand longer than would otherwise have been the case.
Yet another possibility is the seller who retains on hand a greater supply of goods
than can ever be moved in the market. This may reflect poor business judgement
on the seller's part, or it may bespeak the economies of sale associated with the
purchase or, more likely, the manufacture of goods in bulk. As the unit cost of the
goods goes down in such cases in relation to bulk, it cannot be assumed, for example, that a seller who is ultimately able to dispose of forty-nine items out of fifty is
left with an item that cost him as much as any one of the earlier forty-nine or
the first.[433]

Deteriorating goods.   Returning to our example of the goods costing £1,500 to   **12.111**
the buyer, a seller stands to lose, not merely the profit margin guaranteed by the
contract, but also the supply price if he is left with goods in his hands that decline
in value to zero. Such a decline will not happen if his stock figures are modest,
either because few items are kept in hand or the goods are ordered or made as
required, and they do not perish or deteriorate before the next buyer comes along.
Nor, in the case of a manufacturing seller, will it occur if he is able to make adjustments to goods so that they suit the needs of the next buyer. Such action mitigates
the seller's damages by averting the loss of the supply price, though it creates
a smaller loss in the form of the cost of mitigation incurred when the goods are
converted.[434] A further loss will also arise if these same goods are disposed of at a
price that secures a smaller profit margin. This will not occur in a market where
the price, by one method or another, is fixed,[435] but where it does occur, the seller
has suffered an additional recoverable loss.[436]

Secondary markets.   Suppose, however, that the supply price cannot be recouped   **12.112**
in this way and that the seller is left with goods that he cannot sell. The
amount of the supply price, relative to the overall price of the goods in the

---

[433] *Robophone Facilities Ltd v Blank*, n. 56 above, 1443.

[434] These were the facts in *Re Vic Mill Co. Ltd*, n. 422 above, where the sellers recovered as damages the profit margin plus the costs of conversion, since the sellers could instead have manufactured
new goods for the next buyer who came along; see also *Sanford v Senger* [1977] 3 WWR 399.

[435] Like the sale of the cars in *WL Thompson Ltd v Robinson (Gunmakers)Ltd*, n. 298 above, and
Charter v Sullivan, n. 429 above.

[436] This was an additional item allowed in *Re Vic Mill Ltd*, n. 422 above.

contract of sale, will vary according to whether these goods are single items bought or manufactured, or part of a larger quantity purchased or a lengthy run manufactured. If the seller is unable to mitigate, and assuming the goods decline to a zero value, the seller will recover from the buyer both the supply price and the profit margin, and it will not be necessary to quantify their individual contributions to the overall contract price. Nevertheless, mitigation may require the seller to seek out secondary markets to absorb the goods.[437] The most obvious such market is probably the scrap market, but mitigation may require the seller to do better than this.[438] Taking again the example of the goods costing £1,500, a seller may be able to sell them in a secondary market for £1,100. To the extent that the new buyer was not in the market for goods priced at £1,500,[439] the seller has averted the loss of his supply price but has also recouped £100 of the lost profit margin.[440] Consequently, his damages action against the defaulting buyer is reduced to £400 (£1,500—£1,100). On given facts, it may be difficult to know whether the second buyer is in a different market. If the seller is able to dispose of his last 1987 model in the 1988 season, in a market where the supply of goods exceeds demand, it may not be possible to ascertain whether the buyer is someone who would have bought a 1988 model if the 1987 model had not been available. The burden is on the seller suing for damages to prove his loss,[441] but the evidential burden shifts to the defendant buyer to prove that action taken by the seller in fact mitigates his loss. This evidential burden is discharged when the buyer proves the resale of the goods, but the burden thus transferred to the seller is in turn discharged when the seller is able to show the loss of a sale and thus the absence of 'complete mitigation'.[442]

12.113   **Manufacturing sellers and overhead.**   An issue similar to supply price loss arises typically in the case of manufacturing sellers. Suppose that a manufacturer has a limited output capacity and that, in calculating its prices, it allocates to each contract a share of its fixed overhead in respect of mortgage or rental payments,

---

[437] In some cases this will not be possible: see *Robophone Facilities*, n. 433 above.

[438] Some goods will have a negligible, even a non-existent, scrap value, like the answering machines in *Robophone Facilities Ltd v Blank*, n. 56 above, and *Interoffice Telephones Co. Ltd v Robert Freeman Co. Ltd* [1958] 1 QB 190.

[439] Either because he would never have bought at that price, or buys for a particular use that is not worth the price demanded.

[440] *Quaere* the seller who has, besides the buyer's unwanted goods, other goods surplus to demand. Why should it be assumed that mitigation in fact concerns the buyer's goods rather than those other goods? The secondary market, however, may be large enough to absorb all unwanted goods.

[441] Which makes it prudent to insert in the contract a liquidated damages clause.

[442] *Sony Computer Entertainment UK Ltd v Cinram Logistics UK Ltd* [2008] EWCA Civ 955 at [42]–[45] (Rix LJ), relying upon *Re Vic Mill Ltd*, n. 422 above, and *Hill & Sons v Edwin Showell & Sons Ltd*, n. 207 above. See also discussion of mitigation in fact in the text accompanying nn. 156 *et seq.*

commercial rates, employee wages, and similar items. Suppose further that the seller is operating at the limit of its productive capacity. If one purchaser defaults, this attribution of overhead will be lost, along with any net profit, unless a new customer can be found. If a new customer cannot be found and the manufacturing seller in consequence of the breach therefore operates below its capacity, the issue that arises is whether it can recover from the defaulting buyer the latter's contribution to the overhead. The same issue arises when a seller operating below capacity is driven to operate further below capacity as a result of the buyer's breach, except that new customers coming in up to the limit of its productive capacity are not replacing the defaulting buyer's contribution to the seller's overhead. Subject to the rules of remoteness of damage, and although there is little direct authority on the matter, the seller is entitled to recover the loss of overhead. The matter was treated as a simple matter of recovery by the Court of Appeal in a labour and materials case in *Western Web Offset Printers Ltd v Independent Media Ltd*,[443] the court seeing no difference between sale of goods and labour and materials contracts in this respect.[444] The case of the seller evenly allocating its overheads is one thing, but greater difficulty is presented by a seller who attributes overhead in a differential way between its various customers. It is submitted that a buyer having no information about such differential allocation might fairly object on remoteness grounds to any attempt by a seller to charge it with more than its *pro rata* share of the seller's overheads.

Remoteness of damage.   Considerations like those treated in the foregoing paragraphs have emerged in contracts of hire,[445] but hire and sale are alike in the application of principle to this area of law.[446] In particular, it has been convincingly asserted that, in both types of contract, the remoteness of damage rule will support the inference that the defendant buyer, or hirer, ought to have contemplated that the claimant might have lost a profit because of the relationship between supply and demand in the market.[447] This is entirely consistent with the way that the remoteness rule is applied. It will be recalled that the defendant need not actually have considered the consequences of any breach on his part and that, if he had considered them, then the claimant's loss need not be more probable than not as a consequence of breach, still less a certain loss. Accordingly, the decision of the Court of Appeal in *Lazenby Garages Ltd v Wright*[448] repays close and critical examination. **12.114**

---

[443] [1996] CLC 77.

[444] *Ibid.*, 80.

[445] *Robophone Facilities Ltd v Blank*, n. 56 above; *Interoffice Telephones Co. Ltd v Robert Freeman Co. Ltd*, n. 433 above; *W & J Investments Ltd v Bunting* [1984] 1 NSWLR 331.

[446] *Interoffice Telephones Co. Ltd v Robert Freeman Co. Ltd*, n. 438 above.

[447] *Ibid.*, 202.

[448] [1976] 1 WLR 459.

Second-hand Goods

12.115 **Proving loss of bargain.** In that case, a buyer repudiated his contract to purchase a specific used BMW 2002 automobile the day after the contract was concluded. The contract price was £1,670, of which £345 represented the profit margin, but the seller was able to sell the same vehicle two months later for £1,770. The sellers' argument was that they had lost a sale since the second buyer might have bought another of the used BMW 2002s in stock at a later date. Seeing this as a matter of even probability, the trial judge did rough justice by awarding the sellers half of their profit margin on the repudiated transaction. Another possibility that does not seem to have been considered is that the sellers, if paid promptly by the defendant buyer, might then have had the liquidity to purchase another used BMW 2002, or even just another used car. This new acquisition might later have been purchased by one of the individuals, not necessarily the eventual buyer, visiting their showrooms at some future date. In the Court of Appeal, the sellers were denied damages altogether for loss of bargain. Bridge LJ declined to speculate on whether the eventual buyer would have purchased another car if the defendant buyer's BMW 2002 had not been thrown back on the sellers' hands, and so was not convinced that a loss had been shown.[449] Lord Denning went further and denied, contrary to the normal application of the remoteness rule,[450] that the buyer should have contemplated a bargain loss at all.

12.116 **Evidence of loss.** In *Lazenby Garages Ltd*,[451] nevertheless, there was a very real possibility that the sellers had incurred a loss. It is easy enough to talk of supply exceeding demand, or demand exceeding supply, but difficult indeed to apply it to a sales business consisting of similar goods, each of which is unique in its own way. A buyer, not finding the BMW 2002 that he wanted, might purchase instead a Mercedes from another dealer. With the defendant buyer's cash in hand, the seller might have bought a second-hand Mercedes which could later have been resold to a different buyer. If the seller's business is clearly fuelled by his receipts so that turnover is increased with each and every sale, then a buyer's default either costs him an extra sale or the chance of an extra sale. The precise loss should be recoverable if evidence is led by the seller to satisfy the court. As interesting as matters of principle are in damages cases, the issues are often ultimately resolved by the difficulty or impracticability of accumulating the necessary detailed evidence required to bring forth these principles to the point of judicial choice. In cases like *Lazenby Garages Ltd*, the practical answer is that the seller ought to demand a

---

[449] *Ibid.*, 463.
[450] Especially as it was applied in *Interoffice Telephones Co. Ltd v Robert Freeman Co. Ltd*, n. 438 above.
[451] n. 448 above.

deposit and forfeit it if the buyer defaults. This is greatly superior to a difficult damages inquiry,[452] and superior, too, to a liquidated damages clause.

Breach of Warranty by the Seller

Damages for Diminished Value

Price abatement.   According to section 53(1) of the Sale of Goods Act, where   **12.117** the seller commits a breach of warranty or of a condition that the buyer is compelled to treat as a breach of warranty,[453] the buyer may 'set up' his warranty entitlement against a seller suing for the price[454] or bring an action for damages against the seller for breach of warranty.[455] A reading of section 53(1) reveals that it is directed towards general damages of the kind that would flow under the first limb of the rule in *Hadley v Baxendale*,[456] namely, a loss of value in the goods, leaving it to section 54 to pick up special or consequential damages flowing through the second limb of the rule in that case. Section 53(1) therefore does not countenance a breach of warranty claim that exceeds in sum the seller's action for the price, which is why the buyer's defence in section 53(1)(a), against a seller's action for the price, is expressed in alternative form to the buyer's warranty action for damages in section 53(1)(b), the latter designed presumably for cases where the price has already been paid. Nevertheless, section 53(4) does go on to recognize the possibility that a buyer who has not yet paid may wish to do more than defend a price action. By stating that the buyer may both defend and sue for damages, it effectively recognizes the separate damages action in section 54.

Market and defective goods.   The rule for asserting the buyer's general damages   **12.118** where goods fail to accord with the contractual warranty standard is found in section 53(3), after section 53(2) restates the first limb of the rule in *Hadley v Baxendale*. According to section 53(3): 'In the case of breach of warranty of quality, such loss is *prima facie* the difference between the value of the goods at the time of delivery to the buyer and the value they would have had if they had answered to the warranty.' The first point to note is that the contract price does not set the ceiling of recovery, in that the buyer is not to be deprived of a later market rise in the value of goods of the kind supplied. If, therefore, the market has so far risen that, even in their defective state, the goods are still worth more than the contract price,

---

[452] See the radically divergent views in these cases of Denning MR, who fails to see the difference between lost profit and supply price loss, and of Diplock LJ.

[453] Because of his acceptance of the goods.

[454] Sub-s.1(a). This codifies the decision in *Mondel v Steel* (1841) 8 M & W 858, which overturned the earlier rule that a warranty claim of this kind had to be pleaded separately as a counterclaim: see *Poulton v Lattimore* (1829) 9 B & C 259 and *Bostock & Co. Ltd v Nicholson & Sons Ltd*, n. 151 above.

[455] Sub-s.1(b).

[456] n. 1 above.

damages will nevertheless be awarded according to the difference between their present value and the enhanced value they would have had if they had conformed to the contract.[457] Where the market falls, the buyer's margin of recovery will commensurately diminish and he will have to take the market loss.[458] So, where the sellers shipped goods beyond the contract period but the buyers later dealt in them so as to lose their right of rejection, it transpired that the only loss actually suffered by the buyers was adverse market movement that would have occurred even if the goods had been shipped in time; the buyers were therefore confined to nominal damages and could not build up a damages claim to recapture a lost opportunity of rejection and termination.[459]

12.119 **Valuing damaged goods.**   Although section 53(3) does not explicitly mention the market, it appears that in principle value should be determined according to the market,[460] at least in those cases where a sub-sale does not take place.[461] The hypothetical character of the market reference in non-acceptance and non-delivery cases is absent here: the buyer actually does have the contract goods. Valuing damaged goods is not easy if no market exists in goods of that kind. Experienced trade umpires will often award a price allowance, though the method of calculation is not commonly stated.[462] In the case of second-hand goods, it may be necessary to look at the price of new goods and then subtract for depreciation.[463] For manufactured goods, the absence of price fluctuations would point to the use of the contract price for conforming goods as the appropriate comparator.[464] The absence of a market in damaged or otherwise non-conforming goods[465] will in some cases lead to the cost of repairs being equated with the gap in value between the goods the buyer should have received and those he did receive.[466] When the cost of repairs comes into play, difficulties can be posed in those cases where a measure based on the cost of repair parts company with one based on the difference in value.

[457] *Jones v Just* (1868) LR 3 QB 197.
[458] See the facts of *Cehave NV v Bremer Handelsgesellschaft mbH*, n. 413 above. Cf. *Naughton v O'Callaghan* [1990] 3 All ER 191, discussed in the text accompanying nn. 481 *et seq.* below.
[459] *Taylor & Sons Ltd v Bank of Athens* (1922) 91 LJ KB 776.
[460] See *Sealace Shipping Ltd v Oceanvoice Ltd (The Alecos M)* [1991] 1 Lloyd's Rep. 120 (treated as a case of non-delivery: see in the text accompanying nn. 476 *et seq.* below), reversing [1990] 1 Lloyd's Rep. 82; *Slater v Hoyle and Smith Ltd* [1920] 2 KB 11, 17.
[461] See above discussion of the problems posed by sub-sales and the decision in *Bence Graphics International Ltd v Fasson UK Ltd*, n. 405 above.
[462] *Cehave NV v Bremer Handelsgesellschaft mbH*, n. 413 above.
[463] *Butler v Countryside Finance Ltd*, n. 306 above.
[464] See *Dingle v Hare* (1859) 29 LJCP 143 for a reference to price; *Naughton v O'Callaghan*, n. 458 above; *White Arrow Express Ltd v Lamey's Distribution Ltd* [1995] CLC 1251 (services), noted by H. Beale (1996) 112 *LQR* 205.
[465] See *Biggin v Permanite Ltd* [1951] 1 KB 422, 438.
[466] *Minster Trust Ltd v Traps Tractors Ltd* [1954] 3 All ER 136; *Channel Island Ferries Ltd v Cenargo Navigation Ltd (The Rozel)* [1994] 2 Lloyd's Rep. 161, 167 (charterparty); *Peakman v Express Circuits Ltd* [1998] EWCA Civ 135.

Damages should not be awarded to repair the goods if the expenditure is unreasonable, defined as the incurring of costs that are 'disproportionate to the financial consequences of the deficiency'.[467] In a case of this type involving profit-earning chattels, the buyer may face greater operating costs, which ought to be recoverable in the form of lost profits.[468] One reason for disallowing repair damages is that, where the cost of repair outstrips the benefits that the repairs will bring to the claimant, it is likely that the claimant will keep the money and forgo the repairs. The windfall benefit thus received by the claimant is considered to belie the expectancy rule that the award of damages is supposed to vindicate.[469] A court's concerns in this matter, however, may in some cases be assuaged to the point of allowing the cost of repair where the claimant has already incurred repair expenditure or the court is convinced that damages recovered will be applied to that purpose.[470] One difficulty that arises from an award based on diminished value relates to concerns that a court may have about gains made by a defendant from breaching the contract.[471] There may be exceptional cases where a defendant might have to pay damages by way of account,[472] but a disparity between the diminished value of goods and the cost of repair, leading to the award of the former, is unlikely to be one of them.[473] The difficulty faced by courts in choosing between value and repair in those cases where there is a major difference between the two has arisen chiefly in the case of building works done on land.[474] That same difficulty might arise in labour and materials contracts, but it has little part to play in the sale of goods, given the presumptive value rule in section 53(3). A justification for remaining with the value rule in sale of goods cases, when it affords less than a rule based on repair, is that a buyer seeking more is already protected by the ability to reject non-conforming goods for breach of the fitness or satisfactory quality conditions. The strict rules in the Sale of Goods Act are less tolerant of non-conforming performance that the substantial performance rule to be found in the case of labour and materials contracts and contracts concerning work carried out on land.[475]

---

[467] *The Rozel*, n. 466 above, 168. See also *Ruxley Electronics and Constructions Ltd v Forsyth* [1996] AC 344; *Jacob & Youngs v Kent* 129 NE 89 (1921).

[468] Discussed in the text accompanying nn. 494 *et seq.*. below.

[469] See Bridge,, n. 7 above.

[470] *Tito v Waddell (No. 2)*, n. 20 above; *Radford v De Froberville* [1977] 1 WLR 1262.

[471] A good example of this is the strip-mining defendant who failed in breach of contract to restore the land in the American case of *Peevyhouse v Garland Coal Co.* 382 P. 2d 109 (1962).

[472] *Attorney General v Blake* [2001] 1 AC 268.

[473] See discussion above.

[474] In cases involving works on land, there is no statutory text that imposes a diminution of value test: see *Tito v Waddell (No. 2)*, n. 20 above; *Radford v De Froberville*, n. 470 above; *Jacob & Youngs v Kent*, n. 467 above.

[475] *H Dakin & Co. Ltd v Lee* [1916] 1 KB 566; *Hoenig v Isaacs* [1952] 2 All ER 176.

12.120 **Value loss or repair cost?** The question of choosing between value and repair (or completion) arose in *The Alecos M*,[476] where the sellers of a ship failed to supply it with its spare propeller. One issue was whether this was a case of non-delivery or defective delivery. The Court of Appeal, following the trial judge, who had disagreed with the arbitrator on this point, concluded that the case was one of non-delivery under section 51,[477] though the choice between section 51 and section 53 does not seem to have affected the result.[478] The characterization of the case as a section 51 case is somewhat questionable: the contract was for the sale of specific goods and those specific goods were delivered. It was an entire contract for the sale of a ship and not for an assembly of individual specific goods that in their totality amounted to a ship. The buyer's problem was not that it did not receive a propeller, but that it received a ship in a defective state because it was missing a spare propeller. The propeller in and of itself had no intrinsic value to the buyer. It was common ground that there was no market in which the buyers could have procured a spare propeller. The arbitrator, whose award was restored by the Court of Appeal, was not convinced that the buyers would use a large damages award[479] to purchase a spare when there was only a remote possibility that it would be used, and concluded that the buyers' true loss was the scrap value of the propeller.[480] At first instance, Steyn J had considered that there were three possible measures of damages: the market value of the missing propeller, the resale value to the buyer of the spare propeller and the replacement cost of the spare propeller. It is not clear what the differences were that separated these three measures. Steyn J rejected the arbitrator's conclusion that the buyer was entitled only to the scrap value of the spare propeller and awarded instead the reasonable cost of replacing the spare propeller. The arbitrator's conclusion had coincided with the arbitrator's view that the buyer was entitled (under section 53) to the difference in value between the value of the ship with, and the value of the ship without, the spare propeller. The Court of Appeal, applying the remoteness rule in section 51(2) in view of the absence of a market in propellers, reinstated the arbitrator's award of the scrap value of the spare propeller. On the arbitrator's findings, that was the value to the buyer of the spare propeller. It would have been easier to justify that result under section 53.

---

[476] n. 460 above; G. H. Treitel (1991) 107 *LQR* 364.

[477] The arbitrator had treated it as section 53 case. At trial, Steyn J did not see the choice beween s. 51 and s. 53 as being of 'critical importance': [1990] 1 Lloyd's Rep. 82, 85.

[478] What would the position have been if the buyer had sought to recover a fraction of the overall price as representing the purchase price of the spare propeller?

[479] $150,000.

[480] $1,100. *Quaere* apportionment of the price and recovery on a partial failure of consideration? See *Ebrahim Dawood Ltd v Heath (1927) Ltd* [1961] 1 Lloyd's Rep. 512 and authorities therein considered.

Date of discovering breach. Section 53(3) computes damages according to the **12.121**
value of the goods in the buyer's hands at the date of delivery. It was treated as a
prima facie rule in *Naughton v O'Callaghan*,[481] a case of the sale of a racehorse
whose pedigree was misdescribed. The buyer claimed damages for both breach
of warranty and for negligent misrepresentation under section 2(1) of the
Misrepresentation Act 1967, the court in its judgment blending the two
approaches. By the time the buyer discovered the misdescription, he had raced the
horse unsuccessfully and it was worth very much less than the sum he paid for it.[482]
Impressed by the fact that the buyer, had he known the truth, would never have
purchased this horse, so different from its stated pedigree, Waller J took the date
of the buyer's discovery as the reference point for comparison with the price paid
by the buyer, thus departing from the rule in section 53(3). At the time of discovery, the buyer had long since lost the right of rejection for breach of condition and
rescission for innocent misrepresentation, so the substantial effect of the judge's
generous damages award[483] was to restore to him these lost rights. This meant that
the buyer had been racing the horse all along at the seller's risk; had the horse been
successful, it is unlikely that the buyer would have turned over the fruits of this
success to the seller. The decision, it is submitted, departed from the *prima facie*
rule in section 53(3) for no good reason.

Consumer Buyers and Price Reduction

Basis of price reduction. One of the remedies for consumer buyers to whom **12.122**
non-conforming goods are delivered, made available when the EU Directive on
certain aspects of the sale of consumer goods and associated guarantees[484] was
transposed in the form of additions to the Sale of Goods Act, is the right to have
the price reduced. The relationship of this right to the other rights introduced
in the same legislation has been noted.[485] As provided in section 48C(1)(a), 'the
buyer . . . may require the seller to reduce the purchase price of the goods . . . by
an appropriate amount'. The price reduction action originates in the civil law
where it is not regarded as a right to damages[486] and is not something in the

---

[481] n. 458 above. *Naughton v O'Callaghan* was distinguished in *Bramhill v Edwards* [2004]
EWCA Civ 403; [2004] 2 Lloyd's Rep. 653.
[482] The contract price was 26,000 guineas; it would have fetched 23,500 guineas at the sales if its
pedigree had been correctly stated; and it was worth only £1,500 (unworthy to be valued in guineas)
when the buyer made his discovery.
[483] Substantial damages for the upkeep of the horse and its training fees were also awarded to
the claimant, who must have felt his cup was running over. The claimant seems to have sought the
recovery of these sums as a surrogate for the unprovable sums that a winning substitute horse would
have provided: n. 458 above, 198.
[484] 1999/44/EC of the European Parliament and of the Council.
[485] See above.
[486] See, e.g., J. Huet, *Les principaux contrats speciaux* (2nd edn, LGDJ 2001), para. 11363
(action estimatoire).

nature of an abatement of the purchase price claimed by the seller.[487] In the United Nations Convention on the International Sale of Goods 1980, which was a source of inspiration for the Directive, price reduction is expressed as a right granted to the buyer and thus amounts to a form of self-help.[488] The differently expressed right of the buyer to require the seller to reduce the price in section 48C is dependent upon the buyer not being able to require repair or replacement of the goods, except for those cases where the seller has failed to repair or replace within a reasonable time or without significant inconvenience to the buyer.[489] Nothing in the Act gives guidance as to whether the buyer's choice between price reduction and rescission is other than a free choice, though the court may in proceedings decide that price reduction is more appropriate than rescission and *vice versa*.[490] The court's discretion is an unstructured one but is more likely to be exercised in favour of salvaging the bargain by preferring price reduction to rescission.[491] Although the reimbursement due to a buyer on rescission may be reduced to take account of any benefit the buyer has obtained from the goods,[492] no similar provision exists for price reduction. Nevertheless, since the reduction must be an 'appropriate' one, account might thereby be taken of any beneficial use and enjoyment that the buyer has had from the goods. The absence of guidance on what is an appropriate reduction, either in the Act or in the Directive, is unfortunate. Since it is the right of the buyer to ask the seller to reduce the price, this remedy grants the initiative to the seller and puts the burden on the buyer of showing that the reduction offered is not appropriate. Because it is not a damages action, it cannot be assumed that the price will be reduced in the same way that it would be in section 53. Where goods the subject of market movement are sold, the price reduction provision in the United Nations Convention operates quite differently from a damages action under section 53.[493] The price is reduced by the difference in value at the time of delivery between the goods in their delivered state and the goods had they been conforming goods. This formula puts a part of any decline in the market value of the goods on the seller, which is not the case under section 53. This difference, however, is unlikely to matter in consumer cases since market volatility is not a feature of consumer goods in general.

---

[487] As it is in s. 53 of the Sale of Goods Act.

[488] Art. 50. It is not located in that Section of the Convention dealing with damages. It is for the sake of convenience dealt with in this chapter under damages.

[489] Discussed above.

[490] S. 48E(3), (4). See also discussion in Ch. 10 above.

[491] It was noted in Ch. 10 above that no provision is made in the Directive for the existence of this discretion.

[492] S. 48C(3).

[493] See M. Bridge, *The International Sale of Goods[:] Law and Practice* (2nd edn, OUP, 2007), Ch. 12.

Profit-earning Chattels

Lost profits and lost value.   Provided that the buyer's loss falls within the remote-   **12.123**
ness rule, it will in certain cases be appropriate to displace the *prima facie* value
difference rule in section 53(3) and award instead the profits the buyer might reasonably have made, subject to the impact of the mitigation rule. A common case
is that of the profit-earning chattel, namely, goods acquired by the buyer to be put
into productive use and to generate profits. In this case, the buyer's lost profits do
not accompany a lost value claim as consequential damages, which was discussed
earlier. Rather, they are a substitute for lost value based on the assumption that the
price of the contract goods was a cost incurred in earning profits.

Gross profits, net profits, and overhead.   If damages are to be awarded for   **12.124**
lost profits, it is vitally important to clarify the working terminology, for a confusion of thought can only lead to under-compensation or, more likely, double
recovery.[494] For our present purposes, the expression 'gross profits' may be understood as the sum of all the receipts earned by the buyer in operating the chattel.
But it must be recognized that the buyer has to incur certain expenses so as to be
able to earn these profits, notably wages and salaries of employees and the overheads (such as power, lighting, rent or mortgage payments, and commercial rates)
associated with running the buyer's premises. Where the seller delivers a defective
chattel, these expenses ought to be ignored,[495] except to the extent that the seller's
breach of warranty either abates these costs, for example with the shutting
down of the buyer's premises for a period, or increases them, for example by
requiring extra labour to operate the chattel. Similarly, the buyer may incur other
costs, for example, repairs, not normally associated with operating a chattel that
complies with the seller's warranties. One item of expense however, that may
never be ignored is the cost of the chattel itself. If the buyer pays £10,000 for a
widget-making machine that, but for the seller's breach of contract, would have
earned £100,000, the buyer may not recover £110,000, for the £10,000 outlay
was a necessary cost incurred by the buyer in putting himself in a position to earn
the £100,000.[496] Similarly, if the buyer has not yet paid the price, this liability
must be debited against any claim made by the buyer for his gross profits.[497]
Again, for present purposes, the expression 'net profits' may be understood as
the buyer's gross profits minus the expenses necessarily incurred by the buyer to
qualify himself to earn those gross profits.

---

[494] See *Cullinane v British 'Rema' Manufacturing Co. Ltd* [1954] 1 QB 292; *RG McLean Ltd v
Canadian Vickers Ltd* (1970) 15 DLR (3d) 15 (criticism of trial award); *Sunnyside Greenhouses Ltd v
Golden West Seeds Ltd* (1972) 27 DLR (3d) 434.
[495] See *Lay's Transport Ltd v Meadow Lake Consumers' Co-operative Association Ltd* (1982) 20 Sask.
R 8 (Can.).
[496] *Cullinane v British 'Rema' Manufacturing Co.Ltd*, n. 494 above.
[497] *RG McLean Ltd v Canadian Vickers Ltd*, n. 494 above.

12.125 **Gross profits claim and depreciation.** In so far as the buyer claims gross profits over the warranted period, and the mitigation rule does not enter the picture, a buyer claiming gross profits need not worry about the depreciating value of the chattel in his hands, as its value declines to zero by the end of the warranted period. Depreciation is just an accountancy term useful in producing an annual picture of the buyer's financial position, and is conveniently represented by a straight-line decline in value based upon the historic cost of acquisition of the chattel. It is only when mitigation prevents the buyer from absorbing the total value of the chattel in his product-making activities that depreciation comes into play as a useful device for assessing the capital value of the chattel in his hands. If the buyer has resold the chattel, however, then the actual resale price is likely to be a better guide in calculating a benefit in the buyer's hands, cast there by the seller's breach, that has to be offset against the buyer's warranty claim for loss of profits.

12.126 **Other overlapping claims.** Besides the example of price and gross profits stated above, other examples of overlapping claims exist. A buyer, for example, may not recover damages representing both the reduced capital value of a chattel and the loss of production by this chattel, if the reduction in value is but an alternative way of expressing in present terms the loss of future production.[498] Reduced value is realized when the buyer disposes of the chattel and applies his assets to an alternative profit-making venture. Similarly, if the buyer ends up, after receiving an allowance for reduced value, having to pay a lesser sum for the chattel, he may not claim a level of profits associated with a chattel priced at a greater sum.

12.127 **Example.** A useful case study in pointing to the problems of double-counting is the Canadian case of *Sunnyside Greenhouses Ltd v Golden West Seeds Ltd*.[499] It concerned a breach of the sellers' warranty that plastic greenhouse-roof panels would last at least seven years. In fact, half of the panels lasted for only three years (on the south side) while the remaining half lasted for five years (on the north side). The court permitted the buyers to recover four-sevenths of the price paid for the south panels and two-sevenths of the price paid for the north panels. At the same time as it made the award for the south panels, however, it also awarded the buyers damages for the shortfall in gross sales of the buyers' crops in 1969 compared to the crops of other years. Since the buyer was recovering the prorated price of the south panels in that same year, double-counting was clearly taking place; the cost of the panels was the price to be paid for earning gross sales. A further example of double-counting occurred when the court awarded the buyers the whole of their costs in installing the panels, despite the fact that they had a useful

---

[498] *H Parsons (Livestock) Ltd v Uttley Ingham & Co. Ltd*, n. 115 above; *Bunting v Tory*, n. 349 above; *Steele v Maurer* (1977) 79 DLR (3d) 764; *Browning v Brachers* [2004] EWHC 16 (QB); [2004] PNLR 28 at [84], reversed on other grounds [2005] EWCA Civ 753; [2005] PNLR 44.
[499] n. 494 above.

life of three years (on the south side) and five years (on the north side). The extent of over-compensation here is revealed in the diametrically opposite view the court took of the cost of removing the panels. Instead of awarding the cost of removal, the court, recognizing that removal would anyway have occurred after seven years, granted damages based on the accelerated expenditure of this sum, namely, interest on the capital sum thus expended for the balance of the seven-year period. This fails to recognize that, over the life of the buyer's business, the seller's breach may have necessitated one extra removal of panels. Whether such a loss has truly occurred is nevertheless a most difficult speculation, and perhaps the addition of the different sums awarded for installation and premature removal works rough justice.

Loss-making ventures. Given the difficulty sometimes presented of proving **12.128** speculative profit losses, it is understandable that courts permit claimants to claim their wasted capital expenditure in lieu of profits.[500] Nevertheless, this is not permitted where the defendant is able to prove that the claimant was engaged upon a loss-making venture.[501] One issue that has arisen is whether a claimant ought to be able to claim both wasted capital expenses and loss of profits, always provided that double-counting is avoided by thus claiming net profits instead of gross profits. The immediate response to this is to assert that this must be acceptable in principle but a pointless thing to do in practice. To revert to the example given earlier of the £10,000 widget-making machine which fails to generate warranted gross profits of £100,000, a buyer wishing to combine capital and profits in one claim is driven to ask for £10,000 plus (£100,000–£10,000), making £100,000 in all, if he is not to be over-compensated. This calculation is therefore a long-winded way of reproducing a simple £100,000 claim for lost gross profits.

Complex case. As simple as the above position ought to be, however, it is **12.129** complicated by the impact of the mitigation rule and by the Court of Appeal decision in *Cullinane v British 'Rema' Manufacturing Co. Ltd*[502] in which the buyers disposed of[503] a clay-pulverizing machine sold by the sellers, together with ancillary machinery and buildings, after three years instead of keeping it for the ten years for which it was warranted to produce clay at the profitable rate of six tons per hour. The buyers claimed two major items of loss: first of all, their capital loss,

---

[500] *Cullinane*, n. 494 above; *McRae v Commonwealth Disposals Commission* (1950) 84 CLR 377; *CCC Films (London) Ltd v Impact Quadrant Films Ltd* [1985] QB 16; *Anglia Television Ltd v Reed* [1972] 1 QB 60; *Security Stove & Manufacturing Co. v American Railway Express Co.* (1932) 51 SW 2d 572 (US).

[501] *Bowlay Logging Ltd v Domtar Ltd* [1978] 4 WWR 105; *C & P Haulage v Middleton* [1983] 3 All ER 94; *CCC Films*, above; *Commonwealth of Australia v Amann Aviation Pty Ltd* (1991) 66 ALJR 123; *Filobake Ltd v Rondo Ltd* [2005] EWCA Civ 563; Bridge, n. 7 above.

[502] n. 494 above. See *Sunnyside Greenhouses*, n. 494 above; *TC Industrial Plant Pty Ltd v Robert's Queensland Pty Ltd* [1964] ALR 1083; H. Street, *Principles of the Law of Damages* (Sweet & Maxwell, 1962), 243–5; J. Macleod [1970] *JBL* 19; M. Baer (1973) 51 *Can. Bar Rev.* 490.

[503] The damages are calculated that they did so in mitigation.

consisting of the purchase price paid for the warranted machine, as well as for the ancillary machinery and buildings, less the residual, break-up capital value of all three items at the end of the three years from the installation of the machine to the trial of the action; and, secondly, their net profits after certain deductions were made, expressed at an annual rate grossed up to the date of statement of claim and stated to be a continuing claim after that date. These deductions included 10 per cent of the purchase price of the three capital items, offset against the annual statement of profits.

12.130 **Combining lost profits and capital loss claims.**   The majority of the court[504] understood that the buyers were claiming loss of profits only for a three-year period instead of for the ten-year period warranted by the sellers. This may well not have been the natural way to read the buyer's statement of claim; moreover, it hardly accorded with the assumptions of the official referee, whose calculations of the profits that the machine should have made over that three-year period, if true to its warranty, were clearly based on a slow progression to profitability as initial teething problems were overcome. Accepting that interpretation made by the majority, however, it is plain that the buyers were claiming too much; they were asking for a little over 50 per cent of their capital investment, representing their net capital loss after break-up, and were offsetting only 30 per cent of the capital cost in the form of depreciation at 10 per cent per year against the gross profits figure. In other words, over 20 per cent of their capital cost had not been counted in against the gross profits amount.[505] Despite this, the official referee, for unexplained reasons, chose to ignore the depreciation factor altogether: he awarded the buyers their net capital loss together with a sum for lost profits that took no account of the capital investment necessarily incurred to earn these profits. The majority of the Court of Appeal, seeing an overlapping element in the buyer's claim for net capital loss and lost profits, put the buyers to their election and awarded them only their lost gross profits minus an unpaid portion of the purchase price, as this was a larger figure than their capital loss.

12.131 **Submission.**   It is submitted that the dissenting member of the court, Morris LJ, was right, assuming that he correctly interpreted the buyers to be claiming lost profits only for three years, without conceding that the machine would have been unprofitable after that time.[506] Morris LJ would have permitted the combination of capital loss and net profits in the form presented by the claimant buyers, presumably on the ground that the 20 per cent or so of the capital cost, not offset

---

[504] Evershed MR and Jenkins LJ.

[505] This seems to be the point made by the Australian High Court in *TC Industrial Plant pty Ltd v Robert's Queensland pty Ltd*, n. 502 above. See also Jenkins LJ in *Cullinane*, n. 494 above, 309 (capital expenditure wiped out over 10 years at the rate of 10% per year).

[506] See *TC Industrial Plant*, n. 502 above.

against the profits claimed over the three years, could be seen as a substitute unclaimed for the profits lost over the remaining seven years of the warranty period. If one accepts that the disagreement in the Court of Appeal centred on the meaning of the buyer's pleadings with regard to the seven-year period, *Cullinane* should not be read as denying the formulation of a capital-loss claim combined with a net loss of profits claim.[507] Indeed, a claim of just this sort is necessitated by the doctrine of mitigation, which requires the buyer to exit from the clay-pulverizing business before the ten-year period has elapsed. Sir Raymond Evershed was quite prepared to countenance a combined claim, if properly made, when he said:

> Upon the question whether the plaintiff could have claimed for loss of profits up to the date of the hearing and have claimed an additional sum because he was at that date left with a machine which was less valuable than the machine as warranted I say only that the plaintiff has not so claimed.[508]

Conclusion. On this approach, the claimant would be entitled to his gross prof-   **12.132** its for three years plus the difference between the value of his capital items after three years' wear-and-tear, if the clay-pulverizing machine had answered to the warranty, and their actual value after three years, given the breach of warranty. The capital loss should (presumably) be the depreciated expected value of these capital items, if the warranty had been satisfied, less the price that a purchaser of the business would actually be prepared to pay for them given their sub-warranty performance. If no such purchaser could be found, that second figure would have to be the break-up value of the capital items. In the light of this, the attitude of the majority to the buyer's claim, formulated in difficult circumstances, might have been more accommodating.

---

[507] *Cullinane* was distinguished in *JP Morgan Chase Bank v Springwell Navigation Corpn* [2006] EWCA Civ 161; [2006] PNLR 28 at [8] (on the facts claims made were not alternative claims but cumulative claims) and in *4 Eng Ltd v Harper* [2008] EWHC (Ch) at 915 [48]–[49]. See also *Browning v Brachers*, n. 498 above (loss of profits from diseased goats additional to loss of value of the land); *Astea (UK) Ltd v Time Publishing Group Ltd* [2003] EWHC 725 (TCC) at [167]–[168]. On the difficulties arising from pleading damages claims in the alternative, see the concerns expressed in *Filobake Ltd v Rondo Ltd*, n. 501 above at [64], about the forensic difficulties that would arise in those cases where the claimant seeks in the alternative lost profits and the return of reliance expenditure, given that the burden is on the claimant to prove lost profits but on the defendant to prove that reliance expenditure would have been wasted in any event.

[508] *Cullinane*, n. 494 above, 306–7.

Appendices

APPENDIX 1

Sale of Goods Act 1979

PART I
CONTRACTS TO WHICH ACT APPLIES

1 Contracts to which Act applies

(1) This Act applies to contracts of sale of goods made on or after (but not to those made before) 1 January 1894.

(2) In relation to contracts made on certain dates, this Act applies subject to the modification of certain of its sections as mentioned in Schedule 1 below.

(3) Any such modification is indicated in the section concerned by a reference to Schedule 1 below.

(4) Accordingly, where a section does not contain such a reference, this Act applies in relation to the contract concerned without such modification of the section.

PART II
FORMATION OF THE CONTRACT

Contract of sale

2 Contract of sale

(1) A contract of sale of goods is a contract by which the seller transfers or agrees to transfer the property in goods to the buyer for a money consideration, called the price.

(2) There may a contract of sale between one part owner and another.

(3) A contract of sale may be absolute or conditional.

(4) Where under a contract of sale the property in the goods is transferred from the seller to the buyer the contact is called a sale.

(5) Where under a contract of sale the transfer of the property in the goods is to take place at a future time or subject to some condition later to be fulfilled the contract is called an agreement to sell.

(6) An agreement to sell becomes a sale when the time elapses or the conditions are fulfilled subject to which the property in the goods is to be transferred.

3 Capacity to buy and sell

(1) Capacity to buy and sell is regulated by the general law concerning capacity to contract and to transfer and acquire property.

(2) Where necessaries are sold and delivered to a minor or to a person who by reason of mental incapacity or drunkenness is incompetent to contract, he must pay a reasonable price for them.

(3) In subsection (2) above 'necessaries' means goods suitable to the condition in life of the minor or other person concerned and to his actual requirements at the time of the sale and delivery.

Formalities of contract

4 How contract of sale is made

(1) Subject to this and any other Act, a contract of sale may be made in writing (either with or without seal), or by word of mouth, or partly in writing and partly by word of mouth, or may be implied from the conduct of the parties.

(2) Nothing in this section affects the law relating to corporations.

Subject matter of contract

5 Existing or future goods

(1) The goods which form the subject of a contract of sale may be either existing goods, owned or possessed by the seller, or goods to be manufactured or acquired by him after the making of the contract of sale, in this Act called future goods.

(2) There may be a contract for the sale of goods the acquisition of which by the seller depends on a contingency which may or may not happen.

(3) Where by a contract of sale the seller purports to effect a present sale of future goods, the contract operates as an agreement to sell the goods.

6 Goods which have perished

Where there is a contract for the sale of specific goods, and the goods without the knowledge of the seller have perished at the time when a contract is made, the contract is void.

7 Goods perishing before sale but after agreement to sell

Where there is an agreement to sell specific goods and subsequently the goods, without any fault on the part of the seller or buyer, perish before the risk passes to the buyer, the agreement is avoided.

The price

8 Ascertainment of price

(1) The price in a contract of sale may be fixed by the contract, or may be left to be fixed in a manner agreed by the contract, or may be determined by the course of dealing between the parties.

(2) Where the price is not determined as mentioned in subsection (1) above the buyer must pay a reasonable price.

(3) What is a reasonable price is a question of fact dependent on the circumstances of each particular case.

9 Agreement to sell at valuation

(1) Where there is an agreement to sell goods on the terms that the price is to be fixed by the valuation of a third party, and he cannot or does not make the valuation, the agreement is avoided; but if the goods or any part of them have been delivered to and appropriated by the buyer he must pay a reasonable price for them.

(2) Where the third party is prevented from making the valuation by the fault of the seller or buyer, the party not at fault may maintain an action for damages against the party at fault.

Implied terms etc.

10 Stipulations about time

(1) Unless a different intention appears from the terms of the contract, stipulations as to time of payment are not of the essence of a contract of sale.

(2) Whether any other stipulation as to time is or is not of the essence of the contract depends on the terms of the contract.

(3) In a contract of sale 'month' prima facie means calendar month.

11 When condition to be treated as warranty

(1) This section does not apply to Scotland.

(2) Where a contract of sale is subject to a condition to be fulfilled by the seller, the buyer may waive the condition, or may elect to treat the breach of the condition as a breach of warranty and not as a ground for treating the contract as repudiated.

(3) Whether a stipulation in a contract of sale is a condition, the breach of which may give rise to a right to treat the contract as repudiated, or a warranty, the breach of which may give rise to a

claim for damages but not to a right to reject the goods and treat the contract as repudiated, depends in each case on the construction of the contract; and a stipulation may be a condition, though called a warranty in the contract.

(4) Subject to section 35A below where a contract of sale is not severable and the buyer has accepted the goods or part of them, the breach of a condition to be fulfilled by the seller can only be treated as a breach of warranty, and not as a ground for rejecting the goods and treating the contract as repudiated, unless there is an express or implied term of the contract to that effect.

(6) Nothing in this section affects a condition or warranty whose fulfilment is excused by law by reason of impossibility or otherwise.

(7) Paragraph 2 of Schedule 1 below applies in relation to a contract made before 22 April 1967 or (in the application of this Act to Northern Ireland) 28 July 1967.

12 *Implied terms about title, etc.*

(1) In a contract of sale, other than one to which subsection (3) below applies, there is an implied term on the part of the seller that in the case of a sale he has a right to sell the goods, and in the case of an agreement to sell he will have such a right at the time when the property is to pass.

(2) In a contract of sale, other than one to which subsection (3) below applies, there is also an implied [term] that—

   (a) the goods are free, and will remain free until the time when the property is to pass, from any charge or encumbrance not disclosed or known to the buyer before the contract is made, and

   (b) the buyer will enjoy quiet possession of the goods except so far as it may be disturbed by the owner or other person entitled to the benefit of any charge or encumbrance so disclosed or known.

(3) This subsection applies to a contract of sale in the case of which there appears from the contract or is to be inferred from its circumstances an intention that the seller should transfer only such title as he or a third person may have.

(4) In a contract to which subsection (3) above applies there is an implied term that all charges or encumbrances known to the seller and not known to the buyer have been disclosed to the buyer before the contract is made.

(5) In a contract to which subsection (3) above applies there is also an implied term that none of the following will disturb the buyer's quiet possession of the goods, namely—

   (a) the seller;

   (b) in a case where the parties to the contract intend that the seller should transfer only such title as a third person may have, that person;

   (c) anyone claiming through or under the seller or that third person otherwise than under a charge or encumbrance disclosed or known to the buyer before the contract is made.

(5A) As regards England and Wales and Northern Ireland, the term implied by subsection (1) above is a condition and the terms implied by subsections (2), (4) and (5) above are warranties.

(6) Paragraph 3 of Schedule 1 below applies in relation to a contract made before 18 May 1973.

13 *Sale by description*

(1) Where there is a contract for the sale of goods by description, there is an implied term that the goods will correspond with the description.

(1A) As regards England and Wales and Northern Ireland, the term implied by subsection (1) above is a condition.

(2) If the sale is by sample as well as by description it is not sufficient that the bulk of the goods corresponds with the sample if the goods do not also correspond with the description.

(3) A sale of goods is not prevented from being a sale by description by reason only that, being exposed for sale or hire, they are selected by the buyer.

(4) Paragraph 4 of Schedule 1 below applies in relation to a contract made before 18 May 1973.

14 Implied terms about quality or fitness

(1) Except as provided by this section and section 15 below and subject to any other enactment, there is no implied term about the quality or fitness for any particular purpose of goods supplied under a contract of sale.

(2) Where the seller sells goods in the course of a business, there is an implied term that the goods supplied under the contract are of satisfactory quality.

(2A) For the purposes of this Act, goods are of satisfactory quality if they meet the standard that a reasonable person would regard as satisfactory, taking account of any description of the goods, the price (if relevant) and all the other relevant circumstances.

(2B) For the purposes of this Act, the quality of goods includes their state and condition and the following (among others) are in appropriate cases aspects of the quality of goods—

(a) fitness for all the purposes for which goods of the kind in question are commonly supplied,

(b) appearance and finish,

(c) freedom from minor defects,

(d) safety, and

(e) durability.

(2C) The term implied by subsection (2) above does not extend to any matter making the quality of goods unsatisfactory—

(a) which is specifically drawn to the buyer's attention before the contract is made,

(b) where the buyer examines the goods before the contract is made, which that examination ought to reveal, or

(c) in the case of a contract for sale by sample, which would have been apparent on a reasonable examination of the sample.

(2D) If the buyer deals as consumer or, in Scotland, if a contract of sale is a consumer contract, the relevant circumstances mentioned in subsection (2A) above include any public statements on the specific characteristics of the goods made about them by the seller, the producer or his representative, particularly in advertising or on labelling.

(2E) A public statement is not by virtue of subsection (2D) above a relevant circumstance for the purposes of subsection (2A) above in the case of a contract of sale, if the seller shows that—

(a) at the time the contract was made, he was not, and could not reasonably have been aware of the statement,

(b) before the contract was made, the statement had been withdrawn in public or, to the extent that it contained anything which was incorrect or misleading, it had been corrected in public, or

(c) the decision to buy the goods could not have been influenced by the statement.

(2F) Subsections (2D) and (2E) above do not prevent any public statement from being a relevant circumstance for the purposes of subsection (2A) above (whether or not the buyer deals as consumer or, in Scotland, whether or not the contract of sale is a consumer contract) if the statement would have been such a circumstance apart from those subsections.

(3) Where the seller sells goods in the course of a business and the buyer, expressly or by implication, makes known—

(a) to the seller, or

(b) where the purchase price of part of it is payable by instalments and the goods were previously sold by a credit-broker to the seller, to that credit-broker, any particular purpose for which the goods are being bought, there is an implied term that the goods supplied under the contract are reasonably fit for that purpose, whether or not that is a purpose for which such goods are commonly supplied, except where the circumstances show that the buyer does not rely, or that it is unreasonable for him to rely, on the skill or judgment of the seller or credit-broker.

(4) An implied term about quality or fitness for a particular purpose may be annexed to a contract of sale by usage.

(5) The preceding provisions of this section apply to a sale by a person who in the course of a business is acting as agent for another as they apply to a sale by a principal in the course of a business, except where that other is not selling in the course of a business and either the buyer knows that fact or reasonable steps are taken to bring it to the notice of the buyer before the contract is made.

(6) As regards England and Wales and Northern Ireland, the terms implied by subsections (2) and (3) above are conditions.

(7) Paragraph 5 of Schedule 1 below applies in relation to a contract made on or after 18 May 1973 and before the appointed day, and paragraph 6 in relation to one made before 18 May 1973.

(8) In subsection (7) above and paragraph 5 of Schedule 1 below references to the appointed day are to the day appointed for the purposes of those provisions by an order of the Secretary of State made by statutory instrument.

Sale by sample

15 Sale by sample

(1) A contract of sale is a contract for sale by sample where there is an express or implied term to that effect in the contract.

(2) In the case of a contract for sale by sample there is an implied term—

    (a) that the bulk will correspond with the sample in quality;

    [. . .]

    (c) that the goods will be free from any defect, making their quality unsatisfactory, which would not be apparent on reasonable examination of the sample.

(3) As regards England and Wales and Northern Ireland, the term implied by subsection (2) above is a condition.

(4) Paragraph 7 of Schedule 1 below applies in relation to a contract made before 18 May 1973.

Miscellaneous

15A Modification of remedies for breach of condition in non-consumer cases

(1) Where in the case of a contract of sale—

    (a) the buyer would, apart from this subsection, have the right to reject goods by reason of a breach on the part of the seller of a term implied by section 13, 14 or 15 above, but

    (b) the breach is so slight that it would be unreasonable for him to reject them, then, if the buyer does not deal as consumer, the breach is not to be treated as a breach of condition but may be treated as a breach of warranty.

(2) This section applies unless a contrary intention appears in, or is to be implied from, the contract.

(3) It is for the seller to show that a breach fell within subsection (1) (b) above.

(4) This section does not apply to Scotland.

15B Remedies for breach of contract as respects Scotland

(1) Where in a contract of sale the seller is in breach of any term of the contract (express or implied), the buyer shall be entitled—

    (a) to claim damages, and

    (b) if the breach is material, to reject any goods delivered under the contract and treat it as repudiated.

(2) Where a contract of sale is a consumer contract, then, for the purposes of subsection (1) (b) above, breach by the seller of any term (express or implied)—

    (a) as to the quality of the goods or their fitness for a purpose,

    (b) if the goods are, or are to be, sold by description, that the goods will correspond with the description,

    (c) if the goods are, or are to be, sold by reference to a sample, that the bulk will correspond with the sample in quality, shall be deemed to be a material breach.

(3) This section applies to Scotland only.

PART III
EFFECTS OF THE CONTRACT

Transfer of property as between seller and buyer

16 Goods must be ascertained

Subject to section 20A below where there is a contract for the sale of unascertained goods no property in the goods is transferred to the buyer unless and until the goods are ascertained.

17 Property passes when intended to pass

(1) Where there is a contract for the sale of specific or ascertained goods the property in them is transferred to the buyer at such time as the parties to the contract intend it to be transferred.

(2) For the purpose of ascertaining the intention of the parties regard shall be had to the terms of the contract, the conduct of the parties and the circumstances of the case.

18 Rules for ascertaining intention

Unless a different intention appears, the following are rules for ascertaining the intention of the parties as to the time at which the property in the goods is to pass to the buyer.

Rule 1. —Where there is an unconditional contract for the sale of specific goods in a deliverable state the property in the goods passes to the buyer when the contract is made, and it is immaterial whether the time of payment or the time of delivery, or both, be postponed.

Rule 2.—Where there is a contract for the sale of specific goods and the seller is bound to do something to the goods for the purpose of putting them into a deliverable state, the property does not pass until the thing is done and the buyer has notice that it has been done.

Rule 3.—Where there is a contract for the sale of specific goods in a deliverable state but the seller is bound to weigh, measure, test, or do some other act or thing with reference to the goods for the purpose of ascertaining the price, the property does not pass until the act or thing is done and the buyer has notice that it has been done.

Rule 4.—When goods are delivered to the buyer on approval or on sale or return or other similar terms the property in the goods passes to the buyer:—

    (a) when he signifies his approval or acceptance to the seller or does any other act adopting the transaction;

    (b) if he does not signify his approval or acceptance to the seller but retains the goods without giving notice of rejection, then, if a time has been fixed for the return of the goods, on the expiration of that time, and, if no time has been fixed, on the expiration of a reasonable time.

Rule 5.—(1) Where there is a contract for the sale of unascertained or future goods by description, and goods of that description and in a deliverable state are unconditionally appropriated to the contract, either by the seller with the assent of the buyer or by the buyer with the assent of the seller, the property in the goods then passes to the buyer; and the assent may be express or implied, and may be given either before or after the appropriation is made.

(2) Where, in pursuance of the contract, the seller delivers the goods to the buyer or to a carrier or other bailee or custodier (whether named by the buyer or not) for the purpose of transmission to the buyer, and does not reserve the right of disposal, he is to be taken to have unconditionally appropriated the goods to the contract.

(3) Where there is a contract for the sale of a specified quantity of unascertained goods in a deliverable state forming part of a bulk which is identified either in the contract or by subsequent agreement between the parties and the bulk is reduced to (or to less than) that quantity, then, if the buyer under that contract is the only buyer to whom goods are then due out of the bulk—

    (a) the remaining goods are to be taken as appropriated to that contract at the time when the bulk is so reduced; and

    (b) the property in those goods then passes to that buyer.

(4) Paragraph (3) above applies also (with the necessary modifications) where a bulk is reduced to (or to less than) the aggregate of the quantities due to a single buyer under separate contracts relating to that bulk and he is the only buyer to whom goods are then due out of that bulk.

19 Reservation of right of disposal

(1) Where there is a contract for the sale of specific goods or where goods are subsequently appropriated to the contract, the seller may, by the terms of the contract or appropriation, reserve the right of disposal of the goods until certain conditions are fulfilled; and in such a case, notwithstanding the delivery of the goods to the buyer, or to a carrier or other bailee or custodier for the purpose of transmission to the buyer, the property in the goods does not pass to the buyer until the conditions imposed by the seller are fulfilled.

(2) Where goods are shipped, and by the bill of lading the goods are deliverable to the order of the seller or his agent, the seller is prima facie to be taken to reserve the right of disposal.

(3) Where the seller of goods draws on the buyer for the price, and transmits the bill of exchange and bill of lading to the buyer together to secure acceptance or payment of the bill of exchange, the buyer is bound to return the bill of lading if he does not honour the bill of exchange, and if he wrongfully retains the bill of lading the property in the goods does not pass to him.

20 Passing of risk

(1) Unless otherwise agreed, the goods remain at the seller's risk until the property in them is transferred to the buyer, but when the property in them is transferred to the buyer the goods are at the buyer's risk whether delivery has been made or not.

(2) But where delivery has been delayed through the fault of either buyer or seller the goods are at the risk of the party at fault as regards any loss which might not have occurred but for such fault.

(3) Nothing in this section affects the duties or liabilities of either seller or buyer as a bailee or custodier of the goods of the other party.

(4) In a case where the buyer deals as consumer or, in Scotland, where there is a consumer contract in which the buyer is a consumer, subsections (1) to (3) above must be ignored and the goods remain at the seller's risk until they are delivered to the consumer.

20A Undivided shares in goods forming part of a bulk

(1) This section applies to a contract for the sale of a specified quantity of unascertained goods if the following conditions are met—
    (a) the goods or some of them form part of a bulk which is identified either in the contract or by subsequent agreement between the parties; and
    (b) the buyer has paid the price for some or all of the goods which are the subject of the contract and which form part of the bulk.

(2) Where this section applies, then (unless the parties agree otherwise), as soon as the conditions specified in paragraphs (a) and (b) of subsection (1) above are met or at such later time as the parties may agree—
    (a) property in an undivided share in the bulk is transferred to the buyer; and
    (b) the buyer becomes an owner in common of the bulk.

(3) Subject to subsection (4) below, for the purposes of this section, the undivided share of a buyer in a bulk at any time shall be such share as the quantity of goods paid for and due to the buyer out of the bulk bears to the quantity of goods in the bulk at that time.

(4) Where the aggregate of the undivided shares of buyers in a bulk determined under subsection (3) above would at any time exceed the whole of the bulk at that time, the undivided share in the bulk of each buyer shall be reduced proportionately so that the aggregate of the undivided shares is equal to the whole bulk.

(5) Where a buyer has paid the price for only some of the goods due to him out of a bulk, any delivery to the buyer out of the bulk shall, for the purposes of this section, be ascribed in the first place to the goods in respect of which payment has been made.

(6) For the purpose of this section payment of part of the price for any goods shall be treated as payment for a corresponding part of the goods.

20B *Deemed consent by co-owner to dealings in bulk goods*

(1) A person who has become an owner in common of a bulk by virtue of section 20A above shall be deemed to have consented to—
  (a) any delivery of goods out of the bulk to any other owner in common of the bulk, being goods which are due to him under his contract;
  (b) any removal, dealing with, delivery or disposal of goods in the bulk by any other person who is an owner in common of the bulk in so far as the goods fall within that co-owner's undivided share in the bulk at the time of the removal, dealing, delivery or disposal.
(2) No cause of action shall accrue to anyone against a person by reason of that person having acted in accordance with paragraph (a) or (b) of subsection (1) above in reliance on any consent deemed to have been given under that subsection.
(3) Nothing in this section or section 20A above shall—
  (a) impose an obligation on a buyer of goods out of a bulk to compensate any other buyer of goods out of that bulk for any shortfall in the goods received by that other buyer;
  (b) affects any contractual arrangement between buyers of goods out of a bulk for adjustments between themselves; or
  (c) affect the rights of any buyer under his contract.

Transfer of title

21 *Sale by person not the owner*

(1) Subject to this Act, where goods are sold by a person who is not their owner, and who does not sell them under the authority or with the consent of the owner, the buyer acquires no better title to the goods than the seller had, unless the owner of the goods is by his conduct precluded from denying the seller's authority to sell.
(2) Nothing in this Act affects—
  (a) the provisions of the Factors Acts or any enactment enabling the apparent owner of goods to dispose of them as if he were their true owner;
  (b) the validity of any contract of sale under any special common law or statutory power of sale or under the order of a court of competent jurisdiction.

22 *Market overt*

[. . .]
(2) This section does not apply to Scotland.
(3) Paragraph 8 of Schedule 1 below applies in relation to a contract under which goods were sold before 1 January 1968 or (in the application of this Act to Northern Ireland) 29 August 1967.

23 *Sale under voidable title*

When the seller of goods has a voidable title to them, but his title has not been avoided at the time of the sale, the buyer acquires a good title to the goods, provided he buys them in good faith and without notice of the seller's defect of title.

24 *Seller in possession after sale*

Where a person having sold goods continues or is in possession of the goods, or of the documents of title to the goods, the delivery or transfer by that person, or by a mercantile agent acting for him, of the goods or documents of title under any sale, pledge, or other disposition thereof, to any person receiving the same in good faith and without notice of the previous sale, has the same effect as if the person making the delivery or transfer were expressly authorised by the owner of the goods to make the same.

25 *Buyer in possession after sale*

(1) Where a person having bought or agreed to buy goods obtains, with the consent of the seller, possession of the goods or the documents of title to the goods, the delivery or transfer by that person, or by a mercantile agent acting for him, of the goods or documents of title, under any sale, pledge, or other disposition thereof, to any person receiving the same in good faith and without notice of any lien or other right of the original seller in respect of the goods, has the same effect as if the person making the delivery or transfer were a mercantile agent in possession of the goods or documents of title with the consent of the owner.

(2) For the purposes of subsection (1) above—

    (a) the buyer under a conditional sale agreement is to be taken not to be a person who has bought or agreed to buy goods, and

    (b) 'conditional sale agreement' means an agreement for the sale of goods which is a consumer credit agreement within the meaning of the Consumer Credit Act 1974 under which the purchase price or part of it is payable by instalments, and the property in the goods is to remain in the seller (notwithstanding that the buyer is to be in possession of the goods) until such conditions as to the payment of instalments or otherwise as may be specified in the agreement are fulfilled.

(3) Paragraph 9 of Schedule 1 below applies in relation to a contract under which a person buys or agrees to buy goods and which is made before the appointed day.

(4) In subsection (3) above and paragraph 9 of Schedule 1 below references to the appointed day are to the day appointed for the purposes of those provisions by an order of the Secretary of State made by statutory instrument.

26 *Supplementary to sections 24 and 25*

In sections 24 and 25 above 'mercantile agent' means a mercantile agent having in the customary course of his business as such agent authority either—

    (a) to sell goods, or

    (b) to consign goods for the purpose of sale, or

    (c) to buy goods, or

    (d) to raise money on the security of goods.

PART IV
PERFORMANCE OF THE CONTRACT

27 *Duties of seller and buyer*

It is the duty of the seller to deliver the goods, and of the buyer to accept and pay for them, in accordance with the terms of the contract of sale.

28 *Payment and delivery are concurrent conditions*

Unless otherwise agreed, delivery of the goods and payment of the price are concurrent conditions, that is to say, the seller must be ready and willing to give possession of the goods to the buyer in exchange for the price and the buyer must be ready and willing to pay the price in exchange for possession of the goods.

29 *Rules about delivery*

(1) Whether it is for the buyer to take possession of the goods or for the seller to send them to the buyer is a question depending in each case on the contract, express or implied, between the parties.

(2) Apart from any such contract, express or implied, the place of delivery is the seller's place of business if he has one, and if not, his residence; except that, if the contract is for the sale of spe-

cific goods, which to the knowledge of the parties when the contract is made are in some other place, then that place is the place of delivery.

(3) Where under the contract of sale the seller is bound to send the goods to the buyer, but no time for sending them is fixed, the seller is bound to send them within a reasonable time.

(4) Where the goods at the time of sale are in the possession of a third person, there is no delivery by seller to buyer unless and until the third person acknowledges to the buyer that he holds the goods on his behalf; but nothing in this section affects the operation of the issue or transfer of any document of title to goods.

(5) Demand or tender of delivery may be treated as ineffectual unless made at a reasonable hour; and what is a reasonable hour is a question of fact.

(6) Unless otherwise agreed, the expenses of and incidental to putting the goods into a deliverable state must be borne by the seller.

30 *Delivery of wrong quantity*

(1) Where the seller delivers to the buyer a quantity of goods less than he contracted to sell, the buyer may reject them, but if the buyer accepts the goods so delivered he must pay for them at the contract rate.

(2) Where the seller delivers to the buyer a quantity of goods larger than he contracted to sell, the buyer may accept the goods included in the contract and reject the rest, or he may reject the whole.

(2A) A buyer who does not deal as consumer may not—
- (a) where the seller delivers a quantity of goods less than he contracted to sell, reject the goods under subsection (1) above, or
- (b) where the seller delivers a quantity of goods larger than he contracted to sell, reject the whole under subsection (2) above, if the shortfall or, as the case may be, excess is so slight that it would be unreasonable for him to do so.

(2B) It is for the seller to show that a shortfall or excess fell within subsection (2A) above.

(2C) Subsections (2A) and (2B) above do not apply to Scotland.

(2D) Where the seller delivers a quantity of goods—
- (a) less than he contracted to sell, the buyer shall not be entitled to reject the goods under subsection (1) above,
- (b) larger than he contracted to sell, the buyer shall not be entitled to reject the whole under subsection (2) above, unless the shortfall or excess is material.

(2D) Where the seller delivers a quantity of goods—
- (a) less than he contracted to sell, the buyer shall not be entitled to reject the goods under subsection (1) above,
- (b) larger than he contracted to sell, the buyer shall not be entitled to reject the whole under subsection (2) above, unless the shortfall or excess is material.

(2E) Subsection (2D) above applies to Scotland only.

(3) Where the seller delivers to the buyer a quantity of goods larger than he contracted to sell and the buyer accepts the whole of the goods so delivered he must pay for them at the contract rate.

(5) This section is subject to any usage of trade, special agreement, or course of dealing between the parties.

31 *Instalment deliveries*

(1) Unless otherwise agreed, the buyer of goods is not bound to accept delivery of them by instalments.

(2) Where there is a contract for the sale of goods to be delivered by stated instalments, which are to be separately paid for, and the seller makes defective deliveries in respect of one or more instalments, or the buyer neglects or refuses to take delivery of or pay for one or more instalments,

it is a question in each case depending on the terms of the contract and the circumstances of the case whether the breach of contract is a repudiation of the whole contract or whether it is a severable breach giving rise to a claim for compensation but not to a right to treat the whole contract as repudiated.

32 Delivery to carrier

(1) Where, in pursuance of a contract of sale, the seller is authorised or required to send the goods to the buyer, delivery of the goods to a carrier (whether named by the buyer or not) for the purpose of transmission to the buyer is prima facie deemed to be delivery of the goods to the buyer.

(2) Unless otherwise authorised by the buyer, the seller must make such contact with the carrier on behalf of the buyer as may be reasonable having regard to the nature of the goods and the other circumstances of the case; and if the seller omits to do so, and the goods are lost or damaged in course of transit, the buyer may decline to treat the delivery to the carrier as a delivery to himself or may hold the seller responsible in damages.

(3) Unless otherwise agreed, where goods are sent by the seller to the buyer by a route involving sea transit, under circumstances in which it is usual to insure, the seller must give such notice to the buyer as may enable him to insure them during their sea transit, and if the seller fails to do so, the goods are at his risk during such sea transit.

(4) In a case where the buyer deals as consumer or, in Scotland where there is a consumer contract in which the buyer is a consumer, subsections (1) to (3) above must be ignored, but if in pursuance of a contract of sale the seller is authorised or required to send the goods to the buyer, delivery of the goods to the carrier is not delivery of the goods to the buyer.

33 Risk where goods are delivered at distant place

Where the seller of goods agrees to deliver them at his own risk at a place other than that where they are when sold, the buyer must nevertheless (unless otherwise agreed) take any risk of deterioration in the goods necessarily incident to the course of transit.

34 Buyer's right of examining the goods

Unless otherwise agreed, when the seller tenders delivery of goods to the buyer, he is bound on request to afford the buyer a reasonable opportunity of examining the goods for the purpose of ascertaining whether they are in conformity with the contract and, in the case of a contract for sale by sample, of comparing the bulk with the sample.

35 Acceptance

(1) The buyer is deemed to have accepted the goods subject to subsection (2) below—
    (a) when he intimates to the seller that he has accepted them, or
    (b) when the goods have been delivered to him and he does any act in relation to them which is inconsistent with the ownership of the seller.

(2) Where goods are delivered to the buyer, and he has not previously examined them, he is not deemed to have accepted them under subsection (1) above until he has had a reasonable opportunity of examining them for the purpose—
    (a) of ascertaining whether they are in conformity with the contract, and
    (b) in the case of a contract for sale by sample, of comparing the bulk with the sample.

(3) Where the buyer deals as consumer or (in Scotland) the contract of sale is a consumer contract, the buyer cannot lose his right to rely on subsection (2) above by agreement, waiver or otherwise.

(4) The buyer is also deemed to have accepted the goods when after the lapse of a reasonable time he retains the goods without intimating to the seller that he has rejected them.

(5) The questions that are material in determining for the purposes of subsection (4) above whether a reasonable time has elapsed include whether the buyer has had a reasonable opportunity of examining the goods for the purpose mentioned in subsection (2) above.

(6) The buyer is not by virtue of this section deemed to have accepted the goods merely because—

    (a) he asks for, or agrees to, their repair by or under an arrangement with the seller, or

    (b) the goods are delivered to another under a sub-sale or other disposition.

(7) Where the contract is for the sale of goods making one or more commercial units, a buyer accepting any goods included in a unit is deemed to have accepted all the goods making the unit; and in this subsection 'commercial unit' means a unit division of which would materially impair the value of the goods or the character of the unit.

(8) Paragraph 10 of Schedule 1 below applies in relation to a contract made before 22 April 1967 or (in the application of this Act to Northern Ireland) 28 July 1967.

35A *Right of partial rejection*

(1) If the buyer—

    (a) has the right to reject the goods by reason of a breach on the part of the seller that affects some or all of them, but

    (b) accepts some of the goods, including, where there are any goods unaffected by the breach, all such goods, he does not by accepting them lose his right to reject the rest.

(2) In the case of a buyer having the right to reject an instalment of goods, subsection (1) above applies as if references to the goods were references to the goods comprised in the instalment.

(3) For the purposes of subsection (1) above, goods are affected by a breach if by reason of the breach they are not in conformity with the contract.

(4) This section applies unless a contrary intention appears in, or is to be implied from, the contract.

36 *Buyer not bound to return rejected goods*

Unless otherwise agreed, where goods are delivered to the buyer, and he refuses to accept them, having the right to do so, he is not bound to return them to the seller, but it is sufficient if he intimates to the seller that he refuses to accept them.

37 *Buyer's liability for not taking delivery of goods*

(1) When the seller is ready and willing to deliver the goods, and requests the buyer to take delivery, and the buyer does not within a reasonable time after such request take delivery of the goods, he is liable to the seller for any loss occasioned by his neglect or refusal to take delivery, and also for a reasonable charge for the care and custody of the goods.

(2) Nothing in this section affects the rights of the seller where the neglect or refusal of the buyer to take delivery amounts to a repudiation of the contract.

Part V

Rights Of Unpaid Seller Against The Goods

Preliminary

38 *Unpaid seller defined*

(1) The seller of goods is an unpaid seller within the meaning of this Act—

    (a) when the whole of the price has not been paid or tendered;

    (b) when a bill of exchange or other negotiable instrument has been received as conditional payment, and the condition on which it was received has not been fulfilled by reason of the dishonour of the instrument or otherwise.

(2) In this Part of this Act 'seller' includes any person who is in the position of a seller, as, for instance, an agent of the seller to whom the bill of lading has been indorsed, or a consignor or agent who has himself paid (or is directly responsible for) the price.

39 *Unpaid seller's rights*

(1) Subject to this and any other Act, notwithstanding that the property in the goods may have passed to the buyer, the unpaid seller of goods, as such, has by implication of law—

    (a) a lien on the goods or right to retain them for the price while he is in possession of them;

(b) in the case of the insolvency of the buyer, a right of stopping the goods in transit after he has parted with the possession of them;

(c) a right of re-sale as limited by this Act.

(2) Where the property in goods has not passed to the buyer, the unpaid seller has (in addition to his other remedies) a right of withholding delivery similar to and coextensive with his rights of lien or retention and stoppage in transit where the property has passed to the buyer.

Unpaid seller's lien

41 Seller's lien

(1) Subject to this Act, the unpaid seller of goods who is in possession of them is entitled to retain possession of them until payment or tender of the price in the following cases:—

(a) where the goods have been sold without any stipulation as to credit;

(b) where the goods have been sold on credit but the term of credit has expired;

(c) where the buyer becomes insolvent.

(2) The seller may exercise his lien or right of retention notwithstanding that he is in possession of the goods as agent or bailee or custodier for the buyer.

42 Part delivery

Where an unpaid seller has made part delivery of the goods, he may exercise his lien or right of retention on the remainder, unless such part delivery has been made under such circumstances as to show an agreement to waive the lien or right of retention.

43 Termination of lien

(1) The unpaid seller of goods loses his lien or right of retention in respect of them—

(a) when he delivers the goods to a carrier or other bailee or custodier for the purpose of transmission to the buyer without reserving the right of disposal of the goods;

(b) when the buyer or his agent lawfully obtains possession of the goods;

(c) by waiver of the lien or right of retention.

(2) An unpaid seller of goods who has a lien or right of retention in respect of them does not lose his lien or right of retention by reason only that he has obtained judgment or decree for the price of the goods.

Stoppage in transit

44 Right of stoppage in transit

Subject to this Act, when the buyer of goods becomes insolvent the unpaid seller who has parted with the possession of the goods has the right of stopping them in transit, that is to say, he may resume possession of the goods as long as they are in course of transit, and may retain them until payment or tender of the price.

45 Duration of transit

(1) Goods are deemed to be in course of transit from the time when they are delivered to a carrier or other bailee or custodier for the purpose of transmission to the buyer, until the buyer or his agent in that behalf takes delivery of them from the carrier or other bailee or custodier.

(2) If the buyer or his agent in that behalf obtains delivery of the goods before their arrival at the appointed destination, the transit is at an end.

(3) If, after the arrival of the goods at the appointed destination, the carrier or other bailee or custodier acknowledges to the buyer or his agent that he holds the goods on his behalf and continues in possession of them as bailee or custodier for the buyer or his agent, the transit is at an end, and it is immaterial that a further destination for the goods may have been indicated by the buyer.

(4) If the goods are rejected by the buyer, and the carrier or other bailee or custodier continues in possession of them, the transit is not deemed to be at an end, even if the seller has refused to receive them back.

(5) When goods are delivered to a ship chartered by the buyer it is a question depending on the circumstances of the particular case whether they are in the possession of the master as a carrier or as agent to the buyer.

(6) Where the carrier or other bailee or custodier wrongfully refuses to deliver the goods to the buyer or his agent in that behalf, the transit is deemed to be at an end.

(7) Where part delivery of the goods has been made to the buyer or his agent in that behalf, the remainder of the goods may be stopped in transit, unless such part delivery has been made under such circumstances as to show an agreement to give up possession of the whole of the goods.

46 How stoppage in transit is effected

(1) The unpaid seller may exercise his right of stoppage in transit either by taking actual possession of the goods or by giving notice of his claim to the carrier or other bailee or custodier in whose possession the goods are.

(2) The notice may be given either to the person in actual possession of the goods or to his principal.

(3) If given to the principal, the notice is ineffective unless given at such time and under such circumstances that the principal, by the exercise of reasonable diligence, may communicate it to his servant or agent in time to prevent a delivery to the buyer.

(4) When notice of stoppage in transit is given by the seller to the carrier or other bailee or custodier in possession of the goods, he must re-deliver the goods to, or according to the directions of, the seller; and the expenses of the re-delivery must be borne by the seller.

Re-sale etc. by buyer

47 Effect of sub-sale etc. by buyer

(1) Subject to this Act, the unpaid seller's right of lien or retention or stoppage in transit is not affected by any sale or other disposition of the goods which the buyer may have made, unless the seller has assented to it.

(2) Where a document of title to goods has been lawfully transferred to any person as buyer or owner of the goods, and that person transfers the document to a person who takes it in good faith and for valuable consideration, then—

(a) if the last-mentioned transfer was by way of sale the unpaid seller's right of lien or retention or stoppage in transit is defeated; and

(b) if the last-mentioned transfer was made by way of pledge or other disposition for value, the unpaid seller's right of lien or retention of stoppage in transit can only be exercised subject to the rights of the transferee.

Rescission: and re-sale by seller

48 Rescission: and re-sale by seller

(1) Subject to this section, a contract of sale is not rescinded by the mere exercise by an unpaid seller of his right of lien or retention or stoppage in transit.

(2) Where an unpaid seller who has exercised his right of lien or retention or stoppage in transit re-sells the goods, the buyer acquires a good title to them as against the original buyer.

(3) Where the goods are of a perishable nature, or where the unpaid seller gives notice to the buyer of his intention to re-sell, and the buyer does not within a reasonable time pay or tender the price, the unpaid seller may re-sell the goods and recover from the original buyer damages for any loss occasioned by his breach of contract.

(4) Where the seller expressly reserves the right of re-sale in case the buyer should make default, and on the buyer making default re-sells the goods, the original contract of sale is rescinded but without prejudice to any claim the seller may have for damages.

PART VA

ADDITIONAL RIGHTS OF BUYER IN CONSUMER CASES

48A Introductory

(1) This section applies if—
    (a) the buyer deals as consumer or, in Scotland, there is a consumer contract in which the buyer is a consumer, and
    (b) the goods do not conform to the contract of sale at the time of delivery.
(2) If this section applies, the buyer has the right—
    (a) under and in accordance with section 48B below, to require the seller to repair or replace the goods, or
    (b) under and in accordance with section 48C below—
        (i) to require the seller to reduce the purchase price of the goods to the buyer by an appropriate amount, or
        (ii) to rescind the contract with regard to the goods in question.
(3) For the purposes of subsection (1) (b) above goods which do not conform to the contract of sale at any time within the period of six months starting with the date on which the goods were delivered to the buyer must be taken not to have so conformed at that date.
(4) Subsection (3) above does not apply if—
    (a) it is established that the goods did so conform at that date;
    (b) its application is incompatible with the nature of the goods or the nature of the lack of conformity.

48B Repair or replacement of the goods

(1) If section 48A above applies, the buyer may require the seller—
    (a) to repair the goods, or
    (b) to replace the goods.
(2) If the buyer requires the seller to repair or replace the goods, the seller must—
    (a) repair or, as the case may be, replace the goods within a reasonable time but without causing significant inconvenience to the buyer;
    (b) bear any necessary costs incurred in doing so (including in particular the cost of any labour, materials or postage).
(3) The buyer must not require the seller to repair or, as the case may be, replace the goods if that remedy is—
    (a) impossible, or
    (b) disproportionate in comparison to the other of those remedies, or
    (c) disproportionate in comparison to an appropriate reduction in the purchase price under paragraph (a), or rescission under paragraph (b), of section 48C(1) below.
(4) One remedy is disproportionate in comparison to the other if the one imposes costs on the seller which, in comparison to those imposed on him by the other, are unreasonable, taking into account—
    (a) the value which the goods would have if they conformed to the contract of sale,
    (b) the significance of the lack of conformity, and
    (c) whether the other remedy could be effected without significant inconvenience to the buyer.
(5) Any question as to what is a reasonable time or significant inconvenience is to be determined by reference to—
    (a) the nature of the goods, and
    (b) the purpose for which the goods were acquired.

48C Reduction of purchase price or rescission of contract

(1) If section 48A above applies, the buyer may—

    (a) require the seller to reduce the purchase price of the goods in question to the buyer by an appropriate amount, or

    (b) rescind the contract with regard to those goods, if the condition in subsection (2) below is satisfied.

(2) The condition is that—

    (a) by virtue of section 48B(3) above the buyer may require neither repair nor replacement of the goods; or

    (b) the buyer has required the seller to repair or replace the goods, but the seller is in breach of the requirement of section 48B(2) (a) above to do so within a reasonable time and without significant inconvenience to the buyer.

(3) For the purposes of this Part, if the buyer rescinds the contract, any reimbursement to the buyer may be reduced to take account of the use he has had of the goods since they were delivered to him.

48D Relation to other remedies etc.

(1) If the buyer requires the seller to repair or replace the goods the buyer must not act under subsection (2) until he has given the seller a reasonable time in which to repair or replace (as the case may be) the goods.

(2) The buyer acts under this subsection if—

    (a) in England and Wales or Northern Ireland he rejects the goods and terminates the contract for breach of condition;

    (b) in Scotland he rejects any goods delivered under the contract and treats it as repudiated;

    (c) he requires the goods to be replaced or repaired (as the case may be).

48E Powers of the court

(1) In any proceedings in which a remedy is sought by virtue of this Part the court, in addition to any other power it has, may act under this section.

(2) On the application of the buyer the court may make an order requiring specific performance or, in Scotland, specific implement by the seller of any obligation imposed on him by virtue of section 48B above.

(3) Subsection (4) applies if—

    (a) the buyer requires the seller to give effect to a remedy under section 48B or 48C above or has claims to rescind under section 48C, but

    (b) the court decides that another remedy under section 48B or 48C is appropriate.

(4) The court may proceed—

    (a) as if the buyer had required the seller to give effect to the other remedy, or if the other remedy is rescission under section 48C

    (b) as if the buyer had claimed to rescind the contract under that section.

(5) If the buyer has claimed to rescind the contract the court may order that any reimbursement to the buyer is reduced to take account of the use he has had of the goods since they were delivered to him.

(6) The court may make an order under this section unconditionally or on such terms and conditions as to damages, payment of the price and otherwise as it thinks just.

48F Conformity with the contract

For the purposes of this Part, goods do not conform to a contract of sale if there is, in relation to the goods, a breach of an express term of the contract or a term implied by section 13, 14 or 15 above.

PART VI

ACTIONS FOR BREACH OF THE CONTRACT

Seller's remedies

49 Action for price

(1) Where, under a contract of sale, the property in the goods has passed to the buyer and he wrong-fully neglects or refuses to pay for the goods according to the terms of the contract, the seller may maintain an action against him for the price of the goods.

(2) Where, under a contract of sale, the price is payable on a day certain irrespective of delivery and the buyer wrongfully neglects or refuses to pay such price, the seller may maintain an action for the price, although the property in goods has not passed and the goods have not been appropri-ated to the contract.

(3) Nothing in this section prejudices the right of the seller in Scotland to recover interest on the price from the date of tender of the goods, or from the date on which the price was payable, as the case may be.

50 Damages for non-acceptance

(1) Where the buyer wrongfully neglects or refuses to accept and pay for the goods, the seller may maintain an action against him for damages for non-acceptance.

(2) The measure of damages is the estimated loss directly and naturally resulting in the ordinary course of events, from the buyer's breach of contract.

(3) Where there is an available market for the goods in question the measure of damages is prima facie to be ascertained by the difference between the contract price and the market or current price at the time or times when the goods ought to have been accepted or (if no time was fixed for acceptance) at the time of the refusal to accept.

Buyer's remedies

51 Damages for non-delivery

(1) Where the seller wrongfully neglects or refuses to deliver the goods to the buyer, the buyer may maintain an action against the seller for damages for non-delivery.

(2) The measure of damages is the estimated loss directly and naturally resulting, in the ordinary course of events, from the seller's breach of contract.

(3) Where there is an available market for the goods in question the measure of damages is prima facie to be ascertained by the difference between the contract price and the market or current price of the goods at the time or times when they ought to have been delivered or (if no time was fixed) at the time of the refusal to deliver.

52 Specific performance

(1) If any action for breach of contract to deliver specific or ascertained goods the court may, if it thinks fit, on the plaintiff's application, by its judgment or decree direct that the contract shall be performed specifically, without giving the defendant the option of retaining the goods on payment of damages.

(2) The plaintiff's application may be made at any time before judgment or decree.

(3) The judgment or decree may be unconditional, or on such terms and conditions as to damages, payment of the price and otherwise as seem just to the court.

(4) The provisions of this section shall be deemed to be supplementary to, and not in derogation of, the right of specific implement in Scotland.

53 *Remedy for breach of warranty*

(1) Where there is a breach of warranty by the seller, or where the buyer elects (or is compelled) to treat any breach of a condition on the part of the seller as a breach of warranty, the buyer is not by reason only of such breach of warranty entitled to reject the goods; but he may—
  (a) set up against the seller the breach of warranty in diminution of extinction of the price, or
  (b) maintain an action against the seller for damages for the breach of warranty.
(2) The measure of damages for breach of warranty is the estimated loss directly and naturally resulting, in the ordinary course of events, from the breach of warranty.
(3) In the case of breach of warranty of quality such loss is prima facie the difference between the value of the goods at the time of delivery to the buyer and the value they would have had if they had fulfilled the warranty.
(4) The fact that the buyer has set up the breach of warranty in diminution or extinction of the price does not prevent him from maintaining an action for the same breach of warranty if he has suffered further damage.
(5) This section does not apply to Scotland.

53A *Measure of damages as respects Scotland*

(1) The measure of damages for the seller's breach of contract is the estimated loss directly and naturally resulting, in the ordinary course of events, from the breach.
(2) Where the seller's breach consists of the delivery of goods which are not of the quality required by the contract and the buyer retains the goods, such loss as aforesaid is prima facie the difference between the value of the goods at the time of delivery to the buyer and the value they would have had if they had fulfilled the contract.
(3) This section applies to Scotland only.

Interest, etc.

54 *Interest, etc.*

Nothing in this Act affects the right of the buyer or the seller to recover interest or special damages in any case where by law interest or special damages may be recoverable, or to recover money paid where the consideration for the payment of it has failed.

PART VII
SUPPLEMENTARY

55 *Exclusion of implied terms*

(1) Where a right duty or liability would arise under a contract of sale of goods by implication of law, it may (subject to the Unfair Contract Terms Act 1977) be negatived or varied by express agreement, or by the course of dealing between the parties, or by such usage as binds both parties to the contract.
(2) An express [term] does not negative a [term] implied by this Act unless inconsistent with it.
(3) Paragraph 11 of Schedule 1 below applies in relation to a contract made on or after 18 May 1973 and before 1 February 1978, and paragraph 12 in relation to one made before 18 May 1973.

56 *Conflict of laws*

Paragraph 13 of Schedule 1 below applies in relation to a contract made on or after 18 May 1973 and before 1 February 1978, so as to make provision about conflict of laws in relation to such a contract.

57 *Auction sales*

(1) Where goods are put up for sale by auction in lots, each lot is prima facie deemed to be the subject of a separate contract of sale.

(2) A sale by auction is complete when the auctioneer announces its completion by the fall of the hammer, or in other customary manner; and until the announcement is made any bidder may retract his bid.

(3) A sale by auction may be notified to be subject to a reserve or upset price, and a right to bid may also be reserved expressly by or on behalf of the seller.

(4) Where a sale by auction is not notified to be subject to a right to bid by or on behalf of the seller, it is not lawful for the seller to bid himself or to employ any person to bid at the sale, or for the auctioneer knowingly to take any bid from the seller or any such person.

(5) A sale contravening subsection (4) above may be treated as fraudulent by the buyer.

(6) Where, in respect of a sale by auction, a right to bid is expressly reserved (but not otherwise) the seller or any one person on his behalf may bid at the auction.

58 *Payment into court in Scotland*

In Scotland where a buyer has elected to accept goods which he might have rejected, and to treat a breach of contract as only giving rise to a claim for damages, he may, in an action by the seller for the price, be required, in the discretion of the court before which the action depends, to consign or pay into court the price of the goods, or part of the price, or to give other reasonable security for its due payment.

59 *Reasonable time a question of fact*

Where a reference is made in this Act to a reasonable time the question what is a reasonable time is a question of fact.

60 *Rights, etc. enforceable by action*

Where a right, duty or liability is declared by this Act, it may (unless otherwise provided by this Act) be enforced by action.

61 *Interpretation*

(1) In this Act, unless the context or subject matter otherwise requires,— 'action' includes counter-claim and set-off, and in Scotland condescendence and claim and compensation;

'bulk' means a mass or collection of goods of the same kind which—

    (a) is contained in a defined space or area; and

    (b) is such that any goods in the bulk are interchangeable with any other goods therein of the same number or quantity;

'business' includes a profession and the activities of any government department (including a Northern Ireland department) or local or public authority;

'buyer' means a person who buys or agrees to buy goods;

'consumer contract' has the same meaning as in section 25(1) of the Unfair Contract Terms Act 1977; and for the purposes of this Act the onus of proving that a contract is not to be regarded as a consumer contract shall lie on the seller 'contract of sale' includes an agreement to sell as well as a sale,

'credit-broker' means a person acting in the course of a business of credit brokerage carried on by him, that is a business of effecting introductions of individuals desiring to obtain credit—

    (a) to persons carrying on any business so far as it relates to the provision of credit, or

    (b) to other persons engaged in credit brokerage;

'defendant' includes in Scotland defender, respondent, and claimant in a multiple-poinding;

'delivery' means voluntary transfer of possession from one person to another; except that in relation to sections 20A and 20B above it includes such appropriation of goods to the contract as results in property in the goods being transferred to the buyer;

'document of title to goods' has the same meaning as it has in the Factors Acts;

'Factors Acts' means the Factors Act 1889, the Factors (Scotland) Act 1890, and any enactment amending or substituted for the same;

'fault' means wrongful act or default;

'future goods' means goods to be manufactured or acquired by the seller after the making of the contract of sale;

'goods' includes all personal chattels other than things in action and money, and in Scotland all corporeal moveables except money; and in particular 'goods' includes emblements, industrial growing crops, and things attached to or forming part of the land which are agreed to be severed before sale or under the contract of sale; and includes an undivided share in goods;

'plaintiff' includes pursuer, complainer, claimant in a multiple-poinding and defendant or defender counter-claiming;

'producer' means the manufacturer of goods, the importer of goods into the European Economic Area or any person purporting to be a producer by placing his name, trade mark or other distinctive sign on the goods;

'property' means the general property in goods, and not merely a special property;

'repair' means, in cases where there is a lack of conformity in goods for purposes of section 48F of this Act, to bring the goods into conformity with the contract;

'sale' includes a bargain and sale as well as a sale and delivery;

'seller' means a person who sells or agrees to sell goods;

'specific goods' means goods identified and agreed on at the time a contract of sale is made; and includes an undivided share, specified as a fraction or percentage, of goods identified and agreed on as aforesaid;

'warranty' (as regards England and Wales and Northern Ireland) means an agreement with reference to goods which are the subject of a contract of sale, but collateral to the main purpose of such contract, the breach of which gives rise to a claim for damages, but not to a right to reject the goods and treat the contract as repudiated.

(3) A thing is deemed to be done in good faith within the meaning of this Act when it is in fact done honestly, whether it is done negligently or not.

(4) A person is deemed to be insolvent within the meaning of this Act if he has either ceased to pay his debts in the ordinary course of business or he cannot pay his debts as they become due, . . .

(5) Goods are in a deliverable state within the meaning of this Act when they are in such a state that the buyer would under the contract be bound to take delivery of them.

(5A) References in this Act to dealing as consumer are to be construed in accordance with Part I of the Unfair Contract Terms Act 1977; and, for the purposes of this Act, it is for a seller claiming that the buyer does not deal as consumer to show that he does not.

(6) As regards the definition of 'business' in subsection (1) above, paragraph 14 of Schedule 1 below applies in relation to a contract made on or after 18 May 1973 and before 1 February 1978, and paragraph 15 in relation to one made before 18 May 1973.

62 Savings: rules of law, etc.

(1) The rules in bankruptcy relating to contracts of sale apply to those contracts, notwithstanding anything in this Act.

(2) The rules of the common law, including the law merchant, except in so far as they are inconsistent with the provisions of this Act, and in particular the rules relating to the law of principal and agent and the effect of fraud, misrepresentation, duress or coercion, mistake, or other invalidating cause, apply to contracts for the sale of goods.

(3) Nothing in this Act or the Sale of Goods Act 1893 affects the enactments relating to bills of sale, or any enactment relating to the sale of goods which is not expressly repealed or amended by this Act or that.

(4) The provisions of this Act about contracts of sale do not apply to a transaction in the form of a contract of sale which is intended to operate by way of mortgage, pledge, charge, or other security.

(5) Nothing in this Act prejudices or affects the landlord's right of hypothec . . . in Scotland.

Factors Act 1889

Preliminary

1 Definitions

For the purposes of this Act—

(1) The expression 'mercantile agent' shall mean a mercantile agent having in the customary course of his business as such agent authority either to sell goods or to consign goods for the purpose of sale, or to buy goods, or to raise money on the security of goods:

(2) A person shall be deemed to be in possession of goods or of the documents of title to goods, where the goods or documents are in the actual custody or are held by any other person subject to his control or for him or on his behalf:

(3) The expression 'goods' shall include wares and merchandise:

(4) The expression 'document of title' shall include any bill of lading, dock warrant, warehouse-keeper's certificate, and warrant or order for the delivery of goods, and any other document used in the ordinary course of business as proof of the possession or control of goods, or authorising or purporting to authorise, either by endorsement or by delivery, the possessor of the document to transfer or receive goods thereby represented:

(5) The expression 'pledge' shall include any contract pledging, or giving a lien or security on, goods, whether in consideration of an original advance or of any further or continuing advance or of any pecuniary liability:

(6) The expression 'person' shall include any body of persons corporate or unincorporate.

Dispositions by mercantile agents

2 Powers of mercantile agent with respect to disposition of goods

(1) Where a mercantile agent is, with the consent of the owner, in possession of goods or of the documents of title to goods, any sale, pledge, or other disposition of the goods, made by him when acting in the ordinary course of business of a mercantile agent, shall, subject to the provisions of this Act, be as valid as if he were expressly authorised by the owner of the goods to make the same; provided that the person taking under the disposition acts in good faith, and has not at the time of the disposition notice that the person making the disposition has not authority to make the same.

(2) Where a mercantile agent has, with the consent of the owner, been in possession of goods or of the documents of title to goods, any sale, pledge, or other disposition, which would have been valid if the consent had continued, shall be valid notwithstanding the determination of the consent; provided that the person taking under the disposition has not at the time thereof notice that the consent has been determined.

(3) Where a mercantile agent has obtained possession of any documents of title to goods by reason of his being or having been, with the consent of the owner, in possession of the goods represented thereby, or of any other documents of title to the goods, his possession of the first-mentioned documents shall, for the purposes of this Act, be deemed to be with the consent of the owner.

(4) For the purposes of this Act the consent of the owner shall be presumed in the absence of evidence to the contrary.

3 *Effect of pledges of documents of title*

A pledge of the documents of title to goods shall be deemed to be a pledge of the goods.

4 *Pledge for antecedent debt*

Where a mercantile agent pledges goods as security for a debt or liability due from the pledgor to the pledgee before the time of the pledge, the pledgee shall acquire no further right to the goods than could have been enforced by the pledgor at the time of the pledge.

5 *Rights acquired by exchange of goods or documents*

The consideration necessary for the validity of a sale, pledge, or other disposition of goods, in pursuance of this Act, may be either a payment in cash, or the delivery or transfer of other goods, or of a document of title to goods, or of a negotiable security, or any other valuable consideration; but where goods are pledged by a mercantile agent in consideration of the delivery or transfer of other goods, or of a document of title to goods, or of a negotiable security, the pledgee shall acquire no right or interest in the goods so pledged in excess of the value of the goods, documents, or security when so delivered or transferred in exchange.

6 *Agreements through clerks, &c.*

For the purposes of this Act an agreement made with a mercantile agent through a clerk or other person authorised in the ordinary course of business to make contracts of sale or pledge on his behalf shall be deemed to be an agreement with the agent.

7 *Provisions as to consignors and consignees*

(1) Where the owner of goods has given possession of the goods to another person for the purpose of consignment or sale, or has shipped the goods in the name of another person, and the consignee of the goods has not had notice that such person is not the owner of the goods, the consignee shall, in respect of advances made to or for the use of such person, have the same lien on the goods as if such person were the owner of the goods, and may transfer any such lien to another person.

(2) Nothing in this section shall limit or affect the validity of any sale, pledge, or disposition, by a mercantile agent.

Dispositions by sellers and buyers of goods

8 *Disposition by seller remaining in possession*

Where a person, having sold goods, continues, or is, in possession of the goods or of the documents of title to the goods, the delivery or transfer by that person, or by a mercantile agent acting for him, of the goods or documents of title under any sale, pledge, or other disposition thereof, or under any agreement for sale, pledge, or other disposition thereof, to any person receiving the same in good faith and without notice of the previous sale, shall have the same effect as if the person making the delivery or transfer were expressly authorised by the owner of the goods to make the same.

9 *Disposition by buyer obtaining possession*

Where a person, having bought or agreed to buy goods, obtains with the consent of the seller possession of the goods or the documents of title to the goods, the delivery or transfer, by that person or by a mercantile agent acting for him, of the goods or documents of title under any sale, pledge, or other disposition thereof, or under any agreement for sale, pledge, or other disposition thereof, to any person receiving the same in good faith and without notice of any lien or other right of the original seller in respect of the goods, shall have the same effect as if the person making the delivery or transfer were a mercantile agent in possession of the goods or documents of title with the consent of the owner.

For the purposes of this section—

(i) the buyer under a conditional sale agreement shall be deemed not to be a person who has bought or agreed to buy goods, and

(ii) 'conditional sale agreement' means an agreement for the sale of goods which is a consumer credit agreement within the meaning of the Consumer Credit Act 1974 under which the purchase price or part of it is payable in instalments, and the property in the goods is to remain in the seller (notwithstanding that the buyer is to be in possession of the goods) until such conditions as to the payment of instalments or otherwise as maybe specified in the agreement are fulfilled.

10 *Effect of transfer of documents on vendor's lien or right of stoppage in transitu*

Where a document of title to goods has been lawfully transferred to a person as a buyer or owner of the goods, and that person transfers the document to a person who takes the document in good faith and for valuable consideration, the last-mentioned transfer shall have the same effect for defeating any vendor's lien or right of stoppage in transitu as the transfer of a bill of lading has for defeating the right of stoppage in transitu.

Supplemental

11 *Mode of transferring documents*

For the purposes of this Act, the transfer of a document may be by endorsement, or, where the document is by custom or by its express terms transferable by delivery or makes the goods deliverable to the bearer, then by delivery.

12 *Saving for rights of true owner*

(1) Nothing in this Act shall authorise an agent to exceed or depart from his authority as between himself and his principal, or exempt him from any liability, civil or criminal, for so doing.

(2) Nothing in this Act shall prevent the owner of goods from recovering the goods from any agent or his trustee in bankruptcy at any time before the sale or pledge thereof, or shall prevent the owner of goods pledged by an agent from having the right to redeem the goods at any time before the sale thereof, on satisfying the claim for which the goods were pledged, and paying to the agent, if by him required, any money in respect of which the agent would by law be entitled to retain the goods or the documents of title thereto, or any of them, by way of lien as against the owner, or from recovering from any person with whom the goods have been pledged any balance of money remaining in his hands as the produce of the sale of the goods after deducting the amount of his lien.

(3) Nothing in this Act shall prevent the owner of goods sold by an agent from recovering from the buyer the price agreed to be paid for the same, or any part of that price, subject to any right of set off on the part of the buyer against the agent.

13 *Saving for common law powers of agent*

The provisions of this Act shall be construed in amplification and not in derogation of the powers exercisable by an agent independently of this Act.

. . .

16 *Extent of Act*

This Act shall not extend to Scotland.

APPENDIX 3

Unfair Contract Terms Act 1977

PART I

1 Scope of Part I

(1) For the purposes of this Part of this Act, 'negligence' means the breach—

   (a) of any obligation, arising from the express or implied terms of a contract, to take reasonable care or exercise reasonable skill in the performance of the contract;

   (b) of any common law duty to take reasonable care or exercise reasonable skill (but not any stricter duty);

   (c) of the common duty of care imposed by the Occupiers' Liability Act 1957 or the Occupier's Liability Act (Northern Ireland) 1957.

(2) This Part of the Act is subject to Part III; and in relation to contracts, the operation of sections 2 to 4 and 7 is subject to the exceptions made by Schedule I.

(3) In the case of both contract and tort, sections 2 to 7 apply (except where the contrary is stated in section 6(4)) only to business liability, that is liability to breach of obligations or duties arising—

   (a) from things done or to be done by a person in the course of a business (whether his own business or another's); or

   (b) from the occupation of premises used for business purposes of the occupier; and references to liability are to be read accordingly but liability of an occupier of premises for breach of an obligation or duty towards a person obtaining access to the premises for recreational or educational purposes, being liability for loss or damage suffered by reason of the dangerous state of the premises, is not a business liability of the occupier unless granting that person such access for the purposes concerned falls within the business purposes of the occupier.

(4) In relation to any breach of duty or obligation, it is immaterial for any purpose of this Part of this Act whether the breach was inadvertent or intentional, or whether liability for it arises directly or vicariously.

2 Negligence liability

(1) A person cannot by reference to any contract term or to a notice given to persons generally or to particular persons exclude or restrict his liability for death or personal injury resulting from negligence.

(2) In the case of other loss or damage, a person cannot so exclude or restrict his liability for negligence except in so far as the term or notice satisfies the requirement of reasonableness.

(3) Where a contract term or notice purports to exclude or restrict liability for negligence a person's agreement to or awareness of it is not of itself to be taken as indicating his voluntary acceptance of any risk.

3 Liability arising in contract

(1) This section applies as between contracting parties where one of them deals as consumer or on the other's written standard terms of business.

(2) As against that party, the other cannot by reference to any contract term—

   (a) when himself in breach of contract, exclude or restrict any liability of his in respect of the breach; or

(b) claim to be entitled—
  (i) to render a contractual performance substantially different from that which was reasonably expected of him, or
  (ii) in respect of the whole of any part of his contractual obligation, to render no performance at all, except in so far as (in any of the cases mentioned above in this subsection) the contract term satisfies the requirement of reasonableness.

4 Unreasonable indemnity clauses

(1) A person dealing as consumer cannot by reference to any contract term be made to indemnify another person (whether a party to the contract or not) in respect of liability that may be incurred by the other for negligence or breach of contract, except in so far as the contract term satisfies the requirement of reasonableness.
(2) This section applies whether the liability in question—
  (a) is directly that of the person to be indemnified or is incurred by him vicariously;
  (b) is to the person dealing as consumer or to someone else.

5 'Guarantee' of consumer goods

(1) In the case of goods of a type ordinarily supplied for private use of consumption, where loss or damage—
  (a) arises from the goods proving defective while in consumer use; and
  (b) results from the negligence of a person concerned in the manufacture or distribution of the goods, liability for the loss or damage cannot be excluded or restricted by reference to any contract term or notice contained in or operating by reference to a guarantee of the goods.
(2) For these purposes—
  (a) goods are to be regarded as 'in consumer use' when a person is using them, or has them in his possession for use, otherwise than exclusively for the purposes of a business; and
  (b) anything in writing is a guarantee if it contains or purports to contain some promise or assurance (however worded or presented) that defects will be made good by complete or partial replacement, or by repair, monetary compensation or otherwise.
(3) This section does not apply as between the parties to a contract under or in pursuance of which possession or ownership of the goods passed.

6 Sale and hire-purchase

(1) Liability for breach of the obligations arising from—
  (a) section 12 of the Sale of Goods Act 1979 (seller's implied undertakings as to title, etc.);
  (b) section 8 of the Supply of Goods (Implied Terms) Act 1973 (the corresponding thing in relation to hire-purchase), cannot be excluded or restricted by reference to any contract term.
(2) As against a person dealing as consumer, liability for breach of the obligations arising from—
  (a) section 13, 14 or 15 of the [1979] Act (seller's implied undertakings as to conformity of goods with description or sample, or as to their quality of fitness for a particular purpose);
  (b) section 9, 10 or 11 of the 1973 Act (the corresponding things in relation to hire-purchase), cannot be excluded or restricted by reference to any contract term.
(3) As against a person dealing otherwise than as consumer, the liability specified in subsection (2) above can be excluded or restricted by reference to a contract term, but only in so far as the term satisfies the requirement of reasonableness.
(4) The liabilities referred to in this section are not only the business liabilities defined by section 1 (3), but include those arising under any contract of sale of goods or hire-purchase agreement.

7 Miscellaneous contracts under which goods pass

(1) Where the possession or ownership of goods passes under or in pursuance of a contract not governed by the law of sale of goods or hire-purchase, subsections (2) to (4) below apply as regards the effect (if any) to be given to contract terms excluding or restricting liability for breach of obligation arising by implication of law from the nature of the contract.

(2) As against a person dealing as consumer, liability in respect of the goods' correspondence with description or sample, or their quality or fitness for any particular purpose, cannot be excluded or restricted by reference to any such term.

(3) As against a person dealing otherwise than as consumer, that liability can be excluded or restricted by reference to such a term, but only in so far as the term satisfies the requirement of reasonableness.

(3A) Liability for breach of the obligations arising under section 2 of the Supply of Goods and Services Act 1982 (implied terms about title etc. in certain contracts for the transfer of the property in goods) cannot be excluded or restricted by reference to any such term.

(4) Liability in respect of—
   (a) the right to transfer ownership of the goods, or give possession; or
   (b) the assurance of quiet possession to a person taking goods in pursuance of the contract, cannot (in a case to which subsection (3A) above does not apply) be excluded or restricted by reference to any such term except in so far as the term satisfies the requirement of reasonableness.

(5) This section does not apply in the case of goods passing on a redemption of trading stamps within the Trading Stamps Act 1964 or the Tradings Stamps Act (Northern Ireland) 1965.

9 Effect of breach

(1) Where for reliance upon it a contract term has to satisfy the requirement of reasonableness, it may be found to do so and be given effect accordingly notwithstanding that the contract has been terminated either by breach or by a party electing to treat it as repudiated.

(2) Where on a breach the contract is nevertheless affirmed by a party entitled to treat it as repudiated, this does not of itself exclude the requirement of reasonableness in relation to any contract term.

10 Evasion by means of secondary contract

A person is not bound by any contract term prejudicing or taking away rights of his which arise under, or in connection with the performance of, another contract, so far as those rights extend to the enforcement of another's liability which this Part of this Act prevents that other from excluding or restricting.

11 The 'reasonableness' test

(1) In relation to a contract term, the requirement of reasonableness for the purposes of this Part of this Act, section 3 of the Misrepresentation Act 1967 and section 3 of the Misrepresentation Act (Northern Ireland) 1967 is that the term shall have been a fair and reasonable one to be included having regard to the circumstances which were, or ought reasonably to have been, known to or in the contemplation of the parties when the contract was made.

(2) In determining for the purposes of section 6 or 7 above whether a contract term satisfies the requirement of reasonableness, regard shall be had in particular to the matters specified in Schedule 2 to this Act; but this subsection does not prevent the court or arbitrator from holding, in accordance with any rule of law, that a term which purports to exclude or restrict any relevant liability is not a term of the contract.

(3) In relation to a notice (not being a notice having contractual effect), the requirement of reasonableness under this Act is that it should be fair and reasonable to allow reliance on it, having regard to all the circumstances obtaining when the liability arose or (but for the notice) would have arisen.

(4) Where by reference to a contract term or notice a person seeks to restrict liability to a specified sum of money, and the question arises (under this or any other Act) whether the term or notice satisfies the requirement of reasonableness, regard shall be had in particular (but without prejudice to subsection (2) above in the case of contract terms) to—
   (a) the resources which he could expect to be available to him for the purpose of meeting the liability should it arise; and
   (b) how far it was open to him to cover himself by insurance.

(5) It is for those claiming that a contract term or notice satisfies the requirement of reasonableness to show that it does.

12 'Dealing as consumer'

(1) A party to contract 'deals as consumer' in relation to another party if—
  (a) he neither makes the contract in the course of a business nor holds himself out as doing so; and
  (b) the other party does make the contract in the course of a business; and
  (c) in the case of a contract governed by the law of sale of goods or hire-purchase, or by section 7 of this Act, the goods passing under or in pursuance of the contract are of a type ordinarily supplied for private use or consumption.
(1A) But if the first party mentioned in subsection (1) is an individual paragraph (c) of that subsection must be ignored.
(2) But the buyer is not in any circumstances to be regarded as dealing as consumer—
  (a) if he is an individual and the goods are second hand goods sold at public auction at which individuals have the opportunity of attending the sale in person;
  (b) if he is not an individual and the goods are sold by auction or by competitive tender.
(3) Subject to this, it is for those claiming that a party does not deal as consumer to show that he does not.

13 Varieties of exemption clause

(1) To the extent that this Part of this Act prevents the exclusion or restriction of any liability it also prevents—
  (a) making the liability or its enforcement subject to restrictive or onerous conditions;
  (b) excluding or restricting any right or remedy in respect of the liability, or subjecting a person to any prejudice in consequence of his pursuing any such right or remedy;
  (c) excluding or restricting rules of evidence or procedure; and (to that extent) sections 2 and 5 to 7 also prevent excluding or restricting liability by reference to terms and notices which exclude or restrict the relevant obligation or duty.
(2) But an agreement in writing to submit present or future differences to arbitration is not to be treated under this Part of this Act as excluding or restricting any liability.

14 Interpretation of Part I

In this Part of the Act—

'business' includes a profession and the activities of any government department or local or public authority;
'goods' has the same meaning as in the Sales of Goods Act 1979;
'hire-purchase agreement' has the same meaning as in the Consumer Credit Act 1974;
'negligence' has the meaning given by section 1(1);
'notice' includes an announcement, whether or not in writing, and any other communication or pretended communication; and
'personal injury' includes any disease and any impairment of physical or mental condition.

PART II

15 Scope of Part II

(1) This Part of this Act . . . is subject to Part III of this Act and does not affect the validity of any discharge or indemnity given by a person in consideration of the receipt by him of compensation in settlement of any claim which he has.
(2) Subject to subsection (3) below, sections 16 to 18 of this Act apply to any contract only to the extent that the contract—

(a) relates to the transfer of the ownership or possession of goods from one person to another (with or without work having been done on them);

(b) constitutes a contract of service or apprenticeship;

(c) relates to services of whatever kind, including (without prejudice to the foregoing generality) carriage, deposit and pledge, care and custody, mandate, agency, loan and services relating to the use of land;

(d) relates to the liability of an occupier of land to persons entering upon or using that land;

(e) relates to a grant of any right or permission to enter upon or use land not amounting to an estate or interest in the land.

(3) Notwithstanding anything in subsection (2) above, sections 16 to 18—

(a) do not apply to any contract to the extent that the contract—

(i) is a contract of insurance (including a contract to pay an annuity on human life);

(ii) relates to the formation, constitution or dissolution of any body corporate or unincorporated association or partnership;

(b) apply to—

a contract of marine salvage or towage;

a charter party of a ship or hovercraft;

a contract for the carriage of goods by ship or hovercraft;

or a contract to which subsection (4) below relates,

only to the extent that—

(i) both parties deal or hold themselves out as dealing in the course of a business (and then only in so far as the contract purports to exclude or restrict liability for breach of duty in respect of death or personal injury); or

(ii) the contract is a consumer contract (and then only in favour of the consumer).

(4) This subsection relates to a contract in pursuance of which goods are carried by ship or hovercraft and which either—

(a) specifies ship or hovercraft as the means of carriage over part of the journey to be covered; or

(b) makes no provision as to the means of carriage and does not exclude ship or hovercraft as that means,

in so far as the contract operates for and in relation to the carriage of the goods by that means.

16 Liability for breach of duty

(1) Subject to subsection (1A) below, where a term of a contract, or a provision of a notice given to persons generally or to particular persons, purports to exclude or restrict liability for breach of duty arising in the course of any business or from the occupation of any premises used for business purposes of the occupier, that term or provision—

(a) shall be void in any case where such exclusion or restriction is in respect of death or personal injury;

(b) shall, in any other case, have no effect if it was not fair and reasonable to incorporate the term in the contract or, as the case may be, if it is not fair and reasonable to allow reliance on the provision.

(1A) Nothing in paragraph (b) of subsection (1) above shall be taken as implying that a provision of a notice has effect in circumstances where, apart from that paragraph, it would not have effect.

(2) Subsection (1) (a) above does not affect the validity of any discharge and indemnity given by a person, on or in connection with an award to him of compensation for pneumoconiosis attributable to employment in the coal industry, in respect of any further claim arising from his contracting that disease.

(3) Where under subsection (1) above a term of a contract or a provision of a notice is void or has no effect, the fact that a person agreed to, or was aware of, the term or provision shall not of itself be sufficient evidence that he knowingly and voluntarily assumed any risk.

17 Control of unreasonable exemptions in consumer or standard form contracts

(1) Any term of a contract which is a consumer contract or a standard form contract shall have no effect for the purpose of enabling a party to the contract—
    (a) who is in breach of a contractual obligation, to exclude or restrict any liability of his to the consumer or customer in respect of the breach;
    (b) in respect of a contractual obligation, to render no performance, or to render a performance substantially different from that which the consumer or customer reasonably expected from the contract;
if it was not fair and reasonable to incorporate the term in the contract.

(2) In this section 'customer' means a party to a standard form contract who deals on the basis of written standard terms of business of the other party to the contract who himself deals in the course of a business.

18 Unreasonable indemnity clauses in consumer contracts

(1) Any term of a contract which is a consumer contract shall have no effect for the purpose of making the consumer indemnify another person (whether a party to the contract or not) in respect of liability which that other person may incur as a result of breach of duty or breach of contract, if it was not fair and reasonable to incorporate the term in the contract.

(2) In this section 'liability' means liability arising in the course of any business or from the occupation of any premises used for business purposes of the occupier.

19 'Guarantee' of consumer goods

(1) This section applies to a guarantee—
    (a) in relation to goods which are of a type ordinarily supplied for private use or consumption; and
    (b) which is not a guarantee given by one party to the other party to a contract under or in pursuance of which the ownership or possession of the goods to which the guarantee relates is transferred.

(2) A term of a guarantee to which this section applies shall be void in so far as it purports to exclude or restrict liability for loss or damage (including death or personal injury)—
    (a) arising from the goods proving defective while—
        (i) in use otherwise than exclusively for the purposes of a business; or
        (ii) in the possession of a person for such use; and
    (b) resulting from the breach of duty of a person concerned in the manufacture or distribution of the goods.

(3) For the purposes of this section, any document is a guarantee if it contains or purports to contain some promise or assurance (however worded or presented) that defects will be made good by complete or partial replacement, or by repair, monetary compensation or otherwise.

20 Obligations implied by law in sale and hire-purchase contracts

(1) Any term of a contract which purports to exclude or restrict liability for breach of the obligations arising from—
    (a) section 12 of the Sale of Goods Act 1979 (seller's implied undertakings as to title etc.);
    (b) section 8 of the Supply of Goods (Implied Terms) Act 1973 (implied terms as to title in hire-purchase agreements), shall be void.

(2) Any term of a contract which purports to exclude or restrict liability for breach of the obligations arising from—
    (a) section 13, 14 or 15 of the said Act of 1979 (seller's implied undertakings as to conformity of goods with description or sample, or as to their quality or fitness for a particular purpose);
    (b) section 9, 10 or 11 of the said Act of 1973 (the corresponding provisions in relation to hire-purchase), shall—
        (i) in the case of a consumer contract, be void against the consumer;

(ii) in any other case, have no effect if it was not fair and reasonable to incorporate the term in the contract.

21 *Obligations implied by law in other contracts for the supply of goods*

(1) Any term of a contract to which this section applies purporting to exclude or restrict liability for breach of an obligation—
   (a) such as is referred to in subsection (3) (a) below—
      (i) in the case of a consumer contract, shall be void against the consumer, and
      (ii) in any other case, shall have no effect if it was not fair and reasonable to incorporate the term in the contract;
   (b) such as is referred to in subsection (3) (b) below, shall have no effect if it was not fair and reasonable to incorporate the term in the contract.
(2) This section applies to any contract to the extent that it relates to any such matter as is referred to in section 15(2) (a) of this Act, but does not apply to—
   (a) a contract of sale of goods or a hire-purchase agreement; or
   (b) a charterparty of a ship or hovercraft unless it is a consumer contract (and then only in favour of the consumer).
(3) An obligation referred to in this subsection is an obligation incurred under a contract in the course of a business and arising by implication of law from the nature of the contract which relates—
   (a) to the correspondence of goods with description or sample, or to the quality or fitness of goods for any particular purpose; or
   (b) to any right to transfer ownership or possession of goods, or to the enjoyment of quiet possession of goods.
(3A) Notwithstanding anything in the foregoing provisions of this section, any term of a contract which purports to exclude or restrict liability for breach of the obligations arising under section 11B of the Supply of Goods and Services Act 1982 (implied terms about title, freedom from encumbrances and quiet possession in certain contracts for the transfer of property in goods) shall be void.

22 *Consequence of breach*

For the avoidance of doubt, where any provision of this Part of this Act requires that the incorporation of a term in a contract must be fair and reasonable for that term to have effect—
   (a) if that requirement is satisfied, the term may be given effect to notwithstanding that the contract has been terminated in consequence of breach of that contract;
   (b) for the term to be given effect to, that requirement must be satisfied even where a party who is entitled to rescind the contract elects not to rescind it.

23 *Evasion by means of secondary contract*

Any term of any contract shall be void which purports to exclude or restrict, or has the effect of excluding or restricting—
   (a) the exercise, by a party to any other contract, of any right or remedy which arises in respect of that other contract in consequence of breach of duty, or of obligation, liability for which could not by virtue of the provisions of this Part of this Act be excluded or restricted by a term of that other contract;
   (b) the application of the provisions of this Part of this Act in respect of that or any other contract.

24 *The 'reasonableness' test*

(1) In determining for the purposes of this Part of this Act whether it was fair and reasonable to incorporate a term in a contract, regard shall be had only to the circumstances which were, or

ought reasonably to have been, known to or in the contemplation of the parties to the contract at the time the contract was made.

(2) In determining for the purposes of section 20 or 21 of this Act whether it was fair and reasonable to incorporate a term in a contract, regard shall be had in particular to the matters specified in Schedule 2 to this Act; but this sub-section shall not prevent a court or arbiter from holding in accordance with any rule of law, that a term which purports to exclude or restrict any relevant liability is not a term of the contract.

(2A) In determining for the purposes of this Part of this Act whether it is fair and reasonable to allow reliance on a provision of a notice (not being a notice having contractual effect), regard shall be had to all the circumstances obtaining when the liability arose or (but for the provision) would have arisen.

(3) Where a term in a contract or a provision of a notice purports to restrict liability to a specified sum of money, and the question arises for the purposes of this Part of this Act whether it was fair and reasonable to incorporate the term in the contract or whether it is fair and reasonable to allow reliance on the provision, then, without prejudice to subsection (2) above in the case of a term in a contract, regard shall be had in particular to—

(a) the resources which the party seeking to rely on that term or provision could expect to be available to him for the purpose of meeting the liability should it arise;

(b) how far it was open to that party to cover himself by insurance.

(4) The onus of proving that it was fair and reasonable to incorporate a term in a contract or that it is fair and reasonable to allow reliance on a provision of a notice shall lie on the party so contending.

25 Interpretation of Part II

(1) In this Part of this Act—
'breach of duty' means the breach—

(a) of any obligation, arising from the express or implied terms of a contract, to take reasonable care or exercise reasonable skill in the performance of the contract;

(b) of any common law duty to take reasonable care or exercise reasonable skill;

(c) of the duty of reasonable care imposed by section 2(1) of the Occupiers' Liability (Scotland) Act 1960;

'business' includes a profession and the activities of any government department or local or public authority;

'consumer' has the meaning assigned to that expression in the definition in this section of 'consumer contract';

'consumer contract' means [subject to subsections (1A) and (1B) below] a contract . . . in which—

(a) one party to the contract deals, and the other party to the contract ('the consumer') does not deal or hold himself out as dealing, in the course of a business, and

(b) in the case of a contract such as is mentioned in section 15(2) (a) of this Act, the goods are of a type ordinarily supplied for private use or consumption; and for the purposes of this Part of this Act the onus of proving that a contract is not to be regarded as a consumer contract shall lie on the party so contending;

'goods' has the same meaning as in the Sale of Goods Act 1979;

'hire-purchase agreement' has the same meaning as in section 189(1) of the Consumer Credit Act 1974;

'notice' includes an announcement, whether or not in writing, and any other communication or pretended communication;

'personal injury' includes any disease and any impairment of physical or mental condition.

(1A) Where the consumer is an individual, paragraph (b) in the definition of 'consumer contract' in subsection (1) must be disregarded.

(1B) The expression of 'consumer contract' does not include a contract in which—
(a) the buyer is an individual and the goods are second hand goods sold by public auction at which individuals have the opportunity of attending in person; or
(b) the buyer is not an individual and the goods are sold by auction or competitive tender.

(2) In relation to any breach of duty or obligation, it is immaterial for any purpose of this Part of this Act whether the act or omission giving rise to that breach was inadvertent or intentional or whether liability for it arises directly or vicariously.

(3) In this Part of this Act, any reference to excluding or restricting any liability includes—
(a) making the liability or its enforcement subject to any restrictive or onerous conditions;
(b) excluding or restricting any right or remedy in respect of the liability, or subjecting a person to any prejudice in consequence of his pursuing any such right or remedy;
(c) excluding or restricting any rule of evidence or procedure;

. . .

(5) In section 15 and 16 and 19 to 21 of this Act, any reference to excluding or restricting liability for breach of any obligation or duty shall include a reference to excluding or restricting the obligation or duty itself.

PART III

26 *International supply contracts*

(1) The limits imposed by this Act on the extent to which a person may exclude or restrict liability by reference to a contract term do not apply to liability arising under such a contract as is described in subsection (3) below.

(2) The terms of such a contract are not subject to any requirement of reasonableness under section 3 or 4: and nothing in Part II of this Act should require the incorporation of the terms of such a contract to be fair and reasonable for them to have effect.

(3) Subject to subsection (4), that description of contract is one whose characteristics are the following—
(a) either it is a contract of sale of goods or it is one under or in pursuance of which the possession of ownership of goods passes, and
(b) it is made by parties whose places of business (or, if they have none, habitual residences) are in the territories of different States (the Channel Islands and the Isle of Man being treated for this purpose as different States from the United Kingdom).

(4) A contract falls within subsection (3) above only if either—
(a) the goods in question are, at the time of the conclusion of the contract, in the course of carriage, or will be carried, from the territory of one State to the territory of another; or
(b) the acts constituting the offer and acceptance have been done in the territories of different States; or
(c) the contract provides for the goods to be delivered to the territory of a state other than that within whose territory those acts were done.

27 *Choice of law clauses*

(1) Where the law applicable to a contract is the law of any part of the United Kingdom only by choice of the parties (and apart from that choice would be the law of some country outside the United Kingdom) sections 2 to 7 and 16 to 21 of this Act do not operate as part of the law applicable to the contract.

(2) This Act has effect notwithstanding any contract term which applies or purports to apply the law of some country outside the United Kingdom, where (either or both)—
(a) the term appears to the court, or arbitrator or arbiter to have been imposed wholly or mainly for the purpose of enabling the party imposing it to evade the operation of this Act; or

(b) in the making of the contract one of the parties dealt as consumer, and he was then habitually resident in the United Kingdom, and the essential steps necessary for the making of the contract were taken there, whether by him or by others on his behalf.

(3) In the application of subsection (2) above to Scotland, for paragraph (b) there shall be substituted—

'(b) the contract is a consumer contract as defined in Part 11 of this Act, and the consumer at the date when the contract was made was habitually resident in the United Kingdom, and the essential steps necessary for the making of the contract were taken there, whether by him or by others on his behalf.'

28 *Temporary provision for sea carriage of passengers*

(1) This section applies to a contract for carriage by sea of a passenger or of a passenger and his luggage where the provisions of the Athens Convention (with or without modification) do not have, in relation to the contract, the force of law in the United Kingdom.

(2) In a case where—

(a) the contract is not made in the United Kingdom, and

(b) neither the place of departure nor the place of destination under it is in the United Kingdom, a person is not precluded by this Act from excluding or restricting liability for loss or damage, being loss or damage for which the provisions of the Convention would, if they had the force of law in relation to the contract, impose liability on him.

(3) In any other case, a person is not precluded by this Act from excluding or restricting liability for that loss or damage—

(a) in so far as the exclusion or restriction would have been effective in that case had the provisions of the Convention had the force of law in relation to the contract; or

(b) in such circumstances and to such extent as may be prescribed, by reference to a prescribed term of the contract.

(4) For the purposes of subsection (3) (a), the values which shall be taken to be the official values in the United Kingdom of the amounts (expressed in gold francs) by reference to which liability under the provisions of the Convention is limited shall be such amounts in sterling as the Secretary of State may from time to time by order made by statutory instrument specify.

(5) In this section,—

(a) the references to excluding or restricting liability include doing any of those things in relation to the liability which are mentioned in section 13 or section 25(3) and (5); and

(b) 'the Athens Convention' means the Athens Convention relating to the Carriage of Passengers and their Luggage by Sea, 1974; and

(c) 'prescribed' means prescribed by the Secretary of State by regulations made by statutory instrument; and a statutory instrument containing the regulations shall be subject to annulment in pursuance of a resolution of either House of Parliament.

29 *Saving for other relevant legislation*

(1) Nothing in this Act removes or restricts the effect of, or prevents reliance upon, any contractual provision which—

(a) is authorised or required by the express terms or necessary implication of an enactment; or

(b) being made with a view to compliance with an international agreement to which the United Kingdom is a party, does not operate more restrictively than is contemplated by the agreement.

(2) A contract term is to be taken—

(a) for the purposes of Part I of this Act, as satisfying the requirement of reasonableness; and

(b) for those of Part II, to have been fair and reasonable to incorporate, if it is incorporated or approved by, or incorporated pursuant to a decision or ruling of, a competent authority acting in the exercise of any statutory jurisdiction or function and is not a term in a contract to which the competent authority is itself a party.

(3) In this section—

'competent authority' means any court, arbitrator or arbiter, government department or public authority;

'enactment' means any legislation (including subordinate legislation) of the United Kingdom or Northern Ireland and any instrument having effect by virtue of such legislation; and

'statutory' means conferred by an enactment.

SCHEDULES

Section 1(2)

SCHEDULES 1

SCOPE OF SECTIONS 2 TO 4 AND 7

1 Sections 2 to 4 of this Act do not extend to—
  (a) any contract of insurance (including a contract to pay an annuity on human life);
  (b) any contract so far as it relates to the creation or transfer of an interest in land, or to the termination of such an interest, whether by extinction, merger, surrender, forfeiture or otherwise;
  (c) any contract so far as it relates to the creation or transfer of a right or interest in any patent, trade mark, copyright [or design right];
  (d) any contract so far as it relates—
    (i) to the formation or dissolution of a company (which means any body corporate or unincorporated association and includes a partnership), or
    (ii) to its constitution or the rights or obligations of its corporators or members;
  (e) any contract so far as it relates to the creation or transfer of securities or of any right or interest in securities.

2 Section 2(1) extends to—
  (a) any contract of marine salvage or towage;
  (b) any charterparty of a ship or hovercraft; and
  (c) any contract for the carriage of goods by ship or hovercraft; but subject to this sections 2 to 4 and 7 do not extend to any such contract except in favour of a person dealing as a consumer.

3 Where goods are carried by ship or hovercraft in pursuance of a contract which either—
  (a) specifies that as the means of carriage over part of the journey to be covered, or
  (b) makes no provision as to the means of carriage and does not exclude that means, then sections 2(2), 3 and 4 do not, except in favour of a person dealing as consumer, extend to the contract as it operates for and in relation to the carriage of the goods by that means.

4 Section 2(1) and (2) do not extend to a contract of employment, except in favour of the employee.

5 Section 2(1) does not affect the validity of any discharge and indemnity given by a person, on or in connection with an award to him of compensation for pneumoconiosis attributable to employment in the coal industry, in respect of any further claim arising from his contracting the disease.

Sections 11(2) and 24(2)

SCHEDULES 2

'GUIDELINES' FOR APPLICATION OF REASONABLENESS TEST

The matters to which regard is to be had in particular for the purposes of sections 6(3), 7(3) and (4), 20 and 21 are any of the following which appear to be relevant—

(a) the strength of the bargaining positions of the parties relative to each other, taking into account (among other things) alternative means by which the customer's requirements could have been met;

(b) whether the customer received an inducement to agree to the term, or in accepting it had an opportunity of entering into a similar contract with other persons, but without having to accept a similar term;

(c) whether the customer knew or ought reasonably to have known of the existence and extent of the term (having regard, among other things, to any custom of the trade and any previous course of dealing between the parties);

(d) where the term excludes or restricts any relevant liability if some condition is not complied with, whether it was reasonable at the time of the contract to expect that compliance with that condition would be practicable;

(e) whether the goods were manufactured, processed or adapted to the special order of the customer.

APPENDIX 4

Unfair Terms in Consumer Contracts Regulations 1999

SI 1999 No. 2083

3 Interpretation

(1) In these Regulations—

'the Community' means the European Community;

'consumer' means any natural person who, in contracts covered by these Regulations, is acting for purposes which are outside his trade, business or profession;

'court' in relation to England and Wales and Northern Ireland means a county court or the High Court, and in relation to Scotland, the Sheriff or the Court of Session;

'Director' means the Director General of Fair Trading;

'EEA Agreement' means the Agreement on the European Economic Area signed at Oporto on 2nd May 1992 as adjusted by the protocol signed at Brussels on 17th March 1993;

'Member State' means a State which is a contracting party to the EEA Agreement;

'notified' means notified in writing;

'qualifying body' means a person specified in Schedule 1;

'seller or supplier' means any natural or legal person who, in contracts covered by these Regulations, is acting for purposes relating to his trade, business or profession, whether publicly owned or privately owned;

'unfair terms' means the contractual terms referred to in regulation 5.

(1A) The references—

(a) in regulation 4(1) to a seller or a supplier, and

(b) in regulation 8(1) to a seller or supplier, include references to a distance supplier and to an intermediary.

(1B) In paragraph (1A) and regulation 5(6)—

'distance supplier' means—

(a) a supplier under a distance contract within the meaning of the Financial Services (Distance Marketing) Regulations 2004, or

(b) a supplier of unsolicited financial services within regulation 15 of those Regulations; and 'intermediary' has the same meaning as in those Regulations.

(2) In the application of these Regulations to Scotland for references to an 'injunction' or an 'interim injunction' there shall be substituted references to an 'interdict' or 'interim interdict' respectively.

4 Terms to which these Regulations apply

(1) These Regulations aply in relation to unfair terms in contracts concluded between a seller or a supplier and a consumer.

(2) These Regulations do not apply to contractual terms which reflect—

(a) mandatory statutory or regulatory provisions (including such provisions under the law of any Member State or in Community legislation having effect in the United Kingdom without further enactment);

(b) the provisions or principles of international conventions to which the Member States or the Community are party.

5 Unfair Terms

(1) A contractual term which has not been individually negotiated shall be regarded as unfair if, contrary to the requirement of good faith, it causes a significant imbalance in the parties' rights and obligations arising under the contract, to the detriment of the consumer.

(2) A term shall always be regarded as not having been individually negotiated where it has been drafted in advance and the consumer has therefore not been able to influence the substance of the term.

(3) Notwithstanding that a specific term or certain aspects of it in a contract has been individually negotiated, these Regulations shall apply to the rest of a contract if an overall assessment of it indicates that it is a pre-formulated standard contract.

(4) It shall be for any seller or supplier who claims that a term was individually negotiated to show that it was.

(5) Schedule 2 to these Regulations contains an indicative and non-exhaustive list of the terms which may be regarded as unfair.

(6) Any contractual term providing that a consumer bears the burden of proof in respect of showing whether a distance supplier or an intermediary complied with any or all of the obligations placed upon him resulting from the Directive and any rule or enactment implementing it shall always be regarded as unfair.

(7) In paragraph (6)—

'the Directive' means Directive 2002/65/EC of the European Parliament and of the Council of 23 September 2002 concerning the distance marketing of consumer financial services and amending Council Directive 90/619/EEC and Directives 97/7/EC and 98/27/EC; and

'rule' means a rule made by the Financial Services Authority under the Financial Services and Markets Act 2000 or by a designated professional body within the meaning of section 326 (2) of that Act.

6 Assessment of unfair terms

(1) Without prejudice to regulation 12, the unfairness of a contractual term shall be assessed, taking into account the nature of the goods or services for which the contract was concluded and by referring, at the time of conclusion of the contract, to all the circumstances attending the conclusion of the contract and to all the other terms of the contract or of another contract on which it is dependent.

(2) In so far as it is in plain intelligible language, the assessment of fairness of a term shall not relate—
   (a) to the definition of the main subject matter of the contract, or
   (b) to the adequacy of the price or remuneration, as against the goods or services supplied in exchange.

7 Written contracts

(1) A seller or supplier shall ensure that any written term of a contract is expressed in plain, intelligible language.

(2) If there is doubt about the meaning of a written term, the interpretation which is most favourable to the consumer shall prevail but this rule shall not aply in proceedings brought under regulation 12.

8 Effect of unfair term

(1) An unfair term in a contract concluded with a consumer by a seller or supplier shall not be binding on the consumer.

(2) The contract shall continue to bind the parties if it is capable of continuing in existence without the unfair term.

9 Choice of law clauses

These Regulations shall apply notwithstanding any contract term which aplies or purports to aply the law of a non-Member State, if the contract has a close connection with the territory of the Member States.

10 Complaints—consideration by Director

(1) It shall be the duty of the Director to consider any complaint made to him that any contract term drawn up for general use is unfair, unless—
   (a) the complaint apears to the Director to be frivolous or vexatious; or
   (b) a qualifying body has notified the Director that it agrees to consider the complaint.

(2) The Director shall give reasons for his decision to apply or not to apply, as the case may be, for an injunction under regulation 12 in relation to any complaint which these Regulations require him to consider.

(3) In deciding whether or not to aply for an injunction in respect of a term which the Director considers to be unfair, he may, if he considers it apropriate to do so, have regard to any undertakings given to him by or on behalf of any person as to the continued use of such a term in contracts concluded with consumers.

11 Complaints—consideration by qualifying bodies

(1) If a qualifying body specified in Part One of Schedule 1 notifies the Director that it agrees to consider a complaint that any contract term drawn up for general use is unfair, it shall be under a duty to consider that complaint.

(2) Regulation 10(2) and (3) shall apply to a qualifying body which is under a duty to consider a complaint as they apply to the Director.

12 Injunctions to prevent continued use of unfair terms

(1) The Director or, subject to paragraph (2), any qualifying body may apply for an injunction (including an interim injunction) against any person appearing to the Director or that body to be using, or recommending use of, an unfair term drawn up for general use in contracts concluded with consumers.

(2) A qualifying body may apply for an injunction only where—
   (a) it has notified the Director of its intention to apply at least fourteen days before the date on which the application is made, beginning with the date on which the notification was given; or
   (b) the Director consents to the application being made within a shorter period.

(3) The court on an application under this regulation may grant an injunction on such terms as it thinks fit.

(4) An injunction may relate not only to use of a particular contract term drawn up for general use but to any similar term, or a term having like effect, used or recommended for use by any person.

13 Powers of the Director and qualifying bodies to obtain documents and information

(1) The Director may exercise the power conferred by this regulation for the purpose of—
   (a) facilitating his consideration of a complaint that a contract term drawn up for general use is unfair; or
   (b) ascertaining whether a person has complied with an undertaking or court order as to the continued use, or recommendation for use, of a term in contracts concluded with consumers.

(2) A qualifying body specified in Part One of Schedule 1 may exercise the power conferred by this regulation for the purpose of—
   (a) facilitating its consideration of a complaint that a contract term drawn up for general use is unfair; or

    (b) ascertaining whether a person has complied with—

        (i) an undertaking given to it or to the court following an application by that body, or

        (ii) a court order made on an application by that body, as to the continued use, or recommendation for use, of a term in contracts concluded with consumers.

(3) The Director may require any person to supply to him, and a qualifying body specified in Part One of Schedule 1 may require any person to supply to it—

    (a) a copy of any document which that person has used or recommended for use, at the time the notice referred to in paragraph (4) below is given, as a pre-formulated standard contract in dealings with consumers;

    (b) information about the use, or recommendation for use, by that person of that document or any other such document in dealings with consumers.

(4) The power conferred by this regulation is to be exercised by a notice in writing which may—

    (a) specify the way in which and the time within which it is to be complied with; and

    (b) be varied or revoked by a subsequent notice.

(5) Nothing in this regulation compels a person to supply any document or information which he would be entitled to refuse to produce or give in civil proceedings before the court.

(6) If a person makes default in complying with a notice under this regulation, the court may, on the application of the Director or of the qualifying body, make such order as the court thinks fit for requiring the default to be made good, and any such order may provide that all the costs or expenses of and incidental to the application shall be borne by the person in default or by any officers of a company or other association who are responsible for its default.

14 Notification of undertakings and orders to Director

A qualifying body shall notify the Director—

(a) of any undertaking given to it by or on behalf of any person as to the continued use of a term which that body considers to be unfair in contracts concluded with consumers;

(b) of the outcome of any application made by it under regulation 12, and of the terms of any undertaking given to, or order made by, the court;

(c) of the outcome of any application made by it to enforce a previous order of the court.

15 Publication, information and advice

(1) The Director shall arrange for the publication in such form and manner as he considers apropriate, of—

    (a) details of any undertaking or order notified to him under regulation 14;

    (b) details of any undertaking given to him by or on behalf of any person as to the continued use of a term which the Director considers to be unfair in contracts concluded with consumers;

    (c) details of any application made by him under regulation 12, and of the terms of any undertaking given to, or order made by, the court;

    (d) details of any application made by the Director to enforce a previous order of the court.

(2) The Director shall inform any person on request whether a particular term to which these Regulations apply has been—

    (a) the subject of an undertaking given to the Director or notified to him by a qualifying body; or

    (b) the subject of an order of the court made upon application by him or notified to him by a qualifying body; and shall give that person details of the undertaking or a copy of the order, as the case may be, together with a copy of any amendments which the person giving the undertaking has agreed to make to the term in question.

(3) The Director may arrange for the dissemination in such form and manner as he considers apropriate of such information and advice concerning the operation of these Regulations as may appear to him to be expedient to give to the public and to all persons likely to be affected by these Regulations.

16 The functions of the Financial Services Authority

The functions of the Financial Services Authority under these Regulations shall be treated as functions of the Financial Services Authority under the Financial Services and Markets Act 2000.

Regulation 3

Schedules 1

Qualifying Bodies

Part One

1. The Information Commissioner.
2. The Gas and Electricity Markets Authority.
3. The Director General of Electricity Supply for Northern Ireland.
4. The Director General of Gas for Northern Ireland.
5. The Office of Communications.
6. The Water Services Regulation Authority.
7. The Rail Regulator.
8. Every weights and measures authority in Great Britain.
9. The Department of Enterprise, Trade and Investment in Northern Ireland.
10. The Financial Services Authority.

Part Two

11. Consumers' Association.

Regulation 5(5)

Schedules 2

Indicative and Non-Exhaustive List Of Terms Which May Be Regarded As Unfair

1. Terms which have the object or effect of—
   (a) excluding or limiting the legal liability of a seller or supplier in the event of the death of a consumer or personal injury to the latter resulting from an act or omission of that seller or supplier;
   (b) inappropriately excluding or limiting the legal rights of the consumer vis-à-vis the seller or supplier or another party in the event of total or partial non-performance or inadequate performance by the seller or supplier of any of the contractual obligations, including the option of offsetting a debt owed to the seller or supplier against any claim which the consumer may have against him;
   (c) making an agreement binding on the consumer whereas provision of services by the seller or supplier is subject to a condition whose realisation depends on his own will alone;
   (d) permitting the seller or supplier to retain sums paid by the consumer where the latter decides not to conclude or perform the contract, without providing for the consumer to receive compensation of an equivalent amount from the seller or supplier where the latter is the party cancelling the contract;
   (e) requiring any consumer who fails to fulfil his obligation to pay a disproportionately high sum in compensation;
   (f) authorising the seller or supplier to dissolve the contract on a discretionary basis where the same facility is not granted to the consumer, or permitting the seller or supplier to retain the sums paid for services not yet supplied by him where it is the seller or supplier himself who dissolves the contract;
   (g) enabling the seller or supplier to terminate a contract of indeterminate duration without reasonable notice except where there are serious grounds for doing so;

(h) automatically extending a contract of fixed duration where the consumer does not indicate otherwise, when the deadline fixed for the consumer to express his desire not to extend the contract is unreasonably early;

(i) irrevocably binding the consumer to terms with which he had no real opportunity of becoming acquainted before the conclusion of the contract;

(j) enabling the seller or supplier to alter the terms of the contract unilaterally without a valid reason which is specified in the contract;

(k) enabling the seller or supplier to alter unilaterally without a valid reason any characteristics of the product or service to be provided;

(l) providing for the price of goods to be determined at the time of delivery or allowing a seller of goods or supplier of services to increase their price without in both cases giving the consumer the corresponding right to cancel the contract if the final price is too high in relation to the price agreed when the contract was concluded;

(m) giving the seller or supplier the right to determine whether the goods or services supplied are in conformity with the contract, or giving him the exclusive right to interpret any term of the contract;

(n) limiting the seller's or supplier's obligation to respect commitments undertaken by his agents or making his commitments subject to compliance with a particular formality;

(o) obliging the consumer to fulfil all his obligations where the seller or supplier does not perform his;

(p) giving the seller or supplier the possibility of transferring his rights and obligations under the contract, where this may serve to reduce the guarantees for the consumer, without the latter's agreement;

(q) excluding or hindering the consumer's right to take legal action or exercise any other legal remedy, particularly by requiring the consumer to take disputes exclusively to arbitration not covered by legal provisions, unduly restricting the evidence available to him or imposing on him a burden of proof which, according to the applicable law, should lie with another party to the contract.

2. Scope of paragraphs 1 (g), (j) and (l)

(a) Paragraph 1(g) is without hindrance to terms by which a supplier of financial services reserves the right to terminate unilaterally a contract of indeterminate duration without notice where there is a valid reason, provided that the supplier is required to inform the other contracting party or parties thereof immediately.

(b) Paragraph 1(j) is without hindrance to terms under which a supplier of financial services reserves the right to alter the rate of interest payable by the consumer or due to the latter, or the amount of other charges for financial services without notice where there is a valid reason, provided that the supplier is required to inform the other contracting party or parties thereof at the earliest opportunity and that the latter are free to dissolve the contract immediately.

Paragraph 1 (j) is also without hindrance to terms under which a seller or supplier reserves the right to alter unilaterally the conditions of a contract of indeterminate duration, provided that he is required to inform the consumer with reasonable notice and that the consumer is free to dissolve the contract.

(c) Paragraphs 1(g), (j) and (l) do not aply to:

– transactions in transferable securities, financial instruments and other products or services where the price is linked to fluctuations in a stock exchange quotation or index or a financial market rate that the seller or supplier does not control;

– contracts for the purchase or sale of foreign currency, traveller's cheques or international money orders denominated in foreign currency;

(d) Paragraph 1 (l) is without hindrance to price indexation clauses, where lawful, provided that the method by which prices vary is explicitly described.

INDEX

purposes, definition of 7.61, 7.96–97

reasonable 7.108

repair facilities and spare parts, availability of 7.116

second hand goods, of 7.112–113

seller's skill and judgement, reliance on
7.84, 7.118–25

  apportionment of responsibility 7.127

  buyer, expertise of 7.120

  contributory negligence of 7.128

  inferred 7.119

  partial 7.118, 7.126

  trade name, sale of article under 7.129

statutory provision 7.84

strict liability 7.94–95

undertaking, notion of 7.86

unsuitability and defectiveness, distinction
between 7.94

warranty, relation to 7.85

fixtures

meaning of 2.12

f.o.b contract

risk of seller 4.18

force majeure 4.63

formalities

writing requirement 1.23, 2.03–04

forfeiture 1.18

equitable relief against 11.86–90

fraud *see also* deceit

common law 8.16

definition 8.17

exclusion clause, and 9.16

frustration

delayed performance on 4.55

deterioration of goods 4.48

discharging parties from contract 4.50–51

effect of 4.65–4.67

express clauses 4.62–64

fault, effect of 4.45–46

government embargoes 4.44

foresight and 4.49

partial 4.50–58

quality obligations 4.47

risk, relation to 4.42

unascertained goods 4.59–61

fructus industriales 2.08–09

fructus naturales 2.07, 2.09, 2.14

gas

sale of 2.15

gift

nature of 2.80–81

goods

acceptance *see* acceptance

ascertained goods 2.47

passing of property, in 3.06–27

body parts 2.16

  definition of 2.02

energy 2.15

existing and future goods 2.42–43

extended statutory definition 2.09

literal interpretation of 2.10

minerals 2.14

money 2.20

perishable goods

  mistake 4.73–74

  passing of risk 4.13–14

quasi-specific goods 2.45–46

shares 2.19

shares in goods 2.21

  definition of 2.11

specific and unascertained goods 2.44, 2.48

things in action and money 2.19

undivided shares 2.23

  allocation of risk in 4.12

unascertained and future goods

  ascertainment and existence 3.28–34

  frustration 4.59–61

  passing of property in 3.28–73

  shrinkage in bulk 3.54

  tenancy in common 3.46–48

  undivided shares in bulk 3.57–60

guarantees

express warranty, and 8.65–71

hardware *see* computers

hire

acceptance 10.79

implied terms 7.149

seller's obligations to transfer title 5.31–33

hire purchase contract

acceptance 10.79

implied terms 7.148

nature of 2.66

penalty clause, rule against 10.07

seller's obligations to transfer title 5.31–32

human material

for transplantation 2.17

human hair 2.16

human skeletons 2.16

sale of human tissue 2.18

trafficking offences 21.7

inertia selling

nature of 1.26

implied terms

description and satisfactory quality 7.05–07

  sale by description 7.08–11

  words of description 7.12–17